THESAURUS OF
QUOTATIONS

THESAURUS OF
QUOTATIONS

Edited by
EDMUND FULLER

———

A NEW CLASSIFIED COLLECTION OF THE
BEST QUOTATIONS FROM ANCIENT
TIMES TO THE PRESENT DAY

———

How forcible are right words.
JOB VI, 25

CROWN PUBLISHERS :: NEW YORK

PRINTED IN THE UNITED STATES OF AMERICA

CONTENTS

INDEX OF SUBJECTS

v

HOW TO USE THIS BOOK

The quotations in this book are classified according to subject and numbered for cross-reference. The subjects are in alphabetical order. A list of subjects is given on page v.

If you want to find an apt thought or felicitous expression on any subject turn to that subject. You will find there a number of quotations from which to choose. In addition to this you will find, immediately under the heading, a list of Related Subjects. One or more of these may be the guide to what you are seeking. Also, at the end of nearly every subject group you will find a list headed See Also. These represent specific quotations, pertaining to the subject at hand but listed under other headings for more direct meanings. Thus, No. 108:

> Nothing with God can be accidental.

is listed under Accident but is referred to as a See Also under God.

If you want to find any specific quotation either to check the exact words or ascertain its source, proceed in the same way by consulting the possible subjects of the quotation, or with the help of the author index on page 1010.

Finally, read the Introduction: it will help you to get the greatest service and enjoyment from this book.

INTRODUCTION

The purpose of this book is to place before the reader, in dictionary form, a broadly representative collection of the thought, wisdom, and wit of past times and of today. The quotations are classified according to meaning, rather than by author. They are so organized that one may find instantly a number of useful quotations on any given subject. Other books of quotations are extant and, naturally, a large body of classical material is common to all. Yet many fine phrases that appear in other books have become lost in the obscurity of little known authors. Here the almost forgotten authors have the chance to serve, on equal footing with the great, in expressing clear thought on their particular subjects. There are other special functions which this book undertakes which we feel it is important to enumerate. In this connection we must further elaborate the principles that have guided us in compilation.

One standard has governed our selection—the value of a quotation. Value may lie in many aspects of the material. It may be the value of wisdom, clarity, brevity, or beauty; the value of singularly happy phrasing of prose or poetry; the value of colloquialism, historical record, characterization, inspiration, prophecy, religious consolation, sheer wit, fact, propaganda or, in this last connection, the value of outright fallacy, exposed and recorded. Occasionally mere familiarity has an intrinsic, associative value but, although there are thousands of familiar quotations in this book, familiarity has not been a standard of selection.

Also, we have not considered it of paramount importance to claim:

I can tell thee where that saying was born.

This book is not a manual for the tracing of quotations to their original sources. We have tried to concern ourselves not with who said it *first* but who said it *best*. A vast body of material was culled from many sources by our staff. We have been at great pains to verify both authenticity and accuracy. Where the source was original and we had it at hand we have given it. When the source was indirect we have not searched out the origin, though other quotations may chance to have emanated directly from it. In Scriptural quotations chapter and verse are given because of the established custom and special importance in this case. In the Shakespearean quotations the work is always cited but not Act, Scene, or line. But neither in poetry, drama, nor prose, aside from these instances, have we been invariably so specific. If there is any smack of inconsistency about this procedure our purpose, as stated, must be remembered. We have felt, with Emerson, that sometimes

A foolish consistency is the hobgoblin of little minds.

Thousands of new quotations have gone into this book. Naturally a large number of these are contemporary, from the date-line speeches of Roosevelt and Churchill, the timely columns of newspapers, to the works of living poets, dramatists, economists, essayists and novelists. But new material has also been gleaned from the Bible, Greek literature, Shakespeare, Johnson, Ibsen, Dickens, Shaw, and others. Some nearly forgotten men, in the quotation field, have been brought forth, such as John PeterAltgeld, the Eagle of Illinois; Eugene Debs, and the great negro Frederick Douglass. There are new Lincoln quotations. We have stormed such literary citadels as *Moby Dick,* called by some compilers impregnable to quotation seekers, and emerged with a rich haul. There are contributions, accordingly, not only of the latter day, but within the entire scope of the book.

We believe the breadth of our system of categories to be wider, not only actually but in its stimulating implications, than that of any other book. We believe we are the first to offer quotations under such typical headings as Appeasement, Isolation, Neutrality, Inflation, Fascism, Unions (Labor), Advertising, Salesmanship, Real Estate, Psychology, and Psychoanalysis.

Any classification of quotations by subject is bound to be a bit arbitrary. For the sake of latitude and deeper significance the emphasis in classification has been placed on *meaning* more than merely upon key words, though naturally these often coincide. We have further guarded against rigidity by a careful yet simple system of cross-referencing. The reader in search of a quotation on Ability, turning to this heading, is immediately offered the suggestion of the Related Subjects: Cleverness, Craftsmanship, Genius, Power, Skill, Strength, Talent. He may at once feel clarified and say to himself, "Come to think of it, Power is really more exactly the sense of what I'm looking for than Ability." Thus, throughout, in a varying degree, we have sought not only to help the user find what he is looking for but also, if his notion is vague, to be infinitely suggestive of alternatives or clearer expressions of the user's idea.

If the reader culls the nineteen quotations under Ability and does not find a suitable thought he may explore the Related Subjects. But in addition to this, he will find at the end of nearly every category, the more specific cross-reference headed See Also. Here, pursuing our example under the same heading, the user will find listed by number, further quotations pertaining in some way to Ability but listed under more direct headings for different meanings. For example, in the See Alsos of Ability we find No. 4764, quoted from Bacon:

> We take cunning for a sinister or crooked wisdom, and certainly there is a great difference between a cunning man and a wise man, not only in point of honesty, but in point of ability.

This, of course, is classified under Cunning, yet it lends itself to use as a quotation on Ability.

This system has enabled the classification of quotations by category to retain a maximum of flexibility. Accordingly the diligent user, pursuing the resources of the Related Subjects and See Alsos of any subject heading, will rarely, if ever, fail to find something that will serve his purpose.

In a few instances a quotation occurs twice when its applicability to two subjects is so marked as to justify it.

A further usefulness of this material will rest in the ingenuity of the user in recognizing how, in many cases, a portion of a longer quotation may be effectively used quite independently of the rest of it. Take the case of No. 2337, from *Moby Dick*:

> Such, and so magnifying, is the virtue of a large and liberal theme! We expand to its bulk. *To produce a mighty book, you must choose a mighty theme.* No great and enduring volume can ever be written on the flea, though many there be who have tried it.

The italicized sentence, lifted piecemeal from the rest, is a pithy and telling thought. Throughout this book the alert and thoughtful reader will find infinite resources of similar "quotations from quotations."

It will be recognized that quotations can frequently be adapted to meanings and significances remote from their original or literal connotation. No. 8891 is from an essay by Carlyle on Jean Paul Richter.

> Except by name, Jean Paul Friedrich Richter is little known out of Germany. The only thing connected with him, we think, that has reached this country is his saying. . . . "Providence has given to the French the empire of the land; to the English that of the sea; to the Germans that of— the air!"

Naturally this had nothing whatever to do with war and air power. Yet today it lends itself so strikingly to a brand new connotation, fraught with timely interest, that it has been classified under Germany for a value not originally belonging to it. Thus it is a distortion of meaning that has led to its inclusion in these pages. Similarly the editor has taken the liberty, with a certain perversity of humor, of classifying the quotation

> My imaginations are as foul as Vulcan's stithy

under Psychoanalysis, relegating its literal classification to a See Also under Imagination, so that it may be found through this obvious channel. In another case, custom has hitherto classified

> They are the abstract and brief chronicles of the time: after your death you were better have a bad epitaph than their ill report while you live.

under the heading Actors. Notwithstanding the fact that it originally bore this significance we have deemed it much more pertinent to suggest a new meaning suited to our times by classifying it under Columnists.

Thus it will be noted that frequently either the classification or cross-reference is based not upon literal qualities but upon a free and possibly more stimulating application of meanings. This may be called an attempt, within practical limits, partially to interpret the material in the book and to render broad suggestions to its users in every possible way.

Outright repetitions of ideas have been generally avoided in favor of some one or two pithy expressions. It's interesting to see how the ornate (and somewhat spurious)

> Millions for defence, but not one cent for tribute!

of Pinckney gives way to the crisp immediacy of Dorothy Thompson's

> The United States is not a nation of people which in the long run allows itself to be pushed around.

A note is necessary on the numbering of the quotations. These numbers are not for the purpose of counting but of locating. They are reference numbers. In order to keep the book from becoming frozen by numbers it was necessary to break their numerical sequence, leaving "expansion joints." The practice has been followed, at the end of each category, of advancing the numbers to begin the next category with the next decade—thus a 7 to 11, a 16 to 21, a 45 to 51. This has made it editorially practical to readjust and perfect this book up to the last minute. It will permit the expansion of further editions without disrupting the entire editorial organization. It is suggested that the constant user may also avail himself of the opportunity to make his own up-to-date supplementary collection of quotations, using the blank numbers to correlate it with the material in this book—a uniquely useful device.

In the final analysis, it must be admitted that no amount of planned procedure can unfold all the useful possibilities of a collection of this order. The alert and ingenious reader will see the value of simply browsing, of poring over these pages for sheer pleasure, familiarizing himself with its broad scope so that it may yield up its riches easily when he needs them most.

Among those who have helped make this book, special thanks are due to Mr. Nathan Ausubel for his discriminating research, especially in the gathering of contemporary quotations. Appreciation should also be recorded for the painstaking and patient work of Miss Bertha Krantz and Miss Claire Just.

Edmund Fuller

New York
October, 1941

THESAURUS OF
QUOTATIONS

ABILITY

Related Subjects: **Cleverness, Craftsmanship, Genius, Power, Skill, Strength, Talent.**

1. There never was a bad man that had ability for good service. BURKE

2. I add this also, that natural ability without education has oftener raised man to glory and virtue, than education without natural ability. CICERO

3. As we advance in life, we learn the limits of our abilities. FROUDE

4. The winds and waves are always on the side of the ablest navigators.
GIBBON, *Decline and Fall*

5. Everything that enlarges the sphere of human powers, that shows man he can do what he thought he could not do, is valuable.
SAMUEL JOHNSON, *Boswell: Life*

6. He was one of those men who possess almost every gift, except the gift of the power to use them.
CHARLES KINGSLEY

7. God obligeth no man to more than he hath given him ability to perform.
The Koran

8. There is great ability in knowing how to conceal one's ability.
LA ROCHEFOUCAULD, *Maxims*

9. From each according to his abilities, to each according to his needs.
KARL MARX, *The German Ideology*

10. I try all things; I achieve what I can.
HERMAN MELVILLE, *Moby Dick*

11. . . . I was in the middle of dream. I thought that if you succeed, that is to be a great man but when I came here and had so much bad time and asked fairly famous man for help and he said to another man that I had no spirit, when I heard this then suddenly I saw that man cannot stand up in the world by ability alone. Even if you do stand up it is like machinery. It is necessary to have virtue to correspond. And really I have awakened to realize that ability is secondary.
NOGUCHI,
Gustave Eckstein: Noguchi

12. A Traveller at Sparta, standing long upon one leg said to a Lacedaemonian, "I do not believe you can do as much." "True," said he, "but every goose can."
PLUTARCH, *Laconic Apothegms*

13. A man can do no more than he can. *Proverb*

14. No one knows what he can do till he tries.
PUBLILIUS SYRUS, *Sententiae*

15. The ability to deal with people is as purchasable a commodity as sugar or coffee. And I pay more for that ability than for any other under the sun. JOHN D. ROCKEFELLER

16.
Out of my lean and low ability
I'll lend you something.
SHAKESPEARE, *Twelfth Night*

17. So long as a man imagines that he cannot do this or that, so long is he determined not to do it; and consequently so long is it impossible to him that he should do it.

SPINOZA, *Ethics*

18. Men of great abilities are generally of a large and vigorous animal nature.   SIR HENRY TAYLOR

19. Man's capacities have never been measured; nor are we to judge of what he can do by any precedents, so little has been tried.

THOREAU, *Walden*

See also: 820, 4743, 4764, 10722, 11560, 12168.

ABNORMALITY, see Normality

ABSENCE

Related Subjects: Exile, Farewell, Memory, Parting, Separation.

21. Absence makes the heart grow fonder—of somebody else.

Anonymous

22. The Lord watch between me and thee, when we are absent one from another.   *Bible: Genesis, xxxi, 49*

23. Absent in body, but present in spirit.   *Bible: 1 Corinthians, v, 3*

24.
But ay the tear comes in my ee,
To think on him that's far awa.

BURNS,
The Bonie Lad That's Far Awa

25.
Wives in their husbands' absences grow subtler,
And daughters sometimes run off with the butler.

BYRON, *Don Juan*

26. Absence, that common cure of love.   CERVANTES, *Don Quixote*

27. Let no one be willing to speak ill of the absent.   DIOGENES LAERTIUS

28.
Where'er I roam, whatever realms to see,
My heart untravelled, fondly turns to thee;
Still to my brother turns, with ceaseless pain,
And drags at each remove a lengthening chain.

GOLDSMITH, *The Traveller*

29.
The rarer seen, the less in mind,
The less in mind, the lesser pain.

BARNABE GOOGE,
Out of Sight, Out of Mind

30. Achilles absent, was Achilles still.

HOMER, *Iliad*

31.
            In the hope to meet
Shortly again, and make our absence sweet.

BEN JONSON, *Underwoods*

32.
Ever absent, ever near;
Still I see thee, still I hear;
Yet I cannot reach thee, dear!

FRANCIS KAZINCZY, *Separation*

33.
What shall I do with all the days and hours
That must be counted ere I see thy face?

FRANCES KEMBLE, *Absence*

34. Presents, I often say, endear absents.   CHARLES LAMB,
A Dissertation upon Roast Pig

35. Your absence of mind we have borne, till your presence of body came to be called in question by it.

CHARLES LAMB, *Last Essays of Elia*

36. Absence quickens our love and elevates our affections. Absence is the invisible and incorporeal mother of ideal beauty.   W. S. LANDOR,
Imaginary Conversations

37. Absence diminishes little passions and increases great ones, just as the wind blows out a candle and fans a fire.
LA ROUCHEFOUCAULD, *Maxims*

38.
Absence not long enough to root out quite
All love, increases love at second sight.   THOMAS MAY, *Henry II*

39.
For there's nae luck about the house;
There's nae luck at aw;
There's little pleasure in the house
When our gudeman's awa.
Attr. to W. J. MICKLE

40.
But O the heavy change, now thou art gone,
Now thou art gone, and never must return!   MILTON, *Lycidas*

41.
With what a deep devotedness of woe
I wept thy absence—o'er and o'er again
Thinking of thee, still thee, till thought grew pain,
And mem'ry, like a drop that, night and day,
Falls cold and ceaseless, wore my heart away!
THOMAS MOORE, *Lalla Rookh*

42.
A boat at midnight sent alone
To drift upon the moonless sea,
A lute, whose leading chord is gone,
A wounded bird, that hath but one
Imperfect wing to soar upon,
Are like what I am, without thee.
THOMAS MOORE, *Loves of the Angels*

43.
Sweet's the laverock's note and lang,
Lifting wildly up the glen;
But aye to me he sings ae sang,
Will ye no come back again?
CAROLINA OLIPHANT,
Will Ye No Come Back Again?

44. Absence is the enemy of love.
Proverb

45. Absence makes the heart grow fonder.   *Proverb*

46. Absence sharpens love, presence strengthens it.   *Proverb*

47. Absence cools moderate passions, but inflames violent ones.   *Proverb*

48. There is not one among them but I dote on his very absence.
SHAKESPEARE,
The Merchant of Venice

49.
How like a winter hath my absence been
From thee, the pleasure of the fleeting year!
SHAKESPEARE, *Sonnet XLIII*

50. Greater things are believed of those who are absent.
TACITUS, *History*

51.
But O for the touch of a vanished hand,
And the sound of a voice that is still!
TENNYSON, *Break, Break, Break*

52.
She only said, "My life is dreary,
He cometh not," she said;
She said, "I am aweary, aweary,
I would that I were dead!"
TENNYSON, *Mariana*

53.
'Tis said that absence conquers love,
But oh! believe it not;
I've tried, alas! its power to prove,
But thou art not forgot.
F. W. THOMAS, *Song*

54. Nothing reopens the springs of love so fully as absence, and no absence so thoroughly as that which must needs be endless.
ANTHONY TROLLOPE,
The Last Chronicle of Barset

ABSTINENCE

Related Subjects: Prohibition, Self-Control, Temperance.

61. Touch not; taste not; handle not.
Bible: Colossians, ii, 21.

62.
Abstinence sows sand all over
The ruddy limbs and flaming hair,
But Desire gratified
Plants fruits of life and beauty there.
BLAKE, *Gnomic Verses*

63. Abstinence is approved of God.
CHAUCER

64.
Call'd to the temple of impure delight,
He that abstains, and he alone, does right.
If a wish wander that way, call it home;
He cannot long be safe whose wishes roam.
COWPER, *The Progress of Error*

65. Abstaining is favorable both to the head and the pocket.
HORACE GREELEY

66.
Against diseases here the strongest fence
Is the defensive virtue, abstinence.
ROBERT HERRICK, *Abstinence*

67. The more a man denies himself, the more shall he obtain from God.
HORACE

68. Abstinence is as easy to me as temperance would be difficult.
SAMUEL JOHNSON

69. By forbearing to do what may innocently be done, we may add hourly new vigor to resolution.
SAMUEL JOHNSON

70. Abstinence is the surety of temperance.
PLATO

71. Self-abstention, if only it be pure enough, gives a stripped beauty to the soul. There lived in me, as doubtless in many, an unchallenged ascetic who was only too glad to be put to the test.
JULES ROMAINS, *Lucienne*

72. To abstain that we may enjoy is the epicureanism of reason.
ROUSSEAU

73.
                Refrain to-night,
And that shall lend a kind of easiness
To the next abstinence: the next more easy;
For use almost can change the stamp of nature.
SHAKESPEARE, *Hamlet*

74. Abstinence is the great strengthener and clearer of reason.
ROBERT SOUTH

75.
And must I wholly banish hence
    These red and golden juices,
And pay my vows to Abstinence,
    That pallidest of Muses?
WILLIAM WATSON,
*To a Fair Maiden Who
Bade Me Shun Wine*

See also: 3162.

ABSURDITIES

Related Subjects: Foolishness, Mockery, Nonsense, Ridicule.

81. Absurdity refutes itself.
A. BARTHOLINI

82. Do not sanction an absurdity.
MME. DE GENLIS

83. Every absurdity has a champion to defend it.
GOLDSMITH

84. The privilege of absurdity; to which no living creature is subject but man only.
THOMAS HOBBES, *Leviathan*

85. Absurdities are great or small in proportion to custom or insuetude.

W. S. LANDOR

86. There is no absurdity so palpable but that it may be firmly planted in the human head if you only begin to inculcate it before the age of five, by constantly repeating it with an air of great solemnity. SCHOPENHAUER

See also: 1382, 1875.

ABUSE

Related Subjects: Curse, Insult, Offense, Slander, Swearing, Threat.

91. There is a time when the hoary head of inveterate abuse will neither draw reverence nor obtain protection.

BURKE

92.
Some have been beaten till they know
What wood a cudgel's of by th' blow
Some kick'd until they can feel whether
A shoe be Spanish or neat's leather.

SAMUEL BUTLER, *Hudibras*

93. The weak resort of cowardice.

C. C. COLTON

94. Remember that it is not he who gives abuse or blows who affronts, but the view we take of these things as insulting. When, therefore, anyone provokes you, be assured that it is your own opinion which provokes you. EPICTETUS, *Discourses*

95. Abuse is the weapon of the vulgar. S. G. GOODRICH

96. Abuse is often of service. There is nothing so dangerous to an author as silence. His name, like a shuttlecock, must be beat backward and forward, or it falls to the ground.

SAMUEL JOHNSON

97. It is better a man should be abused than forgotten.

SAMUEL JOHNSON

98. There are more people abusive to others than open to abuse themselves; but the humor goes round and he that laughs at me today will have somebody to laugh at him tomorrow.

SENECA

99. The hardest knife ill-used doth lose his edge.

SHAKESPEARE, *Sonnet XCV*

100. Whipping and abuse are like laudanum: you have to double the dose as the sensibilities decline.

HARRIET BEECHER STOWE,
Uncle Tom's Cabin

See also: 1281, 2501, 6785.

ACCIDENT

Related Subjects: Calamity, Chance, Death, Fate, Luck, Possibility, Probability.

101. What men call accident is God's own part. GAMALIEL BAILEY

102.
For things said false and never meant,
Do oft prove true by accident.

SAMUEL BUTLER, *Satire*

103. Accidents will occur in the best regulated families.

DICKENS, *David Copperfield*

104.
Our wanton accidents take root, and grow
To vaunt themselves God's laws.

CHARLES KINGSLEY,
The Saint's Tragedy

105. Sometimes there are accidents in our lives the skillful extrication from which demands a little folly.

LA ROCHEFOUCAULD, *Maxims*

106. There are no accidents so unfortunate from which skillful men will not draw some advantage, nor so fortunate that foolish men will not turn them to their hurt.

LA ROCHEFOUCAULD, *Maxims*

107. Nothing under the sun is accidental.

LESSING, *Emilia Galotti*

108. Nothing with God can be accidental.

LONGFELLOW, *The Golden Legend*

109. The Orientals have another word for accident; it is "kismet,"—fate.   MACAULAY

110. By many a happy accident.

THOMAS MIDDLETON,
No Wit Like a Woman's

111. There is no such thing as accident; it is fate misnamed.

NAPOLEON

112. Promptly improve your accidents.   NAPOLEON

113. There's many a slip 'twixt the cup and the lip.   *Proverb*

114. What the reason of the ant laboriously drags into a heap, the wind of accident will collect in one breath.   SCHILLER, *Fiesco*

See also: 782, 1437, 13003.

ACCURACY

Related Subjects: Exaggeration, Honesty, Skill.

121. Hit the nail on the head.

JOHN FLETCHER, *Love's Cure*

122. Has any reader ever found perfect accuracy in the newspaper account of any event of which he himself had inside knowledge?

E. V. LUCAS, *Of Accuracy*

ACQUAINTANCE

Related Subjects: Friendship, Knowledge, Society.

131. Acquaintance softens prejudice.

AESOP, *Fables*

132. It is good discretion not to make too much of any man at the first; because one cannot hold out that proportion.   BACON

133.
Should auld acquaintance be forgot,
    And never brought to mind?
Should auld acquaintance be forgot,
    And auld lang syne?

BURNS, *Auld Lang Syne*

134. I look upon every day to be lost, in which I do not make a new acquaintance.

SAMUEL JOHNSON, *Boswell: Life*

135. If a man does not make new acquaintances as he advances through life, he will soon find himself left alone.

SAMUEL JOHNSON, *Boswell: Life*

136. The art of life is to keep down acquaintances. One's friends one can manage, but one's acquaintances can be the devil.

E. V. LUCAS, *Over Bemerton's*

137. Short acquaintance brings repentance.   *Proverb*

138. Have but few friends, though much acquaintance.   *Proverb*

139. To you! Stranger! If you, passing, meet me, and desire to speak to me, why should you not speak to me? And why should I not speak to you?   WALT WHITMAN

See also: 268, 3793, 8384.

ACT, ACTION

Related Subjects: Behavior, Deeds, Manners.

141. Action is but coarsened thought—thought become concrete, obscure, and unconscious.   AMIEL, *Journal*

142.
Count that day lost whose low descending sun
Views from thy hand no worthy action done.   *Anonymous*

143. The judgment of the world has been that Pilate did not do enough. There is no vigor in expressing an opinion and then washing your hands. HEYWOOD BROUN, *Sacco and Vanzetti*

144.
Better to sink beneath the shock
Than moulder piecemeal on the rock.
   BYRON, *The Giaour*

145. Produce! Were it but the pitifulest infinitesimal fraction of a product, produce it in God's name.
   CARLYLE, *Sartor Resartus*

146. The best way to keep good acts in memory is to refresh them with new.   CATO THE CENSOR

147. For as action follows speeches and votes in the order of time, so does it precede and rank before them in force.   DEMOSTHENES

148. Why should we be cowed by the name of Action?   EMERSON, *Spiritual Laws*

149. I see how many firm acts have been done; how many valiant *noes* have this day been spoken, when others would have uttered ruinous *yeas*.   EMERSON, *Character*

150. We are taught by great actions that the universe is the property of every individual in it.
   EMERSON, *Beauty*

151. The materials of action are variable but the use we make of them should be constant.
   EPICTETUS, *Discourses*

152. Great actions speak great minds.
JOHN FLETCHER, *The Prophetess*

153.
Our acts our angels are, or good or ill,
Our fatal shadows that walk by us still.
   JOHN FLETCHER,
   An Honest Man's Fortune

154. A man of action, forced into a state of thought, is unhappy until he can get out of it.
   GALSWORTHY, *Maid in Waiting*

155. Great acts grow out of great occasions and great occasions spring from great principles, working changes in society, and tearing it up by the roots.
   HAZLITT, *Table Talk*

156. That action is best which procures the greatest happiness for the greatest numbers.
FRANCIS HUTCHESON, *Inquiry Concerning Moral Good & Evil*

157. The great end of life is not knowledge but action.
   THOMAS H. HUXLEY,
   Technical Education

158. Although men flatter themselves with their great actions, they are usually the result of chance and not of design.
   LA ROCHEFOUCAULD, *Maxims*

159. Every man feels instinctively that all the beautiful sentiments in the world weigh less than a single lovely action.   LOWELL, *Among My Books*

160. The Commons, faithful to their system, remained in a wise and masterly inactivity.
   SIR JAMES MACKINTOSH,
   Vindiciae Gallicae

161. Execute every act of thy life as though it were thy last.

MARCUS AURELIUS, *Meditations*

162. Negation, eternal immobility, mean damnation. I am all for motion. I am one who marches on.

MUSSOLINI,
Ludwig: Talks with Mussolini

163. Inactivity is death.

MUSSOLINI, *Fascism*

164. Better do it than wish it done.

Proverb

165. Actions speak louder than words. *Proverb*

166. Action is the proper fruit of knowledge. *Proverb*

167. I wish to preach, not the doctrine of ignoble ease, but the doctrine of the strenuous life.

THEODORE ROOSEVELT

168. One hour of life, crowded to the full with glorious action, and filled with noble risks, is worth whole years of those mean observances of paltry decorum.

SCOTT, *Count Robert of Paris*

169. Action is eloquence.

SHAKESPEARE, *Coriolanus*

170. It is no act of common passage, but a strain of rareness.

SHAKESPEARE, *Cymbeline*

171. You don't learn to hold your own in the world by standing on guard, but by attacking, and getting well hammered yourself.

BERNARD SHAW, *Getting Married*

172. The urge towards activity (ostensibly so practical, so fruitful, so mundane, and so utilitarian) can, when unduly intensified, lead to a positive frenzy in which the doer is really "beside himself"; with the re-sult that his actions do not merely lack the much-vaunted foundation of reality, but unavoidably and automatically culminate in the realm of the preposterous.

JACOB WASSERMANN, *Stanley*

173. Cannot we study the phenomenon of action dying at the root, of a puzzling loss of the true essence of personality, in the men of action who have been most renowned in history— in Alexander, in Attila, in Caesar, in Napoleon, in Cromwell? At some particular moment in their career we note that, of a sudden, for reasons that at first elude us, madness and destruction overwhelm them.

JACOB WASSERMANN, *Stanley*

174. Almost always in life the lots are parted, so that a man of insight is not a man of action and a man of action is not a man of insight.

STEFAN ZWEIG,
The Right to Heresy

See also: 387, 982, 2179, 3432, 3884, 3936, 4065, 5612, 6655, 11220, 12252, 13508, 13511, 14386, 15867, 16145, 16185, 16385, 16401, 19658.

ACTING AND ACTORS

Related Subjects: Drama, Imitation, Orator and Oratory, Stage.

181. An actor is a sculptor who carves in snow. LAWRENCE BARRETT

182. To see Kean act was like reading Shakespeare by flashes of lightning. COLERIDGE, *Table Talk*

183. Never meddle with actors, for they are a favored class . . . as they are merry folk who give pleasure, everyone favors and protects them.

CERVANTES, *Don Quixote*

184.

On this great stage, the world, no monarch e'er
Was half so haughty as a monarch player.
CHARLES CHURCHILL, *The Apology*

185.

The Poet, to the end of time,
Breathes in his works and lives in rhyme;
But, when the Actor sinks to rest,
And the turf lies upon his breast,
A poor traditionary fame
Is all that's left to grace his name.
WILLIAM COMBE,
Dr. Syntax in Search of the Picturesque

186.

No! I am not Prince Hamlet, nor was meant to be;
Am an attendant lord, one that will do
To swell a progress, start a scene or two.
T. S. ELIOT,
The Love Song of J. Alfred Prufrock

187. Have patience with the jealousies and petulances of actors, for their hour is their eternity.
RICHARD GARNETT,
De Flagello Myrteo

188. Everybody has his own theatre, in which he is manager, actor, prompter, playwright, sceneshifter, boxkeeper, doorkeeper, all in one, and audience into the bargain.
A. W. & J. C. HARE,
Guesses at Truth

189. Actors are the only honest hypocrites.
HAZLITT

190.

It worries me to beat the band
To hear folks say our life is grand;
Wish they'd try some one-night stand—
Ain't it awful, Mabel?
J. E. HAZZARD,
Ain't It Awful, Mabel?

191. Beggars, actors, buffoons, and all that breed.
HORACE, *Satires*

192. What pleases in a great actor, as in all arts that appeal to the imagination, is the unforeseen.
JULES JANIN

193. Though the most be players, some must be spectators.
BEN JONSON, *Timber*

194. Acting is therefore the lowest of arts, if it is an art at all.
GEORGE MOORE, *Mummer-Worship*

195.

Like a dull actor now,
I have forgot my part, and I am out,
Even to a full disgrace.
SHAKESPEARE, *Coriolanus*

196. Speak the speech, I pray you, as I pronounced it to you, trippingly on the tongue: but if you mouth it, as many of your players do, I had as lief the town-crier spoke my lines.
SHAKESPEARE, *Hamlet*

197. Nor do not saw the air too much with your hand, thus; but use all gently: for in the very torrent, tempest, and as I may say the whirlwind of passion, you must acquire and beget a temperance, that may give it smoothness. Oh, it offends me to the soul to hear a robustious periwigpated fellow tear a passion to tatters, to very rags, to split the ears of the groundlings, who for the most part are capable of nothing but inexplicable dumb-shows and noise. I would have such a fellow whipped for o'erdoing Termagant; it out-herods Herod.
SHAKESPEARE, *Hamlet*

198. Suit the action to the word, the word to the action; with this special observance, that you o'erstep not the modesty of nature.
SHAKESPEARE, *Hamlet*

199.
To hold, as 'twere, the mirror up to nature.   SHAKESPEARE, *Hamlet*

200.
To show the very age and body of the time his form and pressure.
SHAKESPEARE, *Hamlet*

201. Now this overdone, or come tardy off, though it make the unskilful laugh, cannot but make the judicious grieve; the censure of the which one must in your allowance o'erweigh a whole theatre of others.
SHAKESPEARE, *Hamlet*

202. O, there be players that I have seen play, and heard others praise, and that highly, not to speak it profanely, that, neither having the accent of Christians nor the gait of Christian, pagan, nor man, have so strutted and bellowed that I have thought some of nature's journeymen had made men and not made them well, they imitated humanity so abominably.
SHAKESPEARE, *Hamlet*

203. The stock actor is a stage calamity.   BERNARD SHAW,
Dramatic Opinions & Essays

204. A character actor is one who cannot act and therefore makes an elaborate study of disguises and stage tricks by which acting can be grotesquely simulated.
BERNARD SHAW,
Dramatic Opinions & Essays

205. Our brains evidently work in the same way. At the same time I begin to doubt whether you can really be an actress. Most of 'em have no brains at all. BERNARD SHAW, *to Ellen Terry*

206. In my ideal company there shall not be an actress who can read.
BERNARD SHAW, *to Ellen Terry*

See also: 285.

ADAM AND EVE

Related Subjects: The Bible, Paradise, Parents, Serpent.

211.
When every pool in Eden was a mirror
That unto Eve her dainty charms proclaimed.
She went undraped without a single fear, or
Thought that she had need to be ashamed.
Anonymous, Needed Apples

212.
The woman was not taken
From Adam's head, you know,
So she must not command him,
'Tis evidently so;
The woman was not taken
From Adam's feet, you see,
So he must not abuse her—
The meaning seems to be.
The woman she was taken
From under Adam's arm,
Whch shows he must protect her
From injury and harm.
*Anonymous,
Old Scotch Nuptial Song*

213.
Whilst Adam slept, Eve from his side arose:
Strange his first sleep should be his last repose.
Anonymous, The Consequence

214.
When Adam dolve and Eve span,
Who was then the gentleman?
JOHN BALL

215. And Adam called his wife's name Eve; because she was the mother of all living.
Bible: Genesis, iii, 20

216. Grant that the Old Adam in these persons may be so buried, that the new man may be raised up in them. *The Book of Common Prayer*

217.
"The serpent tempted me and I did
eat."
So much of paradisal nature, Eve's!
Her daughters ever since prefer to
urge
"Adam so starved me I was fain ac-
cept
The apple any serpent pushed my
way."
BROWNING, *The Ring and the Book*

218. That Adam, called "the happiest
of men." BYRON, *Don Juan*

219.
The High God, when he hadde Adam
maked,
And saw him all alone, belly-naked,
God of his greate goodness sedye
then,
"Let us now make a help unto this
man
Like to himself;" and then he made
him Eve.
CHAUCER, *The Marchantes Tale*

220. The fall of the first Adam was
the end of the beginning; the rise of
the second Adam was the beginning
of the end. S. W. DUFFIELD

221.
It is not fair to visit all
The blame on Eve, for Adam's fall;
The most Eve did was to display
Contributory negligée.
OLIVER HERFORD,
Eve: Apropos de Rien

222.
Her rash hand in evil hour
Forth reaching to the fruit, she
pluck'd, she eat;
Earth felt the wound, and Nature
from her seat
Sighing through all her works gave
signs of woe,
That all was lost.
MILTON, *Paradise Lost*

223.
Adam the goodliest man of men since
born
His sons, the fairest of her daughters
Eve. MILTON, *Paradise Lost*

224.
In Adam's fall
We sinned all.
The New England Primer

225.
From yon blue heavens above us bent,
The grand old gardener and his wife,
Smile at the claims of long descent.
TENNYSON,
Lady Clara Vere de Vere

226. Adam and Eve had many advantages, but the principal one was,
that they escaped teething.
MARK TWAIN,
Pudd'nhead Wilson's Calendar

227. Whoever has lived long enough
to find out what life is, knows how
deep a debt of gratitude we owe to
Adam, the first great benefactor of
our race. He brought death into the
world. MARK TWAIN,
Pudd'nhead Wilson's Calendar

228.
Think how poor Mother Eve was
brought
To being as God's afterthought.
ANNA WICKHAM, *To Men*

See also: 810, 4814, 5067, 8802,
21640.

ADAPTABILITY

Related Subject: Change.

231. Mahomet made the people believe that he would call a hill to him,
and from the top of it offer up his
prayers for the observers of his law.
The people assembled. Mahomet
called the hill to come to him, again
and again; and when the hill stood

still he was never a whit abashed, but said, "If the hill will not come to Mahomet, Mahomet will go to the hill."
BACON, *Of Boldness*

232. Nothing is more politic than to make the wheels of the mind concentric and voluble with the wheels of fortune.
BACON, *Advancement of Learning*

233. I am made all things to all men.
Bible: 1 Corinthians, ix, 22

234. I am of a constitution so general, that it consorts and sympathiseth with all things. I have no antipathy, or rather idiosyncrasy, in diet, humour, air, any thing.
SIR THOMAS BROWNE,
Religio Medici

235. He was capable of adapting himself to place, time, and person, and of playing his part appropriately under whatever circumstances.
DIOGENES LAERTIUS, *Aristippus*

236. The wise man does no wrong in changing his habits with the times.
DIONYSIUS CATO,
Disticha de Moribus

237. Man is a pliable animal, a being who gets accustomed to everything!
DOSTOYEVSKY,
The House of the Dead

238. Were I a nightingale, I would act the part of a nightingale; were I a swan, the part of a swan.
EPICTETUS, *Discourses*

239. We must cut our coat according to our cloth, and adapt ourselves to changing circumstances.
DEAN INGE, *Lay Thoughts*

240. Adapt thyself to the estate which is thy portion.
MARCUS AURELIUS, *Meditations*

241.
Who to mankind will not adapt himself,
For his disdain must pay the penalty.
PHAEDRUS, *Fables*

242. Look for a tough wedge for a tough log.
PUBLILIUS SYRUS, *Sententiae*

243.
My nature is subdued
To what it works in, like the dyer's hand. SHAKESPEARE, *Sonnet CXI*

244. It is safest to be moderately base—to be flexible in shame, and to be always ready for what is generous, good, and just, when anything is to be gained by virtue.
SIDNEY SMITH, *Essays*

See also: 952, 1602, 2813, 3427.

ADDRESS

Related Subjects: Cleverness, Home, Orator and Oratory, Skill, Speech, Talk.

251. Give a boy address and accomplishments, and you give him the mastery of palaces and fortunes where he goes. He has not the trouble of earning or owning them; they solicit him to enter and possess. EMERSON

252. Brahma once asked of Force, "Who is stronger than thou?" She replied, "Address." VICTOR HUGO

Address in the sense of residence

253. A man without an address is a vagabond. A man with two addresses is a libertine. BERNARD SHAW

ADMIRATION

Related Subjects: Applause, Esteem, Fame, Praise, Wonder.

261. Admiration is a very short-lived passion, that immediately decays upon growing familiar with its object, unless it be still fed with such discoveries, and kept alive by a new perpetual succession of miracles rising up to its view.   ADDISON

262. All things are admired either because they are new or because they are great.   BACON

263. A fool always finds a greater fool to admire him.
BOILEAU, L'Art Poetique

264. No nobler feeling than this of admiration for one higher than himself dwells in the breast of man.
CARLYLE, Heroes & Hero-Worship

265. Distance is a great promoter of admiration!   DIDEROT

266. It may be laid down as a general rule, that no woman who hath any great pretensions to admiration is ever well pleased in a company where she perceives herself to fill only the second place.   FIELDING

267. Not to be lost in idle admiration is the only sure means of making and of preserving happiness.   HORACE

268. Admiration begins where acquaintance ceases. SAMUEL JOHNSON

269. There is an admiration which is the daughter of knowledge.
JOUBERT, Pensées

270. We always love those who admire us, and we do not always love those whom we admire.
LA ROCHEFOUCAULD, Maxims

271.
Yet let not each gay turn thy rapture move;
For fools admire, but men of sense approve.
POPE, Essay on Criticism

272. Admiration is the daughter of ignorance.   Proverb

273. To cultivate sympathy you must be among living creatures, and thinking about them; and to cultivate admiration, you must be among beautiful things and looking at them.
RUSKIN

274. Admiration and familiarity are strangers.   GEORGE SAND

275. Season your admiration for a while.   SHAKESPEARE, Hamlet

276. We live by admiration, hope, and love.   WORDSWORTH

See also: 1704, 16794, 17984.

ADULTERY

Related Subjects: Cuckold, Fidelity, Lust, Sin.

281. Thou shalt not commit adultery.
Bible: Exodus, xx, 14

282.
What men call gallantry, and gods adultery,
Is much more common where the climate's sultry.   BYRON, Don Juan

283. When a man says, "Get out of my house! what would you have with my wife?" there's no answer to be made.   CERVANTES, Don Quixote

284. To set your neighbor's bed a-shaking is now an ancient and long-established custom. It was the silver age that saw the first adulterers.
JUVENAL, Satires

285. The actors are, it seems, the usual three: Husband, and wife, and lover.
GEORGE MEREDITH, Modern Love

286. The way of the adulterer is hedged with thorns; full of fears and jealousies, burning desires and impatient waitings, tediousness of delay,

and sufferance of affronts, and amazements of discovery.
JEREMY TAYLOR, *Holy Living*

See also: 1695, 1759, 2665, 6058.

ADVANTAGE

Related Subjects: Opportunity, Power, Profit.

291. It's them as take advantage that get advantage i' this world.
GEORGE ELIOT, *Adam Bede*

292. Human felicity is produc'd not so much by great pieces of good fortune that seldom happen, as by little advantages that occur every day.
FRANKLIN, *Autobiography*

293. Never esteem anything as of advantage to thee that shall make thee break thy word or lose thy self-respect.
MARCUS AURELIUS, *Meditations*

294. Every advantage has its disadvantage.   *Proverb*

295. Advantage is a better soldier than rashness.   *Proverb*

296. It is no advantage for a man in a fever to change his bed.   *Proverb*

297. Let not advantage slip.
SHAKESPEARE, *Venus and Adonis*

See also: 106, 226, 1271, 2718, 3344, 9950, 15159.

ADVENTURE

Related Subjects: Boldness, Danger, Events, Pioneer, Risk, Romance.

301. The adventurer is an outlaw. Adventure must start with running away from home.
WILLIAM BOLITHO,
Twelve Against the Gods

302.
        Are there not, dear Michael,
Two points in the adventure of the diver,
One—when, a beggar, he prepares to plunge,
One—when, a prince, he rises with his pearl?   BROWNING, *Paracelsus*

303. Adventures are to the adventurous.   DISRAELI, *Ixion in Heaven*

304. The thirst for adventure is the vent which Destiny offers; a war, a crusade, a gold mine, a new country, speak to the imagination and offer swing and play to the confined powers.
EMERSON,
Natural History of Intellect

305.
Some bold adventurers disdain
The limits of their little reign,
And unknown regions dare descry.
THOMAS GRAY,
*Ode on a Distant Prospect of
Eton College*

306. Who seeks adventures finds blows.   *Proverb*

307.
Wherein I spake of most disastrous chances,
Of moving accidents by flood and field,
Of hair-breadth 'scapes i' the imminent deadly breach.
SHAKESPEARE, *Othello*

See also: 5040, 17218.

ADVERSITY

Related Subjects: Calamity, Depression, Difficulty, Evil, Fall, Fate, Misery, Misfortune, Poverty, Trials, Trouble, Woe.

311. If thou faint in the day of adversity thy strength is small.
Bible: Proverbs, xxiv, 10

312. Whom the Lord loveth he chasteneth.   *Bible: Hebrews, xii, 6*

313. He that is down needs fear no fall.   BUNYAN, *Pilgrim's Progress*

314. Adversity, if a man is set down to it by degrees, is more supportable with equanimity by most people than any great prosperity arrived at in a single lifetime.
SAMUEL BUTLER,
The Way of All Flesh

315. Adversity is the first path to truth.   BYRON, *Don Juan*

316. Adversity is sometimes hard upon a man; but for one man who can stand prosperity there are a hundred that will stand adversity.
CARLYLE, *Heroes & Hero-Worship*

317.
If aught can teach us aught, Affliction's looks,
(Making us pry into ourselves so near),
Teach us to know ourselves, beyond all books,
Or all the learned schools that ever were.
SIR JOHN DAVIES, *Nosce Teipsum*

318. There is in every true woman's heart a spark of heavenly fire, which lies dormant in the broad daylight of prosperity; but which kindles up, and beams and blazes in the dark hour of adversity.
WASHINGTON IRVING,
The Sketch-Book

319. A man used to vicissitudes is not easily dejected.
SAMUEL JOHNSON, *Rasselas*

320. For a man to rejoice in adversity is not grievous to him who loves; for so to joy is to joy in the cross of Christ.   THOMAS À KEMPIS,
Of the Imitation of Christ

321. In the adversity of our best friends we often find something that is not exactly displeasing.
LA ROCHEFOUCAULD, *Maxims*

322. Adversity reminds men of religion.   LIVY, *History*

323.
Let us be patient! These severe afflictions
Not from the ground arise,
But oftentimes celestial benedictions
Assume this dark disguise.
LONGFELLOW, *Resignation*

324. In adversity a man is saved by hope.   MENANDER, *Fragments*

325. Who would have known of Hector, if Troy had been happy? The road to valor is builded by adversity.
OVID, *Tristia*

326. These are the times that try men's souls.   THOMAS PAINE,
The American Crisis

327.
Whom unmerciful disaster
Followed fast and followed faster.
POE, *The Raven*

328. Adversity makes a man wise, though not rich.   *Proverb*

329. Behold a thing worthy of a God, a brave man matched in conflict with adversity.   SENECA, *De Providentia*

330. Gold is tried by fire, brave men by adversity.
SENECA, *De Providentia*

331. Adversity finds at last the man whom she has often passed by.
SENECA, *Hercules Furens*

332.
Sweet are the uses of adversity;
Which, like the toad, ugly and venomous,

Wears yet a precious jewel in his
head;
And this our life, exempt from public
haunt,
Finds tongues in trees, books in the
running brooks,
Sermons in stones, and good in everything.
SHAKESPEARE, *As You Like It*

333. A wretched soul, bruised with
adversity.   SHAKESPEARE,
The Comedy of Errors

334.
Let me embrace thee, sour adversity,
For wise men say it is the wisest
course. SHAKESPEARE, *Henry VI*

335.
The worst is not
So long as we can say, "This is the
worst." SHAKESPEARE, *King Lear*

336.
Henceforth I'll bear
Affliction till it do cry out itself
"Enough, enough," and die.
SHAKESPEARE, *King Lear*

337.
O benefit of ill! now I find true
That better is by evil still made better.
SHAKESPEARE, *Sonnet CXIX*

338. The Lord gets his best soldiers
out of the highlands of affliction.
C. H. SPURGEON,
Sorrow's Discipline

339.
Count each affliction, whether light or
grave,
God's messenger sent down to thee;
do thou
With courtesy receive him.
AUBREY THOMAS DE VERE, *Sorrow*

See also: 712, 4080, 4345, 8659, 9362,
15163.

ADVERTISING AND PUBLICITY

Related Subjects: Business, Propaganda, Psychology, Salesmanship.

341. Advertising is the mouthpiece of
business.   JAMES R. ADAMS,
More Power to Advertising

342. The cardinal sin of advertising,
without doubt, is boastfulness. *Ibid.*

343. An advertiser who refers to
everything he does in superlatives will
soon be discounted. It is as inevitable
as day and night.   *Ibid.*

344. Many a splendid writer, with a
great gift for arousing people to action, comes out with sand in his mouth
when he tries advertising—simply
because he is instinctively opposed to
the profit motive in business. *Ibid.*

345. The end for which advertising
tries is increased commercial activity
—and if it fails to achieve this end, it
simply does not exist as advertising.
It is just so many words and pictures
printed on paper, or so many syllables
spoken over the air.   *Ibid.*

346. Advertising is not an expense
. . . and should never be thought of
as such . . . Advertising is one of
the tools of salesmanship—and, like
every good tool, should be used to
the limit of its capacity. In fact, advertising is opportunity incarnate, and
every advantage should be taken of it.
Ibid.

347. There are two major problems
in advertising. And there are really
no more.

Problem number one is to say the
right thing in the right way, and is
largely a creative problem.

Problem number two is to get this message before the right type of people, and to reach the proper number of them. JAMES R. ADAMS, *More Power to Advertising*

348. The commercial advertiser is interested in influencing public opinion. Politicians, institutions, and organizations also employ this medium, and their efforts may shade over into propaganda. Business corporations, such as the public utilities, make definite efforts to arouse favorable attitudes, especially when such issues as changes of rates are under consideration. HAROLD E. BURTT, *Psychology of Advertising*

349. Instances may be cited in which advertising has made definite contributions to health. The slogan "A clean tooth never decays" made countless people more conscious of oral hygiene, although it was propounded mainly in order to sell tooth-brushes. The public is more conscious of the need for antiseptics as a result of advertising. *Ibid.*

350. It would be undesirable . . . to present pictures of a slaughterhouse in connection with advertisements for ham and beef. Such copy might be entirely pertinent in showing how carefully the product is prepared, but, on the other hand, it reminds the reader that he is carnivorous. *Ibid.*

351. Advertising is not the driving wheel of the industrial machine, but it is undoubtedly its lubricating box, what Edmund Burke called "the lubricator of the fibres" of international trade. VISCOUNT BURNHAM

352. You can tell the ideals of a nation by its advertisements. NORMAN DOUGLAS, *South Wind*

353. If you don't advertise yourself you will be advertised by your loving enemies. ELBERT HUBBARD, *Advertising and Advertisements*

354. Publicity eliminates pretense. The faker cannot work in a club. *Ibid.*

355. There is no quicker way in the world to lose money than through advertising—therefore the necessity of making advertising a science. *Ibid.*

356. Advertising is telling who you are, where you are, and what you have to offer the world in the way of commodity or service. *Ibid.*

357. It is far easier to write ten passably effective Sonnets, good enough to take in the not too inquiring critic, than one effective advertisement that will take in a few thousand of the uncritical buying public. ALDOUS HUXLEY, *On the Margin*

358. He is one of the many who have made themselves *publick,* without making themselves *known.* SAMUEL JOHNSON, *Boswell: Life*

359. The sign brings customers. LA FONTAINE, *Fables*

360. Business today consists in persuading crowds. GERALD STANLEY LEE, *Crowds*

361. We are advertis'd by our loving friends. SHAKESPEARE, *Henry VI*

ADVICE

Related Subjects: Counsel, Persuasion, Prudence, Teaching, Warning.

371. Always advise a friend to do that which you are sure he is not going to do. Then, if his venture fails, you will receive credit for having

warned him. If it succeeds, he will be happy in the opportunity to tell you that you were dead wrong.

    GEORGE ADE

372. The worst men often give the best advice.

    PHILIP J. BAILEY, *Festus*

373. *Advice:* the smallest current coin.   AMBROSE BIERCE, *The Devil's Dictionary*

374.
In ploughman phrase, "God send you speed,"
  Still daily to grow wiser;
And may ye better reck the rede
  Than ever did th' adviser!

    BURNS, *Epistle to a Young Friend*

375. He loves who advises.

    ROBERT BURTON, *Anatomy of Melancholy*

376. Good but rarely came from good advice.   BYRON, *Don Juan*

377.
She had a good opinion of advice,
Like all who give and eke receive it gratis,
For which small thanks are still the market price.   BYRON, *Cain*

378. Advice is seldom welcome; and those who want it the most always like it the least.

    LORD CHESTERFIELD, *Letters*

379. Nobody can give you wiser advice than yourself.

    CICERO, *Epistulae ad Atticum*

380. To profit from good advice requires more wisdom than to give it.

    CHURTON COLLINS, *Aphorisms*

381. 'Twas good advice, and meant, "My son, be good."

    GEORGE CRABBE, *The Learned Boy*

382. They first condemn that first advis'd the ill.

    DRYDEN, *Absalom and Achitophel*

383. No gift is more precious than good advice.

    ERASMUS, *Convivium Religiosum*

384. Take the advice of a faithful friend, and submit thy inventions to his censure.

    THOMAS FULLER, *Holy State*

385. Extremely foolish advice is likely to be uttered by those who are looking at the labouring vessel from the land.

    ARTHUR HELPS, *Friends in Council*

386. Whatever advice you give, be brief.   HORACE, *Ars Poetica*

387. I lay very little stress either upon asking or giving advice. Generally speaking, they who ask advice know what they wish to do and remain firm in their intentions. A man may allow himself to be enlightened on various points, even upon matters of expediency and duty, but after all he must determine his course of action for himself.   HUMBOLDT

388. Advice is offensive, . . . it shows us that we are known to others as well as to ourselves.

    SAMUEL JOHNSON, *The Rambler*

389. Nothing is given so profusely as advice.

    LA ROCHEFOUCAULD, *Maxims*

390. Hazard not your wealth on a poor man's advice.

    PRINCE DON JUAN MANUEL, *Conde Lucanor*

391.
Ask a woman's advice, and, whate'er she advise,

Do the very reverse and you're sure to be wise. THOMAS MOORE,
How to Make a Good Politician

392. Only when a man is safely ensconced under six feet of earth, with several tons of enlauding granite upon his chest, is he in a position to give advice with any certainty, and then he is silent.
A. EDWARD NEWTON,
Amenities of Book-Collecting

393.
Be niggards of advice on no pretence,
For the worst avarice is that of sense.
POPE, *Essay on Criticism*

394. Write down the advice of him who loves you, though you like it not at present. *Proverb*

395. Take your wife's first advice, not her second. *Proverb*

396. Be slow of giving advice, ready to do a service. *Proverb*

397. It is bad advice that cannot be altered. PUBLILIUS SYRUS, *Sententiae*

398. Many receive advice, few profit by it. PUBLILIUS SYRUS, *Sententiae*

399. Advice comes too late when a thing is done.
SAMUEL RICHARDSON,
Clarissa Harlowe

400. To one who knows, it is superfluous to give advice; to one who does not know, it is insufficient.
SENECA, *Epistulae ad Lucilium*

401.
Here comes a man of comfort whose advice
Hath often still'd my brawling discontent.
SHAKESPEARE, *Measure for Measure*

402. *Good advice* is one of those injuries which a good man ought, if

possible, to forgive, but at all events to forget at once.
HORACE SMITH, *The Tin Trumpet*

403. How is it possible to expect that mankind will take advice, when they will not so much as take warning?
SWIFT,
Thoughts on Various Subjects

404. For my own part, I never did nor do I believe I ever shall give advice to a woman who is setting out on a matrimonial voyage . . . A woman very rarely asks an opinion or seeks advice on such an occasion till her mind is wholly made up, and then it is with the hope and expectation of obtaining a sanction, and not that she means to be governed by your disapproval. WASHINGTON

See also: 1780, 1949, 2872, 4452, 5771, 8164, 9642, 20478.

AFFECTATION

Related Subjects: Appearance, Boasting, Elegance, Fop, Form, Hypocrisy, Vanity.

411. Affectation is the product of falsehood. CARLYLE

412. Avoid all affectation and singularity. What is according to nature is best, and what is contrary to it is always distasteful. Nothing is graceful that is not our own.
JEREMY COLLIER

413. Great vices are the proper objects of our detestation, smaller faults of our pity, but affectation appears to be the only true source of the ridiculous. FIELDING

414. Paltry affectation, strained allusions, and disgusting finery are easily attained by those who choose to wear them; they are but too frequently the badges of ignorance or of stupidity,

whenever it would endeavor to please. GOLDSMITH

415. Don't *attitudenize.*
SAMUEL JOHNSON, *Boswell: Life*

416. Affectation is to be always distinguished from hypocrisy, as being the art of counterfeiting those qualities, which we might with innocence and safety, be known to want. Hypocrisy is the necessary burden of villainy; affectation part of the chosen trappings of folly.
SAMUEL JOHNSON

417. Among the numerous stratagems by which pride endeavors to recommend folly to regard, there is scarcely one that meets with less success than affectation, or a perpetual disguise of the real character by fictitious appearances.
SAMUEL JOHNSON

418. There is a pleasure in affecting affectation. CHARLES LAMB

419. We are never so ridiculous from the habits we have as from those we affect to have.
LA ROCHEFOUCAULD, *Maxims*

420. All affectation is the vain and ridiculous attempt of poverty to appear rich. LAVATER

421. Affectation endeavors to correct natural defects, and has always the laudable aim of pleasing, though always misses it. LOCKE

422. Affectation hides three times as many virtues as charity does sins.
HORACE MANN

423. Die of a rose in aromatic pain.
POPE

424. I will not call vanity and affectation twins, because, more properly, vanity is the mother, and affectation is the darling daughter. Vanity is the

sin, and affectation is the punishment; the first may be called the root of self-love, the other the fruit. Vanity is never at its full growth till it spreadeth into affectation, and then it is complete. SIR H. SAVILLE

See also: 586, 734, 800, 1202, 1393, 3643, 4233, 4551.

AFFECTION

Related Subjects: Friendship, Kiss, Love, Tenderness.

431. There are wonders in true affection: it is a body of enigmas, mysteries, and riddles; wherein two so become one, as they both become two.
SIR THOMAS BROWNE,
Religio Medici

432. What's affection, but the power we give another to torment us?
BULWER-LYTTON, *Darnley*

433.
Alas! our young affections run to waste,
Or water but the desert.
BYRON, *Childe Harold*

434. With affection beaming in one eye and calculation shining out of the other.
DICKENS, *Martin Chuzzlewit*

435. What is so pleasant as these jets of affection which make a young world for me again?
EMERSON, *Essays*

436.
I never heard
Of any true affection but 'twas nipped. THOMAS MIDDLETON,
Blurt, Master-Constable

437.
When affection only speaks,
Truth is not always there.
THOMAS MIDDLETON, *The Old Law*

438. There are two sorts of affection —the love of a woman you respect, and the love for the woman you love.
PINERO,
The Second Mrs. Tanqueray

439. Affection can withstand very severe storms of vigor, but not a long polar frost of indifference. SCOTT

440. My affection hath an unknown bottom like the bay of Portugal.
SHAKESPEARE, *As You Like It*

441.
Affection is a coal that must be cool'd;
Else, suffer'd, it will set the heart on fire.
SHAKESPEARE, *Venus and Adonis*

442.
Of such affection and unbroken faith
As temper life's worst bitterness.
SHELLEY, *The Cenci*

443. One in whose heart Affection had no root. SOUTHEY, *Joan of Arc*

See also: 36, 8981.

AFFLICTION, see Adversity

AGE

Related Subjects: **Antiquity, Babyhood, Childhood, Decay, Past, Time, Youth.**

451. Grow up as soon as you can. It pays. The only time you really live fully is from thirty to sixty.
HERVEY ALLEN, *Anthony Adverse*

452. Alonso of Aragon was wont to say in commendation of age, that age appears to be best in four things,— old wood best to burn, old wine to drink, old friends to trust, and old authors to read. BACON, *Apothegms*

453.
She was not old, nor young, nor at the years
Which certain people call a "certain age,"
Which yet the most uncertain age appears. BYRON, *Beppo*

454.
'Tis said that persons living on annuities
Are longer lived than others.
BYRON, *Don Juan*

455.
A man is as old as he's feeling,
A woman as old as she looks.
MORTIMER COLLINS,
How Old Are You?

456. One of the many things nobody ever tells you about middle age is that it's such a nice change from being young. DOROTHY CANFIELD FISHER

457. I love everything that's old: old friends, old times, old manners, old books, old wine.
GOLDSMITH, *She Stoops to Conquer*

458. Age, like distance, lends a double charm.
O. W. HOLMES, *A Rhymed Lesson*

459. The Grecian ladies counted their age from their marriage, not their birth. HOMER

460. Age is the most terrible misfortune that can happen to any man; other evils will mend, this is every day getting worse.
GEORGE JAMES, *Richelieu*

461. A woman is no older than she looks. *Proverb*

462. As old as the itch. *Proverb*

463. How much more elder art thou

than thy looks.   SHAKESPEARE,
The Merchant of Venice

Old Age

464. Old age is but a second childhood.   ARISTOPHANES, *The Clouds*

465. The hoary head is a crown of glory.   *Bible: Proverbs, xvi, 31*

466. In old age we live under the shadow of Death, which, like a sword of Damocles, may descend at any moment, but we have so long found life to be an affair of being rather frightened than hurt that we have become like the people who live under Vesuvius, and chance it without much misgiving.   SAMUEL BUTLER,
The Way of All Flesh

467. Let him draw out his old age to dotage drop by drop.
CAECILIUS STATIUS, *Hymn*

468. The harvest of old age is the recollection and abundance of blessings previously secured.
CICERO, *De Senectute*

469. Old age, especially an honored old age, has so great authority, that this is of more value than all the pleasures of youth.   *Ibid.*

470. Old age is by nature rather talkative.   *Ibid.*

471. For as I like a young man in whom there is something of the old, so I like an old man in whom there is something of the young; and he who follows this maxim, in body will possibly be an old man, but he will never be an old man in mind.   *Ibid.*

472. Intelligence, and reflection, and judgment, reside in old men, and if there had been none of them, no states could exist at all.   *Ibid.*

473.
Not yet by time completely silver'd o'er,
Bespoke him past the bounds of freakish youth,
But strong for service still, and unimpair'd.   COWPER, *The Task*

474.
Of no distemper, of no blast he died,
But fell like autumn fruit that mellow'd long,—
Even wonder'd at because he dropp'd no sooner.
Fate seem'd to wind him up for fourscore years,
Yet freshly ran he on ten winters more;
Till like a clock worn out with eating time,
The wheels of weary life at last stood still.   DRYDEN, *Oedipus*

475.
Old men in impotence can beget
New wars to kill the lusty young.
Young men can sing: old men forget
That any song was ever sung.
ARTHUR D. FICKE, *Youth and Age*

476. Old age, believe me, is a good and pleasant time. It is true that you are gently shouldered off the stage, but then you are given such a comfortable front stall as spectator, and, if you have really played your part, you are more content to sit down and watch.   JANE E. HARRISON,
Reminiscences of a Student's Life

477. To be seventy years young is sometimes far more cheerful and hopeful than to be forty years old.
O. W. HOLMES

478. Old men are only walking hospitals.   HORACE, *Ars Poetica*

479. When grace is joined with wrinkles, it is adorable. There is an unspeakable dawn in happy old age.
VICTOR HUGO, *Les Misérables*

480. Forty is the old age of youth; fifty is the youth of old age.

VICTOR HUGO

481.
The heads of strong old age are beautiful
Beyond all grace of youth. They have strange quiet,
Integrity, health, soundness, to the full
They've dealt with life and been atempered by it.

ROBINSON JEFFERS, *Promise of Peace*

482. No man is so old but thinks he may yet live another year.

ST. JEROME

483. It is a man's own fault, it is from want of use, if his mind grows torpid in old age.

SAMUEL JOHNSON, *Boswell: Life*

484. The growing infirmities of age manifest themselves in nothing more strongly, than in an inveterate dislike of interruption.

CHARLES LAMB, *That Home is Home Though it is Never so Homely*

485. Old age is the "Front Line" of life, moving into No Man's Land.

STEPHEN LEACOCK,
This Business of Growing Old

486.
Ah, nothing is too late,
Till the tired heart shall cease to palpitate.
Cato learned Greek at eighty; Sophocles
Wrote his grand Oedipus and Simonides
Bore off the prize of verse from his compeers,
When each had numbered more than fourscore years.
Chaucer, at Woodstock with the nightingales,
At sixty wrote the Canterbury Tales;

Goethe at Weimar, toiling to the last,
Completed Faust when eighty years were past.

LONGFELLOW, *Morituri Salutamus*

487.
For age is opportunity no less
Than youth itself, though in another dress,
And as the evening twilight fades away
The sky is filled with stars, invisible by day.

LONGFELLOW, *Morituri Salutamus*

488. As if old age were never kindly as well as frosty; as if it had no reverend graces of its own as good in their way as the noisy impertinence of childhood, the elbowing self-conceit of youth, or the pompous mediocrity of middle life!

LOWELL,
A Good Word for Winter

489. A comely olde man as busie as a bee.

JOHN LYLY,
Euphues & his England

490. Whoever saw old age which did not praise the past time and blame the present?

MONTAIGNE, *Essays*

491. The old men know when an old man dies.

OGDEN NASH, *Old Men*

492. Be old betimes, that thou mayst long be so.

Proverb

493. An old man hath the almanack in his body.

Proverb

494. A man, as he manages himself, may die old at thirty or young at eighty.

Proverb

495. The young man who has not wept is a savage, and the old man who will not laugh is a fool.

SANTAYANA, *Dialogues in Limbo*

496.
Thus aged men, full loth and slow,
The vanities of life forego,

And count their youthful follies o'er,
Till Memory lends her light no more.
SCOTT, *Rokeby*

497.
His withered cheek, and tresses gray,
Seem'd to have known a better day.
SCOTT,
The Lay of the Last Minstrel

498. Therefore my age is as a lusty winter, frosty, but kindly.
SHAKESPEARE, *As You Like It*

499. They say an old man is twice a child. SHAKESPEARE, *Hamlet*

500.
But age, with his stealing steps,
Hath claw'd me in his clutch.
SHAKESPEARE *Hamlet*

501.
An old man, broken with the storms of state,
Is come to lay his weary bones among ye;
Give him a little earth for charity!
SHAKESPEARE, *Henry VIII*

502. A poor, infirm, weak, and despised old man. SHAKESPEARE,
King Lear

503.
          My way of life
Is fall'n into the sere, the yellow leaf;
And that which should accompany old age,
As honour, love, obedience, troops of friends,
I must not look to have.
SHAKESPEARE, *Macbeth*

504. A good old man, sir; he will be talking; as they say, When the age is in, the wit is out.
SHAKESPEARE,
Much Ado About Nothing

505.
          I am declined
Into the vale of years.
SHAKESPEARE, *Othello*

506.
Crabbed age and youth cannot live together,
Youth is full of pleasure, age is full of care. SHAKESPEARE,
The Passionate Pilgrim

507. *Capt. Shotover:* Take care: I am in my dotage. Old men are dangerous: it doesn't matter to them what is going to happen to the world.
BERNARD SHAW, *Heartbreak House*

508.
This is our portion at the close of life,
Strengthless—companionless.
SOPHOCLES, *Oedipus Coloneus*

509. No man loves life like him that's growing old. SOPHOCLES, *Acrisius*

510. What with its crude awakenings can youth know of the rich returns of awareness to elderly people from their afternoon naps; of their ironic thoughts and long retrospections, and the sweetness they taste of not being dead?
LOGAN PEARSALL SMITH,
Afterthoughts

511. Looked as if she had walked straight out of the ark.
SYDNEY SMITH,
Lady Holland's Memoir

512. That sign of old age, extolling the past at the expense of the present.
SYDNEY SMITH,
Lady Holland's Memoir

513. Age in a virtuous person, of either sex, carries in it an authority which makes it preferable to all the pleasures of youth.
SIR RICHARD STEELE, *The Spectator*

514. She's no chicken; she's on the wrong side of thirty, if she be a day.
SWIFT, *Polite Conversation*

515. Every man desires to live long, but no man would be old.

SWIFT,
Thoughts on Various Subjects

516. Age carries all things, even the mind, away.   VERGIL, *Bucolics*

517.
Say what thou wilt, the young are
  happy never.
Give me bless'd Age, beyond the fire
  and fever,—
Past the delight that shatters, hope
  that stings,
And eager flutt'ring of life's ignorant
  wings.
WILLIAM WATSON, *Epigram*

518.
Thanks in old age,—thanks ere I go,
For health, the midday sun, the im-
  palpable air—for life, mere life,
For precious ever-lingering memo-
  ries.
WALT WHITMAN,
Thanks in Old Age

519. I delight in men over seventy. They always offer one the devotion of a lifetime.   OSCAR WILDE,
A Woman of No Importance

520.
But an old age serene and bright,
And lovely as a Lapland night,
  Shall lead thee to thy grave.
WORDSWORTH, *To a Young Lady*

521.
When you are old and gray and full
  of sleep,
And nodding by the fire take down
  this book.
W. B. YEATS, *When You are Old*

Age in the Sense of Period

522. The age of great men is going; the epoch of the ant-hill, of life in multiplicity is beginning.
AMIEL, *Journal*

523. Every age has its pleasures, its style of wit and its own ways.
BOILEAU, *The Art of Poetry*

524.
                    Every age,
Heroic in proportions, double-faced,
Looks backward and before, expects
  a morn
And claims an epos.
ELIZABETH B. BROWNING,
Aurora Leigh

525. To complain of the age we live in, to murmur at the present posses-sors of power, to lament the past, to conceive extravagant hopes of the fu-ture, are the common dispositions of the greatest part of mankind.
BURKE, *Thoughts on the Cause of the Present Discontents*

526. This Age will serve to make a very pretty farce for the next.
SAMUEL BUTLER, *Remains*

527. Oh, this age! how tasteless and ill-bred it is!   CATULLUS, *Odes*

528. Conspire to censure and expose the age.   WENTWORTH DILLON,
Essay on Translated Verse

529. The riddle of the age has for each a private solution.
EMERSON, *Conduct of Life*

530. Ye unborn ages, crowd not on my soul.   THOMAS GRAY, *The Bard*

531. In this Age, when it is said of a man, He knows *how to live,* it may be implied he is not very honest.
LORD HALIFAX, *Works*

532.
                  The ages roll
Forward; and forward with them,
  draw my soul
Into time's infinite sea.
OWEN MEREDITH, *The Wanderer*

533.
For each age is a dream that is dying,
Or one that is coming to birth.
ARTHUR O'SHAUGHNESSY,
The Music-Makers

534. What an age is this and what a world is this! that a man cannot live without playing the knave and dissimulation. SAMUEL PEPYS, *Diary*

535. One is always of his age and especially he who least appears so.
SAINTE-BEUVE

536.
The time is out of joint; O cursed spite,
That ever I was born to set it right!
SHAKESPEARE, *Hamlet*

537. The age is grown so picked that the toe of the peasant comes so near the heel of the courtier he galls his kibe.   SHAKESPEARE, *Hamlet*

538. O miserable age!
SHAKESPEARE, *Henry VI*

539. These most brisk and giddy-paced times.   SHAKESPEARE,
Twelfth Night

540.
The age is dull and mean. Men creep, Not walk.
WHITTER, *Lines Inscribed to Friends under Arrest for Treason Against the Slave Power.*

541. Born in an age more curious than devout.
EDWARD YOUNG, *Night Thoughts*

See also 200, 326, 851, 1171, 1468, 1475, 1576, 1722, 1753, 2722, 2793, 2868, 3068, 3281, 3283, 3467, 4401, 4632, 5124, 8277, 11764, 12284, 15869, 17824, 20485, 21825.

AGITATION

Related Subjects: Distrust, Excitement, Politics, Worry.

551. The chief complaint leveled against the agitator is that he takes people who are content with their lot and makes them dissatisfied . . . Posterity has picked practically all its heroes from its agitators.
HEYWOOD BROUN, *The Agitator*

AGRICULTURE, see Farming

AIM, see Purpose

ALCHEMY

Related Subjects: Gold, Philosophy, Science.

561. Alchemy may be compared to the man who told his sons he had left them gold buried somewhere in his vineyard; where they by digging found no gold but by turning up the mould about the roots of their vines, procured a plentiful vintage. So the search and endeavors to make gold have brought many useful inventions and instructive experiments to light.
BACON

562.
If by fire
Of sooty coal the empiric alchymist
Can turn, or holds it possible to turn,
Metals of drossest ore to perfect gold.
MILTON, *Paradise Lost*

563. The foolish alchymist sought to make gold of iron, and made iron of gold.   *Proverb*

564. No alchymy like saving.
Proverb

565. I have always looked upon alchemy in natural philosophy to be like enthusiasm in divinity, and to have troubled the world much to the same purpose.   SIR WILLIAM TEMPLE

ALE AND BEER

Related Subjects: Drinking, Wine.

571.
I, being dry, sit idly sipping here
My beer.   GEORGE ARNOLD, *Beer*

572. A double glass o' the inwariable.
          DICKENS, *Pickwick Papers*

573. God made yeast, as well as
dough, and loves fermentation just
as dearly as he loves vegetation.
          EMERSON, *Essays*

574.
Oh many a peer of England brews
Livelier liquor than the Muse,
And malt does more than Milton can
To justify God's ways to man.
Ale, man, ale's the stuff to drink,
For fellows whom it hurts to think.
Look into the pewter pot
To see the world as the world's not.
          A. E. HOUSMAN,
              A Shropshire Lad

575. The man who called it "near
beer" was a bad judge of distance.
PHILANDER JOHNSON, *Shooting Stars*

576. Then to the spicy nut-brown ale.
          MILTON, *L'Allegro*

577. Throw all the beer and spirits
into the Irish Channel, the English
Channel, and the North Sea for a year,
and people in England would be infinitely better. It would certainly
solve all the problems with which the
philanthropists, the physicians, and
the politicians have to deal.
          SIR WILLIAM OSLER,
              Life of Sir William Osler

578.
Back and side go bare, go bare,
  Both foot and hand go cold:
But, belly, God send thee good ale
  enough
  Whether it be new or old.
          BISHOP STILL,
              Gammer Gurton's Needle

579.
All-powerful Ale! whose sorrow-
  soothing sweets
Oft I repeat in vacant afternoon.
          THOMAS WARTON,
              A Panegyric on Oxford Ale

See also: 16107 17099.

ALEXANDER THE GREAT

581. Verily, if I were not Alexander,
I would be Diogenes.
          ALEXANDER, TO DIOGENES,
              Plutarch: Alexander

582. A tomb now suffices him for
whom the whole world was not sufficient. *Greek Epigram on Alexander*

583. If Alexander wishes to be a god,
let him set up as a god.
              Greek Epigram

584. Whenever Alexander heard
Philip had taken any town of importance, or won any signal victory,
instead of rejoicing at it altogether,
he would tell his companions that his
father would anticipate everything,
and leave him and them no opportunities of performing great and illustrious actions.   PLUTARCH, *Lives*

585. Alexander wept when he heard
from Anaxarchus that there was an
infinite number of worlds, and his
friends asking him if any accident
had befallen him, he returned this answer: Do you not think it is a matter
worthy of lamentation that, where
there is such a vast multitude of
worlds, we have not yet conquered
one?   PLUTARCH,
              On the Tranquillity of the Mind

586. Alexander was below a man,
when he affected to be a god.
              Proverb

587. Alexander, the conqueror of so many kings and nations, was laid low by anger and grief.   SENECA

See also: 173, 7289, 13398.

ALLEGORY

Related Subjects: Symbol.

591. Allegories, when well chosen, are like so many tracks of light in a discourse, that make everything about them clear and beautiful.   ADDISON

592. A man conversing in earnest, if he watch his intellectual processes, will find that a material image, more or less luminous, arises in his mind, contemporaneous with every thought, which furnishes the vestment of the thought. Hence, good writing and brilliant discourse are perpetual allegories.   EMERSON

ALMS, see Charity

ALTERNATIVE, see Choice

AMBASSADOR

Related Subjects: Diplomacy, Statesman.

601. All ambassadors make love and are very nice and useful to people who travel.   BERNARD SHAW,
Misalliance

602. An ambassador is an honest man sent to lie abroad for the commonwealth.   SIR HENRY WOTTON,
Reliquiae Wottonianae

See also: 15844.

AMBER

611. We see spiders, flies, or ants entombed and preserved forever in amber, a more than royal tomb.
BACON, *Historia Vitae et Mortis*

612.
The bee enclosed and through the amber shown,
Seems buried in the juice which was his own.   MARTIAL, *Epigrams*

613.
Pretty! in amber to observe the forms
Of hairs, or straws, or dirt, or grubs, or worms!
The things, we know, are neither rich nor rare,
But wonder how the devil they got there.
POPE, *Epistle to Dr. Arbuthnot*

AMBITION

Related Subjects: Aspiration, Desire, Fame, Glory, Success, Vanity, Will, Zeal.

621. I commend you to the goddess of ambition. She teaches the great virtues of labor, aggression and perseverance.   JOHN PETER ALTGELD

622. Ambition has no risk.
BULWER-LYTTON, *Richelieu*

623. I would not give a fig for the young man who does not already see himself the partner or the head of an important firm.
ANDREW CARNEGIE,
Empire of Business

624. All ambitions are lawful except those which climb upward on the miseries or credulities of mankind.
JOSEPH CONRAD, *A Personal Record*

625. Low ambition and the thirst of praise.   COWPER, *Table Talk*

626.
I had the ambition, by which sin
The Angels fell;
I climbed and, step by step, O Lord,
Ascended into Hell.
WILLIAM H. DAVIES, *Ambition*

627.

But wild Ambition loves to slide, not stand,
And Fortune's ice prefers to Virtue's land.
DRYDEN, *Absalom and Achitophel*

628. How many "coming men" has one known! Where on earth do they all go to?   PINERO,
The Notorious Mrs. Ebbsmith

629. The trap to the high-born is ambition.   *Proverb*

630. He that hews above his height may have chips in his eyes.   *Proverb*

631. Climb not too high lest the fall be the greater.   *Proverb*

632. That's villainous, and shows a most pitiful ambition in the fool that uses it.   SHAKESPEARE, *Hamlet*

633. Chok'd with ambition of the meaner sort.   SHAKESPEARE,
Henry VI

634.

I charge thee, fling away ambition:
By that sin fell the angels.
SHAKESPEARE, *Henry VIII*

635. From his ambitious finger.
SHAKESPEARE, *Henry VIII*

636. Ambition should be made of sterner stuff.
SHAKESPEARE, *Julius Caesar*

637.

'Tis a common proof,
That lowliness is young ambition's ladder,
Whereto the climber-upward turns his face;
But when he once attains the upmost round,
He then unto the ladder turns his back,

Looks in the clouds, scorning the base degrees
By which he did ascend.
SHAKESPEARE, *Julius Caesar*

638.

I have no spur
To prick the sides of my intent, but only
Vaulting ambition, which o'erleaps itself
And falls on the other.
SHAKESPEARE, *Macbeth*

See also: 585, 1487, 1498, 1699, 2478, 4111, 11925, 18538.

AMERICA

Related Subjects: Constitution, Democracy, History, Patriotism.

641. If we learn to think in terms of the duties which we freely owe to the great society which we in America are building, and also learn to revaluate our lives in terms of what a standard of living is in the fullest, and not merely a material scale of values, then the American Dream may yet come true in a free democracy.   JAMES TRUSLOW ADAMS,
The Record of America

642. Driven from every other corner of the earth, freedom of thought and the right of private judgment in matters of conscience direct their course to this happy country as their last asylum.   SAMUEL ADAMS

643.

Three thousand miles of borderline,—
nor fort nor armed host
On all this frontier neighbor-ground from east to western coast;
A spectacle to conjure with—a thought to stir the blood!
A living proof to all the world of faith in brotherhood.
Anonymous, Our Borderline

644.
America, half-brother of the world!
With something good and bad of
  every land.
       PHILIP J. BAILEY, *Festus*

645.
  America! America!
God shed His grace on thee,
And crown thy good with brother-
  hood
From sea to shining sea!
       KATHARINE LEE BATES,
         America the Beautiful

646.
You can be a Finn or a Dane and an
  American.
You can be German or French and an
  American,
Jew, Bohunk, Nigger, Mick—all the
  dirty names
We call each other—and yet Ameri-
  can.
       STEPHEN VINCENT BENET,
         Nightmare at Noon

647.
Oh yes, I know the faults and the
  other side,
The lyncher's rope, the bought jus-
  tice, the wasted land,
The scale on the leaf, the borers in
  the corn,
The finks with their clubs, the gray
  sky of relief,
All the long shame of our hearts and
  the long disunion.
I am merely remarking—as a country
  we try.
As a country, I think we try.
       STEPHEN VINCENT BENET,
         Nightmare at Noon

648.
I have fallen in love with American
  names,
The sharp names that never get fat,

The snakeskin-titles of mining-
  claims,
The plumed war-bonnet of Medicine
  Hat,
Tucson and Deadwood and Lost
  Mule Flat.
       STEPHEN VINCENT BENET,
         American Names

649.
I shall not rest quiet in Montparnasse
I shall not lie easy at Winchelsea.
You may bury my body in Sussex
  grass,
You may bury my tongue at Champ-
  médy.
I shall not be there. I shall rise and
  pass,
Bury my heart at Wounded Knee.
       STEPHEN VINCENT BENET,
         American Names

650. God Bless America!
      Title of popular song by
      IRVING BERLIN

651. As a matter of fact, very few
of us correctly understand what we
mean by this "Americanism" and
"Americanization" that we have become so wrought up about. We think
of Americanism as something we can
imbibe, understand and practice in
our lives only if we are born in the
United States of America. . . .
Americanism is not alone a matter
of birth or ancestry. The real America is an ideal—a vision yet to be
fulfilled.   EDWARD BOK,
The Americanization of Edward Bok

652. To be "one hundred per cent
American" a man must be one hundred per cent Christian. He must always and everywhere observe the
Golden Rule. He must put in practice the precepts of the Sermon on
the Mount. In all sacred and profane
history there never lived but one Man
who could qualify as a hundred per

cent American; and men who deny or abridge the rights of others for religion or race should remember that that Man was a Jew!

EDWARD BOK,
The Americanization of Edward Bok

653. Our government, conceived in freedom and purchased with blood, can be preserved only by constant vigilance. May we guard it as our children's richest legacy, for what shall it profit our nation if it shall gain the whole world and lose "the spirit that prizes liberty as the heritage of all men in all lands everywhere?"

WILLIAM JENNINGS BRYAN

654.
Here the free spirit of mankind, at length,
   Throws its last fetters off; and who shall place
A limit to the giant's unchained strength,
   Or curb his swiftness in the forward race? BRYANT, *The Ages*

655. Young man, there is America, which at this day serves for little more than to amuse you with stories of savage men and uncouth manners, yet shall, before you taste of death, show itself equal to the whole of that commerce which now attracts the envy of the world. BURKE,
Speech on Conciliation

656. I never use the word "Nation" in speaking of the United States; I always use the word "Union," or "Confederacy." We are not a Nation, but a Union, a confederacy of equal and sovereign States.

JOHN C. CALHOUN

657. There was a state without king or nobles; there was a church without a bishop; there was a people governed by grave magistrates which it had selected, and by equal laws which it had framed. RUFUS CHOATE

658. Our country! in her intercourse with foreign nations may she always be in the right; but our country, right or wrong!

COMMODORE STEPHEN DECATUR

659. The United States of America —the greatest potential force, material, moral, and spiritual, in the world. G. LOWES DICKINSON,
The Choice Before Us

660. U. S. A. is the slice of a continent. U. S. A. is a group of holding companies, some aggregations of trade unions, a set of laws bound in calf, a radio network, a chain of moving picture theatres, a column of stock-quotations rubbed out and written by a Western Union boy on a blackboard, a public library full of old newspapers and dog-eared history books with protests scrawled on the margins in pencil. U. S. A. is the world's greatest river valley fringed with mountains and hills, U. S. A. is a set of big-mouthed officials with too many bank-accounts, U. S. A. is a lot of men buried in their uniforms in Arlington Cemetery, U. S. A. is the letters at the end of an address when you are away from home. But mostly U. S. A. is the speech of the people. JOHN DOS PASSOS,
U. S. A.

661. We in America produce 92 per cent of the world's natural gas, not counting the speeches of Senators and Congressmen on Saving Democracy. THEODORE DREISER

662. America means opportunity, freedom, power. EMERSON, *Lectures*

663. American life storms about us daily, and is slow to find a tongue.
EMERSON, *Letters and Social Aims*

664. America is a country of young men.
EMERSON, *Society and Solitude*

665. Our country has liberty without license and authority without despotism.   CARDINAL GIBBONS

666.
They love their land because it is
    their own,
    And scorn to give aught other rea-
        son why;
Would shake hands with a king upon
    his throne,
And think it kindness to his Maj-
    esty.
FITZ-GREENE HALLECK, *Connecticut*

667. Private journalists, essayists, political philosophers are equally at cross-purposes. They produce torrents of tracts and orations on the American way, the American dream, the American mission, the American destiny. They prove principally—by their conflicts of views—that we are in much doubt today as to what Americanism is.
WILLIAM HARD

668. I am an American. I am conceited enough to think that no better American lives than myself. Equally am I convinced that I am the better American because I am Irish, and the better Irishman, because I am an American.   CARDINAL HAYES

669. An unprotected and feebly defended America should be as unthinkable and undesirable as a military and overarmed America.
CARDINAL HAYES

670. America is the only place where man is full grown!
O. W. HOLMES,
The Professor at the Breakfast Table

671.
I do not know beneath what sky
    Nor on what seas shall be thy fate;
I only know it shall be high,
    I only know it shall be great.
RICHARD HOVEY,
Unmanifest Destiny

672. We shall maintain our constitutional guarantees only so long as they embody the American spirit. The fundamental need is not satisfied by the fundamental law, but only by a tenacious grasp of the fundamental principles which are back of that law —the principles of liberty to be respected, illustrated and applied by law.   CHARLES EVANS HUGHES

673. It's a complex fate, being an American, and one of the responsibilities it entails is fighting against a superstitious valuation of Europe.
HENRY JAMES

674.
While this America settles in the
    mould of its vulgarity, heavily
    thickening to empire,
And protest, only a bubble in the
    molten mass, pops and sighs out,
    and the mass hardens.
ROBINSON JEFFERS,
Shine, Perishing Republic

675. Peace, commerce, and honest friendship with all nations,—entangling alliances with none.
JEFFERSON

676. The less we have to do with the enmities of Europe the better. Not in our day, but at no distant one, we may shake a rod over the heads of all, which may make the stoutest tremble. But I hope our wisdom will grow with our power, and teach us that the less we use our power the greater it will be. JEFFERSON

677. I am willing to love all mankind, except an American.
SAMUEL JOHNSON, *Boswell: Life*

678. It is notable that the tendency to strong presidents coincides with epochs of difficulty in the United States; it is notable, also, that strong presidents have come with greater frequency in more recent times than in early American history.
• HAROLD J. LASKI,
The American Presidency

679. Intellectually I know that America is no better than any other country; emotionally I know she is better than every other country.
SINCLAIR LEWIS

680. I have often inquired of myself what great principle or idea it was, that kept this Confederacy so long together. It was not the mere separation of the colonies from the Motherland—but that sentiment in the Declaration of Independence which gave *liberty,* not alone to the people of this country, but *hope* to all the world, for all future time. It was that which gave promise that in due time the weights would be lifted from the shoulders of *all*—and that *all* should have an equal chance. This is the sentiment embodied in the Declaration of Independence. LINCOLN

681. Let every man honor and love the land of his birth and the race from which he springs and keep their memory green. It is a pious and honorable duty. But let us have done with British-Americans and Irish-Americans and German-Americans, and so on, and all be Americans.
HENRY CABOT LODGE

682. If a man is going to be an American at all let him be so without any qualifying adjectives; and if he is going to be something else, let him drop the word American from his personal description.
HENRY CABOT LODGE

683. Of "Americanism" of the right sort we cannot have too much. Mere vaporing and boasting become a nation as little as a man. But honest, outspoken pride and faith in our country are infinitely better and more to be respected than the cultivated reserve which sets it down as ill-bred and in bad taste ever to refer to our country except by way of deprecation, criticism, or general negation.
HENRY CABOT LODGE

684.
Sail on, O Ship of State!
Sail on, O Union, strong and great!
Humanity with all its fears,
With all the hopes of future years,
Is hanging breathless on thy fate.
LONGFELLOW,
The Building of the Ship

685. No, America needs no instruction in the things that concern democracy. But instruction is one thing —and another is memory, reflection, re-examination, the recall to consciousness of a spiritual and moral possession of which it would be dangerous to feel too secure and too confident. No worth-while possession can be neglected.
THOMAS MANN,
The Coming Victory of Democracy

686. In the wars of the European powers in matters relating to themselves we have never taken any part, nor does it comport with our policy so to do. It is only when our rights are invaded or seriously menaced that we resent injuries or make preparation for our defence.

JAMES MONROE

687. We owe it, therefore, to candor, and to the amicable relations existing between the United States and those [European] powers, to declare that we should consider any attempt on their part to extend their system to any portion of this hemisphere, as dangerous to our peace and safety.

JAMES MONROE

688. The American continents . . . are henceforth not to be considered as subjects for future colonization by any European powers.   JAMES MONROE

689. The American nation is a creative vision sane with straight-lined ideas. When I talk with men of the United States it does not occur to me to use diplomacy for winning or persuading them. The American spirit is crystalline. One has to know how to take her and possibly win her over with a watchful responsiveness rather than with cunning words.

MUSSOLINI, *Autobiography*

690. I believe in the United States of America as a government of the people, by the people, for the people; whose just powers are derived from the consent of the governed; a democracy in a republic; a sovereign nation of many sovereign states; a perfect union, one and inseparable; established upon those principles of freedom, equality, justice and humanity for which American patriots sacrificed their lives and fortunes. I therefore believe it is my duty to my country to love it, to support its constitution, to obey its laws, to respect its flag and to defend it against all enemies.

WILLIAM TYLER PAGE,
The American's Creed

691. Not a place upon earth might be so happy as America. Her situation is remote from all the wrangling world, and she has nothing to do but to trade with them.

THOMAS PAINE,
The American Crisis

692. You cannot conquer America.

WILLIAM PITT

693. If I were an American, as I am an Englishman, while a foreign troop was landed in my country I never would lay down my arms,—never! never! never!   WILLIAM PITT

694. The United States never lost a war or won a conference.

WILL ROGERS

695. For more than three centuries we have been building on this continent a free society, a society in which the promise of the human spirit may find fulfillment. Commingled here are the blood and genius of all the peoples of the world who have sought this promise.

FRANKLIN D. ROOSEVELT,
Fireside Chat, May 26, 1940

696. I, too, pray for peace—that the ways of aggression and force may be banished from the earth—but I am determined to face the fact realistically that this nation requires a toughness of moral and physical fibre. Those qualities, I am convinced, the American people hold to a high degree.

FRANKLIN D. ROOSEVELT, *Message
to Congress, May 16, 1940*

697. It will never be possible for any length of time for any group of the American people, either by reason of wealth or learning or inheritance or economic power, to retain any mandate, any permanent authority to arrogate to itself the political control of American public life.

FRANKLIN D. ROOSEVELT, *Address, Little Rock, Ark., June 10, 1936*

698. Every American takes pride in our tradition of hospitality to men of all races and all creeds. We must be constantly vigilant against the attacks of intolerance and injustice. We must scrupulously guard the civil rights and civil liberties of all citizens, whatever their background. We must remember that any oppression, any injustice, any hatred, is a wedge designed to attack our civilization.

FRANKLIN D. ROOSEVELT

699. There is a homely adage which runs, "Speak softly and carry a big stick; you will go far." If the American nation will speak softly and yet build and keep at a pitch of the highest training a thoroughly efficient navy, the Monroe Doctrine will go far. THEODORE ROOSEVELT

700. I care nothing for a man's creed or his birthplace, or descent—but I regard him as an unworthy citizen unless he is an American and nothing else. THEODORE ROOSEVELT

701. O prairie mother, I am one of your boys. I have loved the prairie as a man with a heart shot full of pain over love.

CARL SANDBURG, *Prairie*

702. The American people never carry an umbrella. They prepare to walk in eternal sunshine.

ALFRED E. SMITH

703. For a steady self-esteem and indomitable confidence in our own courage, greatness, magnanimity, who can compare with Britons, except their children across the Atlantic?

THACKERAY, *The Virginians*

704. A nation of 130,000,000 people does not give up supinely what five generations of its ancestors have maintained—a free Atlantic and a free Pacific.

DOROTHY THOMPSON, *On the Record*

705. The United States is not a nation of people which in the long run allows itself to be pushed around.

DOROTHY THOMPSON, *On the Record*

706. Picture to yourself, my dear friend, if you can, a society which comprises all the nations of the world —English, French, German: people differing from one another in language, in beliefs, in opinions; in a word, a society possessing no roots, no memories, no prejudices, no routine, no common ideas, no national character, yet with a happiness a hundred times greater than our own. . . . What is the connecting link between these so different elements? How are they welded into one people? *By community of interests.* That is the secret.   DE TOCQUEVILLE, *Democracy in America*

707. Don't sell America short.

Traditional

708. 'Tis our true policy to steer clear of permanent alliances, with any portion of the foreign world.

WASHINGTON

709. Thank God! I—I also—am an American!   DANIEL WEBSTER

710. I shall know but one country. The ends I aim at shall be my country's, my God's, and Truth's.

I was born an American; I will live an American; I shall die an American.

DANIEL WEBSTER

711. One country, one constitution, one destiny.   DANIEL WEBSTER

712.

Long, too long America
Traveling roads all even and peaceful
  you learn'd from joys and prosperity only,
But now, ah now, to learn from crises
  of anguish, advancing, grappling
  with direct fate and recoiling not.
      WALT WHITMAN,
      Long, Too Long America

713.

As a strong bird on pinions free,
Joyous, the amplest spaces heaven-
  ward cleaving,
Such be the thought I'd think of thee,
  America,
Such be the recitative I'd bring for
  thee.
    WALT WHITMAN, *Thou Mother*
      with Thy Equal Brood

714.

O America because you build for
  mankind I build for you.
      WALT WHITMAN,
      By Blue Ontario's Shore

715.

I hear America singing, the varied
  carols I hear.
      WALT WHITMAN,
      I Hear America Singing

716. The United States themselves
are essentially the greatest poem. . . .
Here at last is something in the doings
of man that corresponds with the
broadcast doings of the day and
night.   WALT WHITMAN,
    Preface to Leaves of Grass

717.

And thou, America,
Thy offspring towering e'er so high,
  yet higher Thee above all towering,
With Victory on thy left, and at thy
  right hand Law;
Thou Union holding all, fusing, ab-
  sorbing, tolerating all,

Thee, ever thee, I sing.
      WALT WHITMAN,
      Song of the Exposition

718. America is one long expectora-
tion.   OSCAR WILDE

719. The only thing that has ever distinguished America among the nations is that she has shown that all
men are entitled to the benefits of the
law.   WOODROW WILSON

720. Just what is it that America
stands for? If she stands for one thing
more than another, it is for the sovereignty of self-governing people.
      WOODROW WILSON

721. Sometimes people call me an
idealist. Well, that is the way I know
I am an American. America is the
only idealistic nation in the world.
      WOODROW WILSON

722. Americanism consists in utterly
believing in the principles of America.
      WOODROW WILSON

723. Some Americans need hyphens
in their names because only part of
them has come over.
      WOODROW WILSON

724. Our whole duty, for the present,
at any rate, is summed up in the
motto: America First.
      WOODROW WILSON

725.

Pickaxe, shovel, spade, crowbar, hoe,
  and barrow,
Better not invade, Yankees have the
  marrow.
      SAMUEL WOODWORTH,
      The Patriotic Diggers

726. America is God's Crucible, the
great Melting-Pot where all the races
of Europe are melting and re-form-
ing!
ISRAEL ZANGWILL, *The Melting-Pot*

See also: 1492, 2760, 2767, 2816, 3276, 5166, 5615, 5864, 6154, 6155, 6213, 6638, 6900, 7164, 7807, 8152, 8153, 9811, 10893, 11643, 11647, 11667, 11672, 13354, 13855, 13858, 13880, 14300, 14564, 14629, 17698, 20759, 20807, 22063.

AMIABILITY

Related Subjects: Courtesy, Friendship, Good Humor.

731. Good-nature is more agreeable in conversation than wit, and gives a certain air to the countenance which is more amiable than beauty.
ADDISON, *The Spectator*

732. As good-natured a soul as e'er trod on shoe of leather.
CERVANTES, *Don Quixote*

733. We ought to regard amiability as the quality of woman, dignity that of man.   CICERO

734. That constant desire of pleasing, which is the peculiar quality of some, may be called the happiest of all desires in this, that it scarcely ever fails of attaining its ends, when not disgraced by affectation. FIELDING

735. Amiability shines by its own light.   HORACE

736. Good nature without prudence, is foolishness.   *Proverb*

AMUSEMENT

Related Subjects: Cards, Dancing, Fun, Gambling, Holiday, Merriment, Pleasure, Sport, Stage.

741. Encourage innocent amusement.
ADDISON

742. If those who are the enemies of innocent amusements had the direction of the world, they would take away the spring, and youth, the former from the year, the latter from human life.   BALZAC

743. Certain bounds must be observed in our amusements, and we must be careful not to carry things too far and, swept away by our passions, lapse into shameful excess.
CICERO, *De Officiis*

744. Amusement, to an observing mind, is study.   DISRAELI

745. If you would rule the world quietly, you must keep it amused.
EMERSON, *Essays*

746. I am a great friend to public amusements; for they keep people from vice.
SAMUEL JOHNSON, *Boswell: Life*

747. No man is a hypocrite in his pleasures.   SAMUEL JOHNSON

748. You can't live on amusement. It is the froth on water, an inch deep, and then the mud!
GEORGE MACDONALD

749. To find recreation in amusements is not happiness; for this joy springs from alien and extrinsic sources, and is therefore dependent upon and subject to interruption by a thousand accidents, which may minister inevitable affliction. PASCAL

750. Amusement allures and deceives us, and leads us down imperceptibly in thoughtlessness to the grave.
PASCAL

751. Amusement is the happiness of those who cannot think.
POPE, *Thoughts on Various Subjects*

752. The real character of a man is found out by his amusements.
SIR JOSHUA REYNOLDS

753. It is meat and drink to me to see a clown.

SHAKESPEARE, *As You Like It*

754.
What revels are in hand? Is there no play
To ease the anguish of a torturing hour?   SHAKESPEARE,
A Midsummer-Night's Dream

755. We are not amused.

QUEEN VICTORIA

756.
O ye Lorenzos of our age! who deem
One moment unamus'd, a misery.

EDWARD YOUNG, *Night Thoughts*

See also: 1391, 5076.

ANALOGY

Related Subjects: Comparisons, Likeness.

761. Though analogy is often misleading, it is the least misleading thing we have.

SAMUEL BUTLER, *Note-Books*

See also: 913, 20251.

ANARCHY

Related Subjects: Agitation, Chaos, Government, Order, Politics, Rebellion, Revolution.

771. The choking, sweltering, deadly, and killing rule of no rule; the consecration of cupidity and braying of folly, and dim stupidity and baseness, in most of the affairs of men. Slopshirts attainable three-halfpence cheaper by the ruin of living bodies and immortal souls.   CARLYLE

772. There is no grievance that is a fit object of redress by mob law.

LINCOLN

773. If the vicious portion of the population shall be permitted to gather in bands of hundreds and thousands, and burn churches, ravage and rob provision-stores, throw printing presses into rivers, shoot editors, and hang and burn obnoxious persons at pleasure and with impunity, depend on it, this government cannot endure.

LINCOLN

774. In a state of anarchy power is the measure of right.   LUCAN

775. Anarchy is a word which comes from the Greek, and signifies, strictly speaking, *without government:* the state of a people, without any constituted authority, that is, without government.

ENRICO MALATESTA, *Anarchy*

776. Anarchy is the sure consequence of tyranny; or no power that is not limited by laws can ever be protected by them.   MILTON

777. In times of anarchy one may seem a despot in order to be a savior.

MIRABEAU

778. The old cry that Anarchists are haters of mankind, and apostles of wholesale destruction, is beginning to die out. . . Instead of being denounced as human monsters, Anarchists are now accused of being impractical idealists.

JAMES F. MORTON, *Is It All a Dream?*

779. Every anarchist is a baffled dictator.   MUSSOLINI

780. When the rich assemble to concern themselves with the business of the poor it is called charity. When the poor assemble to concern themselves with the business of the rich it is called anarchy.   PAUL RICHARD,
The Scourge of Christ

781.
There lives no greater fiend than Anarchy;
She ruins states, turns houses out of doors,
Breaks up in rout the embattled soldiery.   SOPHOCLES, *Antigone*

782. If the will of man were free, that is, if every man could act as he chose, the whole of history would be a tissue of disconnected accidents.
TOLSTOY, *War and Peace*

See also: 3056, 10522.

ANCESTRY

Related Subjects: Antiquity, Birth, Breeding, Family, Gentleman, Heredity, Nobility, Posterity.

791. He is not from Virginia, we never knew his grandfather.
STEPHEN VINCENT BENET,
John Brown's Body

792.
So that the branch a goodly verdure flings,
I reck not if an acorn gave it birth.
BYRON, *Don Juan*

793. The pride of ancestry increases in the ratio of distance.
G. W. CURTIS, *Prue and I*

794. It is not observed in history that families improve with time. It is rather discovered that the whole matter is like a comet, of which the brightest part is the head; and the tail, although long and luminous, is gradually shaded into obscurity.
G. W. CURTIS, *Prue and I*

795. What! You say a horse is noble because it is good in itself, and the same you say of a falcon or a pearl; but a man shall be called noble because his ancestors were so? Not

with words, but with knives must one answer such a beastly notion.
DANTE

796. *Noblesse oblige.* (Birth compels it. Nobility constrains us. Noble birth imposes the obligation of noble actions.)   DUC DE LEVIS, *Maxims*

797. And seldom three descents continue good.
DRYDEN, *The Wife of Bath*

798. No distinction so little excites envy as that which is derived from ancestors by a long descent.
FENELON, *Telemachus*

799. I am, in point of fact, a particularly haughty and exclusive person, of pre-Adamite ancestral descent. You will understand this when I tell you that I can trace my ancestry back to a protoplasmal primordial atomic globule. W. S. GILBERT, *The Mikado*

800.
Spurn not the nobly born with love affected!
Nor treat with virtuous scorn the well-connected!
W. S. GILBERT, *Iolanthe*

801.
The fairest flower
That ever blossomed on ancestral timber.
W. S. GILBERT, *H. M. S. Pinafore*

802.
Each in his narrow cell forever laid,
The rude forefathers of the hamlet sleep.   THOMAS GRAY,
Elegy in a Country Churchyard

803. Once in every half-century, at longest, a family should be merged into the great, obscure mass of humanity, and forget all about its ancestors.   HAWTHORNE,
The House of the Seven Gables

804. The Jukes were an old family, too.   LILLIAN HELLMAN,
The Children's Hour

805. How convenient it would be to many of our great men and great families of doubtful origin, could they have the privilege of the heroes of yore, who, whenever their origin was involved in obscurity, modestly announced themselves descended from a God.   WASHINGTON IRVING
Knickerbocker's History of New York

806.
Nor stand so much on your gentility,
Which is an airy, and mere borrowed
    thing,
From dead men's dust, and bones,
    and none of yours,
Except you make, or hold it.
    BEN JONSON,
Every Man in His Humour

807. I am my own ancestor.
    MARSHAL JUNOT

808. I don't know who my grandfather was; I am much more concerned to know what his grandson will be.   LINCOLN

809.
i have often noticed that
ancestors never boast
of the descendants who boast
of ancestors i would
rather start a family than
finish one
    DON MARQUIS,
a roach of the taverns

810.
Out of one man a race
Of men innumerable.
    MILTON, *Paradise Lost*

811.
A penniless lass wi' a lang pedigree.
    CAROLINE OLIPHANT,
The Laird o' Cockpen

812. The man who has not anything to boast of but his illustrious ancestors is like a potato—the only good belonging to him is underground.
    SIR THOMAS OVERBURY

813. Every king springs from a race of slaves, and every slave has had kings among his ancestors.
    PLATO, *Thaestetus*

814. It is indeed a desirable thing to be well descended, but the glory belongs to our ancestors.
    PLUTARCH, *Lives*

815. To Harmodius, descended from the ancient Harmodius, when he reviled Iphicrates (a shoemaker's son) for his mean birth, "My nobility," said he, "begins with me, but yours ends in you.   PLUTARCH, *Lives*

816. The younger brother is the ancienter gentleman.   *Proverb*

817. So yourself be good, a fig for your grandfather.   *Proverb*

818. He that boasteth of his ancestors, confesseth he hath no virtue of his own.   *Proverb*

819. From our ancestors come our names; but from our virtues our honours.   *Proverb*

820. Gentility without ability is worse than plain beggary.   *Proverb*

821. As long as a Welsh pedigree.
    Proverb

822.
Depend upon it, my snobbish friend,
Your family thread you can't ascend,
Without good reason to apprehend
You may find it waxed at the farther
    end
    By some plebeian vocation;
Or, worse than that, your boasted
    Line

May end in a loop of stronger twine,
That plagued some worthy relation!
J. G. SAXE,
The Proud Miss MacBride

823. We have all had the same number of forefathers.
SENECA, *Epistulae ad Lucilium*

824. Look in the chronicles; we came in with Richard Conqueror.
SHAKESPEARE,
The Taming of the Shrew

825. The Smiths never had any arms, and have invariably sealed their letters with their thumbs.
SYDNEY SMITH,
Lady Holland's Memoir

826. Each has his own tree of ancestors, but at the top of all sits Probably Arboreal.   STEVENSON,
Memories and Portraits

827. A pedigree reaching as far back as the Deluge.
THACKERAY, *The Rose and the Ring*

828. Whoever serves his country well has no need of ancestors. VOLTAIRE

829.
They that on glorious ancestors enlarge
Produce their debt instead of their discharge.
EDWARD YOUNG, *Love of Fame*

See also: 225, 1382, 11251, 14874.

ANGEL

Related Subjects: Paradise, Saint, Spirit, Vision.

831. He shall give his angels charge over thee, to keep thee in all thy ways.
Bible: Psalms. xci, 11

832. Like angel visits, few and far between.   THOMAS CAMPBELL

833. We are never like angels till our passion dies.   THOMAS DEKKER

834.
In Heaven a spirit doth dwell
  "Whose heart-strings are a lute";
None sing so wildly well
  As the angel Israfel. POE, *Israfel*

835. The guardian angel of life sometimes flies so high that man cannot see it; but he always is looking down upon us, and will soon hover nearer to us.   J. P. RICHTER

836.
A guardian angel o'er his life presiding,
Doubling his pleasures, and his cares dividing.
SAMUEL ROGERS, *Human Life*

837.
An angel! or, if not,
An earthly paragon!
SHAKESPEARE, *Cymbeline*

838. A ministering angel shall my sister be.   SHAKESPEARE, *Hamlet*

839. Angels and ministers of grace defend us!   SHAKESPEARE, *Hamlet*

840. Angels are bright still, though the brightest fell.
SHAKESPEARE, *Macbeth*

841. I'm no angel.
THACKERAY, *Vanity Fair*

See also: 153, 626, 634, 1750, 2668, 3521, 5275, 10062, 12409.

ANGER

Related Subjects: Hatred, Indignation, Irritation, Passion, Resentment, Revenge, Scorn.

851. 'Tis said that wrath is the last thing in a man to grow old.
ALCAEUS, *Scholiast on Sophocles*

852. Anybody can become angry—that is easy; but to be angry with the right person, and to the right degree, and at the right time, and for the right purpose, and in the right way—that is not within everybody's power and is not easy. ARISTOTLE,
Nicomachean Ethics

853. Remember, when you are angry, to say or do nothing until you have repeated the four-and-twenty letters to yourself. ATHENODORUS, *to Caesar Augustus,*
Plutarch: Lives

854. Anger makes dull men witty, but it keeps them poor.
BACON, *Apothegms*

855. Never forget what a man says to you when he is angry.
H. W. BEECHER, *Life Thoughts*

856. A soft answer turneth away wrath: but grievous words stir up anger. *Bible: Proverbs, xv, 1*

857. Let not the sun go down upon your wrath. *Bible: Ephesians, iv, 26*

858.
I was angry with my friend;
I told my wrath, my wrath did end.
I was angry with my foe;
I told it not, my wrath did grow.
BLAKE, *A Poison Tree*

859.
Whare sits our sulky, sullen dame,
Gathering her brows like gathering storm,
Nursing her wrath to keep it warm.
BURNS, *Tam o' Shanter*

860. An angry man opens his mouth and shuts his eyes.
CATO THE CENSOR

861.
He that strives not to stem his anger's tide,

Does a wild horse without a bridle ride.
COLLEY CIBBER, *Love's Last Shift*

862. Rage supplies all with arms. When an angry man thirsts for blood, anything will serve him as a spear.
CLAUDIAN, *Rimanit Telum Ira Facit*

863.
To be wroth with one we love
Doth work like madness in the brain.
COLERIDGE, *Christabel*

864. Whenever you are angry, be assured, that it is not only a present evil, but that you have increased a habit, and added fuel to a fire.
EPICTETUS, *Discourses*

865. Reckon the days in which you have not been angry. I used to be angry every day; now every other day, then every third and fourth day; and if you miss it so long as thirty days, offer a sacrifice of thanksgiving to God. EPICTETUS, *Discourses*

866. Anger and folly walk cheek by jowl; repentance treads on both their heels. FRANKLIN, *Poor Richard*

867. Anger is one of the sinews of the soul; he that wants it hath a maimed mind.
THOMAS FULLER,
Holy and Profane State

868. There ain't no sense in gittin' riled. BRET HARTE, *Jim*

869. Anger, far sweeter than trickling honey, rises like smoke in the breasts of men. HOMER, *Iliad*

870. He who curbs not his anger will wish undone that which vexation and wrath prompted. HORACE, *Epistles*

871.
Anger in its time and place
May assume a kind of grace.

It must have some reason in it,
And not last beyond a minute.
CHARLES AND MARY LAMB, *Anger*

872. The one thet fust gits mad's most ollers wrong.
LOWELL, *The Biglow Papers*

873. Every normal man must be tempted, at times, to spit on his hands, hoist the black flag, and begin slitting throats.
H. L. MENCKEN, *Prejudices*

874. Inextinguishable rage.
MILTON, *Paradise Lost*

875. He best keeps from anger, who remembers that God is always looking upon him.   PLATO

876. Let anger's fire be slow to burn.
Proverb

877. Anger and haste hinder good counsel.   *Proverb*

878. He is a fool who cannot be angry; but he is a wise man who will not.   *Proverb*

879. Two things a man should never be angry at; what he can help, and what he cannot help.   *Proverb*

880. Anger punishes itself. *Proverb*

881. Choler hates a counsellor.
Proverb

882. He that is angry is seldom at ease.   *Proverb*

883. Anger makes a rich man hated, and a poor man scorned.   *Proverb*

884. Anger is often more hurtful than the injury that caused it.   *Proverb*

885. Anger dieth quickly with a good man.   *Proverb*

886. An angry man is again angry with himself, when he returns to reason.
PUBLILIUS SYRUS, *Sententiae*

887. The anger of lovers renews the strength of love.
PUBLILIUS SYRUS, *Sententiae*

888. What, drunk with choler?
SHAKESPEARE, *Henry IV*

889. Men ne'er spend their fury on a child.   SHAKESPEARE, *Henry VI*

890. Touch me with noble anger!
SHAKESPEARE, *King Lear*

891.
Put not another sin upon my head
By urging me to fury.
SHAKESPEARE, *Romeo and Juliet*

892. Not die here in a rage, like a poisoned rat in a hole.   SWIFT

893. When angry, count four; when very angry, swear.
MARK TWAIN,
Pudd'nhead Wilson's Calendar

894.
But, children, you should never let
Such angry passions rise;
Your little hands were never made
To tear each other's eyes.
ISAAC WATTS, *Divine Songs*

See also: 587, 1132, 2715, 2723, 5356, 10155.

ANGLING, see Fishing

ANIMAL

Related Subjects: Ape, Bear, Birds, Cat, Dog, Elephant, Farming, Fox, Horse, Hunting, Instinct, Lion, Mouse, Nature, Ox, Rat, Serpent, Sheep, Snail, Sport, Swine, Tiger, Wolf.

901. Group struggles to the death between animals of the same species, such as occur in human warfare, can hardly be found among nonhuman animals.   W. C. ALLEE,
The Social Life of Animals

902. Men are kinder to animals, on the whole, than they are to their fellows. They select them more wisely, they fit their work more to their shoulders. They do not mistakenly stimulate the beast's discontent . . . they keep every beast in its place— they do not encourage their sheep to yearn, but to grow wool.
           CLARENCE DAY

903. Animals are such agreeable friends; they ask no questions, pass no criticisms.   GEORGE ELIOT

904. Brutality to an animal is cruelty to mankind—it is only the difference in the victim.   LAMARTINE

905. They rejoice each with their kind, lion with lioness, so fitly them in pairs thou hast combined.
           MILTON

906. Both Empedocles and Heraclitus held it for a truth that man could not be altogether cleared from injustice in dealing with beasts as he now does.
           PLUTARCH

907. There is something in the unselfish and self-sacrificing love of a brute, which goes directly to the heart of him who has had frequent occasion to test the paltry friendship and gossamer fidelity of mere Man.
       POE, *The Black Cat*

908. There is in every animal's eye a dim image and gleam of humanity, a flash of strange light through which their life looks out and up to our great mystery of command over them, and claims the fellowship of the creature if not his soul.   RUSKIN

909. I think I could turn and live with animals, they are so placid and self-contain'd.
    WALT WHITMAN, *Song of Myself*

See also: 4708, 12403, 12422, 12478.

ANT

911.
The ant finds kingdoms in a foot of ground.
       STEPHEN VINCENT BENET
           John Brown's Body

912. Go to the ant, thou sluggard; consider her ways, and be wise.
       Bible: Proverbs, vi, 6

913. The instincts of the ant are very unimportant considered as the ant's; but the moment a ray of relation is seen to extend from it to man, and the little drudge is seen to be a monitor, a little body with a mighty heart, then all its habits, even that said to be recently observed, that it never sleeps, become sublime.   EMERSON

914. None preaches better than the ant, and she says nothing.
           FRANKLIN

See also: 114, 522, 611.

ANTICIPATION, see Expectation

ANTIQUITY

Related Subjects: Age, Ancestry, Decay, History, Past, Time.

921. These times are the ancient times, when the world is ancient, and not those which we account ancient *ordine retrogrado,* by a computation backward from ourselves.
    BACON, *Advancement of Learning*

922. Antiquities are history defaced, or some remnants of history which have casually escaped the shipwrecks of time.
    BACON, *Advancement of Learning*

923. Remove not the ancient landmark.   *Bible: Proverbs, xxii, 28*

924. The ancient and honourable.
       Bible: Isaiah, ix, 15

925. I do by no means advise you to throw away your time ransacking, like a dull antiquarian, the minute and unimportant parts of remote and fabulous times. Let blockheads read what blockheads wrote.
LORD CHESTERFIELD

926. Antiquity is the aristocracy of history.   DUMAS

927. How cunningly Nature hides every wrinkle of her inconceivable antiquity under roses and violets and morning dew!   EMERSON

928. The Pyramids themselves, doting with age, have forgotten the names of their founders.
THOMAS FULLER,
Holy and Profane State

929. The ancients built for tomorrow in another world, forgetting that all of us have a today in this. They spent riches and labour to save the souls of their hierarchy, but they kept their laborers so poor that they had no souls to save. They left astounding testimony to human genius and tenacity, but it never seems to have ruffled their consciousness that they fashioned the beautiful with slavery, misery, and blood.
GALSWORTHY, *Castles In Spain*

930. The volumes of antiquity, like medals, may very well serve to amuse the curious; but the works of the moderns, like the current coin of a kingdom, are much better for immediate use.   GOLDSMITH

931. Rich with the spoils of time.
THOMAS GRAY, *Elegy Written in a Country Churchyard*

932. An acute and experienced critic of antiques.   HORACE, *Satires*

933. You praise the fortune and manners of the men of old, and yet, if on a sudden some god were for taking you back to those days, you would refuse every time.   HORACE, *Satires*

934. Antiquity! thou wondrous charm, what art thou? that, being nothing, are everything! When thou *wert,* thou wert not antiquity—then thou wert nothing, but hadst a remoter *antiquity,* as thou calledst it, to look back to with blind veneration; thou thyself being to thyself flat, jejune, modern!
CHARLES LAMB, *Essays of Elia*

935. It is looked upon as insolence for a man to adhere to his own opinion against the current stream of antiquity.   LOCKE

936. Those we call the ancients were really new in everything.   PASCAL

937. The sacred rust of twice ten hundred years!
POPE, *Epistle to Mr. Addison*

938. Antiquity cannot privilege an error, nor novelty prejudice a truth.
Proverb

939. Antiquity is not always a mark of verity.   *Proverb*

940. Time consecrates; and what is gray with age becomes religion.
SCHILLER

941. All those things that are now held to be of the greatest antiquity were at one time new; what we today hold up by example will rank hereafter as precedent.   TACITUS

942.
We are Ancients of the earth,
And in the morning of the times.
TENNYSON, *The Day Dream*

ANVIL

Related Subjects: Blacksmith, Forge.

951.
Hammer away, ye hostile hands,
Your hammers break, God's anvil
   stands.   SAMUEL V. COLE,
             Hammer and Anvil

952. When you are an anvil, hold you
still; when you are a hammer strike
your fill.
GEORGE HERBERT, *Jacula Prudentum*

953.
Lay me on an anvil, O God.
Beat me and hammer me into a crow-
   bar.
Let me pry loose old walls.
Let me lift and loosen old founda-
   tions.
   CARL SANDBURG, *Prayers of Steel*

ANXIETY, see Fear, Worry

APE

Related Subject: Animal.

961. He doth like the ape, that the
higher he climbs the more he shows
his ars.   BACON, *Promus*

962. The ape, vilest of beasts, how
like to us!   QUINTUS ENNIUS

963. It is a trite proverb that an ape
will be an ape, though clad in purple.
ERASMUS, *Praise of Folly*

964. Apes are never more beasts than
when they wear men's clothes.
Proverb

965. An ape is ne'er so like an ape
as when he wears a doctor's cape.
Proverb

966. More new-fangled than an ape;
more giddy in my desires than a
monkey.
   SHAKESPEARE, *As You Like It*

See also: 4778, 7231, 12476.

APOLOGY, see Excuse

APOTHEGMS AND APHORISMS

Related Subjects: Example, Proverbs, Quotation, Wisdom.

971. Collect as pearls the words of
the wise and virtuous.
            ABD-EL-KADER

972. Aphorisms are portable wisdom, the quintessential extracts of
thought and feeling.   W. R. ALGER

973. Proverbs are potted wisdom.
            CHARLES BUXTON

974. A man of maxims only is like
a Cyclops with one eye, and that eye
placed in the back of his head.
            COLERIDGE

975. Books are the beehives of
thought; laconics the honey taken
from them.   JAMES ELLIS

976. Apothegms are, in history, the
same as the pearls of the sand, or the
gold in the mine.   ERASMUS

977. What gems of painting or
statuary are in the world of art, or
what flowers are in the world of
Nature, are gems of thought to the
cultivated and thinking.
            O. W. HOLMES

978. Apothegms form a short cut to
much knowledge.   THOMAS HOOD

979. The excellence of aphorisms
consists not so much in the expression

of some rare or abstruse sentiment, as in the comprehension of some useful truth in few words.
SAMUEL JOHNSON

980. I fancy mankind may come in time to write all aphoristically, except in narration; grow weary of preparation and connection and illustrations, and all those arts by which a big book is made.   SAMUEL JOHNSON

981. Nothing is so useless as a general maxim.
MACAULAY, *On Niccolo Machiavelli*

982. Few of the many wise apothegms which have been uttered, from the time of the seven sages of Greece to that of poor Richard, have prevented a single foolish action.
MACAULAY, *On Niccolo Machiavelli*

983. Abstracts, abridgments, summaries, etc., have the same use with burning glasses,—to collect the diffused rays of wit and learning in authors, and make them point with warmth and quickness upon the reader's imagination.   SWIFT

APPEARANCE

Related Subjects: Affection, Beauty, Dress, Face, Hypocrisy, Ostentation, Scandal, Sight, Worth.

991. Appearances are deceptive.
AESOP, *The Wolf in Sheep's Clothing*

992. Whited sepulchres, which indeed appear beautiful outward, but are within full of dead men's bones.
Bible: Matthew, xxiii, 27

993. Judge not according to the appearance.   *Bible: John, vii, 24*

994. Men are valued not for what they are, but for what they seem to be.
BULWER-LYTTON, *Money*

995. They cover a dunghill with a piece of tapestry when a procession goes by.   CERVANTES, *Don Quixote*

996.
Keep up appearances; there lies the test;
The world will give thee credit for the rest.
Outward be fair, however foul within;
Sin, if thou wilt, but then in secret sin.
CHARLES CHURCHILL, *Night*

997. Good and bad men are each less so than they seem.
COLERIDGE, *Table Talk*

998. Keep up appearances whatever you do.
DICKENS, *Martin Chuzzlewit*

999. Be not hurried away by excitement, but say, "Semblance, wait for me a little. Let me see what you are and what you represent. Let me try you."   EPICTETUS, *Discourses*

1000. Appearances to the mind are of four kinds: Things either are what they appear to be; or they neither are, nor appear to be; or they are, and do not appear to be; or they are not, and yet appear to be. Rightly to aim in all these cases is the wise man's task.   EPICTETUS, *Discourses*

1001.
Things are seldom what they seem,
Skim milk masquerades as cream.
W. S. GILBERT, *H.M.S. Pinafore*

1002. Handsome is that handsome does.
GOLDSMITH, *The Vicar of Wakefield*

1003. Those awful goddesses, Appearances, are to us what the Fates were to the Greeks.
ARTHUR HELPS, *Friends in Council*

1004.

He seem'd
For dignity compos'd and high exploit:
But all was false and hollow.

MILTON, *Paradise Lost*

1005. Things are not always what they seem. PHAEDRUS, *Fables*

1006. O that such an imposing appearance should have no brain!

PHAEDRUS, *Fables*

1007. Handsome is as handsome does.

Proverb

1008. Be as you would seem to be.

Proverb

1009. A straight stick is crooked in the water. *Proverb*

1010.

Thus ornament is but the guiled shore
To a most dangerous sea; the beauteous scarf
Veiling an Indian beauty; in a word,
The seeming truth which cunning time puts on
To entrap the wisest.

SHAKESPEARE,
The Merchant of Venice

1011.

So may the outward shows be least themselves:
The world is still deceived with ornament. SHAKESPEARE,
The Merchant of Venice

1012.

And give to dust that is a little gilt
More laud than gilt o'er-dusted.

SHAKESPEARE,
Troilus and Cressida

1013. By economy and good management,—by a sparing use of ready money and by paying scarcely anybody,—people can manage, for a time

at least, to make a great show with very little means.

THACKERAY, *Vanity Fair*

1014.

Of the terrible doubt of appearances,
Of the uncertainty after all, that we may be deluded,
That may-be reliance and hope are but speculations after all,
That may-be identity beyond the grave is a beautiful fable only,
May-be the things I perceive, the animals, plants, men, hills, shining and flowing waters,
The skies of day and night, colors, densities, forms, may-be these are (as doubtless they are) only apparitions, and the real something has yet to be known.

WALT WHITMAN,
Of the Terrible Doubt of Appearances

1015. It is only shallow people who do not judge by appearances.

OSCAR WILDE,
The Picture of Dorian Gray

See also: 461, 1861, 9104.

APPEASEMENT

Related Subjects: Isolation, Neutrality.

1021. I do not believe that we can make progress in European appeasement . . . if we allow the impression to gain currency abroad that we yield to constant pressure.

ANTHONY EDEN, *Upon resigning from Chamberlain Government, Feb. 21, 1938*

1022. My good friends, this is the second time in our history that there has come back from Germany to Downing Street peace with honor. . . . I believe it is peace for our time.

. . . I recommend you to go home and sleep quietly in your beds.

NEVILLE CHAMBERLAIN, *Alighting from the plane on his return from Munich, Sept. 25, 1938*

1023. Does not the little man know that history will judge him as harshly as the pottiest appeaser? How often can one individual be betrayed without losing a little virtue on his own account? Democracy ought to have a better plot than "Nellie, the Beautiful Cloak Model." It is not enough to say: "That man betrayed me." Why did you let him? Are you a dynamic force or a flower girl?

SAMUEL GRAFTON, *I'd Rather Be Right*

1024. It is useless for the sheep to pass resolutions in favour of vegetarianism, while the wolf remains of a different opinion.   DEAN INGE

See also: 3804, 3810, 11170, 14817, 14840, 14846, 14848, 17372, 21994.

APPETITE

Related Subjects: Desire, Eating, Food, Hunger, Lust.

1031. These appetites are very humiliating weaknesses. That our grace depends so largely upon animal condition is not quite flattering to those who are hyperspiritual.

H. W. BEECHER

1032. That I have appetite, digest, and thrive—that boon's for me.

BROWNING, *Asolando*

1033. The youth who follows his appetites too soon seizes the cup, before it has received its best ingredients, and by anticipating his pleasures, robs the remaining parts of life of their share, so that his eagerness only pro-

duces a manhood of imbecility and an age of pain.   GOLDSMITH

1034. Our appetites, of one or another kind, are excellent spurs to our reason, which might otherwise but feebly set about the great ends of preserving and continuing the species.

CHARLES LAMB

1035.
Why, she would hang on him,
As if increase of appetite had grown
By what it fed on.

SHAKESPEARE, *Hamlet*

1036. Appetite, a universal wolf.
SHAKESPEARE, *Troilus and Cressida*

1037.
'Tis not the meat, but 'tis the appetite
Makes eating a delight.

SIR JOHN SUCKLING, *Of Thee, King Boy*

1038. No man's body is as strong as his appetites, but Heaven has corrected the boundlessness of his voluptuous desires by stinting his strength and contracting his capacities.

JOHN TILLOTSON

1039. Choose rather to punish your appetites than to be punished by them.
TYRIUS MAXIMUS

See also: 5803, 18305.

APPLAUSE

Related Subjects: Admiration, Compliment, Fame, Popularity, Praise.

1041. He too serves a certain purpose who only stands and cheers.

HENRY ADAMS, *The Education of Henry Adams*

1042. When the million applaud you, seriously ask yourself what harm you have done; when they censure you, what good!   C. C. COLTON

1043. Applause is the spur of noble minds, the end and aim of weak ones.

C. C. COLTON

1044.
O popular applause! what heart of man
Is proof against thy sweet, seducing charms? COWPER, *The Task*

1045. The silence that accepts merit as the most natural thing in the world, is the highest applause. EMERSON

1046. Applause waits on success; the fickle multitude, like the light straw that floats along the street, glide with the current still, and follow fortune.

FRANKLIN

1047. The applause of a single human being is of great consequence.

SAMUEL JOHNSON, *Boswell: Life*

1048. The praise we give to new comers into the world arises from the envy we bear to those who are established.

LA ROCHEFOUCAULD, *Maxims*

1049. A slowness to applaud betrays a cold temper or an envious spirit.

HANNAH MORE

1050. Men, steered by popular applause, though they bear the name of governors, are in reality the mere underlings of the multitude.

PLUTARCH, *Lives*

1051. The applause of the people is a blast of air. *Proverb*

1052. Men seek less to be instructed than applauded. *Proverb*

1053. Hail to the chief who in triumph advances!

SCOTT, *The Lady of the Lake*

1054.
I would applaud thee to the very echo,
That should applaud again.

SHAKESPEARE, *Macbeth*

See also: 10391.

APPRECIATION

Related Subjects: Criticism, Esteem, Gratitude, Knowledge.

1061. Men should allow others' excellences, to preserve a modest opinion of their own. ISAAC BARROW

1062.
I have made a great discovery.
What I love belongs to me. Not the chairs and tables in my house, but the masterpieces of the world.
It is only a question of loving them enough.

ELIZABETH A. BIBESCO, *Balloons*

1063. As some stay against this wretched self-distrust, this bankruptcy of confidence, you must have the recognition of others. There are times when your own approval is enough. There are times when it seems as nothing and even so you cannot get it. Then a single word of appreciation may bring heaven to you.

GAMALIEL BRADFORD,
American Portraits

1064. The difference between appreciation and flattery? That is simple. One is sincere and the other insincere. One comes from the heart out; the other from the teeth out. One is unselfish; the other selfish. One is universally admired; the other is universally condemned.

DALE CARNEGIE,
How to Win Friends

1065. Next to invention is the power of interpreting invention; next to beauty, the power of appreciating beauty. MARGARET FULLER

1066. To appreciate the noble is a gain which can never be torn from us.   GOETHE

1067. Nobody, I think, ought to read poetry, or look at pictures or statues, who cannot find a great deal more in them than the poet or artist has actually expressed.

HAWTHORNE, *The Marble Faun*

1068. We are very much what others think of us. The reception our observations meet with gives us courage to proceed or damps our efforts.
                                    HAZLITT

1069.
It shall belong hereafter to all who
    perceive and enjoy it,
Rather than him who made it.

W. D. HOWELLS, *Pordenone*

1070. The deepest principle in human nature is the craving to be appreciated.   WILLIAM JAMES

1071. No good writer was ever long neglected; no great man overlooked by men equally great. Impatience is a proof of inferior strength, and a destroyer of what little there may be.
                          W. S. LANDOR

1072. It is with certain good qualities as with the senses; those who are entirely deprived of them can neither appreciate nor comprehend them.

LA ROCHEFOUCAULD, *Maxims*

1073. He is incapable of a truly good action who knows not the pleasure in contemplating the good actions of others.   LAVATER

1074. The more enlarged is our own mind, the greater number we discover of men of originality. Your commonplace people see no difference between one man and another.   PASCAL

1075. It is a matter of the simplest demonstration, that no man can be really appreciated but by his equal or superior.   RUSKIN

1076. By appreciation we make excellence in others our own property.
                                  VOLTAIRE

1077. She must be seen to be appreciated.

W. H. AINSWORTH, *Old Saint Paul's*

APRIL

Related Subjects: Month, Spring.

1081.
April hieth, April spieth
Everywhere a lover lieth,
Bringeth sweetness, bringeth fever,
Will not stop at "I would liever,"
Will not heed, "Now God a mercy!"
Turneth Moral topsy-versy,
Bringeth he and she to bed,
Bringeth ill to maidenhead,
Bringeth joyance in its stead.

STEPHEN VINCENT BENET
For City Spring

1082.
In April Rome was founded; Shakespeare died;
The shot whose sound rang out from
    Concord town
And brought an avalanche of echoes
    down,
Shaking all thrones of tyranny and
    pride,
Was fired in April; Sumter far and
    wide
Lifted a voice the years will never
    drown;
'Twas April when they laid the martyr's crown
On Lincoln's brow.

SAMUEL V. COLE, *In April*

1083.
And not a girl goes walking
Along the Cotswold lanes
But knows men's eyes in April
Are quicker than their brains.

JOHN DRINKWATER, *Cotswold Love*

1084. The first day of April, you may send a fool whither you will.

Proverb

1085. April borrows three days of March, and they are ill. *Proverb*

1086.
O! how this spring of love resembleth
The uncertain glory of an April day!

SHAKESPEARE,
The Two Gentlemen of Verona

1087.
May never was the month of love,
For May is full of flowers;
But rather April, wet by kind,
For love is full of showers.

ROBERT SOUTHWELL,
Love's Servile Lot

1088.
April, April,
Laugh thy girlish laughter;
Then, the moment after,
Weep thy girlish tears.

WILLIAM WATSON, *Song*
See also: 6895.

ARCHITECTURE

Related Subjects: Art, Building.

1091. Architecture is preëminently the art of significant forms in space—that is, forms significant of their functions. CLAUDE BRAGDON,
Wake Up and Dream

1092. A man who could build a church, as one may say, by squinting at a sheet of paper.
DICKENS, *Martin Chuzzlewit*

1093.
There is no architect
Can build as the Muse can . . .
. . . She lays her beams in music,
In music every one,
To the cadence of the whirling world
Which dances round the sun.

EMERSON, *The House*

1094. An arch never sleeps.
JAMES FERGUSSON, *History of Indian and Eastern Architecture*

1095. Too many stairs and backdoors makes thieves and whores.
BALTHAZAR GERBIER,
Discourse of Building

1096. Architecture is frozen music.
GOETHE,
Conversations with Eckermann

1097.
Architecture,
Existing in itself, and not in seeming
A something it is not, surpasses them
As substance shadow.
LONGFELLOW, *Michael Angelo*

1098.
The architect
Built his great heart into these sculptured stones,
And with him toiled his children, and their lives
Were builded, with his own, into the walls,
As offerings unto God.
LONGFELLOW, *The Golden Legend*

1099. In the architectural structure, man's pride, man's triumph over gravitation, man's will to power, assume a visible form. Architecture is a sort of oratory of power by means of forms.

NIETZSCHE,
The Twilight of the Idols

1100. The surest test of the civilization of a people—at least, as sure as any—afforded by mechanical art is to be found in their architecture, which presents so noble a field for the display of the grand and the beautiful, and which, at the same time, is so intimately connected with the essential comforts of life.

PRESCOTT, *The Conquest of Peru*

1101. Architecture is the work of nations.

RUSKIN, *True and Beautiful*

1102. Whenever men have become skilled architects at all, there has been a tendency in them to build high.

RUSKIN, *Lectures on Architecture and Painting*

1103. Architecture aims at Eternity; and therefore is the only thing incapable of modes and fashions in its principles.

CHRISTOPHER WREN, *Parentalia*

1104. Architectural values are human values or they are not valuable. So any true modern building is born of organic integration and rises, as the modern city rises, enemy to centralization in whatever form. Both building and city are now true sungrowth and true sun-acceptance or not modern. The building itself may be a shaft of light flashing in the sun.

FRANK LLOYD WRIGHT,
The Disappearing City
See also: 11846.

ARGUMENT

Related Subjects: **Controversy, Differences, Discord, Discussion, Facts, Logic, Obstinacy, Opinion, Quarreling, Reason, Words.**

1111. Arguments out of a pretty mouth are unanswerable. ADDISON

1112. The only way to get the best of an argument is to avoid it.

DALE CARNEGIE,
How to Win Friends

1113. Neither irony nor sarcasm is argument. RUFUS CHOATE

1114. A knock-down argument: 'tis but a word and a blow.

DRYDEN, *Amphitryon*

1115. I always get the better when I argue alone. GOLDSMITH

1116. Be calm in arguing; for fierceness makes error a fault, and truth discourtesy.

GEORGE HERBERT, *Jacula Prudentum*

1117. Strong and bitter words indicate a weak cause. VICTOR HUGO

1118. Let argument bear no unmusical sound. BEN JONSON

1119. Gratuitous violence in argument betrays a conscious weakness of the cause, and is usually a signal of despair. JUNIUS

1120.
Myself when young did eagerly frequent
Doctor and Saint, and heard great argument
About it and about: but evermore
Came out by the same door where in I went.

OMAR KHAYYAM, *Rubaiyat*

1121. Argument is not always truth.

LOUIS KOSSUTH

1122. Argument should be politic as well as logical. LAMARTINE

1123. He who establishes his argument by noise and command shows that reason is weak. MONTAIGNE

1124. It were endless to dispute upon everything that is disputable.

WILLIAM PENN

1125. Nothing is more certain than that arguments or instructions depend on their conciseness. POPE

1126. In too much dispute truth is lost. *Proverb*

1127. He will maintain his argument as well as any military man in the world. SHAKESPEARE, *Henry V*

1128. And sheathed their swords for lack of argument.

SHAKESPEARE, *Henry V*

1129. If thou continuest to take delight in idle argumentation, thou mayest be qualified to combat with the sophists but never know how to live with men.   SOCRATES

1130. Argument as usually managed, is the worst sort of conversation; as it is generally in books the worst sort of reading.   SWIFT

1131. Affect not little shifts and subterfuges to avoid the force of an argument.   ISAAC WATTS

1132. Keep cool; anger is not argument.   DANIEL WEBSTER

1133. I am not arguing with you— I am telling you.   WHISTLER

See also: 5260, 8780, 11012, 16696, 18776.

ARISTOCRACY

Related Subjects: Birth, Breeding, Nobility.

1141. To believe in pure blood, in a privileged race, to stand in thought above other men, must we not from birth have measured the distance which divides patricians from the mob?

BALZAC, *The Commission in Lunacy*

1142. Where some think, and others do not, there is developed aristocracy. Where all have come to think we have democracy,—the government of the people by themselves.

H. W. BEECHER

1143. What is Aristocracy? A corporation of the best, of the bravest.

CARLYLE, *Chartism*

1144. Aristocracy has three successive ages,—the age of superiorities, the age of privileges, and the age of vanities; having passed out of the first, it degenerates in the second, and dies away in the third.

CHATEAUBRIAND

1145.
The pedigree of honey
Does not concern the bee;
A clover, any time, to him
Is aristocracy.

EMILY DICKINSON, *Nature*

1146. An aristocracy is the true support of a monarchy.   NAPOLEON

1147. Aristocracy is always cruel.

WENDELL PHILLIPS

1148. I never could believe that Providence had sent a few men into the world, ready booted and spurred to ride, and millions ready saddled and bridled to be ridden.

RICHARD RUMBOLD

1149. Aristocrats (no doubt) still exist; but they are shorn beings, for whom the wind is not tempered— powerless, out of place, and slightly ridiculous. For about a hundred years it has been so. The stages in the history of nobility may be reckoned by the different barricades it has put up to keep off the common multitude.

LYTTON STRACHEY,
Portraits in Miniature

See also: 926, 5432, 10978.

ARMY

Related Subjects: Discipline, Navy, Sailor, Soldier, War.

1151. A man in armor is his armor's slave.   BROWNING, *Herakles*

1152. Nations are quite capable of starving every other side of life,— education, sanitation, housing, public health, everything that contributes to life, physical, intellectual, moral, and spiritual, in order to maintain their armaments.

G. LOWES DICKINSON,
The Choice Before Us

1153. It has been calculated by the ablest politicians that no State, without being soon exhausted, can maintain above the hundredth part of its members in arms and idleness.

GIBBON, *Decline and Fall*

1154. We know that the end of the education provided by our army is not, and never has been, the production of war-like militarists, but rather of good and reliable citizens.

ADOLF HITLER,
Speech, Sept. 15, 1935

1155. It came upon me freshly how the secret of uniform was to make a crowd solid, dignified, impersonal: to give it the singleness and tautness of an upstanding man. This death's livery which walled its bearers from ordinary life, was sign that they had sold their wills and bodies to the State: and contracted themselves into a service not the less abject for that its beginning was voluntary.

LAWRENCE OF ARABIA,
Revolt in the Desert

1156. The nature of arms decides the composition of armies, their plans of campaign, their marches, positions, and encampments, their order of battle, and the design of their fortifications; this sets in constant opposition the military system of the ancients and that of modern times.

NAPOLEON, *Precis of the Wars of Julius Caesar*

1157. The root of the reluctance of the British Army to adopt modern methods of war lies in its snobbery. And this does not only apply to the love of horse-flesh (as compared with the skilled mechanic's love for his machine) it also applies for example to our Territorial Army, whose officers have been chosen or have chosen themselves on a social basis.

TOM WINTRINGHAM,
New Ways of War

1158. An army cannot elect its officers or vote on what its tactics and strategy shall be. It is the raw stuff of democracy that is called for: men who feel free, and feel themselves by natural right the equals of their fellows; men who accept regulations and order—restrictions on their individual actions—because they realize the need for these in strengthening their collective actions; men who accept commands as part of inescapable methods by which they themselves can achieve their own desires and aims—an army of free men.

TOM WINTRINGHAM,
New Ways of War

1159. Totalitarian methods produce an army fit for war. Our own methods of the past have not produced such an army. But we can find ways to make such an army, which will not merely retain democracy but use its vital force to make something far better than the Nazis can ever produce.

TOM WINTRINGHAM,
New Ways of War
See also: 2815, 3593.

ARROGANCE

Related Subjects: Boasting, Ostentation, Pride.

1161. Better to reign in hell than serve in heaven.

MILTON, *Paradise Lost*

1162. The word that is overbearing is a spur unto strife.

PINDAR, *Fragment from Hymns*

1163. Arrogance is the obstruction of wisdom.   *Proverb*

See also: 2319.

ART, ARTISTS

Related Subjects: **Architecture, Beauty, Criticism, Critic, Culture, Genius, Imitation, Literature, Music, Painting, Poets and Poetry, Sculpture, Sing, Skill, Temperament.**

1171. Every art is social. It is the result of a relation between the artist and his time.

JAMES TRUSLOW ADAMS,
Our Business Civilization

1172. Art is man's nature; nature is God's art.

PHILIP J. BAILEY, *Festus*

1173. Art is choice.   BEZARD

1174. The joy of successful creation is shot through with ardor that consumes even while it intoxicates.

GAMALIEL BRADFORD,
American Portraits

1175.
One may do whate'er one likes
In Art: the only thing is, to make sure
That one does like it.

BROWNING, *Pippa Passes*

1176. The fine arts once divorcing themselves from *truth* are quite certain to fall mad, if they do not die.

CARLYLE, *Latter Day Pamphlets*

1177. The whole difference between construction and creation is exactly this: that a thing constructed can only be loved after it is constructed; but a thing created is loved before it exists.

G. K. CHESTERTON,
Preface to Pickwick Papers

1178. Emotion resulting from a work of art is only of value when it is not obtained by sentimental blackmail.

JEAN COCTEAU, *A Call to Order*

1179. When a work of art appears to be in advance of its period, it is really the period that has lagged behind the work of art.

JEAN COCTEAU, *A Call to Order*

1180. A work that aspires, however humbly, to the condition of art should carry its justification in every line.

JOSEPH CONRAD, *Preface to The
Nigger of the Narcissus*

1181. Efficiency of a practically flawless kind may be reached naturally in the struggle for bread. But there is something beyond—a higher point, a subtle and unmistakable touch of love and pride beyond mere skill; almost an inspiration which gives to all work that finish which is almost art—which *is* art.

JOSEPH CONRAD,
The Mirror of the Sea

1182.
All passes. Art alone
Enduring stays to us;
The Bust outlasts the throne,—
The Coin, Tiberius.

AUSTIN DOBSON, *Ars Victrix*

1183. A nation's art-products and its scientific activities are not mere national property; they are international possessions, for the joy and service of the whole world. The nations hold them in trust for humanity.

HAVELOCK ELLIS,
The Task of Social Hygiene

1184.
In the vaunted works of Art
The master-stroke is Nature's part.
EMERSON, *Art*

1185. Art is the surest and safest civilizer.
CHARLES B. FAIRBANKS,
My Unknown Chum

1186. The value of a work of art . . . must . . . depend upon some reference to external reality. In other words, its objectives must be evaluated in accordance with some hierarchy of general values.
JOHN GASSNER,
A Note on Criticism

1187. Nothing so resembles a daub as a masterpiece.
PAUL GAUGUIN, *Intimate Journals*

1188.
Art for Art's sake   Why not?
Art for Life's sake   Why not?
Art for Pleasure's sake   Why not?
What does it matter, as long as it is art?
PAUL GAUGUIN, *Intimate Journals*

1189. The public, in whose good graces lie the sculptor's or the painter's prospects of success, is infinitely smaller than the public to which literary men make their appeal.
HAWTHORNE, *The Marble Faun*

1190. Art is the only clean thing on earth, except holiness.
J. K. HUYSMANS,
Les Foules de Lourdes

1191. There aren't twelve hundred people in the world who understand pictures. The others pretend and don't care.
KIPLING, *The Light That Failed*

1192. 'Tis the fault of all art to seem antiquated and faded in the eyes of the succeeding generation.
ANDREW LANG,
Letters to Dead Authors

1193. We must have no fear. Reason and truth may suffer apparent eclipse. But in us, in our hearts, they are eternally free. And looking down from the bright regions of art, the spirit may laugh at the triumphant folly of the hour. Not forsaken and alone, but secure in the bond uniting it with all that is best on earth.
THOMAS MANN, *This Peace*

1194. The mania for immortality. A masterpiece must disappear with its author. Immortality in Art is a disgrace. The ancestors of our Italian Art, by their constructive power and their ideal of immortality, have built for us a prison of timidity, of imitation and of plagiarism. They sit there on grandfather chairs and forever dominate our creative agonies with their marble frowns: "Take care, children. Mind the motors. Don't go too quick. Wrap yourselves up well. Mind the draughts. Be careful of the lightning." Forward! Hurrah for motors! Hurrah for speed! Hurrah for draughts! Hurrah for lightning!
MARINETTI, *Futurist Manifesto*

1195. The true work of art is but a shadow of the divine perfection.
MICHELANGELO

1196. If you accept art it must be part of your daily lives.
WILLIAM MORRIS

1197. I wish to be thoroughly disassociated from every "new" or "advanced" movement; every form of "ist," "ism," "post," "neo," "academic," or "inacademic." Also I refuse to use the same technical method to express such contradictory forms as a rock or a woman.

C. R. W. NEVINSON

1198. I wish thoroughly to dissociate myself from all geometric mumbo-jumbo mathematical metaphysics, the pretentious Bloomsbury Belles, and *affreux* Intelligentsia, the New Sky, the Biblical Commentators, and all the Illustrators of Art Theorists and Literary Critics, who write endlessly on painting and esthetics, and the pure, pure art of the cocoa pinks and the chocolate browns.

C. R. W. NEVINSON

1199. There are three arts which are concerned with all things; one which uses, another which makes, a third which imitates them.

PLATO, *The Republic*

1200. Art helps nature, and experience art. *Proverb*

1201. The perfection of art is to conceal art. QUINTILIAN

1202.
All loved Art in a seemly way
With an earnest soul and a capital A.
J. J. ROCHE, *The V-A-S-E*

1203. You desire a popular art? Begin by having a 'people' whose minds are liberated, a people not crushed by misery and ceaseless toil, not brutalised by every superstition and every fanaticism, a people master of itself, and victor in the fight that is being waged today.

ROMAIN ROLLAND, *I Will Not Rest*

1204. When love and skill work together expect a masterpiece.

RUSKIN

1205. What garlic is to salad, insanity is to art.

HOMER SAINT-GAUDENS

1206. There is no such thing as experiment. There is only good and bad art. When a good thing appears to be very new, it is more likely that it is only something that has been forgotten, and is now suddenly remembered. A classic is simply a first work, the beginning of a tradition, and an entry into a fresh realm of human experience, understanding, and expression.

WILLIAM SAROYAN, *Preface to My Heart's In the Highlands*

1207. All art is but imitation of nature. SENECA

1208. More matter, with less art.

SHAKESPEARE, *Hamlet*

1209. Architecture, sculpture, painting, music, and poetry, may truly be called the efflorescence of civilized life. HERBERT SPENCER, *Essays on Education*

1210.
All Arts are one, howe'er distributed they stand;
Verse, tone, shape, color, form, are fingers on one hand.
WILLIAM W. STORY, *Couplets*

1211.
A Picture is not wrought
By hands alone, good Padre, but by thought.
In the interior life it first must start,
And grow to form and colour in the soul;
There once conceived and rounded to a whole,
The rest is but the handicraft of art.
WILLIAM W. STORY, *Padre Bandelli Proses*

1212. Art is a human activity having for its purpose the transmission to others of the highest and best feelings to which men have risen.

TOLSTOY, *What is Art?*

1213. To say of a picture, as is often said in its praise, that it shows great and earnest labour, is to say that it is incomplete and unfit for view.

WHISTLER, *The Gentle Art of Making Enemies*

1214. Industry in Art is a necessity —not a virtue—and any evidence of the same, in the production, is a blemish, not a quality; a proof, not of achievement, but of absolutely insufficient work, for work alone will efface the footsteps of work.

WHISTLER, *The Gentle Art of Making Enemies*

1215. Art should be independent of all clap-trap—should stand alone, and appeal to the artistic sense of eye and ear, without confounding this with emotions entirely foreign to it, as devotion, pity, love, patriotism, and the like. All these have no kind of concern with it.

WHISTLER, *The Gentle Art of Making Enemies*

1216. It is through Art, and through Art only, that we can realize our perfection; through Art and Art only that we can shield ourselves from the sordid perils of actual existence.

OSCAR WILDE, *The Critic as Artist*

1217.
In art I pull no high-brow stuff,
I know what I like, and that's enough.

WILLIAM W. WOOLLCOTT

1218. Art is life seen through a temperament.   EMILE ZOLA

Artists

1219. I have an old theory that every one makes a living on an artist except the artist himself and I begin to find both theory and practice tiresome.   F. P. A.,
Diary of Our Own Samuel Pepys

1220. A poet or a painter or a musician does not say to himself, "I will make a million first, and then I will write poetry or paint pictures or compose music." His art is life itself, the best of life, for the genuine artist.

JAMES TRUSLOW ADAMS,
The Art of Living

1221.
In the still air the music lies unheard;
In the rough marble beauty lies unseen;
To wake the music and the beauty needs
The master's touch, the sculptor's chisel keen.

HORATIUS BONAR,
The Master's Touch

1222. But the artist appeals to that part of our being which is not dependent on wisdom; to that in us which is a gift and not an acquisition —and, therefore, more permanently enduring. He speaks to our capacity for delight and wonder, to the sense of mystery surrounding our lives: to our sense of pity, and beauty, and pain.

JOSEPH CONRAD, *Preface to The Nigger of the Narcissus*

1223.
He held his pen in trust
To Art, not serving shame or lust.

AUSTIN DOBSON, *In After Days*

1224. Art is a jealous mistress, and, if a man have a genius for painting, poetry, music, architecture, or philosophy, he makes a bad husband, and an ill-provider.

EMERSON, *Conduct of Life*

1225. You invest the heaven of art with we know not what deadly rays; you create a new shudder.

VICTOR HUGO, *to Baudelaire*

1226. The great artists of the world are never Puritans, and seldom even ordinarily respectable.

H. L. MENCKEN, *Prejudices*

1227. The true function of art is to criticise, embellish and edit nature—particularly to edit it, and so make it coherent and lovely. The artist is a sort of impassioned proof-reader, blue pencilling the bad spelling of God.   H. L. MENCKEN

1228.
If I was made for art, from childhood given
  A prey for burning beauty to devour,
  I blame the mistress I was born to serve.   MICHELANGELO

1229. Alas! That I made art my idol, my monarch!   MICHELANGELO

1230. He that lives with the muses shall die in the straw.   *Proverb*

1231. An artist lives everywhere.
Proverb

1232. It came to pass that after a time the artist was forgotten, but the work lived.
OLIVE SCHREINER, *Dreams*

1233. If you are an artist, may no love of wealth or fame or admiration and no fear of blame or misunderstanding make you ever paint, with pen or brush, an ideal or a picture of external life otherwise than as you see it.   OLIVE SCHREINER,
From Man to Man

1234. Why, if I did not feel in my inmost soul the living light and love of that Christian faith, my works . . . would be the works of a liar and an ape. My art is my prayer.
RICHARD WAGNER

1235. An artist's sphere of influence is the world.   CARL VON WEBER

1236. An artist's career always begins tomorrow.   WHISTLER

1237. The imitator is a poor kind of creature. If the man who paints only the tree, or flower, or other surface he sees before him were an artist, the king of artists would be the photographer. It is for the artist to do something beyond this: in portrait painting to put on canvas something more than the face the model wears for that one day; to paint the man, in short, as well as his features.
WHISTLER, *The Gentle Art
of Making Enemies*

1238. Nature sings her exquisite song to the artist alone, her son and her master—her son in that he loves her, her master in that he knows her.
WHISTLER, *The Gentle Art
of Making Enemies*

1239. It is only through the self-portraiture of great artists that the genius of mankind becomes comprehensible to earthbound mortals.
STEFAN ZWEIG, *Adepts in
Self-Portraiture*

See also: 192, 194, 1067, 1069, 2030, 2373, 2556, 2871, 3042, 3513, 4211, 4504, 4865, 5402, 5901, 10905, 11396, 11750, 11902, 12073, 13347, 13724, 13737, 13754, 14627, 16001.

ASCETICISM

Related Subjects: Fasting, Hermit, Sacrifice, Self-Denial.

1241. An angry and cruel asceticism begins to befog the world. It is no mere accident that Adolf Hitler neither drinks nor spins. . . . Show me a community or a country where all the minor vices are discouraged and

I will show you one bereft of major virtues.

HEYWOOD BROUN, *Saratoga Fades*

1242. Intend to live in continual mortification and never to expect or desire any worldly ease or pleasure.

JONATHAN EDWARDS, *Diary*

1243. The belief that all higher life is governed by the idea of renunciation poisons our moral life by engendering vanity and egotism.

REBECCA WEST, *I Believe*

See also: 71, 3361.

ASPIRATION

Related Subjects: Ambition, Fame, Zeal.

1251.
To bliss unknown my lofty soul aspires,
My lot unequal to my vast desires.

J. ARBUTHNOT, *Gnothi Seaton*

1252.
What I aspired to be,
And was not, comforts me.

BROWNING, *Rabbi Ben Ezra*

1253. 'Tis not what man Does which exalts him, but what man Would do!

BROWNING, *Saul*

1254.
Better have failed in the high aim, as I,
Than vulgarly in the low aim succeed,—
As, God be thanked, I do not!

BROWNING, *The Inn Album*

1255.
Ah, but a man's reach should exceed his grasp,
Or what's a heaven for?

BROWNING, *Andrea del Sarto*

1256. It is not to taste sweet things, but to do noble and true things, and

vindicate himself under God's heaven as a God-made man, that the poorest son of Adam dimly longs. CARLYLE

1257. It . . . appears to me that our aspirations are rooted in our animal impulses, and that our animal impulses flower out into moral passions, poetry, and science.

IRWIN EDMAN, *I Believe*

1258. There is no sorrow I have thought more about than that,—to love what is great, and try to reach it, and yet to fail. GEORGE ELIOT

1259. It seems to me we can never give up longing and wishing while we are thoroughly alive. There are certain things we feel to be beautiful and good, and we must hunger after them.

GEORGE ELIOT

1260.
A banner with the strange device,
Excelsior!

LONGFELLOW, *Excelsior*

1261. He who attends to his greater self becomes a great man, and he who attends to his smaller self becomes a small man. MENCIUS

1262. Lord, grant that I may always desire more than I can accomplish.

MICHELANGELO

1263. Enflamed with the study of learning and the admiration of virtue; stirred up with high hopes of living to be brave men and worthy patriots, dear to God, and famous to all ages.

MILTON, *Tractate of Education*

1264. The mere aspiration is partial realization. ANNA CORA MOWATT

1265. High honor, high rank, which I have been desiring, today in my eye give no impression, and what I hope is to become a real man and to resign myself to things without grief, and when I come back to my native country I want to be near my great teacher and want to help the poor and the suffering and give rest to my old mother so she can go in peace out of this world.

NOGUCHI, *Eckstein: Noguchi*

1266. This race desires the infinite, it thirsts for it, and pursues it at all costs, beyond the tomb—beyond hell itself.   RÉNAN

1267.
We know what we are, but know not
    what we may be.
            SHAKESPEARE, *Hamlet*

1268.
Let this suffice, by this conceive the
    rest,
He should, he could, he would, he did
    the best.
    ROBERT SOUTHWELL, *Look Home*

1269. To be what we are, and to become what we are capable of becoming, is the only end of life.
            STEVENSON,
Familiar Studies of Men and Books

1270.
I held it truth, with him who sings
To one clear harp in divers tones,
That men may rise on stepping-
    stones
Of their dead selves to higher things.
    TENNYSON, *In Memoriam*

1271. Did you ever hear of a man who had striven all his life faithfully and singly towards an object, and in no measure obtained it? If a man constantly aspires, is he not elevated? Did ever a man try heroism, magnanimity, truth, sincerity, and find that there was no advantage in them,— that it was a vain endeavor?
            THOREAU

1272. The heavens are as deep as our aspirations are high.   THOREAU

1273. The world dreams of things to come, and then in due season arouses itself to their realization.
    ALFRED NORTH WHITEHEAD

1274. Too low they build who build beneath the stars.
    EDWARD YOUNG, *Night Thoughts*

See also: 1212, 2636, 3611, 4156, 9808, 10351, 10725.

ASSERTION

Related Subject: Opinion.

1281. Assertion, unsupported by fact, is nugatory; surmise and general abuse, in however elegant language, ought not to pass for proofs. JUNIUS

1282. It is an impudent kind of sorcery to attempt to blind us with the smoke without convincing us that the fire has existed.   JUNIUS

See also: 14014.

ASSOCIATES, ASSOCIATION

Related Subjects: Business, Companions, Friend.

1291. We are far more liable to catch the vices than the virtues of our associates.   DIDEROT

1292. Associate with men of judgment, for judgment is found in conversation, and we make another man's judgment ours by frequenting his company.   THOMAS FULLER,
        Holy & Profane State

1293. It is best to be with those in time that we hope to be with in eternity.   THOMAS FULLER,
        Holy & Profane State

1294. Keep good company, and you shall be of the number.   *Proverb*

1295. Frequent the company of your betters.   THACKERAY

See also: 2055, 3691.

ASTROLOGY

Related Subjects: Astronomy, Fate, Future, The Heavens, Metaphysics, Prophecy, Stars.

1301. Let now the astrologers, the stargazers, the monthly prognosticators, stand up, and save thee from these things that shall come upon thee. Behold, they shall be as stubble; the fire shall burn them; they shall not deliver themselves from the power of the flame: there shall not be a coal to warm at nor fire to sit before it.
Bible: Isaiah, xlvii, 13, 14

1302.
For in the sterres, clerer than is glas,
Is writen, god wot, who-so coude it rede,
The deeth of every man.
     CHAUCER, *Canterbury Tales*

1303. No date prefixed directs me in the starry rubric set.   MILTON

1304. Astrologers that future fates foreshow.   POPE

1305.
         It is the stars,
The stars above us, govern our conditions.
     SHAKESPEARE, *King Lear*

1306.
There's some ill planet reigns:
I must be patient till the heavens look
With an aspect more favourable.
     SHAKESPEARE, *The Winter's Tale.*

1307. Strange an astrologer should die without one wonder in the sky.
     SWIFT

1308. A wise man shall overrule his

stars, and have a greater influence upon his own content than all the constellations and planets of the firmament.   JEREMY TAYLOR

See also: 7882, 13813, 15423.

ASTRONOMY

Related Subjects: Astrology, The Heavens, Science, Stars, Universe.

1311. The contemplation of celestial things will make a man both speak and think more sublimely and magnificently when he descends to human affairs.   CICERO

1312. It does at first appear that an astronomer rapt in abstraction, while he gazes on a star, must feel more exquisite delight than a farmer who is conducting his team.
     ISAAC D'ISRAELI

1313. The narrow sectarian cannot read astronomy with impunity. The creeds of his church shrivel like dried leaves at the door of the observatory.
     EMERSON

1314. Astronomy is one of the sublimest fields of human investigation. The mind that grasps its facts and principles receives something of the enlargement and grandeur belonging to the science itself. It is a quickener of devotion.   HORACE MANN

1315. Even such a minute instrument as the eye has astonishing powers. On a clear, moonless night it can see quite 6,000,000,000,000 miles into space, provided the object glimpsed is of enormous extent and sufficiently luminous. It can discern about 5,000 individual stars.
     G. E. PENDRAY,
     Men, Mirrors and Stars

1316. Astronomy compels the soul to look upwards and leads us from this world to another.

> PLATO, *The Republic*

1317. Astronomy is the science of the harmony of infinite expanse.

> LORD JOHN RUSSELL

1318. Although in the last twenty years our knowledge of the sidereal world has more than doubled, the list of things we want to know has trebled or quadrupled leaving us relatively more ignorant than before.

> DR. HARLOW SHAPLEY

1319. It will indeed be interesting to see how many of the things which astronomers have learned during this last century will have to be unlearned in the next.

> R. L. WATERFIELD,
> *A Hundred Years of Astronomy*

1320. An undevout astronomer is mad.   EDWARD YOUNG,
> *Night Thoughts*

ATHEISM

Related Subjects: Belief, Doubt, God, Gods, Heresy, Piety.

1321. A little philosophy inclineth man's mind to atheism, but depth in philosophy bringeth men's minds about to religion.

> BACON, *Of Atheism*

1322. I had rather believe all the fables in the legends and the Talmud and the Alcoran, than that this universal frame is without a mind.

> BACON, *Of Atheism*

1323. Atheism is rather in the lip than in the heart of man.

> BACON, *Of Atheism*

1324. There was never miracle wrought by God to convert an atheist, because the light of nature might have led him to confess a God.

> BACON, *Advancement of Learning*

1325. Atheism leaves a man to sense, to philosophy, to natural piety, to laws, to reputation; all which may be guides to an outward moral virtue.

> BACON, *Essays*

1326. The fool hath said in his heart, There is no God.

> *Bible: Psalms xiv, 1*

1327. There is no proselyter half so energetic as the hard-shelled atheist . . . Nobody talks so constantly about God as those who insist that there is no God.   HEYWOOD BROUN,
> *Preface to The Fifty-First Dragon*

1328.
An atheist's laugh's a poor exchange
> For Deity offended!
> BURNS, *Epistle to a Young Friend*

1329.
Who seeks perfection in the art
Of driving well an ass and cart,
Or painting mountains in a mist,
Seeks God although an Atheist.
> FRANCIS CARLIN, *Perfection*

1330.
Forth from his dark and lonely hiding-place,
(Portentous sight!) the owlet Atheism,
Sailing on obscene wings athwart the noon,
Drops his blue-fringèd lids, and holds them close,
And hooting at the glorious sun in Heaven,
Cries out "Where is it?"
> COLERIDGE, *Fears in Solitude*

1331. Atheism is the last word of theism.   HEINE

1332.
The fool hath said: There is no God!
No God! Who lights the morning
    sun,
And sends him on his heavenly road,
A far and brilliant course to run?
    WILLIAM KNOX, *The Atheist*

1333. A man cannot become an
atheist merely by wishing it.
    NAPOLEON

1334. Not one of them who took up
in his youth with this opinion that
there are no gods, ever continued until
old age faithful to his conviction.
    PLATO, *Laws*

1335. An atheist is one point beyond
the devil. *Proverb*

1336. Some are atheists only in fair
weather. *Proverb*

1337. My atheism, like that of Spinoza, is true piety towards the universe and denies only gods fashioned
by men in their own image, to be servants of their human interests.
SANTAYANA, *Soliloquies in England*

1338. By night an atheist half believes a God.
    EDWARD YOUNG, *Night Thoughts*

See also: 951, 3349, 3359, 8794,
10202, 15157, 16796, 17826.

ATHLETICS, see Sport

ATTENTION AND INATTENTION

Related Subjects: Indifference, Interest, Listening, Neglect, Watch.

1341. In the power of fixing the attention lies the most precious of the
intellectual habits. ROBERT HALL

1342. Attention is the stuff that memory is made of, and memory is accumulated genius. LOWELL

Inattention

1343. It is a way of calling a man a
fool when no attention is given to
what he says. L'ESTRANGE

1344. It is the disease of not listening,
the malady of not marking, that I am
troubled withal.
    SHAKESPEARE, *Henry IV*

1345. I never knew any man cured
of inattention. SWIFT

See also: 4818, 5101, 5925, 6426.

ATTRACTION

Related Subject: Desire.

1351. There are but two things that
chiefly excite us to love a woman, an
attractive beauty, and unspotted fame.
    CERVANTES, *Don Quixote*

1352. The poetic element lying hidden in most women is the source of
their magnetic attraction.
    VICTOR HUGO

1353. The more sensible a woman is,
supposing her not to be masculine,
the more attractive she is in her proportionate power to entertain.
    LEIGH HUNT

1354. Rarity gives a charm: thus
early fruits are most esteemed; thus
winter roses obtain a higher price;
thus coyness sets off an extravagant
mistress; a door ever open attracts
no young suitor. MARTIAL

See also: 3147, 3201.

AUGUST

Related Subjects: Month, Summer.

1361.
Never return in August to what you
    love;
Along the leaves will be rust

And over the hedges dust,
And in the air vague thunder and
   silence burning . . .
                BERNICE KENYON, *Return*

1362. Dry August and warm, doth
harvest no harm.   *Proverb*

1363. A rainy August makes a hard
bread-crust.   *Proverb*

1364.
In the parching August wind,
Cornfields bow the head
Sheltered in round valley depths,
On low hills outspread.
                CHRISTINA ROSSETTI

AUTHORITY

Related Subjects: Command, Dictatorship, Discipline, Executives, Government, Influence, Leadership, Law, Master, Obedience, Power, Responsibility.

1371. For he taught them as one having authority, and not as the scribes.
                Bible: Matthew, vii, 29

1372. I am a man under authority,
having soldiers under me: and I say
to this man, Go, and he goeth ; and to
another, Come, and he cometh.
                Bible: Matthew, viii, 9

1373.
Authority intoxicates,
And makes mere sots of magistrates;
The fumes of it invade the brain,
And make men giddy, proud, and
   vain.   SAMUEL BUTLER,
                Miscellaneous Thoughts

1374. It is not for a man in authority to sleep a whole night.   HOMER

1375. He who is firmly seated in authority soon learns to think security,
and not progress, the highest lesson
of statecraft.
                LOWELL, *Among My Books*

1376. "I fired the man," said the new
section boss, "not because I had anything agin him but because I had the
authority."
                CARL SANDBURG, *The People, Yes*

1377. There thou mightst behold the
great image of authority; a dog's
obey'd in office.
                SHAKESPEARE, *King Lear*

1378. Drest in a little brief authority.
SHAKESPEARE, *Measure for Measure*

1379.
Thus can the demigod Authority
Make us pay down for our offence by
   weight
The words of heaven.
SHAKESPEARE, *Measure for Measure*

1380. Though authority be a stubborn bear, yet he is oft led by the nose
with gold.
    SHAKESPEARE, *The Winter's Tale*

1381. And art made tongue-tied by
authority.
            SHAKESPEARE, *Sonnet LXVI*

1382. Of all the authorities to which
men can be called to submit, the wisdom of our ancestors is the most
whimsically absurd.
                JEREMY TAYLOR

1383. Authority forgets a dying king.
        TENNYSON, *Idylls of the King*

1384. No power on earth is so worthy
of honor for itself, or of reverential
obedience to the rights which it represents, that I would consent to admit
its uncontrolled and all-predominant
authority. When I see that the right
and the means of absolute command
are conferred on a people or upon a
king, upon an aristocracy or a democracy, a monarchy or a republic, I recognize the germ of tyranny, and I

journey onwards to a land of more hopeful institutions.

DE TOCQUEVILLE,
Democracy in America

1385. Every nation, every epoch, every thoughtful human being, has again and again to establish the landmarks between freedom and authority: for, in the absence of authority, liberty degenerates into license, and chaos ensues; and authority becomes tyranny unless it is tempered by freedom.

STEFAN ZWEIG, *The Right to Heresy*

See also: 469, 513, 665, 697, 775, 12368, 12470, 16494.

AUTHORS, AUTHORSHIP

Related Subjects: Books, Fiction, Language, Literature, Plagiarism, Poets and Poetry, Writing.

1391. Of all the diversions of life, there is none so proper to fill up its empty spaces as the reading of useful and entertaining authors.

ADDISON, *The Spectator*

1392. Authors have established it as a kind of rule, that a man ought to be dull sometimes; as the most severe reader makes allowances for many rests and nodding-places in a voluminous writer.

ADDISON, *The Spectator*

1393. One hates an author that's all author. BYRON, *Beppo*

1394. O thou who art able to write a book, which once in the two centuries or oftener there is a man gifted to do, envy not him whom they name Citybuilder, and inexpressibly pity him whom they name Conqueror or Cityburner. Thou too art a Conqueror and Victor. CARLYLE, *Sartor Resartus*

1395. There are men that will make you books, and turn 'em loose into the world, with as much dispatch as they would do a dish of fritters.

CERVANTES, *Don Quixote*

1396. A dull author, just delivered, and a plain woman about to be so, are two very important animals.

C. C. COLTON

1397.
Drop the bard and stop the punster,
Let the quill stay on the goose;
Take a business trip through Munster,
Shoot a landlord—be of use!

One Irish Poet to Another,
Padraic Colum: A Half Day's Ride

1398.
And choose an author as you choose a friend.

WENTWORTH DILLON,
Essay on Translated Verse

1399. A writer does not have to drool in order to convince us of his humanity; it is in fact the droolers whose humanitarianism is most suspect.

JOHN GASSNER, *Masters of the Drama*

1400. I consider an author's literary reputation to be alive only while his name will insure a good price for his copy from the bookseller's.

GOLDSMITH,
Boswell: Life of Dr. Johnson

1401. Many contemporary authors drink more than they write. GORKY

1402. A serious writer is not to be confounded with a solemn writer. A serious writer may be a hawk or a buzzard or even a popinjay, but a solemn writer is always a bloody owl.

ERNEST HEMINGWAY,
Death in the Afternoon

1403. The praise of ancient authors proceeds not from the reverence of the dead, but from the competition and mutual envy of the living.

THOMAS HOBBES, *Leviathan*

1404. There rise authors now and then, who seem proof against the mutability of language, because they have rooted themselves in the unchanging principles of human nature.

WASHINGTON IRVING,
The Sketch-Book

1405. It was, I think, Huxley who said that six monkeys set to strum unintelligently on typewriters for millions of millions of years, would be bound in time to write all the books in the British Museum . . . if we looked through all the millions of pages the monkeys had turned off in untold millions of years, we might be sure of finding a Shakespeare sonnet somewhere amongst them, the product of the blind play of chance.

SIR JAMES JEANS,
The Mysterious Universe

1406. *Grub Street:* The name of a street near Moorsfield, London, much inhabited by writers of small histories, dictionaries, and temporary poems.

SAMUEL JOHNSON, *Dictionary*

1407. It has happened not seldom that one work of some author has so transcendently surpassed in execution the rest of his compositions, that the world has agreed to pass a sentence of dismissal upon the latter, and to consign them to total neglect and oblivion.   CHARLES LAMB, *Eliana.*

1408. I met Sir Bulwer-Lytton, or Lytton Bulwer. He is anxious about some scheme for some association of literary men. I detest all such associations. I hate the notion of gregarious authors. The less we have to do with each other, the better.   MACAULAY

1409.
Let him be kept from paper, pen and ink
So may he cease to write, and learn to think.

MATTHEW PRIOR

1410. Like author, like book.
Proverb

1411. He was a one-book man. Some men have only one book in them; others, a library.

SYDNEY SMITH,
Lady Holland's Memoir

1412. Authors are born very untidily. They do not live, as they should do, from century to century, or from reign to reign, but rise as and when they will, and do their work unwinkingly regardless of the historian.

FRANK SWINNERTON,
Georgian Literary Scene

1413. The author who succeeds in his work is he who describes the interesting and significant things which it has been given him to observe and experience in his own life.   TOLSTOY

1414. The writer must be a psychologist, but a secret one; he must sense and know the roots of phenomena, but offer only the phenomena themselves, as they blossom or wither.

TURGENIEV

1415. Authors, in general, may be compared to sausage makers who prepare their stuff for others while sedulously not eating any themselves.

ZOLA

Authorship

1416. For several days after my first book was published I carried it about in my pocket, and took surreptitious peeps at it to make sure that the ink had not faded.   J. M. BARRIE

1417. Thou, O Lord, my God, grant me the grace to produce some fine lines which will prove to myself that I am not the least of men, that I am not inferior to those I condemn!

BAUDELAIRE

1418. The author who speaks about his own books is almost as bad as a mother who talks about her own children. DISRAELI

1419. It is a good lesson—though it may often be a hard one—for a man who has dreamed of literary fame, and of making for himself a rank among the world's dignitaries by such means, to step aside out of the narrow circle in which his claims are recognized, and to find how utterly devoid of significance, beyond that circle, is all that he achieves, and all he aims at.   HAWTHORNE,
Preface to The Scarlet Letter

1420. A writer's problem does not change. He himself changes and the world he lives in changes but his problem remains the same. It is always how to write truly and, having found what is true, to project it in such a way that it becomes a part of the experience of the person who reads it.

ERNEST HEMINGWAY,
The Problems of a Writer in War Time

1421. No man but a blockhead ever wrote except for money.

SAMUEL JOHNSON, *Boswell: Life*

1422. I have been an author for 22 years and an ass for 55.

MARK TWAIN

1423.
An author! It's a venerable name;
How few deserve it, and what numbers claim!   EDWARD YOUNG

See also: 96, 344, 1071, 3997, 4620, 6978, 9132, 19791, 20685.

AUTOMOBILE

Related Subject: Wheel.

1431. The automobile has been extensively taken up by society, and during the past season in Newport and Lenox it played a most important part in social life. Women like Mrs. Stuyvesant Fish, Mrs. Herman Oelrichs, Mrs. Wm. K. Vanderbilt, Jr. and others who are noted for their daring in taking up sports which have the merit of unconventionality, will not be satisfied until they have driven their motor carriages through the city streets.
Automobile Topics, Oct. 20, 1900

1432. It will be possible to construct chariots so that without animals they may be moved with incalculable speed.

ROGER BACON, *600 years ago*

1433. And the Lord was with Judah; and he drave out the inhabitants of the mountain; but could not drive out the inhabitants of the valley, because they had chariots of iron.
Bible: Judges, i, 19

1434. The chariots shall rage in the streets, they shall justle one against another in the broad ways: they shall seem like torches, they shall run like the lightnings. *Bible: Nahum, ii, 4*

1435. The automobile released the farmer and the villager from their bondage. More than any other device, it has helped break the monotony.

CHARLES F. KETTERING,
The New Necessity

1436. The Ford car is Henry Ford done in steel, and other things.

SAMUEL S. MARQUIS, *Henry Ford*

1437.
Carriages without horses shall go,
And accidents fill the world with woe.

MOTHER SHIPTON, *Prophecy*

See also: 2611, 3490.

AUTUMN

Related Subjects: Harvest, October, The Seasons.

1441.
O Autumn, laden with fruit, and stained
With the blood of the grape, pass not, but sit
Beneath my shady roof; there thou may'st rest
And tune thy jolly voice to my fresh pipe,
And all the daughters of the year shall dance!   BLAKE, *To Autumn*

1442.
Autumn wins you best by this, its mute
Appeal to sympathy for its decay.
BROWNING, *Paracelsus*

1443.
The melancholy days are come, the saddest of the year,
Of wailing winds, and naked woods, and meadows brown and sear.
BRYANT, *The Death of the Flowers*

1444.
All-cheering Plenty, with her flowing horn,
Led yellow Autumn, wreath'd with nodding corn.
BURNS, *The Brigs of Ayr*

1445.
There is something in the autumn that is native to my blood—
Touch of manner, hint of mood;
And my heart is like a rhyme,
With the yellow and the purple and the crimson keeping time.
BLISS CARMEN, *A Vagabond Song*

1446.
These are the days when skies put on
The old, old sophistries of June,—
A blue and gold mistake.
EMILY DICKINSON, *Indian Summer*

1447.
No spring nor summer beauty hath such grace
As I have seen in one autumnal face.
JOHN DONNE,
Elegie ix, The Autumnal

1448.
I saw old Autumn in the misty morn
Stand shadowless like Silence, listening
To silence, for no lonely bird would sing
Into his hollow ear from woods forlorn.
THOMAS HOOD, *Ode to Autumn*

1449.
How bravely Autumn paints upon the sky
The gorgeous flame of Summer which is fled!   THOMAS HOOD,
Written in a Volume of Shakespeare

1450.
Fruit-bearing autumn.
HORACE, *Odes*

1451.
Season of mists and mellow fruitfulness,
Close bosom-friend of the maturing sun;
Conspiring with him how to load and bless
With fruit the vines that round the thatch eaves run;
To bend with apples the moss's cottage-trees,
And fill all fruit with ripeness to the core.   KEATS, *To Autumn*

1452.
Third act of the eternal play!
In poster-like emblazonries
"Autumn once more begins today"—
RICHARD LE GALLIENNE,
The Eternal Play

1453.

Behold congenial Autumn comes,
The Sabbath of the year!
                JOHN LOGAN,
*Ode Written on a Visit to the Country
                        in Autumn*

1454.

It was Autumn, and incessant
    Piped the quails from shocks and
        sheaves,
And, like living coals, the apples
    Burned among the withering leaves.
        LONGFELLOW, *Pegasus in Pound*

1455.

The teeming autumn, big with rich
    increase. SHAKESPEARE, *Sonnets*

1456.

                There is a harmony
In Autumn, and a lustre in its sky,
Which thro' the Summer is not heard
        or seen,—
As if it could not be, as if it had not
        been!   SHELLEY,
        Hymn to Intellectual Beauty

1457.

Autumnal frosts enchant the pool,
And make the cart-ruts beautiful.
        STEVENSON, *The House Beautiful*

1458.

Cold autumn, wan with wrath of
    wind and rain.   SWINBURNE,
                Autumn and Winter

1459.

While Autumn, nodding o'er the yel-
    low plain,
Comes jovial on.
    JAMES THOMSON, *The Seasons*

1460. The tints of autumn—a mighty
flower garden blossoming under the
spell of the enchanter, Frost.
        WHITTIER, *Patucket Falls*

AVARICE

**Related Subjects: Desire, Envy,
Gold, Lust, Mammon, Miser,
Money, Riches, Selfishness.**

1461. He would skin a flint.
                JOHN BERTHELSON

1462. Not greedy of filthy lucre.
        Bible: I Timothy, iii, 3

1463.

So for a good old-gentlemanly vice
I think I must take up with avarice.
        BYRON, *Don Juan*

1464. I knew once a very covetous,
sordid fellow, who used to say, "Take
care of the pence, for the pounds will
take care of themselves."
        LORD CHESTERFIELD, *Letters*

1465. The very suspicion of avarice
is to be avoided.
        CICERO, *De Officiis*

1466. If you would abolish avarice,
you must abolish its mother, luxury.
        CICERO, *De Oratore*

1467.

        Avarice, envy, pride,
Three fatal sparks.   DANTE, *Inferno*

1468.

No man of elder years than fifty
Should be empowered with lands and
    gold,
It turns them shrewd and over-
    thrifty,
It makes them cruel and blind and
    cold.
    ARTHUR D. FICKE, *Youth and Age*

1469. Avarice and happiness never
saw each other, how then should they
become acquainted?
        FRANKLIN, *Poor Richard*

1470.

Avarice, sphincter of the heart.
        MATTHEW GREEN, *The Spleen*

1471. The covetous man is ever in want.   HORACE, *Epistles*

1472. Avarice, the spur of industry.
DAVID HUME, *Of Civil Liberty*

1473. Avarice is more opposed to economy than liberality is.
LA ROCHEFOUCAULD, *Maxims*

1474. Excess of wealth is cause of covetousness.
CHRISTOPHER MARLOWE,
The Jew of Malta

1475.
Of which all old men sicken,—
Avarice.
THOMAS MIDDLETON,
The Roaring Girl

1476. It is not necessity but abundance which produces avarice.
MONTAIGNE, *Essays*

1477.
Counts his sure gains, and hurries back for more.
JAMES MONTGOMERY,
The West Indies

1478.
The mishief of grudging and the marring of grasping.
WILLIAM MORRIS,
Story of Child Christopher

1479. He who covets what belongs to another deservedly loses his own.
PHAEDRUS, *Fables*

1480. Covetous men's chests are rich, not they.   *Proverb*

1481. Grasp all, lose all.   *Proverb*

1482. Gold and silver were mingled with dirt, till avarice parted them.
Proverb

1483.
I pledge my allegiance,
say the munitions makers and the international bankers,

I pledge my allegiance to this flag,
that flag,
any flag at all, of any country anywhere
paying its bills and meeting interest on loans,
one and indivisible,
coming through with cash in payment as stipulated
with liberty and justice for all,
say the munitions makers and the international bankers.
CARL SANDBURG, *The People, Yes*

1484.
To greed, all nature is insufficient.
SENECA, *Hercules Œtoeus*

1485.
You yourself
Are much condemn'd to have an itching palm.   SHAKESPEARE,
Julius Caesar

1486.
Those that much covet are with gain so fond,
For what they have not, that which they possess
They scatter and unloose it from their bond,
And so, by hoping more, they have but less.   SHAKESPEARE,
The Rape of Lucrece

1487. Avarice, ambition, lust, etc., are nothing but species of madness, although not enumerated among diseases.   SPINOZA, *Ethics*

See also: 393, 16326.

AVIATION

Related Subject: Speed.

1490. The thing aviation has to sell is speed. In a complete survey of passenger flights by day over our Chicago-San Francisco and Seattle-Los Angeles routes, 75 per cent of the travelers are shown to be business men. They fly to save time, primarily to save *daytime*—to save business days.   W. E. BOEING

1491. The nation that controls the air will ultimately rule the world.
ALEXANDER GRAHAM BELL

1492. The United States is the only country in the world which possesses a really great aeronautical industry.
GIANNI CAPRONI

1493. When I am asked to forecast the future of aviation, I speak with reluctance. Always in the past my estimates have been exceeded two or three times over. The future of aviation I believe to be literally beyond comprehension.
ANTHONY H. G. FOKKER

1494. Were I a young man, seeking a career in either science or commerce, I should unhesitatingly turn to aviation. I consider it the greatest road to opportunity which lies before the science and commerce of the civilized countries of the earth today.
DANIEL GUGGENHEIM

1495. Airplanes have a high rate of depreciation, naturally, but a higher rate of obsolescence. There is no reason why a plane need wear out in 2 years; but my guess is that the best passenger plane manufactured today will be obsolete 2 years from now.
HARRY GUGGENHEIM

1496. The element of time saving in transportation has a large economic importance. Today the airplane is the fastest means of transportation.
HERBERT HOOVER

1497. The flying-machine engaged the attention of ambitious inventors long before the hot-air or the gas balloon was suggested as a means of traveling through the air.
WALDEMAR KAEMPFFERT

1498. And as for man's ambition! What jubilation because man had started to fly like a bird! But just look at the way a bird flies, the simple, easy lightness accompanied by a spontaneous, joyful song. Then think of the clumsy, roaring machines and of the anxiety, panic and deadly fear of the man who tries to play the bird's part.   PIRANDELLO

1499. Aviation is an unfinished story —a story scarcely begun. . . But already it touches us so closely; it beckons to our youth and to our dollars.   EARL REEVES,
Aviation's Place in Tomorrow's Business

1500. Careful and studious men created the aeronautical science. These cautious experimenters were the first to fly. The first pilots were pioneers in the field of knowledge.
EARL REEVES,
Aviation's Place in Tomorrow's Business

1501. The whole progress of aviation has been empirical; we build on experience. We know so little. We must feel our way along.
G. A. RENTSCHLER

1502. This seemed to us the principal value of the aeroplane against a trained infantry: it is a sort of artillery *that can be concentrated very quickly* to check an enemy breakthrough or to hammer at a centre of resistance when your enemy is retreating.   TOM WINTRINGHAM,
New Ways of War

See also: 16889, 20824, 20840.

AWKWARDNESS

Related Subjects: Embarrassment, Manners, Stupidity, Timidity.

1511. Awkwardness is a more real disadvantage than it is generally thought to be; it often occasions ridicule, it always lessens dignity.

LORD CHESTERFIELD

1512.
Not all the pumice of the polish'd town
Can smooth the roughness of the barnyard clown;
Rich, honor'd, titled, he betrays his race
By this one mark—he's awkward in his face.

O. W. HOLMES

1513. He is awkward and out of place in the society of his equals.

CHARLES LAMB,
Essays of Elia

B

BABIES AND BABYHOOD

Related Subjects: Age, Birth, Childhood, Father, Mother.

1521. Babies are bits of star-dust blown from the hand of God. Lucky the woman who knows the pangs of birth, for she has held a star.

LARRY BARRETTO,
The Indiscreet Years

1522. Out of the mouth of babes and sucklings hast thou ordained strength.

Bible: Psalms, viii, 2

1523.
"I have no name;
I am but two days old."
What shall I call thee?
"I happy am,
Joy is my name."
Sweet joy befall thee.

BLAKE, *Infant Joy*

1524.
Sweet babe, in thy face
Soft desires I can trace,
Secret joys and secret smiles,
Little pretty infant wiles.

BLAKE, *A Cradle Song*

1525. Every baby born into the world is a finer one than the last.

DICKENS, *Nicholas Nickleby*

1526.
A little child born yesterday
A thing on mother's milk and kisses fed.   HOMER, *Hymn to Hermes*

1527.
Who can tell what a baby thinks?
J. G. HOLLAND, *Cradle Song*

1528. About the only thing we have left that actually discriminates in favor o' the plain people is the stork.

KIN HUBBARD, *Sayings*

1529. Babies do not want to hear about babies; they like to be told of giants and castles, and of somewhat which can stretch and stimulate their little minds.

SAMUEL JOHNSON, *Miscellanies*

1530.
O child! O new-born denizen
Of life's great city! on thy head
The glory of the morn is shed,
Like a celestial benison!

LONGFELLOW, *To a Child*

1531.
Where did you come from, baby dear?
Out of the everywhere into the here.

GEORGE MACDONALD,
At the Back of the North Wind

1532.
Small traveler from an unseen shore,
By mortal eye ne'er seen before,
    To you, good-morrow.
            COSMO MONKHOUSE,
                To a New-Born Child

1533.
                    The infant,
Mewling and puking in the nurse's
    arms.   SHAKESPEARE,
                As You Like It

1534.
Thou wast the prettiest babe that e'er
    I nursed.   SHAKESPEARE,
                Romeo and Juliet

1535. I first gave it a dose of castor-
oil, and then I christened it; so now
the poor child is ready for either
world.   SYDNEY SMITH,
            Lady Holland's Memoir

1536.
Sweetest li'l' feller, everybody knows;
Dunno what to call him, but he's
    mighty lak' a rose.
        FRANK L. STANTON,
            Mighty Lak' a Rose

1537.
The world has no such flower in any
    land,
And no such pearl in any gulf the sea,
As any babe on any mother's knee.
        SWINBURNE, *Pelagius*

1538. A babe in a house is a well-
spring of pleasure.
    MARTIN F. TUPPER, *Of Education*

1539. Among the three or four million
cradles now rocking in the land are
some which this nation would preserve
for ages as sacred things, if we could
know which ones they are.
    MARK TWAIN, *Toast: The Babies*

See also: 3329, 13410, 14015.

BACHELOR

**Related Subjects: Celibacy, Mar-
riage.**

1541. Single gentlemen who would
be double.   BYRON, *Don Juan*

1542. I would not answer for myself
if I could find an affectionate family,
with good shooting and first-rate
claret.   DISRAELI, *Lothair*

1543.
Bachelor's Hall! what a quare-lookin'
    place it is!
Kape me from sich all the days of my
    life!   JOHN FINLEY,
                Bachelor's Hall

1544.
                    A bachelor
May thrive by observation on a little,
A single life's no burthen: but to draw
In yokes is chargeable, and will re-
    quire
A double maintenance.
            JOHN FORD,
        The Fancies Chaste and Noble

1545. We bachelors laugh and show
our teeth, but you married men laugh
till your hearts ache.
    GEORGE HERBERT, *Jacula Prudentum*

1546.
Let sinful bachelors their woes de-
    plore,
Full well they merit all they feel, and
    more.   POPE, *January and May*

1547. Commend a wedded life, but
keep thyself a bachelor.   *Proverb*

1548. A lewd bachelor makes a jealous husband.   *Proverb*

1549. Shall I never see a bachelor of
three-score again?
            SHAKESPEARE,
        Much Ado About Nothing

1550. If you wish the pick of men and women, take a good bachelor and a good wife.   STEVENSON, *Virginibus Puerisque*

1551. The happy marid man dies in good stile at home, surrounded by his weeping wife and children. The old bachelor don't die at all—he sort of rots away, like a pollywog's tail.
ARTEMUS WARD,
The Draft in Baldinsville

1552. Nowadays all the married men live like bachelors, and all the bachelors like married men.
OSCAR WILDE, *Picture of Dorian Gray*

BALDNESS

Related Subjects: Barber, Hair.

1561. A bald head is soon shaven.
Proverb

1562. There's no time for a man to recover his hair that grows bald by nature.   SHAKESPEARE,
The Comedy of Errors

1563. What he hath scanted men in hair, he hath given them in wit.
SHAKESPEARE, *The Comedy of Errors*

1564. Time himself is bald, and therefore to the world's end will have bald followers.   SHAKESPEARE,
The Comedy of Errors

See also: 4692.

BALLAD

Related Subjects: Music, Poetry, Sing, Song.

1571.
The farmer's daughter hath soft brown hair
(*Butter and eggs and a pound of cheese*)

And I met with a ballad, I can't say where,
That wholly consisted of lines like these.
CHARLES S. CALVERLY, *Ballad*

1572.
Thespis, the first professor of our art,
At country wakes sung ballads from a cart.   DRYDEN,
Sophonisba: Prologue

1573. Some people resemble ballads which are only sung for a certain time.   LA ROCHEFOUCAULD,
Maxims

1574. I have a passion for ballads.
LONGFELLOW, *Hyperion*

1575. For a ballad's a thing you expect to find lies in.
SAMUEL LOVER, *Paddy Blake's Echo*

1576. Solid things do not show the complexion of the times so well as ballads and libels.
JOHN SELDEN, *Table-Talk*

1577. An I have not ballads made on you all and sung to filthy tunes, let a cup of sack be my poison.
SHAKESPEARE, *Henry IV*

1578.
I had rather be a kitten and cry mew,
Than one of these same metre ballad-mongers.   SHAKESPEARE,
Henry IV

1579.
Armado: Is there not a ballad, boy, of the King and the Beggar?
Moth: The world was very guilty of such a ballad some three ages since: but I think now 'tis not to be found.
SHAKESPEARE, *Love's Labour's Lost*

1580. I love a ballad in print, a-life, for then we are sure they are true.
SHAKESPEARE, *The Winter's Tale*

1581. I love a ballad but even too well, if it be doleful matter, merrily set down, or a very pleasant thing indeed, and sung lamentably.
SHAKESPEARE, *The Winter's Tale*

1582.
Build, build, but never monument of stone shall last as long
As one old soldier's ballad borne on breath of battle-song.
MAURICE THOMPSON,
The Ballad of Chickamauga

1583.
The ballads of the people are the bulwarks of the State.
E. F. WARE, *The Organ-Grinder*

1584.
A famous man is Robin Hood,
The English ballad-singer's joy.
WORDSWORTH, *Rob Roy's Grave*

BANISHMENT, see Exile

BANK AND BANKER, see Finance

BARBER

Related Subjects: Baldness, Beard, Hair.

1591. And thou, son of man, take thee a sharp knife, take thee a barber's razor, and cause it to pass upon thine head, and upon thy beard.
Bible: Ezekiel, v, 1

1592. 'Tis an office of more trust to shave a man's beard than to saddle a horse. CERVANTES, *Don Quixote*

1593.
With odorous oil thy head and hair are sleek;
And then thou kemb'st the tuzzes on thy cheek:
Of these, my barbers take a costly care. DRYDEN,
Fourth Satire of Persius

1594. To make a fine gentleman several trades are required, but chiefly a barber. GOLDSMITH

1595. A good lather is half the shave.
WILLIAM HONE, *Every-Day Book*

1596. Of a thousand shavers, two do not shave so much alike as not to be distinguished.
SAMUEL JOHNSON, *Boswell: Life*

1597.
But he shaved with a shell when he chose,
'Twas the manner of primitive man.
ANDREW LANG,
Double Ballad of Primitive Man

1598.
Thy boist'rous locks, no worthy match
For valour to assail, nor by the sword.
. . . . ,
But by the barber's razor best subdued. MILTON,
Samson Agonistes

1599.
Barber, barber, shave a pig!
How many hairs make a wig?
Mother Goose

1600. A prating barber asked Archelaus how he would be trimmed. He answered, "In silence."
PLUTARCH, *Lives*

1601. One barber shaves not so close but another finds work. *Proverb*

1602. Like a barber's chair, that fits all buttocks. SHAKESPEARE,
All's Well that Ends Well

1603.
Our courteous Antony,
. . . . ,
Being barber'd ten times o'er, goes to the feast. SHAKESPEARE,
Antony and Cleopatra

1604.
Whose beard they have sing'd off with
  brands of fire;
And ever, as it blaz'd, they threw on
  him
Great pails of puddled mire to quench
  the hair:
My master preaches patience to him
  and the while
His man with scissors nicks him like
  a fool.   SHAKESPEARE,
              The Comedy of Errors

1605.
    And his chin new reap'd,
Show'd like a stubble-land at harvest-
  time. SHAKESPEARE, *Henry IV*

1606. I must to the barber's, monsieur; for methinks I am marvellous
hairy about the face.
              SHAKESPEARE,
      A Midsummer-Night's Dream

1607.
Accept a proverb out of Wisdom's
  schools—
"Barbers first learn to shave by shaving fools."   JOHN WOLCOT

BARGAIN

Related Subjects: Economy, Oath,
Thrift.

1611. It is naught, it is naught, saith
the buyer; but when he is gone his
way, then he boasteth.
          Bible: Proverbs, xx, 14

1612. Here's the rule for bargains:
"Do other men, for they would do
you." That's the true business precept.
  DICKENS, *Martin Chuzzlewit*

1613. Good bargains are pick-pockets.
                      Proverb

1614. He who findeth fault meaneth
to buy.   *Proverb*

1615. It is a bad bargain, where both
are losers.   *Proverb*

1616. Many have been ruin'd by buying good pennyworths.   *Proverb*

1617. Make the best of a bad bargain.   *Proverb*

1618. At a great bargain make a
pause.   *Proverb*

1619.
Make every bargain clear and plain,
That none may afterwards complain.
                      Proverb

1620. A man loseth his time that
comes early to a bad bargain.
                      Proverb

1621. 'Tis ill luck to go back upon a
bargain.   CHARLES READE,
      The Cloister and the Hearth

1622. Her aunt seemed determined to
make the best of a bad bargain.
        SCOTT, *Quentin Durward*

1623.
Lest the bargain should catch cold
  and starve.   SHAKESPEARE,
                      Cymbeline

1624.
But in the way of bargain, mark ye
  me,
I'll cavil on the ninth part of a hair.
      SHAKESPEARE, *Henry IV*

1625. There never was a better bargain driven.
          SIR PHILIP SIDNEY,
      My True Love Hath My Heart

See also: 2612, 16635.

BASENESS

Related Subjects: Character, Coward, Evil, Servility, Villain, Wickedness.

1631. Lewd fellows of the baser sort.
            Bible: Acts, xvii, 5

1632. Blindness we may forgive, but baseness we will smite.

WILLIAM VAUGHN MOODY,
An Ode in Time of Hesitation

1633.
I have lived in such dishonour that the gods
Detest my baseness.

SHAKESPEARE, *Antony and Cleopatra*

1634.
　　　　The time of life is short;
To spend that shortness basely were too long.　　SHAKESPEARE,
Henry IV

1635. Small things make base men proud.　SHAKESPEARE, *Henry VI*

See also: 2570, 2782, 16071, 19180.

BASHFULNESS, see Timidity

BATHING

Related Subjects: Cleanliness, Dirt, Swimming, Washing, Water.

1641. Many recite their writings in the bath. How pleasantly the vaulted space echoes the voice!

HORACE, *Satires*

1642. Madame (de Flahaut) being ill, goes into the bath and when placed there sends for me. It is a strange place to receive a visit, but there is milk mixed with the water, making it opaque.　GOUVERNEUR MORRIS

1643. In the height of this bath, where I was more than half stewed in grease, like a Dutch dish.

SHAKESPEARE,
The Merry Wives of Windsor

1644.
　A seething bath, which yet men prove
Against strange maladies a sovereign
　cure.　SHAKESPEARE,
Sonnet CLIII

BATTLE, see War

BEAR

Related Subject: Animal.

1651. We roar all like bears.
Bible: Isaiah, lix, 11

1652.
Make ye no truce with Adam-zad—
the Bear that walks like a Man!
KIPLING, *The Truce of the Bear*

1653. I trusted so much that I sold the skin before the bear was taken.
JOHN LYLY, *Euphues*

1654. As savage as a bear with a sore head.　FREDERICK MARRYAT,
The King's Own

1655. He is not worthy to carry guts to a bear.　*Proverb*

1656. He hath as many tricks as a dancing bear.　*Proverb*

1657. He must have iron nails that scratcheth with a bear.　*Proverb*

1658.
　Thou'ldst shun a bear;
But if thy flight lay toward the raging
　sea,
Thou'ldst meet the bear i' the mouth.
SHAKESPEARE, *King Lear*

1659. If it had been a bear it would have bit you!　SWIFT,
Polite Conversation

BEARD

Related Subjects: Barber, Hair.

1661. Saw H. Mankiewicz, and he tells me of how difficult it is to hear what a bearded man is saying. Lord, quoth he, he cannot speak above a whisker.　F. P. A.,
*The Diary of Our Own
Samuel Pepys*

1662. A beard creates lice, not brains.
AMMIANUS, *Greek Anthology*

1663. Since I have dealt in suds, I could never discover more than two reasons for shaving; the one is to get a beard, the other is to get rid of one.
FIELDING, *Tom Jones*

1664.
There was an Old Man with a beard,
Who said: "It is just as I feared!
 Two Owls and a Hen,
 Four Larks and a Wren
Have all built their nests in my
 beard." EDWARD LEAR,
Limerick

1665. All the power is with the sex that wears the beard. MOLIÈRE

1666. Wait till I put aside my beard, for that never committed treason.
SIR THOMAS MORE, *At his execution*

1667. Whoever hath a divided beard, the whole world will not prevail against him. *Proverb*

1668. An old goat is never the more reverend for his beard. *Proverb*

1669.
    You should be women,
And yet your beards forbid me to interpret
That you are so.
 SHAKESPEARE, *Macbeth*

1670. The old ornament of his cheek hath already stuffed tennis-balls.
SHAKESPEARE,
Much Ado About Nothing

1671. Lord, I could not endure a husband with a beard on his face: I had rather lie in the woollen.
SHAKESPEARE,
Much Ado About Nothing

1672. He that hath a beard is more than a youth, and he that hath no beard is less than a man.
SHAKESPEARE,
Much Ado About Nothing

1673. Alas, poor chin! many a wart is richer. SHAKESPEARE,
Troilus and Cressida

1674.
Now Jove, in his next commodity of hair, send thee a beard!
SHAKESPEARE, *Twelfth Night*

1675. His beard, all silver white, Wagg'd up and down.
SHAKESPEARE, *The Rape of Lucrece*

1676.
And slight Sir Robert with his watery
 smile
And educated whisker.
 TENNYSON, *Edwin Morris*

See also: 4493, 15156.

BEAUTY

Related Subjects: Appearance, Art, Charm, Delicacy, Face, Glory, Love, Woman, Youth.

1681. Personal beauty is a greater recommendation than any letter of introduction. ARISTOTLE

1682. There is no excellent beauty that hath not some strangeness in the proportion. BACON, *Of Beauty*

1683. I loved her for that she was beautiful. PHILIP J. BAILEY,
Festus

1684.
The mate for beauty should be a man, and not a money-chest.
 BULWER-LYTTON, *Richelieu*

1685.
She walks in beauty, like the night
 Of cloudless climes and starry skies;

And all that's best of dark and bright
Meet in her aspect and her eyes;
Thus mellow'd to that tender light.
Which Heaven to gaudy day denies.
BYRON, *Hebrew Melodies*

1686. The beautiful is not a physical fact, beauty does not belong to things, it belongs wholly to the human esthetic activity, and thus is a mental or spiritual fact.   WILDON CARR

1687. At all events she had always the "power of suggesting things much lovelier than herself," as the perfume of a single flower may call up the whole sweetness of spring.
WILLA CATHER

1688.
Exceeding fair she was not; and yet fair
In that she never studied to be fairer
Than Nature made her.
GEORGE CHAPMAN, *All Fools*

1689.
Her very frowns are fairer far
Than smiles of other maidens are.
HARTLEY COLERIDGE,
Song, She Is Not Fair

1690. Lovely female shapes are terrible complicators of the difficulties and dangers of this earthly life, especially for their owner.
GEORGE DU MAURIER, *Trilby*

1691.
If eyes were made for seeing,
Then Beauty is its own excuse for being.
EMERSON, *The Rhodora*

1692. There is no beautifier of complexion, or form, or behavior, like the wish to scatter joy and not pain around us.
EMERSON, *Conduct of Life*

1693. Truth, and goodness, and beauty are but different faces of the same all.   EMERSON

1694. Beauty is eternity gazing at itself in a mirror.
KAHLIL GIBRAN, *The Prophet*

1695.
Give me a look, give me a face,
That makes simplicity a grace;
Robes loosely flowing, hair as free,
Such sweet neglect more taketh me
Than all the adulteries of art:
They strike mine eyes, but not my
    heart.   BEN JONSON, *Epicoene*

1696.
Beauty is truth, truth beauty,—that
    is all
Ye know on earth, and all ye need
    to know.
KEATS, *Ode on a Grecian Urn*

1697.
A thing of beauty is a joy forever:
Its loveliness increases; it will
    never
Pass into nothingness.
KEATS, *Endymion*

1698.
'Tis beauty calls and glory shows the
    way.   NATHANIEL LEE,
            Alexander the Great

1699.
What is your sex's earliest, latest
    care,
Your heart's supreme ambition? To
    be fair.
LORD LYTTELTON, *Advice to a Lady*

1700. Whatever is in any way beautiful hath its source of beauty in itself, and is complete in itself; praise forms no part of it. So it is none the worse nor the better for being praised.
MARCUS AURELIUS, *Meditations*

1701.
            Euclid alone
Has looked on Beauty bare. Fortunate they
Who, though once only and then but
    far away,

Have heard her massive sandal set on stone.

EDNA ST. VINCENT MILLAY,
Euclid Alone Has Looked on Beauty Bare

1702. Beauty does not lie in the face. It lies in the harmony between man and his industry. Beauty is expression. When I paint a mother I try to render her beautiful by the mere look she gives her child.   JEAN MILLET

1703.
A bevy of fair women.
MILTON, *Paradise Lost*

1704.
Beauty stands
In the admiration only of weak minds
Led captive.
MILTON, *Paradise Regained*

1705.
Yet beauty, though injurious, hath strange power,
After offence returning, to regain
Love once possess'd.
MILTON, *Samson Agonistes*

1706. The beauty of a butterfly's wing, the beauty of all things, is not a slave to purpose, a drudge sold to futurity. It is excrescence, superabundance, random ebullience, and sheer delightful waste to be enjoyed in its own high right.
DONALD CULROSS PEATTIE,
An Almanac for Moderns

1707.
O that beauty should harbour a heart that's so hard!
THOMAS PERCY,
Reliques of Ancient English Poetry

1708.
Fair tresses man's imperial race ensnare,
And beauty draws us with a single hair.
POPE, *The Rape of the Lock*

1709. When the candles are out all women are fair.   *Proverb*

1710. Beauties without fortunes have sweethearts plenty, but husbands none at all.   *Proverb*

1711. Beauty may have fair leaves, yet bitter fruit.   *Proverb*

1712. She who is born a beauty is half married.   *Proverb*

1713. Beauty without virtue is a curse.   *Proverb*

1714. A fair exterior is a silent recommendation.
PUBLILIUS SYRUS, *Sententiae*

1715.
If she undervalue me,
What care I how fair she be?
SIR WALTER RALEIGH, *Poem*

1716. The beauty that addresses itself to the eyes is only the spell of the moment; the eye of the body is not always that of the soul.
GEORGE SAND

1717. Beauty provoketh thieves sooner than gold.
SHAKESPEARE, *As You Like It*

1718.
Could I come near your beauty with my nails
I'd set my ten commandments in your face.   SHAKESPEARE, *Henry VI*

1719.
One fairer than my love! the all-seeing sun
Ne'er saw her match since first the world begun.
SHAKESPEARE, *Romeo and Juliet*

1720.
Who is Sylvia? what is she?
That all our swains commend her?
SHAKESPEARE,
The Two Gentlemen of Verona

1721.
Beauty itself doth of itself persuade
The eyes of men without an orator.
SHAKESPEARE, *The Rape of Lucrece*

1722.
To me, fair friend, you never can be
    old,
For as you were when first your eye
    I ey'd
Such seems your beauty still.
SHAKESPEARE, *Sonnet CIV*

1723. I believe in Michael Angelo,
Velasquez and Rembrandt; in the
might of design, the mystery of color,
the redemption of all things by Beauty
everlasting.   BERNARD SHAW,
The Doctor's Dilemma

1724.
For all that faire is, is by nature good;
That is a signe to know the gentle
    blood.   EDMUND SPENSER,
An Hymne in Honour of Beautie

1725.
A daughter of the gods, divinely tall,
    And most divinely fair.
TENNYSON, *A Dream of Fair Women*

1726. 'Tis hard with respect to
Beauty, that its possessor should not
have even a life-enjoyment of it, but
be compelled to resign it after, at the
most, some forty years' lease.
THACKERAY, *The Virginians*

1727. The sense of beauty is our subjective appreciation of objective qualities in what we see or hear.
SIR ARTHUR THOMSON,
The Beauty of Nature

1728. The beautiful is not necessarily
the pretty or the handsome; it implies
an artistic unity which excites a joyous aesthetic emotion; it may be seen
in a gargoyle as well as in a statue.
SIR ARTHUR THOMSON,
The Beauty of Nature

1729. Beauty is a quality of things
which arouses in us a particular kind
of delight.
SIR ARTHUR THOMSON,
The Beauty of Nature

1730. The perception of beauty is a
moral test.   THOREAU, *Journal*

1731.
All the beauty of the world 'tis but
    skin deep.   RALPH VENNING,
Orthodox Paradoxes

1732. Even virtue is fairer in a fair
body.   VERGIL, *Aeneid*

1733.
She was a phantom of delight
When first she gleamed upon my
    sight;
A lovely apparition, sent
To be a moment's ornament;
Her eyes as stars of twilight fair,
Like twilight's, too, her dusky hair,
But all things else about her drawn
From May-time and the cheerful
    dawn.   WORDSWORTH,
She Was a Phantom of Delight

See also: 36, 481, 1065, 1111, 1228,
1259, 1351, 1447, 2219, 2391, 2558,
2872, 3497, 5133, 6373, 6541, 7721,
11184, 12638.

BED

Related Subjects: Disease, Marriage, Pain, Rest, Rising, Sleep.

1741.
Like feather-bed betwixt a wall
And heavy brunt of cannon ball.
SAMUEL BUTLER, *Hudibras*

1742.
Would you have a settled head,
You must early go to bed;
I tell you, and I tell't again,
You must be in bed at ten.
NICHOLAS CULPEPER

1743. No civilized person ever goes to bed the same day he gets up.
RICHARD HARDING DAVIS, *Gallegher*

1744.
My bed itself is like the grave,
  My sheets the winding-sheet,
My clothes the mould which I must have,
  To cover me most meet.
GEORGE GASCOIGNE, *Good Night*

1745.
O bed! O bed! delicious bed!
That heaven upon earth to the weary head!   THOMAS HOOD,
Miss Kilmansegg and her Precious Leg

1746. Whoever thinks of going to bed before twelve o'clock is a scoundrel.
SAMUEL JOHNSON, *Miscellanies*

1747. The bed comprehends our whole life, for we were born in it, we live in it, and we shall die in it.
MAUPASSANT, *The Bed*

1748. How it is I know not; but there is no place like a bed for confidential disclosures between friends. Man and wife, they say, there open the very bottom of their souls to each other; and some old couples often lie and chat over old times till nearly morning.
HERMAN MELVILLE, *Moby Dick*

1749. The bed has become a place of luxury to me! I would not exchange it for all the thrones in the world.
NAPOLEON

1750.
Matthew, Mark, Luke, and John,
Bless the bed that I lie on;
Four corners to my bed,
Four angels round my head,
One to watch, and one to pray,
And two to bear my soul away.
Nursery Rhyme

1751. And so to bed.
SAMUEL PEPYS, *Diary*

1752. All that are in a bed must not have quiet rest.   *Proverb*

1753. Age and wedlock bring a man to his nightcap.   *Proverb*

1754. Every hour out of bed after midnight is a nail in your coffin.
Proverb

1755. If a bed would tell all it knows, it would put many to the blush.
Proverb

1756. Bed is a medicine.   *Proverb*

1757.
I would 't were bedtime, Hal, and all well.   SHAKESPEARE, *Henry IV*

1758. She knows the heat of luxurious bed.   SHAKESPEARE,
Much Ado About Nothing

1759.
    There's millions now alive
That nightly lie in those unproper beds
Which they dare swear peculiar.
SHAKESPEARE, *Othello*

1760. To go to bed after midnight is to go to bed betimes.
SHAKESPEARE, *Twelfth Night*

1761. The pleasant Land of counterpane.   STEVENSON,
The Land of Counterpane

1762.
In winter I get up at night
And dress by yellow candle-light.
In summer, quite the other way,
I have to go to bed by day.
STEVENSON, *Bed In Summer*

See also: 1810, 2523.

BEE

Related Subject: Flowers.

1771. The busy bee has no time for sorrow.   BLAKE, *Proverbs of Hell*

1772. Nature's confectioner, the bee.
JOHN CLEVELAND, *Fuscara*

1773.
A vagrant bee twanged like an airy lyre
Of one rich-hearted chord.
JOHN DAVIDSON, *The Ordeal*

1774.
How many cups the bee partakes,—
The debauchee of dews!
EMILY DICKINSON, *Nature*

1775. Strange how often they speak to you of bees. The order and sweetness of a hive seem to have made a great impression on the Russians of this age. Again and again in Tiflis people talked of bees with a sort of wistful affection, as if the cool pungence of bees were a tonic to them in the midst of the soggy bleeding chaos of civil war and revolution.
JOHN DOS PASSOS, *Orient Express*

1776.
Burly, dozing bumblebee,
Where thou art is clime for me.
Let them sail for Porto Rique,
Far-off heats through seas to seek.
I will follow thee alone,
Thou animated torrid-zone!
EMERSON, *The Bumble-Bee*

1777.
The careful insect 'midst his works I view,
Now from the flowers exhaust the fragrant dew,
With golden treasures load his little thighs,
And steer his distant journey through the skies. JOHN GAY, *Rural Sports*

1778.
While Honey lies in Every Flower, no doubt,
It takes a Bee to get the Honey out.
ARTHUR GUITERMAN,
A Poet's Proverbs

1779.
Bees work for man, and yet they never bruise
Their Master's flower, but leave it, having done,
As fair as ever and as fit to use;
So both the flower doth stay, and honey run. GEORGE HERBERT,
Jacula Prudentum

1780. No good sensible working bee listens to the advice of a bedbug on the subject of business.
ELBERT HUBBARD, *Epigrams*

1781.
"O bees, sweet bees!" I said; "that nearest field
Is shining white with fragrant immortelles.
Fly swiftly there and drain those honey wells."
HELEN HUNT JACKSON, *My Bees*

1782.
Even bees, the little almsmen of spring bowers,
Know there is richest juice in poison-flowers. KEATS, *Isabella*

1783.
Listen! Oh, listen!
Here ever hum the golden bees
Underneath full-blossomed trees,
At once with glowing fruit and flowers crowned. LOWELL, *The Sirens*

1784. As busie as a Bee.
JOHN LYLY, *Euphues & his England*

1785. That which is not good for the swarm, neither is it good for the bee.
MARCUS AURELIUS, *Meditations*

1786.
In the nice bee, what sense so subtly true
From pois'nous herbs extracts the healing dew?
POPE, *Essay on Man*

1787. A swarm of bees in May is worth a load of hay but a swarm in July is not worth a fly.   *Proverb*

1788. The bee from her industry in the summer eats honey all the winter.   *Proverb*

1789. Bees that have honey in their mouths have stings in their tails.   *Proverb*

1790. He has a bee in his bonnet.   *Proverb*

1791. Honey is sweet, but the bee stings.   *Proverb*

1792.
   For so work the honey-bees,
Creatures that by a rule in nature
      teach
The act of order to a peopled king-
      dom.
They have a king and officers of sorts,
Where some, like merchants, venture
      trade abroad,
Others like soldiers, armed in their
      stings,
Make boot upon the summer's velvet
      buds,
Which pillage they with merry march
      bring home.
          SHAKESPEARE, *Henry V*

1793.
Where the bee sucks, there suck I;
In a cowslip's bell I lie.
          SHAKESPEARE, *The Tempest*

1794.
               The solitary Bee
Whose buzzing was the only sound of
      life,
   Flew there on restless wing,
Seeking in vain one blossom where to
      fix.   SOUTHEY, *Thalaba*

1795.
How doth the little busy bee
   Improve each shining hour,

And gather honey all the day
   From every opening flower!
          ISAAC WATTS, *Divine Songs*

1796.
The wild Bee reels from bough to
      bough
   With his furry coat and his gauzy
      wing,
Now in a lily cup, and now
   Setting a jacinth bell a-swing,
      In his wandering.
          OSCAR WILDE, *Her Voice*

See also: 489, 612, 1145, 2312, 19430, 20975.

BEER, see Ale and Beer

BEGGAR AND BEGGING

Related Subjects: Borrowing, Charity, Favor, Gifts, Hunger, Poverty.

1801. Better it is to die than to beg.
          Apocrypha: Ecclesiasticus

1802. Beggars must be no choosers.
          BEAUMONT & FLETCHER,
                    Scornful Lady

1803. The horseleech hath two daugh-ters, crying, Give, give.
          Bible: Proverbs, xxx, 15

1804. Set a beggar on horseback and he will ride a gallop.
          ROBERT BURTON,
                    Anatomy of Melancholy

1805.
Jacob God's Beggar was, and so we wait
(Though ne'er so rich) all beggars at
      His Gate.
          ROBERT HERRICK, *Beggars*

1806. The petition of an empty hand is dangerous.
          JOHN OF SALISBURY, *Policraticus*

1807. Better a living beggar than a buried emperor.
LA FONTAINE, *La Matrone d'Ephese*

1808. The real beggar is indeed the true and only king.
LESSING, *Nathan der Weise*

1809.
A beggar through the world am I,
From place to place I wander by.
Fill up my pilgrim's scrip for me.
For Christ's sweet sake and charity.
LOWELL, *The Beggar*

1810. Gie a beggar a bed and he'll repay you with a louse.   *Proverb*

1811. Neither beg of him who has been a beggar, nor serve him who has been a servant.   *Proverb*

1812. Better to die a beggar than live a beggar.   *Proverb*

1813. Beggars can never be bankrupts.   *Proverb*

1814. Beggars fear no rebellion.
Proverb

1815. Beggars must not be choosers.
Proverb

1816. Begging a courtesy is selling liberty.   *Proverb*

1817. Beggars breed and rich men feed.   *Proverb*

1818. Beggar that I am, I am even poor in thanks.
SHAKESPEARE, *Hamlet*

1819. Beggars mounted run their horse to death.
SHAKESPEARE, *Henry VI*

1820.
Well, whiles I am a beggar I will rail
And say there is no sin but to be rich;
And being rich, my virtue then shall be
To say there is no vice but beggary.
SHAKESPEARE, *King John*

1821.
I see, Sir, you are liberal in offers:
You taught me first to beg; and now, methinks,
You teach me how a beggar should be answer'd.
SHAKESPEARE, *Merchant of Venice*

See also: 191, 820, 2791, 4372, 4389, 21441.

BEGINNING

Related Subjects: Cause, End.

1831. The beginning, as the proverb says, is half the whole.
ARISTOTLE, *Politics*

1832. It is only the first obstacle which counts to conquer modesty.
BOSSUET,
Pensées Chrétiennes et Morales

1833. My way is to begin with the beginning.   BYRON, *Don Juan*

1834. The beginnings of all things are small.   CICERO,
De Finibus Bonorum et Malorum

1835. A bad beginning makes a bad ending.   EURIPIDES, *Aeolus*

1836. He has half the deed done, who has made a beginning.
HORACE, *Epistles*

1837. Resist beginnings: it is too late to employ medicine when the evil has grown strong by inveterate habit.
OVID, *Remedia Amoris*

1838. The beginning is the most important part of the work.
PLATO, *The Republic*

1839. He who commences many things finishes but few.   *Proverb*

1840. Take care not to begin anything of which you may repent.
PUBLILIUS SYRUS, *Sententiae*

1841. Whatever begins, also ends.
Seneca,
De Consolatione ad Polybium

1842. Things bad begun make strong themselves by ill.
Shakespeare, *Macbeth*

See also: 220, 11797, 15399.

BEHAVIOR

Related Subjects: Act, Deeds, Manners.

1851. For behaviour, men learn it, as they take diseases, one of another.
Bacon, *Advancement of Learning*

1852. Behaviour seemeth to me as a garment of the mind, and to have the conditions of a garment. For it ought to be made in fashion; it ought not to be too curious; it ought to be shaped so as to set forth any good making of the mind, and hide any deformity; and above all, it ought not to be too strait, or restrained for exercise or motion.
Bacon, *Advancement of Learning*

1853. And put himself upon his good behaviour.   Byron, *Don Juan*

1854. No better than she should be.
Cervantes, *Don Quixote*

1855. Behavior which appears superficially correct but is intrinsically corrupt always irritates those who see below the surface.
James Bryant Conant

1856. "And how did little Tim behave?" asked Mrs. Cratchit . . . "As good as gold," said Bob.
Dickens, *A Christmas Carol*

1857. The laws of behavior yield to the energy of the individual.
Emerson, *Essays*

1858. Would to God we had behaved ourselves well in this world, even for one day. Thomas à Kempis,
Of the Imitation of Christ

1859. Students of human behavior are recognizing increasingly . . . that the "different aspects of civilization interlock and intertwine, presenting—in a word—a *continuum.*"
Robert & Helen Lynd, *Middletown*

1860. Nothing is more adroit than irreproachable conduct.
Madame de Maintenon, *Maxims*

1861.
Behave yoursel' before folk;
Whate'er ye do, when out o' view,
Be cautious aye before folk.
Alexander Rodger,
Behave Yoursel' Before Folk

1862. Keep thy foot out of brothels, thy hand out of plackets, thy pen from lenders' books, and defy the foul fiend.   Shakespeare, *King Lear*

1863. There is a fair behaviour in thee.   Shakespeare, *Twelfth Night*

1864.
Four things a man must learn to do
If he would make his record true:
To think without confusion clearly;
To love his fellow-men sincerely;
To act from honest motives purely;
To trust in God and Heaven securely.
Henry Van Dyke, *Four Things*

See also: 4025, 5228, 6652.

BELIEF AND UNBELIEF

Related Subjects: Atheism, Confidence, Credulity, Creeds, Doctrine, Doubt, Faith, Martyr, Opinion, Religion, Superstition, Trust and Distrust.

1865. A belief is not true because it is useful.   Amiel, *Journal*

1866. Strong beliefs win strong men, and then make them stronger.
WALTER BAGEHOT,
Physics and Politics

1867. Jesus saith unto him, Thomas, because thou hast seen me thou hast believed: blessed are they that have not seen, and yet have believed.
Bible: John, xx, 29

1868. It is always easier to believe than to deny. Our minds are naturally affirmative.
JOHN BURROUGHS,
The Light of Day

1869. Men freely believe that which they desire.   JULIUS CAESAR,
Commentaries

1870. No iron chain, or outward force of any kind, could ever compel the soul of man to believe or to disbelieve.
CARLYLE,
Heroes & Hero-Worship

1871.
He was the Word, that spake it:
He took the bread and brake it;
And what that Word did make it,
I do believe and take it.
JOHN DONNE, *Divine Poems*

1872. A man must not swallow more beliefs than he can digest.
HAVELOCK ELLIS,
The Dance of Life

1873. We are born believing. A man bears beliefs, as a tree bears apples.
EMERSON, *Conduct of Life*

1874. The mob that would die for a belief seldom hesitates to inflict death upon any opposing heretical group.
ELLEN GLASGOW, *I Believe*

1875. When once a man is determined to believe, the very absurdity of the doctrine does but confirm him in his faith.   JUNIUS

1876. Here I stand; I can do no otherwise. God help me. Amen!
MARTIN LUTHER

1877. Nothing is so firmly believed as what we least know.
MONTAIGNE, *Essays*

1878. Better believe it than go where it was done to prove it.   *Proverb*

1879. He that believes all, misseth; he that believes nothing, hits not.
Proverb

1880. He does not believe that does not live according to his belief.
Proverb

1881.
For, dear me, why abandon a belief
Merely because it ceases to be true?
Cling to it long enough, and not a doubt
It will turn true again, for so it goes.
E. A. ROBINSON, *The Black Cottage*

1882. Every man, wherever he goes, is encompassed by a cloud of comforting convictions, which move with him like flies on a summer day.
BERTRAND RUSSELL, *Sceptical Essays*

1883. Few would hold nowadays the extreme doctrine of Tertullian— *Credo quia impossibile,* "I believe for the very reason that it is impossible"; but many still say, "I believe although it is impossible."
SIR HERBERT SAMUEL

1884. Mirabeau said of Robespierre, then hardly known: "That man will go far; he believes everything he says."   JOHN S. SMITH, *Mirabeau*

1885.
He in his heart
Felt that misgiving which precedes belief
In what was disbelieved.
SOUTHEY, *Joan of Arc*

1886. You believe that easily which you hope for earnestly.   TERENCE

1887. I believe because it is impossible.   TERTULLIAN,
De Carne Christi

1888. While men believe in the infinite, some ponds will be thought to be bottomless.   THOREAU, *Walden*

1889. Conviction is the Conscience of the Mind.
MRS. HUMPHRY WARD,
Robert Elsmere

Unbelief

1890. Lord, I believe; help thou mine unbelief.   *Bible: Mark, ix, 24*

1891. He who does not believe that God is above all is either a fool or has no experience of life.
CAECILIUS STATIUS

1892. Alas! the fearful Unbelief is unbelief in yourself.   CARLYLE,
Sartor Resartus

1893.
There is no unbelief;
Whoever plants a seed beneath the sod
And waits to see it push away the clod
He trusts in God.
LIZZIE YORK CASE, *Unbelief*

1894.
Blind unbelief is sure to err,
And scan his work in vain;
God is his own interpreter,
And he will make it plain.
COWPER,
Light Shining out of Darkness

1895. There is no strength in unbelief. Even the unbelief of what is false is no source of might. It is the truth shining from behind that gives the strength to disbelieve.
GEORGE MACDONALD,
The Marquis of Lossie

1896. If he be an unbeliever, he will be too profound and large-minded to ridicule religion or to act against it; he is too wise to be dogmatist or fanatic in his infidelity. He respects piety and devotion; he even supports institutions as venerable, beautiful, or useful, to which he does not assent; he honours the ministers of religion, and it contents him to decline its mysteries without assailing or denouncing them.
CARDINAL NEWMAN,
The Idea of a University

1897. Infidelity does not consist in believing or in disbelieving: it consists in professing to believe what one does not believe.
THOMAS PAINE, *The Age of Reason*

1898. I know of a charm by way of a prayer that will preserve a man from the violence of guns and all manner of fire-weapons and engines, but it will do me no good because I do not believe it.   RABELAIS

1899. A thing that nobody believes cannot be proved too often.
BERNARD SHAW,
The Devil's Disciple

1900. The temerity to believe in nothing.   TURGENIEV,
Fathers and Sons

See also: 1723, 3322, 3344, 3372, 7603, 8903, 9002, 11775, 17325.

BELL

Related Subjects: Church, Fire.

1901.
I call the Living—I mourn the Dead—
I break the Lightning.
ANONYMOUS, *Bell Inscription*

1902.

That all-softening, overpowering knell,
The tocsin of the soul,—the dinner bell.   BYRON, *Don Juan*

1903.

How soft the music of those village bells,
Falling at intervals upon the ear
In cadence sweet; now dying all away,
Now pealing loud again, and louder still,
Clear and sonorous, as the gale comes on!
With easy force it opens all the cells
Where Memory slept.
      COWPER, *The Task*

1904.

The vesper bell from far
That seems to mourn for the expiring day.   DANTE, *Purgatorio*

1905.

Dear bells! How sweet the sound of village bells
When on the undulating air they swim!   THOMAS HOOD,
        Ode to Rae Wilson

1906.

While the steeples are loud in their joy,
To the tune of the bells' ring-a-ding,
Let us chime in a peal, one and all,
For we all should be able to sing
Hullahbaloo.   THOMAS HOOD,
        Song for the Million

1907.

The cheerful Sabbath bells, wherever heard,
Strike pleasant on the sense, most like the voice
Of one, who from the far-off hills proclaims
Tidings of good to Zion.
    CHARLES LAMB, *The Sabbath Bells*

1908.

For bells are the voice of the church;
They have tones that touch and search
  The hearts of young and old.
    LONGFELLOW, *Bells of San Blas*

1909.

He heard the convent bell,
Suddenly in the silence ringing
For the service of noonday.
    LONGFELLOW, *Christus*

1910.

The bells themselves are the best of preachers,
Their brazen lips are learned teachers,
From their pulpits of stone, in the upper air,
Sounding aloft, without crack or flaw,
Shriller than trumpets under the Law,
Now a sermon and now a prayer.
    LONGFELLOW, *Christus*

1911.

Bell, thou soundest merrily,
When the bridal party
  To the church doth hie!
Bell, thou soundest solemnly,
When, on Sabbath morning,
  Fields deserted lie!
    LONGFELLOW, *Hyperion*

1912.

Those evening bells; those evening bells!
How many a tale their music tells!
    THOMAS MOORE,
     Those Evening Bells

1913. When thou dost hear a toll or knell, then think upon thy passing bell.   *Proverb*
See also: 10886.

1914. If you love not the noise of the bells, why pull the ropes? *Proverb*

1915. A cracked bell can never sound well.   *Proverb*

1916. Bells call others, but themselves enter not into the Church. *Proverb*

1917. Like sweet bells jangled, out of tune and harsh.

SHAKESPEARE, *Hamlet*

1918.

Then get thee gone and dig my grave thyself,

And bid the merry bells ring to thine ear

That thou art crowned, not that I am dead. SHAKESPEARE, *Hamlet*

1919.

The bell invites me.

Hear it not, Duncan; for it is a knell

That summons thee to heaven or to hell. SHAKESPEARE, *Macbeth*

1920.

Silence that dreadful bell! it frights the isle

From her propriety.

SHAKESPEARE, *Othello*

1921.

Ring out, wild bells, to the wild sky!

TENNYSON, *In Memoriam*

1922.

Ring out the old, ring in the new,

Ring, happy bells, across the snow!

TENNYSON, *In Memoriam*

1923. Curfew must not ring to-night.

ROSA H. THORPE, *Title of Poem*

See also: 2891, 10886.

BELLY

Related Subjects: Digestion, Drinking, Eating, Food, Hunger.

1931. They found that even the Belly, in its dull quiet way, was doing necessary work for the Body, and that all must work together or the Body will go to pieces. AESOP,
The Belly and the Members

1932. Every investigation which is guided by the principles of nature fixes its ultimate aim upon gratifying the stomach. ATHENAEUS,
Deipnosophists

1933. The belly carries the legs, and not the legs the belly.

CERVANTES, *Don Quixote*

1934. I can reason down or deny everything except this perpetual belly: feed he must and will, and I cannot make him respectable.

EMERSON, *Representative Men*

1935. A full belly makes a dull brain.

FRANKLIN, *Poor Richard*

1936. The belly is the commanding part of the body. HOMER

1937. Do not mourn the dead with the belly. HOMER

1938. He who does not mind his belly will hardly mind anything else.

SAMUEL JOHNSON, *Boswell: Life*

1939.

He had a broad face and a little round belly,

That shook, when he laughed, like a bowlful of jelly.

CLEMENT CLARKE MOORE,
A Visit from St. Nicholas

1940. An empty belly hears nobody.

Proverb

1941. The belly robs the back.

Proverb

1942. A gross belly does not produce a refined mind. *Proverb*

1943. If it were not for the belly, the back might wear gold. *Proverb*

1944. The vilest of beasts is the belly.

Proverb

1945. The eye is bigger than the belly. *Proverb*

1946. When the belly is full the mind is amongst the maids. *Proverb*

1947. No clock is more regular than the Belly.   RABELAIS

1948. A bellyfull is a bellyfull.   RABELAIS

1949. The belly will not listen to advice.   SENECA,
Epistulae ad Lucilium

1950. In fair round belly with good capon lined.   SHAKESPEARE,
As You Like It

1951. My belly's as cold as if I had swallowed snowballs for pills.
SHAKESPEARE,
The Merry Wives of Windsor

1952. Who wears his wit in his belly and his guts in his head.
SHAKESPEARE, *Troilus and Cressida*

1953. Did you ever hear of a heroine with a big belly? SIR RICHARD STEELE

1954. Better belly burst than good liquor be lost.   SWIFT,
Polite Conversation

1955. When the belly is full, the bones would be at rest.   SWIFT,
Polite Conversation

See also: 4215, 10150, 10279.

BENEFITS

Related Subjects: Advantage, Gifts, Improvement.

1961. He who confers a benefit on any one loves him better than he is beloved.   ARISTOTLE,
Nicomachean Ethics

1962. If you confer a benefit, never remember it; if you receive one, never forget it.   CHILON,
Septem Sapientum Sententiae

1963. There is a hook in every benefit, that sticks in his jaws that takes that benefit, and draws him whither the benefactor will.
JOHN DONNE, *Sermons*

1964. He that has once done you a kindness will be more ready to do you another, than he whom you yourself have obliged.   FRANKLIN,
Autobiography

1965. A God-send, as our familiarly pious ancestors termed a benefit received where the benefactor was unknown.   CHARLES LAMB,
Valentine's Day

1966. The good things of life are not to be had singly, but come to us with a mixture. CHARLES LAMB,
*That You Must Love
Me and Love My Dog*

1967. Benefits, like flowers, please most when they are fresh.   *Proverb*

1968. He that requites a benefit pays a great deal.   *Proverb*

1969. To accept a benefit is to sell one's freedom.
PUBLILIUS SYRUS, *Sententiae*

1970. A benefit cited by way of reproach is equivalent to an injury.
RACINE, *Iphigénie*

1971. A benefit consists not in what is done or given, but in the intention of the giver or doer.   SENECA,
De Beneficiis

1972. Let him that hath done the good office conceal it; let him that hath received it disclose it.
SENECA, *De Beneficiis*

1973. I benefit myself in aiding him.
SOPHOCLES, *Oedipus Tyrannus*

1974. In refusing benefits caution must be used lest we seem to despise or to refuse them for fear of having to repay them in kind.

SPINOZA, *Ethics*

1975. Benefits are acceptable, while the receiver thinks he may return them; but once exceeding that, hatred is given instead of thanks.

TACITUS, *History*

See also: 337, 5891.

BENEVOLENCE

Related Subjects: Charity, Gifts, Goodness, Kindness, Philanthropy.

1981. To make some nook of God's Creation a little fruitfuller, better, more worthy of God; to make some human hearts a little wiser, manfuller, happier,—more blessed, less accursed! It is work for a God.

CARLYLE, *Past and Present*

1982. Take egotism out, and you would castrate the benefactors.

EMERSON, *Journals*

1983. Benevolent people are very apt to be one-sided and fussy, and not of the sweetest temper if others will not be good and happy in their way.

ARTHUR HELPS, *Friends in Council*

1984. Benevolence is the distinguishing characteristic of man. As embodied in man's conduct, it is called the path of duty.   MENCIUS

1985.
And chiefly for the weaker by the wall,
You bore that lamp of sane benevolence.   GEORGE MEREDITH,
To a Friend Lost

See also: 1692, 3212.

BETRAYAL, see Treachery

BIBLE, THE

Related Subjects: Christ, Christianity, Faith, God, Miracle, Preacher, Prophecy, Religion.

1991. We have been careful that they that will read may have delight, and that they that are desirous to commit to memory might have ease, and that all into whose hands it comes might have profit.

Apocrypha: 2 Maccabees

1992.
Holy Bible, book divine,
Precious treasure, thou art mine;
Mine to teach me whence I came,
Mine to teach me what I am.

JOHN BURTON,
Holy Bible, Book Divine

1993. In the poorest cottage are Books: is one Book, wherein for several thousands of years the spirit of man has found light, and nourishment, and an interpreting response to whatever is Deepest in him.

CARLYLE, *Essays*

1994. His studie was but litel on the bible.   CHAUCER,
The Canterbury Tales

1995.
A glory gilds the sacred page,
Majestic like the sun,
It gives a light to ev'ry age,
It gives, but borrows none.

COWPER, *Olney Hymns*

1996. The text of the Bible is but a feeble symbol of the Revelation held in the text of Men and Women.

HAVELOCK ELLIS,
Impressions and Comments

1997. There are few among us who have not suffered from too early familiarity with the Bible and the conceptions of religion.

HAVELOCK ELLIS,
The Task of Social Hygiene

1998. The Bible is like an old Cremona; it has been played upon by the devotion of thousands of years until every word and particle is public and tunable.   EMERSON,
Letters and Social Aims

1999. My relations were much troubled at me that I would not go with them to hear the priest; for I would get into the orchard or the fields with my Bible by myself.
GEORGE FOX, *Journal*

2000. The book of books, the storehouse and magazine of life and comfort, the Holy Scriptures.
GEORGE HERBERT,
A Priest to the Temple

2001. Bibles laid open, millions of surprises.   GEORGE HERBERT, *Sinne*

2002.
On Bible stilts I don't affect to stalk,
Nor lard with Scripture my familiar
    talk.   THOMAS HOOD,
Ode to Rae Wilson

2003. As long as woman regards the Bible as the charter of her rights, she will be the slave of man. The Bible was not written by a woman. Within its lids there is nothing but humiliation and shame for her.
ROBERT INGERSOLL,
*The Liberty of Man,
Woman and Child*

2004. The English Bible,—a book which if everything else in our language should perish, would alone suffice to show the whole extent of its beauty and power.   MACAULAY,
On John Dryden

2005. The Bible is literature, not dogma.   SANTAYANA,
*Introduction to The
Ethics of Spinoza*

2006.
Within that awful volume lies
The mystery of mysteries!
SCOTT, *The Monastery*

2007. The Scripture, in time of disputes, is like an open town in time of war, which serves indifferently the occasions of both parties. SWIFT,
Thoughts on Various Subjects

2008. O Bible! say I, "What follies and monstrous barbarities are defended in *thy* name."
WALT WHITMAN

See also: 2453, 5666, 16243, 16753, 18896.

BIGOTRY

Related Subjects: Censorship, Dogmatism, Faith, Fanaticism, Obstinacy, Opinion, Prejudice, Reform, Righteousness, Self-Righteousness, Tolerance, Witch.

2011. A man must be both stupid and uncharitable who believes there is no virtue or truth but on his own side.
ADDISON

2012. There is no tariff so injurious as that with which sectarian bigotry guards its commodities.—It dwarfs the soul by shutting out truths from other continents of thought, and checks the circulation of its own.
E. H. CHAPIN

2013. Bigotry murders religion to frighten fools with her ghost.
C. C. COLTON

2014. There is no bigotry like that of "free thought" run to seed.
HORACE GREELEY

2015. The mind of the bigot is like the pupil of the eye; the more light you pour upon it, the more it will contract.   O. W. HOLMES

See also: 3133, 4540, 6644, 8822, 12957.

BIOGRAPHY

Related Subject: History.

2021. There is no heroic poem in the world but is at bottom a biography, the life of a man; also, it may be said, there is no life of a man, faithfully recorded, but is a heroic poem of its sort, rhymed or unrhymed.

CARLYLE, *Sir Walter Scott*

2022. The biographer has this problem set before him: to delineate a likeness of the earthly pilgrimage of a man.   CARLYLE,
Sir Walter Scott

2023. If an individual is really of consequence enough to have his life and character recorded for public remembrance, we have always been of the opinion that the public ought to be made acquainted with all the inward springs and relations of his character.   CARLYLE, *Burns*

2024. The history of the world is but the biography of great men.

CARLYLE,
Heroes & Hero-Worship

2025. Read no history, nothing but biography, for that is life without theory.   DISRAELI

2026. It seems to me much better to read a man's own writing than to read what others say about him, especially when the man is first-rate and the "others" are third-rate.

GEORGE ELIOT, *Life and Letters*

2027. The real source of all biography is the confession of the man himself to somebody.   EMERSON,
Lectures

2028. There is properly no History; only Biography. EMERSON, *History*

2029.
The poor dear dead have been laid
   out in vain;
Turn'd into cash, they are laid out
   again!   THOMAS HOOD,
On Reading a Diary Lately Published

2030. A great interpreter of life ought not himself to need interpretation.   JOHN MORLEY, *Emerson*

2031. What would become of all historical research and all biographies if they were always written with consideration for people's feelings?
R. H. SCHAUFFLER,
The Unknown Brahms

2032. Noble examples stir us up to noble actions, and the very history of large and public souls inspires a man with generous thoughts.   SENECA

2033.
After my death I wish no other
   herald,
No other speaker of my living actions,
To keep mine honour from corruption,
But such an honest chronicler as
   Griffith.   SHAKESPEARE,
Henry VIII

2034. A man who leaves memoirs, whether well or badly written, provided they be sincere, renders a service to future psychologists and writers.   SIENKIEWICZ,
Without Dogma

2035. A good portrait is a kind of biography, and neither painter nor biographer can carry out his task satisfactorily unless he be admitted behind the scenes.

ALEXANDER SMITH, *Dreamthorp*

2036.

Make bare the poor dead secrets of
   his heart,
Strip the stark-naked soul, that all
   may peer,
Spy, smirk, sniff, snap, snort, snivel,
   snarl, and sneer. SWINBURNE,
                    In Sepulcretis

2037. In these days a man is nobody
unless his biography is kept so far
posted up that it may be ready for
the national breakfast-table on the
morning after his demise.
 ANTHONY TROLLOPE, *Doctor Thorne*

See also: 1239, 7448, 8843, 11920.

BIRDS

**Related Subjects: Animals, Crow,
Cuckoo, Dove, Eagle, Eggs, Feath-
er, Goose, Hawk, Lark, Nature,
Nightingale, Owl, Peacock, Peli-
can, Raven, Robin, Sparrow,
Sport, Swallow, Swan, Tree.**

2041. A bird of the air shall carry
the voice, and that which hath wings
shall tell the matter.
            Bible: Ecclesiastes, x, 20

2042.

A light broke in upon my brain,—
   It was the carol of a bird;
It ceased, and then it came again,
   The sweetest song ear ever heard.
                    BYRON,
            The Prisoner of Chillon

2043.

I shall not ask Jean Jacques Rousseau
If birds confabulate or no.
                    COWPER,
            Pairing Time Anticipated

2044.

The nightingale has a lyre of gold,
   The lark's is a clarion call,
And the blackbird plays but a box-
   wood flute,
   But I love him best of all.
            W. E. HENLEY, *Echoes*

2045. I was always a lover of soft-
winged things.   VICTOR HUGO,
            I Was Always a Lover

2046. A rare bird upon the earth,
and exceedingly like a black swan.
                JUVENAL, *Satires*

2047.

A bird appears a thoughtless thing...
No doubt he has his little cares
And very hard he often fares,
The which so patiently he bears.
                CHARLES LAMB,
                Crumbs to the Birds

2048. The birds, God's poor who
cannot wait.   LONGFELLOW,
            The Sermon of St. Francis

2049.

Do you ne'er think what wondrous
   beings these?
   Do you ne'er think who made them,
   and who taught
The dialect they speak, where melodies
   Alone are the interpreters of
   thought?
Whose household words are songs in
   many keys,
   Sweeter than instrument of man
   e'er caught.   LONGFELLOW,
            Tales of a Wayside Inn

2050.

Every bird that upwards swings
Bears the Cross upon its wings.
            Attr. to JOHN M. NEALE

2051. Never look for birds of this
year in the nests of the last. *Proverb*

2052. A feather in hand is better
than a bird in the air.   *Proverb*

2053. Birds pay equal honours to all
men.   *Proverb*

2054. A bird in the hand is worth
two in the bush.   *Proverb*

2055. Birds of a feather flock together.   *Proverb*

2056. To kill two birds with one stone.   *Proverb*

2057. Don't waste too many stones on one bird.   *Proverb*

2058. A little bird told me.
SHAKESPEARE, *Henry IV*

2059.
Gay, guiltless pair,
What seek ye from the fields of
heaven?
Ye have no need of prayer,
Ye have no sins to be forgiven.
CHARLES SPRAGUE,
The Winged Worshippers

See also: 1498, 1664, 2078, 3850,
6281, 7621, 8798, 11866, 14421,
20431, 20432, 21274.

BIRTH AND BIRTHDAY

Related Subjects: Ancestry, Aristocracy, Babies, Breeding, Holiday, Life, Mother.

2061. When I was born I drew in the common air, and fell upon the earth, which is of like nature, and the first voice which I uttered was crying, as all others do.
Apocrypha: Wisdom of Solomon

2062.
Every night and every morn
Some to misery are born;
Every morn and every night
Some are born to sweet delight.
BLAKE, *Proverbs*

2063. Almost in every kingdom the most ancient families have been at first princes' bastards; their worthiest captains, best wits, greatest scholars, bravest spirits in all our annals, have been base (born).
ROBERT BURTON,
Anatomy of Melancholy

2064. He is born naked, and falls a whining at the first.
ROBERT BURTON,
Anatomy of Melancholy

2065.
Of ancient race by birth, but nobler
yet
In his own worth.   DRYDEN,
Absalom & Achitophel

2066. Man alone at the very moment of his birth, cast naked upon the naked earth, does she abandon to cries and lamentations.
PLINY THE ELDER, *Natural History*

2067. Great birth is a very poor dish at table.   *Proverb*

2068. Who is well-born? He who is by nature well fitted for virtue.
SENECA, *Epistulae ad Lucilium*

2069.
A grievous burthen was thy birth to
me;
Tetchy and wayward was thy infancy.
SHAKESPEARE, *Richard III*

2070. "Do you know who made you?"
"Nobody, as I knows on," said the child, with a short laugh. The idea appeared to amuse her considerably; for her eyes twinkled, and she added—
"I 'spect I growed. Don't think nobody never made me."
HARRIET BEECHER STOWE,
Uncle Tom's Cabin

2071.
As some divinely gifted man,
Whose life in low estate began,
And on a simple village green;
Who breaks his birth's invidious bar.
TENNYSON, *In Memoriam*

2072. Why is it that we rejoice at a birth and grieve at a funeral? It is because we are not the person involved.
MARK TWAIN,
Pudd'nhead Wilson's Calendar

2073.

Our birth is but a sleep and a for-
    getting;
The soul that rises with us, our life's
    star,
    Hath had elsewhere its setting,
      And cometh from afar:
                WORDSWORTH,
Ode on Intimations of Immortality

2074.

  Not in entire forgetfulness,
  And not in utter nakedness,
But trailing clouds of glory do we
  come
From God, who is our home:
Heaven lies about us in our infancy!
                WORDSWORTH,
Ode on Intimations of Immortality

2075. Our birth is nothing but our
death begun.   EDWARD YOUNG,
                Night Thoughts

Birthday

2076. Do you count your birthdays
thankfully?   HORACE, *Epistles*

2077.

A birthday:—and now a day that rose
  With much of hope, with meaning
  rife—
A thoughtful day from dawn to close:
  The middle day of human life.
  JEAN INGELOW, *A Birthday Walk*

2078.

And show me your nest with the
    young ones in it,
  I will not steal them away;
I am old! you may trust me, linnet,
    linnet—
  I am seven times one to-day.
  JEAN INGELOW, *Songs of Seven*

2079. The return of my birthday, if
I remember it, fills me with thoughts
which it seems to be the general care
of humanity to escape.
    SAMUEL JOHNSON, *Boswell: Life*

2080.

My birthday!—what a different sound
  That word had in my youthful ears;
And how each time the day comes
  round,
    Less and less white its mark ap-
    pears.   THOMAS MOORE,
                My Birthday

2081.

Is that a birthday? 'tis, alas! too clear;
'Tis but the funeral of the former
  year.   POPE, *To Mrs. M. B.*

2082.

This day I breathed first: time is
  come round;
And where I did begin, there shall I
  end;
My life is run his compass.
    SHAKESPEARE, *Julius Caesar*

See also: 4123.

BLACK

**Related Subjects: Color, Darkness,
Night, Raven.**

2091. Above black there is no colour,
and above salt no savour.
    JOHN FLORIO, *First Fruites*

2092. Black as hell.
          SHAKESPEARE, *Hamlet*

2093. By heaven, thy love is black as
ebony.   SHAKESPEARE,
          Love's Labour's Lost

2094. The hue of dungeons and the
suit of night.   SHAKESPEARE,
          Love's Labour's Lost

2095. Is black so base a hue?
    SHAKESPEARE, *Titus Andronicus*

2096.

Coal-black is better than another hue,
In that it scorns to bear another hue.
    SHAKESPEARE, *Titus Andronicus*

2097. How black?—Why, as black as ink.   SHAKESPEARE,
Two Gentlemen of Verona

See also: 2108, 3066, 5655.

BLACKSMITH

Related Subjects: Anvil, Forge, Iron.

2101.
Curs'd be that wretch (Death's fac-
    tor sure) who brought
Dire swords into the peaceful world,
    and taught
Smiths (who before could only make
The spade, the plough-share, and the
    rake)
Arts, in most cruel wise
Man's left to epitomize!
                ABRAHAM COWLEY,
        In Commendation of the Time

2102. The first smith was the first
murd'rer's son.   COWPER, *The Task*

2103.
And fitfully you still may see the grim
    smiths ranking round,
All clad in leathern panoply, their
    broad hands only bare;
Some rest upon their sledges here,
    some work the windlass there.
                SAMUEL FERGUSON,
        The Forging of the Anchor

2104.
Under a spreading chestnut tree
    The village smithy stands:
The smith, a mighty man is he,
    With large and sinewy hands;
And the muscles of his brawny arms
    Are strong as iron bands.
LONGFELLOW, *The Village Blacksmith*

2105.
As great Pythagoras of yore,
Standing beside the blacksmith's door,
And hearing the hammers, as they
    smote

The anvils with a different note,
Stole from the varying tones that
    hung
Vibrant on every iron tongue,
The secret of the sounding wire,
And formed the seven-chorded lyre.
                LONGFELLOW, *To a Child*

2106.
And he sang: "Hurra for my handi-
    work!"
    And the red sparks lit the air;
Not alone for the blade was the
    bright steel made;
    And he fashioned the first plough-
    share.
        CHARLES MACKAY, *Tubal Cain*

2107.
In other part stood one who, at the
    forge
Labouring, two massy clods of iron
    and brass
Had melted.   MILTON,
                Paradise Lost

2108. The smith and his penny both
are black.   *Proverb*

2109.
From whence came Smith, albe he
    knight or squire,
But from the smith that forgeth at
    the fire?
                RICHARD ROWLANDS,
    Restitution of Decayed Intelligence

2110.
I saw a smith stand with his hammer,
    thus,
The whilst his iron did on the anvil
    cool.   SHAKESPEARE, *King John*

2111.
The painful smith, with force of fer-
    vent heat,
The hardest iron soon doth mollify,
That with his heavy sledge he can it
    beat,
And fashion it to what he it list apply.
        EDMUND SPENSER, *Amoretti*

BLESSING

Related Subjects: Benefit, Prayer.

2121. 'Tis not for mortals always to be blest. JOHN ARMSTRONG,
Art of Preserving Health

2122.
Blessings star forth forever; but a curse
Is like a cloud—it passes.
 PHILIP J. BAILEY, *Festus*

2123. I will not let thee go, except thou bless me.
 Bible: Genesis, xxxii, 26

2124. The Lord bless thee, and keep thee: The Lord make his face shine upon thee, and be gracious unto thee: The Lord lift up his countenance upon thee, and give thee peace.
 Bible: Numbers, vi, 24, 25, 26

2125. Blessed shall be thy basket and thy store.
 Bible: Deuteronomy, xxviii, 5

2126. The grace of the Lord Jesus Christ, and the love of God, and the communion of the Holy Ghost, be with you all.
 Bible: 2 Corinthians, xiii, 14

2127. Bless me in this life with but peace of my conscience, command of my affections, the love of Thyself and my dearest friends, and I shall be happy enough to pity Caesar.
SIR THOMAS BROWNE, *Religio Medici*

2128. Blessed is he who has found his work; let him ask no other blessedness. CARLYLE, *Past and Present*

2129. Blessed are the valiant that have lived in the Lord. CARLYLE,
Cromwell's Letters and Speeches

2130.
A spring of love gush'd from my heart,
And I bless'd them unaware.
 COLERIDGE, *The Ancient Mariner*

2131.
For blessings ever wait on virtuous deeds,
And though a late, a sure reward succeeds. CONGREVE,
The Mourning Bride

2132. "God bless us every one!" said Tiny Tim. DICKENS,
A Christmas Carol

2133.
To heal divisions, to relieve the oppress'd,
In virtue rich; in blessing others, bless'd. HOMER, *Odyssey*

2134. From people who merely pray we must become people who bless.
 NIETZSCHE, *Thus Spake Zarathustra*

2135.
The blest to-day is as completely so,
As who began a thousand years ago.
 POPE, *Essay on Man*

2136. Good health and good sense are two of life's greatest blessings.
 PUBLILIUS SYRUS, *Sententiae*

2137.
God bless us every one, prayed Tiny Tim
 Crippled and dwarfed of body yet so tall
Of soul, we tiptoe earth to look on him,
 High towering over all.
 JAMES WHITCOMB RILEY,
God Bless Us Every One

2138. The dews of heaven fall thick in blessings on her!
 SHAKESPEARE, *Henry VIII*

2139.
I had most need of blessing, and "Amen"
Stuck in my throat.
 SHAKESPEARE, *Macbeth*

2140. Bless thee, Bottom! bless thee! thou art translated.
 SHAKESPEARE,
A Midsummer-Night's Dream

2141. Blessedness is not the reward of virtue but virtue itself.   SPINOZA

2142. The three blessings for which I am most grateful to Fortune are: first, that I was born a human being and not one of the brutes; second, that I was born a man and not a woman; third, that I was born a Greek and not a barbarian.
THALES, *Diogenes Laertius*

2143.
Amid my list of blessings infinite,
Stands this the foremost, "That my
heart has bled."
EDWARD YOUNG, *Night Thoughts*

See also: 468, 1750, 2316, 2406, 2416, 2426, 2522, 2851, 3102, 5015, 5149, 8923, 11144, 15753.

BLINDNESS

Related Subjects: Darkness, Eyes, Sight, Vision.

2151. If the blind lead the blind, both shall fall into the ditch.
Bible: Matthew, xv, 14

2152. How blind must he be that can't see through a sieve.
CERVANTES, *Don Quixote*

2153.
Oh, say! what is that thing call'd light,
Which I must ne'er enjoy?
What are the blessings of the sight?
Oh, tell your poor blind boy!
COLLEY CIBBER, *The Blind Boy*

2154. Your dear friend and servant, Galileo, has been for the last month perfectly blind, so that this heaven, this earth, this universe, which I by my marvellous discoveries and clear demonstrations have enlarged a hundred thousand times beyond the belief of the wise men of bygone years, henceforward is for me shrunk into such a small space as is filled by my own bodily sensations. So it pleases God; so also shall it therefore please me.   GALILEO, *to Diodati (1638)*

2155. None so blind as those that will not see. MATTHEW HENRY,
Commentaries

2156.
O loss of sight, of thee I most complain!
Blind among enemies, O worse than chains,
Dungeon, or beggary, or decrepit age!
MILTON, *Samson Agonistes*

2157.
O dark, dark, dark, amid the blaze of noon,
Irrecoverably dark, total eclipse
Without all hope of day!
MILTON, *Samson Agonistes*

2158.
        These eyes, tho' clear
To outward view of blemish or of spot,
Bereft of light, their seeing have forgot,
Nor to their idle orbs doth sight appear
Of sun, or moon, or star, throughout the year,
Or man, or woman. Yet I argue not
Against Heaven's hand or will, nor bate a jot
Of heart or hope; but still bear up and steer
Right onward.   MILTON,
Sonnet XXII

2159. He has the greatest blind-side, who thinks he has none.   *Proverb*

2160. What matters it to a blind man that his father could see?   *Proverb*

2161. Blind men's wives need no paint.
Proverb

2162. A blind man will not thank you for a looking-glass.   *Proverb*

2163.

He that is strucken blind cannot forget

The precious treasure of his eyesight lost.   SHAKESPEARE,
Romeo and Juliet

2164.

     And when a damp

Fell round the path of Milton, in his hand

The Thing became a trumpet; whence he blew

Soul-animating strains—alas! too few.

WORDSWORTH, *Scorn Not the Sonnet*

See also: 1282, 1632, 9924, 9930, 11150, 12078, 12941.

BLISS

Related Subjects: **Contentment, Delight, Happiness, Joy, Pleasure.**

2171. The bliss e'en of a moment still is bliss.   JOANNA BAILLIE,
The Beacon

2172.

All indistinctly apprehend a bliss,

On which the soul may rest; the hearts of all

Yearn after it.   DANTE, *Purgatorio*

2173.

Is bliss, then, such abyss

I must not put my foot amiss

For fear I spoil my shoe?

EMILY DICKINSON, *Life*

2174.

The hues of bliss more brightly glow,

Chastis'd by sabler tints of woe.

THOMAS GRAY,
*Ode on the Pleasure Arising from
Vicissitude*

2175.

Where, in creation's wide domains,

Can perfect bliss be found?

REGINALD HEBER, *Happiness*

2176.

Alas! by some degree of woe

   We every bliss must gain;

The heart can ne'er a transport know,

   That never feels a pain.

LORD LYTTLETON, *Song*

2177.

But such a sacred and home-felt delight,

Such sober certainty of waking bliss,

I never heard till now.

MILTON, *Comus*

2178. The sum of earthly bliss.

MILTON, *Paradise Lost*

2179.

Some place the bliss in action, some in ease,

Those call it pleasure, and contentment these.   POPE, *Essay on Man*

2180.

Condition, circumstance, is not the thing;

Bliss is the same in subject or in king.

POPE, *Essay on Man*

2181.

The way to bliss lies not on beds of down;

And he that had no cross deserves no crown.   FRANCIS QUARLES,
Esther

2182.

Man looks at his own bliss, considers it,

Weighs it with curious fingers; and 'tis gone.   WILLIAM WATSON,
Epigrams

2183.

The spider's most attenuated thread

Is cord, is cable, to man's tender tie

On earthly bliss; it breaks at every breeze.   EDWARD YOUNG,
Night Thoughts

See also: 1251, 2669, 3164, 10325, 15570, 22064.

BLOOD

Related Subjects: Family, Heredity, Wounds.

2191. The blood is the life.
Bible: Deuteronomy, xii, 23

2192. His blood be on us and on our children.
Bible: Matthew, xxvii, 25

2193. Something will come of this. I hope it mayn't be human gore.
DICKENS, *Barnaby Rudge*

2194. Blood is a juice of rarest quality.   GOETHE, *Faust*

2195. For four years we have had to fight at home against the idea of international Marxistic solidarity. In this so-called international solidarity we saw merely the enemy of any true national attitude of mind, a mere phantom which lured men away from the only intelligent sort of solidarity that there can be, the solidarity which finds its eternal basis in the ties of blood.   ADOLF HITLER

2196. What coast knows not our blood?   HORACE, *Odes*

2197.
And in the midst, 'mong thousand heraldries,
And twilight saints, and dim emblazonings,
A shielded scutcheon blush'd with blood of queens and kings.
KEATS, *Eve of St. Agnes*

2198. First Moloch, horrid King, besmear'd with blood.   MILTON,
Paradise Lost

2199. A compact sealed in blood.
Proverb

2200. Human blood is all of one color.   *Proverb*

2201. Blood is thicker than water.
Proverb

2202. The hey-day in the blood is tame, it's humble.
SHAKESPEARE, *Hamlet*

2203. Yet who would have thought the old man to have had so much blood in him?   SHAKESPEARE,
Macbeth

2204.
I am in blood
Stepp'd in so far, that, should I wade no more,
Returning were as tedious as go o'er.
SHAKESPEARE, *Macbeth*

2205.
Will all great Neptune's ocean wash this blood
Clean from my hand? No, this my hand will rather
The multitudinous seas incarnadine,
Making the green one red.
SHAKESPEARE, *Macbeth*

2206. Nothing like blood, sir, in hosses, dawgs, and men.
THACKERAY, *Vanity Fair*

2207.
Hands across the sea
Feet on English ground,
The old blood is bold blood, the wide world round.
BYRON WEBBER,
Hands Across the Sea

See also: 862, 1141, 1445, 2651, 2831, 6951, 19811.

BLUNDER, see Error, Mistake

BLUSHING

Related Subjects: Chastity, Embarrassment, Face, Innocence, Modesty, Purity and Impurity, Shame.

2211.
Girls blush, sometimes, because they are alive,

Half wishing they were dead to save
  the shame.
The sudden blush devours them, neck
  and brow;
They have drawn too near the fire of
  life, like gnats,
And flare up bodily, wings and all.
      ELIZABETH B. BROWNING,
               Aurora Leigh

2212.
So sweet the blush of bashfulness,
E'en pity scarce can wish it less!
      BYRON, *Bride of Abydos*

2213. Blushed like the waves of hell.
      BYRON, *Devil's Drive*

2214. Pure friendship's well-feigned
blush.   BYRON,
  Stanzas to Her Who Can Best
        Understand Them

2215.
I pity bashful men, who feel the pain
Of fancied scorn and undeserved dis-
  dain,
And bear the marks upon a blushing
  face,
Of needless shame, and self-impos'd
  disgrace.   COWPER, *Conversation*

2216. Once he [Diogenes] saw a
youth blushing, and addressed him,
"Courage my boy! that is the complexion of virtue."
  DIOGENES LAERTIUS, *Diogenes*

2217. A blush is no language; only a
dubious flag-signal which may mean
either of two contradictories.
  GEORGE ELIOT, *Daniel Deronda*

2218.
The rising blushes, which her cheek
  o'erspread,
Are opening roses in the lily's bed.
      JOHN GAY, *Dione*

2219. The blush is beautiful, but it
is sometimes inconvenient.
      GOLDONI, *Pamela*

2220. Blushing is the colour of virtue.
  MATTHEW HENRY, *Commentaries*

2221.
  Such a blush
In the midst of brown was born,
Like red poppies grown with corn.
      THOMAS HOOD, *Ruth*

2222. Men blush less for their crimes
than for their weaknesses and vanity.
  LA BRUYÈRE, *Les Caractères*

2223. Innocence is not accustomed to
blush.   MOLIÈRE,
    Don Garcie de Navarre

2224.
While mantling on the maiden's cheek
Young roses kindled into thought.
THOMAS MOORE, *Evenings in Greece*

2225. To blush at vice shews the
world you are ashamed of it.
              Proverb

2226. Better a blush in the face than
a spot in the heart.   *Proverb*

2227.
  I will go wash;
And when my face is fair, you shall
  perceive
Whether I blush or no.
      SHAKESPEARE, *Coriolanus*

2228.
Lay by all nicety and prolixious
  blushes,
That banish what they sue for.
SHAKESPEARE, *Measure for Measure*

2229.
  I have mark'd
A thousand blushing apparitions
To start into her face; a thousand
  innocent shames
In angel whiteness beat away those
  blushes.
      SHAKESPEARE,
  Much Ado About Nothing

BLUSHING

2230.
And bid the cheek be ready with a blush
Modest as morning when she coldly eyes
The youthful Phoebus.
SHAKESPEARE, *Troilus and Cressida*

2231.
Come, quench your blushes and present yourself
That which you are, mistress o' the feast.   SHAKESPEARE,
The Winter's Tale

2232.
Yet will she blush, here be it said,
To hear her secrets so bewrayed.
SHAKESPEARE,
The Passionate Pilgrim

2233.
Where now I have no one to blush with me,
To cross their arms and hang their heads with mine.
SHAKESPEARE, *The Rape of Lucrece*

2234.
Two red fires in both their faces blazed;
She thought he blush'd . . .
And, blushing with him, wistly on him gazed.
SHAKESPEARE, *The Rape of Lucrece*

2235. He blushes: all is safe.
TERENCE, *Adelphi*

2236. Man is the only animal that blushes. Or needs to.
MARK TWAIN,
Pudd'nhead Wilson's Calendar

2237. The man that blushes is not quite a brute.   EDWARD YOUNG,
Night Thoughts

See also: 1755, 2254, 2643, 10443.

BOASTING

Related Subjects: Arrogance, Braggart, Conceit, Exaggeration, Ostentation, Pride, Vanity, Vulgarity.

2241. Much outcry, little outcome.
AESOP, *The Mountains in Labor*

2242.
I winna blaw about mysel,
As ill I like my faults to tell.
BURNS, *First Epistle to J. Lapraik*

2243.
Yet if thou sin in wine or wantonness,
Boast not thereof; nor make thy shame thy glory.
GEORGE HERBERT, *The Church-Porch*

2244. Ye deedless boasters!
HOMER, *Odyssey*

2245. Every other enjoyment malice may destroy; every other panegyric envy may withhold; but no human power can deprive the boaster of his own encomiums.
SAMUEL JOHNSON, *The Rambler*

2246.
If you stop to consider the work you have done
  And to boast what your labour is worth, dear,
Angels may come for you, Willie, my son,
  But you'll never be wanted on Earth, dear!
KIPLING, *Mary's Son*

2247.
Let him not boast who puts his armor on
As he who puts it off, the battle done.
LONGFELLOW, *Morituri Salutamus*

2248. The empty vessel giveth a greater sound than the full barrel.
JOHN LYLY, *Euphues*

2249. A man destitute of courage, but boasting of his glorious achievements, imposes on strangers, but is the derision of those who know him.

PHAEDRUS, *Fables*

2250. A boaster and a liar are cousins.
Proverb

2251. Great boast, small roast.
Proverb

2252. He that boasteth of himself affronteth his company.   *Proverb*

2253. He that boasts of his own knowledge proclaims his ignorance.
Proverb

2254. He who blushes at riding in a rattle-trap, will boast when he rides in style.   SENECA,
Epistulae ad Lucilium

2255.
We'll have a swashing and a martial outside,
As many other mannish cowards have.
SHAKESPEARE, *As You Like It*

2256. The saying is true, "The empty vessel makes the greatest sound."
SHAKESPEARE, *Henry V*

2257. Where boasting ends, there dignity begins.   EDWARD YOUNG,
Night Thoughts

See also: 342, 683, 809, 812, 818, 1611.

BOAT AND BOATING, see Ship

BODY

Related Subjects: Bone, Flesh, Head, Health, Leg, Mind, Skin, Soul.

2261. The body is but a pair of pincers set over a bellows and a stewpan and the whole fixed upon stilts.
SAMUEL BUTLER, *Note Books*

2262. The precious porcelain of human clay.   BYRON, *Don Juan*

2263.
Nought cared this body for wind or weather,
When youth and I lived in 't together.
COLERIDGE, *Youth and Age*

2264.
I gave my son a palace
   And a kingdom to control:
The palace of his body,
   The kingdom of his soul.
JULIA WARD HOWE,
Palace and Kingdom

2265.
This body is my house—it is not I:
Triumphant in this faith I live and die.
FREDERIC LAWRENCE KNOWLES,
The Tenant

2266. A human being: an ingenious assembly of portable plumbing.
CHRISTOPHER MORLEY, *Human Being*

2267. The body is the socket of the soul.   *Proverb*

2268. Our bodies are our gardens, to the which our wills are gardeners; . . . either to have it sterile with idleness or manured with industry.
SHAKESPEARE, *Othello*

2269.
My body, which my dungeon is,
And yet my parks and palaces.
STEVENSON, *Underwoods*

2270. Body and spirit are twins: God only knows which is which.
SWINBURNE,
The Higher Pantheism in a Nutshell

2271. Every man is the builder of a temple, called his body.
THOREAU, *Walden*

2272. If any thing is sacred the human body is sacred.
WALT WHITMAN, *Children of Adam*

See also: 493, 1038, 1716, 1732, 1931, 5054.

BOLDNESS

Related Subjects: Adventure, Courage, Valor.

2281. Remember the old saying, "Faint heart ne'er won fair lady."
CERVANTES, *Don Quixote*

2282.
Write on your doors the saying wise and old,
"Be bold! be bold!" and everywhere —"Be bold;
Be not too bold!"
LONGFELLOW, *Morituri Salutamus*

2283. Boldness is a mask for fear, however great. LUCAN,
The Civil War

2284. It is better to be bold than too circumspect, because fortune is of a sex which likes not a tardy wooer and repulses all who are not ardent.
MACHIAVELLI

2285. Boldness in business is the first, second, and third thing. *Proverb*

2286.
How over that same dore was likewise writ,
Be bold, be bold, and ever where Be bold, EDMUND SPENSER,
The Faerie Queene

2287.
Another yron dore, on which was writ,
Be not too bold.
EDMUND SPENSER,
The Faerie Queene

See also: 2731, 5329, 14490.

BONAPARTE, see Napoleon

BONE

Related Subjects: Body, Flesh, Skin, Skull.

2291. Making no bones of it.
ROBERT ARMIN, *Nest of Ninnies*

2292. Bone of my bones.
Bible: Genesis, ii, 23

2293. I may tell all my bones: they look and stare upon me.
Bible: Psalms, xxii, 17

2294. It is the soundness of the bones that ultimates itself in the peach-bloom complexion.
EMERSON, *Conduct of Life*

2295. Fair fall the bones that took the pains for me!
SHAKESPEARE, *King John*

2296. Thy bones are marrowless.
SHAKESPEARE, *Macbeth*

2297. I have a bone to pick with you.
Traditional

See also: 1955.

BOOKS

Related Subjects: Authors, Fiction, History, Library, Literature, Press, Printing, Reading, School, Writing.

2301. Books are the legacies that a great genius leaves to mankind, which are delivered down from generation to generation, as presents to the posterity of those who are yet unborn.
ADDISON, *The Spectator*

2302. Some books are to be tasted, others to be swallowed, and some few to be chewed and digested.
BACON, *Of Studies*

2303. Books must follow sciences, and not sciences books. BACON,
Proposition touching Amendment of Laws

2304.

     Worthy books
Are not companions—they are solitudes:
We lose ourselves in them and all our cares. PHILIP J. BAILEY, *Festus*

2305. Where is human nature so weak as in the book-store!
    H. W. BEECHER, *Star Papers*

2306. Nothing marks the increasing wealth of our times and the growth of the public mind toward refinement, more than the demand for books.
    H. W. BEECHER, *Star Papers*

2307. Oh that my words were now written! oh that they were printed in a book! *Bible: Job, xix, 23*

2308. My desire is . . . that mine adversary had written a book.
    Bible: Job, xxxi, 35

2309. How could an actual person fit into the covers of a book? The book is not a continent, not a definite geographical measure, it cannot contain so huge a thing as an actual full-size person. Any person has to be scaled by eliminations to fit the book world. PEARL BUCK,
   Advice to Unborn Novelists

2310. If the whole be greater than a part, a whole man must be greater than that part of him which is found in a book.
  BULWER-LYTTON, *Caxtonia*

2311. Some books are lies frae end to end.
BURNS, *Death and Dr. Hornbook*

2312. I go to books and to nature as a bee goes to the flower, for a nectar that I can make into my own honey.
    JOHN BURROUGHS,
   The Summit of the Years

2313.

'Tis pleasant, sure, to see one's name in print;
A book's a book, although there's nothin' in 't. BYRON,
English Bards and Scotch Reviewers

2314. All that mankind has done, thought, gained or been: it is lying as in magic preservation in the pages of books.
CARLYLE, *Heroes & Hero-Worship*

2315. In books lies the soul of the whole Past Time: the articulate audible voice of the past, when the body and material substance of it has altogether vanished like a dream.
CARLYLE, *Heroes & Hero-Worship*

2316. May blessings be upon the head of Cadmus or the Phoenicians, or whoever invented books!
    CARLYLE

2317. He that publishes a book runs a very great hazard, since nothing can be more impossible than to compose one that may secure the approbation of every reader.
  CERVANTES, *Don Quixote*

2318. Books are the true levelers. They give to all who faithfully use them the society, the spiritual presence, of the best and greatest of our race. W. E. CHANNING

2319. The book originated in the suggestion of a publisher; as many more good books have done than the arrogance of the man of letters is commonly inclined to admit.
   G. K. CHESTERTON,
   Preface to Pickwick Papers

2320.

Books cannot always please, however good;
Minds are not ever craving for their food.
  GEORGE CRABBE, *The Borough*

2321. There are books of which the backs and covers are by far the best parts. DICKENS, *Oliver Twist*

2322. It is a great thing to start life with a small number of really good books which are your very own.
CONAN DOYLE,
Through the Magic Door

2323.
That book is good
Which puts me in a working mood.
Unless to Thought is added Will,
Apollo is an imbecile.
EMERSON, *The Poet*

2324. By burning Luther's books you may rid your book-shelves of him, but you will not rid men's minds of him.
ERASMUS

2325. I would define a book as a work of magic whence escape all kinds of images to trouble the souls and change the hearts of men. ANATOLE FRANCE

2326.
You must know I've resolved and agreed
My books from my room not to lend,
But you may sit by my fire and read.
CAROLINE H. GILMAN,
One Good Turn Deserves Another

2327. He might be a very clever man by nature for aught I know, but he laid so many books upon his head that his brains could not move.
ROBERT HALL

2328.
The readers and the hearers like my books,
But yet some writers cannot them digest;
But what care I? for when I make a feast
I would my guests should praise it, not the cooks.
SIR JOHN HARRINGTON, *Epigrams*

2329. Books without the knowledge of life are useless; for what should books teach but the art of living.
SAMUEL JOHNSON

2330. Books think for me.
CHARLES LAMB,
Detached Thoughts on Books & Reading

2331. To be strong-backed and neat-bound is the *desideratum* of a volume. Magnificence comes after.
CHARLES LAMB,
Detached Thoughts on Books & Reading

2332. Borrowers of books—those mutilators of collections, spoilers of the symmetry of shelves, and creators of odd volumes.
CHARLES LAMB,
The Two Races of Men

2333. A presentation copy . . . is a copy of a book which does not sell, sent you by the author, with his foolish autograph at the beginning of it; for which, if a stranger, he only demands your friendship; if a brother author, he expects a book of yours, which does not sell, in return.
CHARLES LAMB,
Popular Fallacies

2334.
When others fail him, the wise man looks
To the sure companionship of books.
ANDREW LANG, *Old Friends*

2335. You can cover a great deal of country in books.
ANDREW LANG,
To the Gentle Reader

2336.
The love of learning, the sequestered nooks,
And all the sweet serenity of books.
LONGFELLOW, *Morituri Salutamus*

2337. Such, and so magnifying, is the virtue of a large and liberal theme! We expand to its bulk. To produce a mighty book, you must choose a mighty theme. No great and enduring volume can ever be written on the flea, though many there be who have tried it.

HERMAN MELVILLE, *Moby Dick*

2338. God keep me from ever completing anything. This whole book is but a draught—nay, but the draught of a draught. Oh, Time, Strength, Cash, and Patience!

HERMAN MELVILLE, *Moby Dick*

2339. Deep vers'd in books, and shallow in himself.

MILTON, *Paradise Regained*

2340. As good almost kill a man as kill a good book: who kills a man kills a reasonable creature, God's image; but he who destroys a good book kills reason itself. MILTON, *Areopagitica*

2341. A good book is the precious life-blood of a master-spirit, embalmed and treasured up on purpose to a life beyond life.

MILTON, *Areopagitica*

2342. There are some books which cannot be adequately reviewed for twenty or thirty years after they come out. JOHN MORLEY, *Recollections*

2343. A book that remains shut, is but a block. *Proverb*

2344. After love, book collecting is the most exhilarating sport of all.

A. S. W. ROSENBACH,
A Book Hunter's Holiday

2345. He hath not fed of the dainties that are bred in a book; he hath not eat paper, as it were; he hath not drunk ink.

SHAKESPEARE, *Love's Labour's Lost*

2346. You two are book-men.

SHAKESPEARE, *Love's Labour's Lost*

2347.
Knowing I lov'd my books, he furnish'd me
From mine own library with volumes that
I prize above my dukedom.

SHAKESPEARE, *The Tempest*

2348. The great and good do not die even in this world. Embalmed in books, their spirits walk abroad. The book is a living voice. It is an intellect to which one still listens.

SAMUEL SMILES, *Character*

2349.
Some books are drenched sands
On which a great soul's wealth lies all in heaps,
Like a wrecked argosy.

ALEXANDER SMITH, *A Life Drama*

2350. A best-seller is the gilded tomb of a mediocre talent.

LOGAN PEARSALL SMITH,
Afterthoughts

2351. Books are good enough in their own way, but they are a mighty bloodless substitute for life.

STEVENSON, *Virginibus Puerisque*

2352. Books, the children of the brain.   SWIFT, *Tale of a Tub*

2353. Books, like proverbs, receive their chief value from the stamp and esteem of ages through which they have passed.

SIR WILLIAM TEMPLE,
Ancient & Modern Learning

2354. A good book is the best of friends, the same to-day and for ever.

MARTIN TUPPER, *Of Reading*

2355. Man builds no structure which outlives a book.

E. F. WARE, *The Book*

2356.
Camerado, this is no book,
Who touches this touches a man.
WALT WHITMAN, *So Long!*

2357. There is no such thing as a moral or an immoral book. Books are well written, or badly written. That is all.   OSCAR WILDE,
The Picture of Dorian Gray

See also: 521, 930, 975, 980, 1992, 1993, 2000, 2004, 2006, 2386, 2477, 2478, 2554, 2968, 2969, 5205, 7444, 10461, 10462, 10466, 11557, 12088, 15410, 18680, 18984, 20382, 20829.

BOREDOM, BORES

Related Subjects: Satiety, Stupidity.

2361. *Bore, n.* A person who talks when you wish him to listen.
AMBROSE BIERCE,
The Devil's Dictionary

2362.
Society is now one polish'd horde,
Formed of two mighty tribes, the *Bores* and *Bored*.
BYRON, *Don Juan*

2363. I [Sherlock Holmes] abhor the dull routine of existence, I crave for mental exaltation.
CONAN DOYLE, *The Sign of The Four*

2364. The bore is usually considered a harmless creature, or of that class of irrational bipeds who hurt only themselves. MARIA EDGEWORTH,
Thoughts on Bores

2365. He is not only dull himself, but the cause of dullness in others.
SAMUEL JOHNSON, *Boswell: Life*

2366. We often forgive those who bore us but we cannot forgive those whom we bore.
LA ROCHEFOUCAULD, *Maxims*

2367. Got the ill name of augurs, because they were bores.
LOWELL, *A Fable for Critics*

2368. Is not life a hundred times too short for us to bore ourselves?
NIETZSCHE, *Beyond Good & Evil*

2369.
Again I hear that creaking step!—
  He's rapping at the door!
Too well I know the boding sound
  That ushers in a bore.
J. G. SAXE, *My Familiar*

2370. I assure you it requires no small talents to be a decided bore.
SCOTT

2371.
              O, he's as tedious
As is a tir'd horse, a railing wife;
Worse than a smoky house; I had rather live
With cheese and garlic in a windmill, far,
Than feed on cates, and have him talk to me,
In any summer-house in Christendom.   SHAKESPEARE, *Henry IV*

2372. What a bore it is, waking up in the morning always the same person. I wish I were unflinching and emphatic, and had big, bushy eyebrows and a Message for the Age. I wish I were a deep Thinker, or a great Ventriloquist.
LOGAN PEARSALL SMITH, *Trivia*

2373. Many excellent writers, very many painters, and most musicians are so tedious on any subject but their own.   ARTHUR SYMONS,
The Symbolist Movement in Literature

See also: 1392, 6792, 11791, 11814, 14613.

BORROWING AND LENDING

Related Subjects: Beggars, Debt, Gifts, Necessity, Obligation, Plagiarism, Quotation, Usurer, Want.

2381. Be not made a beggar by banqueting upon borrowing.
Apocrypha: Ecclesiasticus

2382. A good man sheweth favour, and lendeth.   *Bible: Psalms, cxii, 5*

2383. The borrower is servant to the lender.   *Bible: Proverbs, xxii, 7*

2384. Give, and you may keep your friend if you lose your money; lend, and the chances are that you lose your friend if ever you get back your money.   BULWER-LYTTON, *Caxtonia*

2385.
I hae naething to lend—
I'll borrow frae naebody.
BURNS, *I Hae a Wife*

2386. Great collections of books are subject to certain accidents besides the damp, the worms, and the rats; one not less common is that of the *borrowers,* not to say a word of the *purloiners.*   ISAAC D'ISRAELI,
Curiosities of Literature

2387. He that goes a borrowing goes a sorrowing.
FRANKLIN, *Poor Richard*

2388. It is better to give than to lend, and it costs about the same.
SIR PHILIP GIBBS

2389. The biggest businessmen in the world today are borrowers.
ELBERT HUBBARD,
Advertising and Advertisements

2390.
Two things thou shalt not long for, if thou love a mind serene:—

A woman to thy wife, though she were a crowned queen;
And the second, borrowed money,—though the smiling lender say
That he will not demand the debt until the Judgment Day
IBN JEMIN, *Epigram*

2391. There can be no freedom or beauty about a home life that depends on borrowing and debt.
IBSEN, *A Doll's House*

2392. The human species, according to the best theory I can form of it, is composed of two distinct races, the men who borrow, and the men who lend.   CHARLES LAMB,
The Two Races of Men

2393. Borrowing is not much better than begging.
LESSING, *Nathan der Weise*

2394. Better buy than borrow.
Proverb

2395. He begs at them that borrowed at him.   *Proverb*

2396. He that borrows must pay again with shame or loss.   *Proverb*

2397. He that lends, gives.   *Proverb*

2398. Believe me, 'tis a godlike thing to lend; to owe is a heroic virtue.
RABELAIS

2399. Borrowers are nearly always ill-spenders, and it is with lent money that all evil is mainly done, and all unjust war protracted.
RUSKIN, *The Crown of Wild Olive*

2400.
Neither a borrower, nor a lender be;
For loan oft loses both itself and friend,
And borrowing dulls the edge of husbandry.   SHAKESPEARE, *Hamlet*

2401.

In low simplicity

He lends out money gratis and brings
down

The rate of usance here with us in
Venice.　　SHAKESPEARE,
The Merchant of Venice

2402.

If thou wilt lend this money, lend it
not

As to thy friends; for when did
friendship take

A breed for barren metal of his
friend?

But lend it rather to thine enemy;

Who, if he break, thou mayst with
better face

Exact the penalty.
　　SHAKESPEARE,
The Merchant of Venice

2403.

Who goeth a borrowing

Goeth a sorrowing.

Few lend (but fools)

Their working tools.
　　THOMAS TUSSER,
500 Points of Good Husbandry

2404. The holy passion of Friendship
is of so sweet and steady and loyal
and enduring a nature that it will last
through a whole lifetime, if not asked
to lend money.　MARK TWAIN,
Pudd'nhead Wilson's Calendar

2405. Let us all be happy and live
within our means, even if we have to
borrow the money to do it with.
　ARTEMUS WARD, *Natural History*

2406.

God bless pawnbrokers!

They are quiet men.
　　MARGUERITE WILKINSON,
Pawnbrokers

See also: 16, 2326, 2332.

BOY AND BOYHOOD

Related　　Subjects:　　Childhood,
Youth.

2411. He was the spirit of boyhood,
tugging at the skirts of this old world
and compelling it to come back to
play.

J. M. BARRIE, *of R. L. Stevenson*

2412. Boys will be boys.
　　BULWER-LYTTON, *Caxtonia*

2413. Ah! happy years! once more
who would not be a boy!
　　BYRON, *Childe Harold*

2414. I only know two sorts of boys.
Mealy boys and beef-faced boys.
　　DICKENS, *Oliver Twist*

2415. The genuine human boy may,
I think, safely be set down as the
noblest work of God.
　　CHARLES B. FAIRBANKS,
My Unknown Chum

2416.

God bless all little boys who look like
Puck,

With wide eyes, wider mouths and
stickout ears,

Rash little boys who stay alive by luck

And heaven's favor in this world
of tears.
　　ARTHUR GUITERMAN,
Blessing on Little Boys

2417.

O for one hour of youthful joy!

Give back my twentieth spring!

I'd rather laugh, a bright-haired boy,

Than reign, a gray-beard king.
　　O. W. HOLMES,
The Old Man Dreams

2418.

The lusty days of long ago,

When you were Bill and I was Joe.
　　O. W. HOLMES, *Bill and Joe*

2419.

Perhaps there lives some dreamy boy, untaught
In schools, some graduate of the field or street,
Who shall become a master of the art,
An admiral sailing the high seas of thought.

LONGFELLOW, *Possibilities*

2420.

A boy's will is the wind's will,
And the thoughts of youth are long, long thoughts.

LONGFELLOW, *My Lost Youth*

2421.

　　　　　O, 'tis a parlous boy;
Bold, quick, ingenious, forward, capable;
He's all the mother's, from the top to toe.

SHAKESPEARE, *Richard III*

2422.

When that I was and a little tiny boy,
　With hey, ho, the wind and the rain,
A foolish thing was but a toy,
　For the rain it raineth every day.

SHAKESPEARE, *Twelfth Night*

2423.

What are little boys made of, made of?
What are little boys made of?
Snips and snails and puppy-dog tails,
And such are little boys made of.

SOUTHEY,
What all the World is Made of.

2424. One of the best things in the world to be is a boy; it requires no experience, but needs some practice to be a good one.

CHARLES DUDLEY WARNER,
Being a Boy

2425. How rude are the boys that throw pebbles and mire.

ISAAC WATTS, *Innocent Play*

2426.

Blessings on thee, little man,
Barefoot boy, with cheek of tan!

WHITTIER, *The Barefoot Boy*

2427. The sweetest roamer is a boy's young heart.

G. E. WOODBERRY, *Agathon*

2428.

O dearest, dearest boy! my heart
For better lore would seldom yearn,
Could I but teach the hundredth part
Of what from thee I learn.

WORDSWORTH, *Anecdote for Fathers*

See also: 251, 3375, 3448, 13656.

BRAGGART

Related Subjects: Boasting, Cowards, Vanity.

2431.

I love to watch the rooster crow,
He's like so many men I know
Who brag and bluster, rant and shout
And beat their manly breasts, without
The first damn thing to crow about.

JOHN KENDRICK BANGS,
The Rooster

2432. Cunning egotism. If I cannot brag of knowing something, then I brag of not knowing it. At any rate, brag.　　EMERSON, *Journals*

2433. Brag's a good dog, but he hath lost his tail.　　*Proverb*

2434. God and men think him a fool who brags of his own great wisdom.
Proverb

2435. Great braggers little doers.
Proverb

2436.

　Who knows himself a braggart,
Let him fear this, for it will come to
　pass

That every braggart shall be found an
ass.   SHAKESPEARE,
       All's Well that Ends Well

2437.
O, I could play the woman with mine
eyes
And braggart with my tongue.
       SHAKESPEARE, *Macbeth*

2438. A good name is seldom got by
giving it one's self; and women, no
more than honour, are compassed by
bragging.
       WILLIAM WYCHERLEY,
       The Country Wife

BRAIN, see Mind

BRAVERY, see Courage

BREAD

Related Subjects: Food, Meat.

2441. Man shall not live by bread
alone.   *Bible: Deuteronomy, viii, 3*

2442. Cast thy bread upon the
waters: for thou shalt find it after
many days. *Bible: Ecclesiastes, xi, 1*

2443. Give us this day our daily
bread.   *Bible: Matthew, vi, 11*

2444. What man is there of you,
whom if his son ask bread, will he
give him a stone?
       Bible: Matthew, vii, 9

2445.
A loaf of bread, the Walrus said,
   Is what we chiefly need.
       LEWIS CARROLL,
   The Walrus and the Carpenter

2446. Secure of bread as of returning
light.   DRYDEN, *Eleonora*

2447. Will it bake bread?
       EMERSON, *Essays*

2448. Here is bread, which strengthens man's heart, and therefore called
the staff of life.
     MATTHEW HENRY, *Commentaries*

2449.
O God! that bread should be so dear,
   And flesh and blood so cheap!
       THOMAS HOOD,
       The Song of the Shirt

2450.
When you came, you were like red
   wine and honey,
And the taste of you burnt my mouth
   with its sweetness.
Now you are like morning bread,
Smooth and pleasant.
I hardly taste you at all, for I know
   your savor;
But I am completely nourished.
       AMY LOWELL, *A Decade*

2451. Eaten bread is forgotten.
       Proverb

2452. Half a loaf is better than no
bread.   *Proverb*

2453. The Bible tells us that "man
does not live by bread alone." To
hear some people talk, you would
think the Bible said that "man does
not live by bread." You and I know
that he does; and if he is to be decent
and civilized, he needs many other
things, a home with several rooms in
it, and clean clothing, and books, and
recreation.   UPTON SINCLAIR

2454. Bread is the staff of life.
       SWIFT, *Tale of a Tub*

2455. What bread men break is broke
to them again.   JOHN TAYLOR

2456. My piece of bread only belongs
to me when I know that everyone else
has a share, and that no one starves
while I eat.   TOLSTOY

See also: 3661, 6336.

BREEDING

Related Subjects: Ancestry, Birth, Gentleman, Heredity, Manners, Refinement.

2461. In good-breeding, which differs, if at all, from high-breeding, only as it gracefully remembers the rights of others, rather than gracefully insists on its own rights, I discern no special connection with wealth or birth.

CARLYLE, *Sartor Resartus*

2462. He who reflects on another man's want of breeding, shows he wants it as much himself.

PLUTARCH, *Lives*

2463. Better unborn than unbred.

Proverb

2464. Birth is much, but breeding is more.

Proverb

See also: 527, 2206, 2978, 3248, 4376, 12842.

BREVITY

Related Subjects: Simplicity.

2471. It is a foolish thing to make a long prologue, and to be short in the story itself.

Apocrypha: 2 Maccabees

2472. Let thy words be few.

Bible: Ecclesiastes, v, 2

2473.
For brevity is very good,
Where we are, or are not understood.

SAMUEL BUTLER, *Hudibras*

2474. Make 'em brief, Finnigin!

STRICKLAND GILLILAN,
Finnigin to Flannigan

2475. Few were his words, but wonderfully clear.   HOMER, *Iliad*

2476. There is need of brevity, that the thought may run on.

HORACE, *Ars Poetica*

2477. But what is the use of brevity, tell me, when there is a whole book of it?   MARTIAL, *Epigrams*

2478. It is my ambition to say in ten sentences what everyone else says in a whole book,—what everyone else does *not* say in a whole book.

NIETZSCHE,
The Twilight of the Idols

2479. As man is now constituted, to be brief is almost a condition of being inspired.   SANTAYANA, *Little Essays*

2480.
Since brevity is the soul of wit,
And tediousness the limbs and outward flourishes,
I will be brief.

SHAKESPEARE, *Hamlet*

2481. Not that the story need be long, but it will take a long while to make it short.

THOREAU, *Letter to a Friend*

See also: 386, 979, 1378, 4179.

BRIBERY

Related Subjects: Corruption, Crime, Gold, Guilt, Honesty, Money, Politics, Temptation.

2491. Every man has his price, I will bribe left and right.

BULWER-LYTTON, *Walpole*

2492.
'Tis pleasant purchasing our fellow-creatures;
   And all are to be sold, if you consider
Their passions, and are dext'rous; some by features
   Are bought up, others by a warlike leader;

Some by a place—as tend their years
   or natures;
   The most by ready cash—but all
    have prices,
From crowns to kicks, according to
   their vices.   BYRON, *Don Juan*

2493.
Those who would gain the votes of
   British tribes,
Must add to force of merit, force of
   bribes.
   CHARLES CHURCHILL, *The Rosciad*

2494. To refuse with the right and
take with the left.
   JOHN CLARKE, *Paroemiologia*

2495.
Too poor for a bribe, and too proud to
   importune,
He had not the method of making a
   fortune.   THOMAS GRAY,
      On His Own Character

2496. Turn from the glitt'ring bribe
thy scornful eye.
   SAMUEL JOHNSON, *London*

2497.
But here more slow, where all are
   slaves to gold,
Where looks are merchandise, and
   smiles are sold.
     SAMUEL JOHNSON, *London*

2498.
Our supple tribes repress their patriot
   throats
And ask no questions but the price of
   votes.   SAMUEL JOHNSON,
     Vanity of Human Wishes

2499.
Alas! the small discredit of a bribe
Scarce hurts the lawyer, but undoes
   the scribe.
    POPE, *Epilogue to Satires*

2500.
Judges and senates have been bought
   for gold;

Esteem and love were never to be
   sold.   POPE, *Essay on Man*

2501. By gold all good faith has been
banished; by gold our rights are
abused; the law itself is influenced by
gold, and soon there will be an end of
every modest restraint.
     PROPERTIUS, *Elegiae*

2502. He that buyeth magistracy
must sell justice.   *Proverb*

2503. Bribes throw dust into cunning
men's eyes.   *Proverb*

2504. Bribes will enter without
knocking.   *Proverb*

2505.
No mortal thing can bear so high a
   price,
But that with mortal thing it may be
   bought.
     SIR WALTER RALEIGH,
    Love the Only Price of Love

2506.
Honesty stands at the gate and
   knocks, and bribery enters in.
    BARNABE RICH, *Irish Hubbub*

2507.
       There is gold for you;
Sell me your good report.
    SHAKESPEARE, *Cymbeline*

2508.
         'Tis gold
Which buys admittance; oft it doth;
   yea, and makes
Diana's rangers false themselves,
   yield up
Their deer to the stand o' the stealer:
   and 'tis gold
Which makes the true man kill'd and
   saves the thief;
Nay, sometimes hangs both thief and
   true man.
    SHAKESPEARE, *Cymbeline*

2509.
Shall we now
Contaminate our fingers with base
bribes?
SHAKESPEARE, *Julius Caesar*

2510. All those men have their price.
SIR ROBERT WALPOLE

2511. Few men have virtue to withstand the highest bidder.
WASHINGTON, *Moral Maxims*

See also: 1380.

BRIDE AND BRIDEGROOM

Related Subjects: **Marriage, Wedding.**

2521.
The bride hath paced into the hall,
Red as a rose is she.
COLERIDGE, *The Ancient Mariner*

2522.
Blest is the Bride on whom the sun
doth shine.
ROBERT HERRICK, *A Nuptial Song*

2523. The bride goes to her marriage-bed, but knows not what shall happen
to her.   *Proverb*

2524. A bonny bride is soon buskit.
Proverb

2525.
And you, brides and bridegrooms all,
With measure heap'd in joy to the
measures fall.
SHAKESPEARE, *As You Like It*

2526. A happy bridesmaid makes a
happy bride.
TENNYSON, *The Bridesmaid*

Bridegroom

2527. As the bridegroom rejoiceth
over the bride.
Bible: Isaiah, lxii, 5

2528.
As are those dulcet sounds in break of
day
That creep into the dreaming bride-groom's ear
And summon him to marriage.
SHAKESPEARE,
The Merchant of Venice

2529. All the women we need are inside, said the bridegroom, and closed
the door on the bride.
THEOCRITUS, *Idyls*

See also: 3159.

BROTHER AND BROTHER-HOOD

Related Subjects: **Acquaintance, Companionship, Family, Friendship, Philanthropy, Sister.**

2531. In charity to all mankind, bearing no malice or ill-will to any human
being, and even compassionating those
who hold in bondage their fellow-men, not knowing what they do.
JOHN QUINCY ADAMS

2532. A new commandment I give
unto you. That ye love one another.
Bible: John, xiii, 24

2533. The right hand of fellowship.
Bible: Galatians, ii, 9

2534. Brotherhood is not just a Bible
word. Out of comradeship can come
and will come the happy life for all.
The underdog can and will lick his
weight in the wildcats of the world.
HEYWOOD BROUN,
The Fifty-First Birthday

2535. A mystic bond of brotherhood
makes all men one.
CARLYLE, *Essays*

2536.
I have stood for the weak and the
poor

I have stood for the men who toil.
CLARENCE DARROW

2537. We owe to man higher succors than food and fire. We owe to man man.
EMERSON, *Society and Solitude*

2538.
Let me live in my house by the side of the road
And be a friend of man.
SAM W. FOSS,
The House by the Side of the Road

2539. I would rather be torn to pieces than disown my brothers of the suppressed classes. MAHATMA GANDHI

2540.
He held his seat; a friend to human race.
Fast by the road, his ever-open door
Obliged the wealthy, and reliev'd the poor. HOMER, *Iliad*

2541. Write me as one who loves his fellow men.
LEIGH HUNT, *Abou Ben Adhem*

2542. Say "we," "us" and "ours" when you're talking instead of "you fellows" and "I."
KIPLING, *Norman and Saxon*

2543.
Others may sing of the wine and the wealth and the mirth,
The portly presence of potentates goodly in girth;
Mine be the dirt and the dross, the dust and the scum of the earth!
Theirs be the music, the color, the glory, the gold;
Mine be a handful of ashes, a mouthful of mould.
Of the maimed, of the halt and the blind in the rain and the cold.
JOHN MASEFIELD, *Consecration*

2544. Be my brother, or I will bash your head in. NAZI PROVERB,
John Gunther: Inside Europe

2545. And I said almost aloud:
'Have you forgotten so soon? Henceforth this is your great curse as well as your great happiness, to see the souls of men naked and even the most foul a brother to your soul, which contains it. Bow down, even like the simple peasant, who kisses the bountiful corn-giving earth. For the most criminal of these gives you a rich gift, the substance of beauty.'
LIAM O'FLAHERTY, *Two Years*

2546. The brother had rather see the sister rich than make her so.
Proverb

2547. We few, we happy few, we band of brothers.
SHAKESPEARE, *Henry V*

2548.
Slav, Teuton, Kelt, I count them all My friends and brother souls,
With all the peoples, great and small, That wheel between the poles.
TENNYSON,
The Charge of the Heavy Brigade

2549. Not till the sun excludes you do I exclude you.
WALT WHITMAN,
To a Common Prostitute

See also: 28, 643, 644, 645, 816, 2456, 3700, 6513, 12148.

BUILDING

Related Subjects: Architecture, House.

2551. To build many houses is the readiest road to poverty.
Anonymous

2552. The stone which the builders refused is become the head stone of the corner.
Bible: Psalms, cxviii, 22

2553. For which of you, intending to build a tower, sitteth not down first and counteth the cost, whether he have sufficient to finish it?

Bible: Luke, xiv, 28

2554. Buildings are the books that everybody unconsciously reads; and if they are a libel on the laws of architecture, they will surely vitiate in time the taste of those who become familiarized to their deformity.

CHARLES B. FAIRBANKS,
My Unknown Chum

2555. To build is to be robbed.

SAMUEL JOHNSON, *The Idler*

2556.
Ah, to build, to build!
That is the noblest art of all the arts.

LONGFELLOW, *Michael Angelo*

2557. Men who love building are their own undoers, and need no other enemies.

MARCUS CRASSUS, *Plutarch: Lives*

2558. The building which is fitted accurately to its end will turn out to be beautiful, though beauty is not intended. GEORGE MOLLER,
Essay on Architecture

2559. Building is a sweet impoverishing.

Proverb

2560. When we build, let us think that we build for ever. RUSKIN,
Seven Lamps of Architecture

See also: 714, 1274, 1582, 2355, 15304.

BURDEN

Related Subjects: Care, Cross, Responsibility, Worry.

2561. Every man shall bear his own burden. *Bible: Galatians, vi, 5*

2562.
Oh, there are moments for us here,
    when seeing
  Life's inequalities, and woe, and
    care,
The burdens laid upon our mortal
    being
  Seem heavier than the human heart
    can bear.

W. G. CLARK, *A Song of May*

2563. I would rather have a big burden and a strong back, than a weak back and a caddy to carry life's luggage.

ELBERT HUBBARD, *The Philistine*

2564. Money and time are the heaviest burdens of life, and the unhappiest of all mortals are those who have more of either than they know how to use. SAMUEL JOHNSON, *The Idler*

2565.
Take up the White Man's burden—
  Send for the best ye breed—
Go bind your sons to exile
  To serve your captives' need.

KIPLING, *The White Man's Burden*

2566. Respect the burden, Madam.

NAPOLEON

2567. It is not the burden, but the over-burden that kills the beast.

Proverb

2568. None knows the weight of another's burden. *Proverb*

2569. Every one thinks his sack heaviest. *Proverb*

2570. It is base to flinch under a burden.

SENECA, *Epistulae ad Lucilium*

2571. The strength will with the burden grow.

TOM TAYLOR, *Abraham Lincoln*

See also: 2069, 2722, 3222, 3343, 9261, 19084, 19183.

BURNS, ROBERT

2581. A Burns is infinitely better educated than a Byron.   CARLYLE

2582. Burns, of all poets, is the most a Man.   ROSSETTI, *On Burns*

2583.
His greatness, not his littleness,
    Concerns mankind.
        WILLIAM WATSON,
            The Tomb of Burns

2584.
Give lettered pomp to teeth of Time,
    So "Bonnie Doon" but tarry:
Blot out the epic's stately rhyme,
    But spare his Highland Mary!
        WHITTIER, *Burns*

2585.
I mourned with thousands, but as one
More deeply grieved, for he was gone
Whose light I hailed when first it
    shone,
    And showed my youth
How verse may build a princely
    throne
    On humble truth.
WORDSWORTH, *At the Grave of Burns*

BUSINESS

Related Subjects: Advertising, Associates, Capitalism, Commerce, Corporation, Credit, Employment, Finance, Industry, Inflation, Insurance, Labor, Occupation, Profit, Real Estate, Wages, Work.

2591. Build your business as you build your life. Have your big moments; but don't try to be spectacular all the time.
        JAMES R. ADAMS,
            More Power to Advertising

2592. A business is safe and sound and durable only when it has back of it a safe and sound and durable public opinion.   JAMES R. ADAMS,
            More Power to Advertising

2593. There is only one way to look upon a business, if you are genuinely interested in its welfare. You must look upon it from a long-range viewpoint; and you must do nothing today that will take a toll out of it tomorrow.
        JAMES R. ADAMS,
            More Power to Advertising

2594. In fact, you can write it down as a truism that the most difficult thing in the world for a business to get is a good reputation—something which sets it apart, in the public consciousness, from other businesses of its kind.   JAMES R. ADAMS,
            More Power to Advertising

2595. What are called business habits were invented to make the life of man run in harmony with the steam engine, and his movements rival the train in punctuality. The factory system was invented, and it was an instantaneous success. Men were clothed with cheapness and uniformity. Their minds grew numerously alike, cheap and uniform also.
A. E., *Cooperation and Nationality*

2596. Talk of nothing but business, and despatch that business quickly.
        ALDUS MANUTIUS

2597. The market is a place set apart where men may deceive each other.
        ANACHARSIS, *Diogenes Laertius*

2598. The playthings of our elders are called business.
        ST. AUGUSTINE, *Confessions*

2599. The business man has steered a veering course. He has favored peace and war, unity and chaos, mystery and science, according to the immediate prospects of profit. Other men, warriors and rulers, may have sought gold more greedily than he, but they could at least pretend to other ends, whereas he was never able to work up a similar, sustained hocus-pocus about his activities, or hold up even an illusory goal. He had no . . . discoverable ultimate purpose.

MIRIAM BEARD,
History of the Business Man

2600. The word Business has attracted a veneration almost equal to that bestowed on Science. But even this has been only a partial triumph, for the mere addition of the word "big" is enough to ruin the atmosphere—the populace will not hear of Big Business as a suitable aim of supreme human effort.

MIRIAM BEARD,
History of the Business Man

2601. Seest thou a man diligent in his business? He shall stand before kings; he shall not stand before mean men.   *Bible: Proverbs, xxii, 29*

2602. In the field of modern business, so rich in opportunity for the exercise of man's finest and most varied mental faculties and moral qualities, mere money-making cannot be regarded as the legitimate end. Neither can mere growth in bulk or power be admitted as a worthy ambition. Nor can a man nobly mindful of his serious responsibilities to society, view business as a game; since with the conduct of business human happiness or misery is inextricably interwoven.

JUSTICE BRANDEIS

2603. Success must be sought in business also in excellence of performance; and in business, excellence of performance manifests itself among other things, in the advancing of methods and processes; in the improvement of products; in more perfect organization, eliminating friction as well as waste; in bettering the condition of the workingmen, developing their faculties and promoting their happiness; and in the establishment of right relations with customers and with the community.

JUSTICE BRANDEIS

2604. Without some dissimulation no business can be carried on at all.

LORD CHESTERFIELD, *Letters*

2605. Despatch is the soul of business.   LORD CHESTERFIELD, *Letters*

2606. I have always recognized that the object of business is to make money in an honorable manner.

PETER COOPER

2607.
A business with an income at its heels
Furnishes always oil for its own
        wheels.   COWPER,
                Retirement

2608. Like inscriptions over the graves of dead businesses.

DICKENS, *Our Mutual Friend*

2609. Business? It's quite simple. It's other people's money.

DUMAS THE YOUNGER,
La Question d'Argent

2610. We must hold a man amenable to reason for the choice of his daily craft or profession. It is not an excuse any longer for his deeds that they are the custom of his trade. What business has he with an evil trade? Has he not a *calling* in his character?

EMERSON, *Essays*

2611. A business, like an automobile, has to be driven, in order to get results.   B. C. FORBES,
                Forbes Epigrams

2612.
And, if you want it, he
Makes a reduction on taking a quantity.   W. S. GILBERT, *The Sorcerer*

2613. Big business makes its money out of by-products.
ELBERT HUBBARD

2614. The aim of all legitimate business is service, for profit, at a risk.
B. C. LEEMING, *Imagination*

2615. There is no better ballast for keeping the mind steady on its keel, and saving it from all risk of crankiness, than business.   LOWELL,
New England Two Centuries Ago

2616. The typical successful American business man was born in the country, where he worked like hell so he could live in the city, where he worked like hell so he could live in the country.   DON MARQUIS

2617. Business is a combination of war and sport.   ANDRÉ MAUROIS

2618. Business is Business.
OCTAVE MIRBEAU, *Title of Play*

2619. Without any sort of business, is forever busy.   MOLIÈRE,
Le Misanthrope

2620. Busy till night, pleasing myself mightily to see what a deal of business goes off a man's hands when he stays by it.   SAMUEL PEPYS, *Diary*

2621. He that thinks his business below him will always be above his business.   *Proverb*

2622. Men that have much business must have much pardon.   *Proverb*

2623. Do business, but be not a slave to it.   *Proverb*

2624. How happy the life unembarrassed by the cares of business!
PUBLILIUS SYRUS, *Sententiae*

2625. We demand that big business give people a square deal.
THEODORE ROOSEVELT

2626. It is easy to escape from business, if you will only despise the rewards of business.   SENECA,
Epistulae ad Lucilium

2627.
To business that we love we rise betime,
And go to 't with delight.
SHAKESPEARE,
Antony and Cleopatra

2628. Every man has business and desire, Such as it is.
SHAKESPEARE, *Hamlet*

2629. Has this fellow no feeling of his business?
SHAKESPEARE, *Hamlet*

2630. Our conclusion is that a business man can, if he so wills, be a man of honor. A physician is engaged in a highly competitive profession. Most physicians must live by their fees, and they do not forget to send in their bills. But the great majority of physicians we venture to believe, fight disease and rejoice in victory not merely for the sake of their own profit but for the sake of their patients also. A business man may, if he will, take precisely the same attitude toward his customers.   SHARP & FOX,
Business Ethics

2631. A reputable concern can remain in existence only as it supplies the needs of a considerable number of persons. And the kind of service it gives and the cost of such service is a matter that may concern these customers deeply. Since their interests are involved, directly or indirectly, in all its transactions, they have a claim not merely to be treated honestly, but also intelligently. SHARP & FOX,
Business Ethics

2632. A man who has no office to go to—I don't care who he is—is a trial of which you can have no conception. BERNARD SHAW, *The Irrational Knot*

2633. Of all the damnable waste of human life that ever was invented, clerking is the very worst.
BERNARD SHAW, *Misalliance*

2634. *Mazzini:* I am afraid all the captains of industry are what *you* call frauds, Mrs. Hushabye. Of course there are some manufacturers who really do understand their own works; but they don't make as high a rate of profit as Mangan does.
BERNARD SHAW, *Heartbreak House*

2635. Perpetual devotion to what a man calls his business, is only to be sustained by perpetual neglect of many other things. STEVENSON,
Virginibus Puerisque

2636. He had talents equal to business, and aspired no higher.
TACITUS, *History*

2637. When two men in a business always agree, one of them is unnecessary. WILLIAM WRIGLEY, JR.

2638. Go to your business, pleasure, whilst I go to my pleasure, business.
WILLIAM WYCHERLEY,
The Country Wife

2639. It is not the crook in modern business that we fear, but the honest man who doesn't know what he is doing. OWEN D. YOUNG

Business in the sense of personal affairs.

2640. "If everybody minded their own business," the Duchess said, in a hoarse growl, "the world would go round a great deal faster than it does."
LEWIS CARROLL,
Alice in Wonderland

2641. Let every man mind his own business. CERVANTES,
Don Quixote

2642. This business will never hold water. COLLEY CIBBER,
She Wou'd and She Wou'd Not

2643. An honest business never blush to tell. HOMER, *Odyssey*

2644. I remember that a wise friend of mine did usually say, "That which is everybody's business is nobody's business." IZAAK WALTON,
The Compleat Angler

See also: 1483, 1491, 1612, 1780, 2285, 2389, 3371, 3601, 3743, 4773, 5848, 9196, 15790, 16141.

BUTCHER

Related Subjects: Meat, Murder.

2651.
Butchers! whose hands are dy'd with
    blood's foul stain,
And always foremost in the hang-
    man's train. JOHN GAY, *Trivia*

2652.
Whoe'er has gone thro' London
    street,
Has seen a butcher gazing at his meat,
    And how he keeps
    Gloating upon a sheep's
Or bullock's personals, as if his own;
    How he admires his halves
    And quarters—and his calves,
As if in truth upon his own legs
    grown. THOMAS HOOD,
A Butcher

2653.
Of brutal juices the whole man is
    full.—
In fact, fulfilling the metempsychosis,
The Butcher is already half a Bull.
THOMAS HOOD, *A Butcher*

2654.
A sturdy man he look'd to fell an ox,

Bull-fronted, ruddy, with a formal
    streak
Of well-greas'd hair down either
    cheek.   THOMAS HOOD,
               Ode to Rae Wilson

2655. Where is that devil's butcher?
        SHAKESPEARE, *Henry VI*

2656.
Who finds the heifer dead and bleed-
    ing fresh
And sees fast by a butcher with an
    axe,
But will suspect 'twas he that made
    the slaughter? SHAKESPEARE,
                     Henry VI

2657. The butcher looked for his
knife and it was in his mouth.
      SWIFT, *Polite Conversation*

2658. The butcher in his killing
clothes.   WALT WHITMAN,
            The Workingmen

BYRON, GEORGE GORDON (LORD)

2661. Thus it is with everything and
everybody for whom I feel anything
like a real attachment.—"War, death
or discord doth lay siege to them." I
never even could keep alive a dog
that I liked or that liked me. . . If
anything happens to my Amica I have
done with the passion forever—it is
my *last* love. . . I can hope no more
to inspire attachment and I trust
never again feel it.   BYRON

2662. My ideas of a character may
run away with me; like all imaginative men I, of course, embody myself
with the character while I *draw* it,
but not a moment after the pen is
from off the paper.   BYRON

2663.
And be the Spartan's epitaph on me—
"Sparta hath many a worthier son
    than he." BYRON, *Childe Harold*

2664. He had a head which statuaries
loved to copy, and a foot the deformity of which the beggars in the street
mimicked.   MACAULAY,
   Essays: Moore's Life of Byron

2665. From the poetry of Lord
Byron they drew a system of ethics,
compounded of misanthropy and vo-
luptuousness,—a system in which the
two great commandments were, to
hate your neighbour, and to love your
neighbour's wife.   MACAULAY,
   Essays: Moore's Life of Byron

2666.
        Yes, Byron, thou art gone,
Gone like a star that through the fir-
    mament
Shot and was lost, in its eccentric
    course
Dazzling, perplexing. Yet thy heart,
    methinks,
Was generous, noble—noble in its
    scorn
Of all things low or little; nothing
    there
Sordid or servile.
    SAMUEL ROGERS, *Italy: Bologna*

2667. I do not write; I have lived
too long near Lord Byron, and the
sun has extinguished the glow-worm.
         SHELLEY, *Of Byron*

2668. Space wondered less at the
swift and fair creations of God when
He grew weary of vacancy, than I at
this spirit of an angel in the mortal
paradise of a decaying body.
         SHELLEY, *Of Byron*

2669.
Too avid of earth's bliss, he was of
    those
  Whom Delight flies because they
    give her chase.
      WILLIAM WATSON,
       Byron the Voluptuary

See also: 2581.

C

CAESAR

Related Subjects: Ambition, Dictatorship.

2671. Caesar, in modesty mixed with greatness, did for his pleasure apply the name of a Commentary to the best history of the world. BACON,
Advancement of Learning

2672. Render therefore unto Caesar the things which are Caesar's, and unto God the things that are God's.
Bible: Matthew, xxii, 21

2673. What millions died — that Caesar might be great!
THOMAS CAMPBELL,
The Pleasures of Hope

2674. Every woman's man and every man's woman.
CURIO, *of Julius Caesar: Suetonius*

2675. The assassination of Julius Caesar was not in good taste.
GOETHE

2676. "It is not," said Caesar, "these well-fed, long-haired men that I fear, but the pale and the hungry looking"; meaning Brutus and Cassius, by whose conspiracy he afterwards fell.
PLUTARCH, *Lives*

2677. Caesar once, seeing some wealthy strangers at Rome, carrying up and down with them in their arms and bosoms young puppy-dogs and monkeys, embracing and making much of them, took occasion not unnaturally to ask whether the women in their country were not used to bear children.
PLUTARCH, *Lives*

2678. When asked why he parted with his wife, Caesar replied, "I wished my wife to be not so much as suspected."
PLUTARCH, *Lives*

2679. Caesar's wife must be above suspicion.
PLUTARCH, *Lives*

2680. Hail Caesar, those who are about to die salute thee!
Salutation of the Gladiators

2681. There be many Caesars, Ere such another Julius.
SHAKESPEARE, *Cymbeline*

2682.
Julius Caesar, whose remembrance yet
Lives in men's eyes and will to ears and tongues
Be theme and hearing ever.
SHAKESPEARE, *Cymbeline*

2683.
Caesar's ambition,
Which swell'd so much that it did almost stretch
The sides o' the world.
SHAKESPEARE, *Cymbeline*

2684.
In the most high and palmy state of Rome,
A little ere the mightiest Julius fell,
The graves stood tenantless and the sheeted dead
Did squeal and gibber in the Roman streets.
SHAKESPEARE, *Hamlet*

2685. No bending knee will call thee Caesar now.
SHAKESPEARE, *Henry VI*

2686.
Upon what meat doth this our Caesar feed,
That he is grown so great? Age, thou art shamed!
Rome, thou hast lost the breed of noble bloods!
SHAKESPEARE, *Julius Caesar*

2687.

                    Great Caesar fell.
O! what a fall was there, my country-
    men;
Then I, and you, and all of us fell
    down,
Whilst bloody treason flourish'd over
    us.   SHAKESPEARE, *Julius Caesar*

2688.
Friends, Romans, Countrymen, lend
    me your ears;
I come to bury Caesar, not to praise
    him.   SHAKESPEARE, *Julius Caesar*

2689.
Caesar had perished from the world
    of men,
Had not his sword been rescued by
    his pen.   HENRY VAUGHAN,
    On Sir Thomas Bodley's Library

See also: 173, 3911, 4221, 5061,
13397, 14773.

CALAMITY

**Related Subjects: Accident, Ad-
versity, Misfortune.**

2691. Calamity is man's true touchstone.   BEAUMONT & FLETCHER,
              The Triumph of Honor

2692. Calamity is the perfect glass
wherein we truly see and know ourselves.   SIR WILLIAM D'AVENANT

2693. He bade me observe it, and I
should always find, that the calamities of life were shared among the
upper and lower part of mankind;
but that the middle station had the
fewest disasters.   DEFOE,
              Robinson Crusoe

2694. When any calamity has been
suffered, the first thing to be remembered, is how much has been escaped.
              SAMUEL JOHNSON

2695. Half a calamity is better than
a whole one.   LAWRENCE OF ARABIA

2696.
Do they not seek occasion of new
    quarrels
On my refusal to distress me more,
Or make a game of my calamities?
              MILTON, *Samson Agonistes*

2697. He who foresees calamities,
suffers them twice over.
                    B. PORTEUS

2698. Learn to see in another's calamity the ills which you should avoid.
          PUBLILIUS SYRUS, *Sententiae*

2699. Fortune is not satisfied with in-
flicting one calamity.
          PUBLILIUS SYRUS, *Sententiae*

2700.
What time to tardy consummation,
    brings,
Calamity, like to a frosty night
That ripeneth the grain, completes at
    once.   SIR HENRY TAYLOR,
              Philip von Artevelde

2701. What region of earth is not
full of our calamities?   VERGIL,
                              Aeneid

See also: 203, 3736, 5152, 17325,
20791.

CALM, CALMNESS

**Related Subjects: Contentment,
Peace, Quiet, Resignation, Rest,
Self-confidence, Serenity.**

2711.
There's nought, no doubt, so much
    the spirit calms
As rum and true religion.
              BYRON, *Don Juan*

2712.
Tranquillity! thou better name
Than all the family of Fame.
              COLERIDGE, *Ode to Tranquillity*

2713.
If e'er his Duty forced him to contend,
Calmness was all his temper, Peace his end.   DEFOE,
Elegy on Annesley

2714. Keep cool: it will be all one a hundred years hence.
EMERSON, *Representative Men*

2715. A man should study ever to to keep cool. He makes his inferiors his superiors by heat.
EMERSON, *Lectures*

2716. The mind which renounces, once and for ever, a futile hope, has its compensation in ever-growing calm.   GEORGE GISSING,
The Private Papers of Henry Ryecroft

2717. Back of tranquillity lies always conquered unhappiness.
DAVID GRAYSON

2718.
Calmness is great advantage: he that lets
Another chafe, may warm him at his fire.   GEORGE HERBERT,
The Church-Porch

2719. Let what will be said or done, preserve your *sang-froid* immovable, and to every obstacle oppose patience, perseverance and soothing language.
JEFFERSON

2720. Calm of mind, all passion spent.
MILTON, *Samson Agonistes*

2721. As calmly detached as nurses in a hospital who smile faintly at what the patients say under ether.
CHRISTOPHER MORLEY,
Thunder on the Left

2722. He who is of a calm and happy nature will hardly feel the pressure of age. but to him who is of an opposite disposition youth and age are equally a burden.   PLATO, *The Republic*

2723. He that can reply calmly to an angry man is too hard for him.
Proverb

2724. It is the nature of a great mind to be calm and undisturbed.
SENECA, *De Clementia*

2725.
If after every tempest come such calms,
May the winds blow till they have waken'd death!
SHAKESPEARE, *Othello*

2726. There is no joy but calm.
TENNYSON, *The Lotos Eaters*

See also: 1116, 1132.

CALUMNY

Related Subjects: Deceit, Lies, Reputation, Scandal, Slander.

2731. Hurl your calumnies boldly, something is sure to stick.   BACON

2732. As long as there are readers to be delighted with calumny, there will be found reviewers to calumniate.
COLERIDGE, *Biographia Literaria*

2733. The upright man, if he suffer calumny to move him, fears the tongue of man more than the eye of God.
C. C. COLTON

2734. Calumny always makes the calumniator worse, but the calumniated—never.   C. C. COLTON

2735. Opposition and calumny are often the brightest tribute that vice and folly can pay to virtue and wisdom.   RUTHERFORD B. HAYES

2736. The calumniator inflicts wrong by slandering the absent; and he who gives credit to the calumny before he knows it is true, is equally guilty. The person traduced is doubly injured; by him who propagates, and by him who credits the slander.

HERODOTUS, *History*

2737.
False praise can please, and calumny affright
None but the vicious and the hypocrite.   HORACE, *Satires*

2738. Calumny differs from most other injuries in this dreadful circumstance: he who commits it can never repair it.   SAMUEL JOHNSON

2739. I am beholden to calumny, that she hath so endeavoured and taken pains to belie me. It shall make me set a surer guard on myself, and keep a better watch upon my actions.

BEN JONSON, *Explorata*

2740. If nobody took calumny in and gave it lodging, it would starve and die of itself. ARCHBISHOP LEIGHTON

2741. He that lends an easy and credulous ear to calumny, is either a man of very ill morals, or he has no more sense and understanding than a child.   MENANDER

2742. I never listen to calumnies; because if they are untrue, I run the risk of being deceived; and if they are true, of hating persons not worth thinking about.   MONTESQUIEU

2743. There are calumnies against which even innocence loses courage.

NAPOLEON

2744. Believe nothing against another but on good authority; and never report what may hurt another, unless it be a greater hurt to some other to conceal it.   WILLIAM PENN

2745. Calumny and conjecture may injure innocency itself.   *Proverb*

2746. When conscience is pure it triumphs o'er bitter malice, o'er dark calumny; but if there be in it one single stain, reproaches beat like hammers in the ears.   PUSHKIN

2747. Close thine ear against him that opens his mouth against another. If thou receive not his words, they fly back and wound him. If thou receive them, they flee forward and wound thee.   FRANCIS QUARLES

2748.
Be thou as chaste as ice, as pure as Snow, thou shalt not escape calumny. Get thee to a nunnery, go.

SHAKESPEARE, *Hamlet*

2749.
My unsoil'd name, the austereness of my life,
My vouch against you, and my place i' the state,
Will so your accusation overweigh,
That you shall stifle in your own report,
And smell of calumny.
SHAKESPEARE, *Measure for Measure*

2750. Neglected calumny soon expires; show that you are hurt, and you give it the appearance of truth.

TACITUS, *History*

2751. To persevere in one's duty and be silent is the best answer to calumny.

WASHINGTON, *Moral Maxims*

See also: 4079.

CALVINISM

Related Subjects: Belief, Protestantism, Reformation, Religion.

2760. He that will not honor the memory, and respect the influence of Calvin, knows but little of the origin of American independence.

BANCROFT

2761. There is no system which equals Calvinism in intensifying, to the last degree, ideas of moral excellence and purity of character. It has always worked for liberty. There never was a system since the world began which puts upon men such motives to holiness or builds batteries which sweep the whole ground of sin with such horrible artillery.   H. W. BEECHER

2762. Wherever Calvinism was established, it brought with it not only truth but liberty and all the great developments which these two fertile principles carry with them.
          J. H. D'AUBIGNÉ

2763.
You can and you can't,
You will and you won't;
You'll be damn'd if you do.
You'll be damn'd if you don't.
LORENZO DOW, *Chain (of Calvinism)*

2764. The promulgation of Calvin's theology was one of the longest steps that mankind has taken toward personal freedom.   JOHN FISKE

2765. Calvinism has produced characters nobler and grander than any which republican Rome ever produced.   FROUDE

2766. Calvin's Institutes, in spite of its imperfections, is, on the whole, one of the noblest edifices ever erected by the mind of man, and one of the mightiest codes of moral law which ever guided him.   GUIZOT

2767. To the Calvinists, more than to any other class of men, the political liberties of Holland, England, and America are due.   J. L. MOTLEY

2768. Calvinism is a democratic and republican religion.   DE TOCQUEVILLE

CANDLE

Related Subject: Light.

2771. Neither do men light a candle, and put it under a bushel, but on a candlestick, and it giveth light unto all that are in the house.
          Bible: Matthew, v, 15

2772. How inferior for *seeing* with, is your brightest train of fireworks to the humblest farthing candle!
          CARLYLE, *Essay: Diderot*

2773. The butler and steward were in a confederacy and burnt the candle at both ends.   LE SAGE, *Gil Blas*

2774.
My candle burns at both ends;
  It will not last the night;
But ah, my foes, and oh, my friends,
  It gives a lovely light!
    EDNA ST. VINCENT MILLAY,
        A Few Figs from Thistles

2775. A candle lights others and consumes itself.   *Proverb*

2776. Thus hath the candle singed the moth.   SHAKESPEARE,
        The Merchant of Venice

See also: 1709, 1762, 2902, 4957, 9156, 11815, 12595, 18816, 20335.

CANDOR

Related Subjects: Honesty, Sincerity, Truth.

2781.
Gracious to all, to none subservient,
Without offence he spake the word
  he meant.   T. B. ALDRICH,
        The Sisters' Tragedy

2782. Always be ready to speak your mind, and a base man will avoid you.
          BLAKE, *Proverbs of Hell*

2783. If people would dare to speak to one another unreservedly, there would be a good deal less sorrow in the world a hundred years hence.

SAMUEL BUTLER,
The Way of All Flesh

2784. I was so free with him as not to mince the matter.

CERVANTES, *Don Quixote*

2785. Candor is the brightest gem of criticism.   DISRAELI

2786. Frankness invites frankness.

EMERSON, *Essays*

2787. I can promise to be candid, though I may not be impartial.

GOETHE

2788. Speak out, hide not thy thoughts.   HOMER, *Iliad*

2789. I cannot say one thing and mean another.   LONGFELLOW,
Giles Corey

2790. I call a fig a fig, a spade a spade.

MENANDER

2791. Plain-dealing is a jewel, and he that useth it shall die a beggar.

HENRY PORTER,
Two Angry Women of Abington

2792. Call a spade a spade.

Proverb

2793.
Just at the age 'twixt boy and youth,
When thought is speech, and speech
   is truth.   SCOTT, *Marmion*

2794.
        His heart's his mouth:
What his breast forges, that his tongue
   must vent.

SHAKESPEARE, *Coriolanus*

2795. He was wont to speak plain and to the purpose.

SHAKESPEARE,
Much Ado About Nothing

2796. He speaks home, madam; you may relish him more in the soldier than in the scholar.

SHAKESPEARE, *Othello*

2797.
    Take note, take note, O world!
To be direct and honest is not safe.

SHAKESPEARE, *Othello*

2798. Speak frankly as the wind.

SHAKESPEARE, *Troilus and Cressida*

2799. Candor and generosity, unless tempered by due moderation, lead to ruin.   TACITUS, *History*

2800.
I think it good plain English, without
   fraud,
To call a spade a spade, a bawd a
   bawd.   JOHN TAYLOR,
A Kicksey Winsey

2801. If he persists in saying to me what he likes, he shall hear what he does not like.   TERENCE, *Andria*

2802. It is great and manly to disdain disguise; it shows our spirit, and proves our strength.

EDWARD YOUNG

See also: 858.

CANT, see Hypocrisy

CAPITALISM

Related Subjects: Business, Economy, Socialism, Society.

2811. Your system was liable to periodical convulsions, overwhelming alike the wise and unwise, the successful cut-throat as well as his victim. I refer to the business crises at intervals of five to ten years, which wrecked the industries of the nation.

EDWARD BELLAMY,
Looking Backward

2812. Capitalism did not arise because capitalists stole the land or the workmen's tools, but because it was more efficient than feudalism. It will perish because it is not merely less efficient than socialism, but actually self-destructive.

J. B. S. HALDANE, *I Believe*

2813. They tell us that capitalism is doomed: Karl Marx, I believe, made the same announcement 80 years ago. He may still be right: but the old clock ticks on; and it does not help very much to throw stones at it. It would be surprising indeed if our system had survived quite unshaken the unprecedented upheaval of a World War. But it is infinitely adaptable and has not, I think, exhausted its resources.   A. P. HERBERT

2814. People have stopped asking, Can capitalism survive? No intelligent individual under forty-five years of age imagines that it can. What is less certain is an answer to the question, Can the human race survive?

LANCELOT HOGBEN,
Dangerous Thoughts

2815. Mr. Chairman, I am pained when I sit in my place in the House and hear members talk about the sacredness of capital; that the interests of money must not be touched. Yes, sir, they will vote six hundred thousand of the flower of American youth for the army to be sacrificed without a blush; but the great interests of capital currency, must not be touched.

SENATOR W. P. KELLOGG *of Illinois,*
Feb. 3, 1862

2816. The evidence makes it plain that capitalism in its phase of contraction will respect no principle, however venerable, in its effort to retain the power of the state in its hands.

That has been the experience of Mr. Blum in France; it has been, also, the experience of Mr. Roosevelt in the United States.

HAROLD J. LASKI, *I Believe*

2817. Capital, created by the labor of the worker, oppresses the worker by undermining the small proprietor and creating an army of the unemployed.

LENIN

2818. When commercial capital occupies a position of unquestioned ascendancy, it everywhere constitutes a system of plunder.

KARL MARX, *Capital*

2819. Capitalist production begets, with the inexorability of a law of nature, its own negation.

KARL MARX, *Capital*

2820. Another universal saying of those days was that "capital and labor should get together," as if the interminable struggle of these conflicting interests could be settled by a conference.

LINCOLN STEFFENS, *Autobiography*

2821. We have depended too long on the hope that private ownership and control would operate somehow for the benefit of society as a whole. That hope has not been realized. Now we are coming to believe that our resources will best be utilized for the benefit of all if we give deliberate study to the needs of society and adjust our land uses to those needs.

REXFORD G. TUGWELL

See also: 11374, 11380.

CAPITAL PUNISHMENT

Related Subjects: Hanging, Justice, Kill, Murder, Punishment.

2831. Whoso sheddeth man's blood, by man shall his blood be shed.

Bible: Genesis, ix, 6

2832. Now, why am I opposed to capital punishment? It is too horrible a thing for a state to undertake. We are told: "Oh, the killer does it; why shouldn't the state?" I would hate to live in a state that I didn't think was better than a murderer.
CLARENCE DARROW

2833. There is nothing in the history of the world that ever cheapened human life like our great war; next to that the indiscriminate killing of men by states. CLARENCE DARROW

2834. And now, having fully expressed our conviction that the punishment of death is one which should sometimes be inflicted, we may add that we would have it resorted to as unfrequently as possible. Nothing, in our view, but cold-blooded, premeditated, unpalliated murder, can fully justify it. Let this continue to be visited with the sternest penalty.
HORACE GREELEY

2835. As lawyer for defendant, as prosecutor for the State and as Judge of the greatest criminal court in all the world, I say that the only thing the criminal fears is the penalty of death that will follow his crime.
JUDGE TALLEY

2836. Must we do away with capital punishment because it is too cruel? Why, the very advocates of doing away with it would be the first to argue that life imprisonment is more cruel than snuffing out, without torture, the life of any individual.
JUDGE TALLEY

CARDS AND CARD PLAYING

Related Subjects: Amusement, Gambling.

2841. It is very wonderful to see persons of the best sense passing hours together in shuffling and dividing a pack of cards with no conversation but what is made up of a few game-phrases, and no other ideas but those of black or red spots ranged together in different figures. Would not a man laugh to hear anyone of his species complaining that life is short?
ADDISON

2842. Cards are the devil's books.
BULWER-LYTTON, *Money*

2843. As much is lost by a card too many as a card too few.
CERVANTES, *Don Quixote*

2844.
Cards were at first for benefits designed,
Sent to amuse, not to enslave the mind. DAVID GARRICK,
Epilogue to Moore's Gamester

2845. It is an old courtesy at the cards, perdy, to let the loser have his word. SIR THOMAS MORE

2846. When you have counted your cards, you'll find you have gained but little. *Proverb*

2847. Many can pack the cards that cannot play. *Proverb*

2848.
Have I not here the best cards for the game,
To win this easy match play'd for a crown? SHAKESPEARE,
King John

2849. As sure a card as ever won the set. SHAKESPEARE,
Titus Andronicus

2850. I must complain the cards are ill shuffled till I have a good hand.
SWIFT,
Thoughts on Various Subjects

See also: 3014, 14721, 15742.

CARE AND CARELESSNESS

Related Subjects: Burden, Economy, Love, Protection, Prudence, Responsibility, Worry.

2851. "Many of our cares," says Scott, "are but a morbid way of looking at our privileges." We let our blessings get mouldy, and then call them curses.   H. W. BEECHER

2852. Care admitted as a guest, quickly turns to be master.
C. N. BOVEE

2853.
Ye banks and braes o' bonny Doon,
    How can ye bloom sae fresh and
        fair?
How can ye chant, ye little birds,
    And I sae weary fu' o' care?
BURNS, The Banks o' Doon

2854. The cares of to-day are seldom those of to-morrow; and when we lie down at night we may safely say to most of our troubles, "Ye have done your worst, and we shall see you no more."   COWPER

2855. Only man clogs his happiness with care, destroying what is, with thoughts of what may be.   DRYDEN

2856.
If the heart of a man is depress'd with cares,
The mist is dispell'd when a woman appears.   JOHN GAY,
The Beggar's Opera

2857.
Begone, dull Care! I prithee begone from me!
Begone, dull Care! thou and I shall never agree.
JOHN PLAYFORD, Musical Companion

2858. A pound of care will not pay an ounce of debt.   Proverb

2859. Too much care may be as bad as downright negligence.   Proverb

2860. Care's no cure.   Proverb

2861. Careless men let their end steal upon them unawares and unprovided.
Proverb

2862. Put off thy cares with thy clothes; so shall thy rest strengthen thy labor, and so thy labor sweeten thy rest.   FRANCIS QUARLES

2863. Cares are often more difficult to throw off than sorrows; the latter die with time; the former grow upon it.   J. P. RICHTER

2864. So shaken as we are, so wan with care.   SHAKESPEARE,
Henry IV

2865.
                        Golden care!
That keep'st the ports of slumber open wide
To many a watchful night!
SHAKESPEARE, Henry IV

2866. His cares are now all ended.
SHAKESPEARE, Henry IV

2867.
Care is no cure, but rather corrosive,
For things that are not to be remedied.   SHAKESPEARE, Henry VI

2868.
Care keeps his watch in every old man's eye,
And where care lodges, sleep will never lie.   SHAKESPEARE,
Romeo and Juliet

2869. I am sure care's an enemy to life.   SHAKESPEARE, Twelfth Night

2870. Providence has given us hope and sleep as a compensation for the many cares of life.   VOLTAIRE

See also: 506, 1699, 2047, 2624, 2984, 3256, 3258, 5523, 13592.

CARICATURE

Related Subjects: Mockery, Satire.

2871. Nothing conveys a more inaccurate idea of a whole truth than a part of a truth so prominently brought forth as to throw the other parts into shadow. This is the art of caricature, by the happy use of which you might caricature the Apollo Belvidere.   BULWER-LYTTON

2872. Take my advice, and never draw caricature. By the long practice of it I have lost the enjoyment of beauty. I never see a face but distorted, and never have the satisfaction to behold the human face divine.
                         HOGARTH

2873. Parodies and caricatures are the most penetrating of criticisms.
                ALDOUS HUXLEY,
           Point Counter Point

CASTLE

Related Subject: Dreams.

2881. Castles in the air cost a vast deal to keep up.
BULWER-LYTTON, *The Lady of Lyons*

2882.
The snail, which everywhere doth roam
Carrying his own house still, still is at home,
Follow (for he is easy paced) this snail,
Be thine own palace, or the world's thy jail.   JOHN DONNE,
Verse Letter to Sir Henry Wotton

2883. I find the gayest castles in the air that were ever piled, far better for comfort and for use, than the dungeons in the air that are daily dug and caverned out by grumbling, discontented people.   EMERSON,
                Conduct of Life

2884. Castles are forests of stone.
GEORGE HERBERT, *Jacula Prudentum*

2885.
When I could not sleep for cold,
   I had fire enough in my brain,
And builded, with roofs of gold,
   My beautiful castles in Spain.
              LOWELL, *Aladdin*

2886. To build castles in Spain.
                   Proverb

2887.
This castle hath a pleasant seat; the air
Nimbly and sweetly recommends itself
Unto our gentle senses.
        SHAKESPEARE, *Macbeth*

2888.
A castle girt about and bound
   With sorrow, like a spell.
      SWINBURNE, *The Tale of Balen*

2889. If you have built castles in the air, your work need not be lost; that is where they should be. Now put the foundations under them.
           THOREAU, *Walden*

See also: 6164.

CAT

Related Subject: Animal.

2891. Who is to bell the Cat? It is easy to propose impossible remedies.
        AESOP, *Belling the Cat*

2892. An old cat laps as much milk as a young.
        WILLIAM CAMDEN, *Remains*

2893. Those who'll play with cats must expect to be scratched.
        CERVANTES, *Don Quixote*

2894. There wasn't room to swing a cat there.   DICKENS,
David Copperfield

2895.
Confound the cats! All cats—alway—
Cats of all colours, black, white, grey;
By night a nuisance and by day—
    Confound the cats!
            ORLANDO DOBBIN,
            A Dithyramb on Cats

2896. The Cat in Gloves catches no Mice.   FRANKLIN, *Poor Richard*

2897. There are more ways of killing a cat than choking her with cream.
CHARLES KINGSLEY, *Westward Ho!*

2898. To pull the chestnuts from the fire with the cat's paw.
            MOLIÈRE, *L'Etourdi*

2899. When I play with my cat, who knows whether I do not make her more sport than she makes me?
            MONTAIGNE, *Essays*

2900. It has been the providence of Nature to give this creature nine lives instead of one.   PILPAY,
            The Greedy Cat

2901. Keep no more cats than will catch mice.   *Proverb*

2902. When all candles be out all cats be grey.   *Proverb*

2903. When the cat's away The mice will play.   *Proverb*

2904. A cat may look on a king.
            Proverb

2905. He's like a cat; fling him which way you will, he'll light on his legs.
            Proverb

2906. A good cat deserves a good rat.
            Proverb

2907. An old cat sports not with her prey.   *Proverb*

2908. Cats hide their claws.
            Proverb

2909. A harmless necessary cat.
            SHAKESPEARE,
            The Merchant of Venice

2910.
I like little Pussy, her coat is so warm,
And if I don't hurt her, she'll do me no harm.   JANE TAYLOR,
            I Like Little Pussy

See also: 1578, 15422.

CAUSE

Related Subjects: Beginning, Consequences, Controversy, Motive, Necessity, Purpose, Reason, Responsibility.

Cause in the sense of causality

2911. Anaximander used to assert that the primary cause of all things was the Infinite,—not defining exactly whether he meant air or water or anything else.
            DIOGENES LAERTIUS,
            Anaximander

2912. Whatever is, is in its causes just.   DRYDEN, *Oedipus*

2913. I assert that nothing ever comes to pass without a cause.
            JONATHAN EDWARDS,
            The Freedom of the Will

2914. Physical science (i.e. physics), together with astronomy and chemistry and mineralogy, are all based on the strict and universal validity of the principle of causality.
            PROF. MAX PLANCK

2915. To infer a creator is to infer a cause, and causal inferences are only admissable in science when they proceed from observed causal laws. Creation out of nothing is an occurrence which has not been observed. There is, therefore, no better reason to suppose that the world was caused by a Creator than to suppose that it was uncaused; either equally contradicts the causal laws that we can observe.

BERTRAND RUSSELL

2916. Every why hath a wherefore.

SHAKESPEARE,
The Comedy of Errors

2917.
Find out the cause of this effect,
Or rather say, the cause of this defect,
For this effect defective comes by cause.   SHAKESPEARE, *Hamlet*

2918. Every cause produces more than one effect.

HERBERT SPENCER,
Essays on Education

2919. Nothing exists from whose nature some effect does not follow.

SPINOZA, *Ethics*

2920. Man thinks himself free because he is conscious of his wishes and appetites, whilst at the same time he is ignorant of the causes by which he is led to wish and desire, not dreaming what they are.

SPINOZA, *Ethics*

2921. Everything has a cause and the cause of anything is everything.

W. J. TURNER

Cause in the sense of principle

2922. It is the cause, and not the death, that makes the martyr.

NAPOLEON

2923.
There must in every cause be some first Martyr
To suffer and to fall;

There must be also those content to barter
Their victory for their all.

JOHN M. NEALE, *Abraham Lincoln*

2924. It is an ill cause that the lawyer thinks shame o'.   *Proverb*

2925. It is a bad cause, that none dares speak in.   *Proverb*

2926. He that has the worst cause makes the most noise.   *Proverb*

2927. Report me and my cause aright.

SHAKESPEARE, *Hamlet*

See also: 3007, 3028, 3752, 4358, 4631, 5181, 10520, 20363.

CAUTION

Related Subjects: Care, Conservatism, Counsel, Discretion, Example, Preparedness, Prudence, Safety, Warning, Watch, Wisdom.

2931. Going as if he trod upon eggs.

ROBERT BURTON,
Anatomy of Melancholy

2932. All is to be feared where all is to be lost.   BYRON

2933. Brer Fox, he lay low.

JOEL CHANDLER HARRIS,
Legends of the Old Plantation

2934.
Better put a strong fence 'round the top of the cliff,
Than an ambulance down in the valley.   JOSEPH MALINES,
A Fence or an Ambulance

2935. In the time of mirth take heed.

Proverb

2936. Sit still rather than rise and fall down.   *Proverb*

2937. It is well to learn caution by the misfortunes of others.

PUBLILIUS SYRUS, *Sententiae*

2938. Take warning by the misfortunes of others, that others may not take example from you.   SAADI

2939. He that is over-cautious will accomplish but very little.   SCHILLER

2940. Spur not an unbroken horse; put not your ploughshare too deep into new land.   SCOTT,
The Monastery

2941.
My ventures are not in one bottom
   trusted,
Nor to one place.
      SHAKESPEARE,
The Merchant of Venice

2942. More firm and sure the hand of courage strikes, when it obeys the watchful eye of caution.
      JAMES THOMSON

2943. Look before you leap; see before you go.   THOMAS TUSSER

See also: 999, 1618, 3165, 3302, 6681.

CELIBACY

Related Subjects: **Bachelor, Chastity, Marriage, Monk and Nun, Virginity.**

2951. Certainly, the best works and of greatest merit for the public, have proceeded from the unmarried or childless men.   BACON, *Essays*

2952. One was never married, and that's his hell; another is, and that's his plague.   ROBERT BURTON,
Anatomy of Melancholy

2953. The senseless practice of celibacy has been ranked from a remote period as a virtue.   DARWIN

2954. There is ample ethical justification for celibacy as a self-imposed and purposive denial, and some few are born to this state.
      W. M. GALLICHAN,
The Great Unmarried

2955. In Greece and Rome, and notably in Sparta, celibacy was regarded almost as a misdemeanor.
      W. M. GALLICHAN,
The Great Unmarried

2956. Celibates replace sentiment by habits.   GEORGE MOORE, *Impressions*

2957. Marriage may often be a stormy lake, but celibacy is almost always a muddy horse-pond.
      T. L. PEACOCK, *Melincourt*

2958.
Thrice-blessed they that master so
   their blood,
To undergo such maiden pilgrimage;
But earthlier happy is the rose distill'd,
Than that which, withering on the
   virgin thorn,
Grows, lives and dies in single blessedness.   SHAKESPEARE,
A Midsummer-Night's Dream

2959. The celibate, like the fly in the heart of an apple, dwells in a perpetual sweetness, but sits alone, and is confined and dies in singularity.
      JEREMY TAYLOR, *Sermons*

See also: 12546.

CENSORSHIP

Related Subjects: **Bigotry, Criticism, Dictatorship, Morality, Prudery, Tyranny.**

2961. Up in season, and so to the office, and read about how there is to be objection to Eugene O'Neill's play "All God's Chillun Got Wings," for that in the play a Negro kisses the hand of a white woman, and I deem

such objection foolish. . . what would the Klan and such people have done about "Othello"?　　F. P. A.,
The Diary of our Own Samuel Pepys

2962. Those expressions are omitted which can not with propriety be read aloud in the family.
　　DR. THOMAS BOWDLER,
　　Preface to his Family Shakespeare

2963. Unfortunately it has been our experience that there is a distinct affinity between fools and censorship. It seems to be one of those treading grounds where they rush in.
　　HEYWOOD BROUN,
　　Censoring the Censor

2964. So many new ideas are at first strange and horrible though ultimately valuable that a very heavy responsibility rests upon those who would prevent their dissemination.
　　J. B. S. HALDANE

2965. I defy anyone to show that one city or state with censorship is any better than other cities or states like our own where there is no censorship.
　　JUDGE BEN LINDSEY,
　　The Child—The Movie—and Censorship

2966. Pontius Pilate was the first great censor and Jesus Christ the first great victim of censorship.
　　JUDGE BEN LINDSEY,
　　The Child—The Movie—and Censorship

2967. It is argued against certain books, by virtuosi of moral alarm, that they depict vice as attractive. This recalls the king who hanged a judge for deciding that an archbishop was a mammal.　　H. L. MENCKEN

2968. Censorship ends in logical completeness when nobody is allowed to read any books except the books nobody can read.　　BERNARD SHAW

2969. Damn all expurgated books, the dirtiest book of all is the expurgated book.　　WALT WHITMAN

See also: 742, 1241, 2324, 6402, 8041.

CENSURE, see Criticism

CEREMONY

Related Subjects: Courtesy, Form, Ostentation.

2971. To dispense with ceremony is the most delicate mode of conferring a compliment.　　BULWER-LYTTON

2972. All ceremonies are, in themselves, very silly things; but yet a man of the world should know them. They are the outworks of manners and decency, which would too often be broken in upon, if it were not for that defence which keeps the enemy at a proper distance.
　　LORD CHESTERFIELD

2973. Ceremonies differ in every country; they are only artificial helps which ignorance assumes to imitate politeness which is the result of good sense and good-nature.　　GOLDSMITH

2974. Ceremony resembles that base coin which circulates through a country by royal mandate; it serves every purpose of real money at home, but is entirely useless if carried abroad. A person who should attempt to circulate his native trash in another country would be thought either ridiculous or culpable.　　GOLDSMITH

2975. If we use no ceremony toward others, we shall be treated without any. People are soon tired of paying trifling attentions to those who receive them with coldness, and return them with neglect.　　HAZLITT

2976.
When love begins to sicken and decay,
It useth an enforced ceremony.
There are no tricks in plain and
simple faith. SHAKESPEARE,
Julius Caesar

2977.
Ceremony was but devis'd at first
To set a gloss on faint deeds, hollow
welcomes,
Recanting goodness, sorry ere 'tis
shown;
But where there is true friendship,
there needs none.
SHAKESPEARE, *Timon of Athens*

2978. Ceremony is the invention of
wise men to keep fools at a distance;
as good breeding is an expedient to
make fools and wise men equals.
SIR RICHARD STEELE

CERTAINTY AND UNCERTAINTY

Related Subjects: Confidence,
Doubt, Security, Surety, Suspense.

2981. *To be positive:* to be mistaken
at the top of one's voice.
AMBROSE BIERCE,
The Devil's Dictionary

2982.
No great deed is done
By falterers who ask for certainty.
GEORGE ELIOT, *The Spanish Gypsy*

2983. As sure as death.
BEN JONSON,
Every Man in His Humour

2984.
All cares of mortal men did they for-
get,
Except the vague desire not to die,

The hopeless wish to flee from certainty,
That sights and sounds we love will
bring on us
In this sweet fleeting world and
piteous. WILLIAM MORRIS,
Life and Death of Jason

2985. The only certainty is that
nothing is certain.
PLINY THE ELDER,
Historia Naturalis

2986. Quit not certainty for hope.
Proverb

2987. Sure as the coat on your back.
Proverb

2988. Sure as God made little apples.
Proverb

Uncertainty

2989. What is more unwise than to
mistake uncertainty for certainty,
falsehood for truth?
CICERO, *De Senectute*

2990.
Uncertain ways unsafest are,
And doubt a greater mischief than
despair. SIR JOHN DENHAM,
Cooper's Hill

2991. Our Constitution is in actual
operation; everything appears to
promise that it will last; but in this
world nothing is certain but death
and taxes.
FRANKLIN, *Letter to M. Leroy*

2992. He is no wise man that will quit
a certainty for an uncertainty.
SAMUEL JOHNSON, *The Idler*

2993. All between the cradle and the
coffin is uncertain. *Proverb*

See also: 5092.

CHANCE

Related Subjects: Accident, Destiny, Fate, Fickleness, Fortune, Gambling, Luck, Opportunity, Risk.

3001.
We do not what we ought,
  What we ought not, we do,
And lean upon the thought
  That Chance will bring us through.
          MATTHEW ARNOLD,
            Empedocles on Etna

3002. He who distrusts the security of chance takes more pains to effect the safety which results from labor. To find what you seek in the road of life, the best proverb of all is that which says: "Leave no stone unturned."   BULWER-LYTTON

3003.
A "strange coincidence," to use a phrase
By which such things are settled nowadays.   BYRON, *Don Juan*

3004. Chance is a nickname of Providence.   DE CHAMFORT

3005. Work and acquire, and thou hast chained the wheel of Chance.
          EMERSON, *Essays*

3006. Chance fights ever on the side of the prudent.   EURIPIDES

3007. By the word chance we merely express our ignorance of the cause of any fact or effect—not that we think that chance was itself the cause.
          HENRY FERGUS

3008. Chance is perhaps the pseudonym of God when He did not want to sign.   ANATOLE FRANCE,
            Le Jardin d'Epicure

3009. There is a master who, without an effort, surpasses us all, and that master is chance.
          GABORIAU, *File 113*

3010. Things do not happen in this world—they are brought about.
          WILL HAYS

3011.
Under the bludgeonings of chance
  My head is bloody, but unbowed.
          W. E. HENLEY, *Invictus*

3012. Be not too presumptuously sure in any business; for things of this world depend on such a train of unseen chances that if it were in man's hands to set the tables, still he would not be certain to win the game.
          GEORGE HERBERT, *Jacula Prudentum*

3013. Chances rule men and not men chances.   HERODOTUS, *History*

3014.
I never saw any difference
Between playing cards for money
And selling real estate,
Practicing law, banking, or anything else.
For everything is chance.
          EDGAR LEE MASTERS,
            Spoon River Anthology

3015. Everlasting Fate shall yield to fickle Chance.
          MILTON, *Paradise Lost*

3016. Chance is always powerful. Let your hook be always cast; in the pool where you least expect it, there will be a fish.   OVID

3017.
All chance, direction, which thou canst not see.   POPE, *Essay on Man*

3018. He who trusts all things to chance, makes a lottery of his life.
          Proverb

3019. A wise man turns chance into good fortune.   *Proverb*

3020. What is chance but the rude stone which receives its life from the sculptor's hand? Providence gives us chance—and man must mould it to his own designs.

SCHILLER, *Don Carlos*

3021.
Chance will not do the work—Chance
    sends the breeze;
But if the pilot slumber at the helm,
The very wind that wafts us towards
    the port
May dash us on the shelves.

SCOTT, *The Fortunes of Nigel*

3022.
Let my disclaiming from a purposed
    evil
Free me so far in your most generous
    thoughts,
That I have shot mine arrow o'er the
    house,
And hurt my brother.

SHAKESPEARE, *Hamlet*

3023. If chance will have me king, why, chance may crown me.

SHAKESPEARE, *Macbeth*

3024. The doctrine of chances is the Bible of the fool. There is no doubt such a thing as chance; but *I see no reason why* Providence should not make use of it.   W. G. SIMMS

3025. Chance is a name for our ignorance.   LESLIE STEPHENS

3026. What can be more foolish than to think that all this rare fabric of heaven and earth could come by chance, when all the skill of art is not able to make an oyster!

JEREMY TAYLOR, *Sermons*

3027. The mines of knowledge are often laid bare by the hazel-wand of chance.   MARTIN F. TUPPER

3028. Chance is a word void of sense; nothing can exist without a cause.

VOLTAIRE

See also: 158, 5923.

CHANGE

Related Subjects: Adaptability, Consistency, Constancy, Conversion, Fickleness, Novelty, Revolution, Variety.

3031. The greatest vicissitude of things amongst men is the vicissitude of sects and religions.

BACON, *Of Vicissitudes of Things*

3032. He that will not apply new remedies must expect new evils.

BACON

3033.
          I detest all change,
And most a change in aught I loved
    long since.

BROWNING, *Paracelsus*

3034. To-day is not yesterday. We ourselves change. How then, can our works and thoughts, if they are always to be the fittest, continue always the same. Change, indeed, is painful, yet ever needful; and if memory have its force and worth, so also has hope.   CARLYLE

3035. The world is a scene of changes; to be constant in nature were inconstancy.   ABRAHAM COWLEY

3036. Perfection is immutable, but for things imperfect, to change is the way to perfect them. Constancy without knowledge cannot be always good; and in things ill, it is not virtue but an absolute vice.

OWEN FELTHAM

3037.
Most of the change we think we see
    in life

Is due to truths being in and out of favour.

ROBERT FROST, *The Black Cottage*

3038. Matters change and morals change; men remain.   GALSWORTHY

3039. All change is not growth; as all movement is not forward.

ELLEN GLASGOW, *I Believe*

3040.
What I possess I would gladly retain
Change amuses the mind, yet scarcely
     profits.   GOETHE

3041.
Thus times do shift,—each thing his
     turn does hold;
New things succeed, as former things
     grow old.   ROBERT HERRICK,
     Ceremonies for Candlemas Eve

3042. Human nature does not change, or, at any rate, history is too short for any changes to be perceptible. The earliest known specimens of art and literature are still comprehensible. In the fine arts it is only the convention, the form, the incidentals that change: the fundamentals of passion, of intellect and imagination remain unaltered.

ALDOUS HUXLEY, *Do What You Will*

3043. Observe always that everything is the result of a change, and get used to thinking that there is nothing Nature loves so well as to change existing forms and to make new ones like them.

MARCUS AURELIUS, *Meditations*

3044. We have changed all that.
MOLIÈRE, *Le Médecin Malgré Lui*

3045. Is't possible that so short a time can alter the condition of a man?

SHAKESPEARE, *Coriolanus*

3046.
Man's yesterday may ne'er be like his
     morrow;
Naught may endure but Mutability.
         SHELLEY, *Mutability*

3047. But Times do change and move continually.   EDMUND SPENSER,
     The Faerie Queene

3048.
The ever-whirling wheele
Of Change, the which all mortall
     things doth sway.
       EDMUND SPENSER,
       The Faerie Queene

3049. In this world of change naught which comes stays, and naught which goes is lost.   MME. SWETCHINE

3050.
The old order changeth, yielding place
     to new;
And God fulfils himself in many
     ways,
Lest one good custom should corrupt the world.
       TENNYSON, *Morte D'Arthur*

See also: 40, 155, 1420, 3302, 5174.

CHAOS

Related Subjects: Anarchy, Desolation, Order, Revolution, Ruin.

3051. Chaos often breeds life, when order breeds habit.
       HENRY ADAMS,
     The Education of Henry Adams

3052.
Temple and tower went down, nor
     left a site:—
Chaos of ruins!
       BYRON, *Childe Harold*

3053. The chaos of events.
       BYRON, *Prophecy of Dante*

3054.

Chaos, that reigns here
In double night of darkness and of
shades.   MILTON, *Comus*

3055.

Chaos umpire sits,
And by decision more embroils the
fray
By which he reigns.
MILTON, *Paradise Lost*

3056.

Lo! thy dread empire, Chaos! is
restor'd;
Light dies before thy uncreating
word:
Thy hand, great Anarch! lets the
curtain fall,
And universal darkness buries all.
POPE, *The Dunciad*

3057.

Nor time nor place
Did then adhere.
SHAKESPEARE, *Macbeth*

3058. Chaos is come again.
SHAKESPEARE, *Othello*

See also: 1385, 12161, 12294, 13771.

CHARACTER

Related Subjects: Baseness, Conscience, Consistency, Dignity, Example, Genius, Goodness, Heredity, Honesty, Honor, Ideals, Name, Personality, Qualities, Reputation, Virtue, Wickedness, Worth.

3061.
When wealth is lost, nothing is lost;
When health is lost, something is
lost;
When character is lost, all is lost!
Anonymous

3062. Happiness is not the end of
life: character is.
H. W. BEECHER, *Life Thoughts*

3063. Character must be kept bright,
as well as clean.
LORD CHESTERFIELD, *Letters*

3064. Those who deserve a good
character, ought to have the satisfaction of knowing that they have it,
both as a reward and as an encouragement.   LORD CHESTERFIELD, *Letters*

3065. It's not the brains that matter
most, but that which guides them—the
character, the heart, generous qualities, progressive ideas.
DOSTOYEVSKY,
The Insulted and the Injured

3066.
Too black for heaven, and yet too
white for hell.
DRYDEN, *The Hind & the Panther*

3067. His courage foes, his friends
his truth proclaim.
DRYDEN, *Absalom & Achitophel*

3068. Character gives splendor to
youth and awe to wrinkled skin and
gray hairs.
EMERSON, *Conduct of Life*

3069. A character is like an acrostic
—read it forward, backward, or
across, it still spells the same thing.
EMERSON, *Essays*

3070. Character is higher than intellect.   EMERSON, *Nature*

3071. Human character evermore
publishes itself. The most fugitive
deed and word, the intimated purpose, expresses character.
EMERSON, *Essays*

3072. Character is that which can do
without succes.   EMERSON

3073. We must have a weak spot or
two in a character before we can love
it much. People that do not laugh or
cry, or take more of anything than is
good for them, or use anything but

dictionary-words, are admirable subjects for biographies. But we don't always care most for those flat pattern-flowers that press best in the herbarium.   O. W. HOLMES,
The Professor at the Breakfast-Table

3074. He has the luck to be unhampered by either character, or conviction, or social position; so that Liberalism is the easiest thing in the world for him.
IBSEN, *The League of Youth*

3075. It is well for the world that in most of us, by the age of thirty, the character has set like plaster, and will never soften again.
WILLIAM JAMES, *Psychology*

3076. Character is like a tree and reputation like its shadow. The shadow is what we think of it; the tree is the real thing.   LINCOLN

3077. Character is what you are in the dark.
DWIGHT L. MOODY, *Sermons*

3078. Character is much easier kept than recovered.
THOMAS PAINE, *The Crisis*

3079. The most glorious exploits do not furnish us with the clearest discoveries of virtue or vice in men; sometimes a matter of less moment, an expression or a jest, informs us better of their characters and inclinations than the most famous sieges, the greatest armaments, or the bloodiest battles whatsoever.
PLUTARCH, *Lives*

3080. Though the wolf may lose his teeth, he never loses his inclinations.
Proverb

3081. His own character is the arbiter of every one's fortune.
PUBLILIUS SYRUS, *Sententiae*

3082. It matters not what you are thought to be, but what you are.
PUBLILIUS SYRUS, *Sententiae*

3083. A man never shows his own character so plainly as by the way he portrays another's.
J. P. RICHTER, *Titan*

3084. Character is the governing element of life, and is above genius.
FREDERICK SAUNDERS, *Stray Leaves*

3085. See thou character.
SHAKESPEARE, *Hamlet*

3086.
There is a kind of character in thy life,
That to the observer doth thy history
Fully unfold.
SHAKESPEARE, *Measure for Measure*

3087. Put more trust in nobility of character than in an oath.
SOLON, *Diogenes Laertius*

3088.
Fame is what you have taken,
    Character's what you give;
When to this truth you waken,
    Then you begin to live.
BAYARD TAYLOR, *Improvisations*

3089. How can we expect a harvest of thought who have not had a seed-time of character?
THOREAU, *Journal*

3090. I am as bad as the worst, but thank God I am as good as the best.
WALT WHITMAN

3091. Character is a by-product; it is produced in the great manufacture of daily duty.   WOODROW WILSON

See also: 752, 2023, 2610, 2662, 2765, 3475, 3611, 11903, 17161, 18572, 19074, 21621.

CHARITY

Related Subjects: Beggar, Benevolence, Gifts, Help, Kindness, Philanthropy, Poverty, Relief.

3101. Private beneficence is totally inadequate to deal with the vast numbers of the city's disinherited.
JANE ADDAMS,
Twenty Years at Hull House

3102. Blessed is he that considereth the poor. *Bible: Psalms, xli, 1*

3103. He that giveth unto the poor shall not lack.
Bible: Proverbs, xxviii, 27

3104. Take heed that ye do not your alms before men, to be seen of them.
Bible: Matthew, vi, 1

3105. When thou doest alms, let not thy left hand know what thy right hand doeth. *Bible: Matthew, vi, 3*

3106. Inasmuch as ye have done it unto one of the least of these my brethren, ye have done it unto me.
Bible: Matthew, xxv, 40

3107. Though I speak with the tongues of men and of angels, and have not charity, I am become as sounding brass, or a tinkling cymbal.
Bible: 1 Corinthians, xiii, 1

3108. Though I have all faith, so that I could remove mountains, and have not charity, I am nothing.
Bible: 1 Corinthians, xiii, 2

3109. Charity suffereth long and is kind; charity envieth not; charity vaunteth not itself, is not puffed up.
Bible: 1 Corinthians, xiii, 4

3110. And now abideth faith, hope, charity, these three; but the greatest of these is charity.
Bible: 1 Corinthians, xiii, 13

3111. Charity shall cover the multitude of sins. *Bible: 1 Peter, iv, 8*

3112. That worldly principle, Charity begins at home.
SIR THOMAS BROWNE, *Religio Medici*

3113.
Alas for the rarity
Of Christian charity
Under the sun!
THOMAS HOOD, *The Bridge of Sighs*

3114. Anticipate charity by preventing poverty; assist the reduced fellowman, either by a considerable gift, or a sum of money, or by teaching him a trade, or by putting him in the way of business, so that he may earn an honest livelihood, and not be forced to the dreadful alternative of holding out his hand for charity. This is the highest step and the summit of charity's golden ladder.
MAIMONIDES,
Charity's Eight Degrees

3115.
They take a paper and they read the headlines,
So they've heard of unemployment and they've heard of breadlines,
And they philanthropically cure them all
By getting up a costume charity ball.
OGDEN NASH,
Pride Goeth Before a Raise

3116.
The organized charity, scrimped and iced,
In the name of a cautious, statistical Christ.
J. B. O'REILLY, *In Bohemia*

3117.
In faith and hope the world will disagree,
But all mankind's concern is charity.
POPE, *Essay on Man*

3118. Whatever is given to the poor, is laid out of the reach of fortune.
Proverb

3119. The charitable give out at the door and God puts in at the window.
Proverb

3120. A charitable man is the true lover of God.   *Proverb*

3121. Charity and pride have different aims, yet both feed the poor.
Proverb

3122. Charity begins at home, but should not end there.   *Proverb*

3123. Charity excuseth not cheating.
Proverb

3124. He that has no charity merits no mercy.   *Proverb*

3125. He that feeds upon charity has a cold dinner and no supper.
Proverb

3126. Charity is the scope of all God's commands.   *Proverb*

3127. You find people ready enough to do the Samaritan, without the oil and two-pence. SYDNEY SMITH,
Lady Holland's Memoir

3128.
He was always found
Among your ten and twenty pound
    subscribers,
Your benefactors in the newspapers.
His alms were money put to interest
In the other world.
SOUTHEY, *The Alderman's Funeral*

3129. Care of the poor is incumbent on society as a whole.
SPINOZA, *Ethics*

3130. If a body's ever took charity, it makes a burn that don't come out.
JOHN STEINBECK,
The Grapes of Wrath

3131. I hate nobody: I am in charity with the world.
SWIFT, *Polite Conversation*

3132. The noblest charity is to prevent a man from accepting charity; and the best alms are to show and to enable a man to dispense with alms.
The Talmud

3133.
Melt not in an acid sect
The Christian pearl of charity.
WHITTIER, *Snow-Bound*

See also: 422, 501, 780, 2531, 12374.

CHARM

Related Subjects: Beauty, Grace, Personality, Smile, Sweetness, Youth.

3141.
Alick: What *is* charm, exactly, Maggie?
Maggie: Oh, it's—it's a sort of bloom on a woman. If you have it, you don't need to have anything else; and if you don't have it, it doesn't much matter what else you have. Some women, the few, have charm for all; and most have charm for one. But some have charm for none.
J. M. BARRIE,
What Every Woman Knows

3142. That is the worst of those dear people who have charm; they are so terrible to do without, when once you have got accustomed to them and all their ways.
DU MAURIER, *Trilby*

3143. "Charm"—which means the power to effect work without employing brute force—is indispensable to women. Charm is a woman's strength just as strength is a man's charm.   HAVELOCK ELLIS,
The Task of Social Hygiene

3144.
To me more dear, congenial to my
  heart,
One native charm, than all the gloss
  of art.
    GOLDSMITH, *The Deserted Village*

3145.
'Well, for my part,' they say, 'I cannot see the charm of Mrs. Jones.'
'Is it not just conceivable,' I feel inclined to answer, 'that Mrs. Jones
hasn't tried to charm you?'
    LOGAN PEARSALL SMITH,
               Afterthoughts

3146.
She is pretty to walk with,
And witty to talk with,
And pleasant, too, to think on.
    SIR JOHN SUCKLING,
    The Tragedy of Brennoralt

3147. All charming people, I fancy,
are spoiled. It is the secret of their
attraction.   OSCAR WILDE,
    The Portrait of Mr. W. H.

See also: 458, 934, 1354, 1898, 4937,
8579, 11816, 12848.

CHASTITY

**Related Subjects: Blushing, Celi-
bacy, Innocence, Marriage, Modesty, Purity, Virgin, Virtue.**

3151. A man defines his standing at
the court of chastity, by his views of
women. He cannot be any man's
friend, nor his own, if not hers.
    BRONSON ALCOTT

3152. Chaste women are often proud
and froward, as presuming upon the
merit of their chastity.
    BACON, *Essays*

3153. That chastity of honor, which
feels a stain like a wound.   BURKE

3154.
But, whatsoe'er she wished, she acted
  right;
And whether coldness, pride, or virtue, dignify
A woman, so she's good, what does
  it signify?   BYRON, *Don Juan*

3155. She is chaste who was never
asked the question.
    CONGREVE, *Love for Love*

3156.
In vain to honour they pretend
Who guard themselves with ramparts
  and with walls.
Them only fame the truly valiant calls
Who can an open breach defend.
    ABRAHAM COWLEY, *Maidenhead*

3157. Beneath this stone I lie, the
famous woman who loosed her zone
to one man only.
  Greek Epigram, Greek Anthology

3158. A woman's chastity consists,
like an onion, of a series of coats.
    HAWTHORNE, *Journals*

3159.
She who keeps chastely to her husband's side
Is not for one but every night his
  bride:
And stealing still with love and fear
  to bed,
Brings him not one, but many a
  maidenhead.
    ROBERT HERRICK, *Julia's Churching*

3160. Chastity enables the soul to
breathe a pure air in the foulest
places.   JOUBERT, *Pensées*

3161. An unattempted woman cannot
boast of her chastity.
    MONTAIGNE, *Essays*

3162. Do I counsel you to chastity?
Chastity is a virtue in some, but in
many almost a vice. These, it is true,
are abstinent; but from all that they

do the bitch of sensuality looks out with envious eyes.

NIETZSCHE, *Thus Spake Zarathustra*

3163. If she is chaste when there is no fear of detection, she is truly chaste; she who sins not because she dares not, does the sin.

OVID, *Amores*

3164.
I envy not their bliss, if he or she
Think fit to live in perfect chastity:
Pure let them be, and free from taint or vice;
I for a few slight spots am not so nice.

POPE, *Wife of Bath: Prologue*

3165. If not chastely, at all events cautiously.   *Proverb*

3166. A chaste eye exiles licentious looks.   *Proverb*

3167.
My chastity's the jewel of our house,
Bequeathed down from many ancestors.   SHAKESPEARE,
All's Well that Ends Well

3168. The very ice of chastity is in them.
SHAKESPEARE, *As You Like It*

3169. As chaste as unsunn'd snow.
SHAKESPEARE, *Cymbeline*

3170. Neither maid, widow, nor wife.
SHAKESPEARE, *Measure for Measure*

3171. I will find you twenty lascivious turtles ere one chaste man.
SHAKESPEARE,
The Merry Wives of Windsor

3172.
You seem to me as Dian in her orb,
As chaste as is the bud ere it be blown.   SHAKESPEARE,
Much Ado About Nothing

3173.
There my white stole of chastity I doff'd,
Shook off my sober guards and civil fears.
SHAKESPEARE, *A Lover's Complaint*

3174.
                    Fruitless chastity,
Love-lacking vestals and self-loving nuns,
That on the earth would breed a scarcity
And barren dearth of daughters and of sons.
SHAKESPEARE, *Venus and Adonis*

3175.
Who doth desire that chaste his wife should be,
First be he true, for truth doth truth deserve.
SIR PHILIP SIDNEY, *Acadia*

3176. There needs not strength to be added to inviolate chastity; the excellency of the mind makes the body impregnable.   SIR PHILIP SIDNEY

3177.
I have been so misused by chaste men with one wife
That I would live with satyrs all my life.
ANNA WICKHAM, *Ship Near Shoals*

3178. A pure mind in a chaste body is the mother of wisdom and deliberation; sober counsels and ingenuous actions; open deportment and sweet carriage; sincere principles and unprejudiced understanding; love of God and self-denial; peace and confidence; holy prayers and spiritual comfort; and a pleasure of spirit infinitely greater than the sottish pleasure of unchastity.
JEREMY TAYLOR, *Sermons*

See also: 2748, 4511, 9457, 14065.

CHEATING

Related Subjects: Deceit, Fidelity, Honesty, Lies.

3181. Like the strawberry wives, that laid two or three great strawberries at the mouth of their pot, and all the rest were little ones.
BACON, *Apothegms*

3182.
The first and worst of all frauds is to cheat
Oneself.   PHILIP J. BAILEY, *Festus*

3183. This is a pretty flim-flam.
BEAUMONT & FLETCHER,
The Little French Lawyer

3184.
Don't steal; thou'lt never thus compete
Successfully in business. Cheat.
AMBROSE BIERCE,
The Devil's Dictionary

3185. Three things are men most likely to be cheated in, a horse, a wig, and a wife.
FRANKLIN, *Poor Richard*

3186. I hope I shall never be deterred from detecting what I think a cheat, by the menaces of a ruffian.
SAMUEL JOHNSON

3187. Little drops of water poured into the milk, give the milkman's daughter lovely gowns of silk. Little grains of sugar mingled with the sand, make the grocer's assets swell to beat the band.
WALT MASON, *Little Things*

3188.
He that will cheat at play
Will cheat you any way.
Proverb

3189. He that's cheated twice by the same man is an accomplice with the cheater.   *Proverb*

3190. Cheating play never thrives.
Proverb

3191. We know that there are chiselers. At the bottom of every case of criticism and obstruction we have found some selfish interest, some private axe to grind.
FRANKLIN D. ROOSEVELT

See also: 2847, 3123, 4770, 11509, 14940, 19813.

CHEERFULNESS

Related Subjects: Contentment, Gayety, Good Humor, Happiness, Joy, Optimism, Smiles, Warmth.

3201. A cheerful temper joined with innocence will make beauty attractive, knowledge delightful, and wit good-natured.   ADDISON, *The Tatler*

3202. Cheerfulness keeps up a kind of daylight in the mind, filling it with a steady and perpetual serenity.
ADDISON

3203. To be free-minded and cheerfully disposed at hours of meals, and of sleep, and of exercise, is one of the best precepts of long-lasting.
BACON

3204. If my heart were not light, I would die.   JOANNA BAILLIE

3205. The cheerful live longest in years and afterwards in our regards. Cheerfulness is the offshoot of goodness.   C. N. BOVEE

3206. Oh, give us the man who sings at his work.   CARLYLE

3207. Wondrous is the strength of cheerfulness, and its power of endurance—the cheerful man will do more in the same time, will do it better, will persevere in it longer, than the sad or sullen.   CARLYLE

3208. So of cheerfulness, or a good temper, the more it is spent, the more of it remains.

EMERSON, *Conduct of Life*

3209. That which befits us is cheerfulness and courage.

EMERSON, *Essays*

3210. To make knowledge valuable, you must have the cheerfulness of wisdom. Goodness smiles to the last.

EMERSON, *Essays*

3211. An ounce of cheerfulness is worth a pound of sadness to serve God with.   THOMAS FULLER

3212. The true source of cheerfulness is benevolence. The soul that perpetually overflows with kindness and sympathy will always be cheerful.

PARKE GODWIN

3213.

Cheerful at morn he wakes from short repose,

Breasts the keen air, and carols as he goes.   GOLDSMITH, *The Traveller*

3214. We ought to feel a deep cheerfulness, as I may say, that a happy Providence kept it from being any worse.   THOMAS HARDY,

Far From the Madding Crowd

3215.

Learn the sweet magic of a cheerful face;

Not always smiling, but at least serene.

O. W. HOLMES, *The Morning Visit*

3216. The mind that is cheerful at present will have no solicitude for the future, and will meet the bitter occurrences of life with a smile.

HORACE

3217. To be happy, the temperament must be cheerful and gay, not gloomy and melancholy. A propensity to hope and joy, is real riches; one to fear and sorrow is real poverty.

DAVID HUME

3218. Honest good humor is the oil and wine of a merry meeting, and there is no jovial companionship equal to that where jokes are rather small and the laughter abundant.

WASHINGTON IRVING

3219. Every one must have felt that a cheerful friend is like a sunny day, which sheds its brightness on all around; and most of us can, as we choose, make of this world either a palace or a prison.

SIR JOHN LUBBOCK

3220. Cheerful looks make every dish a feast; and it is that which crowns a welcome.   MASSINGER

3221. The most manifest sign of wisdom is a continual cheerfulness.

MONTAIGNE, *Essays*

3222. Burdens become light when cheerfully borne.   OVID

3223. The best of healers is good cheer.   PINDAR, *Nemean Ode*

3224. A man of gladness seldom falls into madness.   *Proverb*

3225. A blithe heart makes a blooming visage.   *Proverb*

3226. Cheerfulness is as natural to the heart of a man in strong health, as color to his cheek; and wherever there is habitual gloom, there must be either bad air, unwholesome food, improperly severe labor, or erring habits of life.   RUSKIN

3227.

Lay aside life-harming heaviness

And entertain a cheerful disposition.

SHAKESPEARE, *Richard II*

Children

3228. Every time a man smiles, and much more when he laughs, it adds something to his fragment of life.

STERNE

3229. Cheerfulness in most cheerful people, is the rich and satisfying result of strenuous discipline.

E. P. WHIPPLE,
Success and Its Conditions

See also: 477, 3885.

CHILDHOOD, CHILDREN

Related Subjects: Age, Babies, Boy, Family, Innocence, Parents, Posterity, Youth.

3231. When I was a child, I spake as a child, I understood as a child, I thought as a child; but when I became a man, I put away childish things. *Bible: 1 Corinthians, xiii, 11*

3232. The dreams of childhood—its airy fables; its graceful, beautiful, humane, impossible adornments of the world beyond: so good to be believed in once, so good to be remembered when outgrown.

DICKENS, *Hard Times*

3233. The doll is one of the most imperious necessities, and at the same time one of the most charming instincts of female childhood.

VICTOR HUGO, *Les Misérables*

3234.
The childhood shows the man,
As morning shows the day.

MILTON, *Paradise Regained*

3235.
Sweet childish days, that were as long
As twenty days are now.

WORDSWORTH, *To a Butterfly*

3236. That our sons may be as plants grown up in their youth; that our daughters may be as corner stones.

Bible: Psalms, cxliv, 12

3237. Train up a child in the way he should go: and when he is old he will not depart from it.

Bible: Proverbs, xxii, 6

3238. Golf . . . is a trifling thing beside the privilege of taking a small son to the zoo and letting him see his first lion, his first tiger and, best of all, his first elephant. Probably he will think that they are part of your own handiwork turned out for his pleasure. . . . Cortes on his lonely peak in Darien was a pigmy discoverer beside the child eating his first spoonful of ice-cream.

HEYWOOD BROUN, *Holding a Baby*

3239. If we had paid no more attention to our plants than we have to our children, we would now be living in a jungle of weeds.

LUTHER BURBANK

3240.
Child of the pure, unclouded brow
    And dreaming eyes of wonder!
Though time be fleet and I and thou
    Are half a life asunder,
Thy loving smile will surely hail
The love-gift of a fairy-tale.

LEWIS CARROLL,
Through the Looking-Glass

3241. I shall never marry; and why should you speak of my having children? I am just as likely to give birth to a Nero as to an Augustus.

QUEEN CHRISTINA OF SWEDEN

3242. No one knows what will be the fate of the child he begets, or the child she bears. The fate of the child is the last thing they consider.

CLARENCE DARROW

3243. In the little world in which children have their existence, whosoever brings them up, there is nothing so finely perceived and so finely felt, as injustice.

DICKENS, *Great Expectations*

3244. Who is there whom bright and agreeable children do not attract to play and creep and prattle with them?

EPICTETUS, *Discourses*

3245. If Nature had arranged that husbands and wives should have children alternatively, there would never be more than *three* in a family.

LAURENCE HOUSMAN

3246.
Thou straggler into loving arms,
  Young climber-up of knees.

MARY LAMB, *A Child*

3247.
Children are what the mothers are.
No fondest father's fondest care
Can fashion so the infant heart.

W. S. LANDOR, *Children*

3248. Men are generally more careful of the breed of their horses and dogs than of their children.

WILLIAM PENN,
Fruits of Solitude

3249. The truth is children are not half-men and half-women, or half-boys and half-girls. They are a race of beings to themselves. And it is in the power of this curious race of beings to plunge into the secret of life more deeply than all other mortals.

J. C. POWYS, *Autobiography*

3250. Children do not play ordinary conventional games unless they are encouraged to do so by the older boys and girls. Children's "games", strictly speaking, are not games at all. They are the child's inmost reality! They are the child's life-illusion. They

turn back to them with a sigh of relief from the impertinent intrusive activities of grown-up people.

J. C. POWYS, *Autobiography*

3251. He that has no children knows not what is love. *Proverb*

3252. Late children are early orphans. *Proverb*

3253. A man among children will be long a child, a child among men will be soon a man. *Proverb*

3254. Little children should be seen and not heard. *Proverb*

3255. Many children, and little bread, is a painful pleasure. *Proverb*

3256. Children are certain cares, but uncertain comforts. *Proverb*

3257. Children are poor men's riches. *Proverb*

3258. Children increase the cares of life, but mitigate the remembrance of death. *Proverb*

3259. Hold your hands off other folks' bairns, till you get some of your own. *Proverb*

3260. Give a little love to a child, and you get a great deal back.

RUSKIN,
The Crown of Wild Olive

3261. A mother's pride, a father's joy. SCOTT, *Rokeby*

3262. The very staff of my age, my very prop. SHAKESPEARE,
The Merchant of Venice

3263.
How pleasant is Saturday night,
  When I've tried all the week to be good,
And not spoke a word that was bad,
  And obliged every one that I could.

NANCY D. SPROAT,
Lullabies for Children

3264.

A child should always say what's true
And speak when he is spoken to,
And behave mannerly at table;
At least as far as he is able.

STEVENSON,
The Whole Duty of Children

3265.

No sweeter thing than children's ways
    and wiles,
    Surely, we say, can gladden eyes
    and ears
Yet sometimes sweeter than their
    words or smiles
    Are even their tears.

SWINBURNE, *A Child's Pity*

3266. I do not love him because he
is good, but because he is my little
child.   TAGORE,
The Crescent Moon

3267. When I bring you coloured
toys, my child, I understand why
there is such a play of colours on
clouds, on water, and why flowers are
painted in tints.   TAGORE,
The Crescent Moon

3268.

Monday's child is fair of face,
Tuesday's child is full of grace,
Wednesday's child is loving and giv-
    ing,
Thursday's child works hard for a
    living.
Friday's child is full of woe,
Saturday's child has far to go,
But the child that is born on the Sab-
    bath-day
Is brave and bonny, and good and
    gay.   *Traditional*

3269. The child is father of the man.
WORDSWORTH,
My Heart Leaps Up When I Behold

See also: 464, 889, 894, 3442, 3445, 4541, 4811, 6433, 9291, 11826.

CHINA AND THE CHINESE

Related Subjects: East.

3271.

Which I wish to remark,
    And my language is plain,
That for ways that are dark
    And for tricks that are vain,
The heathen Chinee is peculiar.

BRET HARTE, *Plain Language
from Truthful James*

3272. We are ruined by Chinese
cheap labor.

BRET HARTE, *Plain Language
from Truthful James*

3273.

You'll never plumb the Oriental mind,
And if you did, it isn't worth the toil.

KIPLING, *One Viceroy Resigns*

3274. In China the spiritual values
have not been separated from the
material values, but rather help man
in a keener enjoyment of life as it
falls to our lot. We live the life of
the senses and the life of the spirit
at the same moment and see no necessary conflict.   LIN YUTANG,
My Country & My People

3275. We [Chinese] never force salvation on anybody who does not come
to ask for it. We have no gun-boats
anyway, and even if we had, we would
never care to go up the Thames or the
Mississippi and shoot the English or
the Americans into heaven against
their will.   LIN YUTANG,
My Country & My People

3276. I do not believe in the myth
of the "subtle Oriental": I am convinced that in a game of mutual de-
ception an Englishman or an American can beat a Chinaman nine times
out of ten.   BERTRAND RUSSELL

3277. But owing to the fact that
China became the leading State, and

that the Chinese had before their eyes no example of another state equal to her, conceit, self-satisfaction and arrogance arose. All this entered into our flesh and blood, and we were transformed into a nation apart. We were our own teachers, as in all reconstruction we made use only of our own resources and strength, without resorting to foreign help.

> Sun Yat-Sen, *Memoirs of a Chinese Revolutionary*

See also: 4098.

CHIVALRY

Related Subjects: Courtesy, Dueling, Gentleman, Valor.

3281. But the age of chivalry is gone; that of sophisters, economists, and calculators has succeeded.

> Burke, *Reflections on the Revolution in France*

3282. Cervantes smil'd Spain's chivalry away.   Byron, *Don Juan*

3283. The age of chivalry is never past, so long as there is a wrong left unredressed on earth.

> Charles Kingsley

3284. Collision is as necessary to produce virtue in men, as it is to elicit fire in inanimate matter; and so chivalry is of the essence of virtue.

> Thomas Russell

CHOICE

Related Subjects: Desire, Election, Prudence, Will.

3291. For many are called, but few are chosen. *Bible: Matthew, xxii, 5*

3292. Life too often presents us with a choice of evils, rather than of goods.

> C. C. Colton

3293. Fate makes our relatives, choice makes our friends.

> Jacques Delille, *La Pitie*

3294. The strongest principle of growth lies in human choice.

> George Eliot, *Daniel Deronda*

3295. God offers to every mind its choice between truth and repose.

> Emerson, *Essays*

3296.
But it is said and ever shall,
Between two stools lieth the fall.

> John Gower, *Confessio Amantis*

3297.
            Or fight or fly,
This choice is left you to resist or die.

> Homer, *Odyssey*

3298. The measure of choosing well, is, whether a man likes and finds good in what he has chosen.

> Charles Lamb

3299. Where there is no choice, we do well to make no difficulty.

> George Macdonald, *Sir Gibbie*

3300. The difficulty in life is the choice.   George Moore,
The Bending of the Bough

3301. No choice amongst stinking fish.   *Proverb*

3302. Be slow in choosing, but slower in changing.   *Proverb*

3303. Choose always the way that seems the best however rough it may be; custom will soon render it easy and agreeable.   Pythagoras

3304. There's small choice in rotten apples.   Shakespeare,
The Taming of the Shrew

3305.
Where to elect there is but one,
'Tis Hobson's choice,—take that or none.   Thomas Ward,
England's Reformation

See also: 1173, 1398, 1802, 6607, 7211.

CHRIST

Related Subjects: The Bible, Christianity, Christmas, Cross, Easter, Faith, God, Jew, Judgment Day, Paradise, Religion, Salvation.

3311.
There was no other good enough
  To pay the price of sin;
He only could unlock the gate
  Of heaven and let us in.
          C. F. Alexander,
    There Is a Green Hill Far Away

3312. As the print of the seal on the wax is the express image of the seal itself, so Christ is the express image —the perfect representation of God.
          St. Ambrose

3313. Everyone in the world is Christ and they are all crucified.
      Sherwood Anderson,
        The Philosopher

3314. The name of Christ—the one great word—well worth all languages in earth or heaven.
        Philip J. Bailey

3315. Lo, I am with you alway, even unto the end of the world.
    Bible: Matthew, xxviii, 20

3316. I am the light of the world; he that followeth me shall not walk in darkness, but shall have the light of life.   *Bible: John, viii, 12*

3317. I am the resurrection and the life.   *Bible: John, xi, 25*

3318. Jesus Christ, the condescension of divinity, and the exaltation of humanity.   Phillips Brooks

3319. Jesus Christ was the first and greatest teacher of democracy because his mission in the world was to win belief. He made faith the test of the human soul. Heywood Broun,
        Convention Studies

3320. The difference between Socrates and Jesus Christ? The great Conscious; the immeasurably great Unconscious.   Carlyle

3321.
But Cristes lore, and his apostles twelve,
He taughte, and first he followed it himselve.   Chaucer,
        Canterbury Tales

3322. I believe Plato and Socrates. I believe in Jesus Christ. Coleridge

3323. The martyred Christ of the working class, the inspired evangel of the downtrodden masses, the world's supreme revolutionary leader, whose love for the poor and the children of the poor hallowed all the days of his consecrated life, lighted up and made forever holy the dark tragedy of his death, and gave to the ages his divine inspiration and his deathless name.   Eugene V. Debs

3324. The whole life of Christ was a continual passion; others die martyrs, but Christ was born a martyr. He found a Golgotha (where he was crucified) even in Bethlehem, where he was born; for to his tenderness then the straws were almost as sharp as the thorns after, and the manger as uneasy at first as his cross at last. His birth and his death were but one continual act, and his Christmas-day and his Good Friday are but the evening and morning of one and the same day.   John Donne,
        Sermon on the Nativity

3325. Jesus was called Christ only in the sense that you say, a Godlike man. I am only a Godlike woman, God-anointed, and I have done a work that none others could do.

MARY BAKER EDDY

3326. An era in human history is the life of Jesus, and its immense influence for good leaves all the perversion and superstition that has accrued almost harmless.   EMERSON

3327. We kind o' thought Christ went agin war an 'pillage.

LOWELL, *The Biglow Papers*

3328. To me Jesus—whom I was later to represent as a fighter and prophet—was as worthy of reverence as Socrates, because he died for truth, as men are doing again today.

EMIL LUDWIG, *I Believe*

3329.
They were all looking for a king
    To slay their foes and lift them high;
Thou cam'st, a little baby thing
    That made a woman cry.

GEORGE MACDONALD,
That Holy Thing

3330. God never gave a man a thing to do concerning which it were irreverent to ponder how the Son of God would have done it.

GEORGE MACDONALD

3331. The nature of Christ's existence is mysterious, I admit; but this mystery meets the wants of man. Reject it and the world is an inexplicable riddle; believe it, and the history of our race is satisfactorily explained.

NAPOLEON

3332. Jesus Christ is a God to whom we can approach without pride, and before whom we may abase ourselves without despair.   PASCAL

3333. All history is incomprehensible without Christ.   RÉNAN,
Life of Jesus

3334.
                    In those holy fields
Over whose acres walked those blessed feet
Which fourteen hundred years ago were nail'd
For our advantage on the bitter cross.
SHAKESPEARE, *Henry IV*

See also: 233, 652, 1371, 1867, 1871, 2126, 2966, 3106, 3116, 3489, 3673, 8588, 11844, 13274, 15654, 17941, 19592, 19611, 20199.

CHRISTIANITY

Related Subjects: The Bible, Christ, Church, Conversion, Faith, God, Martyr, Protestantism, Religion, Salvation.

3341. There was never law, or sect, or opinion did so much magnify goodness, as the Christian religion doth.

BACON

3342. A Christian is nothing but a sinful man who has put himself to school to Christ for the honest purpose of becoming better.

H. W. BEECHER

3343. Christians and camels receive their burdens kneeling.

AMBROSE BIERCE

3344. The Christian has greatly the advantage of the unbeliever, having everything to gain and nothing to lose.

BYRON

3345. Considered as a whole, the Christian religion of late ages has been continually dissipating itself into Metaphysics; and threatens now to disappear, as some rivers do, in deserts of barren sand.   CARLYLE,
Sir Walter Scott

3346. Christianity is not a theory or speculation but a life; not a philosophy of life, but a life and a living process.   COLERIDGE

3347. Christianity proves itself, as the sun is seen by its own light. Its evidence is involved in its excellence.   COLERIDGE

3348. Christianity, rightly understood, is identical with the highest philosophy. The essential doctrines of Christianity are necessary and eternal truths of reason.   COLERIDGE

3349. Though a great man may, by a rare possibility, be an infidel, yet an intellect of the highest order must build upon Christianity. DE QUINCEY

3350. His Christianity was muscular.   DISRAELI, *Endymion*

3351. Even those who have renounced Christianity and attack it, in their inmost being still follow the Christian ideal, for hitherto neither their subtlety nor the ardour of their hearts has been able to create a higher ideal of man and of virtue than the ideal given by Christ of old.   DOSTOYEVSKY, *The Brothers Karamazov*

3352. There is no leveler like Christianity but it levels by lifting all who receive it to the lofty table-land of a true character and of undying hope both for this world and the next.   JONATHAN EDWARDS

3353. Christianity is the record of a pure and holy soul, humble, absolutely disinterested, a truth-speaker, and bent on serving, teaching, and uplifting men. It teaches that to love the All-perfect is happiness.   EMERSON

3354. He who shall introduce into public affairs the principles of primitive Christianity, will revolutionize the world.   FRANKLIN

3355. The moral and religious system which Jesus Christ has transmitted to us, is the best the world has ever seen, or can see.   FRANKLIN

3356. Christianity always suits us well enough so long as we suit it. A mere mental difficulty is not hard to deal with. With most of us it is not reason that makes faith hard, but life.   JEAN INGELOW

3357. Sir, I think all Christians, whether Papists or Protestants, agree in the essential articles, and that their differences are trivial, and rather political than religious.   SAMUEL JOHNSON, *Boswell: Life*

3358. Christianity taught men that love is worth more than intelligence. JACQUES MARITAIN, *I Believe*

3359. I call Christianity the one great curse, the one enormous and innermost perversion, the one great instinct of revenge, for which no means are too venomous, too underhand, too underground and too petty,—I call it the one immortal blemish of mankind.   NIETZSCHE, *The Antichrist*

3360. Religion is a process of turning your skull into a tabernacle, not of going up to Jerusalem once a year.   AUSTIN O'MALLEY

3361. Let it not be imagined that the life of a good Christian must be a life of melancholy and gloominess; for he only resigns some pleasures to enjoy others infinitely better. PASCAL

3362. Christianity is more than history. It is also a system of truths. Every event which its history records, either is a truth, or suggests or expresses a truth, which man needs assent to or to put into practice.   NOAH PORTER

3363. You are Christians of the best edition, all picked and culled.

RABELAIS

3364.
O father Abram! what these Christians are,
Whose own hard dealings teaches them suspect
The thoughts of others!

SHAKESPEARE,
The Merchant of Venice

3365. The Christian doctrine of the infinite worth of every single human being was the disguised expression of man's revolt against slavery.

JOHN STRACHEY, *I Believe*

3366. See how these Christians love one another.   TERTULLIAN,
Apologeticus

3367. Christianity is the companion of liberty in its conflicts—the cradle of its infancy, and the divine source of its claims.   DE TOCQUEVILLE

3368. Whatever makes men good Christians, makes them good citizens.

DANIEL WEBSTER

3369. A Christian is the highest style of man.   EDWARD YOUNG,
Night Thoughts

3370. Scratch the Christian and you find the pagan—spoiled.

ISRAEL ZANGWILL

See also: 652, 3113, 3133, 3463, 3764, 4494, 6416, 7062, 7167, 7753, 10207, 13633, 15071.

CHRISTMAS

Related Subjects: Christ, December, Holiday.

3371. Christmas is over and Business is Business.   F. P. A.,
For the Other 364 Days

3372. Not believe in Santa Claus? You might as well not believe in fairies.   FRANCIS P. CHURCH,
Is There a Santa Claus?

3373.
God rest ye, merry gentlemen! Let nothing you dismay,
For Jesus Christ, our Saviour, was born on Christmas Day.
DINAH CRAIK, *A Christmas Carol*

3374. It was always said of him, that he knew how to keep Christmas well.
DICKENS, *A Christmas Carol*

3375.
'Most all the time, the whole year round, there ain't no flies on me,
But jest 'fore Christmas I'm as good as I kin be!   EUGENE FIELD,
Jest 'Fore Christmas

3376.
'Twas the night before Christmas, when all through the house
Not a creature was stirring,—not even a mouse;
The stockings were hung by the chimney with care,
In hopes that St. Nicholas soon would be there.
CLEMENT CLARKE MOORE,
A Visit from St. Nicholas

3377. "Happy Christmas to all, and to all a good-night!"
CLEMENT CLARKE MOORE,
A Visit from St. Nicholas

3378. Christmas comes but once a year.   *Proverb*

3379. They talk of Christmas so long, that it comes.   *Proverb*

3380.
Heap on more wood!—the wind is chill;
But let it whistle as it will,
We'll keep our Christmas merry still.
SCOTT, *Marmion*

3381.

It came upon the midnight clear,
That glorious song of old.
EDMUND SEARS, *The Angels' Song*

CHURCH

Related Subjects: Bell, The Bible, Christianity, God, Graveyard, Meeting, Preacher, Religion, Sabbath, Salvation, Worship.

3391. It is an unanswerable argument that the statistics of new members of the nation's leading churches show great gains when the country is in a depression, and declines when the country, in the midst of a boom period, is throwing away money and burning the candle at both ends!
ROGER BABSON,
Business Fundamentals

3392. Surely the church is a place where one day's truce ought to be allowed to the dissensions and animosities of mankind.   BURKE

3393. Where God hath a temple, the Devil will have a chapel.
ROBERT BURTON,
Anatomy of Melancholy

3394. Built God a church, and laugh'd His word to scorn.
COWPER, *Retirement*

3395.
Wherever God erects a house of prayer,
The Devil always builds a chapel there;
And 'twill be found, upon examination,
The latter has the largest congregation.   DEFOE,
The True-Born Englishman

3396. To be of no church is dangerous.   SAMUEL JOHNSON

3397. The great scandal of the nineteenth century is the divorce between the working classes and the church.   JACQUES MARITAIN,
I Believe

3398.
And storied windows richly dight,
Casting a dim religious light.
MILTON, *Il Penseroso*

3399. When the existence of the Church is threatened, she is released from the commandments of morality. With unity as the end, the use of every means is sanctified, even cunning, treachery, violence, simony, prison, death. For all order is for the sake of the community, and the individual must be sacrificed to the common good.
BISHOP VON NIEHEIM,
De schismate libri, 1411

3400.
Who builds a church to God, and not to fame,
Will never mark the marble with his name.   POPE, *Moral Essays*

3401. Many come to bring their clothes to church rather than themselves.   *Proverb*

3402. Church-work goes on slowly.
Proverb

3403. But do you know what I would tell you? In the primitive church, the chalices were of wood, the prelates of gold. In these days the church has chalices of gold and prelates of wood.
SAVONAROLA

3404. I never weary of great churches. It is my favorite kind of mountain scenery. Mankind was never so happily inspired as when it made a cathedral.   STEVENSON

See also: 1092, 4383, 4700, 5492, 9597.

CIRCLES

Related Subject: Wheel.

3411. The nature of God is a circle whose centre is everywhere and its circumference nowhere.
ST. AUGUSTINE

3412. We all of us live too much in a circle.   DISRAELI, *Sybil*

3413. The eye is the first circle; the horizon which it forms is the second; and throughout nature this primary figure is repeated without end. It is the highest emblem in the cipher of the world.   EMERSON, *Circles*

3414. Every man is the center of a circle, whose fatal circumference he cannot pass.   J. J. INGALLS

3415. We are swinging round the circle.   ANDREW JOHNSON

3416.
He drew a circle that shut me out—
Heretic, rebel, a thing to flout.
But Love and I had the wit to win:
We drew a circle that took him in.
EDWIN MARKHAM, *Outwitted*

3417.
Circles are prais'd not that abound
In largeness, but th' exactly round;
So life we praise, that does excel
Not in much time, but acting well.
EDMUND WALLER,
Long and Short Life

CIRCUMSTANCE

Related Subjects: Chance, Destiny, Events, Fate, Fortune, Luck, Opportunity.

3421.
Circumstance, that unspiritual god
And miscreator, makes and helps along
Our coming evils.   BYRON,
Childe Harold

3422. Man makes the circumstances, and spiritually as well as economically is the artificer of his own fortune. . . . Man's circumstances are the element he is appointed to live and work in; . . . so that in another no less genuine sense, it can be said circumstances make the man.
CARLYLE, *Diderot*

3423. Man is not the creature of circumstances. Circumstances are the creatures of men.   DISRAELI,
Vivian Grey

3424. Tyrannical Circumstance!
EMERSON, *Conduct of Life*

3425. One must follow circumstances, use the forces about us, do in a word what we find to do.
ANATOLE FRANCE

3426. Circumstances alter cases.
T. C. HALIBURTON,
The Old Judge

3427. He is happy whose circumstances suit his temper but he is more excellent who can suit his temper to any circumstances.   DAVID HUME

3428. Occasions do not make a man either strong or weak, but they show what he is.   THOMAS À KEMPIS,
Of the Imitation of Christ

3429. Circumstances are things round about; we are *in* them, not *under* them.   W. S. LANDOR,
Imaginary Conversations

3430. Circumstances are the rulers of the weak; they are but the instruments of the wise.   SAMUEL LOVER

3431. Circumstances! I make circumstances!   NAPOLEON

3432. It is circumstance and proper measure that give an action its character, and make it either good or bad.
PLUTARCH, *Lives*

3433. The happy combination of fortuitous circumstances.   SCOTT, *The Monastery*

3434. People are always blaming their circumstances for what they are. I don't believe in circumstances. The people who get on in this world are the people who get up and look for the circumstances they want, and, if they can't find them, make them.
BERNARD SHAW,
Mrs. Warren's Profession

3435. Men are not altered by their circumstances but as they give them opportunities of exerting what they are in themselves and a powerful clown is a tyrant in the most ugly form in which he can possibly appear.
SIR RICHARD STEELE

3436. Many a time a man cannot be such as he would be, if circumstances do not admit of it.   TERENCE, *Heauton Timoroumenos*

3437. A man is what the winds and tides have made him.   JIM TULLY

3438. Circumstances over which I have no control.
DUKE OF WELLINGTON

See also: 239, 2180.

CITIES

Related Subjects: **Community, Cosmopolitan, London, New York City, Paris, Park, Town, Village.**

3441. I have found by experience, that they who have spent all their lives in cities, improve their talents, but impair their virtues; and strengthen their minds, but weaken their morals.   C. C. COLTON

3442. The larger our great cities grow, the more irresistible becomes the attraction which they exert on the children of the country, who are fascinated by them, as the birds are fascinated by the lighthouse or the moths by the candle. HAVELOCK ELLIS, *The Task of Social Hygiene*

3443. An urban life saps that calm and stolid strength which is necessary for all great effort and stress, physical or intellectual.
HAVELOCK ELLIS,
The Task of Social Hygiene

3444. Cities force growth and make men talkative and entertaining but they make them artificial.   EMERSON

3445.
But for my children, I would have
    them keep their distance from the
    thickening center; corruption
Never has been compulsory, when
    the cities lie at the monster's feet
    there are left the mountains.
ROBINSON JEFFERS,
Shine, Perishing Republic

3446.
To one who has been long in city pent,
'Tis very sweet to look into the fair
And open face of heaven.
KEATS, *Sonnet, To One who Has Been Long in City Pent*

3447. If you suppress the exorbitant love of pleasure and money, idle curiosity, iniquitous purpose, and wanton mirth, what a stillness would there be in the greatest cities.
LA BRUYÈRE

3448.
Proud is the city—She finds a place
    for many a fad to-day,
But she's more than blind if she fails
    to find a place for the boys to play!
DENIS McCARTHY,
Give Them a Place to Play

3449.
As one who long in populous city
    pent,

Where houses thick and sewers annoy
the air.   MILTON, *Paradise Lost*

3450.
Tower'd cities please us then,
And the busy hum of men.
                    MILTON, *L'Allegro*

3451. City gates stand open to the
bad as well as the good.   *Proverb*

3452. A great city, a great solitude.
                                Proverb

3453. What is the city but the people?
                    SHAKESPEARE, *Coriolanus*

3454. The thing generally raised on
city land is taxes.
            CHARLES DUDLEY WARNER,
                    My Summer in a Garden

3455. A great city is that which has
the greatest men and women.
                    WALT WHITMAN,
                    Song of the Broad-Axe

See also: 1104, 4316, 8796, 9743,
9831, 15153.

CIVILIZATION

Related Subjects: Culture, Progress, Refinement.

3461. The origin of civilization is
man's determination to do nothing
for himself which he can get done
for him.   H. C. BAILEY

3462. Civilization is the upward
struggle of mankind, in which millions
are trampled to death that thousands
may mount on their bodies.
                    LORD BALFOUR

3463. No civilization other than that
which is Christian, is worth seeking
or possessing.   BISMARCK

3464. It is the task of civilization to
raise every citizen above want, but
in so doing to permit a free development and avoid the slavery of the
bee-hive and the ant-heap.
                    JOHN BUCHAN,
                Memory Hold-The-Door

3465. Is man's civilization only a
wrappage, through which the savage
nature of him can still burst, infernal
as ever?   CARLYLE,
                The French Revolution

3466. There are few words which
are used more loosely than the word
"Civilization." What does it mean?
It means a society based upon the
opinion of civilians. It means that
violence, the rule of warriors and
despotic chiefs, the conditions of
camps and warfare, of riot and tyranny, give place to parliaments where
laws are made, and independent
courts of justice in which over long
periods those laws are maintained.
That is Civilization—and in its soul
grow continually freedom, comfort
and culture. When Civilization reigns
in any country, a wider and less
harassed life is afforded to the masses
of the people.
                WINSTON CHURCHILL,
                Blood, Sweat & Tears

3467. What a time! What a civilization!   CICERO, *Catiline*

3468. Consider the cannibal. He used
to devour captured warriors instead
of broiled chickens. But as he grew
civilized he lived on his fellows no
more; he cooked other creatures
which he learned in time to make
more delicious. A similar step should
be taken by some modern cannibals.
Men do not eat men but they live
on them, they live on their labor,
they use them for purposes quite as
fatal to their existence.
                    CLARENCE DAY

3469. Increased means and increased leisure are the two civilizers of man.
DISRAELI

3470. Few nations have been able to reach intellectual refinement and esthetic sensitivity without sacrificing so much in virility and unity that their wealth presents an irresistible temptation to impecunious barbarians. Around every Rome hover the Gauls; around every Athens, some Macedon.
WILL DURANT, *The Life of Greece*

3471. Civilizations have died before, but men continued to live, and there arose in turn other civilizations.
IRWIN EDMAN, *I Believe*

3472. The world does not come to an end each time an individual dies, nor does it end each time a form of civilization decays.
IRWIN EDMAN, *I Believe*

3473. The more rapidly a civilization progresses, the sooner it dies for another to arise in its place.
HAVELOCK ELLIS, *The Dance of Life*

3474. If at some period in the course of civilization we seriously find that our science and our religion are antagonistic, then there must be something wrong either with our science or with our religion.
HAVELOCK ELLIS, *The Dance of Life*

3475. The true test of civilization is, not the census, nor the size of cities, nor the crops, but the kind of man that the country turns out.
EMERSON

3476. A sufficient and sure method of civilization is the influence of good women.
EMERSON

3477. The post office, with its educating energy, augmented by cheapness, and guarded by a certain religious sentiment in mankind, so that

the power of a wafer, or a drop of wax guards a letter as it flies over sea and land, and bears it to its address as if a battalion of artillery had brought it, I look upon as a first measure of civilization.
EMERSON

3478. The ultimate tendency of civilization is toward barbarianism.
A. W. & J. C. HARE

3479. I should hardly like to trust pen and ink with all the audacity of my social ideas; but after fifty years of optimistic contact with 'civilization' and its ability to come out all right in the end, I now abhor it, and feel that it is coming out all wrong in the end, unless it bases itself anew on a real equality.
W. D. HOWELLS,
Letter to Henry James

3480. If civilization is to recreate itself after the war it can only do so on the basis of what, for want of a better word, we must call a social outlook.
JULIAN HUXLEY

3481. A decent provision for the poor is the true test of civilization.
SAMUEL JOHNSON, *Boswell: Life*

3482. Nations, like individuals, live or die but civilization cannot perish.
MAZZINI

3483. Civilization, indeed, may be defined as a constructive criticism of nature, and Huxley even called it a conspiracy against nature.
H. L. MENCKEN

3484. Civilization today, such as it is, is not the creation or the monopoly of one people or nation.
JAWAHARLAL NEHRU,
India and the World

3485. The most civilized people are as near to barbarism as the most

polished steed is to rust. Nations, like metals, have only superficial brilliancy.
ANTOINE DE RIVAROL

3486. Civilization is perhaps approaching one of those long winters that overtake it from time to time. Romantic Christendom—picturesque, passionate, unhappy episode—may be coming to an end. Such a catastrophe would be no reason for despair.
SANTAYANA,
Character and Opinion in the United States

3487. Civilization never looks more lovely than when surrounded by barbarism; and yet, strange to say, barbarism never looks so inviting to me as when I am surrounded by civilization.   H. M. STANLEY

3488. In order to civilize a people, it is necessary first to fix it, and this can not be done without inducing it to cultivate the soil.   DE TOCQUEVILLE

3489. All that is best in the civilization of to-day, is the fruit of Christ's appearance among men.
DANIEL WEBSTER

3490. Actually, when every man in America owns his own car, every man in America will wish he didn't. America too will have reached the saturation point where modern civilization, which is only another name for materialism, will appear to her as bleak disillusionment. And at that moment her statesmen no doubt will discover that the national honor is insulted or some high principle involved and another war will be in full blast.
I. A. R. WYLIE

See also: 1100, 1185, 1209, 1743, 3542, 3601, 3619, 3901, 9574, 12285, 17053, 18768, 19082, 20479.

CLEANLINESS

Related Subjects: Bathing, Dirt, Fastidiousness, Purity, Washing.

3491. Cleanliness is next to impossible.   *Anonymous*

3492. Whoever eats bread without first washing his hands is as though he had sinned with a harlot.
The Babylonian Talmud

3493. Cleanness of the body was ever deemed to proceed from a due reverence to God.   BACON,
Advancement of Learning

3494. When a man reproached him [Diogenes] for going into unclean places, he said, "The sun too penetrates into privies, but is not polluted by them."   DIOGENES LAERTIUS,
Diogenes

3495. The daily ablutions of an infant are no more natural nor necessary than would be the process of taking a fish out of water every day and covering it with dirt in order to make it thrive more vigorously in its own element. . . Water is not the natural habitat of humanity.
MARY BAKER EDDY,
Science & Health

3496. Cleanliness is a great virtue; but when it is carried to such an extent that you cannot find your books and papers which you left carefully arranged on your table—when it gets to be a monomania with man or woman—it becomes a bore.
CHARLES B. FAIRBANKS,
My Unknown Chum

3497. Beauty will fade and perish, but personal cleanliness is practically undying, for it can be renewed whenever it discovers symptoms of decay.
W. S. GILBERT, *The Sorcerer*

3498. Let thy mind's sweetness have its operation upon thy body, thy clothes, and thy habitation.
GEORGE HERBERT, *Jacula Prudentum*

3499. Above all things, keep clean. It is not necessary to be a pig in order to raise one.
ROBERT INGERSOLL,
About Farming in Illinois

3500. One keep-clean is better than ten make-cleans. *Proverb*

3501. A new broom sweeps clean. *Proverb*

3502.
Bid them wash their faces,
And keep their teeth clean.
SHAKESPEARE, *Coriolanus*

3503. Certainly this is a duty, not a sin. "Cleanliness is indeed next to godliness." JOHN WESLEY,
Sermons

See also: 1190.

CLERGYMEN, see Preachers

CLEVERNESS

Related Subjects: Ability, Address, Craftsmanship, Epigram, Intellectuals, Intelligence, Originality, Skill, Wit.

3511. Cleverness is serviceable for everything, sufficient for nothing.
AMIEL, *Journal*

3512. Clever men are good, but they are not the best. CARLYLE, *Goethe*

3513. It's clever, but is it art?
KIPLING,
The Conundrum of the Workshops

3514. It is great cleverness to know how to conceal one's cleverness.
LA ROCHEFOUCAULD, *Maxims*

3515. Too clever is dumb.
OGDEN NASH, *When the Moon Shines*

3516.
If all good people were clever,
 And all clever people were good,
The world would be nicer than ever
 We thought that it possibly could.

But somehow, 'tis seldom or never
 The two hit it off as they should;
The good are so harsh to the clever,
 The clever so rude to the good.
ELIZABETH WORDSWORTH,
The Clever and the Good

See also: 2327, 9140.

CLOUDS

Related Subjects: Fog, Heavens, Rain, Shadow, Snow, Storm, Weather, Wind.

3521. That looked as though an angel, in his upward flight, had left his mantle floating in mid-air.
JOANNA BAILLIE

3522.
The hooded clouds, like friars,
 Tell their beads in drops of rain.
LONGFELLOW,
Midnight Mass for the Dying

3523. Clouds, that the sun builds up, darken him. *Proverb*

3524. Every cloud engenders not a storm. SHAKESPEARE, *Henry VI*

CLUB

Related Subjects: Meeting, Snob, Society, Union.

3531.
The member with the face like a pale ham
Settles his stomachs in the leather chair.

The member with the mustard-colored hair
Chats with the member like a curly ram,
Then silence like the shutting of a clam,
Gulps, and slow eating, and the waiter's stare—
Like prosperous leeches settling to their fare
The members gorge, distending as they cram.
STEPHEN VINCENT BENET,
Lunch at a City Club

3532. A very unclubbable man.
SAMUEL JOHNSON, *Boswell: Life*

See also: 354, 1408.

COAL

Related Subjects: Fire, Warmth.

3541. Coal is a portable climate.
EMERSON, *Conduct of Life*

3542. We may well call it black diamonds. Every basket is power and civilization. EMERSON,
Conduct of Life

3543. Coals to Newcastle. *Proverb*

COLLEGE, see University

COLOR

Related Subjects: Black, Painting.

3551.
Every gaudy color
Is a bit of truth.
NATHALIA CRANE, *The Vestal*

3552.
Oh green is the colour of faith and truth,
And rose the colour of love and youth,
And brown of the fruitful clay.
CHARLES KINGSLEY, *Dartside*

See also: 2200, 3267, 9463, 19602.

COLUMBUS, CHRISTOPHER

Related Subject: America.

3561. Columbus! Other title needs he none. FLORENCE E. COATES,
Columbus

3562. Columbus discovered no isle or key so lonely as himself.
EMERSON, *Society and Solitude*

3563.
He gained a world; he gave that world
Its grandest lesson: "On! sail on!"
JOAQUIN MILLER, *Columbus*

3564.
Columbus found a world, and had no chart,
Save one that faith deciphered in the skies;
To trust the soul's invincible surmise
Was all his science and his only art.
SANTAYANA, *O World*

3565. That mathematical, geographical, son-of-a-gun, Columbo.
TRADITIONAL,
Ballad: Christopher Columbo

COLUMNISTS

Related Subjects: News, The Press, Scandal.

3571. A columnist has three main functions—to instruct, to amuse, or to make you mad. And in exercising the make-you-mad function he frequently pops off with some outrageous and flatfooted statement manufactured out of his own personal bias which is designed to arouse uproar and tumult among the readers.
ERNEST L. MEYERS,
Three Functions of a Columnist

3572. It would simplify matters to accept a columnist for what he is: merely an individual, no wiser, though more articulate, than most people who exists as a convenient peg upon which invited guests can hang the cloak of their prejudice, and either pat his head or kick him in the shins.

ERNEST L. MEYERS,
Three Functions of a Columnist

3573. They are the abstracts and brief chronicles of the time: after your death you were better have a bad epitaph than their ill report while you live. SHAKESPEARE, *Hamlet*

3574. I usually get my stuff from people who promised somebody else that they would keep it a secret.

WALTER WINCHELL

COMFORT

Related Subjects: **Consolation, Contentment, Home, Leisure, Luxury, Pleasure, Relief, Rest, Sympathy, Warmth.**

3581. You canna expect to be baith grand and comfortable.

J. M. BARRIE,
The Little Minister

3582. Thy rod and thy staff they comfort me. *Bible: Psalms, xxiii, 4*

3583. We have all sinned and come short of the glory of making ourselves as comfortable as we easily might have done. SAMUEL BUTLER,
The Way of All Flesh

3584. Never does one feel oneself so utterly helpless as in trying to speak comfort for great bereavement. I will not try it. Time is the only comforter for the loss of a mother.

MRS. THOMAS CARLYLE,
Letter to Thomas Carlyle

3585. Giving comfort under affliction requires that penetration into the human mind, joined to that experience which knows how to soothe, how to reason, and how to ridicule, taking the utmost care not to apply those arts improperly.   FIELDING

3586. The lust for comfort, that stealthy thing that enters the house a guest, and then becomes a host, and then a master.

KAHLIL GIBRAN, *The Prophet*

3587. The powers of Time as a comforter can hardly be overstated; but the agency by which he works is exhaustion.   L. E. LANDON

3588.
Thou art all the comfort
The gods will diet me with.

SHAKESPEARE, *Cymbeline*

3589. He receives comfort like cold porridge.   SHAKESPEARE,
The Tempest

3590. Most of our comforts grow up between our crosses.

EDWARD YOUNG, *Night Thoughts*

See also: 401, 1252, 3256, 3664, 19892.

COMMAND, COMMANDER

Related Subjects: **Authority, Dictatorship, Discipline, Leadership, Obedience.**

3591. To command, must we not have never met our equal?
BALZAC, *The Commission in Lunacy*

3592. It is a fine thing to command, even if it only be a herd of cattle.

CERVANTES, *Don Quixote*

3593. It is better to have a lion at the head of an army of sheep, than a sheep at the head of an army of lions.
DEFOE

3594. He that commandeth well shall be obey'd well.   *Proverb*

3595. A brave captain is as a root, out of which as branches, the courage of his soldiers doth spring.

SIR PHILIP SIDNEY

3596. The right of commanding is no longer an advantage transmitted by nature; like an inheritance, it is the fruit of labors, the price of courage.

VOLTAIRE

See also: 1123, 1936, 2532, 3126, 4298, 5919.

COMMERCE

Related Subjects: Business, Competition, Corporations, Custom, Finance, Salesmen.

3601. Commerce is the most important activity on the face of the earth. It is the foundation on which civilization is built. Religion, society, education—all have their roots in business, and would have to be reorganized in their material aspects should business fail. JAMES R. ADAMS,
More Power to Advertising

3602. A well regulated commerce is not like law, physic, or divinity, to be over stocked with hands; but, on the contrary, flourishes by multitudes, and gives employment to all its professors. ADDISON

3603. Our cargoes of meat, drink and cloaths beat the Dutch.
ANONYMOUS

3604. It may almost be held that the hope of commercial gain has done nearly as much for the cause of truth, as even the love of truth itself.
C. N. BOVEE

3605. When we speak of the commerce with our colonies, fiction lags after truth, invention is unfruitful, and imagination cold and barren.
BURKE, *Conciliation with America*

3606. Commerce may well be termed the younger sister for, in all emergencies she looks to agriculture both for defense and for supply.
C. C. COLTON

3607. The crossroads of trade are the meeting place of ideas, the attrition ground of rival customs and beliefs; diversities beget conflict, comparison, thought; superstitions cancel one another, and reason begins.
WILL DURANT, *The Life of Greece*

3608. Commerce has made all winds her messengers; all climes her tributaries; all her people her servants.
TRYON EDWARDS

3609. The extension of trade is a matter of tariffs rather than of war, and in any case the trade of a country with its own acquisitions by conquest is a comparatively insignificant portion of its total trade.
HAVELOCK ELLIS,
The Task of Social Hygiene

3610. The craft of the merchant is this bringing a thing from where it abounds, to where it is costly.
EMERSON, *Conduct of Life*

3611. Commerce is of trivial import; love, faith, truth of character, the aspiration of man, these are sacred.
EMERSON, *Essays*

3612. Commerce is a kind of spring, which, diverted from its natural channel, ceases to flow. There are but two things which invite foreigners—profit and convenience. If you render commerce less convenient, or less gainful, they will insensibly forsake you.
FENELON, *Telemachus*

3613. No nation was ever ruined by trade. FRANKLIN,
Thoughts on Commercial Subjects

3614.
Where wealth and freedom reign contentment fails,
And honour sinks where commerce long prevails.   GOLDSMITH,
The Traveller

3615. Commerce is no missionary to carry more or better than you have at home. But what you have at home, be it gospel, or be it drunkenness, commerce carries the world over.
EDWARD E. HALE

3616. You dare not make war on cotton. Cotton is king.
JAMES H. HAMMOND

3617. Perish commerce. Let the constitution live!   GEORGE HARDKINGE

3618. Perfect freedom is as necessary to the health and vigor of commerce, as it is to the health and vigor of citizenship.   PATRICK HENRY

3619. Commerce is the great civilizer. We exchange ideas when we exchange fabrics.   ROBERT INGERSOLL

3620. The merchant has no country.
JEFFERSON

3621. Free trade, one of the greatest blessings which a government can confer on a people, is in almost every country unpopular.
MACAULAY,
On Mitford's History of Greece

3622. Trade knows neither friends nor kindred.   *Proverb*

3623. There needs a long apprenticeship to understand the mystery of the world's trade.   *Proverb*

3624. A merchant's happiness hangs upon chance, winds, and waves.
Proverb

3625. Trade is the mother of money.
Proverb

3626. A handful of trade is a handful of gold.   *Proverb*

3627.
Hence Commerce springs, the venal interchange
Of all that human art or Nature yield.   SHELLEY, *Queen Mab*

3628.
Commerce! beneath whose poison-breathing shade
No solitary virtue dares to spring,
But Poverty and Wealth with equal hand
Scatter their withering curses.
SHELLEY, *Queen Mab*

3629. "The romance of modern commerce, George!" my uncle would say, rubbing his hands together and drawing in air through his teeth. "The romance of modern commerce, eh? Conquest. Province by Province. Like sogers."   H. G. WELLS,
Tono-Bungay

See also: 345, 1494.

COMMON SENSE

Related Subjects: Intelligence, Sense.

3631. If a man can have only one kind of sense, let him have common sense. If he has that and uncommon sense too, he is not far from genius.
H. W. BEECHER

3632. Common sense is only a modification of talent. Genius is an exaltation of it.   BULWER-LYTTON

3633. Common sense is, of all kinds, the most uncommon. It implies good judgment, sound discretion, and true and practical wisdom applied to common life.   TRYON EDWARDS

3634. Nothing astonishes men so much as common sense and plain dealing.   EMERSON, *Art*

3635. Common Sense, which, one would say, means the shortest line between two points. EMERSON, *Journals*

3636. Sword of Common Sense! Our surest gift. GEORGE MEREDITH, *To the Comic Spirit*

3637. Fine sense, and exalted sense, are not half as useful as common sense. There are forty men of wit to one man of sense. He that will carry nothing about him but gold, will be every day at a loss for readier change. POPE

3638. One pound of learning requires ten pounds of common sense to apply it. *Proverb*

3639. Common sense is the growth of all countries. *Proverb*

3640. A handful of common sense is worth a bushel of learning. *Proverb*

3641. I think that common sense, in a rough, dogged way, is technically sounder than the special schools of philosophy, each of which squints and overlooks half the facts and half the difficulties in its eagerness to find in some detail the key to the whole. SANTAYANA, *Obiter Scripta*

3642. Common sense is not so common. VOLTAIRE

3643. To act with common sense according to the moment, is the best wisdom I know; and the best philosophy is to do one's duties, take the world as it comes, submit respectfully to one's lot; bless the goodness that has given us so much happiness with it, whatever it is; and despise affectation. SIR ROBERT WALPOLE

COMMUNITY

Related Subjects: Cities, Neighbor, Town, Village.

3651. A community is like a ship; every one ought to be prepared to take the helm. IBSEN, *An Enemy of the People*

3652. Those who set themselves the task of making their communities into places in which the average human being may obtain a share, not only of greater physical well-being, but of wider mental and spiritual existence, will lead an active and adventurous life to reach their goal. ELEANOR ROOSEVELT

See also: 3399.

COMPANIONS, COMPANIONSHIP

Related Subjects: Associates, Brotherhood, Friendship.

3661.
Music I heard with you was more than music,
And bread I broke with you was more than bread.
CONRAD AIKEN, *Bread and Music*

3662. A crowd is not company, and faces are but a gallery of pictures. BACON, *Essays*

3663. Endeavour, as much as you can, to keep company with people above you. LORD CHESTERFIELD, *Letters*

3664. It brings comfort and encouragement to have companions in whatever happens. DIO CHRYSOSTOM, *Third Discourse on Kingship*

3665. "My idea of an agreeable person," said Hugo Bohun, "is a person who agrees with me." DISRAELI, *Lothair*

3666. Men who know the same things are not long the best company for each other. EMERSON, *Representative Men*

3667. The company of just and righteous men is better than wealth and a rich estate. EURIPIDES, *Aegens*

3668. Every man is like the company he is wont to keep. EURIPIDES, *Phoenix*

3669. Company makes cuckolds. THOMAS FULLER, *Gnomologia*

3670. His room is better than his company. ROBERT GREENE

3671. The company makes the feast. J. HACKWOOD, *Good Cheer*

3672.
For 'tis always fair weather
When good fellows get together
With a stein on the table and a good song ringing clear.
RICHARD HOVEY, *A Stein Song*

3673. "A man is known by the company he keeps"—it is the motto of a prig. Little men with foot rules six inches long, applied their measuring sticks in this way to One who lived nineteen centuries ago. "He sits at meat with publicans and sinners," they tauntingly said assuming that His character was smirched thereby. ELBERT HUBBARD, *The Philistine*

3674.
And the bright faces of my young companions
Are wrinkled like my own, or are no more. LONGFELLOW, *The Spanish Student*

3675. A merry companion is as good as a wagon. JOHN LYLY, *Woman in the Moon*

3676.
To no man make yourself a boon companion:
Your joy will be less, but less will be your grief. MARTIAL, *Epigrams*

3677. Present company excepted. JOHN O'KEEFFE, *The London Hermit*

3678.
A glass is good, and a lass is good,
And a pipe to smoke in cold weather;
The world is good, and the people are good,
And we're all good fellows together. JOHN O'KEEFFE, *Sprigs of Laurel*

3679. Keep not ill men company lest you increase the number. *Proverb*

3680. He keeps his road well enough who gets rid of bad company. *Proverb*

3681. A good companion makes good company. *Proverb*

3682. An agreeable companion on a journey is as good as a carriage. PUBLILIUS SYRUS, *Sententiae*

3683.
We still have slept together,
Rose at an instant, learn'd, play'd, eat together;
And whatso'er we went, like Juno's swans,
Still we went coupled and inseparable. SHAKESPEARE, *As You Like It*

3684. Company, villainous company, hath been the spoil of me. SHAKESPEARE, *Henry IV*

3685. It is certain that either wise bearing or ignorant carriage is caught, as men take diseases, one of another: therefore let men take heed of their company. SHAKESPEARE, *Henry IV*

3686. No man can be provident of his time that is not prudent in the choice of his company.

JEREMY TAYLOR,
Holy Living and Dying

3687. I never found the companion that was so companionable as solitude.   THOREAU, *Walden*

3688. As the Italians say, Good company in a journey makes the way seem the shorter.

IZAAK WALTON,
The Compleat Angler

3689. The company in which you will improve most will be least expensive to you.   WASHINGTON,
Moral Maxims

See also: 2055, 2334, 3218, 4682, 4980, 5830, 13093, 18573, 20638.

COMPARISONS

Related Subjects: Analogy, Likeness, Qualities.

3691. The superiority of some men is merely local. They are great because their associates are little.
SAMUEL JOHNSON

3692. If we rightly estimate what we call good and evil, we shall find it lies much in comparison.   LOCKE

3693. Comparisons do ofttime great grievance.   JOHN LYDGATE, *Bochas*

3694. Comparisons are odious.
Proverb

3695. Man, woman, and devil, are the three degrees of comparison.
Proverb

3696. If you would compare two men, you must know them both.
Proverb

3697. Comparison, more than reality makes men happy or wretched.
Proverb

3698.
Comparing what thou art,
With what thou mightst have been.
SCOTT, *The Field of Waterloo*

3699.
Look here, upon this picture, and on this,
The counterfeit presentment of two brothers.   SHAKESPEARE, *Hamlet*

3700.
My father's brother, but no more like my father
Than I to Hercules.
SHAKESPEARE, *Hamlet*

3701. Comparisons are odorous.
SHAKESPEARE,
Much Ado About Nothing

3702.
I have been studying how I may compare
This prison where I live unto the world:
And for because the world is populous
And here is not a creature but myself,
I cannot do it.
SHAKESPEARE, *Richard II*

3703. I will make thee think thy swan a crow.   SHAKESPEARE,
Romeo and Juliet

COMPASSION

Related Subjects: Consideration, Forgiveness, Gentleness, Kindness, Mercy, Pity, Tenderness.

3711. The dew of compassion is a tear.   BYRON

3712. Compassion to an offender who has grossly violated the laws, is, in effect, a cruelty to the peaceable subject who has observed them.

JUNIUS

3713. Compassion is the basis of all morality.   SCHOPENHAUER,
Basis of Morality

3714. There never was any heart truly great and generous, that was not also tender and compassionate.

ROBERT SOUTH

COMPENSATION

Related Subjects: Equality, Payment, Profit, Reward.

3721. Whatsoever a man soweth, that shall he also reap.
Bible: Galatians, vi, 7

3722.
Each loss has its compensation;
  There is healing for every pain;
But the bird with the broken pinion
  Never soars so high again.
H. BUTTERWORTH,
The Broken Pinion

3723.
O Lady! we receive but what we give,
And in our life alone doth Nature
  live;
Ours is her wedding-garment, ours
  her shroud!   COLERIDGE,
Dejection

3724. Every sweet has its sour; every evil its good.   EMERSON,
Compensation

3725. For every thing you have missed, you have gained something else; and for every thing you gain, you lose something.   EMERSON,
Compensation

3726. It is a comfort that the medal has two sides. There is much vice and misery in the world, I know; but more virtue and happiness, I believe.

JEFFERSON

3727. Whatever difference may appear in the fortunes of mankind, there is, nevertheless, a certain compensation of good and evil which makes them equal.
LA ROCHEFOUCAULD, *Maxims*

3728.
Alas! by some degree of woe,
  We every bliss must gain;
The heart can ne'er a transport know
  That never feels a pain.
LORD LYTTELTON, *Song*

3729. Ashes follow blaze inevitably as death follows life. Misery treads on the heels of joy; anguish rides swift after pleasure.
D. G. MITCHELL,
Reveries of a Bachelor

3730. Whoever tries for great objects must suffer something.
PLUTARCH, *Lives*

3731. If you would have a hen lay, you must bear with her cackling.
Proverb

3732. There is no evil without its compensation. Avarice promises money; luxury, pleasure; ambition, a purple robe.   SENECA,
Epistulae ad Lucilium

3733. Every way we look we see even-handed nature administering her laws of compensation.
ALEXANDER SMITH, *Dreamthorp*

3734.
No joy so great but runneth to an
  end,
No hap so hard but may in time
  amend.
ROBERT SOUTHWELL,
Times Go by Turns

3735. When fate has allowed to any man more than one great gift, accident or necessity seems usually to contrive that one shall encumber and impede the other.   SWINBURNE

3736. There is no felicity upon earth, which carries not its counterpoise of misfortunes; no happiness which mounts so high, which is not depressed by some calamity.

JEREMY TAYLOR,
Contemplation of the State of Man

3737.
And light is mingled with the gloom,
  And joy with grief;
Divinest compensations come,
Through thorns of judgment mercies
    bloom
  In sweet relief.

WHITTIER, *Anniversary Poem*

See also: 294, 1791, 2455, 2870, 2893, 7479, 8832, 8844.

COMPETITION

Related Subjects: Commerce, Opposition, Rivalry, Salesmen.

3741. Anybody can win unless there happens to be a second entry.

GEORGE ADE

3742. The only competition worthy of a wise man is with himself.

WASHINGTON ALLSTON

3743. Competition is so necessary a force in business that public ownership is imperative wherever competition is impossible. A private monopoly is indefensible and intolerable.

WILLIAM JENNINGS BRYAN

3744. No man lives without jostling and being jostled; in all ways he has to elbow himself through the world, giving and receiving offense.

CARLYLE

3745.
Thou shalt not covet: but tradition
Approves all forms of competition.

A. H. CLOUGH,
The Latest Decalogue

3746. The battle of competition is fought by cheapening of commodities.   KARL MARX, *Capital*

3747. Fair business competition is that form of competition in which success is sought solely on the merits of one's goods or services.

SHARP & FOX, *Business Ethics*

3748. Ignorant competition is most dangerous to the development and success of our country. . . The competition which is most insidious and dangerous is that which results from an inadequate knowledge of costs.

SHARP & FOX, *Business Ethics*

See also: 171, 1403, 3184, 4167.

COMPLACENCY

Related Subject: Self-Righteousness.

3751. Complaisance renders a superior amiable, an equal agreeable, and an inferior acceptable. It smooths distinction, sweetens conversation, and makes every one in the company pleased with himself. It produces good nature and mutual benevolence, encourages the timorous, soothes the turbulent, humanizes the fierce, and distinguishes a society of civilized persons from a confusion of savages.

ADDISON

3752. Self-complacency is pleasure accompanied by the idea of oneself as cause.   SPINOZA, *Ethics*

3753. Complacency is a coin by the aid of which all the world can, for want of essential means, pay its club bill in society. It is necessary, however, that it may lose nothing of its merits, to associate judgment and prudence with it.   VOLTAIRE

See also: 12550.

COMPLAINING, COMPLAINT

Related Subjects: Disease, Kick, Mourning, Sigh.

3761. Those who do not complain are never pitied. JANE AUSTEN, *Pride and Prejudice*

3762. If you know a better 'ole, go to it. BRUCE BAIRNSFATHER

3763.
The wheel that squeaks the loudest
Is the one that gets the grease.
JOSH BILLINGS, *The Kicker*

3764. Murmur at nothing: if our ills are irreparable, it is ungrateful; if remediless, it is vain. A Christian builds his fortitude on a better foundation than stoicism; he is pleased with everything that happens, because he knows it could not happen unless it had first pleased God and that which pleases Him must be the best. C. C. COLTON

3765. I am a lone lorn creetur . . . and everythink goes contrary with me. DICKENS, *David Copperfield*

3766. I will not be as those who spend the day in complaining of headache, and the night in drinking the wine that gives it. GOETHE

3767. Go not for every grief to the physician, nor for every quarrel to the lawyer, nor for every thirst to the pot. GEORGE HERBERT, *Jacula Prudentum*

3768. The usual fortune of complaint is to excite contempt more than pity. SAMUEL JOHNSON

3769.
Nothing to do but work,
  Nothing to eat but food,
Nothing to wear but clothes
  To keep one from going nude.
B. F. KING, JR., *The Pessimist*

3770. Things cannot always go your way. Learn to accept in silence the minor aggravations, cultivate the gift of taciturnity and consume your own smoke with an extra draught of hard work, so that those about you may not be annoyed with the dust and soot of your complaints. SIR WILLIAM OSLER, *Life of Sir William Osler*

3771. The complaint of the present times is the general complaint of all times. *Proverb*

See also: 525, 1619, 2156, 2850, 15686.

COMPLIMENT

Related Subjects: Applause, Flattery, Praise.

3781. Compliments of congratulation are always kindly taken, and cost nothing but pen, ink, and paper. I consider them as draughts upon good breeding, where the exchange is always greatly in favor of the drawer. LORD CHESTERFIELD, *Letters*

3782. A deserved and discriminating compliment is often one of the strongest encouragements and incentives to the diffident and self-distrustful. TRYON EDWARDS

3783.
You're exceedingly polite,
And I think it only right
To return the compliment.
W. S. GILBERT, *H. M. S. Pinafore*

3784. Compliments which we think are deserved, we accept only as debts, with indifference; but those which conscience informs us we do not merit, we receive with the same gratitude that we do favors given away. GOLDSMITH

3785. A compliment is usually accompanied with a bow, as if to beg pardon for paying it.
A. W. & J. C. HARE,
Guesses at Truth

3786. Whenever a man's friends begin to compliment him about looking young, he may be sure that they think he is growing old.
WASHINGTON IRVING,
Bracebridge Hall

3787.
What honour that,
But tedious waste of time, to sit and hear
So many hollow compliments and lies.   MILTON, *Paradise Regained*

3788. Compliments cost nothing, yet many pay dear for them.   *Proverb*

3789. It is safer to commend the dead than the living.   *Proverb*

3790. Manhood is melted into courtesies, valour into compliment.
SHAKESPEARE,
Much Ado About Nothing

3791.
This barren verbiage, current among men,
Light coin, the tinsel clink of compliment.   TENNYSON,
The Princess

3792. I can live for two months on a good compliment.   MARK TWAIN

3793. An acquaintance that begins with a compliment is sure to develop into a real friendship.
OSCAR WILDE, *An Ideal Husband*

3794. Now-a-days we are all of us so hard up, that the only pleasant things to pay are compliments. They're the only things we *can* pay.
OSCAR WILDE,
Lady Windermere's Fan

See also: 2971, 5303.

COMPROMISE

3801. Please all, and you will please none.   AESOP,
The Man, the Boy, and the Donkey

3802. All government—indeed, every human benefit and enjoyment, every virtue and every prudent act—is founded on compromise and barter.   BURKE, *Speech on Conciliation*

3803. Compromise is but the sacrifice of one right or good in the hope of retaining another, too often ending in the loss of both.
TRYON EDWARDS

3804. Every compromise was surrender and invited new demands.
EMERSON, *Miscellanies*

3805. I will be as harsh as truth and as uncompromising as justice.
W. L. GARRISON, *The Liberator*

3806. Life cannot subsist in society but by reciprocal concessions.
SAMUEL JOHNSON, *Boswell: Life*

3807. Man propounds negotiations, Man accepts the compromise.
KIPLING, *The Female of the Species*

3808. A lean compromise is better than a fat lawsuit.   *Proverb*

3809. Your "If" is the only peacemaker; much virtue in "If."
SHAKESPEARE, *As You Like It*

3810.
Basely yielded upon compromise
That which his noble ancestors achieved with blows.
SHAKESPEARE, *Richard II*

3811.
What you cannot as you would achieve,
You must perforce accomplish as you may.   SHAKESPEARE,
Titus Andronicus

3812. All great alterations in human affairs are produced by compromise.
SYDNEY SMITH, *Essays*

3813. From the beginning of our history the country has been afflicted with compromise. It is by compromise that human rights have been abandoned. I insist that this shall cease. The country needs repose after all its trials; it deserves repose. And repose can only be found in everlasting principles.
CHARLES SUMNER

3814. Is not compromise of old a god among you? SWINBURNE,
A Word from the Psalmist

3815.
From compromise and things half done,
    Keep me with stern and stubborn pride;
And when at last the fight is won,
    God, keep me still unsatisfied.
LOUIS UNTERMEYER, *Prayer*

CONCEALMENT

Related Subjects: Cunning, Mystery, Obscurity, Retirement, Secrecy, Trickery.

3821. "Thou shalt not get found out" is not one of God's commandments; and no man can be saved by trying to keep it. LEONARD BACON

3822. To conceal anything from those to whom I am attached, is not in my nature. I can never close my lips where I have opened my heart.
DICKENS

3823. Youk'n hide de fier, but w'at you gwine do wid de smoke?
JOEL CHANDLER HARRIS,
Plantation Proverbs

3824. It is great cleverness to know how to conceal our cleverness.
LA ROCHEFOUCAULD, *Maxims*

3825. He who can conceal his joys, is greater than he who can hide his griefs. LAVATER

3826. He that cannot conceal his own shame will not conceal another's.
Proverb

3827. A bad bush is better than the open field. *Proverb*

3828. Wherefore are these things hid? SHAKESPEARE,
Twelfth-Night

See also: 8, 1201, 3887, 18679.

CONCEIT

Related Subjects: Boasting, Delusion, Illusion, Pride, Selfishness, Vanity.

3831. Self-conceit may lead to self-destruction. AESOP,
The Frog and the Ox

3832. Conceit is God's gift to little men. BRUCE BARTON, *Conceit*

3833. Conceit is the most incurable disease that is known to the human soul. H. W. BEECHER,
Proverbs from Plymouth Pulpit

3834. To say that a man is vain means merely that he is pleased with the effect he produces on other people. A conceited man is satisfied with the effect he produces on himself.
MAX BEERBOHM, *Quia Imperfectum*

3835. Seest thou a man wise in his own conceit? There is more hope of a fool than of him.
Bible: Proverbs, xxvi, 12

3836. Be not wise in your own conceits. *Bible: Romans, xii, 16*

3837. The world tolerates conceit from those who are successful, but not from anybody else.

JOHN BLAKE, *Uncommon Sense*

3838. He is a poor creature who does not believe himself to be better than the whole world else. No matter how ill we may be, or how low we may have fallen, we would not change identity with any other person. Hence our self-conceit sustains and always must sustain us till death takes us and our conceit together so that we need no more sustaining.

SAMUEL BUTLER, *Note Books*

3839. When people get it into their heads that they are being specially favoured by the Almighty, they had better as a general rule mind their p's and q's. SAMUEL BUTLER, *The Way of All Flesh*

3840. Aesop's Fly, sitting on the axle of the chariot, has been much laughed at for exclaiming: What a dust I do raise! CARLYLE, *On Boswell's Life of Johnson*

3841. He was like a cock who thought the sun had risen to hear him crow. GEORGE ELIOT, *Adam Bede*

3842. I've never any pity for conceited people, because I think they carry their comfort about with them. GEORGE ELIOT, *The Mill on the Floss*

3843. What is the first business of one who studies philosophy? To part with self-conceit. For it is impossible for any one to begin to learn what he thinks that he already knows.

EPICTETUS, *Discourses*

3844. We reproach people for talking about themselves; but it is the subject they treat best.

ANATOLE FRANCE, *Journal des Goncourt*

3845. Conceit is the finest armour a man can wear.

JEROME K. JEROME, *Idle Thoughts of an Idle Fellow*

3846. Every man's affairs, however little, are important to himself.

SAMUEL JOHNSON, *Boswell: Life*

3847.
In men this blunder still you find,
All think their little set mankind.

HANNAH MORE, *Florio and His Friend*

3848. Self-praise is no recommendation. *Proverb*

3849. If you love yourself over much, nobody else will love you at all. *Proverb*

3850. Each bird loves to hear himself sing. *Proverb*

3851. Conceit may puff a man up, but never prop him up.

RUSKIN, *True and Beautiful*

3852. Conceit in weakest bodies strongest works.

SHAKESPEARE, *Hamlet*

3853. He that is giddy thinks the world turns round.

SHAKESPEARE, *The Taming of the Shrew*

3854. To love oneself is the beginning of a lifelong romance.

OSCAR WILDE, *An Ideal Husband*

3855. All men think all men mortal but themselves.

EDWARD YOUNG, *Night Thoughts*

See also: 668, 1982, 2159, 2432, 3752, 3946, 8181, 14209.

CONDUCT, see Behavior, Manners

CONFESSION

Related Subjects: **Guilt, Repentance, Sin.**

3861. The confession of evil works is the first beginning of good works. St. Augustine

3862. I freely name myself with those that are ready to own that they have in their extremities and embarrassments in trade done those things which their own principles condemned, which they are not ashamed to blush for, which they look back on with regret, and strive to make reparation for, with their utmost diligence. Defoe

3863. There are some things which men confess with ease, and others with difficulty. Epictetus, *Discourses*

3864. A man should never be ashamed to own he has been in the wrong, which is but saying, in other words, that he is wiser to-day than he was yesterday. Pope

3865. Confess and be hanged. *Proverb*

3866. Open confession is good for the soul. *Proverb*

3867. A generous confession disarms slander. *Proverb*

3868. Confession of our faults is the next thing to innocency. Publilius Syrus, *Sententiae*

3869. If thou wouldst be justified, acknowledge thine injustice. He that confesses his sin, begins his journey toward salvation. He that is sorry for it, mends his pace. He that forsakes it, is at his journey's end. Francis Quarles

3870. It is not our wrong actions which it requires courage to confess, so much as those which are ridiculous and foolish. Rousseau

3871. Why does no man confess his vices? because he is yet in them. It is for a waking man to tell his dream. Seneca

3872. There is no refuge from confession but suicide; and suicide is confession. Daniel Webster

See also: 2027.

CONFIDENCE

Related Subjects: **Belief, Certainty, Credit, Faith, Optimism, Security, Self-Confidence, Superiority, Surety, Suspicion, Trust.**

3873. They can conquer who believe they can. Dryden

3874. Trust men and they will be true to you; treat them greatly and they will show themselves great. Emerson

3875. Self-trust is the essence of heroism. Emerson

3876. Confidence is a plant of slow growth; especially in an aged bosom. Samuel Johnson

3877. Trust him with little, who, without proofs, trusts you with everything, or when he has proved you, with nothing. Lavater

3878. Confidence imparts a wondrous inspiration to its possessor. It bears him on in security, either to meet no danger, or to find matter of glorious trial. Milton

3879. Confidence in another man's virtue is no slight evidence of one's own. Montaigne, *Essays*

3880. Confidence goeth farther in company than good sense.   *Proverb*

3881. Confidence is the companion of success.   *Proverb*

3882. Confidence in one's self, though the chief nurse of magnanimity, doth not leave the care of necessary furniture for it; of all the Grecians, Homer doth make Achilles the best armed. SIR PHILIP SIDNEY

3883. Society is built upon trust, and trust upon confidence in one another's integrity.   ROBERT SOUTH

3884. It is the attitude of a man of action that he will be lost if he does not learn how to mistrust. Measureless confidence at the outset must be a step on the way toward defensiveness and reserve.
JACOB WASSERMANN, *Stanley*

3885.
A man he seems of cheerful yesterdays
And confident to-morrows.
WORDSWORTH, *The Excursion*

Confidence in the sense of disclosure.

3886. Let us have a care not to disclose our hearts to those who shut up theirs against us.
FRANCIS BEAUMONT

3887. All confidence is dangerous, if it is not entire; we ought on most occasions to speak all, or conceal all. We have already too much disclosed our secrets to a man, from whom we think any one single circumstance is to be concealed.   LA BRUYÈRE

3888. If we are truly prudent we shall cherish those noblest and happiest of our tendencies—to love and to confide.   BULWER-LYTTON

3889. There are cases in which a man would be ashamed not to have been imposed upon. There is a confidence necessary to human intercourse, and without which men are often more injured by their own suspicions, than they could be by the perfidy of others.   BURKE

3890. I could never pour out my inmost soul without reserve to any human being, without danger of one day repenting my confidence.
BURNS

3891. The human heart, at whatever age, opens only to the heart that opens in return.
MARIA EDGEWORTH

See also: 1063, 1748, 3574, 16482, 20525, 22046.

CONQUERORS AND CONQUEST

Related Subjects: Defeat, Glory, Imperialism, Self-Control, Soldier, Submission, Success, Victory, War, Waterloo.

3901. The true way for one civilization to "conquer" another is for it to be so obviously superior in this or that point that others desire to imitate it.   G. LOWES DICKINSON,
The Choice Before Us

3902. Conquest brings self-conceit and intolerance, the reckless inflation and dissipation of energies. Defeat brings prudence and concentration, it ennobles and fortifies.
HAVELOCK ELLIS,
The Task of Social Hygiene

3903. Conquest of lands and peoples has lost its beauty. The mastery of time and space accomplished by technical advances has made the subjugation of one people by another absurd.
EMIL LUDWIG, *I Believe*

3904. After he [Caesar] routed Pharnaces Ponticus at the first assault, he wrote thus to his friends: 'I came, I saw, I conquered.'
                    PLUTARCH, *Lives*

3905. To be conquer'd by an hero is an honour.   *Proverb*

3906. The conquered is never called wise, nor the conqueror rash.
                              Proverb

3907. He that will conquer must fight.   *Proverb*

3908. He hath conquered well that hath made his enemies fly. *Proverb*

3909. He conquers twice who conquers himself in victory.
        PUBLILIUS SYRUS, *Sententiae*

3910. The right of conquest has no foundation other than the right of the strongest.   ROUSSEAU,
                   The Social Contract

3911. I may justly say, with the hook-nosed fellow of Rome, "I came, saw, and overcame."
          SHAKESPEARE, *Henry IV*

3912.
Thus far into the bowels of the land Have we marched on without impediment.   SHAKESPEARE,
                        Richard III

See also: 585, 692, 1394, 6844, 6938, 12198, 12968, 18724.

CONSCIENCE

Related Subjects: Character, Confession, Guilt, Remorse, Repentance, Self-Knowledge, Sin.

3921. Rhetorically, yes; conscientiously, no.
        BULWER-LYTTON, *Caxtonia*

3922.
O clear conscience, and upright! How doth a little failing wound thee sore.   DANTE, *Purgatory*

3923. A good conscience is a sweet vessel, and a strong: whatsoever thou layest up in that, shall serve thee all thy life, and after: and that shall be thine acquittance and discharge. At thy last payment, when thou returnest thy spirit, into his hands that gave it; and then thou shalt have rendered to all their dues, when thou hast given the king honor; the poor, alms; thyself, peace; and God, thy soul.
          JOHN DONNE, *Sermons*

3924. The disease of an evil conscience is beyond the practice of all the physicians of all the countries in the world.   GLADSTONE

3925.
          That fierce thing They call a conscience.
          THOMAS HOOD, *Lamia*

3926. The human being is nature's fall from a state of innocency; but it is not a decline, it is rather an ascent, in that a state of conscience is higher than a state of innocence.
          THOMAS MANN, *I Believe*

3927.
     Now conscience wakes despair That slumber'd—wakes the bitter memory
Of what he was, what is, and what must be
Worse.   MILTON, *Paradise Lost*

3928. "As for conscience, Don Nuccio, I've got a conscience. But I'm also the manager of the lottery."
                        PIRANDELLO

3929. Conscience cannot be compelled.   *Proverb*

3930. Conscience is the chamber of justice.   *Proverb*

3931. An evil conscience breaks many a man's neck. *Proverb*

3932. A guilty conscience needs no accuser. *Proverb*

3933. A guilty conscience never feels secure. Publilius Syrus, *Sententiae*

3934. To a friend who defended the behavior of the upper chamber, saying "At least you find consciences there," Talleyrand replied: "Ah, yes, many, many consciences. Semonville, for example, has at least two."
Phillips Russell, *The Glittering Century*

3935.
The play's the thing
Wherein I'll catch the conscience of
the king. Shakespeare, *Hamlet*

3936.
Thus conscience does make cowards of us all;
And thus the native hue of resolution
Is sicklied o'er with the pale cast of thought,
And enterprises of great pith and moment
With this regard their currents turn awry,
And lose the name of action.
Shakespeare, *Hamlet*

3837.
Leave her to heaven
And to those thorns that in her bosom lodge,
To prick and sting her.
Shakespeare, *Hamlet*

3938. Out, damned spot! Out, I say! Shakespeare, *Macbeth*

3939. A very gentle beast, and of a good conscience. Shakespeare, *A Midsummer-Night's Dream*

3940. O coward conscience, how dost thou afflict me! Shakespeare, *Richard III*

3941.
My conscience hath a thousand several tongues,
And every tongue brings in a several tale,
And every tale condemns me for a villain. Shakespeare, *Richard III*

3942. Conscience has no more to do with gallantry than it has with politics. Sheridan, *The Duenna*

3943.
To sit alone with my conscience
Will be judgment enough for me.
Stubbs, *Conscience and Future Judgment*

3944. Labour to keep alive in your breast that little spark of celestial fire, conscience. Washington

3945. Conscience and cowardice are really the same things.
Oscar Wilde, *The Picture of Dorian Gray*

3946. Conscience makes egotists of us all. Oscar Wilde, *The Picture of Dorian Gray*

See also: 1889, 2746, 4336, 4841, 6755, 9115, 16872, 17349, 18055.

CONSEQUENCES

Related Subjects: Cause, End, Responsibility.

3951. In every affair consider what precedes and what follows, and then undertake it. Epictetus, *Discourses*

3952. Logical consequences are the scarecrows of fools and the beacons of wise men.
Thomas H. Huxley, *Animal Automatism*

3953. Some of us will smart for it.
SHAKESPEARE,
Much Ado About Nothing

See also: 2193.

CONSERVATISM

Related Subjects: Caution, Reserve.

3961. We are living in a phase of evolution which is known as the twentieth century and stands for a certain achieved growth of the human mind. But the enormous majority of the human race do not belong to that phase at all.
ROBERT BRIFFAULT,
Rational Evolution

3962. We have a maxim in the House of Commons, and written on the walls of our house, that old ways are the safest and surest ways.
SIR EDWARD COKE

3963. It seems to me a barren thing, this Conservatism—an unhappy cross-breed, the mule of politics that engenders nothing. DISRAELI,
Coningsby

3964. A conservative government is an organized hypocrisy. DISRAELI

3965. All conservatives are such from personal defects. They have been effeminated by position or nature, born halt and blind, through luxury of their parents, and can only, like invalids, act on the defensive.
EMERSON, *Conduct of Life*

3966. We are reformers in spring and summer. In autumn and winter we stand by the old. Reformers in the morning; conservatives at night. Reform is affirmative; conservatism, negative. Conservatism goes for comfort; reform for truth. EMERSON

3967.
I often think it's comical
How Nature always does contrive
That every boy and every gal,
That's born into this world alive,
Is either a little Liberal,
Or else a little Conservative.
W. S. GILBERT, *Iolanthe*

3968. A conservative is a man who is too cowardly to fight and too fat to run. ELBERT HUBBARD,
One Thousand and One Epigrams

3969. A conservative is a man who will not look at the new moon, out of respect for that "ancient institution," the old one. DOUGLAS JERROLD

3970. What is conservatism? Is it not adherence to the old and tried, against the new and untried?
LINCOLN

3971. Conservatism defends those coercive arrangements which a still-lingering savageness makes requisite. Radicalism endeavours to realize a state more in harmony with the character of the ideal man.
HERBERT SPENCER, *Social Statics*

3972. While it is the conservatives' function to be intensely practical, that ought not to be confused with simply being selfish; and while it seems to be the progressives' function to be idealistic, that idealism ought to be based on potential realities rather than on vague mystic emotion. HENRY A. WALLACE

3973. The staid, conservative, Came-over-with-the-Conqueror type of mind. WILLIAM WATSON,
A Study in Contrasts

3974. Generally young men are regarded as radicals. This is a popular misconception. The most conservative persons I ever met are college undergraduates. WOODROW WILSON

See also: 10241.

CONSIDERATION

Related Subjects: Courtesy, Kindness, Reflection, Tact, Thought.

3981. Consideration is the soil in which wisdom may be expected to grow, and strength be given to every up-springing plant of duty.
EMERSON

3982. Look to the essence of a thing, whether it be a point of doctrine, of practice, or of interpretation.
MARCUS AURELIUS, *Meditations*

3983. Consideration gets as many victories as rashness loses. *Proverb*

3984. He that considers in prosperity, will be less afflicted in adversity.
Proverb

3985. Consideration is half conversion.
Proverb

3986. Consideration is the parent of wisdom. *Proverb*

3987. 'Twere to consider too curiously, to consider so.
SHAKESPEARE, *Hamlet*

See also: 5352.

CONSISTENCY AND INCONSISTENCY

Related Subjects: Change, Character, Constancy, Fidelity, Logic.

3991. A foolish consistency is the hobgoblin of little minds, adored by little statesmen and philosophers and divines. EMERSON, *Self-Reliance*

3992. With consistency a great soul has simply nothing to do. He may

as well concern himself with h shadow on the wall.
EMERSON, *Self-Relianc*

3993. Those who honestly mean t be true contradict themselves mo rarely than those who try to be cor sistent. O. W. HOLME

3994. Without consistency there no moral strength. ROBERT OWE

3995. Consistency, thou art a jewe
Prover

Inconsistency

3996. Mutability of temper and i consistency with ourselves is th greatest weakness of human natur
ADDISO

3997. No author ever drew a cha acter consistent to human nature, b he was forced to ascribe to it man inconsistencies. BULWER-LYTTO

3998. Unfortunately, I have neve been able to maintain a consistent a titude toward life or reality, or t ward anything else. This may be er tirely due to nervousness.
JAMES THURBER, *I Belie*

3999. Inconsistencies of opinio arising from changes of circum stances, are often justifiable.
DANIEL WEBSTE

4000. Do I contradict myself? Ver well then I contradict myself. (I a large, I contain multitudes.)
WALT WHITMA

CONSOLATION

Related Subjects: Comfort, Grie Pity, Religion, Sorrow, Sympathy

4001. Quiet and sincere sympathy often the most welcome and efficie consolation to the afflicted. Said wise man to one in deep sorrow, "I did not come to comfort you; God only can do that; but I did come to say how deeply and tenderly I feel for you in your affliction."

TRYON EDWARDS

4002. God has commanded Time to console the unhappy. JOUBERT,
Pensées

4003. Consolation, i n d i s c r e e t l y pressed upon us when we are suffering under affliction, only serves to increase our pain and to render our grief more poignant.

ROUSSEAU

4004. Before an affliction is digested, consolation comes too soon; and after it is digested, it comes too late; but there is a mark between these two, as fine almost as a hair, for a comforter to take aim at. STERNE

CONSPIRACY

Related Subjects: Deceit, Hypocrisy, Malevolence, Treason.

4011. Conspiracies no sooner should be formed than executed. ADDISON

4012. Conspiracy—a game invented for the amusement of unoccupied men of rank. ADDISON

4013. Combinations of wickedness would overwhelm the world by the advantage which licentious principles afford, did not those who have long practiced perfidy grow faithless to each other. SAMUEL JOHNSON

4014. Two may keep counsel when the third's away.

SHAKESPEARE, *Titus Andronicus*

4015. I thought you and he were hand-in-glove. SWIFT,
Polite Conversation

4016.
A man of plots
Craft, poisonous counsels, wayside ambushings. TENNYSON,
Gareth and Lynette

4017. Dirty work at the crossroads.
Traditional

See also: 2676.

CONSTANCY AND INCONSTANCY

Related Subjects: Change, Consistency, Fickleness, Fidelity, Loyalty.

4021. Without constancy there is neither love, friendship, nor virtue in the world. ADDISON

4022.
A good man it is not mine to see. Could I see a man possessed of constancy, that would satisfy me.

CONFUCIUS, *Analects*

4023. The secret of success is constancy of purpose. DISRAELI

4024. Constancy is the complement of all other human virtues. MAZZINI

4025. In their behavior three things are more steadfast than others: suspicion, the wind, and loyalty: the first never leaves a place it has entered; the second never enters when it cannot see a way of escape; the third never returns to a place it has left.

PETRARCH

4026. A fellow of plain and uncoined constancy. SHAKESPEARE,
Henry V

4027.
But I am constant as the northern star,
Of whose true-fix'd and resting quality
There is no fellow in the firmament.

SHAKESPEARE, *Julius Caesar*

4028.

Sigh no more, ladies, sigh no more,
　Men were deceivers ever;
One foot in sea and one on shore;
　To one thing constant never.
　　　　　SHAKESPEARE,
　　　Much Ado About Nothing

Inconstancy

4029.

I loathe inconstancy—I loathe, detest,
　Abhor, condemn, abjure the mortal
　made
Of such quicksilver clay that in his
　breast
　No permanent foundation can be
　laid.　　　BYRON, *Don Juan*

4030.

The world's a scene of changes, and
　to be
Constant, in Nature were incon-
　stancy.　　ABRAHAM COWLEY,
　　　　　　　　　Inconstancy

4031. Constancy to truth and principle may sometimes lead to what the
world calls inconstancy in conduct.
　　　　　TRYON EDWARDS

4032. Inconstancy is but a name to
fright poor lovers from a better
choice.　　　JOHN RUTTER

4033. There is nothing in this world
constant but inconstancy. SWIFT,
　　On the Faculties of the Mind

CONSTITUTION

Related Subjects: America, Democracy, Government, Law, Nation, State.

4041. The theory that the Constitution is a written document is a legal
fiction. The idea that it can be understood by a study of its language
and the history of its past development is equally mythical. It is what
the government and the people who
count in public affairs recognize and
respect as such, what they think it is
. . . It is always becoming something
else, and those who criticize it and
the acts done under it, as well as
those who praise, help to make it
what it will be tomorrow.
　CHARLES A. BEARD, *Economic In-
　terpretation of the American
　Constitution*

4042. The Constitution, in all its pro-
visions, looks to an indestructible
Union composed of indestructible
States.　　　SALMON P. CHASE

4043. As the British Constitution is
the most subtile organism which has
proceeded from the womb and the
long gestation of progressive history,
so the American Constitution is, so
far as I can see, the most wonderful
work ever struck off at a given time
by the brain and purpose of man.
　GLADSTONE, *Kin Beyond Sea*

4044. Some men look at Constitu-
tions with sanctimonious reverence,
and deem them like the ark of the
covenant, too sacred to be touched.
They ascribe to the men of the preceding age a wisdom more than human, and suppose what they did to be
beyond amendment.　　JEFFERSON

4045. When the constitution is openly invaded, when the first original
right of the people, from which all
laws derive their authority, is directly attacked, inferior grievances
naturally lose their force, and are
suffered to pass by without punishment or observation.　　JUNIUS

4046. It cannot be too often remembered that the founders of the Constitution were working in a predominantly agricultural society in which
the consequences of the Industrial

Revolution could not be even dimly realized. They feared the masses. They were adamant about the "rights" of property. Liberty to them predominantly meant protection of vested interests from the invasions of the multitudes.
HAROLD J. LASKI,
The American Presidency

4047. It's got so it is as easy to amend the Constitution of the United States as it used to be to draw a cork.   THOMAS R. MARSHALL

4048. In our country it is especially important now to inquire into our Constitution, above all, our Bill of Rights. We came to a virgin continent and have made money so fast, though we have wasted and squandered our resources, that we have forgotten our constitutional heritage.
MAURY MAVERICK, *Blood & Ink*

4049. Our Constitution does not copy the laws of neighboring states; we are rather a pattern to others than imitators ourselves.   PERICLES

4050. You will find no justification in any of the language of the Constitution for delay in the reforms which the mass of the American people now demand.
FRANKLIN D. ROOSEVELT, *Address: 150th Anniversary of Signing of Constitution*

4051. Once when Mme. de Staël was praising the British Constitution, Talleyrand explained in an aside: "Above all she admires the *habeas corpus.*"   PHILLIPS RUSSELL,
The Glittering Century

4052. There is a higher law than the Constitution.
WILLIAM H. SEWARD

4053. No philosopher's stone of a constitution can produce golden conduct from leaden instincts.
HERBERT SPENCER, *Social Statics*

4054. The Constitution is a great machine—the machine of compromise between liberty and government.   SUN YAT-SEN,
Memoirs of a Chinese Revolutionary

4055. A constitution is not intended to embody a particular economic theory . . . it is made for people of fundamentally differing views.
Opinion, U. S. Supreme Court

See also: 672, 2991, 3617, 5418, 6528.

CONTEMPLATION

Related Subjects: Meditation, Reflection, Reverie, Study, Thought.

4061. A contemplative life has more the appearance of piety than any other; but the divine plan is to bring faith into activity and exercise.
RICHARD CECIL

4062. In order to improve the mind, we ought less to learn, than to contemplate.   DESCARTES

4063. Contemplation is to knowledge, what digestion is to food—the way to get life out of it.
TRYON EDWARDS

4064. All civil mankind have agreed in leaving one day for contemplation against six for practice.
EMERSON, *Lectures and Biographical Studies*

4065. Let us unite contemplation with action. In the harmony of the two, lies the perfection of character. They are not contradictory and incompatible, but mutually helpful to each other. Contemplation will strengthen for action, and action sends us back to contemplation, and thus the inner and outer life will be harmoniously developed.

SAMUEL FOOTE

4066.
Give me, kind Heaven, a private station,
A mind serene for contemplation.

JOHN GAY, *Fables*

4067. He that contemplates hath a day without night.

GEORGE HERBERT, *Jacula Prudentum*

4068.
Contemplation makes a rare turkey-cock of him:
How he jets under his advanced plumes.

SHAKESPEARE, *Twelfth Night*

CONTEMPT

Related Subjects: Disgrace, Hatred, Indifference, Prejudice, Pride, Ridicule, Scorn, Shame, Sneer.

4071. Despise not any man, and do not spurn anything; for there is no man that hath not his hour, nor is there anything that hath not its place.   RABBI BEN-AZAI

4072. Can there any good thing come out of Nazareth?   *Bible: John, i, 46*

4073. Speak with contempt of no man. Every one hath a tender sense of reputation. And every man hath a sting, which he may, if provoked too far, dart out at one time or another.
ROBERT BURTON,
Anatomy of Melancholy

4074. It is often more necessary to conceal contempt than resentment, the former being never forgiven, but the latter sometimes forgot. Wrongs are often forgiven; contempt never.
LORD CHESTERFIELD

4075. The basest and meanest of all human beings are generally the most forward to despise others. So that the most contemptible are generally the most contemptuous.   FIELDING

4076. There is not in human nature a more odious disposition than a proneness to contempt, which is a mixture of pride and ill-nature. Nor is there any which more certainly denotes a bad disposition; for in a good and benign temper, there can be no room for it. It is the truest symptom of a base and bad heart.   FIELDING

4077. He despises men with tenderness.   ANATOLE FRANCE

4078. None but the contemptible are apprehensive of contempt.
LA ROCHEFOUCAULD, *Maxims*

4079. Contempt is the only way to triumph over calumny.
MME. DE MAINTENON

4080. Many can bear adversity, but few contempt.   *Proverb*

4081. If a man sets out to hate all the miserable creatures he meets, he will not have much energy left for anything else; whereas he can despise them, one and all, with the greatest ease.   SCHOPENHAUER

4082. I have unlearned contempt. It is a sin that is engendered earliest in the soul, and doth beset it like a poison worm, feeding on all its beauty.
N. P. WILLIS

See also: 3768, 4910, 7722.

CONTENTMENT AND DISCONTENT

Related Subjects: Bliss, Calm, Cheerfulness, Comfort, Disappointment, Happiness, Peace, Rest, Suspicion.

4091. Be content with your lot; one cannot be first in everything.
AESOP, *The Peacock and Juno*

4092. I have learned, in whatsoever state I am, therewith to be content.
Bible: Philippians, ii, 11

4093. Who lives content with little possesses everything. BOILEAU

4094. Being content with an attic ought not to mean being unable to move from it and resigned to living in it; it ought to mean appreciating all there is in such a position.
G. K. CHESTERTON

4095. I have found some of the best reasons I ever had for remaining at the bottom simply by looking at the men at the top. F. M. COLBY,
Essays

4096.
Sweet are the thoughts that savour of content;
The quiet mind is richer than a crown. ROBERT GREENE,
Farewell to Folly

4097. In this world he who possesses a morsel of bread, and some nest in which to shelter himself, who is master or slave of no man, tell that man to live content; he possesses a very sweet existence.
OMAR KHAYYAM

4098. A strong determination to get the best out of life, a keen desire to enjoy what one has, and no regrets if one fails: this is the secret of the Chinese genius for contentment.
LIN YUTANG,
My Country and My People

4099. He may very well be contented that need not lie nor flatter. *Proverb*

4100.
'Tis better to be lowly born,
And range with humble livers in content,
Than to be perked up in a glistering grief
And wear a golden sorrow.
SHAKESPEARE, *Henry VIII*

4101. Poor and content is rich, and rich enough. SHAKESPEARE, *Othello*

4102.
One honest John Tompkins, a hedger and ditcher,
Although he was poor, did not want to be richer;
For all such vain wishes in him were prevented
By a fortunate habit of being contented. JANE TAYLOR,
Contented John

4103.
Henceforth I ask not good-fortune, I myself am good-fortune,
Henceforth I whimper no more, postpone no more, need nothing,
Done with indoor complaints, libraries, querulous criticisms,
Strong and content I travel the open road. WALT WHITMAN,
Song of the Open Road

Discontent

4104. No form of society can be reasonably stable in which the majority of the people are not fairly content. People cannot be content if they feel that the foundations of their lives are wholly unstable.
JAMES TRUSLOW ADAMS,
The Record of America

4105. We have the comforts brought by labor-saving devices and all the new inventions of one sort and another. We can cross the Atlantic by air in thirty-six hours. We can talk over the telephone to a friend 10,-000 miles away. We have control of power never dreamed of by man until the past few years. Yet we have lost much of our sense of security. We have lost contentment.

> James Truslow Adams,
> *The Record of America*

4106. Dissatisfaction with the world in which we live and determination to realize one that shall be better, are the prevailing characteristics of the modern spirit.

> G. Lowes Dickinson,
> *The Greek View of Life*

4107. There are two kinds of discontent in this world: the discontent that works, and the discontent that wrings its hands. The first gets what it wants, and the second loses what it has. There's no cure for the first but success; and there's no cure at all for the second. Gordon Graham

4108. The world owes all its onward impulses to men ill at ease. The happy man inevitably confines himself within ancient limits. Hawthorne,
> *The House of the Seven Gables*

4109. No one lives content with his condition, whether reason gave it him, or chance threw it in his way.
> Horace, *Satires*

4110. How does it happen, Maecenas, that one is content with that lot in life which he has chosen, or which chance has thrown in his way, but praises those who follow a different course? Horace, *Satires*

4111. Unhappy man! He frets at the narrow limits of the world.
> Juvenal, *Satires*

4112. To be discontented with the divine discontent, and to be ashamed with the noble shame, is the very germ of the first upgrowth of all virtue. Charles Kingsley,
> *Health and Education*

4113.
The toad beneath the harrow knows
Exactly where each tooth-point goes;
The butterfly upon the road
Preaches contentment to that toad.
> Kipling, *Pagett, M.P.*

4114.
To sigh, yet feel no pain,
　To weep, yet scarce know why;
To sport an hour with Beauty's chain,
　Then throw it idly by.
> George Moore, *The Blue Stocking*

4115. Wealth is the parent of luxury and indolence, and poverty of meanness and viciousness, and both of discontent. Plato, *The Republic*

4116. They need much, whom nothing will content. *Proverb*

4117. Discontents arise from our desires oftener than from our wants.
> *Proverb*

4118. For one rich man that is content there are a hundred that are not.
> *Proverb*

4119. He that wants money, means, and content is without three good friends.
> Shakespeare, *As You Like It*

4120. Striving to better, oft we mar what's well. Shakespeare,
> *King Lear*

4121.
I see your brows are full of discontent,
Your hearts of sorrow and your eyes of tears. Shakespeare,
> *Richard III*

4122.
I know a discontented gentleman,
Whose humble means match not his
    haughty mind. SHAKESPEARE,
                      Richard III

4123. I was *born* to other things.
       TENNYSON, *In Memoriam*

4124.
The thirst to know and understand,
  A large and liberal discontent;
These are the goods in life's rich
    hand,
    The things that are more excellent.
       WILLIAM WATSON,
  Things That are More Excellent

4125.
And from the discontent of man
    The world's best progress springs.
      ELLA W. WILCOX,
               Discontent

4126. Discontent is the first step in
the progress of a man or a nation.
       OSCAR WILDE,
  A Woman of No Importance

See also: 240, 401, 551, 1032, 2883,
3614, 6998.

CONTRADICTION

Related Subjects: Paradox, Perversity.

4131. There's difficulty, there's danger, there's the dear spirit of contradiction in it.
      ISAAC BICKERSTAFFE,
            The Hypocrite

4132. There are contradictions in every human intelligence, and without them there would be no natural lights and shades. CHALIAPIN,
           Man and Mask

4133. Contradictions are to be found in every human soul, beyond question, and whoever attempts to unravel them by some abracadabra only destroys their fascinating configurations. EMIL LUDWIG, *I Believe*

4134. Contradiction should awaken attention, not passion. *Proverb*

See also: 4000, 5055, 8034, 21622.

CONTROVERSY

Related Subjects: Argument, Cause, Quarreling.

4141. Most controversies would soon be ended, if those engaged in them would first accurately define their terms, and then adhere to their definitions. TRYON EDWARDS

4142. The evils of controversy are transitory, while its benefits are permanent. ROBERT HALL

4143. There is no learned man but will confess he hath much profited by reading controversies; his senses awakened, his judgment sharpened, and the truth which he holds more firmly established. In logic they teach that contraries laid together more evidently appear; and controversy being permitted, falsehood will appear more false, and truth more true. MILTON

4144. Controversy is wretched when it is only an attempt to prove another wrong. Religious controversy does only harm. It destroys humble inquiry after truth, and throws all the energies into an attempt to prove ourselves right—a spirit in which no man gets at truth. F. W. ROBERTSON

CONVENTIONALITY AND UNCONVENTIONALITY

Related Subjects: Custom, Fashion, Form, Manners, Morality, Society.

4151. How many times do we find

young men of clear and broad minds who see for themselves the error and the ugliness of all of our conventionalisms; and yet they are hemmed in on every side by parents and friends, every idea, every aspiration is screwed into the strait limits of dogmatic belief.

GAMALIEL BRADFORD

4152. The virtue in most respects is conformity. Self-reliance is its aversion. It loves not realities and creators, but names and customs.

EMERSON, *Self-Reliance*

4153. What will Mrs. Grundy say? What will Mrs. Grundy think?

THOMAS MORTON, *Speed the Plough*

4154. Keep the common road, and thou'rt safe.   *Proverb*

4155. The tyranny of Mrs. Grundy is worse than any other tyranny we suffer under.

HERBERT SPENCER,
Essays on Education

Unconventionality

4156. There never was a great character who did not sometimes smash the routine regulations and make new ones for himself. The rule is only suitable for such as have no aspirations. ANDREW CARNEGIE,
Empire of Business

4157. Whoso would be a man must be a non-conformist. EMERSON,
Self-Reliance

4158. Ascend above the restrictions and conventions of the World, but not so high as to lose sight of them.

RICHARD GARNETT,
De Flagello Myrteo

4159. In the extreme instances of reaction against convention, female

murderers get sheaves of offers of marriage.   BERNARD SHAW,
Getting Married

4160. If a man does not keep pace with his companions, perhaps it is because he hears a different drummer. Let him step to the music which he hears, however measured or far away.   THOREAU, *Walden*

See also: 168, 1226, 1431.

CONVERSATION

Related   Subjects: Discussion, Speech, Talk, Wit, Words.

4161. The secret of success in conversation is to be able to disagree without being disagreeable.

Anonymous

4162. I don't like to talk much with people who always agree with me. It is amusing to coquette with an echo for a little while, but one soon tires of it.   CARLYLE

4163. I don't know whether it is custom or inclination but somehow I can never carry on conversation except with men.

CATHERINE THE GREAT

4164. In conversation, avoid the extremes of forwardness and reserve.

CATO THE CENSOR

4165. Never hold any one by the button, or the hand, in order to be heard out; for if people are unwilling to hear you, you had better hold your tongue than them.

LORD CHESTERFIELD

4166. Two may talk and one may hear, but three cannot take part in a conversation of the most sincere and searching sort. EMERSON,
Friendship

4167. Conversation is an art in which a man has all mankind for competitors. EMERSON

4168. Conversation is the laboratory and workshop of the student. EMERSON

4169. Our companions please us less from the charms we find in their conversation, than from those they find in ours. GREVILLE

4170. Silence is one great art of conversation. HAZLITT

4171. Repose is as necessary in conversation as in a picture. HAZLITT

4172. Inject a few raisins of conversation into the tasteless dough of existence. O. HENRY

4173.
And when you stick on conversation's
    burs,
Don't strew your pathway with those
    dreadful *urs*. O. W. HOLMES,
        A Rhymed Lesson

4174. The wit of conversation consists more in finding it in others than in showing a great deal yourself. He who goes from your conversation pleased with himself and his own wit is perfectly well pleased with you. LA BRUYÈRE

4175. The reason why so few people are agreeable in conversation, is, that each is thinking more of what he is intending to say, than of what others are saying; and we never listen when we are planning to speak.
    LA ROCHEFOUCAULD, *Maxims*

4176. There cannot be a greater rudeness than to interrupt another in the current of his discourse. LOCKE

4177. Do you know that conversation is one of the greatest pleasures in life? But it wants leisure.
    SOMERSET MAUGHAM,
        The Trembling of a Leaf

4178. It is good to rub and polish our brain against that of others.
    MONTAIGNE, *Essays*

4179. Be not too brief in conversation, lest you be not understood; nor too diffuse, lest you be troublesome.
    PROTAGORAS

4180. He that converses not, knows nothing. *Proverb*

4181. Conversation teaches more than meditation. *Proverb*

4182. A single conversation across the table with a wise man is worth a month's study of books. *Proverb*

4183. When you fall into a man's conversation, the first thing you should consider is, whether he has a greater inclination to hear you, or that you should hear him.
SIR RICHARD STEELE, *The Spectator*

4184.
Conversation is but carving!
Give no more to every guest
Than he's able to digest.
Give him always of the prime,
And but little at a time.
Carve to all but just enough,
Let them neither starve nor stuff,
And that you may have your due,
Let your neighbor carve for you.
        SWIFT, *Conversation*

4185. One of the best rules in conversation is, never to say a thing which any of the company can reasonably wish had been left unsaid.
        SWIFT

4186. Lettuce is like conversation; it must be fresh and crisp, so sparkling

that you scarcely notice the bitter in it. CHARLES DUDLEY WARNER,
My Summer in a Garden

See also: 592, 731, 1130, 1292, 5328, 11017.

CONVERSION

Related Subjects: Change, Missionary, Persuasion, Religion

4191. In what way, or by what manner of working God changes a soul from evil to good—how he impregnates the barren rock with priceless gems and gold—is, to the human mind, an impenetrable mystery.
COLERIDGE

4192. As to the value of conversions, God only can judge.—He alone can know how wide are the steps which the soul has to take before it can approach to a community with him, to the dwelling of the perfect, or to the intercourse and friendship of higher natures. GOETHE

4193. You have not converted a man because you have silenced him.
JOHN MORLEY, *On Compromise*

4194. Conversion is not implanting eyes, for they exist already; but giving them a right direction, which they have not. PLATO

See also: 1324.

CONVICTION, see Belief

CONVIVIALITY

Related Subjects: Amiability, Feast, Friendship, Jazz, Merriment.

4201.
Let us have wine and women, mirth and laughter,
Sermons and soda-water the day after. BYRON, *Don Juan*

4202. If he be not fellow with the best king, thou shalt find the best king of good fellows.
SHAKESPEARE, *Henry V*

4203. There are few tables where convivial talents will not pass in payment, especially where the host wants brains, or the guest has money.
J. G. ZIMMERMAN

See also: 3672.

COOKS AND COOKING

Related Subjects: Dining, Eating, Feast, Food.

4211. Cookery is become an art, a noble science; cooks are gentlemen.
ROBERT BURTON,
Anatomy of Melancholy

4212. The art of cookery is the art of poisoning mankind, by rendering the appetite still importunate, when the wants of nature are supplied.
FENELON, *Telemachus*

4213. "A cook should be able to rule Russia. That's what Lenin said. He meant that government should be so simple that any member of the country should be able to take over if needed."
"But who would do the cooking."
"Ah, Jayshus! What's the use of explaining things to the likes of you?" O. St. J. GOGARTY,
As I Was Going Down Sackville St.

4214. He makes his cook his merit, and the world visits his dinners and not him. MOLIÈRE, *Le Misanthrope*

4215. The receipts of cookery are swelled to a volume; but a good stomach excels them all.
WILLIAM PENN, *Fruits of Solitude*

4216. The cook was a good cook, as cooks go; and as cooks go she went.
H. H. MUNRO, *Reginald*

4217. He is a sairy cook that mauna lick his ain fingers. *Proverb*

4218. Boil stones in butter, and you may sip the broth. *Proverb*

4219. God sends meat, and the Devil sends cooks. *Proverb*

4220. As testy as an old cook. *Proverb*

4221.

But, first
Or last, your fine Egyptian cookery
Shall have the fame. I have heard
    that Julius Caesar
Grew fat with feasting there.
SHAKESPEARE, *Antony & Cleopatra*

4222. A joint of mutton, and any pretty little tiny kickshaws, tell William cook. SHAKESPEARE, *Henry IV*

See also: 5752, 14534.

COQUETRY

Related Subjects: Courtship, Deceit, Fickleness, Woman.

4231. A coquette is a woman without any heart, who makes a fool of a man that hasn't got any head.
MME. DELUZY

4232. There is one antidote only for coquetry, and that is true love.
MME. DELUZY

4233. The characteristic of coquettes is affectation governed by whim.— Their life is one constant lie; and the only rule by which you can form any judgment of them, is, that they are never what they seem.
FIELDING

4234. An accomplished coquette excites the passions of others, in proportion as she feels none herself.
HAZLITT

4235. A coquette is like a recruiting sergeant, always on the lookout for fresh victims. DOUGLAS JERROLD

4236. A coquette is a young lady of more beauty than sense, more accomplishments than learning, more charms of person than graces of mind, more admirers than friends, more fools than wise men for attendants. LONGFELLOW

4237.
Had we but world enough, and time,
This coyness, lady, were no crime.
ANDREW MARVELL,
To His Coy Mistress

4238. As coy as Croker's mare. *Proverb*

4239. Mme. de Genlis, in order to avoid the scandal of coquetry, always yielded easily. TALLEYRAND

See also: 4162.

CORPORATIONS

Related Subjects: Business, Commerce, Finance, Profit.

4241. I weigh my words when I say that in my judgment the limited liability corporation is the greatest single discovery of modern times, whether you judge it by its social, by its ethical, by its industrial . . . by its political effects.
NICHOLAS MURRAY BUTLER

4242. They [corporations] cannot commit treason nor be outlawed nor excommunicated, for they have no souls. SIR EDWARD COKE,
Case of Sutton's Hospital

4243. A criminal is a person with predatory instincts who has not sufficient capital to form a corporation.
HOWARD SCOTT

4244. The corporation today is slowly but surely ousting all other types of industrial organization for the transaction of business, particularly of an international scope, or any considerable scale.
I. M. WORMSER, *Frankenstein, Inc.*

4245. The great corporation today must be viewed as a public trust.
Ibid.

4246. A corporate system which awards one or two favored leaders in a corporation such yearly sums by way of bonus as a million or two million dollars, and leaves six million men unemployed though they are ready, able and willing to work, necessitates prompt reform. Such a condition of things cannot endure.
Ibid.

4247. Corporations are not natural living persons, but artificial beings, *corpora ficta*. They are created by the nation or state, which endows them with distinct personality in the eye of the law, special privileges and comprehensive powers. Frankenstein's creature developed into a deadly menace to his creator.
Ibid.

4248. Corporations, the creatures of the state, owe a deep duty to the state. A generous liberalism on their part is today the soundest type of conservatism.
Ibid.

See also: 1143.

CORRUPTION

Related Subjects: Bribery, Decay, Dissipation, Evil, Temptation, Vice, Wickedness.

4251. He that toucheth pitch shall be defiled therewith.
Apocrypha: Ecclesiasticus

4252.
Corruption is a tree, whose branches are
Of an unmeasurable length: they spread
Ev'rywhere.
BEAUMONT & FLETCHER,
Honest Man's Fortune

4253. Evil communications corrupt good manners.
Bible: 1 Corinthians, xv, 33

4254. Corrupt influence is itself the perennial spring of all prodigality, and of all disorder: it loads us more than millions of debt; takes away vigor from our arms, wisdom from our councils, and every shadow of authority and credit from the most venerable parts of our constitution.
BURKE

4255. Corruption never has been compulsory. ANTHONY EDEN

4256. Corruption, the most infallible symptom of constitutional liberty.
GIBBON, *Decline and Fall*

4257. He that lies with the dogs, riseth with fleas. *Proverb*

4258. Corruption of the best becomes the worst. *Proverb*

4259. Thou hast damnable iteration, and art indeed able to corrupt a saint. SHAKESPEARE, *Henry IV*

4260. Corruption wins not more than honesty. SHAKESPEARE, *Henry VIII*

4261. They that touch pitch will be defiled. SHAKESPEARE,
Much Ado About Nothing

4262. The corruptions of the country are closely allied to those of the town, with no difference but what is made by another mode of thought and living. SWIFT

See also: 1855, 3050, 3445, 4517, 15082, 15519, 15698, 21034.

COSMOPOLITANISM

Related Subjects: Cities, Worldliness.

4271. If a man be gracious and courteous to strangers, it shows he is a citizen of the world.
BACON, *Essays*

4272. To a resolved mind, his home is everywhere.
BEAUMONT & FLETCHER,
The Knight of the Burning Pestle

4273.
All countries are a wise man's home,
And so are governments to some.
SAMUEL BUTLER, *Hudibras*

4274. I am a citizen of the world.
DIOGENES LAERTIUS, *Diogenes*

4275. My country is the world; my countrymen are mankind.
W. L. GARRISON,
Prospectus of the Public Liberator

4276. To be really cosmopolitan, a man must be at home even in his own country.   T. W. HIGGINSON,
Short Studies of American Authors

4277. I don't set up for being a cosmopolite, which to my mind signifies being polite to every country except your own.
THOMAS HOOD, *Up the Rhine*

4278.
That man's the best cosmopolite
Who loves his native country best.
TENNYSON, *Hands All Around*

COST, see Price

COUNSEL

Related Subjects: Advice, Caution, Prudence, Warning.

4281. Let the counsel of thine own heart stand: for there is no man more faithful unto thee than it. For a man's mind is sometime wont to tell him more than seven watchmen, that sit above in an high tower.
Apocrypha: Ecclesiasticus

4282. Ask counsel of both times: of the ancient time what is best; and of the latter time what is fittest.
BACON, *Essays*

4283. When all is done, the help of good counsel is that which setteth business straight.   BACON, *Essays*

4284. In counsel it is good to see dangers; but in execution, not to see them unless they be very great.
BACON, *Essays*

4285. There is as much difference between the counsel that a friend giveth, and that a man giveth himself, as there is between the counsel of a friend and a flatterer.
BACON, *Essays*

4286. Who is this that darkeneth counsel by words without knowledge?   *Bible: Job, xxxviii, 2*

4287. In the multitude of counsellors there is safety.
Bible: Proverbs, xi, 14

4288. Who cannot give good counsel? 'Tis cheap, it costs them nothing.
ROBERT BURTON,
Anatomy of Melancholy

4289.
My counsel is a kind one; for 'tis even
Given chiefly at my own expense: 'tis true,
'Twill not be followed, so there's little lost.   BYRON, *Cain*

4290. Beware lest clamour be taken for counsel.   ERASMUS, *Senatulus*

4291. He that won't be counselled can't be helped.
FRANKLIN, *Poor Richard*

4292.
Good counsel failing men may give, for why?
He that's aground knows where the shoal doth lie.
FRANKLIN, *Poor Richard*

4293. Good counsels observed, are chains to grace, which, neglected, prove halters to strange, undutiful children.   THOMAS FULLER

4294. A woman's counsel is not worth much, but he that despises it is no wiser than he should be.
Proverb

4295. It is safer to hear and take counsel than to give it.   *Proverb*

4296. Too much consulting confounds.   *Proverb*

4297. If the counsel be good, no matter who gave it.   *Proverb*

4298. Counsel is no command.
Proverb

4299. Counsel must be followed, not praised.   *Proverb*

4300. Counsel over cups is crazy.
Proverb

4301. An enemy may chance to give good counsel.   *Proverb*

4302. Consult your friend on all things, especially on those which respect yourself.—His counsel may then be useful where your own self-love might impair your judgment.
SENECA

4303. Friendly counsel cuts off many foes.   SHAKESPEARE, *Henry VI*

4304.
I pray thee, cease thy counsel,
Which falls into mine ears as profit-less
As water in a sieve.
SHAKESPEARE,
Much Ado About Nothing

4305. Good counsellors lack no clients.   SHAKESPEARE,
Measure for Measure

See also: 877, 881, 13260.

COUNTRY, THE

Related Subjects: Animal, Farming, Flowers, Forest, Grass, Nature, Park, Sport, Tree.

4311. There is virtue in country houses, in gardens and orchards, in fields, streams, and groves, in rustic recreations and plain manners, that neither cities nor universities enjoy.
BRONSON ALCOTT

4312. I consider it the best part of an education to have been born and brought up in the country.
BRONSON ALCOTT

4313.
No one knows the countryside,
Deep and green and sweetly wide,
Until he loves it as a woman,
Something warm and dear and human.   STRUTHERS BURT,
No One Knows the Countryside

4314.
Nor rural sights alone, but rural sounds
Exhilarate the spirit, and restore
The tone of languid nature.
COWPER, *The Task*

4315.
How blessed is he who leads a country life,
Unvexed with anxious cares, and void of strife!   DRYDEN,
To John Driden of Chesterton

4316. Nine-tenths of all the fine things in our literature concerning the charms of country life, have been written, not beneath the shade of over-arching boughs, but within the crowded city's smoke-stained walls.
CHARLES B. FAIRBANKS,
My Unknown Chum

4317. There is nothing good to be had in the country, or, if there be, they will not let you have it.
HAZLITT, *Lectures*

4318. All country people hate each other. They have so little comfort that they envy their neighbours the smallest pleasure or advantage.
HAZLITT, *Round-Table*

4319. No man, I suspect, ever lived long in the country without being bitten by these meteorological ambitions. He likes to be hotter and colder, to have been more deeply snowed up, to have more trees and larger blown down than his neighbors.
LOWELL, *My Garden Acquaintance*

4320. Men are taught virtue and a love of independence, by living in the country.   MENANDER

4321.
Meadows trim, with daisies pied,
Shallow brooks, and rivers wide;
Towers and battlements it sees
Bosom'd high in tufted trees,
Where perhaps some beauty lies,
The cynosure of neighboring eyes.
MILTON, *L'Allegro*

4322. In those vernal seasons of the year when the air is calm and pleasant, it were an injury and sullenness against nature not to go out and see her riches, and partake in her rejoicing with heaven and earth.
MILTON

4323. The country is both the philosopher's garden and his library, in which he reads and contemplates the power, wisdom, and goodness of God.   WILLIAM PENN

4324.
Before green apples blush,
Before green nuts embrown,
Why, one day in the country
Is worth a month in town.
CHRISTINA ROSSETTI, *Summer*

4325. I suppose the pleasure of country life lies really in the eternally renewed evidences of the determination to live. . . . The powers of resistance against adversity are greater than we thought; the germ of life lies hidden even in the midst of apparent death.   V. SACKVILLE-WEST

4326. My living in Yorkshire was so far out of the way, that it was actually twelve miles from a lemon.
SYDNEY SMITH,
Lady Holland's Memoir

4327. I have no relish for the country; it is a kind of healthy grave.
SYDNEY SMITH

4328. Anybody can be good in the country. There are no temptations there.   OSCAR WILDE,
The Picture of Dorian Gray

See also: 4262, 20721.

COURAGE

Related Subjects: Boldness, Defiance, Endurance, Enterprise, Hero, Martyr, Optimism, Resolution, Self-Confidence, Self-Reliance, Spirit, Stoicism, Valor.

4331. Courage that grows from constitution, often forsakes a man when he has occasion for it; courage which arises from a sense of duty, acts in a uniform manner.   ADDISON

4332. It is easy to be brave from a safe distance.

AESOP, *The Wolf and the Kid*

4333. Witness to the world that I die like a man.   MAJOR JOHN ANDRÉ

4334. It is an error to suppose that courage means courage in everything. —Most people are brave only in the dangers to which they accustom themselves, either in imagination or practice.   BULWER-LYTTON

4335. The courage we desire and prize is not the courage to die decently, but to live manfully.

CARLYLE

4336. The courage of New England was the "courage of Conscience." It did not rise to that insane and awful passion, the love of war for itself.

RUFUS CHOATE

4337. To see what is right and not to do it, is want of courage.

CONFUCIUS, *Analects*

4338. Come on, you sons of bitches! Do you want to live forever?
GUNNERY SERGEANT DANIEL DALY, *U. S. Marine Corps, at Belleau Wood, June 4, 1918*

4339. None but the brave deserve the fair.   DRYDEN, *Alexander's Feast*

4340. Courage from hearts and not from numbers grows.   DRYDEN

4341. Any coward can fight a battle when he's sure of winning; but give me the man who has pluck to fight when he's sure of losing. That's my way, sir, and there are many victories worse than a defeat.
GEORGE ELIOT, *Janet's Repentance*

4342. My center is giving way, my right is pushed back—excellent! I'll attack.   MARSHAL FOCH

4343. Courage is, on all hands, considered as an essential of high character.   FROUDE

4344. Brave men were living before Agamemnon.   HORACE, *Odes*

4345. Live undaunted; and oppose gallant breasts against the strokes of adversity.   HORACE, *Satires*

4346. No man can answer for his courage who has never been in danger.   LA ROCHEFOUCAULD, *Maxims*

4347.
Better like Hector in the field to die,
Than like a perfumed Paris turn and fly.
LONGFELLOW, *Morituri Salutamus*

4348. By this, he seemed to mean, not only that the most reliable and useful courage was that which arises from the fair estimation of the encountered peril, but that an utterly fearless man is a far more dangerous comrade than a coward.
HERMAN MELVILLE, *Moby Dick*

4349. The mariner of old said thus to Neptune in a great tempest, "O God! thou mayest save me if thou wilt, and if thou wilt, thou mayest destroy me; but whether or no, I will steer my rudder true."
MONTAIGNE, *Essays*

4350. He who, though he falleth, is stubborn in his courage, and, being in danger of imminent death, is no whit daunted in his assurance; but, in yielding up the ghost, beholds his enemy with a scornful and fierce look —he is vanquished, not by us, but by fortune; he is slain, but not conquered. The most valiant are often the most unfortunate. So are there triumphant losses more to be envied than victories.   MONTAIGNE, *Essays*

4351. Don't give up the ship! You will beat them off!

CAPTAIN JAMES MUGFORD

4352. Courage consists not in hazarding without fear, but being resolutely minded in a just cause.

PLUTARCH

4353. Courage ought to have eyes as well as arms.   *Proverb*

4354. A courageous foe is better than a cowardly friend.   *Proverb*

4355. A stout heart crushes ill luck.

Proverb

4356. Courage consists, not in blindly overlooking danger, but in seeing and conquering it.

J. P. RICHTER

4357. Women and men of retiring timidity are cowardly only in dangers which affect themselves, but are the first to rescue when others are endangered.   J. P. RICHTER

4358. No man is worth his salt who is not ready at all times to risk his body, to risk his well-being, to risk his life, in a great cause.

THEODORE ROOSEVELT

4359.

The blood more stirs
To rouse a lion than to start a hare!

SHAKESPEARE, *Henry IV*

4360. For courage mounteth with occasion.   SHAKESPEARE, *King John*

4361.
I dare do all that may become a man;
Who dares do more is none.

SHAKESPEARE, *Macbeth*

4362. Courage ought to be guided by skill, and skill armed by courage. Hardiness should not darken wit, nor wit cool hardiness. Be valiant as men despising death, but confident as unwonted to be overcome.

SIR PHILIP SIDNEY

4363. A great deal of talent is lost in this world for the want of a little courage.   SYDNEY SMITH

4364. Return with your shield or on it. *Spartan mother's admonition to her departing warrior son*

4365. I refer those actions which work out the good of the agent to courage, and those which work out the good of others to nobility. Therefore temperance, sobriety, and presence of mind in danger, etc., are species of courage; but modesty, clemency, etc., are species of nobility.

SPINOZA, *Ethics*

4366. When you get into a tight place and everything goes against you, 'til it seems as though you could not hold on a minute longer, never give up then, for that is just the place and time that the tide will turn.

HARRIET BEECHER STOWE

4367. Bravery never goes out of fashion.

THACKERAY, *The Four Georges*

4368. True courage is not the brutal force of vulgar heroes, but the firm resolve of virtue and reason.

PAUL WHITEHEAD

4369. She'd fight a rattlesnake and give it the first two bites.

HARRY LEON WILSON,
Ruggles of Red Gap

See also: 329, 1068, 2249, 2942, 3067, 3209, 3593, 3595, 4482, 4489, 4766, 4771, 6358, 6602, 11952, 13861, 16304, 16923, 20780.

COURT AND COURTIER

Related Subjects: Fop, Kings, Nobility, Prince, Queen.

4371.
To laugh, to lie, to flatter to the face,

Four ways in court to win men's grace.

ROGER ASCHAM, *The Schoolmaster*

4372. Young courtiers be beggars in their age.

ALEXANDER BARCLAY, *Egloges*

4373.
Heads bow, knees bend, eyes watch around a throne,
And hands obey—our hearts are still our own. BYRON, *Don Juan*

4374.
The man that has no friend at court,
Must make the laws confine his sport;
But he that has, by dint of flaws,
May make his sport confine the laws.

THOMAS CHATTERTON,
The Revenge

4375. Falsehood and dissimulation are certainly to be found at courts; but where are they not to be found? Cottages have them, as well as courts, only with worse manners.

LORD CHESTERFIELD, *Letters*

4376. Great courts are the seats of true good-breeding.

LORD CHESTERFIELD, *Letters*

4377.
If you think we are worked by strings,
Like a Japanese marionette,
You don't understand these things:
It is simply Court etiquette.

W. S. GILBERT, *The Mikado*

4378. Who has seen the court has seen the world.

LA BRUYÈRE, *Les Caractères*

4379. The court is like a palace built of marble—made up of very hard, and very polished marble.

LA BRUYÈRE, *Les Caractères*

4380.
Court-virtues bear, like gems, the highest rate,
Born where Heaven's influence scarce can penetrate.

POPE, *Moral Essays*

4381.
Sir, I have lived a courtier all my days,
And studied men, their manners, and their ways;
And have observed this useful maxim still,
To let my betters always have their will. POPE, *January and May*

4382. A nod from a lord is a breakfast for a fool. *Proverb*

4383.
Go, tell the court it glows,
And shines like painted wood;
Go, tell the church it shews
What's good, but does no good.
If court and church reply,
Give court and church the lie.

SIR WALTER RALEIGH

4384.
This is the English, not the Turkish court;
Not Amurath an Amurath succeeds,
But Harry Harry.

SHAKESPEARE, *Henry IV*

4385. To dance attendance on their lordships' pleasures.

SHAKESPEARE, *Henry VIII*

4386.
The caterpillars of the commonwealth,
Which I have sworn to weed and pluck away.

SHAKESPEARE, *Richard II*

4387.
Whoso betakes him to a prince's court,
Becomes his slave, albeit of free birth.

SOPHOCLES

4388. The two maxims of any great man at court are, always to keep his countenance, and never to keep his word. SWIFT, *Thoughts on Various Subjects*

4389. A court is an assemblage of noble and distinguished beggars. TALLEYRAND

4390.
O, happy they that never saw the court,
Nor ever knew great men but by report.
JOHN WEBSTER, *The White Devil*

COURTESY

Related Subjects: **Amiability, Breeding, Ceremony, Chivalry, Gentleman, Good Humor, Grace, Hospitality, Manners, Refinement, Service.**

4391. The small courtesies sweeten life; the greater ennoble it. C. N. BOVEE

4392. Do as you would be done by, is the surest method of pleasing. LORD CHESTERFIELD, *Letters*

4393. The courtesies of a small and trivial character are the ones which strike deepest to the grateful and appreciating heart. It is the picayune compliments which are the most appreciated; far more than the double ones we sometimes pay. HENRY CLAY

4394. We must be courteous to a man as we are to a picture, which we are willing to give the advantage of a good light. EMERSON, *Conduct of Life*

4395. The whole of heraldry and chivalry is in courtesy. A man of fine manners shall pronounce your name with all the ornament that titles of nobility could add. EMERSON

4396. Life is not so short but that there is always time for courtesy. EMERSON

4397.
How sweet and gracious, even in common speech,
Is that fine sense which men call Courtesy! J. T. FIELDS, *Courtesy*

4398. As the sword of the best tempered metal is most flexible, so the truly generous are most pliant and courteous in their behavior to their inferiors. THOMAS FULLER

4399. There is a courtesy of the heart; it is allied to love. From it springs the purest courtesy in the outward behavior. GOETHE

4400. There is no outward sign of true courtesy that does not rest on a deep moral foundation. GOETHE

4401. The constant interchange of those thousand little courtesies which imperceptibly sweeten life, has a happy effect upon the features, and spreads a mellow evening charm over the wrinkles of old age. WASHINGTON IRVING, *Wolfert's Roost*

4402. He was so generally civil, that nobody thanked him for it. SAMUEL JOHNSON, *Boswell: Life*

4403. When saluted with a salutation, salute the person with a better salutation, or at least return the same, for God taketh account of all things. *The Koran*

4404. Courtesy is a science of the highest importance. It is like grace and beauty in the body, which charm at first sight and lead on to further intimacy and friendship. MONTAIGNE, *Essays*

4405. He may freely receive courtesies that knows how to requite them.
Proverb

4406. In courtesy, rather pay a penny too much than too little.
Proverb

4407. Less of your courtesy and more of your purse. *Proverb*

4408. It is a rank courtesy, when a man is forced to give thanks for what is his own. *Proverb*

4409. Courtesy is the inseparable companion of virtue. *Proverb*

4410. Courtesy on one side can never last long. *Proverb*

4411. A civil denial is better than a rude grant. *Proverb*

4412. Too much courtesy, too much craft. *Proverb*

4413. A courtesy much entreated is half recompensed. *Proverb*

4414. All doors open to courtesy.
Proverb

4415. I am the very pink of courtesy.
SHAKESPEARE, *Romeo and Juliet*

4416. Keep a good tongue in your head. SHAKESPEARE, *The Tempest*

4417. A churlish courtesy rarely comes but either for gain or falsehood. SIR PHILIP SIDNEY

4418. Hail, ye small, sweet courtesies of life! for smooth do ye make the road of it.
STERNE, *A Sentimental Journey*

4419.
Of Courtesy, it is much less
Than Courage of Heart or Holiness,
Yet in my walks it seems to me
That the Grace of God is in Courtesy.
TARKINGTON, *Courtesy*

4420. The greater man the greater courtesy.
TENNYSON, *Idylls of the King*

4421.
For courtesy wins woman all as well
As valor may.
TENNYSON, *Idylls of the King*

See also: 1816, 2845.

COURTS OF LAW

Related Subjects: Judge, Judgment, Jury, Justice, Law, Lawyers, Trials.

4431. The history of the Supreme Court is not the history of an abstraction, but the analysis of individuals acting as a Court who make decisions and lay down doctrines, and of other individuals, their successors, who refine, modify, and sometimes even overrule the decisions of their predecessors, reinterpreting and transmuting their doctrines.
JUSTICE FRANKFURTER,
Law and Politic.

4432.
The charge is prepar'd, the lawyer are met,
The judges all ranged, a terribl show! JOHN GAY,
The Beggar's Oper.

4433. A dissent in a court of las resort is an appeal to the broodin, spirit of the law, to the intelligenc of a future day, when a later decisio may possibly correct the error int which the dissenting judge believe the court to have been betrayed.
Nor is this appeal always in vai. In a number of cases dissenting opir ions have in time become the law
CHARLES EVANS HUGHE

4434. Go not in and out in the cou of justice, that thy name may n. stink. . *The Wisdom of An*

COURTSHIP

Related Subjects: Coquetry, Cupid, Kiss, Love, Marriage, Wedding.

4441. Those marriages generally abound most with love and constancy that are preceded by a long courtship. ADDISON, *The Spectator*

4442. The pleasantest part of a man's life is generally that which passes in courtship, provided his passion be sincere, and the party beloved, kind, with discretion. Love, desire, hope, all the pleasing motions of the soul, rise in the pursuit. ADDISON

4443. In courtship a man pursues a woman until she catches him.
Anonymous

4444.
Romances paint at full length people's wooings,
But only give a bust of marriages:
For no one cares for matrimonial
   cooings. BYRON, *Don Juan*

4445. If you cannot inspire a woman with love of yourself, fill her above the brim with love of herself; all that runs over will be yours.
C. C. COLTON

4446. Barkis is willin'. DICKENS,
David Copperfield

4447. With women worth being won, the softest lover ever best succeeds.
AARON HILL

4448. I profess not to know how women's hearts are wooed and won. To me they have always been matters of riddle and admiration.
WASHINGTON IRVING

4449. The surest way to hit a woman's heart is to take aim kneeling.
DOUGLAS JERROLD,
Douglas Jerrold's Wit

4450.
Follow a shadow, it still flies you;
  Seem to fly it, it will pursue:
So court a mistress, who denies you;
  Let her alone, she will court you.
BEN JONSON, *Follow a Shadow*

4451. If I am not worth the wooing, I surely am not worth the winning.
LONGFELLOW,
The Courtship of Miles Standish

4452. And with my advice, faith I wish you'd take me.
SAMUEL LOVER, *Widow Machree*

4453.
If I speak to thee in friendship's
  name,
  Thou think'st I speak too coldly;
If I mention love's devoted flame,
  Thou say'st I speak too boldly.
THOMAS MOORE,
How Shall I Woo?

4454. Faint heart never won fair lady. *Proverb*

4455. He that would the daughter win, must with the mother first begin. *Proverb*

4456. Happy's the wooing, that's not long in doing. *Proverb*

4457. Courting and wooing, brings dallying and doing. *Proverb*

4458. Let a woman once give you a task and you are hers, heart and soul; all your care and trouble lend new charms to her for whose sake they are taken—To rescue, to revenge, to instruct, or to protect a woman, is all the same as to love her.
J. P. RICHTER

4459.
My story being done,
She gave me for my pains a world of
  sighs:
She swore, in faith, 'twas strange,
  'twas passing strange,

'Twas pitiful, 'twas wondrous pitiful:
She wish'd she had not heard it, yet
: she wish'd
That Heaven had made her such a
man; she thank'd me,
And bade me, if I had a friend that
loved her,
I should teach him how to tell my
story
And that would woo her.
> SHAKESPEARE,
> *Othello*

4460. Who wooed in haste and means
to wed at leisure.
> SHAKESPEARE,
> *The Taming of the Shrew*

4461.
Lest too light winning
Make the prize light.
> SHAKESPEARE, *The Tempest*

4462.
That man that hath a tongue, I say, is
no man,
If with his tongue he cannot win a
woman. SHAKESPEARE,
> *The Two Gentlemen of Verona*

4463. You think that you are Ann's
suitor: that you are the pursuer and
she the pursued; that it is your part
to woo, to persuade, to prevail, to
overcome. Fool: it is you who are
the pursued, the marked-down
quarry, the destined prey.
> BERNARD SHAW,
> *Man and Superman*

4464. Courtship consists in a number of quiet attentions, not so pointed
as to alarm, nor so vague as not to be
understood. STERNE,
> *Sentimental Journey*

See also: 2281, 4421, 21155, 21161,
21661.

COW

Related Subjects: **Animal, The
Country, Farming, Milk.**

4471.
Everyone to their liking,
As the old woman said when she
kissed her cow. *Anonymous*

4472.
I never saw a purple cow,
I never hope to see one.
But I can tell you, anyhow,
I'd rather see than be one.
> GELETT BURGESS, *The Purple Cow*

4473. Cows are my passion.
> DICKENS, *Dombey and Son*

4474. A cow does not gaze at the
rainbow, or show or affect any interest in the landscape, or a peacock,
or the song of thrushes.
EMERSON, *Letters and Social Aims*

4475. A cow is a very good animal
in the field; but we turn her out of a
garden. SAMUEL JOHNSON,
> *Boswell: Life*

4476. All is not butter that comes
from the cow. *Proverb*

4477. Many a good cow hath an
evil calf. *Proverb*

4478.
An herd of bulls, whom kindly rage
doth sting,
Do for the milky mothers want complain,
And fill the fields with troublous bellowing.
> EDMUND SPENSER,
> *The Faerie Queene*

4479.
The friendly cow all red and white
I love with all my heart:
She gives me cream with all her
might
To eat with apple-tart.
> STEVENSON, *The Cow*

4480.
Thank you, pretty cow, that made
Pleasant milk to soak my bread.
                    ANN TAYLOR, *The Cow*

See also: 9780, 10148.

COWARD AND COWARDICE

**Related Subjects: Baseness, Boast-
ing, Braggart, Fear, Informer,
Servility, Timidity, Weakness.**

4481. Only cowards insult dying
majesty.   AESOP, *The Sick Lion*

4482. Cowards falter, but danger is
often overcome by those who nobly
dare.   QUEEN ELIZABETH

4483. Cowards do not count in battle;
they are there, but not in it.
                    EURIPIDES, *Meleager*

4484. Cowardice is not synonymous
with prudence. It often happens that
the better part of discretion is valor.
                    HAZLITT

4485. The first in banquets, but the
last in fight.   HOMER, *Iliad*

4486. It is the coward who fawns
upon those above him. It is the
coward who is insolent whenever he
dares be so.   JUNIUS

4487. Cowards are cruel. *Proverb*

4488. Cowards run the greatest danger of any men in a battle. *Proverb*

4489. Many would be cowards if they
had courage enough.   *Proverb*

4490. A coward's fear may make a
coward valiant.   *Proverb*

4491. A plague of all cowards, I say.
                    SHAKESPEARE, *Henry IV*

4492.
Thou wear a lion's hide! doff it for
    shame

And hang a calf's-skin on those rec-
reant limbs.   SHAKESPEARE,
                            King John

4493.
How many cowards, whose hearts are
    all as false
As stairs of sand, wear yet upon their
    chins
The beards of Hercules and frown-
    ing Mars,
Who, inward search'd, have livers
    white as milk?
                    SHAKESPEARE,
                    The Merchant of Venice

4494. Not every man is so great a
coward as he thinks he is—nor yet
so good a Christian.
                    STEVENSON,
                    The Master of Ballantrae

4495. The craven's fear is but selfishness, like his merriment.
                    WHITTIER

See also: 93, 2255, 3936, 3940, 3945,
3968, 4341, 4348, 4354, 4707, 5090,
12200, 12824, 13807, 15444.

CRAFTSMANSHIP

Related Subject: Skill.

4501. No man is his craft's master
the first day.   *Proverb*

4502. Show him rather the simple
man-made things that race after race
have fashioned, and that live still, in
our sight and near to our hands.
Tell him of things. He will stand beside you and wonder as you once
stood in Rome by the maker of rope,
or by the potter in Egypt.
Show him how happy a thing can
be, how blameless, how much ours.
                    RAINER M. RILKE

4503. We shall take the bull by the
horns and run the full risks of con-

troversy in our conception of craft as consisting of the *spirit in which,* rather than solely the *means by which,* a production process is carried out.   S. G. WILLIAMSON,
The American Craftsman

4504. Craft is a link which weds science to art, to the benefit of each.   S. G. WILLIAMSON,
The American Craftsman

4505. Craft is the basis of most invention. . . . Craft instinct must still augment, and lend its creative qualities to, the scientific aspects of invention. What is craft but the perception of how to use something, even if that something is a formula?   S. G. WILLIAMSON,
The American Craftsman

4506. Criticism comes easier than craftsmanship.   ZEUXIS

See also: 1174, 1199, 1211

CREATOR, see God

CREDIT, CREDITOR

Related Subjects: **Borrowing, Business, Confidence, Debt, Inflation, Money, Trust, Usurer.**

4511. Credit is like chastity, they can both stand temptation better than suspicion.   JOSH BILLINGS

4512. Nothing so cements and holds together all the parts of a society as faith or credit, which can never be kept up unless men are under some force or necessity of honestly paying what they owe to one another.
           CICERO

4513. A person who can't pay, gets another person who can't pay, to guarantee that he can pay.
       DICKENS, *Little Dorrit*

4514. However gradual may be the growth of confidence, that of credit requires still more time to arrive at maturity.   DISRAELI

4515. The most trifling actions that affect a man's credit are to be regarded. The sound of your hammer at five in the morning or nine at night, heard by a creditor, makes him easier six months longer; but if he sees you at a billiard table, or hears your voice at a tavern when you should be at work, he sends for his money the next day.   FRANKLIN,
Poor Richard

4516.
Ah, take the Cash, and let the Credit go,
Nor heed the rumble of a distant Drum!
       OMAR KHAYYAM,
Rubaiyat

4517.
Blest paper-credit! last and best supply!
That lends corruption lighter wings to fly!   POPE, *Moral Essays*

4518. He getteth a great deal of credit, who payeth but a small debt.
       Proverb

4519. More credit may be thrown down in a moment, than can be built up in an age.   *Proverb*

4520. The credit got by a lie lasts only till the truth comes out.
       Proverb

4521. He that has lost his credit is dead to the world.   *Proverb*

4522. Credit is better than ill won gear.   *Proverb*

4523. Credit is like a looking-glass, which when once sullied by a breath,

may be wiped clear again; but if once cracked can never be repaired.
Scott

4524. So far as my coin would stretch; and where it would not, I have used my credit.
Shakespeare, *Henry IV*

4525. Credit is the life blood of industry and the *control* of credit is the control of all society.
Upton Sinclair

4526. The private control of credit is the modern form of slavery.
Upton Sinclair

4527.
Who quick be to borrow and slow be to pay,
Their credit is naught, go they never
 so gay. Thomas Tusser,
Five Hundred Points of
Good Husbandrie

Creditor

4528. Creditors have better memories than debtors; they are a superstitious sect, great observers of set days and times. Franklin, *Poor Richard*

4529. A creditor is worse than a master; for a master owns only your person, a creditor owns your dignity, and can belabour that.
Victor Hugo,
Les Miserables

4530. The creditor whose appearance gladdens the heart of a debtor may hold his head in sunbeams, and his foot on storms. Lavater

See also: 15674.

CREDULITY AND
  INCREDULITY

Related Subjects: Belief, Doubt, Faith, Possibility, Probability, Simplicity, Trust, Wonder.

4531. He had been kicked in the Head by a Mule when young and believed everything he read in the Sunday Papers. George Ade,
Fables in Slang

4532. The more gross the fraud, the more glibly will it go down and the more greedily will it be swallowed, since folly will always find faith wherever impostors will find impudence. C. N. Bovee

4533. Your noblest natures are most credulous. George Chapman

4534. It is a curious paradox that precisely in proportion to our own intellectual weakness, will be our credulity as to the mysterious powers assumed by others. C. C. Colton

4535. Generous souls are still most subject to credulity.
Sir William D'Avenant

4536. Credulity is belief on slight evidence, with no evidence, or against evidence. In this sense it is the infidel, not the believer, who is credulous. "The simple," says Solomon, "believeth every word."
Tryon Edwards

4537. A little credulity helps one on through life very smoothly.
Mrs. Gaskell, *Cranford*

4538. I cannot spare the luxury of believing that all things beautiful are what they seem.
Fitz-Greene Halleck

4539. Credulity is the common failing of inexperienced virtue; and he who is spontaneously suspicious may justly be charged with radical corruption.   SAMUEL JOHNSON

4540. Some men are bigoted in politics, who are infidels in religion. Ridiculous credulity!   JUNIUS

4541. Credulity is the man's weakness, but the child's strength.
CHARLES LAMB,
Witches, and Other Night Fears

4542. We seek and offer ourselves to be gulled.   MONTAIGNE, *Essays*

4543. This is yet the childhood of the world, and a supine credulity is still the most charming characteristic of man.   SIR WILLIAM OSLER,
Life of Sir William Osler

4544. The most positive men are the most credulous, since they most believe themselves and advise most with their falsest flatterer and worst enemy,—their own self-love.   POPE

4545. Credulity thinks others short sighted.   *Proverb*

4546. Hatred, as well as love, renders its votaries credulous.
ROUSSEAU, *Confessions*

4547. The only disadvantage of an honest heart is credulity.
SIR PHILIP SIDNEY

4548. The general goodness which is nourished in noble hearts, makes every one think that strength of virtue to be in another whereof they find assured foundation in themselves.
SIR PHILIP SIDNEY

4549. As credulity is a more peaceful possession of the mind than curiosity, so preferable is that wisdom which converses about the surface, to that pretended philosophy which enters into the depth of things,

and then comes back gravely with the informations and discoveries that in the inside they are good for nothing.
SWIFT

Incredulity

4550. More persons, on the whole, are humbugged by believing in nothing, than by believing too much.
P. T. BARNUM

4551. Nothing is so contemptible as that affectation of wisdom which some display by universal incredulity.
GOLDSMITH

4552. Incredulity robs us of many pleasures, and gives us nothing in return.   LOWELL

4553. Incredulity should make men advised, not irresolute.   *Proverb*

See also: 50, 4772, 16425, 16426.

CREEDS

Related Subjects: Belief, Doctrine, Faith, Religion, Theology.

4561.
I speak not of men's creeds—they rest between
Man and his Maker.   BYRON,
Childe Harold

4562. In war: Resolution. In defeat: Defiance. In victory: Magnanimity. In peace: Good Will.
WINSTON CHURCHILL

4563. In politics, as in religion, we have less charity for those who believe the half of our creed, than for those who deny the whole of it.
C. C. COLTON

4564.
Justice is the only worship.
Love is the only priest.
Ignorance is the only slavery.
Happiness is the only good.

The time to be happy is now,
The place to be happy is here,
The way to be happy is to make
    others so.
        ROBERT INGERSOLL, *Creed*

4565. Such a creed as mine must
grow and change as knowledge
grows and changes.
        SIR ARTHUR KEITH,
                I Believe

4566.
The world is my country,
All mankind are my brethren,
To do good is my religion,
I believe in one God and no more.
        THOMAS PAINE,
                The Rights of Man

4567.
Creeds grow so thick along the way,
Their boughs hide God.
        LIZETTE W. REESE, *Doubt*

4568.
I would be true, for there are those
    who trust me;
I would be pure, for there are those
    who care;
I would be strong, for there is much
    to suffer;
I would be brave, for there is much
    to dare.   H. A. WALTER,
                My Creed

See also: 1313, 1723, 5255, 6189.

CRIME

Related Subjects: Bribery, Evil,
Guilt, Justice, Law, Morality, Murder, Offence, Police, Prison, Punishment, Repentance, Retribution,
Sin, Thief, Villainy, Wickedness.

4571. Society prepares the crime;
the criminal commits it.   V. ALFIERI

4572. Heaven will permit no man to
secure happiness by crime.
        V. ALFIERI

4573.
            There's not a crime
But takes its proper change out still
    in crime
If once rung on the counter of this
    world.
        ELIZABETH B. BROWNING,
                Aurora Leigh

4574. Crimes not against forms, but
against those eternal laws of justice,
which are our rule and our birth-
right.   BURKE,
    Impeachment of Warren Hastings

4575. Crimes are not to be measured
by the issue of events, but from
the bad intentions of men.
        CICERO, *De Amicitia*

4576.
But many a crime, deem'd innocent
    on earth,
Is registered in Heaven; and these,
    no doubt,
Have each their record, with a curse
    annex'd.   COWPER, *The Task*

4577. With ready-made opinions one
cannot judge of crime. Its philosophy is a little more complicated than
people think. It is acknowledged
that neither convict prisons, nor the
hulks, nor any system of hard labour
ever cured a criminal.
        DOSTOYEVSKY,
            The House of the Dead

4578. Successful crimes alone are
justified.   DRYDEN, *The Medal*

4579. Wherever a man commits a
crime, God finds a witness.
        EMERSON, *Lectures*

4580. There is no den in the wide
world to hide a rogue. Commit a
crime and the earth is made of glass.
Commit a crime, and it seems as if
a coat of snow fell on the ground,
such as reveals in the woods the

track of every partridge, and fox, and squirrel.   EMERSON

4581. It is worse than a crime; it is a blunder—words which I record, because they have been attributed to others.   FOUCHÉ, *Memoirs*

4582. Crime is not punished as an offense against God, but as prejudicial to society.   FROUDE,
Short Studies on Great Subjects

4583. Crimes sometimes shock us too much; vices almost always too little.   A. W. & J. C. HARE,
Guesses at Truth

4584. What man have you ever seen who was contented with one crime only?   JUVENAL, *Satires*

4585. If poverty is the mother of crimes, want of sense is the father of them.   LA BRUYÈRE

4586. We easily forget crimes that are known only to ourselves.
LA ROCHEFOUCAULD,
Maxims

4587. For the credit of virtue it must be admitted that the greatest evils which befall mankind are caused by their crimes.
LA ROCHEFOUCAULD,
Maxims

4588. Those who are themselves incapable of great crimes, are ever backward to suspect others.
LA ROCHEFOUCAULD,
Maxims

4589. The contagion of crime is like that of the plague. Criminals collected together corrupt each other. They are worse than ever when, at the termination of their punishment, they return to society.   NAPOLEON

4590. The greater the man, the greater the crime.   *Proverb*

4591. Crimes may be secret, yet no secure.   *Proverb*

4592. Successful and fortunate crime is called virtue.   SENECA,
Hercules Furens

4593. With all his crimes broad blown, as flush as May.
SHAKESPEARE, *Hamlet*

4594.
If you bethink yourself of any crime
Unreconcil'd as yet to heaven and grace,
Solicit for it straight.
SHAKESPEARE, *Othello*

4595. And who are the greater criminals—those who sell the instruments of death, or those who buy them and use them?
ROBERT E. SHERWOOD,
Idiot's Delight

4596. This dim-seen track-mark of an ancient crime.   SOPHOCLES,
Oedipus Tyrannus

4597.
They, sweet soul, that most impute a crime
Are pronest to it, and impute themselves,
Wanting the mental range.
TENNYSON,
Idylls of the King

See also: 2222, 4243, 11652, 16075, 20604.

CRITICISM AND CRITICS

Related Subjects: Appreciation, Art, Censorship, Judge, Judgment, Opinion, Rebuke, Taste.

4601.
Men might be better if we better deemed

Of them. The worst way to improve the world
Is to condemn it.
PHILIP J. BAILEY, *Festus*

4602. The legitimate aim of criticism is to direct attention to the excellent. The bad will dig its own grave, and the imperfect may safely be left to that final neglect from which no amount of present undeserved popularity can rescue it.
C. N. BOVEE

4603. I think that the revelation of Divine wisdom in regard to books and plays will be even more interesting than the manifestation of heavenly standards in regard to souls. I am more eager to know whether Thackeray was actually greater than Dickens than I am to find out whether Henry Ford was on the whole a better citizen of the cosmos than Napoleon Bonaparte.
HEYWOOD BROUN,
The Last Review

4604. Is it in destroying and pulling down that skill is displayed? The shallowest understanding, the rudest hand, is more than equal to that task.
BURKE

4605. Silence is sometimes the severest criticism.
CHARLES BUXTON

4606. Criticism is futile because it puts a man on the defensive, and usually makes him strive to justify himself. Criticism is dangerous, because it wounds a man's precious pride, hurts his sense of importance, and arouses his resentment.
DALE CARNEGIE,
How to Win Friends

4607. It is much easier to be critical than to be correct.
DISRAELI

4608. The most noble criticism is that in which the critic is not the antagonist so much as the rival of the author.
DISRAELI

4609. The artist, without respect to medium, is interested in criticism because it is a form of public opinion. Also, because it *creates* public opinion.
JOHN GASSNER,
A Note on Criticism

4610. I would rather be attacked than unnoticed. For the worst thing you can do to an author is to be silent as to his works.
SAMUEL JOHNSON,
Boswell: Life

4611. Blown about with every wind of criticism.
SAMUEL JOHNSON,
Boswell: Life

4612. Criticism, as it was first instituted by Aristotle, was meant as a standard of judging well.
SAMUEL JOHNSON,
Boswell: Life

4613. Criticism is as often a trade as a science; requiring more health than wit, more labor than capacity, more practice than genius.
LA BRUYÈRE

4614. The pleasure of criticism takes from us that of being deeply moved by very beautiful things.
LA BRUYÈRE

4615. The strength of criticism lies only in the weakness of the thing criticised.
LONGFELLOW

4616. The opinion of the great body of the reading public, is very materially influenced even by the unsupported assertions of those who assume a right to criticise.
MACAULAY

4617. He who freely magnifies what hath been nobly done, and fears not to declare as freely what might be done better, gives ye the best covenant of his fidelity. MILTON

4618. There is more ado to interpret interpretations than to interpret the things, and more books upon books than upon all other subjects; we do nothing but comment upon one another. MONTAIGNE, *Essays*

4619. Every intellectual product must be judged from the point of view of the age and the people in which it was produced.
WALTER PATER,
The Renaissance

4620.
Some judge of authors' names, not works, and then
Nor praise nor blame the writing, but the men. POPE,
Essay on Criticism

4621. Ten censure wrong, for one that writes amiss. POPE,
Essay on Criticism

4622. Get your enemies to read your works in order to mend them; for your friend is so much your second self that he will judge too much like you. POPE

4623. Every one can keep house better than her mother 'til she trieth.
Proverb

4624. Criticism often takes from the tree caterpillars and blossoms together. J. P. RICHTER

4625. Criticism is the endeavor to find, to know, to love, to recommend, not only the best, but all the good, that has been known and thought and written in the world.
SAINTSBURY, *A History of Criticism*

4626. One of the commonest but most uncritical faults of criticism—the refusal to consider what it is that the author intended to give us.
SAINTSBURY, *Preface to Tom Jones*

4627. Happy are they that hear their detractions, and can put them to mending. SHAKESPEARE,
Much Ado About Nothing

4628. Of all mortals a critic is the silliest; for, inuring himself to examine all things, whether they are of consequence or not, he never looks upon anything but with a design of passing sentence upon it; by which means he is never a companion, but always a censor.
SIR RICHARD STEELE

4629. Of all the cants in this canting world, deliver me from the cant of criticism. STERNE

4630. I have ever held that the rod with which popular fancy invests criticism is properly the rod of divination: a hazel-switch for the discovery of buried treasure, not a birch-twig for the castigation of offenders.
ARTHUR SYMONS,
Introduction to the Study of Browning

4631. All criticism is dominated by the outworn theory that the man is the cause of the work as in the eyes of the law the criminal is the cause of the crime. Far rather are they both the effects.
PAUL VALÉRY,
Introduction to the Method of Leonardo da Vinci

4632. An age that has no criticism is either an age in which art is immobile, hieratic, and confined to the reproduction of formal types, or an age that possesses no art at all.
OSCAR WILDE, *The Critic as Artist*

Critics

4633. It is ridiculous for any man to criticise the works of another if he has not distinguished himself by his own performances.   ADDISON

4634. A true critick ought to dwell rather upon excellencies than imperfections, to discover the concealed beauties of a writer, and communicate to the world such things as are worth their observation.
ADDISON, *The Spectator*

4635. There is scarcely a good critic of books born in our age, and yet every fool thinks himself justified in criticising persons.
BULWER-LYTTON

4636.
He could distinguish and divide
A hair 'twixt south and southwest
side.   SAMUEL BUTLER, *Hudibras*

4637.
                              As soon
Seek roses in December, ice in June;
Hope constancy in wind, or corn in
chaff;
Believe a woman or an epitaph,
Or any other thing that's false, before
You trust in critics.   BYRON,
English Bards & Scotch Reviewers

4638. Reviewers are usually people who would have been poets, historians, biographers, if they could; they have tried their talents at one or the other and have failed; therefore they turn critics.   COLERIDGE,
Lectures on Shakespeare and Milton

4639. You know who critics are?—the men who have failed in literature and art.   DISRAELI, *Lothair*

4640.
He praised the Thing he understood;
'Twere well if every Critic would.
AUSTIN DOBSON,
The 'Squire at Vauxhall

4641. The good critic relates the adventures of his soul among works of art.   ANATOLE FRANCE

4642. The severest critics are always those who have either never attempted, or who have failed in original composition.   HAZLITT

4643. The man who acts the least, upbraids the most.   HOMER, *Iliad*

4644. It behooves the minor critic, who hunts for blemishes, to be a little distrustful of his own sagacity.
JUNIUS

4645.
O haud your hands frae inkhorns,
though a' the Muses woo;
For critics lie, like saumon fry, to
mak' their meals o' you.
CHARLES KINGSLEY, *The Oubit*

4646. The proper function of a critic is to save the tale from the artist who created it.   D. H. LAWRENCE

4647. Critics are sentinels in the grand army of letters, stationed at the corners of newspapers and reviews to challenge every new author.
LONGFELLOW

4648.
Nature fits all her children with something to do,
He who would write and can't write, can surely review.   LOWELL,
A Fable for Critics

4649. Every man is his own best critic. Whatever the learned say about a book, however unanimous they are in their praise of it, unless it interests you it is no business of yours.
SOMERSET MAUGHAM,
Books and You

4650. It is quite cruel that a poet cannot wander through his regions of enchantment without having a critic, forever, like the man of the sea, upon his back.   THOMAS MOORE

4651. He's the kind of a man that gets up a reputation for being clever and artistic by running down the very one particular thing that everyone likes, and cracking up some book or picture or play that no one has ever heard of.   FRANK NORRIS,
The Pit

4652. Critics are like brushers of other men's clothes.   *Proverb*

4653. Every fool can find faults that a great many wise men can't remedy.
Proverb

4654. For I am nothing if not critical.
SHAKESPEARE, *Othello*

4655.
The critic leaves at curtain fall
   To find, in starting to review it,
He scarcely saw the play at all
   For watching his reaction to it.
       E. B. WHITE, *Critic*

See also: 96, 97, 201, 528, 932, 2732, 2785, 2873, 4506, 5416, 6175.

CROSS

Related Subjects: The Bible, Burden, Christ.

4661.
Onward, Christian soldiers!
   Marching as to war,
With the cross of Jesus
   Going on before.
       S. BARING-GOULD,
Onward, Christian Soldiers

4662. Through this sign thou shalt conquer.   CONSTANTINE

4663.
       The Cross! . . . . . .
There, and there only, is the power
   to save.   COWPER,
The Progress of Error

4664. The cross is the ladder of heaven.   THOMAS DRAXE,
Bibliotheca

4665. Carry the cross patiently, and with perfect submission; and in the end it shall carry you.
       THOMAS À KEMPIS,
Of the Imitation of Christ

4666. Each cross hath its inscription.
Proverb

4667.
   The moon of Mahomet
   Arose, and it shall set;
While, blazoned as on heaven's immortal noon,
   The cross leads generations on.
       SHELLEY, *Hellas*

4668. There are no crown-wearers in heaven who were not cross-bearers here below.   C. H. SPURGEON,
Gleanings Among the Sheaves

4669. Christianity without the Cross is nothing. The Cross was the fitting close of a life of rejection, scorn, and defeat. But in no true sense have these things ceased or changed. Jesus is still He whom man despiseth, and the rejected of men.
       JAMES THOMSON,
The Great Argument

See also: 320, 2050, 2181, 3590.

CROW

Related Subject: Birds.

4671. The black crow thinketh her own birds white.
       GAVIN DOUGLAS, *Aeneis*

4672.
Even the blackest of them all, the
   crow,
Renders good service as your man-at-arms,
Crushing the beetle in his coat of mail

And crying havoc on the slug and
snail.   LONGFELLOW,
Birds of Killingworth

4673. Crows bewail the dead sheep,
and then eat them.   *Proverb*

4674. Crows are never the whiter for
washing themselves.   *Proverb*

4675. We'll pluck a crow together.
SHAKESPEARE,
The Comedy of Errors

4676.
The crow may bathe his coal-black
    wings in mire,
And unperceiv'd fly with the filth
    away;
But if the like the snow-white swan
    desire,
The stain upon his silver down will
    stay.   SHAKESPEARE,
The Rape of Lucrece

See also: 3703.

CROWD

Related Subject: The People.

4680. The multitude is always in the
wrong.
WENTWORTH DILLON,
Essay on Translated Verse

4681. I am a member of the rabble
in good standing.
WESTBROOK PEGLER,
The Lynching Story

4682. A crowd is not company.
Proverb

4683. Sea of upturned faces.
SCOTT, *Rob Roy*

4684.
Who o'er the herd would wish to
    reign,
Fantastic, fickle, fierce, and vain!
Vain as the leaf upon the stream,
And fickle as a changeful dream;

Fantastic as a woman's mood,
And fierce as Frenzy's fever'd blood.
Thou many-headed monster thing,
Oh who would wish to be thy King!
SCOTT, *The Lady of the Lake*

4685. The mutable, rank-scented
many.   SHAKESPEARE,
Coriolanus

4686. Many-headed multitude.
SIR PHILIP SIDNEY, *Arcadia*

See also: 360, 3662, 9692.

CROWN

**Related Subjects: Kings, Queen,
Throne.**

4691. There is a crown for us all
somewhere.   J. M. BARRIE,
Tommy and Grizel

4692. Many a crown covers bald
foreheads.
ELIZABETH B. BROWNING,
Aurora Leigh

4693. Every noble crown is, and on
earth will forever be, a crown of
thorns.   CARLYLE, *Past and Present*

4694.
       A crown! what is it?
It is to bear the miseries of a people!
To hear their murmurs, feel their dis-
    contents,
And sink beneath a load of splendid
    care!   HANNAH MORE, *Daniel*

4695. The royal crown cures not the
headache.   *Proverb*

4696. Uneasy lies the head that
wears a crown.   SHAKESPEARE,
Henry IV

4697.
My crown is in my heart, not on my
    head;
Not deck'd with diamonds and Indian
    stones,

Nor to be seen: my crown is call'd content;
A crown it is that seldom kings enjoy.
SHAKESPEARE, *Henry VI*

4698.
Upon my head they placed a fruitless crown,
And put a barren sceptre in my gripe,
Thence to be wrench'd with an un-lineal hand,
No son of mine succeeding.
SHAKESPEARE, *Macbeth*

4699.
For within the hollow crown
That rounds the mortal temples of a king
Keeps Death his court and there the antic sits,
Scoffing his state and grinning at his pomp. SHAKESPEARE, *Richard II*

4700. Woe to the Crown that doth the Cowl obey! WORDSWORTH, *Ecclesiastical Sonnets*

See also: 3023, 9665.

CRUELTY

Related Subjects: **Kindness, Persecution, Revenge, Savagery, Suffering, Tyranny, Wounds, Wrongs.**

4701. Cruelty and fear shake hands together. BALZAC

4702.
Man's inhumanity to man
Makes countless thousands mourn.
BURNS, *Man Was Made to Mourn*

4703.
I would not enter on my list of friends
The man who needlessly sets foot upon a worm. COWPER

4704.
Detested sport, that owes its pleasures to another's pain. COWPER

4705. Cruelty, like every other vice, requires no motive outside of itself; it only requires opportunity.
GEORGE ELIOT

4706. A man of cruelty is God's enemy. THOMAS FULLER, *Gnomologia*

4707. Cruelty ever proceeds from a vile mind, and often from a cowardly heart. SIR JOHN HARRINGTON, *Orlando Furioso*

4708. I believe, after experience and observation, that those people who identify themselves with animals, that is, the almost professional lovers of dogs, and other beasts, are capable of greater cruelty to human beings than those who do not identify themselves readily with animals.
ERNEST HEMINGWAY, *Death in the Afternoon*

4709. Cruelty is a tyrant that is always attended with fear. *Proverb*

4710. Cruelty is the first attribute of the devil. *Proverb*

4711. All cruelty springs from hardheartedness and weakness. SENECA

4712. I must be cruel, only to be kind.
SHAKESPEARE, *Hamlet*

4713. Let me be cruel, not unnatural.
SHAKESPEARE, *Hamlet*

4714.
Fill me from the crown to the toe, top-full
Of direst cruelty! make thick my blood;
Stop up the access and passage to remorse,
That no compunctious visitings of nature
Shake my fell purpose, nor keep peace between
The effect and it!
SHAKESPEARE, *Macbeth*

4715.

A stony adversary, an inhuman wretch
Uncapable of pity, void and empty
From any dram of mercy.
> SHAKESPEARE,
> *The Merchant of Venice*

4716.
I would find grievous ways to have thee slain,
Intense device, and superflux of pain.
> SWINBURNE, *Anactoria*

4717.
As ruthless as a baby with a worm,
As cruel as a school-boy.
> TENNYSON, *Walking to the Mail*

4718. I do not believe people are cruel because they are greedy; I am sure they invent greed as a pretext for cruelty.   REBECCA WEST,
> *I Believe*

See also: 904, 1147, 2836, 4487, 12824, 16310.

CRYING, see Tears

CUCKOLD

Related Subjects: Adultery, Deceit, Fidelity, Husband.

4721. Cuckolds, themselves are the very last that know it.   *Proverb*

4722. It's better to be a cold than a cuckold.   *Proverb*

4723. Call your husband cuckold in jest, and he'll never suspect you.
> *Proverb*

4724.
                That cuckold lives in bliss
Who, certain of his fate, loves not his wronger;
But, O, what damnèd minutes tells he o'er

Who dotes, yet doubts, suspects, yet strongly loves!
> SHAKESPEARE, *Othello*

See also: 25, 3669, 12538, 13486, 21208.

CUCKOO

Related Subjects: Birds, Spring.

4731. As scabbed as a cuckoo.
> *Proverb*

4732. The cuckoo builds not for himself.   SHAKESPEARE,
> *Antony and Cleopatra*

4733.
The cuckoo then, on every tree,
Mocks married men; for thus sings he, Cuckoo!
Cuckoo! Cuckoo! O word of fear,
Unpleasing to a married ear.
> SHAKESPEARE, *Love's Labour's Lost*

4734.
O Cuckoo! shall I call thee bird,
Or but a wandering voice?
> WORDSWORTH, *To the Cuckoo*

See also: 19102.

CULTURE

Related Subjects: Art, Civilization, Education, Knowledge, Learning, Refinement.

4741. Culture is "to know the best that has been said and thought in the world."   MATTHEW ARNOLD,
> *Literature and Dogma*

4742. Culture has one great passion —the passion for sweetness and light. It has one even yet greater, the passion for making them *prevail*.
> MATTHEW ARNOLD,
> *Culture and Anarchy*

4743. The great law of culture is: Let each become all that he was created capable of being.

CARLYLE, *Essays*

4744. Culture is one thing, and varnish another.   EMERSON, *Journals*

4745. Culture implies all that which gives the mind possession of its own powers; as languages to the critic, telescope to the astronomer.

EMERSON, *Letters and Social Aims*

4746. The triumph of culture is to overpower nationality.

EMERSON, *Lectures*

4747.
Rather than by your culture spoiled, Desist, and give us nature wild.

MATTHEW GREEN, *The Spleen*

4748. There was a time, not so long ago, when the stupid and uneducated aspired to be thought intelligent and cultured. The current of aspiration has changed its direction. It is not at all uncommon now to find intelligent and cultured people doing their best to feign stupidity and to conceal the fact that they have received an education.   ALDOUS HUXLEY, *Foreheads Villainous Low*

4749. The present condition of civilization makes it imperative that culture should be strengthened, even by the humblest. Until the modern mind learns to respect those who are trying to construct or create, rather than those who grab and destroy, there is no hope for Western civilization.

C. R. W. NEVINSON

4750. No man, however learned, can be called a cultured man while there remains an unbridged gap between his reading and his life.

J. C. POWYS,
The Meaning of Culture

4751. Culture is on the horns of this dilemma: if profound and noble it must remain rare, if common it must become mean.   SANTAYANA,
The Life of Reason

4752. Addison was more cultivated than Shakespeare; nevertheless Shakespeare is a finer source of culture than Addison.

ALLEN TATE, *Reactionary Essays*

4753. A culture cannot be consciously created. It is an available source of ideas that are imbedded in a complete and homogeneous society.

ALLEN TATE, *Reactionary Essays*

4754. Culture is the habit of being pleased with the best and knowing why.   HENRY VAN DYKE

4755. Those who find beautiful meanings in beautiful things are the cultivated. For these there is hope.

OSCAR WILDE,
The Picture of Dorian Gray

See also: 8898.

CUNNING

Related Subjects: Concealment, Deceit, Fox, Hypocrisy, Policy, Skill, Subtlety, Trickery.

4761. Cunning is only the mimic of discretion, and may pass upon weak men, as vivacity is often mistaken for wit, and gravity for wisdom.

ADDISON

4762. In things that a man would not be seen in himself, it is a point of cunning to borrow the name of the world; as to say, "The world says," or "There is a speech abroad."

BACON, *Of Cunning*

4763. It is a good point of cunning for a man to shape the answer he would have in his own words and propositions, for it makes the other party stick the less.   BACON, *Of Cunning*

4764. We take cunning for a sinister or crooked wisdom, and certainly there is a great difference between a cunning man and a wise man, not only in point of honesty, but in point of ability.   BACON, *Of Cunning*

4765. A cunning man overreaches no one half as much as himself.   H. W. BEECHER

4766. The weak in courage is strong in cunning.   BLAKE, *Proverbs of Hell*

4767. Cunning pays no regard to virtue, and is but the low mimic of wisdom.   BOLINGBROKE

4768. The very cunning conceal their cunning; the indifferently shrewd boast of it.   C. N. BOVEE

4769. There is a cunning which we in England call the turning of the cat in the pan.   BYRON, *Essays*

4770. The certain way to be cheated is to fancy one's self more cunning than others.   P. CHARRON

4771. We should do by our cunning as we do by our courage,—always have it ready to defend ourselves, never to offend others.   GREVILLE

4772. Cunning has effect from the credulity of others. It requires no extraordinary talents to lie and deceive.   SAMUEL JOHNSON

4773. In a great business there is nothing so fatal as cunning management.   JUNIUS

4774. Cunning is none of the best nor worst qualities; it floats between virtue and vice; there is scarce any exigence where it may not, and per-

haps ought not to be supplied by prudence.   LA BRUYÈRE

4775. Cunning leads to knavery. It is but a step from one to the other, and that very slippery. Only lying makes the difference; add that to cunning and it is knavery.
  LA BRUYÈRE

4776. The common practice of cunning is the sign of a small genius. It almost always happens that those who use it to cover themselves in one place, lay themselves open in another.
  LA ROCHEFOUCAULD, *Maxims*

4777. The greatest of all cunning is to seem blind to the snares which we know are laid for us; men are never so easily deceived as while they are endeavoring to deceive others.
  LA ROCHEFOUCAULD, *Maxims*

4778. Cunning is the ape of wisdom.   LOCKE

4779. It is a cunning part to play the fool well.   *Proverb*

4780. As cunning as Craddock & Co.   *Proverb*

4781. Springes to catch woodcocks.   SHAKESPEARE, *Hamlet*

4782.
A still-soliciting eye, and such a tongue
That I am glad I have not.
  SHAKESPEARE, *King Lear*

See also: 244, 927, 1860, 2604, 4412, 7540.

CUPID

Related Subjects: Courtship, Gods and Goddesses, Love, Mythology, Valentine.

4791.
        Archer's ever
Have two strings to a bow; and shall
  great Cupid

(Archer of archers both in men and
   women),
Be worse provided than a common
   archer?   GEORGE CHAPMAN,
                    Bussy d'Ambois

4792. The frivolous bolt of Cupid.
                MILTON, *Comus*

4793. It may be said of him that
Cupid hath clapped him o' the shoulder.   SHAKESPEARE,
                 As You Like It

4794.
This senior-junior, giant-dwarf, Dan
   Cupid;
Regent of love-rhymes, lord of folded
   arms,
The anointed sovereign of sighs and
   groans,
Liege of all loiterers and malcontents.
SHAKESPEARE, *Love's Labour's Lost*

4795.
Cupid is a knavish lad,
Thus to make poor females mad.
            SHAKESPEARE,
   A Midsummer-Night's Dream

4796.
Young Adam Cupid, he that shot so
   trim
When King Cophetua loved the beggar maid.   SHAKESPEARE,
            Romeo and Juliet

4797.
Sweet, rouse yourself; and the weak
   wanton Cupid
Shall from your neck unloose his
   amorous fold,
And, like a dewdrop from the lion's
   mane,
Be shook to air.
SHAKESPEARE, *Troilus and Cressida*

CURIOSITY

Related Subjects: Inquiry, Interest, Knowledge, Meddler, News,
Question.

4801. Too much curiosity lost Paradise.   MRS. APHRA BEHN,
              The Lucky Chance

4802. The first and simplest emotion
which we discover in the human mind,
is curiosity.   BURKE

4803. I loathe that low vice curiosity.
            BYRON, *Don Juan*

4804.
     Curiosity
Does, no less than devotion, pilgrims
   make.   ABRAHAM COWLEY,
        *Ode on a Chair Made of
        Sir Francis Drake's Ship*

4805. Curiosity is a kernel of the
forbidden fruit which still sticketh
in the throat of a natural man, sometimes to the danger of his choking.
            THOMAS FULLER

4806. Curiosity is little more than
another name for hope.
        A. W. & J. C. HARE,
            Guesses at Truth

4807. Curiosity is one of the permanent and certain characteristics of a
vigorous mind.
   SAMUEL JOHNSON, *The Rambler*

4808. The gratification of curiosity
rather frees us from uneasiness, than
confers pleasure. We are more pained
by ignorance than delighted by instruction. Curiosity is the thirst of
the soul.   SAMUEL JOHNSON,
               The Rambler

4809. There are different kinds of
curiosity; one of interest, which
causes us to learn that which would
be useful to us; and the other of

pride, which springs from a desire to know that of which others are ignorant. LA ROCHEFOUCAULD, *Maxims*

4810. Avoid him who, for mere curiosity, asks three questions running about a thing that cannot interest him. LAVATER

4811. Curiosity in children is but an appetite for knowledge. One great reason why children abandon themselves wholly to silly pursuits and trifle away their time insipidly is because they find their curiosity balked, and their inquiries neglected. LOCKE

4812. No state sorrier than that of the man who keeps up a continual round, and pries into "the secrets of the nether world," as saith the poet, and is curious in conjecture of what is in his neighbour's heart. MARCUS AURELIUS, *Meditations*

4813. The over curious are not over wise. MASSINGER

4814.
Eve, with all the fruits of Eden blest, Save only one, rather than leave that one unknown,
Lost all the rest. THOMAS MOORE

4815. A person who is too nice an observer of the business of the crowd, like one who is too curious in observing the labor of bees, will often be stung for his curiosity. POPE

4816. Curiosity will conquer fear even more than bravery will; indeed it has led many people into dangers which mere physical courage would shudder away from, for hunger and love and curiosity are the great impelling forces of life.
JAMES STEPHENS, *The Crock of Gold*

4817. Curiosity is the direct incontinency of the spirit.
JEREMY TAYLOR, *Holy Living*

4818. Curiosity is as much the parent of attention as attention is of memory. RICHARD WHATELY

4819. You know what a woman's curiosity is. Almost as great as a man's! OSCAR WILDE, *An Ideal Husband*

See also: 541, 15892.

CURSE

Related Subjects: Abuse, Insult, Offence, Slander, Swearing, Threat.

4821.
Curse away!
And let me tell thee, Beauseant, a wise proverb
The Arabs have,—"Curses are like young chickens,
And still come home to roost."
BULWER-LYTTON, *The Lady of Lyons*

4822. And oftentimes such cursing wrongfully returneth again to him that curseth, as a bird that returneth again to his own nest.
CHAUCER, *The Personnes Tale*

4823. Curse and be cursed! it is the fruit of cursing.
JOHN FLETCHER, *Rollo*

4824. I shall curse you with book and bell and candle.
SIR THOMAS MALORY, *Morte d'Arthur*

4825. To curse with bell, book, and candle. *Proverb*

4826.
Therefore be gone,
Without our grace, our love, our benizon. SHAKESPEARE, *King Lear*

4827. Out, damned spot! out, I say.
SHAKESPEARE, *Macbeth*

4828.
Let this pernicious hour
Stand aye accursed in the calendar.
SHAKESPEARE, *Macbeth*

4829. Curses, not loud but deep.
SHAKESPEARE, *Macbeth*

See also: 1713, 2122, 2851, 3359, 17815, 17963.

CUSTOM

Related Subjects: Commerce, Conventionality, Fashion, Habit, Precedent, Society.

4831. We think according to nature; we speak according to rules; we act according to custom.   BACON,
De Augmentis Scientiarum

4832.
     What custom hath endeared
We part with sadly, though we prize
   it not.   JOANNA BAILLIE, *Basil*

4833. Custom reconciles us to everything.   BURKE,
On the Sublime and Beautiful

4834.
Cast away the bondage and the fear
Of rotten custom.
HARTLEY COLERIDGE, *Sonnets*

4835.
Custom, that unwritten law,
By which the people keep even kings
   in awe.
SIR WILLIAM D'AVENANT, *Circe*

4836. Customs may not be as wise as laws, but they are always more popular.   DISRAELI

4837. The interrogation of custom at all points is an inevitable stage in the growth of every superior mind.
EMERSON, *Representative Men*

4838. Custom meets us at the cradle and leaves us only at the tomb.
ROBERT INGERSOLL, *Individuality*

4839. Long customs are not easily broken; he that attempts to change the course of his own life very often labors in vain.
SAMUEL JOHNSON, *Rasselas*

4840. The despotism of custom is everywhere the standing hindrance to human advancement.
JOHN STUART MILL, *On Liberty*

4841. The laws of conscience, which we pretend to be derived from nature, proceed from custom.
MONTAIGNE, *Essays*

4842. Nothing is stronger than custom.   OVID, *The Art of Love*

4843. Bad customs are better broke than kept up.   *Proverb*

4844. Custom is the plague of wise men and the idol of fools.   *Proverb*

4845.
     Custom calls me to 't:
What custom wills, in all things should we do 't.
SHAKESPEARE, *Coriolanus*

4846.
But to my mind, though I am native
   here
And to the manner born,—it is a custom
More honoured in the breach than the observance.
SHAKESPEARE, *Hamlet*

4847. Custom hath made it in him a property of easiness.
SHAKESPEARE, *Hamlet*

4848.
     New Customs,
Though they be never so ridiculous,
Nay, let 'em be unmanly, yet are follow'd.   SHAKESPEARE,
Henry VIII.

4849. What we call necessary insitutions are often no more than institutions to which we have grown accustomed.   DE TOCQUEVILLE

See also: 85, 2610, 3050, 3303, 20485.

CYNICISM, CYNICS

Related Subjects: Doubt, Misanthropy, Mockery, Pessimism, Sneer, Worldliness.

4851. The cynic is one who never sees a good quality in a man, and never fails to see a bad one. He is the human owl, vigilant in darkness and blind to light, mousing for vermin, and never seeing noble game.
H. W. BEECHER

4852. It will generally be found that those who sneer habitually at human nature, and affect to despise it, are among its worst and least pleasant examples.   DICKENS

4853. A cynic can chill and dishearten with a single word.
EMERSON, Society and Solitude

4854. Don't be a cynic and bewail and bemoan.   EMERSON

4855. If to look truth in the face and not resent it when it's unpalatable . . . is to be cynical, then I suppose I'm a cynic.
SOMERSET MAUGHAM,
The Back of Beyond

4856. Cynicism is intellectual dandyism.   GEORGE MEREDITH,
The Egoist

4857. I hate cynicism a great deal worse than I do the devil; unless, perhaps, the two were the same thing?
STEVENSON, Walt Whitman

4858. What is a cynic? A man who knows the price of everything, and the value of nothing.
OSCAR WILDE,
Lady Windermere's Fan

D

DANCING

Related Subjects: Amusement, Feast, Jazz, Joy, Merriment, Music.

4861.
On with the dance! let joy be unconfined;
No sleep till morn, when Youth and Pleasure meet
To chase the glowing hours with flying feet.   BYRON,
Childe Harold

4862.
Imperial Waltz! imported from the Rhine
Famed for the growth of pedigrees and wine),
Long be thine import from all duty free,

And hock itself be less esteem'd than thee.   BYRON, The Waltz

4863.
Endearing Waltz—to thy more melting tune
Bow Irish jig, and ancient rigadoon,
Scotch reels, avaunt! and country-dance forego
Your future claims to each fantastic toe!
Waltz—Waltz alone—both legs and arms demands,
Liberal of feet, and lavish of her hands.   BYRON, The Waltz

4864.
Hot from the hands promiscuously applied,
Round the slight waist, or down the glowing side.   BYRON, The Waltz

4865. Dancing is the loftiest, the most moving, the most beautiful of the arts, because it is no mere translation or abstraction from life; it is life itself.
HAVELOCK ELLIS, *The Dance of Life*

4866.
To brisk notes in cadence beating
Glance their many-twinkling feet.
THOMAS GRAY, *Progress of Poesy*

4867.
And the dancing has begun now,
And the dancers whirl round gaily
In the waltz's giddy mazes,
And the ground beneath them
trembles. HEINE, *Book of Songs*

4868.
Deborah danced, when she was two,
As buttercups and daffodils do.
MRS. JOYCE KILMER, *Experience*

4869.
Merrily, merrily whirled the wheels of the dizzying dances
Under the orchard-trees and down
the path to the meadows;
Old folk and young together, and
children mingled among them.
LONGFELLOW, *Evangeline*

4870.
My men, like satyrs grazing on the
lawn,
Shall with their goat feet dance the
antic hay.
CHRISTOPHER MARLOWE, *Edward II*

4871.
Come, knit hands, and beat the
ground
In a light fantastic round.
MILTON, *Comus*

4872.
Come and trip it as ye go,
On the light fantastic toe.
MILTON, *L'Allegro*

4873. Dancing in the chequer'
shade MILTON, *L'Allegr*

4874. Dancing in all its forms can
not be excluded from the curriculur
of all noble education: dancing wit
the feet, with ideas, with words, and
need I add that one must also be abl
to dance with the pen?
NIETZSCHE,
The Twilight of the Idol

4875.
Others import yet nobler arts from
France,
Teach kings to fiddle, and make sen
ates dance. POPE, *Duncia*

4876. When you go to dance, tak
heed whom you take by the hand.
Prover

4877.
They have measured many a mil
To tread a measure with you on thi
grass.
SHAKESPEARE, *Love's Labour's Los*

4878.
He capers nimbly in a lady's chambe
To the lascivious pleasing of a lute.
SHAKESPEARE, *Richard II*

4879. For you and I are past ou
dancing days.
SHAKESPEARE, *Romeo and Julie*

4880.
Come unto these yellow sands,
And then take hands:
Courtsied when you have, and kiss'
The wild waves whist.
SHAKESPEARE, *The Tempes*

4881.
When you do dance, I wish you
A wave o' the sea, that you migh
ever do
Nothing but that.
SHAKESPEARE, *The Winter's Tal*

4882. It is no small thing to have played for mankind to dance.
RICHARD SPECHT, *of Johann Strauss*

See also: 1441, 5901.

DANGER

Related Subjects: Adventure, Boldness, Risk, Warning.

4891. Dangers bring fears, and fears more dangers bring.
RICHARD BAXTER,
Love Breathing Thanks

4892.
Oh pilot, 'tis a fearful night!
There's danger on the deep.
T. H. BAYLY, *The Pilot*

4893.
I have not quailed to danger's brow
When high and happy—need I now?
BYRON, *The Giaour*

4894. In extreme danger, fear turns a deaf ear to every feeling of pity.
CAESAR, *Commentaries*

4895. Danger, the spur of all great minds.
GEORGE CHAPMAN, *Bussy d'Ambois*

4896. As soon as there is life there is danger. EMERSON, *Lectures*

4897.
Danger gleams
Like sunshine to a brave man's eyes.
EURIPIDES, *Iphigenia in Tauris*

4898. Dangers foreseen are the sooner prevented.
RICHARD FRANCK,
Northern Memoirs

4899. He that bringeth himself into needless dangers, dieth the devil's martyr. THOMAS FULLER, *Holy War*

4900.
See what perils do environ
Those who meddle with hot iron.
GALSWORTHY

4901. Great perils have this beauty, that they bring to light the fraternity of strangers.
VICTOR HUGO, *Les Miserables*

4902.
Ye gentlemen of England
That live at home at ease,
Ah! little do you think upon
The dangers of the seas.
MARTYN PARKER, *Song*

4903.
'Twas a dangerous cliff, as they
freely confessed,
Though to walk near its crest was
so pleasant,
But over its terrible edge there had
slipped
A Duke and full many a peasant,
So the people said something would
have to be done,
But their projects did not at all
tally.
Some said: "Put a fence round the
edge of the cliff."
Some: "An ambulance down in the
valley." JOSEPH MALINES

4904. If thy hand be in a lion's mouth, get it out as fast as thou canst. *Proverb*

4905. The danger past and God forgotten. *Proverb*

4906. Beware of a silent dog and still water. *Proverb*

4907. He that seeks danger perisheth therein unpitied. *Proverb*

4908. Better face a danger once than be always in fear. *Proverb*

4909. Dangers are overcome by dangers. *Proverb*

4910. Constant exposure to dangers will breed contempt for them.

SENECA, *De Providentia*

4911. Blind panic is incapable of providing even for its own safety, for it does not avoid danger but runs away. Yet we are more exposed to danger when we turn our backs.

SENECA, *Epistulae ad Lucilium*

4912. No one can with safety expose himself often to danger. The man who has often escaped is caught at last.   SENECA, *Hercules Furens*

4913. Out of this nettle, danger, we pluck this flower, safety.

SHAKESPEARE, *Henry IV*

4914. The path is smooth that leadeth on to danger.

SHAKESPEARE, *Venus and Adonis*

See also: 507, 1690, 1806, 4131, 4284, 4346, 4356, 4482, 4488, 5916, 11565.

DARING, see Boldness

DARKNESS

Related Subjects: Black, Blindness, Ignorance, Night, Nothingness, Oblivion, Obscurity, Shadow, Sight.

4921. Ask what is darkness of the night.   PHILIP J. BAILEY, *Festus*

4922. Darkness which may be felt.
Bible: Exodus, x, 21

4923. Darkness is more productive of sublime ideas than light.

BURKE,
On the Sublime and Beautiful

4924.
Cabin'd, cribb'd, confined
And bred in darkness.
BYRON, *Childe Harold*

4925.
The waves were dead; the tides were in their grave,
The Moon, their Mistress, had expired before;
The winds were wither'd in the stagnant air,
And the clouds perish'd; darkness had no need
Of aid from them—she was the Universe.   BYRON, *Darkness*

4926.
Come, blessed Darkness, come and bring thy balm
For eyes grown weary of the garish day!
JULIA C. R. DORR, *Darkness*

4927.
O radiant Dark! O darkly fostered ray!
Thou hast a joy too deep for shallow Day.   GEORGE ELIOT,
The Spanish Gypsy

4928. Darkness of slumber and death, forever sinking and sinking.
LONGFELLOW, *Evangeline*

4929.
Lo! darkness bends down like a mother of grief
On the limitless plain, and the fall of her hair
It has mantled a world.
JOAQUIN MILLER, *From Sea to Sea*

4930.
Yet from those flames
No light, but rather darkness visible.
MILTON, *Paradise Lost*

4931. And all around was darkness like a wall.   WILLIAM MORRIS,
Life and Death of Jason

4932. Got home well by coach, though as dark as pitch.
SAMUEL PEPYS, *Diary*

4933. Darkness there, and nothing more.   POE, *The Raven*

4934. He that runs in the dark may well stumble.   *Proverb*

4935. As dark as pitch.   *Proverb*

4936. It was so dark, Hal, that thou couldst not see thy hand.
     SHAKESPEARE, *Henry IV*

4937.
       The charm dissolves apace,
And as the morning steals upon the night,
Melting the darkness, so their rising senses
Begin to chase the ignorant fumes that mantle
Their clearer reason.
     SHAKESPEARE, *The Tempest*

4938. I'm afraid to go home in the dark.
     WILLIAMS-VAN ALYSTYNE, *Song*

See also: 1709, 3056, 3077, 13253.

DAUGHTER

Related Subjects: **Family, Father, Girl, Maid, Mother.**

4941.
To a father waxing old nothing is dearer than a daughter. Sons have spirits of higher pitch, but less inclined to sweet, endearing fondness.
     EURIPIDES

4942. A daughter is an embarrassing and ticklish possession.   MENANDER

4943. Fathers, I think, are most apt to appreciate the excellence and attainments of their daughters; mothers, those of their sons.   MENANDER

4944. Marry your daughters betimes, lest they marry themselves.
     Proverb

4945. It is harder to marry a daughter well, than to bring her up well.
     Proverb

4946. O Jephthah, judge of Israel, what a treasure hadst thou!
     SHAKESPEARE, *Hamlet*

4947.
One fair daughter and no more,
The which he loved passing well.
     SHAKESPEARE, *Hamlet*

4948.
Trust not your daughters' minds
By what you see them act.
     SHAKESPEARE, *Othello*

4949.
Thou art thy mother's glass, and she in thee
Calls back the lovely April of her prime.   SHAKESPEARE, *Sonnet III*

4950.
Leodogran, the King of Cameliard
Had one fair daughter and none other child;
Guinevere, and in her his sole delight.
     TENNYSON, *Idylls of the King*

See also: 1571, 1725, 1803, 3236, 4455, 6385.

DAWN

Related Subjects: **Day, Morning, Sunrise.**

4951.
       Yet, behind the night,
Waits for the great unborn, somewhere afar,
Some white tremendous daybreak.
     RUPERT BROOKE, *Second Best*

4952.
Day!
Faster and more fast,
O'er night's brim, day boils at last;
Boils, pure gold, o'er the cloud-cup's brim.   BROWNING, *Pippa Passes*

4953.
On the road to Mandalay
Where the flyin'-fishes play
   An' the dawn comes up like thunder outer
China 'crost the Bay!
                 KIPLING, *Mandalay*

4954.
Out of the shadows of night
The world rolls into light;
It is daybreak everywhere.
LONGFELLOW, *The Bells of San Blas*

4955.
But, look, the morn in russet mantle clad,
Walks o'er the dew of yon high eastern hill.   SHAKESPEARE, *Hamlet*

4956.
The glow-worm shows the matin to be near,
And 'gins to pale his uneffectual fire.
            SHAKESPEARE, *Hamlet*

4957.
Night's candles are burnt out, and jocund day
Stands tiptoe on the misty mountaintops.
SHAKESPEARE, *Romeo and Juliet*

4958. For what human ill does not dawn seem to be an alleviation?
         THORNTON WILDER,
      The Bridge of San Luis Rey

See also: 479, 1733.

DAY

Related Subjects: Dawn, Evening, Hours, Light, Morning, Night, Noon, Sun, Time.

4961.
Day is a snow-white Dove of heaven
   That from the East glad message brings.
     T. B. ALDRICH, *Day and Night*

4962. When shall I see those halcyon days?   ARISTOPHANES, *The Clouds*

4963. The long days are no happier than the short ones.
       PHILIP J. BAILEY, *Festus*

4964. My days are swifter than a weaver's shuttle.
          Bible: Job, vii, 6

4965. Days should speak and multitude of years should teach wisdom.
        Bible: Job, xxxii, 7

4966. Day unto day uttereth speech, and night unto night showeth knowledge.   *Bible: Psalms, xix, 2*

4967.
Tenderly, day that I have loved, I close your eyes,
And smooth your quiet brow, and fold your thin dead hands.
       RUPERT BROOKE,
      Day That I Have Loved

4968.
So here hath been dawning
   Another blue day:
Think, wilt thou let it
   Slip useless away?
          CARLYLE, *Today*

4969. All comes out even at the end of the day.
   Quoted by WINSTON CHURCHILL

4970.
Daughters of Time, the hypocrite Days,
Muffled and dumb like barefoot dervishes,
And marching single in an endless file,
Bring diadems and fagots in their hands.   EMERSON, *Days*

4971.
The curfew tolls the knell of parting day,
   The lowing herd wind slowly o'er the lea,

The ploughman homeward plods his
    weary way
    And leaves the world to darkness
    and to me.
    THOMAS GRAY, *Elegy Written in
        a Country Churchyard*

4972. Hide me from day's garish
eye.   MILTON, *Il Penseroso*

4973.
How troublesome is day!
It calls us from our sleep away;
It bids us from our pleasant dreams
    awake,
And sends us forth to keep or break
Our promises to pay.
           T. L. PEACOCK,
       How Troublesome is Day

4974. A bad day never hath a good
night.   *Proverb*

4975.
         O, such a day,
So fought, so follow'd and so fairly
won.   SHAKESPEARE, *Henry IV*

4976.
The sun is in the heaven, and the
    proud day,
Attended with the pleasures of the
    world,
Is all too wanton.
         SHAKESPEARE, *King John*

4977. What hath this day deserved?
    what hath it done
That it in golden letters should be set
Among the high tides in the calen-
    dar?   SHAKESPEARE, *King John*

4978. In the posteriors of this day,
which the rude multitude call the
afternoon.
SHAKESPEARE, *Love's Labour's Lost*

4979. We burn daylight.
           SHAKESPEARE,
    The Merry Wives of Windsor

4980. He makes a July's day short as
December.
SHAKESPEARE, *The Winter's Tale*

4981. There is nothing more universally commended than a fine day; the
reason is that people can commend
it without envy.   W. SHENSTONE

4982.
A day can prostrate and upraise again
All that is human.   SOPHOCLES, *Ajax*

4983.
I hate the day, because it lendeth light
To see all things, and not my love to
    see. EDMUND SPENSER, *Daphnaida*

4984.
But the tender grace of a day that is
    dead
Will never come back to me.
    TENNYSON, *Break, Break, Break*

4985. A life that leads melodious
    days.   TENNYSON, *In Memoriam*

4986. One of those heavenly days
that cannot die.
         WORDSWORTH, *Nutting*

See also: 142, 865, 1443, 1762, 1904,
3235, 21861.

DEAFNESS

**Related Subjects: Ears, Silence,
Sound.**

4991. He is as deaf as a door.
           NICHOLAS BRETON

4992. None so deaf as those that will
not hear.
MATTHEW HENRY, *Commentaries*

4993. Your tale, sir, would cure
deafness.
        SHAKESPEARE, *The Tempest*

4994. He tells his story to a deaf
ear.
     TERENCE, *Heauton Timorumenos*

DEATH

Related Subjects: Accident, Decay, Disease, End, Epitaphs, Eternity, Fate, Funeral, Grave, Grief, Hell, Kill, Mortality, Murder, Paradise, Poison, Salvation, Skull, Suicide, Tragedy, War.

5001.
O Death the Healer, scorn thou not,
    I pray,
To come to me: of cureless ills thou
    art
The one physician. Pain lays not its
    touch
Upon a corpse.   AESCHYLUS

5002.
When we are dead we shan't thank
    for flowers,
We shan't hear the parson preaching
    for hours,
We shan't be sorry to be white bare
    bone
At last we shan't be hungry and can
    sleep alone.
          AUDEN & ISHERWOOD,
              The Dog Beneath the Skin

5003. Men fear death as children
fear to go in the dark; and as that
natural fear in children is increased
with tales, so is the other.
          BACON, *Of Death*

5004. The valley of the shadow of
death.   *Bible: Psalms, xxiii, 4*

5005. O death, where is thy sting? O
grave, where is thy victory?
          Bible: I Corinthians, xv, 55

5006.
The door of Death is made of gold,
That mortal eyes cannot behold.
          BLAKE

5007. Death has shaken out the sands
of thy glass.   JOHN BRAINARD,
              Lament for Long Tom

5008.
Blow out, you bugles, over the rich
    dead!
    There's none of these so lonely
        and poor of old,
But, dying, has made us rarer gifts
    than gold.
          RUPERT BROOKE, *The Dead*

5009. The worst friend and enemy is
but Death.   RUPERT BROOKE, *Peace*

5010.
Fear death?—to feel the fog in my
    throat,
    The mist in my face.
          BROWNING, *Prospice*

5011. So he passed over, and all the
trumpets sounded for him on the
other side.
          BUNYAN, *Pilgrim's Progress*

5012. The whole life of some people
is a kind of partial death—a long,
lingering death-bed, so to speak, of
stagnation and nonentity on which
death is but the seal, or solemn signing, as the abnegation of all further
act and deed on the part of the
signed.
          SAMUEL BUTLER, *Note Books*

5013. Death, the sable smoke where
vanishes the flame.
          BYRON, *Childe Harold*

5014. Heaven gives its favourites—
early death.
          BYRON, *Childe Harold*

5015.
I die,—but first I have possess'd,
And come what may, I *have been*
    bless'd.   BYRON, *The Giaour*

5016. "Whom the gods love die
young," was said of yore.
          BYRON, *Don Juan*

5017.
Death, so called, is a thing which
    makes men weep,

And yet a third of life is passed in
   sleep.   Byron, *Don Juan*

5018. He who fears death has already lost the life he covets.
        Cato The Censor

5019. Saved from outrage worse
than death.   Coleridge, *Love*

5020.
Ere sin could blight or sorrow fade,
   Death came with friendly care;
The opening bud to heaven conveyed,
   And bade it blossom there.
   Coleridge, *Epitaph on an Infant*

5021.
Deep in my heart I thought with
   pride,
"I know a person who has died."
Frances Cornford, *A Recollection*

5022. I shall ask leave to desist,
when I am interrupted by so great
an experiment as dying.
    Sir William D'Avenant

5023.
Afraid? Of whom am I afraid?
Not death; for who is he?
The porter of my father's lodge
As much abasheth me.
      Emily Dickinson,
        Time and Eternity

5024.
That short, potential stir
That each can make but once,
That bustle so illustrious
'Tis almost consequence,
Is the *eclat* of death.
      Emily Dickinson,
        Time and Eternity

5025.
One short sleep past, we wake eternally;
And death shall be no more; death,
   thou shalt die.
      John Donne, *Death*

5026.
So softly death succeeded life in her,
She did but dream of heaven, and she
   was there.   Dryden, *Eleonora*

5027.
Death in itself is nothing; but we fear
To be we know not what, we know
   not where.   Dryden, *Aurengzebe*

5028.
I, who exulted in sunshine and laughter,
Dreamed not of dying—death is such
   waste of me!   Galsworthy,
        Valley of the Shadow

5029. What is to cease breathing, but
to free the breath from its restless
tides, that it may rise and expand and
seek God unencumbered?
    Kahlil Gibran, *The Prophet*

5030. Death is never at a loss for occasions.   *Greek Anthology*

5031. Death borders upon our birth,
and our cradle stands in the grave.
    Bishop Hall, *Epistles*

5032.
Death rides on every passing breeze,
   He lurks in every flower.
Each season has its own disease,
   Its peril every hour!
   Reginald Heber, *At a Funeral*

5033.
   Leaves have their time to fall,
And flowers to wither at the north-
   wind's breath,
   And stars to set;—but all,
Thou hast *all* seasons for thine own,
   O Death!
   Mrs. Hemans, *The Hour of Death*

5034.
The ways of Death are soothing and
   serene,
And all the words of Death are
   grave and sweet.
      W. E. Henley,
      In Memoriam R.G.C.B.

5035.
I have been half in love with easeful
  Death,
Call'd him soft names in many a
  mused rhyme.
          KEATS, *Ode to a Nightingale*

5036.
When Earth's last picture is painted,
  and the tubes are twisted and dried,
When the oldest colours have faded,
  and the youngest critic has died,
We shall rest, and, faith, we shall
  need it—lie down for an aeon or
  two,
Till the Master of All Good Workmen shall put us to work anew.
                    KIPLING,
When Earth's Last Picture is Painted

5037. Wheresoever ye be, death will
overtake you, although ye be in lofty
towers.   *The Koran*

5038.
                    Gone before
To that unknown and silent shore.
          CHARLES LAMB, *Hester*

5039. Our birth may be "a sleep and
a forgetting," but not our death.
Death releases us from the barrier of
the flesh, introduces us to the glorious company of those who have
gone before and opens out a majestic
vista of love and service.
          SIR OLIVER LODGE,
              Demonstrated Survival

5040. Death is not a foe, but an inevitable adventure.
              SIR OLIVER LODGE

5041.
There is no Death! What seems so
    is transition;
  This life of mortal breath
Is but a suburb of the life elysian,
  Whose portal we call Death.
          LONGFELLOW, *Resignation*

5042. The long mysterious Exodus
of death.   LONGFELLOW,
    The Jewish Cemetery at Newport

5043. This goin' ware glory waits ye
haint one agreeable feetur.
          LOWELL, *The Biglow Papers*

5044.
Around, around the sun we go:
The moon goes round the earth.
We do not die of death:
We die of vertigo.
          ARCHIBALD MACLEISH,
              Mother Goose's Garland

5045. A man's dying is more the sur-
vivors' affair than his own.
              THOMAS MANN,
                  The Magic Mountain

5046. The only religious way to
think of death is as part and parcel of
life; to regard it, with the understanding and the emotions, as the in-
violable condition of life.
              THOMAS MANN,
                  The Magic Mountain

5047. Death, like generation, is a
secret of Nature.
          MARCUS AURELIUS, *Meditations*

5048. Think not disdainfully of
death, but look on it with favour;
for even death is one of the things
that Nature wills.
          MARCUS AURELIUS, *Meditations*

5049.
Cut is the branch that might have
    grown full straight,
And burnéd is Apollo's laurel bough,
That sometime grew within this
    learned man.
          CHRISTOPHER MARLOWE, *Faustus*

5050.
And may we find, when ended is the
    page,
Death but a tavern on our pilgrimage.
          JOHN MASEFIELD, *The Word*

5051. Death hath a thousand doors to let out life.
MASSINGER, *A Very Woman*

5052. Death . . . on his pale horse.
MILTON, *Paradise Lost*

5053. Death's but one more to-morrow. SILAS W. MITCHELL,
Of One Who Seemed to Have Failed

5054.
So we must part, my body, you and I
  Who've spent so many pleasant years together.
'Tis sorry work to lose your company
Who clove to me so close.
COSMO MONKHOUSE,
Any Soul to Any Body

5055. Death is in such strange contradiction to life that it is no matter for wonder that we recoil from it, and turn to remembrances, and find recompense in perceiving that those we have loved live in our memories as intensely as if they were still before our eyes. GEORGE MOORE, *Ave*

5056. In dying I would offer men the richest of my gifts. It was from the sun I learned that, from the sun which when it sets is so rich; out of its inexhaustible riches it flings gold into the sea, so that the poorest fishermen row with golden oars.
NIETZSCHE

5057. Death is nothing. It is only the divine will to remove us from this world of suffering and none can slip either to right or left.
NOGUCHI, *Eckstein: Noguchi*

5058. It makes death more real and imminent to see one's near relations grown old; for brothers and sisters are, as a general rule, only real to us when they are children.
LIAM O'FLAHERTY, *Two Years*

5059.
Life's race well run,
Life's work well done,
Life's victory won,
  Now cometh rest.
E. H. PARKER,
Funeral Ode on James A. Garfield

5060. A dead man cannot bite.
PLUTARCH, *Lives*

5061. As Caesar was at supper the discourse was of death,—which sort was the best. "That," said he, "which is unexpected." PLUTARCH, *Lives*

5062. If death be terrible, the fault is not in death, but thee. *Proverb*

5063. I know of nobody that has a mind to die this year. *Proverb*

5064. Dying is as natural as living.
Proverb

5065. Old men go to death; but death comes to young men. *Proverb*

5066. When you die, your trumpeter will be buried. *Proverb*

5067. He that died half a year ago is as dead as Adam. *Proverb*

5068. He hath liv'd ill that knows not how to die well. *Proverb*

5069. As dead as a door nail.
Proverb

5070. Death and the grave make no distinction of persons. *Proverb*

5071. Death's day is doom's day.
Proverb

5072. I am going to leap into the dark. Let down the curtain. The farce is over. RABELAIS, *On His Deathbed*

5073. Is it so great an ill merely to cease to live? RACINE, *Phèdre*

5074.
I cannot say, and I will not say
That he is dead.—He is just away!
JAMES WHITCOMB RILEY, *Away*

5075. Death sends a radiogram every day. When I want you I'll drop in— and then one day he comes with a master-key and lets himself in and says: We'll go now.
CARL SANDBURG,
Death Snips Proud Men

5076. Death seems to provide the minds of the Anglo-Saxon race with a greater fund of innocent amusement than any other single subject.
DOROTHY L. SAYERS,
Preface: The Third Omnibus of Crime

5077.
Sleep the sleep that knows not breaking,
Morn of toil, nor night of waking.
SCOTT, *The Lady of the Lake*

5078.
I have a rendezvous with Death
At some disputed barricade,
When Spring comes back with rustling shade
And apple-blossoms fill the air.
ALAN SEEGER,
I Have a Rendezvous With Death

5079. They'll give him death by inches. SHAKESPEARE, *Coriolanus*

5080.
To die,—to sleep,—
No more, and by a sleep to say we end
The heart-ache and the thousand natural shocks
That flesh is heir to,—'t is a consummation
Devoutly to be wished.
SHAKESPEARE, *Hamlet*

5081. Dead, for a ducat, dead!
SHAKESPEARE, *Hamlet*

5082.
All that live must die,
Passing through nature to eternity.
SHAKESPEARE, *Hamlet*

5083.
This fell sergeant, death,
Is strict in his arrest.
SHAKESPEARE, *Hamlet*

5084. The end of life cancels all bands. SHAKESPEARE, *Henry IV*

5085. A man can die but once.
SHAKESPEARE, *Henry IV*

5086. Death, as the Psalmist saith, is certain to all; all shall die. How a good yoke of bullocks at Stamford fair? SHAKESPEARE, *Henry IV*

5087. How many of mine old acquaintances are dead!
SHAKESPEARE, *Henry IV*

5088. He dies, and makes no sign.
SHAKESPEARE, *Henry VI*

5089. Just death, kind umpire of men's miseries.
SHAKESPEARE, *Henry VI*

5090.
Cowards die many times before their deaths;
The valiant never taste of death but once.
Of all the wonders that I yet have heard,
It seems to me most strange that men should fear;
Seeing that death, a necessary end,
Will come when it will come.
SHAKESPEARE, *Julius Caesar*

5091. O, amiable lovely death!
SHAKESPEARE, *King John*

5092.
There is no sure foundation set on blood,
No certain life achiev'd by others' death. SHAKESPEARE, *King John*

5093.

Vex not his ghost: O! let him pass!
he hates him
That would upon the rack of this
tough world
Stretch him out longer.

SHAKESPEARE, *King Lear*

5094.

Nothing in his life
Became him like the leaving it; he
died
As one that had been studied in his
death
To throw away the dearest thing he
owed,
As 'twere a careless trifle.

SHAKESPEARE, *Macbeth*

5095. Death's a great disguiser.

SHAKESPEARE, *Measure for Measure*

5096.

The sense of death is most in apprehension;
And the poor beetle, that we tread
upon,
In corporal sufferance finds a pang
as great
As when a giant dies.

SHAKESPEARE, *Measure for Measure*

5097.

Ay, but to die, and go we know not
where;
To lie in cold obstruction and to rot;
This sensible warm motion to become
A kneaded clod: and the delighted
spirit
To bathe in fiery floods, or to reside
In thrilling region of thick-ribbed
ice;
To be imprison'd in the viewless
winds,
And blown with restless violence
round about
The pendent world.

SHAKESPEARE, *Measure for Measure*

5098.

The weariest and most loathed
worldly life
That age, ache, penury, and im-
prisonment
Can lay on nature, is a paradise
To what we fear of death.

SHAKESPEARE, *Measure for Measure*

5099. Speak me fair in death.

SHAKESPEARE,
The Merchant of Venice

5100. Farewell! Othello's occupation's gone!   SHAKESPEARE, *Othello*

5101.

The tongues of dying men
Enforce attention like deep harmony.   SHAKESPEARE, *Richard II*

5102.

And nothing can we call our own
but death;
And that small model of the barren
earth,
Which serves as paste and cover to
our bones.
For God's sake, let us sit upon the
ground,
And tell sad stories of the death of
kings:—
How some have been depos'd; some
slain in war;
Some haunted by the ghosts they
have depos'd;
Some poisoned by their wives; some
sleeping kill'd;
All murdered.

SHAKESPEARE, *Richard II*

5103. The sons of Edward sleep in
Abraham's bosom.

SHAKESPEARE, *Richard III*

5104. He that dies pays all debts.

SHAKESPEARE, *The Tempest*

5105. I would fain die a dry death.

SHAKESPEARE, *The Tempest*

5106. Out of the jaws of death.

SHAKESPEARE, *Twelfth Night*

5107.

He has outsoared the shadow of our
    night;
Envy and calumny and hate and pain,
And that unrest which men miscall
    delight
Can touch him not and torture not
    again;
From the contagion of the world's
    slow stain
He is secure, and now can never
    mourn
A heart grown cold, a head grown
    gray in vain.
        SHELLEY, *Adonais*

5108.

How wonderful is Death,
Death and his brother Sleep.
        SHELLEY, *Queen Mab*

5109.

Death is the veil which those who
    live call life;
They sleep, and it is lifted.
    SHELLEY, *Prometheus Unbound*

5110. Death's a debt; his mandamus
binds all alike—no bail, no demurrer.
    SHERIDAN, *St. Patrick's Day*

5111. Death calls ye to the crowd of
common men.
    JAMES SHIRLEY, *Cupid & Death*

5112. Death is the ugly fact which
Nature has to hide, and she hides it
well.
    ALEXANDER SMITH, *Dreamthorp*

5113.

Death is not the worst; rather, in
    vain
To wish for death, and not to compass it.   SOPHOCLES, *Ajax*

5114.

Come not in terrors clad, to claim
An unresisting prey.
    CAROLINE SOUTHEY, *To Death*

5115.

Is not short paine well borne, that
    brings long ease,
And layes the soul to sleepe in quiet
    grave?
Sleepe after toyle, port after stormie
    seas,
Ease after warre, death after life does
    greatly please.
        EDMUND SPENSER,
            The Faerie Queene

5116. Death slue not him, but he
made death his ladder to the skies.
        EDMUND SPENSER,
  An Epitaph upon Sir Philip Sidney

5117.

Give me to die unwitting of the day
And stricken in Life's brave heat
    with senses clear!
    E. C. STEDMAN, *Mors Benefica*

5118.

Death's no punishment: it is the
    sense,
The pains and fears afore, that make
    a death.
    SIR JOHN SUCKLING, *Aglaura*

5119. For there is no God found
stronger than death; and death is a
sleep.
    SWINBURNE, *Hymn to Proserpine*

5120.

At the door of life, by the gate of
    breath,
    There are worse things waiting for
    men than death.
    SWINBURNE, *The Triumph of Time*

5121.

For life is sweet, but after life is
    death,
    This is the end of every man's de-
    sire.
    SWINBURNE, *A Ballad of Burdens*

5122. God's fingers touch'd him, and
he slept. TENNYSON, *In Memoriam*

5123.
No life that breathes with human
   breath
Has ever truly longed for death.
            TENNYSON, *The Two Voices*

5124. Old men must die, or the world
would grow mouldy, would only breed
the past again.
            TENNYSON, *Becket*

5125.
Sunset and evening star,
   And one clear call for me!
And may there be no moaning of the
   bar
   When I put out to sea.
            TENNYSON, *Crossing the Bar*

5126. Cruel as death, and hungry as
the grave.
            JAMES THOMSON, *The Seasons*

5127.
There is no kind of death to kill
The sands that lie so meek and
   still . . .
But Man is great and strong and
   wise—
   And so he dies.
            LOUIS UNTERMEYER, *Irony*

5128.
   Here's Death, twitching my ear:
"Live," says he, "for I'm coming."
            VERGIL, *Minor Poems*

5129.
We cease to grieve, cease to be for-
   tune's slaves,
Yes, cease to die, by dying.
            JOHN WEBSTER, *The White Devil*

5130.
I know death hath ten thousand sev-
   eral doors
For men to take their exit.
            JOHN WEBSTER, *Duchess of Malfi*

5131.
Come lovely and soothing death,
Undulate round the world, serenely
   arriving, arriving,

In the day, in the night, to all, to
   each,
Sooner or later, delicate death.
            WALT WHITMAN,
*When Lilacs Last in the Dooryard
            Bloom'd*

5132.
All goes onward and outward, nothing collapses
And to die is different from what any
   one supposed, and luckier.
            WALT WHITMAN, *Song of Myself*

5133. Nothing can happen more
beautiful than death.
            WALT WHITMAN,
            Starting from Paumanok

5134.
Happy is he who heareth
   The signal of his release
In the bells of the Holy City,
   The chimes of eternal peace!
            WHITTIER, *The Red River Voyageur*

5135.
How fast has brother followed
   brother,
From sunshine to the sunless land!
            WORDSWORTH,
      Upon the Death of James Hogg

See also: 40, 51, 52, 54, 163, 227,
466, 474, 491, 510, 1302, 1551, 1801,
2075, 2680, 2834, 2835, 2983, 2991,
4699, 5991, 10031, 11194, 13291,
18253, 18664, 19935, 21051.

DEBT

**Related Subjects: Borrowing,
Credit, Gratitude, Money, Obligation, Promise, Usurer.**

5141. I hold every man a debtor to
his profession.
            BACON, *Maxims of the Law*

5142. Owe no man anything, but to
love one another.
            Bible: Romans, xiii, 8

5143. Youth is in danger until it learns to look upon debts as furies. BULWER-LYTTON

5144. Debt is to a man what the serpent is to the bird; its eye fascinates, its breath poisons, its coil crushes sinew and bone, its jaw is the pitiless grave. BULWER-LYTTON

5145. A man who owes a little can clear it off in a little time, and, if he is prudent, he will; whereas a man, who, by long negligence, owes a great deal, despairs of ever being able to pay, and therefore never looks into his accounts at all. LORD CHESTERFIELD

5146. The so-called debtor class : . . are not dishonest because they are in debt. GROVER CLEVELAND

5147.
Anticipated rents, and bills unpaid,
Force many a shining youth into the shade,
Not to redeem his time, but his estate,
And play the fool, but at the cheaper rate. COWPER, *Retirement*

5148. Think what you do when you run in debt; you give to another power over your liberty. If you cannot pay at the time, you will be ashamed to see your creditor; will be in fear when you speak to him; will make poor, pitiful, sneaking excuses, and by degrees come to lose your veracity, and sink into base, downright lying; for the second vice is lying, the first is running in debt. A freeborn man ought not to be ashamed nor afraid to see or speak to any man living, but poverty often deprives a man of all spirit and virtue. It is hard for an empty bag to stand upright. FRANKLIN

5149. A national debt, if it is not excessive, will be to us a national blessing. ALEXANDER HAMILTON

5150. If a man owe a debt and Adad inundate his field and carry away the produce, or, through lack of water, grain have not grown in the field, in that year he shall not make any return of grain to the creditor, he shall alter his contract-tablet and he shall not pay the interest for that year.
HAMMURABI,
The Code of Hammurabi, King of Babylon

5151.
By no means run in debt: take thine own measure.
Who cannot live on twenty pound a year,
Cannot on forty.
GEORGE HERBERT, *The Church Porch*

5152. Do not accustom yourself to consider debt only as an inconvenience; you will find it is a calamity.
SAMUEL JOHNSON

5153. Debts are nowadays like children, begot with pleasure, but brought forth with pain. MOLIÈRE

5154. He who oweth is all in the wrong. *Proverb*

5155. He that gets out of debt, grows rich. *Proverb*

5156. A poor man's debt makes a great noise. *Proverb*

5157. Debt is the worst poverty. *Proverb*

5158. Better go to bed supperless than rise in debt. *Proverb*

5159. It is better to pay, and have but little left, than to have much, and be always in debt. *Proverb*

5160. A small debt produces a debtor; a large one, an enemy.
PUBLILIUS SYRUS,
Sententiae

5161.
The slender debt to Nature's quickly
  paid,
Discharged, perchance with greater
  ease than made.
FRANCIS QUARLES, *Emblems*

5162. Debts and lies are generally
mixed together.   RABELAIS

5163. I have discovered the philosopher's stone, that turns everything
into gold: it is, "Pay as you go".
JOHN RANDOLPH

5164. Poverty is hard, but debt is
horrible. A man might as well have
a smoky house and a scolding wife,
which are said to be the two worst
evils of our life.   C. H. SPURGEON

5165. Everybody in Vanity Fair must
have remarked how well those live
who are comfortably and thoroughly
in debt; how they deny themselves
nothing; how jolly and easy they are
in their minds.   THACKERAY,
Vanity Fair

5166. Germans hold a debt over a
man for forty years. . . In England
a man who fails seldom again rises
above low-water mark. In America,
where ninety-five out of the hundred
come down, everybody floats in on
the flood.   G. F. TRAIN,
Young America in Wall St.

See also: 829, 2858, 4973, 5104, 6498,
10585, 19296, 21747.

DECAY

Related Subjects: **Age, Antiquity,
Corruption, Death, Disease, Mortality, Ruin, Rust, Weakness.**

5171. A gilded halo hovering round
decay.   BYRON, *The Giaour*

5172.
A general flavor of mild decay,
But nothing local, as one might say.
O. W. HOLMES,
The Deacon's Masterpiece

5173.
While in the progress of their long
  decay,
Thrones sink to dust, and nations
  pass away.
FREDERICK HOWARD,
On the Ruins of Paestum

5174. Change and decay in all around
I see.   HYMN: *Abide With Me*

5175.
An age that melts with unperceiv'd
  decay,
And glides in modest innocence away.
SAMUEL JOHNSON,
The Vanity of Human Wishes

5176. There seems to be a constant
decay of all our ideas.   LOCKE,
Human Understanding

5177. Sullen presage of your own decay.   SHAKESPEARE, *King John*

5178.
Ever upon old Decay
The greenest mosses cling.
WHITTIER,
A Dream of Summer
See also: 1442, 8039.

DECEIT

Related Subjects: **Calumny, Cheating, Conspiracy, Coquetry, Cunning, Delusion, Flattery, Hypocrisy, Lies, Quack, Trickery.**

5181. God is not averse to deceit in
a holy cause.   AESCHYLUS

5182. The easiest person to deceive
is one's own self.
BULWER-LYTTON,
The Disowned

5183. If the world will be gulled, let it be gulled.   ROBERT BURTON,
Anatomy of Melancholy

5184. Like the watermen that row one way and look another.
ROBERT BURTON,
Anatomy of Melancholy

5185.
Like to the apples on the Dead Sea's shore,
All ashes to the taste.
·BYRON, *Childe Harold*

5186. We are never deceived; we deceive ourselves.   GOETHE,
Spruche in Prosa

5187. Deceive not thy physician, confessor, nor lawyer.
GEORGE HERBERT,
Jacula Prudentum

5188. The best happiness a woman can boast is that of being most carefully deceived.   GEORGE JAMES,
Richelieu

5189. It is a double pleasure to deceive the deceiver.
LA FONTAINE,
Fables

5190. You can fool some of the people all of the time, and all of the people some of the time, but you cannot fool all of the people all of the time.
LINCOLN

5191. It is vain to find fault with those arts of deceiving, wherein men find pleasure to be deceived.
LOCKE, *Human Understanding*

5192.
But all was false and hollow; though his tongue
Dropp'd manna, and could make the worse appear

The better reason, to perplex and dash
Maturest counsels.   MILTON,
Paradise Lost

5193. Everything that deceives may be said to enchant.   PLATO,
The Republic

5194. Deceit is in haste, but honesty can wait a fair leisure.   *Proverb*

5195. Deceiving of a deceiver is no knavery.   *Proverb*

5196. By art and deceit men live half a year; and by deceit and art the other half.   *Proverb*

5197.
Oh, what a tangled web we weave,
When first we practise to deceive!
SCOTT, *Marmion*

5198. I am falser than vows made in wine.   SHAKESPEARE,
As You Like It

5199.
With an auspicious and a dropping eye,
With mirth in funeral, and with dirge in marriage,
In equal scale weighing delight and dole.   SHAKESPEARE,
Hamlet

5200. A quicksand of deceit.
SHAKESPEARE, *Henry VI*

5201.
The instruments of darkness tell us truths,
Win us with honest trifles, to betray us
In deepest consequence.
SHAKESPEARE, *Macbeth*

5202.
It oft falls out,
To have what we would have, we speak not what we mean.
SHAKESPEARE,
Measure for Measure

5203.

The seeming truth which cunning
   times put on
To entrap the wisest.

SHAKESPEARE,
The Merchant of Venice

5204. Who makes the fairest show
means most deceit.

SHAKESPEARE, *Pericles*

5205.

Was ever book containing such vile
   matter
So fairly bound? O! that deceit
   should dwell
In such a gorgeous palace.

SHAKESPEARE,
Romeo and Juliet

5206.

Oh, that deceit should steal such
   gentle shapes,
And with a virtuous vizard hide foul
   guile.   SHAKESPEARE,

Richard III

See also: 991, 2597, 2604, 3276, 4028,
9683, 21571.

DECEMBER

Related Subjects: Christmas, Winter.

5211.

December drops no weak, relenting
   tear,
   By our fond Summer sympathies
    ensnared,
Nor from the perfect circle of the
   year
   Can even Winter's crystal gems be
    spared.   C. P. CRANCH,

December

5212.

In a drear-nighted December,
   Too happy, happy brook,
Thy bubblings ne'er remember
   Apollo's summer look.

KEATS, *Stanzas*

5213.

Ah, distinctly I remember it was in
   the bleak December.   POE,

The Raven

5214.

In cold December fragrant chaplets
   blow,
And heavy harvests nod beneath the
   snow.   POPE, *Dunciad*

5215.

When we shall hear

The rain and wind beat dark December, how,
In this our pinching cave, shall we
   discourse
The freezing hours away?

SHAKESPEARE, *Cymbeline*

5216.

The sun that brief December day
Rose cheerless over hills of gray,
And, darkly circled, gave at noon
A sadder light than waning moon.

WHITTIER, *Snow-Bound*

DECENCY

Related Subjects: Modesty, Morality, Nudity, Virtue.

5221. Virtue and decency are so
nearly related that it is difficult to
separate them from each other but
in our imagination.   CICERO

5222. Want of decency is want of
sense.   WENTWORTH DILLON

5223. My cares and my inquiries are
for decency and truth, and in this I
am wholly occupied.   HORACE,

Epistles

5224. Decency is the least of all laws,
but yet it is the law which is most
strictly observed.

LA ROCHEFOUCAULD, *Maxims*

5225.
Those thousand decencies, that daily
  flow
From all her words and actions.
        MILTON, *Paradise Lost*

5226. Respectable means rich, and
decent means poor. I should die if
I heard my father called decent.
    T. L. PEACOCK, *Crotchet Castle*

5227. Decency is Indecency's Conspiracy of Silence.
        BERNARD SHAW,
      Maxims for Revolutionists

5228. Decency of behavior in our
lives obtains the approbation of all
with whom we converse, from the
order, consistency, and moderation
of our words and actions.
        SIR RICHARD STEELE

DECISION AND INDECISION

**Related Subjects: Firmness, Hesi-
tation, Judgment, Purpose, Resolution, Will.**

5231. Multitudes, multitudes in the
valley of decision: for the day of the
Lord is near in the valley of decision.
      Bible: Joel, iii, 14

5232. The die is cast.
        JULIUS CAESAR

5233. He only is a well-made man
who has a good determination.
        EMERSON, *Essays*

5234. There is nothing more to be
esteemed than a manly firmness and
decision of character. I like a person
who knows his own mind and sticks
to it; who sees at once what, in given
circumstances, is to be done, and does
it.   HAZLITT

5235.
Decide not rashly. The decision
  made

Can never be recalled.
        LONGFELLOW,
      Masque of Pandora

5236.
Once to every man and nation comes
  the moment to decide,
In the strife of Truth with Falsehood, for the good or evil side.
    LOWELL, *The Present Crisis*

5237. Men must be decided on what
they will not do, and then they are
able to act with vigor in what they
ought to do.   MENCIUS

5238. Deliberate as often as you
please, but when you decide it is
once for all.   PUBLILIUS SYRUS,
          Sententiae

5239.
  Determine on some course,
More than a wild exposure to each
  chance
That starts i' the way before thee.
    SHAKESPEARE, *Coriolanus*

5240.
      Pleasure and revenge
Have ears more deaf than adders to
  the voice
Of any true decision.
        SHAKESPEARE,
      Troilus and Cressida

Indecision.

5241. The wavering mind is but a
base possession.   EURIPIDES

5242. There is nothing in the world
more pitiable than an irresolute man,
oscillating between two feelings, who
would willingly unite the two, and
who does not perceive that nothing
can unite them.   GOETHE

5243. There is no more miserable
human being than one in whom nothing is habitual but indecision.
    WILLIAM JAMES, *Psychology*

5244.

To be, or not to be, that is the question:
Whether 'tis nobler in the mind to suffer
The slings and arrows of outrageous fortune;
Or to take arms against a sea of troubles,
And by opposing end them?

SHAKESPEARE, *Hamlet*

See also: 149, 19304.

DEEDS

Related Subjects: **Act, Behavior, Manners, Words, Work.**

5251.

All your better deeds
Shall be in water writ, but this in marble.

BEAUMONT & FLETCHER,
Philaster

5252. He who has suffer'd you to impose on him, knows you.

BLAKE,
The Marriage of Heaven and Hell

5253. Whatever is worth doing at all, is worth doing well.

LORD CHESTERFIELD, *Letters*

5254. If thou wouldst not be known to do anything, never do it.

EMERSON, *Essays*

5255.

I am only one,
But still I am one,
I cannot do everything,
But still I can do something;
And because I cannot do everything
I will not refuse to do the something
   that I can do. EDWARD E. HALE

5256. Let not the things that you have not accomplished discourage you. It is what you have done that counts. CARDINAL HAYES

5257.

Do noble things, not dream them, all day long;
And so make life, death, and that vast forever
One grand sweet song.

CHARLES KINGSLEY,
A Farewell

5258. Deeds, not words.

JOHN FLETCHER,
The Lover's Progress

5259. Let us do or die.

JOHN FLETCHER,
The Island Princess

5260. His conduct still right, with his argument wrong. GOLDSMITH,
Retaliation

5261. The world will little note nor long remember what we say here, but it can never forget what they did here. LINCOLN
Gettysburg Address

5262.

Something attempted something done,
Has earned a night's repose.

LONGFELLOW,
The Village Blacksmith

5263.

Let us, then, be up and doing,
With a heart for any fate;
Still achieving, still pursuing,
Learn to labour and to wait.

LONGFELLOW, *A Psalm of Life*

5264.

Boast not of what thou would'st have done, but do
What then thou would'st.

MILTON, *Samson Agonistes*

5265. Every noble deed dieth, if supressed in silence. PINDAR,
Eulogy on Alexander, Son of Amyntas

5266. Deeds are fruits, words are leaves.   *Proverb*

5267. Whatever's worth doing is worth doing well.   *Proverb*

5268. It is vain to use words when deeds are expected.   *Proverb*

5269. To do two things at once is to do neither.   Publilius Syrus,
Sententiae

5270.
How oft the sight of means to do ill deeds
Makes ill deeds done!
    Shakespeare,
King John

5271. The attempt and not the deed Confounds us.   Shakespeare,
Macbeth

5272.
If it were done when 'tis done, then 'twere well
It were done quickly;
    Shakespeare, *Macbeth*

5273. If to do were easy as to know what were good to do, chapels had been churches, and poor men's cottages princes' palaces.
    Shakespeare,
The Merchant of Venice

5274.
One good deed, dying tongueless,
Slaughters a thousand waiting upon that.   Shakespeare,
The Winter's Tale

5275. 'Tis strange what a man may do and a woman yet think him an angel.   Thackeray,
Henry Esmond

5276. Do unto the other feller the way he'd like to do unto you an' do it fust.   E. N. Westcott,
David Harum

5277. Long, long are the shadow cast by our deeds . . . and when w are thought to be still in Weimar, w are already in Erfurt.
    Arnold Zweig,
The Crowning of a Kin

See also: 1002, 1253, 1836, 2131 2982, 7624.

DEFEAT

Related Subjects: Conquerors Failure, Flight, Retreat, Submis sion, Waterloo.

5280. Defeat is a school in which truth always grows strong.
    H. W. Beeche

5281. It is defeat that turns bone to flint, and gristle to muscle, and make men invincible, and formed those heroic natures that are now in ascen dency in the world. Do not the be afraid of defeat. You are neve so near to victory as when defeated i a good cause.   H. W. Beeche

5282. We may be personally de feated, but our principles never.
    W. L. Garrison, *Lif*

5283. No man is defeated withou some resentment which will be con tinued with obstinacy while he be lieves himself in the right, and as serted with bitterness, if even to hi own conscience he is detected in the wrong.   Samuel Johnson

5284.
What though the field be lost?
All is not lost—th' unconquerable Will,
And study of revenge, immortal hate
And courage never to submit or yield
    Milton, *Paradise Los*

5285. There are some defeats more triumphant than victories.
    Montaigne, *Essay*

5286. What is defeat? Nothing but education; nothing but the first step to something better.

WENDELL PHILLIPS

See also: 17, 4350, 9969.

DEFENSE

Related Subjects: Defiance, Resistance, Self-Preservation, War.

5291.
What boots it at one gate to make defence,
And at another to let in the foe?

MILTON, *Samson Agonistes*

5292. Nothing would damp the enemy's spirit more than to see the country turned out against him. He knows the strength of our army—regular militia and reserve—and will come prepared to meet and may hope to beat it. But how penetrate or subdue a country where the population are armed and opposed to him?

SIR JOHN MOORE, *when Napoleon threatened invasion of England*

5293. Millions for defence, but not one cent for tribute.

C. C. PINCKNEY

5294. But we build and defend not for our generation alone. We defend the foundations laid by our fathers. We build a life for generations yet unborn. We defend and we build a way of life, not for America alone, but for all mankind.

FRANKLIN D. ROOSEVELT,
Fireside Chat, May 26, 1940

5295. Defense cannot be static. Defense must grow and change from day to day. Defense must be dynamic and flexible, an expression of the vital forces of the nation and

of its resolute will to meet whatever challenge the future may hold.

FRANKLIN D. ROOSEVELT,
Message to Congress, May 16, 1940

5296. An effective defense by its very nature requires the equipment to attack an aggressor on his route before he can establish strong bases within the territory of American vital interests.

FRANKLIN D. ROOSEVELT,
Message to Congress, May 16, 1940

See also: 669, 686, 693, 725, 839, 5402, 6614, 15847.

DEFERENCE

Related Subjects: Duty, Respect, Submission.

5301. Deference is the instinctive respect which we pay to the great and good; the unconscious acknowledgment of the superiority or excellence of others.   TRYON EDWARDS

5302. Deference often shrinks and withers as much upon the approach of intimacy, as the sensitive plant does upon the touch of one's finger.

W. SHENSTONE

5303. Deference is the most delicate, the most indirect, and the most elegant of all compliments, and before company is the genteelest kind of flattery.   W. SHENSTONE

DEFIANCE

Related Subjects: Courage, Defense, Obedience, Resistance, Threat.

5311. We have petitioned and our petitions have been disregarded; we have entreated and our entreaties have been scorned. We beg no more, we petition no longer, we now defy.

WILLIAM JENNINGS BRYAN

5312. Damn the torpedoes! Go ahead! ADMIRAL FARRAGUT

5313. Defiance provokes an enemy.
Proverb

5314.
"Come one, come all! this rock shall fly
From its firm base as soon as I!"
SCOTT, *The Lady of the Lake*

5315. Fear we broadside? no, let the fiend give fire. SHAKESPEARE,
Henry IV

5316.
I do defy him, and I spit at him;
Call him a slanderous coward and a villain;
Which to maintain, I would allow him odds,
And meet him, were I tied to run afoot,
Even to the frozen ridges of the Alps. SHAKESPEARE,
Richard II

5317. He breathed defiance to my ears. SHAKESPEARE,
Romeo and Juliet

See also: 1862, 3011, 5669, 18670.

DEFINITIONS

Related Subjects: Distinction, Limit.

5321. I hate definitions.
DISRAELI, *Vivian Grey*

5322. A large part of the discussions of disputants come from the want of accurate definition. Let one define his terms and then stick to the definition, and half the differences in philosophy and theology would come to an end, and be seen to have no real foundation.
TRYON EDWARDS

5323. He shall be as a god to me who can rightly divide and define.
EMERSON, *Representative Me*

5324. It is one of the maxims of th civil law, that definitions are hazard ous. SAMUEL JOHNSON,
The Ramble

5325. I am apt to think that me find their simple ideas agree, thoug in discourse they confound one an other with different names.
LOCK

5326. All arts acknowledge tha then only we know certainly, whe we can define; for definition is tha which refines the pure essence o things from the circumstances.
MILTO

5327. Define, define, well-educate infant. SHAKESPEARE,
Love's Labour's Los

5328. If you wish to converse wit me, define your terms. VOLTAIR

See also: 4141, 15375.

DEFORMITY

Related Subjects: Ugliness.

5329. Deformity is daring; it is it essence to overtake mankind by hear and soul and make itself the equa aye, the superior of others. BYRO

5330. Deformity of heart I call th worst deformity of all; for what i form, or face, but the soul's index or its case? C. C. COLTO

5331. Physical deformity calls fort our charity. But the infinite mis fortune of moral deformity calls fort nothing but hatred and vengeance.
CLARENCE DARROV

5332. Many a man has risen t eminence under the powerful reactio of his mind against the scorn of the unworthy, daily evoked by his personal defects, who with a handsome person, would have sunk into the luxury of a careless life under the tranquilizing smile of continual admiration.   DE QUINCEY

5333. Do you suppose we owe nothing to Pope's deformity?—He said to himself, "If my person be crooked, my verses shall be straight."
HAZLITT

5334. If all the world were ugly, deformity would be no monster.
Proverb

5335. A deformed body may have a beautiful soul.   *Proverb*

See also: 2664.

DELAY

Related Subjects: Idleness, Lateness, Neglect, Procrastination, Time, Waiting.

5341. One man by delay restored the state, for he preferred the public safety to idle report.
QUINTUS ENNIUS

5342. Delay in vengeance gives a heavier blow.   JOHN FORD,
'Tis a Pity She's a Whore

5343. With sweet, reluctant, amorous delay.   HOMER, *Odyssey*

5344. Delay is preferable to error.
JEFFERSON, *Writings*

5345. When a man's life is at stake, no delay is too long.   JUVENAL,
Satires

5346.
         Do not delay,
Do not delay: the golden moments fly!   LONGFELLOW,
Masque of Pandora

5347. Delay is ever fatal to those who are prepared.   LUCAN,
The Civil War

5348. And sweet reluctant amorous delay.   MILTON, *Paradise Lost*

5349. Delay is a great procuress.
OVID, *Art of Love*

5350. Nothing is more annoying than a tardy friend.   PLAUTUS, *Paenulus*

5351. Delays increase desires, and sometimes extinguish them.
Proverb

5352. Deliberating is not delaying.
Proverb

5353. Better late than never.
       · *Proverb*

5354.
        'Tis wisdom's use
Still to delay what we dare not refuse.   SCOTT,
Harold the Dauntless

5355. Every delay is too long to one who is in a hurry. SENECA,
Agamemnon

5356. Delay is the greatest remedy for anger.   SENECA, *De Ira*

5357. Delays have dangerous ends.
SHAKESPEARE, *Henry VI*

5358. Dull not device by coldness and delay.   SHAKESPEARE, *Othello*

5359. Delay leads impotent and snail-paced beggary.
SHAKESPEARE, *Richard III*

5360.
The excuse that thou dost make in this delay
Is longer than the tale thou dost excuse.   SHAKESPEARE,
Romeo and Juliet

5361.

Late, late, so late! but we can enter
  still.

Too late, too late! ye cannot enter
  now.   TENNYSON,
           Idylls of the King

5362. And Mecca saddens at the
long delay.   JAMES THOMSON,
              The Seasons

See also: 5518, 20767.

DELICACY

Related Subjects: Beauty, Fastidiousness, Luxury, Sensitivity, Tact, Taste.

5371. An appearance of delicacy, and even of fragility, is almost essential to beauty.   BURKE

5372. True delicacy, as true generosity, is more wounded by an act of offence from itself, than to itself.
                  GREVILLE

5373. Weak men, often, from the very principle of their weakness, derive a certain susceptibility, delicacy, and taste, which render them, in these particulars, much superior to men of stronger and more consistent minds, who laugh at them.   GREVILLE

5374. Friendship, love, and piety, ought to be handled with a sort of mysterious secrecy. They ought to be spoken of only in the rare moments of perfect confidence—to be mutually understood in silence. Many things are too delicate to be thought; many more to be spoken.   NOVALIS

5375. If you destroy delicacy and a sense of shame in a young girl you deprave her very fast.
           HARRIET BEECHER STOWE

5376. The finest qualities of our nature, like the bloom on fruits, can be preserved only by the most delicate handling.   THOREAU

See also: 10152, 16716, 20682.

DELIGHT

Related Subjects: Bliss, Happiness, Joy, Merriment, Pleasure, Sweetness.

5381. A sip is the most that mortals are permitted from any goblet of delight.   BRONSON ALCOTT,
                Table Talk

5382. The soul of sweet delight can never be defil'd.   BLAKE,
            Proverbs of Hell

5383. 'Tis never too late for delight, my dear.   THOMAS MOORE,
         The Young May Moon

5384. Excess of delight palls the appetite.   *Proverb*

5385. All unwarrantable delights have an ill farewell.   *Proverb*

5386. Man delights not me; no, nor woman neither, though, by your smiling, you seem to say so.
        SHAKESPEARE, *Hamlet*

5387.

Why, all delights are vain; but that
  most vain,

Which with pain purchas'd, doth inherit pain.   SHAKESPEARE,
          Love's Labour's Lost

5388.

These violent delights have violent
  ends

And in their triumph die, like fire
  and powder,

Which as they kiss consume.
     SHAKESPEARE, *Romeo and Juliet*

5389.

Rarely, rarely, comest thou,
  Spirit of Delight.   SHELLEY,
       Rarely, Rarely, Comest Thou

5390.
Delight, the rootless flower,
And love, the bloomless bower;
Delight that lives an hour,
  And love that lives a day.
        SWINBURNE, *Before Dawn*

See also: 64, 519, 1037, 1729, 1733, 2627, 2669, 12467, 13109.

DELUSION

Related Subjects: Conceit, Deceit, Error, Fool, Illusion, Sense, Vanity.

5391. No man is happy without a delusion of some kind. Delusions are as necessary to our happiness as realities.   C. N. BOVEE

5392. The worst deluded are the self-deluded.   C. N. BOVEE

5393. The disappointment of manhood succeeds the delusion of youth.
        DISRAELI

5394. You think a man to be your dupe. If he pretends to be so, who is the greatest dupe—he or you?
        LA BRUYÈRE

5395. Were we perfectly acquainted with the object, we should never passionately desire it.
    LA ROCHEFOUCAULD, *Maxims*

5396. When our vices quit us, we flatter ourselves with the belief that it is we who quit them.
    LA ROCHEFOUCAULD, *Maxims*

5397. It many times falls out that we deem ourselves much deceived in others, because we are first deceived in ourselves.   SIR PHILIP SIDNEY

See also: 1014, 6023.

DEMOCRACY

Related Subjects: America, Anarchy, Capitalism, Election, Equality, Freedom, Government, Liberty, Majority, Minority, The People, Politics, Propaganda, Right, Vote.

5401. If liberty and equality, as is thought by some, are chiefly to be found in democracy, they will be best attained when all persons alike share in the government to the utmost.
        ARISTOTLE, *Politics*

5402. It is just as important to prove that democracy can foster good plays and short stories and mural paintings as to prove our ability to build airplanes. . . . Happiness should be the chief cornerstone in national defense.
        HEYWOOD BROUN,
        The Federal Theatre

5403. According to the aristocratic idea, the representative thinks *for* his constituents; according to the democratic idea, the representative thinks *with* his constituents. A representative has no right to defeat the wishes of those who elect him, if he knows their wishes.
    WILLIAM JENNINGS BRYAN

5404. A perfect democracy is therefore the most shameless thing in the world.   BURKE,
    Reflections on the Revolution
        in France

5405. Democracy is, by the nature of it, a self-cancelling business; and gives in the long run a net result of zero.   CARLYLE, *Chartism*

5406. You can never have a revolution in order to establish a democracy. You must have a democracy in order to have a revolution.
        G. K. CHESTERTON,
        Tremendous Trifles

5407. The Commonwealth is one. We are all members of one body. The welfare of the weakest and the welfare of the most powerful are inseparably bound together. Industry cannot flourish if labor languish . . . it is well to remember that the benefit of one is the benefit of all, and the neglect of one is the neglect of all.
CALVIN COOLIDGE

5408. Caesarism is democracy without liberty. TAXILE DELORD,
L'Histoire du Second Empire

5409. Democracy is on trial in the world, on a more colossal scale than ever before. C. F. DOLE,
The Spirit of Democracy

5410. Wherever we look we come back to the Declaration of Independence and the Constitution as the anchors of our democracy and welfare. We do not want an empire, we want democracy. The ideal of democracy is the highest humanity ever developed. THEODORE DREISER

5411. To speak of democracy flourishing and being saved or advanced in war is like speaking of a fish flourishing out of water. The only air in which democracy can breathe is peace and it must be free air and abundant air, in which all ideas regardless of labels and origins can be expressed. THEODORE DREISER

5412. The world is weary of statesmen whom democracy has degraded into politicians. DISRAELI, *Lothair*

5413. Drawn to the dregs of a democracy. DRYDEN,
Absalom and Achitophel

5414. Every man is wanted, and no man is wanted much.
EMERSON, *Nominalist and Realist*

5415. The people I admire most are those who are sensitive and want to create something or discover something, and don't see life in terms of power, and such people get more of a chance under a democracy than elsewhere. E. M. FORSTER,
I Believe

5416. Democracy has another merit. It allows criticism, and if there isn't public criticism there are bound to be hushed up scandals. That is why I believe in the press, despite all its lies and vulgarity . . . I believe in the private member (of Parliament) who makes himself a nuisance. He gets snubbed and is told that he is cranky or ill-informed, but he exposes abuses which would otherwise never have been mentioned.
E. M. FORSTER, *I Believe*

5417. Democracy in this country has expanded despite four wars. And only those unfamiliar with what has taken place in Great Britain since September, 1939, will deny that England is more democratic today than she has ever been.
JUSTICE FRANKFURTER

5418. My boy, about 75 years ago I learned that I was not God. And so, when the people of the various states want to do something and I can't find anything in the Constitution expressly forbidding them to do it, I say, whether I like it or not: Damn it, let 'em do it!
SUPREME COURT JUSTICE HOLMES *to Justice Stone, in reference to the function of the Supreme Court.*

5419. Democracy has its own capacity for tyranny. Some of the most menacing encroachments upon liberty invoke the democratic principle and assert the right of the majority to rule. Shall not the people—that is, the majority—have their heart's desire? There is no gainsaying this in the long run, and our only real protection is that it will not be their heart's desire to sweep away our cherished traditions of personal liberty. The interests of liberty are peculiarly those of individuals, and hence of minorities, and freedom is in danger of being slain at her own altars if the passion for uniformity and control of opinion gathers head.

CHARLES EVANS HUGHES

5420. Democracy has not failed; the intelligence of the race has failed before the problems the race has raised.

ROBERT M. HUTCHINS

5421. The most crying need in the humbler ranks of life is that they should be allowed some part in the direction of public affairs. That is what will develop their faculties and intelligence and self-respect.

IBSEN, *An Enemy of the People*

5422. We sit around in our shops denouncing the present order but we perceive that even badly constituted democracies are responsible for fewer disasters than are oligarchies.

ISOCRATES

5423. Democracy is ever eager for rapid progress, and the only progress which can be rapid is progress down hill. SIR JAMES JEANS

5424. The spirit of the times may alter, will alter. Our rulers will become corrupt, our people careless. A single zealot may become persecutor, and better men be his victims. It can never be too often repeated that the time for fixing essential rights, on a legal basis, is while our rulers are honest, ourselves united.

JEFFERSON,
(written during Revolutionary war)

5425. Tyranny and oppression are just as possible under democratic forms as under any other. We are slow to realize that democracy is a life and involves continual struggle. It is only as those of every generation who love democracy resist with all their might the encroachments of its enemies that the ideals of representative government can even be nearly approximated.

ROBERT M. LAFOLLETTE,
Autobiography

5426. At the historical stage we have reached, the will of the people is unable to use the institutions of capitalist democracy for democratic purposes. For at this stage democracy needs to transform class relations in order to affirm itself; and it will not be allowed to do so by the owning class if it is able to prevent that achievement.

HAROLD J. LASKI, *I Believe*

5427. It is, indeed, true that democracy is based on the thesis that no man is indispensable; therein lies one of its most vital differences from a dictatorial regime, which usually finds insoluble the problem of the succession to the dictator.

HAROLD J. LASKI,
The American Presidency

5428. On the whole, with scandalous exceptions, Democracy's given the ordinary worker more dignity than he ever had. SINCLAIR LEWIS,
It Can't Happen Here

5429. As I would not be a slave, so I would not be a master. This expresses my idea of democracy. Whatever differs from this, to the extent of the difference, is no democracy.

LINCOLN

5430.
Democ'acy gives every man
A right to be his own oppressor.
LOWELL, *Biglow Papers*

5431. To one that advised him to set up a democracy in Sparta, "Pray," said Lycurgus, "do you first set up a democracy in your own house."
PLUTARCH, *Lycurgus*

5432. Thus our democracy was from an early period the most aristocratic, and our aristocracy the most democratic. MACAULAY, *History*

5433. I believe that American liberalism must become more liberal, not less liberal, as the danger in Europe becomes more acute. I believe that American democracy must invent and continually reinvent its democracy; that it must attack not defend.
ARCHIBALD MACLEISH,
A Time to Speak

5434. It is the nature of liberalism to ask questions and not to answer them. ARCHIBALD MACLEISH,
A Time to Speak

5435. We must define democracy as that form of government and of society which is inspired above every other, with the feeling and consciousness of the dignity of man.
THOMAS MANN,
The Coming Victory of Democracy

5436. Democracy's resources of vitality and youthfulness cannot be overestimated; in comparison, the youthful insolence of fascism is a mere grimace.
THOMAS MANN,
The Coming Victory of Democracy

5437. Democracy is liberty plus economic security. We Americans want to pray, think as we please—and eat regular. MAURY MAVERICK

5438. Who's over him, he cries—aye, he would be a democrat to all above; look, how he lords it over all below!
HERMAN MELVILLE, *Moby Dick*

5439. Democracy is a kingless regime infested by many kings who are sometimes more exclusive, tyrannical, and destructive than one, if he be a tyrant. MUSSOLINI, *Fascism*

5440. A democracy,—that is a government of all the people, by all the people, for all the people; of course, a government of the principles of eternal justice, the unchanging law of God; for shortness' sake I will call it the idea of Freedom.
THEODORE PARKER,
The American Idea

5441. Democracy, which is a charming form of government, full of variety and disorder, and dispensing a sort of equality to equals and unequals alike. PLATO, *The Republic*

5442. We do not distrust the future of essential democracy.
FRANKLIN D. ROOSEVELT,
First Inaugural Address

5443. Not only our future economic soundness but the very soundness of our democratic institutions depends on the determination of our Government to give employment to idle men. The people of America are in agreement in defending their liberties at any cost, and the first line of that defense lies in the protection of economic security. Your Government, seeking to protect democracy, must prove that Government is stronger than the forces of business depression. FRANKLIN D. ROOSEVELT,
Radio Address, April 14, 1938

5444. Democracy, as you know it, is seldom more than a long word begin-

ning with a capital letter, which we accept reverently or disparage contemptuously without asking any questions.   BERNARD SHAW,
The Apple Cart: Preface

5445. No democratic form of government can last unless its power springs directly from the majority rule of all the people governed.
ALFRED E. SMITH,
Progressive Democracy

5446. The Republican form of government is the highest form of government: but because of this it requires the highest type of human nature—a type nowhere at present existing.   HERBERT SPENCER,
The Americans

5447. No one can be perfectly free till all are free; no one can be perfectly moral till all are happy.
HERBERT SPENCER,
The Evanescence of Evil

5448. If the damned fools want to go to hell it's not our duty to stop them, if that's what they want to do.
Attr. to CHIEF JUSTICE STONE, *in reference to the function of the Supreme Court.*

5449. The more democratic a people is the more it respects the minority and requires a government to explain policies to the people before committing them, and the more important the issue the more vigilant is its public opinion.
CLARENCE STREIT, *Union Now*

5450. Democracy is unfinished business, not fulfilment; it is a process of always advancing toward fulfilment.   RAYMOND GRAM SWING

5451. Democracy is not saved by weakness and incompetence. Democ-

racy is saved by a powerful popular will.   DOROTHY THOMPSON,
On the Record

5452. Because in the administration it hath respect not to the few but to the multitude, our form of government is called a democracy. Wherein there is not only an equality amongst all men in point of law for their private controversies, but in election to public offices we consider neither class nor rank, but each man is preferred according to his virtue or to the esteem in which he is held for some special excellence; nor is any one put back even through poverty, because of the obscurity of his person, so long as he can do good service to the commonwealth.
THUCYDIDES, *History*

5453. In this hour of worldwide crisis, it is time for the men of science to act. It is time for them to band together to spread far and wide the truth about the genetic basis of democracy, and to work together for a better environment so that our political democracy and scientific freedom may survive.
HENRY A. WALLACE,
The Time to Act

5454. A federation of all humanity, together with a sufficient measure of social justice to ensure health, education, and a rough equality of opportunity, would mean such a release and increase of human energy as to open a new phase in human history.
H. G. WELLS,
The Outline of History

5455. Did you, too, O friend, suppose democracy was only for elections, for politics, and for a party name? I say democracy is only of use there that it may pass on and come to its flower and fruit in man-

ners, in the highest forms of inter-action between men, and their beliefs—in religion, literature, colleges, and schools—democracy in all public and private life, and in the army and navy.   WALT WHITMAN,
Democratic Vistas

5456. Political democracy, as it exists and practically works in America, with all its threatening evils, supplies a training-school for making first-class men. It is life's gymnasium, not of good only, but of all.
WALT WHITMAN,
Democratic Vistas

5457.
Sail, sail thy best, ship of Democracy.
Of value is thy freight, 'tis not the Present only,
The Past is also stored in thee.
WALT WHITMAN,
Thou Mother with Thy Equal Brood

5458.
Thunder on! Stride on! Democracy.
Strike with vengeful strokes.
WALT WHITMAN, *Drum-Taps*

5459. I believe in Democracy because it releases the energies of every human being.   WOODROW WILSON

5460. The world must be made safe for democracy.   WOODROW WILSON

5461. Democracy is, in its essence, the way of living, organising ourselves, training and, if necessary, fighting; that includes voluntary, understood and thinking discipline, and methods of work based on elasticity, initiative and independence.
TOM WINTRINGHAM,
New Ways of War

5462. This "new" deal, having lived in the human heart two thousand five hundred years, finally founded this great Union of States. An experiment. If the "Experiment" is to succeed this union must now turn from centralization that was monarchic to the segregation and integration that is democratic. That means to turn toward the greater freedom of a life for the individual as individual, based squarely with the ground.
FRANK LLOYD WRIGHT,
The Disappearing City

See also: 1023, 1142, 1158, 2768, 3319, 5744, 5903, 7828, 13889, 16383, 18852, 20646, 20743, 20806, 21077.

DEPENDENCE AND INDEPENDENCE

Related Subjects: Freedom, Liberty, Security, Self-reliance.

5471. Dependence goes somewhat against the grain of a generous mind; and it is no wonder that it should do so, considering the unreasonable advantage which is often taken of the inequality of fortune.
JEREMY COLLIER

5472. The greatest man living may stand in need of the meanest, as much as the meanest does of him.
THOMAS FULLER

5473. Even in the common affairs of life, in love, friendship, and marriage, how little security have we when we trust our happiness in the hands of others!   HAZLITT,
On Living to One's Self

5474. No degree of knowledge attainable by man is able to set him above the want of hourly assistance.
SAMUEL JOHNSON

5475. Dependence is a poor trade.
Proverb

5476. There is none so great but he may need the help and service, and stand in fear of the power and unkindness, even of the meanest of mortals.   SENECA

5477. Independence? That's middle class blasphemy. We are all dependent on one another, every soul of us on earth.   BERNARD SHAW, *Pygmalion*

5478. The acknowledgment of weakness which we make in imploring to be relieved from hunger and from temptation, is surely wisely put in our prayer. Think of it, you who are rich, and take heed how you turn a beggar away.   THACKERAY

5479. Dependence is a perpetual call upon humanity, and a greater incitement to tenderness and pity than any other motive whatever.

THACKERAY

5480. Heaven's eternal wisdom has decreed that man should ever stand in need of man.   THEOCRITUS

5481.
It's the folk that depend on us for this
And for the other that we most do miss.   MARY WEBB, *Precious Bane*

Independence

5482.
To catch Dame Fortune's golden smile,
   Assiduous wait upon her;
And gather gear by ev'ry wile
   That's justified by honor:
Not for to hide it in a hedge,
   Nor for a train-attendant;
But for the glorious privilege
   Of being independent.
BURNS, *Epistle to a Young Friend*

5483. Each man for himself.
CHAUCER, *Canterbury Tales*

5484. Depend on no man, on no friend but him who can depend on himself. He only who acts conscientiously toward himself, will act so toward others.   LAVATER

5485. A great step towards independence is a good-humored stomach.   SENECA

5486. The man who goes alone can start today; but he who travels with another must wait till that other is ready.   THOREAU, *Walden*

5487. It is my living sentiment, and by the blessing of God it shall be my dying sentiment,—Independence now and Independence forever.
DANIEL WEBSTER

See also: 680.

DEPRESSION

Related Subjects: Adversity, Desolation, Despair, Employment, Inflation, Melancholy, Poverty, Sorrow, Wages.

5491. The seed of panics is sown during the periods of over-expansion which precede them.
ROGER BABSON, *Business Fundamentals*

5492. Depressions may bring people closer to the church—but so do funerals.   CLARENCE DARROW

5493. Bad times have a scientific value. These are occasions a good learner would not miss.
EMERSON, *Conduct of Life*

5494.
'Tis the song, the sigh of the weary
Hard times, come again no more.
STEPHEN FOSTER,
Hard Times Come Again No More

5495. The times are not so bad as they seem; they couldn't be.

JAY FRANKLIN

5496. If we can boon-doggle our way out of the depression, that word is going to be enshrined in the hearts of the American people for years to come.   FRANKLIN D. ROOSEVELT

See also: 712, 2811, 3391, 5443, 16216.

DESERVING

Related Subjects: Honesty, Merit, Worth.

5501. It is better to deserve without receiving, than to receive without deserving.   ROBERT INGERSOLL,
The Children of the Stage

5502. Use every man after his desert, and who should 'scape whipping?
SHAKESPEARE, *Hamlet*

5503.
O, your desert speaks loud; and I
  should wrong it
To lock it in the wards of covert
  bosom,
When it deserves, with characters of
  brass,
A forted residence 'gainst the tooth
  of time,
And razure of oblivion.
SHAKESPEARE, *Measure for Measure*

5504.
All may be well; but, if God sort it so,
'Tis more than we deserve, or I ex-
  pect.   SHAKESPEARE,
Richard III

5505. There is nothing an honest man should fear more timorously than getting and spending more than he deserves.   STEVENSON,
Morality of the Profession of Letters

See also: 5811, 5997, 9907, 11162.

DESIRE

Related Subjects: Ambition, Appe-tite, Attraction, Avarice, Choice, Envy, Fancy, Hope, Hunger, Love, Lust, Passion, Thirst, Will, Wish.

5511. As the hart panteth after the water-brooks.   *Bible: Psalms, xlii, 1*

5512.
Bring me my bow of burning gold!
  Bring me my arrows of desire!
BLAKE *Milton*

5513. He who desires but acts not, breeds pestilence.   BLAKE,
The Marriage of Heaven and Hell

5514. Desire hath no rest.
ROBERT BURTON,
Anatomy of Melancholy

5515. Nothing troubles you for which you do not yearn.   CICERO,
De Senectute

5516. Passing into higher forms of desire, that which slumbered in the plant, and fitfully stirred in the beast, awakes in the man.
HENRY GEORGE, *Progress & Poverty*

5517. The bloom of young desire, and purple light of love.
THOMAS GRAY,
The Progress of Poesy

5518. Desire suffereth no delay.
GABRIEL HARVEY, *Marginalia*

5519. Naked I seek the camp of those who desire nothing.
HORACE, *Carmina*

5520. We live in our desires rather than in our achievements.
GEORGE MOORE, *Ave*

5521. Each man has his own desires; all do not possess the same inclina-tions.   PERSIUS, *Satires*

5522. Shameless craving must have shameful nay.   *Proverb*

5523. If your desires be endless, your cares will be so too.   *Proverb*

5524. He that desires but little has no need of much.   *Proverb*

5525. We desire nothing so much as what we ought not to have.
PUBLILIUS SYRUS, *Sententiae*

5526.
                          I have
Immortal longings in me.
          SHAKESPEARE,
          Antony and Cleopatra

5527. Is it not strange that desire should so many years outlive performance?   SHAKESPEARE,
          Henry IV

5528. The huge army of the world's desires.   SHAKESPEARE,
          Love's Labour's Lost

5529.
At Christmas I no more desire a rose
Than wish a snow in May's newfangled mirth.
SHAKESPEARE, *Love's Labour's Lost*

5530. Methinks I have a great desire to a bottle of hay: good hay, sweet hay, hath no fellow.
          SHAKESPEARE,
          A Midsummer-Night's Dream

5531. Men prize the thing ungain'd more than it is.
SHAKESPEARE, *Troilus and Cressida*

5532. The trustless wings of false desire.   SHAKESPEARE,
          The Rape of Lucrece

5533. The sea hath bounds, but deep desire hath none.
SHAKESPEARE, *Venus and Adonis*

5534.
The desire of love, Joy;
The desire of life, Peace:
The desire of the soul, Heaven:
The desire of God—a flame-white secret forever.
          WILLIAM SHARP, *Desire*

5535. There are two tragedies in life. One is not to get your heart's desire. The other is to get it.
BERNARD SHAW, *Man and Superman*

5536.
The desire of the moth for the star,
          Of the night for the morrow,
The devotion to something afar
          From the sphere of our sorrow.
          SHELLEY,
          One Word is too Often Profaned

See also: 62, 734, 966, 1251, 1262, 1869, 2628, 4117, 5395, 5787, 9261, 10160, 13283.

DESOLATION

Related Subjects: Chaos, Depression, Despair, Grief, Ruin, Solitude, Sorrow.

5541. Abomination of desolation.
          Bible: Matthew, xxiv, 15

5542. All tenantless, save to the crannying wind. BYRON, *Childe Harold*

5543.
None are so desolate but something dear,
Dearer than self, possesses or possess'd
A thought, and claims the homage of a tear.   BYRON, *Childe Harold*

5544.
Desolate—Life is so dreary and desolate—
Women and men in the crowd meet and mingle,

Yet with itself every soul standeth
single,
Deep out of sympathy moaning its
moan—
Holding and having its brief exulta-
tion—
Making its lonesome and low lamentation—
Fighting its terrible conflicts alone.
                    ALICE CARY, *Life*

5545.

No one is accursed by fate,
No one so utterly desolate,
 But some heart, though unknown,
 Responds unto his own.
                    LONGFELLOW, *Endymion*

5546.

My desolation does begin to make
A better life.   SHAKESPEARE,
                    Antony and Cleopatra

5547. Everything about you demon-
strating a careless desolation.
SHAKESPEARE, *As You Like It*

DESPAIR

Related Subjects: Desolation,
Fear, Grief, Misery, Remorse, Sorrow, Suicide.

5551.

I will indulge my sorrows, and give
way
To all the pangs and fury of despair.
                    ADDISON, *Cato*

5552. The nympholepsy of some fond
despair.   BYRON, *Childe Harold*.

5553.

Now a' is done that men can do,
 And a' is done in vain.
                    BURNS,
 It Was a' For Our Rightful King

5554.

Beware of desperate steps! The darkest day,

Live till to-morrow, will have pass'd
away.   COWPER,
                    The Needless Alarm

5555. Despair is a great incentive to
honorable death.
 QUINTUS CURTIUS RUFUS,
 De Rebus Gestis Alexandri Magni

5556. The disappointment of manhood succeeds to the delusion of
youth: let us hope that the heritage
of old age is not despair.
                    DISRAELI, *Vivian Grey*

5557. Despair is the damp of hell, as
joy is the serenity of heaven.
                    JOHN DONNE

5558. What we call despair is often
only the painful eagerness of unfed
hope.   GEORGE ELIOT

5559. Considering the unforeseen
events of this world, we should be
taught that no human condition
should inspire men with absolute
despair.   FIELDING

5560. Despair gives the shocking
ease to the mind that mortification
gives to the body.   GREVILLE

5561. He who despairs wants love
and faith, for faith, hope, and love
are three torches which blend their
light together, nor does the one shine
without the other.   METASTASIO

5562.

 Thus repuls'd, our final hope
Is flat despair.   MILTON,
                    Paradise Lost

5563.

The strongest and the fiercest spirit
That fought in heaven, Now fiercer
 by despair.   MILTON,
                    Paradise Lost

5564.
Discomfort guides my tongue
And bids me speak of nothing but
despair.   SHAKESPEARE,
Richard II

5565. My ending is despair.
SHAKESPEARE, *The Tempest*

5566.
Thou tyrant!
Do not repent these things, for they
are heavier
Than all thy woes can stir: therefore,
betake thee
To nothing but despair.
SHAKESPEARE, *The Winter's Tale*

5567. No change, no pause, no hope!
Yet I endure.   SHELLEY,
Prometheus Unbound

5568.
Then black despair,
The shadow of a starless night, was
thrown
Over the world in which I moved
alone.   SHELLEY, *Revolt of Islam*

5569. The fact that God has pro-
hibited despair gives misfortune the
right to hope all things, and leaves
hope free to dare all things.
MME. SWETCHINE

5570. It is impossible for that man
to despair who remembers that his
Helper is omnipotent.
JEREMY TAYLOR

5571. The only refuge from despair
is to project one's ego into the world.
TOLSTOY

5572. Night was our friend, our leader was Despair.   VERGIL, *Aeneid*

5573.
I can endure my own despair,
But not another's hope.
WILLIAM WALSH, *Song*

See also: 1119, 3927, 5888, 6164,
6178, 6552, 8811.

DESPONDENCY

Related Subjects: **Grief, Melancholy, Pessimism, Sorrow.**

5581. The name of the slough was
Despond.   BUNYAN,
Pilgrim's Progress

5582. Despondency is not a state of
humility. On the contrary, it is the
vexation and despair of a cowardly
pride; nothing is worse. Whether we
stumble, or whether we fall, we must
only think of rising again and going
on in our course.   FENELON

5583. Some persons depress their
own minds, despond at the first difficulty, and conclude that making any
progress in knowledge, further than
serves their ordinary business, is
above their capacity.   LOCKE

5584. As to feel that we can do a
thing is often success, so to doubt
and despond is a sure step to failure.
LOCKE

5585. Life is a warfare; and he who
easily desponds deserts a double duty
—he betrays the noblest property of
man, which is dauntless resolution;
and he rejects the providence of that
all-gracious Being who guides and
rules the universe.   JANE PORTER

5586. In the lottery of life there are
more prizes drawn than blanks, and
to one misfortune there are fifty advantages. Despondency is the most
unprofitable feeling a man can indulge in.   DE WITT TALMAGE

5587. To despond is to be ungrateful beforehand. Be not looking for
evil. Often thou drainest the gall of
fear while evil is passing by thy
dwelling.   MARTIN F. TUPPER

DESPOTISM

Related Subjects: Dictatorship, Government, Kings, Persecution, Slavery, Tyranny.

5591. It is odd to consider the connection between despotism and barbarity, and how the making one person more than man makes the rest less.   ADDISON

5592. Despots govern by terror. They know that he who fears God fears nothing else, and therefore they eradicate from the mind, through their Voltaire and Helvetius, and the rest of that infamous gang, that only sort of fear which generates true courage.
                                    BURKE

5593. Despotism can no more exist in a nation until the liberty of the press be destroyed, than the night can happen before the sun is set.
                          C. C. COLTON

5594. All despotism is bad; but the worst is that which works with the machinery of freedom.   JUNIUS

5595. In times of anarchy one may seem a despot in order to be a savior.
                          MIRABEAU

5596. When the savages wish to have fruit they cut down the tree and gather it. That is exactly a despotic government.   MONTESQUIEU

5597. As virtue is necessary in a republic, and honor in a monarchy, fear is what is required in a despotism. As for virtue, it is not at all necessary, and honor would be dangerous there.   MONTESQUIEU

5598. I will believe in the right of one man to govern a nation despotically when I find a man born into the world with boots and spurs, and a nation born with saddles on their backs.   ALGERNON SIDNEY

See also: 4840, 10527.

DESTINY

Related Subjects: Chance, Circumstance, Fame, Fate, Fortune, Future, Luck, Providence.

5601.
                              Destiny
Waiteth alike for them that men call free,
And them by others mastered.
              AESCHYLUS, *The Choephoroe*

5602.
Sow a Thought, and you reap an Act;
Sow an Act, and you reap a Habit;
Sow a Habit, and you reap a Character;
Sow a Character, and you reap a Destiny.   *Anonymous*

5603. Death and life have their determined appointments; riches and honors depend upon heaven.
                   CONFUCIUS, *Analects*

5604. This is the thing that I was born to do.   SAMUEL DANIEL,
                              Musophilus

5605. Man supposes that he directs his life and govern his actions, when his existence is irretrievably under the control of destiny.   GOETHE

5606.
No living man can send me to the shades
Before my time; no man of woman born,
Coward or brave, can shun his destiny.   HOMER, *Iliad*

5607. That which God writes on thy forehead, thou wilt come to it.
                          The Koran

5608.

The future works out great men's
    destinies:

The present is enough for common
    souls,

Who, never looking forward, are in-
    deed

Mere clay wherein the footprints of
    their age

Are petrified forever.

           LOWELL, *Act for Truth*

5609. If the course of human affairs
be considered, it will be seen that
many things arise against which
heaven does not allow us to guard.
           MACHIAVELLI

5610.

We are but as the instrument of
    Heaven.

Our work is not design, but destiny.
    OWEN MEREDITH, *Clytemnestra*

5611. Destiny has more resources
than the most imaginative composer
of fiction.   F. F. MOORE,
           The Jessamy Bride

5612. The acts of this life are the
destiny of the next.   *Proverb*

5613. Destiny leads the willing, but
drags the unwilling.   *Proverb*

5614. The clew of our destiny, wander where we will, lies at the cradle
foot.   J. P. RICHTER

5615. This generation of Americans
has a rendezvous with destiny.
    FRANKLIN D. ROOSEVELT,
           Address, 1936

5616.

Think you I bear the shears of des-
    tiny?

Have I commandment on the pulse
    of life?   SHAKESPEARE,
           King John

5617.

If he had been as you and you as he,
You would have slipt like him.
SHAKESPEARE, *Measure for Measure*

5618. Hanging and wiving goes by
destiny.   SHAKESPEARE,
           The Merchant of Venice

5619. And all the bustle of departure
—sometimes sad, sometimes intoxicating—just as fear or hope may be inspired by the new chances of coming
destiny.   MADAME DE STAËL,
           Corinne

5620. We bear each one our own
destiny.   VERGIL, *Aeneid*

5621. Human destiny is a race between ordered thought made effective by education, on the one side,
and catastrophe on the other: so far,
catastrophe seems to be leading.
           H. G. WELLS

5622.

The tissue of the Life to be
    We weave with colors all our own,
And in the field of Destiny
    We reap as we have sown.
        WHITTIER, *Raphael*

See also: 304, 671, 10971.

DEVIL, THE

**Related Subjects: Evil, Flesh, God,
Hell, Sin, Temptation.**

5631. How art thou fallen from
heaven, O Lucifer, son of the morning!   *Bible: Isaiah, xiv, 12*

5632. Resist the Devil, and he will
flee from you. *Bible: James, iv, 7*

5633. Be sober, be vigilant; because
your adversary, the Devil, as a roaring lion, walketh about, seeking
whom he may devour.
        Bible: 1 Peter, v, 8

5634. Renounce the Devil and all his works.   *Book of Common Prayer*

5635. The Devil himself, which is the author of confusion and lies.
ROBERT BURTON,
Anatomy of Melancholy

5636. And bid the devil take the hin'most.   SAMUEL BUTLER,
Hudibras

5637.
Nick Machiavel had ne'er a trick
(Though he gave his name to our Old Nick).
SAMUEL BUTLER, *Hudibras*

5638. Here is the devil-and-all to pay.
CERVANTES, *Don Quixote*

5639. Sathan, that ever us waiteth to bigyle.   CHAUCER,
Canterbury Tales

5640. Talk of the devil, and his horns appear, says the proverb.
COLERIDGE, *Biographia Literaria*

5641.
No, no! The devil is an egotist,
And is not apt, without why or wherefore,
"For God's sake," others to assist.
GOETHE, *Faust*

5642.
I call'd the devil, and he came
    And with wonder his form did I closely scan;
He is not ugly, and is not lame,
    But really a handsome and charming man.
A man in the prime of life is the devil,
Obliging, a man of the world, and civil;
A diplomatist too, well skill'd in debate,
He talks quite glibly of church and state.
HEINE, *Pictures of Travels*

5643. Why should the Devil have all the good tunes? ROWLAND HILL

5644. The Devil is an ass, I do acknowledge it.   BEN JONSON,
The Devil is an Ass

5645.
It is Lucifer,
The son of mystery;
And since God suffers him to be,
He, too, is God's minister,
And labors for some good
By us not understood.
LONGFELLOW, *Christus*

5646.
The devil, my friends, is a woman just now.
'Tis a woman that reigns in Hell.
OWEN MEREDITH

5647.
Pandemonium, city and proud seat
Of Lucifer.   MILTON,
Paradise Lost

5648.
The infernal serpent; he it was whose guile
Stirr'd up with envy and revenge, deceived
The mother of mankind.
MILTON, *Paradise Lost*

5649.
His form had not yet lost
All his original brightness, nor appear'd
Less than arch-angel ruined, and th' excess
Of glory obscured.   MILTON,
Paradise Lost

5650.
Satan exalted sat, by merit raised
To that bad eminence.
MILTON, *Paradise Lost*

5651.
Abashed the Devil stood,
And felt how awful goodness is, and saw

Virtue in her own shape how lovely;
saw

And pined his loss.   MILTON,
Paradise Lost

5652.
Satan; so call him now, his former
name
Is heard no more in heaven.
MILTON, *Paradise Lost*

5653. Swings the scaly horror of his
folded tail.   MILTON,
Hymn on Christ's Nativity

5654. As good eat the devil as the
broth he is boiled in.   *Proverb*

5655. Make not even the devil blacker than he is.   *Proverb*

5656. He that hath shipped the devil
must make the best of him.
Proverb

5657. If you don't open the door to
the devil he goes away.   *Proverb*

5658. Away goes the devil when he
finds the door shut against him.
Proverb

5659.
The Devil was sick,—the Devil a
monk would be;
The Devil was well,—the Devil a
monk was he.   RABELAIS

5660. He must needs go that the
devil drives.   SHAKESPEARE,
All's Well that Ends Well

5661.
I charge thee, Satan, hous'd within
this man,
To yield possession to my holy pray-
ers,
And to thy state of darkness hie thee
straight;
I conjure thee by all the saints in
heaven!   SHAKESPEARE,
The Comedy of Errors

5662.
The devil hath power
To assume a pleasing shape.
SHAKESPEARE, *Hamlet*

5663. Nay, then, let the devil wear
black, for I'll have a suit of sables.
SHAKESPEARE, *Hamlet*

5664. He will give the devil his due.
SHAKESPEARE, *Henry IV*

5665. The prince of darkness is a
gentleman.   SHAKESPEARE,
King Lear

5666. The devil can cite Scripture
for his purpose.
SHAKESPEARE,
The Merchant of Venice

5667. Let me say "amen" betimes,
lest the devil cross my prayer.
SHAKESPEARE,
The Merchant of Venice

5668. This is a devil, and no monster; I will leave him; I have no
long spoon.   SHAKESPEARE,
The Tempest

5669. What, man! defy the Devil:
consider, he's an enemy to mankind.
SHAKESPEARE, *Twelfth Night*

5670. He's a very devil.
SHAKESPEARE, *Twelfth Night*

5671. The Devil is the author of
confusion.   SWIFT, *Letters*

See also: 1335, 1862, 2655, 2843,
3393, 3395, 4710, 4857, 6103, 10289.

DEVOTION

**Related Subjects: Holiness, Love,
Loyalty, Piety, Prayer, Religion,
Sacrifice, Worship.**

5681. For "ignorance is the mother
of devotion," as all the world knows.
ROBERT BURTON,
Anatomy of Melancholy

5682. Give me a man that is capable of a devotion to anything, rather than a cold, calculating average of all the virtues!　BRET HARTE,
Two Men of Sandy Bar

5683. At thy command I would change, not merely my costume, but my very soul, so entirely art thou the sole possessor of my body and my spirit. Never, God is my witness, never have I sought anything in thee but thyself; I have sought thee, and not thy gifts. I have not looked to the marriage-bond or dowry.
HELOÏSE, *to Abélard*

5684. All is holy where devotion kneels.　O. W. HOLMES

5685. The most illiterate man who is touched with devotion, and uses frequent exercises of it, contracts a certain greatness of mind, mingled with a noble simplicity, that raises him above others of the same condition. By this, a man in the lowest condition will not appear mean, or in the most splendid fortune insolent.
SAMUEL JOHNSON

5686. That sweet look of devotion which men have never been able altogether to love, and which still makes the born saint an object almost of suspicion to his earthly brethren.
WALTER PATER, *The Renaissance*

5687. The private devotions and secret offices of religion are like the refreshing of a garden with the distilling and petty drops of a waterpot; but addressed from the temple, they are like rain from heaven.
JEREMY TAYLOR

See also: 519, 1314, 1320, 1998, 2635, 10520, 18152, 18167.

DEW

Related Subjects: Flowers, Grass, Morning, Rain, Water.

5691. The Dewdrop slips into the shining sea!　EDWIN ARNOLD,
The Light of Asia

5692.

The dew,
'Tis of the tears which stars weep, sweet with joy.
PHILIP J. BAILEY, *Festus*

5693. He lived upon dew, after the manner of a grasshopper.
SIR THOMAS BROWNE, *Religio Medici*

5694.
The dews of the evening most carefully shun;
Those tears of the sky for the loss of the sun.
LORD CHESTERFIELD,
Advice to a Lady in Autumn

5695.
Dew-drops are the gems of morning,
But the tears of mournful eve!
COLERIDGE, *Youth and Age*

5696.
The dew-bead
Gem of earth and sky begotten.
GEORGE ELIOT, *The Spanish Gypsy*

5697. The world globes itself in a drop of dew.　EMERSON, *Essays*

5698. The lovely varnish of the dew, whereby the old, hard, peaked earth and its old self-same productions are made new every morning, and shining with the last touch of the artist's hand. EMERSON, *Nature, Addresses*

5699.
Brushing with hasty steps the dews away,
To meet the sun upon the upland lawn.　THOMAS GRAY,
Elegy Written in a Country Church-yard

5700.
I've seen the dew-drop clinging
  To the rose just newly born.
CHARLES JEFFERYS, *Mary of Argyle*

5701. Every dew-drop and rain-drop
had a whole heaven within it.
LONGFELLOW, *Hyperion*

5702.
Stars of morning, dew-drops which
  the sun
Impearls on every leaf and every
  flower.   MILTON, *Paradise Lost*

5703. Every blade of grass has its
own drop of dew.   *Proverb*

5704
must go seek some dewdrops here,
And hand a pearl in every cowslip's
  ear.   SHAKESPEARE,
      A Midsummer-Night's Dream

5705. And every dew-drop paints a
bow.   TENNYSON, *In Memoriam*

See also: 1774, 1777, 1786, 2138,
711.

DIAMOND

Related Subject: Jewel.

5711. Better a diamond with a flaw
than a pebble without.
CONFUCIUS, *Analects*

5712. Acres of diamonds.
RUSSELL H. CONWELL,
      Title of lecture

5713. Diamond cut diamond.
JOHN FORD, *The Lover's Melancholy*

5714. The diamond has become notoriously common since every tradesman has taken to wearing it on his
little finger.
J. K. HUYSMANS, *Against the Grain*

5715. A fine diamond may be ill-set.
Proverb

5716. A diamond is valuable tho' it
lie on a dunghill.   *Proverb*

See also: 3542.

DICE

Related Subject: Gambling.

5721. I never hear the rattling of
dice that it does not sound to me like
the funeral bell of the whole family.
DOUGLAS JERROLD

5722. The best throw with the dice,
is to throw them away.   *Proverb*

DICTATORSHIP

Related Subjects: Censorship,
Communism, Despotism, Fascism,
Government, Leader, Persecution,
Power, Propaganda, Tyranny.

5731. Dictatorship is like a great
beech tree, nice to look at, but nothing grows under it.
STANLEY BALDWIN

5732. Dictatorship—the fetish worship of one man—is a passing phase.
A state of society where men may not
speak their minds, where children
denounce their parents to the police,
where a business man or small shop-
keeper ruins his competitor by telling
tales about his private opinions—such
a state of society cannot long endure
if brought into contact with the
healthy outside world.
WINSTON CHURCHILL,
      Blood, Sweat & Tears

5733. One thing has struck me as
very strange, and that is the resur-
gence of the one-man power after all
these centuries of experience and
progress. It is curious how the Eng-
lish-speaking peoples have always
had this horror of one-man power.
They are quite ready to follow a
leader for a time, as long as he is

serviceable to them; but the idea of handing themselves over, lock, stock and barrel, body and soul, to one man, and worshipping him as if he were an idol—that has always been odious to the whole theme and nature of our civilization.
WINSTON CHURCHILL,
Blood, Sweat & Tears

5734. Who is all-powerful should fear everything.   CORNEILLE, *Cinna*

5735. When liberty becomes license, dictatorship is near.
WILL DURANT,
The Life of Greece

5736.
His energetic fist
Should be ready to resist
A dictatorial word.
W. S. GILBERT,
H. M. S. Pinafore

5737. One must never forget that everything that is actually great in this world has not been fought for and won by coalitions, but that it was always the success of one individual victor.   ADOLF HITLER, *Mein Kampf*

5738. The Fuehrer is the Party and the Party is the Fuehrer. Just as I feel myself only as a part of the Party, the Party feels itself only as a part of me.   ADOLF HITLER,
National Soc. Party Congr. 1935

5739. That to live by one man's will became the cause of all men's misery.
RICHARD HOOKER,
Ecclesiastical Polity

5740. When the dignity of the human soul is denied in great parts of the world, and when that denial is made a slogan under which propaganda is set in motion and armies take the field, no one of us can be sure that his country or even his home is safe.   CORDELL HULL

5741. Dictatorship is always merely an aria, never an opera.
EMIL LUDWIG

5742. He who establishes a dictatorship and does not kill Brutus, or he who founds a republic and does not kill the sons of Brutus, will only reign a short time.
MACHIAVELLI, *Discourse*

5743. Dictators always look good until the last ten minutes.
JAN MASARYK

5744. They [people in lands with dictators] have forgotten the lesson of history that the ultimate failure of dictatorships cost humanity far more than any temporary failures of democracy.
FRANKLIN D. ROOSEVELT,
Address, 193

5745.
Like the form of a seen and unheard
    prowler,
like a slow and cruel violence,
is the known unspoken menace:
do what we tell you or go hungry;
listen to us or you don't eat.
CARL SANDBURG, *The People, Ye*

5746.
    Ye gods, it doth amaze me,
A man of such a feeble temper should
So get the start of the majestic
    world
And bear the palm alone.
SHAKESPEARE, *Julius Caesar*

5747. Any fool can govern with a stick in his hand. *I* could govern that way. It is not God's way.
BERNARD SHAW, *Heartbreak House*

5748. A very fair spot but there is no way down from it.
SOLON, *Of Dictatorship*

5749. As I stand aloof and watch there is something profoundly mov ing in great masses of men following the leadership of men who do not believe in men.   WALT WHITMAN

5750. It is a consoling fact that, in the end, the moral independence of mankind remains undestructible. Never has it been possible for a dictatorship to enforce one religion or one philosophy upon the whole world. Nor will it ever be possible, for the spirit always escapes from servitude; refuses to think in accordance with prescribed forms, to become shallow and supine at the word of command, to allow uniformity to be permanently imposed upon it.

STEFAN ZWEIG, *The Right to Heresy*

See also: 779, 1159, 4013, 5408, 5427, 9979, 10517.

DIET

Related Subjects: **Digestion, Eating, Food, Health.**

5751. Food improperly taken, not only produces diseases, but affords those that are already engendered both matter and sustenance; so that, let the father of disease be what it may, intemperance is its mother.

ROBERT BURTON,
Anatomy of Melancholy

5752. In general, mankind, since the improvement of cookery, eat twice as much as nature requires.

FRANKLIN

5753. Now learn what and how great benefits a temperate diet will bring along with it. In the first place you will enjoy good health.

HORACE, *Satires*

5754. Simple diet is best, for many dishes bring many diseases, and rich sauces are worse than even heaping several meats upon each other.

PLINY THE ELDER

5755. Whatsoever was the father of a disease, an ill diet was the mother.

Proverb

5756. All courageous animals are carnivorous, and greater courage is to be expected in a people whose food is strong and hearty, than in the half-starved of other countries.

SIR WILLIAM TEMPLE

See also: 21856.

DIFFERENCES

Related Subjects: **Argument, Discord, Quarreling.**

5761. If men would consider not so much wherein they differ, as wherein they agree, there would be far less of uncharitableness and angry feeling in the world.   ADDISON

5762. It is better to decide a difference between enemies than friends; for one of our friends will certainly become an enemy, and one of our enemies a friend.   BIAS

5763. It is remarkable that men, when they differ in what they think considerable, are apt to differ in almost everything else. Their difference begets contradiction; contradiction begets heat; heat rises into resentment, rage and ill-will. Thus they differ in affection, as they differ in judgment, and the contention which began in pride, ends in anger.

CATO THE CENSOR

5764.
The King can drink the best of wine—
    So can I;
And has enough when he would dine—
    So have I;
And can not order rain or shine—
    Nor can I.

Then where's the difference—Let me
see—
Betwixt my lord the king and me?
CHARLES MACKAY, *Differences*

5765.
The difference is as great between
The optics seeing as the objects seen.
POPE, *Moral Essays*

5766. The difference is wide that the
sheets will not decide.   *Proverb*

5767. O, the difference of man and
man!   SHAKESPEARE, *King Lear*

5768. Like—but oh! how different!
WORDSWORTH, *The Mountain Echo*

See also: 3014, 9320, 11868.

DIFFICULTY

Related Subjects: Adversity, Possibility, Trouble.

5771. Never trust the advice of a
man in difficulties.
AESOP, *The Fox and the Goat*

5772. Difficulty is a severe instructor.   BURKE,
*Reflections on the Revolution
In France*

5773. The block of granite which was
an obstacle in the pathway of the
weak becomes a stepping-stone in the
pathway of the strong.   CARLYLE

5774. What is difficult? To keep a
secret, to employ leisure well, to be
able to bear an injury.   CHILON

5775. Ease with difficulty.
CICERO, *Oratio Pro Publio Sextio*

5776. The lamentable difficulty I
have always experienced in saying
"No."
COLERIDGE, *Biographia Literaria*

5777. It is difficulties which show
what men are.
EPICTETUS, *Discourses*

5778. The greatest difficulties lie
where we are not looking for them
GOETHE, *Spruche in Prose*

5779. Difficulty is the excuse history
never accepts.
SAMUEL GRAFTON,
I'd Rather Be Right

5780. The illustration which solve
one difficulty by raising another
settles nothing.   HORACE, *Satire*

5781. Difficulty is, for the most part
the daughter of idleness.
SAMUEL JOHNSON, *The Rambler*

5782. Many things difficult to design
prove easy to performance.
SAMUEL JOHNSON, *Rassela*

578∪. He who accounts all things eas
will have many difficulties.
LAO-TSZE, *The Simple Wa*

5784.
So he with difficulty and labor har
Mov'd on, with difficulty and labo
he.   MILTON, *Paradise Lo.*

5785. What is worth while mus
needs be difficult.   OVID,
Art of Lo

5786. To blow and swallow at th
same moment is not easy.
PLAUTUS, *Mostellar*

5787. Difficulty makes desire.
Prove

5788. Difficulties are opportunitie
Prove

5789. What a case am I in.
SHAKESPEARE, *As You Like*

5790.
It is as hard to come as for a cam
To thread the postern of a sm
needle's eye.   SHAKESPEARE,
Richard

5791. I have been in such a pickle since I saw you last.

SHAKESPEARE, *The Tempest*

5792.
O Time, thou must untangle this, not I;
It is too hard a knot for me t' untie.

SHAKESPEARE, *Twelfth Night*

5793. There is nothing so easy but that is becomes difficult when you do it with reluctance.   TERENCE,
Heauton Timoroumenos

See also: 678, 3300, 4131.

DIGESTION AND INDIGESTION

Related Subjects: Belly, Diet, Eating, Food.

5801. To eat is human; to digest, divine.   C. T. COPELAND

5802. What avails it us to have our bellies full of meat if it be not digested?   MONTAIGNE, *Essays*

5803.
Now, good digestion wait on appetite,
And health on both!

SHAKESPEARE, *Macbeth*

Indigestion.

5804.
'Tis not *her* coldness, father,
  That chills my labouring breast;
It's that confounded cucumber
  I've ate and can't digest.

R. H. BARHAM, *The Confession*

5805.
  Indigestion is—that inward fate
Which makes all Styx through one
    small liver flow.   BYRON,
Don Juan

5806. Indigestion is charged by God with enforcing morality on the stomach.

VICTOR HUGO, *Les Miserables*

5807. Unquiet meals make ill digestions.   SHAKESPEARE,
The Comedy of Errors

5808. Old friendships are destroyed by toasted cheese, and hard salted meat has led to suicide. Unpleasant feelings of the body produce correspondent sensations of the mind, and a great scene of wretchedness is sketched out by a morsel of indigestible and misguided food.

SYDNEY SMITH

See also: 1032, 1872, 4063, 5485, 15151.

DIGNITY

Related Subjects: Character, Distinction, Greatness, Honor, Nobility, Pride, Rank, Reserve.

5811. Dignity consists not in possessing honors, but in the consciousness that we deserve them.

ARISTOTLE

5812. Dignity of position adds to dignity of character, as well as to dignity of carriage. Give us a proud position, and we are impelled to act up to it.   C. N. BOVEE

5813. There is a certain dignity of manners absolutely necessary, to make even the most valuable character either respected or respectable.

LORD CHESTERFIELD, *Letters*

5814. Dignity is like a perfume: those who use it are scarcely conscious of it.

QUEEN CHRISTINA OF SWEDEN

5815.
  The dignity of truth is lost
With much protesting.

BEN JONSON, *Catiline*

5816. I confess I *am* a little nervous about the gas-bills which must come in, in the course of time . . . but then the dignity of being liable to such things is a very supporting consideration. No man is a Bohemian who has to pay water-rates and a street tax. SIDNEY LANIER

5817. Remember this,—that there is a proper dignity and proportion to be observed in the performance of every act of life.

MARCUS AURELIUS, *Meditations*

5818. Dignity and love do not blend well nor do they continue long together. OVID

5819. Perhaps the only true dignity of man is his capacity to despise himself. SANTAYANA,
Introduction to the Ethics of Spinoza

5820. It is easier to grow in dignity than to make a start. SENECA,
Epistulae ad Lucilium

5821.
But clay and clay differs in dignity,
Whose death is both alike.
SHAKESPEARE, *Cymbeline*

5822.
　　My cloud of dignity
Is held from falling with so weak a wind
That it will quickly drop.
SHAKESPEARE, *Henry IV*

5823.
　　　Let none presume
To wear an undeserved dignity.
SHAKESPEARE,
The Merchant of Venice

5824.
True dignity abides with him alone
Who, in the silent hour of inward thought,
Can still suspect, and still revere himself,
In lowliness of heart.
WORDSWORTH,
*Lines Left upon a Seat in a
Yew Tree*

See also: 733, 1004, 1511, 2257, 4529, 5428, 5435, 7810, 20202.

DILIGENCE, see Industry

DINING, DINNER

Related Subjects: Cooks and Cooking, Eating, Feast, Food.

5830. It isn't so much what's on the table that matters, as what's on the chairs. W. S. GILBERT

5831.
Among the great whom Heaven has
　made to shine,
How few have learned the art of
　arts,—to dine!
O. W. HOLMES,
The Banker's Secret

5832. Ye diners-out from whom we guard our spoons. MACAULAY,
Political Georgics

5833.
He may live without books,—what
　is knowledge but grieving?
He may live without hope,—what is
　hope but deceiving?
He may live without love,—what is
　passion but pining?
But where is the man that can live
　without dining?
OWEN MEREDITH, *Lucile*

5834. The more the merrier; the fewer, the better fare.
JOHN PALSGRAVE, *L'Eclair*

5835. Who depends upon another man's table often dines late.
Proverb

5836. At a round table there's no dispute of place. *Proverb*

5837.
Serenely full, the epicure would say,
Fate cannot harm me,—I have dined
to-day. SIDNEY SMITH,
Lady Holland's Memoir

5838.
Across the walnuts and the wine.
TENNYSON, *The Miller's Daughter*

Dinner

5839. A warmed-up dinner was never worth much.   BOILEAU, *Le Lutrin*

5840.
All human history attests
That happiness for man—the hungry sinner—
Since Eve ate apples, much depends on dinner!   BYRON, *Don Juan*

5841. A man once asked Diogenes what was the proper time for supper, and he made answer, "If you are a rich man, whenever you please; and if you are a poor man, whenever you can."
DIOGENES LAERTIUS, *Diogenes*

5842. When a man is invited to dinner, he is disappointed if he does not get something good.
SAMUEL JOHNSON, *Boswell: Life*

5843. Strange to see how a good dinner and feasting reconciles everybody.   SAMUEL PEPYS, *Diary*

5844. A good dinner, and company.
SAMUEL PEPYS, *Diary*

5845. To the Trinity House, where a very good dinner among the old soakers.   SAMUEL PEPYS, *Diary*

5846. He sups ill, who eats up all at dinner.   *Proverb*

5847. Better a good dinner than a fine coat.   *Proverb*

5848. A dinner lubricates business.
WILLIAM SCOTT

5849. Come, we have a hot venison pasty to dinner.   SHAKESPEARE, *The Merry Wives of Windsor*

5850. I will make an end of my dinner; there's pippins and cheese to come.   SHAKESPEARE, *The Merry Wives of Windsor*

5851. Dinner was made for eatin', not for talkin'.   THACKERAY, *Fashnable Fax*

5852. They make their pride in making their dinner cost much; I make my pride in making my dinner cost little.   THOREAU

See also: 1902.

DIPLOMACY, DIPLOMAT

Related Subjects: Ambassador, Politics, Statesman, Tact.

5861. It is fortunate that diplomats generally have long noses, since usually they cannot see beyond them.
Anonymous

5862. International arbitration may be defined as the substitution of many burning questions for a smouldering one.   AMBROSE BIERCE, *The Devil's Dictionary*

5863. Respect for treaties is a very important matter and it cannot be treated as if it were a matter of no consequence.
WINSTON CHURCHILL, *Blood, Sweat & Tears*

5864. American diplomacy is easy on the brain but hell on the feet.
CHARLES G. DAWES

5865.
Diplomacy is to do and say
The nastiest thing in the nicest way.
ISAAC GOLDBERG, *The Reflex*

5866.
There are three species of creature who when they seem coming are going,

When they seem going they come:
Diplomats, women, and crabs.
JOHN HAY, *Distichs*

5867. Men, like bullets, go farthest
when they are smoothest.
J. P. RICHTER, *Titan*

5868.
Touch you the sourest points with
sweetest terms.
SHAKESPEARE,
Antony and Cleopatra

See also: 675, 689, 694, 708, 1021,
6151, 6920.

DIRT

Related Subjects: Bathing, Cleanliness, Washing.

5871.
To dig and delve in nice clean dirt
Can do a mortal little hurt.
JOHN KENDRICK BANGS,
Gardening

5872. "Ignorance," says Ajax, "is a
painless evil." So, I should think, is
dirt, considering the merry faces that
go along with it.   GEORGE ELIOT

5873. Dirt is not dirt, but only something in the wrong place.
LORD PALMERSTON

5874. He that deals in dirt has ay foul
fingers.   *Proverb*

5875. He that falls in the dirt, the
longer he lies the dirtier he is.
Proverb
See also: 1482.

DISAPPOINTMENT

**Related Subjects: Contentment,
Expectation, Failure, Loss, Regret.**

5881. We mount to heaven mostly on
the ruins of our cherished schemes,
finding our failures were successes.
BRONSON ALCOTT

5882.
There is no disappointment we endure
One half so great as that we are to
ourselves.   PHILIP J. BAILEY,
Festus

5883. It is sometimes of God's mercy
that men in the eager pursuit of
worldly aggrandizement are baffled;
for they are very like a train going
down an inclined plane—putting on
the brake is not pleasant, but it keeps
the car on the track and from ruin.
H. W. BEECHER

5884. Man must be disappointed with
the lesser things of life before he
can comprehend the full value of the
greater.   BULWER-LYTTON

5885.
And still they dream that they shall
still succeed,
And still are disappointed.
COWPER, *The Task*

5886. As for disappointing them, I
should not so much mind; but I can't
abide to disappoint myself.
GOLDSMITH,
She Stoops to Conquer

5887. He who expects much will be
often disappointed; yet disappointment seldom cures us of expectation,
or has any other effect than that of
producing a moral sentence or peevish
exclamation.   SAMUEL JOHNSON

5888. Disappointment, parent of Despair.   KEATS, *To Hope*

5889. How disappointment tracks the
steps of hope.   L. E. LANDON

5890.
But O! as to embrace me she inclin'd,
I wak'd, she fled, and day brought
back my night.   MILTON,
On his Deceased Wife

5891. It is a bitter disappointment when you have sown benefits, to reap injuries.   PLAUTUS, *Epidicus*

5892. Mean spirits under disappointment, like small beer in a thunderstorm, always turn sour.
                    JOHN RANDOLPH

5893.
Two sisters by the goal are set,
Cold Disappointment and Regret;
One disenchants the winner's eyes,
And strips of all its worth the prize,
While one augments its gaudy show,
More to enhance the loser's woe.
                    SCOTT, *Rokeby*

5894.
All is but toys; renown and grace is
    dead;
The wine of life is drawn, and the
    mere lees
Is left this vault to brag of.
          SHAKESPEARE, *Macbeth*

5895. My cake is dough.
              SHAKESPEARE,
          The Taming of the Shrew

5896. Life often seems like a long shipwreck of which the debris are friendship, glory, and love. The shores of existence are strewn with them.   MME. DE STAËL

5897.
For of all sad words of tongue or
    pen,
The saddest are these: "It might have
    been!"   WHITTIER,
              Maud Muller

See also: 5393, 5842, 14941.

DISASTER, see Misfortune

DISCIPLINE

Related Subjects: **Army, Authority, Command, Obedience, Order, Self-Control, Soldier.**

5901. For the artist life is always a discipline, and no discipline can be

without pain. That is so even of dancing, which of all the arts is most associated in the popular mind with pleasure. To learn to dance is the most austere of disciplines.
              HAVELOCK ELLIS,
                  The Dance of Life

5902. A stern discipline pervades all nature, which is a little cruel that it may be very kind.
              HERBERT SPENCER

5903. The essence of democratic discipline is that it is the self-discipline of men who agree. It can be very severe; it can be the very opposite of anarchy. But it cannot exist without a feeling of freedom to discuss, freedom to take responsibility, and a deep and shared understanding of aims held in common.
              TOM WINTRINGHAM,
                  New Ways of War

See also: 3229, 6624, 20838.

DISCONTENT, see Contentment

DISCORD

Related Subjects: **Argument, Differences, Faction, Harmony, Music, Noise, Opposition, Quarreling, Rebellion, War.**

5911.
From hence, let fierce contending nations know
What dire effects from civil discord flow.   ADDISON, *Cato*

5912. If a house be divided against itself, that house cannot stand.
              Bible: Mark, iii, 25

5913. In a case of dissension, never dare to judge till you've heard the other side.   EURIPIDES,
                  Heracleidae

5914.

When dreadful Discord bursts her
  brazen bars,
And shatters locks to thunder forth
  her wars.   HORACE, *Satires*

5915.

Is it, O man, with such discordant
  noises,
  With such accursed instruments as
  these,
Thou drownest Nature's sweet and
  kindly voices,
And jarrest the celestial harmonies?
              LONGFELLOW,
      The Arsenal at Springfield

5916. All your danger is in discord.
    LONGFELLOW, *Hiawatha*

5917. Discord, with a thousand various mouths.   MILTON,
            Paradise Lost

5918. All discord, harmony not understood.   POPE, *Essay on Man*

5919.

              How, in one house,
Should many people, under two com-
  mands,
Hold amity?   SHAKESPEARE,
              King Lear

5920. The Demon of Discord, with
her sooty wings, had breathed her
influence upon our counsels.
    SMOLLETT, *Roderick Random*

DISCOVERY

Related Subjects: Invention, Pioneer, Progress.

5921. It is the modest, not the pre-
sumptuous inquirer, who makes a
real and safe progress in the discovery of divine truths. He follows
God in his works and in his word.
              BOLINGBROKE

5922. Through every rift of discovery some seeming anomaly drops out
of the darkness, and falls, as a golden
link, into the greatest chain of order.
              E. H. CHAPIN

5923. It is a mortifying truth, and
ought to teach the wisest of us humility, that many of the most valuable
discoveries have been the result of
chance rather than of contemplation,
and of accident rather than of design.
              C. C. COLTON

5924. It is a profound mistake to
think that everything has been discovered; as well think the horizon
the boundary of the world.
              LEMIERRE

5925. If I have ever made any valuable discoveries, it has been owing
more to patient attention, than to any
other talent.   SIR ISAAC NEWTON

See also: 1062.

DISCRETION AND INDISCRETION

Related Subjects: Caution, Foolishness, Prudence, Wisdom.

5931. Much that well may be thought
cannot wisely be said.
              Anonymous,
    The Priest & the Mulberry-Tree

5932. As a jewel of gold in a swine's
snout, so is a fair woman which is
without discretion.
        Bible: Proverbs, xxiv, 22

5933. A time to keep silence, and a
time to speak.
        Bible: Ecclesiastes, iii, 7

5934. Be swift to hear, slow to speak,
slow to wrath.   *Bible: James, i, 19*

5935. Least said, soonest mended.
    DICKENS, *David Copperfield*

5936.
Know when to speak—for many
    times it brings
Danger, to give the best advice to
    kings.   ROBERT HERRICK,
                        Caution in Counsel

5937. He that hears much, and
speaks not all, shall be welcome both
in bower and hall.   *Proverb*

5938. He that goes softly goes safely.
                        Proverb

5939. He knows not when to be
silent who knows not when to speak.
        PUBLILIUS SYRUS, *Sententiae*

5940. Wise men say nothing in dangerous times.   JOHN SELDEN,
                        Table Talk

5941. The better part of valour is
discretion.   SHAKESPEARE,
                        Henry IV

5942.
Have more than thou showest,
Speak less than thou knowest.
        SHAKESPEARE, *King Lear*

Indiscretion

5943. An indiscreet man is more
hurtful than an ill-natured one; for
the latter will only attack his enemies,
and those he wishes ill to; the other
injures indifferently both friends and
foes.   ADDISON

5944. That strange impulse of indiscretion, common to men who lead
secret lives, and accounting for the
invariable existence of "compromising documents" in all the plots and
conspiracies of history.
        JOSEPH CONRAD,
                Under Western Eyes

5945.
For good and evil in our actions
    meet;

Wicked is not much worse than in-
    discreet.   JOHN DONNE

5946. A lover without indiscretion is
no lover at all.
        THOMAS HARDY,
                The Hand of Ethelberta

5947. Indiscretion, rashness, falsehood, levity, and malice produce each
other.   LAVATER

5948. Questions are never indiscreet:
answers sometimes are.
                OSCAR WILDE

See also: 132, 4484, 4761, 11618,
14458, 15160.

DISCUSSION

Related Subjects: Argument, Conversation.

5951. Free and fair discussion will
ever be found the firmest friend to
truth.   GEORGE CAMPBELL

5952. The pain of dispute exceeds,
by much, its utility. All disputation
makes the mind deaf, and when
people are deaf I am dumb.
                JOUBERT, *Pensées*

5953. Men are never so likely to
settle a question rightly as when they
discuss it freely.   MACAULAY,
                Southey's Colloquies

5954. He who knows only his own
side of the case, knows little of that.
                J. S. MILL

5955. All bitter feelings are avoided,
or at least greatly reduced by prompt,
face-to-face discussion.
                WALTER B. PITKIN

5956. Whosoever is afraid of sub-
mitting any question, civil or religious, to the test of free discussion,
is more in love with his own opinion
than with truth.   THOMAS WATSON

5957. He that is not open to conviction, is not qualified for discussion.
RICHARD WHATELY

DISDAIN, see Scorn

DISEASE

Related Subjects: Complaint, Death, Decay, Doctors, Health, Hospitals, Medicine, Rat, Sickness.

5961.
Some little bug is going to find you
some day
Some little bug will creep behind you
some day.   ROY ATWELL,
*Some Little Bug Is Going To Find
You Some Day*

5962. The captain of all these men of death that came against him to take him away, was the Consumption, for it was that was that brought him down to the grave.   BUNYAN,
The Life & Death of Mr. Badman

5963. They do not live but linger.
ROBERT BURTON,
Anatomy of Melancholy

5964. [Diseases] crucify the soul of man, attenuate our bodies, dry them, wither them, shrivel them up like old apples, make them as so many anatomies.   ROBERT BURTON,
Anatomy of Melancholy

5965. Disease is an experience of so-called mortal mind. It is fear made manifest on the body. Christian Science takes away this physical sense of discord, just as it removes any other sense of moral or mental inharmony.
MARY BAKER EDDY,
Science and Health

5966. Before you can cure the diseases of the body, you must cure the

diseases of the soul—greed, ignorance, prejudice and intolerance.
PAUL EHRLICH

5967. The number of diseases is a disgrace to mankind.
FENELON, *Telemachus*

5968.
That dire disease, whose ruthless
power
Withers the beauty's transient flower
GOLDSMITH, *Double Transformation*

5969. This solidarity against pathogenic micro-organisms extends beyond the boundaries of nationality race, or even species. Every Rumanian infected with infantile paralysis, every Indian with smallpox every rat with plague, diminishes the probable length of my life.
J. B. S. HALDANE

5970. A bodily disease which we look upon as whole and entire within itself, may, after all, be but a symptom of some ailment in the spiritual part
HAWTHORNE, *Scarlet Letter*

5971. Extreme remedies are very appropriate for extreme diseases.
HIPPOCRATES, *Aphorisms*

5972. Humanity has but three great enemies: fever, famine and war; of these by far the greatest, by far the most terrible, is fever.
SIR WILLIAM OSLER,
Life of Sir William Osler

5973. They do certainly give very strange and new-fangled names to diseases.   PLATO, *The Republic*

5974. And as in men's bodies, so in government, that disease is most serious which proceeds from the head.   PLINY THE YOUNGER

5975. This long disease, my life.
POPE, *Epistle to Dr. Arbuthnot*

5976.

As man, perhaps, the moment of his
   breath,
Receives the lurking principle of
   death,
The young disease, that must subdue
   at length,
Grows with his growth, and strengthens with his strength.
         POPE, *Essay on Man*

5977.

But just disease to luxury succeeds.
And ev'ry death its own avenger
   breeds.   POPE, *Essay on Man*

5978. Diseases are the tax on ill
pleasures.   *Proverb*

5979. A disease known is half cured.
                 Proverb

5980.

O, he's a limb, that has but a disease;
Mortal, to cut it off; to cure it easy.
     SHAKESPEARE, *Coriolanus*

5981.

         Diseases desperate grown
By desperate appliance are relieved,
Or not at all.   SHAKESPEARE,
                   Hamlet

5982. This apoplexy is, as I take it,
a kind of lethargy, an't please your
lordship; a kind of sleeping in the
blood, a whoreson tingling.
     SHAKESPEARE, *Henry IV*

5983.

Before the curing of a strong disease,
Even in the instant of repair and
   health,
The fit is strongest; evils that take
   leave,
On their departure most of all show
   evil.   SHAKESPEARE, *King John*

5984.

             I'll forbear;
And am fallen out with my more
   headier will,

To take the indispos'd and sickly fit
For the sound man.
     SHAKESPEARE, *King Lear*

See also: 66, 1344, 3833, 3924, 6613,
8312, 11821, 13562, 15667.

DISGRACE

Related Subjects: Contempt,
Scorn, Shame.

5991. Come, Death, and snatch me
from disgrace.
     BULWER-LYTTON, *Richelieu*

5992. Infamy was never incurred for
nothing.   BURKE,
   Impeachment of Warren Hastings

5993. The unbought grace of life, the
cheap defence of nations, the nurse of
manly sentiment and heroic enterprise, is gone!   BURKE,
   *Reflections on the Revolution in
                  France*

5994.

Could he with reason murmer at his
   case,
Himself sole author of his own disgrace?   COWPER, *Hope*

5995.

The lowliest men would sooner face
A thousand dreadful deaths, than
   come
Before their loved ones in disgrace.
     JOHN DAVIDSON,
     A Ballad of a Coward

5996. A wise and good man can suffer no disgrace.   FABIUS MAXIMUS

5997. That only is a disgrace to a
man which he has deserved to suffer.
     PHAEDRUS, *Fables*

5998. The pleasure is over, but the
disgrace remains.   *Proverb*

5999.
And wilt thou still be hammering treachery,
To tumble down thy husband and thyself
From top of honour to disgrace's feet?   SHAKESPEARE, *Henry VI*

6000. It is better not to live at all than to live disgraced.
           SOPHOCLES, *Peleus*

See also: 195, 11365, 13743, 20762.

DISHONESTY, see Honesty

DISILLUSION, see Illusion

DISLIKE

Related Subject: Hatred.

6001.
I do not love thee, Doctor Fell,
The reason why I cannot tell;
But this alone I know full well,
I do not love thee, Doctor Fell.
           THOMAS BROWN

6002. Whom she likes, she likes; whom she dislikes, she dislikes.
           PETRONIUS, *Satyricon*

6003. I do desire we may be better strangers.   SHAKESPEARE,
           As You Like It

6004. I see, lady, the gentleman is not in your books.
           SHAKESPEARE,
       Much Ado About Nothing

6005. My aversion, my aversion, my aversion of all aversions.
       WYCHERLEY, *The Plain-Dealer*

DISOBEDIENCE, see Obedience

DISSENSION, see Discord, Quarreling

DISSIPATION

Related Subjects: Corruption, Drinking, Excess, Idleness, Rake, Sensuality, Sin, Vice.

6011. Wine and women will make men of understanding to fall away.
       Apocrypha: Ecclesiasticus

6012. Wasted his substance with riotous living.   *Bible: Luke, xv, 13*

6013. I may not here omit those two main plagues and common dotages of human kind, wine and women, which have infatuated and besotted myriads of people; they go commonly together.   ROBERT BURTON,
       Anatomy of Melancholy

6014. Wild oats will get sown some time, and one of the arts of life is to sow them at the right time.
       RICHARD LE GALLIENNE,
       The Quest of the Golden Girl

6015. Dissipation is absolutely a labor when the round of Vanity Fair has been once made; but fashion makes us think lightly of the toil, and we describe the circles as mechanically as a horse in a mill.
           J. G. ZIMMERMAN

See also: 2774.

DISTANCE

Related Subject: Travel.

6021.
'Tis distance lends enchantment to the view,
And robes the mountain in its azure hue.   THOMAS CAMPBELL,
       Pleasures of Hope

6022. To the vulgar eye, few things are wonderful that are not distant.
       CARLYLE, *Essays*

6023. A delusion that distance creates, and that contiguity destroys.
C. C. COLTON

6024.
The hills of manhood wear a noble face
    When seen from far;
The mist of light from which they take their grace
Hides what they are.
R. M. MILNES, *Carpe Diem*

6025. The distance is nothing; it is only the first step that costs.
MME. DU DEFFAND,
Letter to d'Alembert

6026. There's a magic in the distance, where the sea-line meets the sky.
ALFRED NOYES,
Forty Singing Seamen

6027. Far away fowls have aye fair feathers.   *Proverb*

6028. Respect is greater from a distance.   TACITUS, *History*

6029.
         Sweetest melodies
Are those that are by distance made more sweet.   WORDSWORTH,
Personal Talk

See also: 265, 575, 793, 4332.

DISTINCTION

Related Subjects: Definition, Dignity, Greatness, Honor, Superiority.

6031. Confucius was once asked: "What must a man do in order to be considered distinguished?"

"What do you mean by the term distinguished?" inquired Confucius.

"One whose fame fills his own private circle and the state at large," was the reply.

"That," said Confucius, "is notori-

ety, not distinction. The man of fine distinction is simple, honest, and a lover of justice and duty."
EDWARD W. BOK,
The Americanization of Edward Bok

6032.
It is no act of common passage, but
A strain of rareness.
SHAKESPEARE, *Cymbeline*

6033. A fellow that hath had losses, and one that hath two gowns, and every thing handsome about him.
SHAKESPEARE,
Much Ado About Nothing

6034. All our distinctions are accidental. Beauty and deformity, though personal qualities, are neither entitled to praise or censure; yet it so happens that they color our opinion of those qualities to which mankind have attached importance.
J. G. ZIMMERMAN

See also: 798, 5070, 17994.

DISTRUST, see Trust

DIVIDENDS

Related Subjects: **Profit, Reward.**

6041. Do you know the only thing that gives me pleasure? It's to see my dividends coming in.
JOHN D. ROCKEFELLER

6042.
Through Life's dark road his sordid way he wends,
An incarnation of fat dividends.
CHARLES SPRAGUE, *Curiosity*

DIVORCE

Related Subject: **Marriage.**

6051. If she go not as thou wouldst have her, cut her off from thy flesh, and give her a bill of divorce, and let her go.   *Apocrypha: Ecclesiasticus*

6052. I think I would make any divorce contingent on a review of the situation at the end of a period of three years. If at the end of the three years one of the partners should still demand an annulment of the marriage, let it be so.

WARWICK DEEPING,
Divorce As I See It

6053. As long as legislators insist on placing marital alliances on a pedestal of a mystic sacrament, instead of on the basis of a clean and just contract, so long will our divorce laws be the everlasting cause of spiritual putrefaction.   FEUCHTWANGER,
Divorce As I See It

6054. The marriage laws of all the United States of America do not materially differ. They are practically the same. It is where divorce is concerned that each state chooses to divide human nature into parts divided by an imaginary line known as the State line.   FANNIE HURST,
Divorce As I See It

6055. There should be so many obstacles placed in the way of divorce that those who overcome them are only the ones who truly desire to do so. Otherwise divorce resembles those automatic revolvers which are responsible for so many murders because they require only a light touch, a gesture which almost involuntarily means death.   ANDRÉ MAUROIS,
Divorce As I See It

6056. A Roman divorced from his wife, being highly blamed by his friends, who demanded, "Was she not chaste? Was she not fair? Was she not fruitful?" holding out his shoe, asked them whether it was not new and well made, "Yet," added he, "none of you can tell where it pinches me."   PLUTARCH, *Lives*

6057. Petty repeated annoyances, arising from unpleasantness or incongruity of character, have been the occasion of such estrangement as to make it impossible for man and wife to live together with any content.

PLUTARCH, *Lives*

6058. Where there are no children divorce should be obtainable at the request of either party. Where there are children the usual ground should be mutual consent; other grounds should be insanity, grave crime, habitual drunkenness, and certain other diseases. Adultery *per se* should not be a ground.

BERTRAND RUSSELL,
Divorce As I See It

6059. Marriage laws and divorces even more than economic and belligerent patriotism remind me, as I care less and less to be reminded, of the irrational ruthlessness of mankind.

H. G. WELLS, *Divorce As I See It*

6060. The divorce of married people with children is nearly always an unspeakable calamity. The point is that if a child is deprived of either its father or its mother it feels that it has been cheated out of a right. He may through yearning for the unattainable parent, get himself into a permanent mood of discontent which will last his life long and make him waste every opportunity of love and happiness that comes to him later.
REBECCA WEST, *Divorce As I See It*

DOCTORS

Related Subjects: Disease, Health, Hospitals, Medicine, Quack, Sickness.

6061. Honour a physician with the honour due unto him.
Apocrypha: Ecclesiasticus

6062.
Physicians of the highest rank
(To pay their fees, we need a bank),
Combine all wisdom, art and skill,
Science and sense, in Calomel.
Anonymous, Calomel

6063. Is there no balm in Gilead? Is there no physician there?
Bible: Jeremiah, viii, 22

6064.
But when ill indeed,
E'en dismissing the doctor don't always succeed.
GEORGE COLMAN,
Lodgings for Single Gentlemen

6065. I observe the physician with the same diligence as he the disease.
JOHN DONNE, *Devotions*

6066.
Better to hunt in fields, for health unbought,
Than fee the doctor for a nauseous draught.
The wise, for cure, on exercise depend;
God never made his work for man to mend. DRYDEN,
Epistle to John Driden of Chesterton

6067. A good surgeon operates with his hand, not with his heart.
DUMAS

6068. It's no trifle at her time of life to part with a doctor who knows her constitution. GEORGE ELIOT,
Janet's Repentance

6069. Sometimes give your services for nothing, calling to mind a previous benefaction or present satisfaction. And if there be an opportunity of serving one who is a stranger in financial straits, give full assistance to all such. For where there is love of man, there is also love of the art. For some patients, though conscious that their condition is perilous, recover their health simply through their contentment with the goodness of the physician. And it is well to superintend the sick to make them well, to care for the healthy to keep them well, but also to care for one's own self, so as to observe what is seemly.
HIPPOCRATES, *Precepts*

6070.
Trained in the holy art whose lifted shield
Wards off the darts a never-slumbering foe,
By hearth and wayside lurking, waits to throw. O. W. HOLMES,
Joseph Warren, M.D.

6071.
Now when a doctor's patients are perplexed,
A consultation comes in order next—
You know what that is? In a certain place
Meet certain doctors to discuss a case
And other matters, such as weather, crops,
Potatoes, pumpkins, lager-beer, and hops. O. W. HOLMES,
Rip Van Winkle, M.D.

6072. A doctor shouldn't have to worry about money! That's one disease he's not trained to fight. It either corrupts him or it destroys him.
SIDNEY KINGSLEY, *Men in White*

6073. No physician, in so far as he is a physician, considers his own good in what he prescribes, but the good of his patient; for the true physician is also a ruler having the human body as a subject, and is not a mere money-maker. PLATO,
The Republic

6074. Who shall decide when doctors disagree?   POPE, *Moral Essays*

6075. Doctors make the worst patients.   *Proverb*

6076. God cures and the doctor takes the fee.   *Proverb*

6077. That patient is not like to recover who makes the doctor his heir.   *Proverb*

6078. The best surgeon is he that has been well hacked himself.   *Proverb*

6079. Honour a physician before thou hast need of him.   *Proverb*

6080. If the doctor cures, the sun sees it; but if he kills, the earth hides it.   *Proverb*

6081. A good surgeon must have an eagle's eye, a lion's heart, and a lady's hand.   *Proverb*

6082.
Like a physician who can do no good,
But knows how soon another would
   have his fee
Were he to tell the truth.
    E. A. ROBINSON, *Avon's Harvest*

6083. With the help of a surgeon, he might yet recover.
    SHAKESPEARE,
    A Midsummer-Night's Dream

6084. I had rather follow you to your grave than see you owe your life to any but a regular-bred physician.
    SHERIDAN, *St. Patrick's Day*

6085. Doctors is all swabs.
    STEVENSON, *Treasure Island*

6086. The best doctors in the world are Doctor Diet, Doctor Quiet, and Doctor Merryman.   SWIFT,
    Polite Conversation

See also: 2630.

DOCTRINE

Related Subjects: Belief, Creeds, Dogmatism, Heresy, Religion, Theology.

6091. Doctrine is nothing but the skin of truth set up and stuffed.
    H. W. BEECHER, *Life Thoughts*

6092. Carried about with every wind of doctrine. *Bible: Ephesians, iv, 14*

6093. False doctrine, heresy, and schism.   *Book of Common Prayer*

6094.
And prove their doctrine orthodox,
By apostolic blows and knocks.
    SAMUEL BUTLER, *Hudibras*

6095. Doctrine is the necessary foundation of duty; if the theory is not correct, the practice cannot be right. Tell me what a man believes, and I will tell you what he will do.
    TRYON EDWARDS

6096. Pure doctrine always bears fruit in pure benefits.   EMERSON

6097. The question is not whether a doctrine is beautiful but whether it is true. When we wish to go to a place, we do not ask whether the road leads through a pretty country, but whether it is the right road.
    A. W. & J. C. HARE,
    Guesses at Truth

6098. Any doctrine that will not bear investigation is not a fit tenant for the mind of an honest man.
    ROBERT INGERSOLL,
    Intellectual Development

6099. Though all the winds of doctrine were let loose to play upon the earth, so Truth be in the field, we do ingloriously, by licensing and prohibiting, to misdoubt her strength.
    MILTON, *Areopagitica*

6100.

He who receives
Light from above, from the Fountain
   of Light,
No other doctrine needs, though
   granted true.   Milton,
Paradise Regained

6101. Say what men may, it is doctrine that moves the world. He who takes no position will not sway the human intellect.   W. G. T. Shedd

6102. Orthodoxy is my doxy—heterodoxy is another man's doxy.
William Warburton

6103. You may be as orthodox as the Devil, and as wicked. John Wesley

See also: 167, 3024, 13215, 13430, 16752.

DOG

Related Subject: Animal.

6111.
Give the boy a dog and you've furnished him a playmate
Always true and faithful as can be.
Berton Braley, *A Gift*

6112. Near this spot are deposited the remains of one who possessed Beauty without Vanity, Strength without Insolence, Courage without Ferocity, and all the Virtues of Man, without his Vices. This Praise, which would be unmeaning Flattery if inscribed over human ashes, is but a just tribute to the Memory of Boatswain, a Dog.   Byron

6113.
The poor dog, in life the firmest friend,
The first to welcome, foremost to defend.   Byron

6114. Did you ever stop to think that a dog is the only animal that doesn't have to work for a living? A hen has to lay eggs; a cow has to give milk; and a canary has to sing. But a dog makes his living by giving you nothing but love.   Dale Carnegie,
How to Win Friends

6115.
Every time I come to town
The boys keep kicking my dawg
   around;
Makes no difference if he is a hound,
They've got to quit kicking my dawg
   around.   *Anonymous*

6116. Let sleeping dogs lie.
Dickens, *David Copperfield*

6117.
And in that town a dog was found,
   As many dogs there be,
Both mongrel, puppy, whelp, and
   hound,
And curs of low degree.
Goldsmith,
The Vicar of Wakefield

6118.
The dog, to gain some private ends,
   Went mad, and bit the man
Goldsmith,
The Vicar of Wakefield

6119.
Oh, the saddest of sights in a world
   of sin
Is a little lost pup with his tail tucked
   in!   Arthur Guiterman,
Little Lost Pup

6120.
My dear dumb friend, low lying
   there,
   A willing vassal at my feet,—
Glad partner of my home and fare,
   My shadow in the street.
J. G. Holland, *To My Dog*

6121. Fox-terriers are born with about four times as much original sin in them as other dogs.
Jerome K. Jerome,
Three Men in a Boat

6122. He that strikes my dog, would strike me if he durst. *Proverb*

6123. He cannot be a gentleman that loveth not a dog. *Proverb*

6124. Dogs wag their tails not so much to you as your bread. *Proverb*

6125. Barking dogs seldom bite. *Proverb*

6126. Give a dog an ill name and you may as well hang him. *Proverb*

6127. Flesh never stands so high but a dog will venture his legs. *Proverb*

6128. Recollect that the Almighty, who gave the dog to be companion of our pleasures and our toils, hath invested him with a nature noble and incapable of deceit. SCOTT, *The Talisman*

6129. The son and heir of a mongrel bitch. SHAKESPEARE, *King Lear*

6130.
                    Mine enemy's dog,
Though he had bit me, should have
    stood that night
Against my fire. SHAKESPEARE, *King Lear*

6131. I like a bit of a mongrel myself, whether it's a man or a dog; they're the best for every day. BERNARD SHAW, *Misalliance*

6132. If you pick up a starving dog and make him prosperous, he will not bite you. This is the principal difference between a dog and a man. MARK TWAIN, *Pudd'nhead Wilson's Calendar*

6133. The dog commends himself to our favour by affording play to our propensity for mastery, and as he is also an item of expense, and commonly serves no industrial purpose, he holds a well-assured place in men's regard as a thing of good repute. THORSTEIN VEBLEN, *The Theory of the Leisure Class*

6134. They say a reasonable number of fleas is good fer a dog—keeps him from broodin' over bein' a dog. E. N. WESTCOTT, *David Harum*

6135.
He may look just the same to you,
    And he may be just as fine,
But the next-door dog is the next-
    door dog,
    And mine—is—mine!
DIXIE WILLSON, *Next-Door Dog*

See also: 1377, 2433, 4257, 4906, 15662.

DOGMATISM

Related Subjects: Bigotry, Creeds, Doctrine, Obstinacy.

6141. No dogmas nail your faith. BROWNING, *Bishop Blougram's Apology*

6142. Any stigma will do to beat a dogma. PHILIP GUEDALLA

6143. Nothing can be more unphilosophical than to be positive or dogmatical on any subject. When men are the most sure and arrogant, they are commonly the most mistaken and have there given reins to passion without that proper deliberation and suspense which alone can secure them from the grossest absurdities. DAVID HUME

6144. From the age of fifteen, dogma has been the fundamental principle of my religion. I know of no other religion; I cannot enter into the idea of any other sort of religion; religion, as a mere sentiment, is to me a dream and a mockery. CARDINAL NEWMAN, *Apologia pro Vita Sua*

6145. A dogmatical tone, a pragmatical pate.   *Proverb*

6146. How absolute the knave is! we must speak by the card, or equivocation will undo us.

SHAKESPEARE, *Hamlet*

6147. It has been said of dogmatism, that it is only puppyism come to its full growth, and certainly the worst form this quality can assume is that of opinionativeness and arrogance.

SAMUEL SMILES

6148. A dogmatical spirit inclines a man to be censorious of his neighbors. Every one of his opinions appears to him written as with sunbeams, and he grows angry that his neighbors do not see it in the same light. He is tempted to disdain his correspondents as men of low and dark understanding because they do not believe what he does.

ISAAC WATTS

See also: 2005, 4151.

DOLLAR, THE

Related Subjects: Economy, Money.

6151. Dollar Diplomacy.

Anonymous

6152. However plenty silver dollars may become they will not be distributed as gifts among the people.

GROVER CLEVELAND

6153. All their cares, hopes, joys, affections, virtues, and associations seem to be melted down into dollars . . . Men were weighed by their dollars. Life was auctioneered, appraised, put up, and knocked down for its dollars . . . The more of that worthless ballast, honor and fair-dealing, which any man cast over-board from the ship of his Good Name and Good Intent, the more ample stowage room he had for dollars. Make commerce one huge lie and mighty theft. Deface the banner of the nation for an idle rag; pollute it star by star; and cut out stripe by stripe as from the arm of a degraded soldier. Do anything for dollars! What is a flag to them?

DICKENS, *Martin Chuzzlewit*

6154. "The American nation in the Sixth Ward is a fine people," he says, "They love th' eagle," he says, "on the back iv a dollar."

F. P. DUNNE,
Mr. Dooley in Peace and War

6155. The Americans have little faith. They rely on the power of the dollar.   EMERSON,
Nature, Addresses and Lectures

6156. The almighty dollar, that great object of universal devotion throughout our land.

WASHINGTON IRVING,
Wolfert's Roost

See also: 1499, 20759.

DOUBT

Related Subjects: Atheism, Belief, Certainty, Credulity, Cynicism, Fear, Heresy, Pessimism, Suspense, Suspicion, Trust.

6161.
Who never doubted never half believed.
Where doubt there truth is—'tis her shadow.   PHILIP J. BAILEY,
Festus

6162. And he that doubteth is damned if he eat.

Bible: Romans, xiv, 23

6163. Doubt whom you will, but never doubt yourself.   C. N. BOVEE

6164. A castle called Doubting Castle, the owner whereof was Giant Despair.   BUNYAN, *Pilgrim's Progress*

6165.
I've stood upon Achilles' tomb,
And heard Troy doubted: time will
  doubt of Rome.   BYRON,
                    Don Juan

6166.
He would not, with a peremptory
  tone,
Assert the nose upon his face his own.
            COWPER, *Conversation*

6167. Doubting charms me not less than knowledge.   DANTE, *Inferno*

6168. Just think of the tragedy of teaching children not to doubt.
            CLARENCE DARROW

6169. In order to reach the Truth, it is necessary, once in one's life, to put everything in doubt—so far as possible.   DESCARTES

6170. Scepticism is the first step on the road to philosophy.   DIDEROT

6171. The faculty of doubting is rare among men. A few choice spirits carry the germs of it in them, but these do not develop without training.   ANATOLE FRANCE,
                    Penguin Island

6172.
Of that there is no manner of doubt—
No probable, possible shadow of
  doubt—
No possible doubt whatever.
        W. S. GILBERT, *The Gondoliers*

6173. Doubt indulged soon becomes doubt realized.
        F. R. HAVERGAL, *Royal Bounty*

6174. When in doubt, win the trick.
                        HOYLE,
    Twenty-four Rules for Learners

6175. A wise scepticism is the first attribute of a good critic.
        LOWELL, *Shakespeare Once More*

6176. Doubts of all things earthly, and intuitions of some things heavenly; this combination makes neither believer nor infidel, but makes a man who regards them both with equal eye.   HERMAN MELVILLE,
                    Moby Dick

6177. Doubts are more cruel than the worst of truths.   MOLIÈRE,
                    Le Misanthrope

6178. Doubt is brother-devil to Despair.   J. B. O'REILLY, *Prometheus*

6179. O Lord—if there is a Lord; save my soul—if I have soul. Amen.
        RÉNAN, *Prayer of a Skeptic*

6180. In all affairs, love, religion, politics, or business—it's a healthy idea, now and then, to hang a question mark on the things you have long taken for granted.
            BERTRAND RUSSELL

6181.
And better had they ne'er been born,
Who read to doubt, or read to scorn.
            SCOTT, *The Monastery*

6182.
But yet, madam— . . .
I do not like, "but yet," it does allay
The good precedence; fie upon "but
  yet!"
"But yet" is a gaoler to bring forth
Some monstrous malefactor.
    SHAKESPEARE, *Antony and Cleopatra*

6183.
Doubt thou the stars are fire;
Doubt that the sun doth move;
Doubt truth to be a liar;
But never doubt I love.
            SHAKESPEARE, *Hamlet*

6184.
But now I am cabin'd, cribb'd, confin'd bound in
To saucy doubts and fears.
SHAKESPEARE, *Macbeth*

6185.
Our doubts are traitors,
And make us lose the good we oft might win
By fearing to attempt.
SHAKESPEARE, *Measure for Measure*

6186.
No hinge nor loop,
To hang a doubt on;
SHAKESPEARE, *Othello*

6187.
To be once in doubt
Is once to be resolv'd.
SHAKESPEARE, *Othello*

6188.
Modest doubt is call'd
The beacon of the wise, the tent that searches
To the bottom of the worst.
SHAKESPEARE, *Troilus and Cressida*

6189.
There lives more faith in honest doubt,
Believe me, than in half the creeds.
TENNYSON, *In Memoriam*

6190. I come from a State that raises corn and cotton and cockleburs and Democrats, and frothy eloquence neither convinces nor satisfies me. I am from Missouri. You have got to show me.   W. D. VANDIVER

See also: 1014, 4724, 7630, 9077, 10940.

DOVE

Related Subjects: Birds, Peace.

6201.
And there my little dove did sit
With feathers softly brown.
ELIZABETH B. BROWNING, *My Doves*

6202.
As when the dove returning bore the mark
Of earth restor'd to the long lab'ring ark,
The relics of mankind, secure of rest,
Oped every window to receive the guest,
And the fair bearer of the message bless'd.
DRYDEN, *To Her Grace of Ormond*

6203. But who does hawk at eagles with a dove?
GEORGE HERBERT, *The Sacrifice*

6204.
See how that pair of billing doves
With open murmurs own their loves
And, heedless of censorious eyes,
Pursue their unpolluted joys:
MARY W. MONTAGU,
Verses Written in a Garden

6205. As patient as the female dove.
SHAKESPEARE, *Hamlet*

6206. Doves will peck in safeguard of their brood.
SHAKESPEARE, *Henry VI*

6207. Who will not change a raven for a dove?   SHAKESPEARE,
A Midsummer-Night's Dream

6208. I will roar you as gently as any sucking dove; I will roar you, as 'twere any nightingale.
SHAKESPEARE,
A Midsummer-Night's Dream

6209. In the spring a livelier iris changes on the burnish'd dove.
TENNYSON, *Lockesley Hall*

See also: 4961.

DRAMA

Related Subjects: Acting, Literature, Poetry, The Stage, Tragedy.

6211.
All tragedies are finished by a death,

All comedies are ended by a marriage.   BYRON, *Don Juan*

6212. We achieved a criticism of life without which the drama is nothing but evanescent showmanship.

JOHN GASSNER,
Introduction: Twenty Best Plays

6213. Athens crowned the theatre with glory while fighting for its existence against a host of enemies. Germany advanced stagecraft by leaps and bounds at a time when it suffered the miseries of inflation and national humiliation. America, struggling through a decade of economic distress, likewise affirmed the strength of the human spirit that often proves so painfully blind and bestial under the whiplash of accumulated errors.

JOHN GASSNER,
Introduction: Twenty Best Plays

6214.
Life's moving-pictures, well-wrought plays,
To others' grief attention raise.

MATTHEW GREEN, *The Spleen*

6215. I would like to see the boys who really know how to write plays really write them, instead of throwing them together out of the shabby devices which they have come to believe are sure-fire. I would like them to remember, for instance, that nothing has ever been more sure-fire than truth and integrity.

WILLIAM SAROYAN,
Preface: My Heart's In the Highlands

6216. The play, I remember, pleased not the million; 'twas caviare to the general.   SHAKESPEARE, *Hamlet*

6217. This writing of plays is a great matter, forming as it does the minds and affections of men in such sort that whatsoever they see done in show on the stage, they will presently be doing in earnest in the world, which is but a larger stage.   BERNARD SHAW,
The Dark Lady of the Sonnets

6218. As long as more people will pay admission to a theatre to see a naked body than to see a naked brain the drama will languish.

BERNARD SHAW, *When asked by a burlesque queen to supply a more graceful word than "strip teaser" to the profession.*

6219. From time to time dramatic art gets a germinal impulse. There follows in the theatre a spring which flourishes into a glorious summer. This becomes stale almost before its arrival is generally recognized; and the sequel is not a new golden age but a barren winter that may last any time from fifteen years to a hundred and fifty. Then comes a new impulse and the cycle begins again.

BERNARD SHAW

6220.
Be patient. Our Playwright may show
In some fifth act what this wild Drama means.

TENNYSON, *The Play*

See also: 5402.

DREAMS

Related Subjects: Castle, Imagination, Psychoanalysis, Psychology, Sleep, Vision.

6221.
When to soft Sleep we give ourselves away,
  And in a dream as in a fairy bark
Drift on and on through the enchanted dark
To purple daybreak—little thought we pay

To that sweet bitter world we know
  by day.   T. B. ALDRICH, *Sleep*

6222.
If there were dreams to sell,
  What would you buy?
      T. L. BEDDOES, *Dream-Pedlary*

6223. As a dream when one awaketh.
      Bible: Psalms, lxxiii, 20

6224. Your old men shall dream
dreams, your young men shall see
visions.   *Bible: Joel, ii, 28*

6225.
I dreamt that I dwelt in marble halls,
With vassals and serfs at my side.
  ALFRED BUNN, *The Bohemian Girl*

6226. I had a dream, which was not
all a dream.   BYRON, *Darkness*

6227.
And dreams in their development
  have breath,
And tears, and tortures, and the
  touch of joy;
They have a weight upon our waking
  thoughts,
They take a weight from off our
  waking toils,
They do divide our being.
      BYRON, *The Dream*

6228. A change came o'er the spirit
of my dream.   BYRON, *The Dream*

6229. My eyes make pictures, when
they are shut.
      COLERIDGE, *A Day Dream*

6230.
And so, his senses gradually wrapt
In a half sleep, he dreams of better
  worlds,
And dreaming hears thee still, O
  singing lark;
That singest like an angel in the
  clouds.
      COLERIDGE, *Fears in Solitude*

6231. A sight to dream of, not to
tell!   COLERIDGE, *Christabel*

6232.
      Dream after dream ensues;
And still they dream that they shall
  still succeed;
And still are disappointed.
      COWPER, *The Task*

6233.
In blissful dream, in silent night,
There came to me, with magic might,
With magic might, my own sweet
  love,
Into my little room above.
      HEINE, *Youthful Sorrows*

6234.
Some dreams we have are nothing
    else but dreams
    Unnatural and full of contradic-
    tions;
Yet others of our most romantic
    schemes
  Are something more than fictions.
THOMAS HOOD, *The Haunted House*

6235.
Abou Ben Adhem (may his tribe increase!)
Awoke one night from a deep dream
  of peace.
    LEIGH HUNT, *Abou Ben Adhem*

6236. Those who dream by night in
the dusty recesses of their minds,
wake in the day to find that it was
vanity: but the dreamers of the day
are dangerous men, for they may act
their dreams with open eyes, to make
it possible.   LAWRENCE OF ARABIA

6237.
Tell me not, in mournful numbers,
  Life is but an empty dream!
    LONGFELLOW, *The Psalm of Life*

6238.
Is this a dream? O, if it be a dream,
Let me sleep on, and do not wake me
  yet!
LONGFELLOW, *The Spanish Student*

6239. For dhrames always go by contraries, my dear.
SAMUEL LOVER, *Rory O'More*

6240. Ground not upon dreams, you know they are ever contrary.
THOMAS MIDDLETON,
The Family of Love

6241. I believe it to be true that Dreams are the true Interpreters of our Inclinations; but there is Art required to sort and understand them.
MONTAIGNE, *Essays*

6242.
Oh! that a dream so sweet, so long enjoy'd,
Should be so sadly, cruelly destroy'd!
THOMAS MOORE, *Lalla Rookh*

6243.
Dreamer of dreams, born out of my due time,
Why should I strive to set the crooked straight?
WILLIAM MORRIS,
The Earthly Paradise

6244.
A thousand creeds and battle cries,
　A thousand warring social schemes,
A thousand new moralities
　And twenty thousand, thousand dreams.　ALFRED NOYES,
Forward

6245. Those dreams are true which we have in the morning, as the lamp begins to flicker.　OVID, *Epistles*

6246.
All that we see or seem
Is but a dream within a dream.
POE, *A Dream Within a Dream*

6247. Those who dream by day are cognizant of many things which escape those who dream only by night.
POE, *Eleonora*

6248. You eat, in dreams, the custard of the day.　POPE, *The Dunciad*

6249.
Till their own dreams at length deceive 'em,
And oft repeating, they believe 'em.
MATTHEW PRIOR, *Alma*

6250.
The republic is a dream.
Nothing happens unless first a dream.
CARL SANDBURG,
Washington Monument by Night

6251.
I'll dream no more—my manly mind
Not even in sleep is well resigned.
My midnight orisons said o'er,
I'll turn to rest and dream no more.
SCOTT, *Lady of the Lake*

6252.
　　　　Thou hast beat me out
Twelve several times, and I have nightly since
Dreamt of encounters 'twixt thyself and me. SHAKESPEARE, *Coriolanus*

6253.
There is some ill a-brewing towards my rest,
For I did dream of money-bags to-night.　SHAKESPEARE,
The Merchant of Venice

6254. I have an exposition of sleep come upon me.　SHAKESPEARE,
A Midsummer-Night's Dream

6255. I have had a dream, past the wit of man to say what dream it was.
SHAKESPEARE,
A Midsummer-Night's Dream

6256. The eye of man hath not heard, the ear of man hath not seen, man's hand is not able to taste, his tongue to conceive, nor his heart to report, what my dream was.
SHAKESPEARE,
A Midsummer-Night's Dream

6257.

This is the rarest dream that e'er dull
   sleep
Did mock sad fools withal.
               SHAKESPEARE, *Pericles*

6258.

Oh, I have pass'd a miserable night,
So full of ugly sights, of ghastly
   dreams,
That, as I am a Christian faithful
   man,
I would not spend another such a
   night,
Though 'twere to buy a world of
   happy days.
               SHAKESPEARE, *Richard III*

6259.

For never yet one hour in his bed
Have I enjoyed the golden dew of
   sleep,
But have been waked by his timorous
   dreams.
               SHAKESPEARE, *Richard III*

6260.

               True, I talk of dreams,
Which are the children of an idle
   brain,
Begot of nothing but vain fantasy.
               SHAKESPEARE, *Romeo and Juliet*

6261.

If I may trust the flattering truth of
   sleep,
My dreams presage some joyful news
   at hand;
My bosom's lord sits lightly in his
   throne;
And all this day an unaccustom'd
   spirit
Lifts me above the ground with cheerful thoughts.
               SHAKESPEARE, *Romeo and Juliet*

6262. Sits as one new-risen from a
dream.   SHAKESPEARE,
               The Taming of the Shrew

6263.

   We are such stuff
As dreams are made on, and our little
   life
   Is rounded with a sleep.
               SHAKESPEARE, *The Tempest*

6264.

We rest. A dream has power to
   poison sleep;
We rise. One wandering thought pollutes the day.
               SHELLEY, *Mutability*

6265. In an ocean of dreams without a sound.
               SHELLEY, *The Sensitive Plant*

6266. Many's the long night I've
dreamed of cheese—toasted, mostly.
               STEVENSON, *Treasure Island*

6267.

Those dreams, that on the silent night
   intrude,
And with false flitting shades our
   minds delude,
Jove never sends us downward from
   the skies;
Nor can they from infernal mansions
   rise;
But are all mere productions of the
   brain,
And fools consult interpreters in vain.
               SWIFT, *On Dreams*

6268.

               The dream
Dreamed by a happy man, when the
   dark East,
Unseen, is brightening to his bridal
   morn.   TENNYSON,
               The Gardener's Daughter

6269. Like glimpses of forgotten
dreams.
               TENNYSON, *The Two Voices*

6270.

Seeing, I saw not, hearing not, I
   heard.

Tho', if I saw not, yet they told me all
So often that I spake as having seen.
　　　TENNYSON, *The Princess*

6271. If one advances confidently in
the direction of his dreams, and endeavors to live the life which he has
imagined, he will meet with a success
unexpected in common hours.
　　　THOREAU, *Walden*

6272. Did You Ever See a Dream
Walking?　*Title of Popular Song*

6273. Saddle your dreams afore you
ride 'em.
　　　MARY WEBB, *Precious Bane*

6274. Hunt half a day for a forgotten dream.
　　　WORDSWORTH, *Hart-Leap Well*

6275.
But I, being poor, have only my
　　dreams;
I have spread my dreams under your
　　feet;
Tread softly, for you tread on my
　　dreams.　　W. B. YEATS,
　　　The Cloths of Heaven

See also: 533, 1273, 3232.

DRESS

Related Subjects: Appearance,
Fashion, Hat, Modesty, Nudity,
Ornament, Shoe, Style, Tailor,
Vanity.

6281. It is not only fine feathers that
make fine birds.
　　　AESOP, *The Jay and the Peacock*

6282. *Garter:* an elastic band intended to keep a woman from coming
out of her stockings and desolating
the country.　AMBROSE BIERCE,
　　　The Devil's Dictionary

6283. Trust not the heart of that
man for whom old clothes are not venerable.　CARLYLE, *Sartor Resartus*

6284. Any man may be in good
spirits and good temper when he's
well dressed. There ain't much credit
in that.
　　　DICKENS, *Martin Chuzzlewit*

6285. Strip the bishop of his apron,
or the beadle of his hat and lace;
what are they? Men. Mere men. Dignity; and even holiness, too, sometimes are more questions of coat and
waistcoat than some people imagine.
　　　DICKENS

6286.
A sweet disorder in the dress
Kindles in clothes a wantonness.
　　　ROBERT HERRICK,
　　　Delight in Disorder

6287. It is principally for the sake of
the leg that a change in the dress of
man is so much to be desired. . . .
The leg is the best part of the figure
. . . and the best leg is the man's.
Man should no longer disguise the
long lines, the strong forms, in those
lengths of piping or tubing that are of
all garments the most stupid.
　　　ALICE MEYNELL, *Essays*

6288. I hate to see men overdressed.
. . . A man ought to look like he's
put together by accident, not added
up on purpose.
CHRISTOPHER MORLEY, *Kitty Foyle*

6289.
Where's the man could ease a heart
Like a satin gown?
DOROTHY PARKER, *The Satin Dress*

6290.
The wasting moth ne'er spoil'd my
　　best array;
The cause was this, I wore it every
　　day.
　　　POPE, *Paraphrases from Chaucer*

6291. Fine clothes oftentimes hide a
base descent.　　　*Proverb*

6292. Better go to heaven in rags than to hell in embroidery. *Proverb*

6293. Borrowed garments never sit well. *Proverb*

6294.
Fond pride of dress is sure a very curse;
Ere fancy you consult, consult your purse. *Proverb*

6295. When you have bought one fine thing you must buy ten more, that your appearance may be all of a piece. *Proverb*

6296. We are all Adam's children, but silk makes the difference.
Proverb

6297. Good clothes open all doors.
Proverb

6298. Motley's the only wear.
SHAKESPEARE, *As You Like It*

6299.
Costly thy habit as thy purse can buy,
But not express'd in fancy; rich, not gaudy;
For the apparel oft proclaims the man. SHAKESPEARE, *Hamlet*

6300.
In nothing am I chang'd
But in my garments.
SHAKESPEARE, *King Lear*

6301.
Through tatter'd clothes small vices do appear;
Robes and furr'd gowns hide all.
SHAKESPEARE, *King Lear*

6302. She wears her clothes as if they were thrown on with a pitchfork. SWIFT, *Polite Conversation*

6303. Beware of all enterprises that require new clothes.
THOREAU, *Walden*

6304. Much of the charm that invests the patent-leather shoe, the stainless linen, the lustrous cylindrical hat, and the walking-stick, which so greatly enhance the native dignity of a gentleman, comes of their pointedly suggesting that the wearer cannot when so attired bear a hand in any employment that is directly or immediately of any human use.
THORSTEIN VEBLEN,
The Theory of the Leisure Class

6305. The womanliness of woman's apparel resolves itself into the more effective hindrance to useful exertion offered by the garments peculiar to women. THORSTEIN VEBLEN,
The Theory of the Leisure Class

6306. The corset is, in economic theory, substantially a mutilation, undergone for the purpose of lowering the subject's vitality and rendering her permanently and obviously unfit for work. It is true, the corset impairs the personal attractions of the wearer, but the loss suffered on that score is offset by the gain in reputability which comes of her visibly increased expensiveness and infirmity.
THORSTEIN VEBLEN,
The Theory of the Leisure Class

6307.
All his reverend wit
Lies in his wardrobe.
JOHN WEBSTER, *The White Devil*

See also: 1155, 2658, 6377, 6942, 13279.

DRINKING AND DRUNKENNESS

Related Subjects: Ale and Beer, Conviviality, Crime, Debauchery, Dissipation, Merriment, Temperance, Thirst, Toast, Wine.

6311. Were I to prescribe a rule for drinking, it should be formed upon a saying quoted by Sir William Temple: the first glass for myself, the second for my friends, the third for good humour, and the forth for mine enemies.　ADDISON, *The Spectator*

6312.
If all be true that I do think,
There are five reasons we should drink;
Good wine—a friend—or being dry—
Or lest we should be by and by—
Or any other reason why.
　　　　　HENRY ALDRICH,
　　　Five Reasons for Drinking

6313.
Inspiring bold John Barleycorn,
What dangers thou canst make us
　scorn!　BURNS, *Tam o' Shanter*

6314.
　What's drinking?
A mere pause from thinking!
BYRON, *The Deformed Transformed*

6315.
For dronkenesse is verray sepulture
Of mannes wit and his discrecioun.
　　　CHAUCER, *Canterbury Tales*

6316.
Fill all the glasses there, for why
Should every creature drink but I?
Why, man of morals, tell me why?
ABRAHAM COWLEY, *Anacreon II*

6317. All learned, and all drunk!
　　　　　COWPER, *The Task*

6318. Gloriously drunk, obey the important call.　COWPER, *The Task*

6319.
All Nature wears one universal grin.
To-day it is our pleasure to be drunk;
And this our queen shall be as drunk
　as we.
FIELDING, *Tom Thumb the Great*

6320. Call things by their right names. . . . Glass of brandy and

water! That is the current but not the appropriate name; ask for a glass of liquid fire and distilled damnation.
　　　　　ROBERT HALL

6321.
　Brain and heart
　Alike depart
From him who worships gin or
　brandy.
　　C. G. HALPINE, *Holland Gin*

6322. Licker talks mighty loud w'en it gits loose from de jug.
　　JOEL CHANDLER HARRIS,
　　　　Plantation Proverbs

6323.
Oh, yer's yer good old whiskey,
　Drink it down.
BRET HARTE, *Two Men of Sandy Bar*

6324.
Teetot'lers seem to die the same as
　others,
So what's the use of knocking off the
　beer?
　A. P. HERBERT, *The Ladies' Bar*

6325.
Drink not the third glass, which thou
　canst not tame,
When once it is within thee.
　　　GEORGE HERBERT,
　　　　The Church Porch

6326.
　　　"While you live,
Drink!—for, once dead, you never
　shall return."
　　OMAR KHAYYAM, *Rubaiyat*

6327.
Candy
Is dandy
But liquor
Is quicker.　OGDEN NASH,
　　　Reflection on Ice-Breaking

6328.
Not drunk is he who from the floor
Can rise alone and still drink more;

But drunk is he, who prostrate lies,
Without the power to drink or rise.
         T. L. PEACOCK,
    The Misfortunes of Elphin

6329. Of all meat in the world, drink goes down the best.   *Proverb*

6330. A drink is shorter than a tale.   *Proverb*

6331. Drunkenness is a pair of spectacles to see the devil and all his works.   *Proverb*

6332. When your companions get drunk and fight, take up your hat and wish them good night.   *Proverb*

6333. Drunkenness turns a man out of himself, and leaves a beast in his room.   *Proverb*

6334. He is not drunk gratis, who pays his reason for his shot.   *Proverb*

6335. As drunk as a lord.   *Proverb*

6336. O, monstrous! but one halfpenny-worth of bread to this intolerable deal of sack!
      SHAKESPEARE, *Henry IV*

6337. If I had a thousand sons, the first human principle I would teach them should be, to forswear thin potations and to addict themselves to sack.   SHAKESPEARE, *Henry IV*

6338. It (drink) provokes the desire, but it takes away the performance.
      SHAKESPEARE, *Macbeth*

6339. O God! that men should put an enemy in their mouths to steal away their brains!
      SHAKESPEARE, *Othello*

6340. I have very poor and unhappy brains for drinking.
      SHAKESPEARE, *Othello*

6341. One draught above heat makes him a fool, the second mads him, and a third drowns him.
      SHAKESPEARE, *Twelfth Night*

6342.
A bumper of good liquor
Will end a contest quicker
Than justice, judge, or vicar.
      SHERIDAN, *The Duenna*

6343.
At the punch-bowl's brink
Let the thirsty think
   What they say in Japan:
"First the man takes a drink,
Then the drink takes a drink,
   Then the drink takes the man!"
         E. R. SILL,
    An Adage from the Orient

6344. A little in drink, but at all times yr. faithfull husband.
      SIR RICHARD STEELE,
        Letter to his wife

6345.
I cannot eat but little meat,
   My stomach is not good;
But sure I think that I can drink
   With him that wears a hood.
         BISHOP STILL,
    Gammer Gurton's Needle

6346. There are two things that will be believed of any man whatsoever, and one of them is that he has taken to drink.   TARKINGTON, *Penrod*

6347. Drink, pretty creature, drink!
    WORDSWORTH, *The Pet Lamb*

6348.
The word must be spoken that bids
   you depart—
Though the effort to speak it should
   shatter my heart—
Though in silence, with blighted affection I pine,

Yet the lips that touch liquor must never touch mine!

G. W. Young,
The Lips that Touch Liquor

See also: 888, 1401, 1954, 2711, 7330, 12694, 14156, 16107.

DUELING

Related Subjects: Chivalry, Fight, Honor, Quarreling, Sword.

6351. If all seconds were as averse to duels as their principals, very little blood would be shed in that way.

C. C. Colton

6352. A duellist is only a Cain in high life. Douglas Jerrold,
Douglas Jerrold's Wit

6353.

I never in my life
Did hear a challenge urg'd more modestly,
Unless a brother should a brother dare
To gentle exercise and proof of arms.

Shakespeare, *Henry IV*

6354. The passado he respects not, the duello he regards not.

Shakespeare, *Love's Labour's Lost*

6355. If I were young again, the sword should end it.

Shakespeare,
The Merry Wives of Windsor

6356.

There I throw my gage,
To prove it on thee to the extremest point
Of mortal breathing.

Shakespeare, *Richard II*

6357. An I thought he had been valiant, and so cunning in fence, I'd have seen him damned ere I'd have challenged him.

Shakespeare, *Twelfth Night*

6358. When you meet your antagonist, do everything in a mild and agreeable manner. Let your courage be as keen, but at the same time as polished, as your sword.

Sheridan, *The Rivals*

6359. Duelling, though barbarous in civilized countries, is a highly civilizing institution among barbarous people; and when compared to assassination is a prodigious victory gained over human passions.

Sydney Smith

DUTY

Related Subjects: Deference, Loyalty, Obligation, Patriotism, Responsibility, Taxes, Trust.

6361. Thanks to the gods! my boy has done his duty. Addison, *Cato*

6362. In doing what we ought we deserve no praise, because it is our duty.

St. Augustine

6363. He who is false to present duty breaks a thread in the loom, and will find the flaw when he may have forgotten its cause.

H. W. Beecher, *Life Thoughts*

6364. Let us hear the conclusion of the whole matter: Fear God, and keep his commandments; for this is the whole duty of man.

Bible: Ecclesiastes, xii, 13

6365. To do my duty in that state of life unto which it shall please God to call me. *Book of Common Prayer*

6366. Do your duty, and leave the rest to heaven. Corneille, *Horace*

6367. The reward of one duty is the power to fulfil another.

George Eliot, *Daniel Deronda*

6368.

So nigh is grandeur to our dust,
  So near is God to man.
When Duty whispers low, *Thou must,*
  The youth replies, *I can.*
                EMERSON, *Voluntaries*

6369.

When I'm not thank'd at all, I'm thank'd enough:
I've done my duty, and I've done no more.   FIELDING, *Tom Thumb*

6370. In common things the law of sacrifice takes the form of positive duty.   FROUDE,
  Short Studies on Great Subjects

6371. The gratifying feeling that our duty has been done.
  W. S. GILBERT, *The Gondoliers*

6372. But what is your duty? What the day demands.
        GOETHE, *Spruche in Prosa*

6373.

Straight is the line of duty;
Curved is the line of beauty;
Follow the straight line, thou shalt see
The curved line ever follow thee.
        WILLIAM MACCALL, *Duty*

6374. Every mission constitutes a pledge of duty. Every man is bound to consecrate his every faculty to its fulfilment. He will derive his rule of action from the profound conviction of that duty.   MAZZINI

6375.

Knowledge is the hill which few may wish to climb;
Duty is the path that all may tread.
    LEWIS MORRIS, *Epic of Hades*

6376. England expects every man to do his duty.   HORATIO NELSON

6377. It is the prime duty of a woman of this terrestrial world to look well. Neatness is the asepsis of clothes.   SIR WILLIAM OSLER,
      Life of Sir William Osler

6378.

O, good old man; how well in thee appears
The constant service of the antique world,
When service sweat for duty, not for meed!
Thou art not for the fashion of these times,
Where none will sweat but for promotion.
    SHAKESPEARE, *As You Like It*

6379. I do perceive here a divided duty.   SHAKESPEARE, *Othello*

6380.

I thought the remnant of mine age
Should have been cherish'd by her child-like duty.
          SHAKESPEARE,
    Two Gentlemen of Verona

6381. There is no duty we underrate so much as the duty of being happy.
    STEVENSON, *Virginibus Puerisque*

6382. Not snow, nor rain, nor heat, nor gloom of night stays these couriers from the swift completion of their appointed rounds.
      U. S. Postal Service: Motto

6383. A sense of duty pursues us ever. It is omnipresent, like the Deity. If we take to ourselves the wings of the morning, and dwell in the uttermost parts of the sea, duty performed or duty violated is still with us, for our happiness or our misery. If we say the darkness shall cover us, in the darkness as in the light our obligations are yet with us.
          DANIEL WEBSTER

6384. Simple duty hath no place for fear.

    WHITTIER, *Tent on the Beach*

6385. Stern Daughter of the Voice

of God!   WORDSWORTH,
        Ode to Duty

See also: 1984, 2713, 2751, 3503, 8935, 9506, 16186.

E

EAGLE

Related Subject: Birds.

6391.
So, in the Libyan fable it is told
That once an eagle, stricken with a
    dart,
Said, when he saw the fashion of the
    shaft,
"With our own feathers, not by
    others' hand
Are we now smitten."   AESCHYLUS

6392. They shall mount up with wings as eagles. *Bible: Isaiah, xl, 31*

6393. Wheresoever the carcass is, there will the eagles be gathered together. *Bible: Matthew, xxiv, 28*

6394. When thou seest an eagle, thou seest a portion of Genius; lift up thy head!   BLAKE, *Proverbs of Hell*

6395.
            Tho' he inherit
Nor the pride, nor ample pinion,
    That the Theban eagle bear,
Sailing with supreme dominion
    Thro' the azure deep of air.
THOMAS GRAY, *Progress of Poesy*

6396.
King of the peak and glacier,
    King of the cold, white scalps,
He lifts his head at that close tread,
    The eagle of the Alps.
    VICTOR HUGO, *Swiss Mercenaries*

6397.
The bird of Jove, stoop'd from his
    aery tour,
Two birds of gayest plume before
    him drove. MILTON, *Paradise Lost*

6398. And little eagles wave their wings in gold. POPE, *Moral Essays*

6399. The eagle does not catch flies.
                  Proverb

6400. I saw Jove's bird, the Roman eagle. SHAKESPEARE, *Cymbeline*

6401.
But flies an eagle flight, bold and
    forth on,
Leaving no track behind.
    SHAKESPEARE, *Timon of Athens*

6402.
The eagle suffers little birds to sing,
And is not careful what they mean
    thereby.   SHAKESPEARE,
             Titus Andronicus

6403.
Gnats are unnoted whereso'er they
    fly,
But eagles gaz'd upon with every eye.
SHAKESPEARE, *The Rape of Lucrece*

6404.
Around, around, in ceaseless circles
    wheeling
With clangs of wings and scream, the
    Eagle sailed
Incessantly.
    SHELLEY, *Revolt of Islam*

6405. Thus the fable tells us, that the wren mounted as high as the eagle, by getting upon his back.
    SIR RICHARD STEELE, *The Tatler*

6406.
Shall eagles not be eagles? wrens be
    wrens?
If all the world were falcons, what
    of that?

The wonder of the eagle were the less,
But he not less the eagle.

TENNYSON, *Golden Year*

EARNESTNESS

Related Subjects: Gravity, Industry, Resolution, Zeal.

6411. Earnestness is the devotion of all the faculties. It is the cause of patience; gives endurance; overcomes pain; strengthens weakness; braves dangers; sustains hope; makes light of difficulties, and lessens the sense of weariness in overcoming them.

C. N. BOVEE

6412. A man in earnest finds means, or if he cannot find, creates them.

W. E. CHANNING

6413. The superior man is slow in his words and earnest in his conduct.

CONFUCIUS, *Analects*

6414. There is no substitute for thorough-going, ardent and sincere earnestness.   DICKENS

6415. I am in earnest. I will not equivocate; I will not excuse; I will not retreat a single inch; and I will be heard!   W. L. GARRISON,
Salutatory of the Liberator

6416. Earnestness commands the respect of mankind. A wavering, vacillating, dead-and-alive Christian does not get the respect of the Church or of the world.   JOHN HALL

6417. Earnestness is enthusiasm tempered by reason.   PASCAL

EARS

Related Subjects: Deafness, Listening, Silence, Sound.

6421. He that hath ears to hear, let him hear.   *Bible: Matthew, iv, 9*

6422. Nature has given to men one tongue, but two ears, that we may hear from others twice as much as we speak.   EPICTETUS, *Discourses*

6423.
                    I was all ear,
And took in strains that might create a soul
Under the ribs of death.

MILTON, *Comus*

6424.
Of Forests, and enchantments drear,
Where more is meant than meets the ear.   MILTON, *Il Penseroso*

6425. If your ear burns, some one is talking about you.

PLINY THE ELDER,
Historia Naturalis

6426. Went in at the one ear and out at the other.   *Proverb*

6427. One pair of ears draws dry a hundred tongues.   *Proverb*

6428. Give every man thy ear, but few thy voice. SHAKESPEARE, *Hamlet*

6429. Friends, Romans, countrymen, lend me your ears.

SHAKESPEARE, *Julius Caesar*

6430. What fire is in mine ears? Can this be true?   SHAKESPEARE,
Much Ado About Nothing

6431. You have a quick ear.

SHAKESPEARE,
Two Gentlemen of Verona

6432. Take heed what you say. Walls have ears.   JAMES SHIRLEY,
A Bird in a Cage

6433. Little pitchers have big ears.
Traditional

EARTH

Related Subjects: The Heavens, World, Worm, Real Estate.

6441. Speak to the earth, and it shall teach thee.   *Bible: Job, xii, 8*

6442. One generation passeth away, and another generation cometh; but the earth abideth for ever.

Bible: Ecclesiastes, i, 4

6443. The first man is of the earth, earthy. *Bible: I Corinthians, xv, 47*

6444.
So simple is the earth we tread,
  So quick with love and life her frame:
Ten thousand years have dawned and fled,
  And still her magic is the same.
S. A. BROOKE, *The Earth and Man*

6445. O earth, so full of dreary noises!
ELIZABETH B. BROWNING,
  The Cry of the Children

6446. Earth, with her thousand voices, praises God. COLERIDGE,
  Hymn Before Sunrise

6447.
The thirsty earth soaks up the rain,
And drinks, and gapes for drink again.
The plants suck in the earth, and are
With constant drinking fresh and fair.
ABRAHAM COWLEY, *Anacreon, II*

6448.
The earth was made so various, that the mind
Of desultory man, studious of change
And pleased with novelty, might be indulged. COWPER, *The Task*

6449. The earth produces all things, and receives all again.
THOMAS FULLER, *Gnomologia*

6450. Earth is but the frozen echo of the silent voice of God.
S. M. HAGEMAN, *Silence*

6451.
The poetry of earth is never dead
The poetry of earth is ceasing never
KEATS,
  On the Grasshopper and Cricket

6452. I am in love with this green earth.
CHARLES LAMB, *Essays of Elia*

6453. O maternal earth which rocks the fallen leaf to sleep!
EDGAR LEE MASTERS,
  Spoon River Anthology

6454. Hail earth, Mother of all!
MELEAGER

6455.
Above the smoke and stir of this dim spot
Which men call Earth.
MILTON, *Comus*

6456.
              Earth now
Seemed like to Heav'n, a seat where gods might dwell.
MILTON, *Paradise Lost*

6457. Earth is the best shelter.
Proverb

6458. The little O, the earth.
SHAKESPEARE, *Antony and Cleopatra*

6459.
              The earth's a thief,
That feeds and breeds by a composture stolen
From general excrement.
SHAKESPEARE, *Timon of Athens*

6460. Earth, Ocean, Air, beloved brotherhood. SHELLEY, *Alastor*

6461.
The green earth sends her incense up
  From many a mountain shrine;
From folded leaf and dewy cup
  She pours her sacred wine.
WHITTIER, *The Worship of Nature*

6462.

The common growth of mother-earth
Suffices me—her tears, her mirth,
Her humblest mirth and tears.
                WORDSWORTH, *Peter Bell*

See also: 9018.

EARTHQUAKE

6471.

Diseased nature oftentimes breaks
    forth
In strange eruptions; oft the teeming
    earth
Is with a kind of colic pinch'd and
    vex'd
By the imprisoning of unruly wind
Within her womb; which, for en-
    largement striving,
Shakes the old beldam earth and
    topples down
Steeples and moss-grown towers.
            SHAKESPEARE, *Henry IV*

6472.

With hue like that when some great
    painter dips
His pencil in the gloom of earthquake
    and eclipse.
            SHELLEY, *Revolt of Islam*

6473.

            With a voice, that like a bell
Toll'd by an earthquake in a trem-
    bling tower,
Rang ruin. TENNYSON, *The Princess*

EASE, see Leisure

EAST

Related Subjects: China, North,
West.

6481.

Oh, East is East, and West is West,
    and never the twain shall meet,
Till Earth and Sky stand presently at
    God's great Judgment Seat;
                KIPLING,
        The Ballad of East and West

6482.

Ship me somewheres east of Suez,
    where the best is like the worst,
Where there aren't no Ten Com-
    mandments, an' a man can raise a
    thirst.   KIPLING, *Mandalay*

6483.

An' I'm learnin' 'ere in London what
    the ten-year soldier tells:
"If you've 'eard the East a-callin',
    you won't never 'eed naught else."
                KIPLING, *Mandalay*

6484.

And the end of the fight is a tomb-
    stone white with the name of the
    late deceased,
And the epitaph drear: "A Fool lies
    here who tried to hustle the East."
            KIPLING, *The Naulahka*

6485.

Big perilous theorem, hard for king
    and priest:
Pursue the West but long enough, 'tis
    East.
    SIDNEY LANIER, *Psalm of the West*

EASTER

Related Subjects: Christ, Holiday.

6491.

Faith and Hope triumphant say
Christ will rise on Easter Day.
PHILLIPS BROOKS, *An Easter Carol*

6492.

Hail, Day of days! in peals of praise
    Throughout all ages owned,
When Christ, our God, hell's empire
    trod,
    And high O'er heaven was throned.
                FORTUNATUS,
Hail, Day of Days! in Peals of Praise

6493.

'Twas Easter Sunday. The full blos-
    somed trees

Filled all the air with fragrance and
  with joy.
Longfellow, *The Spanish Student*

6494.

O chime of sweet Saint Charity,
  Peal soon that Easter morn
When Christ for all shall risen be,
  And in all hearts new-born!
          Lowell, *Godminster Chimes*

6495.

In the bonds of Death He lay
  Who for our offence was slain;
But the Lord is risen to-day,
  Christ hath brought us life again,
Wherefore let us all rejoice,
Singing loud, with cheerful voice,
          Hallelujah!
          Martin Luther,
  Christ Lay In the Bonds of Death

6496.

I think of the garden after the rain;
  And hope to my heart comes sing-
    ing,
"At morn the cherry-blooms will be
    white,
  And the Easter bells be ringing!"
          Edna D. Proctor, *Easter Bells*

6497.

The fasts are done; the Aves said;
  The moon has filled her horn
And in the solemn night I watch
  Before the Easter morn.
Edna D. Proctor, *Easter Morning*

6498. He has but a short Lent that
must pay money at Easter. *Proverb*

6499. I'll warrant you for an egg at
Easter.   *Proverb*

6500.

Spring bursts to-day,
For Christ is risen and all the earth's
    at play.
Christina Rossetti, *Easter Carol*

6501.

"Christ the Lord is risen to-day,"
Sons of men and angels say:

Raise your joys and triumphs high
Sing, ye heavens, and earth, reply.
          Charles Wesley,
          Christ the Lord Is Risen

EATING

**Related Subjects: Appetite, Belly,
Cooks and Cooking, Diet, Digestion, Dining, Feast, Food, Hunger.**

6511. What most moved him was a
certain meal on beans.
          Browning, *Asolando*

6512.

Man is a carnivorous production,
  And must have meals, at least one
    meal a day;
He cannot live, like woodcocks, upon
    suction
  But, like the shark and tiger, must
    have prey;
Although his anatomical construction
  Bears vegetables, in a grumbling
    way,
Your laboring people think beyond all
    question
Beef, veal, and mutton better for di-
    gestion.   Byron, *Don Juan*

6513. Men that can have communion
in nothing else, can sympathetically
eat together, can still rise into some
glow of brotherhood over food and
wine.
          Carlyle, *The French Revolution*

6514.

A loaf of bread, the Walrus said,
  Is what we chiefly need:
Pepper and vinegar besides
  Are very good indeed—
Now if you're ready, Oysters, dear,
  We can begin to feed!
          Lewis Carroll,
          Through the Looking-Glass

6515.

When I demanded of my friend what
  viands he preferred,

He quoth: "A large cold bottle, and a small hot bird!"
EUGENE FIELD,
The Bottle and the Bird

6516. One should eat to live, not live to eat. FRANKLIN

6517. Life, within doors, has few pleasanter prospects than a neatly arranged and well-provisioned breakfast-table. HAWTHORNE,
The House of the Seven Gables

6518. Wouldst thou both eat thy cake and have it? GEORGE HERBERT,
The Size

6519. By suppers more have been killed than Galen ever cured.
GEORGE HERBERT,
Jacula Prudentum

6520.
Go to your banquet, then, but use delight,
So as to rise still with an appetite.
ROBERT HERRICK

6521.
"An't it please your Honour," quoth the Peasant,
"This same Dessert is not so pleasant:
Give me again my hollow Tree,
A crust of Bread, and Liberty."
HORACE

6522. Eat a bit before you drink.
Proverb

6523. Eat and drink measurely, and defy the mediciners. *Proverb*

6524. You dig your grave with your teeth. *Proverb*

6525. It is a great pleasure to eat, and have nothing to pay. *Proverb*

6526. Eat-well is drink-well's brother.
Proverb

6527. The difference between a rich man and a poor man, is this—the former eats when he pleases, and the latter when he can get it.
SIR WALTER RALEIGH

6528.
We have to eat, don't we?
You can't eat promises, can you?
You can't eat the constitution, can you? CARL SANDBURG,
The People, Yes

6529. Sit down and feed, and welcome to our table.
SHAKESPEARE, *As You Like It*

6530. He hath eaten me out of house and home. SHAKESPEARE,
Henry IV

6531. A very valiant trencher-man.
SHAKESPEARE,
Much Ado About Nothing

See also: 1037, 10910, 14490.

ECCENTRICITY

Related Subjects: Individuality, Personality, Sanity and Insanity.

6541. Even beauty cannot palliate eccentricity. BALZAC

6542. Eccentricity has always abounded when and where strength of character has abounded. And the amount of eccentricity in a society has been proportional to the amount of genius, mental vigor, and moral courage it contained. J. S. MILL

6543. All the world is queer save thee and me, and even thou art a little queer. ROBERT OWEN

6544. Oddities and singularities of behavior may attend genius, but when they do, they are its misfortunes and blemishes. The man of true genius will be ashamed of them, or, at least, will never affect to be distinguished by them. SIR WILLIAM TEMPLE

See also: 234, 2615, 4471, 6622.

ECHO

Related Subjects: Imitation, Sound, Voice.

6551.
Let echo, too, perform her part,
Prolonging every note with art;
And in a low expiring strain,
Play all th' concert o'er again.
ADDISON,
Ode for St. Cecilia's Day

6552.
Hark! to the hurried question of Despair:
"Where is my child?" An Echo answers—
"Where?"
BYRON, *The Bride of Abydos*

6553. Even Echo speaks not on these radiant moors.
BARRY CORNWALL,
*English Songs and Other Small
Poems*

6554.
Mysterious haunts of echoes old and far,
The voice divine of human loyalty.
GEORGE ELIOT,
The Spanish Gypsy

6555. Echo is the voice of a reflection in the mirror.   HAWTHORNE,
American Note-Books

6556. And when the echoes had ceased, like a sense of pain was the silence.   LONGFELLOW, *Evangeline*

6557.
Sweetest Echo, sweetest nymph, that liv'st unseen
Within thy airy shell,
By slow Meander's margent green,
And in the violet-embroidered vale.
MILTON, *Comus*

6558. That tuneful nymph, the babbling echo, who has not learned to conceal what is told her, nor yet is able to speak till another speaks.
OVID

6559. And more than echoes talk along the walls.   POPE,
Eloisa to Abelard

6560.
It seemed the harmonious echo
From our discordant life.
ADELAIDE A. PROCTER,
The Lost Chord

6561.
Thy hounds shall make the welkin answer them,
And fetch shrill echoes from the hollow earth.   SHAKESPEARE,
The Taming of the Shrew

6562.
The babbling echo mocks the hounds,
Replying shrilly to the well-tun'd horns,
As if a double hunt were heard at once.   SHAKESPEARE,
Titus Andronicus

6563.
Halloo your name to the reverberate hills,
And make the babbling gossip of the air
Cry out, "Olivia."
SHAKESPEARE, *Twelfth Night*

6564.
Lost Echo sits among the voiceless mountains,
And feeds her grief.   SHELLEY,
Adonais

6565.
Blow, bugle, blow, set the wild echoes flying,
And answer, echoes, answer, dying, dying, dying.   TENNYSON,
The Princess

6566.
And a million horrible bellowing echoes broke

'rom the red-ribb'd hollow behind the
  wood,
\nd thunder'd up into Heaven.
             TENNYSON, *Maud*

567.
he melancholy ghosts of dead renown,
Vhispering faint echoes of the
  world's applause.
           EDWARD YOUNG,
               Night Thoughts

ee also: 1054, 1641, 4162.

ECONOMY

\elated Subjects: Bargain, Capi-
\alism, Care, The Dollar, Money,
'rudence, Thrift, Waste.

571. A man's ordinary expenses
ught to be but to the half of his
eceipts, and if he think to wax rich,
ut to the third part.   BACON

572. Economy before competence is
\neanness after it; therefore economy
; for the poor; the rich may dis-
ense with it.   C. N. BOVEE

573. Mere parsimony is not econ-
my. . . . Expense, and great ex-
ense, may be an essential part of
\:ue economy.   BURKE,
         Letter to a Noble Lord

574. Economy is a distributive vir-
\1e, and consists not in saving but in
election. Parsimony requires no pro-
idence, no sagacity, no powers of
ombination, no comparison, no judg-
\1ent.   BURKE,
         Letter to a Noble Lord

575. To make three guineas do the
\:ork of five.   BURNS

576. Not to be covetous, is money;
ot to be a purchaser, is a revenue.
               CICERO

6577. We tend to think of economic
welfare in terms of more income,
higher prices, more dollars, rather
than in terms of more production and
more consumption. Economic policies
are all too often selected and judged
by their ability to create dollars,
rather than to create goods.
        MORDECAI EZEKIEL,
              $2500 a Year

6578. Our present economic system
inherited from the past, tends to obscure the simple physical aspects of
the problem. By centering attention
on making money, it distracts us from
the primary importance of making
more goods and creating more services.   MORDECAI EZEKIEL,
              $2500 a Year

6579. If you know how to spend less
than you get, you have the philosopher's stone.   FRANKLIN

6580. Let honesty and industry be
thy constant companions, and spend
one penny less than thy clear gains;
then shall thy pockets begin to thrive;
creditors will not insult, nor want oppress, nor hunger bite, nor nakedness freeze thee.   FRANKLIN

6581. Each economic system develops
its own system of thought, law,
ethics, and politics. We can't think
like medieval men today, even though
we try to.   J. B. S. HALDANE,
              I Believe

6582. They are a Tower of Babel of
different Economic languages.
         WILLIAM HARD

6583. Without economy none can be
rich and with it few will be poor.
         SAMUEL JOHNSON

6584. Economists have not yet earned
the right to be listened to attentively.
         J. M. KEYNES

6585. A sound economy is a sound understanding brought into action. It is calculation realized; it is the doctrine of proportion reduced to practice; it is foreseeing contingencies and providing against them; it is contingencies and being prepared for them. HANNAH MORE

6586. Proportion and propriety are among the best secrets of domestic wisdom; and there is no surer test of integrity than a well-proportioned expenditure. HANNAH MORE

6587. He who is taught to live upon little owes more to his father's wisdom than he that has a great deal left him does to his father's care.
WILLIAM PENN

6588. Economy, which in things inanimate is but money-making, when exercised over men becomes policy.
PLUTARCH, *Lives*

6589. Nothing is cheap that is superfluous, for what one does not need, is dear at a penny. PLUTARCH

6590. Spend not, where you may save; spare not, where you must spend. *Proverb*

6591. Lay thy hand upon thy halfpenny twice before thou partest with it. *Proverb*

6592. He that regards not a penny will lavish a pound. *Proverb*

6593. He that has but four and spends five, has no need of a purse.
Proverb

6594. Ask thy purse what thou shouldest buy. *Proverb*

6595. There is no gain so certain as that which arises from sparing what you have. PUBLILIUS SYRUS,
Sententiae

6596. Economy is in itself a sourc of great revenue. SENEC

6597. The regard one shows econom is like that we show an old aunt, wh is to leave us something at last.
W. SHENSTON

6598. Every single economic fact always related to some other equall important fact—and the practic man's job is to measure the relatio ship between the two.
R. D. SKINNER,
Seven Kinds of Inflatio

See also: 1013, 1473, 15496, 1782

EDUCATION

Related Subjects: Culture, Gram mar, Intelligence, Knowledg Learning, Pedantry, Readin Scholar, School, Study, Teache Teaching, University.

6601. Nothing in education is so a tonishing as the amount of ignoran it accumulates in the form of ine facts. HENRY ADAMS,
The Education of Henry Adam

6602. There can be but a single go of education, and that—education courage. ALFRED ADLI

6603. Observation more than book experience rather than persons, a the prime educators.
BRONSON ALCO

6604. The whole object of educatio is, or should be, to develop mind. T mind should be a thing that work It should be able to pass judgmer on events as they arise, make d cisions. SHERWOOD ANDERSO

6605. They who educate childre well, are more to be honoured tha they who produce them; for the

ıly gave them life, those the art of
ving well.   ARISTOTLE

606. All who have meditated on the
t of governing mankind have been
ɔnvinced that the fate of empires de-
ɔnds on the education of youth.
      ARISTOTLE

607. It is by education, I learn to
ɔ by choice, what other men do by
ıe constraint of fear.   ARISTOTLE

608. Unless an individual is free to
ɔtain the fullest education with
hich his society can provide him, he
being injured by society.
      W. H. AUDEN, *I Believe*

609. The standards of a genuinely
ɔeral education, as they have been
ıderstood, more or less from the
ɪne of Aristotle, are being progres-
vely undermined by the utilitarians
ıd the sentimentalists.
      IRVING BABBITT

610. Brought up in this city at the
ɛt of Gamaliel.
      Bible: Acts, xxii, 3

611.
ut to go to school in a summer
   morn,
ɔh, it drives all joy away!
ɪnder a cruel eye outworn,
he little ones spend the day—
ı sighing and dismay.
      BLAKE, *The Schoolboy*

612. Education makes a people easy
ɔ lead, but difficult to drive; easy
ɔ govern, but impossible to enslave.
      LORD BROUGHAM

613. Education is the only cure for
ɛrtain diseases the modern world has
ɪgendered, but if you don't find the
sease, the remedy is superfluous.
      JOHN BUCHAN

6614. Education is the cheap defense
of nations.   BURKE

6615. An educated man stands, as it
were in the midst of a boundless
arsenal and magazine, filled with all
the weapons and engines which man's
skill has been able to devise from the
earliest time.   CARLYLE, *Burns*

6616. Of good natural parts, and of
a liberal education.
      CERVANTES, *Don Quixote*

6617. Do not ask if a man has been
through college; ask if a college has
been through him—if he is a walking
university.   E. H. CHAPIN

6618. What greater or better gift can
we offer the republic than to teach
and instruct our youth?
      CICERO, *De Divinatione*

6619. The foundation of every state
is the education of its youth.
      DIOGENES

6620. On one occasion Aristotle was
asked how much educated men were
superior to those uneducated; "As
much," said he, "as the living are to
the dead."
      DIOGENES LAERTIUS, *Aristotle*

6621. It was a saying of his [Aris-
totle] that education was an ornament in prosperity and a refuge in
adversity.   DIOGENES LAERTIUS,
      Aristotle

6622. The Self-Educated are marked
by stubborn peculiarities.
      ISAAC D'ISRAELI,
      Literary Character

6623. By education most have been
misled.   DRYDEN,
      The Hind & the Panther

6624. The great end of education is,
to discipline rather than to furnish

the mind; to train it to the use of its own powers, rather than fill it with the accumulations of others.

TRYON EDWARDS

6625. That which we are we are all the while teaching, not voluntarily, but involuntarily.   EMERSON

6626. The secret of education lies in respecting the pupil.   EMERSON

6627. Education begins with life. Before we are aware the foundations of characters are laid, and subsequent teaching avails but little to remove or alter them.   FRANKLIN

6628. States should spend money and effort on this great all-underlying matter of spiritual education as they have hitherto spent them on beating and destroying each other.

GALSWORTHY

6629. Education is a thing of which only the few are capable; teach as you will only a small percentage will profit by your most zealous energy.

GEORGE GISSING,
*The Private Papers of
Henry Ryecroft*

6630. A college education shows a man how little other people know.

T. C. HALIBURTON

6631. Persons without education certainly do not want either acuteness or strength of mind in what concerns themselves, or in things immediately within their observation; but they have no power of abstraction, no general standard of taste, or scale of opinion. They see their objects always near, and never in the horizon. Hence arises that egotism which has been remarked as the characteristic of self-taught men.   HAZLITT,
The Round Table

6632. Education is the ability to me life's situations.

DR. JOHN C. HIBBE

6633. Periods of intellectual renai sance are periods when education *about something,* when it has a topic relation to social needs and to soci aspirations which dominate the liv of men and women.

LANCELOT HOGBEN,
Dangerous Though

6634. Education in its widest sen includes everything that exerts formative influence, and causes young person to be, at a given poi what he is.   MARK HOPKI

6635. There is no science to educ tion. You may send your boy Phillips Exeter for two years a Harvard for four, and when he com back you may have to support hi the rest of his life.

ELBERT HUBBA

6636. Education is the instruction the intellect in the laws of Natu under which name I include n merely things and their forces, b men and their ways; and the fashio ing of the affections and of the w into an earnest and loving desire move in harmony with these laws.

THOMAS H. HUXLEY,
A Liberal Educati

6637. He that has found a way keep a child's spirit easy, active, a free, and yet at the same time to r strain him from many things th are uneasy to him, has, in my opinic got the true secret of education.

LOCK

6638. It was in making education n only common to all, but in some sen compulsory on all, that the destiny

e free republics of America was
actically settled.   LOWELL,
New England Two Centuries Ago

639. Jails and prisons are the com-
.ement of schools; so many less as
ou have of the latter, so many more
ust you have of the former.
                    HORACE MANN

640. Schoolhouses are the republican
ne of fortifications.   HORACE MANN

641. Education is our only political
afety.   Outside of this ark all is
eluge.   HORACE MANN

642. Finally, education alone can
onduct us to that enjoyment which
s, at once, best in quality and in-
inite in quantity.   HORACE MANN

643. Public instruction should be the
irst object of government.
                      NAPOLEON

644. If I have any inclination above
all others it is for the truthful educa-
ion of the youth of America. The
fundamentalist movement had not previously given me a moment's thought
or concern, but when it began thus to
interfere with the teachings in our
schools and colleges, to deceive the
youth of our country, our boys and
girls, our young men and women in
the formative stage, on whose right
thinking and right conduct the whole
future of America depends, I was
thoroughly aroused.
           HENRY F. OSBORN,
Evolution and Religion in Education

6645. Education—a debt due from
present to future generations.
                 GEORGE PEABODY

6646. Education is the only interest
worthy the deep, controlling anxiety
of the thoughtful man.
                 WENDELL PHILLIPS

6647. Educational institutions will become, more and more purely, institutions for educating people; and, as
they become this, they will cease to
be seats of scientific inquiry save on
the very lowest level.
             WALTER B. PITKIN

6648. The direction in which education starts a man will determine his
future life.   PLATO, *The Republic*

6649.
'Tis education forms the common
    mind:
Just as the twig is bent the tree's
    inclined.   POPE, *Moral Essays*

6650. It is only the ignorant who despise education.
         PUBLILIUS SYRUS, *Sententiae*

6651. Educational relations make the
strongest tie.   CECIL RHODES

6652. Education does not mean
teaching people to know what they
do not know; it means teaching them
to behave as they do not behave.
                       RUSKIN

6653. The more purely intellectual
aim of education should be the endeavor to make us see and imagine
the world in an objective manner as
far as possible as it really is in itself,
and not merely through the distorting
medium of personal desires.
                BERTRAND RUSSELL

6654. Manhood, not scholarship, is
the first aim of education.
                ERNEST T. SETON

6655. The great aim of education is
not knowledge but action.
                HERBERT SPENCER

6656. Only the refined and delicate
pleasures that spring from research
and education can build up barriers
between different ranks.
             MME. DE STAËL, *Corinne*

6657. Every school-boy knows it.
> JEREMY TAYLOR,
> *On the Real Presence*

6658. It made me gladsome to be getting some education, it being like a big window opening.
> MARY WEBB, *Precious Bane*

6659. Men are born but citizens are made. A child takes to itself what is brought to it. It accepts example, usage, traditions and general ideas. All the forms of its social reactions and most of its emotional interpretations are provided by its education.
> H. G. WELLS,
> *The Shape of Things to Come*

6660. Slavery is but half abolished, emancipation is but half completed, while millions of freemen with votes in their hands are left without education. Justice to them, the welfare of the States in which they live, the safety of the whole Republic, the dignity of the elective franchise,— all alike demand that the still remaining bonds of ignorance shall be unloosed and broken, and the minds as well as the bodies of the emancipated go free. R. C. WINTHROP

6661. The more a man is educated, the more it is necessary, for the welfare of the State, to instruct him how to make a proper use of his talents. Education is like a double-edged sword. It may be turned to dangerous usages if it is not properly handled. WU TING-FANG

See also: 2, 86, 251, 1154, 1676, 2581, 3237, 4312, 10423, 18493.

EFFORT

Related Subjects: **Labor, Sweat, Work.**

6671. If you would relish food, labor for it before you take it; if enjoy clothing, pay for it before you wear it; if you would sleep soundly, take a clear conscience to bed with you.
> FRANKLI

6672. Things don't turn up in th world until somebody turns them u
> JAMES A. GARFIEL

6673.
Somebody said that it couldn't b
  done
But he with a chuckle replied
That "maybe it couldn't," but h
  would be one
Who wouldn't say so till he'd tried.
> EDGAR GUEST,
> *It Couldn't Be Don*

6674.
Attempt the end and never stand t
  doubt;
Nothing's so hard but search will fin
  it out.
> ROBERT HERRICK, *Seek and Fin*

6675. The lab'ring mountain scarc brings forth a mouse.
> HORACE, *Ars Poetic*

6676.
No endeavor is in vain;
Its reward is in the doing,
And the rapture of pursuing
Is the prize the vanquished gain.
> LONGFELLOW,
> *The Wind Over the Chimne*

6677. To have striven, to have mad an effort, to have been true to certai ideals—this alone is worth th struggle.
> SIR WILLIAM OSLER,
> *Life of Sir William Osle*

See also: 10, 14, 647, 1271, 758 18681.

EGGS

Related Subject: **Birds.**

6681. Going as if he trod upon egg
> ROBERT BURTON,
> *Anatomy of Melanchol*

6682. A hen is only an egg's way of making another egg.
SAMUEL BUTLER, *Life and Habit*

6683. All the goodness of a good egg cannot make up for the badness of a bad one. CHARLES A. DANA,
The Making of a Newspaper Man

6684. There is always a best way of doing everything, if it be to boil an egg. EMERSON, *Conduct of Life*

6685. It is very hard to shave an egg. GEORGE HERBERT,
Jacula Prudentum

6686. Can you unscramble eggs?
J. P. MORGAN

6687. A black hen lays a white egg.
Proverb

6688. As full as an egg is of meat.
Proverb

6689. Don't put all your eggs in one basket. *Proverb*

6690. Omelettes are not made without breaking eggs. ROBESPIERRE

6691.
Think him as a serpent's egg
Which, hatch'd, would, as his kind, grow mischievous
And kill him in the shell.
SHAKESPEARE, *Julius Caesar*

6692. Will you take eggs for money?
SHAKESPEARE, *The Winter's Tale*

6693. Put all your eggs in one basket, and—watch the basket.
MARK TWAIN,
Pudd'nhead Wilson's Calendar

See also: 2931, 10681.

ELECTION

Related Subjects: Choice, Democracy, Government, Majority, Office, Politics, Vote.

6701. I have fought up to the present fourteen contested elections, which

take about a month of one's life apiece. It is melancholy when one reflects upon our brief span, to think that no less than fourteen months of life have been passed in this wearing clatter. WINSTON CHURCHILL,
A Roving Commission

6702. Popp'd in between the election and my hopes. SHAKESPEARE,
Hamlet

6703. What imports the nomination of this gentleman?
SHAKESPEARE, *Hamlet*

6704. But I do prophesy the election lights on Fortinbras. He has my dying voice. SHAKESPEARE,
Hamlet

See also: 1158.

ELECTRICITY

Related Subjects: Light, Machinery, Power, Radio, Science, Thunder and Lightning.

6711. Man could not study the behavior of electrical currents until he found some way of producing and controlling them. It is no wonder, therefore, that we have not developed an "electrical common-sense" like the mechanical common sense which has become almost instinctive. There is really nothing more mysterious about electrical forces than about the forces which lift weights or pull trains, in fact it is the latter which are the more complicated. W. L. BRAGG,
Electricity

6712. Striking the electric chain wherewith we are darkly bound.
BYRON, *Childe Harold*

6713. Not to make a large or a blinding light, but a small light having the mildness of gas.

Object: Edison to effect exact imitation of all done by gas, so as to replace lighting by gas by lighting by electricity.   THOMAS EDISON,
Note-Book

6714. Electricity—carrier of light and power, devourer of time and space, bearer of human speech over land and sea, greatest servant of man, itself unknown.   CHARLES W. ELIOT

6715. A machine that is like the tools of the Titans put in your hands.
CHARLES FERGUSON

6716. Is it a fact—or have I dreamt it—that by means of electricity, the world of matter has become a great nerve, vibrating thousands of miles in a breathless point of time? Rather, the round globe is a vast head, a brain, instinct with intelligence: or shall we say it is itself a thought, nothing but thought, and no longer the substance which we dreamed it.   HAWTHORNE,
The House of the Seven Gables

6717. The phansy of Amber delights to allect straws, chaffe and other festucous bodies by an attraction, we confess, obscure and weake enough, yet sufficiently manifest and strong to attest an *Electricity* or attractive nature.
HELMONTS, *Ternary of Paradoxes* (*London, 1650*). *First appearance of the word "Electricity."*

6718. The narrative of that particular branch of science which we call *Electricity* commences with a pretty trinket—a *yellow necklace* of amber beads. Therein begins the story of the telephone, of the X-ray, of radio. . . . The power of amber to attract and "clutch" light bodies is due to the fact that it becomes *electrified* when it is rubbed or subjected

to friction. That strange behavior of amber which earned it the name of "clutcher" was probably *the first intelligent observation of an electric action.*   ALFRED P. MORGAN,
The Pageant of Electricity

6719. Some readers may expect me at this stage to tell them what electricity "really is." The fact is that I have already said what it is. It is not a thing like St. Paul's Cathedral; *it is a way in which things behave.* . . . When I say that an electron has a certain amount of negative electricity, I mean merely that it behaves in a certain way. Electricity is not like red paint, a substance which can be put on to the electron and taken off again, it is merely a convenient name for certain physical laws.
BERTRAND RUSSELL,
A B C of Atoms

ELEGANCE

Related Subjects: Affectation, Fastidiousness, Fop, Vanity.

6721. Taste and elegance, though they are reckoned only among the smaller and secondary morals, are of no mean importance in the regulation of life. A moral taste is not of force to turn vice into virtue; but it recommends virtue with something like the blandishments of pleasure and it infinitely abates the evils of vice.   BURKE

6722. Elegance is something more than ease—more than a freedom from awkwardness and restraint. It implies a precision, a polish, and a sparkling which is spirited, yet delicate.   HAZLITT

6723. When the mind loses its feeling for elegance, it grows corrupt an

grovelling, and seeks in the crowds
what ought to be found at home.
W. S. LANDOR

See also: 18986.

ELEPHANT

Related Subect: Animal.

6731.
Th' unwieldy elephant,
To make them mirth, us'd all his
    might, and wreath'd
His lithe proboscis.
MILTON, Paradise Lost

6732. Slow as the elephant.
SHAKESPEARE,
Troilus and Cressida

6733. The elephant hath joints, but
none for courtesy: his legs are legs
for necessity, not for flexure.
SHAKESPEARE,
Troilus and Cressida

6734. An elephant never forgets.
Traditional

6735. The elephant is never won with
anger.   JOHN WILMOT,
Valentinian

See also: 21629.

ELOQUENCE

Related Subjects: Language, Orator, Persuasion, Preacher, Speech, Tongue, Words.

6741. Eloquence is logic on fire.
LYMAN BEECHER

6742. The truest eloquence is that
which holds us too mute for applause.   BULWER-LYTTON

6743. Eloquence is vehement simplicity.
RICHARD CECIL

6744. The manner of speaking is full
as important as the matter, as more
people have ears to be tickled than
understandings to judge.
LORD CHESTERFIELD

6745. There is no eloquence without
a man behind it.   EMERSON

6746. The pleasure of eloquence is in
greatest part owing often to the stimulus of the occasion which produces
it—to the magic of sympathy which
exalts the feeling of each, by radiating on him the feeling of all.
EMERSON

6747. Honesty is one part of eloquence. We persuade others by being
in earnest ourselves.   HAZLITT

6748.
Talking and eloquence are not the
    same.
To speak and to speak well are two
    things.
A fool may talk, but a wise man
    speaks.   BEN JONSON

6749. There is not less eloquence in
the voice, the eye, the gesture, than
in words.   LA ROCHEFOUCAULD,
Maxims

6750. True eloquence consists in saying all that is proper, and nothing
more.   LA ROCHEFOUCAULD,
Maxims

6751. There was no man of his time
like Antony for addressing a multitude, or for carrying soldiers with
him by the force of words.
PLUTARCH, Lives

6752. As the grace of man is in the
mind, so the beauty of the mind is
eloquence.   Proverb

6753. He that has no silver in his
purse, should have silver on his
tongue.   Proverb

4. Unprofitable eloquence is like the cypress, which is great and tall, but bears no fruit.   *Proverb*

6755. A grand eloquence, little conscience.   *Proverb*

6756. It is but a poor eloquence which only shows that the orator can talk.   Sir Joshua Reynolds

6757. *Rev. Samuel J. May:* Mr. Garrison, you are too excited—you are on fire!
William Lloyd Garrison: I have need to be on fire, for I have icebergs around me to melt.
    Sandburg: *Abraham Lincoln*

6758.
Turn him to any cause of policy,
The Gordian knot of it he will unloose,
Familiar as his garter: that when he speaks,
The air, a chartered libertine, is still.
    Shakespeare, *Henry V*

6759. Bid me discourse, I will enchant thine ear.
    Shakespeare, *Venus and Adonis*

6760. True eloquence does not consist in speech. It cannot be brought from far. Labor and learning may toil for it in vain. Words and phrases may be marshalled in every way, but they cannot compass it. It must consist in the man, in the subject, and in the occasion.   Daniel Webster

6761.
Choice word and measured phrase, above the reach
Of ordinary men.
    Wordsworth,
Resolution and Independence

See also: 169.

EMBARRASSMENT

Related Subjects: **Awkwardness, Blushing, Timidity.**

6771.
He scratch'd his ear, the infallible resource
To which embarrass'd people have recourse.   Byron, *Don Juan*

6772.
He stood a spell on one foot fust,
   Then stood a spell on t'other,
An' on which one he felt the wust
   He couldn't ha' told ye nuther.
    Lowell, *The Courtin'*

See also: 2624, 13675.

EMOTION, see Feeling

EMPEROR, see King

EMPIRE

Related Subjects: **Imperialism, Kings.**

6781. What are your empires but brigandage and rapine?
    St. Augustine

6782.
Whose game was empires and whose stakes were thrones,
Whose table earth, whose dice were human bones.   Byron,
The Age of Bronze

6783. The only way to save our empires from the encroachment of the people is to engage in war, and thus substitute national passions for social aspirations.   Catherine the Great

6784. The day of small nations has passed away; the day of Empires has come.   Joseph Chamberlain

6785. It is not their long reigns, nor their frequent changes which occasion the fall of empires, but their abuse of power.   GEORGE CRABBE

6786. All empire is no more than power in trust.   DRYDEN,
Absalom & Achitophel

6787. The Napoleonic Empire itself was no more than neutral ground for men of the most diverse ideas, a useful bridge to people who climbed out of the revolutionary floodwaters, and ran to and fro upon it for twenty years undecided whether to land on the right banks of contemporary opinion.   HEINE

6788. Extended empire, like expanded gold, exchanges solid strength for feeble splendor.
SAMUEL JOHNSON

6789. To make an empire durable, the magistrates must obey the laws, and the people the magistrates.
SOLON

6790. As a general truth, nothing is more opposed to the well-being and freedom of men, than vast empires.
DE TOCQUEVILLE

See also: 674, 3056, 19869.

EMPLOYMENT AND UNEMPLOYMENT

Related Subjects: Business, Depression, Labor, Occupation, Poverty, Profit, Wages, Work.

6791. The outstanding mistake of the employer is his failure to realize that he is dealing with human material.
ROGER BABSON,
Business Fundamentals

6792. Employment and ennui are simply incompatible.
MME. DELUZY

6793. Employment is nature's physician, and is essential to human happiness.   GALEN

6794. A man who qualifies himself well for his calling, never fails of employment.   JEFFERSON

6795. Be always employed about some rational thing, that the devil find thee not idle.   ST. JEROME

6796. The wise prove, and the foolish confess, by their conduct, that a life of employment is the only life worth leading.   WILLIAM PALEY

6797. Employment gives health, sobriety, and morals. Constant employment and well-paid labor produce, in a country like ours, general prosperity, content, and cheerfulness.
DANIEL WEBSTER

Unemployment.

6798. I have known people to stop and buy an apple on the corner and then walk away as if they had solved the whole unemployment problem.
HEYWOOD BROUN,
It Seems to Me

6799. Here are all kinds of employers wanting all sorts of servants, and all sorts of servants wanting all kinds of employers, and they never seem to come together.
DICKENS, *Martin Chuzzlewit*

6800. When men are employed, they are best contented; for on the days they worked they were good-natured and cheerful, and, with the consciousness of having done a good day's work, they spent the evening jollily; but on our idle days they were mutinous and quarrelsome.
FRANKLIN, *Autobiography*

6801. Stocks are property, yes. Bonds are property, yes.

Machines, land, buildings, are property, yes.
A job is property,
No, nix, nah nah!
CARL SANDBURG,
The People, Yes

6802. What is a man to do who is starving, and cannot find work?
God knows. WILLIAM H. TAFT

See also: 2817, 5443, 12613.

ENCOURAGEMENT

Related Subjects: Help, Hope, Patronage.

6811. Correction does much, but encouragement does more. Encouragement after censure is as the sun after a shower. GOETHE

6812. We ought not to raise expectations which it is not in our power to satisfy. It is more pleasing to see smoke brightening into flame, than flame sinking into smoke.
SAMUEL JOHNSON

6813. I believe that any man's life will be filled with constant and unexpected encouragement, if he makes up his mind to do his level best each day and as nearly as possible reaching the highwater mark of pure and useful living. BOOKER T. WASHINGTON

See also: 3664, 3782.

END

Related Subjects: Beginning, Consequences, Death, Extremes, Intention, Limit, Purpose.

6821. Better never begin than never make an end.
GEORGE HERBERT,
Jacula Prudentum

6822. You began better than you end.
OVID, *Heroides*

6823. The end must justify the means. MATTHEW PRIOR,
Hans Carvel

6824. The end justifies the means.
PUBLILIUS SYRUS, *Sententiae*

6825. All's well that ends well.
SHAKESPEARE,
All's Well that Ends Well

6826. Let the end try the man.
SHAKESPEARE, *Henry IV*

6827.
O, that a man might know
The end of this day's business, ere it come.
SHAKESPEARE, *Julius Caesar*

6828. The true beginning of our end.
SHAKESPEARE,
A Midsummer-Night's Dream

6829.
The daintiest last, to make the end most sweet. SHAKESPEARE,
Richard II

6830.
The end crowns all,
And that old common arbitrator, Time,
Will one day end it.
SHAKESPEARE,
Troilus and Cressida

See also: 220, 2861.

ENDURANCE

Related Subjects: Courage, Martyr, Stoicism, Suffering, Trials.

6841. What can't be cured must be endured. ROBERT BURTON,
Anatomy of Melancholy

6842. Not in the achievement, but in the endurance of the human soul, does it show its divine grandeur, and its alliance with the infinite God.
E. H. CHAPIN

6843.

The troubles of our proud and angry
    dust
  Are from eternity, and shall not
    fail.
Bear them we can, and if we can
    we must.
  Shoulder the sky, my lad, and
    drink your ale.
        A. E. HOUSMAN, *Last Poems*

6844. He conquers who endures.
                        PERSIUS

6845. By bravely enduring, an evil
which cannot be avoided is overcome.
                        Proverb

6846. He that endureth is not overcome.   *Proverb*

6847. This and a great deal more
like it I have had to put up with.
        TERENCE, *Eunuchus*

6848. I am not good at knives and
curses but better at flying to lovers
and enduring a good deal in the way
of rocks and shocks.
        ELLEN TERRY, to Bernard Shaw

6849. To endure is greater than to
dare; to tire out hostile fortune; to be
daunted by no difficulty; to keep
heart when all have lost it; to go
through intrigue spotless; to forego
even ambition when the end is gained
—who can say this is not greatness?
        THACKERAY, *The Virginians*

See also: 336, 1182, 2562, 3011, 3046,
3207, 5567.

ENEMY

Related Subjects: **Hatred, Jealousy, Opposition, Revenge, Rivalry, War.**

6851. While I see many hoof-marks
going in, I see none coming out. It is
easier to get into the enemy's toils
than out again.   AESOP,
        The Lion, the Fox, and the Beasts

6852. You will only injure yourself
if you take notice of despicable enemies.   AESOP,
        The Bald Man and the Fly

6853. Never soar aloft on an enemy's
pinions.   AESOP,
        The Tortoise and the Birds

6854. Rejoice not over thy greatest
enemy being dead, but remember that
we die all.
        Apocrypha: Ecclesiasticus

6855.

Believe me, a thousand friends suf-
    fice thee not;
In a single enemy thou hast more
    than enough.
        ALI BEN ABOU TALEB

6856. If thine enemy hunger, feed
him; if he thirst, give him drink: for
in so doing thou shalt heap coals of
fire on his head.
        Bible: Romans, xii, 20

6857.

A man's worst enemies are those
  Of his own house and family.
        BLAKE, *Jerusalem*

6858. They love him most for the
enemies he has made.   E. S. BRAGG

6859. You shall judge of a man by
his foes as well as by his friends.
        JOSEPH CONRAD, *Lord Jim*

6860. Nobody's enemy but his own.
        DICKENS, *David Copperfield*

6861. Life'd not be worth livin' if
we didn't keep our inimies.
        F. P. DUNNE,
        On New Year's Resolutions

6862. One enemy is too much.
        GEORGE HERBERT, *Jacula Prudentum*

⊽3. If we could read the secret history of our enemies, we should find in each man's life sorrow and suffering enough to disarm all hostility.

LONGFELLOW, *Driftwood*

6864.
You have no enemies, you say?
  Alas! my friend, the boast is poor—
He who has mingled in the fray
  Of duty, that the brave endure,
Must have made foes! If you have none,
Small is the work that you have done;
You've hit no traitor on the hip;
You've dashed no cup from perjured lip;
You've never turned the wrong to right—
You've been a coward in the fight!

CHARLES MACKAY

6865.
My nearest
And dearest enemy.

THOMAS MIDDLETON,
Anything for a Quiet Life

6866. The enemy has no definite name, though in a certain degree we all know him. He who puts always the body before the spirit, the dead before the living; who makes things only in order to sell them; who has forgotten that there is such a thing as truth, and measures the world by advertisement or by money; who daily defiles the beauty that surrounds him and makes vulgar the tragedy.

GILBERT MURRAY,
Religio Grammatici

6867. Though thy enemy seem a mouse, yet watch him like a lion.
Proverb

6868. One adversary may do us more harm than a great many friends can do us good.   *Proverb*

6869. Make a golden bridge for a flying enemy.   *Proverb*

6870. If we are bound to forgive an enemy, we are not bound to trust him.
Proverb

6871. It is good to strike the serpent's head with your enemy's hand.
Proverb

6872. If we be enemies to ourselves, whither shall we fly?   *Proverb*

6873. He that dallies with his enemy gives him leave to kill him. *Proverb*

6874. Best dealing with an enemy when you take him at his weakest.
Proverb

6875. All men think their enemies ill men.   *Proverb*

6876. No tears are shed when an enemy dies.   PUBLILIUS SYRUS,
Sententiae

6877. It is an unhappy lot which finds no enemies.
PUBLILIUS SYRUS, *Sententiae*

6878. He makes no friend who never made a foe.   TENNYSON,
Idylls of the King

See also: 353, 858, 4301, 4622, 4706, 5160, 5972, 8057, 8654, 17964.

ENERGY

Related Subjects: Enterprise, Enthusiasm, Exercise, Force, Impulse, Power, Violence, Zeal.

6881. This world belongs to the energetic.   EMERSON

6882. Energy will do anything that can be done in the world; and no talents, no circumstances, no opportunities will make a two-legged animal a man without it.   GOETHE

6883. He alone has energy who cannot be deprived of it.   LAVATER

6884. There is no genius in life like the genius of energy and activity.
D. G. MITCHELL

6885. It is energy—the central element of which is will—that produces the miracles of enthusiasm in all ages. Everywhere it is the main-spring of what is called force of character, and the sustaining power of all great action.   SAMUEL SMILES, *Self-Help*

See also: 18, 1857.

ENGLAND AND THE ENGLISH

Related Subjects: Europe, Ireland, Island, London, Scotland.

6891. Sir Roger made several reflections on the greatness of the British Nation; as, that one Englishman could beat three Frenchmen; that we could never be in danger of Popery so long as we took care of our fleet; that the Thames was the noblest river in Europe . . . with many other honest prejudices, which naturally cleave to the heart of a true Englishman.   ADDISON, *The Spectator*

6892. The royal navy of England hath ever been its greatest defence and ornament; it is its ancient and natural strength,—the floating bulwark of our island.
SIR WILLIAM BLACKSTONE,
Commentaries

6893. O England! long, long may it be ere the sun of thy glory sink beneath the wave of darkness! Though gloomy and portentous clouds are now gathering rapidly around thee, still, still may it please the Almighty to disperse them, and to grant thee a futurity longer in duration and still brighter in renown than thy past! Or, if thy doom be at hand, may that doom be a noble one, and worthy of her who has been styled the Old Queen of the waters! May thou sink, if thou dost sink, amidst blood and flame, with a mighty noise, causing more than one nation to participate in thy downfall!
GEORGE BORROW, The Bible in Spain

6894.
If I should die, think only this of me:
 That there's some corner of a foreign field
That is forever England.
RUPERT BROOKE, The Soldier

6895.
Oh, to be in England,
Now that April's there.
BROWNING,
Home—Thoughts from Abroad

6896. England is a paradise for women and hell for horses; Italy a paradise for horses, hell for women, as the diverb goes.
ROBERT BURTON,
Anatomy of Melancholy

6897.
Ye mariners of England,
That guard our native seas;
Whose flag has braved, a thousand years,
The battle and the breeze!
THOMAS CAMPBELL,
Ye Mariners of England

6898.
Britannia needs no bulwarks,
No towers along the steep;
Her march is o'er the mountain waves,
Her home is on the deep.
THOMAS CAMPBELL,
Ye Mariners of England

6899.

Be England what she will,
With all her faults she is my country
    still. CHARLES CHURCHILL,
                    The Farewell

6900. The whole fury and might of
the enemy must very soon be turned
on us. Hitler knows that he will have
to break us in this Island or lose the
war. If we can stand up to him, all
Europe may be free and the life of
the world may move forward into
broad, sunlit uplands. But if we fail,
then the whole world, including the
United States, including all that we
have known and cared for, will sink
into the abyss of a new Dark Age
made more sinister and perhaps more
protracted, by the lights of perverted
science. WINSTON CHURCHILL,
                    Blood, Sweat & Tears

6901. Today is Trinity Sunday. Centuries ago words were written to be
a call and a spur to the faithful
servants of Truth and Justice:
"Arm yourselves and be ye men of
valor, and be in readiness for the conflict for it is better for us to perish in
battle than to look upon the outrage
of our nation and our altar."
            WINSTON CHURCHILL,
                Blood, Sweat & Tears

6902.

Dash the bomb on the dome of
    Paul's—
Deem ye the fame of the Admiral
    falls?
Pry the stone from the chancel
    floor,—
Dream ye that Shakespeare shall live
    no more?
Where is the giant shot that kills
Wordsworth walking the old green
    hills?   HELEN G. CONE,
        A Chant of Love for England

6903. For Englishmen especially, of
all the races of the earth, a task, any
task, undertaken in an adventurous
spirit acquires the merit of romance.
JOSEPH CONRAD, *A Personal Record*

6904.

England, with all thy faults I love
    thee still,
My country!   COWPER, *The Task*

6905.

Slaves cannot breathe in England; if
    their lungs
Receive our air, that moment they
    are free!
They touch our country, and their
    shackles fall.   COWPER, *The Task*

6906. You have only got to look at
the pages of British imperial history
to hide your head in shame that you
are British.   SIR STAFFORD CRIPPS

6907.

Nay, nay sweet England, do not
    grieve!
    Not one of these poor men who
        died
But did within his soul believe
    That death for thee was glorified.
            WALTER DE LA MARE,
                How Sleep the Brave

6908. Things they don't understand
always cause a sensation among the
English.   ALFRED DE MUSSET,
                The White Blackbird

6909.

Vain, mightiest fleets of iron framed,
    Vain, those all-shattering guns;
Unless proud England keep, untamed,
    The strong heart of her sons.
            SIR F. H. DOYLE,
                The Private of the Buffs

6910. The Englishman's reverence
for the individual's rights goes beyond the Frenchman's, for in France
there is a tendency to subordinate the

individual to the family, and in England the interests of the individual predominate. HAVELOCK ELLIS, *The Task of Social Hygiene*

6911. I find the Englishman to be him of all men who stands firmest in his shoes. EMERSON, *English Traits*

6912. Materialism is a rock on which to build any edifice, even a temple of dreams. On materialism Englishmen. . . . built the British Empire.
O. ST. J. GOGARTY

6913. An Englishman is a man who lives on an island in the North Sea governed by Scotsmen.
PHILIP GUEDALLA,
Supers & Supermen

6914. "The English," says Froissart, "amused themselves sadly after the fashion of their country." They have indeed a way of their own. Their mirth is a relaxation from gravity, a challenge to dull care to be gone; and one is not always clear at first, whether the appeal is successful.
HAZLITT, *Merry England*

6915.
The stately homes of England!
How beautiful they stand,
Amidst their tall ancestral trees,
O'er all the pleasant land!
MRS. HEMANS,
The Homes of England

6916. I shall examine with some suspicion any proposals that may be made for the distribution of the British Empire among foreign countries, whatever their birthrate, insolence or inefficiency.
A. P. HERBERT

6917.
Oh England is a pleasant place for them that's rich and high,

But England is a cruel place for such poor folks as I.
CHARLES KINGSLEY,
The Last Buccaneer

6918.
Our England is a garden, and such gardens are not made
By singing:—"Oh, how beautiful!" and sitting in the shade.
KIPLING, *The Glory of the Garden*

6919. For what there is of it—for such as it is—and for what it may be worth—will you drink to England and the English? KIPLING

6920. Mr. Baldwin has the Englishman's genius for appearing an amateur in a game in which, in fact, he is a superb professional.
HAROLD J. LASKI

6921. A certain incomprehensible reticence of soul which is peculiar to the English. WILLIAM McFEE,
Command

6922. We know no spectacle so ridiculous as the British public in one of its periodical fits of morality.
MACAULAY,
On Moore's Life of Lord Byron

6923. English nationalism was a creed which defined Americans as cads, Frenchmen as libertines, and the rest of the European races as a great deal worse—with the possible exceptions of Germans, who were regarded merely as dangerous rivals in trade. C. R. W. NEVINSON

6924. I attended endless divine services—listened to strange sermons delivered by doctors of divinity in which Englishmen were confused with God, Nelson with Jesus Christ, Lady Hamilton with the Virgin Mary.
C. R. W. NEVINSON

6925. There'll Always Be an England.

ROSS PARKER & HUEY CHARLES,
Title of Song

6926. When Good Friday falls in a lady's lap, to England will happen some mishap. *Proverb*

6927. When the sand doth feed the clay, England woe and well a day; but when the clay doth feed the sand, then it's well with old England.
Proverb

6928. He that would England win, must with Ireland first begin.
Proverb

6929. A famine in England begins at the horse-manger. *Proverb*

6930. England is the paradise of individuality, eccentricity, heresy, anomalies, hobbies, and humours.
SANTAYANA, *Soliloquies in England*

6931. It was always yet the trick of our English nation, if they have a good thing, to make it too common.
SHAKESPEARE, *Henry IV*

6932.
O England! model to thy inward greatness,
Like little body with a mighty heart,
What mightst thou do, that honour would thee do,
Were all thy children kind and natural! SHAKESPEARE, *Henry V*

6933.
I thought upon one pair of English legs
Did march three Frenchmen.
SHAKESPEARE, *Henry V*

6934. That island of England breeds very valiant creatures: their mastiffs are of unmatchable courage.
SHAKESPEARE, *Henry V*

6935.
Once more unto the breach, dear friends, once more;
Or close the wall up with our English dead! SHAKESPEARE,
Henry V

6936.
Let us be back'd with God and with the seas
Which he hath given for fence impregnable,
And with their helps only defend ourselves;
In them and in ourselves our safety lies. SHAKESPEARE, *Henry VI*

6937. There shall be in England seven half-penny loaves sold for a penny; the three-hooped pot shall have ten hoops; and I will make it felony to drink small beer.
SHAKESPEARE, *Henry VI*

6938.
This England never did, nor never shall,
Lie at the proud foot of a conqueror.
SHAKESPEARE, *King John*

6939.
Come the three corners of the world in arms,
And we shall shock them. Nought shall make us rue,
If England to itself do rest but true.
SHAKESPEARE, *King John*

6940. Heaven take my soul, and England keep my bones.
SHAKESPEARE, *King John*

6941.
This royal throne of kings, this sceptred isle,
This earth of majesty, this seat of Mars,
This other Eden, demi-paradise,
This fortress built by Nature for herself

Against infection and the hand of war,

This happy breed of men, this little world,

This precious stone set in the silver sea,

Which serves it in the office of a wall

Or as a moat defensive to a house,

Against the envy of less happier lands,

This blessed plot, this earth, this realm, this England.

      SHAKESPEARE, *Richard II*

6942. We don't bother much about dress and manners in England, because, as a nation we don't dress well and we've no manners.

BERNARD SHAW, *You Never Can Tell*

6943. In England we always let an institution strain itself until it breaks.

   BERNARD SHAW, *Getting Married*

6944. The whole strength of England lies in the fact that the enormous majority of the English people are snobs.   BERNARD SHAW,

              Getting Married

6945. There are only two classes in good society in England: the equestrian classes and the neurotic classes.

BERNARD SHAW, *Heartbreak House*

6946.

Hector: and this ship we are all in? This soul's prison we call England? *Capt. Shotover:* The captain is in his bunk, drinking bottled ditch-water; and the crew is gambling in the forecastle. She will strike and split and sink. Do you think the laws of God will be suspended in favor of England because you were born in it?

BERNARD SHAW, *Heartbreak House*

6947. There is nothing so bad or so good that you will not find an Englishman doing it: but you will never find an Englishman in the wrong.

He does everything on principles; he robs you on business principles; he enslaves you on imperial principles.

BERNARD SHAW, *The Man of Destiny*

6948. War with the world, and peace with England.   *Spanish Proverb*

6949.

Gorgonized me from head to foot, With a stony British stare.

      TENNYSON, *Maud*

6950.

Rule, Britannia! Britannia rules the waves!

Britons never shall be slaves.

      JAMES THOMSON, *Alfred*

6951.

Fee, fi, fo, fum!

I smell the blood of an Englishman.

Be he live or be he dead

I'll grind his bones to make my bread.

Traditional, Jack and the Bean Stalk

6952. In England we have come to rely upon a comfortable time-lag of fifty years or a century intervening between the perception that something ought to be done and a serious attempt to do it.   H. G. WELLS,

The Work, Wealth & Happiness of

                       Mankind

6953. Those who say that this war is a war between two great Empires, each fighting for the right to rule and exploit other peoples without the latter's consent, are speaking of a war that is past. They are, to be exact, speaking of Mr. Chamberlain's war. Mr. Chamberlain lost that war. It is over. We are now engaged on quite a different struggle, and it is time we woke up to that fact, and made it clear to the whole world.

      TOM WINTRINGHAM,

            New Ways of War

6954. We will stick by whatever we find to do or are told to do, in spite of invasion, bombardment, wounds, hunger or whatever may be the price of victory. We will take all that comes courageously; and we will not do anything that may endanger victory.

Tom Wintringham,
New Ways of War

6955. Whatever the future may hold we will continue our war for liberty by every means, open or secret, that we can use; we shall go on, stubbornly and doggedly, until we have overthrown Fascism, with the aid of all free men who seek freedom anywhere across the earth.

Tom Wintringham,
New Ways of War

6956. Those comfortably padded lunatic asylums which are known, euphemistically, as the stately homes of England. Virginia Woolf,
The Common Reader

6957.
Oh, it's a snug little island!
A right little, tight little island.

Wordsworth,
The Snug Little Island

6958.
They called thee Merry England in old time;
A happy people won for thee that name
With envy heard in many a distant clime. Wordsworth,
They Called Thee Merry England

6959.
A Briton, even in love, should be
A subject, not a slave!

Wordsworth,
Ere With Cold Beads of Midnight

6960.
We must be free or die, who speak the tongue

That Shakespeare spake; the faith and morals hold
Which Milton held.

Wordsworth,
It is Not to be Thought Of

See also: 574, 577, 703, 1022, 1157, 1584, 2207, 2493, 2767, 3276, 4043, 4384, 4902, 5166, 5417, 5733, 6376, 8382, 8536, 8891, 10873, 11672, 12595, 12662, 12947, 13791, 13792, 13977, 14564, 14782, 16751, 18874, 20524, 20529, 20944, 20986, 21084.

ENTERPRISE

Related Subjects: Business, Courage, Energy, Self-reliance.

6961.
It is always good
When a man has two irons in the fire.

Francis Beaumont,
On the Tombs in Westminster Abbey

6962. The method of the enterprising is to plan with audacity, and execute with vigor; to sketch out a map of possibilities, and then to treat them as probabilities.   C. N. Bovee

6963. Plough deep while sluggards sleep.   Franklin, *Poor Richard*

6964. An ounce of enterprise is worth a pound of privilege.

F. R. Marvin,
The Companionship of Books

6965. To do anything in this world worth doing, we must not stand back shivering and thinking of the cold and danger, but jump in, and scramble through as well as we can.

Sydney Smith

6966. What people say you cannot do, you try and find that you can.

Thoreau, *Walden*

See also: 112, 171, 291, 6303.

ENTHUSIASM

Related Subjects: Energy, Youth, Zeal.

6971. It is unfortunate, considering that enthusiasm moves the world, that so few enthusiasts can be trusted to speak the truth.   LORD BALFOUR

6972. Great designs are not accomplished without enthusiasm of some sort. It is the inspiration of everything great. Without it no man is to be feared, and with it none despised.
C. N. BOVEE

6973. Enthusiasm is the genius of sincerity, and truth accomplishes no victories without it.
BULWER-LYTTON,
The Last Days of Pompeii

6974.
Rash enthusiasm in good society
Were nothing but a moral inebriety.
BYRON, *Don Juan*

6975. Enlist the interests of stern morality and religious enthusiasm in the cause of political liberty, as in the time of the old Puritans, and it will be irresistible.   COLERIDGE

6976.
No wild enthusiast ever yet could rest,
Till half mankind were, like himself, possest.   COWPER

6977. Every production of genius must be the production of enthusiasm.
DISRAELI

6978. Truth is never to be expected from authors whose understandings are warped with enthusiasm; for they judge all actions and their causes by their own perverse principles, and a crooked line can never be the measure of a straight one.   DRYDEN

6979. Nothing great was ever achieved without enthusiasm.
EMERSON, *Circles*

6980. Every great and commanding movement in the annals of the world is the triumph of enthusiasm. Nothing great was ever achieved without it.   EMERSON

6981. The fellow who isn't fired with enthusiasm is apt to be fired.
B. C. FORBES, *Forbes Epigrams*

6982. Enthusiasts soon understand each other.   WASHINGTON IRVING

6983. The world belongs to the Enthusiast who keeps cool.
WILLIAM MCFEE, *Casuals of the Sea*

6984. No virtue is safe that is not enthusiastic.   J. R. SEELEY

6985. The sense of this word among the Greeks affords the noblest definition of it; enthusiasm signifies "God in us."   MME. DE STAËL

See also: 6417.

ENVIRONMENT

Related Subjects: Influence, Limit, Opportunity, Society.

6991. Man's advance in control over his environment is making it more and more difficult for him, at least in the industrialized countries with a high standard of living, like America or England, to lead a naturally good life, and easier and easier to lead a morally bad one.
W. H. AUDEN, *I Believe*

6992. Language and customs are determined far more by the environment in which the child grows up than by its descent, because the physical attributes, so far as they have any influence at all, occur with

extraordinary variety within every group.   FRANZ BOAS,
Aryans & Non-Aryans

6993. Mankind has the latent power deliberately to adjust its environment in the interest of a fuller and happier life for all. We are not the helpless creatures of blind forces forever beyond our control.
STUART CHASE, *Are Radicals Crazy?*

6994. Complete adaptation to environment means death. The essential point in all response is the desire to control environment.   JOHN DEWEY

6995. Men resemble their contemporaries even more than their progenitors.   EMERSON, *Representative Men*

6996.
Hearts just as pure and fair
May bloom in Belgrave Square
As in the lowly air of Seven Dials.
          W. S. GILBERT, *Iolanthe*

6997. Human nature will not flourish, any more than a potato, if it be planted and replanted, for too long a series of generations, in the same worn-out soil.   HAWTHORNE,
The Scarlet Letter

6998.
There's many a life of sweet content
Whose virtue is environment.
          WALTER LEARNED

6999. They that live in a trading street are not disturbed at the passage of carts.   SIR RICHARD STEELE,
The Spectator

See also: 5453.

ENVY

Related Subjects: Avarice, Desire, Jealousy, Rivalry.

7001.
For not many men, the proverb saith,
Can love a friend whom fortune prospereth
Unenvying.   AESCHYLUS,
Agamemnon

7002. A man that hath no virtue in himself ever envieth virtue in others; for men's minds will either feed upon their own good, or upon others' evil; and who wanteth the one will prey upon the other; and whoso is out of hope to attain to another's virtue, will seek to come at even hand by depressing another's fortune.   BACON

7003. Envy's a coal comes hissing hot from hell.
          PHILIP J. BAILEY, *Festus*

7004. Thou shalt not covet thy neighbour's house, thou shalt not covet thy neighbour's wife, nor his manservant, nor his maidservant, nor his ox, nor his ass, nor any thing that is thy neighbour's.   *Bible: Exodus, xx, 17*

7005. Envy is like a fly that passes all a body's sounder parts, and dwells upon the sores.   GEORGE CHAPMAN

7006. Antisthenes used to say that envious people were devoured by their own disposition, just as iron is by rust.   DIOGENES LAERTIUS,
Antisthenes

7007.
Fools may our scorn, not envy raise,
For envy is a kind of praise.
          JOHN GAY

7008. Envy feels not its own happiness but when it may be compared with the misery of others.
          SAMUEL JOHNSON

7009. All envy is proportionate to desire; we are uneasy at the attainments of another, according as we think our own happiness would be advanced by the addition of that which he withholds from us; and therefore whatever depresses immoderate wishes, will, at the same time, set the heart free from the corrosion of envy, and exempt us from that vice which is, above most others, tormenting to ourselves, hateful to the world, and productive of mean artifices and sordid projects.   SAMUEL JOHNSON

7010. Envy sets the stronger seal on desert; if he have no enemies, I should esteem his fortune most wretched.   BEN JONSON

7011. The truest mark of being born with great qualities, is being born without envy.
          LA ROCHEFOUCAULD, Maxims

7012. Envy has no other quality but that of detracting from virtue.
          . LIVY, History

7013. Other passions have objects to flatter them, and which seem to content and satisfy them for a while. There is power in ambition, pleasure in luxury, and pelf in covetousness; but envy can gain nothing but vexation.   MONTAIGNE, Essays

7014. Envy is a pain of mind that successful men cause their neighbors.
          ONASANDER, The General

7015. Envy always implies conscious inferiority wherever it resides.
          PLINY THE ELDER

7016. Better be envied than pitied.
          Proverb

7017. Envy shoots at others, and wounds herself.   Proverb

7018. An envious man waxes lean with the fatness of his neighbour.
          Proverb

7019. It is difficult keeping that which is admired by many.
          PUBLILIUS SYRUS, Sententiae

7020. How bitter a thing it is to look into happiness through another man's eyes! SHAKESPEARE, As You Like It

7021. There is not a passion so strongly rooted in the human heart as envy.   SHERIDAN, The Critic

7022. If we did but know how little some enjoy of the great things that they possess, there would not be much envy in the world. EDWARD YOUNG

See also: 1048, 1049, 1394, 1403, 1467, 4318, 4981, 7954, 15544.

EPIGRAM, THE

Related Subjects: Cleverness, Humor, Joke, Pun, Wit.

7031.
What is an Epigram? A dwarfish whole,
Its body brevity, and wit its soul.
          COLERIDGE, An Epigram

7032. In general I don't see how an epigram, being a pure bolt from the blue, with no introduction or cue, gets itself writ.
          WILLIAM JAMES, Letters

7033. The sharp, the rapier-pointed epigram.   KEATS, Letters

7034. An epigram is a gag that's played Carnegie Hall.
          OSCAR LEVANT

7035. No epigram contains the whole truth.   C. W. THOMPSON,
          Presidents I've Known

7036. Somewhere in the world there is an epigram for every dilemma.
          H. W. VAN LOON, Tolerance

7037. An epigram often flashes light into regions where reason shines but dimly.   E. C. WHIPPLE

EPITAPHS

Related Subjects: Death, Funeral, Grave, Monument.

7041. Do ye not laugh, O listening friends, when men praise those dead whose virtues they discovered not when living. It takes much marble to build the sepulchre. How little of lath and plaster would have repaired the garret!   BULWER-LYTTON

7042.
Green be the turf above thee,
    Friend of my better days!
None knew thee but to love thee,
    Nor named thee but to praise.
    FITZ-GREENE HALLECK,
    On the Death of Joseph Rodman Drake

7043.
He lies below, correct in cypress wood,
And entertains the most exclusive worms.
    DOROTHY PARKER,
    The Very Rich Man

7044. On my father's tombstone the legend reads: "A wit, a journalist and gentleman unafraid." My mother's epitaph says: "She ate of life as if it were fruit."   DONALD C. PEATTIE

7045. If all would speak as kindly of the living as in epitaphs they do of the dead, slander and censorious gossip would soon be strangers in the world.   PLATO

7046.
Thy ignominy sleep with thee in the grave,
But not remember'd in thy epitaph!
    SHAKESPEARE, *Henry IV*

7047.
This be the verse you grave for me:
Here he lies where he longed to be;
Home is the sailor, home from sea,
And the hunter home from the hill.
    STEVENSON, *Requiem*

See also: 2663, 3573, 8563, 10964.

EQUALITY AND INEQUALITY

Related Subjects: Compensation, Democracy, Freedom, Law, Liberty, The People, Rights.

7051. The sole equality on earth is death.   PHILIP J. BAILEY, *Festus*

7052. Whatever difference there may appear to be in men's fortunes, there is still a certain compensation of good and ill in all, that makes them equal.
    P. CHARRON

7053. When the Lord sent me forth into the world, He forbade me to put off my hat to any, high or low.
    GEORGE FOX, *Journal*

7054. Society is a more level surface than we imagine. Wise men or absolute fools are hard to be met with; and there are few giants or dwarfs.
    HAZLITT

7055. We shall not produce equality by turning everything upside down.
    A. P. HERBERT

7056. We hold these truths to be self-evident,—that all men are created equal; that they are endowed by their Creator with certain unalienable rights; that among these are life, liberty, and the pursuit of happiness.
    JEFFERSON,
    Declaration of Independence

7057. Sir, your levelers wish to level down as far as themselves. But they cannot bear leveling up to themselves. They would all have some people under them. Why not then have some people above them?
    SAMUEL JOHNSON, *Boswell: Life*

7058. By the law of God, given by him to humanity, all men are free, are brothers, and are equals.

MAZZINI

7059. All men are by nature equal, made, all of the same earth by the same Creator, and however we deceive ourselves, as dear to God is the poor peasant as the mighty prince.

PLATO

7060. As men, we are all equal in the presence of death.

PUBLILIUS SYRUS, *Sententiae*

7061. In the gates of eternity the black hand and the white hold each other with an equal clasp.

HARRIET BEECHER STOWE

7062. The equality of conditions is more complete in the Christian countries of the present day, than it has been at any time, or in any part of the world. Its gradual development is a providential fact, and it possesses all the characteristics of a divine decree; it is universal, it is durable, and it constantly eludes all human interference; and all events, as well as all men, contribute to its progress.

DE TOCQUEVILLE

Inequality

7063. Our inequality materializes our upper class, vulgarizes our middle class, brutalizes our lower class.

MATTHEW ARNOLD

7064. Let them ease their hearts with prate of equal rights, which man never knew.

BYRON

7065. Men are by nature unequal. It is vain, therefore, to treat them as if they were equal.

FROUDE

7066. So far is it from being true that men are naturally equal, that no two people can be half an hour together but one shall acquire an evident superiority over the other.

SAMUEL JOHNSON, *Boswell: Life*

7067.
Some must follow, and some command,
Though all are made of clay.

LONGFELLOW

7068.
Among unequals in society
Can sort, what harmony or true delight?   MILTON, *Paradise Lost*

7069. It is not true that equality is a law of nature. Nature has no equality. Its sovereign law is subordination and dependence.   VAUVENARGUES

See also: 823, 1075, 1513, 3090, 3479, 3591, 18293, 18493, 21452.

EQUITY, see Law

ERROR

Related Subjects: Delusion, Faults, Fool, Guilt, Heresy, Illusion, Lies, Mistake, Sin, Understanding, Wickedness, Wrongs.

7071. It is only an error of judgment to make a mistake, but it argues an infirmity of character to adhere to it when discovered.   C. N. BOVEE

7072. An old and gray-headed error.
SIR THOMAS BROWNE, *Vulgar Errors*

7073.
Then gently scan your brother man,
  Still gentler sister woman;
Though they may gang a kennin wrang,
To step aside is human.

BURNS, *Address to the Unco Guid*

7074. He that errs in so considerable a passage, may well be suspected to have committed many gross errors through the whole history.

CERVANTES, *Don Quixote*

7075. Honest error is to be pitied, not ridiculed.   LORD CHESTERFIELD

7076. There are errors which no wise man will treat with rudeness, while there is a probability that they may be the refraction of some great truth still below the horizon.   COLERIDGE

7077. Ignorance has no light, but error follows a false one. The consequence is, that error, when she retraces her steps, has farther to go before she can arrive at truth, than ignorance.   C. C. COLTON

7078. Most of us, if you will pardon me for betraying the universal secret, have, at some time or other, discovered in ourselves a readiness to stray far, ever so far, on the wrong road.   JOSEPH CONRAD,
Notes on Life and Letters

7079.
What can we know? or what can we discern,
When error chokes the windows of the mind?   SIR JOHN DAVIES,
The Vanity of Human Learning

7080.
Errors, like straws, upon the surface flow;
He who would search for pearls must dive below.   DRYDEN, *All for Love*

7081. That men may err was never yet denied.   DRYDEN,
The Hind & the Panther

7082. When a man covers a vast field many errors may be forgiven him if the result adds to our comprehension of life.   DURANT,
The Life of Greece

7083.
Our truest steps are human still,—
To walk unswerving were divine.   O. W. HOLMES,
The Crooked Footpath

7084. Error of opinion may be tolerated where reason is left free to combat it.   JEFFERSON,
First Inaugural Address

7085. Find earth where grows no weed, and you may find a heart wherein no error grows.
THOMAS KNOWLES

7086. I shall try to correct errors where shown to be errors, and I shall adopt new views as fast as they shall appear to be true views.   LINCOLN

7087. Error is not a fault of our knowledge, but a mistake of our judgment giving assent to that which is not true.   LOCKE

7088.
Were half the power, that fills the world with terror,
  Were half the wealth, bestowed on camps and courts,
Given to redeem the human mind from error,
  There were no need of arsenals or forts.   LONGFELLOW,
The Arsenal At Springfield

7089. Sometimes we may learn more from a man's errors, than from his virtues.   LONGFELLOW

7090. Our understandings are always liable to error. Nature and certainty are very hard to come at, and infallibility is mere vanity and pretence.   MARCUS AURELIUS,
Meditations

7091. Error commonly has some truth in what it affirms, is wrong generally in what it denies.
F. L. PATTON

7092. For to err in opinion, though it be not the part of wise men, is at least human.   PLUTARCH

7093. A man should never be ashamed to own he has been in the wrong, which is but saying, in other words, that he is wiser to-day than he was yesterday.   POPE,
Thoughts on Various Subjects

7094. Thinks what ne'er was, nor is, nor e'er shall be.   POPE,
Essay on Criticism

7095. To err is human, to forgive divine.   POPE, *Essay on Criticism*

7096. Error is always in haste.
Proverb

7097. It is a manly act to forsake an error.   *Proverb*

7098. Every age confutes old errors, and begets new.   *Proverb*

7099. Error, though blind herself, sometimes bringeth forth children that can see.   *Proverb*

7100. From the errors of others a wise man corrects his own.
PUBLILIUS SYRUS, *Sententiae*

7101. Above the pitch, out of tune, and off the hinges.   RABELAIS

7102.
If this be error and upon me proved never writ, nor no man ever loved.
SHAKESPEARE, *Sonnet CXVI*

7103. Errors to be dangerous must have a great deal of truth mingled with them. It is only from this alliance that they can ever obtain an extensive circulation. From pure extravagance, and genuine, unmingled falsehood, the world never has, and never can sustain any mischief.
SYDNEY SMITH

7104. Few practical errors in the world are embraced on conviction, but on inclination; for though the judgment may err on account of weakness, yet, where one error enters at this door, ten are let into it through the will; that, for the most part, being set upon those things which truth is a direct obstacle to the enjoyment of; and where both cannot be had, a man will be sure to buy his enjoyment, though he pays down truth for the purchase.
ROBERT SOUTH

7105. Men err from selfishness; women because they are weak.
MME. DE STAËL

7106. An expert is a person who avoids the small errors as he sweeps on to the grand fallacy.
BENJAMIN STOLBERG

7107.
To err
From the right path is common to mankind. SOPHOCLES, *Antigone*

7108. Men are apt to prefer a prosperous error to an afflicted truth.
JEREMY TAYLOR

7109. Error is the force that welds men together; truth is communicated to men only by deeds of truth.
TOLSTOY, *My Religion*

7110. Error is a hardy plant: it flourisheth in every soil.
MARTIN F. TUPPER,
Of Truth in Things False

7111. There is nothing so true that the damps of error have not warped it.   MARTIN F. TUPPER

7112. There is no error so crooked but it hath in it some lines of truth, nor is any poison so deadly that it serveth not some wholesome use.

Spurn not a seeming error, but dig below its surface for the truth.

MARTIN F. TUPPER

See also: 938, 1116, 5344, 7474, 8584, 10696, 11318, 13326, 14184, 15826, 17627, 20201.

ESTEEM

Related Subjects: Admiration, Appreciation, Honor, Judgment, Popularity, Respect.

7121. The chief ingredients in the composition of those qualities that gain esteem and praise, are good nature, truth, good sense, and good breeding.   ADDISON

7122. The esteem of wise and good men is the greatest of all temporal encouragements to virtue; and it is a mark of an abandoned spirit to have no regard to it.   BURKE

7123.
Then take what gold could never buy—
An honest bard's esteem.

BURNS, *To John McMurdo*

7124. Esteem cannot be where there is no confidence; and there can be no confidence where there is no respect.

HENRY GILES

7125. Esteem has more engaging charms than friendship and even love. It captivates hearts better, and never makes ingrates.

LA ROCHEFOUCAULD, *Maxims*

7126. We have so exalted a notion of the human soul that we cannot bear to be despised, or even not to be esteemed by it. Man, in fact, places all his happiness in this esteem.

PASCAL

7127. Even a nod from a person who is esteemed is of more force than a thousand arguments or studied sentences from others.

PLUTARCH, *Lives*

See also: 2500.

ETERNITY

Related Subjects: Death, Hell, Judgment Day, Mortality, Paradise, Salvation, Soul, Time.

7131. Eternity, thou pleasing dreadful thought! through what variety of untried being! through what new scenes and changes must we pass. The wide, the unbounded prospect lies before me; but shadows, clouds and darkness rest upon it.   ADDISON

7132. The things which are seen are temporal; but the things which are not seen are eternal.

Bible: 2 Corinthians, iv, 18

7133. Yesterday, and to-day, and forever.   *Bible: Hebrews, xiii,*

7134. What we call eternity may be but an endless series of the transitions which men call deaths, abandonments of home, going ever to fairer scenes and loftier heights. Age after age, the spirit—that glorious nomad —may shift its tent, carrying with it evermore its elements, activity and desire.   BULWER-LYTTON

7135. Eternity looks grander and kinder if time grows meaner and more hostile.   CARLYLE

7136. He that will often put eternity and the world before him, and will dare to look steadfastly at both of them, will find that the more he contemplates them, the former will grow greater and the latter less.

C. C. COLTON

7137. All great natures delight in stability; all great men find eternity affirmed in the very promise of their faculties.   EMERSON

7138. For ever wilt thou love, and she be fair!
KEATS, *Ode on a Grecian Urn*

7139.
The horologe of Eternity
Sayeth this incessantly,—
"Forever—never!
Never—forever!"
LONGFELLOW, *Clock on the Stairs*

7140. Eternity is the ocean; time is the wave.   MAETERLINCK,
Before the Great Silence

7141. Eternity has no gray hairs.
Proverb

7142. For ever and a day.
SHAKESPEARE, *As You Like It*

7143.
I saw Eternity the other night
Like a great ring of pure and endless light.
HENRY VAUGHAN, *The World*

See also: 1103, 1293, 1694, 7061, 9054, 11795, 11822, 18674, 19649.

EUPHEMISM

Related Subject: Evasion.

7151. It is good to find modest words to express immodest things.
Anonymous

7152. This instinct of politeness in speech—euphemism, as it is called—which seeks to hint at an unpleasant or indelicate thing rather than name it directly, has had much to do with making words acquire new meanings and lose old ones.
ROBERT CHAMBERS,
Information for the People

7153. The ancient Athenians used to cover up the ugliness of things with auspicious and kindly terms, giving them polite and endearing names. Thus they called harlots "companions," taxes "contributions," and the prison a "chamber."
PLUTARCH, *Lives*

7154. I will but look upon the hedge and follow you.
SHAKESPEARE, *The Winter's Tale*

See also: 21088.

EUROPE

Related Subjects: England, France, Germany, History, Holland, Italy, Poland, Rome, Spain.

7161. Without so much as pausing to wipe her feet, which are dipped in blood to the ankle, hasn't Europe always been willing to recommence hostilities?   BALZAC

7162.
There is not a nation in Europe but labours
To toady itself and to humbug its neighbours.
R. H. BARHAM, *The Auto-da-Fé*

7163.
Europe is given a prey to sterner fates,
And writhes in shackles; strong the arms that chain
To earth her struggling multitude of states.   BRYANT, *The Ages*

7164. Can we never extract the tapeworm of Europe from the brain of our countrymen?
EMERSON, *Conduct of Life*

7165. Man is the only animal which devours his own kind, for I can apply no milder term to the governments of Europe, and the general prey of the rich on the poor.   JEFFERSON

7166. We appear to be in a dissolving period of history, when the world is in labor and out of her travail will give birth to a new order . . . The brief day of European domination is already approaching its end. Europe has ceased to be the centre of activity and interest. The future lies with America and Asia.
            JAWAHARLAL NEHRU,
                India and the World

7167. Two great European narcotics, alcohol and Christianity.
            NIETZSCHE,
                The Twilight of the Idols

7168.
People cry: "More light!"
I say: "More Warmth!"
The heart of Europe is freezing to
    death.   UNAMUNO

7169. The mines of Mexico and Potosi furnished the means of buying the liberty of Europe.   VOLTAIRE

7170.
Nor red from Europe's old dynastic
    slaughterhouse,
(Area of murder-plots of thrones,
    with scent left yet of wars and
    scaffolds everywhere).
            WALT WHITMAN,
                Song of the Redwood Tree

See also: 673, 676, 686, 687, 688, 726, 1021, 10886, 14826.

EVASION

Related Subjects: Euphemism, Excuse, Sophistry.

7171. Evasion is unworthy of us, and is always the intimate of equivocation.   BALZAC

7172. Evasions are the common shelter of the hard-hearted, the false, and the impotent when called upon to as-

sist; the real great, alone, plan instantaneous help, even when their looks or words presage difficulties.
                LAVATER

7173. Evasion, like equivocation comes generally from a cowardly or a deceiving spirit, or from both afraid to speak out its sentiments, or from guile concealing them.
                MILTON

7174. Crafty evasions save not veracity.   *Proverb*

7175. 'Tis neither here nor there.
        SHAKESPEARE, *Othello*

EVE, see Adam

EVENING

Related Subjects: Day, Sunset, Twilight.

7181. The death-bed of a day, how beautiful! PHILIP J. BAILEY, *Festus*

7182.
To me at least was never evening yet
But seemed far beautifuller than its
    day.
BROWNING, *The Ring and the Book*

7183.
Hath not thy heart within thee
    burned
At evening's calm and holy hour?
        S. G. BULFINCH, *Meditation*

7184. So let us welcome peaceful evening in.   COWPER, *The Task*

7185. Welcome sweet night! the evening crowns the day.
            JOHN FORD,
                'Tis a Pity She's a Whore

7186.
Now fades the glimmering landscape
    on the sight,

And all the air a solemn stillness
holds.   THOMAS GRAY,
*Elegy Written in a Country
Churchyard*

7187. Day, like a weary pilgrim, had
reached the western gate of heaven,
and Evening stooped down to unloose
the latchets of his sandal shoon.
          LONGFELLOW, *Hyperion*

7188.
Now came still evening on, and twi-
    light gray
Had in her sober livery all things
    clad.   MILTON, *Paradise Lost*

7189.
It is a beauteous evening, calm and
    free;
The holy time is quiet as a Nun
Breathless with adoration.
          WORDSWORTH,
          It Is a Beauteous Evening

EVENTS

Related Subjects: Adventure, Circumstance, Fate.

7191. The signs of the times.
          Bible: Matthew, xvi, 3

7192. There are certain events which
to each man's life are as comets to
the earth, seemingly strange and er-
ratic portents; distinct from the ordinary lights which guide our course
and mark our seasons, yet true to
their own laws, potent in their own
influences.   BULWER-LYTTON,
          What Will He Do With It

7193.
          Often do the spirits
Of great events stride on before the
    events,
And in to-day already walks tomor-
    row.   COLERIDGE, *Wallenstein*

7194. Events of all sorts creep or fly
exactly as God pleases.   COWPER

7195. Whatever happens at all happens as it should; thou wilt find this
true, if thou shouldst watch narrowly.
MARCUS AURELIUS, *Meditations*

7196. There is no faith, and no stoicism, and no philosophy, that a mortal
man can possibly evoke, which will
stand the final test in a real impassioned onset of Life and Passion
upon him. Faith and philosophy are
air, but events are brass.
          HERMAN MELVILLE, *Pierre*

7197. Everything happens to everybody sooner or later if there is time
enough.
BERNARD SHAW, *Back to Methuselah*

7198. There is a rhythm of events
thanks to which a man, having completed what he set out to do, lingers
amid the gestures of activity; he finds
it hard to realize that his day is over;
in fantasy he still pursues the round
of active movement. He cannot accept repose; he does not know that
he is dreaming; the harmony formed
by doing and being eludes him.
          JACOB WASSERMANN, *Stanley*

See also: 3053, 19819.

EVIDENCE, see Proof

EVIL

Related Subjects: Adversity, Baseness, Crime, The Devil, Goodness,
Malevolence, Mischief, Misfortune,
Sin and Sinners, Villainy, Wickedness.

7200. Evil and good are God's right
hand and left.
          PHILIP J. BAILEY, *Festus*

7201. Woe unto them that call evil
good, and good evil.
          Bible: Isaiah, v, 20

7202. For the good that I would I do not; but the evil which I would not, that I do.
Bible: Romans, vii, 19

7203. Recompense to no man evil for evil. *Bible: Romans, xii, 17*

7204. Be not overcome of evil, but overcome evil with good.
Bible: Romans, xii, 21

7205. There is nothing that is evil except because a man has not mastery over it; and there is no good thing that is not evil if it have a mastery over a man.
EDWARD CARPENTER,
Towards Democracy

7206. When God sends us evil, He sends with it the weapon to conquer it.   PAUL V. CARROLL,
Shadow and Substance

7207. The belief in a supernatural source of evil is not necessary: men alone are quite capable of every wickedness.   JOSEPH CONRAD,
Under Western Eyes

7208. Oft hath even a whole city reaped the evil fruit of a bad man.
HESIOD, *Works and Days*

7209. For himself doth a man work evil in working evils for another.
HESIOD, *Works and Days*

7210.
But evil is wrought by want of thought,
As well as want of heart.
THOMAS HOOD, *The Lady's Dream*

7211. Of two evils, the less is always to be chosen.
THOMAS À KEMPIS,
Of the Imitation of Christ

7212. And out of good still to find means of evil.
MILTON, *Paradise Lost*

7213.
More safe I sing with mortal voice, unchang'd
To hoarse or mute, though fall'n on evil days,
On evil days though fall'n, and evil tongues.   MILTON, *Paradise Lost*

7214. He that helpeth the evil hurteth the good.   *Proverb*

7215. A bad thing never dies.
Proverb

7216. Who would do ill ne'er wants occasion.   *Proverb*

7217. He who is bent on doing evil can never want occasion.
PUBLILIUS SYRUS, *Sententiae*

7218. God makes all things good; man meddles with them and they become evil.
ROUSSEAU, *Emile, or Education*

7219. Ill deeds are doubled with an evil word.   SHAKESPEARE,
The Comedy of Errors

7220.
The evil that men do lives after them,
The good is oft interred with their bones.
SHAKESPEARE, *Julius Caesar*

7221. No evil can happen to a good man, either in life or after death.
SOCRATES

7222. Evil perpetually tends to disappear.   HERBERT SPENCER,
The Evanescence of Evil

7223. There are a thousand hacking at the branches of evil to one who is striking at the root.
THOREAU, *Walden*

7224. No evil deed live oN.
E. F. WARE, *The Palindrome*

7225. Perish with him the folly that seeks through evil good.

WHITTIER, *Brown of Ossawatomie*

See also: 337, 864, 2399, 2610, 3022, 3032, 3292, 13214, 15149, 21435.

EVOLUTION

Related Subjects: Life, Man, Progress, Science.

7231.
There was an ape in days that were earlier;
Centuries passed and his hair became curlier;
Centuries more and his thumb gave a twist,
And he was a man and a Positivist.
Anonymous, Parody on Evolution

7232.
Some call it Evolution,
And others call it God.
W. H. CARRUTH,
Each in His Own Tongue

7233. Today there isn't a single professor who dares to say what he thinks. Evolution is taught as a "theory" while the Jonah and the whale incident is given as a "fact"; and so on throughout the fields of religion and science.
CLARENCE DARROW

7234. The expression often used by Mr. Herbert Spencer, of the Survival of the Fittest, is more accurate, and is sometimes equally convenient.
DARWIN, *Origin of Species*

7235. We will now discuss in a little more detail the Struggle for Existence. DARWIN, *Origin of Species*

7236. It has taken God—or Nature, if we will—unknown millions of years of painful struggle to evolve Man, and to raise the human species above that helpless bondage to reproduction which marks the lower animals. HAVELOCK ELLIS,
Little Essays on Love and Virtue

7237.
And striving to be man, the worm
Mounts through all the spires of form. EMERSON, *May-Day*

7238.
Darwinian Man, though well-behaved,
At best is only a monkey shaved!
W. S. GILBERT, *Princess Ida*

7239. It [cosmic radiation] falls on the earth in large quantities, and its powers of destruction are immense. Every second it breaks up about twenty atoms in every cubic inch of our atmosphere, and millions of atoms in each of our bodies. It has been suggested that this radiation, falling on germ-plasm, may produce the spasmodic biological variations which the modern theory of evolution demands; it may have been cosmic radiation that turned monkeys into men. SIR JAMES JEANS,
The Mysterious Universe

7240. Evolution is not a force but a process; not a cause but a law.
JOHN MORLEY, *On Compromise*

7241. Every man of us has all the centuries in him.
JOHN MORLEY, *Life of Gladstone*

7242.
To
John Thomas Scopes
and
Other Courageous Teachers of the
United States
Who elect to face squarely the issue
that
The youth of America should be
Freely taught the truth of evolution
and the

Fact that this great law of living
   nature,
Is consistent with the highest
   ideals
Of religion and conduct.
              HENRY F. OSBORN,
   *Dedication: Evolution and Re-
              ligion in Education*

7243. If a single cell, under appropriate conditions, becomes a man in
the space of a few years, there can
surely be no difficulty in understanding how, under appropriate conditions, a cell may, in the course of untold millions of years, give origin to
the human race.
              HERBERT SPENCER,
              Principles of Biology

7244. There must be, one cannot help
thinking, some evolutionary urge or
nisus, élan, or impulse, rather subtler
than has been yet analyzed into either
mechanical or chemical or biological
terms. I mean nothing mystical, but
something more than tendencies to
aggregate, to colloidify, to incorpo-
rate, to grow, to multiply, and so on,
with all the involved catalysts, hor-
mones and organisers—I mean a psychical urge, the subjective side of endeavour.   SIR ARTHUR THOMPSON

7245.
I am an anti-Darwin intellectual:
The man that says any nice young
   boy or gal
Is a descendant of the ape
Shall never from Hell's fire escape.
              W. W. WOOLLCOTT
See also: 3961.

EXAGGERATION

**Related Subjects: Accuracy,
Boasting, Excess, Extravagance,
Honesty, Imagination.**

7251. We exaggerate misfortune and
happiness alike. We are never either

so wretched or so happy as we say we
are.   BALZAC

7252. They make of a fly an elephant, and of a molehill a mountain.
         THOMAS BECON, *Catechism*

7253. Some persons are exaggerators
by temperament. They do not mean
untruth, but their feelings are strong,
and their imaginations vivid, so that
their statements are largely discounted by those of calm judgment
and cooler temperament. They do not
realize that "we always weaken what
we exaggerate."   TRYON EDWARDS

7254. An exaggeration is a truth that
has lost its temper.
      KAHLIL GIBRAN, *Sand and Foam*

7255. There is a sort of harmless
liars, frequently to be met with in
company, who deal much in the marvellous. Their usual intention is to
please and entertain: but as men are
most delighted with what they conceive to be truth, these people mistake
the means of pleasing, and incur universal blame.   DAVID HUME

7256. To make a mountain of a molehill.   *Proverb*

7257. The reports of my death are
greatly exaggerated.
              MARK TWAIN,
      *Cable from Europe to the
              Associated Press*

See also: 343, 20604.

EXAMPLE AND PRECEPT

**Related Subjects: Apothegms,
Caution, Character, Influence, Imitation, Proverbs, Quotation, Wisdom.**

7261. Do but set the example yourself, and I will follow you. Example
is the best precept.
              AESOP, *The Two Crabs*

7262. For precept must be upon precept, precept upon precept; line upon line, line upon line; here a little, and there a little.
Bible: Isaiah, xxviii, 10, 13

7263. Example has more followers than reason. We unconsciously imitate what pleases us, and approximate to the characters we most admire. A generous habit of thought and action carries with it an incalculable influence.   C. N. Bovee

7264. Example is the school of mankind and they will learn at no other.
Burke, *On a Regicide Peace*

7265. Example is more forcible than precept. People look at my six days in the week to see what I mean on the seventh.   Richard Cecil

7266.
     So our lives
In acts exemplary, not only win
Ourselves good names, but doth to others give
Matter for virtuous deeds, by which we live.
George Chapman, *Bussy D'Ambois*

7267. No man is so insignificant as to be sure his example can do no hurt.
Lord Clarendon

7268. Of all commentaries upon the Scriptures, good examples are the best and the liveliest.   John Donne

7269. Though "the words of the wise be as nails fastened by the masters of assemblies", yet their examples are the hammer to drive them in to take the deeper hold. A father that whipped his son for swearing, and swore himself whilst he whipped him, did more harm by his example than good by his correction.
Thomas Fuller

7270. You can preach a better sermon with your life than with your lips.   Goldsmith

7271. People seldom improve when they have no model but themselves to copy after.   Goldsmith

7272.
I'd rather see a sermon than hear one any day;
I'd rather one should walk with me than merely tell the way.
Edgar Guest, *Sermons We See*

7273. The innocence of the intention abates nothing of the mischief of the example.   Robert Hall

7274. Four precepts: to break off customs; to shake off spirits ill-disposed; to meditate on youth; to do nothing against one's genius.
Hawthorne,
American Note-Books

7275. We can do more good by being good, than in any other way.
Rowland Hill

7276. Example is always more efficacious than precept.
Samuel Johnson, *Rasselas*

7277. So act that your principle of action might safely be made a law for the whole world.   Kant

7278. A wise and good man will turn examples of all sorts to his own advantage. The good he will make his patterns, and strive to equal or excel them. The bad he will by all means avoid.   Thomas À Kempis,
Of the Imitation of Christ

7279. Nothing is so infectious as example.   Charles Kingsley

7280.
Lives of great men all remind us
   We can make our lives sublime,

And, departing, leave behind us
  Footprints on the sands of time.
      LONGFELLOW, *A Psalm of Life*

7281. Every one is bound to bear patiently the results of his own example.   PHAEDRUS, *Fables*

7282. Cato used to assert that wise men profited more by fools, than fools by wise men; for that wise men avoided the faults of fools, but the fools would not imitate the good examples of wise men.
      PLUTARCH, *Lives*

7283. When old age is evil, youth can learn no good.   *Proverb*

7284. One ill example spoils many good.   *Proverb*

7285. The example of good men is visible philosophy.   *Proverb*

7286. Ill examples are like contagious diseases.   *Proverb*

7287. Men trust rather to their eyes than to their ears. The effect of precepts is, therefore, slow and tedious, while that of examples is summary and effectual.   SENECA

7288.
       He arrests him on it;
And follows close the rigour of the
  statute,
To make him an example.
SHAKESPEARE, *Measure for Measure*

7289. Alexander received more bravery of mind by the pattern of Achilles, than by hearing the definition of fortitude.
      SIR PHILIP SIDNEY

7290. There is a transcendent power in example. We reform others unconsciously, when we walk uprightly.
      MME. SWETCHINE

7291. My advice is to consult the lives of other men, as one would a looking-glass, and from thence fetch examples for imitation.   TERENCE

7292. Few things are harder to put up with than the annoyance of a good example.   MARK TWAIN,
    Pudd'nhead Wilson's Calendar

7293. He or she is greatest who contributes the greatest original practical example. WALT WHITMAN,
    By Blue Ontario's Shore

See also: 912, 941, 1851, 2032, 3321, 7100, 14131, 14608.

EXCELLENCE

Related Subjects: Goodness, Merit, Virtue, Worth.

7301. I assure you I had rather excel others in the knowledge of what is excellent, than in the extent of my power and dominion.
    ALEXANDER THE GREAT,
    Plutarch, Lives

7302. There is no surer mark of the absence of the highest moral and intellectual qualities than a cold reception of excellence. PHILIP J. BAILEY

7303. There is a moral excellence attainable by all who have the will to strive for it; but there is an intellectual and physical superiority which is above the reach of our wishes, and is granted to only a few.
    GEORGE CRABBE

7304. There has nothing been more without a definition than Excellency; although it be what we are most concerned with: yea, we are concerned with nothing else.
    JONATHAN EDWARDS

7305. Excellence is the perfect excuse. Do it well, and it matters little what.   EMERSON, *Journal*

EXCESS

Related Subjects: Dissipation, Exaggeration, Extravagance, Extremes, Gluttony, Moderation, Prodigality, Recklessness, Waste.

7306. One that desires to excel should endeavor it in those things that are in themselves most excellent.

EPICTETUS, *Discourses*

7307. Behold, thou mayest choose vice easily even in heaps; for the path is plain, and she dwells very near. But before excellence the immortal gods have placed the sweat of toil; long and steep is the road that leads to her, and rough it is at first; but when you reach the height then truly it is easy, though so hard before.

HESIOD, *Works and Days*

7308. Those who attain to any excellence commonly spend life in some one single pursuit, for excellence is not often gained upon easier terms.

SAMUEL JOHNSON

7309.
Consider first, that great
Or bright infers not excellence.

MILTON, *Paradise Lost*

7310. It takes a long time to bring excellence to maturity.

PUBLILIUS SYRUS, *Sententiae*

7311. Excellence is never granted to man but as the reward of labor. It argues no small strength of mind to persevere in habits of industry without the pleasure of perceiving those advances, which, like the hand of a clock, whilst they make hourly approaches to their point, yet proceed so slowly as to escape observation.

SIR JOSHUA REYNOLDS

7312.
It is the witness still of excellency
To put a strange face on his own perfection.

SHAKESPEARE,
Much Ado About Nothing

See also: 1076, 3347, 4124, 4602.

7321. The desire of power in excess caused angels to fall; the desire of knowledge in excess caused man to fall; but in charity is no excess, neither can man or angels come into danger by it.

BACON

7322. All excess brings on its own punishment, even here. By certain fixed, settled, and established laws of Him who is the God of nature, excess of every kind destroys that constitution which temperance would preserve. The debauchee offers up his body a living sacrifice to sin.

C. C. COLTON

7323.
Nor too much wealth nor wit come to thee,
So much of either may undo thee.

BISHOP CORBET

7324. There can be no excess to love, to knowledge, to beauty, when these attributes are considered in the purest sense.

EMERSON

7325. The best things beyond their measure cloy.

HOMER, *Iliad*

7326. Too much noise deafens us; too much light blinds us; too great a distance, or too much of proximity equally prevents us from being able to see; too long or too short a discourse obscures our knowledge of a subject; too much of truth stuns us.

PASCAL

7327. Excess generally causes reaction and produces a change in the opposite direction, whether it be in the seasons, or in individuals, or in government.

PLATO

7328. Too much is stark naught.
Proverb

7329. Too much is a vanity; enough is a feast.   FRANCIS QUARLES

7330. 'Tis not the drinking that is to be blamed, but the excess.
JOHN SELDEN, *Table Talk*

7331. Can one desire too much of a good thing?
SHAKESPEARE, *As You Like It*

7332.
To gild refined gold, to paint the lily,
To throw a perfume on the violet
To smooth the ice, or add another hue
Unto the rainbow, or with taper-light
To seek the beauteous eye of heaven to garnish,
Is wasteful and ridiculous excess.
SHAKESPEARE, *King John*

7333. They are as sick that surfeit with too much, as they that starve with nothing.   SHAKESPEARE,
The Merchant of Venice

See also: 1474, 2567, 5384, 9186, 13170, 15394.

EXCITEMENT

Related Subject: Agitation.

7341. Excitement in the higher realm of thought and feeling does not wear out or waste men. The moral sentiments nourish and feed us.
H. W. BEECHER

7342. Never be afraid because the community teems with excitement. Silence and death are dreadful. The rush of life, the vigor of earnest men, and the conflict of realities, invigorate, cleanse, and establish the truth.
H. W. BEECHER

7343. Violent excitement exhausts the mind, and leaves it withered and sterile.   FENELON

7344. The language of excitement is at best but picturesque merely. You must be calm before you can utter oracles.   THOREAU

See also: 999.

EXCUSE

Related Subjects: Evasion, Forgiveness, Sophistry.

7351. Better a bad excuse, than none at all.   WILLIAM CAMDEN, *Remains*

7352. Apologizing—a very desperate habit—one that is rarely cured. Apology is only egotism wrong side out.
O. W. HOLMES,
The Professor at the Breakfast-Table

7353. Don't make excuses—make good.   ELBERT HUBBARD, *Epigrams*

7354. Contests allow no excuses, no more do friendships.   IBYCUS

7355. He who excuses himself accuses himself.
GABRIEL MEURIER,
Trésor des Sentences

7356. Hence with denial vain, and coy excuse.   MILTON, *Lycidas*

7357.
To him she hasted, in her face excuse
Came prologue, and apology too prompt.   MILTON, *Paradise Lost*

7358. Bad excuses are worse than none.   *Proverb*

7359. You may often make excuses for another, never for yourself.
PUBLILIUS SYRUS, *Sententiae*

7360. You patch'd up your excuses.
SHAKESPEARE, *Antony and Cleopatra*

7361.
And oftentimes excusing of a fault
Doth make the fault the worse by the
   excuse. SHAKESPEARE, *King John*

7362.
I do not trouble my spirit to vindicate
   itself or be understood,
I see that the elementary laws never
   apologize.
WALT WHITMAN, *Song of Myself*

See also: 1691, 2610, 3123, 5360,
5779, 7305, 7585, 11497, 20291.

EXECUTIVES

Related Subjects: Authority, Responsibility.

7371. Executive duties represent applied thinking. They consist in taking past experience, analyzing it and bringing it to bear upon an existing situation. That the personnel entrusted with this important function shall be the very best available, is the objective of progressive management.
R. E. BELL, *Selecting an Executive*

7372. The ultimate aim of management policy is the reduction of executive turnover to the vanishing point.
R. E. BELL, *Selecting an Executive*

7373. An executive is a person who is responsible for the efforts of others, makes decisions on questions both as to policy and practice, and exercises authority in seeing that decisions are carried out.
CLEETON & MASON,
Executive Ability

7374. What the future holds for all of us depends in a large measure on the intelligence, breadth of vision, and leadership of those in executive positions. *Ibid.*

7375. An executive who lacks those personal qualities which instantly secure whole-hearted response from subordinates may be considered a failure as a leader, but if he recognizes this shortcoming, and selects subordinates who have the qualities of leadership necessary to facilitate carrying out his plans, he may still be a success as an executive.
CLEETON & MASON,
Executive Ability

7376. The tyrant and autocrat who succeeded a generation ago, would be a failure today. . . . Try to picture Alexander the Great, Cheops, the builder of the Pyramids, Disraeli, Andrew Jackson, or E. H. Harriman using the conference method of executive control. *Ibid.*

7377. Executive ability is deciding quickly and getting somebody else to do the work. J. G. POLLARD

7378. Better direct well than work hard. *Proverb*

See also: 15, 11533.

EXERCISE

Related Subjects: Energy, Recreation, Sport, Walking.

7381. Whenever I feel the urge to exercise coming on I lie down until it passes over. *Anonymous*

7382. For bodily exercise profiteth little: but godliness is profitable unto all things. *Bible: I Timothy, iv, 8*

7383. Exercise and temperance can preserve something of our early strength even in old age. CICERO

7384. By constant exercise one develops freedom of movement—for virtuous deeds. DIOGENES

7385. The wise for cure on exercise depend.

> DRYDEN, *Epistle to John Driden*

7386.
To cure the mind's wrong bias,
   Spleen,
Some recommend the bowling green;
Some, hilly walks; all, exercise;
Fling but a stone, the giant dies.

> MATTHEW GREEN, *The Spleen*

7387. Games played with the ball, and others of that nature, are too violent for the body and stamp no character on the mind.   JEFFERSON

7388. I take the true definition of exercise to be, labor without weariness.   SAMUEL JOHNSON

7389. Such is the constitution of man, that labor may be styled its own reward. Nor will any external incitements be requisite if it be considered how much happiness is gained, and how much misery escaped, by frequent and violent agitation of the body.   SAMUEL JOHNSON

7390. The rich advantage of good exercise.   SHAKESPEARE, *King John*

7391. Health is the vital principle of bliss; and exercise, of health.

> JAMES THOMSON

See also: 17081.

EXILE

Related Subjects: Absence, Punishment, Separation.

7401. I know how men in exile feed on dreams. AESCHYLUS, *Agamemnon*

7402.
They bore within their breasts the
   grief
That fame can never heal—

The deep, unutterable woe
  Which none save exiles feel.

> W. E. AYTOUN,
> *The Island of the Scots*

7403. Exile is terrible to those who have, as it were, a circumscribed habitation; but not to those who look upon the whole globe as one city.

> CICERO, *Paradoxa*

7404. Whosoever flieth from his country for the sake of God's true religion, shall find in the earth many forced to do the same, and plenty of provisions.   *The Koran*

7405.
The world was all before them
   where to choose
Their place of rest, and Providence
   their guide:
They, hand in hand, with wand'ring
   steps and slow,
Through Eden took their solitary
   way.   MILTON, *Paradise Lost*

7406. No, my good lord: banish Peto, banish Bardolph, banish Poins; but for sweet Jack Falstaff, kind Jack Falstaff, true Jack Falstaff, valiant Jack Falstaff, and therefore more valiant, being, as he is, old Jack Falstaff, banish not him thy Harry's company: banish plump Jack and banish all the world.

> SHAKESPEARE, *Henry IV*

7407.
The sly slow hours shall not determinate
The dateless limit of thy dear exile
The hopeless word of "never to return"
Breathe I against thee, upon pain of life.   SHAKESPEARE, *Richard II*

7408. Eating the bitter bread of banishment.   SHAKESPEARE, *Richard II*

7409.
For exile hath more terror in his look,
Much more than death.
SHAKESPEARE, *Romeo and Juliet*

7410.
They are free men, but I am banished.
And say'st thou yet that exile is not death?
SHAKESPEARE, *Romeo and Juliet*

7411.
                              Banished?
O friar, the damned use that word in hell;
Howlings attend it: how hast thou the heart,
Being a divine, a ghostly confessor,
A sin-absolver, and my friend profess'd,
To mangle me with that word "banished"?
SHAKESPEARE, *Romeo and Juliet*

7412. Since they would not listen to you at home in your own lands, happy he that goes into exile. For banishment is often the only means of saving the nobler possessions of the world. And if the spirit of man has set forth on the flight into Egypt, because the executioner is at hand, it is better to be the ass on which the foster-father rides, or the Virgin who bore him, than Herod in his purple and his crown.
ARNOLD ZWEIG,
The Crowning of a King

See also: 2565.

EXPECTATION

Related Subjects: Disappointment, Failure, Hope, Waiting.

7421. Do not count your chickens before they are hatched.
AESOP, *The Milkmaid and Her Pail*

7422. Uncertainty and expectation are the joys of life. Security is an insipid thing, though the overtaking and possessing of a wish discovers the folly of the chase.   CONGREVE

7423. What we anticipate seldom occurs; what we least expected generally happens.
DISRAELI, *Henrietta Temple*

7424. Nothing is so good as it seems beforehand.
GEORGE ELIOT, *Silas Marner*

7425. It has been a thousand times observed, and I must observe it once more, that the hours we pass with happy prospects in view, are more pleasing than those crowned with fruition.   GOLDSMITH,
The Vicar of Wakefield

7426. Blessed is he who expects nothing, for he shall never be disappointed.   POPE, *Letter to Gay*

7427. Long looked-for comes at last.
Proverb

7428.
Oft expectation fails, and most oft there
Where most it promises.
SHAKESPEARE,
All's Well that Ends Well

7429. He hath indeed better bettered expectation.   SHAKESPEARE,
Much Ado About Nothing

7430.
'Tis expectation makes a blessing dear,
Heaven were not heaven, if we knew what it were.
SIR JOHN SUCKLING,
Against Fruition

See also: 6812, 7802, 13658, 15339.

EXPERIENCE

Related Subjects: Innocence, Knowledge, Life, Observation, Wisdom.

7441. All experience is an arch, to build upon.   HENRY ADAMS,
The Education of Henry Adams

7442. Experience, the universal Mother of Sciences.
CERVANTES, *Don Quixote*

7443. I am fully aware that the fact of my not being a man of letters may cause certain arrogant persons to think that they may with reason censure me, alleging that I am a man ignorant of book-learning. . . Do they not know that my subjects require for their exposition Experience rather than Words of Others? And sure Experience has been the Mistress of whoever has written well, I take her as my mistress and to her in all points make my appeal.
DA VINCI, *Notebooks*

7444. Experience is the child of Thought, and Thought is the child of Action. We can not learn men from books.   DISRAELI,
Vivian Grey

7445. Experience keeps a dear school, but fools will learn in no other.
FRANKLIN, *Poor Richard*

7446. I have but one lamp by which my feet are guided, and that is the lamp of experience.
PATRICK HENRY

7447. Experience is not what happens to a man; it is what a man does with what happens to him. It is a gift for dealing with the accidents of existence, not the accidents themselves.   ALDOUS HUXLEY

7448. The story of any one man's real experience finds its startling parallel in that of every one of us.
LOWELL, *Spenser*

7449.
Till old experience do attain
To something like prophetic strain.
MILTON, *Il Penseroso*

7450. Experience without learning is better than learning without experience.   *Proverb*

7451. Experience is the great baffler of speculation.   *Proverb*

7452. Experience is good if not bought too dear.   *Proverb*

7453. All is but lip-wisdom, that wanteth experience.   *Proverb*

7454. A burnt child dreads the fire.
Proverb

7455. Practice is the best of all instructors.   PUBLILIUS SYRUS,
Sententiae

7456. What! wouldst thou have a serpent sting thee twice?
SHAKESPEARE,
The Merchant of Venice

7457. Unless experience be a jewel.
SHAKESPEARE,
The Merry Wives of Windsor

7458.
One must learn
By doing the thing; for though you think you know it
You have no certainty, until you try.
SOPHOCLES, *Trachiniae*

7459.
Others' follies teach us not,
Nor much their wisdom teaches;
And most, of sterling worth, is what
Our own experience preaches.
TENNYSON,
*Will Waterproof's
Lyrical Monologue*

7460. Experience is the name everyone gives to his mistakes.
OSCAR WILDE,
Lady Windermere's Fan

See also: 1200, 1501, 4501, 6603, 10005, 10353, 16260.

EXTRAVAGANCE

Related Subjects: **Exaggeration, Excess, Prodigality, Waste.**

7461. The passion of acquiring riches in order to support a vain expense, corrupts the purest souls. FENELON

7462. Laws cannot prevent extravagance; and this perhaps is not always an evil to the public. A shilling spent idly by a fool may be picked up by a wiser person, who knows better what to do with it; it is, therefore, not lost. FRANKLIN

7463. He calls his extravagance, generosity; and his trusting everybody, universal Benevolence.
GOLDSMITH,
The Good-Natur'd Man

7464. He that is extravagant will soon become poor, and poverty will enforce dependence, and invite corruption. SAMUEL JOHNSON

7465. He that runs out by extravagancy, must retrieve by parsimony.
Proverb

7466. Prodigality is the vice of a weak nature, as avarice is of a strong one. It comes of a weak craving for those blandishments of the world which are easily had for money.
SIR HENRY TAYLOR

7467. Waste of time is the most extravagant and costly of all expenses.
THEOPHRASTUS

7468. That is suitable to a man, in point of ornamental expense, not which he can afford to have, but which he can afford to lose.
RICHARD WHATELY

EXTREMES

Related Subjects: **End, Excess.**

7471. We must remember how apt man is to extremes—rushing from credulity and weakness, to suspicion and distrust. BULWER-LYTTON

7472. Men are as much blinded by the extremes of misery as by the extremes of poverty. BURKE

7473. The fierce extremes of good and ill to brook.
THOMAS CAMPBELL,
Gertrude of Wyoming

7474. All extremes are error. The reverse of error is not truth, but error still. Truth lies between these extremes. RICHARD CECIL

7475. That extremes beget extremes, is an apothegm built on the most profound observation of the human mind. C. C. COLTON

7476.
Thus each extreme to equal danger tends,
Plenty, as well as Want, can sep'rate friends.
ABRAHAM COWLEY, *Davideis*

7477.
Extremes of fortune are true wisdom's test.
And he's of men most wise who bears them best.
BISHOP CUMBERLAND, *Philemon*

7478. Extremes meet, and there is no better example than the haughtiness of humility. EMERSON,
Letters and Social Aims

7479. Extremes are vicious and proceed from men; compensation is just, and proceeds from God.

LA BRUYÈRE

7480. Both in individuals, and in masses, violent excitement is always followed by remission, and often by reaction. We are all inclined to depreciate what we have over-praised, and, on the other hand, to show undue indulgence where we have shown undue rigor. MACAULAY

7481.
Perfect good sense shuns all extremity,
Content to couple wisdom with
 sobriety. MOLIÈRE,
    Le Misanthrope

7482.
Avoid extremes, and shun the fault of such,
Who still are pleas'd too little or too much. POPE, *Essay on Criticism*

7483.
 The fate of all extremes is such:
Men may be read, as well as books,
  too much. POPE, *Moral Essays*

7484.
Like to the time o' the year between the extremes
Of hot and cold, he was nor sad nor
 merry. SHAKESPEARE,
   Antony and Cleopatra

7485. Who can be patient in such extremes? SHAKESPEARE, *Henry VI*

EYES

Related Subjects: Blindness, Face, Sight, Tears, Vision.

7491. A beautiful eye makes silence eloquent; a kind eye makes contradiction an assent; an enraged eye makes beauty deformed. This little member gives life to every other part about us. ADDISON

7492.
The light that lies
In woman's eyes . . .
And lies, and lies, and lies.
 Anonymous, Parody of Moore

7493. The light of the body is the eye. *Bible: Matthew, vi, 22*

7494.
The look in your eyes
Was as soft as the underside of soap in a soap-dish.
 WITTER BYNNER, *I Evade*

7495. The eyes those silent tongues of Love. CERVANTES, *Don Quixote*

7496. Black is a pearl in a woman's eye. GEORGE CHAPMAN,
   An Humorous Day's Mirth

7497. The eyes of the dead are closed gently; we also have to open gently the eyes of the living.
 JEAN COCTEAU, *A Call to Order*

7498. One of the most wonderful things in nature is a glance of the eye; it transcends speech; it is the bodily symbol of identity.
 EMERSON

7499. Our eyes, when gazing on sinful objects, are out of their calling, and out of God's keeping.
 THOMAS FULLER

7500. One's eyes are what one is, one's mouth what one becomes.
 GALSWORTHY,
   Flowering Wilderness

7501. Men of cold passions have quick eyes. HAWTHORNE

7502. The balls of sight are so formed, that one man's eyes are spectacles to another, to read his heart with. SAMUEL JOHNSON

7503. Lovers are angry, reconciled,

entreat, thank, appoint, and finally speak all things by their eyes.
MONTAIGNE, *Essays*

7504.
The light that lies
In woman's eyes.
THOMAS MOORE,
The Time I've Lost in Wooing

7505. Four eyes see more than two.
Proverb

7506. The eye that sees all things else sees not itself.   *Proverb*

7507. He that has but one eye had need look well to that.   *Proverb*

7508. A small hurt in the eye is a great one.   *Proverb*

7509. The eye is bigger than the belly.   *Proverb*

7510. The buyer needs a hundred eyes, the seller not one.   *Proverb*

7511. A man may see how this world goes with no eyes. Look with thine ears; see how yond justice rails upon yon simple thief. Hark, in thine ear: change places; and, handy-dandy, which is the justice, which is the thief?   SHAKESPEARE, *King Lear*

7512. I have a good eye, uncle; I can see a church by daylight.
SHAKESPEARE,
Much Ado About Nothing

7513. Stabbed with a white wench's black eye.   SHAKESPEARE,
Romeo and Juliet

7514.
Alack! there lies more peril in thine eye
Than twenty of their swords.
SHAKESPEARE, *Romeo and Juliet*

7515. An unforgiving eye, and a damned disinheriting countenance.
SHERIDAN,
The School for Scandal

7516. The dearest things in the world are our neighbor's eyes; they cost everybody more than anything else in housekeeping.   SYDNEY SMITH

7517.
Eyes of pure women, wholesome stars of love.   TENNYSON,
Idylls of the King

See also: 860, 908, 1083, 1315, 1685, 1691, 1716, 1722, 1733, 2015, 3166, 3413, 4194, 12060, 21642.

F

FACE

Related Subjects: Appearance, Beauty, Blushing, Eyes, Head, Lip, Mouth, Nose, Tongue.

7521. To put a tempting face aside when duty demands every faculty, it is a lesson which takes most men longest to learn.
GERTRUDE ATHERTON,
The Conqueror

7522. A beautiful face is a silent commendation.   BACON,
Ornamenta Rationalia

7523. It is the common wonder of all men, how among so many millions of faces there should be none alike.   SIR THOMAS BROWNE,
Religio Medici

7524.
As a white candle
In a holy place
So is the beauty
Of an aged face.
JOSEPH CAMPBELL,
The Old Woman

7525.
There is a garden in her face
Where roses and white lilies blow;

A heavenly paradise that place,
  Wherein all pleasant fruits do
    grow;
There cherries grow that none may
  buy,
Till Cherry-Ripe themselves do cry.
        THOMAS CAMPION, *Cherry-Ripe*

7526. The magic of a face.
        THOMAS CAREW,
          Epitaph on the Lady S—

7527. Every line in her face is the
line of least resistance.   IRVIN COBB

7528. It matters more what's in a
woman's face than what's on it.
        CLAUDETTE COLBERT

7529. To be plain with you, friend,
you don't carry in your countenance a
letter of recommendation.
        DICKENS, *Barnaby Rudge*

7530.
  Her pure and eloquent blood
Spoke in her cheeks, and so distinctly
  wrought
That one might almost say her body
  thought.   JOHN DONNE,
            Funeral Elegies

7531.
As a beauty I'm not a great star.
Others are handsomer far;
  But my face—I don't mind it
  Because I'm behind it;
It's the folks out in front that I jar.
        ANTHONY EUWER, *Limerick*

7532.
Is this the face that launched a thou-
  sand ships
And burnt the topless towers of
  Ilium?
  CHRISTOPHER MARLOWE, *Faustus*

7533.
The might of one fair face sublimes
  my love,
For it hath weaned my heart from low
  desires.   MICHELANGELO

7534.
If to her share some female errors
  fall,
Look on her face, and you'll forget
  'em all.   POPE,
            The Rape of the Lock

7535. A fair face may hide a foul
heart.   *Proverb*

7536. I have heard of your paintings
too, well enough; God has given you
one face, and you make yourselves
another.   SHAKESPEARE, *Hamlet*

7537. My comfort is, that old age,
that ill layer-up of beauty, can do no
more spoil upon my face.
        SHAKESPEARE, *Henry V*

7538.
            In thy face I see
The map of honour, truth, and
  loyalty.   SHAKESPEARE, *Henry VI*

7539.
I have seen better faces in my time
Than stands on any shoulder that I
  see
Before me at this instant.
        SHAKESPEARE, *King Lear*

7540.
Your face, my thane, is as a book
  where men
May read strange matters. To be-
  guile the time,
Look like the time; bear welcome in
  your eye,
Your hand, your tongue: look like the
  innocent flower,
But be the serpent under 't.
        SHAKESPEARE, *Macbeth*

7541.
            There's no art
To find the mind's construction in
  the face:
He was a gentleman on whom I built
An absolute trust.
        SHAKESPEARE, *Macbeth*

7542. His face is the worst thing about him. SHAKESPEARE,
Measure for Measure

7543. It is not night when I do see your face. SHAKESPEARE,
A Midsummer-Night's Dream

See also: 33, 1447, 1512, 1524, 1939, 2872, 3215, 3662, 4683, 10205, 12204, 12471, 20311, 21565, 21895.

FACTION

Related Subjects: Discord, Opposition, Politics.

7551. Faction is the excess and abuse of party. It begins when the first idea of private interest, preferred to public good, gets footing in the heart. It is always dangerous, yet always contemptible. RICHARD CHENEVIX

7552. Faction is the demon of discord armed with power to do endless mischief, and intent only on destroying whatever opposes its progress. Woe to that state in which it has found an entrance. GEORGE CRABBE

FACTS

Related Subjects: Argument, Realism and Reality, Statistics, Theories, Truth.

7561. The facts will promptly blunt his ardor. CAECILIUS STATIUS,
The Changeling

7562. False facts are highly injurious to the progress of science, for they often endure long; but false views, if supported by some evidence, do little harm, for every one takes a salutary pleasure in proving their falseness. DARWIN, *Descent of Man*

7563. Facts and Figures! Put 'em down! DICKENS, *The Chimes*

7564. God give me strength to face a fact though it slay me.
THOMAS H. HUXLEY

7565. The healthy human intellect will never believe that the same proposition may be true for faith and untrue in fact. DEAN INGE

7566. Facts are apt to alarm us more than the most dangerous principles.
JUNIUS

7567. A single fact is worth a shipload of argument. *Proverb*

7568. There is no adding to fundamentals. *Proverb*

7569. I am inclined to think that if a question as serious as going to war were presented to our nation we would demand facts unvarnished by interpretation. Whether we, even in our free democracy, could obtain them is another matter.
ELEANOR ROOSEVELT

7570. Seems, madam! Nay, it is; I know not seems.
SHAKESPEARE, *Hamlet*

7571. As the old hermit of Prague, that never saw pen and ink, very wittily said to a niece of King Gorboduc, "That that is, is."
SHAKESPEARE, *Twelfth Night*

7572. Don't tell me of facts, I never believe facts; you know Canning said nothing was so fallacious as facts, except figures. SYDNEY SMITH,
Lady Holland's Memoir

7573. Facts are stubborn things.
SMOLLETT, *Translation of Gil Blas*

7574. It is as fatal as it is cowardly to blink facts because they are not to our taste. JOHN TYNDALL,
Fragments of Science

7575. The fact can't be no longer disgised that a Krysis is onto us.
ARTEMUS WARD, *The Crisis*

7576. Two and two continue to make four, in spite of the whine of the amateur for three, or the cry of the critic for five. WHISTLER,
The Gentle Art of Making Enemies

See also: 1281, 1686, 6601, 7772, 11134, 11463, 16174, 19483, 19686, 19803.

FAILURE

Related Subjects: Defeat, Disappointment, Expectation, Fall, Faults, Ruin, Weakness.

7581.
They fail, and they alone, who have not striven. T. B. ALDRICH,
Enamored Architect of Airy Rhyme

7582.
To a man who has not succeeded we say,
"You made a mistake."
To one who lost at the lottery,
"You had bad luck."
PAUL GAUGUIN, *Intimate Journals*

7583. There is the greatest practical benefit in making a few failures early in life. THOMAS H. HUXLEY,
On Medical Education

7584.
There is not a fiercer hell than the failure in a great object.
KEATS, *Preface to Endymion*

7585. We have forty million reasons for failure, but not a single excuse.
KIPLING, *The Lesson*

7586. Of all failures, to fail in a witticism is the worst, and the mis-

hap is the more calamitous in a drawn out and detailed one.
W. S. LANDOR,
Imaginary Conversations

7587. Never give a man up until he has failed at something he likes.
LEWIS E. LAWES

7588. Not failure, but low aim, is crime. LOWELL, *For an Autograph*

7589. *Important.* When we can begin to take our failures non-seriously, it means we are ceasing to be afraid of them. It is of immense importance to learn to *laugh at ourselves.*
KATHERINE MANSFIELD, *Journals*

7590. There are few pains so grievous as to have seen, divined, or experienced how an exceptional man has missed his way and deteriorated.
NIETZSCHE, *Beyond Good and Evil*

7591.
Macbeth. If we should fail,—
Lady Macbeth. We fail
But screw your courage to the sticking-place,
And we'll not fail.
SHAKESPEARE, *Macbeth*

See also: 1254, 1258, 4639, 5584, 7882, 22036.

FAIRIES

Related Subjects: Imagination, Superstition, Tale, Vision.

7601.
Up the airy mountain,
Down the rushy glen,
We daren't go a-hunting
For fear of little men;
Wee folk, good folk,
Trooping all together;
Green jacket, red cap,
And white owl's feather!
WILLIAM ALLINGHAM,
The Fairies

7602. When the first baby laughed for the first time, his laugh broke into a million pieces, and they all went skipping about. That was the beginning of fairies.

J. M. BARRIE, *Little White Bird*

7603. Whenever a child says "I don't believe in fairies" there's a little fairy somewhere that falls right down dead.

J. M. BARRIE, *Peter Pan*

7604.
Children born of fairy stock
Never need for shirt or frock,
Never want for food or fire,
Always get their heart's desire.

ROBERT GRAVES,
I'd Love to Be a Fairy's Child

7605.
A little fairy comes at night,
    Her eyes are blue, her hair is brown,
With silver spots upon her wings,
    And from the moon she flutters down.   THOMAS HOOD,
                    Queen Mab

7606.
I took it for a faery vision
Of some gay creatures of the element,
That in the colours of the rainbow live,
And play i' th' plighted clouds.

MILTON, *Comus*

7607.
                    Faery elves,
Whose midnight revels by a forest-side,
Or fountain, some belated peasant sees,
Or dreams he sees, while overhead the Moon
Sits arbitress.   MILTON,
                Paradise Lost

7608. There never was a merry world since the fairies left dancing and the parson left conjuring.

JOHN SELDEN, *Table-Talk*

7609.
This is the fairy land; O spite of spites!
We talk with goblins, owls and sprites.   SHAKESPEARE,
            The Comedy of Errors

7610.
They are fairies; he that speaks to them shall die:
I'll wink and couch: no man their works must eye.

SHAKESPEARE,
The Merry Wives of Windsor

7611.
Over hill, over dale,
    Through brush, through brier,
Over park, over pale,
    Through flood, through fire.

SHAKESPEARE,
A Midsummer-Night's Dream

7612.
O, then, I see Queen Mab hath been with you.
She is the fairies' midwife, and she comes
In shape no bigger than an agate-stone
On the forefinger of an alderman,
Drawn with a team of little atomies
Athwart men's noses as they lie asleep: . . .
Her chariot is an empty hazel-nut
Made by the joiner squirrel, or old grub,
Time out o' mind the fairies' coach-makers.   SHAKESPEARE,
                Romeo and Juliet

7613.
Where the bee sucks, there suck I:
In a cowslip's bell I lie;
There I couch when owls do cry.
On the bat's back I do fly
After summer merrily.

SHAKESPEARE, *The Tempest*

7614. Or like a fairy trip upon the green.   SHAKESPEARE,
                Venus and Adonis

7615. The horns of Elfland faintly blowing. TENNYSON, *The Princess*

7616. Ye fairies, from all evil keep her! WORDSWORTH, *Peter Bell*

See also: 3372.

FAITH

Related Subjects: **Belief, The Bible, Christianity, Confidence, Credulity, Creeds, God, Hope, Ideals, Martyr, Miracle, Prayer, Prophecy, Religion, Trust.**

7621. The reason birds can fly and we can't is simply that they have perfect faith, for to have faith is to have wings. J. M. BARRIE, *The Little White Bird*

7622. He hath denied the faith, and is worse than an infidel.
Bible: 1 Timothy, v, 8

7623. Faith is the substance of things hoped for, the evidence of things not seen. *Bible: Hebrews, xi, 1*

7624. Faith without works is dead.
Bible: James, ii, 26

7625. Man is not sufficient unto himself. He must have a rallying cry, a slogan by which to die and by which to live. . . Even an empty slogan is better than no slogan at all.
HEYWOOD BROUN,
Preface to The Fifty-First Dragon

7626. Do you know how I would live if I renounced religion and was illogical enough to disbelieve in a life beyond—in the real life? Why, if I threw away and denounced my faith, I would surround myself with the most adroit hijackers, learn every trick of the highest banking and stock manipulations, avail myself of the laws under which to hide my own crimes, create a smoke-screen to throw into the eyes of men, and—believe me, I would become the world's champion crook.
FATHER COUGHLIN

7627.
His *faith,* perhaps, in some nice tenets might
Be wrong; his *life,* I'm sure, was in the right.
ABRAHAM COWLEY,
On the Death of Crashaw

7628. The cleverest defenders of a faith are its greatest enemies; for their subtleties engender doubt and stimulate the mind.
WILL DURANT,
The Story of Philosophy

7629. If we are certain our faith rests on the sure foundation of reality, we must be content to understand that the failure of others to accept it in no way destroys its truth.
GEORGE LANSBURY,
My Pilgrimage for Peace

7630. If a man have a strong faith he can indulge in the luxury of scepticism. NIETZSCHE,
The Twilight of the Idols

7631. Nothing in life is more wonderful than faith—the one great moving force which we can neither weigh in the balance nor test in the crucible. SIR WILLIAM OSLER,
Life of Sir William Osler

7632. One may lose one's faith for any number of reasons; and, as a general rule, a man who loses his faith is convinced, at any rate at the beginning, that he has obtained some gain in exchange for it.
PIRANDELLO

7633. Love asks faith, and faith asks firmness. *Proverb*

7634. He wears his faith but as the fashion of his hat.

SHAKESPEARE,
Much Ado About Nothing

7635. In the harsh face of life faith can read a bracing gospel.

STEVENSON, *Pulvis et Umbra*

7636.
Faith in faith established evermore
Stands a sea-mark in the tides of
time.   SWINBURNE, *A Sea-Mark*

7637.
Faith and unfaith can ne'er be equal
powers;
Unfaith in aught is want of faith in
all.   TENNYSON,
Idylls of the King

7638.
Cleave ever to the sunnier side of
doubt,
And cling to Faith beyond the forms
of Faith.   TENNYSON,
The Ancient Sage

7639. Give me faith, Lord, and let me help others to find it.   TOLSTOY

7640. I have no faith in the sense of comforting beliefs which persuade me that all my troubles are blessings in disguise. REBECCA WEST, *I Believe*

7641.
When faith is lost, when honor dies,
The man is dead!
WHITTIER, *Ichabod*

7642.
Talk Faith.   The world is better off
without
Your uttered ignorance and morbid
doubt.   ELLA W. WILCOX,
Speech

7643.
One in whom persuasion and belief

Had ripened into faith, and faith become
A passionate intuition.

WORDSWORTH, *The Excursion*

See also: 442, 1234, 2501, 2976, 3108, 3110, 3117, 3564, 6155, 7196, 7565, 7761, 8062, 11775, 16670, 18281, 18691.

FALCON, see Hawk

FALL

Related Subjects: Adversity, Failure, Ruin, Sin.

7651. A rich man beginning to fall is held up of his friends; but a poor man being down is thrust also away by his friends.

Apocrypha: Ecclesiasticus

7652. How are the mighty fallen!
Bible: II Samuel, I, 52

7653. How art thou fallen from heaven, O Lucifer, son of the morning!   *Bible: Isaiah, xiv, 12*

7654.
He that is down needs fear no fall,
He that is low, no pride.
BUNYAN, *The Pilgrim's Progress*

7655.
Who falls from all he knows of bliss,
Cares little into what abyss.
BYRON, *The Giaour*

7656. He that falls to-day may be up again tomorrow.
CERVANTES, *Don Quixote*

7657. Our greatest glory is not in never falling but in rising every time we fall.   CONFUCIUS, *Analects*

7658.
Fallen, fallen, fallen, fallen,
Fallen from his high estate,
And welt'ring in his blood;

Deserted at his utmost need,
By those his former bounty fed;
On the bare earth expos'd he lies,
With not a friend to close his eyes.
      DRYDEN, *Alexander's Feast*

7659.

           From morn
To noon he fell, from noon to dewy
    eve,
A summer's day; and with the set-
    ting sun
Dropt from the zenith like a falling
    star.   MILTON, *Paradise Lost*

7660. Awake, arise, or be forever
fallen!   MILTON, *Paradise Lost*

7661.

      I made him just and right,
Sufficient to have stood, though free
    to fall.
Such I created all th' ethereal Powers
And Spirits, both them who stood,
    and them who fail'd:
Freely they stood who stood, and fell
    who fell.   MILTON, *Paradise Lost*

7662. As he rose like a rocket, he
fell like a stick.
         THOMAS PAINE,
        Said of Edmund Burke

7663. Keeping from falling, is better
than helping up.   *Proverb*

7664. If a man once fall, all will
tread on him.   *Proverb*

7665. Hasty climbers have sudden
falls.   *Proverb*

7666. He that's down, down with
him, cries the world.   *Proverb*

7667. Every slip is not a fall.
                     Proverb

7668. He that is fallen cannot help
him that is down.   *Proverb*

7669.
Forget not that no fellow-being yet
May fall so low but love may lift
    his head.
    JAMES WHITCOMB RILEY,
    Let Something Good Be Said

7670. Some falls are means the happier to arise.   SHAKESPEARE,
              Cymbeline

7671.
O Hamlet, what a falling-off was
there!   SHAKESPEARE, *Hamlet*

7672.

           I shall fall,
Like a bright exhalation in the eve-
    ning,
And no man see me more.
      SHAKESPEARE, *Henry VIII*

7673. Press not a falling man too
far!   SHAKESPEARE, *Henry VIII*

7674.
I see thy glory like a shooting star
Fall to the base earth from the firma-
    ment.
Thy sun sets weeping in the lowly
    west.   SHAKESPEARE, *Richard II*

7675.
"Yea," quoth he, "dost thou fall upon
    thy face?
Thou wilt fall backward when thou
    hast more wit."
    SHAKESPEARE, *Romeo and Juliet*

7676.
Well, chile, de slip may come to all,
    But den de diff'ence foller;
For, if you watch him when he fall,
    De jus' man do not *waller*.
    JOHN B. TABB, *The Difference*

See also: 220, 221, 224, 631, 840,
2687, 3296, 5631, 15939.

FALSEHOOD, see Lies and Lying

FAME

Related Subjects: Admiration, Ambition, Applause, Destiny, Fortune, Glory, Greatness, Hero, Honor, Monument, Name, Praise, Reputation, Vanity, Zeal.

7681.
Oh, who shall lightly say that fame
Is nothing but an empty name,
When but for those, our mighty dead,
All ages past a blank would be.
JOANNA BAILLIE,
The Worth of Fame

7682. His fame was noised throughout all the country.
Bible: Joshua, vi, 27

7683. Happy is the man who hath never known what it is to taste of fame—to have it is a purgatory, to want it is a hell.
BULWER-LYTTON,
The Last of the Barons

7684. Doubt the permanent fame of any work of science which makes immediate reputation with the ignorant multitude; doubt the permanent fame of any work of imagination which is at once applauded by a convention clique that styles itself "the critical few." BULWER-LYTTON, *Caxtonia*

7685. Fame is the thirst of youth.
BYRON, *Childe Harold*

7686. I awoke one morning and found myself famous. BYRON

7687. Fame, we may understand, is no sure test of merit, but only a probability of such. CARLYLE,
Goethe

7688.
Fame is the breath of power?
What valid work was ever for itself
Wrought solely, be it war, art, statesmanship? JOHN DAVIDSON,
Smith

7689.
How dreary to be somebody!
How public, like a frog
To tell your name the livelong day
To an admiring bog!
EMILY DICKINSON, *Life*

7690. Most men are so completely corrupted by opinion that they would rather be notorious for the greatest calamities than suffer no ill and be unknown. DIO CHRYSOSTOM

7691.
Fame is a food that dead men eat,—
I have no stomach for such meat.
AUSTIN DOBSON,
*Fame Is a Food that
Dead Men Eat*

7692. What's fame, afther all, me la-ad? 'Tis as apt to be what some wan writes on ye'er tombstone.
F. P. DUNNE, *Fame*

7693.
Herein the only royal road to fame and fortune lies:
Put not your trust in vinegar—molasses catches flies!
EUGENE FIELD, *Uncle Eph*

7694. Fame sometimes hath created something of nothing.
THOMAS FULLER,
Holy and Profane State

7695.
I hate the man who builds his name
On ruins of another's fame.
JOHN GAY, *The Poet and the Rose*

7696. When a man is dead, they put money in his coffin, erect monuments to his memory, and celebrate the anniversary of his birthday in set speeches. Would they take any notice of him if he were living? No!

HAZLITT, *On Living to One's Self*

7697. The temple of fame is the shortest passage to riches and preferment. JUNIUS

7698.
Fame, like a wayward girl, will still be coy
To those who woo her with too slavish knees. KEATS, *Sonnet on Fame*

7699. Notoriety may be achieved in a narrow sphere, but fame demands for its evidence a more distant and prolonged reverberation.

LOWELL, *A Great Public Character*

7700. All is ephemeral,—fame and the famous as well.

MARCUS AURELIUS, *Meditations*

7701.
Fame is the spur that the clear spirit doth raise
(That last infirmity of noble mind)
To scorn delights, and live laborious days;
But the fair guerdon when we hope to find,
And think to burst out into sudden blaze,
Comes the blind Fury with th' abhorred shears
And slits the thin-spun life.

MILTON, *Lycidas*
(*Source of title of novel by Howard Spring.*)

7702.
Fame is no plant that grows on mortal soil. MILTON, *Lycidas*

7703.
Fame, if not double-faced, is double-mouthed,
And with contrary blast proclaims most deeds;

On both his wings, one black, the other white,
Bears greatest names in his wild aery flight. MILTON,
Samson Agonistes

7704.
Nor Fame I slight, nor for her favours call;
She comes unlooked for, if she comes at all. POPE,
The Temple of Fame

7705.
Unblemish'd let me live or die unknown;
Oh, grant an honest fame or grant me none! POPE,
The Temple of Fame

7706. Fame is a magnifying glass.
Proverb

7707. Fame is but the breath of the people, and that often unwholesome. *Proverb*

7708. Fame, like a river, is narrowest at its source and broadest afar off.
Proverb

7709. All fame is dangerous; good bringeth envy; bad, shame.
Proverb

7710.
The honorable orators, the gazettes of thunder,
the tycoons, big shots and dictators,
flicker in the mirror a few moments
and Fade through the glass of death
for discussion in an autocracy of worms. CARL SANDBURG,
The People, Yes

7711. I would give all my fame for a pot of ale and safety.
SHAKESPEARE, *Henry V*

7712. He lives in fame that died in virtue's cause. SHAKESPEARE,
Titus Andronicus

7713. How men long for celebrity! Some would willingly sacrifice their lives for fame, and not a few would rather be known by their crimes than not known at all.

SIR JOHN SINCLAIR

7714. Fame is the perfume of heroic deeds.   SOCRATES

7715. Fame has also this great drawback, that if we pursue it we must direct our lives in such a way as to please the fancy of men, avoiding what they dislike and seeking what is pleasing to them.   SPINOZA, *Tractatus de Intellectus*

7716. Censure is the tax a man pays to the public for being eminent.

SWIFT,
Thoughts on Various Subjects

7717. To famous men all the earth is a sepulchre.   THUCYDIDES, *History*

7718.
I won a noble fame,
But, with a sudden frown,
The people snatched my crown,
And in the mire trod down
    My lofty name.

THEODORE TILTON,
Sir Marmaduke's Musings

7719.
When I peruse the conquer'd fame
    of heroes and victories of mighty
    generals, I do not envy the gen-
    erals.   WALT WHITMAN,
When I Peruse the Conquer'd Fame

7720.
There's not a thing on earth that I
    can name,
So foolish, and so false, as common
    fame.   JOHN WILMOT,
Did E'er This Saucy World

See also: 185, 358, 1419, 2712, 3088, 3400, 11184.

FAMILIARITY

Related Subjects: Form, Friend, Impertinence, Impudence, Knowledge.

7721.
Beauty soon grows familiar to the
    lover,
Fades in his eye, and palls upon the
    sense.   ADDISON, *Cato*

7722. Familiarity breeds contempt.
AESOP, *The Fox and the Lion*

7723. I hold he loves me best that calls me Tom.

THOMAS HEYWOOD,
Hierarchie of the Blessed Angells

7724. I hope upon familiarity will grow more contempt.

SHAKESPEARE,
The Merry Wives of Windsor

7725. The coach jumbled us insensibly into some sort of familiarity.
SIR RICHARD STEELE, *The Spectator*

7726. Staled by frequence, shrunk by usage into commonest commonplace!   TENNYSON, *Locksley Hall Sixty Years After*

See also: 274, 20684.

FAMILY

Related Subjects: Ancestry, Brother, Children, Daughter, Father, Heredity, Home, Husband, Marriage, Mother, Name, Parents, Sister, Son, Wife.

7731. He that hath wife and children hath given hostages to fortune; for they are impediments to great enterprises, either of virtue or mischief.
BACON, *Of Marriage and Single Life*

7732. Family jokes, though rightly

cursed by strangers, are the bond that keeps most families alive.
STELLA BENSON,
Pipers and a Dancer

7733. A medley of kindred, that 'twould puzzle a convocation of casuists to resolve their degrees of consanguinity. CERVANTES,
Don Quixote

7734. And so do his sisters, and his cousins, and his aunts.
W. S. GILBERT, *H.M.S. Pinafore*

7735. My family have done me far more harm than I have been able to do them good. NAPOLEON

7736.
One would be in less danger
From the wiles of the stranger
If one's own kin and kith
Were more fun to be with
OGDEN NASH, *Family Court*

7737. A family is but too often a commonwealth of malignants. POPE

7738. It is a poor family that hath neither a whore nor a thief in it.
Proverb

7739. He that is poor all his kindred scorn him, he that is rich all are kin to him. *Proverb*

7740. Many kinsfolk, few friends.
Proverb

7741. He that hath a wife and children must not sit with his fingers in his mouth. *Proverb*

7742. He that has no fools, knaves, or beggars in his family, was begot by a flash of lightning. *Proverb*

7743. Better have one plough going than two cradles. *Proverb*

7744.
We have careful thought for the stranger,

And smiles for the sometime guest,
But oft for our own the bitter tone,
Though we love our own the best.
MARGARET E. SANGSTER, *Our Own*

7745. A family enjoying the unspeakable peace and freedom of being orphans. BERNARD SHAW,
You Never Can Tell

7746. All happy families resemble one another; every unhappy family is unhappy in its own fashion.
TOLSTOY, *Anna Karenina*

7747.
We flatter those we scarcely know
  We please the fleeting guest,
And deal full many a thoughtless blow
  To those who love us best.
ELLA W. WILCOX, *Life's Scars*

See also: 103, 1542, 2063, 3293, 6857, 17642.

FANATICISM

Related Subjects: Belief, Bigotry, Opinion, Prejudice, Reform, Tolerance, Witch.

7751. Of all things wisdom is the most terrified of epidemical fanaticism, because, of all enemies, it is that against which she is the least able to furnish any kind of resource.
BURKE

7752. Just as every conviction begins as a whim so does every emancipator serve his apprenticeship as a crank. A fanatic is a great leader who is just entering the room.
HEYWOOD BROUN, *Whims*

7753.
Christians have burnt each other, quite persuaded
That all the Apostles would have done as they did. BYRON, *Don Juan*

7754. The downright fanatic is nearer to the heart of things than the cool and slippery disputant.
                                        E. H. CHAPIN

7755. Fanaticism, the false fire of an overheated mind.   COWPER

7756.
So over violent, or over civil,
That every man with him was God or
    Devil.   DRYDEN,
                    Absalom & Achitophel

7757. Fanaticism is the child of false zeal and superstition, the father of intolerance and persecution.
                    SAMUEL FLETCHER

7758. The blind fanaticism of one foolish honest man may cause more evil than the united efforts of twenty rogues.   FRIEDRICH GRIMM

7759. Fanaticism is such an overwhelming impression of the ideas relating to the future world as disqualifies for the duties of this.
                    ROBERT HALL

7760. We often excuse our own want of philanthropy by giving the name of fanaticism to the more ardent zeal of others.   LONGFELLOW

7761.
But Faith, fanatic Faith, once wedded fast
To some dear falsehood, hugs it to the last.   THOMAS MOORE,
                    Lalla Rookh

7762.
Fire in each eye, and papers in each hand,
They rave, recite, and madden round the land.   POPE,
                    Epistle to Dr. Arbuthnot

7763. Fanaticism consists in redoubling your effort when you have forgotten your aim.   SANTAYANA

See also: 172, 1203, 1874, 12598, 15032, 16386.

FANCY

Related Subjects: Desire, Fantasy, Idea, Imagination.

7771.
    Exalted ideas of fancy require
To be clothed in a suitable vesture of
        phrase.   ARISTOPHANES,
                    The Frogs

7772. Oh, fancies that might be, oh, facts that are!   BROWNING, *Asolando*

7773. Most marvellous and enviable is that fecundity of fancy which can adorn whatever it touches, which can invest naked fact and dry reasoning with unlooked for beauty, make flowers bloom even on the brow of the precipice, and turn even the rock itself into moss and lichens. This faculty is most important for the vivid and attractive exhibition of truth to the minds of men.   THOMAS FULLER

7774.
Ever let the Fancy roam,
Pleasure never is at home.
                    KEATS, *Fancy*

7775. Thou wilt find rest from vain fancies if thou doest every act in life as though it were thy last.
                    MARCUS AURELIUS, *Meditations*

7776. Fancy rules over two thirds of the universe, the past and future, while reality is confined to the present.   J. P. RICHTER

7777. Chewing the food of sweet and bitter fancy.   SHAKESPEARE,
                    As You Like It

7778. Fancy and humor, early and constantly indulged, may expect an old age overrun with follies.
                    ISAAC WATTS

See also: 17481.

FAREWELL

Related Subjects: Absence, Parting.

7781.
Once more, farewell!
If e'er we meet hereafter, we shall
    meet
In happier climes, and on a safer
    shore.   ADDISON, *Cato*

7782. All farewells should be sudden.
                BYRON, *Sardanapalus*

7783.
Farewell! a word that must be, and
    hath been—
A sound which makes us linger;—
    yet—farewell!   BYRON,
                Childe Harold

7784.
Fare thee well! and if forever,
    Still forever, fare thee well.
            BYRON, *Fare Thee Well*

7785.
            Farewell happy fields,
Where joy for ever dwells.
        MILTON, *Paradise Lost*

7786. The last farewell. OVID,
                Metamorphoses

7787.
            Fare thee well;
The elements be kind to thee, and
    make
Thy spirits all of comfort!
SHAKESPEARE, *Antony and Cleopatra*

7788. Sweets to the sweet: farewell!
        SHAKESPEARE, *Hamlet*

7789. Farewell, and stand fast.
        SHAKESPEARE, *Henry IV*

7790.
For ever, and for ever, farewell,
    Cassius!
If we do meet again, why, we shall
    smile;

If not, why then this parting was well
    made.   SHAKESPEARE,
                Julius Caesar

7791.
            O, now, for ever
Farewell the tranquil mind! farewell
    content!
Farewell the plumed troop, and the
    big wars,
That make ambition virtue! O, farewell!
Farewell the neighing steed, and the
    shrill trump,
The spirit-stirring drum, the ear-
    piercing fife,
The royal banner and all quality,
Pride, pomp, and circumstance of
    glorious war!
And, O you mortal engines, whose
    rude throats
The immortal Jove's dread clamours
    counterfeit,
Farewell! Othello's occupation 's
    gone!   SHAKESPEARE, *Othello*

7792.
            Welcome ever smiles,
And farewell goes out sighing.
SHAKESPEARE, *Troilus and Cressida*

7793. Farewell! thou art too dear for
my possessing.   SHAKESPEARE,
                Sonnet LXXXVII

FARMING

Related Subjects: Animal, The
Country, Cow, Fruit, Garden, Harvest, Ox.

7801. "Gentlemen farmers"—a race
worn out quite. BYRON, *Don Juan*

7802. A man learns not to expect
much after he's farmed cotton most
of his life. ERSKINE CALDWELL,
        You Have Seen Their Faces

7803. Farm tenancy, and particularly
sharecropping, is not self-perpetu-

ating. It can survive only by feeding upon itself, like an animal in a trap eating its own flesh and bone. The only persons interested in its continuation are the landlords who accumulate wealth by extracting tribute not from the products of the earth but from the labor of the men, women and children who till the earth.

ERSKINE CALDWELL,
You Have Seen Their Faces

7804.
"God speed the plough!" be this a prayer
To find its echo everywhere.
ELIZA COOK, *God Speed the Plough*

7805. The farmer is covetous of his dollar, and with reason. . . . He knows how many strokes of labor it represents. His bones ache with the day's work that earned it.
EMERSON, *Conduct of Life*

7806.
Wisdom, Power and Goodness meet
In the bounteous field of wheat.
HANNAH F. GOULD, *The Wheatfield*

7807.
Uncle Sam is rich enough
To give us all a farm.
JESSE HUTCHINSON, JR.,
Uncle Sam's Farm

7808. The agricultural population, says Cato, produces the bravest men, the most valiant soldiers, and a class of citizens the least given of all to evil designs. PLINY THE ELDER,
Natural History

7809.
The farmer works the soil,
The agriculturist works the farmer.
E. F. WARE, *The Kansas Bandit*

7810. No race can prosper till it learns that there is as much dignity in tilling a field as in writing a poem.
BOOKER T. WASHINGTON,
Up From Slavery

7811. When tillage begins, other arts follow. The farmers therefore are the founders of human civilization.
DANIEL WEBSTER

See also: 3488, 3606.

FASCISM

Related Subjects: Capitalism, Dictatorship, Government, Socialism.

7821. Definition of corporate state: A method by which complete power is given to the capitalist to produce that scarcity which will insure him a share of the national wealth, out of all proportion to his efforts, and which will enable him to enslave the workers by substituting for their freedom and right to combine a nominal and ineffective minority voice in the government of industry.
SIR STAFFORD CRIPPS

7822. No taunt has hurt us so much as the one that national socialism is tantamount to intellectual barbarism.
GOEBBELS

7823. I, as a National Socialist, and all my followers, absolutely refuse, however, by reason of our national principles, to acquire at the cost of the life-blood of those who love and are dear to us, subjects of a foreign nation, who, in any case, will never love us.   ADOLF HITLER,
Oct. 14, 1933

7824. All we wish is to be left alone in peace so that we can work.
ADOLF HITLER, *Oct. 22, 1933*

7825. National Socialism does not harbor the slightest aggressive intent towards any European nation.
ADOLF HITLER,
Nat'l. Soc. Party Congress, 1935

7826. We National Socialists, however, have no desire for our Army to

be used to force on other nations something that they have no wish for.
ADOLF HITLER,
Nat'l. Soc. Party Congress, 1936

7827. What is denied to amity the fist must take. . . The very first essential for success is a perpetually constant and regular employment of violence. . . Success is the sole earthly judge of the right and wrong. . . Terrorism can be broken only by terrorism.   ADOLF HITLER,
Mein Kampf

7828. Cure the evils of Democracy by the evils of Fascism! Funny therapeutics. I've heard of their curing syphilis by giving the patient malaria, but I've never heard of their curing malaria by giving the patient syphilis.
SINCLAIR LEWIS,
It Can't Happen Here

7829. We are . . . a State which controls all forces acting in Nature. We control political forces, we control moral forces, we control economic forces, therefore, we are a full-blown Corporative State.
MUSSOLINI, *April 7, 1926*

7830. The Fascist State claims its ethical character: it is Catholic but above all it is fascist. In fact it is exclusively and essentially fascist. Catholicism completes Fascism, and this we openly declare, but let no one think they can turn the tables on us, under cover of metaphysics or philosophy.   MUSSOLINI,
Chamber of Deputies, May 13, 1929

7831. Fascism, in short, is not only a law-giver and a founder of institutions, but an educator and a promoter of spiritual life. It aims at refashioning not only the forms of life but their content—man, his character, and his faith. To achieve this purpose it en-

forces discipline and uses authority, entering into the soul and ruling with undisputed sway.   MUSSOLINI,
Fascism

7832. Fascism will have nothing to do with universal embraces.
MUSSOLINI, *Fascism*

7833. Revealed truths we have torn to shreds, dogmas we have spat upon; we have rejected all thrones of paradise; we have baffled charlatans—white, red, black charlatans who placed miraculous drugs on the market to give "happiness" to mankind. We do not believe in programs, in plans, in saints or apostles, above all, we do not believe in happiness, in salvation, in the promised land.
MUSSOLINI, *Fascism*

7834. These ideologies are all based upon myths, such as the personification of the state; upon unrealities, such as that of the superiority of the Nordic race; upon superstitions, such as the peculiar sanctity to be attached to Teutonic "Blud und Boden." The essence of madness is in them, and they are impelling their adherents to anti-social conduct as mad as it is cruel.   H. C. ROBBINS

7835. Now it is, whether they realize it or not, the object of the Nazi leaders to drive the mass of mankind back to a new form of slavery, as a condition necessary to the continuance of the private ownership of fields, factories, and mines!
JOHN STRACHEY, *I Believe*

7836. We are going to fight Fascism, and its friends wherever we find them, until Fascism is destroyed throughout the earth. We shall do this because Fascism organises oppression, delights in warfare, and lays

waste homes and arts, sciences and
the ordinary lives of men.
Tom Wintringham,
New Ways of War

See also: 1159, 5436, 6955, 8892,
9771, 9772, 10981, 11650, 11707.

FASHION

**Related Subjects: Conventionality,
Custom, Dress, Fashion, Fop,
Form, Habit, Method, Society,
Style.**

7841. The fashion of this world
passeth away.
Bible: 1 Corinthians, vii, 31

7842. As good be out of the world
as out of the fashion
Colley Cibber, *Love's Last Shift*

7843. Better be dead as out o' fashion.
Proverb

7844. Tailors and writers must mind
the fashion. *Proverb*

7845. Fine clothes wear soonest out
of fashion. *Proverb*

7846.
The glass of fashion and the mould
of form,
The observed of all observers!
Shakespeare, *Hamlet*

7847.
He was indeed the glass
Wherein the noble youth did dress
themselves. Shakespeare,
Henry IV

7848. The fashion wears out more
apparel than the man.
Shakespeare,
Much Ado About Nothing

7849. Old fashions please me best.
Shakespeare,
The Taming of the Shrew

See also: 4367, 13236.

FASTIDIOUSNESS

**Related Subjects: Cleanliness,
Delicacy, Elegance, Prudery.**

7851. Fastidiousness is the envelope
of indelicacy. T. C. Haliburton

7852. Fastidiousness is only another
form of egotism; and all men who
know not where to look for truth, save
in the narrow well of self, will find
their own image at the bottom, and
mistake it for what they are seeking.
Lowell

FASTING

Related Subjects: Asceticism, Hunger, Self-Denial.

7861.
Whoso will pray, he must fast and
be clean,
And fat his soul, and make his body
lean. Chaucer,
The Somnours Tale

7862. He fasts enough who eats with
reason. A. J. Cronin,
Grand Canary

7863. He fasts enough whose wife
scolds all dinnertime. *Proverb*

7864. Surfeit is the father of much
fast. Shakespeare,
Measure for Measure

7865. And therein fasting, hast thou
made me gaunt. Shakespeare,
Richard II

FATE

**Related Subjects: Accident,
Chance, Death, Destiny, Fortune,
Future, Gods, Luck, Misfortune,
Necessity, Providence.**

7871. Resolved to take Fate by the
throat and shake a living out of her.
Louisa M. Alcott,
Life, Letters & Journals

7872.

We, in some unknown Power's employ,
    Move on a rigorous line;
Can neither, when we will, enjoy;
    Nor, when we will, resign.
           MATTHEW ARNOLD

7873.

Night and the curtains drawn
The household still
Fate with appointed strength
Hath worked its will.
     HELEN GRANVILLE-BARKER,
       Night and the Curtains Drawn

7874.

It's odd to think we might have been
    Sun, moon and stars unto each
        other—
Only, I turned down one little street
    As you went up another.
         FANNY H. LEA, *Fate*

7875. Oh, busy weaver! Unseen
weaver! pause! one word! whither
flows the fabric? What palace may it
deck? Wherefore all these ceaseless
toilings? Speak, weaver! Stay thy
hand! But one single word with thee!
Nay—the shuttle flies—the figures
float from forth the loom; the freshet
—rushing carpet forever slides away.
     HERMAN MELVILLE, *Moby Dick*

7876. Our hour is marked, and no
one can claim a moment of life beyond what fate has predestined.
            NAPOLEON

7877.

Heaven from all creatures hides the
    book of Fate,
All but the page prescrib'd, their
    present state. POPE, *Essay on Man*

7878. Heaven know its time; the
bullet has its billet. SCOTT,
        Count Robert of Paris

7879.

Our remedies oft in ourselves do lie
Which we ascribe to Heaven.
          SHAKESPEARE,
       All's Well that Ends We

7880.

There's a divinity that shapes ou
    ends
Rough-hew them how we will.
       SHAKESPEARE, *Hamle*

7881.

What fates impose, that men mus
    needs abide;
It boots not to resist both wind an
    tide. SHAKESPEARE, *Henry V*

7882.

Men at some time are masters o
    their fates:
The fault, dear Brutus, is not in ou
    stars,
But in ourselves, that we are u
    derlings. SHAKESPEARE,
           Julius Caes

7883.

    I'll make assurance doubly sur
And take a bond of fate.
       SHAKESPEARE, *Macbe*

7884. A pair of star-cross'd lovers
    SHAKESPEARE, *Romeo and Juli*

7885. For man is man and master o
his fate. TENNYSON,
         Idylls of the Ki

See also: 474, 3293, 3735, 1603
16655, 17867.

FATHER AND FATHERHOO

Related Subjects: Babies, Famil
Mother.

7891.

    There's a blessing on the heart
A special providence for fatherhoo
BROWNING, *The Ring and the Bo*

7892. Diogenes struck the father when the son swore.

ROBERT BURTON,
Anatomy of Melancholy

7893.
The child whom many fathers share
Hath seldom known a father's care.
JOHN GAY, *Fables*

7894. One father is more than a hundred schoolmasters.
GEORGE HERBERT,
Jacula Prudentum

7895. It is impossible to please all the world and one's father.
LA FONTAINE, *Fables*

7896. Directly after God in heaven comes Papa. THE BOY MOZART

7897. It is a wise child that knows its own father. *Proverb*

7898. To be the father unto many sons. SHAKESPEARE, *Henry VI*

7899. It is wise father that knows his own child. SHAKESPEARE,
The Merchant of Venice

7900.
Father, dear Father, come home with me now,
The clock in the steeple strikes one;
You said you were coming right home from the shop
As soon as your day's work was done. H. C. WORK,
Come Home, Father

See also: 3247, 3269, 10615, 14011.

FATNESS

Related Subjects: **Flesh, Weight.**

7901. I am resolved to grow fat, and look young till forty. DRYDEN,
The Maiden Queen

7902. Who ever hears of fat men leading a riot, or herding together in turbulent mobs?—no—no, 'tis your lean, hungry men who are continually worrying society, and setting the whole community by the ears.
WASHINGTON IRVING,
Knickerbocker's History of New York

7903. A fat paunch never breeds fine thoughts. ST. JEROME

7904. A soul in a fat body lieth soft, and is loth to rise. *Proverb*

7905. Fat, fair, and forty.
SCOTT, *St. Roman's Well*

7906.
Let me have men about me that are fat;
Sleek-headed men, and such as sleep O' nights.
Yond Cassius has a lean and hungry look;
He thinks too much: such men are dangerous. SHAKESPEARE,
Julius Caesar

7907.
Fat paunches have lean pates, and dainty bits
Make rich the ribs, but bankrupt quite the wits.
SHAKESPEARE, *Love's Labour's Lost*

See also: 19254.

FAULTS

Related Subjects: **Error, Failure, Perfection, Weakness.**

7911. The greatest of faults, I should say, is to be conscious of none.
CARLYLE, *Heroes & Hero-Worship*

7912. All his faults were such that one loved him still the better for them. GOLDSMITH,
The Good-Natur'd Man

7913. If we were without faults, we should not take so much pleasure in remarking them in others.
LA ROCHEFOUCAULD, *Maxims*

7914. The flaw which is hidden is deemed greater than it is. MARTIAL

7915.
Whoe'er it be
That tells my faults, I hate him mortally! POPE,
Paraphrases from Chaucer

7916. A wilful fault has no excuse, and deserves no pardon. *Proverb*

7917. The first faults are theirs that commit them; the second theirs that permit them. *Proverb*

7918. Forget others' faults by remembering your own. *Proverb*

7919. Every one puts his faults on the times. *Proverb*

7920. In every fault there is folly. *Proverb*

7921. By others' faults wise men correct their own. *Proverb*

7922. If nobody takes notice of our faults, we easily forget them ourselves. *Proverb*

7923. If the best man's faults were written on his forehead, it would make him pull his hat over his eyes. *Proverb*

7924. It is weel that our fau'ts are na written on our face. *Proverb*

7925. Lifeless, faultless. *Proverb*

7926. A fault, once denied, is twice committed. *Proverb*

7927. Every one fault seeming monstrous till his fellow fault came to match it. SHAKESPEARE,
As You Like It

7928. Every man has his fault, and honesty is his. SHAKESPEARE,
Timon of Athens

7929.
But friend, to me
He is all fault who hath no fault at all.
For he who loves me must have a touch of earth. TENNYSON,
Idylls of the King

See also: 413, 647, 1192, 2242, 7361, 7882, 11602, 20617.

FAVOR

Related Subjects: Gifts, Influence Kindness, Service.

7931. Regarding the innumerable applicants for favors, the President [Lincoln] made the remark that "There are too many pigs for the teats." This is said to have been uttered by the ladies, who blushingly hid their faces behind their handkerchiefs. L. P. CLARK, *Lincoln*

7932. I am a great foe of favouritism in public life, in private life, and even in the delicate relationship of an author to his works.
JOSEPH CONRAD,
Lord Jim: Author's Note

7933. To remind a man of the good turns you have done him is very much like a reproach. DEMOSTHENES,
De Coron

7934. One good turn deserves another. *Prover*

7935. A favour ill-placed is great waste. *Prover*

7936. You roll my log, and I will roll yours. SENEC

937. Favors cease to be favors when here are conditions attached to them.
THORNTON WILDER,
The Woman of Andros

See also: 8642, 11170.

FEAR

Related Subjects: Cowardice, Despair, Doubt, Flight, Imagination, Timidity.

7941. Throw fear to the wind.
ARISTOPHANES, *The Wasps*

7942. There is no fear in love; but perfect love casteth out fear.
Bible: 1 John, iv, 18

7943. We must get rid of Fear.
CARLYLE, *Heroes & Hero-Worship*

7944. Fear is sharp-sighted, and can see things under ground, and much more in the skies.   CERVANTES,
Don Quixote

7945.
We listen'd and look'd sideways up!
Fear at my heart, as at a cup,
My life-blood seem'd to sip.
COLERIDGE, *The Ancient Mariner*

7946.
Like one that on a lonesome road
Doth walk in fear and dread,
And having once turned round, walks on,
And turns no more his head;
Because he knows a frightful fiend
Doth close behind him tread.
COLERIDGE, *The Ancient Mariner*

7947. Whistling to keep myself from being afraid.   DRYDEN, *Amphitryon*

7948.
The thing that numbs the heart is this:
That men cannot devise

Some scheme of life to banish fear
That lurks in most men's eyes.
JAMES N. HALL, *Fear*

7949.
Fear of the lack of shelter, food,
And fire for winter's cold;
Fear of their children's lacking these,
This in a world so old.
JAMES N. HALL, *Fear*

7950.
Fear and amazement beat upon my heart,
Even as a madman beats upon a drum.
THOMAS HEYWOOD,
A Woman Killed With Kindness

7951. Many may not love us, but all shall fear us.   HEINRICH HIMMLER

7952.
And how am I to face the odds
Of man's bedevilment and God's?
I, a stranger and afraid
In a world I never made.
A. E. HOUSMAN, *Last Poems*

7953. When I have fears that I may cease to be.   KEATS,
When I Have Fears

7954.
Alike were they free from
Fear, that reigns with the tyrant, and
envy, the vice of republics.
LONGFELLOW, *Evangeline*

7955. There's nae medicine for fear.
Proverb

7956. Two things ought to be the object of our fear, the envy of friends, and the hatred of enemies.   *Proverb*

7957. Fear can keep a man out of danger, but courage only can support him in it.   *Proverb*

7958. Fear is one part of prudence.
Proverb

7959. Fear is stronger than love.
Proverb

7960. He that's afraid to do good would do ill if he durst.   *Proverb*

7961. He that fears leaves must not come into a wood.   *Proverb*

7962. He that fears you present will hate you absent.   *Proverb*

7963. He is miserable once who feels it, but twice who fears it before it comes.   *Proverb*

7964. The fear of death is more to be dreaded than death itself.
PUBLILIUS SYRUS, *Sententiae*

7965. The only thing we have to fear is fear itself.
FRANKLIN D. ROOSEVELT,
First Inaugural Address

7966. Scared out of his seven senses.
SCOTT, *Rob Roy*

7967.
         So slippery that
The fear's as bad as falling.
SHAKESPEARE, *Cymbeline*

7968.
         Distill'd
Almost to jelly with the act of fear.
SHAKESPEARE, *Hamlet*

7969. Of all base passions, fear is most accurs'd.   SHAKESPEARE,
Henry VI

7970. Fie, my lord, fie! a soldier, and afeard!   SHAKESPEARE, *Macbeth*

7971.
         When our actions do not,
Our fears do make us traitors.
SHAKESPEARE, *Macbeth*

7972.
But now I am cabin'd, cribb'd, confined, bound in
To saucy doubts and fears.
SHAKESPEARE, *Macbeth*

7973. Tush, tush! fear boys with bugs.   SHAKESPEARE,
The Taming of the Shrew

7974. To fear the worst oft cures the worse.   SHAKESPEARE,
Troilus and Cressida

7975. To him who is in fear everything rustles.   SOPHOCLES

7976.
The very hair on my head
Stands up for dread.
SOPHOCLES, *Oedipus Coloneus*

7977. Fear, like pain, looks and sounds worse than it feels.
REBECCA WEST

7978. To teach people not to be afraid of being afraid is one of the most necessary and most neglected things in war. Youngsters who feel as almost all soldiers feel during battle imagine that these feelings are abnormal and become obsessed with the idea that they have a yellow streak in them. If they can be reassured on this point they will do their job well.
TOM WINTRINGHAM,
New Ways of War

See also: 1193, 2283, 2932, 4701, 4709, 4816, 4891, 4908, 4938, 5003, 5018, 5023, 5592, 5597, 5734, 6384, 9624, 14121, 17435, 20803, 20840, 21538.

FEAST AND FESTIVAL

Related Subjects: Conviviality, Cooks and Cooking, Dancing, Dining, Eating, Food, Guests, Holiday, Music, Thanksgiving Day, Toast.

7981. Let us eat and drink; for tomorrow we shall die.
Bible: Isaiah, xxii, 13

7982. Bring hither the fatted calf.
Bible: Luke, xv, 23

7983. Enough is equal to a feast.
FIELDING,
The Covent Garden Tragedy

7984. Fools make feasts and wise men eat them.   FRANKLIN,
Poor Richard

7985. A feast is not made of mushrooms only.   *Proverb*

7986. Feasting is the physician's harvest.   *Proverb*

7987.
Who risest from a feast
With that keen appetite that he sits
down?   SHAKESPEARE,
The Merchant of Venice

7988.
Feast, and your halls are crowded;
Fast, and the world goes by.
ELLA W. WILCOX, *Solitude*

See also: 1603, 2231, 3671, 8736, 8991, 10065, 20442.

FEATHER

Related Subject: **Birds.**

7991. Horsefeathers!
Epithet coined by BILLY DEBECK, *in the cartoon, "Barney Google." It enjoyed a considerable currency.*

7992. It hath been an ancient custom among them [The Hungarians] that none should wear a feather but he who had killed a Turk, to whom only it was lawful to show the number of his slain enemies by the number of feathers in his cap.
RICHARD HANSARD,
A Description of Hungary

7993. Feather by feather, birds build nests.
MIDDLETON & ROWLEY,
The Spanish Gypsy

7994. I am a feather for each wind that blows.   SHAKESPEARE,
The Winter's Tale

FEBRUARY

Related Subjects: **Month, Winter.**

8001.
While the slant sun of February pours
Into the bowers a flood of light.
BRYANT, *A Winter Palace*

8002.
Late February days; and now, at last,
Might you have thought that Winter's woe was past;
So fair the sky was and so soft the air.   WILLIAM MORRIS,
The Earthly Paradise

8003. February makes a bridge, and March breaks it.   *Proverb*

8004. February sun is dearly won.
Proverb

8005. All the months in the year curse a fair Februeer.   *Proverb*

8006.
So, in a single night,
Fair February came,
Bidding my lips to sing
Or whisper their surprise,
With all the joys of spring
And morning in her eyes.
FRANCIS B. YOUNG, *February*

FEELING

Related Subjects: **Heart, Impressions, Sense, Sensitivity, Sympathy.**

8011. The barrenest of all mortals is the sentimentalist.   CARLYLE,
Sir Walter Scott

8012. The human spirit is compounded of reason and feeling. Feeling is the unifying, the inclusive principle in the world, and leads, in the end, to universalism.
COHEN-PORTHEIM

8013.

They are not long, the weeping and
    the laughter,
  Love and desire and hate :
I think they have no portion in us
    after
  We pass the gate.
      ERNEST DOWSON,
        Vitae Summa Brevis

8014. I have something more to do
than feel.   CHARLES LAMB

8015.

      Who lets his feelings run
In soft luxurious flow,
Shrinks when hard service must be
  done,
And faints at every woe.
      CARDINAL NEWMAN,
        Flowers Without Fruit

8016. Seeing's believing, but feeling's
the truth.   *Proverb*

8017.

Some feelings are to mortals given,
With less of earth in them than
  heaven.   SCOTT,
    The Lady of the Lake

8018. It is high time, it seems to me,
that a moral game-law were passed
for the preservation of the wild and
vagrant feelings of human nature.
      SMITH, *Dreamthorp*

See also: 1178, 1212, 2031, 9806,
15127, 21550.

FICKLENESS

**Related Subjects: Chance, Change,
Constancy, Coquetry, Fidelity,
Resolution, Variety.**

8021. Had sigh'd to many, though he
loved but one.   BYRON,
      Childe Harold

8022. I'm going away to-day with a
handsomer man than you.
      WILL CARLETON,
    Gone With a Handsomer Man

8023.

How happy could I be with either,
Were t'other dear charmer away!
    JOHN GAY, *The Beggar's Opera*

8024.

I know I am but summer to your
  heart,
And not the full four seasons of the
  year.
    EDNA ST. VINCENT MILLAY,
        Two Seasons

8025.

And if I loved you Wednesday,
  Well, what is that to you?
I do not love you Thursday—
  So much is true.
    EDNA ST. VINCENT MILLAY,
        Thursday

8026.

'Tis sweet to think, that, where'er we
  rove,
  We are sure to find something bliss-
    ful and dear ;
And that when we're far from the
  lips we love,
  We've but to make love to the lips
    we are near.
THOMAS MOORE, *'Tis Sweet to Think*

8027.

My merry, merry merry roundelay
  Concludes with Cupid's curse ;
They that do change old love for new,
  Pray gods, they change for worse !
    GEORGE PEELE, *Cupid's Curse*

8028. The fickleness of women I
love is only equaled by the infernal
constancy of the women who love me.
  BERNARD SHAW, *The Philanderer*

8029. The only difference between a caprice and a lifelong passion is that the caprice lasts a little longer.
OSCAR WILDE,
The Picture of Dorian Gray

See also: 21, 12188.

FICTION

Related Subjects: Authors, Books, Tale, Truth, Writing.

8031. The phantasmagorical world of novels and of opium.
MATTHEW ARNOLD,
Literature and Dogma

8032.
True fiction hath a higher end, and scope
Wider than fact; it is nature's possible,
Contrasted with life's actual mean.
PHILIP J. BAILEY, *Festus*

8033. In the march up to the heights of fame there comes a spot close to the summit in which a man reads "nothing but detective stories." It is the Antaean touch which distinguishes all Olympians.
HEYWOOD BROUN, *G. K. C.*

8034.
When we risk no contradiction,
It prompts the tongue to deal in fiction. JOHN GAY,
The Elephant & the Bookseller

8035. Novels (receipts to make a whore). MATTHEW GREEN,
The Spleen

8036. Fictions meant to please should be close to the real. HORACE,
Ars Poetica

8037. A little attention to the nature of the human mind evinces that the entertainments of fiction are useful as well as pleasant. JEFFERSON

8038. Where there is leisure for fiction there is little grief.
SAMUEL JOHNSON

8039. Character in decay is the theme of the great bulk of superior fiction.
H. L. MENCKEN, *Prejudices*

8040. The first thing will be to have a censorship of the writers of fiction, to accept the good and reject the bad.
PLATO, *The Republic*

8041. Make them laugh, make them cry, make them wait.
CHARLES READE,
Recipe for Writing Novels

8042. The reason that fiction is more interesting than any other form of literature to those of us who really like to study people, is that in fiction the author can really tell the truth without hurting anyone and without humiliating himself too much.
ELEANOR ROOSEVELT

8043. If this were played upon a stage now, I could condemn it as an improbable fiction.
SHAKESPEARE, *Twelfth Night*

8044. The most influential books, and the truest in their influence, are works of fiction. STEVENSON

8045. Fiction carries a greater amount of truth in solution than the volume which purports to be all true.
THACKERAY,
The English Humourists

8046. The only real people are the people who never existed.
OSCAR WILDE, *The Decay of Lying*

See also: 5611, 11972, 13977, 20179, 20181.

FIDELITY AND INFIDELITY

Related Subjects: Adultery, Cheating, Constancy, Cuckold, Faith, Fickleness, Loyalty, Martyr, Virtue.

8051.
Ah, love, let us be true
To one another!
MATTHEW ARNOLD, *Dover Beach*

8052. *Jupiter:* You know, Mercury, most faithful wives are unfaithful to their husbands with everything except men; with jewels, with perfumes, with reading, with religion and with the contemplation of Spring, with everything in fact, except a man.
S. N. BEHRMAN, *Amphitryon 38*

8053. Be thou faithful unto death.
Bible: Revelation, ii, 10

8054.
I have been faithful to thee, Cynara! in my fashion.
ERNEST DOWSON, *Cynara*

8055.
The temper of chums, the love of your wife, and a new piano's tune—
Which of the three will you trust at the end of an Indian June?
KIPLING, *Certain Maxims of Hafiz*

8056.
No, the heart that has truly lov'd never forgets,
But as truly loves on to the close;
As the sunflower turns on her god, when he sets,
The same look which she turn'd when he rose.
THOMAS MOORE,
*Believe Me, if all Those
Endearing Young Charms*

8057.
Then if my friendships break and bend,
There's little need to cry

The while I know that every foe
Is faithful till I die.
DOROTHY PARKER, *The Leal*

See also: 907, 3349, 19134.

FIGHT, FIGHTING

Related Subjects: Dueling, Sword, War.

8061. Fight the good fight.
Bible: 1 Timothy, vi, 12

8062. I have fought a good fight, I have finished my course, I have kept the faith. *Bible: 2 Timothy, iv, 7*

8063.
When the fight begins within himself,
A man's worth something.
BROWNING,
Bishop Blougram's Apology

8064.
Strike—till the last armed foe expires;
Strike—for your altars and your fires;
Strike—for the green graves of your sires;
God—and your native land!
FITZ-GREENE HALLECK,
Marco Bozzaris

8065. You should never wear your best trousers when you go out to fight for freedom and truth.
IBSEN, *An Enemy of the People*

8066. I have not yet begun to fight.
JOHN PAUL JONES

8067. Friends, how goes the fight?
MACAULAY,
The Battle of Lake Regillus

8068. But the truth is—and that is the fatal paradox—we mortals are so pathetically heroic that it will have to be made clear to us that it is more heroic to fight against fighting than to fight, before we have the guts to defy these leaders who, after all, are only ourselves turned into prime ministers and dictators.

J. C. Powys, *Autobiography*

8069. Fight till the last gasp.
SHAKESPEARE, *Henry VI*

8070.
Lay on, Macduff,
And damn'd be him that first cries
"Hold, enough!"
SHAKESPEARE, *Macbeth*

8071.
"Oh, anywhere! Forward! 'Tis all the same, Colonel:
You'll find lovely fighting along the whole line!" E. C. STEDMAN,
Kearny at Seven Pines

8072. A man will fight for himself because if he does not he will go under. JOHN STRACHEY, *I Believe*

See also: 3907, 15045, 15964, 21551.

FINANCE

Related Subjects: Business, Commerce, Corporations, Economy, Inflation, Profit.

8081. The plain high-road of finance.
BURKE, *On American Taxation*

8082. What good, honest, generous men at home will be wolves and foxes on change!
EMERSON, *Conduct of Life*

8083. This bank-note world.
FITZ-GREENE HALLECK,
Alnwick Castle

8084. These heroes of finance are like beads on a string—when one slips off, all the rest follow.
IBSEN, *A Doll's House*

8085. I sincerely believe that banking establishments are more dangerous than standing armies, and that the principle of spending money to be paid by posterity, under the name of funding, is but swindling futurity on a large scale. JEFFERSON

8086. One-third of the people in the United States promote, while the other two-thirds provide.
WILL ROGERS, *The Illiterate Digest*

8087. Economic Royalists.
Expression coined by FRANKLIN D.
ROOSEVELT *in his Addresses*

8088. Let him look to his bond.
SHAKESPEARE,
The Merchant of Venice

8089. Our present system of "high finance" is a soap-bubble, which differs from other soap-bubbles in just one respect—it is as big as the world.
UPTON SINCLAIR

8090. The American banking system is the most perfect contrivance yet devised by the human brain for making the rich richer and the poor poorer. UPTON SINCLAIR

8091. Where are the c-c-c-customers' yachts? W. R. TRAVERS,
When shown the broker's yachts anchored off the foot of Wall St.

8092. The way to stop financial joyriding is to arrest the chauffeur, not the automobile. WOODROW WILSON

See also: 1483.

FINGERS

Related Subject: Hand.

8101. From his ambitious finger.
SHAKESPEARE, *Henry VIII*

8102. At my fingers' ends.
SHAKESPEARE, *Twelfth Night*

8103. Fingers were made before forks, and hands before knives.

SWIFT, *Polite Conversation*

See also: 2509, 19815.

FIRE

Related Subjects: Coal, Warmth.

8111. Can a man take fire in his bosom, and his clothes not be burned?

Bible: Proverbs, vi, 27

8112. The hand that kindles cannot quench the flame. BYRON, *Lara*

8113. Fire is the best of servants; but what a master!

CARLYLE, *Past and Present*

8114. Three removes are as bad as a fire. FRANKLIN, *Poor Richard*

8115. A fireside is a great opiate.

LEIGH HUNT, *A Few Thoughts on Sleep*

8116. There can be no great smoke arise, but there must be some fire.

JOHN LYLY, *Euphues and his Euphoebus*

8117.
A little fire is quickly trodden out; Which, being suffered, rivers cannot quench.

SHAKESPEARE, *Henry VI*

8118. Fire is the most tolerable third party. THOREAU, *Journal*

See also: 876, 1282, 3823, 7454, 10225, 18125.

FIRMNESS

Related Subjects: Decision, Resolution, Strength, Will.

8121. Firmness, both in suffering and exertion, is a character which I would wish to possess. I have always despised the whining yelp of complaint, and the cowardly feeble resolve. BURNS

8122. I will neither yield to the song of the siren nor the voice of the hyena, the tears of the crocodile nor the howling of the wolf.

GEORGE CHAPMAN, *Eastward Ho*

8123. Firmness of purpose is one of the most necessary sinews of character, and one of the best instruments of success. Without it genius wastes its efforts in a maze of inconsistencies. LORD CHESTERFIELD

8124. Not to go back is somewhat to advance. HORACE

8125. The firm, without pliancy, and the pliant, without firmness, resemble vessels without water, and water without vessels. LAVATER

8126. I hope to stand firm enough not to go backward. LINCOLN

8127. The greatest firmness is the greatest mercy. LONGFELLOW

8128. When firmness is sufficient, rashness is unnecessary. NAPOLEON

8129. The purpose firm is equal to the deed. EDWARD YOUNG

See also: 8884.

FISH AND FISHING

Related Subjects: Oyster, River, Sea, Sport, Water.

8131. Here's a pretty kettle of fish!

W. S. GILBERT, *Iolanthe*

8132. Fish dinners will make a man spring like a flea. THOMAS JORDAN

8133. Fish are not to be caught with a bird-call. *Proverb*

8134. It is good fish, if it were but caught. *Proverb*

8135. It is good fishing in troubled waters.   *Proverb*

8136. Still he fisheth that catcheth one.   *Proverb*

8137. A hook's well lost to catch a salmon.   *Proverb*

8138. It's no fish ye're buying, it's men's lives.   SCOTT, *The Antiquary*

8139. Bait the hook well; this fish will bite.   SHAKESPEARE,
Much Ado About Nothing

8140.
The pleasant'st angling is to see the fish
Cut with her golden oars the silver stream,
And greedily devour the treacherous bait.   SHAKESPEARE,
Much Ado About Nothing

8141.
3rd Fisherman. Master, I marvel how the fishes live in the sea.
1st Fisherman. Why, as men do a-land; the great ones eat up the little ones.   SHAKESPEARE,
Pericles

8142.
Oh, the gallant fisher's life!
   It is the best of any;
'Tis full of pleasure, void of strife,
   And 'tis beloved by many.
     IZAAK WALTON, *The Angler*

8143. We may say of angling as Dr. Boteler said of strawberries: "Doubtless God could have made a better berry, but doubtless God never did;" and so, if I might be judge, God never did make a more calm, quiet, innocent recreation than angling.
     IZAAK WALTON,
The Compleat Angler

8144. An excellent angler, and now with God.   *Ibid.*

8145. You will find angling to be like the virtue of humility, which has a calmness of spirit and a world of other blessings attending upon it.
     IZAAK WALTON,
The Compleat Angler

8146. Doubt not but angling will prove to be so pleasant that it will prove to be, like virtue, a reward to itself.   *Ibid.*

8147. As no man is born an artist, so no man is born an angler.   *Ibid.*

8148. Angling may be said to be like the mathematics that it can never be fully learnt.   *Ibid.*

8149. I have laid aside business, and gone a-fishing.   *Ibid.*

See also: 3301, 8198, 9414, 11255, 14256, 14565, 16402.

FLAG

Related Subject: Patriotism.

8151. A thoughtful mind, when it sees a Nation's flag, sees not the flag only, but the Nation itself; and whatever may be its symbols, its insignia, he reads chiefly in the flag the Government, the principles, the truths, the history which belong to the Nation that sets it forth.
H. W. BEECHER, *The American Flag*

8152. I pledge allegiance to the flag of the United States and to the republic for which it stands, one nation, indivisible, with liberty and justice for all.   F. M. BELLAMY,
The Pledge of Allegiance to the Flag

8153. If any one attempts to haul down the American flag, shoot him on the spot.   JOHN ADAMS DIX

8154.
And the star-spangled banner, oh long may it wave

O'er the land of the free and the home of the brave.

FRANCIS S. KEY,
The Star-Spangled Banner

8155. There is the National flag. He must be cold, indeed, who can look upon its folds rippling in the breeze without pride of country. If in a foreign land, the flag is companionship, and country itself, with all its endearments.

CHARLES SUMNER,
Are We a Nation?

8156.
"Shoot, if you must, this old gray head,
But spare your country's flag," she said.

WHITTIER, *Barbara Frietchie*

8157. The things that the flag stands for were created by the experiences of a great people. Everything that it stands for was written by their lives. The flag is the embodiment, not of sentiment, but of history. It represents the experiences made by men and women, the experiences of those who do and live under that flag.

WOODROW WILSON

See also: 1260, 1483, 20759.

FLATTERY

Related Subjects: **Compliment, Deceit, Praise, Trickery, Vanity.**

8161. Woe unto you, when all men shall speak well of you!

Bible: Luke, vi, 26

8162. And wrinkles (the damned democrats) won't flatter.

BYRON, *Don Juan*

8163. There is no greater bane to friendship than adulation, fawning, and flattery. CICERO, *De Amicitia*

8164. To ask advice is in nine cases out of ten to tout for flattery.

CHURTON COLLINS, *Maxims*

8165.
'Tis hard to find a man of great estate,
That can distinguish flatterers from friends. HORACE

8166. Madam, before you flatter a man so grossly to his face, you should consider whether your flattery is worth his having.

SAMUEL JOHNSON

8167. Men are not flattered by being shown that there has been a difference of purpose between the Almighty and them. LINCOLN

8168. Flatterers haunt not cottages.
Proverb

8169. He that rewards flattery, begs it.
Proverb

8170. He that is open to flattery is fenced against admonition.
Proverb

8171. If we did not flatter ourselves, nobody else could. *Proverb*

8172. Flattery displays a braver flag than humility. *Proverb*

8173. Flattery sits in the parlour, when plain dealing is kicked out of doors. *Proverb*

8174. Lay not that flattering unction to your soul. SHAKESPEARE, *Hamlet*

8175.
No; let the candied tongue lick absurd pomp,
And crook the pregnant hinges of the knee
Where thrift may follow fawning.
SHAKESPEARE, *Hamlet*

8176.
But when I tell him he hates flatterers,
He says he does, being then most flattered.
SHAKESPEARE, *Julius Caesar*

8177. Flattery is like friendship in show, but not in fruit.   SOCRATES

8178. None are more taken in by flattery than the proud, who wish to be the first and are not.
SPINOZA, *Ethics*

8179. Among all the diseases of the mind there is not one more epidemical or more pernicious than the love of flattery.
SIR RICHARD STEELE, *The Spectator*

8180.
'Tis an old maxim in the schools,
That flattery's the food of fools;
Yet now and then your men of wit
Will condescend to take a bit.
SWIFT, *Cadenus and Vanessa*

8181. Self-love is the greatest of all flatterers.   VOLTAIRE

See also: 158, 1064, 4371, 10393, 15418.

FLESH

Related Subjects: **Body, Bone, Devil, Father, Sin, Skin, Weight.**

8191. All flesh is grass.
Bible: Isaiah, xl, 6

8192. The world, the flesh, and the devil.   *Book of Common Prayer*

8193. Alas! It is my fate. The flesh, in my cosmos, is a little thing. It is the soul that is everything. I love the flesh as the Greeks loved it, and yet it is a form of love that is almost, if not quite, artistic in nature.
JACK LONDON

8194. Her fair and unpolluted flesh.
SHAKESPEARE, *Hamlet*

8195. Such is the simplicity of man to hearken after the flesh.
SHAKESPEARE,
Love's Labour's Lost

8196.
The words expressly are "a pound of flesh;"
Take then thy bond, take thou thy pound of flesh. SHAKESPEARE,
The Merchant of Venice

8197. As pretty a piece of flesh as any is in Messina.
SHAKESPEARE,
Much Ado About Nothing

8198. O flesh, flesh, how art thou fishified!
SHAKESPEARE, *Romeo and Juliet*

8199. As witty a piece of Eve's flesh as any in Illyria.
SHAKESPEARE, *Twelfth Night*

8200. I saw him now going the way of all flesh.
JOHN WEBSTER, *Westward Ho!*

See also: 20852, 20954.

FLIGHT

Related Subjects: **Defeat, Fear, Retreat.**

8201. In fleeing the ashes he's fallen into the coals.   ALCAEUS

8202. The wicked flee when no man pursueth; but the righteous are bold as a lion.   *Bible: Proverbs, xxviii, 1*

8203.
For those that fly may fight again,
Which he can never do that's slain.
SAMUEL BUTLER, *Hudibras*

8204. And brave men fled who never fled before.
G. H. CALVERT, *Bunker Hill*

8205. Love is conquered only by flight. Against such an enemy, true courage consists in fear and retreat, in retreat without deliberation, and without looking back.
FENELON, *Telemachus*

8206.
For he who fights and runs away
May live to fight another day;
But he who is in battle slain
Can never rise and fight again.
GOLDSMITH,
The Art of Poetry on a New Plan

8207. He who flees from trial confesses his guilt.
PUBLILIUS SYRUS, *Sententiae*

8208. Let us fly and save our bacon.
RABELAIS

8209. Show it a fair pair of heels and run for it. SHAKESPEARE, *Henry IV*

8210.
To fly the boar before the boar pursues,
Were to incense the boar to follow us
And make pursuit where he did mean no chase.
SHAKESPEARE, *Richard III*

8211. I girded up my Lions and fled the Seen. ARTEMUS WARD,
A Visit to Brigham Young

See also: 1658, 4911, 13801.

FLIRTATION, see Coquetry

FLOWERS

Related Subjects: **Bee, Country, Dew, Garden, Hyacinth, Lilac, Lily, Lotus, Park, Poppy, Rose, Spring, Sunflower, Violet, Weed.**

8221.
The daisy lives, and strikes its little root

Into the lap of time: centuries may come,
And pass away into the silent tomb,
And still the child, hid in the womb of time,
Shall smile and pluck them, when this simple rhyme
Shall be forgotten.
JOHN CLARE, *The Daisy's Eternity*

8222. The Flower that once has blown forever dies.
OMAR KHAYYAM, *Rubaiyat*

8223. Say it with flowers.
P. F. O'KEEFE,
Slogan for the Society of American Florists

8224. One flower makes no garland.
Proverb

8225. There's rosemary, that's for remembrance; . . . and there is pansies, that's for thoughts.
SHAKESPEARE, *Hamlet*

8226. I know a bank whereon the wild thyme blows.
SHAKESPEARE,
A Midsummer-Night's Dream

8227.
When you walk in a field,
Look down
Lest you tramp
On a daisy's crown!
JAMES STEPHENS, *When You Walk*

8228.
To me the meanest flower that blows can give
Thoughts that do often lie too deep for tears. WORDSWORTH,
Ode on Intimations of Immortality

8229.
A primrose by a river's brim
A yellow primrose was to him,
And it was nothing more.
WORDSWORTH, *Peter Bell*

See also: 1537, 1687, 1967, 3267.

FLY

8231. Dead flies cause the ointment of the apothecary to send forth a stinking savour: so doth a little folly him that is in reputation for wisdom and honour. *Bible: Ecclesiastes, x, 1*

8232.
The wanton boy that kills a fly
Shall feel the spider's enmity.
BLAKE, *Auguries of Innocence*

8233. A fly is as untamable as a hyena. EMERSON, *Conduct of Life*

8234. An actually existing fly is more important than a possibly existing angel. EMERSON

8235. The fly that sips treacle is lost in the sweets.
JOHN GAY, *The Beggar's Opera*

8236. I killed a fly this morning—it buzzed, and I wouldn't have it!
W. S. GILBERT, *Ruddigore*

8237. And so we plough along, as the fly said to the ox.
LONGFELLOW, *The Spanish Student*

8238. Flies come to feasts unasked.
Proverb

8239. To a boiling pot flies come not.
Proverb

8240. King James said to the fly,
Have I three kingdoms, and thou must needs fly into my eye?
JOHN SELDEN, *Table-Talk*

8241.
Though he in a fertile climate dwell,
Plague him with flies.
SHAKESPEARE, *Othello*

8242. As willingly as one would kill a fly.
SHAKESPEARE, *Titus Andronicus*

8243.
Baby bye, Here's a fly,
Let us watch him, you and I,

How he crawls up the walls
Yet he never falls.
THEODORE TILTON, *Baby Bye*

See also: 611, 3840.

FOG

Related Subjects: Clouds, Obscurity, Rain, Storm, Weather.

8251.
Wrapped in a cloak
Of grey mystery
Fog, the Magician,
Steals tip-toe out of the sea.
MELVILLE CANE, *Fog, the Magician*

8252. This is a London particular— a fog, miss. DICKENS, *Bleak House*

8253. A fog cannot be dispelled by a fan. *Proverb*

8254.
The fog comes
on little cat feet.
It sits looking
over the harbor and city
on silent haunches
and then, moves on.
CARL SANDBURG, *Fog*

8255. To lose itself in a fog.
SHAKESPEARE, *Coriolanus*

8256.
The starry welkin cover thou anon
With drooping fog as black as Acheron. SHAKESPEARE,
A Midsummer-Night's Dream

FOOD

Related Subjects: Appetite, Bread, Cooks, Diet, Digestion, Dining, Drink, Eating, Hunger, Inn, Meat.

8261. I suppose there is plenty to eat somewhere if you can find it; the cat always does.
ERSKINE CALDWELL,
You Have Seen Their Faces

8262. What is food to one man may be fierce poison to others.

　　Lucretius, *De Rerum Natura*

8263. i have noticed that when chickens quit quarrelling over their food they often find that there is enough for all of them i wonder if it might not be the same way with the human race　　Don Marquis,
　　archys life of mehitabel

8264.
　　　　　　The gods sent not
Corn for the rich men only.
　　Shakespeare, *Coriolanus*

8265.
But mice, and rats, and such small deer,
Have been Tom's food for seven long year.　　Shakespeare, *King Lear*

8266. The food that to him now is as luscious as locusts, shall be to him shortly as bitter as coloquintida.
　　Shakespeare, *Othello*

See also: 8982.

FOOL, FOLLY

Related Subjects: **Absurdities, Goose, Mockery, Nonsense, Ridicule.**

8271. A prosperous fool is a grievous burden.　　Aeschylus

8272. Answer a fool according to his folly.　　*Bible: Proverbs, xxvi, 5*

8273. And every one that heareth these sayings of mine, and doeth them not, shall be likened unto a foolish man, which built his house upon the sand: And the rain descended, and the floods came, and the winds blew, and beat upon that house; and it fell: and great was the fall of it.
　　Bible: Matthew, vii, 26, 27

8274. God hath chosen the foolish things of the world to confound the wise; and God hath chosen the weak things of the world to confound the things which are mighty.
　　Bible: 1 Corinthians, i, 27

8275. If others had not been foolish, we should be so.
　　Blake, *Proverbs of Hell*

8276. The most artful part in a play is the fool's.
　　Cervantes, *Don Quixote*

8277.
Young men think old men are fools;
But old men know young men are fools.　　George Chapman,
　　All Fools

8278. Nobody can describe a fool to the life, without much patient self-inspection. Frank M. Colby, *Essays*

8279. A fool must now and then be right by chance.
　　Cowper, *Conversation*

8280. I love fools' experiments. I am always making them.　　Darwin

8281.
This age thinks better of a gilded fool
Than of a threadbare saint in wisdom's school.
　　Thomas Dekker, *Old Fortunatus*

8282.
A fool there was and he made his prayer
　　(Even as you and I!)
To a rag and a bone and a hank of hair.
　　(We called her the woman who did not care)
But the fool he called her his lady fair—
　　(Even as you and I!)
　　Kipling, *The Vampire*

8283. Look ye, pudding-heads should never grant premises.
HERMAN MELVILLE, *Moby Dick*

8284. To foolish men belongeth a love for things afar. PINDAR, *Paean*

8285. For fools rush in where angels fear to tread.
POPE, *Essay on Criticism*

8286. No creature smarts so little as a fool.
POPE, *Epistle to Dr. Arbuthnot*

8287. He who is born a fool is never cured.   *Proverb*

8288. If wise men play the fool, they do it with a vengeance.   *Proverb*

8289. He is na the fool that the fool is, but he that wi' the fool deals.
Proverb

8290. A fool may make money, but it requires a wise man to spend it.
Proverb

8291. No one is a fool always, every one sometimes.   *Proverb*

8292. Unless a fool knows latin he is never a great fool.   *Proverb*

8293. If fools went not to market, bad wares would not be sold. *Proverb*

8294. Fools grow without watering.
Proverb

8295. A fool's bolt may sometimes hit the mark.   *Proverb*

8296. Let a fool hold his tongue and he will pass for a sage.
PUBLILIUS SYRUS, *Sententiae*

8297. Always the dulness of the fool is the whetstone of the wits.
SHAKESPEARE, *As You Like It*

8298. I had rather have a fool to make me merry than experience to make me sad.
SHAKESPEARE, *As You Like It*

8299. The fool doth think he is wise, but the wise man knows himself to be a fool.
SHAKESPEARE, *As You Like It*

8300. Here comes a pair of very strange beasts, which in all tongues are called fools.
SHAKESPEARE, *As You Like It*

8301. How ill white hairs become a fool and jester.
SHAKESPEARE, *Henry IV*

8302. Lord, what fools these mortals be! SHAKESPEARE,
A Midsummer-Night's Dream

8303. O that he were here to write me down an ass! SHAKESPEARE,
Much Ado About Nothing

8304. A fool's paradise.
SHAKESPEARE, *Romeo and Juliet*

8305. Foolery, sir, does walk about the orb like the sun, it shines everywhere.   SHAKESPEARE,
Twelfth Night

8306.
But of all burdens, that a man can beare,
Moste is, a fooles talke to beare and to heare. EDMUND SPENSER,
The Shepheardes Calender

8307. Give me the young man who has brains enough to make a fool of himself.   STEVENSON,
Virginibus Puerisque

Folly

8308. A good folly is worth what you pay for it.   GEORGE ADE,
Fables in Slang

8309. The folly of one man is the fortune of another. BACON, *Essays*

8310. Folly in youth is sin, in age 'tis madness. SAMUEL DANIEL,
The Tragedy of Cleopatra

8311. The folly of others is ever most ridiculous to those who are themselves most foolish.
GOLDSMITH,
The Citizen of the World

8312. The chief disease that reigns this year is folly.
GEORGE HERBERT,
Jacula Prudentum

8313. Who lives without folly is not so wise as he thinks.
LA ROCHEFOUCAULD,
Maxims

8314. Happy is the man who sees his folly in his youth.   *Proverb*

8315. A man's folly ought to be his greatest secret.   *Proverb*

8316. The most exquisite folly is made of wisdom too fine spun.
Proverb

8317. Natural folly is bad enough; but learned folly is intolerable.
Proverb

8318. The common curse of mankind—folly and ignorance.
SHAKESPEARE,
Troilus and Cressida

8319. Foolery, sir, does walk about the orb like the sun; it shines everywhere.   SHAKESPEARE,
Twelfth Night

8320.
You may as well
Forbid the sea for to obey the moon,
As or by oath remove or counsel shake
The fabric of his folly.
SHAKESPEARE,
The Winter's Tale

8321. Folly is the direct pursuit of Happiness and Beauty.
BERNARD SHAW,
Maxims for Revolutionists

See also: 105, 263, 271, 385, 866, 878, 982, 1084, 1193, 1326, 1332, 1343, 1607, 2434, 2963, 2978, 4653, 4779, 4844, 5448, 7225, 7984, 8231, 10325, 11518, 11571, 12672, 14929, 15158, 16924, 17482, 17912, 19053, 20195, 21469.

FOOT

Related Subjects: **Leg, Shoe, Walking.**

8331.
My feet, they haul me Round the House,
  They Hoist me up the Stairs;
I only have to steer them, and
  They Ride me Everywheres.
GELETT BURGESS, *My Feet*

8332.
Her treading would not bend a blade of grass
Or shake the downy blue-ball from his stalk,
And where she went, the flowers took thickest root,
As she had sow'd them with her odorous foot.   BEN JONSON,
The Sad Shepherd

8333. Feet that run on willing errands!   LONGFELLOW, *Hiawatha*

8334.
A foot more light, a step more true,
Ne'er from the heath-flower dashed the dew;
E'en the slight harebell raised its head,
Elastic from her airy tread.
SCOTT, *The Lady of the Lake*

8335. Toes unplagu'd with corns.
SHAKESPEARE, *Romeo and Juliet*

8336.
Here comes the lady! O, so light a foot

Will ne'er wear out the everlasting
flint.   SHAKESPEARE,
                    Romeo and Juliet

8337. Nay, her foot speaks.
                SHAKESPEARE,
            Troilus and Cressida

8338.
O happy earth,
Whereon thy innocent feet do ever
tread!   EDMUND SPENSER,
                The Faerie Queene

8339.
Her feet beneath her petticoat,
Like little mice, stole in and out,
    As if they feared the light.
        SIR JOHN SUCKLING,
            A Ballad Upon a Wedding

See also: 2664, 6772.

FOP

**Related Subjects: Affectation,
Courtier, Elegance, Fashion, Snob,
Vanity.**

8341.
Foppery atones
For folly, gallantry for ev'ry vice.
            COWPER, *The Task*

8342.
The solemn fop; significant and
    budge;
A fool with judges, amongst fools a
    judge.   COWPER,
                Conversation

8343.
True fops help nature's work, and
    go to school
To file and finish God Almighty's
    fool.   DRYDEN, *Men of Mode*

8344.
A greenery-yallery, Grosvenor Gal-
lery
Foot-in-the-grave young man!
            W. S. GILBERT, *Patience*

8345.
There's Bardus, a six-foot column of
    fop,
A lighthouse without any light atop.
            THOMAS HOOD,
                Miss Kilmansegg

8346.
Nature made ev'ry fop to plague his
    brother,
Just as one beauty mortifies another.
                POPE,
        Satires of Dr. John Donne

8347. A fop of fashion is the mercer's
friend, the tailor's fool, and his own
foe.   *Proverb*

8348.
He was perfumed like a milliner;
And 'twixt his finger and his thumb
    he held
A pouncet-box, which ever and anon
He gave his nose, and took 't away
    again.   SHAKESPEARE,
                    Henry IV

8349. A beardless boy, A cocker'd
silken wanton.   SHAKESPEARE,
                    King John

8350. The weathy curled darlings of
our nation.
            SHAKESPEARE, *Othello*

8351. A man who can dominate a
London dinner table can dominate the
world. The future belongs to the
dandy. It is the exquisites who are
going to rule.   OSCAR WILDE,
            A Woman of No Importance

See also: 756.

FORCE

**Related Subjects: Energy, Im-
pulse, Might, Necessity, Power,
Strength, Violence, War.**

8361. Force is no remedy.
                JOHN BRIGHT,
                On the Irish Troubles

8362. What force cannot effect, fraud shall devise.

RICHARD CRASHAW,
Sospetto d'Herode

8363. Force is of brutes.

DRYDEN, *Palamon and Arcite*

8364. We love force and we care very little how it is exhibited.

EMERSON, *Journal*

8365. What about force, though? ... Doesn't all society rest on force? If a government can't count upon the police and the army, how can it hope to rule? And if an individual gets knocked on the head or sent to a labor camp, of what significance are his opinions? E. M. FORSTER,
I Believe

8366. Force works on servile natures, not the free. BEN JONSON,
Every Man in His Humour

8367.
Who overcomes
By force hath overcome but half his foe. MILTON, *Paradise Lost*

8368. Every body perseveres in its state of rest or of uniform motion in a straight line, except in so far as it is compelled to change that state by impressed forces.

SIR ISAAC NEWTON,
First Law of Motion

8369. Force without fore-cast is of little avail. *Proverb*

8370.
Men must reap the things they sow,
Force from force must ever flow.
SHELLEY,
*Lines Written Among the
Euganean Hills*

8371. Hence no force, however great, can stretch a cord, however fine, into

a horizontal line which is accurately straight. WILLIAM WHEWELL,
*Elementary Treatise on Mechanics.
(A celebrated instance of accidental
versification)*

See also: 147, 252, 1870, 8886, 11336.

FOREIGNERS

Related Subject: Novelty.

8381. I have been a stranger in a strange land.

Bible: Exodus, ii, 22

8382. An English lady on the Rhine hearing a German speaking of her party as foreigners, exclaimed, "No, we are not foreigners; we are English; it is you that are foreigners."

EMERSON, *English Traits*

8383. And I'll wager in their joy they kissed each other's cheek
(Which is what them furriners do).
W. S. GILBERT, *Ruddigore*

8384. People have prejudices against a nation in which they have no acquaintance.

PHILIP HAMERTON,
Modern Frenchmen

8385.
Father, Mother and Me,
Sister and Auntie say
All the people like us are We,
And every one else is They.
KIPLING, *We and They*

8386. Hope nothing from foreign governments. They will never be really willing to aid you until you have shown that you are strong enough to conquer without them.
MAZZINI, *Life and Writings*

8387.
At the gate of the West I stand,
On the isle where the nations throng,
We call them "scum o' the earth."
R. H. SCHAUFFLER,
Scum o' the Earth

8388. A foreigner can photograph the exteriors of a nation, but I think that is as far as he can get. No foreigner can report its interior—its soul, its life, its speech, its thought.
MARK TWAIN,
What Paul Bourget Thinks of Us

8389. They spell it Vinci and pronounce it Vinchy; foreigners always spell better than they pronounce.
MARK TWAIN,
Innocents Abroad
See also: 708, 3612.

FOREST

Related Subjects: Animal, Country, Nature, Tree.

8391. The groves were God's first temples. BRYANT, *A Forest Hymn*

8392. Among the scenes which are deeply impressed on my mind, none exceed in sublimity the primeval forests undefaced by the hand of man. No one can stand in these solitudes unmoved, and not feel that there is more in man than the mere breath of his body. DARWIN

8393. This is the forest primeval.
LONGFELLOW, *Evangeline*

8394.
Woods have tongues
As walls have ears.
TENNYSON, *Idylls of the King*

8395. The whole wood-world is one full peal of praise. TENNYSON,
Idylls of the King

8396. I went to the woods because I wished to live deliberately, to front only the essential facts of life, and see if I could not learn what it had to teach, and not, when I came to die, discover that I had not lived.
THOREAU, *Walden*

8397.
One impulse from a vernal wood
May teach you more of man,
Of moral evil and of good,
Than all the sages can.
WORDSWORTH,
The Tables Turned
See also: 2884.

FORGETFULNESS

Related Subjects: Forgiveness, Gratitude, Memory, Neglect, Oblivion.

8401.
My mind lets go a thousand things,
Like dates of wars and deaths of kings. T. B. ALDRICH,
Memory

8402. Life cannot go on without much forgetting. BALZAC

8403.
I have forgot much, Cynara! gone with the wind,
Flung roses, roses riotously with the throng. ERNEST DOWSON,
Cynara
(*Source of title of novel by Margaret Mitchell*)

8404. Lest we forget—lest we forget!
KIPLING, *Recessional*

8405. I have confessed to you my utter inability to remember in any comprehensive way what I read. I can vehemently applaud, or perversely stickle, at *parts;* but I cannot grasp at a whole. CHARLES LAMB

8406.
Were it not better to forget
Than but remember and regret?
L. E. LANDON, *Despondency*

8407. Blessed are the forgetful: for they get the better even of their blunders. NIETZSCHE,
Beyond Good and Evil

8408. We have all forgotten more than we remember.   *Proverb*

8409. Forgetting of a wrong is a mild revenge.   *Proverb*

8410. It is sometimes expedient to forget who we are.
PUBLILIUS SYRUS, *Sententiae*

8411. We may with advantage at times forget what we know.
PUBLILIUS SYRUS, *Sententiae*

See also: 35, 53, 402, 855, 2073, 2074, 2545, 4586, 6734, 12479, 15750, 15945.

FORGIVENESS

Related Subjects: Compassion, Excuse, Forgetfulness, Mercy.

8421. They who forgive most shall be most forgiven.
PHILIP J. BAILEY, *Festus*

8422. "I can forgive, but I cannot forget," is only another way of saying, "I cannot forgive."
H. W. BEECHER, *Life Thoughts*

8423.
And throughout all Eternity
I forgive you, you forgive me.
BLAKE, *Broken Love*

8424. Now may the good God pardon all good men!
ELIZABETH B. BROWNING,
Aurora Leigh

8425.
But to have power to forgive,
Is empire and prerogative;
And 'tis in crowns a nobler gem
To grant a pardon than condemn.
SAMUEL BUTLER, *Hudibras*

8426. He who forgives readily only invites offense.   CORNEILLE, *Cinna*

8427.
Forgiveness to the injured doth belong,
But they ne'er pardon who have done the wrong.   DRYDEN,
Conquest of Granada

8428. Bless the hand that gave the blow.   DRYDEN, *The Spanish Friar*

8429. God may forgive you, but I never can.
QUEEN ELIZABETH, *to the Countess of Nottingham.*

8430. Forgiveness is better than revenge; for forgiveness is the sign of a gentle nature, but revenge the sign of a savage nature.
EPICTETUS, *Discourses*

8431. Nobuddy ever fergits where he buried a hatchet.   KIN HUBBARD

8432. We pardon in the degree that we love.   LA ROCHEFOUCAULD,
Maxims

8433. A brave man thinks no one is superior who does him an injury; for he has it then in his power to make himself superior to the other by forgiving it.   POPE,
Thoughts on Various Subjects

8434.
Only heaven
Means crowned, not conquered, when it says "Forgiven."
ADELAIDE A. PROCTOR,
A Legend of Provence

8435. Forgive any sooner than thyself.   *Proverb*

8436. An injury forgiven is better than an injury avenged.   *Proverb*

8437. Pardon's the word to all.
SHAKESPEARE, *Cymbeline*

8438. May one be pardoned, and retain the offence?
SHAKESPEARE, *Hamlet*

8439. Pray you now, forget and forgive.　SHAKESPEARE, *King Lear*

8440. I pardon him, as God shall pardon me.　SHAKESPEARE, *Richard II*

8441. Not to relent is beastly, savage, devilish.　SHAKESPEARE, *Richard III*

8442. Only the brave know how to forgive.　STERNE, *Sermons*

8443.
The sin forgiven by Christ in Heaven
By man is cursed alway.
　N. P. WILLIS, *Unseen Spirits*

See also: 402, 2366, 2622, 8618, 19611, 21609.

FORM, FORMALITY, INFORMALITY

Related Subjects: Affectation, Ceremony, Conventionality, Familiarity, Ostentation.

8451. Form may be just as tough in fiber as rebellion. Not all the steadfastness of the world belongs to heretics.　HEYWOOD BROUN, *The Orthodox Champion*

8452. I had not time to lick it into form, as a bear doth her young ones.　ROBERT BURTON, *Anatomy of Melancholy*

8453. Of what use are forms, seeing at times they are empty? Of the same use as barrels, which, at times, are empty too.　A. W. & J. C. HARE, *Guesses At Truth*

8454. Informal's what women always say they're going to be and never are.　CHRISTOPHER MORLEY, *Thunder on the Left*

See also: 1091, 1099.

FORTUNE

Related Subjects: Chance, Circumstance, Destiny, Fame, Fate, Luck, Misfortune, Opportunity, Providence, Prosperity, Riches.

8461. Fortune is a god and rules men's lives.　AESCHYLUS, *The Choephoroe*

8462. If a man look sharply and attentively, he shall see Fortune; for though she is blind, she is not invisible.　BACON, *Of Fortune*

8463. Chiefly the mould of a man's fortune is in his own hands.　BACON, *Of Fortune*

8464. Fortune is like the market, where many times, if you can stay a little, the price will fall.　BACON, *Of Delays*

8465.
We cannot be more faithful to ourselves,
In anything that's manly, than to make
Ill fortune as contemptible to us
As it makes us to others.
　BEAUMONT & FLETCHER, *Honest Man's Fortune*

8466.
I am not now in fortune's power;
He that is down can fall no lower.
　SAMUEL BUTLER, *Hudibras*

8467. The brave man carves out his fortune, and every man is the son of his own works.　CERVANTES, *Don Quixote*

8468. Every man was not born with a silver spoon in his mouth.　CERVANTES, *Don Quixote*

8469. Fortune may have yet a better success in reserve for you, and they who lose to-day may win to-morrow.　CERVANTES, *Don Quixote*

8470.
Fortune, the great commandress of the world,
Hath divers ways to advance her followers:
To some she gives honour without deserving,
To other some, deserving without honour. GEORGE CHAPMAN,
All Fools

8471. Do Fortune as she list, I stand prepared. DANTE, *Inferno*

8472. A man must take the fat with the lean. DICKENS,
David Copperfield

8473. We make our fortunes and we call them fate. DISRAELI

8474.
I think that Fortune watcheth o'er our lives,
Surer than we. But well said: he who strives
Will find his gods strive for him equally. EURIPIDES,
Iphigenia in Tauris

8475. Hairbreadth missings of happiness looks like the insults of Fortune. FIELDING, *Tom Jones*

8476. Vicissitudes of fortune, which spares neither man nor the proudest of his works, which buries empires and cities in a common grave.
GIBBON, *Decline and Fall*

8477. To what fortuitous concurrence do we not owe every pleasure and convenience of our lives.
GOLDSMITH,
The Vicar of Wakefield

8478.
Fortune, men say, doth give too much to many,
But yet she never gave enough to any. SIR JOHN HARRINGTON,
Epigrams

8479. Some believe that all things are subject to the chances of fortune, and that the world has no governor to move it. JUVENAL, *Satires*

8480. I am unwilling to mix my fortune with him that is going down the wind. SAMUEL PEPYS,
Diary

8481. Good fortune will elevate even petty minds, and give them the appearance of a certain greatness and stateliness, as from their high place they look down upon the world; but the truly noble and resolved spirit raises itself, and becomes more conspicuous in times of disaster and ill fortune. PLUTARCH, *Lives*

8482. Fortune can take from us nothing but what she gave us. *Proverb*

8483. If you are too fortunate you will not know yourself. *Proverb*

8484. Fortune is like glass,—the brighter the glitter, the more easily broken. PUBLILIUS SYRUS,
Sententiae

8435. When Fortune flatters, she does it to betray.
PUBLILIUS SYRUS, *Sententiae*

8486. It is more easy to get a favour from fortune than to keep it.
PUBLILIUS SYRUS, *Sententiae*

8487. Fortune dreads the brave, and is only terrible to the coward.
SENECA

8488. I am a man whom Fortune hath cruelly scratched.
SHAKESPEARE,
All's Well that Ends Well

8489. Fortune brings in some boats that are not steer'd.
SHAKESPEARE, *Cymbeline*

8490.
A man that fortune's buffets and re-
wards
Hast ta'en with equal thanks.
SHAKESPEARE, *Hamlet*

8491.
Will Fortune never come with both
hands full
But write her fair words still in
foulest letters?
She either gives a stomach and no
food;
Such are the poor in health; or else
a feast
And takes away the stomach.
SHAKESPEARE, *Henry IV*

8492. We are ready to try our fortunes to the last man.
SHAKESPEARE, *Henry IV*

8493.
Yield not thy neck
To fortune's yoke, but let thy daunt-
less mind
Still ride in triumph over all mis-
chance. SHAKESPEARE,
Henry VI

8494.
When Fortune means to men most
good,
She looks upon them with a threaten-
ing eye. SHAKESPEARE,
King John

8495.
The lowest and most dejected thing
of fortune. SHAKESPEARE,
King Lear

8496.
Fortune, good night, smile once
more; turn thy wheel.
SHAKESPEARE, *King Lear*

8497.
Things at the worst will cease, or
else climb upward
To what they were before.
SHAKESPEARE, *Macbeth*

8498. To be a well-favoured man is
the gift of fortune; but to write and
read comes by nature.
SHAKESPEARE,
Much Ado About Nothing

8499. It makes us, or it mars us.
SHAKESPEARE, *Othello*

8500. We have seen better days.
SHAKESPEARE, *Timon of Athens*

8501.
All states with others' ruin built
To ruin run amain.
No chance of Fortune's calms
Can cast my fortune down.
When Fortune smiles, I smile to
think
How quickly she will frown.
ROBERT SOUTHWELL,
I Envy Not Their Hap

See also: 232, 292, 627, 2495, 2699,
3081, 3118, 10554, 13107, 15548.

FOX

Related Subjects: Animal, Cunning, Hunting.

8511. The little foxes, that spoil the
vines. *Bible: The Song of Solomon,*
ii, 15
(*Source of title of play by*
Lillian Hellman.)

8512. Like Aesop's fox, when he had
lost his tail, would have all his fellow foxes cut off theirs.
ROBERT BURTON,
Anatomy of Melancholy

8513. The more the fox is cursed,
the better he fares.
ROBERT GREENE, *Friar Bacon*

8514. Where the lion's skin will not
reach, a little of the fox's must be
used. LYSANDER,
Plutarch: Lives

8515. A fox should not be of the jury at a goose's trial. *Proverb*

8516. He that will outwit the fox must rise betimes. *Proverb*

8517. The fox may grow grey but never good. *Proverb*

8518. At length the fox is brought to the furrier. *Proverb*

8519. Foxes dig not their own holes. *Proverb*

8520. Foxes never fare better than when they are curst. *Proverb*

8521. The fox barks not when he would steal the lamb.
SHAKESPEARE, *Henry VI*

8522. The fox which lives by subtlety.
SHAKESPEARE, *Venus and Adonis*

8523. The fox changes his fur, but not his habits. SUETONIUS,
Lives of the Twelve Caesars

See also: 2933, 11931.

FRANCE AND THE FRENCH

Related Subjects: Europe, Paris.

8531. The thirst for truth is not a French passion. AMIEL, *Journal*

8532. France is an absolute monarchy, tempered by songs.
Anonymous

8533.
The King of France went up the hill
　With twenty thousand men;
The King of France came down the
　hill,
　And ne'er went up again.
Anonymous, Old Tarleton's Song

8534. France, fam'd in all great arts, in none supreme.
MATTHEW ARNOLD,
To A Republican Friend

8535. The most frivolous and fickle of civilised nations—they pass from the game of war to the game of peace, from the game of science to the game of art, from the game of liberty to the game of slavery, from the game of slavery to the game of licence. WALTER BAGEHOT,
Literary Studies

8536. The further off from England the nearer is to France.
LEWIS CARROLL,
Alice in Wonderland

8537. Frenchmen are like gunpowder, each by itself smutty and contemptible; but mass them together, they are terrible indeed!
COLERIDGE, *Table Talk*

8538. Citizen, I have just arrived from Caen. Your love for your native place doubtless makes you wish to learn the events which have occurred in that part of the republic. I shall call at your residence in about an hour. Be so good as to receive me and give me a brief interview. I will put you in such condition [she planned to assassinate him] as to render great service to France.
CHARLOTTE CORDAY,
Letter to Marat

8539. The French woman says, "I am a woman and a Parisienne, and nothing foreign to me appears altogether human." EMERSON,
Lectures

8540. No country in the world is so passionately enamored of literary and art movements as France, and no nation is so partial to labels.
JOHN GASSNER,
Masters of the Drama

8541.
Gay sprightly land of mirth and social ease,

Pleas'd with thyself, whom all the world can please.
GOLDSMITH, *The Traveller*

8542. Fifty million Frenchmen can't be wrong.
Attributed to TEXAS GUINAN

8543.
Never go to France
Unless you know the lingo,
If you do, like me,
You will repent, by jingo.
THOMAS HOOD,
French and English

8544. Never was there a country where the practice of governing too much had taken deeper root and done more mischief.   JEFFERSON

8545. The French are excellent in this, they have a book on every subject.   SAMUEL JOHNSON,
Boswell: Life

8546. A Frenchman loves his mother —in the abstract.
H. S. MERRIMAN,
The Sowers

8547. Have the French for friends, but not for neighbors.
EMPEROR NICEPHORUS

8548. My thoughts and wishes bend again toward France.
SHAKESPEARE, *Hamlet*

8549. 'Tis better using France than trusting France.   SHAKESPEARE,
Henry VI

8550. That sweet enemy, France.
SIR PHILIP SIDNEY,
Astrophel and Stella

8551. A nation of monkeys with the throat of parrots.   JOSEPH SIÈYES

8552. Lafayette, we are here.
CHARLES E. STANTON,
Said at the disembarking of the A. E. F. in France.

8553. "They order," said I, "this matter better in France."
STERNE, *A Sentimental Journey*

8554. If they have a fault, they are too serious.   STERNE,
A Sentimental Journey

8555. It [French] is the true and native language of insincerity.
ALFRED SUTRO,
A Marriage Has Been Arranged

8556. The cross of the Legion of Honor has. been conferred upon me. However, few escape that distinction.
MARK TWAIN,
A Tramp Abroad

8557. I do not dislike the French from the vulgar antipathy between neighbouring nations, but for their insolent and unfounded airs of superiority.   SIR ROBERT WALPOLE

See also: 2816, 4875, 6910, 6933, 8870, 8891, 10873, 10977, 11073, 11672, 13686, 15608, 21383.

FRANKLIN, BENJAMIN

8561.
While Franklin's quiet memory climbs to heaven,
Calming the lightning which he thence hath riven.   BYRON,
The Age of Bronze

8562. Benjamin Franklin, incarnation of the peddling, tuppeny Yankee.
JEFFERSON DAVIS

8563. The body of Benjamin Franklin, Printer (like the cover of an old book, its contents torn out and stripped of its lettering and gilding), lies here, food for worms; but the work shall not be lost, for it will (as he believed) appear once more in a new and more elegant edition, revised and corrected by the Author.
FRANKLIN: *Epitaph for Himself*

8564. I succeed him; no one could replace him.   JEFFERSON,
When it was said that he replaced Franklin as Ambassador to France.

8565. "What is the use of this new invention?" some one asked Franklin. "What is the use of a new-born child?" was his reply.
            JAMES PARTON,
The Life and Times of Benjamin Franklin

FRANKNESS, see Candor

FRAUD, see Deceit

FREEDOM

Related Subjects: **Democracy, Dependence, Equality, Government, Liberty, The People, Rights, Security.**

8571. The free man is he who does not fear to go to the end of his thought.   LEON BLUM

8572.
"Freedom!" their battle-cry,—
"Freedom! or leave to die!"
            G. H. BOKER,
The Black Regiment

8573. Without free speech no search for truth is possible, without free speech no discovery of truth is useful, without free speech progress is checked and the nations no longer march forward toward the nobler life which the future holds for man. Better a thousand-fold abuse of free speech than a denial of free speech. The abuse dies in a day, but the denial slays the life of the people, and entombs the hope of the race.
            CHARLES BRADLAUGH

8574. A man can be free even within prison walls. Freedom is something spiritual. Whoever has once had it,

can never lose it. There are some people who are never free outside a prison. The body can be bound with chains, the spirit never. One's thoughts are free.
            BERT BRECHT,
A Penny for the Poor

8575. We have suddenly discovered that what we took for the enduring presuppositions of our life are in danger of being destroyed. Today we value freedom, I think, as we have not valued it before. Just as a man never appreciates his home so much as when he is compelled to leave it so now we realize our inestimable blessings when they are threatened. We have been shaken out of our smugness and warned of a great peril, and in that warning lies our salvation.   JOHN BUCHAN,
Pilgrim's Way

8576.
Yet, Freedom! yet thy banner, torn, but flying,
Streams like the thunder-storm against the wind.   BYRON,
Childe Harold

8577.
For freedom's battle, once begun,
Bequeath'd by bleeding sire to son,
Though baffled oft, is ever won.
            BYRON, *The Giaour*

8578. I would have nobody to control me, I would be absolute; and who but I? Now, he that is absolute can do what he likes; he that can do what he likes, can take his pleasure; he that can take his pleasure, can be content; and he that can be content, has no more to desire. So the matter's over; and come what will come, I am satisfied.   CERVANTES,
Don Quixote

8579.
Freedom has a thousand charms to
  show,
That slaves, howe'er contented, never
  know.   COWPER, *Table Talk*

8580.
I am as free as Nature first made
  man,
Ere the base laws of servitude began,
When wild in woods the noble savage
  ran.   DRYDEN,
          The Conquest of Granada

8581.
For what avail the plough or sail,
Or land or life, if freedom fail?
          EMERSON, *Boston*

8582. There were some who said that
a man at the point of death was
more free than all others, because
death breaks every bond, and over
the dead the united world has no
power.   FENELON, *Telemachus*

8583. Without freedom of thought
there can be no such thing as wisdom; and no such thing as public
liberty without freedom of speech;
which is the right of every man as
far as by it he does not hurt or control the right of another; and this
is the only check it ought to suffer
and the only bounds it ought to
know.   FRANKLIN

8584. Freedom is not worth having
if it does not connote freedom to
err.   MAHATMA GANDHI

8585. Freedom is the recognition of
necessity.   J. B. S. HALDANE,
          I Believe

8586. The seed of liberal principles
sprouts first in green abstraction and
must be allowed to grow slowly into
concrete, knotty actuality. Freedom,
which hitherto has become man only

here and there, must enter the very
masses, must pass into the lowest
classes of society and become *the
people.*   HEINE

8587. In the course of history no
people has ever been made a present
of freedom, and if freedom did cost
nothing no people would ever keep
it! Freedom has a high price, and
men must ever struggle to preserve
it.   ADOLF HITLER,
          Nat'l Soc. Party Congress, 1935

8588. As He died to make men holy,
let us die to make men free.
          JULIA WARD HOWE,
          Battle Hymn of the Republic

8589. That this nation, under God,
shall have a new birth of freedom,
and that government of the people,
by the people, for the people, shall
not perish from the earth.
          LINCOLN, *Gettysburg Address*

8590. In giving freedom to the slave
we assure freedom to the free,—
honorable alike in what we give and
what we preserve.   LINCOLN

8591. Among freemen there can be
no successful appeal from the ballot
to the bullet, and . . . they who take
such appeal are sure to lose their case
and pay the cost.   LINCOLN

8592.
If I have freedom in my love,
  And in my soul am free,
Angels alone that soar above
  Enjoy such liberty.
          RICHARD LOVELACE,
          To Althea in Prison

8593.
And I honor the man who is willing
  to sink
Half his present repute for the freedom to think.

And, when he has thought, be his
cause strong or weak,
Will risk t' other half for the freedom to speak.   LOWELL,
A Fable for Critics

8594. The life of nations and of
states must in the future be dominated
by a new idea of freedom, as of a
limited individualism constrained by
social forces. Only through the victory of this idea of freedom, the idea
of super-national democracy, can happiness, peace, and order be secured
for Europe—in the place of an anarchy
which leads again and again to
bloody wars and is destroying civilization.   THOMAS MANN,
This War

8595. Liberal institutions straightway cease from being liberal the moment they are soundly established:
once this is attained no more grievous
and more thorough enemies of freedom exist than liberal institutions.
     NIETZSCHE,
The Twilight of the Idols

8596. Blandishments will not fasci-
nate us, nor will threats of a "halter"
intimidate. For, under God, we are
determined that wheresoever, when-
soever, or howsoever we shall be
called to make our exit, we will die
free men.   JOSIAH QUINCY

8597. The people who settled in New
England came here for religious freedom, but religious freedom to them
meant freedom only for their kind of
religion. They were not going to be
any more liberal to others who dif-
fered with them in this new country,
than others had been with them in
the countries from which they came.

This attitude seems to be our attitude
in many situations today.
     ELEANOR ROOSEVELT

8598. Man is born free, and everywhere he is in irons.   ROUSSEAU,
The Social Contract

8599. I saw a woman sleeping. In her
sleep she dreamt Life stood before
her, and held in each hand a gift—in
the one Love, in the other Freedom.
And she said to the woman, "Choose!"
And the woman waited long: and she
said, "Freedom!"
     OLIVE SCHREINER, *Dreams*

8600. Can the individual man standing on his own right make secure his
freedom by means of free speech, free
discussion, a free press, and in the
last resort by the invocation of the
aid of an independent judiciary? Or
on the other hand, do all his rights
come from his government and does
his security depend solely upon the
privileges which that government sees
fit to grant him? These are the two
essential conceptions of individual
rights which have been fighting in
this world during the past thousand
years.   HENRY L. STIMSON,
*Democracy and Nationalism In
Europe*

8601. We know all this, and in our
hearts we know, too, that for each
of us to gain the most freedom we
must keep all the doors to life forever
freely open to every man and woman.
     CLARENCE STREIT, *Union Now*

8602. Freedom is not saved by powerlessness. Freedom is inseparably
linked with power and the will and
capacity to use it.
DOROTHY THOMPSON, *On the Record*

8603. There are times in the lives of all people when freedom is the twin of duty, sacrifice the companion of happiness, and when courage—parent of fortitude, endurance, determination—is the first virtue.
DOROTHY THOMPSON, *On the Record*

8604. Now, the very idea of freedom rests on a profound respect for humanity. It rests in a profound conception of human dignity. It rests in the belief in human brotherhood. It is deeply religious, or, if you prefer, ethical and moral in its basis.
DOROTHY THOMPSON,
Let the Record Speak

8605. I do not agree with a word that you say, But I will defend to the death your right to say it.
VOLTAIRE

8606. We cannot be free at home unless we are free to go and come across the world. Our continent cannot confine the dynamite of democratic opportunity. WILLIAM A. WHITE,
Defense for America

8607. Are we preserving freedom in this land of ours, the hope of all the earth? Have we, inheritors of this continent and of the ideals to which the fathers consecrated it,—have we maintained them, realizing them, as each generation must, anew? Are we, in the consciousness that the life of man is pledged to higher levels here than elsewhere, striving still to bear aloft the standards of liberty and hope; or, disillusioned and defeated, are we feeling the disgrace of having had a free field in which to do new things and of not having done them?
WOODROW WILSON,
The New Freedom

See also: 642, 654, 662, 695, 704, 782, 1158, 1385, 1969, 2391, 2764, 2920, 3618, 5594, 6790, 9893, 11468, 17055, 20175, 20217.

FRIEND, FRIENDSHIP

Related Subjects: Acquaintance, Affection, Associates, Brotherhood, Companions, Conviviality, Familiarity, Guests, Hospitality, Love, Neighbor, Warmth.

8611. A friend in power is a friend lost. HENRY ADAMS,
The Education of Henry Adams

8612. One friend in a lifetime is much; two are many; three are hardly possible. Friendship needs a certain parallelism of life, a community of thought, a rivalry of aim.
HENRY ADAMS,
The Education of Henry Adams

8613. Little friends may prove great friends. AESOP,
The Lion and the Mouse

8614. A faithful friend is a strong defence: and he that hath found such an one hath found a treasure.
Apocrypha: Ecclesiasticus

8615. Forsake not an old friend, for the new is not comparable to him. A new friend is as new wine: when it is old, thou shalt drink it with pleasure. *Apocrypha: Ecclesiasticus*

8616. My friends! There are no friends. ARISTOTLE

8617. The perfect friendship of two men is the deepest and highest sentiment of which the finite mind is capable; women miss the best in life.
GERTRUDE ATHERTON,
The Conqueror

8618. Cosmus, Duke of Florence, was wont to say of perfidious friends, that "We read that we ought to forgive our enemies; but we do not read that we ought to forgive our friends." BACON, *Apothegms*

8619. Friends, they say, are the thieves of time. BACON

8620. A man that hath friends must show himself friendly; and there is a friend that sticketh closer than a brother. *Bible: Proverbs, xviii, 24*

8621.
Gif ye want ae friend that's true,
   I'm on your list. BURNS,
     First Epistle to J. Lapraik

8622.
The social, friendly, honest man,
   Whate'er he be,
'Tis he fulfils great Nature's plan,
   And none but he. BURNS,
     Second Epistle to J. Lapraik

8623. Friendship is Love without his wings. BYRON,
   L'Amitie est l'Amour sans Ailes

8624. You can make more friends in two months by becoming interested in other people than you can in two years by trying to get other people interested in you.
   DALE CARNEGIE,
     How to Win Friends

8625. It is a true saying, that a man must eat a peck of salt with his friend, before he knows him.
   CERVANTES, *Don Quixote*

8626. Most people enjoy the inferiority of their best friends.
   LORD CHESTERFIELD

8627. Friends are good,—good if well chosen. DEFOE

8628. The only way to have a friend is to be one. EMERSON, *Friendship*

8629. A friend may well be reckoned the masterpiece of Nature.
   EMERSON, *Friendship*

8630. A friend is a person with whom I may be sincere. Before him, I may think aloud. EMERSON,
     Friendship

8631. Happy is the house that shelters a friend. EMERSON, *Friendship*

8632. I do then with my friends as I do with my books. I would have them where I can find them, but I seldom use them. EMERSON,
     Friendship

8633. Friendship is a disinterested commerce between equals; love, an abject intercourse between tyrants and slaves. GOLDSMITH,
     The Good-Natur'd Man

8634.
There's never a bond, old friend, like this,—
We have drunk from the same canteen! C. G. HALPINE,
     The Canteen

8635.
Fame is the scentless sunflower, with gaudy crown of gold;
But friendship is the breathing rose with sweets in every fold.
   O. W. HOLMES,
     No Time Like the Old Time

8636.
True friendship's laws are by this rule express'd,
Welcome the coming, speed the parting guest. HOMER, *Odyssey*

8637.
True friends appear less mov'd than counterfeit;
As men that truly grieve at funeral
Are not so loud, as those that cry for hire. HORACE, *Ars Poetica*

8638. Blessed are they who have the gift of making friends, for it is one of God's best gifts. It involves many things, but above all, the power of going out of one's self, and appreciating whatever is noble and loving in another. THOMAS HUGHES

8639. To let friendship die away by negligence and silence, is certainly not wise. It is voluntarily to throw away one of the greatest comforts of this weary pilgrimage.

SAMUEL JOHNSON, *Boswell: Life*

8640. A man, sir, should keep his friendship in a constant repair.

SAMUEL JOHNSON

8641. Friendship is only a reciprocal conciliation of interests, and an exchange of good offices; it is a species of commerce out of which self-love always expects to gain something.

LA ROCHEFOUCAULD, *Maxims*

8642. If you want to make a dangerous man your friend, let him do you a favor. LEWIS E. LAWES

8643.
How many friends I loved are gone!
Death delicately takes the best:
O Death, be careful of the rest!
I cannot spare another one.
RICHARD LE GALLIENNE,
How Many Friends

8644.
Each year to ancient friendships adds a ring
As to an oak. LOWELL,
Under the Willows

8645.
You ask me "why I like him." Nay, I cannot; nay, I would not, say.
I think it vile to pigeonhole
The pros and cons of a kindred soul.
E. V. LUCAS, *Friends*

8646. Women, like princes, find few real friends. LORD LYTTELTON,
Advice to a Lady

8647. One of the most mawkish of human delusions is the notion that friendship should be lifelong. The fact is that a man of resilient mind outwears his friendships just as certainly as he outwears his love affairs and his politics.

H. L. MENCKEN,
Selected Prejudices

8648.
Friend after friend departs;
Who hath not lost a friend?
There is no union here of hearts
That finds not here an end.
JAMES MONTGOMERY,
The Little Cloud

8649. Came but for Friendship and took away Love.
THOMAS MOORE,
A Temple to Friendship

8650.
A friendship that like love is warm;
A love like friendship steady.
THOMAS MOORE, *How Shall I Woo?*

8651.
Oh, call it by some better name,
For friendship sounds too cold.
THOMAS MOORE,
Oh, Call It by Some Better Name

8652. In the life of a young man the most essential thing for happiness is the gift of friendship.
SIR WILLIAM OSLER,
Life of Sir William Osler

8653. Thou wert my guide, philosopher, and friend. POPE,
Essay on Man

8654. A reconciled friend is a double enemy. *Proverb*

8655. A true friend does sometimes venture to be offensive. *Proverb*

8656. A true friend should be like a privy, open in necessity. *Proverb*

8657. A man may see his freend need, but winna see him bleed. *Proverb*

8658. A friend in need is a friend indeed. *Proverb*

8659. A friend is best found in adversity. *Proverb*

8660. A friend that you buy, will be bought from you. *Proverb*

8661. A friend is not so soon gotten as lost. *Proverb*

8662. Few there are that will endure a true friend. *Proverb*

8663. Friends need no formal invitation. *Proverb*

8664. Friendship consists not in saying, What's the best news? *Proverb*

8665. Friendship increases in visiting friends, but more in visiting them seldom. *Proverb*

8666. Friendship is not to be bought at a fair. *Proverb*

8667. Friendship that flames, goes out in a flash. *Proverb*

8668. Friendship, the older it grows, the stronger it is. *Proverb*

8669. Go slowly to the entertainments of thy friends, but quickly to their misfortunes. *Proverb*

8670. By requiting one friend we invite many. *Proverb*

8671. Happy is he whose friends were born before him. *Proverb*

8672. Make not thy friend too cheap to thee, nor thyself to thy friend. *Proverb*

8673. He that ceaseth to be a friend never was a good one. *Proverb*

8674. Before you make a friend, eat a bushel of salt with him. *Proverb*

8675. Treat your friend as if he might become an enemy.
PUBLILIUS SYRUS, *Sententiae*

8676. Prosperity makes friends, adversity tries them.
PUBLILIUS SYRUS, *Sententiae*

8677.
Strange that I did not know him then,
  That friend of mine.
I did not even show him then
  One friendly sign. . . .
I would have rid the earth of him
  Once, in my pride.
I 'never knew the worth of him
  Until he died.   E. A. ROBINSON

8678. The principal task of friendship is to foster one's friends' illusions.   ARTHUR SCHNITZLER,
Anatole

8679. Old friends are best. King James used to call for his old shoes; they were easiest for his feet.
JOHN SELDEN, *Table Talk*

8680. I have some friends, some honest friends, and honest friends are few; My pipe of briar, my open fire, a book that's not too new.
R. W. SERVICE,
I Have Some Friends

8681. My friends were poor, but honest.   SHAKESPEARE,
All's Well that Ends Well

8682. A back-friend, a shoulder-clapper.   SHAKESPEARE,
The Comedy of Errors

8683.
Be thou familiar, but by no means vulgar;
Those friends thou hast, and their adoption tried,

Grapple them to thy soul with hoops
of steel.   SHAKESPEARE, *Hamlet*

8684. Here is a dear and true industrious friend.   SHAKESPEARE,
Henry IV

8685.
I count myself in nothing else so
happy
As in a soul remembering my good
friends.   SHAKESPEARE,
Richard II

8686.
And do as adversaries do in law,
Strive mightily, but eat and drink as
friends.   SHAKESPEARE,
The Taming of the Shrew

8687.
While I think on thee, dear friend,
All losses are restor'd and sorrows
end.   SHAKESPEARE, *Sonnet XXX*

8688.
I'm very lonely now, Mary,
    For the poor make no new friends;
But, oh! they love the better still
    The few our Father sends.
        HELEN S. SHERIDAN,
    Lament of the Irish Emigrant

8689. We need new friends; some of
us are cannibals who have eaten their
old friends up: others must have ever-
renewed audiences before whom to
re-enact an ideal version of their lives.
    LOGAN PEARSALL SMITH,
        Afterthoughts

8690. Now am I hail-fellow-well-
met with all.   SOPHOCLES,
        Oedipus Tyrannus

8691.
Desiderata:
1. Good Health.
2. 2 to 3 hundred (pounds) a year.
3. O du lieber Gott, *friends!*
        Amen.   STEVENSON

8692.
Hast thou a friend, as heart may wish
    at will?
Then use him so, to have his friend-
    ship still.
Wouldst have a friend, wouldst know
    what friend is best?
Have God thy friend, who passeth
    all the rest.   THOMAS TUSSER,
        Posies for a Parlour

8693. Friendship is the only cement
that will ever hold the world together.   WOODROW WILSON

See also: 321, 361, 384, 858, 903,
907, 1398, 2214, 2354, 2384, 2400,
2402, 2404, 2977, 4285, 4302, 11458.

FROST

Related Subjects: Ice, Snow, Winter.

8701.
These Winter nights against my
    window-pane
    Nature with busy pencil draws de-
        signs
Of ferns and blossoms and fine spray
    of pines,
    Oak-leaf and acorn and fantastic
        vines.   T. B. ALDRICH,
            Frost-Work

8702.
The frost performs its secret ministry,
Unhelped by any wind.
    COLERIDGE, *Frost at Midnight*

8703. The frost which kills the harvest of a year, saves the harvests of
a century, by destroying the weevil
or the locust.   EMERSON,
        Conduct of Life

8704.
On a lone winter evening, when the
    frost
Has wrought a silence.   KEATS,
    On the Grasshopper and Cricket

8705.

An envious sneaping frost,
That bites the first-born infants of
the spring.   SHAKESPEARE,
Love's Labour's Lost

8706.

What miracle of weird transforming
Is this wild work of frost and light,
This glimpse of glory infinite?
     WHITTIER, *The Pageant*

See also: 1457, 1460.

FRUIT

Related Subjects: Farming, Garden, Grapes, Harvest, Tree.

8711. The kindly fruits of the earth.
Book of Common Prayer

8712. He that would have the fruit
must climb the tree.   *Proverb*

8713. A black plum is as sweet as a
white.   *Proverb*

8714. You should go to a pear-tree
for pears, not to an elm.
     PUBLILIUS SYRUS, *Sententiae*

8715.

Fruit unripe, sticks on the tree;
But fall, unshaken, when they mellow
be.   SHAKESPEARE, *Hamlet*

8716.

Before thee stands this fair Hesperides,
With golden fruit, but dangerous to
be touched.   SHAKESPEARE,
Pericles

8717. The ripest fruit first falls.
     SHAKESPEARE, *Richard II*

8718.

       Superfluous branches
We lop away that bearing boughs
may live.   SHAKESPEARE,
Richard II

8719.

Fair fruit in an unwholesome dish
Are like to rot untasted.
   SHAKESPEARE, *Troilus and Cressida*

See also: 222, 1450, 1451, 1711, 5266.

FUN

Related Subjects: Amusement, Joy, Laughter, Merriment, Pleasure, Sport.

8721. It takes all the fun out of a
bracelet if you have to buy it yourself.
     PEGGY JOYCE

8722. I've taken my fun where I've
found it.   KIPLING, *The Ladies*

FUNERAL

Related Subjects: Death, Epitaphs, Grave, Monument, Mourning, Preacher.

8731. The care of funeral, the manner of burial, the pomp of obsequies,
are rather a consolation to the living
than of any service to the dead.
     ST. AUGUSTINE

8732.

Of all The fools who flocked to swell
or see the show,
Who cared about the corpse? The
funeral
Made the attraction, and the black the
woe.   BYRON,
The Vision of Judgment

8733.

       As grand
And griefless as a rich man's funeral.
     SIDNEY DOBELL,
A Musing on a Victory

8734. Worldly faces never look so
worldly as at a funeral.
   GEORGE ELIOT, *Janet's Repentance*

8735. What men prize most is a privilege, even if it be that of chief mourner at a funeral. LOWELL,
Democracy

8736. After a funeral, a feast.
Proverb

8737.
His obscure funeral,
No trophy, sword, nor hatchment o'er his bones,
No noble rite, nor formal ostentation.
SHAKESPEARE, *Hamlet*

8738.
All things that we ordained festival,
Turn from their office to black funeral;
Our instruments to melancholy bells,
Our wedding cheer to a sad burial feast.   SHAKESPEARE,
Romeo and Juliet

8739. Nay, if you be an undertaker, I am for you.   SHAKESPEARE,
Twelfth Night

See also: 11451, 19726.

FUTILITY

Related Subjects: Idleness, Waste.

8741. It's but little good you'll do, a-watering the last year's crop.
GEORGE ELIOT, *Adam Bede*

8742.
For none upon earth can achieve his scheme;
The best as the worst are futile here.
VICTOR HUGO,
Early Love Revisited

8743. Great cry and little wool, as the Devil said when he sheared the hogs.   *Proverb*

8744. An emmet may work its heart out, but can never make honey.
Proverb

8745.
Saint George, that swinged the dragon, and e'er since
Sits on his horse back at mine hostess' door.   SHAKESPEARE, *King John*

8746. He has spent all his life in letting down empty buckets into empty wells; and he is frittering away his age in trying to draw them up again.   SYDNEY SMITH,
Lady Holland's Memoir

8747.
But what am I?
An infant crying in the night:
An infant crying for the light,
And with no language but a cry.
TENNYSON, *In Memoriam*

8748.
Thy leaf has perished in the green
And, while we breathe beneath the sun,
The world which credits what is done
Is cold to all that might have been.
TENNYSON, *In Memoriam*

See also: 1024, 16765, 22024.

FUTURE

Related Subjects: Destiny, Fate, Progress, Providence, Tomorrow.

8751. The old frontier called chiefly for muscle, physical endurance, courage, individualism, and a vision of the future. The conquest of the new frontier will demand the highest qualities of thought and character. Success can be won only by wisdom, knowledge, willingness for sacrifice, and the strongest possible sense of social justice and obligation.
JAMES TRUSLOW ADAMS,
The Record of America

8752. You can never plan the future by the past.   BURKE

8753. I am pleading for the future; I am pleading for a time when hatred and cruelty will not control the hearts of men. When we can learn by reason and judgment and understanding and faith that all life is worth saving, and that mercy is the highest attribute of man.   CLARENCE DARROW

8754. All hopes for the future and, so to say, restfulness of outlook, lie in our having something at last built up, instead of this everlasting destruction, instead of chips flying in all directions, rubbish and disorder which has led to nothing for two hundred years.   DOSTOYEVSKY,
A Raw Youth

8755. I never think of the future. It comes soon enough.
ALBERT EINSTEIN

8756.
On the thirty-second day of the thirteenth month of the eighth day of the week,
On the twenty-fifth hour and the sixty-first minute, we'll find all things we seek.
SAM W. FOSS,
The Eighth Day of the Week

8757. The future is a convenient place for dreams.
ANATOLE FRANCE

8758. I know of no way of judging of the future but by the past.
PATRICK HENRY

8759. Remember this also, and be well persuaded of its truth: the future is not in the hands of Fate, but in ours.   JULES JUSSERAND

8760. If the future belongs to anybody it belongs to those to whom it has always belonged, to those, that is to say, too absorbed in living to feel the need for thought and they will come, as the barbarians have always come, absorbed in the processes for their own sake, eating without asking if it is worth while to eat, begetting children without asking why they should produce them, and conquering without asking why they should conquer. J. W. KRUTCH,
The Modern Temper

8761. The future is a world limited by ourselves; in it we discover only what concerns us and, sometimes, by chance, what interests those whom we love the most.
MAETERLINCK, *Joyzelle*

8762.
                    The never-ending flight
Of future days.   MILTON,
Paradise Lost

8763. I believe the future is only the past again, entered through another gate.   PINERO,
The Second Mrs. Tanqueray

8764. No one can walk backwards into the future.   *Proverb*

8765. The golden age is before us not behind us.   SAINT-SIMON

8766.
            How many ages hence
Shall this our lofty scene be acted o'er,
In states unborn and accents yet unknown!   SHAKESPEARE,
Julius Caesar

8767.
The baby figure of the giant mass Of things to come.
SHAKESPEARE, *Troilus and Cressida*

See also: 1493, 10465, 12448, 15622.

G

GAMBLING

Related Subjects: **Adventure, Amusement, Cards, Chance, Dice, Luck, Risk, Sport.**

8771. The gambling passion lurks . . . at the bottom of every heart, be it a girl's heart, a provincial's, a diplomatist's; everybody longs to have money without working for it; you may hedge the desire about with restrictions, but the gambling mania immediately breaks out in another form. BALZAC,
The Firm of Nucingen

8772. Gaming is a principle inherent in human nature.   BURKE

8773.
For most men (till by losing rendered sager)
Will back their own opinions by a wager.   BYRON, *Beppo*

8774. Death and the dice level all distinctions. SAMUEL FOOTE,
The Minor

8775.
Could fools to keep their own contrive,
On what, on whom could gamesters thrive?   JOHN GAY, *Fables*

8776. The strength of Monaco is the weakness of the world.
HERBERT A. GIBBONS, *Riviera Towns*

8777.
Play not for gain but sport. Who plays for more
Than he can lose with pleasure, stakes his heart,—
Perhaps his wife's too, and whom she hath bore. GEORGE HERBERT,
The Church-Porch

8778. Gambling is a disease of barbarians superficially civilized.
DEAN INGE

8779. Gie o'er when the play is gude.
Proverb

8780. A wager is a fool's argument.
Proverb

8781. The devil is in the dice.
Proverb

8782. The most patient man in loss, the most coldest that ever turned up ace. SHAKESPEARE, *Cymbeline*

8783.
       Were it good
To set the exact wealth of all our states
All at one cast? to set so rich a main
On the nice hazard of one doubtful hour? SHAKESPEARE, *Henry IV*

8784. A wise player ought to accept his throws and score them, not bewail his luck.   SOPHOCLES

8785. If there were two birds sitting on a fence, he would bet you which one would fly first.
MARK TWAIN, *The Jumping Frog*

8786.
And once or twice to throw the dice
   Is a gentlemanly game,
But he does not win who plays with Sin
   In the secret House of Shame.
OSCAR WILDE,
The Ballad of Reading Gaol

GAME, see Sport

GARDEN

Related Subjects: **Farming, Flowers, Fruit, Grass, Nature, Tree, Weed.**

8791.
"Fine for the flowers
The lovely showers,"

Is pretty reading,
But, oh, the weeding!   F. P. A.

8792.

Who loves a garden still his Eden
  keeps,
Perennial pleasures plants, and wholesome harvests reaps.
          BRONSON ALCOTT, *Tablets*

8793. God Almighty first planted a
garden.   BACON, *Of Gardens*

8794.

A Garden is a lovesome thing, God
    wot!
  Rose plot,
  Fringed pool,
  Ferned grot—
  The veriest school
  Of Peace; and yet the fool
Contends that God is not—
Not God! in Gardens! when the eve
  is cool?
Nay, but I have a sign;
'Tis very sure God walks in mine.
          THOMAS E. BROWN, *My Garden*

8795.

These are the gardens of the Desert,
  these
The unshorn fields, boundless and
  beautiful
For which the speech of England has
  no name—
The Prairies.   BRYANT, *The Prairies*

8796. God the first garden made, and
the first city Cain.
          ABRAHAM COWLEY, *The Garden*

8797. Who loves a garden loves a
greenhouse too.   COWPER, *The Task*

8798. He that hires one garden eats
birds; he that hires more than one
will be eaten by the birds.   *Proverb*

8799. This rule in gardening never
forget, to sow dry and set wet.
          Proverb

8800. Many things grow in the garden, that were never sowed there.
          Proverb

8801. A good garden may have some
weeds.   *Proverb*

8802. There is no ancient gentlemen
but gardeners . . . they hold up
Adam's profession.
          SHAKESPEARE, *Hamlet*

8803. How deeply seated in the human heart is the liking for gardens
and gardening.
          ALEXANDER SMITH, *Dreamthorp*

8804.

Let first the onion flourish there,
Rose among roots, the maiden-fair
Wine-scented and poetic soul
Of the capacious salad bowl.
          STEVENSON, *To a Gardener*

8805. What a man needs in gardening is a cast-iron back, with a hinge
in it.
          CHARLES DUDLEY WARNER,
                My Summer in a Garden

8806. To own a bit of ground, to
scratch it with a hoe, to plant seeds,
and watch the renewal of life,—this
is the commonest delight of the race,
the most satisfactory thing a man can
do.   CHARLES DUDLEY WARNER,
                My Summer in a Garden

See also: 2268, 4475.

GAYETY

Related   Subjects: Cheerfulness,
Good Humor, Happiness, Joy.

8811. Gayety is often the reckless
ripple over depths of despair.
          E. H. CHAPIN

8812. Gayety is not a proof that the
heart is at ease, for often in the midst
of laughter the heart is sad.
          MME. DE GENLIS

8813. The gayety of the wicked is like the flowery surface of Mount Aetna, beneath which materials are gathering for an eruption that will one day reduce all its beauties to ruin and desolation.   LEIGH HUNT

8814. Leaves seem light, useless, idle, wavering, and changeable—they even dance; yet God has made them part of the oak. So he has given us a lesson, not to deny stout-heartedness within, because we see lightsomeness without.   LEIGH HUNT

8815. Gayety is to good humor, as animal perfumes to vegetable fragrance: the one overpowers weak spirits, the other recreates and revives them.   SAMUEL JOHNSON

GENERALIZATION

8821. To generalize is to be an idiot.
        BLAKE

8822. The narrower the mind, the broader the statement.   TED COOK

8823. All generalizations are dangerous, even this one.
        DUMAS, THE YOUNGER

8824. Crafty men deal in generals.
        Proverb

See also: 981.

GENEROSITY, see Gifts

GENIUS

Related Subjects: Ability, Art, Character, Inspiration, Intelligence, Mind, Skill, Talent, Temperament.

8831.
Genius, that power which dazzles mortal eyes,
Is oft but perseverance in disguise.
        HENRY W. AUSTIN,
        Perseverance Conquers All

8832. I have known no man of genius who had not to pay, in some affliction or defect either physical or spiritual, for what the gods had given him.
        MAX BEERBOHM, *The Pines*

8833. What is the fierce sting, the cruel driving spur that urges the artist onward, till one is sometimes almost tempted to conclude that genius consists in the sting itself even more than in the gifts and powers that it forces to its service?
        GAMALIEL BRADFORD,
        American Portraits

8834. Since when was genius found respectable?
        ELIZABETH B. BROWNING,
        Aurora Leigh

8835.
Talk not of genius baffled. Genius is master of man.
Genius does what it must, and talent does what it can.
        BULWER-LYTTON, *Last Words*

8836. Talent may be in time forgiven, but genius never!   BYRON

8837.
Genius hath electric power
    Which earth can never tame,
Bright suns may scorch and dark clouds lower,
    Its flash is still the same.
        LYDIA M. CHILD,
        Marius Amid the Ruins of Carthage

8838. Genius must be born, and never can be taught.   DRYDEN,
        Epistle to Congreve

8839.
Great wits are sure to madness near allied,
And thin partitions do their bounds divide.   DRYDEN,
        Absalom & Achitophel

8840.
Our builders were with want of
genius curst,
The second temple was not like the
first. DRYDEN

8841. Genius is one per cent inspiration and ninety-nine per cent perspi-
ration. THOMAS A. EDISON

8842. Every man of genius sees the
world at a different angle from his
fellows, and there is his tragedy.
HAVELOCK ELLIS, *The Dance of Life*

8843. Great geniuses have the shortest biographies. EMERSON,
Representative Men

8844. For precocity some great price
is always demanded sooner or later
in life. MARGARET FULLER, *Diary*

8845. Genius will live and thrive
without training, but it does not the
less reward the watering-pot and
pruning-knife. MARGARET FULLER

8846. Men of genius do not excel in
any profession because they labour
in it, but they labour in it, because
they excel. HAZLITT,
Characteristics

8847. Genius, in truth, means little
more than the faculty of perceiving in
an unhabitual way.
WILLIAM JAMES, *Psychology*

8848. A man of genius has been seldom ruined but by himself.
SAMUEL JOHNSON, *Boswell: Life*

8849. When your Daemon is in
charge, do not try to think consciously. Drift, wait, and obey.
KIPLING, *Something of Myself*

8850. Contemporary spites do not
harm true genius.
ANDREW LANG,
Letters to Dead Authors

8851. Not only is fame (and until
recent years even liberty), denied to
men of genius during their lives, but
even the means of subsistence. After
death they receive monuments and
rhetoric by way of compensation.
LOMBROSO, *The Man of Genius*

8852. The appearance of a single
great genius is more than equivalent
to the birth of a hundred mediocrities.
LOMBROSO, *The Man of Genius*

8853. Good sense travels on the well-
worn paths; genius, never. And that
is why the crowd, not altogether
without reason, is so ready to treat
great men as lunatics.
LOMBROSO, *The Man of Genius*

8854. I do not believe that there is
such a thing as thwarted genius, or
that a man may die before his time
. . . I have no sympathy for the
baffled poet or statesman who blames
his failure on the misunderstanding
of the rest of the world.
EMIL LUDWIG, *I Believe*

8855. If we are to have genius we
must put up with the inconvenience
of genius, a thing the world will never
do; it wants geniuses, but would like
them just like other people.
GEORGE MOORE

8856.
One science only will one genius fit;
So vast is art, so narrow human wit.
POPE, *Essay on Criticism*

8857. The comfort and the delight
found by genius in itself and its creations, and the inferiority under
which other men appear to it, give it
so lofty a strain as to make it wholly
indifferent to fame among them.
SCHOPENHAUER

8858. There is no great genius without some touch of madness. SENECA

8859. The work of the master reeks not of the sweat of the brow—suggests no effort and is finished from the beginning.   WHISTLER, *The Gentle Art of Making Enemies*

See also: 170, 1342, 2301, 3084, 3631, 3632, 6394, 6544, 6884, 6977, 8123, 10431, 10541, 12288, 15403, 18557, 19677, 20193.

GENTLEMAN

Related Subjects: Ancestry, Breeding, Chivalry, Courtesy, Honor, Manners, Nobility.

8861. One of the embarrassments of being a gentleman is that you are not permitted to be violent in asserting your rights.
          NICHOLAS MURRAY BUTLER

8862.
Loke who that is most vertuous alway,
Privee and apert, and most entendeth ay
To do the gentil dedes that he can,
And tak him for the grettest gentilman.   CHAUCER, *Canterbury Tales*

8863.
Whom do we dub as Gentlemen? The knave, the fool, the brute—
If they but own full tithe of gold, and wear a courtly suit.
          ELIZA COOK, *Nature's Gentleman*

8864. A gentleman will not insult me, and no man not a gentleman can insult me.   FREDERICK DOUGLASS

8865. His tribe were God Almighty's gentlemen.   DRYDEN, *Absalom & Achitophel*

8866. A gentleman is one who never hurts anyone's feeling unintentionally.   OLIVER HERFORD

8867. It is almost a definition of a gentleman to say he is one who never inflicts pain.
          CARDINAL NEWMAN, *The Idea of a University*

8868.
"My father's trade!—why, blockhead, art thou mad?
My father, sir, did never stoop so low;
He was a Gentleman, I'd have you know."
     "Excuse the liberty I take,"
          Modestus said, with archness on his brow—
     "Pray, why did not your father make
          A Gentleman of you?"
SELLECK OSBORN, *The Modest Retort*

8869. What is a gentleman but his word?   *Proverb*

8870. Jack would be a gentleman, if he could but speak French. *Proverb*

8871. He's a gentleman: look at his boots. BERNARD SHAW, *Pygmalion*

8872. I entreat you rather send but 30 carpenters, husbandmen, gardeners, fishermen, blacksmiths, masons, and diggers up of trees' roots, well provided, than a thousand [gentlemen] such as we have.
          CAPTAIN JOHN SMITH, *Letter from Virginia to The London Co.*

8873.
And thus he bore without abuse
     The grand old name of gentleman,
     Defamed by every charlatan,
And soiled with all ignoble use.
          TENNYSON, *In Memoriam*

See also: 214, 1541, 1594, 4211, 5665, 6123, 8802, 14753, 17397, 19614.

GENTLENESS

Related Subjects: Compassion, Grace, Kindness, Manners, Tact, Tenderness.

8881.
The great mind knows the power of gentleness,
Only tries force because persuasion fails. BROWNING,
Prince Hohenstiel-Schwangau

8882. Gentle of speech, beneficent of mind. HOMER, *Odyssey*

8883.
Speak gently! 'tis a little thing
Dropped in the heart's deep well;
The good, the joy that it may bring
Eternity shall tell.
G. W. LANGFORD, *Speak Gently*

8884. It is only people who possess firmness who can possess true gentleness. Those who appear gentle generally possess nothing but weakness, which is readily converted into harshness. LA ROCHEFOUCAULD, *Maxims*

8885. A gentle heart is tied with an easy thread. *Proverb*

8886.
What would you have? Your gentleness shall force
More than your force moves us to gentleness. SHAKESPEARE,
As You Like It

8887. Touch'd with human gentleness and love. SHAKESPEARE,
The Merchant of Venice

8888. The gentleness of all the gods go with thee. SHAKESPEARE,
Twelfth Night

See also: 3939, 22096.

GERMANY AND THE GERMANS

Related Subjects: Europe.

8891. Except by name, Jean Paul Friedrich Richter is little known out of Germany. The only thing connected with him, we think, that has reached this country is his saying,— "Providence has given to the French the empire of the land; to the English that of the sea; to the Germans that of—the air!" CARLYLE, *Richter*

8892. Even in Germany itself there are millions who stand aloof from the seething mass of criminality and corruption constituted by the Nazi Party machine. Let them take courage amid perplexities and perils, for it may well be that the final extinction of a baleful domination will pave the way to a broader solidarity of all the men in all the lands than we could ever have planned if we had not marched together through the fire.
WINSTON CHURCHILL,
Blood, Sweat & Tears

8893. On my left sat a scientist's wife who showed equal freedom. She said, "German universities are about to be ruined. Half their professors would migrate to the United States if it were possible to get positions." I felt keenly for her and her husband, one of the foremost authorities in his field in Europe. This sort of talk comes to us almost every week.
WILLIAM E. DODD, *Diary*

8894. [German] women send their only sons of fifteen to fight, and no mourning is worn and it is etiquette to congratulate a family who has lost a son on the battle-field.
JAMES W. GERARD,
to Colonel E. M. House, Berlin,
Nov. 1914

8895. O Lord, thou seest that we have become different, that the German nation is no more a nation without honor, a nation covered with shame, a nation at war within itself, a nation of little courage, a nation of little faith. No, Lord, the German nation is strong again in its own will, strong in perseverance and strong to make every sacrifice. Lord, we will not let thee go! Bless our fight for our freedom, and bless our German people and fatherland.
ADOLF HITLER, *May 1, 1933*

8896. Our love of peace is perhaps greater than that of other nations, for we suffered most from this unhappy war. No one of us has the intention of threatening anybody.
ADOLF HITLER, *May 21, 1935*

8897. Today there is no more class struggle in Germany, for there is no longer any one left here who is in a position to lead it . . . There may perhaps be an odd person or so wandering round with such ideas in his head and hoping for "better times" —which would in reality be worse times—when he will once more be in a position to mobilize this instinct. But let such people make no mistake —we have the power to prevent such a happening.   ADOLF HITLER,
Oct. 6, 1935

8898. Wherever Germany extends her sway, she ruins culture.
NIETZSCHE, *Ecce Homo*

8899. The only way to treat a Prussian is to step on his toes until he apologizes.   *Austrian Proverb,*
John Gunther: Inside Europe

8900. The situation in Germany is serious but not hopeless; the situation in Austria is hopeless but not serious.
Viennese Saying,
John Gunther: Inside Europe

See also: 1021, 5166, 6213, 9771, 9772, 10977, 17641.

GHOST

Related Subjects: Imagination, Spirit, Superstition, Vision.

8901. Ghosts, like ladies, never speak till spoke to.   R. H. BARHAM,
The Ghost

8902. The only ghosts, I believe, who creep into this world, are dead young mothers, returned to see how their children fare. There is no other inducement great enough to bring the departed back.   J. M. BARRIE,
The Little White Bird

8903. I don't believe in ghosts, but I've been afraid of them all my life.
CHARLES A. DANA

8904. Thin, airy shoals of visionary ghosts.   HOMER, *Odyssey*

8905.
O'er all there hung a shadow and a fear;
A sense of mystery the spirit daunted,
And said as plain as whisper in the ear,
The place is Haunted.
THOMAS HOOD, *The Haunted House*

8906. Alas, poor ghost!
SHAKESPEARE, *Hamlet*

8907.
  I am thy father's spirit,
Doom'd for a certain term to walk the night.   SHAKESPEARE,
Hamlet

8908. It is an honest ghost, that let me tell you.   SHAKESPEARE,
Hamlet

8909.
              The times have been
That, when the brains were out, the man would die,

And there an end; but now they rise
   again,
With twenty mortal murders on their
   crowns,
And push us from our stools.
            SHAKESPEARE, *Macbeth*

8910.
I seem'd to move among a world of
   ghosts,
And feel myself the shadow of a
   dream.   TENNYSON,
                     The Princess

See also: 5093, 9775, 19992.

GIANT

Related   Subjects: **Mythology,
Tale.**

8911. I say with Didacus Stella, a
dwarf standing on the shoulders of a
giant may see farther than a giant
himself.   ROBERT BURTON,
            Anatomy of Melancholy

8912. A giant will starve on what will
surfeit a dwarf.   *Proverb*

8913.
        O, it is excellent
To have a giant's strength; but it is
   tyrannous
To use it like a giant.
SHAKESPEARE, *Measure for Measure*

See also: 1529.

GIFTS AND GIVING

Related Subjects: **Beggar, Benefits,
Benevolence, Borrowing and Lending, Charity, Favor, Kindness,
Patronage, Philanthropy, Selfishness.**

8921. The Lord gave, and the Lord
hath taken away; blessed be the name
of the Lord.   *Bible: Job, i, 21*

8922. A gift is as a precious stone in
the eyes of him that hath it.
         Bible: Proverbs, xvii, 8

8923. It is more blessed to give than
to receive.   *Bible: Acts, xx, 35*

8924. God loveth a cheerful giver.
         Bible: 2 Corinthians, ix, 7

8925.
He ne'er consider'd it, as loth
To look a gift-horse in the mouth.
      SAMUEL BUTLER, *Hudibras*

8926. The manner of giving is worth
more than the gift.
         CORNEILLE, *Le Menteur*

8927. Let him give on till he can
give no more.
      DRYDEN, *Absalom & Achitophel*

8928. One can know nothing of giving aught that is worthy to give unless one also knows how to take.
         HAVELOCK ELLIS,
      Little Essays of Love & Virtue

8929. The only gift is a portion of
thyself.   EMERSON, *Gifts*

8930. The gifts of a bad man bring
no good with them.
         EURIPIDES, *Medea*

8931. Give not Saint Peter so much,
to leave Saint Paul nothing.
         GEORGE HERBERT,
            Jacula Prudentum

8932. Bounty always receives part of
its value from the manner in which
it is bestowed.
      SAMUEL JOHNSON, *Boswell: Life*

8933. Liberality consists less in giving a great deal than in gifts well-
timed.
      LA BRUYÈRE, *Les Caractères*

8934. Give what you have. To some
one, it may be better than you dare to
think.   LONGFELLOW, *Kavanagh*

8935.
He gives only the worthless gold
Who gives from a sense of duty.
LOWELL,
The Vision of Sir Launfal

8936.
The gift without the giver is bare;
Who gives himself with his alms
feeds three,—
Himself, his hungering neighbor, and
me.   LOWELL,
The Vision of Sir Launfal

8937. I did give ten shillings and no
more, though I believe most of the
rest did give more, and did believe
that I did so too.
SAMUEL PEPYS, *Diary*

8938. He giveth twice that gives in
a trice.   *Proverb*

8939. He that gives to be seen will
believe none in the dark. *Proverb*

8940. He that giveth to a good man
selleth well.   *Proverb*

8941. Give a thing and take again,
and you shall ride in hell's wain.
Proverb

8942. A man's gift makes room for
him.   *Proverb*

8943. The most important thing in
any relationship is not what you get
but what you give. It does not hurt to
worship at a shrine which is quite
unconscious, for out of it may grow
an inner development in yourself and
sometimes a relationship of real value.
In any case the giving of love is an
education in itself.
ELEANOR ROOSEVELT

8944. Rich gifts wax poor when giv-
ers prove unkind.
SHAKESPEARE, *Hamlet*

8945. What's mine is yours, and what
is yours is mine.
SHAKESPEARE, *Measure for Measure*

8946. Seven hundred pounds and
possibilities is goot gifts.
SHAKESPEARE,
The Merry Wives of Windsor

8947. My good will is great, though
the gift small.
SHAKESPEARE, *Pericles*

8948.
Let the man who has and doesn't give
Break his neck, and cease to live!
Let him who gives without a care
Gather rubies from the air!
JAMES STEPHENS,
In the Imperative Mood

8949. You must be fit to give before
you can be fit to receive.
JAMES STEPHENS, *The Crock of Gold*

8950. I am in the habit of looking
not so much to the nature of a gift as
to the spirit in which it is offered.
STEVENSON, *New Arabian Nights*

8951. God gave them Youth, God
gave them Love and even God can
give no more.
RIDGELY TORRENCE,
The Young Lovers

8952.
Behold, I do not give lectures or a
little charity,
When I give I give myself.
WALT WHITMAN, *Song of Myself*

See also: 6, 34, 383, 389, 2545, 3832,
9390, 12332, 17800.

GIRL

Related Subjects: Daughter, Maid.

8961.
Of all the girls that are so smart,
There's none like pretty Sally.

She is the darling of my heart,
And she lives in our alley.
HENRY CAREY,
Sally in Our Alley

8962.
What do little girls talk about?
What is their mystic theme?
Those still too young for puppy love,
Yet old enough to dream.
WILLIAM HERSCHELL,
What Do Little Girls Talk About

8963.
There was a little girl
Who had a little curl
Right in the middle of her forehead;
And when she was good
She was very, very good,
But when she was bad she was horrid.
LONGFELLOW,
There Was a Little Girl

8964.
Men seldom make passes
At girls who wear glasses.
DOROTHY PARKER, *News Item*

8965.
You may tempt the upper classes
With your villainous demi-tasses,
But Heaven will protect the Working
Girl.   EDGAR SMITH,
*Heaven Will Protect the
Working Girl*

8966.
What are young women made of? . . .
Sugar and spice and all things nice,
And such are young women made of.
SOUTHEY,
What All the World Is Made Of

See also: 811, 1083, 2211, 5375,
9642.

GLORY

**Related   Subjects: Ambition,
Beauty, Conquerors, Fame, Hero,
Honor, Light, Martyr.**

8971.
And glory long has made the sages
smile,

'Tis something, nothing, words, illusion, wind—
Depending more upon the historian's
style
Than on the name a person leaves
behind.   BYRON, *Don Juan*

8972. There is no glory in outstrip-
ping donkeys.   MARTIAL

8973. But the desire for glory has
great power in washing the tincture
of philosophy out of the souls of men
PLUTARCH

8974. The man who is completely
wise and virtuous has no need at all
of glory, except so far as it disposes
and eases his way of action by the
greater trust that it procures him.
PLUTARCH

8975. Sudden glory soon goes out.
Prover

8976. Desire of glory is the last garment that even wise men put off.
Prover

8977.
Glory is like a circle in the water,
Which never ceaseth to enlarge itself
Till by broad spreading it dispers
to nought.
SHAKESPEARE, *Henry V*

8978.
I see thy glory like a shooting star
Fall to the base earth from the fi
mament.
SHAKESPEARE, *Richard*

8979.
The glories of our blood and state
Are   shadows,   not   substant
things;
There is no armour against fate;
Death lays his icy hand on king
JAMES SHIRLEY,
Contention of Ajax & Ulys.

3980. Avoid shame, but do not seek glory,—nothing so expensive as glory. SYDNEY SMITH, *Lady Holland's Memoir*

3981. Of all the affections which attend human life, the love of glory is the most ardent. SIR RICHARD STEELE, *The Spectator*

3982.

His food
Was glory, which was poison to his mind
And peril to his body.
SIR HENRY TAYLOR, *Philip Van Artevelde*

3983. Where is it now, the glory and the dream? WORDSWORTH, *Ode On Intimations of Immortality*

See also: 465, 814, 1698, 1995, 9388, 15134, 15142, 15545, 20199.

GLUTTONY

Related Subjects: **Eating, Excess, Hunger.**

3991.
Some men are born to feast, and not to fight;
Whose sluggish minds, e'en in fair honor's field,
Still on their dinner turn—
Let such pot-boiling varlets stay at home,
And wield a flesh-hook rather than a sword. JOANNA BAILLIE, *Basil*

3992. Whose God is their belly, and whose glory is in their shame.
Bible: Philippians, iii, 19

3993. More die by food than famine.
Proverb

3994. Better fill a glutton's belly than eye. *Proverb*

8995. A bellyful of gluttony will never study willingly. *Proverb*

8996.
Who with a body filled and vacant mind
Gets him to rest, crammed with distressful bread.
SHAKESPEARE, *Henry V*

8997. Lord, Madame, I have fed like a farmer; I shall grow as fat as a porpoise.
SWIFT, *Polite Conversation*

See also: 1944, 6516.

GOD

Related Subjects: **Atheism, Bible, Christ, Christianity, Church, Devil, Faith, Gods, Paradise, Prayer, Providence, Religion, Universe, Worship.**

9001. God's mouth knows not to utter falsehood, but he will perform each word. AESCHYLUS, *Prometheus*

9002. I believe in the incomprehensibility of God. BALZAC

9003. Underneath are the everlasting arms.
Bible: Deuteronomy, xxxiii, 27

9004. Lead me to the rock that is higher than I. *Bible: Psalms, lxi, 2*

9005. I will say of the Lord, He is my refuge and my fortress: my God; in Him will I trust.
Bible: Psalms, xci, 2

9006. Have we not all one father? hath not one God created us?
Bible: Malachi, ii, 10

9007. For God so loved the world, that He gave His only begotten Son, that whosoever believeth in Him should not perish, but have everlasting life. *Bible: John, iii, 16*

9008. God is love.
Bible: 1 John, iv, 8

9009. I found an altar with this inscription, To the Unknown God.
Bible: Acts, xix, 28

9010. If God be for us, who can be against us? *Bible: Romans, viii, 31*

9011. I am Alpha and Omega, the beginning and the end, the first and the last. *Bible: Revelation, xxi, 6*

9012. God, as some cynic has said, is always on the side which has the best football coach.
HEYWOOD BROUN,
Some of My Best Friends Are Yale Men

9013. God only, who made us rich, can make us poor.
ELIZABETH B. BROWNING,
Sonnets from the Portuguese

9014.
God's in His heaven:
All's right with the world.
BROWNING, *Pippa Passes*

9015.
I recognize
Power passing mine, immeasurable,
God. BROWNING,
Prince Hohenstiel-Schwangau

9016.
What I call God,
And fools call Nature.
BROWNING, *The Ring and the Book*

9017.
Beneath the shadow of the Great Protection,
The soul sits, hushed and calm.
J. F. CLARKE, *The Shadow*

9018. Earth, with her thousand voices, praises God.
COLERIDGE,
Hymn in the Vale of Chamouni

9019. Gangway for de Lawd God Jehovah! MARC CONNELLY,
The Green Pastures

9020. Even bein' Gawd ain't a bed o roses. MARC CONNELLY,
The Green Pastures

9021.
God moves in a mysterious way
His wonders to perform;
He plants His footsteps in the sea
And rides upon the storm.
COWPER,
Light Shining out of Darkness

9022. Father expected a good deal of God. He didn't actually accuse God of inefficiency, but when he prayed his tone was loud and angry, like that of a dissatisfied guest in a carelessly managed hotel.
CLARENCE DAY, *God and My Father*

9023. Job felt the hand of destruction upon him, and he felt the hand of preservation too; and it was all one hand; this is God's method, and His alone, to preserve by destroying.
JOHN DONNE, *Sermons*

9024. Divine Love always has met and always will meet every human need. MARY BAKER EDDY,
Science and Health

9025.
Is not God upon the ocean,
Just the same as on the land?
J. T. FIELDS, *Ballad of the Tempest*

9026. Why the people of Israel, however, adhered to their God all the more devotedly the worse they were treated by Him, that is a question we must leave open.
SIGMUND FREUD,
Moses and Monotheism

9027. Love is God's essence; Power but His attribute; therefore is His love greater than His power.
RICHARD GARNETT,
De Flagello Myrteo

9028. Man proposeth, God disposeth.
George Herbert,
Jacula Prudentum

9029. To lift up the hands in prayer gives God glory, but a man with a dungfork in his hands, a woman with a slop-pail, give Him glory too. He is so great that all things give Him glory if you mean they should. So then, my brethren, live.
G. M. Hopkins

9030. An honest God is the noblest work of man.
Robert Ingersoll, *Epigram*

9031.
From Thee, great God, we spring, to Thee we tend,—
Path, motive, guide, original and end.
Samuel Johnson,
Motto of the Rambler

9032.
O servant, where dost thou seek Me?
Lo! I am beside thee.
I am neither in temple nor in mosque:
I am neither in Kaaba nor in Kailash:
Neither am I in rites and ceremonies,
Nor in Yoga and renunciation.
If thou art a true seeker, thou shalt at once see Me: thou shalt meet Me in a moment of time. Kabir says, "O Sadhu! God is the breath of all breath."
Kabir: *Songs*

9033.
Praise God, from whom all blessings flow!
Praise Him, all creatures here below!
Praise Him above, ye heavenly host!
Praise Father, Son, and Holy Ghost!
Bishop Thomas Ken,
Morning & Evening Hymn

9034. The Almighty has His own purposes.
Lincoln

9035. Trusting to Him who can go with me, and remains with you, and be everywhere for good, let us confidently hope that all will yet be well.
Lincoln

9036.
'Tis heaven alone that is given away;
'Tis only God may be had for the asking.
Lowell,
The Vision of Sir Launfal

9037.
You've got to git up airly
Ef you want to take in God.
Lowell, *The Biglow Papers*

9038.
A mighty fortress is our God,
A bulwark never failing;
Our helper He amid the flood
Of mortal ills prevailing.
Martin Luther, *Ein' Feste Burg*

9039. I live and love in God's peculiar light.
Michelangelo

9040.
How vain
Against the Omnipotent to rise in arms.
Milton, *Paradise Lost*

9041.
Just are the ways of God,
And justifiable to men;
Unless there be who think not God at all.
Milton, *Samson Agonistes*

9042. It is ridiculous to suppose that the great head of things, whatever it be, pays any regard to human affairs.
Pliny the Elder, *Natural History*

9043.
Can it be fancied that Deity ever vindictively
Made in His image a mannikin merely to madden it?
Poe, *The Rationale of Verse*

9044.
Father of all! in every age,
In every clime adored,

By saint, by savage, and by sage,
Jehovah, Jove, or Lord!
POPE, *The Universal Prayer*

9045. Beware of him whom God hath marked.   *Proverb*

9046. Who hath God, hath all; who hath Him not, hath less than nothing.
Proverb

9047. God reaches us good things by our own hands.   *Proverb*

9048. God giveth His wrath by weight, but His mercy without measure.   *Proverb*

9049. God comes at last when we think He is farthest off.   *Proverb*

9050. Against God's wrath no castle is thunder proof.   *Proverb*

9051. We are in God's hand.
SHAKESPEARE, *Henry V*

9052.
God be prais'd, that to believing souls
Gives light in darkness, comfort in despair!
SHAKESPEARE, *Henry VI*

9053.
Had I but served my God with half the zeal
I served my king, He would not in mine age
Have left me naked to mine enemies.
SHAKESPEARE, *Henry VIII*

9054. God and all the attributes of God are eternal.   SPINOZA, *Ethics*

9055. Cast all your cares on God; that anchor holds.
TENNYSON, *Enoch Arden*

9056.
I found Him in the shining of the stars,
I mark'd Him in the flowering of His fields,
But in His ways with men I find Him not.
TENNYSON, *Idylls of the King*

9057. If God were not a necessary Being of Himself, He might almost seem to be made for the use and benefit of men.
JOHN TILLOTSON, *Sermon*

9058. But I always think, that the best way to know God is to love many things. Love a friend, a wife, something, whatever you like . . . To give you an example: someone loves Rembrandt, but seriously,— that man will know that there is a God, he will surely believe it.
VAN GOGH, *Letters*

9059. If there were no God, it would be necessary to invent Him.
VOLTAIRE

9060. In the faces of men and women I see God.
WALT WHITMAN, *Song of Myself*

9061. God is and all is well.
WHITTIER, *My Birthday*

9062.
God's ways seem dark, but, soon or late,
They touch the shining hills of day.
WHITTIER

See also: 7, 22, 63, 67, 101, 104, 108, 219, 228, 312, 329, 338, 339, 650, 726, 831, 875, 951, 1098, 1172, 1227, 1256, 1433, 1521, 1805, 1864, 1891, 1893, 1894, 1981, 2048, 2074, 2124, 2129, 2415, 2672, 3008, 3050, 3120, 3411, 3493, 4706, 4905, 5570, 6385, 6446, 7232, 8793, 9721, 16681, 16976.

GODS AND GODDESSES

Related Subjects: Atheism, Cupid, Fate, God, Idolatry, Mythology, Pan, Superstition, Venus, Worship.

9071. Slowly but surely moveth the might of the gods.
EURIPIDES, *Bacchae*

9072. These things surely lie on the knees of the gods.
HOMER, *Odyssey*

9073. Little Tin Gods on Wheels.
KIPLING, *Public Waste*

9074. Man is certainly stark mad; he cannot make a worm, and yet he will be making gods by dozens.
MONTAIGNE, *Essays*

9075. And this which you deem of no moment is the very highest of all: that is whether you have a right idea of the gods, whereby you may live your life well or ill.   PLATO, *Laws*

9076. The great god Pan is dead.
PLUTARCH

9077. With regard to the gods I know not whether they exist or not, or what they are like. Many things prevent our knowing: the subject is obscure, and brief is the span of our mortal life.   PROTAGORAS

9078.
In Paestum's ancient fanes I trod,
    And mused on those strange men of old,
Whose dark religion could unfold
So many gods, and yet no God.
R. W. RAYMOND,
Ramblings in Greece

9079.
The saying is wise, though it sounds like a jest,
    That "the gods don't allow us to be in their debt,"
For though we may think we are specially blest,
We are certain to pay for the favors we get!   J. G. SAXE,
The Gifts of the Gods

9080.
The gods are just, and of our pleasant vices
Make instruments to plague us.
SHAKESPEARE, *King Lear*

9081.
As flies to wanton boys are we to the gods;
They kill us for their sport.
SHAKESPEARE, *King Lear*

9082. I call the gods to witness.
SHAKESPEARE, *Timon of Athens*

9083.
        To the gods alone
Belongs it never to be old or die,
But all things else melt with all-powerful Time.
SOPHOCLES, *Oedipus Coloneus*

9084. Men have always made their gods in their own images—The Greeks like the Greeks, the Ethiopians like the Ethiopians.
XENOPHANES

See also: 583, 586, 621, 805, 1003, 1633, 1725, 3421, 3814, 5119, 15175.

GOLD

Related Subjects: Alchemy, Avarice, Bribery, Mammon, Miser, Money, Rainbow, Riches.

9091. Thinking to get at once all the gold the Goose could give, he killed it and opened it only to find,—nothing.   AESOP,
The Goose With the Golden Eggs

9092. To a shower of gold most things are penetrable.
CARLYLE, *The French Revolution*

9093. If golde ruste, what shal iren do?
CHAUCER, *Canterbury Tales*

9094.
Gold! Gold! Gold! Gold!
Bright and yellow, hard and cold.
THOMAS HOOD,
Miss Kilmansegg and Her Precious Leg

9095.
The gold is thar, most anywhar,
  And they dig it out with an iron
    bar.
         JESSE HUTCHINSON, JR.,
           Ho for California

9096.
That for which all virtue now is sold,
And almost every vice,—almighty
gold.   BEN JONSON

9097. It is extraordinary how many emotional storms one may weather in safety if one is ballasted with ever so little gold.   WILLIAM MCFEE,
         Casuals of the Sea

9098. They wonder much to hear that gold, which in itself is so useless a thing, should be everywhere so much esteemed, that even Men for whom it was made, and by whom it has its value, should yet be thought of less value than it is.
       SIR THOMAS MORE, *Utopia*

9099. Whereas gold is the kindest of all hosts when it shines in the sky, it comes an evil guest into those that receive it in their hand.
       SIMONIDES, *Plutarch: Lives*

9100. Gold goes in at any gate except heaven's.   *Proverb*

9101. Chains of gold are stronger than chains of iron.   *Proverb*

9102. Gold is no balm to a wounded spirit.   *Proverb*

9103.
How quickly nature falls into revolt
When gold becomes her object!
       SHAKESPEARE, *Henry IV*

9104. All that glisters is not gold.
         SHAKESPEARE,
     The Merchant of Venice

9105.
There is thy gold, worse poison to
  men's souls,

Doing more murders in this loath-
  some world,
Than these poor compounds that thou
  mayst not sell.
I sell thee poison, thou hast sold me
  none.
     SHAKESPEARE, *Romeo and Juliet*

9106. Saint-seducing gold.
     SHAKESPEARE, *Romeo and Juliet*

See also: 330, 976, 1380, 1717, 3626, 3637.

THE GOLDEN RULE

Related Subjects: Goodness, Morality.

9111. Therefore all things whatsoever ye would that men should do to you, do ye even so to them: for this is the law and the prophets.
       Bible: Matthew, vii, 12

9112. Do as you would be done by is the surest method that I know of pleasing.
     LORD CHESTERFIELD, *Letters*

9113. Every man takes care that his neighbor does not cheat him. But a day comes when he begins to care that he do not cheat his neighbor. Then all goes well.
     EMERSON, *Conduct of Life*

9114. Therefore if anyone would take these two words to heart and use them for his own guidance, he will be almost without sin. These two words are bear and forbear.
     EPICTETUS, *Discourses*

9115. The discovery of the golden rule finds its beginnings in "the dawn of conscience."
       ROBERT A. MILLIKAN

9116. Thence arises that Golden Rule of dealing with others as we would have others deal with us.
     ISAAC WATTS, *Logic*

See also: 652, 4392, 5276.

GOOD HUMOR

Related Subjects: **Amiability, Cheerfulness, Gayety, Laughter, Merriment, Smile.**

9121. Good humor will sometimes conquer ill humor, but ill humor will conquer it oftener; and for this plain reason, good humor must operate on generosity; ill humor on meanness.　GREVILLE

9122. Honest good humor is the oil and wine of a merry meeting, and there is no jovial companionship equal to that where the jokes are rather small, and the laughter abundant.　WASHINGTON IRVING

9123. Some people are commended for a giddy kind of good humor, which is no more a virtue than drunkenness.　POPE

9124. Good humor is the health of the soul; sadness is its poison.　KING STANISLAUS

9125. This portable quality of good humor seasons all the parts and occurrences we meet with in such a manner that there are no moments lost, but they all pass with so much satisfaction that the heaviest of loads, when it is a load, that of time, is never felt by us.　SIR RICHARD STEELE

GOODNESS

Related Subjects: **Benevolence, Character, Evil, Excellence, Holiness, Ideals, Kindness, Morality, Philanthropy, Virtue.**

9131. What makes men good is held by some to be nature, by others habit or training, by others instruction.

As for the goodness that comes by nature, this is plainly not within our control, but is bestowed by some divine agency on certain people who truly deserve to be called fortunate.　ARISTOTLE, *Nicomachean Ethics*

9132. Goodness is easier to recognize than to define; only the greatest novelists can portray good people.　W. H. AUDEN, *I Believe*

9133. It is as hard for the good to suspect evil, as it is for the bad to suspect good.　CICERO

9134. Good Will is the mightiest practical force in the universe.　C. F. DOLE

9135.
Look round the habitable world: how few
Know their own good, or knowing it, pursue.　DRYDEN, *Juvenal*

9136.
When good men die their goodness does not perish,
But lives though they are gone. As for the bad,
All that was theirs dies, and is buried with them.　EURIPIDES, *Temenidae*

9137. Men don't become good by being kept in cotton-wool, but by fighting difficulties and temptations.　J. B. S. HALDANE, *I Believe*

9138. He is so good that no one can be a better man.　HORACE, *Satires*

9139. Do good by stealth, and blush to find it fame.　HORACE

9140. Be good, sweet maid, and let who will be clever.　CHARLES KINGSLEY, *A Farewell*

9141. The greatest pleasure I know is to do a good action by stealth, and to have it found out by accident.　CHARLES LAMB

9142.
> Abash'd the devil stood,
> And felt how awful goodness is, and saw
> Virtue in her shape how lovely.
> MILTON, *Paradise Lost*

9143.
> Good, the more
> Communicated, more abundant grows. MILTON, *Paradise Lost*

9144. There is no man so good, who, were he to submit all his thoughts and actions to the laws, would not deserve hanging ten times in his life.
MONTAIGNE, *Essays*

9145. The good you do is not lost, though you forget it. *Proverb*

9146. If they say you are good, ask yourself if it be true. *Proverb*

9147. It is goodness, not greatness, that will do thee good. *Proverb*

9148. Gude fowk are scarce, tak' care o' ane. *Proverb*

9149. Good men must die, but death cannot kill their names. *Proverb*

9150. Do all you can to be good, and you'll be so. *Proverb*

9151. Concealed goodness is a sort of vice. *Proverb*

9152. It is not nor it cannot come to good. SHAKESPEARE, *Hamlet*

9153.
> There is some soul of goodness in things evil,
> Would men observingly distil it out.
> SHAKESPEARE, *Henry V*

9154. The hand that hath made you fair hath made you good.
SHAKESPEARE, *Measure for Measure*

9155.
> They say best men are moulded out of faults
> And, for the most, become much more the better
> For being a little bad.
> SHAKESPEARE, *Measure for Measure*

9156.
> How far that little candle throws his beams!
> So shines a good deed in a naughty world. SHAKESPEARE,
> *The Merchant of Venice*

9157. Are you Good men and true?
SHAKESPEARE,
Much Ado About Nothing

9158. He hath a daily beauty in his life. SHAKESPEARE, *Othello*

9159.
> Who does not befriend himself
> By doing good?
> SOPHOCLES, *Oedipus Coloneus*

9160. We too often forget that not only is there "a soul of goodness in things evil." but very generally a soul of truth in things erroneous.
HERBERT SPENCER,
First Principles

9161. She has more goodness in her little finger than he has in his whole body. SWIFT, *Polite Conversation*

9162. Howe'er it be, it seems to me,
'Tis only noble to be good.
> Kind hearts are more than coronets,
> And simple faith than Norman blood. TENNYSON,
> *Lady Clara Vere de Vere*

9163. Goodness is the only investment that never fails.
THOREAU, *Walden*

9164.
> Do all the good you can,
> By all the means you can,

In all the ways you can,
In all the places you can,
At all the times you can,
To all the people you can,
As long as ever you can.
JOHN WESLEY, *John Wesley's Rule*

9165.
       The good die first,
And they whose hearts are dry as
    summer dust
Burn to the socket.
      WORDSWORTH, *The Excursion*

See also: 332, 381, 817, 885, 1073, 1693, 1724, 3205, 3210, 3341, 3375, 3516, 4022, 4328, 4548, 5651, 11596, 17152.

GOOSE

Related Subjects: Birds, Fool.

9171. To kill the goose that laid the golden eggs.   AESOP, *Fables*

9172. A wild goose never laid a tame egg.   *Proverb*

9173. Gae shoe the goose.   *Proverb*

9174. He is not able to say boo to a goose.   *Proverb*

9175.
       Thou cream-faced loon,
Where got'st thou that goose look?
      SHAKESPEARE, *Macbeth*

9176. Sauce for the goose is sauce for the gander.
      SWIFT, *Journal to Stella*

9177. A goose is a goose still, dress it as you will.   THOREAU, *Walden*

See also: 12, 9091.

GOSSIP, see Scandal

GOVERNMENT

Related Subjects: Anarchy, Authority, Constitution, Democracy, Despotism, Dictatorship, Election, Fascism, Kings, Law, Nation, Office, Order, People, Politics, Propaganda, Revolution, Rule, State, Taxes, Tyranny, Vote.

9181. And having looked to Government for bread, on the very first scarcity they will turn and bite the hand that fed them.   BURKE,
     Thoughts & Details on Scarcity

9182. The office of government is not to confer happiness, but to give men opportunity to work out happiness for themselves.   W. E. CHANNING,
      *The Life & Character of
        Napoleon Bonaparte*

9183. The final end of Government is not to exert restraint but to do good.
      RUFUS CHOATE

9184. Government is a trust, and the officers of the government are trustees; and both the trust and the trustees are created for the benefit of the people.   HENRY CLAY

9185. I would have been glad to have lived under my woodside, and to have kept a flock of sheep, rather than to have undertaken this government.   OLIVER CROMWELL

9186. Every form of government tends to perish by excess of its basic principle.   WILL DURANT,
      The Story of Philosophy

9187. The less government we have, the better—the fewer laws, and the less confided power.
      EMERSON, *Politics*

9188. More and more government is conceived as the biggest organized social effort for dealing with social problems. Our whole evolutionary thinking leads to the conclusion that economic independence lies at the very foundation of social and moral well-being.

JUSTICE FRANKFURTER,
Law and Politics

9189. The history of a nation's spiritual development is but the tale of its wistful groping toward the provision of a machinery of State, which shall, as nearly as may be, accord with the demand of this spirit of Equity. GALSWORTHY

9190. I can retain neither respect nor affection for a Government which has been moving from wrong to wrong in order to defend its immorality.

MAHATMA GANDHI

9191. You cannot possibly have a broader basis for any government than that which includes all the people, with all their rights in their hands, and with an equal power to maintain their rights.

W. L. GARRISON, *Life*

9192. What is the best government? That which teaches us to govern ourselves. GOETHE

9193.
For just experience tells, in every soil,
That those that think must govern those that toil.

GOLDSMITH, *The Traveller*

9194. A decent and manly examination of the acts of Government should be not only tolerated, but encouraged.

WILLIAM HENRY HARRISON,
Inaugural Address

9195. We admit of no government by divine right. . . . the only legitimate right to govern is an express grant of power from the governed.

WILLIAM HENRY HARRISON,
Inaugural Address

9196. You can't run a government solely on a business basis.

HERBERT H. LEHMAN

9197. It has long been a grave question whether any government, not too strong for the liberties of its people, can be strong enough to maintain its existence in great emergencies. LINCOLN

9198. This government, with its institutions, belongs to the people who inhabit it. Whenever they shall grow weary of the existing government, they can exercise their constitutional right of amending it, or their revolutionary right to dismember or overthrow it. LINCOLN

9199. No government proper ever had a provision in its organic law for its own termination. LINCOLN

9200. While the people retain their virtue and vigilance, no administration, by any extreme of wickedness or folly, can very seriously injure the government in the short space of four years. LINCOLN

9201. I go for all sharing the privileges of the government who assist in bearing its burden. LINCOLN

9202. That is the best government which desires to make the people happy, and knows how to make them happy. MACAULAY,
On Mitford's History of Greece

9203. Nothing is so galling to a people, not broken in from the birth, as a paternal or, in other words, a meddling government, a government which tells them what to read and say and eat and drink and wear.

MACAULAY, *Southey's Colloquies*

9204.
there is bound to be a certain amount of trouble running any country

if you are president the trouble happens to you
but if you are a tyrant you can ar-
range things so
that most of the trouble happens to
other people   DON MARQUIS,
archys newest deal

9205. There is one thing better than
good government, and that is government in which all the people have a
part.   W. H. PAGE, *Life and Letters*

9206. Government, like dress, is the
badge of lost innocence.
THOMAS PAINE

9207. Governments, like clocks, go
from the motion men give them; and
as governments are made and moved
by men, so by them they are ruined
too.   Wherefore governments rather
depend upon men than men upon
governments.   WILLIAM PENN,
*Preface to Pennsylvania's
Frame of Government*

9208. Oligarchy: A government resting on a valuation of property, in
which the rich have power and the
poor man is deprived of it.
PLATO, *The Republic*

9209. Such is the government, such
are the people.   *Proverb*

9210. Rewards and punishments are
the basis of good government.
Proverb

9211. When any man ventures to
scoff at the use of brains in government he should be asked to explain
by what part of the anatomy he believes human affairs should be conducted.   DONALD RICHBERG

9212. I hope that calm counsel and
constructive leadership will provide
the steadying influence and the time
necessary for the coming of new and

more practical forms of representative
government throughout the world
wherein privilege will occupy a lesser
place and welfare a greater.
FRANKLIN D. ROOSEVELT

9213. To do what any honest government of any country would do; to
try to increase the security and the
happiness of a larger number of people in all occupations of life and in all
parts of the country; to give them
more of the good things of life; to
give them a greater distribution, not
only of wealth in the narrow terms
but of wealth in the wider terms;
. . . to give them assurance that they
are not going to starve in their old
age; to give honest business a chance
to go ahead and make a reasonable
profit, and to give everyone a chance
to earn a living.
FRANKLIN D. ROOSEVELT

9214. No greater obligation faces the
Government than to justify the faith
of its young people in the fundamental rightness of our democratic
institutions and to preserve their
strength, loyalty and idealism against
the time when they must assume the
responsibilities of citizenship.
FRANKLIN D. ROOSEVELT,
Letter to NYA, June 26, 1936.

9215. Thou little thinkest what a little
foolery governs the world.
JOHN SELDEN, *Table Talk*

9216. They that govern the most
make the least noise.
JOHN SELDEN, *Table Talk*

9217. Old forms of government
finally grow so oppressive that they
must be thrown off even at the risk
of reigns of terror.
HERBERT SPENCER,
Essays on Education

9218. The most urgent problem of civilized mankind is to constitute effective means of governing itself where its civilization has already made its world practically one.

CLARENCE STREIT, *Union Now*

9219. The power of the government is a living power, constantly changing and developing to meet new conditions and accomplish new purposes.

Opinion: U. S. Supreme Court

9220. The people's government, made for the people, made by the people, and answerable to the people.

DANIEL WEBSTER

See also: 160, 3802, 3964, 4213, 5974, 6606, 6643, 8544, 12361, 12367, 16192.

GRACE, GRACEFULNESS

Related Subjects: Charm, Courtesy, Gentleness.

9221. An outward and visible sign of an inward and spiritual grace.

Book of Common Prayer

9222.
Some hae meat and canna eat,
  And some wad eat that ant it;
But we hae meat, and we can eat,
  And sae the Lord be thankit.

BURNS, *The Selkirk Grace*

9223.
Whate'er he did was done with so much ease,
In him alone, 'twas natural to please.

DRYDEN, *Absalom & Achitophel*

9224. Grace is given of God, but knowledge is bought in the market.

A. H. CLOUGH,
The Bothie of Tober-na-Vuolich

9225. The custom of saying grace at meals had, probably, its origin in the early times of the world, and the

hunter state of man, when dinners were precarious things, and a full meal was something more than a common blessing.

CHARLES LAMB,
Grace Before Meat

9226.
See, what a grace was seated on this
  brow;
Hyperion's curls; the front of Jove
  himself;
An eye like Mars, to threaten and
  command,
A station like the herald Mercury
New-lighted on a heaven-kissing hill,
A combination and a form indeed,
Where every god did seem to set his
  seal,
To give the world assurance of a
  man.   SHAKESPEARE, *Hamlet*

9227. He does it with a better grace, but I do it more natural.

SHAKESPEARE, *Twelfth Night*

9228.
              Long graces do
But keep good stomachs off, that
  would fall to.
      SIR JOHN SUCKLING,
          To Lord Lepington

See also: 479, 645, 839, 1031, 1447, 2126, 12339.

GRAMMAR

Related Subjects: Education, Language, Pedantry, Rule, School, Speech, Teacher, Words, Writing.

9231. I am king of the Romans, and above grammar.

EMPEROR SIGISMUND

9232. Why care for grammar as long as we are good?

ARTEMUS WARD, *Natural History*

9233. Heedless of grammar, they all cried, *that's him!*

R. H. BARHAM,
The Jackdaw of Rheims

9234.

The grammar has a rule absurd
  Which I would call an outworn myth
"A preposition is a word
  You mustn't end a sentence with!"
BERTON BRALEY,
No Rule To Be Afraid Of

9235. A heretic in grammar.
ERASMUS

9236. Grammar is the grave of letters.
ELBERT HUBBARD

9237. Grammar, which knows how to lord it over kings, and with high hands makes them obey its laws.
MOLIÈRE, *Les Femmes Savantes*

GRAPES

Related Subjects: Fruit, Wine.

9241. I am sure the grapes are sour.
AESOP, *The Fox and the Grapes*

9242.

The Grape that can with Logic absolute
The Two-and-Seventy jarring Sects
  confute.   OMAR KHAYYAM,
Rubaiyat

See also: 15055, 20199.

GRASS

Related Subjects: Country, Dew, Garden, Grasshopper, Park, Straw, Weed.

9251.

A common thing is a grass blade small,
  Crushed by the feet that pass,
But all the dwarfs and giants tall,

Working till doomsday shadows fall
  Can't make a blade of grass.
J. S. CUTLER, *Wonderful*

9252. Next in profusion to the divine profusion of water, light and air, those three physical facts which render existence possible, may be reckoned the universal beneficence of grass.   J. J. INGALLS, *Blue Grass*

9253. Grass is the forgiveness of nature—her constant benediction. Fields trampled with battle, saturated with blood, torn with the ruts of the cannon, grow green again with grass, and carnage is forgotten.   Forests decay, harvests perish, flowers vanish, but grass is immortal.

J. J. INGALLS, *Blue Grass*

9254.

Grass that is made each year equals
  the mountains in her past and future;
Fashionable and momentary things
  we need not see nor speak of.
ROBINSON JEFFERS, *Point Joe*

9255.

Pile the bodies high at Austerlitz and Waterloo,
Shovel them under and let me work—
I am the grass; I cover all.
CARL SANDBURG, *Grass*

9256. If grass look green in Janiveer, 'twill look the worser all the year.
Proverb

9257. Grass grows not upon the highway.   *Proverb*

9258. The grass stoops not, she treads on it so light.   SHAKESPEARE,
Venus and Adonis

9259.

Grass nibbling inward
  Like green fire.
MARK VAN DOREN,
Former Barn Lot

9260. I believe a leaf of grass is no less than the journey-work of the stars.   WALT WHITMAN, *Song of Myself*

See also: 8191, 12410, 14927.

GRASSHOPPER

Related Subject: Grass.

9261. The grasshopper shall be a burden, and desire shall fail; because man goeth to his long home, and the mourners go about the streets.
Bible: Ecclesiastes, xii, 5

9262.
Happy insect! what can be
In happiness compared to thee?
ABRAHAM COWLEY,
The Grasshopper

9263.
The Grasshopper, the Grasshopper,
   I will explain to you:—
He is the Brownies' Racehorse,
   The Fairies' Kangaroo.
VACHEL LINDSAY,
The Grasshopper

See also: 5693.

GRATITUDE AND INGRATITUDE

Related Subjects: Appreciation, Debt, Forgetfulness, Obligation, Praise.

9271. Gratitude is the sign of noble souls.   AESOP, *Androcles*

9272. He that proclaims the kindnesses he has received, shows his disposition to repay 'em if he could.
CERVANTES, *Don Quixote*

9273. Gratitude to benefactors is a well recognized virtue, and to express it in some form or other, however imperfectly, is a duty to ourselves as well as to those who have helped us.
FREDERICK DOUGLASS,
Autobiography

9274. The still small voice of gratitude.   THOMAS GRAY,
Ode for Music

9275. Gratitude is a fruit of great cultivation; you do not find it among gross people. SAMUEL JOHNSON,
Tour to the Hebrides

9276. The gratitude of most men is but a secret desire of receiving greater benefits.
LA ROCHEFOUCAULD, *Maxims*

9277.
                A grateful mind
By owing owes not, but still pays, at once
Indebted and discharg'd.
MILTON, *Paradise Lost*

9278.
Two kinds of gratitude: the sudden kind
We feel for what we take, the larger kind
We feel for what we give.
E. A. ROBINSON, *Captain Craig*

9279. He who receives a benefit with gratitude, repays the first instalment on his debt.   SENECA

9280.
O Lord! that lends me life,
Lend me a heart replete with thankfulness!   SHAKESPEARE,
Henry VI

9281. Evermore thanks, the exchequer of the poor.
SHAKESPEARE, *Richard II*

9282.
I can no other answer make but thanks,
And thanks, and ever thanks.
SHAKESPEARE, *Twelfth Night*

9283. Gratitude is but a lame sentiment; thanks, when they are expressed, are often more embarrassing than welcome. STEVENSON, *Underwoods*

Ingratitude.

9284. A man is very apt to complain of the ingratitude of those who have risen far above him. SAMUEL JOHNSON, *Boswell: Life*

9285. A man who is ungrateful is often less to blame than his benefactor. LA ROCHEFOUCAULD, *Maxims*

9286. Gratitude is the least of virtues, but ingratitude the worst of vices. *Proverb*

9287. Ingratitude is the daughter of pride. *Proverb*

9288. Ingratitude makes the receiver worse, but the benefactor better. *Proverb*

9289. Be not ungrateful to your old friend. *Proverb*

9290.
Blow, blow, thou winter wind!
Thou art not so unkind
As man's ingratitude.
SHAKESPEARE, *As You Like It*

9291.
How sharper than a serpent's tooth it is
To have a thankless child!
SHAKESPEARE, *King Lear*

9292. Ingratitude, thou marble-hearted fiend! SHAKESPEARE, *King Lear*

9293.
I hate ingratitude more in a man
Than lying, vainness, babbling drunkenness,

Or any taint of vice whose strong corruption
Inhabits our frail blood.
SHAKESPEARE, *Twelfth Night*

See also: 227, 518, 1818, 1962, 19618.

GRAVE, GRAVEYARD

Related Subjects: Church, Death, Epitaphs, Funeral, Monument.

9301. Only on the edge of the grave can man conclude anything.
HENRY ADAMS,
The Education of Henry Adams

9302. One foot in the grave.
BEAUMONT & FLETCHER,
The Little French Lawyer

9303.
All that tread
The globe are but a handful to the tribes
That slumber in its bosom.
BRYANT, *Thanatopsis*

9304. As James J. Hill used to say: "There'll be no pockets in your shroud." B. C. FORBES

9305.
The boast of heraldry, the pomp of pow'r,
And all that beauty, all that wealth e'er gave,
Await alike the inevitable hour:
The paths of glory lead but to the grave. THOMAS GRAY,
Elegy Written in a Country Churchyard

9306. Caskets!—a vile modern phrase, which compels a person of sense and good taste to shrink more disgustfully than ever before from the idea of being buried at all.
HAWTHORNE, *Our Old Home*

9307. Wrapt in the cold embraces of the tomb. HOMER, *Iliad*

9308. In the democracy of the dead, all men at last are equal. There is neither rank nor station nor prerogative in the republic of the grave.
                    J. J. INGALLS

9309.
Teach me to live, that I may dread
The grave as little as my bed.
            BISHOP THOMAS KEN,
            Morning and Evening Hymn

9310.
I like that ancient Saxon phrase, which calls
The burial-ground God's-Acre!
            LONGFELLOW, *God's-Acre*

9311.
The grave itself is but a covered bridge
Leading from light to light, through a brief darkness.
            LONGFELLOW, *The Golden Legend*

9312.
All, all are sleeping, sleeping, sleeping on the hill.   MASTERS,
            Spoon River Anthology

9313.
O Lady, he is dead and gone!
    Lady, he's dead and gone!
And at his head a green grass turfe,
    And at his heels a stone.
    THOMAS PERCY, *Reliques of A. P.*

9314. The grave is the general meeting-place.   *Proverb*

9315.
            Lay her i' the earth;
And from her fair and unpolluted flesh
May violets spring.
            SHAKESPEARE, *Hamlet*

9316.
Let's talk of graves, of worms, and epitaphs;

Make dust our paper, and with rainy eyes
Write sorrow on the bosom of the earth.   SHAKESPEARE,
                    Richard II

9317.
And my large kingdom for a little grave,
A little little grave, an obscure grave.
            SHAKESPEARE, *Richard II*

9318.
What will they give me, when journey's done?
Your own room to be quiet in, Son!
        HUMBERT WOLFE, *Journey's End*

9319.
One that would peep and botanize
Upon his mother's grave.
        WORDSWORTH, *A Poet's Epitaph*

9320.
She lived unknown, and few could know
    When Lucy ceased to be;
But she is in her grave, and, oh
    The difference to me.
            WORDSWORTH, *Lucy*

See also: 392, 520, 750, 802, 1744, 1918, 2684, 4327, 20575.

GRAVITY

Related Subjects: Earnestness.

9321. Gravity is only the bark of wisdom's tree, but it preserves it.
            CONFUCIUS, *Analects*

9322. His smile is sweetened by his gravity.   GEORGE ELIOT,
                    The Spanish Gypsy

9323. Gravity is the ballast of the soul, which keeps the mind steady.
            THOMAS FULLER,
            Holy and Profane State

9324. Gravity is a trick of the body devised to conceal deficiencies of the mind. LA ROCHEFOUCAULD, *Maxims*

9325. What doth gravity out of his bed at midnight? SHAKESPEARE, *Henry IV*

9326. 'Tis not for gravity to play at cherry-pit with Satan.
SHAKESPEARE, *Twelfth Night*

9327. As grave as judge that's giving charge. SAMUEL WESLEY, *Maggots*

GREATNESS

Related Subjects: **Dignity, Distinction, Fame, Honor, Power, Reputation.**

9331. Great men are the real men, the men in whom nature has been fortunate. They are not extraordinary—they are in the true order. It is the little men who are not what they ought to be.   AMIEL

9332. Men in great place are thrice servants,—servants of the sovereign or state, servants of fame, and servants of business.   BACON, *Of Great Place*

9333. Great men are not always wise.
Bible: Job, xxxii, 9

9334.
When the dust of death has choked
A great man's voice, the common words he said
Turn oracles.
ELIZABETH B. BROWNING, *Casa Guidi Windows*

9335.
Beneath the rule of men entirely great,
The pen is mightier than the sword.
BULWER-LYTTON, *Richelieu*

9336. All greatness is unconscious, or it is little and naught.
CARLYLE, *Sir Walter Scott*

9337. No sadder proof can be given by a man of his own littleness than disbelief in great men.
CARLYLE, *Heroes & Hero-Worship*

9338. They're only truly great who are truly good.
GEORGE CHAPMAN, *Revenge for Honour*

9339.
Greatness and goodness are not means,—but ends!
Hath he not always treasures, always friends,
The good great man? Three treasures,—love, and light,
And calm thoughts, regular as infant's breath;—
And three firm friends, more sure than day and night,—
Himself, his Maker, and the angel Death.   COLERIDGE, *Complaint*

9340. Some great men owe most of their greatness to the ability of detecting in those they destine for their tools the exact quality of strength that matters for their work.
JOSEPH CONRAD, *Lord Jim*

9341. No great man is ever born too soon or too late. When we say that the time is not ripe for this or that celebrity, we confess by implication that this very man, and no other, is required. NORMAN DOUGLAS, *South Wind*

9342.
When the high heart we magnify,
And the clear vision celebrate,
And worship greatness passing by,
Ourselves are great.
JOHN DRINKWATER, *Abraham Lincoln*

9343. It is only the great men who are truly obscene. It is that touch which stamps their genius. It gives profundity and truth to their vision of life. If they had not dared to be obscene they could never have dared to be great. Their vision of the world would have remained fatally marred.   HAVELOCK ELLIS,
The Art of Life

9344. To be great is to be misunderstood.   EMERSON, *Self-Reliance*

9345. When nature removes a great man, people explore the horizon for a successor; but none comes, and none will. His class is extinguished with him. In some other and quite different field, the next man will appear.   EMERSON,
Representative Men

9346. He is great who is what he is from Nature, and who never reminds us of others.   EMERSON,
Representative Men

9347. Great men are they who see that spiritual is stronger than any material force; that thoughts rule the world.   EMERSON,
Progress of Culture

9348. No, I distrust Great Men. They produce a desert of uniformity around them and often a pool of blood, too.   E. M. FORSTER,
I Believe

9349. The world cannot live at the level of its great men.
SIR JAMES G. FRAZER,
The Golden Bough

9350. Greatness is so often a courteous synonym for great success.
PHILIP GUEDALLA

9351. The union of theorizer, organizer, and leader in one man is the rarest phenomenon on earth; therein lies greatness.   ADOLF HITLER

9352. Great minds have purposes, others have wishes. Little minds are tamed and subdued by misfortune; but great minds rise above them.
WASHINGTON IRVING

9353.
Thou'rt an ass, Robin, thou'rt an ass,
  To think that great men be
More gay than I that lie on the grass
  Under the greenwood tree.
I tell thee no, I tell thee no,
The Great are slaves to their gilded
  show.   GEORGE JAMES, *Richelieu*

9354. He seemed to me ever by his work one of the greatest men, and most worthy of admiration. In his adversity I ever prayed that God would give him strength; for greatness he could not want.
BEN JONSON, *Of Francis Bacon*

9355. Greatness of name in the father oft-times overwhelms the son they stand too near one another The shadow kills the growth: so much, that we see the grandchild come more and oftener to be heir of the first.   BEN JONSON, *Timber*

9356.
So when a great man dies,
For years beyond our ken,
The light he leaves behind him lies
Upon the paths of men.
LONGFELLOW, *Charles Sumner*

9357.
Great thoughts, great feelings, came
  to them,
  Like instincts unawares.
  R. M. MILNE, *The Men of Old*

9358. Great men are meteors designed to burn so that the earth may be lighted.   NAPOLEON

9359. Pathetic attitudes are not in keeping with greatness.
NIETZSCHE, *Ecce Homo*

9360. Serve a great man, and you will know what sorrow is.   *Proverb*

9361. A great man's foolish sayings pass for wise ones.   *Proverb*

9362. Great men rejoice in adversity just as brave soldiers triumph in war.   SENECA, *De Providentia*

9363. It is a rough road that leads to the heights of greatness.   SENECA

9364. There's hope a great man's memory may outlive his life half a year.   SHAKESPEARE, *Hamlet*

9365.
    Rightly to be great
Is not to stir without great argument,
But greatly to find quarrel in a straw
When honour's at the stake.
    SHAKESPEARE, *Hamlet*

9366.
I have touched the highest point of all my greatness;
And from that full meridian of my glory,
I haste now to my setting: I shall fall
Like a bright exhalation in the evening,
And no man see me more.
    SHAKESPEARE, *Henry VIII*

9367. The choice and master spirits of this age.   SHAKESPEARE, *Julius Caesar*

9368. They that stand high have many blasts to shake them.
    SHAKESPEARE, *Richard III*

9369. Some are born great, some achieve greatness, and some have greatness thrust upon them.
    SHAKESPEARE, *Twelfth Night*

9370. The great man is the man who does a thing for the first time.
    ALEXANDER SMITH, *Dreamthorp*

9371. Great men hallow a whole people, and lift up all who live in their time.   SYDNEY SMITH, *Lady Holland's Memoir*

9372. The world knows nothing of its greatest men.
    SIR HENRY TAYLOR, *Philip Van Artevelde*

9373.
    In me there dwells
No greatness, save it be some far-off touch
Of greatness to know well I am not great.   TENNYSON, *Idylls of the King*

9374. I wish the rulers would try a little more to make great men; that they would set less value on the work, and more on the workmen; that they would never forget that a nation cannot long remain strong when every man belonging to it is individually weak, and that no form or combination or social policy has yet been devised to make an energetic people of a community of pusillanimous and enfeebled citizens.
    DE TOCQUEVILLE, *Democracy in America*

9375. The death of a great man begins another history, of his continuing influence, his changing renown, the legend which takes the place of fact.   CARL VAN DOREN, *Benjamin Franklin*

9376. The great things are not done only by impulse, but are a series of small things brought together. . . And great things are not something accidental but certainly must be willed.
    VAN GOGH, *Letters*

9377.
Men are we, and must grieve when even the shade

Of that which once was great, is
  passed away. WORDSWORTH,
*On the Extinction of the Venetian
Republic*

See also: 150, 152, 155, 158, 522,
1071, 1226, 1261, 2583, 2724, 3349,
3455, 3874, 3992, 4156, 4420, 4590,
4895, 19434.

GREECE AND THE GREEKS

Related Subjects: Europe, History,
Rome and the Romans, Troy.

9380.
The isles of Greece, the isles of
  Greece!
Where burning Sappho loved and
  sung. . . .
Eternal summer gilds them yet,
But all, except their sun, is set.
          BYRON, *Don Juan*

9381. Put not thy faith in any Greek.
    EURIPIDES, *Iphigenia in Tauris*

9382. The Attic Greek culture which
drew material inspiration from the
surplus wealth created by slave labor
in the silver mines was scientifically
sterile, because it was the culture of
a leisured class divorced from contact with the instruments of production.   LANCELOT HOGBEN,
        Dangerous Thoughts

9383. When Greeks joined Greeks,
then was the tug of war.
        NATHANIEL LEE,
        Alexander the Great

9384.
Athens, the eye of Greece, mother of
  arts
And eloquence.
      MILTON, *Paradise Lost*

9385. I think that a knowledge of
Greek thought and life, and of the
arts in which the Greeks expressed

their thought and sentiment, essential
to high culture. A man may know
everything else, but without this
knowledge he remains ignorant of the
best intellectual and moral achievements of his own race.
        CHARLES E. NORTON

9386. It is perhaps the highest distinction of the Greeks that they recognized the indissoluble connection of
beauty and goodness.
        CHARLES E. NORTON

9387. When we compare Austable's
Historia Animalium of the fourth
century B. C. with the stupendous
volumes of research of the present
day . . . we realize the wide contrast
and wonder the more that the Greeks,
with their comparatively meagre and
limited knowledge, came so near the
truth.   HENRY F. OSBORN,
      From the Greeks to Darwin

9388.
To the glory that was Greece,
And the grandeur that was Rome.
        POE, *To Helen*

9389. But, for my own part, it was
Greek to me.   SHAKESPEARE,
        Julius Caesar

9390. I fear the Greeks, even when
bringing gifts.   VERGIL, *Aeneid*

See also: 459, 1003, 2142, 2955,
3470, 4049, 6213, 7153, 20826.

GRIEF

Related Subjects: Consolation,
Death, Desolation, Despair, Despondency, Loss, Melancholy, Misery, Mourning, Regret, Sorrow,
Sympathy, Tears, Woe.

9391.
           I think the slain
Care little if they sleep or rise again;

And we, the living, wherefore should
  we ache
With counting all our lost ones?
            AESCHYLUS, *Agamemnon*

9392. 'Twill grieve me so to the
heart, that I shall cry my eyes out.
            CERVANTES, *Don Quixote*

9393. Grief tires more than anything, and brings a deeper slumber.
      GEORGE DU MAURIER, *Trilby*

9394. One gives people in grief their
own way.   MRS. GASKELL,
                  Cranford

9395. In all the silent manliness of
grief.   GOLDSMITH,
            The Deserted Village

9396. Great grief is a divine and
terrible radiance which transfigures
the wretched.   VICTOR HUGO,
                  Les Miserables

9397. While grief is fresh, every attempt to divert only irritates.
    SAMUEL JOHNSON, *Boswell: Life*

9398. Love hath no physic for a grief
too deep.   ROBERT NATHAN,
                  A Cedar Box

9399.
Because my grief seems quiet and
    apart,
  Think not for such a reason it is
    less.
True sorrow makes a silence in the
    heart,
  Joy has its friends, but grief its
    loneliness.
    ROBERT NATHAN, *A Cedar Box*

9400.
Was there love once? I have for-
    gotten her.
Was there grief once? grief yet is
    mine.   ROBERT NICHOLS,
                  Fulfilment

9401. Happiness is beneficial for the
body but it is grief that develops the
powers of the mind.
            MARCEL PROUST,
            The Past Recaptured

9402. The bitter past, more welcome
is the sweet.   SHAKESPEARE,
            All's Well that Ends Well

9403. A plague of sighing and grief!
It blows a man up like a bladder.
      SHAKESPEARE, *Henry IV*

9404. What private griefs they have,
alas! I know not.
      SHAKESPEARE, *Julius Caesar*

9405.
Grief fills the room up of my absent
    child,
Lies in his bed, walks up and down
    with me,
Puts on his pretty looks, repeats his
    words,
Remembers me of all his gracious
    parts,
Stuffs out his vacant garments with
    his form.   SHAKESPEARE,
                  King John

9406.
I will instruct my sorrows to be
    proud;
For grief is proud, and makes his
    owner stoop. SHAKESPEARE,
                  King John

9407. Every one can master a grief
but he that has it.
            SHAKESPEARE,
      Much Ado About Nothing

9408. Patch grief with proverbs.
            SHAKESPEARE,
      Much Ado About Nothing

9409.
                  Men
Can counsel and speak comfort to
    that grief

Which they themselves not feel.
SHAKESPEARE,
Much Ado About Nothing

9410. My grief lies onward, and my joy behind.   SHAKESPEARE,
Sonnet L

See also: 40, 587, 2072.

GUESTS

Related Subjects: Feast, Friend, Hospitality, Inn.

9411. People are either born hosts or born guests.   MAX BEERBOHM

9412.
Hail Guest! We ask not what thou art:
If Friend, we greet thee, hand and heart;
If Stranger, such no longer be;
If Foe, our love shall conquer thee.
ARTHUR GUITERMAN, *Door Verse*

9413. Ye diners-out from whom we guard our spoons.
MACAULAY, *Political Georgics*

9414. Fish and guests smell at three days old.   *Proverb*

9415. Unbidden guests are welcomest when they are gone.
Proverb

9416. Leave weelcome a-hent ye.
Proverb

9417. He is an ill guest that never drinks to his host.   *Proverb*

9418. A constant guest is never welcome.   *Proverb*

See also: 2852, 12203.

GUILT

Related Subjects: Bribery, Confession, Conscience, Crime, Error, Law, Murder, Punishment, Remorse, Repentance, Sin.

9421. The pot calls the kettle black.
CERVANTES, *Don Quixote*

9422. Guilt is present in the very hesitation, even though the deed be not committed.   CICERO, *De Officiis*

9423. Secret guilt by silence is betrayed.   DRYDEN,
The Hind & the Panther

9424. Guilt has very quick ears to an accusation.   FIELDING, *Amelia*

9425. Let no guilty man escape, if it can be avoided. No personal considerations should stand in the way of performing a public duty.
ULYSSES S. GRANT

9426.
But Guilt was my grim Chamberlain
That lighted me to bed,
And drew my midnight curtains round,
With fingers bloody red!
THOMAS HOOD,
The Dream of Eugene Aram

9427.
How guilt, once harbour'd in the conscious breast,
Intimidates the brave, degrades the rest.   SAMUEL JOHNSON, *Irene*

9428. He that knows no guilt can know no fear.   MASSINGER,
The Great Duke of Florence

9429.
These false pretexts and varnish'd colours failing,
Bare in thy guilt how foul must thou appear.   MILTON,
Samson Agonistes

9430. Whose house is of glass, must not throw stones at another.
Proverb

9431. Successful guilt is the bane of society.   PUBLILIUS SYRUS,
Sententiae

9432.
And then it started like a guilty thing
Upon a fearful summons.
       SHAKESPEARE, *Hamlet*

9433. The lady doth protest too
much, methinks. SHAKESPEARE,
                  Hamlet

9434. My stronger guilt defeats my
strong intent.   SHAKESPEARE,
                  Hamlet

9435.
So full of artless jealousy is guilt,
It spills itself in fearing to be spilt.
       SHAKESPEARE, *Hamlet*

9436.
Thou canst not say I did it; never
  shake
Thy gory locks at me.
       SHAKESPEARE, *Macbeth*

9437.
               Guiltiness will speak
Though tongues were out of use.
       SHAKESPEARE, *Othello*

See also: 2192, 9478, 11137, 19216,
20096.

GYPSIES, see Wanderlust

H

HABIT

Related Subjects: Custom, Fashion, Manners, Order, Rule.

9441. Habit is thus the enormous flywheel of society, its most precious conservative agent. It alone is what keeps us all within the bounds of ordinance.   WILLIAM JAMES,
                 Psychology

9442. Habit is a cable; we weave a thread of it every day, and at last we cannot break it.   HORACE MANN

9443. Moral habits, induced by public practices, are far quicker in making their way into men's private lives, than the failings and faults of individuals are in infecting the city at large.   PLUTARCH, *Lives*

9444. Powerful indeed is the empire of habit.   PUBLILIUS SYRUS,
               Sententiae

9445. How use doth breed a habit in a man!   SHAKESPEARE,
   The Two Gentlemen of Verona

9446. Habit is habit, and not to be flung out of the window by any man,
but coaxed down-stairs a step at a time.   MARK TWAIN,
   Pudd'nhead Wilson's Calendar

9447. The formation of right habits is essential to your permanent security. They diminish your chance of falling when assailed, and they augment your chance of recovery when overthrown.   JOHN TYNDALL,
     Fragments of Science

See also: 73, 236, 419, 864, 1837, 2595, 2956, 3051.

HAIR

Related Subjects: Baldness, Barber, Beard, Head.

9451. If a woman have long hair, it is a glory to her.
   Bible: 1 Corinthians, xi, 15

9452. It is foolish to pluck out one's hair for sorrow, as if grief could be assuaged by baldness.   BION,
               Sententiae

9453.
And yonder sits a maiden,
  The fairest of the fair,

With gold in her garment glittering,
And she combs her golden hair.
HEINE, *The Lorelei*

9454.
But she is vanish'd to her shady home
Under the deep, inscrutable; and there
Weeps in a midnight made of her own hair. THOMAS HOOD,
Hero and Leander

9455.
When friends leave we're down-hearted;
Hair knows what 'tis to be parted!
W. S. LAPSLEY, *Parting*

9456. A fine head of hair adds beauty to a good face, and terror to an ugly one. LYCURGUS,
Plutarch: Lives

9457. A chaste woman ought not to dye her hair yellow. MENANDER

9458. Long hair and short wit.
Proverb

9459. To split a hair. *Proverb*

9460.
Rosalind: His hair is of a good colour.
Celia: An excellent colour: your chestnut was ever the only colour.
SHAKESPEARE, *As You Like It*

9461.
Bind up those tresses. O, what love I note
In the fair multitude of those her hairs!
Where but by chance a silver drop hath fallen. SHAKESPEARE,
King John

9462.
And her sunny locks
Hang on her temples like a golden fleece. SHAKESPEARE,
The Merchant of Venice

9463. Her hair shall be of what colour it please God.
SHAKESPEARE,
Much Ado About Nothing

9464.
Rising up,
Robed in the long night of her deep hair. TENNYSON, *The Princess*

See also: 1708, 2654.

HAND

Related Subjects: Fingers, Hospitality.

9471.
My wife's hands are long and thin,
Fit to catch a spirit in,
Fit to set a subtle snare
For something lighter than the air.
STEPHEN VINCENT BENET,
Hands

9472.
Tools were made, and born were hands,
Every farmer understands.
BLAKE, *Proverbs*

9473.
Give me the hand that is honest and hearty,
Free as the breeze and unshackled by party. JAMES MONTGOMERY,
Give Me The Hand

9474. Many hands make light work.
Proverb

9475. Give me your hand and let me feel your pulse. SHAKESPEARE,
The Comedy of Errors

9476. The hand of little employment hath the daintier sense.
SHAKESPEARE, *Hamlet*

9477. Now join your hands, and with your hands your hearts.
SHAKESPEARE, *Henry VI*

9478. All the perfumes of Arabia will not sweeten this little hand.
SHAKESPEARE, *Macbeth*

9479.
See, how she leans her cheek upon her hand.
O! that I were a glove upon that hand,
That I might touch that cheek.
SHAKESPEARE, *Romeo and Juliet*

9480. To kiss the tender inward of thy hand.   SHAKESPEARE,
Sonnet CXXVIII

See also: 51, 951, 1485, 2207, 2533, 2651, 9709.

HANGING

Related Subjects: **Capital Punishment, Justice, Murder, Punishment.**

9481. Gaols, fetters, and gibbets are odd melancholy things; for a gentleman to dangle out of the world in a string has something so ugly, so awkward, and so disagreeable in it, that you cannot think of it without some regret.
DANIEL DEFOE, *to his enemies who wanted to see him hang.*

9482.
Three merry boys, and three merry boys,
And three merry boys are we,
As ever did sing in a hempen string
Under the gallows-tree.
JOHN FLETCHER,
The Bloody Brother

9483. Give him but rope enough, and he'll hang himself.   *Proverb*

9484. He that hath one of his family hanged, may not say to his neighbour, Hang up this fish.   *Proverb*

9485. If I be hanged, I'll choose my gallows.   *Proverb*

9486. A hangman is a good trade, he doth his work by daylight. *Proverb*

9487.
Mr. Harris: In behalf of Virginia I wish to say that her people never hung a northern man except John Brown and his friends; and then they hung, not by scores, but by law.
Mr. Stevens: You hung them exactly right, sir.
Mr. Harris: Yes; they were well hung.   CARL SANDBURG,
Abraham Lincoln; War Years

9488. That would hang us, every mother's son.   SHAKESPEARE,
A Midsummer-Night's Dream

9489. Let them hang themselves in their own straps.
SHAKESPEARE, *Twelfth Night*

9490. Hanging was the worst use a man could be put to.
SIR HENRY WOTTON,
The Disparity between Buckingham and Essex

9491. Hang me if you like—but stop shoving me! ART YOUNG, *to Sheriff*

See also: 822, 2651, 3865, 5618, 17216, 19342, 20364.

HAPPINESS AND UNHAPPINESS

Related Subjects: **Bliss, Cheerfulness, Contentment, Delight, Grief, Joy, Misery, Pleasure, Sorrow.**

9501. All cannot be happy at once for the glory of one state depends upon the ruin of another.
SIR THOMAS BROWNE,
Religio Medici

9502. The happiness of life is made up of minute fractions—the little soon forgotten charities of a kiss or smile, a kind look, a heartfelt compliment, and the countless infinitesimals of pleasurable and genial feeling.

COLERIDGE, *The Friend*

9503.
And there is even a happiness
That makes the heart afraid.

THOMAS HOOD,
Ode to Melancholy

9504. The supreme happiness of life is the conviction that we are loved.

VICTOR HUGO, *Les Miserables*

9505. To crave for happiness in this world is simply to be possessed by a spirit of revolt. What right have we to happiness? IBSEN, *Ghosts*

9506. The world would be better and brighter if our teachers would dwell on the Duty of Happiness as well as on the Happiness of Duty, for we ought to be as cheerful as we can, if only because to be happy ourselves is a most effectual contribution to the happiness of others.

SIR JOHN LUBBOCK,
The Pleasures of Life

9507. Remember this: that very little is needed to make a happy life.

MARCUS AURELIUS, *Meditations*

9508. The days that make us happy make us wise.

JOHN MASEFIELD, *Biography*

9509.
Live while ye may,
Yet happy pair. MILTON,
Paradise Lost

9510. As happy a man as any in the world, for the whole world seems to smile upon me. SAMUEL PEPYS,
Diary

9511. Happy go lucky. *Proverb*

9512. All worldly happiness consists in opinion. *Proverb*

9513.
Glad that I live am I;
That the sky is blue;
Glad for the country lanes,
And the fall of dew.

LIZETTE W. REESE,
A Little Song of Life

9514.
Silence is the perfectest herald of joy;
I were but little happy, if I could say How much. SHAKESPEARE,
Much Ado About Nothing

9515. We have no more right to consume happiness without producing it than to consume wealth without producing it. BERNARD SHAW, *Candida*

9516. A lifetime of happiness! No man alive could bear it: it would be hell on earth. BERNARD SHAW,
Man and Superman

9517. Happiness is a wine of the rarest vintage, and seems insipid to a vulgar taste.

LOGAN PEARSALL SMITH,
Afterthoughts

9518. Why are happy people not afraid of Death, while the insatiable and the unhappy so abhor that grim feature?

LOGAN PEARSALL SMITH,
Afterthoughts

9519. That here on earth is no sure happiness. EDMUND SPENSER,
The Faerie Queene

9520.
The world is so full of a number of things,
I'm sure we should all be as happy as kings. STEVENSON,
Happy Thought

9521.
Happiness is the shadow of things past,

Which fools still take for that which
is to be!
FRANCIS THOMPSON,
From the Night of Forebeing

9522.
Talk happiness. The world is sad
enough
Without your woe. No path is wholly
rough.   ELLA W. WILCOX,
Speech

Unhappiness

9523.
Let no one till his death
Be called unhappy. Measure not the
work
Until the day's out and the labor
done.
ELIZABETH B. BROWNING,
Aurora Leigh

9524. It seldom happens that any
felicity comes so pure as not to be
tempered and allayed by some mixture of sorrow.   CERVANTES,
Don Quixote

9525. Call no man happy till you
know the nature of his death! he is at
best but fortunate.   HERODOTUS

9526. No man is happy who does not
think himself so.
PUBLILIUS SYRUS, *Sententiae*

9527. Ah! *Vanitas Vanitatum!* which
of us is happy in this world? Which
of us has his desire? or, having it, is
satisfied?   THACKERAY, *Vanity Fair*

See also: 156, 218, 267, 292, 325,
517, 749, 751, 1469, 1523, 2127, 2717,
2855, 3062, 3736, 4572, 4962, 5391,
6381, 7020, 9666, 10665, 15862,
17937.

HARLOT, see Whore

HARMONY

**Related Subjects: Discord, Melo-
dy, Music, Song.**

9531. Where all was harmony, and
calm and quiet.   BYRON, *Don Juan*

9532. Harmony arises from the contest of opposites.   COHEN-PORTHEIM

9533.
From Harmony, from heav'nly Har-
mony,
This universal Frame began:
From Harmony to Harmony
Through all the compass of the notes
it ran,
The diapason closing full in Man.
DRYDEN,
A Song for St. Cecilia's Day

9534.
By harmony our souls are swayed;
By harmony the world was made.
GEORGE GRANVILLE,
The British Enchanters

9535.
Many have held the soul to be
Nearly allied to harmony.
MATTHEW GREEN, *The Spleen*

9536. Sentimentally I am disposed
to harmony; but organically I am incapable of a tune.
CHARLES LAMB, *A Chapter on Ears*

9537.
Seeing more harmony In her bright
eye
Than now you hear.
RICHARD LOVELACE,
Orpheus to the Beasts

9538.
The melting voice through mazes
running
Untwisting all the chains that tie
The hidden soul of harmony.
MILTON, *L'Allegro*

9539. If only the whole world could
feel the power of harmony . . . But

it is impossible for the world to feel it, for under that divine influence, the world would cease to be; humanity could not endure the paltriness of existence.
MOZART, *to Salieri*

9540.
How irksome is this music to my heart!
When such strings jar, what hope of harmony?   SHAKESPEARE,
Henry VI

9541.
            Soft stillness and the night
Become the touches of sweet harmony.   SHAKESPEARE,
The Merchant of Venice

9542. Weave harmonies divine, yet ever new.   SHELLEY,
Prometheus Unbound

9543.
No sound is uttered,—but a deep
And solemn harmony pervades
The hollow vale from steep to steep,
And penetrates the glades.
WORDSWORTH

9544.
Rapt Cecilia, seraph-haunted Queen
Of Harmony.   WORDSWORTH,
Ecclesiastical Sonnets

See also: 1317, 1456, 1702, 6560.

HARVEST

Related Subjects: Autumn, Farming, Fruit, Thanksgiving Day.

9551.
And the ripe harvest of the new-mown hay
Gives it a sweet and wholesome odour.
COLLEY CIBBER,
Richard III (Adaptation)

9552.
Fear not that I shall mar so fair an harvest

By putting in my sickle ere 'tis ripe.
JOHN HOME, *Douglas*

9553. A long harvest for a little corn.   *Proverb*

9554. He that hath a good harvest may be content with some thistles.
Proverb

9555. Harvest will come, and then every farmer's rich.   *Proverb*

9556. Harvest comes not every day, though it comes every year.
Proverb

9557.
Who eat their corn while yet 'tis green,
At the true harvest can but glean.
SAADI, *Gulistan*

9558.
            The seedsman
Upon the slime and ooze scatters his grain,
And shortly comes to harvest.
SHAKESPEARE, *Antony and Cleopatra*

9559.
To glean the broken ears after the man
That the main harvest reaps.
SHAKESPEARE, *As You Like It*

9560.
            Think, oh! grateful think
How good the God of Harvest is to you!   JAMES THOMSON,
The Seasons: Autumn

9561.
In harvest time, harvest-folk, servants and all,
Should make altogether good cheer in the hall.   THOMAS TUSSER,
Five Hundred Points of Good Husbandrie

9562.
Once more the liberal year laughs out

O'er richer stores than gems of
gold;
Once more with harvest song and
shout
Is nature's boldest triumph told.
WHITTIER, *Harvest Hymn*

See also: 468, 1362, 3089.

HASTE

Related Subjects: Patience,
Promptness, Speed.

9571. Sir Amice Pawlet, when he
saw too much haste made in any matter, was wont to say, "Stay a while,
that we may make an end the sooner."
BACON, *Apothegms*

9572. He is invariably in a hurry.
Being in a hurry is one of the tributes
he pays to life.
ELIZABETH A. BIBESCO, *Balloons*

9573.
Ther nis no werkman, what-so-ever
he be,
That may bothe werke wel and
hastily;
This wol be doon at leyser parfitly.
CHAUCER, *Canterbury Tales*

9574. No man who is in a hurry is
quite civilized.   WILL DURANT,
The Life of Greece

9575. A hasty man never wants woe.
Proverb

9576. Haste makes waste, and waste
makes want, and want makes strife
between the goodman and his wife.
Proverb

9577. Nothing can be done at once
hastily and prudently.
PUBLILIUS SYRUS, *Sententiae*

9578. He gets through too late who
goes too fast.
PUBLILIUS SYRUS, *Sententiae*

9579.
                   This sweaty haste
Doth make the night joint-labourer
with the day.   SHAKESPEARE,
Hamlet

9580. Make haste; the better foot
before.   SHAKESPEARE, *King John*

9581. Too swift arrives as tardy as
too slow.   SHAKESPEARE,
Romeo and Juliet

9582. Wisely and slow; they stumble
that run fast.   SHAKESPEARE,
Romeo and Juliet

9583. Though I am always in haste,
I am never in a hurry.
JOHN WESLEY, *Letters*

See also: 877, 6484, 7096, 9592,
16562.

HAT

Related Subjects: Dress, Head.

9591. There is not so variable thing
in nature as a lady's head-dress.
ADDISON, *The Spectator*

9592. Here's your hat, what's your
hurry?   B. C. COSTELLO,
Title of Song

9593. A hat not much the worse for
wear.   COWPER,
History of John Gilpin

9594. "If I knew as little of life as
that, I'd eat my hat and swallow the
buckle whole," said the clerical gentleman.   DICKENS, *Pickwick Papers*

9595. Pull down thy hat on the windy
side.   *Proverb*

9596. The hat is the *ultimatum mori-
ens* of respectability.
O. W. HOLMES,
The Autocrat of the Breakfast-Table

9597. The only place a new hat can be carried into with safety is a church, for there is plenty of room there.
LEIGH HUNT, *A Chapter on Hats*

9598. A broad hat does not always cover a venerable head.   *Proverb*

9599. Put your bonnet to its right use; 'tis for the head.
SHAKESPEARE, *Hamlet*

9600. Their hats are pluck'd about their ears.   SHAKESPEARE,
Julius Caesar

9601. If he be not in love with some woman, there is no believing old signs : a' brushes his hat o' mornings; what should that bode?
SHAKESPEARE,
Much Ado About Nothing

9602. An old hat and "the humour of forty fancies" prick'd in 't for a feather.   SHAKESPEARE,
The Taming of the Shrew

9603. Where did you get that hat, that collar and that tie?
J. J. SULLIVAN,
Where Did You Get that Hat?

HATRED

Related Subjects: Anger, Contempt, Dislike, Enemy, Jealousy, Malevolence, Murder, Passion, Revenge.

9611. A healthy hatred of scoundrels.
CARLYLE, *Latter Day Pamphlets*

9612.
Heaven has no rage like love to hatred turned,
Nor hell a fury like a woman scorned.
CONGREVE, *The Mourning Bride*

9613. You can't hate something that means nothing.   GALSWORTHY,
The Roof

9614. He was a very good hater.
SAMUEL JOHNSON

9615. Folks never understand the folks they hate.
LOWELL, *The Biglow Papers*

9616. In appearance, at least, he being on all occasions glad to be at friendship with me, though we hate one another, and know it on both sides.   SAMUEL PEPYS, *Diary*

9617.
Years of love have been forgot
In the hatred of a minute.
POE, *To* ———

9618. He who hath bitter in his breast spits no sweet.   *Proverb*

9619. As the best wine makes the sharpest vinegar, so the deepest love turns to the deadliest hatred. *Proverb*

9620. The fires of hatred are cinders of affection. SIR WALTER RALEIGH

9621.
'Tis not my speeches that you do mislike,
But 'tis my presence that doth trouble ye.
Rancour will out.
SHAKESPEARE, *Henry VI*

9622.
Heat not a furnace for your foe so hot
That it do singe yourself.
SHAKESPEARE, *Henry VIII*

9623.
There is no sport in hate when all the rage
Is on one side.
SHELLEY, *Lines to a Reviewer*

9624.
As love, if love be perfect, casts out fear,
So hate, if hate be perfect, casts out fear.
TENNYSON, *Idylls of the King*

See also: 1975, 3131, 4546, 10639, 11095, 12053, 13037.

HAWK AND HAWKING

Related Subjects: Birds, Hunting, Sport.

9631. Pretty pastime, nephew! 'Tis royal sport.
MASSINGER, *The Guardian*

9632. We hate the hawk because he always lives in arms.
OVID, *Art of Love*

9633. The first point of hawking is hold fast.   *Proverb*

9634.
A falcon, tow'ring in her pride of place,
Was by a mousing owl hawk'd at and kill'd.   SHAKESPEARE, *Macbeth*

9635. I have a fine hawk for the bush.   SHAKESPEARE,
The Merry Wives of Windsor

9636.
Dost thou love hawking? thou hast hawks will soar.
Above the morning lark.
SHAKESPEARE,
The Taming of the Shrew

See also: 11350.

HEAD

Related Subjects: Body, Face, Hair, Hat, Heart, Mind, Neck, Skull.

9641.
Such as take lodgings in a head
That's to be let unfurnished.
SAMUEL BUTLER, *Hudibras*

9642. It's my old girl that advises. She has the head.
DICKENS, *Bleak House*

9643. As the saying is, So many heads, so many wits.
QUEEN ELIZABETH

9644. Some men's heads are as easily blown away as their hats.
LORD HALIFAX

9645. O human head! Majestic box! O wondrous can, from labels free! If man is craving fame or rocks, he'll get them if he uses thee!
WALT MASON, *The Human Head*

9646. From the crown of our head to the sole of our foot.
THOMAS MIDDLETON,
A Mad World, My Masters

9647. Hang the pensive head.
MILTON, *Lycidas*

9648. Better be the head of an ass, than the tail of a horse.   *Proverb*

9649. He that has no head deserves not a laced hat.   *Proverb*

9650. When the head acheth, all the body is the worse.   *Proverb*

9651. It is a fortunate head that never ached.   *Proverb*

9652. Two heads are better than one.
Proverb

9653. A great head and a little wit.
Proverb

9654. It's better to be the head of a lizard than the tail of a lion. *Proverb*

9655. He that hath a head of wax must not walk in the sun.   *Proverb*

9656. I never knew so young a body with so old a head.
SHAKESPEARE,
The Merchant of Venice

9657. Faith, thou hast some crotchets in thy head.   SHAKESPEARE,
The Merry Wives of Windsor

9658. Thou hast a head, and so has a pin.   SWIFT, *Polite Conversation*

See also: 481, 2664, 3011, 5974, 20048.

HEALTH

Related Subjects: Body, Diet, Disease, Doctors, Hospitals, Life, Medicine, Sickness, Strength.

9661. A man's own observation, what he finds good of and what he finds hurt of, is the best physic to preserve health.
                    BACON, *Of Regimen of Health*

9662. Blessed is the healthy nature; it is the coherent, sweetly co-operative, not incoherent, self-distracting, self-destructive one!
                    CARLYLE, *Sir Walter Scott*

9663. Ill-health, of body or of mind, is defeat . . . Health alone is victory. Let all men, if they can manage it, contrive to be healthy!
                    CARLYLE, *Sir Walter Scott*

9664. The health of the people is really the foundation upon which all their happiness and all their powers as a State depend.   DISRAELI

9665.
The head that wears a crown may be
Inclined to some anxiety,
But, on the other hand, I know
A derby domes its meed of woe.
          SAMUEL HOFFENSTEIN,
          Songs of Faith in the Year After

9666. The groundwork of all happiness is health.   LEIGH HUNT,
                    Deaths of Little Children

9667.
Joy and Temperance and Repose
Slam the door on the doctor's nose.
          LONGFELLOW, *The Best Medicines*

9668. Health without wealth is half a sickness.   *Proverb*

9669. The head and feet kept warm, the rest will take no harm.   *Proverb*

9670. He that wants health wants everything.   *Proverb*

9671. As fit as a fiddle.   *Proverb*

9672. Hygiene is the only useful part of medicine, and hygiene is rather a virtue than a science.
                    ROUSSEAU,
                    Emile, or Education

9673. There's no joy even in beautiful Wisdom, unless one have holy Health.   SIMONIDES

9674. I have gout, asthma, and seven other maladies, but am otherwise very well.   SYDNEY SMITH,
                    Lady Holland's Memoir

9675.
Health is the vital principle of bliss,
And exercise, of health.
          JAMES THOMSON,
          The Castle of Indolence

9676. Health is the second blessing that we mortals are capable of,—a blessing that money cannot buy.
                    IZAAK WALTON,
                    The Compleat Angler

See also: 349, 2136, 2294, 3061.

HEARING, see Ears

HEART

Related Subjects: Feeling, Head, Love, Mind.

9681. A wise and an understanding heart.   *Bible: 1 Kings, iii, 12*

9682. There are many devices in a man's heart; nevertheless the counsel of the Lord, that shall stand.
                    Bible: Proverbs, xix, 21

9683. The heart is deceitful above all things, and desperately wicked: who can know it? *Bible: Jeremiah, xvii, 9*

9684.
The human heart has hidden treasures,
In secret kept, in silence sealed;—
The thoughts, the hopes, the dreams, the pleasures,
Whose charms were broken if revealed.
CHARLOTTE BRONTË, *Evening Solace*

9685.
The heart of man is the place the Devil dwells in; I feel sometimes a hell within myself.
SIR THOMAS BROWNE,
Religio Medici

9686. If a good face is a letter of recommendation, a good heart is a letter of credit.
BULWER-LYTTON,
What Will He Do With It

9687. A good heart is better than all the heads in the world.
BULWER-LYTTON, *The Disowned*

9688.
In many ways doth the full heart reveal
The presence of the love it would conceal.   COLERIDGE,
Motto to Poems Written in Later Life

9689. What other dungeon is so dark as one's own heart! What jailer so inexorable as one's self!
HAWTHORNE,
The House of the Seven Gables

9690.
The heart's dead
Are never buried.
SAMUEL HOFFENSTEIN,
Summer Day

9691.
The tumult and the shouting dies;
The Captains and the Kings depart:
Still stands Thine ancient sacrifice,
An humble and a contrite heart.
KIPLING, *Recessional*

9692. Cannot the heart in the midst of crowds feel frightfully alone?
CHARLES LAMB, *Eliana*

9693.
The beating of my own heart
Was all the sound I heard.
R. M. MILNES, *The Brookside*

9694.
When true hearts lie wither'd
And fond ones are flown
Oh, who would inhabit
This bleak world alone?
THOMAS MOORE,
The Last Rose of Summer

9695.
Ah! little they think who delight in her strains,
How the heart of the Minstrel is breaking.   THOMAS MOORE,
She is Far From the Land

9696. There are chords in the hearts of the most reckless which cannot be touched without emotion. Even with the utterly lost, to whom life and death are equally jests, there are matters of which no jest can be made.
POE, *The Masque of the Red Death*

9697. He that gives his heart will not deny his money.   *Proverb*

9698. Hearts may agree, though heads differ.   *Proverb*

9699. When the heart is a-fire, some sparks will fly out of the mouth.
Proverb

9700. Deep lies the heart's language.
Proverb

9701. Every heart hath its own ache.
Proverb

9702. It was written: "In the sweat of thy brow," but it was never written: "In the breaking of thy heart."
RUSKIN

9703. I'll warrant him heart-whole.
SHAKESPEARE, *As You Like It*

9704.
And let me wring your heart; for so I shall,
If it be made of penetrable stuff.
SHAKESPEARE, *Hamlet*

9705. Now cracks a noble heart.
SHAKESPEARE, *Hamlet*

9706.
A habitation giddy and unsure
Hath he that buildeth on the vulgar heart.   SHAKESPEARE, *Henry IV*

9707. He hath a heart as sound as a bell.   SHAKESPEARE,
Much Ado About Nothing

9708.
I will wear my heart upon my sleeve
For daws to peck at.
SHAKESPEARE, *Othello*

9709.
Ferdinand. Here's my hand.
Miranda. And mine, with my heart in't.
SHAKESPEARE, *The Tempest*

9710.
A merry heart goes all the day,
Your sad tires in a mile-a.
SHAKESPEARE, *The Winter's Tale*

9711. My heart is a lonely hunter that hunts on a lonely hill.
WILLIAM SHARP,
The Lonely Hunter
(Source of title of novel by Carson McCullers.)

9712.
My true-love hath my heart, and I have his,

By just exchange one for the other given:
I hold his dear, and mine he cannot miss,
There never was a better bargain driven.
SIR PHILIP SIDNEY, *The Bargain*

9713. There is a bonfire in my heart but no one comes to warm himself at it.   VAN GOGH

See also: 45, 443, 1326, 1445, 1470, 1699, 1707, 2130, 2143, 2176, 2226, 2281, 2427, 2794, 2856, 3204, 3225, 3714, 3886, 3891, 4281, 4330, 4355, 4449, 5330, 9162, 12311, 12320, 14082, 16535, 17012, 17193.

HEAVEN, see Paradise

THE HEAVENS

Related Subjects: Astrology, Astronomy, Clouds, Earth, Moon, Stars, Sun, Universe, Weather, World.

9721. The heavens declare the glory of God; and the firmament showeth his handiwork. *Bible: Psalms, xix, 1*

9722.
That inverted Bowl they call the Sky,
Whereunder crawling coop'd we live and die.
OMAR KHAYYAM, *Rubaiyat*

See also: 225, 1272.

HEIR, see Inheritance

HELL

Related Subjects: Death, Devil, Eternity, Judgment Day, Pain, Punishment, Salvation, Suffering.

9731.
    To appreciate heaven well
'Tis good for a man to have some fifteen minutes of hell.
WILL CARLETON,
Gone With a Handsomer Man

9732. I found the original of my hell in the world which we inhabit.

DANTE

9733.

Hell hath no limit, nor is circumscribed

In one self-place; for where we are is Hell,

And where Hell is, there must we ever be.

CHRISTOPHER MARLOWE, *Faustus*

9734.

When all the world dissolves,

And every creature shall be purified,

All places shall be hell that are not heaven.

CHRISTOPHER MARLOWE, *Faustus*

9735.

Long is the way

And hard, that out of hell leads up to light.   MILTON, *Paradise Lost*

9736. The hell within him.

MILTON, *Paradise Lost*

9737.

Which way shall I fly

Infinite wrath and infinite despair?

Which way I fly is hell; myself am hell;

And in the lowest deep a lower deep,

Still threat'ning to devour me, opens wide,

To which the hell I suffer seems a heaven.   MILTON, *Paradise Lost*

9738. All hell broke loose.

MILTON, *Paradise Lost*

9739. The most frightful idea that has ever corroded human nature— the idea of eternal punishment.

JOHN MORLEY, *Vauvenargues*

9740.

To rest, the cushion and soft dean invite,

Who never mentions hell to ears polite.   POPE, *Moral Essays*

9741. All hell shall stir for this.

SHAKESPEARE, *Henry V*

9742. Go the primrose way to the everlasting bonfire.

SHAKESPEARE, *Macbeth*

9743.

Hell is a city much like London—

A populous and smoky city.

SHELLEY, *Peter Bell the Third*

See also: 626, 1161, 2092, 2213, 3066, 9612, 10783, 17116, 21127.

HELP

Related Subjects: **Charity, Encouragement, Improvement, Kindness, Patronage, Philanthropy, Relief, Sympathy.**

9751. The gods help them that help themselves.   AESOP,
Hercules and the Waggoner

9752. God is our refuge and strength, a very present help in trouble.
Bible: Psalms, xlvi, 1

9753. Vain is the help of man.
Bible: Psalms, lx, 11

9754. They helped every one his neighbour: and every one said to his brother, Be of good courage.
Bible: Isaiah, xli, 6

9755. I would help others, out of a fellow-feeling.   ROBERT BURTON,
Anatomy of Melancholy

9756.

Try first thyself, and after call in God;

For to the worker God himself lends aid.   EURIPIDES, *Hippolytus*

9757. God helps them that help themselves.   FRANKLIN, *Poor Richard*

9758. It is a wonderful thing to go among the people and to help them.
ADOLF HITLER, *Oct. 4, 1936*

9759. The hands that help are holier than the lips that pray.
ROBERT INGERSOLL,
The Children of the Stage

9760. Assist me up, and in coming down I will shift for myself.
SIR THOMAS MORE, *at his execution*

9761. He is my friend that succoureth me, not he that pitieth me.
Proverb

9762. Call you that backing of your friends? A plague upon such backing!
SHAKESPEARE, *Henry IV*

9763. Help me, Cassius, or I sink!
SHAKESPEARE, *Julius Caesar*

9764.
'Tis not enough to help the feeble up,
But to support him after.
SHAKESPEARE, *Timon of Athens*

9765. I'm learnin' one thing good. Learnin' it all a time, ever' day. If you're in trouble, or hurt or need— go to the poor people. They're the only ones that'll help—the only ones.
JOHN STEINBECK,
The Grapes of Wrath

9766. Something between a hindrance and a help.
WORDSWORTH, *Michael*

See also: 1200, 4291.

HEREDITY

Related Subjects: Ancestry, Blood, Breeding, Character, Family, Posterity.

9771. The present policies of the German government are based on the assumption that an "Aryan" has certain biologically determined qualities that are entirely foreign to every "Non-Aryan." All members of each race, it is claimed, have certain unescapable hereditary characteristics which determine their mental life and their social behavior. These beliefs are based on a complete misunderstanding of what constitutes a race and of the way in which we arrive at the concept of a racial type.
FRANZ BOAS, *Aryans & Non-Aryans*

9772. That unity of race, which is the foundation of the policies of the German government, does not exist. A race consists of individuals diverse in bodily build; and heredity is a matter that is important in the study of the forms of the offspring, but there is no such thing as racial heredity even in relatively pure groups in regard to those traits that occur in many different forms in that group.
FRANZ BOAS,
Aryans & Non-Aryans

9773. How shall a man escape from his ancestors, or draw off from his veins the black drop which he drew from his father's or his mother's life?
EMERSON, *Conduct of Life*

9774.
A hundred little things make likenesses
In brethen born, and shows the father's blood. EURIPIDES, *Electra*

9775. What we have inherited from our fathers and mothers is not all that "walks" in us. There are all sorts of dead ideas and lifeless old beliefs. They have no tangibility but they haunt us all the same and we cannot get rid of them. Whenever I take up a newspaper I seem to see Ghosts gliding between the ·lines. Ghosts must be all over the country, as thick as the sands of the sea.
IBSEN, *Ghosts*

9776. The proper time to influence the character of a child is about a hundred years before he is born.

DEAN INGE

9777. There are some hereditary strokes of character by which a family may be as clearly distinguished as by the blackest features of the human face.

JUNIUS

9778. The error of the eugenists lies in the assumption that a physically healthy man is the best fitted to survive. . . . Imagine estimating philosophers by their chest expansions, their blood pressures, their Wassermann reactions.

H. L. MENCKEN

9779. It will not out of the flesh that is bred in the bone.

Proverb

9780.
Bull Jove, sir, had an amiable low;
And some such strange bull leap'd your father's cow,
And got a calf in that same noble feat
Much like to you, for you have just his bleat.

SHAKESPEARE,
Much Ado About Nothing

See also: 4477, 6997, 10533, 18028, 18583, 18588.

HERESY

Related Subjects: Atheism, Doctrine, Doubt, Error, Piety, Treason.

9781. You who sentence me are in greater fear than I who am condemned. I have fought, that is much —victory is in the hands of fate. Be that as it may, this at least future ages will not deny me, be the victor who he may—that I did not fear to die. I yielded to none of my fellows in constancy and preferred a spiritual death to a cowardly life.

GIORDANO BRUNO, *at the stake*

9782. False doctrine does not necessarily make a man a heretic, but an evil heart can make any doctrine heretical.

COLERIDGE

9783. But because I have been enjoined by this Holy Office altogether to abandon the false opinion which maintains that the sun is the centre and immovable, and forbidden to hold, defend, or teach the said false doctrine in any manner, and after it had been signified to me that the said doctrine is repugnant with the Holy Scripture . . . I abjure, curse, and detest the said heresies and errors . . . and I swear that I will never more in future say or assert anything verbally, or in writing, which may give rise to a similar suspicion of me.

GALILEO,
Recantation before the Holy Inquisition

9784. Society can overlook murder, adultery or swindling; it never forgives the preaching of a new gospel.

FREDERIC HARRISON

9785. Heresy is what the minority believe; it is the name given by the powerful to the doctrine of the weak.

ROBERT INGERSOLL,
Liberty of Man, Woman and Child

9786. A man may be a heretic in the truth; and if he believe things only because his pastor says so, or the assembly so determines, without knowing other reason, though his belief be true, yet the very truth he holds becomes his heresy.

MILTON, *Areopagitica*

9787. Heresy is the school of pride.

Proverb

9788.
In our windy world
What's up is faith, what's down is heresy.

TENNYSON, *Harold*

9789. Better heresy of doctrine, than heresy of heart.

WHITTIER, *Mary Garvin*

See also: 1874, 20200.

HERMIT

Related Subjects: Asceticism, Monk, Solitude.

9791. The hermit thinks the sun shines nowhere but in his cell.

Proverb

9792. People who live to themselves are generally left to themselves.

GEORGE KELLY, *Craig's Wife*

9793. The peculiarity of the New England hermit has not been his desire to get near to God, but his anxiety to get away from man.

H. W. MABIE,
Backgrounds of Literature

9794.
Shall I, like a hermit, dwell
On a rock or in a cell?

SIR WALTER RALEIGH,
Shall I, Like a Hermit, Dwell

HERO AND HEROISM

Related Subjects: Courage, Fame, Glory, Martyr, Sacrifice, Valor.

9801.
These, who desired to live, went out to death:
Dark underground their golden youth is lying.
We live: and there is brightness in our breath
They could not know—the splendour of their dying.

LASCELLES ABERCROMBIE, *Epitaph*

9802.
But whether on the scaffold high
Or in the battle's van,

The fittest place where man can die
Is where he dies for man!

M. J. BARRY,
The Place Where Men Should Die

9803. Brave men were living before Agamemnon.   BYRON, *Don Juan*

9804. When ye build yer triumphal arch to yer conquerin' hero, Hinnissey, build it out of bricks so the people will have somethin' convanient to throw at him as he passes through.

F. P. DUNNE, *Fame*

9805. Those persons who are burning to display heroism may rest assured that the course of social evolution will offer them every opportunity.   HAVELOCK ELLIS,
The Task of Social Hygiene

9806. Heroism feels and never reasons and therefore is always right.

EMERSON, *Heroism*

9807. Every hero becomes a bore at last.   EMERSON, *Representative Men*

9808. He who aspires to be a hero must drink brandy.

SAMUEL JOHNSON

9809. It is one's duty to youth to point out that there are ways of living heroically during peace times. I do not imagine that Monsieur and Madame Curie ever felt the lack of adventure in their lives, for there is nothing more adventurous than experimentation with an unknown element. Their purpose was to find something of benefit to the human race. They jeopardized no lives but their own.   ELEANOR ROOSEVELT

9810.
There are heroes then—among the plain people—Heroes, did you say? And why not? They give all they've got and ask no questions and take

what comes and what more do you
want?   CARL SANDBURG,
The People, Yes

9811.
I will put in my poems that with you
is heroism upon land and sea,
And I will report all heroism from an
American point of view.
WALT WHITMAN,
Starting from Paumanok

See also: 522, 551, 805, 1953, 3875,
3905, 12429, 17752.

HESITATION

**Related Subjects: Decision, Doubt,
Resolution, Suspense.**

9821. No man, having put his hand
to the plough, and looking back, is fit
for the kingdom of God.
Bible: Luke, ix, 62

9822. He who dallies is a dastard, he
who doubts is damned.
Attributed to GEORGE MCDUFFLE

9823. Infirm of purpose!
SHAKESPEARE, *Macbeth*

9824.
Letting "I dare not" wait upon "I
would,"
Like the por cat i' the adage.
SHAKESPEARE, *Macbeth*

9825. We would, and we would not.
SHAKESPEARE, *Measure for Measure*

See also: 9422.

HILLS

Related Subject: Mountains.

9831. A city that is set on an hill cannot be hid.   *Bible: Matthew, v, 14*

9832.
         The hills,
Rock-ribbed, and ancient as the sun.
BRYANT, *Thanatopsis*

9833. The first range of hills that en-
circles the scanty vale of human life
is the horizon for the majority of its
inhabitants. On *its* ridges the common
sun is born and departs. From *them*
the stars rise, and touching *them,* they
vanish.
COLERIDGE, *Biographia Literaria*

9834. Over the hills and far away.
JOHN GAY, *The Beggar's Opera*

9835.
Praise be to you, O hills, that you
   can breathe
Into our souls the secret of your
   power!
RICHARD HOVEY, *Comrades*

9836.
But on and up, where Nature's heart
Beats strong amid the hills.
R. M. MILNES,
Tragedy of the Lac de Gaube

9837. For we were nursed upon the
self-same hill.   MILTON, *Lycidas*

9838. The higher the hill the lower
the grass.   *Proverb*

9839. He that stays in the valley shall
never get over the hill.   *Proverb*

9840.
         To climb steep hills
Requires slow pace at first.
SHAKESPEARE, *Henry VIII*

9841. Hills whose heads touch
heaven.   SHAKESPEARE, *King Lear*

9842.
What if the bridge men built goes
   down,
What if the torrent sweeps the town,
The hills are safe, the hills remain,
And hills are happy in the rain.
SARA TEASDALE, *Even To-Day*

9843.
Come, heart, where hill is heaped
upon hill:

For there the mystical brotherhood
Of sun and moon and hollow and
   wood
And river and stream work out their
   will.   W. B. YEATS,
                   Into the Twilight

See also: 231.

HISTORY

Related Subjects: America, Antiquity, Biography, Books, Europe, Greece, Memory, Past, Rome, Yesterday.

9851.
The horrid tale of perjury and strife,
Murder and spoil, which men call
   history.   BRYANT, *Earth*

9852. History's purchased page to
call them great.
            BYRON, *Childe Harold*

9853.
'Tis but the same rehearsal of the
   past . . .
And History, with all her volumes
   vast,
Hath but one page.
            BYRON, *Childe Harold*

9854. Happy the people whose annals
are blank in history-books.
            CARLYLE,
      Life of Frederick the Great

9855. All the historical books which
contain no lies are extremely tedious.
            ANATOLE FRANCE,
   The Crime of Sylvestre Bonnard

9856. The reign of Antoninus is
marked by the rare advantage of furnishing very few materials for history; which is indeed little more than
the register of the crimes, follies, and
misfortunes of mankind.
            GIBBON, *Decline and Fall*

9857. The history of science is
science itself; the history of the individual, the individual.
            GOETHE, *Elective Affinities*

9858. Peoples and governments
never have learned anything from
history, or acted on principles deduced from it.   HEGEL

9859. Very few things happen at the
right time, and the rest do not happen at all. The conscientious historian
will correct these defects.
            HERODOTUS, *History*

9860. The only good histories are
those that have been written by the
persons themselves who commanded
in the affairs whereof they write.
            MONTAIGNE, *Essays*

9861.
        How oft we sigh
When histories charm to think that
   histories lie!
            THOMAS MOORE, *The Sceptic*

9862. So very difficult a matter is it
to trace and find out the truth of anything by history.   PLUTARCH, *Lives*

9863. The long historian of my country's woes.
            POPE, *The Odyssey of Homer*

9864. There is a history in all men's
lives.   SHAKESPEARE, *Henry IV*

9865. History is little else than a
picture of human crimes and misfortunes.   VOLTAIRE, *L'Ingenu*

9866. Human history is in essence a
history of ideas.
      H. G. WELLS, *The Outline of History*

9867. History is merely gossip.
            OSCAR WILDE,
      Lady Windermere's Fan

9868. History has no time to be just.
It is her business, as impartial chron-

icler, to record successes, but she rarely appraises their moral worth. She keeps her eyes fixed on the victorious, and leaves the vanquished in the shadows.

STEFAN ZWEIG, *The Right to Heresy*

See also: 782, 2671, 3086, 3333, 3362, 20777.

HOLIDAY

Related Subjects: Amusement, Birth, Christmas, Easter, Feast, Thanksgiving Day.

9871. Butcher'd to make a Roman holiday!   BYRON, *Childe Harold*

9872. That vague kind of penitence which holidays awaken next morning.
DICKENS, *The Old Curiosity Shop*

9873. The maid-servant, the sailor, and the schoolboy, are the three beings that enjoy a holiday beyond all the rest of the world.
LEIGH HUNT, *The Maid-Servant*

9874.
The holiest of all holidays are those
Kept by ourselves in silence and apart;
The secret anniversaries of the heart.
LONGFELLOW, *Holidays*

9875.
If all the year were playing holidays,
To sport would be as tedious as to work.   SHAKESPEARE, *Henry IV*

See also: 4977.

HOLINESS

Related Subjects: Devotion, Goodness, Piety, Religion.

9881. Put off thy shoes from off thy feet, for the place whereon thou standest is holy ground.
Bible: Exodus, iii, 25

9882. In the beauties of holiness.
Bible: Psalms, cx, 3

9883. Everything that lives is holy.
BLAKE

9884. Things sacred should not only be untouched with the hands, but unviolated in thought.
CICERO, *In Verrem*

9885. Holiness appeared to me to be of a sweet, pleasant, charming, serene, calm nature; which brought an inexpressible purity, brightness, peacefulness and ravishment to the soul.
JONATHAN EDWARDS, *Holiness*

9886. We believe that holiness confers a certain insight, because not by private, but by our public force can we share and know the nature of things.   EMERSON, *Conduct of Life*

9887.
And many a holy text around she strews
That teach the rustic moralist to die.
THOMAS GRAY,
Elegy Written in a Country Church-Yard

9888.
But all his mind is bent to holiness
To number Ave-Maries on his beads.
SHAKESPEARE, *Henry VI*

9889.
What thou wouldst highly
That wouldst thou holily.
SHAKESPEARE, *Macbeth*

9890. Our holy lives must win a new world's crown.
SHAKESPEARE, *Richard II*

See also: 1190, 16488.

HOLLAND AND THE HOLLANDERS

Related Subject: Europe.

9891.
A country that draws fifty foot of water,

In which men live as in the hold of
Nature,
And when the sea does in upon them
break,
And drowns a province, does but
spring a leak.
SAMUEL BUTLER,
Description of Holland

9892. That water-land of Dutchmen
and of ditches. BYRON, *Don Juan*

9893. Holland is one of the traditional lands of freedom; it was the
home of independent intellect, of free
religion, of autonomous morals, when
every other country in Europe was
closed to these manifestations of the
spirit. HAVELOCK ELLIS,
The Task of Social Hygiene

9894.
Embosom'd in the deep where Hol-
land lies,
Methinks her patient sons before me
stand,
Where the broad ocean leans against
the land. GOLDSMITH,
The Traveller

See also: 2767, 3603, 10873, 14564.

HOME

Related Subjects: Address, Comfort, Family, Hospitality, House,
Marriage.

9901. They shall sit every man under
his vine and under his fig-tree.
Bible: Micah, iv, 4

9902.
Name me no names for my disease
With uninforming breath;
I tell you I am none of these,
But homesick unto death.
WITTER BYNNER,
The Patient to the Doctors

9903. You are a King by your own

Fireside, as much as any Monarch
on his Throne. CERVANTES,
Don Quixote

9904. In love of home, the love of
country has its rise. DICKENS,
The Old Curiosity Shop

9905. Many a man who thinks to
found a home discovers that he has
merely opened a tavern for his
friends. NORMAN DOUGLAS,
South Wind

9906. The domestic hearth. There
only is real happiness.
ANATOLE FRANCE,
The Crime of Sylvestre Bonnard

9907.
"Home is the place where, when you
have to go there
They have to take you in." "I should
have called it
Something you somehow haven't to
deserve." ROBERT FROST,
The Death of the Hired Man

9908. He is the happiest, be he king
or peasant, who finds peace in his
home. GOETHE

9909.
A world of care without,
A world of strife shut out,
A world of love shut in.
DORA GREENWELL, *Home*

9910.
Peace and rest at length have come,
All the day's long toil is past,
And each heart is whispering, "Home,
Home at last."
THOMAS HOOD, *Home at Last*

9911.
Stay, stay at home, my heart, and
rest;
Home-keeping hearts are happiest.
LONGFELLOW, *Song*

9912. Be it ever so humble, there's no place like home.
> JOHN H. PAYNE,
> *Home Sweet Home*

9913. The poorest man may in his cottage bid defiance to all the force of the Crown. It may be frail; its roof may shake; the wind may blow through it; the storms may enter, the rain may enter,—but the King of England cannot enter; all his forces dare not cross the threshold of the ruined tenement.   WILLIAM PITT

9914. East or west, home is best.
> *Proverb*

9915.
There's nothing half so pleasant
As coming home again.
> MARGARET E. SANGSTER,
> *The Joy of Coming Home*

9916.
Ay, now am I in Arden: the more
  fool I.
When I was at home I was in a
  better place;
But travellers must be content.
> SHAKESPEARE, *As You Like It*

9917. Home life as we understand it is no more natural to us than a cage is natural to a cockatoo.
> BERNARD SHAW, *Getting Married*

See also: 253, 301, 2391, 3112, 3122, 4272, 4273, 5431, 10675.

HOMER

9921. A very pretty poem, Mr. Pope, but it's not Homer.
> RICHARD BENTLEY,
> *Comment upon Pope's translation*
> *of the Iliad*

9922. Wayfarer, though the tomb be small, pass me not by, but pour on me a libation, and venerate me as

thou dost the gods. For I hold the divine Homer, the poet of the epic, honored exceedingly by the Pierian muses.   *Anonymous: Epitaph*

9923. A man who has not read Homer is like a man who has not seen the ocean. There is a great object of which he has no idea.
> WALTER BAGEHOT, *Literary Studies*

9924.
I can no more believe old Homer
  blind,
Than those who say the sun hath
  never shin'd:
The age wherein he liv'd was dark,
  but he
Could not want sight who taught the
  world to see.
> SIR JOHN DENHAM,
> *Progress of Learning*

9925. Homer himself hath been observ'd to nod.   HORACE, *Ars Poetica*

9926. Every novel is a debtor to Homer.
> EMERSON,
> *Representative Men*

9927.
Seven cities warred for Homer being
  dead
Who living had no roofe to shrowd
  his head.
> THOMAS HEYWOOD,
> *Hierarchie of the Blessed Angells*

9928. Here the earth covers the sacred head of divine Homer, the glorifier of hero-men.
> HOMER, *his own epitaph*

9929.
When 'Omer smote 'is blooming lyre,
He'd 'eard men sing by land an' sea;
An' what he thought 'e might require,
'E went an' took—the same as me!
> KIPLING,
> *When 'Omer Smote 'Is Bloomin'*
> *Lyre*

9930.
There's a blind man here with a brow
As big and white as a cloud.
And all we fiddlers, from highest to
  lowest,
Writers of music and tellers of
  stories,
Sit at his feet,
And hear him sing of the fall of Troy.
        EDGAR LEE MASTERS,
            Spoon River Anthology

See also: 14581.

HONESTY AND DISHONESTY

Related Subjects: Accuracy, Bribery, Candor, Character, Cheating, Deserving, Exaggeration, Honor, Realism and Reality, Sincerity, Temptation, Thief, Trust, Truth.

9931. Make yourself an honest man, and then you may be sure that there is one rascal less in the world.
        CARLYLE

9932. I ever loved to see everything upon the square.   CERVANTES,
            Don Quixote

9933. A few honest men are better than numbers. If you choose godly, honest men to be captains of horse, honest men will follow them.
        CROMWELL,
    Reorganization of the Army

9934. You are an honest man, you say. I pray, sir, was you ever tried? Have you seen yourself, wife, and dear children ready to perish for food, and having your neighbor's loaf in your cupboard, *or his money in your hands,* for 'tis all one, refused to touch it, and let them starve rather than taste it, because it was none of your own?   DEFOE

9935. An honest man, like the true religion, appeals to the understand-

ing, or modestly confides in the internal evidence of his conscience. The imposter employs force instead of argument, imposes silence where he cannot convince, and propagates his character by the sword.   JUNIUS

9936. Honesty is praised and starves.
        JUVENAL

9937.
A wit's a feather, and a chief a rod;
An honest man's the noblest work of
  God.   POPE, *Essay on Man*

9938. Honest men never have the love of a rogue.   *Proverb*

9939. Honesty is the best policy.
        Proverb

9940. A man never surfeits of too much honesty.   *Proverb*

9941. A good honest man, now-a-days, is but a civil word for a fool.
        Proverb

9942. No legacy is so rich as honesty.
        SHAKESPEARE,
        All's Well that Ends Well

9943. Rich honesty dwells like a miser, sir, in a poor house; as your pearl in your foul oyster.
    SHAKESPEARE, *As You Like It*

9944. To be honest, as this world goes, is to be one man picked out of ten thousand.   SHAKESPEARE,
            Hamlet

9945. You lie in your throat if you say I am other than an honest man.
    SHAKESPEARE, *Henry IV*

9946. As upright as the cedar.
        SHAKESPEARE,
        Love's Labour's Lost

9947. An honest, exceeding poor man.
        SHAKESPEARE,
        The Merchant of Venice

9948. I thank God, I am as honest as any man living, that is an old man and no honester than I.
SHAKESPEARE,
Much Ado About Nothing

Dishonesty.

9949. Thou shalt not steal.
Bible: Exodus, xx, 15

9950. Dishonesty is a forsaking of permanent for temporary advantages.
C. N. BOVEE

9951. I have known a vast quantity of nonsense talked about bad men not looking you in the face. Don't trust that conventional idea. Dishonesty will stare honesty out of countenance, any day in the week, if there is anything to be got by it. DICKENS,
Hunted Down

9952.
He who sells what isn't his'n,
Must buy it back or go to prison.
DANIEL DREW

9953. A shady business never yields a sunny life.   B. C. FORBES,
Forbes Epigrams

9954. He who purposely cheats his friend, would cheat his God.
LAVATER

9955. For de little stealin' dey gits you in jail soon or late. For de big stealin' dey makes you emperor and puts you in de Hall o' Fame when you croaks. If dey's one thing I learns in ten years on de Pullman cars listenin' to de white quality talk, it's dat same fact.
EUGENE O'NEILL,
The Emperor Jones

9956. He that steals an egg will steal an ox.   *Proverb*

9957. It is not a sin to sell dear, but it is to make ill measure.   *Proverb*

9958. There's neither honesty, manhood, nor good fellowship in thee.
SHAKESPEARE, *Henry IV*

9959. "Convey," the wise it call. "Steal!" foh! a fico for the phrase!
SHAKESPEARE,
The Merry Wives of Windsor

See also: 531, 602, 2639, 2643, 4260, 4547, 5146, 5194, 7927, 11291, 11719, 12340, 14094, 15499, 19700, 20560.

HONOR

Related Subjects: Dignity, Distinction, Dueling, Esteem, Fame, Gentleman, Glory, Greatness, Honesty, Oath, Reputation, Respect, Virgin.

9961. The man whom the king delighteth to honour.
Bible: Esther, vi, 6

9962.
Honour has come back, as a king, to earth,
And paid his subjects with a royal wage;
And Nobleness walks in our ways again;
And we have come into our heritage.
RUPERT BROOKE, *The Dead*

9963.
The fear o' hell's a hangman's whip
To haud the wretch in order;
But where ye feel your honour grip,
Let that ay be your border.
BURNS, *Epistle to a Young Friend*

9964. Two men I honour, and no third. First, the toilworn craftsman that with earth-made implement laboriously conquers the earth, and makes her man's. . . . A second man I honour, and still more highly: Him who is seen toiling for the spiritually indispensable; not daily bread, but the bread of life. 　CARLYLE, *Sartor Resartus*

9965. My honour is dearer to me than my life. 　CERVANTES, *Don Quixote*

9966. Solon gave the following advice: "Consider your honour, as a gentleman, of more weight than an oath." 　DIOGENES LAERTIUS, *Solon*

9967. One that will not plead that cause wherein his tongue must be confuted by his conscience. 　THOMAS FULLER, *Holy & Profane State*

9968. Honour is to be useful without vanity. 　ARTHUR KOESTLER, *Darkness at Noon*

9969. There could be no honour in a sure success, but much might be wrested from a sure defeat. 　LAWRENCE OF ARABIA, *Revolt in the Desert*

9970. To die with honour when one can no longer live with honour. 　J. L. LONG, *Madam Butterfly*

9971. National honor is national property of the highest value. 　JAMES MONROE

9972. It is a worthier thing to deserve honour, than to possess it. 　*Proverb*

9973. Honour and profit will not keep in one sack. 　*Proverb*

9974. What is left when honour is lost? 　PUBLILIUS SYRUS, *Sententiae*

9975.
This above all: to thine own self be true,
And it must follow, as the night the day,
Thou canst not then be false to any man. 　SHAKESPEARE, *Hamlet*

9976. Honour pricks me on. Yea, but how if honour prick me off when I come on,—how then? Can honour set to a leg? no: or an arm? no: or take away the grief of a wound? no. Honour hath no skill in surgery, then? no. What is honour? a word. What is in that word honour; what is that honour? air. A trim reckoning! Who hath it? he that died o' Wednesday. Doth he feel it? no. Doth he hear it? no. It is insensible, then? yea, to the dead. But will it not live with the living? no. Why? detraction will not suffer it. Therefore I'll none of it. Honour is a mere scutcheon. And so ends my catechism. 　SHAKESPEARE, *Henry IV*

9977. But if it be a sin to covet honour I am the most offending soul alive. 　SHAKESPEARE, *Henry V*

9978.
For Brutus is an honourable man;
So are they all, all honourable men. 　SHAKESPEARE, *Julius Caesar*

9979.
Well, honour is the subject of my story.
I cannot tell what you and other men
Think of this life; but, for my single self,
I had as lief not be as live to be
In awe of such a thing as I myself. 　SHAKESPEARE, *Julius Caesar*

9980.
Mine honour is my life; both grow in one;
Take honour from me, and my life is done. 　SHAKESPEARE, *Richard II*

9981.
And as the sun breaks through the darkest clouds,
So honour peereth in the meanest habit. 　SHAKESPEARE, *The Taming of the Shrew*

9982.
Truly, to tell lies is not honourable
But when the truth entails tremendous
    ruin,
To speak dishonourably is pardonable.
         SOPHOCLES, *Creusa*

9983.
The shackles of an old love straitened
    him,
His honour rooted in dishonour stood,
And faith unfaithful kept him falsely
    true.   TENNYSON,
        Idylls of the King

See also: 819, 924, 1022, 1633, 2606,
2630, 3153, 3156, 3614, 6061, 12102,
13261, 21143.

HOPE

Related Subjects: Desire, Encouragement, Expectation, Faith, Optimism, Wish.

9991. Hope deferred maketh the
heart sick.   *Bible: Proverbs, xiii, 12*

9992. Who against hope believed in
hope.   *Bible: Romans, iv, 18*

9993. We have such hope, we use
great plainness of speech.
      Bible: 2 Corinthians, iii, 12

9994. Hope to the end.
        Bible: 1 Peter, i, 13

9995. There are no hopeless situations; there are only men who have
grown hopeless about them.
    Quoted by CLARE BOOTHE,
      Europe in the Spring

9996.
I live on hope and that I think do all
Who come into this world.
      ROBERT BRIDGES,
      The Growth of Love

9997.
Our hope is ever livelier than despair,
    our joy

Livelier and more abiding than our
    sorrows are.
      ROBERT BRIDGES,
      The Testament of Beauty

9998. There is no place more delightful than hope.   CICERO,
        Epistolae

9999. All hope abandon, ye who
enter here.   DANTE, *Inferno*

10000. The question was put to him,
[Aristotle] what hope is; and his answer was, "The dream of a waking
man."   DIOGENES LAERTIUS,
        Aristotle

10001. "While there is life there's
hope," he cried.   JOHN GAY,
    The Sick Man and the Angel

10002.
To the last moment of his breath,
    On hope the wretch relies;
And even the pang preceding death
    Bids expectation rise.
      GOLDSMITH, *The Captivity*

10003.
Hope, like the gleaming taper's light,
    Adorns and cheers our way;
And still, as darker grows the night,
    Emits a brighter ray.
      GOLDSMITH, *The Captivity*

10004. There is nothing so well
known as that we should not expect
something for nothing—but we all
do and call it Hope.
        E. W. HOWE,
      Country Town Sayings

10005. The triumph of hope over experience.   SAMUEL JOHNSON,
        Boswell: Life

10006. A Hope beyond the shadow
of a dream.   KEATS, *Endymion*

10007.
Sweet Hope, ethereal balm upon me
    shed,

And wave thy silver pinions o'er my
head.   KEATS, *To Hope*

10008.
The Worldly Hope men set their
Hearts upon
Turns Ashes—or it prospers; and
anon,
Like Snow upon the Desert's dusty
Face,
Lighting a little hour or two—is gone.
            OMAR KHAYYAM, *Rubaiyat*

10009.
So farewell hope, and, with hope,
farewell fear,
Farewell remorse; all good to me is
lost.
Evil, be thou my good.   MILTON,
            Paradise Lost

10010. Hope against hope, and ask
till ye receive.
            JAMES MONTGOMERY,
            The World Before the Flood

10011. A man will already be in no
mean Paradise if at the hour of sunset a ray of good hope may fall upon
him like harmonies of music.
            JOHN MORLEY, *Voltaire*

10012. Things which you do not hope
happen more frequently than things
which you do hope.   PLAUTUS,
            Mostellaria

10013.
Hope springs eternal in the human
breast:
Man never is, but always to be, blest.
            POPE, *Essay on Man*

10014. It is hope alone that makes us
willing to live.   *Proverb*

10015. He that lives on hope has but
a slender diet.   *Proverb*

10016. A good hope is better than a
bad possession.   *Proverb*

10017.
            Fair be all thy hopes,
And prosperous be thy life in peace
and war!   SHAKESPEARE,
            Henry VI

10018.
The miserable have no other medicine,
But only hope.   SHAKESPEARE,
            Measure for Measure

10019.
True hope is swift, and flies with
swallow's wings;
Kings it makes gods, and meaner
creatures kings.
            SHAKESPEARE, *Richard III*

10020. Past hope, past cure, past
help!   SHAKESPEARE,
            Romeo and Juliet

10021. Take short views, hope for
the best and trust in God.
            SYDNEY SMITH,
            Lady Holland's Memoir

10022.
Full little knowest thou that hast not
tride,
What hell it is, in suing long to bide:
To lose good dayes, that might be
better spent;
To waste long nights in pensive dis-
content;
To speed to-day, to be put back to-
morrow;
To feed on hope, to pine with feare
and sorrow.
            EDMUND SPENSER,
            Mother Hubberds Tale

10023.
Never go gloomily, man with a mind!
Hope is a better companion than
fear.   MARTIN F. TUPPER,
            Cheer Up

10024.
Ah, well! for us all some sweet hope
lies
Deeply buried from human eyes.
            WHITTIER, *Maud Muller*

See also: 276, 324, 680, 1886, 2716, 2821, 2986, 3034, 3110, 3117, 4806, 5558, 5562, 5573, 5889, 13401, 14732.

HORSE, HORSEMANSHIP

Related Subjects: Animal, Hunting, Sport.

10031. A pale horse: and his name that sat on him was Death.
Bible: Revelation, vi, 8

10032.
A horse misused upon the road
Calls to heaven for human blood.
BLAKE, *Proverb*

10033. From the horsemen we might all learn something of high respect for adjectives. The true follower of the turf enforces a precision of speech which is not known elsewhere in the country. HEYWOOD BROUN,
Be-Kind-to-Adjectives Week

10034. One of Lord Palmerston's aphorisms was: "The best thing for the inside of a man is the outside of a horse." WILLIAM FRASER,
Disraeli and His Day

10035. God forbid that I should go to any heaven in which there are no horses. CUNNINGHAME GRAHAM

10036. It makes men imperious to sit a horse. O. W. HOLMES,
Elsie Venner

10037. If you hit a pony over the nose at the outset of your acquaintance, he may not love you, but he will take a deep interest in your movements ever afterwards.
KIPLING, *Plain Tales*

10038. A gift horse should not be look't in the mouth. *Proverb*

10039. It is ill to set spurs to a flying horse. *Proverb*

10040. Restive horses must be roughly dealt with. *Proverb*

10041. Up hill spare me, down hill forbear me; plain way, spare me not, nor let me drink when I'm hot.
Proverb

10042. A horse is neither better nor worse for his trappings. *Proverb*

10043. A man may lead his horse to water, but cannot make him drink.
Proverb

10044.
A full-hot horse, who being allow'd his way,
Self-mettle tires him.
SHAKESPEARE, *Henry VIII*

10045. He doth nothing but talk of his horse. SHAKESPEARE,
The Merchant of Venice

10046. A horse! a horse! my kingdom for a horse!
SHAKESPEARE, *Richard III*

10047. Give me another horse! bind up my wounds.
SHAKESPEARE, *Richard III*

See also: 795, 1437, 1804, 1819, 2940, 3185, 14312, 15386.

HOSPITAL

Related Subjects: Disease, Doctors, Health, Medicine, Sickness.

10051. The importance of social work in connection with hospitals and dispensaries has been established, and is now recognized as a necessary factor in completing the hospital's service as a social agent in the community.
LUCY C. CATLIN,
The Hospital as a Social Agent

10052. What social worker is better able to know the menace of physical defects and disease to the individual and society than the nurse doing social work in the hospital? And who is in a better position to remedy these defects, and to bring about the cure or isolation of these diseases than this nurse?

LUCY C. CATLIN,
The Hospital as a Social Agent

10053. If the last decade of the nineteenth century saw the significant change in nomenclature from "asylum" to "hospital", the twentieth century has witnessed a transformation in fact as well as in name. The process is by no means complete; some "hospitals" have as little right to their title as certain "universities" have to theirs.

ALBERT DEUTSCH,
Treatment of the Mentally Ill in America

10054. There are institutions for the mentally ill that are actually abandoned prisons, remodelled for the reception of a new group of "inmates."

ALBERT DEUTSCH,
Treatment of the Mentally Ill In America

10055.
The Hospital, grey, quiet, old,
Where Life and Death like friendly chafferers meet.

W. E. HENLEY, *In Hospital*

See also: 478, 2721.

HOSPITALITY

Related Subjects: Courtesy, Friend, Guests, Hand, Home, Inn.

10061.
Pleasantest
Of all ties is the tie of host and guest.

AESCHYLUS, *The Choephoroe*

10062. Be not forgetful to entertain strangers, for thereby some have entertained angels unawares.

Bible: Hebrews, xiii, 2

10063. The reception one meets with from the women of a family generally determines the tenor of one's whole entertainment.

DE QUINCEY,
Confessions of an English Opium-Eater

10064. It is a sin against hospitability, to open your doors, and shut up your countenance.   *Proverb*

10065. Small cheer and great welcome makes a merry feast.

SHAKESPEARE,
The Comedy of Errors

10066. I had three chairs in my house: one for solitude, two for friendship, three for society.

THOREAU, *Walden*

See also: 698, 14625.

HOURS

Related Subjects: Day, Minute, Time.

10071. We reckon hours and minutes to be dollars and cents.

T. C. HALIBURTON,
The Clockmaker

10072. Lost, yesterday, somewhere between sunrise and sunset, two golden hours, each set with sixty diamond minutes. No reward is offered for they are gone forever.

HORACE MANN

10073.
The lazy leaden-stepping Hours,
Whose speed is but the heavy plummet's pace.   MILTON, *On Time*

10074. An hour of pain is as long as a day of pleasure.   *Proverb*

10075. It chanceth in an hour, that comes not in seven years.   *Proverb*

0076. An hour may destroy what n age was building.   *Proverb*

0077.
Tis but an hour ago since it was nine,
And after one hour more 'twill be eleven.
And so, from hour to hour, we ripe and ripe,
And then, from hour to hour, we rot and rot;
And thereby hangs a tale.
SHAKESPEARE, *As You Like It*

10078. Pleasure and action make the hours seem short.
SHAKESPEARE, *Othello*

See also: 168, 1754.

HOUSE

Related Subjects: Address, Building, Home, Window.

10081.
The beauty of the house is order;
The blessing of the house is contentment;
The glory of the house is hospitality;
The crown of the house is godliness.
Anonymous, Fireplace Motto

10082. Houses are built to live in, and not to look on; therefore let use be preferred before uniformity.
BACON, *Essays*

10083. Except the Lord build the house, they labour in vain that build it.   *Bible: Psalm, cxxvii, 1*

10084.
Old houses mended,
Cost little less than new before they're ended.   COLLEY CIBBER,
The Double Gallant

10085. The house of every one is to him as his castle and fortress, as well for his defence against injury and violence as for his repose.
SIR EDWARD COKE,
Semayne's Case

10086.
Oh, to have a little house
To own the hearth and stool and all!
PADRAIC COLUM,
An Old Woman of the Roads

10087.
And I am praying God on high,
And I am praying Him night and day,
For a little house—a house of my own—
Out of the wind's and the rain's way.
PADRAIC COLUM,
An Old Woman of the Roads

10088.
All houses wherein men have lived and died
Are haunted houses.
LONGFELLOW, *Haunted Houses*

10089.
I in mine own house am an emperor
And will defend what's mine.
MASSINGER, *The Roman Actor*

10090. My house, my house, though thou art small, thou art to me the Escurial.   *Proverb*

10091. Burn not your house to fright away the mice.   *Proverb*

10092. Better one's house be too little one day than too big all the year after.   *Proverb*

10093.
As if the story of a house
Were told, or ever could be.
E. A. ROBINSON, *Eros Tyrannos*

10094. This house is turned upside down.   SHAKESPEARE, *Henry IV*

10095. A plague o' both your houses!
SHAKESPEARE, *Romeo and Juliet*

10096. When you dwell in a house you mis-like, you will look out of window a deal more than those that are content with their dwelling.

MARY WEBB, *Precious Bane*

See also: 39, 2265, 2882, 5912, 9430, 11817, 12560.

HUMANITY, see Man

HUMILITY

Related Subjects: Inferiority, Meekness, Modesty, Resignation, Self-Knowledge, Submission, Timidity.

10100. Whosoever shall exalt himself shall be abased; and he that shall humble himself shall be exalted.
Bible: Matthew, xxiii, 12

10101.
God knows, I'm no the thing I should be,
Nor am I even the thing I could be.
BURNS,
To the Reverend John M'Math

10102. I'm a very 'umble person.
DICKENS, *David Copperfield*

10103. I ate umble pie with an appetite.   DICKENS,
David Copperfield

10104. At moments she discovered she was grotesquely wrong, and then she treated herself to a week of passionate humility.
HENRY JAMES,
The Portrait of a Lady

10105. One may be humble out of pride.   MONTAIGNE, *Essays*

10106.
Humility, that low, sweet root
From which all heavenly virtues shoot.   THOMAS MOORE,
The Loves of the Angels

10107. Humility often gains mor than pride.   *Prover*

10108. It is not a sign of humility t declaim against pride.   *Prover*

10109. The highest condition take rise in the lowest.
PUBLILIUS SYRUS, *Sententia*

10110. Humility is a virtue all preach none practice; and yet everybody i content to hear. JOHN SELDEN,
Table Tal

10111. One who despises himself i the nearest to a proud man.
SPINOZ

See also: 1061, 5824, 5923, 747 9691, 15935, 15937, 21389.

HUMOR

Related Subjects: Epigram, Joke Laughter, Limericks, Merrimen Nonsense, Paradox, Pun, Satire Wit.

10121. The humourist's like a ma firin' at a target—he doesna ke whether he hits or no till them a the target tells 'im.
J. M. BARRIE,
A Window in Thrum

10122. The sharpest humor thes days is the briefest, the most visual.
WHIT BURNETT,
The Literary Life & the Hell With I

10123. True humour springs no more from the head than from th heart; it is not contempt, its essenc is love; it issues not in laughter, bu in still smiles, which lie far deeper.
CARLYLE, *Richte*

10124. Men will confess to treaso murder, arson, false teeth, or a wig How many of them will own up to lack of humor?
FRANK M. COLBY, *Essay*

10125. Humour is a drug which it's the fashion to abuse.

W. S. GILBERT, *His Excellency*

10126. The sense of humour is the just balance of all the faculties of man, the best security against the pride of knowledge and the conceits of the imagination, the strongest inducement to submit with a wise and pious patience to the vicissitudes of human existence.

R. M. MILNES,
Memoir of Thomas Hood

10127. Lift up one hand to heaven and thank your stars if they have given you the proper sense to enable you to appreciate the inconceivably droll situations in which we catch our fellow creatures.

SIR WILLIAM OSLER,
Life of Sir William Osler

10128. Democratic humour is the spleen of the normal in the presence of the abnormal. J. C. POWYS,
In Defence of Sensuality

10129.
He must not laugh at his own wheeze:
A snuff box has no right to sneeze.
KEITH PRESTON, *The Humorist*

10130. There's the humour of it.
SHAKESPEARE,
The Merry Wives of Windsor

10131. If a person desires to be a humorist it is necessary that the people around him shall be at least as wise as he is, otherwise, his humor will not be comprehended.

JAMES STEPHENS, *The Demi-Gods*

10132. Everything human is pathetic. The secret source of humor itself is not joy, but sorrow. There is no humor in heaven. MARK TWAIN

See also: 755, 17280.

HUNGER

Related Subjects: Appetite, Beggar, Eating, Fasting, Food, Gluttony, Poverty, Thirst.

10141. Hunger is sharper than the sword.
BEAUMONT & FLETCHER,
The Honest Man's Fortune

10142. There's no sauce in the world like hunger. CERVANTES,
Don Quixote

10143. Oliver Twist has asked for more. DICKENS, *Oliver Twist*

10144. An empty stomach is not a good political adviser.
ALBERT EINSTEIN, *Cosmic Religion*

10145. Hungry rooster don't cackle w'en he fine a wum.
JOEL CHANDLER HARRIS,
Plantation Proverbs

10146. They that die by famine die by inches. MATTHEW HENRY,
Commentaries

10147. Hunger is insolent, and will be fed. HOMER, *Odyssey*

10148. Any of us would kill a cow rather than not have beef.
SAMUEL JOHNSON, *Boswell: Life*

10149. No hunger of an empty, food-entreating belly gives such an ache as the coward heart, which cries for comfort in distress.
LIAM O'FLAHERTY, *Two Years*

10150.
So if unprejudiced you scan
The goings of this clock-work, man,
You find a hundred movements made
By fine devices in his head;
But 'tis the stomach's solid stroke
That tells his being what's o'clock.
MATTHEW PRIOR, *Alma*

10151. A hungry man smells meat afar off.   *Proverb*

10152. Hunger is not dainty.
                    Proverb

10153. Hunger makes hard beans sweet.   *Proverb*

10154. Hunger and cold deliver a man up to his enemy.   *Proverb*

10155. A hungry man is an angry man.   *Proverb*

10156. Oppress'd by two weak evils, age and hunger.   SHAKESPEARE,
                    As You Like It

10157. Famine is in thy cheeks.
    SHAKESPEARE, *Romeo and Juliet*

10158. The awful phantom of the hungry poor.
            HARRIET P. SPOFFORD,
                    A Winter's Night

10159. The fields were fruitful, and starving men moved on the roads. The granaries were full and the children of the poor grew up rachitic, and the pustules of pellagra swelled on their sides. The great companies did not know that the line between hunger and anger is a thin line.
            JOHN STEINBECK,
                    The Grapes of Wrath

10160.
Because of body's hunger are we born,
And by contriving hunger are we fed;
Because of hunger is our work well done,
As so are songs well sung, and things well said.
Desire and longing are the whips of God.   ANNA WICKHAM,
                    Sehnsucht

See also: 1259.

HUNTING

Related Subjects: Animal, Bear Birds, Dog, Elephant, Fox, Hawk, Horse, Kill, Sport.

10161.
                    Detested sport,
That owes its pleasures to another's pain.   COWPER, *The Task*

10162. There is a passion for *hunting something* deeply implanted in the human breast.   DICKENS,
                    Oliver Twist

10163.
The dusky night rides down the sky,
And ushers in the morn;
The hounds all join in glorious cry,
The huntsman winds his horn,
And a-hunting we will go.
    FIELDING, *A-hunting We Will Go*

10164. Don't think to hunt two hares with one dog.   FRANKLIN,
                    Poor Richard

10165. Wild animals never kill for sport. Man is the only one to whom the torture and death of his fellow creatures is amusing in itself.
                    FROUDE, *Oceana*

10166.
Soon as Aurora drives away the night,
And edges eastern clouds with rosy light,
The healthy huntsman, with the cheerful horn,
Summons the dogs, and greets the dappled Morn.   JOHN GAY,
                    Rural Sports

10167.
Oh, who will stay indoor, indoor,
When the horn is on the hill?
With the crisp air stinging, and the huntsmen singing,
And a ten-tined buck to kill!
            RICHARD HOVEY, *King Arthur*

10168. It is very strange, and very melancholy, that the paucity of human pleasures should persuade us ever to call hunting one of them.
SAMUEL JOHNSON, *Miscellanies*

10169. Hunting was the labour of the savages of North America, but the amusement of the gentlemen of England.   SAMUEL JOHNSON

10170. Good and much company, and a good dinner; most of their discourse was about hunting, in a dialect I understand very little.
SAMUEL PEPYS, *Diary*

10171. Hunting—the least honourable form of war on the weak.
PAUL RICHARD,
The Scourge of Christ

10172.
The chase I follow far,
Tis mimicry of noble war.
SCOTT, *The Lady of the Lake*

10173. Huntsman, rest! thy chase is done.   SCOTT, *The Lady of the Lake*

10174.
The horn, the horn, the lusty horn
Is not a thing to laugh to scorn.
SHAKESPEARE, *As You Like It*

10175.
Hold, Warwick, seek thee out some other chase,
For I myself must hunt this deer to death.   SHAKESPEARE, *Henry VI*

10176.
Rose-cheeked Adonis hied him to the chase;
Hunting he loved, but love he laughed to scorn.
SHAKESPEARE, *Venus and Adonis*

10177. Everybody can see that the people who hunt are the right people, and the people who don't are the wrong ones.   BERNARD SHAW,
Heartbreak House

10178. When a man wants to murder a tiger he calls it sport: when the tiger wants to murder him he calls it ferocity.
BERNARD SHAW,
Maxims for Revolutionists

See also: 9711.

HUSBAND

Related Subjects: Family, Marriage, Wife.

10181. The Fraternity of the Henpeck'd.   ADDISON, *The Spectator*

10182.
But, oh! ye lords of ladies intellectual,
Inform us truly,—have they not henpeck'd you all?   BYRON,
Don Juan

10183. Those men are most apt to be obsequious and conciliating abroad, who are under the discipline of shrews at home.
WASHINGTON IRVING,
The Sketch-Book

10184. This is worth remembering. Speaking to, or crying over, a husband never did any good yet.
KIPLING, *Plain Tales*

10185. The lover in the husband may be lost.   LORD LYTTELTON,
Advice to a Lady

10186. Better have an old man to humour than a young rake to break your heart.   *Proverb*

See also: 1224, 1548, 1671, 1710, 6344, 12326, 15631, 16544, 17396, 21154.

HYACINTH

Related Subject: Flowers.

10191. The hyacinth's for constancy wi' its unchanging blue.
BURNS, *The Posie*

10192.
Here hyacinths of heavenly blue
Shook their rich tresses to the morn.
                    JAMES MONTGOMERY,
                    The Adventure of a Star

10193.
If of thy mortal goods thou art bereft,
And from thy slender store two loaves
  alone to thee are left,
Sell one, and with the dole
Buy hyacinths to feed thy soul.
                    SAADI, *Gulistan*

10194.
And the hyacinth purple, and white,
  and blue,
Which flung from its bells a sweet
  peal anew
Of music so delicate, soft, and intense,
It was felt like an odour within the
  sense.
          SHELLEY, *The Sensitive Plant*

HYPOCRISY

**Related Subjects: Affectation, Ap-
pearance, Concealment, Conspiracy, Cunning, Deceit, Lies, Sincerity, Trickery.**

10201. I will have nought to do with
a man who can blow hot and cold
with the same breath.   AESOP,
                    The Man and the Satyr

10202. Great hypocrites are the real
atheists.   BACON,
                    De Augmentis Scientiarum

10203. The words of his mouth were
smoother than butter, but war was in
his heart.   *Bible: Psalms, lv, 21*

10204. Smile with an intent to do
mischief, or cozen him whom he salutes.   ROBERT BURTON,
                    Anatomy of Melancholy

10205. No man, for any considerable
period, can wear one face to himself,

and another to the multitude, withou
finally getting bewildered as to whic
may be the true.   HAWTHORNE,
                    The Scarlet Lette

10206. We are not hypocrites in ou
sleep.   HAZLITT, *On Dream*

10207. It is no fault of Christianit
if a hypocrite falls into sin.
                    ST. JEROM

10208. Woe be unto those who pray
and who are negligent at their prayer
who play the hypocrites, and den
necessaries to the needy.
                    The Kora

10209. Hypocrisy is a homage vic
pays to virtue.
          LA ROCHEFOUCAULD, *Maxim*

10210. He that praiseth publicly wi
slander privately.   *Prover*

10211. Many kiss the hands the
wish to see cut off.   *Prover*

10212. May the man be damned an
never grow fat, who wears two face
under one hat.   *Prover*

10213. Hypocritical honesty goe
upon stilts.   *Prover*

10214. Hypocritical piety is doubl
iniquity.   *Prover*

10215. It is easy for men to talk on
thing and think another.
          PUBLILIUS SYRUS, *Sententia*

10216. To appear the friend of
man, when in reality we are no longe
so, is to reserve to ourselves th
means of doing him an injury by su
prising honest men into an error.
                ROUSSEAU, *Confession*

10217.
          With devotion's visag
And pious action we do sugar o'er
The devil himself.
                SHAKESPEARE, *Haml*

0218.
      I want that glib and oily art,
To speak and purpose not.
      SHAKESPEARE, *King Lear*

0219.
O, what may man within him hide,
Though angel on the outward side!
      SHAKESPEARE,
      Measure for Measure

10220.
And thus I clothe my naked villainy
With odd old ends stolen forth of
  holy writ,
And seem a saint when most I play
  the devil.   SHAKESPEARE,
      Richard III

See also: 189, 434, 747, 1897, 3964, 8682, 10619, 11296, 14070, 14442.

I

ICE

Related Subjects: Frost, Snow, Winter.

0221. In things that are tender and unpleasing, it is good to break the ice, by some whose words are of less weight, and to reserve the more weighty voice, to come in, as by chance.   BACON, *Essays*

0222. Motionless torrents! silent cataracts!   COLERIDGE,
*Hymn Before Sunrise in the Vale
      of Chamouni*

0223.
And ice, mast-high, came floating by
As green as emerald.
  COLERIDGE, *The Ancient Mariner*

0224. In skating over thin ice our safety is in our speed.
      EMERSON, *Essays*

0225.
Some say the world will end in fire,
Some say in ice.
From what I've tasted of desire,
I hold with those who favor fire.
But if it had to perish twice,
I think I know enough of hate
To say that for destruction ice
Is also great
And would suffice.
  ROBERT FROST, *Fire and Ice*

0226. Trust not one night's ice.
      Proverb

10227. What a sea of melting ice I walk on!   MASSINGER,
      Maid of Honour

10228. When it cracks, it bears; when it bends, it breaks.   *Proverb*

See also: 3168, 18781.

IDEA

Related Subjects: Fancy, Intelligence, Knowledge, Principle, Speculation, Theories, Thought.

10231. I am convinced that a person's behavior springs from his ideas. . . How we interpret the great and important facts of existence depends upon our style of life.
   ALFRED ADLER, *Social Interest*

10232. If the ancients left us ideas, to our credit be it spoken that we moderns are building houses for them.
   BRONSON ALCOTT, *Table Talk*

10233. One of the greatest pains to human nature is the pain of a new idea.   WALTER BAGEHOT,
      Physics and Politics

10234. Only the wise possess ideas; the greater part of mankind are possessed by them.   COLERIDGE,
      Miscellanies

10235. God screens us evermore from premature ideas. EMERSON, *Essays*

10236. Ideas must work through the brains and the arms of good and brave men, or they are no better than dreams. EMERSON, *Miscellanies*

10237. When we are exalted by ideas, we do not owe this to Plato, but to the idea, to which also Plato was debtor. EMERSON, *Representative Men*

10238. Men possessed with an idea cannot be reasoned with. FROUDE, *Short Studies*

10239. One can only oppose an Idea with a better Idea. ADOLF HITLER, *Mein Kampf*

10240. Every idea must have a visual enfolding. VICTOR HUGO

10241. The public doesn't require any new ideas. The public is best served by the good, old-fashioned ideas it already has. IBSEN, *An Enemy of the People*

10242. Ideas are, in truth, forces. Infinite, too, is the power of personality. A union of the two always makes history. HENRY JAMES, *Charles W. Eliot*

10243. An idea, to be suggestive, must come to the individual with the force of a revelation. WILLIAM JAMES, *Varieties of Religious Experience*

10244. Let me exhort everyone to do their utmost to think outside and beyond our present circle of ideas. For every idea gained is a hundred years of slavery remitted. RICHARD JEFFERIES, *The Story of My Heart*

10245. He who receives an idea from me, receives instruction himself without lessening mine; as he who lights his taper at mine receives light without darkening me. JEFFERSON

10246. That fellow seems to posses but one idea, and that is a wrong on SAMUEL JOHNSON, *Boswell: Lif*

10247. I do not believe in salvatio through an idea, because every ide must perish as it succeeds. EMIL LUDWIG, *I Believ*

10248. An Idea isn't responsible fo the people who believe in it. DON MARQUIS, *The Sun Di*

10249. The ruling ideas of each ag have ever been the ideas of its rulin class. KARL MARX, *Manifesto of the Communist Part*

10250. To die for an idea: it is ur questionably noble. But how muc nobler it would be if men died fo ideas that were true! H. L. MENCKEN, *Prejudice*

10251. For an idea ever to be fasl ionable is ominous, since it must after wards be always old-fashioned. SANTAYANA, *Words of Doctrin*

10252. The best ideas are commo property. SENEC

10253. This creature man, who in h own selfish affairs is a coward to th backbone, will fight for an idea lik a hero. BERNARD SHAW, *Man and Superma*

10254.
To pull you through. Avoid ideas— they're common
And might crack through the varnis of your smile,
Impinge upon your worship of Go Mammon
Filling your soul with pity, and thin vile. OSBERT SITWELL, *Collected Satir*

10255. Early ideas are not usuall true ideas. HERBERT SPENCER, *Principles of Biolog*

10256. I require three or four cubic feet of new ideas per day, as a steamboat requires coal.   STENDHAL

10257. It's bad form to think, feel, or have an idea. ALFRED SUTRO,
The Walls of Jericho

10258.
Ten thousand great ideas filled his mind;
But with the clouds they fled, and left no trace behind.
JAMES THOMSON,
Castle of Indolence

10259.
Through thy idea, lo, the immortal reality!
Through thy reality, lo, the immortal idea!   WALT WHITMAN,
Thou Mother With Thy Equal Brood

See also: 1790, 2964, 3607, 3619, 4923, 5176, 9866, 11399, 14622, 19483, 20219.

IDEALS, IDEALISM

Related Subjects: Character, Faith, Goodness, Honor, Principle.

10261. Our ideals are our better selves.   BRONSON ALCOTT,
Table Talk

10262. An idealist is a person who helps other people to be prosperous.
HENRY FORD

10263. People talk a great deal about idealizing nowadays, whatever that may mean. MRS. GASKELL, *Cranford*

10264. Idealism increases in direct proportion to one's distance from the problem.   GALSWORTHY

10265. Be it said to his [Russell Sage] credit that he was unshakenly faithful to his sordid ideals.
GUSTAVUS MYERS,
History of the Great American Fortunes

10266. Ideals are like the stars—we never reach them, but like the mariners on the sea, we chart our course by them.   CARL SCHURZ

10267. When they come downstairs from their Ivory Towers, Idealists are apt to walk straight into the gutter.   LOGAN PEARSALL SMITH,
Afterthoughts

10268. To nurse a blind ideal like a girl.   TENNYSON, *The Princess*

10269. Though vanquished, those who lived before the time was ripe have found significance in the fulfillment of a timeless ideal; for an idea is quickened to life in the real world only through the endeavors of those who conceived it where none could witness the conception, and were ready for its sake to advance along the road to dusty death.
STEFAN ZWEIG, *The Right to Heresy*

10270. When the ideals of one generation have lost their fire, their zest, their vivid tints, it is enough for a man (or woman) equipped with strong powers of suggestion to declare peremptorily that he and he alone has discovered the new and true formulas, and myriads will confidently accept the teachings of the *nth* Messiah.   STEFAN ZWEIG,
The Right to Heresy

See also: 352, 651, 721, 778, 3351, 3972, 5410, 16386.

IDLENESS

Related Subjects: Delay, Futility, Indifference, Leisure, Neglect, Waste.

10271. The terrible burden of having nothing to do.   BOILEAU

10272. Idleness is an appendix to nobility.   ROBERT BURTON,
Anatomy of Melancholy

10273.
As idle as a painted ship
Upon a painted ocean.
COLERIDGE, *The Ancient Mariner*

10274.
An idler is a watch that wants both
  hands,
As useless if it goes as if it stands.
COWPER, *Retirement*

10275.
How various his employments, whom
  the world
Calls idle, and who justly in return
Esteems that busy world an idler too!
COWPER, *The Task*

10276. Idleness and lack of occupation are the best things in the world to ruin the foolish.
DIO CHRYSOSTOM

10277. That indolent but agreeable condition of doing nothing.
EPICTETUS, *Discourses*

10278. There is no place in civilization for the idler. None of us has any right to ease.   HENRY FORD

10279. Lazy folk's stummucks don't git tired.
JOEL CHANDLER HARRIS,
Plantation Proverbs

10280. That happy age when a man can be idle with impunity.
WASHINGTON IRVING,
The Sketch-Book

10281. The frivolous work of polished idleness.
SIR JAMES MACKINTOSH,
Dissertation on Ethical Philosophy

10282. An idle brain is the devil's workshop.   *Proverb*

10283. An idle youth, a needy age.
Proverb

10284. A slothfu' man is a beggar's brither.   *Proverb*

10285. Better to be idle than not well occupied.   *Proverb*

10286. He that is busy is tempted but by one devil; he that is idle, by a legion.   *Proverb*

10287. By doing nothing we learn to do ill.   *Proverb*

10288. A sluggard takes an hundred steps because he would not take one in due time.   *Proverb*

10289. He is not only idle who does nothing but he is idle who might be better employed.   SOCRATES

10290.
For Satan finds some mischief still
  For idle hands to do.
ISAAC WATTS, *Divine Songs*

10291.
'Tis the voice of the sluggard; I heard
  him complain,
"You have wak'd me too soon, I must
  slumber again."
ISAAC WATTS, *The Sluggard*

10292. Only the lowest type of humanity can endure idleness without wanting to kill themselves, and they usually end by killing one another.
I. A. R. WYLIE

See also: 144, 162, 163, 756, 1153, 2268, 5781, 6795, 18698, 19662, 21074.

IDOLATRY

Related Subjects: Gods and Goddesses, Worship.

10301. Four species of idols beset the human mind: idols of the tribe; idols of the den; idols of the market; and idols of the theatre.
BACON, *Novum Organum*

10302. Thou shalt not make unto thee any graven image, or any likeness of anything that is in heaven above, or that is in the earth beneath, or that is in the water under the earth.   *Bible: Exodus, xx, 4*

10303.
Her overpowering presence made you feel
It would not be idolatry to kneel.
                          BYRON, *Don Juan*

10304.
Ah, spare your idol! think him human still.
Charms he may have, but he has frailties too!
Dote not too much, nor spoil what ye admire.   COWPER, *The Task*

10305.
The 'eathen in 'is blindness bows down to wood an' stone;
'E don't obey no orders unless they is 'is own.   KIPLING, *The 'Eathen*

10306. Yet, if he would, man cannot live all to this world. If not religious, he will be superstitious. If he worship not the true God, he will have his idols.   THEODORE PARKER,
Critical and Miscellaneous Writings

10307. He begs a blessing of a wooden god.   *Proverb*

10308. The god of my idolatry.
    SHAKESPEARE, *Romeo and Juliet*

10309. An idiot holds his bauble for a god.   SHAKESPEARE,
                    Titus Andronicus

10310.
                'Tis mad idolatry
To make the service greater than the god.   SHAKESPEARE,
                Troilus and Cressida

10311. Was this the idol that you worship so?   SHAKESPEARE,
        Two Gentlemen of Verona

10312. He who slays a king and he who dies for him are alike idolaters.
                    BERNARD SHAW,
            Maxims for Revolutionists

See also: 1229, 18048.

IGNORANCE

Related Subjects: Darkness, Prejudice, Stupidity, Superstition.

10321. Ignorance is the night of the mind, but a night without moon or star.   CONFUCIUS, *Analects*

10322. He [Socrates] declared that he knew nothing, except the fact of his ignorance.
    DIOGENES LAERTIUS, *Socrates*

10323. Mr. Kremlin was distinguished for ignorance; for he had only one idea, and that was wrong.
                    DISRAELI, *Sybil*

10324. Ignorance never settles a question.   DISRAELI

10325.
No more; where ignorance is bliss,
    'Tis folly to be wise.
                    THOMAS GRAY,
        On a Distant Prospect of Eton College

10326. Ignorance is preferable to error; and he is less remote from truth who believes nothing, than he who believes what is wrong.   JEFFERSON

10327. A Smattering of Ignorance.
    OSCAR LEVANT, *Title of Book*

10328. By ignorance we mistake, and by mistakes we learn.   *Proverb*

10329. Faults of ignorance are excusable only where the ignorance itself is so.   *Proverb*

10330. Ignorance is a voluntary misfortune.   *Proverb*

10331. Better be ignorant of a matter than half know it.
PUBLILIUS SYRUS, *Sententiae*

10332. Ignorance is degrading only when found in company with riches.
SCHOPENHAUER

10333. That unlettered small-knowing soul.   SHAKESPEARE,
Love's Labour's Lost

10334. A very superficial, ignorant, unweighing fellow.
SHAKESPEARE,
Measure for Measure

10335. What you don't know would make a great book.
SYDNEY SMITH,
Lady Holland's Memoir

10336.
The happiest life consists in ignorance,
Before you learn to grieve and to rejoice.   SOPHOCLES, *Ajax*

10337.
        Blind and naked Ignorance
Delivers brawling judgments, unashamed,
On all things all day long.
TENNYSON, *Idylls of the King*

10338. I envy the beasts two things —their ignorance of evil to come, and their ignorance of what is said about them.   VOLTAIRE

See also: 272, 414, 1318, 2253, 3025, 4808, 5681, 5872, 6650, 7077, 10444, 11497, 15762, 21393, 21679.

ILL-NATURE

Related Subject: Temper.

10341. Ill-humor is but the inward feeling of our own want of merit; a dissatisfaction with ourselves which is always united with an envy that foolish vanity excites.   GOETHE

10342. It is impossible that an ill-natured man can have a public spirit; for how should he love ten thousand men who has never loved one?
POPE

ILLUSION AND DISILLUSION

Related Subjects: Delusion, Error, Fantasy, Imagination, Mistake, Sense, Vision.

10351. I drink the wine of aspiration and the drug of illusion. Thus I am never dull.   GALSWORTHY,
The White Horn Mountain

10352.
Death only grasps; to live is to pursue,—
Dream on! there's nothing but illusion true!   O. W. HOLMES,
The Old Player

10353. Nothing can justly be called an illusion which is a permanent and universal human experience.
J. C. POWYS, *The Complex Vision*

10354.
And here we wander in illusions;
Some blessed power deliver us from hence!   SHAKESPEARE,
The Comedy of Errors

10355. Don't part with your illusions. When they are gone you may still exist, but you have ceased to live.
MARK TWAIN

Disillusion

10356.
We strip illusion of her veil;
We vivisect the nightingale
To probe the secret of his note.
T. B. ALDRICH, *Realism*

10357.
But time strips our illusions of their hue,

And one by one in turn, some grand
  mistake
Casts off its bright skin yearly, like
  a snake.   BYRON, *Don Juan*

10358. Rob the average man of his
life-illusion, and you rob him of his
happiness at the same stroke.
          IBSEN, *The Wild Duck*

10359. Better a dish of illusion and
a hearty appetite for life, than a feast
of reality and indigestion therewith.
          H. A. OVERSTREET,
              The Enduring Quest

10360. I was never afraid of disillusion and I have chosen it.
          SANTAYANA, *I Believe*

10361. Wisdom comes by disillusionment.   SANTAYANA

10362. If they make you not then
the better answer, you may say they
are not the men you took them for.
          SHAKESPEARE,
          Much Ado About Nothing

See also: 14685.

IMAGINATION

Related Subjects: Dreams, Exaggeration, Fairies, Fancy, Fear,
Ghost, Illusion, Invention, Originality, Sense, Tale, Vision.

10371. Only in men's imagination
does every truth find an effective and
undeniable existence. Imagination,
not invention, is the supreme master
of art as of life.
JOSEPH CONRAD, *A Personal Record*

10372. That faculty of beholding at
a hint the face of his desire and the
shape of his dream, without which the
earth would know no lover and no
adventurer.   JOSEPH CONRAD,
              Lord Jim

10373. Imagination is as good as
many voyages—and how much cheaper.   G. W. CURTIS, *Prue and I*

10374.
That minister of ministers,
  Imagination, gathers up
The undiscovered Universe,
  Like jewels in a jasper cup.
          JOHN DAVIDSON,
      There Is a Dish to Hold the Sea

10375. To know is nothing at all; to
imagine is everything.
          ANATOLE FRANCE,
      The Crime of Sylvestre Bonnard

10376. As a rule, indeed, grown-up
people are fairly correct on matters
of fact; it is in the higher gift of
imagination that they are so sadly to
seek.   KENNETH GRAHAME,
              The Golden Age

10377. Were it not for imagination,
Sir, a man would be as happy in the
arms of a chambermaid as of a
Duchess.   SAMUEL JOHNSON

10378. I am certain of nothing but of
the holiness of the heart's affections,
and the truth of Imagination. What
the Imagination seizes as Beauty
must be Truth.   KEATS

10379. Man consists of body, mind
and imagination. His body is faulty,
his mind untrustworthy, but his
imagination has made him remarkable. In some centuries, his imagination has made life on this planet an
intense practice of all the lovelier
energies.   JOHN MASEFIELD,
              Shakespeare

10380. Give me an ounce of civet,
good apothecary, to sweeten my
imagination.   SHAKESPEARE,
              King Lear

10381.
The lunatic, the lover, and the poet
Are of imagination all compact:
One sees more devils than vast hell
　can hold,
That is, the madman: the lover, all as
　frantic
Sees Helen's beauty in a brow of
　Egypt:
The poet's eye, in a fine frenzy rolling,
Doth glance from heaven to earth,
　from earth to heaven;
And as imagination bodies forth
The form of things unknown, the
　poet's pen
Turns them to shapes, and gives to
　airy nothing
A local habitation and a name.
Such tricks hath strong imagination,
That if it would but apprehend some
　joy,
It comprehends some bringer of that
　joy;
Or in the night, imagining some fear,
How easy is a bush supposed a bear!
　　　　　SHAKESPEARE,
　　　A Midsummer-Night's Dream

10382.
Joan: I hear voices telling me what
　to do. They come from God.
Robert: They come from your imagi-
　nation.
Joan: Of course. That is how the
　messages of God come to us.
　　　BERNARD SHAW, *Saint Joan*

See also: 304, 7684, 12634, 16334,
18561.

IMITATION

**Related Subjects: Acting, Art,
Echo, Example, Plagiarism.**

10391. Men often applaud an imita-
tion, and hiss the real thing.
　　　　　　　　AESOP,
　　The Buffoon and the Countryman

10392. As large as life and twice as
natural.　　　LEWIS CARROLL,
　　　Through the Looking-Glass

10393. Imitation is the sincerest flattery.　　　　　C. C. COLTON

10394. Almost all absurdity of conduct arises from the imitation of
those whom we can not resemble.
SAMUEL JOHNSON, *The Rambler*

10395. Agesilaus being invited once
to hear a man who admirably imitated the nightingale, he declined,
saying he had heard the nightingale
itself.　　　　PLUTARCH, *Lives*

10396. With the exception of the instinct of self-preservation, the propensity for emulation is probably the
strongest and most alert and persistent of the economic motives proper.
　　　　THORSTEIN VEBLEN,
　　The Theory of the Leisure Class

See also: 14527.

IMMODESTY, see Modesty

IMMORALITY, see Morality

IMMORTALITY, see Mortality

IMPATIENCE, see Patience

IMPERFECTION, see Perfection

IMPERIALISM

**Related Subjects: Conquerors,
Empire, Kings, War.**

10401. Imperialism finds no warrant
in the Bible. The command, "go ye
into all the world and preach the
gospel to every creature," has no
gatling gun attachment.
　　　WILLIAM JENNINGS BRYAN

10402. Learn to think imperially.
　　　　JOSEPH CHAMBERLAIN

10403. In every part of the world the good desire of men for peace and decency is undermined by the dynamite of jingoism. And it needs only one spark, set off anywhere by one egomaniac to send it all up in one final fatal explosion.

ROBERT E. SHERWOOD,
Idiot's Delight

See also: 2565, 3609, 6906.

IMPERTINENCE

Related Subjects: Familiarity, Impudence, Mockery.

10411. He is guilty of impertinence who considers not the circumstances of time, or engrosses the conversation, or makes himself the subject of his discourse, or pays no regard to the company he is in. CICERO

10412. There is both an impertinence and a lack of taste in any man's laying bare to the public eye—to any eye —the bliss that has come to him through the love of a devoted woman, with whose life his own has been bound up.

GEORGE DU MAURIER,
Peter Ibbetson

10413. Receive no satisfaction for premeditated impertinence; forget it, and forgive it, but keep inexorably at a distance him who offered it.

LAVATER

IMPIETY, see Piety

IMPOSSIBILITY, see Possibility

IMPRESSIONS

Related Subjects: Feeling, Opinion, Reaction.

10421. If you would stand well with a great mind, leave him with a favor-able impression of yourself; if with a little mind, leave him with a favorable opinion of himself. COLERIDGE

10422. The least and most imperceptible impressions received in our infancy have consequences very important and of long duration. It is with these first impressions as with a river, whose waters we can easily turn at its source; with the same facility we may turn the minds of children to what direction we please.
LOCKE

10423. The mind unlearns with difficulty what has long been impressed on it. SENECA

IMPROVEMENT

Related Subjects: Benefits, Help, Progress, Reform, Reformation.

10431. Improvement makes straight roads, but the crooked roads without improvement are the roads of genius.
BLAKE, *Proverbs of Hell*

10432. Where we cannot invent, we may at least improve; we may give somewhat of novelty to that which was old, condensation to that which was diffuse, perspicuity to that which was obscure, and currency to that which was recondite. C. C. COLTON

10433. Judge of thine improvement, not by what thou speakest or writest, but by the firmness of thy mind, and the government of thy passions and affections. THOMAS FULLER

10434. If a better system is thine, import it; if not, make use of mine.
HORACE

10435. Slumber not in the tents of your fathers. The world is advancing. Advance with it. MAZZINI

See also: 794, 7271.

IMPRUDENCE, see Prudence

IMPUDENCE

Related Subjects: Familiarity, Impertinence.

10441. The way to avoid the imputation of impudence is, not to be ashamed of what we do, but never to do what we ought to be ashamed of.
CICERO

10442. An impudent fellow may counterfeit modesty, but I'll be hanged if a modest man can ever counterfeit impudence.
GOLDSMITH, *She Stoops to Conquer*

10443. The man who cannot blush, and who has no feelings of fear, has reached the acme of impudence.
MENANDER

10444. Ignorance is the mother of impudence.   *Proverb*

10445. He that knows the world will not be bashful; he who knows himself will not be impudent.
C. SIMMONS

10446. A true and genuine impudence is ever the effect of ignorance, without the least sense of it.
SIR RICHARD STEELE

See also: 1282.

IMPULSE

Related Subjects: Energy, Force, Motive, Passion, Rashness.

10451. A thing of impulse and a child of song.   BYRON, *Don Juan*

10452. He's sudden if a thing comes in his head.   SHAKESPEARE,
Henry VI

10453. Impulse manages all things badly.   STATIUS, *Thebais*

10454. Mistrust first impulses, they are always good.   TALLEYRAND

See also: 1257, 8397, 12845.

IMPURITY, see Purity

INATTENTION, see Attention

INCONSISTENCY, see Consistency

INCONSTANCY, see Constancy

INCREDULITY, see Credulity

INDECISION, see Decision

INDEPENDENCE, see Dependence

INDEX

Related Subject: Statistics.

10461. A book without an index is much like a compass-box, without the needle, perplexing instead of directive to the point we would reach.
Anonymous

10462. I certainly think the best book in the world would owe the most to a good index; and the worst book, if it had in it but a single good thought, might be kept alive by it.
HORACE BINNEY

10463. The making of indexes is what gives editors that haggard and querulous look.   SAXE COMMINS

10464. An index is a necessary implement, without which a large author is but a labyrinth without a clue to direct the readers within.
THOMAS FULLER

10465.
And in such indexes, although small pricks

To their subsequent volumes, there is
 seen
The baby figure of the giant mass
Of things to come at large.
SHAKESPEARE, *Troilus and Cressida*

10466. Get thorough insight into the
index, by which the whole book is
governed. SWIFT

See also: 18772.

INDIAN

Related Subject: Savagery.

10471. Send me wives for my Ca-
nadians. They are running in the
woods after Indian girls.
BIENVILLE,
Letter to the French Government

10472.
Lo, the poor Indian! whose untutor'd
 mind
Sees God in clouds, or hears him in
 the wind;
His soul proud Science never taught
to stray
Far as the solar walk or milky way.
POPE, *Essay on Man*

10473.
Ye say they all have passed away,
 That noble race and brave;
That their light canoes have vanished
From off the crested wave;
That mid the forests where they
 roamed
There rings no hunter's shout;
But their name is on your waters;
Ye may not wash it out.
LYDIA H. SIGOURNEY,
Indian Names

INDIFFERENCE

**Related Subjects: Attention, Con-
tempt, Idleness, Mediocrity, Neglect, Neutrality, Scorn.**

10481.
The earth revolves with me, yet
makes no motion,

The stars pale silently in a coral sky,
In a whistling void I stand before my
 mirror,
Unconcerned, and tie my tie.
CONRAD AIKEN,
Morning Song of Senlin

10482. Moral indifference is the
malady of the cultivated classes.
AMIEL, *Journal*

10483.
The cat is in the parlor, the dog is
 in the lake;
The cow is in the hammock—what
 difference does it make?
Anonymous

10484. I care not two-pence.
BEAUMONT & FLETCHER,
The Coxcomb

10485. The whole frame of things
preaches indifferency.
EMERSON, *Essays*

10486. The tragedy of love is indifference. SOMERSET MAUGHAM,
The Trembling of a Leaf

10487. Happy are the men whom
nature has buttressed with indifference and cased in stoicism.
MAUPASSANT, *After*

10488. Indifference is the invincible
giant of the world. OUIDA

10489. Diffidence is the right eye of
prudence. *Proverb*

10490. At length the morn and cold
indifference came.
NICHOLAS ROWE, *The Fair Penitent*

10491.
 A man whose blood
Is very snow-broth; one who never
 feels
The wanton stings and motions of
 the sense. SHAKESPEARE,
Measure for Measure

10492. I am a man, and nothing that concerns a man do I deem a matter of indifference to me.

TERENCE, *Heauton Timoroumenos*

See also: 439, 18878, 19281.

INDIGESTION, see Digestion

INDIGNATION

Related Subjects: Anger, Resentment.

10501. I see no wisdom in saving up indignation for a rainy day . . . Fighters who pull their punches lose their fights. HEYWOOD BROUN,
Sacco and Vanzetti

10502. No one is such a liar as the indignant man. NIETZSCHE,
Beyond Good and Evil

10503. There is something among men more capable of shaking despotic power than lightning, whirlwind, or earthquake; that is the threatened indignation of the whole civilized world. DANIEL WEBSTER

INDISCRETION, see Discretion

INDIVIDUALITY

Related Subjects: Eccentricity, Originality, Personality.

10511. If I thought mottoes and slogans did any good I would replace the "God bless our happy home" of a generation or two ago, and the "Say it quick" of our offices today, with old Emerson's "Be Yourself." That is what every artist, every civilized man and woman has got to be, as the very foundation of an art of living. It is indeed only the foundation, but it is essential.

JAMES TRUSLOW ADAMS,
Our Business Civilization

10512. If we unlock the rooms of the far past we can peer in and see ourselves, busily occupied in beginning to become you and me.

J. M. BARRIE

10513. There has never been a time or place where the individual was free to follow his own whims. He had to accept certain limitations set by the society in which he lived.

FRANZ BOAS, *I Believe*

10514. Individuals will always be the center and the consummation of experience, but what the individual actually *is* in his life experience depends upon the nature and movement of associated life.

JOHN DEWEY, *I Believe*

10515. In the light of the rise of totalitarian states, I am led to emphasize the idea that only the voluntary initiative and voluntary cooperation of individuals can produce social institutions that will protect the liberties necessary for achieving development of genuine individuality.

JOHN DEWEY, *I Believe*

10516. The individual is always mistaken. EMERSON, *Essays*

10517. The dictator-hero can grind down his citizens till they are all alike, but he can't melt them into a single man. That is beyond his power.

E. M. FORSTER, *I Believe*

10518. What another would have done as well as you, do not do it. What another would have said as well as you, do not say it; written as well, do not write it. Be faithful to that which exists nowhere but in yourself—and thus make yourself indispensable. ANDRÉ GIDE,
Les Nourritures Terrestres

10519. Rugged individualism.
HERBERT HOOVER, *The New Day*

10520. An individual may believe that he should devote himself entirely to a cause, even sacrifice himself to it—his country, truth, art, love. It is in the devotion or the sacrifice that he becomes most himself, it is because of the devotion or sacrifice of individuals that causes become of value.
JULIAN HUXLEY, *I Believe*

10521. The man whom God wills to slay in the struggle of life He first individualizes.   IBSEN, *Brand*

10522. Individualism, is in theory a kind of Anarchy without Socialism. It is, therefore, no better than a lie, because, liberty is not possible without equality, and true Anarchy cannot be without Solidarity, without Socialism.
ENRICO MALATESTA, *Anarchy*

10523. A man lives not only his personal life, as an individual, but also, consciously or unconsciously, the life of his epoch and his contemporaries.
THOMAS MANN,
The Magic Mountain

10524. "Do you know what individuality is?"
"No."
"Consciousness of will. To be conscious that you have a will and can act."
Yes, it is. It's a glorious saying.
KATHERINE MANSFIELD, *Journals*

10525.
The earth keeps some vibration going
There in your heart, and that is you.
EDGAR LEE MASTERS,
Spoon River Anthology

10526. A people, it appears, may be progressive for a certain length of time, and then stop. When does it stop? When it ceases to possess individuality.   J. S. MILL,
On Liberty

10527. Whatever crushes individuality is despotism, by whatever name it may be called.   J. S. MILL,
On Liberty

10528. How glorious it is—and also how painful—to be an exception.
ALFRED DE MUSSET,
The White Blackbird

10529. Have you ever considered that if every thumb print is different, perhaps everything else is different? No two people are alike. Yet originals, individualists, bright intellects, and the gang who lead the laughter and point the way, are alarmed by an idea that we are becoming standardized.
FELIX RIESENBERG, *Endless River*

10530.
No, I am that I am, and they that level
At my abuses reckon up their own.
SHAKESPEARE, *Sonnet CXXI*

10531. The worst cliques are those which consist of one man.
BERNARD SHAW,
Back to Methuselah

10532. I have ever hated all nations, professions, and communities, and all my love is toward individuals . . . Principally I hate and detest that animal called man.   SWIFT

10533. One's self is, first of all, the sum of one's inheritance, not only one's biological but of one's social inheritance. It is the complex of all that one believes, and all that one longs for, of what one knows, and of what one hopes, some day, somehow, to find out, if only people will let you go on trying to find out.
DOROTHY THOMPSON,
Let the Record Speak

10534. The individual is the end of the Universe.
UNAMUNO, *Tragic Sense of Life*

10535. Individuality is the salt of common life. You may have to live in a crowd, but you do not have to live like it, nor subsist on its food.
HENRY VAN DYKE,
The School of Life

10536. The whole theory of the universe is directed unerringly to one single individual—namely to You.
WALT WHITMAN,
By Blue Ontario's Shore

10537. I announce the great individual, fluid as Nature, chaste, affectionate, compassionate, fully arm'd.
WALT WHITMAN, *So Long!*

10538.
I wear my hat as I please indoors or out.
Why should I pray? why should I venerate and be ceremonious?
Having pried through the strata, analyzed to a hair, counsel'd with doctors and calculated close,
I find no sweeter fat than sticks to my own bones.
WALT WHITMAN, *Song of Myself*

10539.
I know I am solid and sound,
To me the converging objects of the universe perpetually flow,
All are written to me.
WALT WHITMAN, *Song of Myself*

See also: 150, 1857, 11637, 15731, 18876, 18899, 21882.

INDUSTRY

Related Subjects: Business, Earnestness, Labor, Machinery, Mass Production, Science, Wages, Work, Zeal.

Industry in the sense of diligence

10541. In the ordinary business of life, industry can do anything which

genius can do, and very many things which it cannot.
H. W. BEECHER,
Proverbs from Plymouth Pulpit

10542. She looketh well to the ways of her household, and eateth not the bread of idleness.
Bible: Proverbs, xxxi, 27

10543. The dog that trots about finds a bone.   GEORGE BORROW,
The Bible in Spain

10544. Industry is a loadstone to draw all good things.
ROBERT BURTON,
Anatomy of Melancholy

10545. Keep thy shop, and thy shop will keep thee. Light gains make heavy purses. 'Tis good to be merry and wise.
GEORGE CHAPMAN, *Eastward Ho*

10546. Industry is the soul of business and the keystone of prosperity.
DICKENS, *Barnaby Rudge*

10547. Leave no stone unturned.
EURIPIDES, *Heracleidae*

10548.
Plough deep while Sluggards sleep,
And you shall have Corn to sell and to keep. FRANKLIN, *Poor Richard*

10549. Industry need not wish.
FRANKLIN, *Poor Richard*

10550. Let us, then, be up and doing.
LONGFELLOW, *A Psalm of Life*

10551. Push on—keep moving.
THOMAS MORTON,
A Cure for the Heart-Ache

10552. Industry is fortune's right hand, and frugality her left. *Proverb*

10553. Much industry and little conscience make a man rich. *Proverb*

10554. Industry is the mother of fortune. *Proverb*

10555. If you have great talents, industry will improve them; if you have but moderate abilities, industry will supply their deficiencies.
SIR JOSHUA REYNOLDS,
Discourses on Painting

10556. Life without industry is guilt, industry without art is brutality.
RUSKIN, *Lectures on Art*

10557. Love of bustle is not industry.
SENECA

10558. The best of me is diligence.
SHAKESPEARE, *King Lear*

10559. Nothing is achieved before it be thoroughly attempted.
SIR PHILIP SIDNEY, *Arcadia*

Modern industry

10560. And if the industrialists who own or manage it [industry] cannot make it work, cannot avoid ruinous crashes periodically, cannot provide employment for the millions of idle who beg for a chance to live, then the Government of the United States can assume sovereignty over it, engage competent engineers to set it in motion with the aid of management and labor. CHARLES A. BEARD,
The Open Door at Home

10561. The prosperous industry no longer just "grows," like Topsy. Success is spelled not only by superior manufacturing methods, but by the labor market, the transportation costs and many other elements that have to do with location.
H. S. COLBURN, *Industrial Properties*

10562. The great masses of our working people depend upon industry for their life and happiness. Industry has a duty to them. It must be con-

ducted in a manner which will promote the common good.
CARDINAL HAYES

10563. We have utterly failed to adopt our economic and political machinery to the complete technical revolution in industrial and agricultural production.
MAURY MAVERICK, *Blood & Ink*

10564. The accumulated knowledge resulting from modern scientific and technical discoveries is so great that were it rapidly and continuously applied to the improvement of productive processes, we could have a rate of industrial advancement, and attain a level of production in the not distant future, that would dwarf anything that has been known in the past.
H. G. MOULTON,
Income & Economic Progress

See also: 561, 1472, 1702, 1784, 1788, 1795, 2268, 4525.

INFERIORITY

Related Subjects: Humility, Mediocrity, Timidity.

10571. The feeling of inferiority rules the mental life and can be clearly recognized in the sense of incompleteness and unfulfilment, and in the uninterrupted struggle both of individuals and of humanity.
ALFRED ADLER, *Social Interest*

10572. Exaggerated sensitiveness is an expression of the feeling of inferiority.
ALFRED ADLER, *Social Interest*

10573. There is no inherently inferior race, and the white men's burden accordingly is an adventure in impertinence.
STUART CHASE, *Are Radicals Crazy?*

10574. No one can make you feel inferior without your consent.

ELEANOR ROOSEVELT

10575. With a higher moral nature will come a restriction on the multiplication of the inferior.

HERBERT SPENCER, *First Principles*

See also: 7882, 10906.

INFIDELITY, see Fidelity

INFLATION

Related Subjects: Business, Credit, Depression, Finance, Money, Wages.

10581. To the office, and heard a vast amount of discussion about the inflation of currency, and for all of me they may inflate it till it bursts, or deflate it to flatness. For I have found that no matter what happens to the national currency, there is only one thing that happens to mine: it vanishes.   F. P. A.,
The Diary of Our Own Samuel Pepys

10582. Shall I count them pure with the wicked balances, and with the bag of deceitful weights?

Bible: Micah, vi, 10

10583. Abundance and scarcity of goods have never substantially moved the price level.

Inflation and deflation of the circulating medium have, from time immemorial, moved it up and down like a child's skipping rope.

IRVING FISHER, *Inflation*

10584. During the French Revolution, heads were not only bloody, they were cut off. For "after the paper money machine comes the guillotine" —such was one of the aphorisms of that day.   IRVING FISHER, *Inflation*

10585. The inescapable conclusion of any factual study of the major kinds of inflation is that debt, in its many forms, moves restlessly and relentlessly beneath all of them.

R. D. SKINNER,
Seven Kinds of Inflation

See also: 13707.

INFLUENCE

Related Subjects: Associates, Authority, Companions, Environment, Example and Precept, Favor, Motive, Power.

10591. Why doth one man's yawning make another yawn?

ROBERT BURTON,
Anatomy of Melancholy

10592. Nothing in human life is more to be lamented, than that a wise man should have so little influence.

HERODOTUS, *Calliope*

10593. The finest edge is made with the blunt whetstone.

JOHN LYLY, *Euphues*

10594. Men are not easily taken by frontal assault; it is only stratagem that can quickly knock them down. To be a blonde, pink, soft, and delicate, is to be a stratagem.   H. L. MENCKEN

10595. Under the influence either of poverty or of wealth, workmen and their work are equally liable to degenerate.   PLATO, *The Republic*

10596.
Manners with fortunes, humours turn with climes,
Tenets with books, and principles with times.   POPE, *Moral Essays*

10597. Do you think, I am easier to be played on than a pipe?

SHAKESPEARE, *Hamlet*

10598. O, thou hast damnable iteration, and art indeed able to corrupt a saint. Thou hast done much harm upon me, Hal; God forgive thee for it! Before I knew thee, Hal, I knew nothing; and now am I, if a man should speak truly, little better than one of the wicked.

SHAKESPEARE, *Henry IV*

10599. The only way in which one human being can properly attempt to influence another is encouraging him to think for himself, instead of endeavoring to instil ready-made opinions into his head. LESLIE STEPHENS

See also: 1235, 1291, 1308, 2501, 3247, 11968, 14299, 15381.

INFORMALITY, see Form, Formality

INFORMER

Related Subjects: Cowards, Spying, Treachery.

10601. The informer is the worst rogue of the two. *Proverb*

INGRATITUDE, see Gratitude

INHERITANCE

Related Subjects: Will and Testament.

10611. The fool inherits, but the wise must get.
WILLIAM CARTWRIGHT,
The Ordinary

10612. There is a strange charm in the thoughts of a good legacy, or the hopes of an estate, which wondrously alleviates the sorrow that men would otherwise feel for the death of friends. CERVANTES, *Don Quixote*

10613.
How seldom, friend! a good great man inherits
Honor or wealth, with all his worth and pains!
It sounds like stories from the land of spirits
If any man obtains that which he merits,
Or any merit that which he obtains.
COLERIDGE, *The Knight's Tomb*

10614. Say not you know another entirely, till you have divided an inheritance with him. LAVATER

10615. A son could bear complacently the death of his father, while the loss of his inheritance might drive him to despair.
MACHIAVELLI, *The Prince*

10616. Lest, selling that noble inheritance for a poor mess of perishing pottage, you never enter into His eternal rest.
WILLIAM PENN, *No Cross No Crown*

10617. He is no great heir that inherits not his ancestor's virtues.
Proverb

10618. Who wait for dead men's shoes shall go long barefoot. *Proverb*

10619. The tears of an heir are laughter under a mask.
PUBLILIUS SYRUS, *Sententiae*

10620. I owe much; I have nothing; the rest I leave to the poor.
RABELAIS, *Will*

10621.
Happy always was it for that son
Whose father for his hoarding went to hell. SHAKESPEARE, *Henry VI*

10622. To inherit property is not to be born—is to be still-born, rather.
THOREAU, *Journal*

INJURY

Related Subjects: **Abuse, Insult, Mischief, Slander, Threat, Violence, Wounds, Wrongs.**

10630. The injuries we do and those we suffer are seldom weighed in the same scales.   AESOP, *Fables*

10631. It is better to receive than to do an injury.   CICERO

10632. Christianity commands us to pass by injuries; policy, to let them pass by us. FRANKLIN, *Poor Richard*

10633.
What a fool
An injury may make of a staid man.
KEATS, *Otho the Great*

10634. The noblest remedy of injuries is oblivion.   *Proverb*

10635. He that defends an injury is next to him that commits it. *Proverb*

10636. No one is injured except by himself.   *Proverb*

10637. It is the mark of a good man not to know how to do an injury.
PUBLILIUS SYRUS, *Sententiae*

10638. He who has injured thee was either stronger or weaker. If weaker, spare him; if stronger, spare thyself.
SENECA, *De Ira*

10639. Whom they have injured they also hate.   SENECA

10640.
To wilful men
The injuries that they themselves procure
Must be their schoolmasters.
SHAKESPEARE, *King Lear*

10641. A readiness to resent injuries is a virtue only in those who are slow to injure.
SHERIDAN, *A Trip to Scarborough*

10642. Kindnesses are easily forgotten; but injuries?—what worthy man does not keep *those* in mind.
THACKERAY, *Lovel the Widower*

See also: 402, 884, 1705, 1970, 12377, 16363, 21629.

INJUSTICE, see Justice

INK

Related Subjects: **Pen, Printing, Writing.**

10651. Let there be gall enough in thy ink; though thou write with a goose-pen, no matter.
SHAKESPEARE, *Twelfth Night*

See also: 1416, 2097, 2345.

INN AND INNKEEPER

Related Subjects: **Food, Guests, Hospitality.**

10661.
Lodgings,—free from bugs and fleas, if possible,
If you know any such.
ARISTOPHANES, *The Frogs*

10662. Oh that I had in the wilderness a lodging-place of wayfaring men!   *Bible: Jeremiah, ix, 2*

10663. Though I am an innkeeper, thank Heaven I am a Christian.
CERVANTES, *Don Quixote*

10664. He knew the taverns well in every town.
CHAUCER, *Canterbury Tales*

10665. There is nothing which has yet been contrived by man by which so much happiness is produced as by a good tavern or inn.
SAMUEL JOHNSON, *Boswell: Life*

10666.
Souls of Poets dead and gone,
What Elysium have ye known,

Happy field or mossy cavern,
Choicer than the Mermaid Tavern?
KEATS, *Lines on the Mermaid Tavern*

10667.
But I'm for toleration and for drink-
ing at an inn,
Says the old bold mate of Henry
Morgan.   JOHN MASEFIELD,
            Captain Stratton's Fancy

10668. He goes not out of his way,
that goes to a good inn.   *Proverb*

10669. A handsome hostess is bad
for the purse.   *Proverb*

10670. Shall I not take mine ease in
mine inn?   SHAKESPEARE, *Henry IV*

10671. The red-nosed innkeeper of
Daventry.   SHAKESPEARE, *Henry IV*

10672.
Now spurs the lated traveller apace
To gain the timely inn.
            SHAKESPEARE, *Macbeth*

10673. Lastly and finally, mine host
of the Garter.   SHAKESPEARE,
        The Merry Wives of Windsor

10674. I reckon this always, that a
man is never undone till he be hanged,
nor never welcome to a place till
some certain shot be paid and the
hostess say "Welcome!"
                SHAKESPEARE,
        The Two Gentlemen of Verona

10675. The great advantage of a
hotel is that it's a refuge from home
life.   BERNARD SHAW,
                You Never Can Tell

10676.
Whoe'er has travelled life's dull
    round,
Where'er his stages may have been,
May sigh to think he still has found
The warmest welcome at an inn.
                W. SHENSTONE,
        Written at an Inn at Henley

INNOCENCE

**Related Subjects: Blushing, Chas-
tity, Childhood, Experience, Maid,
Modesty, Purity, Simplicity, Virtue.**

10681. As innocent as a new-laid
egg.   W. S. GILBERT, *Engaged*

10682. He's armed without that's innocent within.   HORACE

10683. Live innocently; God is here.
                        LINNAEUS

10684. The mind, conscious of recti-
tude laughed to scorn the falsehood
of report.   OVID, *Fasti*

10685. The breast-plate of innocence
is not always scandal-proof. *Proverb*

10686. Innocence is no protection.
                        Proverb

10687. Innocence itself, sometimes
hath need of a mask.   *Proverb*

10688. He that is innocent may well
be confident.   *Proverb*

10689. All are presumed good till
they are found in a fault.   *Proverb*

10690. It is better to risk saving a
guilty person than to condemn an innocent one.   VOLTAIRE, *Zadig*

See also: 2059, 2743, 2745, 3201,
3868, 3926, 16372.

INQUIRY, INQUISITIVENESS

**Related Subjects: Curiosity, Ques-
tion, Research, Study.**

10691. It is a shameful thing to be
weary of inquiry when what we
search for is excellent.   CICERO

10692. Free inquiry, if restrained
within due bounds, and applied to
proper subjects, is a most important

privilege of the human mind; and if well conducted, is one of the greatest friends to truth. But when reason knows neither its office nor its limits, and when employed on subjects foreign to its jurisdiction, it then becomes a privilege dangerous to exercise.   J. H. D'AUBIGNÉ

10693. The man who is inquisitive into the secrets of your affairs, with which he has no concern, should be an object of your caution. Men no more desire another's secrets to conceal them, than they would another's purse for the pleasure only of carrying it.   FIELDING

10694. Inquisitiveness or curiosity is a kernel of the forbidden fruit, which still sticketh in the throat of a natural man, and sometimes to the danger of his choking.   THOMAS FULLER

10695. Shun the inquisitive, for you will be sure to find him leaky. Open ears do not keep conscientiously what has been intrusted to them, and a word once spoken flies, never to be recalled.   HORACE

10696. It is error only, and not truth, that shrinks from inquiry.
     THOMAS PAINE

10697. An inquisitive man is a creature naturally very vacant of thought itself, and therefore forced to apply to foreign assistance.
     SIR RICHARD STEELE

10698. Inquisitive people are the funnels of conversation; they do not take anything for their own use, but merely to pass it on to others.
     SIR RICHARD STEELE

INSANITY, see Sanity

INSENSITIVITY, see Sensitivity

INSPIRATION

Related Subjects: Art, Genius Skill.

10701. 'Tis inspiration expounds experience.   PHILIP J. BAILEY, Festus

10702. My themes come to me in flash. They are intuitive. Long after their arrival I take them up and work very hard over them.   BRAHMS,
     Schauffler: The Unknown Brahms

10703. No man was ever great without some portion of divine inspiration.   CICERO, De Natura Deorum

10704. Fill'd with fury, rapt, inspired.
     WILLIAM COLLINS, The Passions

10705. The text inspires not them but they the text inspire.
     DRYDEN, The Medal

10706. We cannot carry on inspiration and make it consecutive. One day there is no electricity in the air, and the next the world bristles with sparks like a cat's back.
     EMERSON, Lecture

10707.
Poet greets Inspiration with a curse
"I will be damned," cries he, "if write verse."   GILBERT FRANKAU

10708. Out of my entire annual output of songs, perhaps two—or at the most, three—come as a result of inspiration. We can never rely on inspiration. When we most want it, it does not come. Therefore the composer does not sit around and wait for an inspiration to walk up and introduce itself. What he substitutes for it is nothing more than talent plus his knowledge. If his endowment is great enough, the song is made to sound as if it were truly inspired.
     GEORGE GERSHWIN

10709. If there were such a thing as inspiration from a higher realm, it might well be that the neurotic temperament would furnish the chief condition for the requisite receptivity.

WILLIAM JAMES,
Varieties of Religious Experience

10710.
If there be good in that I wrought,
Thy hand compelled it, Master,
Thine—
Where I have failed to meet Thy
Thought
I know, through Thee, the blame
was mine.
KIPLING, *My New-Cut Ashlar*

10711.
Earth's fiery core alone can feed the
bough
That blooms between Orion and the
Plough.
EDNA ST. VINCENT MILLAY, *Sonnet*

10712.
O! for a Muse of fire, that would as-
cend
The brightest heaven of invention!
SHAKESPEARE, *Henry V*

10713.
Spirits are not finely touch'd
But to fine issues.
SHAKESPEARE,
The Merry Wives of Windsor

10714. No more inspiration in her than in a plate of muffins.
BERNARD SHAW, *Man and Superman*

10715.
All around him Patmos lies
Who hath spirit-gifted eyes.
EDITH M. THOMAS, *Patmos*

10716.
Who with one breath attunes the
spheres,
And also my poor human heart.
THOREAU, *Inspiration*

10717. It seems to me that this one [one of Mary Baker Eddy's revisions of the Lord's Prayer] is distinctly superior to the one that was inspired for last year's edition. It is strange, but to my mind plain, that inspiring is an art which does improve with practice.   MARK TWAIN
Christian Science

10718.
Great God! I'd rather be
A Pagan suckled in a creed outworn;
So might I, standing on this pleas-
ant lea,
Have glimpses that would make me
less forlorn;
Have sight of Proteus rising from the
sea,
Or hear old Triton blow his wreathed
horn.   WORDSWORTH,
The World Is Too Much With Us

10719.
There's not a man
That lives who hath not known his
godlike hours.
WORDSWORTH, *The Prelude*

See also: 1181, 2479.

INSTINCT

Related Subjects: Animal, Intelligence, Nature, Perception, Sense.

10721. That which is imprinted upon the spirit of man by an inward instinct.
BACON, *Advancement of Learning*

10722. Instinct is untaught ability.
A. BAIN, *Senses and Intellect*

10723. An unfathomable Somewhat, which is *Not we.*
CARLYLE, *French Revolution*

10724. Instinct needs to be trained by method; but instinct alone helps us to discover a method which will suit us, and thanks to which our instinct may be trained.

    JEAN COCTEAU, *A Call to Order*

10725.

A good man, through obscurest aspirations,

Has still an instinct of the one true way.   GOETHE, *Faust*

10726. A moment's insight is sometimes worth a life's experience.

    O. W. HOLMES,
The Professor at the Breakfast-Table

10727.

       Instinct preceded wisdom
Even in the wisest men, and may sometimes

Be much the better guide.

    GEORGE LILLO, *Fatal Curiosity*

10728. Man's natural instinct is never toward what is sound and true; it is toward what is specious and false. H. L. MENCKEN, *Prejudices*

10729.

Reason, however able, cool at best,

Cares not for service, or but serves when prest,

Stays till we call, and then not often near;

But honest instinct comes a volunteer;

Sure never to o'er-shoot, but just to hit,

While still too wide or short is human wit.   POPE, *Essay on Man*

10730.

         I'll never
Be such a gosling to obey instinct.

    SHAKESPEARE, *Coriolanus*

10731. Beware instinct.

    SHAKESPEARE, *Henry IV*

10732. Instinct is a great matter; I was now a coward on instinct.

    SHAKESPEARE, *Henry IV*

10733. Upon instinct.—I grant ye, upon instinct.

    SHAKESPEARE, *Henry IV*

10734.

By a divine instinct men's minds mistrust

Ensuing dangers.

    SHAKESPEARE, *Richard III*

10735. A few strong instincts, and a few plain rules. WORDSWORTH,
    *Alas! What Boots the
    Long Laborious Quest?*

10736.

High instincts before which our mortal nature

Did tremble like a guilty thing surprised.   WORDSWORTH,
Ode on Intimations of Immortality

10737.

Reason progressive, instinct is complete;

Swift instinct leaps; slow reason feebly climbs.

    EDWARD YOUNG, *Night Thoughts*

See also: 913, 4053, 20178.

INSULT

Related Subjects: Abuse, Curse, Injury, Offence, Slander, Sneer.

10741. An injury is much sooner forgiven than an insult.

    LORD CHESTERFIELD, *Letters*

10742. He who allows himself to be insulted deserves to be.

    CORNEILLE, *Héraclius*

10743.

Am I to set my life upon a throw

Because a bear is rude and surly? No—

A moral, sensible, and well-bred man

Will not affront me, and no other can.

    COWPER, *Conversation*

10744. If he is insulted, he can be insulted; all his affair is not to insult.

EMERSON, *Conduct of Life*

10745. The way to procure insults is to submit to them.

HAZLITT, *Characteristics*

10746. To add insult to injury.

PHAEDRUS, *Fables*

10747. Insults are like bad coins; we cannot help their being offered to us, but we need not take them.

C. H. SPURGEON, *Salt-Cellars*

See also: 8864.

INSURANCE

Related Subjects: Business, Protection, Safety, Security, Surety.

10751. All insurance is based on the law of averages. H. H. RICHARDSON

INTELLECTUALS

Related Subjects: Cleverness, Intelligence, Reason, Snob.

10761. There is no inherent reason why the miner, plowman, and milkmaid should not be as intellectual as the poet, auditor, or school teacher. STUART CHASE, *Are Radicals Crazy?*

10762. The presence of a body of well-instructed men, who have not to labor for their daily bread, is important to a degree which cannot be overestimated; as all high intellectual work is carried on by them, and on such work material progress of all kinds mainly depends, not to mention other and higher advantages.

DARWIN, *Descent of Man*

10763. It has been my observation that the so-called intellectuals are more easily taken in by mass-suggestion than others, because their ex-

perience is drawn not from life but—more comfortably—from printed paper. EINSTEIN

10764.
We are the hollow men
We are the stuffed men
Leaning together
Headpiece filled with straw. Alas!
Our dried voices, when
We whisper together
Are quiet and meaningless
As wind in dry grass
Or rats' feet over broken glass
In our dry cellar.

T. S. ELIOT, *The Hollow Men*

10765. Profundity is not a mere matter of intellect. JOHN GASSNER,
Masters of the Drama

10766. A highbrow is the kind of person who looks at a sausage and thinks of Picasso. A. P. HERBERT

10767. What a revelation this crisis has been to me in regard to human nature, above all, of the intellectual *élite*. How quickly and totally have these thinkers, so proud, so jealous of their reason, so imbued with the great principles of liberty and humanity, renounced them and toppled them in the dust! I will not forget it in the sequel when, with peace once more established, I shall be seeing them again professing their ideas, flaunting their spirit, its liberality and its kinships with all that is human

ROMAIN ROLLAND, *I Will Not Rest*

10768. The progress of the world depends upon us. Let us not weary in hope and action: let the intellectuals illuminate the road that the workers have to build. There are different labour gangs. But the object of labour is the same.

ROMAIN ROLLAND, *I Will Not Rest*

See also: 1198, 1202, 2339, 5327, 6317, 8316, 8317, 11576, 13771, 14176, 14890, 19397, 21407.

INTELLIGENCE

Related Subjects: Cleverness, Common Sense, Education, Genius, Idea, Instinct, Intellectuals, Knowledge, Metaphysics, Mind, Philosophy, Reason, Thought, Wisdom.

10771. Intelligence is characterized by a natural lack of comprehension of life.   BERGSON

10772. A man known to us only as a celebrity in politics or in trade, gains largely in our esteem if we discover that he has some intellectual taste or skill.   EMERSON, *Conduct of Life*

10773. There are three classes of intellects: one which comprehends by itself; another which appreciates what others comprehend; and a third which neither comprehends by itself nor by the showing of others; the first is the most excellent, the second is good, the third is useless.
         MACHIAVELLI, *The Prince*

10774. The controlling Intelligence understands its own nature, and what it does, and whereon it works.
     MARCUS AURELIUS, *Meditations*

10775. Intellect is invisible to the man who has none.   SCHOPENHAUER

10776. He has not so much brain as ear-wax.   SHAKESPEARE,
          Troilus and Cressida

10777. The march of intellect.
              SOUTHEY, *Colloquies*

10778. Intelligence appears to be the thing that enables a man to get along without education. Education appears to be the thing that enables a

man to get along without the use of intelligence.   A. E. WIGGAM,
       The New Decalogue of Science

See also: 472, 3070, 3358, 4132, 4534, 14141.

INTENTION

Related Subjects: End, Motive, Purpose, Will.

10781. Stain not fair acts with foul intentions.
          SIR THOMAS BROWNE,
                 Christian Morals

10782. A good intention clothes itself with sudden power.   EMERSON,
               Conduct of Life

10783. Hell is paved with good intentions.   SAMUEL JOHNSON,
                 Boswell: Life

10784. One often sees good intentions, if pushed beyond moderation, bring about very vicious results.
              MONTAIGNE, *Essays*

10785. "He means well" is useless unless he does well.   PLAUTUS,
                     Trinummus

10786. Man punishes the action, but God the intention.   *Proverb*

10787. We will take the good will for the deed.   RABELAIS

10788. All men mean well.
               BERNARD SHAW,
         Maxims for Revolutionists

See also: 1971, 3022, 4575, 7273.

INTEREST

Related Subjects: Attention, Curiosity, Selfishness, Usurer.

10791. Interest speaks all sorts of tongues, and plays all sorts of parts, even that of disinterestedness.
          LA ROCHEFOUCAULD, *Maxims*

10792. It makes a difference whose ox is gored. MARTIN LUTHER

10793. Young man, get a hobby; preferably get two, one for indoors and one for out; get a pair of hobby-horses that can safely be ridden in opposite directions.
A. EDWARD NEWTON,
Amenities of Book-Collecting

10794. To know when one's self is interested, is the first condition of interesting other people.
WALTER PATER,
Marius the Epicurean

10795. We are interested in others when they are interested in us.
PUBLILIUS SYRUS, *Sententiae*

10796. A man's interest in the world is only the overflow of his interest in himself. BERNARD SHAW,
Heartbreak House

Interest on investment.

10797.
With loves and doves, at all events
With money in the Three per Cents.
BROWNING, *Dis Aliter Visum*

10798.
Year after year they voted cent. per cent.,
Blood, sweat, and tear-wrung millions—why? for rent!
BYRON, *The Age of Bronze*

10799. Where interests are high, in any investment, the risk is greater.
H. L. SIMPSON,
The Financing of Real Estate

10800. It is always better policy to earn an interest than to make a thousand pounds. STEVENSON,
Lay Morals
See also: 1483, 3128.

INVENTION

Related Subjects: Discovery, Imagination, Machinery, Originality, Progress, Science, Skill.

10801. A tool is but the extension of a man's hand, and a machine is but a complex tool. And he that invents a machine augments the power of a man and the well-being of mankind.
H. W. BEECHER,
Proverbs from Plymouth Pulpit

10802. God hath made man upright; but they have sought out many inventions. *Bible: Ecclesiastes, vii, 29*

10803. A weak invention of the enemy. COLLEY CIBBER,
Richard III (adaptation)

10804. 'Tis frivolous to fix pedantically the date of particular inventions. They have all been invented over and over fifty times. Man is the arch machine, of which all these shifts drawn from himself are toy models.
EMERSON, *Conduct of Life*

10805. Only an inventor knows how to borrow, and every man is or should be an inventor.
EMERSON, *Letters and Social Aims*

10806. Invention breeds invention.
EMERSON, *Society and Solitude*

10807. Invention came that men might have life and that they might have it more abundantly.
GLENN FRANK

10808. The social reformer fights wealth. The inventor fights want. The social reformer fights slave drivers. The inventor fights slavery.
GLENN FRANK

10809. The inventor is not the bought-and-paid-for slave of business and industry. He is blood-brother of the scientist and the artist. He is animated by the itch to invent as the scientist is animated by the itch to know and the artist by the itch to create.   GLENN FRANK

10810. The great inventors have been the great surprisers. Again and again they have shamed our limited outlook. They have done the things we have said could not be done. They have been experts in the impossible.
GLENN FRANK

10811. The final goal of inventor and engineer is to make available to the masses comforts and conveniences that now only the wealthy may have. In other words, whether we realize it or not, the inventors and the engineers are waging a war of human liberation.   GLENN FRANK

10812. Take the advice of a faithful friend, and submit thy inventions to his censure.   THOMAS FULLER,
Holy and Profane State

10813. Invention by accident rather than design has been a common phenomenon.   JOHN A. MALONEY

10814. Inventions are usually the results of synthesis. JOHN A. MALONEY

10815. Gladstone, seeing one of Faraday's inventions, asked of what possible use it could be. "Why, Mr. Prime Minister," answered Faraday, "You will soon be able to tax it!"
JOHN A. MALONEY

10816.
Th' invention all admir'd, and each, how he
To be th' inventor miss'd, so easy it seem'd,
Once found, which yet unfound most would have thought
Impossible.   MILTON, Paradise Lost

10817.
Some one invented the telephone,

And interrupted a nation's slumbers,
Ringing wrong but similar numbers.
OGDEN NASH,
Look What you Did, Christopher

10818. Nothing is invented and perfected at the same time.   Proverb

10819. Rarely does it happen that any device or invention of importance is made by one man alone. The threads of inquiry are taken up and traced, one labor succeeding another, each tracing it a little further, often without apparent result. This goes on sometimes for centuries, until at length one man, greater perhaps than his fellows, seeking to fulfil the needs of his time, gathers the various threads together, treasures up the gain of past successes and failures, and uses them as the means for some solid achievement.   SAMUEL SMILES

10820. The greatest inventions were produced in times of ignorance; as the use of the compass, gunpowder, and printing; and by the dullest nation, as the Germans.   SWIFT,
Thoughts on Various Subjects

10821. Science, for one thing, has greatly systematized the processes of invention. It might be said that invention has become more self-conscious since the advent of scientific perception of the attributes and uses of materials.
S. G. WILLIAMSON,
The American Craftsman

See also: 561, 1065, 1497, 2316, 4505, 8565, 13804.

IRELAND AND THE IRISH

Related Subjects: England, Island.

10831. We Irishmen are apt to think something and nothing are near neighbors.   BISHOP BERKELEY

10832. Politics is the chloroform of the Irish People, or, rather, the hashish. O. St. J. Gogarty, *As I Was Going Down Sackville St.*

10833. Ireland gives England her soldiers, her generals too. George Meredith, *Diana of the Crossways*

10834. English, Scotchmen, Jews, do well in Ireland—Irishmen never; even the patriot has to leave Ireland to get a hearing. George Moore, *Ave*

10835. It is the plain duty of every Irishman to disassociate himself from memories of Ireland—Ireland being a fatal disease, fatal to Englishmen and doubly fatal to Irishmen. George Moore, *Ave*

10836. They think they have pacified Ireland; think they have foreseen everything; but the fools, the fools, the fools!—they have left us our Fenian dead, and while Ireland holds these graves, Ireland, unfree, shall never be at peace! Sean O'Casey, *The Plough and the Stars*

10837. Give an Irishman lager for a month, and he's a dead man. An Irishman is lined with copper, and the beer corrodes it. But whiskey polishes the copper and is the saving of him. Mark Twain, *Life on the Mississippi*

See also: 668, 13658, 14564.

IRON

Related Subjects: Blacksmith, Rust.

10841. Strike while the iron is hot. Addaeus, *Epigram*

10842.
"Gold is for the mistress—silver for the maid—
Copper for the craftsman cunning at his trade."
"Good!" said the Baron, sitting in his hall,
"But Iron—Cold Iron—is master of them all." Kipling, *Cold Iron*

10843. He is teaching iron to swim. *Proverb*

10844. Put up your iron. Shakespeare, *Twelfth Night*

10845. This extraordinary metal, the soul of every manufacture, and the mainspring perhaps, of civilised society. Samuel Smiles, *Invention and Industry*

10846. I saw the iron enter into his soul. Sterne, *Sentimental Journey*

See also: 14492.

IRONY

Related Subjects: Ridicule, Sarcasm, Satire.

10851. Irony is the foundation of the character of Providence. Balzac, *Eugénie Grandet*

10852. Irony is to the high-bred what billingsgate is to the vulgar; and when one gentleman thinks another gentleman an ass, he does not say it point-blank; he implies it in the politest terms he can invent. Bulwer-Lytton

10853. Life's Little Ironies. Thomas Hardy, *Title of Collection of Short Stories*

10854. Clap an extinguisher upon your irony if you are unhappily blessed with a vein of it. Charles Lamb

10855. Irony is jesting hidden behind gravity.   JOHN WEISS,
Wit, Humor and Shakespeare

See also: 1113.

IRRESOLUTION, see Resolution

IRRITATION

Related Subjects: Anger, Resentment.

10861.
too many creatures
both insects and humans
estimate their own value
by the amount of minor irritation
they are able to cause
to greater personalities than themselves   DON MARQUIS, *pride*

ISLAND

Related Subjects: England, Ireland, Water.

10871.
Sprinkled along the waste of years
Full many a soft green isle appears.
JOHN KEBLE, *The Christian Year*

10872.
There is no lover like an island shore
For lingering embrace;
No tryst so faithful as the turning tide
At its accustomed place.
MRS. DWIGHT MORROW,
Islands

10873. In settling an island, the first building erected by a Spaniard would be a church; by a Frenchman, a fort; by a Dutchman, a warehouse; and by an Englishman, an alehouse.
Proverb

10874.
Many a green isle needs must be
In the deep wide sea of Misery,

Or the mariner, worn and wan,
Never thus could voyage on.
SHELLEY, *Lines Written Among
the Euganean Hill*

10875. Summer isles of Eden lyin
in dark-purple spheres of sea.
TENNYSON, *Locksley Ha*

10876.
I will arise and go now, and go t
Innisfree,
And a small cabin build there, of cla
and wattles made;
Nine bean-rows will I have there,
hive for the honey-bee,
And live alone in the bee-loud glad
W. B. YEATS,
The Lake Isle of Innisfre

See also: 10886.

ISOLATION

Related Subjects: Responsibility
Society, Solitude.

10881. "Let them stew in their ow
juice," but that juice is the lifebloo
of all mankind, and it is thicker tha
the mountains and deeper than th
seas which are supposed to insure u
a private prosperity and a separat
peace. . . . Look well . . . upon thi
world in which you ask us to dis
claim all citizenship. Already th
tramping of the millions across th
sea sets up a tremor in the whea
fields of Nebraska.
HEYWOOD BROUN,
New Lamps for Ol

10882. But it was Cain who firs
voiced and set the philosophy of isola
tion and rugged individualism . .
Will it be well for us to wash ou
hands and say with the cynicism o
Cain, "Am I my brother's keeper?
HEYWOOD BROUN,
My Brother's Keepe

0883. But we will be useless even
ɔ our own interests if we close our
yes and pretend our world ends at
ne misty line where some wooded
american hill keeps its rendezvous
·ith the sky. This is not the end
f the world or the end of the road.
·here are sounds louder than the tick-
ng of the clock. Time and space
annot be discarded, nor can we
nrow off the circumstances that we
re citizens of the world. The blood
f one is the blood of all. Our Lord
ies once again.
HEYWOOD BROUN,
There is no Hiding Place

0884. Whenever our neighbor's
ouse is on fire, it cannot be amiss
or the engines to play a little on our
wn. Better to be despised for too
nxious apprehensions, than ruined
y too confident security.　BURKE

0885. If you wish to avoid foreign
ɔllision, you had better abandon the
cean.　HENRY CLAY

0886. No man is an *Iland,* intire of
. selfe; everyman is a peece of the
ontinent, a part of the *maine,* if a
·lod bee washed away by the *Sea,*
urope is the lesse, as well as if a
·romontorie were, as well as if a
·lannor of thy *friends* or of *thine*
·wne were; any mans *death* dimi-
ishes *me,* because I am involved in
·lankinde; and therefore never send
ɔ know for whom the *bell* tolls; It
ɔlls for *thee.*　JOHN DONNE,
Devotions
(Source of title of novel by
Ernest Hemingway.)

0887. We cannot now be isolated
·rom the wars, depressions, ideas,
niseries, and cruelties of an unor-
anized world. We cannot be isolated
·rom the structure of a world whose
nighty industrial framework gathers

up wars and depressions anywhere
and implicates men everywhere.
FRANK P. GRAHAM,
Democracy and the Second
World War

10888. Instead of minding their own
business, the Fathers of the Republic
never lost an opportunity to declare
in favor of democratic movements, no
matter in what part of the world.
They had the vision to see that the
clash between democratic government
and autocratic government was not
local but universal, and that the battle
was not merely for a day but the
struggle everlasting.
GEORGE CREEL,
The "Isolation" Myth

10889. None of us has the honour of
living a life all to himself.
VICTOR HUGO

10890. Half the world knows not
how the other half lives.　*Proverb*

10891. One cannot teach a nation
that it must depend on itself for
everything without teaching it to distrust other nations and regard them
as potential enemies.
CLARENCE STREIT, *Union Now*

10892. The Atlantic Ocean may still
be our bulwark. But this world is,
despite all we can do, one economic
unit.　WILLIAM A. WHITE,
Defense for America

10893. America cannot be an ostrich
with its head in the sand.
WOODROW WILSON

See also: 691, 11667, 19693.

ITALY AND THE ITALIANS

**Related Subjects: Europe, Rome
and Romans.**

10901.
Oh, woman-country, wooed, not wed,

Loved all the more by earth's male-
   lands
Laid to their hearts instead!
        BROWNING, *By the Fireside*

10902. Italy a paradise for horses,
hell for women, as the proverb goes.
        ROBERT BURTON,
        Anatomy of Melancholy

10903.
Italia! O Italia! thou who hast
The fatal gift of beauty.
        BYRON, *Childe Harold*

10904.
Ah, slavish Italy! thou inn of grief!
Vessel without a pilot in loud storm!
Lady no longer of fair provinces,
But brothel-house impure!
        DANTE, *Purgatorio*

10905.
Home of the Arts! where glory's
   faded smile
Sheds lingering light o'er many a
   mouldering pile.
        MRS. HEMANS,
   *Restoration of the Works of Art
                     to Italy*

10906. A man who has not been i
Italy is always conscious of an in
feriority.   SAMUEL JOHNSON,
                 Boswell: Lif

10907. Beyond the Alps lies Italy.
              LIVY, *Histor*

10908. Italy is only a geographica
expression.   METTERNICH,
   Memorandum to the Great Power

10909. I am desperately Italian. I be
lieve in the function of Latinity.
        MUSSOLINI, *Autobiograph*

10910. Fortunately the Italian peopl
is not yet accustomed to eating sev
eral times per day.   MUSSOLIN

10911. All Italians are plunderers.
              NAPOLEO

10912. The story is extant, and wr
in choice Italian. SHAKESPEARE,
                      Haml

10913. A paradise inhabited wit
devils.   SIR HENRY WOTTON,
              Letters from Ital

See also: 1194, 6896.

J

JAZZ

**Related Subjects: Conviviality,
Dancing, Music, Merriment.**

10921. I should say: "Hot music
shall last forever." There'll probably
be new names for it, that's all. There
have been several names since I can
remember way back to the good ol'
days in New Orleans, Louisiana,
when Hot Music was called 'rag-
time music,' 'jazz-music,' 'gut-bucket
music,' 'swing-music,' and now 'hot
music.' So you see instead of dying
out, it only gets new names.
        LOUIS ARMSTRONG,
   Introduction to "Le Jazz Hot"

10922. [Jazz] is a sickness that ha
come upon music . . . a rash upo
the times . . . no more importai
than was the polka to Bohemia, th
waltz to Germany.
        SIR THOMAS BEECHAI

10923. There is no reason why yo
should renounce classical music; it
simply necessary that you learn t
take along with classical music, a
entirely different set of emotion
those belonging to jazz.
        STEPHANE MAUGI

10924. It is often said that jazz
"sensual" music. This does not mea
very much. As a matter of fact, a

music is "sensual", if by this word you mean that it affects the senses. Certainly, hot music, by reason of the intonations used, does attack the senses of the listener more violently, perhaps, than other music.
HUGUES PANASSIÉ, *Le Jazz Hot*

10925. Swing is "a gift"—either you have it deep within yourself, or you don't have it at all. If you can play with absolute correctness, you can hold a place in a good symphony orchestra; and you can attain this skill by study and hard work. But neither long study nor hard work will get you anywhere in jazz if you do not naturally know how to play with a swing. You can't learn swing.
HUGUES PANASSIÉ, *Le Jazz Hot*

10926. The sources of swing music are unquestionably Negroid. It is that expression of sadness, of the melancholy of the soul of the oppressed Negro which gives swing music its intensely moving accent.
HUGUES PANASSIÉ, *Le Jazz Hot*

10927. American music is not jazz, and jazz is not music.
PAUL ROSENFELD

10928. Jazz will endure as long as people hear it through their feet instead of their brains. SOUSA

10929. We learned syncopation from three different teachers: the Indians, the Negroes, and our neighbors in Mexico. It had become firmly established before the Civil War. The dance craze of the last 25 years has simply exaggerated it.
VIRGIL THOMPSON

10930. Jazz is not yet the thing said; it is the manner of saying it.
PAUL WHITEMAN

JEALOUSY

Related Subjects: Enemy, Envy, Hatred, Love, Rivalry, Suspicion.

10931. Love is strong as death; jealousy is cruel as the grave.
Bible: The Song of Solomon, viii, 6

10932.
Yet he was jealous, though he did not show it,
For jealousy dislikes the world to know it. BYRON, *Don Juan*

10933.
Thou tyrant, tyrant Jealousy,
Thou tyrant of the mind!
DRYDEN, *Song of Jealousy*

10934. Jealousy, the jaundice of the soul. DRYDEN,
The Hind & the Panther

10935. Jealousy is inborn in women's hearts. EURIPIDES, *Andromache*

10936. A jealous woman believes everything her passion suggests.
JOHN GAY, *The Beggar's Opera*

10937. Jealousy is said to be the offspring of Love. Yet, unless the parent makes haste to strangle the child, the child will not rest till it has poisoned the parent.
A. W. & J. C. HARE,
Guesses at Truth

10938.
First, then, a woman will or won't, depend on 't;
If she will do 't she will; and there's an end on 't,
But if she won't, since safe and sound your trust is,
Fear is affront, and jealousy injustice.
AARON HILL, *Zara*

10939. There is more self-love than love in jealousy.
LA ROCHEFOUCAULD, *Maxims*

10940. Jealousy is nourished by doubt, and becomes madness or ends when it passes from doubt to certainty.   LA ROCHEFOUCAULD, *Maxims*

10941.
>   Nor jealousy
> Was understood, the injur'd lover's hell.   MILTON, *Paradise Lost*

10942.
> Can't I another's face commend,
> And to her virtues be a friend,
> But instantly your forehead lowers,
> As if *her* merit lessen'd *yours?*
>   EDWARD MOORE,
> *The Farmer, the Spaniel, and the Cat*

10943. All jealous women are mad.
>   PINERO,
> *The Second Mrs. Tanqueray*

10944. Love being jealous, makes a good eye look asquint.   *Proverb*

10945. A jealous man's horns hang in his eyes.   *Proverb*

10946. O jealousy thou magnifier of trifles!   SCHILLER, *Fiesco*

10947. I will be more jealous of thee than a Barbery cock-pigeon over his hen. SHAKESPEARE, *As You Like It*

10948.
> The venom clamours of a jealous woman
> Poisons more deadly than a mad dog's tooth.   SHAKESPEARE,
>   *The Comedy of Errors*

10949.
> Think'st thou I'ld make of life a jealousy
> To follow still the changes of the moon
> With fresh suspicions?
>   SHAKESPEARE, *Othello*

10950.
> Though I perchance am vicious in my guess,

> As, I confess, it is my nature's plagu
> To spy into abuses, and oft m
>   jealousy
> Shapes faults that are not.
>   SHAKESPEARE, *Othell*

10951.
> One not easily jealous, but, bein wrought,
> Perplexed in the extreme.
>   SHAKESPEARE, *Othell*

10952.
>   'Tis not to make me jealous
> To say my wife is fair, feeds wel loves company,
> Is free of speech, sings, plays an dances well.   SHAKESPEARE,
>   *Othell*

10953.
> Jealous souls will not be answer'd sc
> They are not jealous for the cause,
> But jealous for they are jealous: 't a monster
> Begot upon itself, born on itself.
>   SHAKESPEARE, *Othell*

10954.
>   Trifles light as air
> Are to the jealous confirmatior strong
> As proofs of holy writ.
>   SHAKESPEARE, *Othell*

10955.
> O! beware, my lord, of jealousy;
> It is the green-eyed monster whic doth mock
> The meat it feeds on.
>   SHAKESPEARE, *Othell*

10956. Jealousy's eyes are green.
>   SHELLEY, *Swellfoot the Tyra*

10957. Jealousy, at any rate, is or of the consequences of love; you ma like it or not, at pleasure; but ther it is.   STEVENSON,
>   *On Falling in Lo*

0958. Plain women are always ealous of their husbands, beautiful omen never are!
OSCAR WILDE,
A Woman of No Importance

0959.
Iunger, Revenge, to sleep are petty foes,
ut only Death the jealous eyes can close. WILLIAM WYCHERLEY,
Love in a Wood

ee also: 1224, 1548.

JEFFERSON, THOMAS

0961. Were Jefferson alive today, is voice would be heard from ocean ocean demanding that the people hemselves must own the monopolies.
JOHN PETER ALTGELD

0962. He was called a demagogue nd his followers a mob, but the imortal Jefferson dared to follow the est promptings of his heart. He laced man above matter, humanity bove property, and, spurning the ribes of wealth and power, pleaded he cause of the common people.
WILLIAM JENNINGS BRYAN

0963. In his ripest life [Jefferson] ave no more conspicuous evidence f his foresight and statesmanship han in the inauguration of a policy hich comprehended in its scope the xploration and settlement of the enre trans-Mississippi region.
GENERAL GREELY,
Explorers & Travellers

0964. Here was buried Thomas efferson, author of the Declaration f American Independence, of the tatute of Virginia for religious freeom, and father of the University of irginia. JEFFERSON *Epitaph,*
written for himself

10965. Since the days when Jefferson expounded his code of political philosophy, the whole world has become his pupil.
MICHAEL MACWHITE

10966. A gentleman of thirty-two who could calculate an eclipse, survey an estate, tie an artery, plan an edifice, try a cause, break a horse, dance a minuet and play the violin.
JAMES PARTON, *Life of Jefferson*

10967. The immortality of Thomas Jefferson does not lie in any one of his achievements, but in his attitude toward mankind.
WOODROW WILSON

JESUS, see Christ

JEW

Related Subject: Christ.

10971. To be a Jew is a destiny.
VICKI BAUM, *And Life Goes On*

10972. And Israel shall be a proverb and a by-word among all people.
Bible: I Kings, ix, 7

10973. Behold an Israelite indeed, in whom is no guile! *Bible: John, i, 47*

10974. Since the Jews are considered as a thoroughly different element, we must define their racial position. There is no more a Semitic than there is an Aryan race, since both terms define linguistic groups, not human beings. . . . It is well known that dark Syroid Jews are often taken for Spaniards or Italians, Armenoids for South Slavs or other Alpines, and blond, blue-eyed Jews for Northwest Europeans. FRANZ BOAS,
Aryans & Non-Aryans

10975. Have Mercy upon Jews, Turks, Infidels, and Heretics.
Book of Common Prayer

10976. Yes, I am a Jew, and when the ancestors of the right honourable gentlemen were brutal savages in an unknown island, mine were priests in the temple of Solomon.   DISRAELI

10977. If my theory of relativity is proven successful, Germany will claim me as a German and France will declare that I am a citizen of the world. Should my theory prove untrue, France will say that I am a German and Germany will declare that I am a Jew.   EINSTEIN

10978. The Jews are among the aristocracy of every land; if a literature is called rich in the possession of a few classic tragedies, what shall we say to a national tragedy lasting for fifteen hundred years, in which the poets and the actors were also the heroes.   GEORGE ELIOT, *Daniel Deronda*

10979. The sufferance, which is the badge of the Jew, has made him, in these days, the ruler of the rulers of the earth.   EMERSON, *Conduct of Life*

10980. The political misfortunes of the nation [Jews] taught them to appreciate the only possession they had retained, their written records, at its true value. Immediately after the destruction of the Temple in Jerusalem by Titus, Rabbi Jochanaan ben Sakkai asked for permission to open at Jabne the first school for the study of the Torah. From now on it was the Holy Book, and the study of it, that kept the scattered people together.   SIGMUND FREUD, *Moses and Monotheism*

10981. A Jew is for me an object of physical disgust. I vomit when I see one . . . Christ cannot possibly have been a Jew. I don't have to prove that scientifically. It is a fact . . . treasure an ordinary prostitute abov a married Jewess.   GOEBBELS, *John Gunther: Inside Europ*

10982. When people talk about wealthy man of my creed, they ca him an Israelite; but if he is poo they call him a Jew.   HEIN

10983.
Pride and humiliation hand in han
   Walked with them through th
     world where'er they went;
Trampled and beaten were they a
     the sand,
   And yet unshaken as the continen
       LONGFELLOW,
   The Jewish Cemetery at Newpor

10984.
Who taught you tender Bible tales
Of honey-lands, of milk and wine?
Of happy, peaceful Palestine?
Of Jordan's holy harvest vales?
Who gave the patient Christ? I say
Who gave your Christian creed? Yea
   yea,
Who gave your very God to you?
Your Jew! Your Jew! Your hate
Jew!   JOAQUIN MILLER,
            To Russi

10985. I am a Jew else, an Ebre
Jew.   SHAKESPEARE, *Henry I*

10986.
You call me misbeliever, cut-throa
   dog,
And spit upon my Jewish gaberdin
       SHAKESPEARE,
   The Merchant of Venic

10987. For sufferance is the badge o
all our tribe.   SHAKESPEARE,
   The Merchant of Venic

10988. I am a Jew. Hath not a Je
eyes? Hath not a Jew hands, or
gans, dimensions, senses, affection
passions?   SHAKESPEARE,
   The Merchant of Venic

10989.
A second Daniel, a Daniel, Jew!
Now, infidel, I have thee on the hip.
SHAKESPEARE,
The Merchant of Venice

10990. The Jews generally give value.
They make you pay; but they deliver
the goods. In my experience the men
who want something for nothing are
invariably Christians.
BERNARD SHAW, *Saint Joan*

See also: 652, 13455, 15821.

JEWEL

Related Subjects: Diamond, Luxury, Pearl, Riches.

10991. Have you ever noticed, Harry,
that many jewels make women either
incredibly fat or incredibly thin?
J. M. BARRIE,
The Twelve-Pound Look

10992.
Jewels, orators of Love,
Which, ah! too well men know, do
women move.
SAMUEL DANIEL,
Complaint of Rosamond

10993.
These gems have life in them: their
colours speak,
Say what words fail of.
GEORGE ELIOT, *The Spanish Gypsy*

10994.
How many a thing which we cast to
the ground,
When others pick it up, becomes a
gem! GEORGE MEREDITH,
Modern Love

10995.
Rich and rare were the gems she
wore,
And a bright gold ring on her wand
she bore. THOMAS MOORE,
*Rich & Rare Were the Gems She
Wore*

10996. The Utopians wonder how
any man should be so much taken
with the glaring doubtful lustre of a
jewel or stone, that can look up to a
star, or to the sun.
SIR THOMAS MORE, *Utopia*

10997.
From the east to western Ind,
No jewel is like Rosalind.
SHAKESPEARE, *As You Like It*

10998.
'Tis plate of rare device, and jewels
Of rich and exquisite form; their
value's great. SHAKESPEARE,
Cymbeline

10999.
I took a costly jewel from my neck,
A heart it was, bound in with diamonds. SHAKESPEARE,
Henry VI

11000.
It seems she hangs upon the cheek
of night
Like a rich jewel in an Ethiope's ear.
SHAKESPEARE, *Romeo and Juliet*

11001. The best of us has our weaknesses, & if a man has gewelry let
him show it. ARTEMUS WARD,
Edwin Forrest as Othello

See also: 332, 2791, 3167, 3995.

JOHNSON, SAMUEL

11011. Rough Johnson, the great
moralist. BYRON, *Don Juan*

11012. There is no arguing with
Johnson: for if his pistol misses fire,
he knocks you down with the butt
end of it. GOLDSMITH,
Boswell: Life

11013. The great English moralist.
Never was a descriptive epithet more
nicely appropriate than that! Dr.

Johnson's morality was as English an article as a beefsteak.
HAWTHORNE, *Our Old Home*

11014.
Here lies poor Johnson; reader have a care;
Tread lightly, lest you rouse a sleeping bear.
Religious, moral, generous, and humane
He was; but self-sufficient, rude, and vain;
Ill-bred, and overbearing in dispute,
A scholar and a Christian and a brute.
SOAME JENYNS,
Epitaph on Samuel Johnson

11015. You must not mind me, madam; I say strange things, but I mean no harm.   SAMUEL JOHNSON

11016. What a singular destiny has been that of this remarkable man! To be regarded in his own age as a classic, and in ours as a companion! To receive from his contemporaries that full homage which men of genius have in general received from posterity; to be more intimately known to posterity than other men are known to their contemporaries.   MACAULAY

11017. The conversation of Johnson is strong and clear, and may be compared to an antique statue, where every vein and muscle is distinct and bold. Ordinary conversation resembles an inferior cast.
THOMAS PERCY

11018. I have not wasted my life trifling with literary fools in taverns as Johnson did when he should have been shaking England with the thunder of his spirit.
BERNARD SHAW,
Parents and Children

11019. The great Cham of literature.
SMOLLETT

JOKE, JOKING

Related Subjects: Epigram, Humor, Laughter, Merriment, Pun, Wit.

11021.
Master, shall I begin with the usual jokes
That the audience always laugh at?
ARISTOPHANES, *The Frogs*

11022. He'd rather lose his dinner than his jest.
BEAUMONT & FLETCHER,
Wit at Several Weapons

11023. The ordinary and over-worn trade of jesting.
BEAUMONT & FLETCHER,
The Woman Hater

11024. There is no jesting with edge tools. BEAUMONT & FLETCHER,
The Little French Lawyer

11025. Jests that give pain are no jests.   CERVANTES, *Don Quixote*

11026. A good joke is the one ultimate and sacred thing which cannot be criticized. Our relations with a good joke are direct and even divine relations.   G. K. CHESTERTON,
Preface to Pickwick Papers

11027.
My son was killed while laughing at some jest. I would I knew
What it was, and it might serve me in a time when jests are few.
KIPLING, *Epitaphs of the War*

11028. Suppress me if you can! I am a Merry Jest!   ANDREW LANG,
Ballade of the Primitive Jest

11029.
The saddest ones are those that wear
The jester's motley garb.
DON MARQUIS,
The Tavern of Despair

11030.
Haste thee, Nymph, and bring with
  thee
Jest and youthful Jollity,
Quips and Cranks, and wanton Wiles,
Nods, and Becks, and wreathed
  Smiles.   MILTON, *L'Allegro*

11031.
Joking decides great things,
Stronglier, and better oft than earnest
  can. MILTON, *Imitation of Horace*

11032. Good jests bite like lambs, not
like dogs.   *Proverb*

11033. That's the cream of the jest.
                        Proverb

11034. Many a true word is spoken
in jest.   *Proverb*

11035. The wise make jests and fools
repeat them.   *Proverb*

11036. A jest driven too far brings
home hate.   *Proverb*

11037. A jest loses its point when
the jester laughs himself.
                  SCHILLER, *Fiesco*

11038. Alas, poor Yorick! I knew
him, Horatio: a fellow of infinite jest,
of most excellent fancy.
            SHAKESPEARE, *Hamlet*

11039. It would be argument for a
week, laughter for a month, and a
good jest for ever.
          SHAKESPEARE, *Henry IV*

11040.
A jest's prosperity lies in the ear
Of him that hears it, never in the
  tongue
Of him that makes it.
          SHAKESPEARE,
            Love's Labour's Lost

11041.
My way of joking is telling the truth.
That is the funniest joke in the world.
                  BERNARD SHAW

11042. You could read Kant by yourself, if you wanted; but you must
share a joke with some one else.
      STEVENSON, *Virginibus Puerisque*

11043. A college joke to cure the
dumps.   SWIFT, *Cassinus and Peter*

11044. I tried him with mild jokes,
then with severe ones.
        MARK TWAIN, *A Deception*

See also: 3218, 7586, 7732.

JOURNALISM, see Press

JOY

**Related Subjects: Bliss, Cheerful-
ness, Dancing, Delight, Fun, Happiness, Laughter, Merriment,
Pleasure, Tears.**

11051. Weeping may endure for a
night, but joy cometh in the morning.
          Bible: Psalms, xxx, 5

11052.
          Every joy is gain
And gain is gain, however small.
        BROWNING, *Paracelsus*

11053.
    All who joy would win
Must share it,—happiness was born
  a twin.   BYRON, *Don Juan*

11054. My joys have far exceeded
my sorrows and my friends have
brought me far more than my enemies
have taken from me.
          FREDERICK DOUGLASS,
                  Autobiography

11055. Joys are not the property of
the rich alone: nor has he lived ill,
who at his birth and at his death has
passed unnoticed. HORACE, *Epistles*

11056.
Vain deluding Joys,
The brood of Folly without father
  bred!   MILTON, *Il Penseroso*

11057.
Oh stay! oh stay!
Joy so seldom weaves a chain
Like this to-night, that oh, 'tis pain
To break its links so soon.
THOMAS MOORE, *Fly Not Yet*

11058.
And the stern joy which warriors feel
In foemen worthy of their steel.
SCOTT, *The Lady of the Lake*

11059.
Make the coming hour o'erflow with
joy,
And pleasure drown the brim.
SHAKESPEARE,
All's Well that Ends Well

11060. Eat with the Rich, but go to
the play with the Poor, who are
capable of Joy.
LOGAN PEARSALL SMITH,
Afterthoughts

11061. Joy is not in things; it is in
us.   RICHARD WAGNER

11062. For he who gives joy to the
world is raised higher among men
than he who conquers the world.
RICHARD WAGNER

See also: 320, 905, 1174, 1523, 1692,
1697, 2072, 2726, 3825, 9667, 15782.

JUDGE

**Related Subjects: Criticism, Judg-
ment, Judgment Day, Jury, Justice,
Law, Lawyers, Precedent.**

11071. That judges of important
causes should hold office for life is
not a good thing, for the mind grows
old as well as the body.
ARISTOTLE, *Politics*

11072. A judge is not God; his duty
is to adapt facts to principles, to
judge cases of infinite variety while
measuring them by a fixed standard.
BALZAC, *The Commission in Lunacy*

11073. France employs about six
thousand judges; no generation has
six thousand great men at her command, much less can she find them
in the legal profession.   BALZAC,
The Commission in Lunacy

11074. I am as sober as a judge.
FIELDING,
Don Quixote in England

11075. A judge ought to go through
a term of hard labor, of penal servitude, three strokes of the "cat" and
a partial hanging before being fit to
pass any sentence. Who would be a
judge on these terms, I wonder?
LAURENCE HOUSMAN

11076. The judge should not be
young; he should have learned to
know evil, not from his own soul,
but from late and long observation of
the nature of evil in others; knowledge should be his guide, not personal
experience.   PLATO, *The Republic*

11077.
The hungry judges soon the sentence
sign,
And wretches hang that jurymen
may dine.   POPE,
The Rape of the Lock

11078. Magistrates are to obey as
well as execute laws.   *Proverb*

11079. An upright judge has more
regard to justice than to men.
Proverb

11080. The judge is condemned when
the criminal is absolved.
PUBLILIUS SYRUS, *Sententiae*

11081. No one should be judge in his
own cause.   PUBLILIUS SYRUS,
Sententiae

11082.
Heaven is above all yet; there sits a judge
That no king can corrupt.
SHAKESPEARE, *Henry VIII*

11083. An upright judge, a learned judge. SHAKESPEARE,
The Merchant of Venice

11084.
                 Fill the seats of justice
With good men, not so absolute in goodness
As to forget what human frailty is.
SIR T. N. TALFOURD, *Ion*

See also: 1373, 2500, 2502, 4946, 9327.

JUDGMENT

Related Subjects: Courts of Law, Criticism, Decision, Esteem, Judge, Judgment Day, Jury, Justice, Law, Opinion, Trials.

11091. Thou art weighed in the balances, and art found wanting.
Bible: Daniel, v, 27

11092. By their fruits ye shall know them. *Bible: Matthew, vii, 20*

11093. Out of thine own mouth will I judge thee. *Bible: Luke, xix, 22*

11094. Wherein thou judgest another, thou condemnest thyself.
Bible: Romans, ii, 1

11095. Strike through the varnish of any judgment seat and what will you strike but hate thick-clotted from centuries of angry verdicts?
HEYWOOD BROUN,
Sacco and Vanzetti

11096. God himself, sir, does not propose to judge man until the end of his days. SAMUEL JOHNSON

11097. Everyone complains of his memory, and no one complains of his judgment.
LA ROCHEFOUCAULD, *Maxims*

11098. Most people judge men only by success or by fortune.
LA ROCHEFOUCAULD, *Maxims*

11099.
'Tis with our judgments as our watches, none
Go just alike, yet each believes his own. POPE, *Essay on Criticism*

11100. You cannot judge of a man till you know his whole story.
Proverb

11101. He hath a good judgment, that relieth not wholly on his own.
Proverb

11102. Commonly we say a judgment falls upon a man for something in him we cannot abide.
JOHN SELDEN, *Table Talk*

11103. When I was green in judgment. SHAKESPEARE,
Antony and Cleopatra

11104.
Give every man thy ear, but few thy voice;
Take each man's censure, but reserve thy judgment. SHAKESPEARE,
Hamlet

11105.
O judgment! thou art fled to brutish beasts,
And men have lost their reason.
SHAKESPEARE, *Julius Caesar*

11106.
Why, all the souls that were, were forfeit once;
And He that might the vantage best have took
Found out the remedy. How would you be,

If He, which is the top of judgment,
should
But judge you as you are?
SHAKESPEARE,
Measure for Measure

11107. A Daniel come to judgment!
yea, a Daniel!   SHAKESPEARE,
The Merchant of Venice

11108. The number of those who
undergo the fatigue of judging for
themselves is very small indeed.
SHERIDAN, *The Critic*

11109.
But as when an authentic watch is
shown,
Each man winds up and rectifies his
own,
So in our very judgments.
SIR JOHN SUCKLING, *Aglaura*

See also: 271, 472, 993, 1015, 1292,
3633, 3943, 7087.

JUDGMENT DAY

Related Subjects: Christ, Eternity,
Hell, Judge, Judgment, Mortality,
Paradise, Repentance, Salvation,
Soul.

11111. In that day a man shall cast
his idols . . . to the moles and to the
bats.   *Bible: Isaiah, ii, 20*

11112. Be ye also ready; for in such
an hour as ye think not, the Son of
man cometh.
Bible: Matthew, xxiv, 44

11113.
The last loud trumpet's wondrous
sound,
Shall thro' the rending tombs re-
bound,
And wake the nations under ground.
WENTWORTH DILLON,
On the Day of Judgment

11114.
When rattling bones together fly
From the four corners of the sky.
DRYDEN

11115. God will not look you over
for medals, degrees or diplomas, but
for scars.   ELBERT HUBBARD,
Epigrams

11116. That fellow would vulgarize
the day of judgment.
DOUGLAS JERROLD, *A Comic Author*

11117.
That day of wrath, that dreadful day,
When heaven and earth shall pass
away.   SCOTT,
The Lay of the Last Minstrel

11118.
I see the judge enthron'd! the flam-
ing guard!
The volume open'd!—open'd ev'ry
heart!   EDWARD YOUNG,
Night Thoughts

See also: 3937, 17156, 20683.

JUNE

Related Subject: Spring.

11121. Knee-deep in June.
ALFRED AUSTIN, *A Wild Rose*

11122. Flame-flowered, yellow-pet-
alled June.   DON BLANDING,
Hawaiian June

11123. June's twice June since she
breathed it with me. BROWNING,
The Flower's Name

11124. The leafy month of June.
COLERIDGE, *The Ancient Mariner*

11125.
And what is so rare as a day in June?
Then, if ever, come perfect days;
Then Heaven tries the earth if it be
in tune,

And over it softly her warm ear
lays.   LOWELL,
The Vision of Sir Launfal

11126. Calm weather in June sets
corn in tune.   *Proverb*

11127.
How softly runs the afternoon
Beneath the billowy clouds of June!
C. H. TOWNE, *How Softly Runs*

See also: 1446.

JURY

**Related Subjects: Courts of Law,
Judge, Judgment, Justice, Law,
Lawyers, Trials.**

11131. Wise men plead causes, but
fools decide them.
ANACHARSIS, *Plutarch: Lives*

11132. In my mind, he was guilty of
no error, he was chargeable with no
exaggeration, he was betrayed by his
fancy into no metaphor, who once
said that all we see about us, kings,
lords, and Commons, the whole machinery of the State, all the apparatus
of the system, and its varied work-
ings, end in simply bringing twelve
good men into a box.
LORD BROUGHAM,
Present State of the Law

11133. As harsh as a prejudiced jury.
THOMAS HOOD, *For the New Year*

11134.
Since twelve honest men have de-
cided the cause,
And were judges of fact, though not
judges of laws.
SIR W. PULTENEY,
The Honest Jury

11135.
For twelve honest men have decided
the cause,

Who are judges alike of the facts and
the laws. SIR W. PULTENEY,
The Honest Jury

11136.
The hungry judges soon the sentence
sign,
And wretches hang that jurymen may
dine.   POPE, *Rape of the Lock*

11137.
The jury, passing on the prisoner's
life,
May in the sworn twelve have a thief
or two
Guiltier than him they try.
SHAKESPEARE,
Measure for Measure

11138. They have been grand-jury-
men since before Noah was a sailor.
SHAKESPEARE, *Twelfth Night*

See also: 8515.

JUSTICE AND INJUSTICE

**Related Subjects: Capital Punish-
ment, Courts of Law, Crime, Hang-
ing, Judge, Judgment, Judgment
Day, Law, Lawyers, Murder,
Prison, Punishment, Retribution,
Right, Rights, Trial.**

11141. Much may be said on both
sides.   ADDISON, *The Spectator*

11142. Any structure must be plumb
if it is to endure or the building will
fall. So it is with nations. Wrong
may seem to triumph. Right may
seem to be defeated. But the gravitation of eternal justice is upward
toward the throne of God. Any political institution if it is to endure
must be plumb with that line of
justice.   JOHN PETER ALTGELD

11143. The path of the just is as
the shining light, that shineth more
and more unto the perfect day.
Bible: Proverbs, iv, 18

11144. The memory of the just is blessed.   *Bible: Proverbs, x, 7*

11145. It would not be thought very just or wise to arraign the honorable professions of law and physic because the one produces the pettifogger and the other the quack.   HENRY CLAY

11146. Justice is something that man knows little about. He may know something about charity and understanding and mercy, and he should cling to these as far as he can.
CLARENCE DARROW

11147. The term "social justice" has been dangerously distorted by Father Coughlin. What possible social justice can there be in ideas of division, hatred, racial strife, bigotry and sympathy for totalitarian systems where freedom is lost and economic oppression rife? Social justice has no meaning apart from tolerance, racial friendliness, brotherhood, freedom and peace under democracy.
DALE DE WITT,
Genuine Social Justice

11148. Justice is truth in action.
DISRAELI

11149. Justice is a machine that, when some one has once given it the starting push, rolls on of itself.
GALSWORTHY, *Justice*

11150. Justice was known by the ancients to be blind; by ourselves is admitted blind; will be acclaimed blind by the tongues of our descendents. It is blind because it is depart— or rather compartmental.
GALSWORTHY

11151. Hindus, Parsees, Christians, or Jews, if we wish to live as one nation, the interest of anyone of us must be the interest of all. The only

deciding consideration can be the justice of a particular cause.
MAHATMA GANDHI

11152. I have always proclaimed that there can be nothing finer than to be the advocate of those who cannot defend themselves.
ADOLF HITLER, *May 1, 1937*

11153. Indeed, I tremble for my country when I reflect that God is just. JEFFERSON, *Notes on Virginia*

11154. Why should there not be a patient confidence in the ultimate justice of the people? Is there any better or equal hope in the world?
LINCOLN

11155. What we call Justice is but the organization of our egoism, which would be more noxious if it were not cabined and confined.
MAETERLINCK,
Before the Great Silence

11156.
I'm armed with more than complete steel,—
The justice of my quarrel.
CHRISTOPHER MARLOWE,
Lust's Dominion

11157. Justice is the having and doing what is one's own.   PLATO

11158. Asking him if Aristides had ever done him any injury, "None at all," said he, "neither know I the man; but I am tired of hearing him everywhere called the Just."
PLUTARCH, *Lives*

11159. The love of justice is, in the majority of men, the fear of suffering injustice. LA ROCHEFOUCAULD,
Maxims

11160. Every man loves justice at another man's house; nobody cares for it at his own.   *Proverb*

11161.
Horatio, thou art e'en as just a man
As e'er my conversation coped withal.
SHAKESPEARE, *Hamlet*

11162. Use every man after his
deserts, and who should 'scape whipping?   SHAKESPEARE, *Hamlet*

11163.
What stronger breastplate than a
heart untainted!
Thrice is he armed that hath his
quarrel just,
And he but naked, though locked up
in steel,
Whose conscience with injustice is
corrupted.   SHAKESPEARE,
Henry VI

11164. Be just before you're generous.   SHERIDAN,
The School for Scandal

11165. While the cardinal principles
of justice are immutable, the methods
by which justice is administered are
subject to constant fluctuations.
Opinion: U. S. Supreme Court

11166.
The sweet remembrance of the just
Shall flourish when he sleeps in dust.
TATE & BRADY, *Psalms*

11167. Justice, sir, is the great interest of man on earth.
DANIEL WEBSTER

Injustice

11168. It appears to be taken for
granted that it is a principle of
American jurisprudence that men
who are victims of a popular outcry
are not entitled to a fair trial.
JOHN PETER ALTGELD

11169. A great outrage on the spirit

of Justice breaks down all barriers of
race and nationality.
HALL CAINE, *The Eternal City*

11170. When one has been threatened
with a great injustice, one accepts a
smaller as a favour.
MRS. THOMAS CARLYLE, *Journal*

11171. National injustice is the surest
road to national downfall.
GLADSTONE

11172. The injustice to an individual
is sometimes of service to the public.
JUNIUS

11173. Mankind censure injustice,
fearing that they may be the victims
of it and not because they shrink
from committing it.   PLATO,
The Republic

11174. Much law, but little justice.
Proverb

11175. If it had not been for [the
Sacco and Vanzetti case] I might
have live out my life, talking on
street corners to scorning men. I
might have die, unmarked, unknown,
a failure. Now we are not a failure.
This is our career and our triumph.
Never in our full life can we do such
a work for tolerance, for joostice, for
man's onderstanding of man, as now
we do by an accident. Our words—
our lives—our pains—nothing! The
taking of our lives—lives of a good
shoemaker and a poor fishpeddler—
all! The last moment belongs to us
—that agony is our triumph!
BARTOLOMEO VANZETTI,
Letter to his son, April 9, 1927

See also: 698, 906, 2502, 2625, 2912,
3243, 3805, 3869, 3930, 12915, 13704,
17021, 20217, 20441, 20562.

K

KEATS, JOHN

11181. Keats did not postpone writing his poetry until he could retire from mixing drugs and find a cottage in the country. If he had there would have been no poetry to make his name immortal.
JAMES TRUSLOW ADAMS,
The Art of Living

11182.
And Keats the real
Adonis with the hymeneal
Fresh vernal buds half sunk between
His youthful curls, kissed straight and sheen
In his Rome-grave, by Venus queen.
BROWNING, *A Vision of Poets*

11183. That dirty little blackguard Keats. BYRON

11184. I have loved the principle of beauty in all things, and if I had had time I would have made myself remembered. KEATS

11185. Here lies one whose name was writ in water. KEATS, *Epitaph*

11186. I weep for Adonais—he is dead! SHELLEY, *Adonais*

11187.
The soul of Adonais, like a star,
Beacons from the abode where the Eternal are. SHELLEY, *Adonais*

KICK

Related Subject: Complaining.

11191. It is human nature to kick a fallen man. AESCHYLUS,
Agamemnon

11192.
I hate to be a kicker, I always long for peace,

But the wheel that does the squeaking is the one that gets the grease.
Anonymous, The Kicker

11193.
But Hudibras gave him a twitch
As quick as lightning in the breech,
Just in the place where honour's lodg'd,
As wise philosophers have judg'd;
Because a kick in that part more
Hurts honour than deep wounds before. SAMUEL BUTLER, *Hudibras*

11194. To kick the bucket, an unfeeling phrase for to die.
WILDON CARR, *Craven Dialect*

11195. I am going to be an absolute wreck astern. PLAUTUS, *Epidicus*

11196. I should kick, being kick'd.
SHAKESPEARE,
The Comedy of Errors

KILL, KILLING

Related Subjects: Capital Punishment, Death, Hunting, Murder, War.

10201. Thou shalt not kill.
Bible: Exodus, xx, 13

11202. Saul hath slain his thousands, and David his ten thousands.
Bible: 1 Samuel, xviii, 7

11203. Personally, I never killed anybody that I know of. But I've had a great deal of satisfaction now and then reading obituary notices and I used to delight with the rest of my hundred per cent patriotic friends, when I saw that ten or fifteen thousand Germans had been killed in a day. Everybody loves killing, some of them think it too mussy for them.
CLARENCE DARROW

11204. The flea, though he kill none, he does all the harm he can.

> JOHN DONNE, *Devotions VI*

11205. He that kills a man when he's drunk must be hang'd when he's sober.   *Proverb*

11206. He kills a man that saves not his life when he can.   *Proverb*

See also: 2340, 11524, 12200.

KINDNESS AND UNKINDNESS

Related Subjects: Beggar, Benevolence, Cruelty, Favor, Gentleness, Gifts, Help, Mercy, Philanthropy, Sympathy, Tenderness.

11211. Shall we make a new rule of life from tonight: always to try to be a little kinder than is necessary? J. M. BARRIE, *The Little White Bird*

11212.
Have you had a kindness shown?
> Pass it on.
> HENRY BURTON, *Pass It On*

11213.
A kindness loses its grace by being noised abroad,
Who desires it to be remembered should forget it.
> CORNEILLE, *Théodore*

11214. In scattering the seed, scattering your 'charity,' your kind deeds, you are giving away in one form or another, part of your personality, and taking into yourself part of another. He who has received them from you will hand them on to another. And how can you tell what part you may have in the future determination of the destinies of humanity? DOSTOYEVSKY, *The Idiot*

11215. Humane treatment may raise up one in whom the divine image has long been obscured. It is with the unfortunate, above all, that humane conduct is necessary.

> DOSTOYEVSKY,
> *The House of the Dead*

11216.
Strew gladness on the paths of men—
You will not pass this way again.
> SAM W. FOSS,
> *I Shall Not Pass This Way Again*

11217. The cheerful clatter of Sir James Barrie's cans as he went round with the milk of human kindness.

> PHILIP GUEDALLA, *Some Critics*

11218.
She doeth little kindnesses
Which most leave undone, or despise.
> LOWELL, *My Love*

11219. Many men have been capable of doing a wise thing, more a cunning thing, but very few a generous thing. POPE, *Thoughts on Various Subjects*

11220.
Not always actions show the man: we find
Who does a kindness is not therefore kind.   POPE, *Moral Essays*

11221. He merits no thanks that does a kindness for his own mind.

> *Proverb*

11222. Unkindness has no remedy at Law.   *Proverb*

11223. He that is kinder than he was wont, hath a design upon thee.

> *Proverb*

11224. A forced kindness deserves no thanks.   *Proverb*

11225. What wisdom can you find that is greater than kindness?

> ROUSSEAU, *Emile, or Education*

11226. A little more than kin, and less than kind.

> SHAKESPEARE, *Hamlet*

11227. This was the most unkindest cut of all.
SHAKESPEARE, *Julius Caesar*

11228.
Yet do I fear thy nature;
It is too full o' the milk of human kindness. SHAKESPEARE, *Macbeth*

11229.
The kindest man,
The best-condition'd and unwearied spirit
In doing courtesies.
SHAKESPEARE,
The Merchant of Venice

11230. To kill a wife with kindness.
SHAKESPEARE,
The Taming of the Shrew

11231.
Kindness in women, not their beauteous looks,
Shall win my love.
SHAKESPEARE,
The Taming of the Shrew

11232. If you stop to be kind, you must swerve often from your path.
MARY WEBB, *Precious Bane*

11233.
That best portion of a good man's life,—
His little, nameless, unremembered, acts
Of kindness and of love.
WORDSWORTH

See also: 902, 1964, 10642, 11243.

KINGS

Related Subjects: **Court, Crown, Despotism, Empire, Government, Imperialism, Nobility, Prince, Queen, Throne, Tyranny.**

11241. And all the people shouted, and said, God save the king.
Bible: 1 Samuel, x, 24

11242.
God save our gracious king!
Long live our noble king!
God save the king.
HENRY CAREY,
God Save the King

11243. And kind as kings upon their coronation day.
DRYDEN, *The Hind and the Panther*

11244. At long last I am able to say a few words of my own. I have never wanted to withold anything, but until now it has not been constitutionally possible for me to speak.
KING EDWARD VIII
Abdication Speech

11245. But you must believe me when I tell you that I have found it impossible to carry the heavy burden of responsibility and to discharge my duties as King as I would wish to do without the help and support of the woman I love.
KING EDWARD VIII,
Abdication Speech

11246.
God said, I am tired of Kings,
I suffer them no more.
EMERSON, *Boston Hymn*

11247.
On the king's gate the moss grew gray;
The king came not. They called him dead
And made his eldest son one day
Slave in his father's stead.
HELEN HUNT JACKSON, *Coronation*

11248. Certain I am, however, that a king's head is solemnly oiled at his coronation, even as a head of salad. Can it be, though, that they anoint it with a view of making its interior run well, as they anoint machinery?
HERMAN MELVILLE, *Moby Dick*

11249. The right divine of kings to govern wrong.   POPE, *The Dunciad*

11250. Good kings never make war, but for the sake of peace.   *Proverb*

11251. What can they see in the longest kingly line in Europe, save that it runs back to a successful soldier?   SCOTT, *Woodstock*

11252. Never king dropped out of the clouds. JOHN SELDEN, *Table Talk*

11253. A King is a thing men have made for their own sakes, for quietness' sake. Just as in a Family one man is appointed to buy the meat.   JOHN SELDEN, *Table Talk*

11254. A king of shreds and patches.   SHAKESPEARE, *Hamlet*

11255. A man may fish with the worm that hath eat of a king, and eat of the fish that hath fed of that worm.   SHAKESPEARE, *Hamlet*

11256.
There's such divinity doth hedge a king,
That reason can but peep to what it would.   SHAKESPEARE, *Hamlet*

11257.
There was a Brutus once that would have brook'd
The eternal devil to keep his state in Rome
As easily as a king.
     SHAKESPEARE, *Julius Caesar*

11258. Ay, every inch a king.   SHAKESPEARE, *King Lear*

11259.
Not all the water in the rough rude sea
Can wash the balm off from an anointed king.
     SHAKESPEARE, *Richard II*

11260. The king's name is a tower of strength. SHAKESPEARE, *Richard III*

11261. Kings are not born: they are made by universal hallucination.
     BERNARD SHAW,
     The Revolutionist's Handbook

11262.
Kings are like stars—they rise and set, they have
The worship of the world, but no repose.   SHELLEY, *Hellas*

11263. The Emperor reasoned with him: "Why should you desire to be a pirate?" And the other replied: "Why call me a pirate? Because you see me going about in a little galley? If I could arm myself like you, like you I would be an emperor."
     VILLON,
     Diomedes the Pirate to Alexander

See also: 184, 666, 813, 1146, 1383, 1808, 2180, 2198, 2417, 2904, 3023, 3329, 3616, 4202, 4684, 4835, 5102, 5439, 5474, 5764, 8533, 9231, 10312.

KISS AND KISSING

Related Subjects: Affection, Courtship, Lip, Love, Mouth, Parting, Passion, Tenderness.

11271. Kiss till the cow comes home.
     BEAUMONT & FLETCHER,
     Scornful Lady

11272.
Kiss me, though you make believe;
Kiss me, though I almost know
You are kissing to deceive.
     ALICE CARY, *Make Believe*

11273.
What is a kiss? Why this, as some approve:
The sure, sweet cement, glue, and lime of love.
     ROBERT HERRICK, *A Kiss*

11274.
Being used but sisterly salutes to feel,
Insipid things—like sandwiches of veal.
     THOMAS HOOD, *Bianca's Dream*

11275.

Say I'm weary, say I'm sad,
Say that health and wealth have
    missed me.
Say I'm growing old, but add,
    Jenny kissed me.
LEIGH HUNT, Rondeau

11276.

Her lips were so near
That—what else could I do?
WALTER LEARNED, An Explanation

11277.

I couldn't stand it, sir, at all,
But up and kissed her on the spot!
W. P. PALMER,
The Smack in School

11278. If you can kiss the mistress, never kiss the maid.   *Proverb*

11279. A kiss of the mouth often touches not the heart.   *Proverb*

11280.

Then come kiss me, sweet and twenty,
Youth's a stuff will not endure.
SHAKESPEARE, Twelfth Night

11281.

See the mountains kiss high Heaven
  And the waves clasp one another.
No sister-flower would be forgiven
  If it disdained its brother;
And the sunlight clasps the earth
  And the moonbeams kiss the sea:
What is all this sweet work worth
  If thou kiss not me?
SHELLEY, Love's Philosophy

11282. Lord! I wonder what fool it was that first invented kissing.
SWIFT, Polite Conversation

11283.

O love, O fire! once he drew
With one long kiss my whole soul
    through
My lips, as sunlight drinketh dew.
TENNYSON, Fatima

See also: 2524, 4471, 8383, 9480, 12200.

KNAVE AND KNAVERY

Related Subjects: Perversity, Quack, Trickery, Villain, Wickedness.

11291. He who says there is no such thing as an honest man, you may be sure is himself a knave.
BISHOP BERKELEY,
Maxims Concerning Patriotism

11292. For every inch that is not fool is rogue.
DRYDEN, Absalom & Achitophel

11293. Now will I show myself to have more of the serpent than the dove; that is, more knave than fool.
CHRISTOPHER MARLOWE,
The Jew of Malta

11294. Knavery, without luck, is the worst trade in the world.   *Proverb*

11295. The first of the nine orders of knaves is he that tells his errand before he goes it.   *Proverb*

11296. No rogue like the godly rogue.   *Proverb*

11297. If there were no knaves and fools, all the world would be alike.
Proverb

11298. He is doubly sinful who congratulates a successful knave.
Proverb

11299. As good a knave I know as a knave I know not.   *Proverb*

11300. An artful fellow is a devil in a doublet.   *Proverb*

11301. A knave discovered is a great fool.   *Proverb*

11302. A cunning knave needs no broker.   *Proverb*

11303. Three misbegotten knaves in Kendal green.
SHAKESPEARE, *Henry IV*

11304. Masters, it is proved already that you are little better than false knaves; and it will go near to be thought so shortly.
SHAKESPEARE,
Much Ado About Nothing

See also: 534, 4775, 4795, 5195, 6146.

KNOWLEDGE

Related Subjects: **Acquaintance, Appreciation, Culture, Curiosity, Education, Experience, Familiarity, Idea, Learning, Observation, Perception, School, Science, Study, University, Wisdom.**

11311. What one knows is, in youth, of little moment; they know enough who know how to learn.
HENRY ADAMS,
The Education of Henry Adams

11312. Man knows much more than he understands.
ALFRED ADLER, *Social Interest*

11313.
He who knows not, and knows not that he knows not, is a fool. Shun him.
He who knows not, and knows that he knows not, is simple. Teach him.
He who knows, and knows not that he knows, is asleep. Waken him.
He who knows, and knows that he knows, is wise. Follow him.
Arabic Apothegm

11314. Knowledge is power.
BACON

11315. He multiplieth words without knowledge. *Bible: Job, xxxv, 16*

11316. He that increaseth knowledge increaseth sorrow.
Bible: Ecclesiastes, i, 18

11317. Many shall run to and fro, and knowledge shall be increased.
Bible: Daniel, xii, 4

11318. It is better to know nothing than to know what ain't so.
JOSH BILLINGS, *Proverb*

11319.
Knowledge by suffering entereth,
And life is perfected by death.
ELIZABETH B. BROWNING,
A Vision of Poets

11320. An expert is one who knows more and more about less and less.
NICHOLAS MURRAY BUTLER

11321.
He knew what's what, and that's as high
As metaphysic wit can fly.
SAMUEL BUTLER, *Hudibras*

11322. It is far safer to know too little than too much. People will condemn the one, though they will resent being called upon to exert themselves to follow the other.
SAMUEL BUTLER,
The Way of All Flesh

11323. It is surprising, approaching the final enlightenment, how little one really has to know or feel sure about.
ADMIRAL BYRD, *Alone*

11324. I know what's what.
CERVANTES, *Don Quixote*

11325.
Knowledge is proud that he has learn'd so much;
Wisdom is humble that he knows no more.   COWPER, *The Task*

11326.
Since knowledge is but sorrow's spy,
It is not safe to know.
SIR WILLIAM D'AVENANT,
The Just Italian

11327. He [Socrates] said that there was one only good, namely, knowledge; and one only evil, namely, ignorance.

DIOGENES LAERTIUS, *Socrates*

11328. All knowledge of physical objects is inferential . . . Familiar objects which we handle are just as much inferential as a remote star inferred from an image on a photographic plate.

SIR ARTHUR EDDINGTON

11329. Revelation is always measured by capacity.

MICHAEL FAIRLESS,
The Roadmender

11330. If you have knowledge, let others light their candles at it.

MARGARET FULLER

11331. Excepting for knowledge nothing has any meaning, and to have no meaning is to be non-existent.

LORD HALDANE

11332. Nothing exists because it is known, but things are known because they exist. L. T. HOBHOUSE

11333. Knowledge and timber shouldn't be much used till they are seasoned. O. W. HOLMES,
The Autocrat of the Breakfast-Table

11334. If a little knowledge is dangerous, where is the man who has so much as to be out of danger?

THOMAS H. HUXLEY,
*On Elemental Instruction
in Physiology*

11335. Knowledge is of two kinds: we know a subject ourselves, or we know where we can find information upon it.

SAMUEL JOHNSON, *Boswell: Life*

11336. Knowledge is more than equivalent to force.

SAMUEL JOHNSON, *Rasselas*

11337. Diffused knowledge immortalizes itself.

SIR JAMES MACKINTOSH,
Vindiciae Gallicae

11338. No one knows what is good who knows not what is evil; and no one knows what is true who knows not what is false.

EDGAR LEE MASTERS,
Spoon River Anthology

11339. In many ways the saying "Know thyself" is not well said. It were more practical to say "Know other people."

MENANDER, *Thrasyleon*

11340. No one can draw more out of things, books included, than he already knows. A man has no ears for that to which experience has given him no access.

NIETZSCHE, *Ecce Homo*

11341. Knowledge which is acquired under compulsion obtains no hold on the mind. PLATO, *The Republic*

11342. He that imagines he hath knowledge enough hath none.
Proverb

11343. He that knows least commonly presumes most. *Proverb*

11344. Knowledge is a treasure, but practice is the key to it. *Proverb*

11345. One part of knowledge consists in being ignorant of such things as are not worthy to be known.
Proverb

11346. He that knows little soon repeats it. *Proverb*

11347. He who knows nothing is confident in everything. *Proverb*

11348. All I know is just what I read in the papers. WILL ROGERS

11349. It is better, of course, to know useless things than to know nothing.
SENECA

11350. When the wind is southerly, I know a hawk from a handsaw.
SHAKESPEARE, *Hamlet*

11351. Knows not which is which.
SHAKESPEARE,
A Midsummer-Night's Dream

11352. Knowledge, in truth, is the great sun in the firmament. Life and

power are scattered with all its beams.
DANIEL WEBSTER

11353. To me the charm of an encyclopedia is that it knows—and I needn't.   FRANCIS YEATS-BROWN

See also: 157, 166, 269, 400, 978, 1267, 1318, 1500, 1696, 1755, 1877, 2253, 2329, 2432, 3027, 3036, 3210, 3666, 4180, 4286, 4565, 4966, 6375, 10375, 10564, 10614, 11900, 12072, 14884, 18755, 21421, 22065, 22074.

L

LABOR

Related Subjects: Business, Effort, Employment, Industry, Sweat, Union, Wages, Work.

11361. *Labor:* one of the processes by which A acquires property for B.
AMBROSE BIERCE,
The Devil's Dictionary

11362. Even in the meanest sorts of labor, the whole soul of a man is composed into a kind of real harmony the instant he sets himself to work.
CARLYLE, *Past and Present*

11363. Honest labour bears a lovely face.
THOMAS DEKKER, *Patient Grissell*

11364. By labor Wisdom gives poignancy to pleasure, and by pleasure he restores vigor to labor.
FENELON, *Telemachus*

11365. Labor disgraces no man; unfortunately you occasionally find men disgrace labor.   ULYSSES S. GRANT

11366. Nothing is more dangerous than discontinued labour; it is habit lost. A habit easy to abandon, difficult to resume.
VICTOR HUGO, *Les Miserables*

11367. Everything in the world is purchased by labor, and our passions are the only causes of labor.
DAVID HUME

11368. The most extraordinary spectacle is the vast expenditure of labor and time wasted in obtaining mere subsistence.
RICHARD JEFFERIES,
The Story of My Heart

11369. Bodily labour earns not much.
Proverb

11370. Labor was the first price, the original purchase money that was paid for all things.
ADAM SMITH,
The Wealth of Nations

11371.

           Ah, why
Should life all labour be?
TENNYSON, *The Lotos-Eaters*

11372. Labour preserves us from three great evils—weariness, vice, and want.   VOLTAIRE, *Candide*

Labor as a social group

11373. I am not a labor leader. I don't want you to follow me or anyone else. If you are looking for a Moses to lead you out of the capitalist wilderness you will stay right where you are. I would not lead you into this promised land if I could, because if I could lead you in, someone else would lead you out.

EUGENE V. DEBS

11374. Labor is prior to, and independent of, capital. Capital is only the fruit of labor, and could never have existed if labor had not first existed.   LINCOLN

11375. Inasmuch as most good things are produced by labor, it follows that all such things ought to belong to those whose labor has produced them. But it has happened in all ages of the world that some have labored, and others, without labor, have enjoyed a large proportion of the fruits. This is wrong, and should not continue. To secure to each laborer the whole product of his labor as nearly as possible is a worthy object of any good government.   LINCOLN

11376.
Bowed by the weight of centuries he leans
Upon his hoe and gazes on the ground,
The emptiness of ages in his face,
And on his back the burden of the world.   EDWIN MARKHAM,
The Man With the Hoe

11377.
Heart of the people! Workingmen!
Marrow and nerve of human powers;
Who on your sturdy backs sustain
Through streaming time this world of ours.   R. M. MILNES, *Labor*

11378. All their devices for cheapening labour simply resulted in increasing the burden of labour.
WILLIAM MORRIS,
News from Nowhere

11379. I am a true labourer: I earn that I eat, get that I wear, owe no man hate, envy no man's happiness glad of other men's good.
SHAKESPEARE, *As You Like It*

11380. Labor in this country is independent and proud. It has not to ask the patronage of capital, but capital solicits the aid of labor.
DANIEL WEBSTER

11381. Labor and work are quite different matters. Labor is a commodity in terms of applied energy; work is an activity wherein the worker's personality effects or shapes his product
S. G. WILLIAMSON,
The American Craftsman

See also: 621, 1213, 3272, 5428 17207.

LAMB, see Sheep and Shepherd

LANGUAGE

Related Subjects: Authors, Eloquence, Grammar, Speech, Words Writing.

11391. An Aryan is anyone who speaks an Aryan language, Swede as well as American Negro or Hindu In other words Aryan is a linguistic term and has nothing to do with race
FRANZ BOAS,
Aryans and Non-Aryans

11392. The immense value of becoming acquainted with a foreign language is that we are thereby led into a new world of tradition and thought and feeling.   HAVELOCK ELLIS,
The Task of Social Hygiene

11393.
I like the Anglo-Saxon speech
With its direct revealings;

It takes a hold, and seems to reach
'Way down into your feelings.
EUGENE FIELD,
"Good-by—God Bless You!"

11394. We shall never understand one another until we reduce the language to seven words.
KAHLIL GIBRAN, *Sand and Foam*

11395. Language develops by the felicitous misapplication of words.
J. B. GREENOUGH

11396. Language is as much an art and as sure a refuge as painting or music or literature.
JANE E. HARRISON,
Reminiscences of a Student's Life

11397. Language gradually varies, and with it fade away the writings of authors who have flourished their allotted time.
WASHINGTON IRVING,
The Sketch-Book

11398. We would not be at the trouble to learn a language, if we could have all that is written in it just as well in a translation.
SAMUEL JOHNSON, *Boswell: Life*

11399. I could not sleep . . . when I got on a hunt for an idea, until I had caught it; and when I thought I had got it I was not satisfied until I had repeated it over and over again, until I had put it in language plain enough, as I thought, for any boy I knew to comprehend. This was a kind of passion with me, and it has stuck by me.   LINCOLN

11400. The English language is being impoverished by bloodless people who can't stand words that really mean things. "Belly" for example; t became "stomach" and now in Eng-

land they've begun to think that wrong and call it "tummy."
SEAN O'CASEY

11401. That's not good language that all understand not.   *Proverb*

11402. They have been at a great feast of languages, and stolen the scraps.
SHAKESPEARE, *Love's Labour's Lost*

11403. Here will be an old abusing of God's patience and the King's English.   SHAKESPEARE,
The Merry Wives of Windsor

11404. There's language in her eye, her cheek, her lip.
SHAKESPEARE,
Troilus and Cressida

11405. Perhaps of all the creations of man language is the most astonishing.
LYTTON STRACHEY,
Words and Poetry

11406. The first among languages is that which possesses the largest number of excellent works.   VOLTAIRE

See also: 2004, 2217, 2800, 3314, 8543, 8555, 9700, 13593, 14529.

LARK

Related Subject: Birds.

11411.
The music soars within the little lark,
And the lark soars.
ELIZABETH B. BROWNING,
Aurora Leigh

11412. The busy lark, the messenger of day. CHAUCER, *The Knightes Tale*

11413.
The lark now leaves his wat'ry nest
And, climbing, shakes his dewy wings.
SIR WILLIAM D'AVENANT,
Who Look for Day

11414. When the sky falleth we shall have Larks.   *Proverb*

11415. It were better to hear the lark sing, than the mouse cheep. *Proverb*

11416.
Hark, hark! the lark at heaven's gate sings,
And Phoebus 'gins arise.
          SHAKESPEARE, *Cymbeline*

11417. Merry larks are ploughmen's clocks.
SHAKESPEARE, *Love's Labour's Lost*

11418. It was the lark, the herald of the morn.
          SHAKESPEARE, *Romeo and Juliet*

11419.
It is the lark that sings so out of tune,
Straining harsh discords and unpleasing sharps.
          SHAKESPEARE, *Romeo and Juliet*

11420.
Lo! here the gentle lark, weary of rest,
From his moist cabinet mounts up on high
And wakes the morning.
          SHAKESPEARE, *Venus and Adonis*

11421.
Hail to thee, blithe Spirit!—
     Bird thou never wert!—
That from Heaven, or near it,
     Pourest thy full heart
In profuse strains of unpremeditated
     art.   SHELLEY, *To a Skylark*

LATENESS

Related Subjects: Delay, Procrastination, Time.

11431. Five minutes—Zounds! I have been five minutes too late all my lifetime.
HANNAH COWLEY, *Belle's Stratagem*

11432.
Ah! nothing is too late
Till the tired heart shall cease to palpitate.
     LONGFELLOW, *Morituri Salutamus*

11433. Better late than never.
          Proverb

11434. Never too late to mend.
          Proverb

11435. Too early seen unknown, and known too late!
          SHAKESPEARE, *Romeo and Juliet*

11436.
Late, late, so late! but we can enter still.
Too late, too late! ye cannot enter now.   TENNYSON, *Guinevere*

11437. If you're there before it's over, you're on time.   JAMES J. WALKER

11438. He was always late on principle, his principle being that punctuality is the thief of time.
          OSCAR WILDE,
     The Picture of Dorian Gray

See also: 399, 486.

LAUGHTER

Related Subjects: Delight, Fun, Humor, Joke, Joy, Merriment, Pleasure, Smile, Wit.

11441. I laugh'd till I cried.
          ARISTOPHANES, *The Frogs*

11442. It wasn't nice in those days to laugh. To get a real responsive audience, said [Mark] Twain, give him "the 850 unmixed male inmates of Elmira Reformatory."
          WHIT BURNETT,
     *The Literary Life & The
          Hell With I*

11443.
And if I laugh at any mortal thing,
'Tis that I may not weep.
         BYRON, *Don Juan*

11444. The man who cannot laugh is not only fit for treasons, strategems and spoils; but his whole life is already a treason and a stratagem.
         CARLYLE, *Sartor Resartus*

11445. No man who has once heartily and wholly laughed can be altogether irreclaimably bad.
         CARLYLE, *Sartor Resartus*

11446.
On this hapless earth
There's small sincerity of mirth,
And laughter oft is but an art
To drown the outcry of the heart.
         HARTLEY COLERIDGE,
      Address to Certain Gold-fishes

11447. And unextinguish'd laughter shakes the sky.   HOMER, *Iliad*

11448. The laugh will then be mine.
         HORACE, *Epodes*

11449.
Laugh then at any but at fools or foes;
These you but anger, and you mend not those.
Laugh at your friends, and if your friends are sore,
So much the better, you may laugh the more.   HORACE

11450. To laugh at men of sense is the privilege of fools.
         LA BRUYÈRE, *Les Caractères*

11451. Anything awful makes me laugh, I misbehaved once at a funeral.
         CHARLES LAMB

11452. Laughter is the joyous, universal evergreen of life.   LINCOLN

11453. A fit of laughter which has been indulged to excess almost always produces a violent reaction.
         PLATO, *The Republic*

11454. He is not laughed at, that laughs at himself first.   *Proverb*

11455. Laugh yourself into stitches.
         SHAKESPEARE, *Twelfth Night*

11456. Laugh and be fat.
         JOHN TAYLOR

11457.
Laugh, and the world laughs with you;
   Weep, and you weep alone;
For the sad old earth must borrow its mirth,
   But has trouble enough of its own.
         ELLA W. WILCOX, *Solitude*

11458. Laughter is not at all a bad beginning for a friendship, and it is far the best ending for one.
         OSCAR WILDE,
      The Picture of Dorian Gray

See also: 495, 1328, 1545, 1939, 2417, 7602, 12331.

LAW

Related Subjects: Authority, Constitution, Courts of Law, Crime, Equality, Government, Guilt, Judge, Judgment, Jury, Justice, Lawyers, Murder, Police, Possession, Precedent, Punishment, Trials.

11461. Even when laws have been written down, they ought not always to remain unaltered.
         ARISTOTLE, *Politics*

11462. The law has no power to command obedience except that of habit, which can only be given by time, so that a readiness to change from old to new laws enfeebles the power of the law.   ARISTOTLE, *Politics*

11463. Equity is the outcome of facts, law is the application of principles to facts.   BALZAC, *The Commission in Lunacy*

11464. It becomes not a law-maker to be a law-breaker.   BIAS

11465. The law is good, if a man use it lawfully. *Bible: I Timothy, i, 8*

11466. In spite of all the cynics say, the infallible way of inducing a sense of wrongdoing is by making laws.   WILLIAM BOLITHO

11467. Solon used to say . . . that laws were like cobwebs,—for that if any trifling or powerless thing fell into them, they held it fast; while if it were something weightier, it broke through them and was off.   DIOGENES LAERTIUS, *Solon*

11468. Man became free when he recognized that he was subject to law.   WILL DURANT, *The Life of Greece*

11469. The law, in its majestic equality, forbids the rich as well as the poor to sleep under bridges, to beg in the streets, and to steal bread.   ANATOLE FRANCE

11470. To be sure judicial doctrine is one thing, practice another. The pressure of so-called great cases is sometimes too much for judicial self-restraint, and the Supreme Court from time to time in its history has forgotten its own doctrines when they should have been most remembered.   JUSTICE FRANKFURTER, *Law and Politics*

11471. If facts are changing law cannot be static. So-called immutable principles must accommodate themselves to facts of life, for facts are stubborn and will not yield. In truth, what are now deemed immutable principles once, themselves, grew out of living conditions.   JUSTICE FRANKFURTER, *Law and Politics*

11472.
The Law is the true embodiment
Of everything that's excellent.
It has no kind of fault or flaw,
And I, my Lords, embody the Law.
          W. S. GILBERT, *Iolanthe*

11473. Laws grind the poor, and rich men rule the law.   GOLDSMITH, *The Traveller*

11474. I know no method to secure the repeal of bad or obnoxious laws so effective as their stringent execution.   ULYSSES S. GRANT

11475. The felt necessities of the time, the prevalent moral and political theories, institutions of public policy, avowed or unconscious, even the prejudices which judges share with their fellow men, have had a good deal more to do than the syllogism in determining the rules by which men should be governed.   JUSTICE HOLMES

11476.
The laws of God, the laws of man,
He may keep that will and can;
Not I: let God and man decree
Laws for themselves and not for me.
          A. E. HOUSMAN, *Last Poems*

11477. Laws and institutions must go hand in hand with the progress of the human mind.   JEFFERSON

11478. The law is the last result of human wisdom acting upon human experience for the benefit of the public.   SAMUEL JOHNSON

11479. Make laws as though all men were good: The wicked triumph, the good are crushed.
     Make laws as though all men were

evil: The wicked slip through them or circumvent them. Only the good obey them and suffer.

MAETERLINCK,
Before the Great Silence

11480. Men of most renowned virtue have sometimes by transgressing most truly kept the law.

MILTON, *Tetrachordon*

11481. Where law ends, tyranny begins. WILLIAM PITT

11482. Marius said that the law spoke too softly to be heard in such a noise of war. PLUTARCH, *Lives*

11483. In a thousand pounds of law there's not an ounce of love. *Proverb*

11484. Human laws reach not thoughts. *Proverb*

11485. He that is suffered to do more than is fitting, will do more than is lawful. *Proverb*

11486. Where there are many laws, there are many enormities. *Proverb*

11487. The worst of law is that one suit breeds twenty. *Proverb*

11488. Some go to law for the wagging of a straw. *Proverb*

11489. He that would thrive by law must see his enemy's counsel as well as his own. *Proverb*

11490. Good men want the laws only for their defence. *Proverb*

11491. Law cannot persuade where it cannot punish. *Proverb*

11492. Laws catch flies, but let hornets go free. *Proverb*

11493. Agree, for the law is costly. *Proverb*

11494. An ill plea should be well pleaded. *Proverb*

11495. Good laws lead to the making of better ones; bad ones bring about worse.

ROUSSEAU, *The Social Contract*

11496. Equity is a roguish thing. For law we have a measure, know what to trust to; Equity is according to the conscience of him that is Chancellor, and as that is larger or narrower, so is Equity. 'Tis all one as if they should make the standard for the measure we call a "foot" a Chancellor's foot; what an uncertain measure would this be! One Chancellor has a long foot, another a short foot, a third an indifferent foot. 'Tis the same thing in the Chancellor's conscience. JOHN SELDEN, *Table Talk*

11497. Ignorance of the law excuses no man; not that all men know the law, but because 'tis an excuse every man will plead, and no man can tell how to refute him.

JOHN SELDEN, *Table Talk*

11498. Old father antic the law.
SHAKESPEARE, *Henry IV*

11499. Is not this a lamentable thing, that of the skin of an innocent lamb should be made parchment? that parchment, being scribbled o'er, should undo a man?

SHAKESPEARE, *Henry VI*

11500. The law hath not been dead, though it hath slept.
SHAKESPEARE, *Measure for Measure*

11501.
In law, what plea so tainted and corrupt
But being season'd with a gracious voice,
Obscures the show of evil?

SHAKESPEARE,
The Merchant of Venice

11502. Is it so nominated in the bond?   SHAKESPEARE,
The Merchant of Venice

11503. 'Tis not in the bond.
SHAKESPEARE,
The Merchant of Venice

11504. Still you keep o' the windy side of the law.
SHAKESPEARE, *Twelfth Night*

11505. The laws are with us, and God on our side.
SOUTHEY, *Popular Disaffection*

11506. Law is the mechanism of human affairs.   SUN YAT-SEN,
Memoirs of a Chinese Revolutionary

11507.
Mastering the lawless science of our law,
That codeless myriad of precedent,
That wilderness of single instances.
TENNYSON, *Aylmer's Field*

11508. Rigorous law is often rigorous injustice.
TERENCE, *Heauton Timoroumenos*

11509.
Gentlemen:
You have undertaken to cheat me. I will not sue you, for law takes too long. I will ruin you.
Sincerely yours,
CORNELIUS VANDERBILT,
Josephson: The Robber Barons

11510. The law: It has honored us; may we honor it.   DANIEL WEBSTER

See also: 719, 776, 2501, 2766, 4836, 5224, 6789, 8686, 12121, 13810, 14123, 15706, 16106, 18595.

LAWYERS

Related Subjects: Courts of Law, Judge, Jury, Justice, Law, Trials.

11511. A lawyer is a learned gentle-man who rescues your estate from your enemies and keeps it himself.
LORD BROUGHAM

11512.
And summed it so well that it came to far more
Than the Witnesses ever had said!
LEWIS CARROLL,
The Hunting of the Snark

11513. The trouble with law and government is lawyers.
CLARENCE DARROW

11514. A barrister's profession is such an uncertain thing, especially if he won't undertake unsavoury cases.
IBSEN, *A Doll's House*

11515. Litigious terms, fat contentions, and flowing fees.
MILTON, *Tractate of Education*

11516. They have no lawyers among them, for they consider them as a sort of people whose profession it is to disguise matters.
SIR THOMAS MORE, *Utopia*

11517. Lawyers' gowns are lined with the wilfulness of their clients.
Proverb

11518. Lawyers' houses are built on the heads of fools.   *Proverb*

11519. Woe be to him whose advocate becomes his accuser.   *Proverb*

11520. A good lawyer makes an evil neighbour.   *Proverb*

11521. A wise lawyer never goes to law himself.   *Proverb*

11522. A lawyer without history or literature is a mechanic, a mere working mason; if he possesses some knowledge of these, he may venture to call himself an architect.
SCOTT, *Guy Mannering*

11523. Why may not that be the skull of a lawyer? Where be his quiddities now, his quillets, his cases, his tenures, and his tricks?

SHAKESPEARE, *Hamlet*

11524. The first thing we do, let's kill all the lawyers.

SHAKESPEARE, *Henry VI*

11525. I cannot believe that a republic could subsist at the present time if the influence of lawyers in public business did not increase in proportion to the power of the people.

DE TOCQUEVILLE,
Democracy in America

11526. The profession of law is the only aristocratic element which can be amalgamated without violence with the natural elements of democracy, and which can be advantageously and permanently combined with them. DE TOCQUEVILLE,
Democracy in America

11527. Always remember that when you go into an attorney's office door you will have to pay for it, first or last. ANTHONY TROLLOPE,
The Last Chronicle of Barset

See also: 2499, 2924.

LAZINESS, see Idleness

LEADER, LEADERSHIP

Related Subjects: Authority, Command, Dictatorship, Master, Teacher.

11531. For if the trumpet give an uncertain sound, who shall prepare himself to the battle?
Bible: I Corinthians, xiv, 8

11532. And when we think we lead we most are led.
BYRON, *The Two Foscari*

11533. Leadership does not imply the making of wise decisions or proper use of power in influencing men. Gandhi is an outstanding leader lacking in executive ability; Andrew Jackson was a good executive but a failure as a leader.
CLEETON & MASON,
Executive Ability

11534. To be a leader of men one must turn one's back on men.
HAVELOCK ELLIS,
*Introduction to J. K. Huysmans'
"Against the Grain"*

11535. The people have always some champion whom they set over them and nurse into greatness.
PLATO, *The Republic*

11536. When it is evident that a leader's day is past, the one service he can render is to step aside and leave the ground clear for the development of a successor.
THEODORE ROOSEVELT,
Letter to W. A. White

11537. A great pilot can sail even when his canvas is rent. SENECA

11538.
What though the mast be now blown over-board,
The cable broke, the holding anchor lost,
And half our sailors swallow'd in the flood?
Yet lives our pilot still.
SHAKESPEARE, *Henry VI*

11539. Thou marshall'st me the way that I was going.
SHAKESPEARE, *Macbeth*

11540.
That pilot of the state
Who sets no hand to the best policy,

But remains tongue-tied through
some terror, seems
Vilest of men.
          SOPHOCLES, *Antigone*

11541.
          The fire of God
Fills him. I never saw his like; there
lives
No greater leader.
          TENNYSON, *Lancelot and Elaine*

See also: 2151.

LEARNING

**Related Subjects: Culture, Educa-
tion, Knowledge, Mathematics,
School, Science, Study, Teacher,
University, Wisdom.**

11551. Learning is an ornament in
prosperity, a refuge in adversity, and
a provision in old age.   ARISTOTLE

11552. Much learning doth make thee
mad.   *Bible: Acts, xxvi, 24*

11553. Learning will be cast into the
mire and trodden down under the
hoofs of a swinish multitude.
          BURKE,
     *Reflections on the Revolution in
                         France*

11554. Out of too much learning become mad.   ROBERT BURTON,
          Anatomy of Melancholy

11555. He is sufficiently learned, that
knows how to do well, and has power
enough to refrain from evil.
                    CICERO

11556. Great contest follows, and
much learned dust.
          COWPER, *The Task*

11557. Learning hath gained most by
those books by which the printers
have lost.   THOMAS FULLER,
          Holy & Profane State

11558. To unlearn the taken-for-
granted is harder than to learn the
hitherto unsuspected.
          IRVING FISHER

11559. Take care not to step on the
foot of a learned idiot. His bite is
incurable.   PAUL GAUGUIN,
          Intimate Journals

11560. It is better to be able neither
to read nor write than to be able to
do nothing else.   HAZLITT,
     On the Ignorance of the Learned

11561. It is no shame for a man to
learn that which he knoweth not,
whatever be his age.   ISOCRATES

11562. Let ignorance talk as it will,
learning has its value.
          LA FONTAINE, *Fables*

11563. Solon was under a delusion
when he said that a man when he
grows old may learn many things—
for he can no more learn much than
he can run much; youth is the time
for any extraordinary toil.
          PLATO, *The Republic*

11564.
Love seldom haunts the breast where
     learning lies,
And Venus sets ere Mercury can rise.
     POPE, *Paraphrases from Chaucer*

11565.
A little learning is a dangerous thing;
Drink deep, or taste not the Pierian
     spring;
There shallow draughts intoxicate the
     brain,
And drinking largely sobers us again.
          POPE, *Essay on Criticism*

11566. It is less painful to learn in
youth than to be ignorant in age.
                    Proverb

11567. 'Tis harder to unlearn than
learn.   *Proverb*

11568. There is much more learning than knowledge in the world.
Proverb

11569. Learning makes a man fit company for himself. *Proverb*

11570. Learning makes a good man better, and an ill man worse. *Proverb*

11571. Folly and learning often dwell together. *Proverb*

11572. A wise man gets learning from those who have none themselves.
Proverb

11573. It is better to learn late than never. PUBLILIUS SYRUS, *Sententiae*

11574. No man is the wiser for his learning. JOHN SELDEN, *Table Talk*

11575. Few men make themselves masters of the things they write or speak. JOHN SELDEN, *Table Talk*

11576. All the learned and authentic fellows. SHAKESPEARE,
All's Well that Ends Well

11577.
Wearing all that weight
Of learning lightly like a flower.
TENNYSON, *In Memoriam*

See also: 1263, 1319, 2336, 2428, 3638, 3640, 5493, 6317, 7450, 8317, 10328, 16493, 17838.

LEG

Related Subjects: Body, Foot, Walking.

11581.
The centipede was happy quite
Until a toad in fun
Said, "Prey, which leg goes after which?"
That worked her mind to such a pitch,
She lay distracted in a ditch,
Considering how to run.
MRS. E. CRASTER

11582. Legs are staple articles and will never go out of fashion while the world lasts. JARRETT & PALMER

11583. A wooden leg is better than no leg. *Proverb*

11584. He hasn't a leg to stand on.
Proverb

See also: 1933, 6287, 20895.

LEISURE

Related Subjects: Comfort, Idleness, Luxury, Rest.

11591.
When a man's busy, why, leisure
Strikes him as wonderful pleasure:
'Faith, and at leisure once is he?
Straightway he wants to be busy.
BROWNING, *The Glove*

11592. He is never less at leisure than when at leisure. CICERO, *De Officiis*

11593. He hath no leisure who useth it not. *Proverb*

11594.
No blessed leisure for love or hope,
But only time for grief.
THOMAS HOOD,
The Song of the Shirt

11595. I hope succeeding generations will be able to be idle. I hope that nine-tenths of their time will be leisure time; that they may enjoy their days, and the earth, and the beauty of this beautiful world; that they may rest by the sea and dream; that they may dance and sing, and eat and drink.
RICHARD JEFFERIES,
The Story of My Heart

11596. Be always at leisure to do good.
MARCUS AURELIUS, *Meditations*

11597.
And add to these retired Leisure,
That in trim gardens takes his
    pleasure.   Milton, *Il Penseroso*

11598. Dionysius the Elder, being
asked whether he was at leisure, he
replied, "God forbid that it should
ever befall me!" Plutarch, *Lives*

11599. A life of leisure and a life of
laziness are two things.   *Proverb*

See also: 3469, 4177, 13097, 21452.

LENDING, see Borrowing

LENIENCY

**Related Subjects: Magnanimity,
Mercy, Tolerance.**

11601. Man may dismiss compassion
from his heart, but God will never.
                      Cowper

11602. It is only necessary to grow
old to become more indulgent. I see
no fault committed that I have not
committed myself.   Goethe

11603. And what makes robbers bold
but too much lenity?
       Shakespeare, *Henry VI*

11604. Lenity will operate with
greater force in some instances than
rigor. It is, therefore, my first wish
to have all my conduct distinguished
by it.   Washington

LETTERS

**Related Subjects: Literature,
Writing.**

11611. [Napoleon] directed Bour-
rienne to leave all his letters unopened
for three weeks, and then observed
with satisfaction how large a part of

the correspondence had thus disposed
of itself, and no longer required an
answer.   Emerson,
         Representative Men

11612. It has been said of ladies
when they write letters, that they
put their minds in their postscripts—
let out the real objects of their writing, as if it were a second thought,
or a thing comparatively indifferent.
      Leigh Hunt, *Anacreon*

11613. A short letter to a distant
friend is, in my opinion, an insult like
that of a slight bow or cursory salutation.   Samuel Johnson,
         Boswell: Life

11614. Blessed be letters—they are
the monitors, they are also the com-
forters, and they are the only true
heart-talkers. D. G. Mitchell,
      Reveries of a Bachelor

11615.
Lives of great men all remind us
As their pages o'er we turn,
That we're apt to leave behind us
Letters that we ought to burn.
Quoted by Dr. A. S. W. Rosenbach

11616. Correspondences are like
small-clothes before the invention of
suspenders; it is impossible to keep
them up.   Sydney Smith

11617. I beg of you to burn it when
you've read it.
     Sir Richard Steele,
        The Spectator

11618. The best way is to make your
letters safe. I never wrote a letter
in all my life that would commit me,
and demmy, sir, I have had some
experience of women.
     Thackeray, *Pendennis*

See also: 18752.

LIBERTY

Related Subjects: Democracy, Dependence, Equality, Freedom, Rights.

11621. The tree of liberty only grows when watered by the blood of tyrants.
BERTRAND BARÈRE

11622. Experience should teach us to be most on our guard to protect liberty when the Government's purposes are beneficial. Men born to freedom are naturally alert to repel invasion of their liberty by evil minded rulers. The greatest dangers to liberty lurk in insidious encroachment by men of zeal, well-meaning, but without understanding.
JUSTICE BRANDEIS

11623. "Liberty!" he snorted. "That is but a catch-word of those blasted agitators, mostly foreigners, to appeal to so-called workers. Workers! A worker is a blighter who goes on strike. Liberty means liberty to go on strike. Let those damned shirkers come over here and try to go on strike. We'd soon teach them. No eight hours' day in the army.
ROBERT BRIFFAULT,
Europa In Limbo

11624.
But little do or can the best of us:
That little is achieved through Liberty. BROWNING,
Why I Am a Liberal

11625. The people never give up their liberties but under some delusion.
BURKE

11626.
Liberty's in every blow!
Let us do, or die. BURNS,
Scots Wha Hae Wi, Wallace Bled

11627. Looking at the Statue of Liberty which stands there, she says bitterly: "O Liberty, what things are done in thy name!" CARLYLE,
The French Revolution

11628. Liberty is impossible without order, order without law, and the carrying out of law depends on force.
COHEN-PORTHEIM

11629. Magna Charta is such a fellow that he will have no sovereign.
SIR EDWARD COKE,
Debate in Commons

11630. It is the common fate of the indolent to see their rights become a prey to the active. The condition upon which God hath given liberty to man is eternal vigilance; which condition if he break, servitude is at once the consequence of his crime and the punishment of his guilt.
J. P. CURRAN

11631. Spinoza was not primarily interested in politics, but he insisted with great force on civil liberty as a condition of spiritual freedom. And civil liberty, we know now, is only insured by economic equality and freedom. IRWIN EDMAN, *I Believe*

11632. They that can give up essential liberty to obtain a little temporary safety deserve neither liberty nor safety. FRANKLIN,
Historical Review of Pennsylvania

11633. God grant that not only the love of liberty but a thorough knowledge of the rights of man may pervade all the nations of the earth, so that a philosopher may set his foot anywhere on its surface and say: "This is my country." FRANKLIN

11634. When liberty is mentioned, we must always be careful to observe whether it is not really the assertion of private interests which is thereby designated. HEGEL

11635. Is life so dear, or peace so sweet, as to be purchased at the price of chains and slavery? Forbid it, Almighty God! I know not what course others may take, but as for me, give me liberty, or give me death!
PATRICK HENRY

11636. The continuous adjustment of our society to new forces introduced by advancing science, the unending battle against economic domination, all require constant reform and amendment of our laws if we are to preserve Liberty.
HERBERT HOOVER,
The Challenge of Liberty

11637. Liberty conceives that the mind and spirit of men can be free only if the individual is free to choose his own calling, to develop his talents, to win and to keep a home sacred from intrusion, to rear children in ordered security. It holds he must be free to earn, to spend, to save, to accumulate property that may give protection in old age and to loved ones. HERBERT HOOVER,
The Challenge of Liberty

11638.
Give me again my hollow tree,
A crust of bread, and liberty.
HORACE

11639. Our institutions were not devised to bring about uniformity of opinion; if they had been, we might well abandon hope. It is important to remember, as has well been said, that "the essential characteristic of true liberty is, that under its shelter many different types of life and character and opinion and belief can develop unmolested and unobstructed."
CHARLES EVANS HUGHES

11640. The God who gave us life, gave us liberty at the same time.
JEFFERSON

11641. What country before ever existed a century and a half without a rebellion? The tree of liberty must be refreshed from time to time with the blood of patriots and tyrants. It is its natural manure. JEFFERSON

11642. It is true that liberty is precious—so precious that it must be rationed. LENIN

11643. The world has never had a good definition of the word liberty, and the American people, just now, are much in want of one. LINCOLN

11644. Liberty is not merely a privilege to be conferred; it is a habit to be acquired. LLOYD GEORGE

11645.
Did it ever occur to you that personal liberty
Is liberty of the mind,
Rather than of the belly?
EDGAR LEE MASTERS,
Spoon River Anthology

11646. We have left our liberties mainly to judges and lawyers.
MAURY MAVERICK, *Blood & Ink*

11647. Thus as a matter of common sense, all the people, no matter what their viewpoint and no matter what their economic status, should insist upon the preservation of civil liberties. This is practical. It is sensible. It is, as a matter of fact, fair play, a means of protecting orderly government. It is one of the foundation stones of the American system—of our living constitution. MAURY MAVERICK,
Blood & Ink

11648. The mountain nymph, sweet Liberty. MILTON, *L'Allegro*

11649.
License they mean when they cry Liberty;

For who loves that must first be wise
and good.   MILTON,
*On the Detraction which Followed
Upon My Writing Certain Treatises*

11650. We have buried the putrid
corpse of liberty.   MUSSOLINI

11651. Lean liberty is better than fat
slavery.   *Proverb*

11652. O Liberty! Liberty! how
many crimes are committed in thy
name!   MME. ROLAND

11653. I personally am very averse
to abridging the civil liberties of any
group in this country, primarily because I am afraid that, once started,
anything of this kind makes it possible to abridge the civil liberties of
every group and every individual.
          ELEANOR ROOSEVELT

11654. We would rather die on our
feet than live on our knees.
          FRANKLIN D. ROOSEVELT

11655.
I must have liberty
Withal, as large a charter as the wind,
To blow on whom I please.
          SHAKESPEARE, *As You Like It*

11656. What is liberty? Liberty is
an elusive thing. It isn't a thing that
you can lock up in the safe, turn the
key and go away, and expect to find
there when you come back. Eternal
vigilance alone is the price that you
pay for that liberty and there devolves
upon every citizen who believes in
that Declaration and in the Constitution . . . to conduct himself with that
regard for his neighbor that his neighbor as well as himself may have the
full enjoyment of the blessings of
liberty that grow from a free republic.
          ALFRED E. SMITH,
          Progressive Democracy

11657.
What more felicitie can fall to crea-
ture,
Than to enjoy delight with libertie.
          EDMUND SPENSER, *Muiopotmos*

11658. So long as a man rides his
hobby-horse peaceably and quietly
along the King's highway, and neither
compels you or me to get up behind
him,—pray, Sir, what have either you
or I to do with it?   STERNE,
          Tristram Shandy

11659. Liberalism, therefore, should
have held constantly before its eyes
the twin ideas of freedom and responsibility; self-expression and self-
control, extreme tolerance of others,
with extreme demands upon oneself.
          DOROTHY THOMPSON,
          Political Guide

11660. I have shown, and shall continue to show, a lively and rational
passion for liberty, and this for two
reasons. In the first place it is my
profound conviction, and in the second I do not wish to be identified
with those lovers of order who are
ready to sell free will and our laws
cheap for the sake of sleeping safely
in their beds. There are enough of
them already, and I dare to prophesy
that they will never achieve anything
great or durable.
          DE TOCQUEVILLE,
          Democracy in America

11661. Liberty of thought is the life
of the soul.   VOLTAIRE

11662. For the combating of "racism"
before it sinks its poison fangs deep
in our body politic, the scientist has
both a special motive and a special
responsibility. His motive comes from
the fact that when personal liberty
disappears scientific liberty also disappears.   HENRY A. WALLACE,
          The Time to Act

11663. God grants liberty only to those who love it, and are always ready to guard and defend it.

DANIEL WEBSTER

11664. Liberty and Union, now and forever, one and inseparable.

DANIEL WEBSTER

11665. Liberty exists in proportion to wholesome restraint.

DANIEL WEBSTER

11666. The modern view, with its deepening insistence upon individuality and upon the significance of its uniqueness, steadily intensifies the value of freedom, until at last we begin to see liberty as the very substance of life, that indeed it is life, and that only the dead things, the choiceless things, live in absolute obedience to law. H. G. WELLS,

A Modern Utopia

11667. Wherever a free man is in chains we are threatened also. Whoever is fighting for liberty is defending America.

WILLIAM A. WHITE,
Defense for America

11668. Liberty is the one thing you can't have unless you give it to others.

WILLIAM A. WHITE

11669. When you define liberty you limit it, and when you limit it you destroy it.   BRAND WHITLOCK

11670.
When liberty goes out of a place, it
    is not the first to go, nor the second
    or third to go,
It waits for all the rest to go—it is
    the last.   WALT WHITMAN

11671. Liberty is to be subserved whatever occurs.

WALT WHITMAN,
To a Foil'd European Revolutionary

11672. The English love liberty, Heine has said, as a legitimate wife—not too caressingly but with a sense of ownership and protectiveness: the French, he said, love her as a mistress —always to be wooed in order to be retained. The Americans, my father added, treat her like a familiar drudge —so sure of her that they may abuse and neglect her. She will grow old and feeble in time and will perhaps die altogether. HANS ZINSSER,

As I Remember Him

See also: 653, 665, 672, 680, 698, 1385, 1816, 2762, 2767, 3367, 4046, 4256, 5148, 5735, 6521, 6975, 14300, 15789, 15890.

LIBRARY

Related Subjects: Books, Literature, Reading, Research, Study.

11681. The richest minds need not large libraries.

BRONSON ALCOTT, *Table Talk*

11682. Libraries, which are as the shrines where all the relics of the ancient saints, full of true virtue, and that without delusion or imposture, are preserved and reposed.

BACON, *Advancement of Learning*

11683. A library is but the soul's burial-ground. It is the land of shadows.   H. W. BEECHER,

Star Papers

11684. Good as it is to inherit a library, it is better to collect one.

AUGUSTINE BIRRELL, *Obiter Dicta*

11685. Libraries are not made; they grow.   AUGUSTINE BIRRELL,

Obiter Dicta

11686. How much are we bound to those munificent Ptolemies, bountiful Maecenates, heroical patrons, divine

spirits, that have provided for us so many well-furnished libraries.
> ROBERT BURTON,
> *Anatomy of Melancholy*

11687. A great library contains the diary of the human race.
> REV. GEORGE DAWSON

11688. Meek young men grow up in libraries.   EMERSON,
> *Nature, Addresses and Lectures*

11689. Consider what you have in the smallest chosen library. A company of the wisest and wittiest men that could be picked out of all civil countries, in a thousand years, have set in best order the results of their learning and wisdom.   EMERSON,
> *Society and Solitude*

11690. It is a vanity to persuade the world one hath much learning, by getting a great library.
> THOMAS FULLER,
> *Holy and Profane State*

11691. He that revels in a well-chosen library, has innumerable dishes, and all of admirable flavour.
> WILLIAM GODWIN, *The Enquirer*

11692. Every library should try to be complete on something, if it were only the history of pinheads.
> O. W. HOLMES,
> *The Poet at the Breakfast-Table*

11693. I have often thought that nothing would do more extensive good at small expense than the establishment of a small circulating library in every county, to consist of a few well-chosen books, to be lent to the people of the county, under such regulations as would secure their safe return in due time.   JEFFERSON

11694. A man will turn over half a library to make one book.
> SAMUEL JOHNSON, *Boswell: Life*

11695. Money invested in a library gives much better returns than mining stock. SIR WILLIAM OSLER,
> *Life of Sir William Osler*

11696. Lucullus' furnishing a library, however deserves praise and record, for he collected very many choice manuscripts; and the use they were put to was even more magnificent than the purchase, the library being always open, and the walks and reading-rooms about it free to all Greeks.
> PLUTARCH, *Lives*

11697. My library was dukedom large enough.   SHAKESPEARE,
> *The Tempest*

11698.
Come, and take choice of all my library,
And so beguile thy sorrow.
> SHAKESPEARE, *Titus Andronicus*

11699.
Shut not your doors to me proud libraries,
For that which was lacking on all your well-fill'd shelves, yet needed most, I bring.
> WALT WHITMAN,
> *Shut Not Your Doors*

11700.
Unlearned men of books assume the care,
As eunuchs are the guardians of the fair.   EDWARD YOUNG,
> *Love of Fame*

See also: 1411.

LIES AND LYING

Related Subjects: Cheating, Deceit, Error, Hypocrisy, Oath, Slander, Trickery, Truth.

11701. A liar will not be believed, even when he speaks the truth.
> AESOP, *The Shepherd's Boy*

11702. Thou shalt not bear false witness against thy neighbour.
Bible: Exodus, xx, 16

11703. I said in my haste, All men are liars.   *Bible: Psalms, cxvi, 11*

11704. The best liar is he who makes the smallest amount of lying go the longest way—who husbands it too carefully to waste it where it can be dispensed with.
SAMUEL BUTLER,
The Way of All Flesh

11705. Thou liar of the first magnitude.   CONGREVE, *Love for Love*

11706. I think a lie with a purpose is wan iv th' worst kind an' th' mos' profitable.   F. P. DUNNE,
On Lying

11707. The lie was raised to the dignity of a political instrument.
EINSTEIN, *I Believe*

11708. Sin has many tools, but a lie is the handle which fits them all.
O. W. HOLMES,
The Autocrat at the Breakfast-Table

11709. When I meet with a falsehood, I care not who the great persons who proclaim it may be, I do not try to like it or believe it or mimic the fashionable prattle of the world about it.   W. H. HUDSON,
The Purple Land

11710. A lie, turned topsy-turvy, can be prinked and tinselled out, decked in plumage new and fine, till none knows its lean old carcass.
IBSEN, *Peer Gynt*

11711. If I accustom a servant to tell a lie for *me,* have I not reason to apprehend that he will tell many lies for *himself?*
SAMUEL JOHNSON, *Boswell: Life*

11712. Whoever has even once become notorious by base fraud, even if he speaks the truth, gains no belief.   PHAEDRUS, *Fables*

11713. Jesting lies bring serious sorrows.   *Proverb*

11714. A liar is not believed when he speaks the truth.   *Proverb*

11715. Show me a liar, and I will show thee a thief.   *Proverb*

11716. False folk should have many witnesses.   *Proverb*

11717. Almost and very nigh saves many a lie.   *Proverb*

11718. A lie begets a lie till they come to generations.   *Proverb*

11719. A very honest woman, but something given to lie.
SHAKESPEARE,
Antony and Cleopatra

11720.
I had rather seal my lips, than, to my peril,
Speak that which is not.
SHAKESPEARE,
Antony and Cleopatra

11721. Mark now, how a plain tale shall put you down.
SHAKESPEARE, *Henry IV*

11722. Lord, Lord, how this world is given to lying! I grant you I was down and out of breath; and so was he. But we rose both at an instant, and fought a long hour by Shrewsbury clock.   SHAKESPEARE, *Henry IV*

11723.
A goodly apple rotten at the heart:
O, what a goodly outside falsehood
    hath!   SHAKESPEARE,
The Merchant of Venice

11724.
> By telling of it,
> Make such a sinner of his memory,
> To credit his own lie.
>> SHAKESPEARE, *The Tempest*

11725. Let me have no lying; it becomes none but tradesmen.
> SHAKESPEARE, *The Winter's Tale*

11726. Liars ought to have good memories. ALGERNON SIDNEY,
> *Discourses on Government*

11727. False words are not only evil in themselves, but they infect the soul with evil.   SOCRATES,
> *Dialogues of Plato*

11728. The cruellest lies are often told in silence.   STEVENSON,
> *Virginibus Puerisque*

11729.
> That a lie which is half a truth is ever the blackest of lies,
> That a lie which is all a lie may be met and fought with outright,
> But a lie which is part a truth is a harder matter to fight.
>> TENNYSON, *The Grandmother*

11730. An experienced, industrious, ambitious, and often quite picturesque liar.   MARK TWAIN,
> *My Military Campaign*

11731. It is often the case that the man who can't tell a lie thinks he is the best judge of one.
> MARK TWAIN,
> *Pudd'nhead Wilson's Calendar*

See also: 102, 411, 602, 1575, 2250, 2311, 4233, 4375, 4520, 5162, 9855, 9861, 9945, 10502, 15494, 18912, 20026, 20888.

LIFE

Related Subjects: Birth, Evolution, Experience, Health, Mortality, Realism, Soul, Strength.

11741. Life is my college. May I graduate well, and earn some honors.
> LOUISA ALCOTT,
> *Life, Letters and Journals*

11742. All men have one entrance into life, and the like going out.
> *Apocrypha: Wisdom of Solomon*

11743.
> He most lives
> Who thinks most—feels the noblest
> —acts the best.
>> PHILIP J. BAILEY, *Festus*

11744. The life of every man is a diary in which he means to write one story, and writes another; and his humblest hour is when he compares the volume as it is with what he vowed to make it. J. M. BARRIE,
> *The Little Minister*

11745. Life, Crichton is like a cup of tea; the more heavily we drink the sooner we reach the dregs.
> J. M. BARRIE,
> *The Admirable Crichton*

11746. Our days on the earth are as a shadow.
> *Bible: 1 Chronicles, xxix, 15*

11747. All that a man hath, will he give for his life.   *Bible: Job, ii, 4*

11748. There's night and day, brother, both sweet things; sun, moon, and stars, brother, all sweet things; there's likewise a wind on the heath. Life is very sweet, brother; who would wish to die?
> GEORGE BORROW, *Lavengro*

11749. Life comes before literature, as the material always comes before the work. The hills are full of marble before the world blooms with statues.
PHILLIPS BROOKS,
Literature and Life

11750. Life is a copycat and can be bullied into following the master artist who bids it come to heel.
HEYWOOD BROUN, *It Seems to Me*

11751. A little sunburnt by the glare of life.
ELIZABETH B. BROWNING,
Aurora Leigh

11752.
How good is man's life, the mere living! how fit to employ
All the heart and the soul and the senses forever in joy!
BROWNING, *Saul*

11753.
So live, that when thy summons comes to join
The innumerable caravan which moves
To that mysterious realm, where each shall take
His chamber in the silent halls of death,
Thou go not, like the quarry-slave at night,
Scourged to his dungeon, but, sustained and soothed
By an unfaltering trust, approach thy grave,
Like one that wraps the drapery of his couch
About him, and lies down to pleasant dreams.   BRYANT, *Thanatopsis*

11754.
O Life! thou art a galling load,
Along a rough, a weary road,
    To wretches such as I!
BURNS, *Despondency*

11755. Life is a struggle, but not a warfare.   JOHN BURROUGHS,
The Summit of the Years

11756.
How short this Life, how long withal;
    how false its weal, how true its woes,
This fever-fit with paroxysms to mark its opening and its close.
RICHARD BURTON,
The Kasidah of Haji Abdu

11757. Is life worth living? This is a question for an embryo, not for a man. SAMUEL BUTLER, *Note-Books*

11758. Life is the art of drawing sufficient conclusions from insufficient premises.   SAMUEL BUTLER,
Note-Books

11759.
'Tis very certain the desire of life
Prolongs it.   BYRON, *Don Juan*

11760. Life, be it happy or unhappy, fortunate or unfortunate, is the only good man possesses, and he who does not love life is unworthy of life.
CASANOVA

11761. The short period of life is long enough for living well and honourably.   CICERO, *De Senectute*

11762. If life had a second edition, how I would correct the proofs.
JOHN CLARE

11763. In life we are strangled between two doors, of which the one is labelled *Too Soon* and the other *Too Late*.   BARBEY D'AUREVILLY

11764. Youth is a blunder; manhood a struggle; old age a regret.
DISRAELI, *Coningsby*

11765. All the art of living lies in a fine mingling of letting go and holding in.   HAVELOCK ELLIS,
The Art of Life

11766.

Life is too short to waste
In critic peep or cynic bark,
Quarrel or reprimand;
'Twill soon be dark;
Up! mind thine own aim, and
God speed the mark!   EMERSON

11767.

Life's a pudding full of plums;
Care's a canker that benumbs,
Wherefore waste our elocution
On impossible solution?
Life's a pleasant institution,
Let us take it as it comes!
          W. S. GILBERT, *The Gondoliers*

11768.

Life's perhaps the only riddle
That we shrink from giving up.
          W. S. GILBERT, *The Gondoliers*

11769. Life is made up of marble
and mud.   HAWTHORNE,
          The House of the Seven Gables

11770. Life is (I think) a blunder
and a shame.   W. E. HENLEY,
                    In Hospital

11771. Life is an end in itself and
the only question whether it is worth
living is whether you have had enough
of it.   JUSTICE HOLMES

11772. There are two ways of living:
a man may be casual and simply exist,
or constructive and deliberately try
to do something with his life. The
constructive idea implies construc-
tiveness not only about one's own life,
but about that of society, and the
future possibilities of humanity.
          JULIAN HUXLEY,
          Essays of a Biologist

11773. Men are educated to be self-
reliant and enterprising in the details of life, but dependent, unre-

flective, *laissez-faire* about life itself.
The idea that the basis of living could
be really and radically altered is outside most people's orbit; and if it is
forced upon their notice, they often
as not find it in some way immoral.
          JULIAN HUXLEY,
          Essays of a Biologist

11774. We have the fact that ninety-
nine people out of a hundred are concerned with getting a living rather
than with living, and that if for any
reason they are liberated from this
necessity, they generally have not the
remotest idea how to employ their
time with either pleasure or profit to
themselves or to others.
          JULIAN HUXLEY,
          Essays of a Biologist

11775. The only faith that is both
concrete and comprehensive is in life,
its abundance and its progress. My
final belief is in life.
          JULIAN HUXLEY, *I Believe*

11776. I believe that life can be worth
living. I believe this in spite of pain,
squalor, cruelty, unhappiness, and
death. I do not believe that it is
necessarily worth living, but only that
for most people it can be.
          JULIAN HUXLEY, *I Believe*

11777. Be not afraid of life, Believe
that life *is* worth living, and your belief will help create the fact.
          WILLIAM JAMES,
          The Will to Believe

11778. Life is very short, and very
uncertain; let us spend it as well as
we can.   SAMUEL JOHNSON,
                    Boswell: Life

11779. Life is a progress from want
to want, not from enjoyment to enjoyment.   SAMUEL JOHNSON,
                    Boswell: Life

11780. Life is not long, and too much of it must not pass in idle deliberation how it shall be spent.

SAMUEL JOHNSON, *Boswell: Life*

11781. It matters not how a man dies, but how he lives.

SAMUEL JOHNSON, *Boswell: Life*

11782. Life is the rose's hope while yet unblown. KEATS, *Sleep and Poetry*

11783.

Life is but a day; .
A fragile dewdrop on its perilous way
From a tree's summit.

KEATS, *Sleep and Poetry*

11784. Life to be enjoyed has to be decorated. Bare subsistence is not enough. SIR ARTHUR KEITH, *I Believe*

11785. All efforts to find a rational justification of life, to declare it worth the living for this reason or that, are, in themselves, a confession of weakness, since life at its strongest never feels the need of any such justification and since the most optimistic philosopher is less optimistic than that man or animal who, his belief that life is good being too immediate to require the interposition of thought, is no philosopher at all.

J. W. KRUTCH,
The Modern Temper

11786. What is this chemical ferment called life all about? Small wonder that small men down the ages have conjured gods in answer. A little god is a snug little possession and explains it all. But how about you and me who have no God? There's damned little satisfaction in being a materialistic monist. JACK LONDON

11787. For a long life be moderate in all things, but don't miss anything.

DR. ADOLF LORENZ

11788. Though thou be destined to live three thousand years and as many myriads besides, yet remember that no man loseth other life than that which he liveth, nor liveth other than that which he loseth.

MARCUS AURELIUS, *Meditations*

11789. Deem not life a thing of consequence. For look at the yawning void of the future, and at that other limitless space, the past.

MARCUS AURELIUS, *Meditations*

11790. All life is an attempt to get beyond the barriers of self: some attempt it by drunkenness or devotion, some by love, drugs, danger or the arts: others by one of the churches or by service: many attempt it, blindly, many more under guidance which may be blind. They attempt because they hope that beyond their own personal nature they may touch the nature of the world.

JOHN MASEFIELD

11791. The basic fact about human existence is not that it is a tragedy, but that it is a bore. H. L. MENCKEN

11792. It seems that I must live by that which causes others to die.

MICHELANGELO

11793. The breath of life.

MILTON, *Paradise Lost*

11794.

Nor love thy life, nor hate; but what thou liv'st
Live well; how long or short permit to Heaven. MILTON,
Paradise Lost

11795.

This narrow isthmus 'twixt two boundless seas,
The past, the future,—two eternities

THOMAS MOORE, *Lalla Rookh*

11796. The great business of life is to be, to do, to do without, and to depart.   JOHN MORLEY,
Address on Aphorisms

11797. Fear not that thy life shall come to an end, but rather fear that it shall never have a beginning.
    CARDINAL NEWMAN

11798. Life always gets harder toward the summit—the cold increases, responsibility increases.
    NIETZSCHE, *The Antichrist*

11799. Life is just one damned thing after another.   F. W. O'MALLEY

11800. The Leaves of Life keep falling one by one.
    OMAR KHAYYAM, *Rubaiyat*

11801. Strange interlude! Yes, our lives are merely strange dark interludes in the electrical display of God the Father!   EUGENE O'NEILL,
Strange Interlude

11802. What is the prime of life? May it not be defined as a period of about twenty years in a woman's life, and thirty in a man's?   PLATO,
The Republic

11803.
The fever called "Living"
  Is conquered at last.   POE,
For Annie

11804. Live, and let live.   *Proverb*

11805. Those that God loves do not live long.   *Proverb*

11806. Life is half spent before we know what it is.   *Proverb*

11807. It matters not how long you live, but how well.
    PUBLILIUS SYRUS, *Sententiae*

11808.
In the cup of life, 'tis true,
Dwells a draught of bitter dew . . .
Yet no other cup I know
Where such radiant waters glow.
    AGNES ROBINSON, *Epilogue*

11809. Only those are fit to live who do not fear to die; and none are fit to die who have shrunk from the joy of life and the duty of life.
    THEODORE ROOSEVELT,
The Great Adventure

11810. There is no Wealth but Life.
    RUSKIN, *Unto This Last*

11811.
Sound, sound the clarion, fill the fife!
  To all the sensual world proclaim,
One crowded hour of glorious life
  Is worth an age without a name.
    SCOTT, *Old Mortality*

11812. The web of our life is of a mingled yarn, good and ill together.
    SHAKESPEARE,
All's Well that Ends Well

11813. I do not set my life at a pin's fee.   SHAKESPEARE, *Hamlet*

11814.
Life is as tedious as a twice-told tale,
Vexing the dull ear of a drowsy man.
    SHAKESPEARE, *King John*

11815.
    Out, out brief candle!
Life's but a walking shadow, a poor player
That struts and frets his hour upon the stage
And then is heard no more: it is a tale
Told by an idiot, full of sound and fury,
Signifying nothing.
    SHAKESPEARE, *Macbeth*

11816. I bear a charmed life.
    SHAKESPEARE, *Macbeth*

11817.
You take my house, when you do take the prop

That doth sustain my house; you take my life,
When you do take the means whereby I live.   SHAKESPEARE,
The Merchant of Venice

11818. Life is a shuttle.
      SHAKESPEARE,
The Merry Wives of Windsor

11819.
Gonzalo. Here is everything advantageous to life.
Antonio. True; save means to live.
      SHAKESPEARE, *The Tempest*

11820. Those who do not know how to live must make a merit of dying.
      BERNARD SHAW,
Heartbreak House: Preface

11821. Life is a disease; and the only difference between one man and another is the stage of the disease at which he lives.
      BERNARD SHAW,
Back to Methuselah

11822.
Life like a dome of many-coloured glass,
Stains the white radiance of eternity.
      SHELLEY, *Adonais*

11823. I fall upon the thorns of life!
I bleed!   SHELLEY,
Ode to the West Wind

11824. May you live all the days of your life.   SWIFT,
Polite Conversation

11825.
Life is a dream in the night, a fear among fears,
A naked runner lost in a storm of spears.   ARTHUR SYMONS,
In the Wood of Finvara

11826. When all is done, human life is, at the greatest and the best, but like a froward child, that must be played with and humoured a little to keep it quiet till it falls asleep, and then the care is over.
      SIR WILLIAM TEMPLE, *Miscellanea*

11827. To be awake is to be alive.
      THOREAU, *Walden*

11828. Let us endeavor so to live that when we come to die even the undertaker will be sorry.
      MARK TWAIN,
Pudd'nhead Wilson's Calendar

11829. All say, "How hard it is that we have to die"—a strange complaint to come from the mouths of people who have had to live.
      MARK TWAIN,
Pudd'nhead Wilson's Calendar

11830. I advise you to go on living solely to enrage those who are paying your annuities. It is the only pleasure I have left.   VOLTAIRE

11831.
Life is ever lord of Death
And Love can never lose its own.
      WHITTIER, *Snow-Bound*

11832.
For he who lives more lives than one
More deaths than one must die.
      OSCAR WILDE,
The Ballad of Reading Gaol

See also: 157, 167, 168, 227, 451, 454, 466, 481, 482, 485, 503, 508, 509, 515, 531, 1196, 1218, 1220, 1634, 1747, 2025, 2191, 2329, 2351, 2869, 2900, 3051, 3346, 4865, 4896, 5585, 5975, 16404, 17026, 19807.

LIGHT

Related Subjects: Candle, Day, Electricity, Glory, Shadow, Sight.

11841. Light, even though it passes through pollution, is not polluted.
      ST. AUGUSTINE

11842. God's first creature, which was light.   BACON, *New Atlantis*

11843. And God said, Let there be light: and there was light.
Bible: Genesis, i, 3

11844. Ye are the light of the world.
Bible: Matthew, v, 14

11845. Light is the first of painters. There is no object so foul that intense light will not make it beautiful.
EMERSON, *Nature*

11846. Light, God's eldest daughter, is a principal beauty in a building.
THOMAS FULLER,
Holy and Profane State

11847. Lamps make oil-spots, and candles need snuffing; it is only the light of heaven that shines pure and leaves no stain.   GOETHE,
Spruche in Prosa

11848.
The tolerance and equity of light
That gives as freely to the shrinking flower
As to the great oak flaring to the wind.   EDWIN MARKHAM,
Lincoln, the Man of the People

11849.
Where glowing embers through the room,
Teach light to counterfeit a gloom.
MILTON, *Il Penseroso*

11850.
He that has light within his own clear breast
May sit i' the center and enjoy bright day;
But he that hides a dark soul and foul thoughts
Benighted walks under the mid-day sun.   MILTON, *Comus*

11851.
Lead, kindly Light, amid the encircling gloom;
Lead thou me on!
CARDINAL NEWMAN,
The Pillar of the Cloud

11852. If you desire to see my light, you must minister oil to my lamp.
Proverb

11853. You stand in your own light.
Proverb

11854. Light seeking light doth light of light beguile.   SHAKESPEARE,
Love's Labour's Lost

11855.
Put out the light, and then put out the light:
If I quench thee, thou flaming minister,
I can again thy former light restore
Should I repent me; but once put out thy light,
Thou cunning'st pattern of excelling nature,
I know not where is that Promethean heat
That can thy light relume.
SHAKESPEARE, *Othello*

11856. The two noblest things, which are sweetness and light.
SWIFT, *The Battle of the Books*

11857.
There are two ways of spreading light: to be
The candle or the mirror that reflects it.   EDITH WHARTON,
Vesalius in Zante

11858. The thing to do is to supply light and not heat.
WOODROW WILSON

11859.
A light to guide, a rod
To check the erring, and reprove.
WORDSWORTH, *Ode to Duty*

See also: 735, 1995, 2153, 3316.

LIGHTNING, see Thunder

LIKENESS

Related Subjects: Analogy, Comparisons, Contrast.

11861. Like father, like son.
WILLIAM LANGLAND,
Piers Plowman

11862. Things that have a common quality ever quickly seek their kind.
MARCUS AURELIUS, *Meditations*

11863. Like master, like man.
PETRONIUS, *Satyricon*

11864. As like as peas in a pod.
Proverb

11865.
The one so like the other
As could not be distinguish'd but by names.   SHAKESPEARE,
The Comedy of Errors

11866. Both of you are birds of self-same feather.   SHAKESPEARE,
Henry VI

11867. Almost as like as eggs.
SHAKESPEARE, *The Winter's Tale*

11868. Like,—but oh how different!
WORDSWORTH,
Yes, It Was the Mountain Echo

See also: 962, 1410, 5768.

LILAC

Related Subject: Flowers.

11871.
Lilacs, False blue, White, Purple,
Colour of lilac,
Your great puffs of flowers
Are everywhere in this my New England.   AMY LOWELL, *Lilacs*

11872.
Go down to Kew in lilac-time, in lilac-time, in lilac-time;
Go down to Kew in lilac-time (it isn't far from London!)
ALFRED NOYES, *The Barrel-Organ*

11873.
When lilacs last in the dooryard bloom'd,   .
And the great star early droop'd in the western sky in the night,
I mourn'd, and yet shall mourn with ever-returning spring.
WALT WHITMAN,
When Lilacs Last in the Dooryard Bloom'd

11874.
The Lilac-bush tall-growing with heart-shaped leaves of rich green,
With many a pointed blossom rising delicate, with the perfume strong I love,
With every leaf a miracle.
WALT WHITMAN,
When Lilacs Last in the Dooryard Bloom'd

11875. Warble me now for joy of lilac-time.   WALT WHITMAN,
Warble for Lilac-Time

LILY

Related Subject: Flowers.

11881.
I like the chaliced lilies,
The heavy Eastern lilies,
The gorgeous tiger-lilies,
   That in our garden grow.
T. B. ALDRICH, *Tiger-Lilies*

11882.
Consider the lilies of the field, how they grow; they toil not, neither do they spin: And yet I say unto you, That even Solomon in all his glory was not arrayed like one of these.
Bible: Matthew, vi, 28,29

11883.
          And lilies are still lilies, pulled
By smutty hands, though spotted
   from their white.
          ELIZABETH B. BROWNING,
                    Aurora Leigh

11884.
By cool Siloam's shady rill
   How sweet the lily grows!
          REGINALD HEBER,
          First Sunday after Epiphany

11885.
Like these cool lilies may our loves
   remain,
Perfect and pure, and know not any
   stain.   ANDREW LANG,
          A Vow to Heavenly Venus

11886.
          The lilies
Contending with the roses in her
   cheeks,
Who shall most set them off.
          MASSINGER,
          The Great Duke of Florence

11887. Lilies are whitest in a blacka-
moor's hand.   *Proverb*

11888. How bravely thou becomest
thy bed, fresh lily.
          SHAKESPEARE, *Cymbeline*

LIMERICKS

Related Subjects: Humor, Nonsense, Poets and Poetry.

11891.
There was an old man of Nantucket
Who kept all his cash in a bucket;
   But his daughter, named Nan,
   Ran away with a man—
And as for the bucket, Nantucket.
          Anonymous

11892.
There once was a brainy baboon
Who always breathed down a bas-
   soon,

For he said, "It appears
That in billions of years
I shall certainly hit on a tune.
          SIR ARTHUR EDDINGTON

11893. There are three kinds of limericks; limericks to be told when
ladies are present; limericks to be
told when ladies are absent but clergymen are present;—and limericks.
          DON MARQUIS

11894.
There was a young lady named
   Bright
Whose movements were faster than
   light;
   She ran off one day
   In a relative way,
And returned on the previous night.
          Limerick on the
          Einstein Theory of Relativity

See also: 1664, 14893.

LIMIT, LIMITATION

Related Subjects: Definitions,
End, Environment.

11900. We know in part, and we
prophesy in part.
          Bible: I Corinthians, xiii, 9

11901. Whoso belongs only to his
own age, and reverences only its gilt
Popinjays or soot-smeared Mumbo-
jumbos, must needs die with it.
          CARLYLE, *On Boswell*

11902. Art is limitation; the essence
of every picture is the frame.
          G. K. CHESTERTON, *Orthodoxy*

11903. No man can climb out beyond
the limitations of his own character.
          JOHN MORLEY, *Robespierre*

11904. The most perfect types of
manhood are always in revolt against
the limitations of man's nature, his
position on the face of the earth, and

his ignorance. Towards the end of remedying these defects in man's structure and powers, good men have always struggled, and always shall struggle, to cleanse the blurred compass of man's intellect that it may make manifest all the degrees of knowledge in the universe.

LIAM O'FLAHERTY, *Two Years*

See also: 3, 13.

LINCOLN, ABRAHAM

11911.
No king this man, by grace of God's intent;
No, something better, freeman,—President!
A nature, modeled on a higher plan,
Lord of himself, an inborn gentleman!

G. H. BOKER, *Our Heroic Themes*

11912.
Our pastoral captain, skilled to crook
The spear into the pruning hook,
The simple, kindly man,
Lincoln, American.

J. V. CHENEY, *Lincoln*

11913.
O Uncommon Commoner! may your name
Forever lead like a living flame!
Unschooled scholar! how did you learn
The wisdom a lifetime may not earn?

E. V. COOKE,
The Uncommon Commoner

11914.
Hail, Lincoln! As the swift years lengthen
Still more majestic grows thy fame;
The ties that bind us to thee strengthen;
Starlike-immortal shines thy name.

M. H. DOLE,
Lincoln's Birthday

11915. His heart was as great as the world, but there was no room in it to hold the memory of a wrong.

EMERSON

11916. We are coming, Father Abraham, three hundred thousand more.

J. S. GIBBONS

11917. Lincoln had faith in time, and time has justified his faith.

BENJAMIN HARRISON

11918. Abraham Lincoln was as just and generous to the rich and well-born as to the poor and humble—a rare thing among politicians.

JOHN HAY

11919. In the heroic figure of Abraham Lincoln who in life and death consecrated himself to the purest ideals of the nation, the law of the "charity of brotherhood" shall ever find inspiration: "With charity toward all, with malice toward none."

CARDINAL HAYES

11920. Another expense we didn' used to have wuz buyin' an entirely new life of Lincoln ever' month or so.   KIN HUBBARD

11921. Lincoln was not a type. He stands alone—no ancestors, no fellows, no successors.

ROBERT INGERSOLL

11922. Nobody ever expected me to be President. In my poor, lean, lank face nobody has ever seen that any cabbages were sprouting.

LINCOLN, *Campaign Speech, 1860*

11923. The Union must live, or I shall die.   LINCOLN

11924. My Cabinet, like Caesar's wife, must be above suspicion.

LINCOLN

11925. I had my ambitions—yes—as every American boy worth his salt

has. And I dared to dream this vision
of the White House,—I, the humblest of the humble, born in a lowly
pioneer's cabin in the woods of Ken-
tucky. My dream came true, and
where is its glory? Ashes and blood.
I . . . have lived with aching heart
through it all and envied the dead
their rest on the battlefields.

LINCOLN

11926.
His grave a nation's heart shall be,
His monument a people free!

CAROLINE A. MASON
President Lincoln's Grave

11927.
I am Ann Rutledge who sleeps be-
neath these weeds,
Beloved in life of Abraham Lincoln,
Wedded to him, not through union,
But through separation.
Bloom forever, O Republic,
From the dust of my bosom.

EDGAR LEE MASTERS,
Spoon River Anthology

11928. When Abraham Lincoln was
shoveled into the tombs, he forgot
the copperheads and the assassin
. . . in the dust, in the cool tombs.

CARL SANDBURG, *Cool Tombs*

11929.
O Captain! My Captain! our fearful
trip is done,
The ship has weather'd every rack,
the prize we sought is won,
The port is near, the bells I hear, the
people all exulting,
While follow eyes the steady keel, the
vessel grim and daring;
But O heart! heart! heart!
O the bleeding drops of red,
Where on the deck my Captain
lies,
Fallen cold and dead.

WALT WHITMAN,
O Captain! My Captain!

11930.
This dust was once the man,
Gentle, plain, just and resolute, un-
der whose cautious hand,
Against the foulest crime in history
known in any land or age,
Was saved the Union of these States.

WALT WHITMAN,
This Dust Was Once the Man

See also: 14941.

LION:

Related Subject: Animal.

11931. Where the lion's skin will
not reach, you must patch it out with
the fox's.   PLUTARCH, *Lives*

11932. The lion is not so fierce as
they paint him.   *Proverb*

11933. Kill the lion's whelp; thou'lt
strive in vain when he's grown.
Proverb

11934. A man is a lion in his own
cause.   *Proverb*

11935. It's not good to wake a sleeping lion.   *Proverb*

11936.
When the lion fawns upon the lamb,
The lamb will never cease to follow
him.   SHAKESPEARE, *Henry VI*

11937.
Talks as familiarly of roaring lions
As maids of thirteen do of puppy-
dogs!   SHAKESPEARE,
King John

11938. A lion among ladies is a most
dreadful thing.   SHAKESPEARE,
A Midsummer-Night's Dream

See also: 3593, 4359, 4492, 4904,
12250.

LIP

Related Subjects: Face, Kiss, Mouth, Speech, Tongue.

11941.
Those cherries fairly do enclose
  Of orient pearl a double row,
Which when her lovely laughter
    shows,
  They look like rosebuds fill'd with
    snow.   THOMAS CAMPION,
                       Cherry-Ripe

11942. Oh that those lips had language!   COWPER,
           On the Receipt of
      My Mother's Picture

11943. Lips are no part of the head, only made for a double-leaf door for the mouth.   JOHN LYLY, *Midas*

11944. Lips, however rosy, must be fed.   *Proverb*

11945.
Take, O, take those lips away,
That so sweetly were forsworn.
SHAKESPEARE, *Measure for Measure*

11946.
        O, how ripe in show
Thy lips, those kissing cherries, tempting grow!
            SHAKESPEARE,
  A Midsummer-Night's Dream

11947.
Teach not thy lips such scorn, for
  they were made
For kissing, lady, not for such contempt.   SHAKESPEARE,
             Richard III

11948.
Their lips were four red roses on a
  stalk,
Which in their summer beauty kiss'd
  each other.   SHAKESPEARE,
             Richard III

11949.
Romeo: Have not saints lips, and
  holy palmers too?
Juliet: Ay, pilgrim lips that they
  must use in prayer.
  SHAKESPEARE, *Romeo and Juliet*

11950.
And steal immortal blessing from her
  lips,
Who, even in pure and vestal
  modesty,
Still blush, as thinking their own
  kisses sin.   SHAKESPEARE,
        Romeo and Juliet

11951.
Oh, what a deal of scorn looks beautiful
In the contempt and anger of his lip!
  SHAKESPEARE, *Twelfth Night*

11952. Keep a stiff upper lip.
                Traditional

See also: 113, 8026.

LISTENING

Related Subjects: Attention, Ears, Spying.

11961.
But yet she listen'd—'tis enough—
Who listens once will listen twice.
         BYRON, *Mazeppa*

11962. And listens like a three years' child.   COLERIDGE,
      The Ancient Mariner

11963.
It takes a great man to make a good listener.
    ARTHUR HELPS, *Brevia*

11964. Listen, my children, and you shall hear.   LONGFELLOW,
    Tales of a Wayside Inn

11965. Eurybiades lifting up his staff as if he were going to strike, Themistocles said, "Strike, if you will, but hear."   PLUTARCH, *Lives*

11966. Know how to listen, and you will profit even from those who talk badly.   PLUTARCH

11967. Hear a' parties.   *Proverb*

11968. To listen well, is as powerful a means of influence as to talk well, and is as essential to all true conversation.   *Proverb*

11969. And this cuff was but to knock at your ear, and beseech listening.   SHAKESPEARE,
The Taming of the Shrew

See also: 4175, 15541.

LITERATURE

Related Subjects: Art, Authors, Books, Drama, Letters, Poets, Reading, Writing.

11971. Only the more rugged mortals should attempt to keep up with current literature.
GEORGE ADE, *Fables in Slang*

11972. "Only a novel" . . . in short, only some work in which the greatest powers of the mind are displayed, in which the most thorough knowledge of human nature, the happiest delineation of its varieties, are conveyed to the world in the best chosen language.   JANE AUSTEN,
Northanger Abbey

11973. A national literature ought to be built, as the robin builds its nest, out of the twigs and straws of one's native meadows.
VAN WYCK BROOKS,
The Flowering of New England

11974. I think it is entirely possible that a number of things which have

been established as classics through sheer persistency are no great shakes . . . A thing is neither true nor beautiful because the world has clung to it for a thousand years.
HEYWOOD BROUN, *The Last Review*

11975. In science, read, by preference, the newest works; in literature, the oldest. The classic literature is always modern.
BULWER-LYTTON, *Caxtonia*

11976. Literature is an investment of genius which pays dividends to all subsequent times.
JOHN BURROUGHS, *Literary Fame*

11977. There is a great discovery still to be made in Literature, that of paying literary men by the quantity they do not write.   CARLYLE, *Scott*

11978. To have lived in vain must be a painful thought to any man, and especially so to him who has made literature his profession.
COLERIDGE, *Biographia Literaria*

11979. Never pursue literature as a trade.
COLERIDGE, *Biographia Literaria*

11980. Literature is the greatest of all sources of refined pleasure, and one of the great uses of a liberal education is to enable us to enjoy that pleasure.   THOMAS H. HUXLEY,
A Liberal Education

11981. "The literary world," said he, "is made up of little confederacies, each looking upon its own members as the lights of the universe; and considering all others as mere transient meteors, doomed soon to fall and be forgotten, while its own luminaries are to shine steadily on to immortality."   WASHINGTON IRVING,
Tales of a Traveller

11982. It is amazing how little literature there is in the world.

SAMUEL JOHNSON, *Boswell: Life*

11983. There are masterpieces which are acknowledged to be such by all the best critics and to which the historians of literature devote considerable space, yet which no ordinary person can now read with enjoyment . . . I have read George Eliot's *Adam Bede,* but I cannot put my hand on my heart and say that it was with pleasure. I read it from a sense of duty: I finished it with a sigh of relief.

SOMERSET MAUGHAM,
Books and You

11984. Literature—the most seductive, the most deceiving, the most dangerous of professions.

JOHN MORLEY, *Burke*

11985. After all, there is no such literature as a dictionary.

SIR WILLIAM OSLER,
Life of Sir William Osler

11986. It is with literature as with law or empire—an established name is an estate in tenure, or a throne in possession.   POE

11987. So complex and various are the elements of literature that no writer can be damned on a mere enumeration of faults. He may always possess merits which make up for everything; if he loses on the swings, he may win on the roundabouts.

LYTTON STRACHEY,
Portraits in Miniature

11988. A classic is something that everybody wants to have read and nobody wants to read.

MARK TWAIN
The Disappearance of Literature

11989. In the civilization of to-day it is undeniable that, over all the arts, literature dominates, serves beyond all.   WALT WHITMAN,
Democratic Vistas

11990. That complete statement which is literature.

VIRGINIA WOOLF,
The Common Reader

See also: 930, 2005, 4316, 19018, 21076.

LITTLE THINGS

Related Subject: Trifles.

11991. A little thing in hand is worth more than a great thing in prospect.

AESOP,
The Fisher and the Little Fish

11992. Little by little does the trick.

AESOP, *The Crow and the Pitcher*

11993. He that is faithful in that which is least is faithful also in much; and he that is unjust in the least is unjust also in much.

Bible: Luke, xvi, 10

11994.
Little drops of water, little grains of sand,
Make the mighty ocean and the pleasant land.
So the little moments, humble though they be,
Make the mighty ages of eternity.

JULIA CARNEY, *Little Things*

11995. Little things affect little minds.   DISRAELI, *Sybil*

11996.
Large streams from little fountains flow,
Tall oaks from little acorns grow.

DAVID EVERETT

11997. A little house well filled, a little land well tilled, and a little wife well willed, are great riches.

Proverb

11998. Little things attract light minds.   *Proverb*

11999. A whole bushel of wheat is made up of single grains.   *Proverb*

12000. It is better to have a little than nothing.
PUBLILIUS SYRUS, *Sententiae*

12001. Thought she be but little, she is fierce.   SHAKESPEARE,
A Midsummer-Night's Dream

12002.
He that high growth on cedars did
   bestow,
Gave also lowly mushrumps leave to
   grow.   ROBERT SOUTHWELL,
Scorn Not the Least

12003.
Hereby I learned have, not to de-
   spise,
Whatever thing seemes small in com-
   mon eyes.
EDMUND SPENSER,
Visions of the Worlds Vanitie

12004.
Forgive us all our trespasses,
Little creatures, everywhere!
JAMES STEPHENS, *Little Things*

See also: 1635.

LOGIC

Related Subjects: **Argument, Consistency, Order, Reason.**

12011. Logic and rhetoric make men able to contend. Logic differeth from rhetoric as the fist from the palm; the one close, the other at large.   BACON

12012. Logic is a large drawer, containing some needful instruments, and many more that are superfluous. A wise man will look into it for two purposes, to avail himself of those instruments that are really useful, and to admire the ingenuity with which those that are not so are assorted and arranged.
C. C. COLTON

12013. Ethics make one's soul mannerly and wise, but logic is the armory of reason, furnished with all offensive and defensive weapons.
THOMAS FULLER

12014. Logic is the art of convincing us of some truth.   LA BRUYÈRE

12015. A thing may sound so logical you are convinced it must be wrong. The moment a philosophical system becomes too impressive or logically beautiful, I become suspicious.
LIN YUTANG, *I Believe*

12016. Syllogism is of necessary use, even to the lovers of truth, to show them the fallacies that are often concealed in florid, witty, or involved discourses.   LOCKE

12017. Logic is neither an art nor a science but a dodge.   STENDHAL

12018. It was a saying of the ancients, that "truth lies in a well"; and to carry on the metaphor, we may justly say, that logic supplies us with steps whereby we may go down to reach the water.   ISAAC WATTS

See also: 4143, 6741, 12882, 17480, 21660.

LONDON

Related Subjects: **Cities, England.**

12021.
Lo, where huge London, huger day
   by day,
O'er six fair counties spreads it hideous sway!   ALFRED AUSTIN,
The Golden Age

12022.

As I came down the Highgate Hill
I met the sun's bravado,
And saw below me, fold on fold
Grey to pearl and pearl to gold,
This London like a land of old,
The land of Eldorado.

     H. H. BASHFORD, *Romance*

12023. London is the clearing-house
of the world.

     JOSEPH CHAMBERLAIN

12024.

Let but thy wicked men from out
    thee go,
And all the fools that crowd thee so,
Even thou, who dost thy millions
    boast,
A village less than Islington will
    grow,
A solitude almost.

     ABRAHAM COWLEY, *Of Solitude*

12025.

The finest thing in London is the
    Bobby;
Benignant information is his hobby.

     ARTHUR GUITERMAN,
         The Lyric Baedeker

12026. When a man is tired of London, he is tired of life; for there is
in London all that life can afford.

     SAMUEL JOHNSON, *Boswell: Life*

12027.

Oh London Town's a fine town, and
    London sights are rare,
And London ale is right ale, and
    brisk's the London air.

     JOHN MASEFIELD, *London Town*

12028. Dear, damn'd, distracting
town.   POPE, *A Farewell to London*

12029. I hope to see London once
ere I die.

     SHAKESPEARE, *Henry IV*

12030.

In London, that great sea, whose ebb
and flow

At once is deaf and loud, and on the
    shore
Vomits its wrecks, and still howls on
    for more.   SHELLEY

See also: 9743, 14929.

LONELINESS, see Solitude

LOSS

**Related Subjects: Disappoint-
ment, Grief, Misfortune, Sorrow.**

12031. There are occasions when it
is undoubtedly better to incur loss
than to make gain.

     PLAUTUS, *Aulularia*

12032. A wise man's loss is his secret.   *Proverb*

12033. He loseth indeed that loseth
at last.   *Proverb*

12034. Losers are always in the
wrong.   *Proverb*

12035. He that goeth out with often
loss, at last comes home by weeping
cross.   *Proverb*

12036. The loss which is unknown is
no loss at all.

     PUBLILIUS SYRUS, *Sententiae*

12037. Whatever you can lose, you
should reckon of no account.

     PUBLILIUS SYRUS, *Sententiae*

12038.

Praising what is lost
Makes the remembrance dear.

     SHAKESPEARE,
     All's Well that Ends Well

12039.

He that is robb'd, not wanting what
    is stolen,
Let him not know 't and he's not
    robb'd at all.

     SHAKESPEARE, *Othello*

12040. No man can lose what he never had.   IZAAK WALTON,
The Compleat Angler

See also: 3061, 3722, 6033.

LOTUS

Related Subject: Flowers.

12041. Lotos the name: divine, nectareous juice!
HOMER, *Odyssey*

12042.
They wove the lotus band to deck
And fan with pensile wreath their
   neck.   THOMAS MOORE,
Odes of Anacreon

12043.
Thro' every hollow cave and alley
   lone,
Round and round the spicy downs the
   yellow
     Lotos-dust is blown.
TENNYSON, *The Lotos-Eaters*

12044.
In that dark land of mystic dream
   Where dark Osiris sprung,
It bloomed beside his sacred stream
   While yet the world was young;
And every secret Nature told,
   Of golden wisdom's power,
Is nestled still in every fold,
   Within the Lotos flower.
WILLIAM WINTER, *A Lotos Flower*

LOVE

Related Subjects: Affection, Beauty, Courtship, Cupid, Desire, Devotion, Friendship, Heart, Jealousy, Kiss, Loyalty, Lust, Marriage, Mistress, Passion, Romance, The Sexes, Tenderness, Valentine.

12051. Above all, true love lives by the memory. The woman whose soul is not engraved upon, either by an excess of pleasure or a strength of feeling, can she ever be said to be in love?   BALZAC,
The Girl With the Golden Eyes

12052. Let no one who loves be called altogether unhappy. Even love unreturned has its rainbow.
J. M. BARRIE, *The Little Minister*

12053. Better is a dinner of herbs where love is, than a stalled ox and hatred therewith.
Bible: Proverbs, xv, 17

12054. Many waters cannot quench love, neither can the floods drown it.
Bible: The Song of Solomon, viii, 7

12055. Love is the fulfilling of the law.   *Bible: Romans, xiii, 10*

12056. He that loveth not abideth in fear.   *Bible: 1 John, iii, 14*

12057. Love iz like the meazles; we kant have it bad but onst, and the later in life we have it the tuffer it goes with us.
JOSH BILLINGS, *Affurisms*

12058. Never seek to tell thy love.
BLAKE, *Love's Secret*

12059.
Love seeketh not itself to please,
   Nor for itself hath any care,
But for another gives its ease,
   And builds a heaven in hell's de-
     spair.   BLAKE,
The Clod and the Pebble

12060.
The mind has a thousand eyes,
   And the heart but one;
Yet the light of a whole life dies,
   When love is done.
F. W. BOURDILLON, *Light*

12061.
I thought when love for you died, I should die.

It's dead. Alone, most strangely, I
 live on.
RUPERT BROOKE, *The Life Beyond*

12062. The ability to make love
frivolously is the chief characteristic
which distinguishes human beings
from the beasts.
HEYWOOD BROUN, *It Seems to Me*

12063.
If thou must love me, let it be for
 nought
Except for love's sake only.
ELIZABETH B. BROWNING,
Sonnets from the Portuguese

12064.
Love, like Death,
Levels all ranks, and lays the shep-
 herd's crook
Beside the sceptre.
BULWER-LYTTON,
The Lady of Lyons

12065.
Oh, my luve is like a red, red rose,
 That's newly sprung in June;
Oh, my luve is like the melodie,
 That's sweetly played in tune.
BURNS, *A Red, Red Rose*

12066.
But to see her was to love her,
Love but her, and love forever.
BURNS, *Ae Fond Kiss*

12067.
Had we never loved sae kindly,
Had we never loved sae blindly,
Never met—or never parted—
We had ne'er been broken-hearted!
BURNS, *Ae Fond Kiss*

12068. To enlarge or illustrate this
power and effect of love is to set a
candle in the sun.
ROBERT BURTON,
Anatomy of Melancholy

12069.
The cold in clime are cold in blood,
Their love can scarce deserve the
 name.   BYRON, *The Giaour*

12070.
Man's love is of man's life a thing
 apart;
'Tis woman's whole existence.
BYRON, *Don Juan*

12071.
Then fly betimes, for only they
Conquer Love that run away.
THOMAS CAREW, *Conquest by Flight*

12072. Love is ever the beginning of
Knowledge, as fire is of light.
CARLYLE, *Essays*

12073. Love is an Art, and the great-
est of the Arts.
EDWARD CARPENTER,
The Drama of Love and Death

12074. My love and hers have always
been purely Platonick.
CERVANTES, *Don Quixote*

12075. Love and War are the same
thing, and stratagems and policy are
as allowable in the one as in the other.
CERVANTES, *Don Quixote*

12076.
I tell thee Love is Nature's second
 sun,
Causing a spring of virtues where he
 shines.
GEORGE CHAPMAN, *All Fools*

12077. None ever loved but at first
sight they loved.
GEORGE CHAPMAN,
The Blind Beggar of Alexandria

12078. Love is blind.
CHAUCER, *Canterbury Tales*

12079. Servant in love, and lord in
marriage.
CHAUCER, *Canterbury Tales*

12080.
All thoughts, all passions, all delights,
Whatever stirs this mortal frame,
   All are but ministers of Love,
     And feed his sacred flame.
            COLERIDGE, *Love*

12081.
If there's delight in love, 'tis when I
   see
That heart which others bleed for,
   bleed for me.
CONGREVE, *The Way of the World*

12082.
A mighty pain to love it is,
And 'tis a pain that pain to miss;
But of all pains, the greatest pain
It is to love, but love in vain.
      ABRAHAM COWLEY, *Anacreon*

12083.
Love is a sickness full of woes,
All remedies refusing.
        SAMUEL DANIEL,
          Hymen's Triumph

12084. Love comes unseen; we only
see it go.   AUSTIN DOBSON

12085.
Fool, not to know that love endures
   no tie,
And Jove but laughs at lovers' perjury.   DRYDEN,
        Palamon and Arcite

12086.
Pains of love be sweeter far
Than all other pleasures are.
      DRYDEN, *Tyrannic Love*

12087. No man ever forgot the vis-
itations of that power to his heart
and brain, which created all things
new; which was the dawn in him of
music, poetry, and art.
          EMERSON, *Love*

12088. "Perhaps they were right in
putting love into books," he thought
quietly. "Perhaps it could not live
anywhere else."
      WILLIAM FAULKNER,
          Light in August

12089. The days of romantic love are
gone by. The scientific spirit has put
an end to that kind of self-deception.
What we think of now is moral and
intellectual and physical compatibil-
ity.   GEORGE GISSING,
          New Grub Street

12090. It is to the credit of human
nature, that, except where its selfishness is brought into play, it loves
more readily than it hates.
    HAWTHORNE, *The Scarlet Letter*

12091.
You say to me-wards your affection's strong;
Pray love me little, so you love me
   long.   ROBERT HERRICK,
      Love me Little, Love me Long

12092.
Love is like a dizziness,
It winna let a poor body
Gang about his bizziness.
         JAMES HOGG,
      Love is Like a Dizziness

12093.
Love is a proud and gentle thing, a
   better thing to own
Than all of the wide impossible stars
   over the heavens blown.
    ROBINSON JEFFERS, *The Door*

12094.
'Tis the pest
Of love, that fairest joys give most
   unrest.   KEATS, *Endymion*

12095. Lovers are never tired of each
other, though they always speak of
themselves.
    LA ROCHEFOUCAULD, *Maxims*

12096. In their first passion women

love their lovers, in all the others they love love.

LA ROCHEFOUCAULD, *Maxims*

12097. There are few people who would not be ashamed of being loved when they love no longer.

LA ROCHEFOUCAULD, *Maxims*

12098. The pleasure of love is in loving. We are happier in the passion we feel than in that we inspire.

LA ROCHEFOUCAULD, *Maxims*

12099. Love is the selfishness of two persons. LA SALLE

12100.
Love in my bosom like a bee
Doth suck his sweet.

THOMAS LODGE, *Rosalind*

12101. There was never any yet that wholly could escape love, and never shall there be any, never so long as beauty shall be, never so long as eyes can see. LONGUS,
Daphnis and Chloe

12102.
I could not love thee, dear, so much,
Lov'd I not honour more.

RICHARD LOVELACE, *To Lucasta,
on Going to the Wars*

12103.
He reckoneth without his Hostesse.
Love knoweth no laws.

JOHN LYLY, *Euphues*

12104.
Come live with me, and be my love;
And we will all the pleasures prove
That hills and valleys, dales and fields,
Woods or steepy mountain yields.

CHRISTOPHER MARLOWE, *The
Passionate Shepherd to His Love*

12105.
Love is flame to burn out human wills,

Love is a flame to set the will on fire,
Love is a flame to cheat men into mire.
One of the three, we make Love what we choose.

JOHN MASEFIELD,
The Widow in the Bye Street

12106. He who loves well is consumed in the flames of his love.

MICHELANGELO

12107.
Whether or not we find what we are seeking
Is idle, biologically speaking.

EDNA ST. VINCENT MILLAY,
I Shall Forget You Presently

12108.
Love-quarrels oft in pleasing concord end;
Not wedlock-treachery.

MILTON, *Samson Agonistes*

12109.
So dear I love him that with him all deaths
I could endure, without him live no life. MILTON, *Paradise Lost*

12110. It is a wonderful seasoning of all enjoyments to think of those we love. MOLIÈRE, *Le Misanthrope*

12111.
I know not, I ask not, if guilt's in that heart,
I but know that I love thee, whatever thou art. THOMAS MOORE,
Come, Rest in This Bosom

12112.
But there's nothing half so sweet in life
As love's young dream.

THOMAS MOORE,
Love's Young Dream

12113.
Young Love may go,
For aught I care,
To Jericho!   THOMAS MOORE,
When Love is Kind

12114. Love is enough, though the
world be a-waning.
   WILLIAM MORRIS, *Love is Enough*

12115.
Youth's for an hour,
Beauty's a flower,
But love is the jewel that wins the
   world.   MOIRA O'NEILL,
Beauty's a Flower

12116. Scratch a lover, and find a
foe.   DOROTHY PARKER,
Ballade of a Great Weariness

12117. It is not true that Love will
do no wrong.
COVENTRY PATMORE, *If I Were Dead*

12118.
Thou wast all that to me, love,
   For which my soul did pine—
A green isle in the sea, love,
   A fountain and a shrine,
All wreathed with fairy fruits and
   flowers,
   And all the flowers were mine.
     POE, *To One in Paradise*

12119.
O, human love! thou spirit given,
On Earth, of all we hope in Heaven!
     POE, *Tamerlane*

12120. How vast a memory has
Love!   POPE, *The Dunciad*

12121.
Curse on all laws but those which
   love has made!
Love, free as air at sight of human
   ties,
Spreads his light wings, and in a
   moment flies.   POPE,
Eloisa to Abelard

12122.
Ye Gods! annihilate but space and
   time,
And make two lovers happy.   POPE

12123.
Love is something so divine,
   Description would but make it less;
'Tis what I feel, but can't define,
   'Tis what I know, but can't ex-
     press.   B. PORTEUS, *On Love*

12124. In love is no lack.   *Proverb*

12125. In Love's wars, he who flieth
is conqueror.   *Proverb*

12126. Love can neither be bought
nor sold; its only price being love.
     Proverb

12127. Love comes in at the windows, and goes out at the doors.
     Proverb

12128. Love is as warm among cot-
tagers as courtiers.   *Proverb*

12129. Love is a sweet tyranny, because the lover endureth his torments
willingly.   *Proverb*

12130. Love is blind.   *Proverb*

12131. Love is the touchstone of virtue.   *Proverb*

12132. Love laughs at locksmiths.
     Proverb

12133. Love me little, and love me
long.   *Proverb*

12134. He that hath love in his breast
hath spurs at his heels.   *Proverb*

12135. Love, and a cough, cannot be
hid.   *Proverb*

12136. Love is incompatible with
fear.   PUBLILIUS SYRUS, *Sententiae*

12137. The approaches of love must
be resisted at the first assault, lest
they undermine at the second.
     PYTHAGORAS

12138.

Love that's wise
Will not say all it means.
> E. A. ROBINSON, *Tristram*

12139.

True love's the gift which God has
　　given,
To man alone beneath the heaven:
　It is not fantasy's hot fire,
　　Whose wishes, soon as granted,
　　　fly;
　It liveth not in fierce desire,
　　With dead desire it doth not die;
It is the secret sympathy,
The silver link, the silken tie,
Which heart to heart and mind to
　　mind
In body and in soul can bind.
SCOTT, *The Lay of the Last Minstrel*

12140.

The hind that would be mated by the
　　lion
Must die for love.
> SHAKESPEARE,
> *All's Well that Ends Well*

12141.

It were all one
That I should love a bright particular
　　star
And think to wed it.
> SHAKESPEARE,
> *All's Well that Ends Well*

12142. There's beggary in the love
that can be reckon'd.
> SHAKESPEARE,
> *Antony and Cleopatra*

12143.

Down on your knees,
And thank Heaven fasting, for a
　good man's love.
> SHAKESPEARE, *As You Like It*

12144.

If thou remember'st not the slightest
　folly

That ever love did make thee run
　into,
Thou hast not lov'd.
> SHAKESPEARE, *As You Like It*

12145. Men have died from time to
time, and worms have eaten them,
but not for love.
> SHAKESPEARE, *As You Like It*

12146.

Under the greenwood tree
Who loves to lie with me.
> SHAKESPEARE, *As You Like It*

12147. No sooner met but they
looked; no sooner looked but they
loved; no sooner loved but they
sighed; no sooner sighed but they
asked one another the reason; no
sooner knew the reason but they
sought the remedy.
> SHAKESPEARE, *As You Like It*

12148.

　　　　　Forty thousand brothers
Could not, with all their quantity of
　love,
Make up my sum.
> SHAKESPEARE, *Hamlet*

12149.

When the blood burns, how prodigal
　the soul
Lends the tongue vows.
> SHAKESPEARE, *Hamlet*

12150. If the rascal have not given
me medicines to make me love him,
I'll be hanged.　SHAKESPEARE,
> *Henry IV*

12151. A man that I love and Honour with my soul, and my heart, and
my duty, and my life, and my living,
and my uttermost power.
> SHAKESPEARE, *Henry V*

12152. This word "love", which
greybeards call divine.
> SHAKESPEARE, *Henry VI*

12153. Though last, not least in love.
SHAKESPEARE, *Julius Caesar*

12154.
My love's
More richer than my tongue.
SHAKESPEARE, *King Lear*

12155.
But love is blind, and lovers cannot see
The pretty follies that themselves commit. SHAKESPEARE,
The Merchant of Venice

12156.
Friendship is constant in all other things
Save in the office and affairs of love;
Therefore, all hearts in love use their own tongues;
Let every eye negotiate for itself,
And trust no agent.
SHAKESPEARE,
Much Ado About Nothing

12157. Speak low, if you speak love.
SHAKESPEARE,
Much Ado About Nothing

12158.
Love looks not with the eyes, but with the mind,
And therefore is winged Cupid painted blind. SHAKESPEARE,
A Midsummer-Night's Dream

12159.
For Aught that I could ever read,
Could ever hear by tale or history,
The course of true love never did run smooth. SHAKESPEARE,
A Midsummer-Night's Dream

12160.
She loved me for the dangers I had passed,
And I loved her that she did pity them.
This only is the witchcraft I have used. SHAKESPEARE,
Othello

12161.
Excellent wretch! Perdition catch my soul,
But I do love thee! and when I love thee not,
Chaos is come again.
SHAKESPEARE, *Othello*

12162.
Base men being in love have then a nobility in their natures more than is native to them. SHAKESPEARE,
Othello

12163.
How silver-sweet sound lovers' tongues by night,
Like softest music to attending ears!
SHAKESPEARE, *Romeo and Juliet*

12164.
At lovers' perjuries,
They say, Jove laughs.
SHAKESPEARE, *Romeo and Juliet*

12165. For stony limits cannot hold love out. SHAKESPEARE,
Romeo and Juliet

12166.
This bud of love, by summer's ripening breath,
May prove a beauteous flower when next we meet. SHAKESPEARE,
Romeo and Juliet

12167.
Do not give dalliance
Too much rein. SHAKESPEARE,
The Tempest

12168. All lovers swear more performance than they are able, and yet reserve an ability that they never perform; vowing more than the perfection of ten, and discharging less than the tenth part of one.
SHAKESPEARE, *Troilus and Cressida*

12169.
Duke: And what's her history?
Viola: A blank, my lord. She never told her love,

But let concealment, like a worm i'
   the bud,
Feed on her damask cheek: she pined
   in thought,
And with a green and yellow melancholy
She sat like patience on a monument,
Smiling at grief.
      SHAKESPEARE, *Twelfth Night*

12170.
Journeys end in lovers meeting,
Every wise man's son doth know.
      SHAKESPEARE, *Twelfth Night*

12171. Love sought is good, but
given unsought, is better.
      SHAKESPEARE, *Twelfth Night*

12172.
Then let thy love be younger than
   thyself,
Or thy affection cannot hold the bent.
      SHAKESPEARE, *Twelfth Night*

12173. O! they love least that let
men know their love.
      SHAKESPEARE,
      Two Gentlemen of Verona

12174. They do not love that do not
show their love. SHAKESPEARE,
      Two Gentlemen of Verona

12175. Love's best habit is a soothing tongue. SHAKESPEARE,
      The Passionate Pilgrim

12176.
When my love swears that she is
   made of truth,
I do believe her, though I know she
   lies. SHAKESPEARE,
      The Passionate Pilgrim

12177.
That love is merchandiz'd whose rich
   esteeming
The owner's tongue doth publish
   every where. SHAKESPEARE,
      Sonnet CII

12178.
For thy sweet love remember'd such
   wealth brings
That then I scorn to change my state
   with kings. SHAKESPEARE,
      Sonnet XXIX

12179.
Love is my sin, and thy dear virtue
   hate,
Hate of my sin, grounded on sinful
   loving. SHAKESPEARE,
      Sonnet CXLII

12180. Love is a spirit all compact of
fire. SHAKESPEARE,
      Venus and Adonis

12181. Love comforteth like sunshine after rain. SHAKESPEARE,
      Venus and Adonis

12182. Love gilds the scene, and
women guide the plot.
      SHERIDAN, *The Rivals*

12183. I loved him for himself alone.
      SHERIDAN, *The Duenna*

12184.
They sin who tell us love can die;
With life all other passions fly,
   All others are but vanity.
      SOUTHEY, *The Curse of Kehama*

12185. All for love, and nothing for
reward. EDMUND SPENSER,
      The Faerie Queene

12186. So long as we love we serve;
so long as we are loved by others, I
would almost say that we are indispensable; and no man is useless while
he has a friend. STEVENSON,
      Lay Morals

12187. To love is the great Amulet
that makes this world a garden.
STEVENSON, *Travels With a Donkey*

12188.
Out upon it, I have loved
   Three whole days together;

And am like to love three more,
  If it prove fair weather.
        SIR JOHN SUCKLING,
          A Poem With the Answer

12189.
Why so pale and wan, fond lover?
  Prithee, why so pale?
Will, when looking well can't move
    her,
  Looking ill prevail?
        SIR JOHN SUCKLING, *Song*

12190. To have known love, how bitter a thing it is.   SWINBURNE,
                Laus Veneris

12191.
And I would have, now love is over,
  An end to all, an end:
I cannot, having been your lover,
  Stoop to become your friend!
        ARTHUR SYMONS, *After Love*

12192.
God gives us love. Something to love
  He lends us; but when love is
    grown
To ripeness, that on which it throve
Falls off, and love is left alone.
        TENNYSON, *To J. S.*

12193.
'Tis better to have loved and lost
Than never to have loved at all.
        TENNYSON, *In Memoriam*

12194.
Sweet is true love tho' given in vain,
    in vain;
And sweet is death who puts an end
    to pain.   TENNYSON,
                Idylls of the King

12195.
The love of my life came not
  As love unto others is cast;
For mine was a secret wound—
  But the wound grew a pearl, at
    last.   EDITH M. THOMAS,
                The Deep-Sea Pearl

12196. There is no remedy for love
but to love more.   THOREAU

12197.
Make channels for the stream of love
Where they may broadly run,
And love has overflowing streams
To fill them every one.
        R. C. TRENCH, *The Law of Love*

12198. Love conquers all.
            VERGIL, *Eclogues*

12199.
O, rank is good, and gold is fair,
  And high and low mate ill;
But love has never known a law
  Beyond its own sweet will!
        WHITTIER, *Amy Wentworth*

12200.
Yet each man kills the thing he loves,
  By each let this be heard,
Some do it with a bitter look,
  Some with a flattering word,
The coward does it with a kiss,
  The brave man with a sword!
        OSCAR WILDE,
          The Ballad of Reading Gaol

12201.
                    Mightier far
Than strength of nerve and sinew, or
    the sway
Of magic potent over sun and star,
Is Love, though oft to agony distrest,
And though his favorite seat be
    feeble woman's breast.
        WORDSWORTH, *Laodamia*

12202.
And you must love him, ere to you
He will seem worthy of your love.
        WORDSWORTH, *A Poet's Epitaph*

12203.
Love lodged in a woman's breast
Is but a guest.
        SIR HENRY WOTTON,
                A Woman's Heart

12204.
How many loved your moments of
   glad grace,
And loved your beauty, with love
   false or true;
But one man loved the pilgrim soul in
   you,
And loved the sorrows of your chang-
   ing face.
   W. B. YEATS, *When You Are Old*

12205. In how many lives does Love
really play a dominant part? The
average taxpayer is no more capable
of a "grand passion" than of a grand
opera.   ISRAEL ZANGWILL,
        Romeo and Juliet and
        Other Love Stories

12206. There are certain kinds of
love that few but the very wise fully
understand until they have become
memories.   HANS ZINSSER,
        As I Remember Him

See also: 26, 36, 38, 44, 46, 53, 54,
270, 276, 375, 394, 701, 863, 887,
1062, 1086, 1087, 1204, 1351, 1361,
1864, 1961, 2130, 2344, 2500, 2532,
2976, 3251, 3260, 3266, 3358, 3849,
3854, 4232, 7942, 9008, 9027, 9601,
11564, 13608, 14489, 16321, 18828.

LOYALTY

**Related Subjects: Constancy, De-
votion, Duty, Fidelity, Love, Patriotism, Unity.**

12211. Oh whistle, and I'll come to
ye, my lad.   BURNS,
   Whistle, and I'll Come to Ye
12212.
Loyal be to loyal friends;
Make them pay you dividends;
Work, like the industrious bee,
Your friends and foes impartially.
        SAMUEL HOFFENSTEIN,
        A Garden of Verses for the
        Little Ones

12213.
While fortune smiles you'll have a
   host of friends,
But they'll desert you when the
   storm descends.   OVID, *Tristia*

12214.
I will follow thee
To the last gasp with truth and loy-
   alty.   SHAKESPEARE,
        As You Like It

12215. My man's as true as steel.
   SHAKESPEARE, *Romeo and Juliet*

See also: 1483.

LUCK

**Related Subjects: Accident,
Chance, Destiny, Fate, Fortune,
Gambling, Misfortune, Opportu-
nity, Providence.**

12221. The best you get is an even
break.   F. P. A., *Ballade of*
        Schopenhauer's Philosophy

12222. Now up, now doun, as boket
in a welle.   CHAUCER,
        Canterbury Tales

12223. Watch out w'en you er gittin'
all you want. Fattenin' hogs ain't in
luck.   JOEL CHANDLER HARRIS,
        Plantation Proverbs

12224.
True luck consists not in holding the
   best of the cards at the table:
Luckiest he who knows just when to
   rise and go home. JOHN HAY,
        Distichs

12225.
          so unlucky
that he runs into accidents
which started out to happen
to somebody else.
        DON MARQUIS, *archys life*
        of mehitabel

12226. Good luck reaches farther than long arms. *Proverb*

12227. When ill luck falls asleep, let nobody wake her. *Proverb*

12228. Bad luck often brings good luck. *Proverb*

12229. Lucky at cards, unlucky at love. *Proverb*

12230. Better be born lucky than rich. *Proverb*

12231. Even ill luck itself is good for something in a wise man's hand.
Proverb

12232. As good luck would have it.
SHAKESPEARE,
The Merry Wives of Windsor

12233.
For what is virtue, courage, wit,
In all men, but a lucky hit?
WILLIAM SOMERVILLE,
The Lucky Hit

12234. In the queer mess of human destiny the determining factor is Luck. For every important place in life there are many men of fairly equal capacities. Among them Luck decides who shall accomplish the great work who shall be crowned with Laurel, and who shall fall back into obscurity and silence.
W. E. WOODWARD,
George Washington

See also: 1621, 3074, 4355, 9511, 11294, 12982, 13683, 18143.

LUST

Related Subjects: Adultery, Appetite, Avarice, Desire, Love, Passion, Sin, Vice, Whore.

12241.
To couple is a custom,
All things thereto agree:

Why should not I then love,
Since love to all is free?
Anonymous

12242. To be carnally minded is death. *Bible: Romans, viii, 6*

12243.
For men have ever a likerous appetite
On lower things to perform their delight
Than on their wives, be they never so fair,
Nor never so true, nor so debonair.
Flesh is so newfangel, with mischaunce,
That we can in no thing have pleasaunce
That tendeth unto virtue any while.
CHAUCER, *Canterbury Tales*

12244.
There's times when you'll think that you mightn't,
    There's times when you'll know that you might;
But the things you will learn from the Yellow an' Brown,
    They'll 'elp you a lot with the White!   KIPLING, *The Ladies*

12245. The new lust gives the lecher the new thrill. JOHN MASEFIELD,
The Widow in the Bye Street

12246.
              When Lust
By unchaste looks, loose gestures, and foul talk,
But most by lewd and lavish act of sin,
Lets in defilement to the inward parts,
The soul grows clotted by contagion,
Imbodies and imbrutes.
MILTON, *Comus*

12247.
Lust, thro' some certain strainers well refin'd,

Is gentle love, and charms all wom-
ankind.　　Pope, *Essay on Man*

12248.

There goes a saying, and 'twas
shrewdly said,
Old fish at table, but young flesh in
bed.
My soul abhors the tasteless dry em-
brace
Of a stale virgin with a winter face.
　　Pope, *January and May*

12249.

Though Argus hundred eyes in
watch doth keep,
Yet lust at length will lull them all
asleep.　　Francis Rous, *Thule*

12250. Lust is the oldest lion of them
all. Marjorie Allen Seifert,
　　An Italian Chest

12251. I'll canvass thee between a
pair of sheets.　Shakespeare,
　　Henry IV

12252.

The expense of spirit in a waste of
shame
Is lust in action; and till action, lust
Is perjured, murderous, bloody, full
of blame,
Savage, extreme, rude, cruel, not to
trust;
Enjoyed no sooner but despised
straight;
Past reason hunted; and no sooner
had,
Past reason hated, as a swallowed
bait,
On purpose laid to make the taker
mad.　　Shakespeare,
　　Sonnet CXXIX

12253.

Love comforteth like sunshine after
rain,
But Lust's effect is tempest after
sun;

Love's gentle spring doth always
fresh remain,
Lust's winter comes ere summer half
be done:
Love surfeits not. Lust like a glutton
dies;
Love is all truth, Lust full of forged
lies.
　　Shakespeare, *Venus and Adonis*

12254. The lusts and greeds of the
Body scandalize the Soul; but it has
to come to heel.
　　Logan Pearsall Smith,
　　Afterthoughts

See also: 1223, 1759, 1946.

LUXURY

**Related Subjects: Comfort, Deli-
cacy, Jewel, Leisure, Pleasure,
Riches.**

12261. Too much plenty makes
mouth dainty.　　Franklin,
　　Poor Richard

12262.

What will not Luxury taste? Earth,
sea, and air,
Are daily ransacked for the bill of
fare!　　John Gay, *Trivia*

12263. O Luxury! thou curst by
Heaven's decree!　Goldsmith,
　　The Deserted Village

12264. We can do without any article of luxury we have never had;
but when once obtained, it is not in
human natur' to surrender it voluntarily.　　T. C. Halliburton,
　　The Clockmaker

12265. There is a limit to luxury.
　　Elbert Hubbard, *The Philistine*

12266. Luxury is like a wild beast,
first made fiercer with tying and then
let loose.　　Montaigne, *Essays*

12267.
Impatient of a scene whose luxuries
   stole,
Spite of himself, too deep into his
   soul.   THOMAS MOORE,
Lalla Rookh

12268.
Fell luxury! more perilous to youth
Than storms or quicksands, poverty
   or chains.   HANNAH MORE,
Belshazzar

12269. Give us the luxuries of life,
and we will dispense with its necessaries.   J. L. MOTLEY

12270. It is the superfluous things
for which men sweat.   SENECA,
Epistulae ad Lucilium

12271. Falsely luxurious! will not
man awake?   JAMES THOMSON,
The Seasons

12272. Most of the luxuries, and
many of the so-called comforts, of
life are not only not indispensable,
but positive hindrances to the elevation of mankind.   THOREAU, *Walden*

12273. The superfluous, a very necessary thing.   VOLTAIRE, *Le Mondain*

See also: 167, 1466, 1749, 1758, 5977.

M

MACHINERY

Related Subjects: Electricity, Industry, Invention, Mass Production, Power, Science, Steam.

12281. Only the most machine-like
race could win custom. After a while
every country felt it had to be drilled
or become extinct. Some made themselves into machines to enter the
English market, some to preserve
their own markets. Even the indolent
Oriental is getting keyed up, and in
another fifty years the Bedouin of
the desert will be at his desk and
the wild horseman of Tartary will be
oiling his engines.   A. E.,
Cooperation and Nationality

12282. A tool is but the extension of
a man's hand and a machine is but a
complex tool; and he that invents a
machine augments the power of man
and the well-being of mankind.
           H. W. BEECHER

12283. Man is a tool-using animal.
Feeblest of bipeds! . . . Nowhere do
you find him without tools. Without
tools he is nothing; with tools he is
all.   CARLYLE

12284. It is the Age of Machinery, in
every outward and inward sense of
that word.   CARLYLE,
Signs of the Times

12285. The greatest task before civilization at present is to make machines what they ought to be, the
slaves, instead of the masters of
men.   HAVELOCK ELLIS,
Little Essays on Love & Virtue

12286. Armed with his machinery
man can dive, can fly, can see atoms
like a gnat; he can peer into Uranus
with his telescope, or knock down
cities with his fists of gunpowder.
        EMERSON, *Lectures*

12287. Stop the machines and half
the people in the world would perish
in a month.   RAYMOND FOSDICK

12288. One machine can do the work
of fifty ordinary men. No machine
can do the work of one extraordinary
man.   ELBERT HUBBARD,
The Philistine

12289. Let us not despise machinery
in our zeal for fullness of life any
more than we should dream that ma-

chinery can ever automatically grind out perfection of living.

JULIAN HUXLEY, *I Believe*

12290. Don't throw a monkey-wrench into the machinery.

PHILANDER JOHNSON

12291. It is never the machines that are dead. It is only the mechanically-minded men that are dead.

GERALD STANLEY LEE, *Crowds*

12292. It is questionable if all the mechanical inventions yet made have lightened the day's toil of any human being. J. S. MILL, *Principles of Political Economy*

12293. As I read history the machine age taken in its entirety has actually freed, educated, and inspired mankind, rather than enslaved it! ROBERT A. MILLIKAN, *Alleged Sins of Science*

12294. The prosy modern piston imitates the Olympian deities; it transforms a chaos into a cosmos.

MICHAEL PUPIN

12295. Machines are worshipped because they are beautiful, and valued because they confer power; they are hated because they are hideous, and loathed because they impose slavery.

BERTRAND RUSSELL, *Sceptical Essays*

12296. You're not a man, you're a machine. BERNARD SHAW, *Arms and the Man*

12297. There will be little drudgery in this better ordered world. Natural power harnessed in machines will be the general drudge.

H. G. WELLS, *Outline of History*

12298. The citizen's entire life is exaggerated but sterilized by machinery —and medicine: were motor oil and castor oil to dry up, the city would cease to function and promptly perish. FRANK LLOYD WRIGHT, *The Disappearing City*

See also: 11378.

MADNESS, see Sanity

MAGNANIMITY

Related Subjects: Leniency, Nobility, Selfishness, Tolerance.

12301. A brave man knows no malice; but forgets, in peace, the injuries of war, and gives his direst foe a friend's embrace. COWPER

12302. Of all virtues magnanimity is the rarest; there are a hundred persons of merit for one who willingly acknowledges it in another.

HAZLITT

12303. Magnanimity is sufficiently defined by its name; yet we may say of it, that it is the good sense of pride, and the noblest way of acquiring applause.

LA ROCHEFOUCAULD, *Maxims*

12304. If you desire to be magnanimous, undertake nothing rashly, and fear nothing thou undertakest. Fear nothing but infamy; dare anything but injury; the measure of magnanimity is to be neither rash nor timorous. FRANCIS QUARLES

MAID, MAIDENHOOD

Related Subjects: Daughter, Girl, Innocence, Virgin.

12311.
Maidens' hearts are always soft:
Would that men's were truer!

BRYANT, *Song*

12312.
I once was a maid, though I cannot tell when,

And still my delight is in proper
   young men.   BURNS,
            The Jolly Beggars

12313.
Maidens, like moths, are ever caught
   by glare,
And Mammon wins his way where
   seraphs might despair.
       BYRON, *Childe Harold*

12314.
Maid of Athens, ere we part,
Give, oh give me back my heart!
      BYRON, *Maid of Athens*

12315.
A lovely being, scarcely formed or
   moulded,
A rose with all its sweetest leaves yet
   folded.   BYRON, *Don Juan*

12316. Is a maiden all the better
when she's tough?
    W. S. GILBERT, *The Mikado*

12317.
Maids' nays are nothing; they are
   shy
But do desire what they deny.
     ROBERT HERRICK,
      Maids' Nays are Nothing

12318.
My Son, if a maiden deny thee and
   scufflingly bid thee give o'er,
Yet lip meets with lip at the lastward.
   Get out! She has been there before.
   KIPLING, *Certain Maxims of Hafiz*

12319.
Standing, with reluctant feet,
Where the brook and river meet,
Womanhood and childhood fleet!
     LONGFELLOW, *Maidenhood*

12320.
And, when once the young heart of
   a maiden is stolen,
The maiden herself will steal after it
   soon.   THOMAS MOORE, *Ill Omens*

12321.
The rare and radiant maiden, whom
   the angels name Lenore—
Nameless here for evermore.
      POE, *The Raven*

12322.
Warn'd by the Sylph, O pious maid,
   beware!
This to disclose is all thy guardian
   can:
Beware of all, but most beware of
   man!   POPE,
      The Rape of the Lock

12323. And she who scorns a man
must die a maid.   POPE,
      The Rape of the Lock

12324. While the tall maid is stoop-
ing, the little one hath swept the
house.   *Proverb*

12325. When maidens sue, men live
like gods.   *Proverb*

12326. Maids want nothing but husbands, and when they have them,
they want every thing.   *Proverb*

12327. Do as the maids do, say no,
and take it.   *Proverb*

12328. Maidens should be mild and
meek, swift to hear and slow to
speak.   *Proverb*

12329. All are good maids, but
whence come the bad wives? *Proverb*

12330. Glasses and lasses are brittle
ware.   *Proverb*

12331. A maid that laughs is half
taken.   *Proverb*

12332. A maid that giveth yieldeth.
      Proverb

12333.
I am a simple maid, and therein
   wealthiest,
That I protest I simply am a maid.
     SHAKESPEARE,
      All's Well that Ends Well

12334. Be somewhat scanter of your maiden presence.

SHAKESPEARE, *Hamlet*

12335.
The chariest maid is prodigal enough,
If she unmask her beauty to the moon.　SHAKESPEARE, *Hamlet*

12336. A maid yet rosed over with the virgin crimson of modesty.

SHAKESPEARE, *Henry V*

12337.
Not all the dukes of waterish Burgundy
Can buy this unprized precious maid of me.　SHAKESPEARE, *King Lear*

12338.
She that's a maid now, and laughs at my departure,
Shall not be a maid long, unless things be cut shorter.

SHAKESPEARE, *King Lear*

12339. A maid of grace and complete majesty.　SHAKESPEARE,
Love's Labour's Lost

12340. An honest maid as ever broke bread.　SHAKESPEARE,
The Merry Wives of Windsor

12341.
A maiden never bold;
Of spirit so still and quiet, that her motion
Blush'd at itself.　SHAKESPEARE,
Othello

12342. Tell me, pretty maiden, are there any more at home like you?

LESLIE STUART,
*Tell Me, Pretty Maiden:
Refrain of the Floradora Sextette*

12343.
A simple maiden in her flower
Is worth a hundred coats-of-arms.

TENNYSON, *Lady Clara Vere de Vere*

12344.
Mother, a maiden is a tender thing
And best by her that bore her understood.　TENNYSON,
Idylls of the King

12345. Here by God's rood is the one maid for me.　TENNYSON,
Idylls of the King

12346. The sweetest garland to the sweetest maid.

THOMAS TICKELL,
To a Lady with a Present of Flowers

12347. Maidens withering on the stalk.　WORDSWORTH, *Personal Talk*

12348.
She dwelt among the untrodden ways
　Beside the springs of Dove,
A maid whom there were none to praise
And very few to love.

WORDSWORTH, *Lucy*

See also: 1946, 15398.

MAJORITY, MINORITY

Related Subjects: Democracy, Election, Politics.

Majority

12351. When great changes occur in history, when great principles are involved, as a rule the majority are wrong.　EUGENE V. DEBS

12352. No one can expect a majority to be stirred by motives other than ignoble.　NORMAN DOUGLAS,
South Wind

12353. The oppression of a majority is detestable and odious: the oppression of a minority is only by one degree less detestable and odious.

GLADSTONE

12354. Decision by majorities is as much an expedient as lighting by gas. GLADSTONE

12355. The most dangerous foe to truth and freedom in our midst is the compact majority. Yes, the damned, compact, liberal majority. IBSEN, *An Enemy of the People*

12356. One man with courage makes a majority. ANDREW JACKSON

12357. One on God's side is a majority. WENDELL PHILLIPS

12358. The fact disclosed by a survey of the past that majorities have been wrong must not blind us to the complementary fact that majorities have usually not been entirely wrong. HERBERT SPENCER, *First Principles*

12359. A majority, with a good cause, are negligent and supine. SWIFT

12360. Any man more right than his neighbors, constitutes a majority of one. THOREAU, *The Duty of Civil Disobedience*

Minority

12361. Government is everywhere to a great extent controlled by powerful minorities, with an interest distinct from that of the mass of the people. G. LOWES DICKINSON, *The Choice Before Us*

12362. Shall we judge a country by the majority, or by the minority? By the minority, surely. EMERSON, *Conduct of Life*

12363. All history is a record of the power of minorities, and of minorities of one. EMERSON, *Letters and Social Aims*

12364. What is a minority? The chosen heroes of this earth have been in a minority. There is not a social, political, or religious privilege that you enjoy to-day that was not bought for you by the blood and tears and patient suffering of the minority. It is the minority that have stood in the van of every moral conflict, and achieved all that is noble in the history of the world. J. B. GOUGH, *What Is a Minority*

12365.
Minority is no disproof:
Wisdom is not so strong and fleet
As never to have known defeat.
LAURENCE HOUSMAN, *Advocatus Diaboli*

12366. The minority is always in the right. IBSEN, *An Enemy of the People*

12367. Governments exist to protect the rights of minorities. The loved and the rich need no protection,—they have many friends and few enemies. WENDELL PHILLIPS

12368.
How a minority,
Reaching majority,
Seizing authority,
Hates a minority.
L. H. ROBBINS, *Minorities*

12369. A little group of willful men, representing no opinion but their own. WOODROW WILSON

See also: 156.

MALEVOLENCE, MALICE

Related Subjects: **Conspiracy, Evil, Hatred, Revenge, Slander, Villain, Wickedness.**

12371. Malice never spoke well. WILLIAM CAMDEN, *Remains*

12372. Malice hath a strong memory. THOMAS FULLER, *Pisgah Sight*

12373. The malicious have a dark happiness.　VICTOR HUGO, *Les Miserables*

12374. With malice toward none, with charity for all, with firmness in the right, as God gives us to see the right.　LINCOLN

12375. There is no rampart that will hold out against malice.
MOLIÈRE, *Tartuffe*

12376. Accusing is proving, where malice and force sit judges. *Proverb*

12377. Injury is to be measured by malice.　*Proverb*

12378. Malice drinketh its own poison.　*Proverb*

12379. Malice hath a sharp sight and a strong memory.　*Proverb*

12380. Malice seldom wants a mark to shoot at.　*Proverb*

12381.
Men that make
Envy and crooked malice nourishment,
Dare bite the best.
SHAKESPEARE, *Henry VIII*

12382.
Speak of me as I am; nothing extenuate,
Nor set down aught in malice.
SHAKESPEARE, *Othello*

12383. Wit larded with malice, and malice forced with wit.
SHAKESPEARE, *Troilus and Cressida*

12384. The malice of a good thing is the barb that makes it stick.
SHERIDAN, *The School for Scandal*

12385.
Yet malice never was his aim;
He lashed the vice, but spared the name.

No individual could resent,
Where thousands equally were meant.
SWIFT, *On the Death of Dr. Swift*

See also: 11830, 12301, 14673.

MAMMON

Related Subjects: Avarice, Gold, Money, Riches, World.

12391.
No man can serve two masters ...
Ye cannot serve God and Mammon.
Bible: Matthew, vi, 24

12392.
Pray'st thou for riches? Away, away!
This is the throne of Mammon grey.
BLAKE, *I Rose Up at the Dawn of Day*

12393.
Cursed Mammon be, when he with treasures
To restless action spurs our fate!
Cursed when for soft, indulgent leisures,
He lays for us the pillows straight.
GOETHE, *Faust*

12394.
Mammon led them on,
Mammon, the least erected spirit that fell
From heaven; for ev'n in heaven his looks and thoughts
Were always downward bent, admiring more
The riches of heaven's pavement, trodden gold,
Than aught divine or holy else enjoy'd
In vision beatific.　MILTON, *Paradise Lost*

12395.
Who sees pale Mammon pine amidst his store,
Sees but a backward steward for the poor.　POPE, *Moral Essays*

12396. Thou canst not serve God, unless thy mammon serve thee.

Proverb

MAN

Related Subjects: Evolution, The Sexes, Woman.

12401. The human, to use a euphuism, race has gone crazy. Millions of its members are engaged now in hating other millions and in trying to kill them. Now the human race has its good points; among its members, active, honorary, and life, we count some of our best friends. But if these things against humanity continue, we warn the House Committee that we shall send in our resignation, or at least, ask to be transferred to non-resident membership.

F. P. A.,
The Diary of Our Own Samuel Pepys

12402. Man is the merriest species of the creation; all above or below him are serious.   ADDISON

12403. Man is an animal and until his immediate material and economic needs are satisfied, he cannot develop further.   W. H. AUDEN, *I Believe*

12404. Men are born neither free nor good.   W. H. AUDEN, *I Believe*

12405.
Man is a military animal,
Glories in gunpowder, and loves parades.   PHILIP J. BAILEY, *Festus*

12406.
Then, my good girls, be more than women wise;
At least be more than I was; and be sure

You credit any thing the light gives life to,
Before a man.

BEAUMONT & FLETCHER,
The Maid's Tragedy

12407. Man that is born of a woman is of few days, and full of trouble.

Bible: Job, xiv, 1

12408. What is man, that thou art mindful of him? *Bible: Psalms, viii, 4*

12409. Thou hast made him a little lower than the angels.

Bible: Psalms, viii, 5

12410. As for man, his days are as grass: as a flower of the field, so he flourisheth.   *Bible: Psalms, ciii, 15*

12411. I am fearfully and wonderfully made. *Bible: Psalms, cxxxix, 14*

12412.
Of all the creatures that creep, swim, or fly,
Peopling the earth, the waters, and the sky,
From Rome to Iceland, Paris to Japan,
I really think the greatest fool is man.

BOILEAU, *Satires*

12413. Man is a noble animal, splendid in ashes and pompous in the grave.

SIR THOMAS BROWNE,
Urn-Burial

12414. Man has staggered and bled and reeled from hammer blows, but he hasn't been counted out as yet. Until the final ten has been tolled who dares to say that he is puny?

HEYWOOD BROUN,
In the Image of God

12415.
Here the free spirit of mankind, at length,
Throws its last fetters off; and who shall place

A limit to the giant's unchained strength,
Or curb his swiftness in the forward race? BRYANT, *The Ages*

12416. O poor mortals, how ye make this earth bitter for each other.
CARLYLE, *The French Revolution*

12417.
What is Man? A foolish baby,
  Vainly strives, and fights, and frets.
Demanding all, deserving nothing,
  One small grave is what he gets.
CARLYLE, *Qui Bono*

12418. Every man is as Heaven made him, and sometimes a great deal worse. CERVANTES, *Don Quixote*

12419. I thank God that my lot is bound up with that of the human race. W. E. CHANNING

12420.
Unless above himself he can
Erect himself, how poor a thing is man! SAMUEL DANIEL,
To the Countess of Cumberland

12421.
I know my life's a pain, and but a span;
I know my sense is mock'd in ev'ry thing:
And to conclude, I know myself a man,
Which is a proud, and yet a wretched thing. SIR JOHN DAVIES,
The Vanity of Human Learning

12422. Human beings themselves are wild animals when they are born— more helpless than other species, but by no means more tame. If they seem tamer it is only because they are brought up in that way. Don't you realize if you can tame boys you can tame almost anything? Wild horses from the range can be tamed quickly

in a few weeks, but it takes years of patience and effort to tame young human beings. CLARENCE DAY,
Animals in a Machine Age

12423. Plato having defined man to be a two-legged animal without feathers, Diogenes plucked a cock and brought it into the Academy, and said, "This is Plato's man." On which account this addition was made to the definition,—"With broad flat nails."
DIOGENES LAERTIUS, *Diogenes*

12424. Diogenes lighted a candle in the daytime, and went round saying, "I am looking for a man."
DIOGENES LAERTIUS, *Diogenes*

12425. Man derives a sense of his consequence in the world not merely subjectively, but objectively. If from the cradle through life the outside world brands a class unfit for this or that work, the character of the class will come to resemble and conform to the character described.
FREDERICK DOUGLASS, *Autobiography*

12426. Men are but children of a larger growth. DRYDEN,
All for Love

12427. This is the porcelain clay of humankind. DRYDEN, *Don Sebastian*

12428. A man is a bundle of relations, a knot of roots, whose flower and fruitage is the world.
EMERSON, *History*

12429.
The plain man is the basic clod
From which we grow the demigod;
And in the average man is curled
The hero stuff that rules the world.
SAM W. FOSS,
The Man from the Crowd

12430. A man is *so* in the way in the house. MRS. GASKELL, *Cranford*

12431. Man seems the only growth that dwindles here.

GOLDSMITH, *The Traveller*

12432. O wearisome condition of humanity!   GREVILLE

12433. Man is the only animal that laughs and weeps; for he is the only animal that is struck with the difference between what things are and what they ought to be.   HAZLITT

12434.
Though every prospect pleases,
  And only man is vile.

REGINALD HEBER, *Missionary Hymn*

12435. In the busy haunts of men.

MRS. HEMANS,
Tale of the Secret Tribunal

12436.
God give us men! A time like this demands
  Strong minds, great hearts, true faith, and ready hands;
Men whom the lust of office does not kill;
  Men whom the spoils of office cannot buy;
Men who possess opinions and a will;
  Men who have honor; men who will not lie;
Men who can stand before a demagogue
  And damn his treacherous flatteries without winking;
Tall men, sun-crowned, who live above the fog
  In public duty and in private thinking.   J. G. HOLLAND,
The Day's Demand

12437. The lot of man; to suffer and to die.   HOMER, *Odyssey*

12438. To aspire to be superhuman is a most discreditable admission that you lack the guts, the wit, the moderating judgment to be successfully and consummately human.

ALDOUS HUXLEY,
Do What You Will

12439. The complete human being is no longer a product of nature, he is an artificial product like corn, and fruit-trees, and the Creole race and thoroughbred horses and dogs, the vine, etc.   IBSEN, *Ghosts: Notes*

12440. It seems incredible that the universe can have been designed primarily to produce life like our own; had it been so, surely we might have expected to find a better proportion between the magnitude of the mechanism and the amount of the product. At first glance at least, life seems to be an utterly unimportant by-product; we living things are somehow off the main line.

SIR JAMES JEANS,
The Mysterious Universe

12441. Man must reconcile himself to the humble position of the inhabitant of a speck of dust, and adjust his views on the meaning of human life accordingly.   SIR JAMES JEANS,
The Mysterious Universe

12442. By learning the sufferings and burden of men, I became aware as never before of the life-power that has survived the forces of darkness—the power which, though never completely victorious, is continuously conquering. The very fact that we are still here carrying on the contest against the hosts of annihilation proves that on the whole the battle has gone for humanity.

HELEN KELLER

12443. Man proposes, but God disposes.   THOMAS À KEMPIS,
Of the Imitation of Christ

12444. If death for us and our kind is the inevitable result of our stubbornness then we can only say, "So be it." Ours is a lost cause and there is no place for us in the natural universe, but we are not, for all that, sorry to be human. We should rather die as men than live as animals.

J. W. KRUTCH, *Modern Temper*

12445. All through history men were the masters, women the inferiors. Now they are nearly equal—but men still have them licked.

SINCLAIR LEWIS

12446. Human nature will not change. In any future great national trial, compared with the men of this, we shall have as weak and as strong, as silly and as wise, as bad and as good.

LINCOLN

12447. Today more than ever—I feel we must not, however well-founded our doubts, be betrayed into mere cynicism and contempt for the human race. We must not—despite all the evidence of its fantastic vileness—forget its great and honorable traits, revealed in the shape of art, science, the quest for truth, the creation of beauty, the conception of justice.

THOMAS MANN, *I Believe*

12448. All love of humanity is bound up with the future.

THOMAS MANN, *I Believe*

12449. This Being of mine, whatever it really is, consists of a little flesh, a little breath, and the part which governs.

MARCUS AURELIUS, *Meditations*

12450. Bread, beauty and brotherhood are the three great needs of man.

EDWIN MARKHAM

12451. A man says to himself before he goes out, "What shall I say?" A

woman meditates, "What shall I wear?" METTERNICH

12452. After all there is but one race —humanity. GEORGE MOORE, *The Bending of the Bough*

12453. A grain of manhood.

MILTON, *Samson Agonistes*

12454.
Our days begin with trouble here,
   Our life is but a span,
And cruel death is always near,
   So frail a thing is man.
The New England Primer

12455. Man is a rope stretched between the animal and the Superman —a rope over an abyss.

NIETZSCHE, *Thus Spake Zarathustra*

12456. Man never falls so low that he can see nothing higher than himself. THEODORE PARKER, *A Lesson for the Day*

12457. Man is but a reed, the weakest in nature, but he is a thinking reed. PASCAL, *Thoughts*

12458. What a chimera, then, is man! what a novelty, what a monster, what a chaos, what a subject of contradiction, what a prodigy! A judge of all things, feeble worm of the earth, depositary of the truth, cloaca of uncertainty and error, the glory and the shame of the universe!

PASCAL, *Thoughts*

12459. No human thing is of serious importance. PLATO, *The Republic*

12460. The forgotten man at the bottom of the economic pyramid.

FRANKLIN D. ROOSEVELT

12461. It is a mighty good thing to know men, not from looking at them, but from having been one of them. When you have worked with them, when you have lived with them, you do not have to wonder how they feel, because you feel it yourself.

THEODORE ROOSEVELT

12462. A man is young if a lady can make him happy or unhappy. He enters middle age when a lady can make him happy, but can no longer make him unhappy. He is old and gone if a lady can make him neither happy nor unhappy.

MORITZ ROSENTHAL

12463. A man's truest monument must be a man.

M. J. SAVAGE, *The Song of a Man*

12464. Man individually and as a race is possible on earth only because, not for weeks or months but for years, love and the guardianship of the strong over the weak has existed.

OLIVE SCHREINER,
From Man to Man

12465.
He was a man, take him for all in all, I shall not look upon his like again.

SHAKESPEARE, *Hamlet*

12466. What a piece of work is a man! how noble in reason! how infinite in faculty! in form and moving how express and admirable! in action how like an angel! in apprehension how like a god!

SHAKESPEARE, *Hamlet*

12467. Man delights not me; no, nor woman neither.

SHAKESPEARE, *Hamlet*

12468.
His life was gentle, and the elements So mix'd in him that Nature might stand up
And say to all the world, "This was a man!"   SHAKESPEARE,
Julius Caesar

12469. As proper men as ever trod upon neat's leather.

SHAKESPEARE, *Julius Caesar*

12470.
But man, proud man,
Drest in a little brief authority,
Most ignorant of what he's most assured,
His glassy essence, like an angry ape,
Plays such fantastic tricks before high heaven
As make the angels weep.

SHAKESPEARE, *Measure for Measure*

12471.
There are a sort of men whose visages
Do cream and mantle like a standing pond.   SHAKESPEARE,
The Merchant of Venice

12472. When he is best, he is a little worse than a man; and when he is worst, he is little better than a beast.

SHAKESPEARE,
The Merchant of Venice

12473. God made him, and therefore let him pass for a man.

SHAKESPEARE,
The Merchant of Venice

12474. But men are men; the best sometimes forget.

SHAKESPEARE, *Othello*

12475. Men should be what they seem.   SHAKESPEARE, *Othello*

12476.
But I know that Man is still
An ape at heart,
A talkative, chattering ape.
His curiosity shall discover many strange secrets,
But he will use them solely
For his two recreations,
Lying and killing,

Or—as he calls them—
Conversation and sport.

> OSBERT SITWELL,
> *Subtlety of the Serpent*

12477.
To eate thy heart through comfort-
lesse dispaires,
To fawne, to crowche, to waite, to
ride, to ronne,
To spend, to give, to want, to be un-
donne.
Unhappie wight, born to disastrous
end,
That doth his life in so long tendance
spend.   EDMUND SPENSER,
> *Mother Hubberds Tale*

12478. Man is a social animal.
> SPINOZA, *Ethics*

12479. The Forgotten Man works and
votes—generally he prays—but his
chief business in life is to pay. . . .
Who and where is the Forgotten Man
in this case, who will have to pay for
it all?   W. G. SUMNER,
> *The Forgotten Man*

12480. I am a man; nothing human
is alien to me.   TERENCE

12481.
I am a parcel of vain strivings tied
  By a chance bond together.
> THOREAU, *Sic Vita*

12482. For some curious reason Man
has always assumed that his is the
highest form of life in the universe.
There is, of course, nothing at all
with which to sustain this view.
> JAMES THURBER, *I Believe*

12483. The lower animals cooperate
in the interest of the preservation of
the species. Man no longer has the
natural, earthy sense which would interest him in the preservation of the
species.   JAMES THURBER, *I Believe*

12484. Just now I am going through
one of those periods when I believe
that the black panther and the cedar
waxwing have a higher hope of
Heaven than Man has.
> JAMES THURBER, *I Believe*

12485.
The man that lays his hand upon a
  woman,
Save in the way of kindness, is a
  wretch
Whom 'twere gross flattery to name
  a coward.
> JOHN TOBIN, *The Honeymoon*

12486. All that I care to know is that
a man is a human being—that is
enough for me; he can't be any
worse.   MARK TWAIN

12487. I can imagine no better news
than to hear that there had emerged
from the South American forest or
the Australian desert specimens of a
new species which would, by reason
of some new organ or adaptation of
an organ, be able to dominate man as
man has dominated the other animals.
> REBECCA WEST, *I Believe*

12488.
Ah, how unjust to Nature and himself
Is thoughtless, thankless, inconsistent
  man!
> EDWARD YOUNG, *Night Thoughts*

12489. The more a man lives the life
of his generation, the more likely is
he to die when his generation passes
away. The more a man lives within
himself, is sufficient unto himself, so
much the more likely is his memory
to remain green.
> STEFAN ZWEIG,
> *Adepts in Self-Portraiture*

See also: 84, 237, 241, 455, 670, 684,
714, 733, 902, 1266, 1672, 1684, 1984,
1996, 2066, 2142, 2236, 2356, 2441,

2537, 3231, 3423, 4157, 6132, 6289, 10532, 17840.

MANNERS

Related Subjects: Act, Awkwardness, Behavior, Breeding, Courtesy, Conventionality, Custom, Deeds, Gentleman, Gentleness, Habit, Refinement.

12491. Manners must adorn knowledge, and smooth its way through the world. Like a great rough diamond, it may do very well in a closet by way of curiosity, and also for its intrinsic value.
LORD CHESTERFIELD, *Letters*

12492. There is always a best way of doing everything, if it be to boil an egg. Manners are the happy ways of doing things.
EMERSON, *Conduct of Life*

12493. Your manners are always under examination, and by committees little suspected,—a police in citizens' clothes,—but are awarding or denying you very high prizes when you least think of it.
EMERSON, *Conduct of Life*

12494. Fine manners need the support of fine manners in others.
EMERSON, *Conduct of Life*

12495. Manner, not gold, is woman's best adornment.   MENANDER

12496. Good laws often proceed from bad manners.   *Proverb*

12497.
Men's evil manners live in brass; their virtues
We write in water.
SHAKESPEARE, *Henry VIII*

12498. The great secret, Eliza, is not having bad manners or good manners or any other particular sort of manners, but having the same manner for all human souls: in short, behaving as if you were in Heaven, where there are no third-class carriages, and one soul is as good as another.
BERNARD SHAW, *Pygmalion*

12499.
The gentle minde by gentle deeds is knowne
For a man by nothing is so well bewrayed,
As by his manners.
EDMUND SPENSER,
The Faerie Queene

12500. They say fingers were made before forks, and hands before knives.   SWIFT, *Polite Conversation*

12501.
For manners are not idle, but the fruit
Of loyal nature and of noble mind.
TENNYSON, *Idylls of the King*

See also: 2972, 6942.

MARCH

Related Subject: Month.

12511.
The stormy March has come at last,
    With winds and clouds and changing skies;
I hear the rushing of the blast
    That through the snowy valley flies.   BRYANT, *March*

12512.
March winds and April showers
Bring forth May flowers.
F. T. ELWORTHY,
West Somersetshire Word-Book

12513. Like the month of March, in like a lion and out like a lamb.
ROGER NORTH, *Lives of the Norths*

12514.

Ah, March! we know thou art
Kind-hearted, 'spite of ugly looks and
    threats,
And, out of sight, art nursing April's
    violets!
    HELEN HUNT JACKSON, *March*

12515. Beware the ides of March.
    SHAKESPEARE, *Julius Caesar*

12516.

Up from the sea the wild north wind
    is blowing
  Under the sky's gray arch;
Smiling, I watch the shaken elm
    boughs, knowing
  It is the wind of March.
    WHITTIER, *March*

12517.

The braggart March stood in the sea-
    son's door
With his broad shoulders blocking up
    the way.
R. B. WILSON, *The Passing of March*

See also: 1085.

MARRIAGE

**Related Subjects: Bride, Court-
ship, Divorce, Family, Home, Husband, Love, Wedding, Widow,
Wife.**

12521. Marriage is that relation between man and woman in which the
independence is equal, the dependence
mutual and the obligation reciprocal.
    L. K. ANSPACHER

12522. What therefore God hath
joined together, let no man put
asunder.   *Bible: Matthew, xix, 6*

12523. *Marriage:* a community consisting of a master, a mistress, and
two slaves, making in all, two.
    AMBROSE BIERCE,
    The Devil's Dictionary

12524. Marriage and hanging go by
destiny; matches are made in heaven.
    ROBERT BURTON,
    Anatomy of Melancholy

12525.

Thus grief still treads upon the heels
of pleasure;
Married in haste, we may repent at
leisure.
    CONGREVE, *The Old Bachelor*

12526.

Misses! the tale that I relate
  This lesson seems to carry,—
Choose not alone a proper mate
  But proper time to marry.
    COWPER, *Pairing Time Anticipated*

12527.

Wedlock, indeed, hath oft compared
  been
To public feasts, where meet a public
  rout,—
Where they that are without would
  fain go in,
And they that are within would fain
  go out.   SIR JOHN DAVIES,
    Contention Betwixt a Wife

12528. The wictim o' connubiality.
    DICKENS, *Pickwick Papers*

12529. Being asked whether it was
better to marry or not, he [Socrates]
replied, "Whichever you do you will
repent it."
    DIOGENES LAERTIUS, *Socrates*

12530. Every woman should marry—
and no man.   DISRAELI, *Lothair*

12531. I may commit many follies in
life but I never intend to marry for
love.   DISRAELI

12532. The chain of wedlock is so
heavy that it takes two to carry it—
sometimes three.   DUMAS

12533. "Ye know a lot about marriage, but ye niver marrid," said Mr.
Hennessy.

"No," said Mr. Dooley, "No, say I, givin' three cheers, I know about marriage th' way an astronomer knows about th' stars."

F. P. Dunne, *Marriage*

12534. A single Man has not nearly the value he would have in the State of Union. He is an incomplete Animal. He resembles the odd half of a pair of scissors.   Franklin

12535. The awe and dread with which the untutored savage contemplates his mother-in-law are amongst the most familiar facts of anthropology.
Sir J. G. Frazer, *The Golden Bough*

12536. Deceive not thy self by over-expecting happiness in the married estate. Remember the nightingales which sing only some months in the spring, but commonly are silent when they have hatched their eggs.
Thomas Fuller,
Holy & Profane State

12537. They that marry ancient people, merely in expectation to bury them, hang themselves in hope that one will come and cut the halter.
Thomas Fuller,
Holy & Profane State

12538. In marriage, the greater cuckold of the two is the lover.
Paul Gauguin, *Intimate Journals*

12539. As a rule, marriage is the result of a mild preference, encouraged by circumstances, and deliberately heightened into strong sexual feeling. When it rises to the point of frenzy people may strictly be said to be in love.
George Gissing, *New Grub Street*

12540. The sum which two married people owe to one another defies calculation. It is an infinite debt, which can only be discharged through all eternity. Goethe, *Elective Affinities*

12541.
One pairing is as good as another
Where all is venture!
Thomas Hardy, *The Contretemps*

12542. Here's to matrimony, the high sea for which no compass has yet been invented.   Heine

12543. Marriage for external reasons, even when these are religious or moral, brings a Nemesis upon the offspring.   Ibsen, *Ghosts: Notes*

12544. Marriage is a thing you've got to give your whole mind to.
Ibsen, *The League of Youth*

12545. Were he not to marry again, it might be concluded that his first wife had given him a disgust to marriage; but by taking a second wife he pays the highest compliment to the first, by showing that she made him so happy as a married man, that he wishes to be so a second time.
Samuel Johnson, *Boswell: Life*

12546. Marriage has many pains, but celibacy has few pleasures.
Samuel Johnson

12547.
Pleasant the snaffle of Courtship, improving the manners and carriage;
But the colt who is wise will abstain from the terrible thorn-bit of Marriage.
Kipling, *Certain Maxims of Hafiz*

12548.
The married man must sink or swim
An'—'e can't afford to sink!
Kipling, *The Married Man*

12549. After marriage arrives a reaction, sometimes a big, sometimes a little, one; but it comes sooner or later, and must be tided over by both parties if they desire the rest of their lives to go with the current.

KIPLING, *Plain Tales*

12550. Nothing is to me more distasteful than that entire complacency and satisfaction which beam in the countenances of a new-married couple.   CHARLES LAMB, *The Behaviour of Married People*

12551.
Hail, wedded love, mysterious law, true source
Of human offspring.

MILTON, *Paradise Lost*

12552. He that marrieth for wealth sells his liberty.   *Proverb*

12553. Better be half hang'd, than ill wed.   *Proverb*

12554. More belongs to marriage than four bare legs in a bed.   *Proverb*

12555. Like blood, like good, and like age, make the happiest marriages.   *Proverb*

12556. Marriage, with peace, is the world's paradise; with strife, this life's purgatory.   *Proverb*

12557. Wedlock's a padlock. *Proverb*

12558. The married man must turn his staff into a stake.   *Proverb*

12559. It is a sad house where the hen crows louder than the cock. *Proverb*

12560. Be sure before you marry, of a house wherein to tarry.   *Proverb*

12561. An ill marriage is a spring of ill fortune.   *Proverb*

12562. When we are handfasted, as we term it, we are man and wife for a year and day; that space gone by, each may choose another mate, or, at their pleasure, may call the priest to marry them for life; and this we call handfasting.   SCOTT, *The Monastery*

12563. Marriage is a desperate thing.

JOHN SELDEN, *Table Talk*

12564. A young man married is a man that's marr'd.

SHAKESPEARE, *All's Well that Ends Well*

12565. Men are April when they woo, December when they wed: maids are May when they are maids, but the sky changes when they are wives.

SHAKESPEARE, *As You Like It*

12566.
For what is wedlock forced, but a hell,
An age of discord and continual strife?
Whereas the contrary bringeth bliss,
And is a pattern of celestial peace.

SHAKESPEARE, *Henry VI*

12567. Hasty marriage seldom proveth well.   SHAKESPEARE, *Henry VI*

12568. If there be no great love in the beginning, yet heaven may decrease it upon better acquaintance, when we are married and have more occasion to know one another; I hope, upon familiarity will grow more contempt.

SHAKESPEARE, *The Merry Wives of Windsor*

12569.
But earthlier happy is the rose distill'd
Than that which withering on the virgin thorn,
Grows, lives, and dies in single blessedness.   SHAKESPEARE, *A Midsummer-Night's Dream*

12570. Benedick the married man.

SHAKESPEARE, *Much Ado About Nothing*

12571. Shall quips and sentences and these paper bullets of the brain awe a

man from the career of his humour?
No; the world must be peopled.
When I said I would die a bachelor,
I did not think I should live till I
were married.   SHAKESPEARE,
Much Ado About Nothing

12572.

O curse of marriage!
That we can call these delicate crea-
            tures ours,
And not their appetites.
                    SHAKESPEARE, *Othello*

12573.
Let me not to the marriage of true
            minds
Admit impediments. Love is not love
Which alters when it alteration finds.
            SHAKESPEARE, *Sonnet CXVI*

12574. When two people are under
the influence of the most violent, most
insane, most delusive, and most transient of passions, they are required
to swear that they will remain in that
excited, abnormal, and exhausting
condition continuously until death do
them part.
    BERNARD SHAW, *Getting Married*

12575. You had no taste when you
married me.
    SHERIDAN, *The School for Scandal*

12576. Marriage resembles a pair of
shears, so joined that they can not be
separated; often moving in opposite
directions, yet always punishing anyone who comes between them.
            SYDNEY SMITH,
            Lady Holland's Memoir

12577.
Some pray to marry the man they
            love,
My prayer will somewhat vary:
I humbly pray to Heaven above
That I love the man I marry.
    ROSE P. STOKES, *My Prayer*

12578. Marriages are made in
Heaven. TENNYSON, *Aylmer's Field*

12579.

                    A mastiff dog
May love a puppy cur for no more
            reason
Than that the twain have been tied
            up together.
    TENNYSON, *Queen Mary*

12580. This I set down as a positive
truth. A woman with fair opportunities, and without an absolute hump,
may marry whom she likes.
            THACKERAY, *Vanity Fair*

12581. Remember, it's as easy to
marry a rich woman as a poor woman.
            THACKERAY, *Pendennis*

12582. How I do hate those words,
"an excellent marriage." In them is
contained more of wicked worldliness
than any other words one ever hears
spoken.   ANTHONY TROLLOPE,
    The Small House at Allington

12583. He is dreadfully married.
"He's the most married man I ever
saw in my life."
    ARTEMUS WARD, *Moses, the Sassy*

12584. When a woman marries again
it is because she detested her first husband. When a man marries again, it
is because he adored his first wife.
Women try their luck; men risk
theirs.   OSCAR WILDE,
    The Picture of Dorian Gray

See also: 404, 459, 1712, 3241, 4159,
4733, 4944, 4945, 5618, 17942.

MARTYR AND MARTYRDOM

**Related Subjects: Belief, Chris-
tianity, Courage, Endurance, Faith,
Fidelity, Glory, Hero, Sacrifice,
Saint, Suffering, Trials.**

12591. Men reject their prophets and
slay them, but they love their mar-

tyrs and honour those whom they have slain.   DOSTOYEVSKY,
The Brothers Karamazov

12592. All have not the gift of martyrdom.   DRYDEN,
The Hind and the Panther

12593. We have not all strength for martyrdom and I fear that if trouble comes I shall act like Peter.
ERASMUS

12594. The blood of the martyrs is the seed of the church.   ST. JEROME

12595. Play the man, Master Ridley; we shall this day light such a candle, by God's grace, in England, as I trust shall never be put out.
HUGH LATIMER, *At the Stake*

12596. The commandments have made as many good martyrs as the creed.   *Proverb*

12597. Like a pale martyr in his shirt of fire.
ALEXANDER SMITH, *A Life Drama*

12598. It is computed, that eleven thousand persons have, at several times, suffered death, rather than submit to break their eggs at the smaller end.   SWIFT, *Gulliver's Travels*

See also: 2922, 2923, 3323, 3324, 4899, 10250.

MASS PRODUCTION

Related Subjects: Industry, Machinery.

12601. The tremendous national machine of American economy must be fed by mass-orders, which depend in turn upon mass-prosperity, and, to a very much greater degree than in even a European democracy, upon free speech and good spirits.
MIRIAM BEARD,
History of the Business Man

12602. Mass production depends on the attenuation of overhead charges and, above all; upon the prevalence of low and even prices of raw material and mechanical power—that is to say, on the cheapness of original values.   VISCOUNT BURNHAM

12603. The changes to mass production and mass distribution can be made most rapidly through big advertising. The great profits of mass production and mass distribution will go almost wholly to big advertisers and big advertising.   E. A. FILENE

MASTER

Related Subjects: Authority, Leader, Servant, Slavery, Teacher.

12611. The measure of a master is his success in bringing all men round to his opinion twenty years later.
EMERSON, *Conduct of Life*

12612. The eye of a master will do more work than both his hands.
FRANKLIN, *Poor Richard*

12613. The man who gives me employment, which I must have or suffer, that man is my master, let me call him what I will.
HENRY GEORGE, *Social Problems*

12614.
O masters, lords and rulers in all lands,
Is this the handiwork you give to God?   EDWIN MARKHAM,
The Man With the Hoe

12615. No man is good enough to be another man's master.
WILLIAM MORRIS

12616. He that is a master must serve.   *Proverb*

12617. The master absent and the house dead.   *Proverb*

12618. Masters should be sometimes blind and sometimes deaf. *Proverb*

12619. He that is master of himself will soon be master of others.

Proverb

12620. Better a master be feared than despised. *Proverb*

12621.
Most potent, grave, and reverend signiors,
My very noble and approv'd good masters. Shakespeare, *Othello*

12622.
We cannot all be masters, nor all masters
Cannot be truly followed.
Shakespeare, *Othello*

12623.
He is master and lord of his brothers
Who is worthier and wiser than they.
Swinburne,
A Word for the Country

See also: 3009, 4501, 4529, 5429, 12391.

MATHEMATICS

Related Subjects: Learning, Numbers, Science.

12631. The mathematician has reached the highest rung on the ladder of human thought.
Havelock Ellis, *The Dance of Life*

12632. Mathematics is the science which uses easy words for hard ideas.
Kasner & Newman,
Mathematics & the Imagination

12633. When the Greek philosophers found that the square root of 2 is not a rational number, they celebrated the discovery by sacrificing 100 oxen.
Kasner & Newman,
Mathematics & the Imagination

12634. Ultimately mathematics reaches pinnacles as high as those attained by the imagination in its most daring reconnoiters.
Kasner & Newman,
Mathematics & the Imagination

12635. Geometry is the purest realization of human reason; but Euclid's axioms cannot be proved. He who does not believe in them sees the whole building crash.
Arthur Koestler,
Darkness at Noon

12636. O King, for traveling over the country there are both royal roads and roads for common citizens; but in geometry there is one road for all.
Menaechmus, *to Alexander*

12637. I have hardly ever known a mathematician who was capable of reasoning. Plato, *The Republic*

12638. Mathematics possesses not only truth, but supreme beauty—a beauty cold and austere, like that of sculpture, without appeal to any part of our weaker nature, sublimely pure, and capable of a stern perfection such as only the greatest art can show. Bertrand Russell,
The Study of Mathematics

12639. In pure mathematics the maximum of detachment appears to be reached: the mind moves in an infinitely complicated pattern, which is absolutely free from temporal considerations. Yet this very freedom—the essential condition of the mathematician's activity—perhaps gives him an unfair advantage. He can only be wrong—he cannot cheat.
Lytton Strachey,
Portraits in Miniature

12640. Let us grant that the pursuit of mathematics is a divine madness of the human spirit, a refuge from the goading urgency of contingent happenings.

ALFRED NORTH WHITEHEAD,
Science and the Modern World

See also: 3565, 12884.

MAY

Related Subjects: Month, Spring.

12641.
As it fell upon a day
In the merry month of May,
Sitting in a pleasant shade
Which a grove of myrtles made.
RICHARD BARNFIELD,
Address to the Nightingales

12642.
Which May had painted with his softe showers
This garden full of leaves and of flowers.
CHAUCER, *Canterbury Tales*

12643.
Hard is his herte that loveth nought in May.
CHAUCER, *The Romaunt of the Rose*

12644. What potent blood hath modest May!   EMERSON, *May-Day*

12645. There was no month but May.
GEORGE HERBERT, *Affliction*

12646. Oh! that we two were Maying.   CHARLES KINGSLEY,
The Saint's Tragedy

12647. The hawthorne-scented dusks of May.
DON MARQUIS, *An Open Fire*

12648. As tall as a May-pole.
Proverb

12649. Be sure of hay till the end of May.   *Proverb*

12650. A May flood never did good.
Proverb

12651.
No doubt they rose up early to observe
The rite of May.
SHAKESPEARE,
A Midsummer-Night's Dream

12652.
When May, with cowslip-braided locks,
Walks through the land in green attire.
BAYARD TAYLOR, *The Lost May*

12653.
God ripes the wines and corn, I say,
And wenches for the marriage-day,
And boys to teach love's comely play.
By Goddes fay, by Goddes fay!
It is the month, the jolly month,
It is the jolly month of May.
FRANCIS THOMPSON, *A May Burden*

See also: 1087, 1787, 4593.

MEAT

Related Subjects: Bread, Butcher, Drink, Food, Salt.

12661. Strong meat belongeth to them that are of full age.
Bible: Hebrews, v, 14

12662.
When mighty roast beef was the Englishman's food
It ennobled our hearts and enriched our blood.
Our soldiers were brave and our courtiers were good.
Oh! the roast beef of England,
And Old England's roast beef.
FIELDING,
The Roast Beef of Old England

12663. Meat eaten without either mirth or music is ill of digestion.
SCOTT, *The Monastery*

12664. I wished your venison better; it was ill kill'd.
SHAKESPEARE,
The Merry Wives of Windsor

12665. I am a great eater of beef, and I believe that does harm to my wit.   SHAKESPEARE, *Twelfth Night*

See also: 1037, 6329.

MEDDLER

Related Subjects: Curiosity, Scandal, Spying.

12671. Thus everybody meddled with what they had nothing to do.
MRS. APHRA BEHN, *The Fair Jilt*

12672. Every fool will be meddling.
Bible: Proverbs, xx, 3

12673. I never thrust my nose into other men's porridge. It is no bread and butter of mine.
CERVANTES, *Don Quixote*

12674. Meddle with what you have to do.   JOHN CLARKE

12675. Meddling with another man's folly is always thankless work.
KIPLING, *Plain Tales*

12676. Be not busybodies: meddle not with other folks' matters but when in conscience and duty prest; for it procures troubles and ill-manners, and is very unseemly to wise men.
WILLIAM PENN,
Letters to His Wife & Child

12677. Busy-bodies never want a bad day.   *Proverb*

12678. Never thrust your own sickle into another's corn.
PUBLILIUS SYRUS, *Sententiae*

12679. Thou find'st to be too busy is some danger. SHAKESPEARE, *Hamlet*

12680. For my part, I'll not meddle.
SHAKESPEARE, *Troilus and Cressida*

See also: 2619.

MEDICINE

Related Subjects: Disease, Doctors, Health, Hospitals, Sickness.

12681. Physick, for the most part, is nothing else but the substitute of exercise or temperance.
ADDISON, *The Spectator*

12682. The remedy is worse than the disease.   BACON, *Of Seditions*

12683. Medicine, the only profession that labours incessantly to destroy the reason for its own existence.
LORD BRYCE

12684. Desperate cures must be to desperate ills applied.
DRYDEN, *The Hind & the Panther*

12685. Healing is a matter of time, but it is sometimes also a matter of opportunity. HIPPOCRATES, *Precepts*

12686. Life is short and the art long.
HIPPOCRATES, *Aphorisms*

12687. I firmly believe that if the whole *materia medica* as now used could be sunk to the bottom of the sea, it would be all the better for mankind—and all the worse for the fishes.   O. W. HOLMES

12688. To live by medicine is to live horribly. LINNAEUS, *Diaeta Naturalis*

12689. Do I believe in medicine alone? No, never. In science alone? No, never. It seems to me childish and ridiculous to suppose one can be cured like a cow if one is not a cow.
KATHERINE MANSFIELD, *Journals*

12690. Nearly all men die of their remedies, and not of their illnesses.
MOLIÈRE, *Le Malade Imaginaire*

12691. Medical science today is infantile, only half explored, and of all the sicknesses the curable are few and to find more cures for others we must depend on the progress of pathology and the responsibility on us pathologists is great and we ought not to waste a single day.

NOGUCHI, *Eckstein: Noguchi*

12692. The desire to take medicine is perhaps the greatest feature which distinguishes man from animals.

SIR WILLIAM OSLER,
Life of Sir William Osler

12693. Medicine, to produce health, has to examine disease, and music, to create harmony, must investigate discord.   PLUTARCH, *Lives*

12694. Take a hair of the same dog that bit you.   *Proverb*

12695. I was well, would be better, took physic, and died.   *Proverb*

12696. If physic do not work, prepare for the kirk.   *Proverb*

12697. Bitter pills may have wholesome effects.   *Proverb*

12698. Better use medicines at the outset than at the last moment.

PUBLILIUS SYRUS, *Sententiae*

12699.
By medicine life may be prolong'd,
      yet death
Will seize the doctor too.

SHAKESPEARE, *Cymbeline*

See also: 1756, 1837, 3223, 7955, 12150, 15443, 16427.

MEDIOCRITY

Related Subjects: Indifference, Inferiority.

12701. Mediocrity is safest.
NICHOLAS BACON

12702. Commonplace and cringing, one gets everywhere.

BEAUMARCHAIS,
The Barber of Seville

12703. The universal subjugator, the commonplace.   GOETHE

12704. Mediocre minds generally condemn everything which passes their understanding.

LA ROCHEFOUCAULD, *Maxims*

12705.
For where is he that, knowing the
      height
And depth of ascertain'd delight,
Inhumanly henceforward lies
Content with mediocrities!

COVENTRY PATMORE,
The Victories of Love

12706. Mediocrity is praised in all cases.   RABELAIS

12707. "So so" is good, very good, very excellent good; and yet it is not; it is but so so.

SHAKESPEARE, *As You Like It*

12708. I do now remember the poor creature, small beer.

SHAKESPEARE, *Henry IV*

12709. A fellow of no mark nor likelihood. SHAKESPEARE, *Henry IV*

See also: 488, 1074, 1261, 2350, 7882, 8852.

MEDITATION

Related Subjects: Contemplation, Reflection, Reverie, Solitude, Thought.

12711. Let the words of my mouth, and the meditation of my heart, be acceptable in thy sight.

Bible: Psalms, xix, 14

12712. Meditation may think down hours to moments. The heart may give most useful lessons to the head, and learning wiser grow without his books.   COWPER

12713. Meditation is the soul's perspective glass, whereby, in her long removes, she discerneth God, as if he were nearer at hand.
          OWEN FELTHAM

12714. It is easier to walk six miles to hear a sermon, than to spend one quarter of an hour in meditating on it when I come home. PHILIP HENRY

12715. He that can read and meditate, will not find his evenings long, or life tedious.   *Proverb*

12716. Meditation is the life of the soul; action is the soul of meditation; honor is the reward of action: so meditate, that thou mayst do; so do, that thou mayst purchase honor; for which purchase, give God the glory.
          FRANCIS QUARLES

12717. Reading and conversation may furnish us with many ideas of men and things, yet it is our own meditation that must form our judgment.   ISAAC WATTS

12718. 'Tis greatly wise to talk with our past hours and ask them what report they bore to heaven, and how they might have borne more welcome news.   EDWARD YOUNG

See also: 4181.

MEEKNESS

Related Subjects: Humility, Submission, Timidity.

12721.
          Keep quiet by the fire
And never say "no" when the world
    says "ay."
          ELIZABETH B. BROWNING,
                    Aurora Leigh

12722.
Wisdom has taught us to be calm
    and meek,
To take one blow, and turn the other
    cheek.   O. W. HOLMES,
                    Non-Resistance

12723. It's goin' t' be fun t' watch an' see how long th' meek kin keep the earth after they inherit it.
          KIN HUBBARD

12724. Meekness is not weakness.
                    Proverb

12725. They can be meek that have no other cause.   SHAKESPEARE,
                    Richard III

See also: 13452.

MEETING

Related Subjects: Church, Club, Union, Worship.

12731.
If e'er we meet hereafter, we shall
    meet
In happier climes, and on a safer
    shore.   ADDISON, *Cato*

12732.
Like driftwood spars which meet and
    pass
    Upon the boundless ocean-plain,
So on the sea of life, alas!
    Man nears man, meets, and leaves
        again. MATTHEW ARNOLD,
                    The Terrace at Berne

12733. Why meet on the bridge of Time to 'change one greeting and to part?   RICHARD BURTON,
                    The Kasidah

12734. Between cultivated minds the first interview is the best.
                    EMERSON

12735.
Ships that pass in the night, and speak each other in passing,

Only a signal shown and a distant
  voice in the darkness;
So on the ocean of life we pass and
  speak one another,
Only a look and a voice; then darkness again and a silence.
                    LONGFELLOW,
              Tales of a Wayside Inn

12736. The joy of meeting not unmixed with pain. LONGFELLOW,
                Morituri Salutamus

12737.
In life there are meetings which seem
Like a fate. OWEN MEREDITH,
                              Lucile

12738.
Some day, some day of days, thread-
    ing the street
  With idle, heedless pace,
  Unlooking for such grace,
  I shall behold your face!
Some day, some day of days, thus
  may we meet. NORA PERRY,
                  Some Day of Days

12739.
The joys of meeting pay the pangs of
  absence;
Else who could bear it?
        NICHOLAS ROWE, *Tamerlane*

12740.
The meeting of these champions
  proud
Seemed like the bursting thunder-
  cloud.   SCOTT,
          The Lay of the Last Minstrel

12741.
1 Witch. When shall we three meet
      again
    In thunder, lightning, or in rain?
2 Witch. When the hurlyburly's done,
    When the battle's lost and won.
            SHAKESPEARE, *Macbeth*

12742. Hail fellow, well met.
      SWIFT, *My Lady's Lamentation*

See also: 31, 139, 3218.

MELANCHOLY

**Related Subjects: Depression, De-
spondency, Pessimism, Sigh, Sorrow.**

12751. That which Pythagoras said
to his scholars of old, may be for
ever applied to melancholy men, eat
no beans.   ROBERT BURTON,
                Anatomy of Melancholy

12752. Naught so sweet as melancholy.   ROBERT BURTON,
                Anatomy of Melancholy

12753. The   chronic   melancholy
which is taking hold of the civilized
races with the decline of belief in a
beneficent power.
                    THOMAS HARDY,
              Tess of the D'Urbervilles

12754.
There's not a string attuned to mirth
But has its chord in melancholy.
    THOMAS HOOD, *Ode to Melancholy*

12755.
Ay, in the very temple of Delight
Veil'd Melancholy has her sovran
  shrine. KEATS, *Ode on Melancholy*

12756. My mind is gay but my soul
is melancholy.   ANDREW LANG

12757.
    Moping melancholy,
And moon-struck madness.
        MILTON, *Paradise Lost*

12758.
Hence, loathéd Melancholy,
Of Cerberus and blackest midnight
  born.   MILTON, *L'Allegro*

12759. It is a melancholy of mine
own, compounded of many simples,
extracted from many objects, and indeed the sundry contemplation of my
travels, in which my often rumina-

tion wraps me in a most humorous sadness.   SHAKESPEARE,
As You Like It

12760. He is of a very melancholy disposition.   SHAKESPEARE,
Much Ado About Nothing

12761. Never give way to melancholy; resist it steadily, for the habit will encroach.   SYDNEY SMITH,
Lady Holland's Memoir

See also: 319, 1443, 3226, 20533, 21453.

MELODY

Related Subjects: Harmony, Music, Sing, Song.

12771.
Heard melodies are sweet, but those unheard
  Are sweeter.   KEATS,
Ode on a Grecian Urn

12772. The song is ended, but the melody lingers on.   *Popular song*

See also: 6029.

MEMORY

Related Subjects: Absence, Forgetfulness, History, Monument, Neglect, Oblivion, Past, Reflection, Time, Yesterday.

12781.
Friends depart, and memory takes them
  To her caverns, pure and deep.
      T. H. BAYLY,
Teach Me to Forget

12782. Memory, no less than hope, owes its charm to "the far away."
BULWER-LYTTON, *A Lament*

12783.
While Memory watches o'er the sad review

Of joys that faded like the morning dew.   THOMAS CAMPBELL,
Pleasures of Hope

12784.
To live in hearts we leave behind.
Is not to die.
    THOMAS CAMPBELL,
Hallowed Ground

12785. My memory is so bad, that many times I forget my own name!
CERVANTES, *Don Quixote*

12786.
A man should choose with careful eye
The things to be remembered by.
    ROBERT P. T. COFFIN,
The Weather Vane

12787. In plucking the fruit of memory one runs the risk of spoiling its bloom.   JOSEPH CONRAD,
The Arrow of Gold

12788. It is notorious that the memory strengthens as you lay burdens upon it, and becomes trustworthy as you trust it.   DE QUINCEY,
Confessions of an English Opium-Eater

12789. O Memory! thou fond deceiver.   GOLDSMITH, *The Captivity*

12790.
A place in thy memory, dearest,
  Is all that I claim;
To pause and look back when thou hearest
The sound of my name.
    GERALD GRIFFIN,
A Place in Thy Memory

12791.
I remember, I remember
The house where I was born,
The little window where the sun
Came peeping in at morn;

He never came a wink too soon
Nor brought too long a day.
                    THOMAS HOOD,
        I Remember, I Remember

12792.
Tho' lost to sight, to memory dear
    Thou ever wilt remain;
One only hope my heart can cheer,—
    The hope to meet again.
                    GEORGE LINLEY, *Song*

12793.
Oft in the stilly night,
    Ere slumber's chain has bound me,
Fond memory brings the light
    Of other days around me;
        The smiles, the tears,
        Of boyhood's years,
The words of love then spoken;
        The eyes that shone
        Now dimmed and gone,
The cheerful hearts now broken.
                    THOMAS MOORE,
            Oft in the Stilly Night

12794. The proper memory for a politician is one that knows what to remember and what to forget.
            JOHN MORLEY, *Recollections*

12795. A great memory does not make a philosopher, any more than a dictionary can be called a grammar.
                    CARDINAL NEWMAN,
            The Idea of a University

12796.
Remembrance and reflection how allied!
What thin partitions sense from
    thought divide!   POPE,
                    Essay on Man

12797. Memory is the treasurer of the mind.   *Proverb*

12798. Memory tempers prosperity, mitigates adversity, controls youth, and delights old age.   *Proverb*

12799.
Sweet Memory! wafted by thy gentle
    gale,
Oft up the stream of Time I turn
    my sail.   SAMUEL ROGERS,
            The Pleasures of Memory

12800. Still are the thoughts to memory dear.   SCOTT, *Rokeby*

12801.
When, musing on companions gone,
We doubly feel ourselves alone.
                    SCOTT, *Marmion*

12802. The memory be green.
                    SHAKESPEARE, *Hamlet*

12803.
    While memory holds a seat
In this distracted globe. Remember
    thee!
Yea, from the table of my memory
I'll wipe away all trivial fond records.
                    SHAKESPEARE, *Hamlet*

12804. I'll note you in my book of memory.   SHAKESPEARE, *Henry VI*

12805. Memory, the warder of the brain.   SHAKESPEARE, *Macbeth*

12806.
When to the sessions of sweet silent
    thought
I summon up remembrance of things
    past,
I sigh the lack of many a thing I
    sought,
And with old woes new wail my dear
    times' waste.   SHAKESPEARE,
                    Sonnet XXX

12807. The Right Honorable gentleman is indebted to his memory for his jests, and to his imagination for his facts.   SHERIDAN

12808. A man's real possession is his memory. In nothing else is he rich, in nothing else is he poor.
            ALEXANDER SMITH, *Dreamthorp*

12809.
    Some mindfulness
A man should surely keep, of any
    thing
That pleased him once.
SOPHOCLES, Ajax

12810. Memory is the diary that we
all carry about with us.
OSCAR WILDE,
The Importance of Being Earnest

12811.
How dear to this heart are the scenes
    of my childhood,
When fond recollection presents
    them to view.
SAMUEL WOODWORTH,
The Old Oaken Bucket

See also: 41, 133, 146, 468, 496, 518,
1342, 1903, 1991, 4528, 11144,
11726, 12051, 12120, 14252, 16494,
19364, 20467.

MERCY

Related Subjects: **Compassion,
Forgiveness, Justice, Kindness,
Leniency, Pity.**

12821.
For Mercy, Courage, Kindness,
    Mirth,
    There is no measure upon earth;
Nay, they wither, root and stem,
    If an end be set to them.
LAURENCE BINYON, A Song

12822. Mercy is for the merciful.
BYRON

12823. We hand folks over to God's
mercy, and show none ourselves.
GEORGE ELIOT

12824.
Cowards are cruel, but the brave
Love mercy and delight to save.
JOHN GAY, Fables

12825. And shut the gates of mercy
on mankind.   THOMAS GRAY,
Elegy Written in a Coun-
try Church-Yard

12826.
Mercy the wise Athenians held to be
Not an affection, but a Deity.
ROBERT HERRICK, Mercy

12827.
Teach me to feel another's woe,
    To hide the fault I see;
That mercy I to others show,
    That mercy show to me. POPE,
The Universal Prayer

12828.
No ceremony that to great ones
    'longs,
Not the king's crown, nor the dis-
    put'd sword,
The marshal's truncheon, nor the
    judge's robe,
Become them with one half so good
    a grace
As mercy does.
SHAKESPEARE, Measure for Measure

12829.
The quality of mercy is not strain'd,
It droppeth as the gentle rain from
    heaven
Upon the place beneath. It is twice
    bless'd:
It blesseth him that gives and him
    that takes.
'Tis mightiest in the mightiest: it be-
    comes
The throned monarch better than his
    crown;
His sceptre shows the force of tem-
    poral power,
The attribute to awe and majesty,
Wherein doth sit the dread and fear
    of kings;
But mercy is above this sceptred
    sway,
It is enthroned in the hearts of kings,
It is an attribute to God himself;

And earthly power doth then show
  likest God's
When mercy seasons justice. Therefore, Jew,
Though justice be thy plea, consider
  this,
That in the course of justice, none of
  us should see salvation: we do
  pray for mercy;
And that same prayer doth teach us
  all to render
The deeds of mercy.
                SHAKESPEARE,
          The Merchant of Venice

12830.
Wilt thou draw near the nature of
  the gods?
Draw near them then in being merci-
  ful:
Sweet mercy is nobility's true badge.
    SHAKESPEARE, *Titus Andronicus*

12831.
Brother, you have a vice of mercy
  in you,
Which better fits a lion than a man.
SHAKESPEARE, *Troilus and Cressida*

See also: 3124, 8127, 9048, 10975,
19731.

MERIT

Related Subjects: Deserving, Excellence, H o n e s t y , Qualities,
Worth.

12841. Merit is worthier than fame.
                        BACON

12842. Merit and good-breeding will
make their way everywhere.
      LORD CHESTERFIELD, *Letters*

12843.
The little merit man can plead
In doing well, dependeth still
Upon his power of doing ill.
    CHARLES CHURCHILL, *The Ghost*

12844.
No farther seek his merits to disclose.
  Or draw his frailties from their
    dread abode,
(There they alike in trembling hope
    repose)
  The bosom of his Father and his
    God.   THOMAS GRAY,
          *Elegy Written in a Coun-
                try Church-Yard*

12845. Man's chief merit consists in
resisting the impulses of his nature.
    SAMUEL JOHNSON, *Miscellanies*

12846.
What merit to be dropped on for-
  tune's hill?
The honour is to mount it!
    J. S. KNOWLES, *The Hunchback*

12847. The world more often rewards the appearance of merit than
merit itself.
    LA ROCHEFOUCAULD, *Maxims*

12848. Charms strike the sight, but
merit wins the soul.   POPE,
          The Rape of the Lock

12849. O, if men were to be saved
by merit, what hole in hell were hot
enough for him? SHAKESPEARE,
                        Henry IV

12850. The force of his own merit
makes his way. SHAKESPEARE,
                        Henry VIII

See also: 792, 1045, 4214, 13657.

MERRIMENT

Related Subjects: Amusement,
Conviviality, Dancing, Delight,
Fun, Humor, Jazz, Joke, Joy,
Laughter, Pleasure.

12851. Mirth is like a flash of
lightning, that breaks through a
gloom of clouds, and glitters for a
moment; cheerfulness keeps up a

kind of daylight in the mind, and fills it with a steady and perpetual serenity.   ADDISON, *The Spectator*

12852. A merry heart doeth good like a medicine. *Bible: Proverbs, xvii, 22*

12853. There are times when the mirth of others only saddens us, especially the mirth of children with high spirits, that jar on our own quiet mood.   BULWER-LYTTON,
Kenelm Chillingly

12854. Vex'd with mirth the drowsy ear of night.   BYRON,
Childe Harold

12855.
A very merry, dancing, drinking,
Laughing, quaffing, and unthinking
    time.   DRYDEN,
The Secular Masque

12856. There'll be a hot time in the old town to-night.
JOSEPH HAYDEN,
A Hot Time in the Old Town

12857.
And more than wisdom, more than wealth,—
A merry heart that laughs at care.
H. H. MILMAN, *The Merry Heart*

12858.
Haste thee, Nymph, and bring with thee
Jest, and youthful Jollity,
Quips and Cranks and wanton Wiles,
Nods and Becks and wreathed Smiles.   MILTON, *L'Allegro*

12859.
Far from all resort of mirth,
Save the cricket on the hearth.
MILTON, *Il Penseroso*

12860. Be always as merry as you can, for no one delights in a sorrowful man.   *Proverb*

12861. As merry as a cricket.
Proverb

12862.
Where lives the man that has not tried
How mirth can into folly glide,
    And folly into sin!   SCOTT,
The Bridal of Triermain

12863.
                'Tis ever common
That men are merriest when they are from home.   SHAKESPEARE,
Henry V

12864.
    A merrier man,
Within the limit of becoming mirth,
I never spent an hour's talk withal.
SHAKESPEARE, *Love's Labour's Lost*

12865. As merry as the day is long.
SHAKESPEARE,
Much Ado About Nothing

12866. From the crown of his head to the sole of his foot, he is all mirth.
SHAKESPEARE,
Much Ado About Nothing

12867.
How oft when men are at the point of death
Have they been merry.
SHAKESPEARE, *Romeo and Juliet*

See also: 2935, 12402.

METAPHYSICS

Related Subjects: Astrology, Intelligence, Philosophy, Sophistry.

12871. Metaphysicians are whetstones, on which to sharpen dull intellects.   H. W. BEECHER

12872. Metaphysics is the anatomy of the soul.   BOUFFLERS

12873. The metaphysical aim is to rectify our fundamental ideas so as

to make them consistent with themselves and adequate to their function.
B. P. Bowne, *Metaphysics*

12874. Metaphysicians are apt to think, with Schelling, that philosophy is not everybody's affair; and if others find their writings useless or superfluous, they reply, with Fichte, that such persons do not belong to those for whom they wrote.
B. P. Bowne, *Metaphysics*

12875. There is an immanent metaphysics in all thinking and in all science. Physics is founded on metaphysics. Its basal ideas are not given in experience, but are metaphysical notions whereby we seek to interpret experience.   B. P. Bowne,
Metaphysics

12876. Metaphysicians can unsettle things, but they can erect nothing. They can pull down a church, but they cannot build a hovel.
Richard Cecil

12877. Logic and metaphysics make use of more tools than all the rest of the sciences put together, and they do the least work.   C. C. Colton

12878. Metaphysicians have been learning their lesson for the last four thousand years; and it is now high time that they should begin to teach us something. Can any of the tribe inform us why all the operations of the mind are carried on with undiminished strength and activity in dreams, except the judgment, which alone is suspended and dormant?
C. C. Colton

12879. The metaphysician is not justified in leaving the subjects of the Universe and Life just as they are in this present world; he is to enquire into the possibility of a further interpretation.
W. Tudor Jones,
Metaphysics of Life & Death

12880. Metaphysics simply means, on the scientific level, the science of general principles or concepts which have been brought into existence by objects perceived in the external world being seen in the form of mental relations.
W. Tudor Jones,
Metaphysics of Life & Death

12881. The individual who looks beyond the events to the causes that have brought the events into existence, and reads those causes in the light of the events, will obtain a Metaphysic of Nature—a Metaphysic which is an all-important adjunct to a Metaphysic of Life, and which in reality is an actual part of the Metaphysic of Life itself.
W. Tudor Jones,
Metaphysics of Life & Death

12882. Logic   works;   metaphysics contemplates.   Joubert, *Pensées*

12883. Metaphysics is the art of bewildering oneself methodically.
Michelet

12884. Algebra is the metaphysics of arithmetic.   Sterne

12885. When he that speaks, and he to whom he speaks, neither of them understand what is meant, that is metaphysics.   Voltaire

See also: 3345.

METHOD

Related Subjects: **Fashion, Order, Plan, System.**

12891.
There is a method in man's wickedness,—

It grows up by degrees.
> BEAUMONT & FLETCHER,
> *A King and No King*

12892. The methods by which a people forces its way upward are of no moment. Only the goal is important.
> GOEBBELS,
> *John Gunther: Inside Europe*

12893.
There are nine and sixty ways of constructing tribal lays,
    And every single one of them is
    right.   KIPLING,
> *In the Neolithic Age*

12894. Though this be madness, yet there is method in 't.
> SHAKESPEARE, *Hamlet*

12895. Method is good in all things.
> SWIFT, *Letters*

See also: 6823, 10724.

MIDNIGHT

Related Subject: Night.

12901. That hour, o' night's black arch the keystane.   BURNS,
> *Tam o' Shanter*

12902.
The midnight train is slow and old,
But of it let this thing be told,
To its high honor be it said,
It carries people home to bed.
My cottage lamp shines white and
    clear.
God bless the train that brought me
    here.   JOYCE KILMER,
> *The Twelve-Forty-Five*

12903.
Midnight brought on the dusky hour
Friendliest to sleep and silence.
> MILTON, *Paradise Lost*

12904.
'Tis now the very witching time of
    night,

When churchyards yawn and hell itself breathes out
Contagion to this world.
> SHAKESPEARE, *Hamlet*

12905. The iron tongue of midnight hath told twelve. SHAKESPEARE,
> *A Midsummer-Night's Dream*

See also: 1754, 1760.

MIGHT

Related Subjects: Force, Power. Strength, Violence.

12911.
Shrine of the mighty! can it be
That this is all remains of thee?
> BYRON, *The Giaour*

12912. That makes a Title, where there is no Right.
> SAMUEL DANIEL, *Civil War*

12913.
For who can be secure of private
    right,
If sovereign sway may be dissolv'd
    by might?   DRYDEN,
> *Absalom & Achitophel*

12914. It has been said of the world's history hitherto that might makes right. It is for us and for our time to reverse the maxim, and to say that right makes might. LINCOLN

12915. I proclaim that might is right, justice the interest of the stronger.   PLATO, *The Republic*

12916. Might overcometh right.
> *Proverb*

12917.
Where might is, the right is:
    Long purses make strong swords.
Let weakness learn meekness:
    God save the House of Lords.
> SWINBURNE,
> *A Word for the Country*

MILK

Related Subject: Cow.

12921. Such as have need of milk, and not of strong meat.
Bible: Hebrews, v, 12

12922. It's no good crying over spilt milk, because all the forces of the universe were bent on spilling it.
SOMERSET MAUGHAM,
Of Human Bondage

12923. Don't cry over spilt milk.
Proverb

12924.
If you would live forever,
You must wash milk from your liver.
Proverb

12925.
      Come to my woman's breasts
And take my milk for gall.
SHAKESPEARE, *Macbeth*

See also: 11217.

MILL AND MILLER

12931. The miller sees not all the water that goes by his mill.
ROBERT BURTON,
Anatomy of Melancholy

12932.
The mill goes toiling slowly around
   With steady and solemn creak,
And my little one hears in the kindly
   sound
   The voice of the old mill speak.
EUGENE FIELD,
Nightfall in Dordrecht

12933. The same water that drives the mill, decayeth it.
STEPHEN GOSSON,
The Schoole of Abuse

12934.
Though the mills of God grind slowly,
   yet they grind exceeding small;

Though with patience He stands waiting, with exactness grinds He all.   LONGFELLOW, *Retribution*

12935. The miller grinds more men's corn than one.   THOMAS NASHE

12936. God's mill grinds slow, but sure.   *Proverb*

12937. Honest millers have golden thumbs.   *Proverb*

See also: 14692.

MILTON, JOHN

12941.
On his anointed eyes, God set his seal
And gave him blindness—and the inward light,
That he, repining not at lack of sight,
Might see as never man saw.
R. R. BOWKER, *Milton*

12942.
Milton's the prince of poets—so we
   say;
   A little heavy, but no less divine;
An independent being in his day—
   Learn'd, pious, temperate in love
      and wine.   BYRON, *Don Juan*

12943.
Three Poets, in three distant Ages
   born,
Greece, Italy, and England did adorn.
The first in loftiness of thought surpass'd,
The next in majesty, in both the last;
The force of nature could no farther
   go;
To make the third she join'd the
   former two.   DRYDEN

12944. There are no mute, inglorious Miltons, save in the hallucinations of poets. The one sound test of a Milton is that he function like a Milton.
H. L. MENCKEN, *Prejudices*

12945. By labour and intent study (which I take to be my portion in this life), joined with the strong propensity of nature, I might perhaps leave something so written to after times as they should not willingly let it die.   MILTON,
The Reason of Church Government

12946. That mighty orb of song, The divine Milton.   WORDSWORTH,
The Excursion

12947.
Milton! thou shouldst be living at this hour:
England hath need of thee.
            WORDSWORTH, *Sonnet*

12948.
Thy soul was like a Star, and dwelt apart:
Thou hadst a voice whose sound was like the sea:
Pure as the naked heavens, majestic, free,
So didst thou travel on life's common way,
In cheerful godliness: and yet thy heart
The lowliest duties on herself did lay.
            WORDSWORTH, *Sonnet*

See also: 574, 2164, 15406.

MIND

Related Subjects: Body, Genius, Head, Heart, Intelligence, Sense, Soul, Spirit.

12951.
The world must have great minds, even as great spheres
Or suns, to govern lesser restless minds.   PHILIP J. BAILEY,
Festus

12952. The dark side of a man's mind seems to be a sort of antenna tuned to catch gloomy thoughts from all directions. ADMIRAL BYRD, *Alone*

12953. Experience informs us that the first defence of weak minds is to recriminate.   COLERIDGE,
Biographia Literaria

12954.
One need not be a chamber to be haunted;
One need not be a house;
The brain has corridors surpassing Material place.
        EMILY DICKINSON,
Time and Eternity

12955.
My mind to me a kingdom is;
    Such present joys therein I find,
That it excels all other bliss
    That earth affords or grows by kind:
Though much I want which most would have,
Yet still my mind forbids to crave.
            EDWARD DYER

12956. The rich mind lies in the sun and sleeps, and is Nature.
        EMERSON, *Spiritual Laws*

12957. A fellow that makes no figure in company, and has a mind as narrow as the neck of a vinegar-cruet.
        SAMUEL JOHNSON,
Tour to the Hebrides

12958. It is by presence of mind in untried emergencies that the native metal of a man is tested.
        LOWELL, *Abraham Lincoln*

12959. A well-ordered mind is early trained.   MARCUS AURELIUS,
Meditations

12960.
A mind not to be chang'd by place or time,
The mind is its own place, and in itself
Can make a heaven of hell, a hell of heaven.   MILTON, *Paradise Lost*

12961. Whose little body lodg'd a mighty mind.   POPE,
The Iliad of Homer

12962. Little minds, like weak liquors, are soonest soured. *Proverb*

12963. As sight in the eye, so is the mind in the soul.   *Proverb*

12964. A good mind possesses a kingdom.   SENECA, *Thyestes*

12965.
O! what a noble mind is here o'erthrown;
The courtier's, soldier's, scholar's eye, tongue, sword.
    SHAKESPEARE, *Hamlet*

12966.
My mind is troubled, like a fountain stirr'd;
And I myself see not the bottom of it.
    SHAKESPEARE, *Troilus and Cressida*

12967. Not body enough to cover his mind decently with; his intellect is improperly exposed.
    SYDNEY SMITH,
Lady Holland's Memoir

12968. Minds are conquered not by arms but by greatness of soul.
    SPINOZA

12969. It is difficult to think of a germ-cell, of a higher animal at least, as being without its psychical aspect. Unless we think of "the mind" as entering in at a later stage in development, the germ-cell must have a dim primordium of the subjective, the promise and potency of mentality.
    SIR ARTHUR THOMPSON

12970.
Companion none is like
Unto the mind alone;

For many have been harmed by speech,
Through thinking, few or none.
    SIR THOMAS VAUX,
Of a Contented Mind

12971. Mind is the great lever of all things; human thought is the process by which human ends are ultimately answered.   DANIEL WEBSTER

12972.
Minds that have nothing to confer
Find little to perceive.
    WORDSWORTH, *Yes, Thou Art Fair*

12973.
Strongest minds
Are often those of whom the noisy world
Hears least.
    WORDSWORTH, *The Excursion*

See also: 232, 483, 516, 1074, 1322, 1529, 1704, 1852, 1868, 1935, 1942, 1946, 2015, 2595, 2615, 3065, 3273, 3441, 6604, 9211, 11645, 12158, 12573, 16081, 18772.

MINORITY, see Majority

MINUTE

Related Subjects: Hours, Time.

12981.
But yet what minutes! Moments like to these
Rend men's lives into immortalities.
    BYRON, *The Island*

12982. Myself and the lucky moment.
    CHARLES V.

12983. I recommend you to take care of the minutes, for the hours will take care of themselves.
    LORD CHESTERFIELD, *Letters*

12984. Since our office is with moments, let us husband them. Five minutes of today are worth as much to me as five minutes in the next millennium.   EMERSON, *Essays*

12985. An old French sentence says, "God works in moments." We ask for long life, but 'tis deep life, or grand moments, that signify.
EMERSON, *Society and Solitude*

12986. There are moments in life worth purchasing with worlds.
FIELDING, *Amelia*

12987.
Like coral insects multitudinous
The Minutes are whereof our life is made.   JEAN INGELOW, *Work*

12988. O moments big as years!
KEATS, *Hyperion*

12989. Take hold of a good minute.
Proverb

12990.
Like as the waves make toward the pebbled shore,
So do our minutes hasten to their end.
SHAKESPEARE, *Sonnet LX*

12991. He who governed the world before I was born shall take care of it likewise when I am dead. My part is to improve the present moment.
JOHN WESLEY

MIRACLE

Related Subjects: The Bible, Faith, Superstition, Wonder.

13001. The Ages of Miracles is forever here!
CARLYLE, *Heroes & Hero-Worship*

13002. The Miracles of the Church seem to me to rest not so much upon faces or voices or healing power coming suddenly near to us from afar off, but upon our perceptions being made finer so that for a moment our eyes can see and our ears can hear what is there about us always.
WILLA CATHER,
Death Comes for the Archbishop

13003. Miracles are propitious accidents, the natural causes of which are too complicated to be readily understood.   SANTAYANA,
Introduction to The Ethics of Spinoza

13004. They say miracles are past.
SHAKESPEARE,
All's Well that Ends Well

13005.
To me every hour of the light and dark is a miracle,
Every cubic inch of space is a miracle.   WALT WHITMAN, *Miracles*

13006.
Why, who makes much of a miracle?
As to me, I know of nothing else but miracles.   WALT WHITMAN

See also: 1324, 15769, 17421.

MIRROR

Related Subjects: Reflection, Vanity.

13011. Bronze is the mirror of the form; wine, of the heart. AESCHYLUS

13012.
I change, and so do women too;
But I reflect, which women never do.
Anonymous

13013.
Be sure to keep a mirror always nigh
In some convenient, handy sort of place,
And now and then look squarely in thine eye,
And with thyself keep ever face to face.
JOHN KENDRICK BANGS,
Face to Face

13014. The mirror reflects all objects without being sullied.

　　　　CONFUCIUS, *Analects*

13015.
　　What I admire most in men—
To sit opposite a mirror at dinner
　　and not look in it.

　　　　RICHARD HARDING DAVIS

13016. When her mother tends her, before the laughing mirror.

　　　　GEORGE MEREDITH,
　　　　　Love in the Valley

13017.
My mother says I must not pass
Too near that glass;
She is afraid that I will see
A little witch that looks like me,
With a red mouth to whisper low
The very thing I should not know.

　　　　SARAH PIATT,
　　　　　The Witch in the Glass

13018. Your looking-glass will tell you what none of your friends will.

　　　　Proverb

13019.
When such a spacious mirror's set before him,
He needs must see himself.

SHAKESPEARE, *Antony and Cleopatra*

13020. To hold as 'twere, the mirror up to nature. SHAKESPEARE, *Hamlet*

13021.
You have no such mirrors as will turn
Your hidden worthiness into your
eye. SHAKESPEARE, *Julius Caesar*

13022. Go some of you and fetch a looking-glass.

　　　　SHAKESPEARE, *Richard II*

13023.
An if my word be sterling yet in
　　England,
Let it command a mirror hither
　　straight,

That it may show me what a face I
　　have.　SHAKESPEARE, *Richard II*

13024.
　　She's adorned
Amply that in her husband's eye
　　looks lovely,—
The truest mirror that an honest wife
Can see her beauty in.

　　　　JOHN TOBIN, *The Honeymoon*

13025. The devil's behind the glass.

　　　　J. C. WALL, *Devils*

See also: 199, 211, 1694, 2162, 2692, 4523, 4949.

MISANTHROPY

Related Subjects: Cynicism, Self-ishness.

13031.
And this the burden of his song for-
　　ever used to be,—
"I care for nobody, no, not I, if no-
　　body cares for me."

　　　　ISAAC BICKERSTAFF,
　　　　　Love in a Village

13032.
Naebody cares for me,
I care for naebody.

　　　　BURNS, *I Hae a Wife o' my Ain*

13033. To fly from, need not be to hate mankind. BYRON, *Childe Harold*

13034. Landscape painting is the obvious resource of misanthropy.

　　　　HAZLITT, *Criticisms on Art*

13035. Lean, hungry, savage, anti-everythings.

　　　　O. W. HOLMES, *A Modest Request*

13036. To be the friend of the human race is not at all in my line.

　　　　MOLIÈRE, *Le Misanthrope*

13037. I am Misanthropos, and hate mankind.

　　　　SHAKESPEARE, *Timon of Athens*

13038. A misanthrope I can understand—a womanthrope never.

OSCAR WILDE,
The Importance of Being Earnest

See also: 2665.

MISCHIEF

Related Subjects: Evil, Fool, Injury, Trouble.

13041. He that mischief hatcheth, mischief catcheth.

WILLIAM CAMDEN, *Remains*

13042. He'll find money for mischief, when he can find none for corn.

Proverb

13043.
Let them call it mischief:
When it is past and prospered 'twill
    be virtue. BEN JONSON, *Catiline*

13044. No one returns with good-will to the place which has done him a mischief.   PHAEDRUS, *Fables*

13045.
But when to mischief mortals bend
    their will,
How soon they find fit instruments of
    ill!   POPE, *Rape of the Lock*

13046. That mischief comes justly that is of your own seeking.   *Proverb*

13047. Little mischief, too much.

Proverb

13048. He that hinders not a mischief when it is in his power, is guilty of it.   *Proverb*

13049. This is miching mallecho; it means mischief.

SHAKESPEARE, *Hamlet*

13050.
To mourn a mischief that is past and
    gone,
Is the next way to draw new mischief
    on.   SHAKESPEARE, *Othello*

13051.
     O mischief, thou art swift
To enter in the thoughts of desperate
    men!

SHAKESPEARE, *Romeo and Juliet*

See also: 20636.

MISER

Related Subjects: Avarice, Gold, Money, Possessions.

13061. He heapeth up riches, and knoweth not who shall gather them.

Bible: Psalms, xxxix, 6

13062. He has not acquired a fortune; the fortune has acquired him.

BION

13063.
A ful gret fool is he, y-wis,
That bothe riche and nigard is.
CHAUCER, *The Romaunt of the Rose*

13064. A mere madness, to live like a wretch and die rich.

ROBERT BURTON,
Anatomy of Melancholy

13065. Punishment of a miser,—to pay the drafts of his heir in his tomb.
HAWTHORNE, *American Note-Books*

13066. The miser acquires, yet fears to use his gains.

HORACE, *Ars Poetica*

13067. The unsunn'd heaps of miser's treasures.   MILTON, *Comus*

13068. The beautiful eyes of my money-box!   MOLIÈRE, *L'Avare*

13069.
Which is the happier or the wiser,
A man of merit, or a miser?
POPE, *Imitations of Horace*

13070. The devil lies brooding in the miser's chest.   *Proverb*

13071. As good beg of a naked man as of a miser.   *Proverb*

13072. His money comes from him like drops of blood.   *Proverb*

13073. The miser is as much in want of what he has as of what he has not.
PUBLILIUS SYRUS, *Sententiae*

13074.
Doth, like a miser, spoil his coat with
    scanting
A little cloth.
SHAKESPEARE, *Henry V*

MISERY

Related Subjects: Adversity, Despair, Grief, Happiness, Pain, Poverty, Suffering, Woe.

13081. It is a miserable state of mind to have few things to desire, and many things to fear.   BACON, *Essays*

13082.
        Nothing is a misery,
Unless our weakness apprehend it so.
BEAUMONT & FLETCHER,
        Honest Man's Fortune

13083. To have a stomach and lack meat, to have meat and lack a stomach, to lie in bed and cannot rest are great miseries.
WILLIAM CAMDEN, *Remains*

13084. 'Tis the only comfort of the miserable to have partners in their woes.   CERVANTES, *Don Quixote*

13085. If in this world there is one misery having no relief, it is the pressure on the heart from the Incommunicable.
DE QUINCEY, *Confessions of an English Opium-Eater*

13086. It would be far better to work at the prevention of misery, than to multiply places of refuge for the miserable.
DIDEROT, *The Encyclopedia*

13087. There are a good many real miseries in life that we cannot help smiling at, but they are the smiles that make wrinkles and not dimples.
O. W. HOLMES,
        The Poet at the Breakfast Table

13088.
This, this is misery! the last, the
    worst,
That man can feel.   HOMER, *Iliad*

13089. He that wanders about the world sees new forms of human misery, and if he chances to meet an old friend, meets a face darkened with troubles.   SAMUEL JOHNSON, *Letters*

13090. Misery is but the shadow of happiness. Happiness is but the cloak of misery.
LAO-TSZE, *The Simple Way*

13091.
Me miserable! which way shall I fly
Infinite wrath and infinite despair?
MILTON, *Paradise Lost*

13092. He bears misery best that hides it most.   *Proverb*

13093. Misery loves company.
        Proverb

13094. Nothing almost sees miracles
But misery.
SHAKESPEARE, *King Lear*

13095.
        Meagre were his looks,
Sharp misery had worn him to the
    bones.
SHAKESPEARE, *Romeo and Juliet*

13096. Misery acquaints a man with strange bedfellows.
SHAKESPEARE, *The Tempest*

13097. The secret of being miserable is to have leisure to bother about whether you are happy or not. The cure for it is occupation.
BERNARD SHAW,
Parents and Children

13098. If misery loves company, misery has company enough.
THOREAU, *Journal*

See also: 756, 10018, 10874.

MISFORTUNE

Related Subjects: Accident, Adversity, Calamity, Chance, Fate, Loss, Luck, Poverty, Ruin, Tragedy.

13101. There is always someone worse off than yourself.
AESOP, *The Hares and the Frogs*

13102. The worst thing that can happen to a man is to lose his money, the next worst his health, the next worst his reputation.
SAMUEL .BUTLER, *Note-books*

13103. The very remembrance of my former misfortune proves a new one to me.   CERVANTES, *Don Quixote*

13104. Mishaps are like knives, that either serve us or cut us, as we grasp them by the blade or the handle.
LOWELL,
Cambridge Thirty Years Ago

13105. The worst comes to the worst.
THOMAS MIDDLETON, *The Phoenix*

13106. With man, most of his misfortunes are occasioned by man.
PLINY THE ELDER, *Natural History*

13107. No fence against ill fortune.
Proverb

13108. If you are too unfortunate nobody will know you.   *Proverb*

13109. Never find your delight in another's misfortune.
PUBLILIUS SYRUS, *Sententiae*

13110. To tell sad stories of my own mishaps.   SHAKESPEARE,
The Comedy of Errors

13111. That it should come to this.
SHAKESPEARE, *Hamlet*

13112. On horror's head horrors accumulate.   SHAKESPEARE, *Othello*

13113. One writ with me in sour misfortune's book.
SHAKESPEARE, *Romeo and Juliet*

See also: 460, 2937, 2938, 16563.

MISSIONARY

Related Subjects: The Bible, Christianity, Church, Conversion, God, Religion.

13121. Go ye therefore, and teach all nations. *Bible: Matthew, xxviii, 19*

13122. Come over into Macedonia, and help us.   *Bible: Acts, xvi, 9*

13123. Our noble society for providing the infant negroes in the West Indies with flannel waistcoats and moral pocket-handkerchiefs.
DICKENS, *Pickwick Papers*

13124. Every cause in Nature is nothing but a disguised missionary.
EMERSON, *Lectures*

13125.
From Greenland's icy mountains,
From India's coral strand,
Where Afric's sunny fountains
Roll down their golden sand;
From many an ancient river,
From many a palmy plain,
They call us to deliver
Their land from error's chain.
REGINALD HEBER, *Missionary Hymn*

13126. Men go to the East to convert the infidels. And the infidels pervert them.   BERNARD SHAW, *Saint Joan*

13127.
If I were a Cassowary
  On the plains of Timbuctoo,
I would eat a missionary,
  Coat and bands and hymn-book too.
     BISHOP WILBERFORCE, *Epigram*

See also: 3275, 3615, 16162, 16809, 18084.

MISTAKE

Related Subjects: Delusion, Error, Fool, Illusion, Understanding.

13131.
And one by one in turn, some grand mistake,
Casts off its bright skin yearly like the snake.   BYRON, *Don Juan*

13132. Any man may make a mistake; none but a fool will persist in it.
     CICERO, *Philippicae*

13133. Half our mistakes in life arise from feeling where we ought to think, and thinking where we ought to feel.
     CHURTON COLLINS, *Aphorisms*

13134.
There is a glory
  In a great mistake.
     NATHALIA CRANE, *Imperfection*

13135. Mistakes are often the best teachers.   FROUDE,
     Short Studies on Great Subjects

13136. Great blunders are often made, like large ropes, of a multitude of fibres.
     VICTOR HUGO, *Les Miserables*

13137. Senator, I ordinarily make good appointments. I think I have made very few mistakes. But when I make a mistake, it's a beaut.
     FIORELLO H. LaGUARDIA, *Commenting before a Senate Comm.; referring to Judge Herbert A. O'Brien.*

13138. To make no mistakes is not in the power of man; but from their errors and mistakes the wise and good learn wisdom for the future.
     PLUTARCH

13139. The wrong sow by the ear.
     Proverb

13140. Wise men learn by other men's mistakes, fools by their own.
     Proverb

13141. A miss is as good as a mile.
     Proverb

13142. Leave no rubs nor botches in the work.   SHAKESPEARE, *Macbeth*

13143. To make mistakes as we are on the way to knowledge is far more honourable than to escape making them through never having set out to seek knowledge.
     R. C. TRENCH, *The Study of Words*

13144. There is no mistake; there has been no mistake; and there shall be no mistake.   DUKE OF WELLINGTON

13145. The only things one never regrets are one's mistakes.
     OSCAR WILDE,
     Picture of Dorian Gray

See also: 1446, 2981, 5924, 7460, 10328, 10516, 13595.

MISTRESS

Related Subjects: Love, Passion, Romance, Wife.

13151.
As Juan mused on mutability
Or on his mistress—terms synonymous.   BYRON, *Don Juan*

13152.

Not that he had no cares to vex,
He loved the muses and the sex;
And sometimes these so froward are,
They made him wish himself at war;
But soon his wrath being o'er, he took
Another mistress, or new book.
                    BYRON, *Mazeppa*

13153.

A mistress moderately fair,
And good as guardian angels are,
    Only belov'd and loving me.
        ABRAHAM COWLEY, *The Wish*

13154. Through more Experience they [elderly mistresses] are more prudent and discreet in conducting an Intrigue to prevent Suspicion. The Commerce with them is therefore safer with regard to your Reputation.
    FRANKLIN, *Advice to a Young Man on the Choice of a Mistress*

13155. A poet's Mistress is a hallowed thing.   R. M. MILNES, *Tempe*

13156. Few men have wedded their sweethearts, their paramours or mistresses, but have come home by Weeping Cross, and ere long repented their bargain.   MONTAIGNE, *Essays*

13157. To each of you one fair and virtuous mistress.
            SHAKESPEARE,
        All's Well that Ends Well

13158.

And every one his love-feat will advance
Unto his several mistress.
SHAKESPEARE, *Love's Labour's Lost*

13159. A mistress should be like a little country retreat near the town; not to dwell in constantly, but only for a night and away.
        WILLIAM WYCHERLEY,
            The Country Wife

13160. Next to the pleasure of making a new mistress is that of being rid of an old one.
        WILLIAM WYCHERLEY,
            The Country Wife

See also: 1224, 1228, 1354, 4450, 11278.

MISUNDERSTANDING, see Understanding

MOCKERY

Related Subjects: **Absurdities, Caricature, Cynicism, Fool, Impertinence, Ridicule, Satire.**

13161. Mocking is catching. *Proverb*

13162. Mockery is the fume of little hearts.
        TENNYSON, *Idylls of the King*

MODERATION

Related Subjects: **Self-Control, Temperance.**

13170. There is moderation even in excess.   DISRAELI, *Vivian Grey*

13171. Moderation, the noblest gift of Heaven.   EURIPIDES, *Medea*

13172. Moderation is the silken string running through the pearl chain of all virtues.   BISHOP HALL

13173. Observe moderation. In all, the fitting season is best.
        HESIOD, *Works and Days*

13174. The rule of *not too much.*
        MILTON, *Paradise Lost*

13175. Moderation is best, and to avoid all extremes. PLUTARCH, *Lives*

13176. Moderate riches will carry you; if you have more, you must carry them.   *Proverb*

13177. Moderation in prosperity argues a great mind. *Proverb*

13178. Be moderate, be moderate.
SHAKESPEARE, *Troilus and Cressida*

See also: 743, 2799, 11787.

MODESTY AND IMMODESTY

Related Subjects: Blushing, Chastity, Decency, Dress, Humility, Innocence, Nudity, Virtue.

13181. Modesty cannot properly be described as a virtue, for it is a feeling rather than a disposition—a kind of fear of disrepute.
ARISTOTLE, *Nicomachean Ethics*

13182. Modesty is the only sure bait when you angle for praise.
LORD CHESTERFIELD, *Letters*

13183. On their own merits modest men are dumb.
GEORGE COLMAN,
Epilogue to the Heir at Law

13184.
I have done one braver thing
  Than all the Worthies did;
And yet a braver thence doth spring,
  Which is, to keep that hid.
JOHN DONNE, *The Undertaking*

13185. Modesty becomes a young man. PLAUTUS, *Asinaria*

13186. Modesty ruins all that bring it to court. *Proverb*

13187. Modest dogs miss much meat. *Proverb*

13188. As demure as an old whore at a christening. *Proverb*

13189. When one remains modest, not after praise but after blame, then is he really so.
J. P. RICHTER, *Hesperus*

13190.
Me of my lawful pleasure she restrain'd
And pray'd me oft forbearance; did it with
A pudency so rosy the sweet view on 't
Might well have warm'd old Saturn.
SHAKESPEARE, *Cymbeline*

13191.
Modesty may more betray our sense
Than woman's lightness.
SHAKESPEARE, *Measure for Measure*

13192. Not stepping o'er the bounds of modesty.
SHAKESPEARE, *Romeo and Juliet*

13193.
Since maids, in modesty say "No" to that
Which they would have the profferer construe, "Ay."
SHAKESPEARE,
Two Gentlemen of Verona

13194. Oh, if people only would be modest enough to believe in themselves!
BERNARD SHAW, *to Ellen Terry*

13195. Modesty antedates clothes and will be resumed when clothes are no more. Modesty died when clothes were born. Modesty died when false modesty was born. MARK TWAIN

13196. Modesty in a man is a crime. Don't be modest. It is a woman's virtue. FREDERICK WARDE

13197.
Naked in nothing should a woman be
But veil her very wit with modesty
Let man discover, let her not display
But yield her charms of mind with sweet delay.
EDWARD YOUNG, *Love of Fame*

Immodesty

13198.
Immodest words admit of no defence,
For want of decency is want of sense.
WENTWORTH DILLON,
Essay on Translated Verse

13199. He that has no modesty has all the town for his own.   *Proverb*

13200.
     An act
That blurs the grace and blush of modesty.   SHAKESPEARE, *Hamlet*

13201.
Have you no modesty, no maiden shame,
No touch of bashfulness?
SHAKESPEARE,
A Midsummer-Night's Dream

See also: 1061, 1832, 2671, 7151, 10442, 12336, 15369, 20479, 21588.

MONARCH, see Kings

MONEY

Related Subjects: Avarice, Bribery, Credit, Debt, The Dollar, Gold, Inflation, Mammon, Miser, Patronage, Profit, Riches.

13211. What this country needs is a good five cent nickel.   F. P. A.

13212. Money and freedom may be pleasant and useful but they are not the essence of any art, that of life any more than any other.
JAMES TRUSLOW ADAMS,
The Art of Living

13213. Money—the desire for money—the need of money has always been hurtful to me and to all men and women I have known.
SHERWOOD ANDERSON, *Notebook*

13214. The love of money is the root of all evil.   *Bible: I Timothy, vi, 10*

13215.
What makes all doctrines plain and clear?
About two hundred pounds a year.
And that which was prov'd true before
Prove false again? Two hundred more.   SAMUEL BUTLER, *Hudibras*

13216. Ready money is Aladdin's lamp.   BYRON, *Don Juan*

13217. Annual income twenty pounds, annual expenditure nineteen nineteen six, result happiness. Annual income twenty pounds, annual expenditure twenty pounds ought and six, result misery. DICKENS, *David Copperfield*

13218. Money, which represents the prose of life, and which is hardly spoken of in parlors without an apology, is, in its effects and laws, as beautiful as roses.
EMERSON, *Nominalist and Realist*

13219. The world is his, who has money to go over it.
EMERSON, *Conduct of Life*

13220. He knew that there was only one reality in this world—money. War and peace, life and death, the virtue of women, the Pope's power to bind or to loose, the Estates' enthusiasm for liberty, the purity of the Augsburg Confession, the ships on the sea, the coercive power of princes, the Christianizing of the New World, love, piety, cowardice, wantonness, blasphemy and virtue, they were all derived from money and they would all turn into money, and they could all be expressed in plain figures.
FEUCHTWANGER, *Power*

13221. A penny will hide the biggest star in the universe if you hold it close enough to your eye.
SAMUEL GRAFTON
I'd Rather Be Right

13222. The darkest hour in any man's life is when he sits down to plan how to get money without earning it.
HORACE GREELEY

13223. This bank-note world.
FITZ-GREENE HALLECK,
Alnwick Castle

13224.
Never ask of money spent
Where the spender thinks it went.
Nobody was ever meant
To remember or invent
What he did with every cent.
ROBERT FROST,
The Hardship of Accounting

13225. In order to make money the first thing is to have no need of it.
LUDOVIC HALÉVY,
The Abbé Constantin

13226. Put not your trust in money, but put your money in trust.
O. W. HOLMES,
The Autocrat of the Breakfast-Table

13227. How pleasant it is to have money! A. H. CLOUGH, *Dipsychus*

13228.
Get money; still get money, boy,
No matter by what means.
BEN JONSON,
Every Man in His Humour

13229. The love of pelf increases with the pelf. JUVENAL, *Satires*

13230. It's money I want, or rather the things money will buy; and I can never possibly have too much. As to living on practically nothing, I propose to do as little of that as I possibly can. It's the feed not the breed that makes the man. More money means more life to me. The habit of getting money will never become one of my vices, but the habit of spending money, ah God! I shall always be its victim. If cash comes with fame,

come, fame; if cash comes without fame, then come cash. JACK LONDON

13231. It's good to have money and the things that money can buy, but it's good, too, to check up once in a while and make sure you haven't lost the things that money can't buy.
GEORGE H. LORIMER

13232. If a man runs after money, he's money-mad; if he keeps it he's a capitalist; if he spends it, he's a play-boy; if he doesn't try to get it, he lacks ambition. If he gets it without working for it, he's a parasite; and if he accumulates it after a life-time of hard work, people call him a fool who never got anything out of life.
VIC OLIVER

13233. How little you know about the age you live in if you fancy that honey is sweeter than cash in hand.
OVID, *Fasti*

13234. This morning came home my fine camlet cloak, with gold buttons, and a silk suit, which cost me much money, and I pray God to make me able to pay for it.
SAMUEL PEPYS, *Diary*

13235.
For without money, George,
    A man is but a beast:
But bringing money, thou shalt be
    Always my welcome guest.
THOMAS PERCY, *George Barnwell*

13236. Money in purse will be always in fashion. *Proverb*

13237. Talk is but talk; but 'tis money that buys land. *Proverb*

13238. Ready money is ready medicine. *Proverb*

13239. Money is often lost for want of money. *Proverb*

13240. Money is the best bait to fish for men with.   *Proverb*

13241. Money, like manure, does no good till it is spread.   *Proverb*

13242. Money makes not so many true friends as real enemies. *Proverb*

13243. If money be not thy servant, it will be thy master.   *Proverb*

13244. He that shews his purse, longs to be rid of it.   *Proverb*

13245.
He that gets money before he gets wit,
Will be but a short while master of it.
    Proverb

13246. A fool and his money are soon parted.   *Proverb*

13247. Money alone sets all the world in motion.
    PUBLILIUS SYRUS, *Sententiae*

13248. Money is the seed of money, and the first guinea is sometimes more difficult to acquire than the second million.   ROUSSEAU,
A Discourse on Political Economy

13249. Remuneration! O! that's the Latin word for three farthings.
SHAKESPEARE, *Love's Labour's Lost*

13250. Put money in thy purse.
    SHAKESPEARE, *Othello*

13251. Nothing comes amiss, so money comes withal.
    SHAKESPEARE,
The Taming of the Shrew

13252. The pursuit of women is impossible without pocket money.
    BERNARD SHAW

13253.
Hector: Shall I turn up the light for you?

Capt. Shotover: No. Give me deeper darkness. Money is not made in the light.
BERNARD SHAW, *Heartbreak House*

13254. Money talks: money prints: money broadcasts: money reigns; and kings and labor leaders alike have to register its decrees, and even, by a staggering paradox, to finance its enterprises and guarantee its profits.   BERNARD SHAW,
The Apple Cart: Preface

13255. What money *should* be—and what any honest money system should try to make it—is just this: a debt owed by the community in exchange for actual goods or services delivered to the community and exchangeable at some later date for an *equivalent value* of goods or services.
    R. D. SKINNER,
Seven Kinds of Inflation

13256.
Let all the learned say what they can,
'Tis ready money makes the man.
    WILLIAM SOMERVILLE,
Ready Money

13257. For money you would sell your soul.   SOPHOCLES, *Antigone*

13258.
Ah, search the wide world wherever you can,
There is no open door for the moneyless man!
    H. T. STANTON,
The Moneyless Man

13259. 'Tis as cheap sitting as standing.   SWIFT, *Polite Conversation*

13260. No man will take counsel, but every man will take money. Therefore, money is better than counsel.
    SWIFT

13261. But the jingling of the guinea
helps the hurt that Honour feels.
> TENNYSON, *Locksley Hall*

13262.
If you have money, it doth not stay,
But this way and that it wastes
  amain:
What does it profit you, anyway?
Ill-gotten good is nobody's gain.
> VILLON, *The Greater Testament*

See also: 1421, 1684, 2404, 2564,
2606, 2609, 2613, 2815, 3469, 3625,
6072, 6692, 8290, 9304, 9697, 11695,
15357, 15659, 19806, 20892.

MONK AND NUN

Related Subjects: Celibacy, Hermit, Religion.

13271.
There was also a Nonne, a Prioresse,
That of her smiling was full simple
  and coy.
> CHAUCER, *Canterbury Tales*

13272.
If you become a nun, dear,
  A friar I will be;
In any cell you run, dear,
  Pray look behind for me.
The roses all turn pale, too;
The doves all take the veil, too;
  The blind will see the show;
What! you become a nun, my dear,
  I'll not believe it, no!
> LEIGH HUNT, *The Nun*

13273.
I envy them, those monks of old,
Their books they read, and their beads
  they told.
> GEORGE JAMES, *The Monks of Old*

13274. Thou must be contented for
Christ's sake to be esteemed as a fool
in this world, if thou desire to lead
the life of a monk.
> THOMAS À KEMPIS,
> *Of the Imitation of Christ*

13275. Dress and tonsure profit little;
but change of heart and perfect mortification of the passions make a true
monk.   THOMAS À KEMPIS,
> *Of the Imitation of Christ*

13276.
It was a friar of orders gray
Walked forth to tell his beads.
> THOMAS PERCY,
> *The Friar of Orders Gray*

13277.
I think that friars and their hoods,
Their doctrines and their maggots,
Have lighted up too many feuds,
And far too many faggots.
> W. M. PRAED, *Chant of Brazen Head*

13278. As fit as a fritter for a friar's
mouth.   *Proverb*

13279. The habit does not make the
monk.   RABELAIS

See also: 2748, 3174.

MONTH

Related Subjects: April, August,
December, February, June, March,
May, October, Time, Year.

13281.
Thirty days hath November,
April, June, and September,
February hath twenty-eight alone,
And all the rest have thirty-one.
> RICHARD GRAFTON, *Abridgement
> of the Chronicles of England*

13282.
For hark! the last chime of the dial
  has ceased,
  And Old Time, who his leisure to
    cozen,
Has finished the Months, like the
  flasks at a feast,
  Is preparing to tap a fresh dozen.
> THOMAS HOOD, *For the New Year*

13283. When people earnestly desire a thing, they frequently say, they have a month's mind to it.

FRANCIS PECK

13284. A little month.

SHAKESPEARE, *Hamlet*

MONUMENT

Related Subjects: Epitaphs, Fame, Grave, Memory.

13291. Death comes even to the monumental stones and the names inscribed thereon. AUSONIUS, *Epitaphs*

13292. Gods for themselves are monuments enough.

ALFRED AUSTIN, *On the Proposal to Erect a Statue to Shakespeare in London*

13293.
Let not a monument give you or me hopes,
Since not a pinch of dust remains of Cheops.   BYRON, *Don Juan*

13294. Monuments are made for victories over strangers: domestic troubles should be covered with the veil of sadness.   JULIUS CAESAR

13295. Th' dead ar-re always pop'lar. I knowed a society wanst to vote a monyment to a man an' refuse to help his fam'ly, all in wan night.

F. P. DUNNE, *On Charity*

13296. Tombs are the clothes of the dead; a grave is but a plain suit, and a rich monument is one embroidered.

THOMAS FULLER, *The Holy State*

13297. In lapidary inscriptions a man is not upon oath.

SAMUEL JOHNSON, *Boswell: Life*

13298.
See nations slowly wise, and meanly just,

To buried merit raise the tardy bust.

SAMUEL JOHNSON,
The Vanity of Human Wishes

13299. The erection of a monument is superfluous; our memory will endure if our lives have deserved it.

PLINY THE YOUNGER, *Epistles*

13300. Cato said, "I had rather men should ask why my statue is not set up, than why it is."   PLUTARCH

13301. The most lasting monuments are doubtless paper-monuments.

Proverb

13302. There's hope a great man's memory may outlive his life half a year: but, by 'r lady, he must build churches, then; or else shall he suffer not thinking on.

SHAKESPEARE, *Hamlet*

13303. This grave shall have a living monument.   SHAKESPEARE, *Hamlet*

13304.
And when old time shall lead him to his end,
Goodness and he fill up one monument! SHAKESPEARE, *Henry VIII*

13305. And sleep in dull cold marble.
SHAKESPEARE, *Henry VIII*

13306.
If charnel-houses and our graves must send
Those that we bury back, our monuments
Shall be the maws of kites.

SHAKESPEARE, *Macbeth*

See also: 1582, 12463, 13525, 15424, 15425, 21451.

MOON, THE

Related Subjects: Heavens, Night, Romance, Stars, Sun.

13311.
Late, late yestreen I saw the new moon,

Wi' the auld moon in her arm.
Anonymous

13312.
The moon, like a flower,
In heaven's high bower
With silent delight
Sits and smiles on the night.
BLAKE, *Night*

13313.
The devil's in the moon for mischief;
they
  Who call'd her chaste, methinks,
    began too soon
Their nomenclature; there is not a
  day,
  The longest, not the twenty-first of
    June,
Sees half the business in a wicked
  way,
  On which three single hours of
    moonshine smile—
And then she looks so modest all the
  while!   BYRON, *Don Juan*

13314.
The moving Moon went up the sky,
  And no where did abide:
Softly she was going up,
  And a star or two beside.
COLERIDGE, *The Ancient Mariner*

13315. The man who has seen the rising moon break out of the clouds at
midnight, has been present like an
archangel at the creation of light and
of the world. EMERSON, *Essays*

13316.
What is there in thee, Moon! that
  thou should'st move
My heart so potently?
KEATS, *Endymion*

13317. The moon was a ghostly gal-
leon tossed upon cloudy seas.
ALFRED NOYES, *The Highwayman*

13318. Clear moon, frost soon.
Proverb

13319. You gazed at the moon and
fell in a gutter. *Proverb*

13320. The moon does not heed the
barking of dogs. *Proverb*

13321. Or think that the moon is
made of a green cheese. *Proverb*

13322. O sovereign mistress of true
melancholy. SHAKESPEARE,
Antony and Cleopatra

13323.
Upon the corner of the moon,
There hangs a vaporous drop pro-
found. SHAKESPEARE, *Macbeth*

13324. How sweet the moonlight
sleeps upon this bank!
SHAKESPEARE,
The Merchant of Venice

13325.
          How slow
This old moon wanes! she lingers my
  desires,
Like to a step-dame or a dowager
Long withering out a young man's
  revenue. SHAKESPEARE,
A Midsummer-Night's Dream

13326.
It is the very error of the moon;
She comes more nearer earth than
  she was wont,
And makes men mad.
SHAKESPEARE, *Othello*

13327.
Romeo. Lady, by yonder blessed
  moon I swear,
That tips with silver all these fruit-
  tree tops,—
Juliet. O! swear not by the moon,
  the inconstant moon,
That monthly changes in her circled
  orb,
Lest that thy love prove likewise
  variable.
SHAKESPEARE, *Romeo and Juliet*

13328.
Arise, fair sun, and kill the envious
   moon,
Who is already sick and pale with
   grief,
That thou her maid art far more fair
   than she:
Be not her maid, since she is envious.
   SHAKESPEARE, *Romeo and Juliet*

13329. How now, moon-calf? How
dost thine ague?
   SHAKESPEARE, *The Tempest*

13330. Everyone is a moon, and has
a dark side which he never shows to
anybody.   MARK TWAIN,
Pudd'nhead Wilson's New Calendar

13331. Meet me by moonlight alone.
   J. A. WADE,
   Meet Me by Moonlight Alone

13332.
Lo, the moon ascending,
Up from the east the silvery round
   moon,
Beautiful   over   the   house-tops,
   ghastly, phantom moon,
Immense and silent moon.
   WALT WHITMAN,
   Dirge for Two Veterans

See also: 3969, 4667.

MORALITY AND IMMORALITY

**Related Subjects: Censorship,
Conventionality, Crime, Decency,
Golden Rule, Goodness, Principle,
Prudery, Right, Righteousness,
Sin, Vice, Virtue, Wickedness.**

13341. Morality is a private and
costly luxury.   HENRY ADAMS,
   The Education of Henry Adams

13342. I shall endeavor to enliven
morality with wit, and to temper wit
with morality.
   ADDISON, *The Spectator*

13343.
Morality, thou deadly bane,
Thy tens o' thousands thou hast
   slain!   BURNS,
   A Dedication to Gavin Hamilton

13344. The foundations of morality.
These are like all other foundations,
if you dig too much about them the
superstructure will come tumbling
down. SAMUEL BUTLER, *Note-Books*

13345.
And finds, with keen, discriminating
   sight,
Black's not so black,—nor white so
   very white.
   GEORGE CANNING, *New Morality*

13346.
If good men were only better,
   Would the wicked be so bad?
   J. W. CHADWICK,
   A Timely Question

13347. Nothing sublimely artistic has
ever arisen out of mere art, any more
than anything essentially reasonable
has ever arisen out of the pure reason.
There must always be a rich moral
soil for any great aesthetic growth.
   G. K. CHESTERTON,
   A Defence of Nonsense

13348. The highest possible stage in
moral culture is when we recognize
that we ought to control our thoughts.
   DARWIN, *Descent of Man*

13349. What we call "morals" is
simply blind obedience to words of
command.   HAVELOCK ELLIS,
   The Dance of Life

13350. He who wears his morality
but as his best garment were better
naked.
   KAHLIL GIBRAN, *The Prophet*

13351. So far, about morals, I know
only that what is moral is what you

feel good after and what is immoral is what you feel bad after and judged by these moral standards, which I do not defend, the bullfight is very moral to me because I feel very fine while it is going on and have a feeling of life and death and mortality and immortality, and after it is over I feel very sad but very fine.

ERNEST HEMINGWAY,
Death in the Afternoon

13352. Man is so essentially, so necessarily, a moral being that, when he denies the existence of all morality, that very denial already becomes the foundation of a new morality.

MAETERLINCK

13353. Where there is no free agency, there can be no morality. Where there is no temptation, there can be little claim to virtue. Where the routine is rigorously proscribed by law, the law, and not the man, must have the credit of the conduct.

PRESCOTT, *The Conquest of Peru*

13354. The change in the moral climate of America.

FRANKLIN D. ROOSEVELT

13355. Every intelligent person is interested in the possibility of moral progress, if for no other than egoistic reasons. Equally as a producer and as a consumer, he can fare best in a community where business is conducted efficiently, honestly and with fairness.

SHARP & FOX, *Business Ethics*

13356. I have to live for others and not for myself; that's middle class morality.

BERNARD SHAW, *Pygmalion*

13357. Morality knows nothing of geographical boundaries or distinctions of race. HERBERT SPENCER,
The Evanescence of Evil

13358. The important thing is, not the moral perfection to which a man attains, but the process of attainment.

TOLSTOY, *Diary*

Immorality

13359. It is at least as difficult to stay a moral infection as a physical one.   DICKENS, *Little Dorrit*

13360. This story is slightly immoral, but so, I guess, are all stories based on truth.   RING LARDNER

13361. No man's religion ever survives his morals.   *Proverb*

13362. It would be difficult to find a more shattering refutation of the lessons of cheap morality than the life of James Boswell. One of the most extraordinary successes in the history of civilization was achieved by an idler, a lecher, a drunkard, and a snob . . . Boswell triumphed by dint of abandoning himself, through fifty years, to his instincts.

LYTTON STRACHEY,
Portraits in Miniature

See also: 1257, 1325, 1730, 2357, 2761, 2766, 3399, 3441, 3713, 3994, 4400, 5331, 5806, 6922, 6991, 9190, 11013, 13509, 15512, 17913, 21229.

MORNING

Related Subjects: Dawn, Dew, Rising, Sunrise.

13371.
The morn is up again, the dewy morn,
With breath all incense.
BYRON, *Childe Harold*

13372.
The morn,
All unconcerned with our unrest, begins
Her rosy progress smiling.
MILTON, *Paradise Lost*

13373. Do not shorten the morning by getting up late; look upon it as the quintessence of life, as to a certain extent sacred.   SCHOPENHAUER

13374. Full many a glorious morning have I seen.

SHAKESPEARE, *Sonnet XXXIII*

13375.
The lark is up to greet the sun,
    The bee is on the wing;
The ant its labor has begun,
    The woods with music ring.

JANE TAYLOR, *The Sun is Up*

See also: 3213.

MORTALITY AND IMMORTALITY

Related Subjects: Death, Decay, Eternity, Judgment Day, Life, Salvation, Soul.

13381.
Mortality, behold and fear!
What a change of flesh is here!

FRANCIS BEAUMONT,
On the Tombs in Westminster Abbey

13382. For dust thou art, and unto dust shalt thou return.

Bible: Genesis, iii, 19

13383. Man being in honour abideth not; he is like the beasts that perish.

Bible: Psalms, xlix, 12, 20

13384. In the midst of life we are in death.   *Book of Common Prayer*

13385.
If there's another world, he lives in
    bliss;
If there is none, he made the best of
    this.

BURNS, *Epitaph on William Muir*

13386. I . . . feel death is the finis to mortal life but that mortal men may, while briefly living, experience immortal things.

IRWIN EDMAN, *I Believe*

13387. I shall pass through this world but once; any good things therefore that I can do, or any kindness that I can show to any human being or dumb animal, let me do it now. Let me not defer it or neglect it for I shall not pass this way again.

GALSWORTHY

13388.
Can storied urn, or animated bust
    Back to its mansion call the fleet-
        ing breath?
Can honour's voice provoke the silent
    dust,
    Or flatt'ry soothe the dull cold ear
        of death?   THOMAS GRAY,
            *Elegy Written in a
            Country Churchyard*

13389.
Though now she be pleasant and
    sweet to the sense,
Will be damnably mouldy a hundred
    years hence.   THOMAS JORDAN

13390.
                    Mortality
Weighs heavily on me like unwilling
    sleep.
KEATS, *On Seeing the Elgin Marbles*

13391.
Strange, is it not? that of the myriads
    who
Before us pass'd the door of Dark-
    ness through,
    Not one returns to tell us of the
        Road,
Which to discover we must travel too.
OMAR KHAYYAM, *Rubaiyat*

13392.
Art is long, and Time is fleeting,
    And our hearts, though stout and
        brave,
Still, like muffled drums, are beating
    Funeral marches to the grave.
LONGFELLOW, *The Psalm of Life*

13393. Practically all the progress that man has made is due to the fact that he is mortal. If man knew that his days on earth were to be endless, all incentive to bestir himself—except to seek food and clothing—would be lost. There would be no desire to make his mark in the world; no stimulating ambition to leave the world a little better than he found it; no hungry aspiration to be remembered after he is dead. If there were no death, life would become a thing stagnant, monotonous and unspeakably burdensome.

R. W. MACKENNA, *The Adventure*

13394.
How gladly would I meet
Mortality, my sentence, and be earth
Insensible! how glad would lay me
  down
As in my mother's lap!
MILTON, *Paradise Lost*

13395. Dust thou art, and shalt to dust return. MILTON, *Paradise Lost*

13396.
Golden lads and girls all must,
As chimney-sweepers, come to dust.
SHAKESPEARE, *Cymbeline*

13397.
Imperious Caesar, dead and turn'd to
  clay,
Might stop a hole to keep the wind
  away. SHAKESPEARE, *Hamlet*

13398. To what base uses we may return, Horatio! Why may not imagination trace the noble dust of Alexander, till he find it stopping a bunghole? SHAKESPEARE, *Hamlet*

13399.
What is pomp, rule, reign, but earth
  and dust?
And, live we how we can, yet die we
  must. SHAKESPEARE, *Henry VI*

13400. We cannot hold mortality's strong hand.
SHAKESPEARE, *King John*

Immortality

13401.
That divinest hope, which none can
  know of
Who have not laid their dearest in
  the grave.
T. L. BEDDOES, *Death's Jest Book*

13402. Or ever the silver cord be loosed or the golden bowl be broken, or the pitcher be broken at the fountain or the wheel broken at the cistern. Then shall the dust return to the earth as it was: and the spirit shall return unto God who gave it.
Bible: Ecclesiastes, xii, 6

13403. If a man die, shall he live again? *Bible: Job, xiv, 14*

13404. Set your affections on things above, not on things on the earth.
Bible: Colossians, iii, 2

13405. Earth to earth, ashes to ashes, dust to dust; in sure and certain hope of the Resurrection unto eternal life.
Book of Common Prayer

13406. If the Father deigns to touch with divine power the cold and pulseless heart of the buried acorn and to make it burst forth from its prison walls, will He leave neglected in the earth the soul of man made in the image of his Creator?
WILLIAM JENNINGS BRYAN,
The Prince of Peace

13407. If matter mute and inanimate, though changed by the forces of Nature into a multitude of forms, can never die, will the spirit of man suffer annihilation when it has paid a brief visit, like a royal guest, to this tenement of clay? No. I am as sure that there is another life as I am that I live to-day.

WILLIAM JENNINGS BRYAN,
The Prince of Peace

13408.
The voice of Nature loudly cries,
And many a message from the skies,
That something in us never dies.
BURNS, *New Year's Day*

13409. An immortal like Shakespeare knows nothing of his own immortality about which we are so keenly conscious. As he knows nothing of it when it is in its highest vitality, centuries, it may be, after his apparent death, so it is best and happiest if during his bodily life he should think little or nothing about it and perhaps hardly suspect that he will live after his death at all.
SAMUEL BUTLER, *Note-Books*

13410. Every mother who has lost an infant, has gained a child of immortal youth.   G. W. CURTIS, *Prue and I*

13411.
A voice within us speaks the startling word,
"Man, thou shalt never die!"
R. H. DANA, *Immortality*

13412. Believing as I do that man in the distant future will be a far more perfect creature than he now is, it is an intolerable thought that he and all other sentient beings are doomed to complete annihilation after such long-continued slow progress. To those who fully admit the immortality of the human soul, the destruction of our world will not appear so dreadful.
DARWIN, *Life and Letters*

13413. As for a future life, every man must judge for himself between conflicting vague probabilities.
DARWIN, *Life and Letters*

13414. Several incidents in my life have convinced me of spiritual interposition—of the promptings of some beneficent force outside ourselves, which tries to help us where it can.
CONAN DOYLE,
Through the Magic Door

13415.
O may I join the choir invisible
Of those immortal dead who live again
In minds made better by their presence.   GEORGE ELIOT,
O May I Join the Choir Invisible

13416.
Who knows but life be that which men call death,
And death what men call life?
EURIPIDES, *Phrixus*

13417. Our Creator would never have made such lovely days, and have given us the deep hearts to enjoy them, above and beyond all thought, unless we were meant to be immortal.   HAWTHORNE,
Mosses from an Old Manse

13418. Not lost, but gone before.
MATTHEW HENRY, *Commentaries*

13419.
I shall not wholly die. What's best of me
Shall 'scape the tomb.
HORACE,   *Odes*

13420.
Is there beyond the silent night
An endless day?
Is death a door that leads to light?
We cannot say.
ROBERT INGERSOLL,
Declaration of the Free

13421. Every   cradle   asks   us, "Whence?"   and   every   coffin, "Whither?"   The   poor   barbarian, weeping above his dead, can answer these questions as intelligently as the robed priest of the most authentic creed.   ROBERT INGERSOLL

13422.
Oh, write of me, not "Died in bitter pains,"
But, "Emigrated to another star!"
HELEN HUNT JACKSON, *Emigravit*

13423. If survival is a reality, and if, by actual demonstration, the continued existence of higher or mental attributes is proved to be true, then we may expect that life itself even of a low grade, never really goes out of existence—though it need not have an individual or personal existence except in its higher grades—and the whole province of biology becomes revolutionized.
SIR OLIVER LODGE,
Demonstrated Survival

13424.
Dust thou art to dust returnest,
    Was not spoken of the soul.
LONGFELLOW, *The Psalm of Life*

13425. There will come another era when it shall be light and man will awaken from his lofty dreams, and find his dreams all there, and nothing is gone save his sleep.
H. W. MABIE, *The Awakening*

13426.
There is no such thing as death,
    In Nature nothing dies.
From each sad remnant of decay
    Some forms of life arise.
CHARLES MACKAY,
There Is No Such Thing as Death

13427.
If there be any life beyond the grave,
It must be near the men and things we love.
JOHN MASEFIELD, *August 1914*

13428.
Immortality is not a gift,
Immortality is an achievement;
And only those who strive mightily
Shall possess it.
EDGAR LEE MASTERS,
Spoon River Anthology

13429.
'Tis not the whole of life to live,
    Nor all of death to die.
JAMES MONTGOMERY,
The Issues of Life and Death

13430. My doctrine is: Live that thou mayest desire to live again,— that is thy duty,—for in any case thou wilt live again!
NIETZSCHE, *Eternal Recurrence*

13431. All men desire to be immortal.
THEODORE PARKER,
A Sermon on the Immortal Life

13432.
Is there no bright reversion in the sky
For those who greatly think, or bravely die?   POPE,
To the Memory of an Unfortunate Lady

13433. Our birth made us mortal, our death will make us immortal.
Proverb

13434. Life is eternal; and love is immortal; and death is only a horizon, and a horizon is nothing save the limit of our sight.   R. W. RAYMOND,
A Commendatory Prayer

13435.
                    To die,—to sleep,—
To sleep! perchance to dream! ay, there's the rub;
For in that sleep of death what dreams may come
When we have shuffled off this mortal coil,
Must give us pause: there's the respect

That makes calamity of so long life;
For who would bear the whips and
    scorns of time,
The oppressor's wrong, the proud
    man's contumely,
The pangs of dispriz'd love, the
    law's delay,
The insolence of office, and the spurns
That patient merit of the unworthy
    takes,
When he himself might his quietus
    make
With a bare bodkin? who would
    fardels bear,
To grunt and sweat under a weary
    life,
But that the dread of something after
    death,
The undiscover'd country from whose
    bourn
No traveller returns, puzzles the will,
And makes us rather bear those ills
    we have
Than fly to others that we know not
    of?   SHAKESPEARE, *Hamlet*

13436.
Peace, Peace! he is not dead, he doth
    not sleep—
He hath awakened from the dream of
    life.   SHELLEY, *Adonais*

13437. He seems so near, and yet so
far.   TENNYSON, *In Memoriam*

13438. How fares it with the happy
dead?   TENNYSON, *In Memoriam*

13439.
Ah Christ, that it were possible
    For one short hour to see
The souls we loved, that they might
    tell us
    What and where they be.
              TENNYSON, *Maud*

13440.
I hope to meet my Pilot face to face
When I have crossed the bar.
          TENNYSON, *Crossing the Bar*

13441. I swear I think there is nothing but immortality!
WALT WHITMAN, *To Think of Time*

13442.
              The life to be
Is still the unguessed mystery:
Unscaled, unpierced the cloudy walls
    remain,
We beat, with dream and wish, the
    soundless doors in vain.
              WHITTIER,
      *Interlude after The Grave
              by the Lake*

13443.
And, lucid in that second birth,
    I shall discern
What all the sages of the earth
    Have died to learn.
WILLIAM WINTER, *The Rubicon*

13444.
              And, when the stream
Which overflowed the soul was
    passed away,
A consciousness remained that it had
    left,
Deposited upon the silent shore
Of memory, images and precious
    thoughts,
That shall not die, and cannot be de-
    stroyed.
          WORDSWORTH, *The Excursion*

See also: 1194, 2348, 3855, 18585.

MOSES

13451.
By Nebo's lonely mountain,
    On this side Jordan's wave,
In a vale in the land of Moab,
    There lies a lonely grave;
But no man built that sepulcher,
    And no man saw it e'er,
For the angels of God upturned the
    sod
    And laid the dead man there.
          C. F. ALEXANDER,
          The Burial of Moses

13452. Now the man Moses was very meek, above all the men which were upon the face of the earth.
Bible: Numbers, xii, 3

13453. And he buried him in a valley in the land of Moab, over against Beth-peor: but no man knoweth of his sepulcher unto this day.
Bible: Deuteronomy, xxxiv, 6

13454. Without doubt it must have been a tremendous father image that stooped in the person of Moses to tell the poor Jewish laborers that they were his dear children . . . Probably they did not find it easy to separate the image of the man Moses from that of his God, and their instinct was right in this, since Moses might very well have incorporated into the character of his God some of his own traits, such as his irascibility and implacability.   SIGMUND FREUD,
Moses and Monotheism

13455. And since we know that behind the God who chose the Jews and delivered them from Egypt stood the man Moses who achieved that deed, ostensibly at God's command, we venture to say this: it was one man, the man Moses, who created the Jews.
SIGMUND FREUD,
Moses and Monotheism

MOTHER AND MOTHERHOOD

Related Subjects: Babies, Child, Family, Father.

13461. Where there is a mother in the house, matters speed well.
BRONSON ALCOTT, *Table Talk*

13462. God could not be everywhere and therefore he made mothers.
Anonymous

13463. Does your mother know you're out? *Anonymous*

13464.
Don't poets know
Better than others?
God can't be always everywhere: and, so,
Invented Mothers.
SIR EDWIN ARNOLD, *Mothers*

13465.
Lord, who ordainest for mankind
  Benignant toils and tender cares!
We thank Thee for the ties that bind
  The mother to the child she bears.
BRYANT, *The Mother's Hymn*

13466. Motherhood is, after all, woman's great and incomparable work.   EDWARD CARPENTER,
Love's Coming-of-Age

13467.
A mother is a mother still,
  The holiest thing alive.
COLERIDGE, *The Three Graves*

13468. Do you perhaps think that nature gave women nipples as a kind of beauty spot, not for the purpose of nourishing their children?
FAVORINUS

13469. Our women have a proverb, "It is a sad burden to carry a dead man's child."
THOMAS FULLER, *Church History*

13470.
Where yet was ever found a mother
Who'd give her booby for another?
JOHN GAY,
The Mother, the Nurse, and the Fairy

13471. These women of the present day, ill-used as daughters, as sisters, as wives, not educated according to their gifts, prevented from following their inclination, deprived of their inheritance, embittered in temper—it is these who furnish the mothers of the new generation.

IBSEN, *Ghosts: Notes*

13472.
Maids must be wives and mothers, to fulfil
Th' entire and holiest end of women's being.

FRANCES KEMBLE, *Woman's Heart*

13473. A mother loves her child more than the father does, because she knows it's her own, while the father only thinks it's his.

MENANDER, *Fragments*

13474.
The bravest battle that ever was fought;
Shall I tell you where and when?
On the maps of the world you will find it not;
It was fought by the mothers of men.

JOAQUIN MILLER, *The Bravest Battle*

13475. The future destiny of the child is always the work of the mother.   NAPOLEON

13476.
I feel that, in the Heavens above,
The angels, whispering to one another,
Can find, among their burning terms of love,
None so devotional as that of "Mother."

POE, *To My Mother*

13477. Light-heel'd mothers make leaden-heel'd daughters.   *Proverb*

13478. No mother is so wicked but desires to have good children.   *Proverb*

13479. The mother-in-law remembers not that she was a daughter-in-law.   *Proverb*

13480. The mother knows best, whether the child be like the father.   *Proverb*

13481. A child may have too much of mother's blessing.   *Proverb*

13482.
So loving to my mother
That he might not beteem the winds of heaven
Visit her face too roughly.

SHAKESPEARE, *Hamlet*

13483.
A grandam's name is little less in love,
Than is the doting title of a mother.

SHAKESPEARE, *Richard III*

13484. Simply having children does not make mothers.

A. SHEDD, *Salt from My Attic*

13485. Children are the anchors that hold a mother to life.

SOPHOCLES, *Phaedra*

13486. A lady who had gallantries and several children, told her husband he was like the austere man, who reaped where he did not sow.

SWIFT,
Thoughts on Various Subjects

13487.
Who ran to help me when I fell,
And would some pretty story tell,
Or kiss the place to make it well?
My mother.

JANE TAYLOR, *My Mother*

13488. Is not a young mother one of the sweetest sights life shows us?

THACKERAY, *The Newcomes*

13489. Mother is the name for God in the lips and hearts of little children.   THACKERAY, *Vanity Fair*

13490. The hand that rocks the cradle is the hand that rules the world. WILLIAM R. WALLACE,

The Hand That Rules the World

13491.
Years to a mother bring distress
But do not make her love the less.
WORDSWORTH,
The Affliction of Margaret

See also: 215, 228, 701, 1418, 1702, 3247, 3584, 8546, 8902, 12344, 19514, 21159, 21182, 21598, 21605.

MOTIVE

Related Subjects: Cause, Impulse, Influence, Intention, Necessity, Purpose, Reason.

13501. God made man to go by motives, and he will not go without them, any more than a boat without steam, or a balloon without gas.
H. W. BEECHER

13502. Motives are better than actions. Men drift into crime. Of evil they do more than they contemplate, and of good they contemplate more than they do.   C. N. BOVEE

13503. Our best conjectures, as to the true spring of actions, are very uncertain; the actions themselves are all we know from history. That Caesar was murdered by twenty-four conspirators, I doubt not; but I very much doubt whether their love of liberty was the sole cause.
LORD CHESTERFIELD

13504. Iago's soliloquy, the motive-hunting of a motiveless malignity—how awful it is!   COLERIDGE

13505. Motives imply weakness, and the existence of evil and temptation. Angelic natures would act from impulse alone.   COLERIDGE

13506. The true motives of our actions, like the real pipes of an organ, are usually concealed; but the gilded and hollow pretext is pompously placed in the front for show.
C. C. COLTON

13507. We must not inquire too curiously into motives. They are apt to become feeble in the utterance: the aroma is mixed with the grosser air. We must keep the germinating grain away from the light.   GEORGE ELIOT

13508. A man's acts are usually right, but his reasons seldom are.
ELBERT HUBBARD

13509. The morality of an action depends upon the motive from which we act.   SAMUEL JOHNSON

13510. It is motive alone that gives character to the actions of men.
LA BRUYÈRE

13511. However brilliant an action, it should not be esteemed great unless the result of a great and good motive.
LA ROCHEFOUCAULD, *Maxims*

13512. We should often have reason to be ashamed of our most brilliant actions if the world could see the motives from which they spring.
LA ROCHEFOUCAULD, *Maxims*

13513. One will rarely err if extreme actions be ascribed to vanity, ordinary actions to habit, and mean actions to fear.   NIETZSCHE,
Human, All Too Human

13514. He that does good for good's sake, seeks neither praise nor reward, but he is sure of both in the end.
WILLIAM PENN

13515. The noblest motive is the public good.   VERGIL

See also: 1864, 4705, 12352, 13682.

MOUNTAINS

Related Subjects: Hills, Nature.

13521. They came to the Delectable Mountains.
BUNYAN, *The Pilgrim's Progress*

13522.
Mountains are good to look upon
But do not look too long.
They are made of granite. They will
    break your heart.
              GRACE CONKLING, *Mountains*

13523. On every mountain height is
rest.   GOETHE, *Ein Gleiches*

13524. Mountains never shake hands.
Their roots may touch: they may keep
together some way up; but at length
they part company, and rise into individual, insulated peaks. So it is
with great men.
              A. W. & J. C. HARE,
                    Guesses at Truth

13525. Mountains are earth's unde-
caying monuments.
              HAWTHORNE,
                Sketches from Memory

13526.
              They were setting
Ossa upon Olympus, and upon
Steep Ossa leafy Pelius.
              HOMER, *Odyssey*

13527. A mountain and a river are
good neighbours.   *Proverb*

13528. If the mountain will not go
to Mahomet, let Mahomet go to the
mountain.   *Proverb*

13529. I would have you call to mind
the strength of the ancient giants, that
undertook to lay the high mountain
Pelion on the top of Ossa, and set
among those the shady Olympus.
              RABELAIS

13530. Mountains are the beginning
and the end of all natural scenery.
              RUSKIN, *True and Beautiful*

13531.
Who digs hills because they do as-
    pire,

Throws down one mountain to cast
up a higher.
              SHAKESPEARE, *Pericles*

See also: 3445, 6675.

MOURNING

**Related Subjects: Complaining,
Death, Funeral, Grief, Sigh, Sorrow, Woe.**

13541. Ah, surely nothing dies but
something mourns.
              BYRON, *Don Juan*

13542.
The air is full of farewells to the
    dying,
And mournings for the dead.
              LONGFELLOW, *Resignation*

13543. What we call mourning for
our dead is perhaps not so much grief
at not being able to call them back as
it is grief at not being able to want
to do so.   THOMAS MANN,
                The Magic Mountain

13544.
Too innocent for coquetry, too fond
    for idle scorning—
O friend, I fear the lightest heart
    makes sometimes heaviest mourn-
    ing.   CAROLINE NORTON,
                Bingen on the Rhine

13545. A dirge for her, the doubly
dead in that she died so young.
              POE, *Lenore*

13546. Absent thee from felicity
awhile.   SHAKESPEARE, *Hamlet*

13547.
        I count it crime
To mourn for any overmuch.
              TENNYSON, *In Memoriam*

13548. He mourns the dead who lives
as they desire.
              EDWARD YOUNG, *Night Thoughts*

See also: 1937, 2585, 4702.

MOUSE

Related Subjects: Animal, Rat.

13551. Better a mouse in the pot than no flesh at all.   *Proverb*

13552. It must be a wily mouse that can breed in a cat's ear.   *Proverb*

13553. As merry as mice in malt.
Proverb

13554. A mouse must not think to cast a shadow like an elephant.
Proverb

13555. Not a mouse stirring.
SHAKESPEARE, *Hamlet*

See also: 2903, 3376, 11415, 16308.

MOUTH

Related Subjects: Face, Kiss, Lip, Smile, Speech, Tongue, Tooth.

13561. Nature has given us two ears but only one mouth.
DISRAELI, *Henrietta Temple*

13562. Look to thy mouth: diseases enter there.   *Proverb*

13563.
Mouth he remembered: the quaint orifice
From which came heat that flamed upon the kiss.
J. C. RANSOM, *The Equilibrists*

13564. He that hath a mouth of his own should not say to another, blow.
Proverb

13565.
               I wear not
My dagger in my mouth.
SHAKESPEARE, *Cymbeline*

13566. She looks as if butter wouldn't melt in her mouth.
SWIFT, *Polite Conversation*

See also: 860, 1111, 2657, 9699.

MURDER, MURDERER

Related Subjects: Butcher, Capital Punishment, Crime, Death, Guilt, Hanging, Hatred, Kill, Law, Mystery, Poison, Revenge.

13571.
Lizzie Borden took an axe
And gave her mother forty whacks;
When she saw what she had done
She gave her father forty-one.
Anonymous

13572. If once a man indulges himself in murder, very soon he comes to think little of robbing; and from robbing he next comes to drinking and Sabbath-breaking, and from that to incivility and procrastination.
DE QUINCEY, *On Murder*

13573.
O! my offence is rank, it smells to heaven;
It hath the primal eldest curse upon 't,
A brother's murder.
SHAKESPEARE, *Hamlet*

13574. How easily murder is discovered!   SHAKESPEARE,
Titus Andronicus

13575. Other sins only speak; murder shrieks out.   JOHN WEBSTER,
The Duchess of Malfi

See also: 2102, 20242, 20841.

MUSIC

Related Subjects: Art, Ballad, Dancing, Discord, Harmony, Jazz, Melody, Sing, Song.

13581. If we could have devised an arrangement for providing everybody with music in their homes, perfect in quality, unlimited in quantity, suited to every mood, and beginning and ceasing at will, we should have considered the limit of human felicity already attained.

EDWARD BELLAMY,
Looking Backward

13582.

We are all but fellow-travellers
  Along Life's weary way;
If any man can play the pipes,
  In God's name, let him play.

JOHN BENNETT

13583. It is not hard to compose but it is wonderfully hard to let the superfluous notes fall under the table.

BRAHMS,
Schauffler: The Unknown Brahms

13584. There is music even in the beauty, and the silent note which Cupid strikes, far sweeter than the sound of an instrument; for there is music wherever there is harmony, order, or proportion; and thus far we may maintain the music of the spheres. SIR THOMAS BROWNE,
Religio Medici

13585. The first string that the musician usually touches is the bass, when he intends to put all in tune. God also plays upon this string first, when he sets the soul in tune for himself. BUNYAN, *Pilgrim's Progress*

13586.

O Music, sphere-descended maid,
Friend of Pleasure, Wisdom's aid!
WILLIAM COLLINS, *The Passions*

13587.

Music hath charms to soothe the savage breast,
To soften rocks, or bend a knotted
  oak.   CONGREVE,
The Mourning Bride

13588.

Music the beautiful disturber of the
  air,
Drew near,

Saying: Come with me into my country of air
Out of the querulous and uncivil clay;
Fling down its aching members into
  a chair,
And come away.
GEORGE DILLON, *The Constant One*

13589.

Let me go where'er I will,
I hear a sky-born music still.

EMERSON

13590.

Some cry up Haydn, some Mozart,
Just as the whim bites. For my part,
I do not care a farthing candle
For either of them, nor for Handel.
CHARLES LAMB,
*Free Thoughts on Several Eminent
Composers*

13591. When she had passed, it seemed like the ceasing of exquisite music. LONGFELLOW, *Evangeline*

13592.

And the night shall be filled with
  music,
  And the cares that infest the day,
Shall fold their tents, like the Arabs,
  And as silently steal away.
LONGFELLOW, *The Day is Done*

13593. Music is the universal language of mankind,—poetry their universal pastime and delight.
LONGFELLOW, *Outre-Mer*

13594. Music my rampart, and my only one.
EDNA ST. VINCENT MILLAY,
*On Hearing a Symphony of
Beethoven*

13595. Without music life would be a mistake. NIETZSCHE,
The Twilight of the Idols

13596. The music's not immortal, but the world has made it sweet.
ALFRED NOYES,
The Barrel-Organ

13597. Piano playing is more difficult than statesmanship. It is harder to awake emotions in ivory keys than it is in human beings. PADEREWSKI

13598. All art constantly aspires towards the condition of music.
WALTER PATER, *The Renaissance*

13599. Musick and women I cannot but give way to, whatever my business is. SAMUEL PEPYS, *Diary*

13600. Musical training is a more potent instrument than any other, because rhythm and harmony find their way into the inward places of the soul.
PLATO, *The Republic*

13601.
Music resembles poetry; in each
Are nameless graces which no methods teach,
And which a master-hand alone can reach. POPE, *Essay on Criticism*

13602. As in politics, so in music, revolutionary changes penetrate into all homes, great and small. In music the new influence is perceptible even where its sensual ties with life are strongest, that is, in the dance.
ROBERT SCHUMANN

13603.
The man that hath no music in himself,
Nor is not moved with concord of sweet sounds,
Is fit for Treasons, stratagems, and spoils;
The motions of his spirit are dull as night,
And his affections dark as Erebus.
Let no such man be trusted.
SHAKESPEARE,
The Merchant of Venice

13604. I am never merry when I hear sweet music. SHAKESPEARE,
The Merchant of Venice

13605. And the vile squealing of the wry-necked fife. SHAKESPEARE,
The Merchant of Venice

13606.
How sour sweet music is
When time is broke and no proportion kept!
So is it in the music of men's lives.
SHAKESPEARE, *Richard II*

13607. This music mads me!
SHAKESPEARE, *Richard II*

13608.
If music be the food of love, play on;
Give me excess of it, that, surfeiting,
The appetite may sicken, and so die.
That strain again! it had a dying fall:
O! it came o'er my ear like the sweet sound
That breathes upon a bank of violets,
Stealing and giving odour!
SHAKESPEARE, *Twelfth Night*

13609.
Music, when soft voices die,
Vibrates in the memory.
SHELLEY,
Music, When Soft Voices Die

13610. Music must take rank as the highest of the fine arts—as the one which, more than any other, ministers to human welfare.
HERBERT SPENCER,
Essays on Education

13611.
It is the little rift within the lute,
That by and by will make the music mute,
And ever widening slowly silence all.
TENNYSON, *Idylls of the King*

13612.
There is sweet music here that softer falls
Than petals from blown roses on the grass. TENNYSON,
The Lotos-Eaters

13613.
Music that gentlier on the spirit lies,
Than tir'd eyelids upon tir'd eyes;
Music that brings sweet sleep down
    from the blissful skies.
        TENNYSON, *The Lotos-Eaters*

13614. The god of music dwelleth
out of doors.
        EDITH M. THOMAS, *Music*

13615. All music is what awakes from
you when you are reminded by the
instruments. WALT WHITMAN,
        A Song for Occupations

13616.
The orchestra whirls me wider than
    Uranus flies,
It wrenches such ardors from me I
    did not know I possess'd them.
    WALT WHITMAN, *Song of Myself*

13617. Over the piano was printed a
notice: "Please do not shoot the
pianist. He is doing his best."
        OSCAR WILDE,
        Impressions of America

13618.
The music in my heart I bore
Long after it was heard no more.
        WORDSWORTH,
        The Solitary Reaper

13619. The still, sad music of humanity.   WORDSWORTH

See also: 1093, 1096, 1903, 2105,
3661, 4160, 5643, 11411.

MYSTERY

Related Subjects: Concealment,
Murder, Obscurity, Secrecy, Superstition.

13621. A proper secrecy is the only
mystery of able men; mystery is the
only secrecy of weak and cunning
ones.   LORD CHESTERFIELD

13622. We injure mysteries, which
are matters of faith, by any attempt
at explanation, in order to make them
matters of reason. Could they be explained, they would cease to be mysteries; and it has been well said that
a thing is not necessarily against reason, because it happens to be above
it.   C. C. COLTON

13623. Mystery is but another name
for our ignorance; if we were omnis-
cient, all would be perfectly plain.
        TRYON EDWARDS

13624.
My name is John Wellington Wells,
I'm a dealer in magic and spells,
In blessings and curses
And ever-filled purses,
And prophecies, witches, and knells.
        W. S. GILBERT, *The Sorcerer*

13625. The most consistent materialist
is willing to admit that there is an
unknown and possibly unknowable
mystery surrounding existence, of
which he stands in some awe, without presuming to formulate any idea
of the nature of that mystery.
        SIR OLIVER LODGE,
        Demonstrated Survival

13626. It is the dim haze of mystery
that adds enchantment to pursuit.
        ANTOINE DE RIVAROL

13627. Pluck out the heart of my
mystery.   SHAKESPEARE, *Hamlet*

13628. The mystic too full of God to
speak intelligibly to the world.
        ARTHUR SYMONS,
        *The Symbolist Movement in
        Literature*

13629. A religion without mystery
must be a religion without God.
        JEREMY TAYLOR

See also: 2006, 3331, 4191.

MYTHOLOGY

Related Subjects: Cupid, Giant, Gods and Goddesses, Oracle, Pan, Superstition, Tale, Venus.

13631. Mythology is not religion. It may rather be regarded as the ancient substitute, the poetical counterpart for dogmatic theology.
A. W. & J. C. Hare,
Guesses at Truth

13632. Mythology is the religious sentiment growing wild. Schelling

13633. The heathen mythology not only was not true, but it was not even supported as true; it not only deserved no faith, but it demanded none. The very pretension to truth, the very demand of faith, were characteristics of Christianity. Richard Whately

See also: 14953.

N

NAIL

13641. A nail in the wound.
Cicero, Pro Domo Sua

13642. With tooth and nail.
G. Du Bartas,
Devine Weekes and Workes

13643. Nail is driven out by nail.
Proverb

13644. To hit the nail on the head.
Proverb

13645.
I'll never see't; for, I am sure, my nails
Are stronger than mine eyes.
Shakespeare,
Antony and Cleopatra

13646.
Falstaff: What, is the old king dead?
Pistol: As nail in door.
Shakespeare, Henry IV

13647.
Could I come near your beauty with my nails,
I'd set my ten commandments in your face. Shakespeare, Henry VI

See also: 121, 1657, 1718, 1754.

NAKEDNESS, see Nudity

NAME

Related Subjects: Character, Fame, Family, Rank, Reputation, Titles.

13651. I name no parties.
Beaumont & Fletcher,
Wit at Several Weapons

13652. A good name is rather to be chosen than great riches.
Bible: Proverbs, xxii, 1

13653. A good name is better than precious ointment.
Bible: Ecclesiastes, vii, 1

13654.
Who hath not own'd, with rapture-smitten frame,
The power of grace, the magic of a name? Thomas Campbell,
Pleasures of Hope

13655.
Some to the fascination of a name,
Surrender judgment hoodwink'd.
Cowper, The Task

13656.
Father calls me William, sister calls me Will,
Mother calls me Willie, but the fellers call me Bill!
Eugene Field,
Jest 'Fore Christmas

13657. How vain, without the merit, is the name! Homer, Iliad

13658.
Stephen Dedalus is my name,
Ireland is my nation,
Clongowes is my dwellingplace
And heaven's my expectation.

JAMES JOYCE,
*Portrait of the Artist as a
Young Man*
*(A variant of this traditional jingle
concludes with "destination." Thornton Wilder used the latter form as
title source for a novel.)*

13659. "My name," said I, in a clear
and respectful voice, "is Algernon
Sidney Potts. If I be pushed to the
avowal, I am sorry it *is* Potts! . . .
Can a man hope to make such a name
illustrious? Can he aspire to the notion of a time when people will allude
to the great Potts, the celebrated
Potts, the immortal Potts?" . . . I
suddenly bethought me of Mr. Pitt
and I said aloud, "And if Pitt, why
not Potts?"

CHARLES LEVER, *A Day's Ride*

13660. He that has an ill name is half
hang'd.   *Proverb*

13661. There are two very difficult
things in the world. One is to make
a name for oneself and the other is
to keep it.   ROBERT SCHUMANN

13662.
And if his name be George, I'll call
  him Peter;
For new-made honour doth forget
  men's names.

SHAKESPEARE, *King John*

13663. I cannot tell what the dickens
his name is.   SHAKESPEARE,
The Merry Wives of Windsor

13664.
          Your name is great
In mouths of wisest censure.

SHAKESPEARE, *Othello*

13665.
What's in a name? That which we
  call a rose
By any other name would smell as
  sweet.   SHAKESPEARE,
Romeo and Juliet

13666.
The sweetest name that ever love
Waxed weary of.

SWINBURNE, *Félise*

See also: 215, 646, 648, 649, 819,
1400, 1423, 1523, 2109, 2313, 2438,
2749, 3314, 4434, 6320, 8651, 11986,
17645.

NAPOLEON

13671. The instinct of active, brave,
able men, throughout the middle class
everywhere, has pointed out Napoleon
as the incarnate Democrat.

EMERSON

13672. Napoleon is thoroughly modern, and, at the highest point of his
fortunes, has the very spirit of the
newspapers.   EMERSON

13673. Napoleon was a man! His
life was the stride of a demigod.

GOETHE

13674. Napoleon was whipped because he carried a chip on his shoulder: this is the one thing that the
gods who write the laws of nations
will not palliate nor excuse.

ELBERT HUBBARD

13675. . . . There was no longer any
room for Napoleon. . . . Smoking
blood, over-filled cemeteries, mothers
in tears,—these are formidable plead-
ers . . . Napoleon had been denounced
in the infinite, and his fall had been
decided on. He embarrassed God.

VICTOR HUGO, *Les Miserables*

13676. A little while ago, I stood by
the grave of Napoleon . . . I would

rather have been a French peasant and worn wooden shoes ... and gone down to the tongueless silence of the dreamless dust, than to have been that imperial impersonation of force and murder known as "Napoleon the Great." ROBERT INGERSOLL

13677. I saw none but you, I admired none but you; I desire only you. Answer at once, and calm the impatient ardor of— N.,
NAPOLEON, *to Marie Walewska*

13678. It is my great privilege to be a leader of nations. Once I was an acorn; now I am an oak. Yet when I am the oak to all others, I am glad to become the acorn to you.
NAPOLEON, *to Marie Walewska*

13679. There are times when all splendors become oppressive, as I feel but too deeply at the present moment. How can I satisfy the desires of a heart that yearns to cast itself at your feet, when its impulses are checked at every point by considerations of the highest moment? Oh, if you would, you alone might overcome the obstacles that keep us apart. *My friend Duroc will make all easy for you.* Oh, come, come! Your every wish shall be gratified! Your country will be dearer to me when you take pity on my poor heart.
NAPOLEON, *to Marie Walewska*

13680. The first Napoleon, dining at a table full of monarchs, when he heard one of them deferentially alluding to the Bonaparte family as being very old and noble, exclaimed:
"Pish! My nobility dates from the day of Marengo!"

13681. No one but myself can be blamed for my fall. I have been my own greatest enemy, the cause of my disastrous fate. NAPOLEON,
Ludwig: Napoleon

13682. There are two motives to action: self-interest and fear. Believe me love is a foolish blindness! ... I love no one, not even my brothers ... Let us leave sensibilities to women. Men should be firm of heart and strong of will ... I have an iron heart. I never really loved ... I incline to the view of Gassion, who once said to me that he did not love life well enough to give it to another being.
NAPOLEON, *Ludwig: Napoleon*

13683. I have had no luck since I gave up Josephine. NAPOLEON

13684. I am neither an atheist nor a rationalist; I believe in God, and am of the religion of my father. I was born a Catholic, and will fulfil all the duties of that church, and receive the assistance which she administers.
NAPOLEON

13685. I desire that you preserve my heart in spirits of wine, and that you carry it to Parma to my dear Marie Louise. NAPOLEON,
To Dr. Antommarchi, at death

13686. I wish my ashes to repose on the banks of the Seine, in the midst of the French people I have loved so well. NAPOLEON'S WILL

13687. I foresee that he [Napoleon] will bring disaster on himself and all his family. He should be content with what he has. He tries to grasp too much, and will lose all.
NAPOLEON'S MOTHER,
Ludwig: Napoleon

13688. Grand, gloomy, and peculiar, he sat upon the throne a sceptred hermit, wrapped in the solitude of his own originality. CHARLES PHILLIPS

13689. Although too much of a soldier among sovereigns, no one could claim with better right to be a sovereign among soldiers.

Scott, *Life of Napoleon*

13690. What! alive, and so bold, O earth?   Shelley,
Upon hearing of Napoleon's death

13691. He [Napoleon] neither hates nor loves; for him, no one exists but himself; all other people are merely 'number so-and-so.' A great chess-player, for whom humanity-at-large is the adversary he hopes to check-mate. His success is quite as much due to the qualities he lacks as to the qualities he possesses . . . Where his own interest is involved, he pursues it as the just man seeks virtue; if his aim were good, his perseverance would be exemplary. . . . I have never been able to breathe freely in his presence.   Mme. de Staël

13692.
Though more than half the world
     was his,
   He died without a rood his own;
And borrowed from his enemies
   Six feet of ground to lie upon.
            Thackeray,
     The Chronicle of the Drum

13693. I don't care a twopenny damn what becomes of the ashes of Napoleon Bonaparte.

Attr. to Duke of Wellington

See also: *173, 18923.*

NATION

Related Subects: **Constitution, Government, Patriotism, State.**

13701. Nation after nation, when at the zenith of its power, has pro-claimed itself invincible because its army could shake the earth with its tread, and its ships could fill the seas, but these nations are dead, and we must build upon a different founda-tion if we would avoid their fate.

William Jennings Bryan

13702. The strength of a nation does not lie in forts, nor in navies, nor yet in great standing armies, but in happy and contented citizens, who are ever ready to protect for themselves and to preserve for posterity the blessings which they enjoy.

William Jennings Bryan

13703. Individualities may form com-munities, but it is institutions alone that can create a nation.   Disraeli

13704. Justice is as strictly due be-tween neighbor nations as between neighbor citizens. A highwayman is as much a robber when he plunders in a gang, as when single; and a nation that makes an unjust war is only a great gang.   Franklin

13705. It is because nations tend to stupidity and baseness that mankind moves so slowly; it is because in-dividuals have a capacity for better things that it moves at all.

George Gissing,
*The Private Papers of
Henry Ryecroft*

13706.
Ill fares the land, to hastening ills a
     prey,
Where wealth accumulates, and men
     decay;
Princes and lords may flourish or may
     fade;
A breath can make them, as a breath
     has made;
But a bold peasantry, their country's
     pride,
When once destroy'd, can never be
     supplied.
   Goldsmith, *The Deserted Village*

13707. The first panacea for a mis-managed nation is inflation of the currency; the second is war. Both bring a temporary prosperity; both bring a permanent ruin. But both are the refuge of political and economic opportunists.

ERNEST HEMINGWAY,
Notes on the Next War

13708. Size is not grandeur, and territory does not make a nation.

THOMAS H. HUXLEY,
On University Education

13709. Methinks I see in my mind a noble and puissant nation rousing herself like a strong man after sleep, and shaking her invincible locks: methinks I see her as an eagle mewing her mighty youth, and kindling her undazzled eyes at the full midday beam.　　MILTON, *Areopagitica*

13710.
Not with dreams, but with blood and with iron,
Shall a nation be moulded to last.

SWINBURNE,
A Word for the Country

13711. If a nation wants prosperity more than freedom, wealth more than dignity, pleasure more than strength, brilliance more than character; if it considers that all the creative sacrifices have been endured by its ancestors; if it forgets that the individual holds his freedom as a trust for the nation, and the nation exists in service to humanity, individual freedom will be short-lived and so will the free nation.

DOROTHY THOMPSON,
On the Record

13712. The only nations which ever come to be called historic are those which recognize the importance and worth of their own institutions.

TOLSTOY, *Anna Karenina*

13713. Our true nationality is mankind.　　H. G. WELLS,
The Outline of History

See also: 352, 653, 656, 704, 705, 721, 1101, 1152, 1183, 1385, 3482, 3613, 4173, 8151, 10891, 16255, 21822.

NATURE

Related Subjects: Animal, Birds, Country, Forest, Garden, Grass, Instinct, Mountains, Tree.

13721. Nature will out.
AESOP, *The Cat-Maiden*

13722. Nature is thought immersed in matter.　　BRONSON ALCOTT,
Sonnet to Louisa May Alcott

13723. Rich with the spoils of Nature.　　SIR THOMAS BROWNE,
Religio Medici

13724. Nature is the art of God.
SIR THOMAS BROWNE,
Religio Medici

13725.
To him who in the love of Nature holds
Communion with her visible forms, she speaks
A various language.　　BRYANT,
Thanatopsis

13726.
Go forth, under the open sky, and list
To Nature's teachings.
BRYANT, *Thanatopsis*

13727.
Gie me ae spark o' Nature's fire,
I'm on your list.　　BURNS,
First Epistle to J. Lapraik

13728.
When Nature her great masterpiece design'd,
And fram'd her last, best work, the human mind,
Her eye intent on all the wondrous plan,
She form'd of various stuff the various Man.　　BURNS,
To Robert Graham

13729. Nature teaches more than she preaches. There are no sermons in stones. It is easier to get a spark out of a stone than a moral.
JOHN BURROUGHS,
Time and Change

13730.
How often we forget all time, when lone,
Admiring Nature's universal throne,
Her woods her wilds, her waters, the intense
Reply of hers to our intelligence.
BYRON, *The Island*

13731. And muse on Nature with a poet's eye. THOMAS CAMPBELL,
Pleasures of Hope

13732. Nature, the vicaire of th' almyghty lorde.   CHAUCER,
The Parlement of Foules

13733. It is agayns the proces of nature.   CHAUCER,
Canterbury Tales

13734. An elemental force is ruthlessly frank.   JOSEPH CONRAD,
Typhoon

13735. Nature, that is the seal to mortal wax.   DANTE, *Purgatory*

13736. I have called this principle, by which each slight variation, if useful, is preserved, by the term Natural Selection.   DARWIN,
The Origin of Species

13737. For Art may err, but Nature cannot miss.   DRYDEN,
The Cock and the Fox

13738. He needed not the spectacles of Books to read Nature; he looked inwards, and found her there.
DRYDEN, *Essay of Dramatic Poesy*

13739.
Hast thou named all the birds without a gun;

Loved the wood-rose, and left it on its stalk?   EMERSON,
Forbearance

13740.
Love not the flower they pluck, and know it not,
And all their botany is Latin names.
EMERSON, *Blight*

13741. Nature is a mutable cloud, which is always and never the same.
EMERSON, *History*

13742. Everything in Nature contains all the powers of Nature. Everything is made of one hidden stuff.
EMERSON, *Compensation*

13743. What is natural is never disgraceful.   EURIPIDES

13744.
For Nature forms, and softens us within,
And writes our fortune's changes in our face.   HORACE, *Ars Poetica*

13745. You may drive out nature with a fork, yet still she will return.
HORACE, *Epistles*

13746. "Nature" will no longer do the work unaided.   Nature—if by that we mean blind and non-conscious forces—has, marvellously, produced man and consciousness; they must carry on the task to new results which she alone can never reach.
JULIAN HUXLEY,
Essays of a Biologist

13747. To a person uninstructed in natural history, his country or seaside stroll is a walk through a gallery filled with wonderful works of art, nine-tenths of which have their faces turned to the wall.
THOMAS H. HUXLEY

13748. There remains no reason for supposing that the present laws were specially selected in order to produce life. They are just as likely, for instance, to have been selected in order to produce magnetism or radio-activity—indeed more likely, since to all appearances physics plays an incomparably greater part in the universe than biology.

SIR JAMES JEANS,
The Mysterious Universe

13749.
So Nature deals with us, and takes away
Our playthings one by one, and by the hand
Leads us to rest.

LONGFELLOW, *Nature*

13750. In those vernal seasons of the year, when the air is calm and pleasant, it were an injury and sullenness against Nature not to go out and see her riches, and partake in her rejoicing with heaven and earth.

MILTON, *Tractate of Education*

13751.
Accuse not Nature! she hath done her part;
Do thou but thine!   MILTON,
Paradise Lost

13752. Let us a little permit Nature to take her own way; she better understands her own affairs than we.

MONTAIGNE, *Essays*

13753.
Living Nature, not dull Art
Shall plan my ways and rule my heart.   CARDINAL NEWMAN,
Nature and Art

13754.
All Nature is but Art, unknown to thee;
All Chance, Direction, which thou canst not see.   POPE,
Essay on Man

13755.
Eye Nature's walks, shoot folly as it flies,
And catch the manners living as they rise;
Laugh where we must, be candid where we can,
But vindicate the ways of God to man.   POPE, *Essay on Man*

13756.
All are but parts of one stupendous whole,
Whose body Nature is, and God the soul.   POPE, *Essay on Man*

13757. Nature is beyond all teaching.
Proverb

13758. Nature must obey necessity.
Proverb

13759. Nature passes nurture.
Proverb

13760. He that follows nature is never out of his way.   *Proverb*

13761. Nature teaches beasts to know their friends.   SHAKESPEARE,
Coriolanus

13762. There is something in this more than natural, if philosophy could find it out.   SHAKESPEARE, *Hamlet*

13763.
          Nature her custom holds,
Let shame say what it will.
SHAKESPEARE, *Hamlet*

13764.
Diseased Nature oftentimes breaks forth
In strange eruptions.
SHAKESPEARE, *Henry IV*

13765. Nature's above art in that respect.   SHAKESPEARE, *King Lear*

13766.
Now, by two-headed Janus,
Nature hath framed strange fellows
in her time.
SHAKESPEARE,
The Merchant of Venice

13767. Framed in the prodigality of nature. SHAKESPEARE, *Richard III*

13768. One touch of nature makes the whole world kin. SHAKESPEARE,
Troilus and Cressida

13769. This is the true joy in life, the being used for a purpose recognized by yourself as a mighty one; the being thoroughly worn out before you are thrown on the scrap heap; the being a force of Nature instead of a feverish selfish little clod of ailments and grievances complaining that the world will not devote itself to making you happy.
BERNARD SHAW,
Man and Superman

13770. Certainly nothing is unnatural that is not physically impossible.
SHERIDAN, *The Critic*

13771. Do you realize what it is that is causing world chaos? ... it's Nature hitting back. Not with the old weapons—floods, plagues, holocausts. We can neutralize them. She's fighting back with strange instruments called neuroses. She's deliberately afflicting mankind with the jitters. Nature is proving that she can't be beaten—not by the likes of us. She's taking the world away from the intellectuals and giving it back to the apes. ROBERT E. SHERWOOD,
The Petrified Forest

13772. Nature abhors a vacuum.
SPINOZA, *Ethics*

13773. I warn you that I do not attribute to nature either beauty or deformity, order or confusion. Only in relation to our imagination can things be called beautiful or ugly, well-ordered or confused. SPINOZA

13774.
So, naturalists observe, a flea
Hath smaller fleas that on him prey;
And these have smaller still to bite
'em;
And so proceed *ad infinitum*.
SWIFT, *On Poetry*

13775.
By acting on nature outside himself,
and changing it
Man simultaneously changes his own
nature. GENEVIEVE TAGGARD

13776.
So careful of the type she seems.
So careless of the single life.
TENNYSON, *In Memoriam*

13777. There is a fundamental tendency in the stones and mortar of Nature to grow from more to more—atoms building up molecules, molecules uniting in micellae, these forming higher units or wholes, and so on. SIR ARTHUR THOMSON,
The Beauty of Nature

13778.
Like Nature? Can imagination boast,
Amid its gay creation, hues like hers?
JAMES THOMSON, *The Seasons*

13779.
Let dogs delight to bark and bite,
For God hath made them so;
Let bears and lions growl and fight,
For 'tis their nature too.
ISAAC WAATS, *Divine Songs*

13780. After you have exhausted what there is in business, politics, conviviality, and so on—have found that none of these finally satisfy, or permanently wear—what remains? Nature remains.
WALT WHITMAN, *Specimen Days*

13781. You must not know too much, or be too precise or scientific about birds and trees and flowers and water-craft; a certain free margin, and even vagueness—perhaps ignorance, cre-dulity—helps your enjoyment of these things.

WALT WHITMAN, *Specimen Days*

13782. Nature speaks in symbols and in signs. WHITTIER,
To Charles Sumner

13783.
Thou unassuming commonplace
Of Nature. WORDSWORTH,
To the Daisy

13784.
Come forth into the light of things,
Let Nature be your teacher.
WORDSWORTH, *The Tables Turned*

13785.
Knowing that Nature never did be-
tray
The heart that loved her.
WORDSWORTH

13786. The course of Nature is the art of God. EDWARD YOUNG,
Night Thoughts

See also: 199, 222, 412, 927, 1172, 1184, 1200, 1207, 1227, 1238, 1324, 1484, 1688, 1772, 1932, 2066, 2312, 2900, 3043, 3245, 3483, 3723, 3733, 4030, 4747, 5047, 5112, 5161, 5902, 6471, 7069, 9016, 9103, 17683.

NAVY

Related Subjects: Army, Sailor, Sea, Ship, Soldier, War.

13791. Not only is the British Em-pire the first of naval powers, it is also the first of colonial powers. One attribute is closely connected with the other; neither, without the other, would be applicable.
ADMIRAL BRIDGE

13792. The true objective in naval warfare is the enemy's navy. That must be destroyed or decisively de-feated, or intimidated into remaining in its ports. The British Empire may fall to pieces from causes as yet un-known or unsuspected: it cannot be kept together if it loses the power of gaining command of the Sea.
ADMIRAL BRIDGE

13793. The high antiquity of decisive naval campaigns is amongst the most interesting features of international conflicts. Notwithstanding the much greater frequency of land wars, the course of history has been profoundly changed more often by contests on the water. ADMIRAL BRIDGE

13794.
Stick close to your desks and never
go to sea,
And you all may be rulers of the
Queen's Navee!
W. S. GILBERT, *Pinafore*

13795. Theories about the naval war-fare of the future are almost wholly presumptive.
CAPT. A. T. MAHAN (U.S.N.)

13796. It is particularly in the field of naval strategy that the teachings of the past have a value which is in no degree lessened.
CAPT. A. T. MAHAN (U.S.N.)

13797. A vague feeling of contempt for the past, supposed to be obsolete, combines with natural indolence to blind men even to those permanent strategic lessons which lie close to the surface of naval history.
CAPT. A. T. MAHAN (U.S.N.)

13798. The history of Sea Power is largely, though by no means solely, a narrative of contests between nations, of mutual rivalries, of violence frequently culminating in war.

CAPT. A. T. MAHAN (U.S.N.)

13799. Naval tactics are based upon conditions the chief causes of which, namely the arms, may change; which in turn causes necessarily a change in the construction of ships, in the manner of handling them, and so finally in the disposition and handling of fleets. ADMIRAL MOROGUES

See also: 699, 6892.

NAZISM, see Fascism

NECESSITY

Related Subjects: Cause, Fate, Force, Motive, Poverty, Want.

13801. Flying for life, one does not stickle about the vehicle.

CARLYLE, *The French Revolution*

13802. One of his [Pittacus] sayings was, "Even the gods cannot strive against necessity."

DIOGENES LAERTIUS, *Pittacus*

13803. Necessity can set me helpless on my back, but she cannot keep me there; nor can four walls limit my vision. MICHAEL FAIRLESS,
The Roadmender

13804. Necessity, the mother of invention. GEORGE FARQUHAR,
The Twin Rivals

13805.
And with necessity,
The tyrant's plea, excus'd his devilish deeds. MILTON, *Paradise Lost*

13806. Where necessity pinches, boldness is prudence *Proverb*

13807. Necessity and opportunity may make a coward valiant. *Proverb*

13808. It is a fair degree of plenty to have what is necessary. *Proverb*

13809. A wise man never refuses anything to necessity.

PUBLILIUS SYRUS, *Sententiae*

13810. Necessity knows no law except to conquer.

PUBLILIUS SYRUS, *Sententiae*

13811.
He that stands upon a slippery place
Makes nice of no vile hold to stay
him up. SHAKESPEARE,
King John

13812. Necessity's sharp pinch!
SHAKESPEARE, *King Lear*

13813. As if we were villains by necessity; fools by heavenly compulsion. SHAKESPEARE, *King Lear*

13814. To make a virtue of necessity.
SHAKESPEARE,
The Two Gentlemen of Verona

13815.
In the ills of men
There is none sorer than Necessity.
SOPHOCLES, *Ajax*

13816.
Human hopes and human creeds
Have their root in human needs.
E. F. WARE,
The Washerwoman's Song

13817.
Who, doomed to go in company with
Pain,
And Fear, and Bloodshed, miserable
train!
Turns his necessity to glorious gain.
WORDSWORTH,
Character of the Happy Warrior

See also: 9, 1214, 1476, 2139, 2445, 2453, 5421, 8585, 12269, 12273, 13758, 20608, 20804.

NECK

Related Subject: Head.

13821.

The stately neck is manhood's man-
    liest part;
It takes the life-blood freshest from
    the heart
With short, curled ringlets close
    around it spread,
How light and strong it lifts the
    Grecian head!
    O. W. Holmes, *A Rhymed Lesson*

13822. Anger wishes all mankind had
only one neck; love, that it had only
one heart.   J. P. Richter,
    Flowers, Fruit and Thorns

13823. Bending down His corrigible
neck.   Shakespeare,
    Antony and Cleopatra

13824. I had as lief thou didst break
his neck as his finger.
    Shakespeare, *As You Like It*

13825.

Falls not the axe upon the humblest
    neck
But first begs pardon.
    Shakespeare, *As You Like It*

13826. And thus I set my foot on's
neck.   Shakespeare, *Cymbeline*

NEEDLE

Related Subject: Tailor.

13831.

With fingers weary and worn,
    With eyelids heavy and red,
A woman sat in unwomanly rags
    Plying her needle and thread,—
    Stitch! Stitch! Stitch!
         Thomas Hood,
    The Song of the Shirt

13832. To look for a needle in a hay-
stack.   *Proverb*

13833. So delicate with her needle.
    Shakespeare, *Othello*

13834.

As hard to come as for a camel
To thread the postern of a small
    needle's eye.   Shakespeare,
         Richard II

13835.

The bright little needle—the swift-
    flying needle,
The needle directed by beauty and
    art.   Samuel Woodworth,
         The Needle

See also: 5790, 17097.

NEGLECT

**Related Subjects: Attention, De-
lay, Forgetfulness, Idleness, Indifference, Procrastination.**

13841. A wise and salutary neglect.
    Burke

13842. Whose most tender mercy is
neglect.   George Crabbe,
         The Village

13843. A little neglect may breed
mischief: for want of a nail the shoe
was lost; for want of a shoe the
horse was lost; and for want of a
horse the rider was lost.
    Franklin, *Poor Richard*

13844. There is something inexplicable about me which brings ill luck
on the governments that neglect me.
    Talleyrand, *to Louis XVIII*

See also: 1071, 1695, 2635, 2750,
2859.

NEGRO

Related Subject: Slavery.

13851. Can the Ethiopian change his
skin, or the leopard his spots?
    Bible: Jeremiah, xiii, 23

13852.

My mother bore me in the southern
wild,
And I am black, but O my soul is
white!   BLAKE,
The Little Black Boy

13853. The Negro tenant farmer on
a plantation is still a slave.
ERSKINE CALDWELL,
You Have Seen Their Faces

13854. The Negro, thanks to his
temperament, appears to make the
greatest amount of happiness out of
the smallest capital. EMERSON,
Journal

13855. The influence of the Negro,
upon the psychology of the American
has been tremendous. The white may
have educated the black; but that
education has been returned in a
dozen subtle ways. We taught him
things; he taught us feelings. We
gave him knowledge; he has helped
to give us passion which is not the
meaner of the gifts. From the first,
the white has been under some psy-
chologic compulsion to mimic the
Negro, at first in ridicule and superiority, then in understanding and
sympathy. The Negro, at almost
every step, has participated in the
making of our popular song.
ISAAC GOLDBERG, *Tin-Pan Alley*

13856.

To fling my arms wide
In the face of the sun,
Dance! whirl! whirl!
Till the quick day is done.
Rest at pale evening . . .
A tall slim tree. . . .
Night coming tenderly
  Black like me.
LANGSTON HUGHES,
Dream Variation

13857.

The night is beautiful

So the faces of my people.

The stars are beautiful
So the eyes of my people.

Beautiful, also, is the sun.
Beautiful, also, are the souls of my
  people. LANGSTON HUGHES,
My People

13858.

I, too, sing America.
I am the darker brother.
They send me to eat in the kitchen
When company comes,
But I laugh,
And eat well,
And grow strong.

Tomorrow,
I'll sit at the table
When company comes.
Nobody'll dare
Say to me,
"Eat in the kitchen,"
Then . . .
I, too am America.
LANGSTON HUGHES, *I Too*

13859. All I ask for the negro is that
if you do not like him, let him alone.
If God gave him but little, that little
let him enjoy.   LINCOLN

13860. In the right to eat the bread
. . . . which his own hand earns, he
[the negro] *is my equal and the equal
of Judge Douglas, and the equal of
every living man.* LINCOLN, *Debate*

13861. Some doubt the courage of
the Negro. Go to Haiti and stand on
those fifty thousand graves of the
best soldiers France ever had, and
ask them what they think of the
Negro's sword. WENDELL PHILLIPS

13862. I said to the mulatto delegate:
"That's what Negroes need in Ameri-
can politics—a highly organized all-
Negro group. When you have that
. . . you will be getting somewhere.
We may feel inflated as *individual*
Negroes sitting in on the councils of

the whites, but it means very little if our people are not organized. Otherwise the whites will want to tell us what is right for our people even against our better thinking.

CLAUDE McKAY,
A Long Way From Home

13863. "When I was a slave, if I fell off a boat they would stop and pick me up and put me by a fire to dry. I was worth money. Now if I fall off a boat they calls out, 'It's only a damned nigger—let him go under.'"

A NEWLY FREED NEGRO,
Sandburg: Abraham Lincoln, the War Years

See also: 2961, 10926, 15821.

NEIGHBOR

Related Subjects: Community, Friend, Village.

13871. Better is a neighbour that is near than a brother far off
Bible: Proverbs, xxvii, 10

13872. Love thy neighbour as thyself. *Bible: Matthew, xix, 19*

13873.
A man may tak a neebor's part,
  Yet hae nae cash to spare him.
BURNS, *Epistle to a Young Friend*

13874. What we've got to do, is to keep up our spirits, and be neighbourly. We shall come all right in the end, never fear. DICKENS,
Martin Chuzzlewit

13875. Man's plan it is to aid his neighbors in every respect; that is the nucleus of all morals.
FREDERICK THE GREAT,
to d'Alembert

13876. A bad neighbour is as great a misfortune as a good one is a great blessing. HESIOD, *Works and Days*

13877. We can live without our friends, but not without our neighbours. *Proverb*

13878. Love your neighbour, yet pull not down your hedge. *Proverb*

13879. Good neighbours and true friends are two things. *Proverb*

13880. In the field of world policy I would dedicate this nation to the policy of the good neighbor.
FRANKLIN D. ROOSEVELT,
First Inaugural Address

See also: 2665, 7516, 10884, 11520, 13527.

NEUTRALITY

Related Subject: Indifference.

13881. People who live on the fence gather a great many rocks.
HEYWOOD BROUN

13882. The cold neutrality of an impartial judge. BURKE,
Preface to Brissot's Address

13883. Neutral men are the devil's allies. E. H. CHAPIN

13884. Neutrality is no favorite with Providence, for we are so formed that it is scarcely possible for us to stand neuter in our hearts, although we may deem it prudent to appear so in our actions. C. C. COLTON

13885. There is in some men a dispassionate neutrality of mind, which, though it generally passes for good temper, can neither gratify nor warm us; it must indeed be granted that these men can only negatively offend; but then it should also be remembered that they cannot positively please.
GREVILLE

13886. Neutrality, as a lasting principle, is an evidence of weakness.
LOUIS KOSSUTH

13887. A wise neuter joins with neither, but uses both as his honest interest leads him. WILLIAM PENN

13888. The neutrals must be dynamic. They must not be passive or disinterested observers but an active force, working for the only kind of future world that will have any stability at all—a peaceful world whose policies are based on reason, intelligence, realism and humanity.
DOROTHY THOMPSON,
On the Record

13889. The neutrality act was a typical gesture of a Congress dominated by weak men who believed that safety lay in powerlessness and that democracy is threatened whenever it sticks up for its rights.
DOROTHY THOMPSON,
On the Record

NEWS

Related Subjects: **Columnists, Curiosity, The Press, Rumor, Scandal, Tale.**

13891. As cold waters to a thirsty soul, so is good news from a far country. *Bible: Proverbs, xxv, 25*

13892. When a dog bites a man, that is not news, because it happens so often. But if a man bites a dog, that is news. JOHN B. BOGART

13893. Mails from the North—the East—the West—the South—whence, according to some curious etymologists, comes the magical word NEWS. DE QUINCEY,
Confessions of an English Opium-Eater

13894. It is good news, worthy of all acceptation; and yet not too good to be true. MATTHEW HENRY,
Commentaries

13895. For evil news rides post, while good news baits. MILTON,
Samson Agonistes

13896.
Though it be honest, it is never good
To bring bad news.
SHAKESPEARE,
Antony and Cleopatra

13897.
Yet the first bringer of unwelcome news
Hath but a losing office, and his tongue
Sounds ever after as a sullen bell,
Remember'd knolling a departing friend. SHAKESPEARE, *Henry IV*

13898.
I saw a smith stand with his hammer thus,
The whilst his iron did on the anvil cool,
With open mouth swallowing a tailor's news. SHAKESPEARE,
King John

13899. This news is old enough, yet it is every day's news.
SHAKESPEARE,
Measure for Measure

13900. I wouldst thou hadst my bones, and I thy news.
SHAKESPEARE, *Romeo and Juliet*

13901. None love the messenger who brings bad news. SOPHOCLES,
Antigone

13902. In the case of news, we should always wait for the sacrament of confirmation. VOLTAIRE

See also: 122.

NEWSPAPER, see Press

NEW YORK CITY

Related Subject: Cities.

13911. New York, the hussy, was taken in sin again!
THOMAS BEER, *The Mauve Decade*

13912. The Sidewalks of New York.
BLAKE & LAWLOR, *Song*

13913. Give my regards to Broadway.   GEORGE M. COHAN, *Song*

13914. I think any man who can afford a hall bedroom and a gas stove in New York City is better off than he would be as the owner of 160 acres on the prairie or in one of those small so-called cities.
RICHARD HARDING DAVIS

13915. New York is a sucked orange.
EMERSON, *Conduct of Life*

13916. In dress, habits, manners, provincialism, routine and narrowness, he acquired that charming insolence, that irritating completeness, that sophisticated crassness, that overbalanced poise that makes the Manhattan gentleman so delightfully small in his greatness.   O. HENRY, *The Voice of the City*

13917. What else can you expect from a town that's shut off from the world by the ocean on one side and New Jersey on the other?
O'HENRY, *The Gentle Grafter*

13918. Well, little old Noisyville-on-the-Subway is good enough for me.
O'HENRY, *Strictly Business*

13919. The renowned and ancient city of Gotham.
WASHINGTON IRVING, *Salmagundi*

13920.
Manhattan's a hell where culture
rarely grew;

But it lets two lives do all they care to do.   ALFRED KREYMBORG, *Two Lives and Six Million*

13921.
City of hurried and sparkling waters! city of spires and masts!
City nested in bays! my city!
WALT WHITMAN, *Mannahatta*

13922. A little strip of an island with a row of well-fed folks up and down the middle, and a lot of hungry folks on each side.
HARRY LEON WILSON, *The Spenders*

NIGHT

Related Subjects: Darkness, Day, Evening, Midnight, Moon, Sleep, Stars.

13931. There shall be no night there.
Bible: Revelation, xxii, 5
(Source of title of a Pulitzer Prize play by Robert E. Sherwood)

13932.
The night
Is the safe time for robbers, as the light
For just men.   EURIPIDES, *Iphigenia in Tauris*

13933. I have been one acquainted with the night.   ROBERT FROST, *Acquainted With the Night*

13934.
Night with her train of stars
And her great gift of sleep.
W. E. HENLEY, *In Memoriam Margaritae Sorori*

13935.
When night
Darkens the streets, then wander forth the sons
Of Belial, flown with insolence and wine.   MILTON, *Paradise Lost*

13936. Sum up at night, what thou hast done by day.   *Proverb*

13937. Let's have one other gaudy night.   SHAKESPEARE, *Antony and Cleopatra*

13938. In the dead vast and middle of the night.   SHAKESPEARE, *Hamlet*

13939.
This will last out a night in Russia
When nights are longest there.
          SHAKESPEARE, *Measure for Measure*

13940. This night, methinks, is but the daylight sick.
          SHAKESPEARE, *The Merchant of Venice*

13941.
                    This is the night
That either makes me or fordoes me
    quite.   SHAKESPEARE, *Othello*

13942.
I was thinking the day most splendid till I saw what the not-day exhibited,
I was thinking this globe enough till there sprang out so noiseless around me myriads of other globes.
          WALT WHITMAN, *Night on the Prairies*

See also: 1338, 1685, 13592.

NIGHTINGALE

Related Subject: Birds.

13951. A nightingale dies for shame if another bird sings better.
          ROBERT BURTON, *Anatomy of Melancholy*

13952.
Oh nightingale! What doth she ail?
    And is she sad or jolly?
For ne'er on earth was sound of mirth
    So like to melancholy.
          HARTLEY COLERIDGE, *Song*

13953.
The nightingale among the thick-leaved spring
That sits alone in sorrow, and doth sing
Whole nights away in mourning.
          JOHN FLETCHER, *The Faithful Shepherdess*

13954.
Thou wast not born for death, immortal Bird!
    No hungry generations tread thee down;
The voice I hear this passing night was heard
    In ancient days by emperor and clown:
Perhaps the self-same song that found a path
    Through the sad heart of Ruth, when, sick for home,
She stood in tears amid the alien corn;
    The same that oft-times hath
Charm'd magic casements, opening on the foam
    Of perilous seas, in faery lands forlorn.   KEATS, *Ode to a Nightingale*

13955.
    All but the wakeful nightingale;
She all night long her amorous descant sung.   MILTON, *Paradise Lost*

13956. Thy liquid notes that close the eye of day.   MILTON, *To the Nightingale*

13957.
There's a bower of roses by Bendemeer's stream
And the nightingale sings round it all day long.   THOMAS MOORE, *Lalla Rookh*

13958.
The Nightingale that in the branches sang,

Ah whence and whither flown again,
who knows!
OMAR KHAYYAM, Rubaiyat

13959.

The nightingale, if she should sing
by day,
When every goose is cackling, would
be thought
No better a musician than the wren.
How many things by season season'd
are
To their right praise and true per-
fection!   SHAKESPEARE,
The Merchant of Venice

13960.

It was the nightingale, and not the
lark,
That pierced the fearful hollow of
thine ear;
Nightly she sings on yon pomegranate
tree.   SHAKESPEARE,
Romeo and Juliet

See also: 238, 6208, 10395.

NOBILITY

**Related Subjects: Ancestry, Aris-
tocracy, Breeding, Court, Dignity,
Gentleman, Kings, Magnanimity,
Name, Prince, Queen, Rank, Titles.**

13961.

Be noble! and the nobleness that lies
In other men, sleeping, but never
dead,
Will rise in majesty to meet thine
own.   LOWELL, Sonnet

13962. He is more noble that deserves, than he that confers benefits.
Proverb

13963. He is noble that hath noble
conditions.   Proverb

13964. Men do not care how nobly
they live, but only how long, although

it is within the reach of every man
to live nobly, but within no man's
power to live long.   SENECA

13965. True nobility is exempt from
fear.   SHAKESPEARE, Henry VI

Nobility of birth

13966. Nobility of birth commonly
abateth industry; and he that is not
industrious envieth him that is. Besides, noble persons cannot go much
higher; and he that standeth at a
stay when others rise can hardly avoid
motions of envy.   BACON, Essays

13967. Nobility is a graceful orna-
ment to the civil order. It is the
Corinthian capital of polished society.
BURKE,
Reflections on the Revolution in
France

13968. It becomes noblemen to do
nothing well.
GEORGE CHAPMAN,
The Gentleman Usher

13969. The nobly born must nobly
meet his fate.   EURIPIDES, Alcymene

13970.

Blue blood! Blue blood!
  Of what avail art thou
  To serve us now?
Though dating from the flood,
  Blue blood! Ah, blue blood!
W. S. GILBERT, Iolanthe

13971. Hereditary nobility is due to
the presumption that we shall do well
because our fathers have done well.
JOUBERT, Pensées

13972.

Let wealth and commerce, laws and
learning die,
But leave us still our old nobility.
LORD MANNERS, England's Trust

13973.
To be nobly born
Is now a crime   MASSINGER,
The Roman Actor

13974. Send your noble blood to
market and see what it will buy.
Proverb

13975.
Nature's own Nobleman, friendly
    and frank,
    Is a man with his heart in his hand!
           MARTIN TUPPER,
         Nature's Nobleman

13976. Those transparent swindles—
transmissible nobility and kingship.
          MARK TWAIN,
    A Connecticut Yankee

13977. You should study the Peerage
. . . It is the best thing in fiction the
English have ever done.
        OSCAR WILDE,
    A Woman of No Importance

See also: 264, 890, 1066, 2032, 2065,
3087, 4365, 4533, 10272, 13680,
21801.

NOISE

Related Subjects: Discord, Sound.

13981.
    The small, dim noises, thousand-
        fold,
That all old houses and forests hold.
    STEPHEN VINCENT BENET,
        John Brown's Body

13982. Loud clamor is always more
or less insane.   CARLYLE,
On Boswell's Life of Johnson

13983. He who sleeps in continual
noise is wakened by silence.
    W. D. HOWELLS, *Pordenone*

13984. People who make no noise are
dangerous.   LA FONTAINE, *Fables*

13985. Fill'd the air with barbarous
dissonance.   MILTON, *Comus*

13986. Splitting the air with noise.
    SHAKESPEARE, *Coriolanus*

See also: 1123, 2926, 6445.

NONSENSE

**Related Subjects: Absurdities,
Foolishness, Humor, Limericks,
Mockery, Ridiculousness.**

13991.
For daring nonsense seldom fails to
    hit,
Like scattered shot, and pass with
    some for wit.
        SAMUEL BUTLER,
        On Modern Critics

13992. A doosed fine gal—well educated too—with no biggodd nonsense
about her.   DICKENS, *Little Dorrit*

13993. So she went into the garden
to cut a cabbage-leaf to make an
apple-pie; and at the same time a
great she-bear, coming down the
street, pops its head into the shop.
What! no soap? So he died, and she
very imprudently married the Barber; and there were present the Pic-
ninnies, and the Joblillies, and the
Garyulies, and the grand Panjan-
drum himself, with the little round
button at top; and they all fell to
playing the game of catch-as-catch-
can, till the gun powder ran out at
the heels of their boots.
        SAMUEL FOOTE,
    *Traditionally supposed to have been
    written to challenge the memory of
    Charles Macklin, the actor, who
    prided himself upon rapid study.*

13994. No one is exempt from talking nonsense; the misfortune is to do
it solemnly.   MONTAIGNE, *Essays*

13995.
A little nonsense now and then
Is relished by the wisest men.
Nursery Rhyme

13996. And such a deal of skimble-skamble stuff.   SHAKESPEARE,
Henry IV

NOON

Related Subject: Day.

14001. Clearer than the noonday.
Bible: Job, xi, 17

14002. Another morn Ris'n on mid-noon.   MILTON, *Paradise Lost*

14003.
With twelve great shocks of sound,
    the shameless noon
Was clash'd and hammer'd from a
    hundred towers.   TENNYSON,
Godiva

NOSE

Related Subjects: Face, Odor, Perfume, Sneezing.

14011. My father was a freedman who wiped his nose on his sleeve.
BION

14012. Any nose May ravage with impunity a rose.   BROWNING,
Sordello

14013. As clear and as manifest as the nose on a man's face.
ROBERT BURTON,
Anatomy of Melancholy

14014.
He would not with a peremptory
    tone,
Assert the nose upon his face his own.
COWPER, *Conversation*

14015. Another tumble! That's his precious nose!   THOMAS HOOD,
Ode to My Infant Son

14016. When I want any good head-work done, I always choose a man, if suitable otherwise, with a long nose.
NAPOLEON

14017. Cleopatra's nose: had it been shorter, the whole aspect of the world would have been altered.
PASCAL, *Pensées*

14018. The King is well enough pleased with her; which, I fear, will put Madam Castlemaine's nose out of joint.   SAMUEL PEPYS, *Diary*

14019. Paying through the nose.
Proverb

14020. He that has a great nose thinks everybody is speaking of it.
Proverb

14021. Hold their noses to the grindstone.   *Proverb*

14022. An inch in a man's nose is much.   *Proverb*

14023. To cut off one's nose to spite one's face.   PUBLILIUS SYRUS,
Sententiae

14024.
Nose, nose, nose, nose!
And who gave thee that jolly red
    nose?
Sinament and Ginger, Nutmegs and
    Cloves,
And that gave me my jolly red nose.
THOMAS RAVENSCROFT,
Deuteromela

14025.
I like the saucy retroussé,
    Admire the Roman, love the Greek;
But hers is none of these—it's a
      Beak.   E. M. ROBINSON,
A Disagreeable Feature

14026.
A great nose indicates a great man—
Genial, courteous, intellectual,
Virile, courageous.
EDMOND ROSTAND,
Cyrano de Bergerac

14027. His nose was as sharp as a pen.   SHAKESPEARE, *Henry V*

14028. Take my advice and seek no further than the end of your nose. You will always know that there is something beyond that; and in that knowledge you will be hopeful and happy.   BERNARD SHAW, *The Adventures of the Black Girl*

See also: 5861.

NOTHINGNESS

Related Subjects: **Darkness, Oblivion.**

14031. From nothing I was born, and soon again I shall be nothing as at first.   *Anonymous*

14032. We brought nothing into this world, and it is certain we can carry nothing out. *Bible: 1 Timothy, vi, 7*

14033. They that have nothing need fear to lose nothing.
JOHN CLARKE, *Paroemiologia*

14034. I hear nothing, I speak nothing, I take interest in nothing, and from nothing to nothing I travel gently down the dull way which leads to becoming nothing.
MME. DU DEFFAND

14035. It began of nothing and in nothing it ends.   GALLUS

14036. A world where nothing is had for nothing.   A. H. CLOUGH

14037. Nothing can come out of nothing, any more than a thing can go back to nothing.
MARCUS AURELIUS, *Meditations*

14038. Naught is never in danger.
Proverb

14039. A man may live upon little, but he cannot live upon nothing.
Proverb

14040. To say nothing, to do nothing, to know nothing, and to have nothing.
SHAKESPEARE,
All's Well that Ends Well

14041. Nothing will come of nothing.
SHAKESPEARE, *King Lear*

14042. Thou art an O without a figure.   SHAKESPEARE, *King Lear*

14043.
Where every something, being blent together
Turns to a wild of nothing.
SHAKESPEARE,
The Merchant of Venice

14044.
A life of nothings, nothing worth,
From that first nothing ere his birth
To that last nothing under earth.
TENNYSON, *The Two Voices*

14045. Nothing exists.   ZENO

See also: 1697, 3769.

NOVELTY

Related Subjects: **Change, Foreigners, Originality, Variety.**

14051. There is no new thing under the sun.   *Bible: Ecclesiastes, i, 9*

14052. Is there anything whereof it may be said, See, this is new? It hath been already of old time, which was before us.
Bible: Ecclesiastes, i, 10

14053. Every new movement or manifestation of human activity, when unfamiliar to people's minds, is sure to be misrepresented and misunderstood.
EDWARD CARPENTER,
The Drama of Love and Death

14054. The earth was made so various, that the mind of desultory man, studious of change, and pleased with novelty, might be indulged.
COWPER

14055. Such is the nature of novelty that where anything pleases it becomes doubly agreeable if new; but if it displeases, it is doubly displeasing on that very account.

DAVID HUME

14056. It is not only old and early impressions that deceive us; the charms of novelty have the same power. PASCAL

14057. Novelty always appears handsome. *Proverb*

14058. 'Tis novelty that sets people a-gaping. *Proverb*

14059.
There is nothing left remarkable
Beneath the visiting moon.

SHAKESPEARE,
Antony and Cleopatra

14060. Novelty has charms that our minds can hardly withstand. The most valuable things, if they have for a long while appeared among us, do not make any impression as they are good, but give us a distaste as they are old. But when the influence of this fantastical humor is over, the same men or things will come to be admired again, by a happy return of our good taste. THACKERAY

See also: 262, 936, 941, 966, 1206, 6448, 20184.

NUDITY

Related Subjects: Decency, Dress, Modesty.

14061. Naked came we into the world, and naked shall we depart from it. AESOP, *Fables*

14062. The nakedness of woman is the work of God. BLAKE,
Proverbs of Hell

14063. Lives the man that can figure a naked Duke of Windlestraw addressing a naked House of Lords?

CARLYLE, *Sartor Resartus*

14064.
Her gentle limbs did she undress,
And lay down in her loveliness.

COLERIDGE, *Christabel*

14065. Nothing is so chaste as nudity. Venus herself, as she drops her garments and steps on to the model-throne, leaves behind her on the floor every weapon in her armory by which she can pierce to the grosser passions of man. GEORGE DU MAURIER,
Trilby

14066.
In naked beauty more adorn'd,
More lovely, than Pandora.

MILTON, *Paradise Lost*

14067. I always forget the interpretation the average member of the public puts on a nude. Nothing startles me more than when the Mayor and his aldermen representing various municipal galleries come to my studio to choose a picture, and they arrive all agog and begin lifting the curtains and peering into cubbyholes in the hope of seeing a naked girl.

C. R. W. NEVINSON

14068. Without clothes, but with all her insides. PLAUTUS, *Pseudolus*

14069.
With presented nakedness out-face
The winds and persecutions of the
sky. SHAKESPEARE, *King Lear*

14070.
Othello: Naked in bed, Iago, and not
mean harm!
It is hypocrisy against the devil.

SHAKESPEARE, *Othello*

See also: 211, 219, 2064, 2066, 2074.

NUMBERS

Related Subject: Mathematics.

14071. Who can number the sands of the sea, and the drops of rain, and the days of eternity?

Apocrypha: Ecclesiasticus

14072. Round numbers are always false.   SAMUEL JOHNSON

14073. This is the third time; I hope good luck lies in odd numbers . . . There is divinity in odd numbers, either in nativity, chance, or death.

SHAKESPEARE,
Merry Wives of Windsor

See also: 19046.

NUN, see Monk

O

OAK

Related Subject: Tree.

14081. The oak grows silently, in the forest, a thousand years; only in the thousandth year, when the woodman arrives with his axe is there heard an echoing through the solitudes; and the oak announces itself when, with far-sounding crash, it falls.

CARLYLE,
The French Revolution

14082. Heart of oak.

CERVANTES, *Don Quixote*

14083.
The oak, when living, monarch of the wood;
The English oak, which, dead, commands the flood.

CHARLES CHURCHILL, *Gotham*

14084.
The talking oak To the ancient spoke.
But any tree Will talk to me.

CAROLYN DAVIES,
Be Different to Trees

14085.
The monarch oak, the patriarch of the trees,
Shoots rising up, and spreads by slow degrees.
Three centuries he grows, and three he stays
Supreme in state; and in three more decays.   DRYDEN,
Palamon and Arcite

14086. Every oak must be an acorn.

EDWARD FITZGERALD, *Polonius*

14087. Oaks may fall when reeds stand the storm.

THOMAS FULLER, *Gnomologia*

14088. An oak whose antique root peeps out.   SHAKESPEARE,
As You Like It

See also: 15057.

OATH

Related Subjects: Bargain, Honor, Lies, Obligation, Patriotism, Promise, Swearing, Vow.

14091. It is not the oath that makes us believe the man, but the man the oath.   AESCHYLUS

14092.
He that imposes an oath makes it,
Not he that for convenience takes it;
Then how can any man be said
To break an oath he never made?

SAMUEL BUTLER, *Hudibras*

14093. Oaths are but words, and words but wind.

SAMUEL BUTLER, *Hudibras*

14094. An honest man's word is as good as his bond.   CERVANTES,
Don Quixote

14095. I will take my corporal oath on it.   CERVANTES, *Don Quixote*

14096. You may depend upon it, the more oath-taking, the more lying generally among the people.

COLERIDGE, *Table Talk*

14097. Oaths, used as playthings or convenient tools. COWPER,
Expostulation

14098. We mutually pledge to each other our lives, our fortunes, and our sacred honor. JEFFERSON,
Declaration of Independence

14099. I take the official oath to-day with no mental reservations and with no purpose to construe the Constitution by any hypercritical rules.
LINCOLN

14100. Better break your word than do worse in keeping it. *Proverb*

14101. An unlawful oath is better broke than kept. *Proverb*

14102. Oaths are the fossils of piety.
SANTAYANA,
Interpretations of Poetry

14103. False as dicers' oaths.
SHAKESPEARE, *Hamlet*

14104. A good mouth-filling oath.
SHAKESPEARE, *Henry IV*

14105.
　　What fool is not so wise
To break an oath, to win a paradise?
SHAKESPEARE,
Love's Labour's Lost

14106.
Having sworn too hard a keeping oath,
Study to break it and not break my troth. SHAKESPEARE,
Love's Labour's Lost

14107. Thou swear'st thy gods in vain. SHAKESPEARE,
Love's Labour's Lost

14108.
An oath, an oath, I have an oath in heaven:
Shall I lay perjury upon my soul?
No, not for Venice.
SHAKESPEARE, *Merchant of Venice*

14109.
I'll take thy word for faith, not ask thine oath;
Who shuns not to break one will sure crack both. SHAKESPEARE,
Pericles

14110.
　　The strongest oaths are straw
To the fire i' the blood.
SHAKESPEARE, *The Tempest*

14111. If it be ne'er so false, a true gentleman may swear it in the behalf of his friend. SHAKESPEARE,
The Winter's Tale

14112. I write a woman's oaths in water. SOPHOCLES

See also: 3087, 8869, 13297.

OBEDIENCE AND DISOBEDIENCE

Related Subjects: Authority, Command, Defiance, Discipline, Submission, Treason.

14121. The fear of some divine and supreme powers keeps men in obedience. ROBERT BURTON,
Anatomy of Melancholy

14122. My son Hannibal will be a great general, because of all my soldiers he best knows how to obey.
HAMILCAR

14123.
Now these are the Laws of the Jungle, and many and mighty are they;
But the head and the hoof of the Law and the haunch and the hump is—Obey! KIPLING,
The Law of the Jungle

14124.

We must do the thing we *must*
Before the thing we may;
We are unfit for any trust
Till we can and do obey.
GEORGE MACDONALD,
Willie's Question

14125. They that are bound must obey.   *Proverb*

14126.

Obedience,
Bane of all genius, virtue, freedom, truth,
Makes slaves of men, and, of the human frame,
A mechanized automaton.
SHELLEY, *Queen Mab*

14127.

Theirs not to make reply,
Theirs not to reason why,
Theirs but to do and die.
TENNYSON,
The Charge of the Light Brigade

Disobedience

14128. Disobedient children, if preserved from the gallows, are reserved for the rack, to be tortured by their own posterity. One complaining, that never father had so undutiful a child as he had, yes, said his son, with less grace than truth, my grandfather had.
THOMAS FULLER

14129. Wherever there is authority, there is a natural inclination to disobedience.   T. C. HALIBURTON

14130. That men so universally disobey God bespeaks alienation and enmity of mind, for as obedience proceeds from love so disobedience proceeds from enmity.   JOHN HOWE

14131.

Let it profit thee to have heard,

By terrible example, the reward
Of disobedience.   MILTON,
Paradise Lost

14132. Rogues differ little. Each begun first as a disobedient son.
Proverb

OBLIGATION

Related Subjects: Borrowing, Debt, Duty, Gratitude, Oath, Responsibility, Trust.

14141. The Moral Obligation to Be Intelligent.   JOHN ERSKINE,
Title of book

14142. It is well known to all great men, that by conferring an obligation they do not always procure a friend, but are certain of creating many enemies.   FIELDING

14143. Obligation is thraldom, and thraldom is hateful.
THOMAS HOBBES

14144. Too great haste to repay an obligation is a kind of ingratitude.
LA ROCHEFOUCAULD, *Maxims*

14145. We are always much better pleased to see those whom we have obliged, than those who have obliged us.   LA ROCHEFOUCAULD, *Maxims*

14146. Excess of obligations may lose a friend.   *Proverb*

14147. If you oblige those who can never pay you, you make Providence your debtor.   *Proverb*

14148. Up to a certain point it is good for us to know that there are people in the world who will give us love and unquestioned loyalty to the limit of their ability. I doubt, however, if it is good for us to feel assured of this without the accompanying obligation of having to justify this devotion by our behavior.

ELEANOR ROOSEVELT,
This is My Story

14149. In some there is a kind of graceless modesty that makes a man ashamed of requiting an obligation, because it is a confession that he has received one.   SENECA

See also: 7, 796, 1964, 5084.

OBLIVION

Related Subjects: Darkness, Forgetfulness, Memory, Nothingness.

14151. Our name shall be forgotten in time, and no man shall have our works in remembrance, and our life shall pass away as the trace of a cloud, and shall be dispersed as a mist.
Apocrypha: Wisdom of Solomon

14152. Oblivion is not to be hired: the greater part must be content to be as though they had not been.
SIR THOMAS BROWNE, *Urn-Burial*

14153. Oblivion is the dark page whereon memory writes her light-beam characters, and makes them legible; were it all light, nothing could be read there, any more than if it were all darkness.   CARLYLE, *Essays*

14154. And o'er the past Oblivion stretch her wing.   HOMER, *Odyssey*

14155. As for life, it is a battle and sojourning in a strange land; but the fame that comes after is oblivion.
MARCUS AURELIUS, *Meditations*

14156.
And if I drink oblivion of a day,
So shorten I the stature of my soul.
GEORGE MEREDITH, *Modern Love*

14157.
Far off from these, a slow and silent stream,

Lethe, the River of Oblivion, rolls
Her wat'ry labyrinth, whereof who drinks
Forthwith his former state and being forgets.   MILTON, *Paradise Lost*

14158.
Cancell'd from Heav'n and sacred memory,
Nameless in dark oblivion let them dwell.   MILTON, *Paradise Lost*

14159.
Where dust and damned oblivion is the tomb
Of honour'd bones.
SHAKESPEARE,
All's Well that Ends Well

14160. And blind oblivion swallow'd cities up.   SHAKESPEARE,
Troilus and Cressida

14161.
What's past and what's to come is strew'd with husks
And formless ruin of oblivion.
SHAKESPEARE,
Troilus and Cressida

See also: 10634.

OBSCURITY

Related Subjects: Concealment, Darkness, Fog, Mystery, Secrecy.

14171. Obscurity often brings safety.
AESOP, *The Tree and the Road*

14172. Now we see through a glass, darkly.   *Bible: 1 Corinthians, xiii, 12*

14173.
I give the fight up; let there be an end,
A privacy, an obscure nook for me,
I want to be forgotten even by God.
BROWNING, *Paracelsus*

14174. Of all outward evils Obscurity is perhaps in itself the least.
CARLYLE,
On Boswell's Life of Johnson

14175. Thy greatest praise had been to live unknown.
CHARLES CHURCHILL, *The Rosciad*

14176.
If this young man expresses himself
    in terms too deep for *me,*
Why, what a very singularly deep
    young man this deep young man
    must be! W. S. GILBERT, *Patience*

14177.
Some village Hampden, that with
    dauntless breast
    The little tyrant of his fields with-
    stood;
Some mute, inglorious Milton here
    may rest,
    Some Cromwell guiltless of his
    country's blood.
          THOMAS GRAY,
    Elegy Written in a Country
              Churchyard

14178.
Full many a gem of purest ray serene
    The dark unfathom'd caves of
    ocean bear:
Full many a flower is born to blush
    unseen,
    And waste its sweetness on the
    desert air. THOMAS GRAY,
    Elegy Written in a Country
              Churchyard

14179. You banter me by discoursing obscurely.   HORACE, *Satires*

14180. He has lived well who has lived obscurely.   OVID, *Tristia*

14181.
Thus let me live, unseen, unknown,
    Thus unlamented let me die;
Steal from the world, and not a stone
    Tell where I lie.
        POPE, *Ode on Solitude*

14182. A long list of the illustrious obscure.   SHELLEY, *Adonais*

14183. Sweet were the days when I was all unknown.
    TENNYSON, *Idylls of the King*

14184. Obscurity is the realm of error.   VAUVENARGUES

See also: 794, 805, 8737, 9317, 15374.

OBSERVATION

Related Subjects: Experience, Knowledge, Perception, Sophistication.

14191. Seeing many things, but thou observest not; opening the ears, but he heareth not.
    Bible: Isaiah, xlii, 20

14192. Shakespeare says, we are creatures that look before and after: the more surprising that we do not look round a little, and see what is passing under our very eyes.
    CARLYLE, *Sartor Resartus*

14193. The difference between landscape and landscape is small, but there is great difference in the beholders.
    EMERSON, *Essays*

14194. I do love to note and to observe.   BEN JONSON, *Volpone*

14195. I have seen the outward appearance of the city, but I have observed the manners of men too little.
    PLAUTUS, *Persa*

14196.
To observations which ourselves we
    make,
We grow more partial, for th' ob-
    server's sake.
        POPE, *Moral Essays*

14197. Observation, not old age, brings wisdom.
    PUBLILIUS SYRUS, *Sententiae*

14198.
For he is but a bastard to the time
That doth not smack of observation.
SHAKESPEARE, *King John*

See also: 744, 4815, 6603.

OBSTINACY

Related Subjects: Argument, Bigotry, Dogmatism, Opinion, Perseverance, Perversity, Resolution.

14201. Obstinacy in a bad cause is but constancy in a good.
SIR THOMAS BROWNE,
Religio Medici

14202.
Where Obstinacy takes his sturdy stand,
To disconcert what Policy has plann'd. COWPER, *Expostulation*

14203.
Man is a creature of a wilful head,
And hardly driven is, but eas'ly led.
SAMUEL DANIEL, *Queen's Arcadia*

14204. Oh, my dear Kepler, how I wish that we could have one hearty laugh together. Here at Padua, is the principal professor of philosophy whom I have repeatedly and urgently requested to look at the moon and planets through my glass, which he pertinaciously refuses to do. Why are you not here? What shouts of laughter we should have at this glorious folly. GALILEO, *to John Kepler*

14205.
The gods that unrelenting breast have steel'd,
And curs'd thee with a mind that cannot yield. HOMER, *Iliad*

14206. Obstinacy and heat of opinion are the surest proof of stupidity.
MONTAIGNE, *Essays*

14207. Fools and obstinate men make lawyers rich. *Proverb*

14208. You may bring a horse to the river, but he will drink when and what he pleaseth. *Proverb*

14209. It is self-conceit that makes opinion obstinate. *Proverb*

14210. A wilful man never wants woe. *Proverb*

14211. Let it be virtuous to be obstinate. SHAKESPEARE, *Coriolanus*

14212. I'll not budge an inch.
SHAKESPEARE,
The Taming of the Shrew

See also: 2155, 4992, 11517, 15060.

OCCUPATION

Related Subjects: Business, Employment, Work.

14221.
Oh, let us love our occupations,
Bless the squire and his relations,
Live upon our daily rations,
And always know our proper stations.
DICKENS, *The Chimes*

14222. What I advise is that each contentedly practise the trade he understands. HORACE, *Epistles*

14223. Occupation is one great source of enjoyment. No man, properly occupied, was ever miserable.
L. E. LANDON

14224. He who busies himself in mean occupations produces, in the very pains he takes about things of little or no use, an evidence against himself of his negligence and indisposition to what is really good.
PLUTARCH, *Lives*

14225. Constant occupation prevents temptation. *Proverb*

14226. He that brings up his son to nothing breeds a thief. *Proverb*

14227. A man of many trades begs his bread on Sundays. *Proverb*

14228. When men are rightly occupied, their amusement grows out of their work, as the colour-petals out of a fruitful flower.

RUSKIN, *Sesame and Lilies*

14229. 'Tis my vocation, Hal; 'tis no sin for a man to labour in his vocation. SHAKESPEARE, *Henry IV*

14230. Farewell! Othello's occupation's gone! SHAKESPEARE, *Othello*

14231.
No profit grows where is no pleasure ta'en;
In brief, sir, study what you most affect. SHAKESPEARE,
The Taming of the Shrew

See also: 10285, 13097.

OCEAN, see Sea

OCTOBER

Related Subjects: Autumn, Month.

14241. There is something in October sets the gypsy blood astir.
BLISS CARMAN, *A Vagabond Song*

14242. There is no season when such pleasant and sunny spots may be lighted on, and produce so pleasant an effect on the feelings, as now in October.
HAWTHORNE, *American Notebooks*

14243.
The skies they were ashen and sober;
The leaves they were crispéd and sere—

The leaves they were withering and sere;
It was night in the lonesome October
Of my most immemorial year.
POE, *Ulalume*

14244.
And close at hand, the basket stood
With nuts from brown October's wood. WHITTIER, *Snow-Bound*

ODOR

Related Subjects: Perfume, Nose.

14251.
I counted two-and-seventy stenches,
All well defined, and several stinks.
COLERIDGE, *Cologne*

14252. There is nothing like an odour to stir memories.
WILLIAM MCFEE, *The Market*

14253. To stink like a pole-cat.
Proverb

14254. The rankest compound of villainous smell that ever offended nostril. SHAKESPEARE,
The Merry Wives of Windsor

14255. Eat no onions nor garlic, for we are to utter sweet breath.
SHAKESPEARE,
A Midsummer-Night's Dream

14256. A very ancient and fish-like smell. SHAKESPEARE, *The Tempest*

14257.
Odours, when sweet violets sicken,
Live within the sense they quicken.
SHELLEY,
Music, When Soft Voices Die

14258. There is no odor so bad as that which arises from goodness tainted. THOREAU, *Walden*

OFFENCE

Related Subjects: Abuse, Crime, Curse, Injury, Insult, Slander, Threat.

14261. What dire offence from am'-rous causes springs.

POPE, *Rape of the Lock*

14262. And love the offender, yet detest the offence.

POPE, *Eloisa to Abelard*

14263. The multitude of offenders is their protection.   *Proverb*

14264. The offender never pardons.

Proverb

14265. No offence taken where none is meant.   *Proverb*

14266.
In such a time as this it is not meet
That every nice offence should bear
    his comment.

SHAKESPEARE, *Julius Caesar*

14267.
All's not offence that indiscretion
    finds
And dotage terms so.

SHAKESPEARE, *King Lear*

14268.
The very head and front of my of-
    fending
Hath this extent, no more.

SHAKESPEARE, *Othello*

14269. My remembrance is very free and clear from any image of offence done to any man.

SHAKESPEARE, *Twelfth Night*

See also: 388, 1379, 1705, 3744, 8438, 13573, 21578, 21955.

OFFICE

Related Subjects: Election, Government, Place, Politics, Rank.

14271. Public life is a situation of power and energy; he trespasses against his duty who sleeps upon his watch, as well as he that goes over to the enemy.   BURKE,
*Thoughts on the Cause
of the Present Discontent*

14272. It ought to be the happiness and glory of a representative to live in the strictest union, the closest correspondence, and the most unreserved communication with his constituents. Their wishes ought to have great weight with him; their opinion high respect, their business unremitted attention. It is his duty to sacrifice his repose, his pleasures, his satisfaction, to theirs; and above all, ever, and in all cases, to prefer their interests to his own.   BURKE,
Speech to the Electors of Bristol

14273. Your representative owes you, not his industry only, but his judgment; and he betrays instead of serving you if he sacrifices it to your opinion.   BURKE,
Speech to the Electors of Bristol

14274. Governing persons, were they never so insignificant intrinsically, have for most part plenty of memoir-writers.

CARLYLE, *The French Revolution*

14275. Public officers are the servants and agents of the people, to execute the laws which the people have made.   GROVER CLEVELAND

14276. A man ain't got no right to be a public man, unless he meets the public views.

DICKENS, *Martin Chuzzlewit*

14277. I shall never ask, never refuse, nor ever resign an office.

FRANKLIN, *Autobiography*

14278. Never with my consent shall an officer of the people, compensated for his services out of their pockets, become the pliant instrument of the Executive will.

WILLIAM HENRY HARRISON,
Inaugural Address

14279. It is not fit the public trusts should be lodged in the hands of any, till they are first proved and found fit for the business they are to be entrusted with.

MATTHEW HENRY, *Commentaries*

14280. When a man assumes a public trust, he should consider himself as a public property.   JEFFERSON

14281.
Trust me, To-day's Most Indispensables,
Five hundred men can take your place or mine.

KIPLING, *The Last Department*

14282. No important institution, moreover, is ever merely what the law makes it. It accumulates about itself traditions, conventions, ways of behavior, which, without ever attaining the status of formal law, are not less formidable in their influence than law itself could require.

HAROLD J. LASKI,
The American Presidency

14283. Every time I fill a vacant office, I make ten malcontents and one ingrate.   LOUIS XIV

14284. To be turned from one's course by men's opinions, by blame, and by misrepresentation, shows a man unfit to hold an office.

PLUTARCH, *Lives*

14285. He that puts on a public gown must put off a private person.
Proverb

14286. We must remember not to judge any public servant by any one act, and especially should we beware of attacking the men who are merely

the occasions and not the causes of disaster.   THEODORE ROOSEVELT

14287. They who are in highest places, and have the most power, have the least liberty, because they are most observed.

JOHN TILLOTSON, *Reflections*

See also: 1377, 2632.

OPINION

Related Subjects: Argument, Assertions, Belief, Bigotry, Criticism, Fanaticism, Impressions, Judgment, Obstinacy, Propaganda.

14291.
Men get opinions as boys learn to spell
By reiteration chiefly.

ELIZABETH B. BROWNING,
Aurora Leigh

14292.
He that complies against his will
Is of his own opinion still.

SAMUEL BUTLER, *Hudibras*

14293. Them's my sentiments, tew.
WILL CARLETON,
The Schoolmaster's Guests

14294. They that approve a private opinion, call it opinion; but they that mislike it, heresy: and yet heresy signifies no more than private opinion.

THOMAS HOBBES, *Leviathan*

14295. Opinions is a species of property I am always desirous of sharing.
CHARLES LAMB

14296. We hardly find any persons of good sense save those who agree with us. LA ROUCHEFOUCAULD, *Maxims*

14297. Opinions cannot survive if one has no chance to fight for them.
THOMAS MANN,
The Magic Mountain

14298. Remember that to change thy mind and to follow him that sets thee right, is to be none the less the free agent that thou wast before.

MARCUS AURELIUS, *Meditations*

14299. If any man can convince me and bring home to me that I do not think or act aright, gladly will I change; for I search after truth, by which man never yet was harmed.

MARCUS AURELIUS, *Meditations*

14300. The principal thing is for all Americans to find a way to hang on to what our forefathers called *liberty*. Conservative or radical, you have the right to any opinion you like—that's inherent in Americanism. Free opinion is one of the blessings of our Constitution.

MAURY MAVERICK, *Blood & Ink*

14301. What we have to do is to be forever curiously testing new opinions and courting new impressions.

WALTER PATER, *The Renaissance*

14302. You are young, my son, and, as the years go by, time will change, and even reverse many of your present opinions. Refrain therefore awhile from setting yourself up as a judge of the highest matters.

PLATO, *Laws*

14303. Two Sir Positives can scarce meet without a skirmish. *Proverb*

14304. He that seeks a' opinions, comes ill speed. *Proverb*

14305. A wise man changes his mind, a fool never. *Proverb*

14306.
I have bought
Golden opinions from all sorts of people. SHAKESPEARE, *Macbeth*

14307.
Fish not, with this melancholy bait,

For this fool gudgeon, this opinion.

SHAKESPEARE,
The Merchant of Venice

14308. Has it ever occurred to you that a man with an open mind must be a bit of a scoundrel? . . . I like a man who makes up his mind once for all as to what's right and what's wrong and then sticks to it.

BERNARD SHAW, *Misalliance*

14309. "That was excellently observed," say I when I read a passage in another where his opinion agrees with mine. When we differ, then I pronounce him to be mistaken.

SWIFT,
Thoughts on Various Subjects

14310. Them's my sentiments.

THACKERAY, *Vanity Fair*

14311. I agree with no man's opinions. I have some of my own.

TURGENIEV, *Fathers and Sons*

14312. It is difference of opinion that makes horse races.

MARK TWAIN,
Pudd'nhead Wilson's Calendar

14313. It is difficult to be emphatic when no one is emphatic on the other side.

CHARLES DUDLEY WARNER,
My Summer in a Garden

Public Opinion

14314. The machinery for weighing or measuring the popular will from week to week, or month to month has not been, and is not likely to be, invented. LORD BRYCE,
The American Commonwealth

14315. Public opinion's always in advance of the Law.

GALSWORTHY, *Windows*

14316. It is now a commonplace that

the dissenting opinions of one generation become the prevailing interpretation of the next.

BURTON J. HENDRICK,
Bulwark of the Republic

14317. That mysterious independent variable of political calculation, Public Opinion.

THOMAS H. HUXLEY,
Universities, Actual and Ideal

14318. Opinion is like a pendulum and obeys the same law. If it goes past the centre of gravity on one side, it must go a like distance on the other; and it is only after a certain time that it finds the true point at which it can remain at rest.

SCHOPENHAUER

14319. You deal in the raw material of opinion, and, if my convictions have any validity, opinion ultimately governs the world.

WOODROW WILSON

See also: 94, 143, 348, 935, 1334, 2592, 3999, 4433, 5449, 7084, 9512, 11639, 18895.

OPPORTUNITY

Related Subjects: **Advantage, Chance, Circumstance, Environment, Fortune, Luck.**

14321.
With doubt and dismay you are
  smitten
You think there's no chance for you
  son?
Why, the best books haven't been
  written,
The best race hasn't been run.

BERTON BRALEY, *Opportunity*

14322.
Gather ye rosebuds while ye may,
  Old Time is still a-flying,

And this same flower that smiles today
  Tomorrow will be dying.

ROBERT HERRICK,
*To the Virgins to Make
Much of Time*

14323. Seize now and here the hour that is, nor trust some later day.

HORACE, *Odes*

14324.
I knock unbidden once at every gate!
If sleeping, wake; if feasting, rise
  before
I turn away. It is the hour of fate.

J. J. INGALLS, *Opportunity*

14325. I don't think I regret a single "excess" of my responsive youth—I only regret in my chilled age, certain occasions and possibilities I didn't embrace.   HENRY JAMES

14326.
They do me wrong who say I come
  no more
    When once I knock and fail to find
      you in;
For every day I stand outside your
  door,
    And bid you wake, and rise to
      fight and win.

WALTER MALONE, *Opportunity*

14327. Never refuse a good offer.
Proverb

14328. There is an hour wherein a man might be happy all his life could he find it.   *Proverb*

14329. A wise man will make more opportunities than he finds.
Proverb

14330. An occasion lost cannot be redeemed.   *Proverb*

14331. While we stop to think, we often miss our opportunity.

PUBLILIUS SYRUS, *Sententiae*

14332. You should hammer your iron when it is glowing hot.

PUBLILIUS SYRUS, *Sententiae*

14333.
We must take the current when it
    serves,
Or lose our ventures.

SHAKESPEARE, *Julius Caesar*

14334. I am busy about the main chance.   SIR RICHARD STEELE

14335. Now or never was the time.

STERNE, *Tristram Shandy*

14336.
To every life there comes a time
    supreme;
One day, one night, one morning, or
    one noon,
One freighted hour, one moment op-
    portune,
One rift through which sublime ful-
    filments gleam.

MARY A. TOWNSEND,
Opportunity

See also: 106, 112, 155, 251, 346, 487, 584, 662, 1494, 4705, 5270, 5712, 5788, 10841, 19775, 21053.

OPPOSITION

Related Subjects: Competition, Discord, Enemy, Faction, Rivalry.

14341. He that is not with me is against me.   *Bible: Luke, xi, 23*

14342. He that wrestles with us strengthens our nerves and sharpens our skill. Our antagonist is our helper.   BURKE,
*Reflections on the Revolution
in France*

14343. Opposition may become sweet to a man when he has christened it persecution.   GEORGE ELIOT,
Janet's Repentance

14344. The effects of opposition are wonderful. There are men who rise refreshed on hearing of a threat,— men to whom a crisis which intimidates and paralyzes the majority, comes graceful and beloved as a bride!   EMERSON

14345. The coldest bodies warm with opposition; the hardest sparkle in collision.   JUNIUS

14346. Opposition always inflames the enthusiast, never converts him.

SCHILLER

14347.
Have you not learn'd great lessons
    from those who reject you, and
    brace themselves against you? or
    who treat you with contempt, or
    dispute the passage with you?

WALT WHITMAN, *Stronger Lessons*

See also: 2735.

OPPRESSION, see Tyranny

OPTIMISM

Related Subjects: Cheerfulness, Confidence, Courage, Faith, Hope.

14351.
The barren optimistic sophistries
Of comfortable moles.

MATTHEW ARNOLD,
To a Republican Friend

14352.
I find earth not grey but rosy
Heaven not grim but fair of hue.

BROWNING, *At the "Mermaid"*

14353.
God's in his Heaven
All's right with the world!

BROWNING, *Pippa Passes*

14354. The optimist proclaims that we live in the best of all possible

worlds; and the pessimist fears this is true.   BRANCH CABELL,
The Silver Stallion

14355. The noble temptation to see too much in everything.
G. K. CHESTERTON,
Robert Browning

14356. In short, if anything turns up.
DICKENS, *David Copperfield*

14357. The place where optimism most flourishes is the lunatic asylum.
HAVELOCK ELLIS,
The Dance of Life

14358. Optimism is a kind of heart stimulant—the digitalis of failure.
ELBERT HUBBARD,
A Thousand and One Epigrams

14359. The habit of looking on the best side of every event is worth more than a thousand pounds a year.
SAMUEL JOHNSON

14360.
There's a good time coming, boys!
A good time coming.
CHARLES MACKAY,
The Good Time Coming

14361. All is for the best in the best of all possible worlds.
VOLTAIRE, *Candide*

14362. Optimism is the madness of maintaining that everything is right when it is wrong.   VOLTAIRE,
Candide

14363. What will be will be well, for what is is well.
WALT WHITMAN,
To Think of Time

14364.
Say you are well, or all is well with you,
And God shall hear your words and make them true.
ELLA W. WILCOX, *Speech*

14365.
'Twixt optimist and pessimist
The difference is droll:
The optimist sees the doughnut,
The pessimist, the hole.
McLANDBURGH WILSON,
Optimist and Pessimist

See also: 482, 702.

ORACLE

Related Subjects: **Mythology, Priest, Prophecy, Superstition, Wisdom.**

14371.
I am Sir Oracle,
And when I ope my lips, let no dog
bark!   SHAKESPEARE,
The Merchant of Venice

14372. Bold as an oracle.
SHAKESPEARE,
Troilus and Cressida

14373. There is no truth at all i' the oracle.   SHAKESPEARE,
The Winter's Tale

See also: 7344, 9334.

ORATOR AND ORATORY

Related Subjects: **Acting, Eloquence, Politics, Preacher, Speech.**

14381. I commend the old proverb, "For we must look about under every stone, lest an orator bite us."
ARISTOPHANES

14382. All epoch-making revolutionary events have been produced not by the written but by the spoken word.   ADOLF HITLER,
Mein Kampf

14383. Declamation roar'd, while Passion slept.   SAMUEL JOHNSON

14384.
There was an old man at a Station,
Who made a promiscuous oration.
EDWARD LEAR, *Limerick*

14385. Whoso can speak well is a man.   MARTIN LUTHER

14386. When Demosthenes was asked what was the first part of oratory, he answered, "Action"; and which was the second, he replied, "Action"; and which was the third, he still answered, "Action."   PLUTARCH, *Lives*

14387. Cicero said loud-bawling orators were driven by their weakness to noise, as lame men to take horse.
PLUTARCH, *Lives*

14388. It is a thing of no great difficulty to raise objections against another man's oration,—nay, it is a very easy matter; but to produce a better in its place is a work extremely troublesome.   PLUTARCH

14389. He is a good orator who convinces himself.   *Proverb*

14390. Good orators, when they are out, they will spit.
SHAKESPEARE, *As You Like It*

14391.
A man in all the world's new fashion planted,
That hath a mint of phrases in his brain.   SHAKESPEARE,
Love's Labour's Lost

14392. If ever a woman feels proud of her lover, it is when she sees him as a successful public speaker.
HARRIET BEECHER STOWE

See also: 1099, 1721, 14435, 20795.

ORDER

Related Subjects: Anarchy, Chaos, Discipline, Government, Habit, Logic, Method, Plan, Police, Reason, System.

14401. Order means light and peace, inward liberty and free command over oneself; order is power.
AMIEL, *Journal*

14402. Let all things be done decently and in order.
Bible: I Corinthians, xiv, 40

14403.
Order is a lovely thing; . . . .
It has a meek and lowly grace,
Quiet as a nun's face.
ANNA H. BRANCH,
The Monk in the Kitchen

14404. Good order is the foundation of all good things.   BURKE,
*Reflections on the Revolution in
France*

14405.
For the world was built in order
And the atoms march in tune.
EMERSON, *Monadnock*

14406. Order and simplification are the first steps toward the mastery of a subject—the actual enemy is the unknown.   THOMAS MANN,
The Magic Mountain

14407.
Confusion heard his voice, and wild uproar
Stood rul'd, stood vast infinitude confin'd;
Till at his second bidding darkness fled,
Light shone, and order from disorder sprung.   MILTON, *Paradise Lost*

14408. Order is Heav'n's first law.
POPE, *Essay on Man*

14409. All is soon ready in an orderly house.   *Proverb*

14410. Order gave each thing view.
SHAKESPEARE, *Henry VIII*

14411.
The heavens themselves, the planets and this centre
Observe degree, priority, and place,
Insisture, course, proportion, season, form,

Office and custom, in all line of order.
SHAKESPEARE,
Troilus and Cressida

14412. Order governs the world.
SWIFT, Letters

14413.
Large elements in order brought,
  And tracts of calm from tempest made,
And world-wide fluctuation sway'd,
In vassal tides that follow'd thought.
TENNYSON, In Memoriam

See also: 1792, 5922.

ORIGINALITY

Related Subjects: Cleverness, Imagination, Individuality, Invention, Novelty, Wit.

14421.
No bird has ever uttered note
That was not in some first bird's throat;
Since Eden's freshness and man's fall
No rose has been original.
T. B. ALDRICH, Originality

14422. Not picked from the leaves of any author, but bred amongst the weeds and tares of mine own brain.
SIR THOMAS BROWNE,
Religio Medici

14423. The merit of originality is not novelty; it is sincerity. The believing man is the original man.
CARLYLE, Heroes & Hero-Worship

14424. What is originality? It is being one's self, and reporting accurately what we see and are.
EMERSON,
Letters and Social Aims

14425. Originality provokes originality.
GOETHE, Spruche in Prosa

14426. A thought is often original, though you have uttered it a hundred times.
O. W. HOLMES,
The Autocrat of the Breakfast-Table

14427. Originality is undetected plagiarism.
DEAN INGE

14428. He has left off reading altogether, to the great improvement of his originality. CHARLES LAMB,
Detached Thoughts on Books &
Reading

14429. Originality is the one thing which unoriginal minds cannot feel the use of. J. S. MILL, <i>On Liberty</i>

14430. All good things which exist are the fruits of originality.
J. S. MILL, On Liberty

See also: 1074, 15323, 15381, 20193.

ORNAMENT

Related Subjects: Dress, Ostentation, Vanity.

14431. Ornaments were invented by modesty.   JOUBERT, <i>Pensées</i>

14432. The true ornament of matrons is virtue, not apparel.   JUSTIN

14433. Show is not substance; realities govern wise men.
WILLIAM PENN

14434.
The world is still deceiv'd with ornament,
In law, what plea so tainted and corrupt,
But, being season'd with a gracious voice,
Obscures the show of evil? In religion,
What damned error, but some sober brow
Will bless it and approve it with a text,

Hiding the grossness with fair ornament?   SHAKESPEARE,
The Merchant of Venice

14435. Orators and stage-coachmen,
when the one wants argument and
the other a coat of arms, adorn their
cause and their coaches with rhetoric
and flower-pots.   W. SHENSTONE

14436.
                  Loveliness
Needs not the foreign aid of orna-
      ment,
·But is when unadorn'd, adorn'd the
      most.
JAMES THOMSON, *The Seasons*

14437. We all originally came from
the woods; it is hard to eradicate
from any of us the old taste for the
tattoo and the war-paint; and the
moment that money gets into our
pockets, it somehow or another breaks
out in ornaments on our person, without always giving refinement to our
manners.   E. P. WHIPPLE

See also: 1010, 1011, 1670, 1733.

OSTENTATION

**Related Subjects: Appearance, Ar-
rogance, Boasting, Ceremony, Ornament, Pride, Vanity, Vulgarity.**

14441. An ostentatious man will
rather relate a blunder or an absurdity
he has committed, than be debarred
from talking of his own dear person.
                        ADDISON

14442. Ostentation is the signal flag
of hypocrisy. The charlatan is ver-
bose and assumptive; the Pharisee is
ostentatious, because he is a hypocrite.
Pride is the master sin of the devil,
and the devil is the father of lies.
                    E. H. CHAPIN

14443. Whatever is done without ostentation, and without the people being

witnesses of it, is, in my opinion, most
praiseworthy: not that the public eye
should be entirely avoided, for good
actions desire to be placed in the
light; but notwithstanding this, the
greatest theatre for virtue is conscience.   CICERO

14444. Where there is much pretension, much has been borrowed; nature
never pretends.   LAVATER

OWL

Related Subject: Birds.

14451. An owl is the king of the
night.   THOMAS DRAXE, *Bibliotheca*

14452.
Can grave and formal pass for wise
When men the solemn owl despise?
                JOHN GAY, *Fables*

14453.
    From yonder ivy-mantled tow'r
The moping owl does to the Moon
      complain.   THOMAS GRAY,
        *Elegy Written in a Country
                    Church-yard*

14454.
St. Agnes' Eve—Ah, bitter chill it
      was!
The owl, for all his feathers, was
      a-cold.   KEATS,
            The Eve of St. Agnes

14455.
The Owl and the Pussy-Cat went to
      sea
In a beautiful pea-green boat.
                EDWARD LEAR,
        The Owl and the Pussy-Cat

14456.
The screech-owl, with ill-boding cry,
    Portends strange things, old women
      say;
Stops every fool that passes by,
    And frights the school-boy from
      his play.
            MARY W. MONTAGU,
                The Politicians

14457. The owl is not accounted the wiser for living retiredly.   *Proverb*

14458.
A wise old owl sat on an oak,
  The more he saw the less he spoke;
The less he spoke the more he heard;
  Why aren't we like that wise old
    bird?   E. H. RICHARDS,
            A Wise Old Owl

14459. They say the owl was a baker's daughter.
            SHAKESPEARE, *Hamlet*

14460.
Then nightly sings the staring owl,
Tu-whit; Tu-who, a merry note.
            SHAKESPEARE,
            Love's Labour's Lost

14461.
It was the owl that shriek'd, the fatal bellman,
Which gives the stern'st good-night.
            SHAKESPEARE, *Macbeth*

14462. Do you think I was born in a wood to be afraid of an owl?
            SWIFT, *Polite Conversation*

14463. Like an owl in an ivy bush.
            SWIFT, *Polite Conversation*

See also: 1330, 1402, 1664, 4851.

OX

Related Subjects: Animal, Farming.

14471. As an ox goeth to the slaughter.   *Bible: Proverbs, vii, 22*

14472. The ox knoweth his owner, and the ass his master's crib.
            Bible: Isaiah, i, 3

14473. Thou shalt not muzzle the mouth of the ox that treadeth out the corn.   *Bible: 1 Corinthians, ix, 9*

14474. An ox is taken by the horns, and a man by the tongue.   *Proverb*

14475. The old ox makes the straightest furrow.   *Proverb*

14476. Where shall the ox go, but he must labour?   *Proverb*

14477.
Oxen that rattle the yoke and chain or halt in the leafy shade, what is it that you express in your eyes?
It seems to me more than all the print I have read in my life.
            WALT WHITMAN, *Song of Myself*

14478.
The cattle are grazing,
Their heads never raising;
There are forty feeding like one!
            WORDSWORTH, *Written in March*

OYSTER

Related Subjects: Fish, Pearl.

14481.
Nor brighter was his eye, nor moister
Than a too-long opened oyster.
            BROWNING, *The Pied Piper*

14482. It is unseasonable and unwholesome in all months that have not an *R* in their name to eat an oyster.
            WILLIAM BUTLER,
            Dyet's Dry Dinner

14483.
But four young Oysters hurried up,
  All eager for the treat:
Their coats were brushed, their faces washed,
  Their shoes were clean and neat—
And this was odd, because, you know,
  They hadn't any feet.
            LEWIS CARROLL,
            Through the Looking-Glass

14484. "Wery good power o' suction, Sammy," said Mr. Weller the elder. . . . "You'd ha' made an uncommon fine oyster, Sammy, if you'd been born in that station o' life."
            DICKENS, *Pickwick Papers*

14485. "It's a wery remarkable circumstance, sir," said Sam, "that poverty and oysters always seem to go together." DICKENS, *Pickwick Papers*

14486. How do you after your oysters? *Proverb*

14487.
Why, then the world's mine oyster,
Which I with sword will open.
SHAKESPEARE,
The Merry Wives of Windsor

14488. I will not be sworn but love may transform me to an oyster; but I'll take my oath on it, till he have made an oyster of me, he shall never make me such a fool.
SHAKESPEARE,
Much Ado About Nothing

14489. An oyster may be crossed in love! SHERIDAN, *The Critic*

14490. He was a bold man that first eat an oyster. SWIFT,
Polite Conversation

See also: 3026.

P

PAIN

Related Subjects: Bed, Disease, Misery, Suffering, Tears.

14491. The fiercest agonies have shortest reign. BRYANT, *Mutation*

14492.
Iron, left in the rain
    And fog and dew,
With rust is covered.—Pain
    Rusts into beauty too.
CAROLYN DAVIES, *Rust*

14493. He has seen but half the universe who never has been shewn the house of Pain. EMERSON,
Natural History of the Intellect

14494. So great was the extremity of his pain and anguish, that he did not only sigh but roar.
MATTHEW HENRY, *Commentaries*

14495. Those who do not feel pain seldom think that it is felt.
SAMUEL JOHNSON, *The Rambler*

14496.
Pleasure is oft a visitant; but pain
Clings cruelly to us. KEATS,
Endymion

14497.
Pain is perfect misery, the worst
Of evils, and excessive, overturns
All patience. MILTON, *Paradise Lost*

14498. An hour of pain is as long as a day of pleasure. *Proverb*

14499. No pains, no gains. *Proverb*

14500. Pain is the price that God putteth upon all things. *Proverb*

14501. Past pain is pleasure.
Proverb

14502. Lord, how we lose our pains!
SHAKESPEARE,
All's Well that Ends Well

14503.
One fire burns out another's burning,
One pain is lessen'd by another's anguish. SHAKESPEARE,
Romeo and Juliet

14504.
I'll rack thee with old cramps,
Fill all thy bones with aches, make thee roar
That beasts shall tremble at thy din.
SHAKESPEARE, *The Tempest*

14505. And painful pleasure turns to pleasing pain.
EDMUND SPENSER,
The Faerie Queene

14506. He loves to make parade of pain.   TENNYSON, *In Memoriam*

14507.
Nothing begins, and nothing ends,
  That is not paid with moan;
For we are born in other's pain,
  And perish in our own.
FRANCIS THOMPSON, *Daisy*

14508. Pain with the thousand teeth.
WILLIAM WATSON,
The Dream of Man

14509.
It changed the soul of one to sour
  And passionate regret;
To one it gave unselfish power
  To love and to forget.
S. L. WHITCOMB, *Pain*

See also: 2176, 4716, 5001, 8867, 10074, 11025, 12082, 17484.

PAINTING

Related Subjects: **Art, Color, Sculpture.**

14511. The love of gain never made a painter, but it has marred many.
WASHINGTON ALLSTON,
Lectures on Art

14512. What has reasoning to do with the art of painting?   BLAKE

14513. I can look for a whole day with delight upon a handsome picture, though it be but of an horse.
SIR THOMAS BROWNE,
Religio Medici

14514. Nobody will ever know the harm that chemistry has done to the art of painting. Look how the color has cracked in that canvas; what do you suppose they could have put into it?   DEGAS

14515. There are only two styles of portrait painting, the serious and the smirk.   DICKENS,
Nicholas Nickleby

14516. Pictures must not be too picturesque.   EMERSON, *Essays*

14517. Painting is the language of the uncertainties, the outbursts and retreats of the heart.   ELIE FAURE

14518. One picture in ten thousand, perhaps, ought to live in the applause of mankind, from generation to generation until the colors fade and blacken out of sight or the canvas rot entirely away.   HAWTHORNE,
The Marble Faun

14519.
The picture that approaches sculpture nearest
Is the best picture.
LONGFELLOW, *Michael Angelo*

14520. I am not a painter.
MICHELANGELO

14521. Modern painting is uninteresting because there is no innocency left in it.   GEORGE MOORE, *Ave*

14522. The dreary, bare walls of to-day are due to intellectual prigs writing and writing that painting is too difficult to be understood by any but the writer and his tiny clique of "superior persons." For the complete enjoyment of any art, knowledge of its works or backstage is dangerous. Pictures are painted to be looked at, not explained.   C. R. W. NEVINSON

14523. He best can paint them who shall feel them most.   POPE,
Eloisa to Abelard

14524. On painting and fighting look afar off.   *Proverb*

14525. Painters an' poets hae liberty to lie. *Proverb*

14526. A mere copier of nature can never produce anything great.
SIR JOSHUA REYNOLDS,
Discourses on Painting

14527. No picture can be good which deceives by its imitation, for the very reason that nothing can be beautiful which is not true. RUSKIN,
Modern Painters

14528. They are good furniture pictures, unworthy of praise, and undeserving of blame. RUSKIN,
Modern Painters

14529. Painting with all its technicalities, difficulties, and peculiar ends, is nothing but a noble and expressive language, invaluable as the vehicle of thought, but by itself is nothing.
RUSKIN, *True and Beautiful*

14530. Every time I paint a portrait I lose a friend. JOHN SARGENT

14531. Wrought he not well that painted it? SHAKESPEARE,
Timon of Athens

14532. Painting is silent poetry, and poetry is painting with the gift of speech. SIMONIDES, *Plutarch: Lives*

14533. To sit for one's portrait is like being present at one's own creation. ALEXANDER SMITH,
Dreamthorp

14534. Good painting is like good cooking: it can be tasted, but not explained. VLAMINCK, *On Painting*

14535. A life passed among pictures makes not a painter—else the policeman in the National Gallery might assert himself. As well allege that he who lives in a library must needs be a poet. WHISTLER,
The Gentle Art of Making Enemies

14536. Every portrait that is painted with feeling is a portrait of the artist, not of the sitter. OSCAR WILDE,
The Picture of Dorian Gray

See also: 1702, 2035, 11845, 14781.

PALM

Related Subject: Tree.

14541.
Ye gods, it doth amaze me
A man of such a feeble temper should
So get the start of the majestic world,
And bear the palm alone.
SHAKESPEARE, *Julius Caesar*

14542. You shall see him a palm in Athens again. SHAKESPEARE,
Timon of Athens

14543.
First the high palm-trees, with branches fair,
Out of the lowly valleys did arise,
And high shoot up their heads into the skies. SPENSER, *Virgil's Gnat*

14544.
I love the Palm,
With his leaves of beauty, his fruit of balm. BAYARD TAYLOR,
The Arab to the Palm

14545.
"Allah il Allah!" he sings his psalm,
On the Indian Sea, by the isles of balm;
"Thanks to Allah, who gives the palm!" WHITTIER, *The Palm-Tree*

PAN

Related Subjects: Gods and Goddesses, Mythology, Superstition.

14551.
Yet half a beast is the great god Pan,
To laugh as he sits by the river.
ELIZABETH B. BROWNING,
A Musical Instrument

14552.

And that dismal cry rose slowly
And sank slowly through the air,
Full of spirit's melancholy
And eternity's despair!
And they heard the words it said—
"Pan is dead!—Great Pan is dead—
   Pan, Pan is dead."
     ELIZABETH B. BROWNING,
       The Dead Pan

14553.

Of Pan we sing, the best of leaders
   Pan,
   That leads the Naiads and the
    Dryads forth;
And to their dances more than
   Hermes can,
   Hear, O you groves, and hills re-
    sound his worth.
       BEN JONSON,
     Pan's Anniversary Hymn

14554.

       Pan himself,
The simple shepherd's awe-inspiring
   god!   WORDSWORTH,
       The Excursion

PARADISE

Related Subjects: Adam and Eve,
Angel, Death, Eternity, Judgment
Day, Reward, Saint, Salvation,
Serpent, Soul.

14561. A land flowing with milk and
honey.   *Bible: Exodus, xxxiii, 3*

14562. Lay up for yourselves treasures in heaven.
     Bible: Matthew, vi, 20

14563. In my Father's house are
many mansions.   *Bible: John, xiv, 2*

14564. Put an Englishman into the
garden of Eden, and he would find
fault with the whole blarsted consarn;
—put a Yankee in, and he would see
where he could alter it to advantage;
—put an Irishman in, and he would
want tew boss the thing;—put a
Dutchman in, and he would proceed
tew plant it.   JOSH BILLINGS,
      Affurisms

14565.

And in that Heaven of all their wish,
There shall be no more land, say fish.
     RUPERT BROOKE, *Heaven*

14566. All places are distant from
heaven alike. ROBERT BURTON,
     Anatomy of Melancholy

14567.

For he on honey-dew hath fed,
And drunk the milk of Paradise.
     COLERIDGE, *Kubla Khan*

14568. What matter if it be a fool's
paradise? Paradise is paradise, for
whoever owns it!
GEORGE DU MAURIER, *Peter Ibbetson*

14569. Man and Woman may only
enter Paradise hand in hand. Together, the myth tells us, they left it
and together must they return.
     RICHARD GARNETT,
      De Flagello Myrteo

14570.

A Book of Verses underneath the
   Bough
A Jug of Wine, a Loaf of Bread—
   and Thou
   Beside me singing in the Wilder-
    ness—
Oh, Wilderness were Paradise enow!
     OMAR KHAYYAM, *Rubaiyat*

14571.

Heav'n but the Vision of fulfill'd Desire,
And Hell the Shadow from a Soul
   on fire.   OMAR KHAYYAM,
      Rubaiyat

14572.

And only the Master shall praise us,
   and only the Master shall blame;

And no one shall work for money,
    and no one shall work for fame;
But each for the joy of the working,
    and each, in his separate star,
Shall draw the Thing as he sees It for
    the God of Things as They Are!
            KIPLING,
       When Earth's Last Picture is
               Painted

14573.
Must I thus leave thee, Paradise?
    thus leave
Thee, native soil? these happy walks
    and shades?   MILTON,
              Paradise Lost

14574.
                Since call'd
The Paradise of Fools, to few unknown.   MILTON, *Paradise Lost*

14575. Imparadis'd in one another's
arms.   MILTON, *Paradise Lost*

14576. The heaven of each is but
what each desires.
       THOMAS MOORE, *Lalla Rookh*

14577.
A Persian's heaven is easily made:
'Tis but black eyes and lemonade.
  THOMAS MOORE, *Intercepted Letters*

14578. A good key is necessary to
enter Paradise.   *Proverb*

14579. Heaven without good society
cannot be heaven.   *Proverb*

14580.
The old road to Paradise
Easy it is missed!
      MARGARET WIDDEMER,
        The Old Road to Paradise

14581.
How each hath back what once he
    stayed to weep;
Homer his sight, David his little lad!
       LIZETTE W. REESE, *Tears*

14582. The kingdom of heaven is of
the childlike, of those who are easy to
please, who love and give pleasure.
    STEVENSON, *Across the Plains*

14583. Heaven does not choose its
elect from among the great and
wealthy.   THACKERAY,
              The Virginians

14584.
There is a land of pure delight,
    Where saints immortal reign;
Infinite day excludes the night,
    And pleasures banish pain.
        ISAAC WATTS,
       Hymns & Spiritual Songs

14585.
Heaven-gates are not so highly arch'd
As princes' palaces; they that enter
    there
Must go upon their knees.
        JOHN WEBSTER,
        The Duchess of Malfy

14586.
  Heaven's gate is shut to him who
    comes alone;
Save thou a soul, and it shall save
    thy own!   WHITTIER,
           The Two Rabbis

See also: 1161, 1225, 1255, 2074,
3066, 4801, 8304, 9731, 10011, 10035,
10132, 13658.

PARADOX

Related Subjects: **Contradiction,
Humor.**

14591. Paradoxes are useful to attract attention to ideas.
      MANDELL CREIGHTON

14592. The paradoxes of conduct begin to twinkle into sight; sugar is
good, but there is a time to refrain
from taking it though you can; a lie
will easily get you out of a scrape,
and yet, strangely and beautifully,

rapture possesses you when you have taken the scrape and left out the lie.
C. E. MONTAGUE, *Disenchantment*

14593. These are old fond paradoxes to make fools laugh i' the alehouse.
SHAKESPEARE, *Othello*

PARDON, see Forgiveness

PARENTS

Related Subjects: Adam and Eve, C h i l d h o o d, Family, Father, Mother.

14601. Reverence for parents—this standeth written third among the statutes of Justice to whom supreme honor is due.   AESCHYLUS,
The Suppliants

14602. Honour thy father and thy mother: that thy days may be long upon the land which the Lord thy God giveth thee.
Bible: Exodus, xx, 12

14603. My son, hear the instruction of thy father, and forsake not the law of thy mother.   *Bible: Proverbs, i, 8*

14604. The eye that mocketh at his father, and despiseth to obey his mother, the ravens of the valley shall pick it out, and the young eagles shall eat it.   *Bible: Proverbs, xxiii, 22*

14605.
Lovers grow cold, men learn to hate their wives,
And only parents' love can last our lives.   BROWNING, *Pippa Passes*

14606.
The childless cherubs well might envy thee
The pleasures of a parent.
BYRON, *Cain*

14607. In general those parents have the most reverence who deserve it;

for he that lives well cannot be despised.   SAMUEL JOHNSON, *Rasselas*

14608. Few parents act in such a manner as much to enforce their maxims by the credit of their lives.
SAMUEL JOHNSON

14609. The notion that parents are entitled to respect simply because they are parents is preposterous. The stream of obligation runs strongly the other way. A child owes its parents no gratitude whatever for bringing him into the world (as Swift sardonically said, while they were thinking of something else).
JOHN MACY, *About Women*

14610. He is too experienced a parent ever to make positive promises.
CHRISTOPHER MORLEY,
Thunder on the Left

14611.
One moment makes a father, but a mother
Is made by endless moments, load on load.   JOHN G. NEIHARDT,
Eight Hundred Rubles

14612. Thus when I shun Scylla, your father, I fall into Charybdis, your mother.   SHAKESPEARE,
The Merchant of Venice

14613. If parents would only realize how they bore their children!
BERNARD SHAW, *Misalliance*

14614. I tell you there's a wall ten feet thick and ten miles high between parent and child.
BERNARD SHAW, *Misalliance*

14615. The relation between parent and child may be an affectionate relation. It may be a useful relation. It may be a necessary relation. But it can never be an innocent relation.
BERNARD SHAW, *Misalliance*

14616. He argued that the principal duty which a parent owed to a child was to make him happy.
ANTHONY TROLLOPE, *Doctor Thorne*

14617. Children begin by loving their parents; as they grow older they judge them; sometimes they forgive them. OSCAR WILDE,
The Picture of Dorian Gray

PARIS

Related Subjects: Cities, France.

14621. Is not Paris a vast meadow incessantly stirred by a storm of whirling diverse interests, its crop of men mowed down by death, at an earlier age than elsewhere.
BALZAC,
The Girl With the Golden Eyes

14622. It [Paris] is a city where great ideas perish, done to death by a witticism. BALZAC

14623. Fair, fantastic Paris.
ELIZABETH B. BROWNING,
Aurora Leigh

14624. Paris is terribly derisive of all absurd pretensions but its own.
EMERSON

14625. Paris is nothing but an immense hospitality. VICTOR HUGO

14626. Secrets travel fast in Paris.
NAPOLEON

14627. As an artist, a man has no home in Europe save in Paris.
NIETZSCHE, *Ecce Homo*

14628.
You who have ever been to Paris, know;
And you who have not been to Paris —go!
RUSKIN, *A Tour Through France*

14629. They say that when good Americans die they go to Paris.
OSCAR WILDE,
A Woman of No Importance

PARK

Related Subjects: Cities, Country, Flowers, Grass, Tree.

14631. Public money is scarcely ever so well employed as in securing bits of waste ground and keeping them as open spaces.
ARTHUR HELPS, *Friends in Council*

14632. What had been the delights of the lord are now the delights of the people. MARTIAL, *De Spectaculis*

PARTING

Related Subjects: Absence, Farewell, Kiss, Separation.

14641. When shall we three meet again? *Anonymous,*
Parting Friends (Dartmouth College Song)

14642. Technique of saying good bye: two persons who do not part with kisses should part with haste.
RALPH BERGENGREN

14643. It is never any good dwelling on good-byes. It is not the being together that it prolongs, it is the parting. ELIZABETH A. BIBESCO,
The Fir and the Palm

14644.
Go from me. Yet I feel that I shall stand
Henceforward in thy shadow.
ELIZABETH B. BROWNING,
Sonnets from the Portuguese

14645.
God be with you.
I bear you company no more.
DANTE, *Purgatory*

14646. Since there's no help, come let us kiss and part.
MICHAEL DRAYTON, *Love's Farewell*

14647. We only part to meet again.
JOHN GAY, *Sweet William's Farewell*

14648. Adieu, she cried, and waved her lily hand.
JOHN GAY, *Sweet William's Farewell*

14649. Leave-takings are but wasted sadness. Let me pass out quietly.
JEROME K. JEROME,
The Passing of the Third Floor Back

14650. Gude nicht, and joy be wi' you a'.   CAROLINA OLIPHANT,
Gude Nicht

14651. Well, good bye, Jim, Take keer of yourself.
JAMES WHITCOMB RILEY,
The Old Man and Jim

14652.
To all, to each, a fair good-night,
And pleasing dreams, and slumbers light.   SCOTT, *Marmion*

14653.
So part we sadly in this troublous world
To meet with joy in sweet Jerusalem.
SHAKESPEARE, *Henry VI*

14654.
Stand not upon the order of your going,
But go at once.
SHAKESPEARE, *Macbeth*

14655. A thousand times good-night!
SHAKESPEARE, *Romeo and Juliet*

14656.
Good night, good night! parting is such sweet sorrow,
That I shall say good night till it be morrow.
SHAKESPEARE, *Romeo and Juliet*

14657.
Eyes, look your last!
Arms, take your last embrace!
SHAKESPEARE, *Romeo and Juliet*

PASSION

Related Subjects: Anger, Desire, Hatred, Impulse, Kiss, Love, Lust, Mistress, Revenge.

14661. A man without passion is only a latent force, only a possibility, like a stone waiting for the blow from the iron to give forth sparks.
AMIEL

14662.
In her first passion woman loves her lover,
In all the others, all she loves is love.   BYRON, *Don Juan*

14663. We are ne'er like angels till our passion dies.
THOMAS DEKKER,
The Honest Whore

14664. We may affirm absolutely that nothing great in the world has been accomplished without passion.
HEGEL

14665. The passions are the only orators that always persuade; they are, as it were, a natural art, the rules of which are infallible; and the simplest man with passion is more persuasive than the most eloquent without it.
LA ROCHEFOUCAULD, *Maxims*

14666. Terrible and sublime thought, that every moment is supreme for some man and woman, every hour the apotheosis of some passion!
WILLIAM McFEE, *Casuals of the Sea*

14667. All passions that suffer themselves to be relished and digested are but moderate.   MONTAIGNE, *Essays*

14668. Passion is a sort of fever in the mind, which ever leaves us weaker than it found us.

WILLIAM PENN,
Fruits of Solitude

14669.
On life's vast ocean diversely we sail,
Reason the card, but passion is the
  gale.   POPE, *Essay on Man*

14670.
And hence one master-passion in the
  breast,
Like Aaron's serpent, swallows up the
  rest.   POPE, *Essay on Man*

14671.
The ruling passion, be it what it will,
The ruling passion conquers reason
  still.   POPE, *Moral Essays*

14672. He that shews a passion, tells his enemy where he may hit him.
Proverb

14673. Passionate people lay up no malice.   *Proverb*

14674. He that overcomes his passions overcomes his greatest enemies.
Proverb

14675.
Give me that man
That is not passion's slave, and I
  will wear him   •
In my heart's core, ay, in my heart of
  hearts,
As I do thee.   SHAKESPEARE,
Hamlet

14676.
        Nay, an thou'lt mouth,
I'll rant as well as thou.
SHAKESPEARE, *Hamlet*

14677. This passion, and the death of a dear friend, would go near to make a man look sad.   SHAKESPEARE,
A Midsummer-Night's Dream

14678. All great passion makes us dumb, and the highest happiness as well as the highest grief seizes us too violently to be expressed by our words.   SIR RICHARD STEELE

14679.
No more subtle master under
  heaven
Than is the maiden passion for a
  maid,
Not only to keep down the base in
  man
But teach high thought, and amiable
  words,
And courtliness, and the desire of
  fame
And love of truth, and all that makes
  a man.   TENNYSON,
Idylls of the King

14680.
He will hold thee, when his passion
  shall have spent its novel force,
Something better than his dog, a little
  dearer than his horse.
TENNYSON, *Locksley Hall*

See also: 37, 47, 743, 833, 894, 1574, 2450, 2720, 4473, 4742, 8029, 12574, 19574, 22079.

PAST

Related Subjects: Age, Antiquity, History, Memory, Yesterday.

14681. I have small patience with the antiquarian habit which magnifies the past and belittles the present. It is a vicious business to look backward unless the feet are set steadfastly on a forward road. Change is inevitable, at once a penalty and a privilege.

JOHN BUCHAN,
Memory Hold-the-Door

14682. The "good old times"—all times when old are good.
BYRON, *The Age of Bronze*

14683. I reject the monstrous theory that while a man may redeem the past a woman never can.

HALL CAINE, *The Eternal City*

14684.
Not heaven itself upon the past has power;
But what has been, has been, and I have had my hour.   DRYDEN,
Imitation of Horace

14685. The illusion that times that were are better than those that are, has probably pervaded all ages.

HORACE GREELEY,
The American Conflict

14686.
What is to come we know not. But we know
That what has been was good.
W. E. HENLEY, *What Is To Come*

14687.
I have had playmates, I have had companions,
In my days of childhood, in my joyful school-days,
All, all are gone, the old familiar faces.   CHARLES LAMB,
Old Familiar Faces

14688.
Things bygone are the only things that last:
The present is mere grass, quickmown away;
The past is stone, and stands for ever fast.   E. LEE-HAMILTON,
Roman Baths

14689. Look not mournfully into the Past. It comes not back again. Wisely improve the Present. It is thine. Go forth to meet the shadowy Future, without fear, and with a manly heart.
LONGFELLOW, *Hyperion*

14690. From the days of the first grandfather, everybody has remembered a golden age behind him!

LOWELL, *Carlyle*

14691. Those who compare the age in which their lot has fallen with a golden age which exists only in imagination, may talk of degeneracy and decay; but no man who is correctly informed as to the past, will be disposed to make a morose or desponding view of the present.

MACAULAY, *History of England*

14692. The mill cannot grind with water that's past.   *Proverb*

14693. I tell you the past is a bucket of ashes.   CARL SANDBURG, *Prairie*

14694. Those who cannot remember the past are condemned to repeat it.
SANTAYANA

14695.
There was—and O! how many sorrows crowd
Into these two brief words!
SCOTT, *The Lord of the Isles*

14696.
Still linger, in our northern clime,
Some remnants of the good old time.
SCOTT, *Marmion*

14697. True is it that we have seen better days.   SHAKESPEARE,
As You Like It

14698.
Let us not burden our remembrances
With a heaviness that's gone.
SHAKESPEARE, *The Tempest*

14699. Through the centuries the people have dreamed of a Golden Age and longed for its return, unconscious that they dreamed of a day that had never been.   DR. GUY E. SHIPLER

14700. The past is only the present become invisible and mute; and because it is invisible and mute, its memoried glances and its murmurs are infinitely precious. We are to-morrow's past. MARY WEBB, *Precious Bane*

14701. The past and the present are in deadly grapple and the peoples of the world are being done to death between them. WOODROW WILSON

See also: 2315, 2418, 8752, 8758, 8763, 9521.

PATIENCE AND IMPATIENCE

Related Subjects: **Haste, Philosophy, Resignation, Rest, Waiting, Worry.**

14711. Patience is so like fortitude, that she seems either her sister or her daughter. ARISTOTLE

14712. There is, however, a limit at which forbearance ceases to be a virtue. BURKE

14713. Pacience is an heigh vertu certeyn. CHAUCER, *Canterbury Tales*

14714.
No state of life but must to patience bow:
  The tradesman must have patience for his bill;
He must have patience who to law will go;
  And should he lose his right, more patience still;
Yea, to prevent or heal full many a strife,
How oft, how long must man have patience with his wife.
  ROBERT DODSLEY, *To Patience*

14715. Possess your soul with patience. DRYDEN, *The Hind & the Panther*

14716. Beware the fury of a patient man. DRYDEN, *Absalom & Achitophel*

14717. Patience, that blending of moral courage with physical timidity. THOMAS HARDY, *Tess of the D'Urbervilles*

14718.
        Arm th' obdur'd breast
With stubborn patience as with triple steel. MILTON, *Paradise Lost*

14719. Patience is the best remedy for every trouble. PLAUTUS, *Rudens*

14720. Job was not so miserable in his sufferings, as happy in his patience. *Proverb*

14721. Patience, and shuffle the cards. *Proverb*

14722. Be patient, and you shall have patient children. *Proverb*

14723. Patience is a remedy for every sorrow. PUBLILIUS SYRUS, *Sententiae*

14724. He that has patience may compass anything. RABELAIS

14725. Patience is bitter, but its fruit sweet. ROUSSEAU

14726. But patience, cousin, and shuffle the cards, till our hand is a stronger one. SCOTT, *Quentin Durward*

14727. The most patient man in loss, the most coldest that ever turned up ace. SHAKESPEARE, *Cymbeline*

14728. You tread upon my patience. SHAKESPEARE, *Henry IV*

14729. I will be the pattern of all patience. SHAKESPEARE, *King Lear*

14730.
'Tis all men's office to speak patience
To those that wring under the load of sorrow;
But no man's virtue nor sufficiency

To be so moral when he shall endure
The like himself. SHAKESPEARE,
Much Ado About Nothing

14731. How poor are they that have
not patience! SHAKESPEARE, *Othello*

14732. Patience is the art of hoping.
VAUVENARGUES

14733.
Whether I come to my own to-day or
   in ten thousand or ten million years,
I can cheerfully take it now, or with
   equal cheerfulness I can wait.
WALT WHITMAN, *Song of Myself*

14734. I can be pushed just so far.
HARRY LEON WILSON,
Ruggles Of Red Gap

Impatience

14735. Whoever is out of patience is
out of possession of his soul. Men
must not turn bees, and kill themselves in stinging others. BACON

14736. I have not so great a struggle
with my vices, great and numerous
as they are, as I have with my impatience. My efforts are not absolutely useless; yet I have never been
able to conquer this ferocious wild
beast. JOHN CALVIN

14737. Impatience dries the blood
sooner than age or sorrow. CLEON

14738. In all evils which admit a
remedy, impatience should be avoided,
because it wastes that time and attention in complaints which, if properly
applied, might remove the cause.
SAMUEL JOHNSON

14739. Such is our impatience, our
hatred of procrastination in everything but the amendment of our practices and the adornment of our nature,

one would imagine we were dragging
time along by force, and not he us.
W. S. LANDOR

14740. Impatience does not diminish,
but augments the evil. *Proverb*

14741. Impatience turns an ague
into a fever, a fever to the plague,
fear into despair, anger into rage, loss
into madness, and sorrow to amazement. JEREMY TAYLOR

See also: 323, 1071, 2047, 2719, 6205,
7485, 12169, 21176.

PATRIOTISM

**Related Subjects: America, Duty,
Flag, Loyalty, Nation, Oath,
Unity.**

14751.
      What pity is it
That we can die but once to save our
   country! ADDISON, *Cato*

14752. No man can be a patriot on
an empty stomach. BRANN,
The Iconoclast

14753. So to be patriots as not to
forget we are gentlemen.
BURKE,
*Thoughts on the Cause of the
Present Discontents*

14754. I only regret that I have but
one life to lose for my country.
NATHAN HALE

14755. The really patriotic citizen is
the one who loves.
CARDINAL HAYES

14756. I am not a Virginian, but an
American. PATRICK HENRY

14757. And for our country 'tis a
bliss to die. HOMER, *Iliad*

14758.
Without a sign, his sword the brave
   man draws,
And asks no omen but his country's
   cause.   HOMER, *Iliad*

14759. A patriot is a fool in ev'ry
age.   HORACE

14760. Patriotism is the last refuge
of a scoundrel.
   SAMUEL JOHNSON, *Boswell: Life*

14761. The least considerable man
among us has an interest equal to the
proudest nobleman, in the laws and
constitution of his country, and is
equally called upon to make a generous contribution in support of them;
—whether it be the heart to conceive,
the understanding to direct, or the
hand to execute.   JUNIUS

14762.
When a nation's life's at hazard,
   We've no time to think of men!
GEORGE LIPPARD, *Independence Bell*

14763. It is a deliberate and discern-
ing love of a nation that appeals to
me, not the indiscriminate love that
assumes everything to be right because it bears a national label.
          THOMAS MASARYK

14764. Love of one's own nation
should not entail non-love of other
nations . . . Institutions by themselves are not enough.
          THOMAS MASARYK

14765. Who dare to love their country, and be poor.   POPE,
   On His Grotto at Twickenham

14766. We should behave toward
our country as women behave toward
the men they love. A loving wife will
do anything for her husband except
stop criticizing and trying to improve
him. We should cast the same affectionate but sharp glance at our country. We should love it, but also insist
upon telling it all its faults. The noisy,
empty "patriot," not the critic, is
the dangerous citizen.
          J. B. PRIESTLEY

14767. A man who is good enough to
shed his blood for his country is good
enough to be given a square deal
afterward. More than that no man is
entitled to, and less than that no man
shall have.   THEODORE ROOSEVELT

14768. Where is the man who owes
nothing to the land in which he lives?
Whatever the land may be, he owes
to it the most precious thing possessed
by man, the morality of his actions
and the love of virtue.
   ROUSSEAU, *Emile, or Education*

14769. Our country, right or wrong.
When right, to be kept right; when
wrong, to be put right.
          CARL SCHURZ

14770.
Breathes there the man, with soul so
   dead,
Who never to himself hath said
   This is my own, my native land!
Whose heart hath ne'er within him
   burn'd
As home his footsteps he hath turn'd,
   From wandering on a foreign
     strand?   SCOTT,
   The Lay of the Last Minstrel

14771.
Stood for his country's glory fast,
And nail'd her colors to the mast!
        SCOTT, *Marmion*

14772.
          I do love
My country's good with a respect
   more tender,
More holy, more profound, than
   mine own life.
   SHAKESPEARE, *Coriolanus*

14773. Not that I loved Caesar less, but that I loved Rome more.

SHAKESPEARE, *Julius Caesar*

14774. Sleep in peace, slain in your country's wars! SHAKESPEARE, *Titus Andronicus*

14775. Such is the condition of human affairs, that to wish for the greatness of one's own country, is to wish for the harm of its neighbors.

VOLTAIRE

14776. I have alreddy given Two cousins to the war, & I stand reddy to sacrifiss my wife's brother ruther 'n not see the rebelyin krusht. And if wuss comes to wuss, I'll shed ev'ry drop of blud my able-bodid relations has got. ARTEMUS WARD, *To the Prince of Wales*

14777. Let our object be our country, our whole country, and nothing but our country. DANIEL WEBSTER

14778. There is one certain means by which I can be sure never to see my country's ruin,—I will die in the last ditch. WILLIAM OF ORANGE

See also: 828, 1263, 2498, 4278, 9904, 15119, 17995.

PATRONAGE

Related Subjects: Encouragement, Gifts, Help, Money, Philanthropy.

14781.
"O dear Mother Outline! of wisdom
  most sage,
What's the first part of painting?"
  She said, "Patronage."
"And what is the second, to please
  and engage?"
She frowned like a fury, and said:
  "Patronage." BLAKE,
On Art and Artists

14782.
The mud of English patronage
Grows round his feet, and keeps him
  down. ROBERT BUCHANAN,
Edward Crowhurst

14783. *Patron:* Commonly a wretch who supports with insolence, and is paid with flattery.

SAMUEL JOHNSON, *Dictionary*

14784. Is not a patron, my lord [Chesterfield], one who looks with unconcern on a man struggling for life in the water, and when he has reached ground encumbers him with help? SAMUEL JOHNSON,
Boswell: Life

14785. No man's talents, however brilliant, can raise him from obscurity, unless they find scope, opportunity, and also a patron to commend them.

PLINY THE YOUNGER

14786.
  What would you have me do?
Seek for the patronage of some great
  man,
And like a creeping vine on a tall tree
Crawl upward, where I cannot stand
  alone? EDMOND ROSTAND,
Cyrano De Bergerac

14787. Getting Patronage is the whole art of life. A man cannot have a career without it.

BERNARD SHAW,
Captain Brassbound's Conversion

PAYMENT

Related Subjects: Compensation, Debt, Reward, Wages.

14791. I would pay him in his own coin. MRS. APHRA BEHN,
Lucky Chance

14792. What you will have, quoth God, pay for it and take it.

EMERSON

14793. If I can't pay, why I can owe.
JOHN HEYWOOD, *Be Merry, Friends*

14794. Pass the hat for your credit's sake, and pay, pay, pay!
KIPLING,
The Absent-Minded Beggar

14795.
The time for payment comes, early or
late,
No earthly debtor but accounts to
Fate.   JOHN MASEFIELD,
The Widow in the Bye Street

14796. He that pays last never pays twice.   *Proverb*

14797. Who cannot pay with money, must pay with his body.   *Proverb*

14798. Pay beforehand and your work will be behindhand.   *Proverb*

14799. He who pays the piper can call the tune.   *Proverb*

14800. Base is the slave that pays.
SHAKESPEARE, *Henry V*

14801. He is well paid that is well satisfied.   SHAKESPEARE,
The Merchant of Venice

14802. She pays him in his own coin.
SWIFT, *Polite Conversation*

See also: 2396, 3794, 11527, 13249.

PEACE

Related Subjects: Calm, Contentment, Dove, Quiet, Serenity.

14811. Better beans and bacon in peace than cakes and ale in fear.
AESOP,
*The Town Mouse and the Country
Mouse*

14812.
Peace, peace is what I seek, and public calm;

Endless extinction of unhappy hates.
MATTHEW ARNOLD, *Merope*

14813.
Sosie: At least what passes for peace
—the breathing-spell between wars.
S. N. BEHRMAN, *Amphitryon 38*

14814. They shall beat their swords into plowshares, and their spears into pruning-hooks; nation shall not lift up sword against nation, neither shall they learn war any more.
Bible: Isaiah, ii, 4

14815. There is no peace, saith the Lord, unto the wicked.
Bible: Isaiah, xlviii, 22

14816. How beautiful upon the mountains are the feet of him that bringeth good tidings, that publisheth peace.   *Bible: Isaiah, lii, 7*

14817. They have healed also the hurt of the daughter of my people slightly, saying, Peace, peace; when there is no peace.
Bible: Jeremiah, vi, 14

14818. Behold, the prophets say unto them, Ye shall not see the sword, neither shall ye have famine; but I will give you assured peace in this place. Then the Lord said unto me, The prophets prophesy lies in my name: I sent them not, neither have I commanded them, neither spake unto them: they prophesy unto you a false vision and divination, and a thing of nought, and the deceit of their heart.
Bible: Jeremiah, xiv, 13, 14

14819. Can two walk together, except they be agreed?   *Bible: Amos, iii, 3*

14820. Glory to God in the highest, and on earth peace, good will toward men.   *Bible: Luke, ii, 14*

14821. If it be possible, as much as lieth in you, live peaceably with all men.   *Bible: Romans, xii, 18*

14822. Let us therefore follow after the things which make for peace.
Bible: Romans, xiv, 19

14823. The peace of God, which passeth all understanding.
Bible: Philippians, iv, 7

14824. We confine our love of peace to paper; our war spirit finds its expression in deeds. We profess tolerance, and practice intolerance. We profess friendship, and practice vengeance . . . I would rather have just now one ounce of practice than tons of profession in the cause of peace.
WILLIAM E. BORAH,
How to End War

14825. What all men are really after is some form, or perhaps only some formula, of peace.
JOSEPH CONRAD,
Under Western Eyes

14826. It is now in the power of the present confederacy for ever to prevent any more war in Europe. It is in their power to make themselves arbiters of all the differences and disputes that ever can happen in Europe, whether between kingdom and kingdom, or between sovereign and subjects. A congress of this alliance may be made a Court of Appeals for all the injured and oppressed, whether they are princes or people that are or ever shall be in Europe to the end of the world. Here the petty states and princes shall be protected against the terror of their powerful neighbors, the great shall no more oppress the small, or the mighty devour the weak; this very confederacy have at this time, and, if they please, may preserve to themselves, the power of banishing war out of Europe.
DEFOE, *Plan for a League of Nations*

14827.
"Peace upon earth!" was said. We
   sing it,
And pay a million priests to bring it.
After two thousand years of mass,
We've got as far as poison-gas.
THOMAS HARDY

14828. "To disarm" appears to be an irregular verb with no first person singular and only a future tense.
EDUARD HERRIOT,
*At the Disarmament Conference in
Geneva*

14829. With malice toward none; with charity for all; with firmness in the right, as God gives us to see the right, let us strive on to finish the work we are in; to bind up the nation's wounds; to care for him who shall have borne the battle, and for his widow and his orphan—to do all which may achieve and cherish a just and lasting peace among ourselves and with all nations.   LINCOLN

14830.
Ef you want peace, the thing you've
   gut tu du
Is jes' to show you're up to fightin',
   tu.   LOWELL, *The Biglow Papers*

14831. In proportion as the antagonism between classes within the nation vanishes, the hostility of one nation to another will come to an end.
KARL MARX,
Manifesto of the Communist Party

14832. An olive-leaf he brings, pacific sign.   MILTON, *Paradise Lost*

14833.
   Peace hath her victories
No less renown'd than war.
MILTON,
To the Lord General Cromwell

14834. Peace can only come when the causes of war are removed. So long as there is the domination of one country over another, or the exploitation of one class by another, there will always be attempts to subvert the existing order, and no stable equilibrium can endure. Out of imperialism and capitalism peace can never come.   JAWAHARLAL NEHRU,
India and the World

14835. Blessed is the peace-maker, not the conqueror.   *Proverb*

14836. It is madness for a sheep to treat of peace with a wolf.   *Proverb*

14837. Nobody can live longer in peace than his neighbour pleases.
Proverb

14838. He that makes a good war makes a good peace.   *Proverb*

14839. Better an egg in peace than an ox in war.   *Proverb*

14840. A deceitful peace is more hurtful than open war.   *Proverb*

14841. We will have to want Peace, want it enough to pay for it, before it becomes an accepted rule.
ELEANOR ROOSEVELT

14842. We wish peace; but we wish the peace of justice, the peace of righteousness. We wish it because we think it is right, and not because we are afraid.
THEODORE ROOSEVELT,
Inaugural Address

14843. And after the strife of war begins the strife of peace.
CARL SANDBURG, *The People, Yes*

14844.
That it shall hold companionship in peace
With honour, as in war.
SHAKESPEARE, *Coriolanus*

14845. Blessed are the peacemakers on earth.   SHAKESPEARE, *Henry VI*

14846. They make desolation, which they call peace.   TACITUS, *Agricola*

14847. Peace has to be created, in order to be maintained. It is the product of Faith, Strength, Energy, Will, Sympathy, Justice, Imagination and the triumph of principle. It will never be achieved by passivity and quietism. Passivity and quietism are invitations to war.
DOROTHY THOMPSON,
On the Record

14848. They have not wanted *Peace* at all; they have wanted to be spared war—as though the absence of war was the same as peace.
DOROTHY THOMPSON,
On the Record

14849. Let us work without disputing; it is the only way to render life tolerable.   VOLTAIRE, *Candide*

14850. To be prepared for war is one of the most effectual means of preserving peace.   WASHINGTON

14851. Open covenants of peace openly arrived at.
WOODROW WILSON

14852. The world can be at peace only if its life is stable, and there can be no stability where the will is in rebellion, where there is not tranquillity of spirit and the sense of justice, of freedom, and of right.
WOODROW WILSON

14853. No peace can last, or ought to last, which does not recognize and accept the principle that governments derive all their just power from the consent of the governed, and that no right anywhere exists to hand peoples about from sovereignty to sovereignty as if they were property.   WOODROW WILSON

14854. Only a peace between equals can last. Only a peace the very principle of which is equality and a common participation in a common benefit. The right state of mind, the right feeling between nations, is as necessary for a lasting peace as is the just settlement of vexed questions of territory or of racial and national allegiance.   WOODROW WILSON

14855. The whole family of nations will have to guarantee to each nation that no nation shall violate its political independence or its territorial integrity. That is the basis, the only conceivable basis for the future peace of the world.   WOODROW WILSON

See also: 696, 1022, 2124, 5411, 15783, 15850, 15857, 15859, 17183, 20781, 20800, 20825, 21678.

PEACOCK

Related Subjects: Birds, Vanity.

14861.
Like an imperial peacock stalk abroad
(That royal bird, whose tail's a diadem).   BYRON, *Don Juan*

14862. Like a peacock whose eyes are inclin'd to his tail.
    THOMAS HOOD, *A Parthian Glance*

14863. She is a peacock in everything but beauty.   OSCAR WILDE,
       Picture of Dorian Gray

See also: 15952.

PEARL

Related Subjects: Jewel, Oyster.

14871. Give not that which is holy unto the dogs, neither cast ye your pearls before swine, lest they trample them under their feet, and turn again and rend you. *Bible: Matthew, vii, 6*

14872. When he had found one pearl of great price.
    Bible: Matthew, xiii, 46

14873. They [the Russians] came to the court balls dropping pearls and vermin.
    MACAULAY, *History of England*

14874.
Has a pearl less whiteness
Because of its birth?
    THOMAS MOORE, *Desmond's Song*

14875. This treasure of an oyster.
    SHAKESPEARE, *Antony and Cleopatra*

14876.
       One whose hand
Like the base Indian, threw a pearl away
Richer than all his tribe.
    SHAKESPEARE, *Othello*

See also: 302, 971, 976, 1537, 3133, 7496.

PEDANTRY

Related Subjects: Education, Grammar, Teacher, School.

14881.
A Babylonish dialect
Which learned pedants much affect.
    SAMUEL BUTLER, *Hudibras*

14882.
The languages, especially the dead,
   The sciences, and most of all the abstruse,
The arts, at least all such as could be said
   To be the most remote from common use.   BYRON, *Don Juan*

14883. Pedantry consists in the use of words unsuitable to the time, place, and company.
    COLERIDGE, *Biographia Literaria*

14884. Pedantry is the dotage of knowledge. HOLBROOK JACKSON, *Anatomy of Bibliomania*

14885.
Such labour'd nothings, in so strange a style,
Amaze th' unlearn'd, and make the learned smile.
POPE, *Essay on Criticism*

14886.
The bookful blockhead, ignorantly read,
With loads of learned lumber in his head. POPE, *Essay on Criticism*

14887. An artist may visit a museum, but only a pedant can live there.
SANTAYANA, *Life of Reason*

14888.
Bold in thy applause,
The Bard shall scorn pedantic laws.
SCOTT, *Marmion*

14889. Figures pedantical.
SHAKESPEARE, *Love's Labour's Lost*

14890.
A reasoning, self-sufficing thing,
An intellectual All-in-all.
WORDSWORTH, *A Poet's Epitaph*

PELICAN

Related Subject: Birds.

14891.
By them there sat, the loving pelican,
Whose young ones, poison'd by the serpent's sting,
With her own blood to life again doth bring.
MICHAEL DRAYTON, *Noah's Flood*

14892.
Like the kind, life-retiring pelican,
Repast them with my blood.
SHAKESPEARE, *Hamlet*

14893.
A wonderful bird is the pelican;

His bill holds more than his bellican;
He takes in his beak
Enough food for a week,
And I don't know how in the hellican.
Traditional

PEN

Related Subjects: Ink, Writing.

14901.
Art thou a pen, whose task shall be
To drown in ink What writers think?
Oh, wisely write, That pages white
Be not the worse for ink and thee!
ETHEL L. BEERS, *The Gold Nugget*

14902. I had rather stand in the shock of a basilisk, than in the fury of a merciless pen.
SIR THOMAS BROWNE, *Religio Medici*

14903.
Beneath the rule of men entirely great,
The pen is mightier than the sword.
BULWER-LYTTON, *Richelieu*

14904.
Oh! nature's noblest gift, my grey goose-quill!
Slave of my thoughts, obedient to my will,
Torn from thy parent-bird to form a pen,
That mighty instrument of little men!
BYRON,
English Bards & Scotch Reviewers

14905. Pen and ink is wit's plough.
JOHN CLARKE, *Paroemiologia*

14906.
I dip my pen in the blackest ink, because
I am not afraid of falling into my inkpot.
EMERSON, *Conduct of Life*

14907. The pen became a clarion.

LONGFELLOW, *Monte Cassino*

14908. Many wearing rapiers are afraid of goose-quills.

SHAKESPEARE, *Hamlet*

14909. One that excels the quirks of blazoning pens.

SHAKESPEARE, *Othello*

14910. Ask my pen,—it governs me, —I govern not it.

STERNE, *Tristram Shandy*

14911.
Pens are most dangerous tools, more sharp by odds
Than swords, and cut more keen than whips or rods.

JOHN TAYLOR,
News from Hell, Hull, and Halifax

14912.
There's no wound deeper than a pen can give,
It makes men living dead, and dead men live.

JOHN TAYLOR, *A Kicksey-Winsey*

14913.
     The feather, whence the pen
Was shaped that traced the lives of these good men,
Dropped from an Angel's wing.

WORDSWORTH, *Ecclesiastical Sonnets*

See also: 1223, 2689, 15352.

PEOPLE, THE

Related Subjects: **Crowd, Democracy, Equality, Freedom, Government.**

14921. Early up, and reading in the publick prints about the oil inquiry in Washington, I was struck with the lack of indignation it arouseth, and I wondered what it would be that would be important enough to make a people angry, and I thought it would be something not worth getting angry about, like in the days when the big, strong Americans made so great a stir about German opera a year or so after the war. But of official perfidy they seem oblivious.   F. P. A.,
*The Diary of Our Own
Samuel Pepys*

14922. It was we, the people; not we, the white male citizens; nor yet we, the male citizens; but we, the whole people, who formed the Union. And we formed it, not to give the blessings of liberty, but to secure them; not to the half of ourselves and the half of our posterity, but to the whole people—women as well as men.

SUSAN B. ANTHONY,
Woman's Right to Suffrage

14923.
The General Public has no notion
Of what's behind the scenes.
They vote at times with some emotion
But don't know what it means.
Doctored information
Is all they have to judge things by;
The hidden situation
Develops secretly.

AUDEN & ISHERWOOD,
The Dog Beneath the Skin

14924. No doubt but ye are the people.   *Bible: Job, xii, 2*

14925. I do not know the method of drawing up an indictment against an whole people.

BURKE, *Speech on Conciliation*

14926. A people who are still, as it were, but in the gristle, and not yet hardened into the bone of manhood.

BURKE, *Speech on Conciliation*

14927. "The people may eat grass": hasty words, which fly abroad irrevocable,—and will send back tidings.

CARLYLE, *The French Revolution*

14928. The Public is an old woman. Let her maunder and mumble.

CARLYLE, *Journal*

14929. Four thousand people cross London Bridge every day, mostly fools.   CARLYLE

14930. When dealing with people, let us remember we are not dealing with creatures of logic. We are dealing with creatures of emotion, creatures bustling with prejudices and motivated by pride and vanity.

DALE CARNEGIE,
How to Win Friends

14931. People may be divided into two classes: the people who like to drink the dregs of their cup, and the people whose instinctive preference it is to leave the dregs. This is a distinction which cuts deep into the moral life. The people of the first class are usually counted the more interesting, and necessarily they are able to extract more out of life, more pain, and possibly more pleasure, though one may question the quality of the extract.

HAVELOCK ELLIS, *The Art of Life*

14932. I painfully reflect that in almost every political controversy of the last fifty years the leisured classes, the educated classes, the wealthy classes, the titled classes have been in the wrong. The common people— the toilers, the men of uncommon sense—these have been responsible for nearly all of the social reform measures which the world accepts today.   GLADSTONE

14933. If you inquire what the people are like here, I must answer, "The same as everywhere!"

GOETHE, *The Sorrows of Werther*

14934. There is not a more mean, stupid, dastardly, pitiful, selfish, spiteful, envious, ungrateful animal than the Public. It is the greatest of cowards, for it is afraid of itself.

HAZLITT, *On Living to One's Self*

14935. When, in the course of human events, it becomes necessary for one people to dissolve the political bands which have connected them with another, and to assume among the powers of the earth the separate and equal station to which the laws of nature and of nature's God entitle them, a decent respect to the opinions of mankind requires that they should declare the causes which impel them to the separation.

JEFFERSON,
Declaration of Independence

14936. Cherish the spirit of our people and keep alive their attention. Do not be too severe upon their errors, but reclaim them by enlightening them. If once they become inattentive to public affairs, you and I, and Congress and assemblies, judges and governors, shall all become wolves.

JEFFERSON, *The Price of Liberty*

14937. Two things only the people anxiously desire—bread and circus games.   JUVENAL, *Satires*

14938.
No doubt but ye are the People—absolute, strong, and wise;
Whatever your heart has desired ye have not withheld from your eyes.
On your own heads, in your own hands, the sin and the saving lies!

KIPLING, *The Islanders*

14939. The public seldom forgives twice.   LAVATER

14940. It is true that you may fool all the people some of the time; you can even fool some of the people all the time; but you can't fool all of the people all the time.   LINCOLN

14941. If the good people, in their wisdom, shall see fit to keep me in the background, I have been too familiar with disappointments to be very much chagrined.   LINCOLN

14942. If the people are poor, I am the poorest.   EMPEROR NINTOKU

14943. The People! They live in the abyss, the poet lives on the mountain top. To the people the end of life is the life created for them; to the poet the end of life is the life that he creates for himself; life has a stifling grip upon the people's throat,—it is the poet's musician. The poet ever strives to save the people; the people ever strive to destroy the poet.
SEAN O'CASEY,
The Shadow of a Gunman

14944. He that does anything for the public is accounted to do it for nobody.   *Proverb*

14945. Tactics are important, but we could not exist if the majority of the people did not support us. We are nothing but the fist of the people beating their oppressors.
PENG TEH-HUAI,
Snow: Red Star Over China

14946. The public must and will be served.
WILLIAM PENN, *Fruits of Solitude*

14947. Most people would die sooner than think; in fact, they do so.
BERTRAND RUSSELL

14948.
The people, yes, the people,
Everyone who got a letter today
And those the mail-carrier missed.
The women at the cookstoves preparing meals, in a sewing corner

mending, in a basement laundering, woman the homemaker,
The woman at the factory tending a stitching machine, some of them the mainstay of the jobless man at home cooking, laundering,
Streetwalking jobhunter, walkers alive and keen, sleepwalkers drifting along, the stupefied and hopeless down-and-outs, the game fighters who will die fighting. . . .
CARL SANDBURG, *The People, Yes*

14949.
The people is a lighted believer and hoper—and this is to be held against them?
The panderers and cheaters are to have their way in trading on these lights of the People?
Not always, no, not always, for the people is a knower too.
CARL SANDBURG, *The People, Yes*

14950.
The people is a monolith,
A mover, a dirt farmer,
A desperate hoper.
CARL SANDBURG, *The People, Yes*

14951.
The people have come far and can look back and say, "We will go farther yet."
The people is a plucked goose and a shorn sheep of legalized fraud
And the people is one of those mountain slopes holding a volcano of retribution,
Slow in all things, slow in its gathered wrath, slow in its onward heave,
Slow in its asking: "Where are we now? What time is it?"
CARL SANDBURG, *The People, Yes*

14952.
The people is Everyman, everybody.
Everybody is you and me and all others.

What everybody says is what we all
say.

CARL SANDBURG, *The People, Yes*

14953.
"The people is a myth, an abstraction."
And what myth would you put in
place of the people?
And what abstraction would you exchange for this one?
And when has creative man not toiled
deep in myth?
And who fights for a belly full only
and where is any name worth remembering for anything else than
the human abstraction woven
through it with invisible things?

CARL SANDBURG, *The People, Yes*

14954. Sweep on, you fat and greasy
citizens.

SHAKESPEARE, *As You Like It*

14955. Each man of you, individually, walketh with the tread of a fox,
but collectively ye are geese.

SOLON, *Of the Athenians allow-
ing themselves to be duped into
dictatorship by Peisistratus.*

14956. You got to have patience.
Why Tom, us people will go on livin'
when all them people is gone . . .
Rich fellas come up an' they die, an'
their kids ain't no good, an' they die
out. But we keep a-comin'.

JOHN STEINBACK,
The Grapes of Wrath

14957. In matters of sentiment, the
public has very crude ideas; and the
most shocking fault of women is that
they make the public the supreme
judge of their lives.   STENDHAL

14958. No organizations of peoples
have a permanent ownership of even
the land they collectively live on.
They have only a lease.

DOROTHY THOMPSON,
On the Record

14959. I have found out that ther
ain't no surer way to find out whethe
you like people or hate them than t
travel with them.   MARK TWAI⟩

14960. The public be damned.
WILLIAM H. VANDERBIL⟩

14961.
The two kinds of people on earth th⟩
I mean
Are the people who lift and the peop⟩
who lean.   ELLA W. WILCOX,
To Lift or to Lea⟩

14962. The thought of the pla⟩
people here and everywhere through⟩
out the world, the people who e⟩
joy no privilege and have very simp⟩
and unsophisticated standards ⟨
right and wrong is the air all gover⟩
ments must henceforth breathe
they would live.   WOODROW WILSO⟩

See also: 1203, 1528, 1583, 254
3453, 8046, 9810, 11154, 1626
20833, 21840.

PERCEPTION

**Related Subjects: Instinct, Know⟩
edge, Observation, Understandin⟩
Wisdom.**

14971.
Earth's crammed with heaven,
And every common bush afire wi⟩
God;
But only he who sees, takes off h⟩
shoes.   ELIZABETH B. BROWNI⟩

14972. You can see farther into
millstone than he.
CERVANTES, *Don Quixo⟩*

14973. Penetration seems a kind ⟨
inspiration; it gives me an idea ⟨
prophecy.   GREVIL⟩

14974. Simple creatures, who⟩
thoughts are not taken up, like tho⟩
of educated people, with the care of

reat museum of dead phrases, are
ery quick to see the live facts which
re going on about them.
                    O. W. HOLMES

4975. The heart has eyes that the
rain knows nothing of.
                    C. H. PARKHURST

see also: 1069, 1730.

PERFECTION AND
IMPERFECTION

Related Subjects: Faults, Purity.

4981. Be ye therefore perfect, even
s your Father which is in heaven is
perfect.   *Bible: Matthew, v, 48*

4982.
All his perfections were so rare,
The wit of man could not declare
Which single virtue, or which grace
Above the rest had any place.
SAMUEL BUTLER, *Hudibras's Elegy*

4983.
Oh! she was perfect past all paral-
    lel—
Of any modern female saint's com-
    parison.   BYRON, *Don Juan*

4984. Everything splendid is rare,
and nothing is harder to find than perfection.   CICERO, *De Amicitia*

14985. The microscope cannot find
the animalcule which is less perfect
for being little.   EMERSON, *Essays*

14986. The desire of perfection is the
worst disease that ever afflicted the
human mind.   FONTANES

14987. The very pink of perfection.
GOLDSMITH, *She Stoops to Conquer*

14988. Were she perfect, one would
admire her more, but love her less.
              C. HARTLEY GRATTAN

14989. Trifles make perfection, and
perfection is no trifle.
                  MICHELANGELO

14990. God made thee perfect, not
immutable.   MILTON, *Paradise Lost*

14991.
'Tis true, perfection none must hope
    to find
In all the world, much less in woman-
    kind.   POPE, *January and May*

14992.
Whose dear perfection hearts that
    scorn'd to serve
Humbly call'd mistress.
                    SHAKESPEARE,
              All's Well that Ends Well

14993. She did make defect perfection.
SHAKESPEARE, *Antony and Cleopatra*

14994. Thou art the nonpareil.
              SHAKESPEARE, *Macbeth*
14995.
        I had else been perfect,
Whole as the marble, founded as the
    rock,
As broad and general as the casing
    air.   SHAKESPEARE, *Macbeth*

14996.
How many things by season season'd
    are
To their right praise and true per-
    fection!   SHAKESPEARE,
              The Merchant of Venice
14997.
            But you, O you,
So perfect and so peerless, are
    created
Of every creature's best!
           SHAKESPEARE, *The Tempest*

14998.
If, one by one, you wedded all the
    world,
Or from the all that are took some-
    thing good,
To make a perfect woman, she you
    kill'd
Would be unparallel'd.
       SHAKESPEARE, *The Winter's Tale*

14999.

Every thing that grows
Holds in perfection but a little mo-
    ment.   SHAKESPEARE, *Sonnet XV*

15000. No perfect thing is too small
for eternal recollection.

ARTHUR SYMONS

15001.

I thought I could not breathe in that
    fine air,
That pure severity of perfect light.

TENNYSON, *Idylls of the King*

15002.

In this broad earth of ours,
Amid the measureless grossness and
    the slag,
Enclosed and safe within its central
    heart,
Nestles the seed Perfection.

WALT WHITMAN,
Song of the Universal

Imperfection

15003. What an absurd thing it is to
pass over all the valuable parts of a
man, and fix our attention on his infirmities.   ADDISON

15004. He censures God who quarrels with the imperfections of men.

BURKE

15005. It is only imperfection that
complains of what is imperfect. The
more perfect we are, the more gentle
and quiet we become toward the defects of others.   FENELON

15006. The finer the nature, the more
flaws will show through the clearness
of it; and it is a law of this universe
that the best things shall be seldomest
seen in their best forms.   RUSKIN

15007.

No perfection is so absolute,
That some impurity doth not pollute.
SHAKESPEARE, *The Rape of Lucrece*

15008. Our erected wit maketh u
know what perfection is, and yet ou
infected will keepeth us from reachin
unto it.   SIR PHILIP SIDNEY,
The Defense of Poes

15009.

To keep in sight Perfection, an
    adore
    The vision, is the artist's best d
        light;
His bitterest pang, that he can ne'
    do more
    Than keep her long'd-for lovel
        ness in sight.
WILLIAM WATSON, *Epigran*

15010. Even the vainest among
feels that he is not perfect, not s
perfect as he would like others
think him.   STEFAN ZWE

See also: 1195, 1201, 1216, 132
3036, 10818, 19904.

PERFUME

Related Subjects: Nose, Odor.

15011.

Gentle and noble are their tempe:
    framed,
That can be quickened with perfum
    and sounds.
GEORGE CHAPMAN,
Ovid's Banquet of Sen

15012.

I cannot talk with civet in the roor
A fine puss-gentleman that's all pe
    fume;
The sight's enough—no need to sm
    a beau.   COWPER, *Conversatio*

15013. The sweetest essences are a
ways confined in the smallest glasse
DRYDEN, *Essa*

15014. He does not smell well wl
always has a nice scent upon him.
MARTIAL, *Epigran*

5015. A stream of rich distill'd per-umes.   MILTON, *Comus*

5016. They that smell least, smell est.   *Proverb*

5017. Look not for musk in a dog-ennel.   *Proverb*

5018. A strange invisible perfume its the sense.
SHAKESPEARE, *Antony and Cleopatra*

5019. So perfumed that The winds were love-sick.
SHAKESPEARE, *Antony and Cleopatra*

5020. All the perfumes of Arabia will not sweeten this little hand.
SHAKESPEARE, *Macbeth*

5021.
Let me have them very well per-fumed;
For she is sweeter than perfume itself
To whom they go to.
SHAKESPEARE,
The Taming of the Shrew

15022. Perfume for a lady's cham-ber.
SHAKESPEARE, *The Winter's Tale*

15023. The perfumed tincture of the roses.   SHAKESPEARE, *Sonnets*

PERSECUTION

Related Subjects: Cruelty, Des-potism, Dictatorship, Prison, Tol-erance, Tyranny.

15031. Persecution of whole groups of people, based solely upon disap-proval of the beliefs they hold and express, is wholly un-American and can only be destructive of the very foundations of democracy.
JOHN M. COFFEE

15032. In all places, and in all times, those religionists who have believed too much, have been more inclined to violence and persecution than those who have believed too little.
C. C. COLTON

15033. Transgressors . . . that dis-compose, and tear the body of man with violence, are those inhuman per-secutors, who with racks, and tor-tures, and prisons, and fires, and ex-quisite inquisitions, throw down the bodies of the true God's true serv-ants, to the idolatrous worship of their imaginary gods; that torture men into hell, and carry them through the inquisition into damnation.
JOHN DONNE, *Sermons*

15034. The history of persecution is a history of endeavors to cheat na-ture, to make water run uphill, to twist a rope of sand. It makes no dif-ference whether the actors be many or one, a tyrant or a mob.
EMERSON

15035. Persecution does not make people more affable or more enter-taining. That is a sufficient reason for not persecuting people.
LANCELOT HOGBEN,
Dangerous Thoughts

15036. Wherever you see persecu-tion, there is more than a probability that truth is on the persecuted side.
HUGH LATIMER

15037. For belief or practice in reli-gion no man ought to be punished or molested by any outward force what-ever.   MILTON

15038. The resource of bigotry and intolerance, when convicted of error, is always the same; silenced by argu-ment, it endeavors to silence by per-secution, in old times by fire and sword, in modern days by the tongue.
C. SIMMONS

See also: 92, 15173, 17417.

PERSEVERANCE, PERSISTENCE

Related Subjects: Obstinacy, Resolution.

15041. Plodding wins the race.
AESOP, *The Hare and the Tortoise*

15042. Life is not easy for any of us. But what of that? We must have perseverance and above all confidence in ourselves. We must believe that we are gifted for something, and that this thing, at whatever cost, must be attained.   MARIE CURIE,
Curie: Madame Curie

15043. Little strokes fell great oaks.
FRANKLIN, *Poor Richard*

15044. The best way out is always through.   ROBERT FROST,
A Servant to Servants

15045. I propose to fight it out on this line, if it takes all summer.
ULYSSES S. GRANT

15046.
'Tis a lesson you should heed,
    Try, try, try again.
If at first you don't succeed,
    Try, try, try again.
W. E. HICKSON, *Try and Try Again*

15047.
The heights by great men reached
    and kept
Were not attained by sudden flight,
But they, while their companions
    slept,
Were toiling upward in the night.
         LONGFELLOW,
The Ladder of Saint Augustine

15048. Forward, as occasion offers. Never look round to see whether any shall note it.
MARCUS AURELIUS, *Meditations*

15049.
        Yet I argue not
Against Heav'n's hand or will, n[
    bate a jot
Of heart or hope; but still bear ι
    and steer
Right onward. MILTON, *Sonnet XX.*

15050. Perseverance is more prevai[
ing than violence; and many thin[
which cannot be overcome when th[
are together, yield themselves ι
when taken little by little.
        PLUTARCH, *Liv[*

15051. If you would be a pope, y[
must think of nothing else. *Prove[*

15052. It's dogged as does it.
Prove[

15053. A rolling stone gathers [
moss. PUBLILIUS SYRUS, *Sententi[*

15054. Do not turn back when y[
are just at the goal.
PUBLILIUS SYRUS, *Sententi[*

15055. De man what keeps pullin' [
grapevine shakes down a few bunch[
at leas'.   IRWIN RUSSELL,
Precepts at Parti[

15056. Neither to the right of m[
nor to the left of me, nor behind [
—but ever forward. Some people w[
say: "Turn this way," or "turn th[
way." But I say, "Neither to t[
right of me, nor to the left of me, n[
behind me—but ever forward!"
        ARNOLD SCHOENBE[

15057.
And many strokes, though with [
    little axe,
Hew down and fell the harde[
    timbered oak.
        SHAKESPEARE, *Henry [*

15058. Harp not on that string.
        SHAKESPEARE, *Richard [*

15059. A man must not swerve from his path because of the barkings of dogs.   H. M. STANLEY

15060. 'Tis known by the name of perseverance in a good cause,—and of obstinacy in a bad one.
STERNE, *Tristram Shandy*

See also: 621, 2751, 8831, 15605.

PERSONALITY

Related Subjects: Character, Charm, Eccentricity, Individuality.

15061. Every individual represents both a unity of personality and the individual fashioning of that unity. The individual is thus both the picture and the artist. He is the artist of his own personality, but as an artist he is neither an infallible worker, nor a person with a complete understanding of soul and body—he is rather a weak, extremely fallible and imperfect human being.
ALFRED ADLER,
Education of Children

15062. Hannibal, as he had mighty virtues, so had he many vices; he had two distinct persons in him.
ROBERT BURTON,
Anatomy of Melancholy

15063. 'Tisn't beauty, so to speak, nor good talk necessarily. It's just It.
KIPLING, *Traffics & Discoveries*

15064. Put thyself into the trick of singularity.
SHAKESPEARE, *Twelfth Night*

15065. For more than a century poets have been bred on the romantic notion that the individual is capable of godlike perfection. This is poison food, and those who eat it die a lingering and pallid death. But before he dies the poet repeats the doctrine that has poisoned him. He feeds his audience on the gigantic fiction of a *Free Personality*.
GENEVIEVE TAGGARD

15066. As I conceive it, liberalism is pre-eminently a type of mind, a kind of spirit and a sort of behavior, the basis of which is an enormous respect for personality. It is, therefore, above everything else, human and humane.
DOROTHY THOMPSON,
Political Guide

15067. It is native personality, and that alone, that endows a man to stand before presidents or generals, or in any distinguish'd collection, with *aplomb*—and *not* culture, or any knowledge or intellect whatever.
WALT WHITMAN, *Democratic Vistas*

See also: 173, 412.

PERSUASION

Related Subjects: Advice, Conversion, Counsel, Eloquence, Warning.

15071. Almost thou persuadest me to be a Christian. *Bible: Acts, xxvi, 28*

15072. Let every man be fully persuaded in his own mind.
Bible: Romans, xiv, 5

15073. He, from whose lips divine persuasion flows.   HOMER, *Iliad*

15074.
Yet hold it more humane, more heav'nly, first,
By winning words to conquer willing hearts,
And make persuasion do the work of fear. MILTON, *Paradise Regained*

15075. The persuasion of the fortunate sways the doubtful.   *Proverb*

15076. He did entreat me, past all saying nay.   SHAKESPEARE, *The Merchant of Venice*

15077. Persuasion hung upon his lips.   STERNE, *Tristram Shandy*

See also: 360, 1721.

PERVERSITY

Related Subjects: Contradiction, Knave, Obstinacy, Wickedness.

15081. Men take more pains to lose themselves than would be requisite to keep them in the right road.
K. H. DIGBY,
The Broad Stone of Honour

15082. All things can corrupt perverted minds.   OVID, *Tristia*

15083. 'Zounds, sir, you are one of those that will not serve God if the devil bid you.
SHAKESPEARE, *Othello*

15084.
Men of perverse opinion do not know
The excellence of what is in their hands,
Till some one dash it from them.
SOPHOCLES, *Ajax*

PESSIMISM

Related Subjects: Cynicism, Despondency, Doubt, Melancholy.

15091. A man that could look no way but downwards with a muck-rake in his hand.
BUNYAN, *Pilgrim's Progress*

15092.
It's hardly in a body's pow'r,
To keep, at times, frae being sour.
BURNS, *Epistle to Davie*

15093. Pessimism is only the name that men of weak nerves give to wisdom.
BERNARD DE VOTO, *Mark Twain*

15094. In the end—pessimism is always the victim of its own deceit. I disregards the great law which migh be called the law of the double energ movement of history.
JACQUES MARITAIN, *I Believ*

15095. She not only expects th worst, but makes the most of it whe it happens.   HUGH MEARN

15096. The refuge from pessimism is the good men and women at an time existing in the world,—they kee faith and happiness alive.
CHARLES E. NORTO

15097.
Who breathes, must suffer, and wh
    thinks must mourn;
And he alone is bless'd who ne'er wa
    born.   MATTHEW PRIOR,
Solomon on the Vanity of the Worl

15098. It is a poor heart that neve rejoices.   *Prover*

15099.
Never to have been born is much th
    best;
    And the next best, by far,
To return thence, by the way speed
    iest,
    Where our beginnings are.
SOPHOCLES, *Oedipus Coloneu*

15100. The worst is yet to come.
TENNYSON, *Sea Dream*

15101.
Not to be born, never to see th
    sun—
No worldly blessing is a greater one
And the next best is speedily to die
And lapt beneath a load of earth t
    lie.   THEOGNI

PHILANTHROPY

Related Subjects: Benevolence Brotherhood, Charity, Gifts, Help Kindness, Patronage.

15111. Gifts and alms are the ex

pressions, not the essence, of this virtue.   ADDISON, *The Guardian*

15112.
There are, while human miseries
    abound,
A thousand ways to waste superfluous
    wealth,
Without one fool or flatterer at your
    board,
Without one hour of sickness or dis-
    gust.   JOHN ARMSTRONG,
                Art of Preserving Health

15113. I was eyes to the blind, and feet was I to the lame.
    Bible: Job, xxix, 15

15114. However, while I crawl upon this planet, I think myself obliged to do what good I can in my narrow domestic sphere, to all my fellow-creatures, and to wish them all the good I cannot do.
    LORD CHESTERFIELD

15115. In nothing do men more nearly approach the gods than in doing good to their fellowmen.
    CICERO, *Pro Ligario*

15116.
Youth, beauty, graceful action seldom
    fail:
But common interest always will pre-
    vail;
And pity never ceases to be shown
To him who makes the people's
    wrongs his own.   DRYDEN,
              Absalom & Achitophel

15117. I tell thee, thou foolish philanthropist, that I grudge the dollar, the dime, the cent I give to such men as do not belong to me and to whom I do not belong.   EMERSON, *Essays*

15118. It is easy to live for others; everybody does.   EMERSON,
                      Journals

15119. I love my country better than my family, but I love human nature better than my country.
    FENELON, *Telemaque*

15120. The most acceptable service of God is doing good to man.
    FRANKLIN, *Autobiography*

15121.
A kind and gentle heart he had,
    To comfort friends and foes;
The naked every day he clad,
    When he put on his clothes.
          GOLDSMITH,
    Elegy on the Death of a Mad Dog

15122. He held his seat; a friend to human race.   HOMER, *Iliad*

15123.
        "I pray thee, then,
Write me as one that loves his fellow
    men."   LEIGH HUNT,
              Abou Ben Adhem

15124. He is one of those wise philanthropists who in a time of famine would vote for nothing but a supply of toothpicks.
    DOUGLAS JERROLD,
          Douglas Jerrold's Wit

15125.
Officious, innocent, sincere,
    Of every friendless name the
    friend.   SAMUEL JOHNSON,
    On the Death of Dr. Robert Levet

15126.
          For his bounty
There was no winter in 't; an autumn
    'twas
That grew the more by reaping.
        SHAKESPEARE,
      Antony and Cleopatra

15127. Feel for others—in your pocket.   C. H. SPURGEON,
                Salt-Cellars

15128. Philanthropy is almost the only virtue which is sufficiently appreciated by mankind.
THOREAU, *Walden*

15129. As for doing good, that is one of the professions that are full.
THOREAU, *Walden*

15130. Philanthropy seems to me to have become simply the refuge of people who wish to annoy their fellow-creatures. OSCAR WILDE,
An Ideal Husband

15131. Philanthropists don't give their lives, they give their names—they have them carved in stone over their institutes and libraries.
JESSIE L. WILLIAMS, *Why Marry?*

15132.
For thou wert still the poor man's stay,
The poor man's heart, the poor man's hand;
And all the oppressed, who wanted strength,
Had thine at their command.
WORDSWORTH, *Rob Roy's Grave*

PHILOSOPHY

Related Subjects: **Intelligence, Metaphysics, Patience, Principle, Resignation, Sophistry, Theories, Thought.**

15141.
Be his
My special thanks, whose even-balanced soul,
From first youth tested up to extreme old age,
Business could not make dull, nor Passion wild:
Who saw life steadily and saw it whole. MATTHEW ARNOLD,
To A Friend

15142. Though they [philosophers] write *contemptu gloriae,* yet as Hieron observes, they will put their names to their books. ROBERT BURTON,
Anatomy of Melancholy

15143.
Cheer'd up himself with ends of verse
And sayings of philosophers.
SAMUEL BUTLER, *Hudibras*

15144. The Philosopher is he to whom the Highest has descended, and the Lowest has mounted up; who is the equal and kindly brother of all.
CARLYLE, *Sartor Resartus*

15145. Not for Philosophy does this rose give a damn. E. E. CUMMINGS

15146. Asked what he gained from philosophy, he [Aristotle] answered, "To do without being commanded what others do from fear of the laws." DIOGENES LAERTIUS,
Aristotle

15147. The race of men is a race of partisans feeding their pigeon-holes with contradictory reports of life, and when a fellow comes and lays a summary on the desk, they look at him askance; but the future pays attention, for the impartial is all that it has time for. GALSWORTHY

15148. Philosophy is the microscope of thought. VICTOR HUGO,
Les Miserables

15149. Philosophy triumphs easily over past evils and future evils; but present evils triumph over it.
LA ROCHEFOUCAULD, *Maxims*

15150. Stated in the simplest terms, science is but a sense of curiosity about life, religion is a sense of reverence for life, literature is a sense of wonder at life, art is a taste for life, while philosophy is an attitude toward life, based on a greater or lesser, but always limited, comprehension of the universe as far as we happen to know it.   LIN YUTANG, *I Believe*

15151. So soon as I hear that such or such a man gives himself out for a philosopher, I conclude that, like the dyspeptic old woman, he must have "broken his digester."
HERMAN MELVILLE, *Moby Dick*

15152.
How charming is divine philosophy!
Not harsh and crabbed, as dull fools
    suppose,
But musical as is Apollo's lute,
And a perpetual feast of nectar'd
    sweets
Where no crude surfeit reigns.
MILTON, *Comus*

15153. Philosophers, who need most quiet for their meditations, are the greatest proof that man, when sane, vigorous, and in full possession of his faculties, needs to be in a crowd in order to be happy. They always live in cities.   LIAM O'FLAHERTY,
Two Years

15154. Philosophy is toleration, and it is only one step from toleration to forgiveness.   PINERO,
The Second Mrs. Tanqueray

15155. Many talk like philosophers, and live like fools.   *Proverb*

15156. Tis not the beard that makes the philosopher.   *Proverb*

15157. If you sit down a mere philosopher, you will rise almost an atheist.   *Proverb*

15158. Fools and philosophers were made out of the same metal.
Proverb

15159. It is a great advantage for a system of philosophy to be substantially true.   SANTAYANA,
The Unknowable

15160. Philosophy is nothing but discretion.   JOHN SELDEN, *Table Talk*

15161.
There are more things in heaven and
    earth, Horatio,
Than are dreamt of in your philoso-
    phy.   SHAKESPEARE, *Hamlet*

15162.
For there was never yet philosopher
That could endure the toothache pa-
    tiently.   SHAKESPEARE,
Much Ado About Nothing

15163. Adversity's sweet milk, philosophy.   SHAKESPEARE,
Romeo and Juliet

15164. The greater philosopher a man is, the more difficult it is for him to answer the questions of common people.   SIENKIEWICZ, *Quo Vadis*

15165. The upper classes pay the philosopher, in order that he may discover only such truths as are expedient in their eyes.
And suppose uncomfortable truths should be discovered?
They are called lies, and the philosopher gets no pay.
AUGUST STRINDBERG,
A Catechism for Workers

15166. Philosophers must deal with ideas, but the trouble with most nineteenth-century poets is too much philosophy; they are nearer to being philosophers than poets, without being in the true sense either.
ALLEN TATE, *Reactionary Essays*

15167.
I make the most of all that comes,
    And the least of all that goes.
SARA TEASDALE, *The Philosopher*

15168. Philosophy offers the rather cold consolation that perhaps we and our planet do not actually exist; religion presents the contradictory and scarcely more comforting thought that we exist but that we cannot hope to get anywhere until we cease to exist.   JAMES THURBER, *I Believe*

15169. It is easier to write ten volumes of philosophy than to put one principle into practice.
TOLSTOY, *Diary*

15170. The true philosophers are the young men of their age. Not . . . because they do it very well; but because they rush upon ideas with their whole soul. Later one philosophizes for praise, or for apology, or because it is a complicated intellectual game.
THORNTON WILDER,
The Woman of Andros

See also: 1321, 1325, 3348, 3641, 3643, 3843, 4323, 4549, 6170, 7285, 8973, 11042, 13762, 15324, 15326, 17843, 21395.

PIETY AND IMPIETY

Related Subjects: Atheism, Devotion, Goodness, Heresy, Holiness, Prayer, Religion.

15171. One's piety is best displayed in his pursuits.
BRONSON ALCOTT, *Table Talk*

15172. One day lived after the perfect rule of piety, is to be preferred before sinning immortality.
SIR THOMAS BROWNE,
To a Friend

15173. Religious persecution may shield itself under the guise of a mistaken and overzealous piety. BURKE

15174. Piety is the foundation of all virtues. CICERO, *Pro Cnaeo Plancio*

15175. The Gods are mortal, but piety is everlasting. WILL DURANT,
The Life of Greece

15176. Although I am a pious man, I am not the less a man.
MOLIÈRE, *Tartuffe*

15177. Glistening semblances of piety.
SHAKESPEARE, *Henry V*

15178. O cruel, irreligious piety!
SHAKESPEARE, *Titus Andronicus*

Impiety.

15179. *Impiety:* Your irreverence toward my deity.
AMBROSE BIERCE,
The Devil's Dictionary

15180.
No solemn, sanctimonious face I pull,
Nor think I'm pious when I'm only
  bilious.   THOMAS HOOD,
Ode to Rae Wilson

15181. There is no piety but amongst the poor. THOMAS RANDOLPH,
*On the Content He Enjoys in the
Muses*

15182. Volumes might be written upon the impiety of the pious.
HERBERT SPENCER, *First Principles*

See also: 4061, 10214.

PILGRIM-FATHERS

Related Subjects: Pioneer, Puritans.

15191.
Wild was the day; the wintry sea
  Moaned sadly on New England's
    strand,
When first the thoughtful and the
  free,
  Our fathers, trod the desert land.
BRYANT,
The Twenty-Second of December

15192. They cultivated industry and frugality at the same time—which is the real foundation of the greatness of the Pilgrims. ULYSSES S. GRANT

15193.
The Pilgrims landed, worthy men,
    And saved from wreck on raging
        seas,
They fell upon their knees, and then
    Upon the Aborigines.
            ARTHUR GUITERMAN,
            The Pilgrims' Thanksgiving

15194.
Ay, call it holy ground,
    The soil where first they trod!
They have left unstained what there
        they found—
    Freedom to worship God.
            MRS. HEMANS,
The Landing of the Pilgrim Fathers

15195. God had sifted three kingdoms to find the wheat for this plant-
ing.   LONGFELLOW,
    The Courtship of Miles Standish

15196.
Down to the Plymouth Rock, that
        had been to their feet as a door-
        step
Into a world unknown,—the corner-
    stone of a nation!
            LONGFELLOW,
    The Courtship of Miles Standish

15197. Give it only the fulcrum of
Plymouth Rock, an idea will upheave
the continent.   WENDELL PHILLIPS

15198.
The Pilgrim spirit has not fled:
    It walks in noon's broad light;
And it watches the bed of the glori-
        ous dead,
    With the holy stars by night.
            JOHN PIERPONT,
            The Pilgrim Fathers

PINE

Related Subject: Tree.

15201.
Desert-loving pine, whose emerald
        scalp

Nods to the storm.   BYRON,
            Prophecy of Dante

15202.
As sunbeams stream through liberal
        space
And nothing jostle or displace,
So waved the pine-tree through my
        thought
And fanned the dreams it never
        brought.   EMERSON, *Wood Notes*

15203. The pine wishes herself a
shrub when the axe is at her root.
            Proverb

15204.
Like two cathedral towers these
        stately pines
Uplift their fretted summits tipped
    with cones.   LONGFELLOW,
            My Cathedral

15205. Yes, the pine is the mother of
legends.   LOWELL,
            The Growth of the Legend

15206.
The arched walks of twilight groves,
And shadows brown that Sylvan
        loves,
Of pine.   MILTON, *Il Penseroso*

15207.
Ay me! the bark peel'd from the lofty
        pine,
His leaves will wither and his sap
    decay.   SHAKESPEARE,
            The Rape of Lucrece

15208.
And wind, that grand old harper,
        smote
His thunder-harp of pines.
    ALEXANDER SMITH, *A Life Drama*

15209.
Here also grew the rougher rinded
        pine
The great Argoan ship's brave orna-
    ment.   EDMUND SPENSER,
            Virgil's Gnat

15210. The sailing pine.
EDMUND SPENSER,
The Faerie Queene

15211.
Ancient Pines,
Ye bear no record of the years of
man.
Spring is your sole historian.
BAYARD TAYLOR,
The Pine Forest of Monterey

See also: 15940.

PIONEER

Related Subjects: Adventure, Discovery, Pilgrim-Fathers, Progress.

15221. It is sometimes the man who
opens the door who is the last to
enter the room.
ELIZABETH A. BIBESCO,
The Fir and the Palm

15222. Pioneering does not pay.
ANDREW CARNEGIE

15223.
There are pioneer souls that blaze
their paths
Where highways never ran.
SAM W. FOSS,
The House by the Side of the Road

15224. Not only have you opened up
a new continent to our view, but you
have given impetus to scientific and
philanthropic enterprises which will
have its effect on the progress of the
world. GAMBETTA, *to Stanley*

15225. The history of America for
two hundred years after the voyage
of Joliet has been the history of
courageous, persistent, and successful exploration, wherein the track of
the explorer, instantly serving as a
trail for the pioneer, has speedily
broadened into the wagon-road of in-
vading immigrants.
GENERAL GREELY,
Explorers & Travellers

15226. The man who makes the experiment deservedly claims the honour
and the reward. HORACE, *Epistles*

15227.
O willing hearts turned quick to clay,
Glad lovers holding death in scorn
Out of the lives ye cast away
The coming race is born.
LAURENCE HOUSMAN, *The Settler*

15228. Look history over and you
will see. The missionary comes after
the whiskey—I mean he arrives after
the whiskey has arrived. Next comes
the poor immigrant with ax and hoe
and rifle; next, the trader, next the
miscellaneous rush; next the gambler,
the desperado, the highwayman, and
all their kindred in sin of both sexes
and next the smart chap who has
bought up an old grant that covers
all the land; this brings in the lawyer
tribe; the vigilance committee brings
the undertakers. All these interests
bring the newspaper; the newspaper
starts up politics and a railroad; all
hands turn to and build a church and
a jail—and behold, civilization is established forever in the land.
MARK TWAIN, *Hell-On-Wheels*

15229.
Conquering, holding, daring, ventur-
ing as we go the unknown ways
Pioneers! O pioneers!
WALT WHITMAN,
Pioneers! O Pioneers

15230.
The paths to the house I seek to make,
But leave to those to come the house
itself. WALT WHITMAN,
*Thou Mother with Thy
Equal Brood*

15231.
We cross the prairie as of old
The pilgrims crossed the sea,

To make the West, as they the East,
The homestead of the free!
WHITTIER,
The Kansas Emigrants

See also: 1500.

PITY

Related Subjects: Compassion,
Consolation, Mercy, Sympathy.

15241.
Him who pitieth suffering men
Zeus pitieth, and his ways are sweet
on earth.   AESCHYLUS,
The Eumenides

15242.
Of all the paths (that) lead to a
woman's love
Pity's the straightest.
BEAUMONT & FLETCHER,
The Knight of Malta

15243. He that hath pity upon the
poor lendeth unto the Lord.
Bible: Proverbs, xix, 17

15244. What humanity needs is not
the promise of scientific immortality,
but compassionate pity in this life and
infinite mercy on the Day of Judgment.   JOSEPH CONRAD,
Notes on Life and Letters

15245. Man, man, one cannot live
quite without pity.
DOSTOYEVSKY,
Crime and Punishment

15246. For pity melts the mind to
love.   DRYDEN, Alexander's Feast

15247. Pity is the feeling which ar-
rests the mind in the presence of whatever is grave and constant in human
sufferings and unites it with the human sufferer.   JAMES JOYCE,
A Portrait of the Artist as a
Young Man

15248.
I never saw a wild thing
Sorry for itself.
D. H. LAWRENCE, Self-Pity

15249.
Some undone widow sits upon mine
arm,
And takes away the use of it, and
my sword,
Glued to my scabbard with wronged
orphans' tears,
Will not be drawn.
MASSINGER,
A New Way to Pay Old Debts

15250. We may pity, though not pardon thee.   SHAKESPEARE,
The Comedy of Errors

15251.
Some of you with Pilate wash your
hands
Showing an outward pity.
SHAKESPEARE, Richard II

See also: 3761, 3842, 4894, 17487,
18462, 21685.

PLACE

Related Subjects: Office, Rank.

15261. It is not the places that grace
men, but men the places.
AGESILAUS

15262. Nothing is more annoying
than a low man raised to a high position.   CLAUDIAN, In Eutropium

15263. Accept the place the divine
providence has found for you.
EMERSON, Essays

15264. When the whole world is nodding to its fall, happy the man who
has been able to learn already the
lowly place appointed for him.
LUCAN, The Civil War

15265.
God attributes to place
No sanctity, if none be thither
　brought
By men who there frequent.
MILTON, Paradise Lost

15266. There is no greater immorality than to occupy a place you cannot fill.
NAPOLEON

15267. All things have their place, knew we how to place them.
Proverb

15268. Sit in your place, and none can make you rise. 　Proverb

15269. Have a place for everything and have everything in its place.
Proverb

15270. High places have their precipices. 　Proverb

15271. Where Macgregor sits, there is the head of the table.
SCOTT, Rob Roy

15272. The place is dignified by the doer's deed. 　SHAKESPEARE,
All's Well that Ends Well

15273. There's place and means for every man alive.
SHAKESPEARE,
All's Well that Ends Well

15274. In the world I fill up a place, which may be better supplied when I have made it empty.
SHAKESPEARE, As You Like It

15275.
O place and greatness! millions of
　false eyes
Are stuck upon thee.
SHAKESPEARE,
Measure for Measure

15276.
O place, O form,
How often dost thou with thy case
　thy habit,
Wrench awe from fools!
SHAKESPEARE,
Measure for Measure

15277. I know my place, as I would they should do theirs.
SHAKESPEARE, Twelfth Night

15278. It is a maxim, that those to whom everybody allows the second place have an undoubted title to the first. 　SWIFT, <i>Tale of a Tub</i>

PLAGIARISM

Related Subjects: Authors, Borrowing, Imitation.

15281. They lard their lean books with the fat of others' works.
ROBERT BURTON,
Anatomy of Melancholy

15282. We can say nothing but what hath been said. Our poets steal from Homer. . . . Our story-dressers do as much; he that comes last is commonly best. 　ROBERT BURTON,
Anatomy of Melancholy

15283. The Eighth Commandment was not made for bards.
COLERIDGE, The Reproof and Reply

15284. *Pirate:* A sea robber, and robber; particularly a bookseller who seizes the copies of other men.
SAMUEL JOHNSON, Dictionary

15285. They copied all they could follow, but they couldn't copy my mind. 　KIPLING,
The "Mary Gloster"

15286. For such kind of borrowing as this, if it be not bettered by the

borrower, among good authors is accounted plagiarè.   MILTON,
Iconoclastes XXIII

15287. Take the whole range of imaginative literature, and we are all wholesale borrowers. In every matter that relates to invention, to use, or beauty or form, we are borrowers.
WENDELL PHILLIPS

15288. In comparing various authors with one another, I have discovered that some of the gravest and latest writers have transcribed, word for word, from former works, without making acknowledgment.
PLINY THE ELDER, *Natural History*

15289.
Or where the pictures for the page atone,
And Quarles is sav'd by beauties not his own.   POPE, *The Dunciad*

15290.
Next o'er his books his eyes begin to roll,
In pleasing memory of all he stole.
POPE, *The Dunciad*

15291. Steal! to be sure they may; and, egad, serve your best thoughts as gypsies do stolen children,—disfigure them to make 'em pass for their own.   SHERIDAN, *The Critic*

See also: 1194, 9929, 14427.

PLAN

Related Subjects: Method, Order, Policy, System.

15301. Which of you, intending to build a tower, sitteth not down first, and counteth the cost, whether he have sufficient to finish it.
Bible: Luke, xiv, 28

15302. All human plans and projects come to naught.   BROWNING,
The Ring and the Book

15303.
The best laid schemes o' mice and men
Gang aft a-gley;
An' lea'e us nought but grief and pain,
For promis'd joy.
BURNS, *To a Mouse*
(*Source of title of novel by John Steinbeck*)

15304. I should rather walk the sidewalk in front of a man's office for two hours before an interview, than step into his office without a perfectly clear idea of what I am going to say and what he—from my knowledge of his interest and motives—is likely to answer.   DEAN DONHAM

15305. Make a model before thou buildest.   *Proverb*

15306. It is a bad plan that admits of no modification.
PUBLILIUS SYRUS, *Sententiae*

15307.
When we mean to build,
We first survey the plot, then draw the model;
And when we see the figure of the house,
Then must we rate the cost of the erection.   SHAKESPEARE,
Henry IV

See also: 2553.

PLATITUDE

Related Subjects: Proverbs, Quotation.

15311.
The spell was broken, the key denied me
And at length your flat clear voice beside me
Mouthed cheerful clear flat platitudes.   RUPERT BROOKE,
The Voice

15312. You came and quacked beside me in the wood.
>>> RUPERT BROOKE, *The Voice*

15313.
I am *not* fond of uttering platitudes
In stained-glass attitudes.
>>> W. S. GILBERT, *Patience*

15314. The moral commonplaces.
>>> SIR PHILIP SIDNEY,
>>> *Apology for Poetry*

15315. The everlasting platitudes.
>>> R. H. STODDARD,
>>> *Proverbial Philosophy*

15316. Nothing produces such an effect as a good platitude.
>>> OSCAR WILDE, *An Ideal Husband*

PLATO

15321. He, if anyone, had the highest meed of praise for wisdom, and was too great for envy.
>>> *Anonymous, Greek Anthology*

15322.
Oh, Plato! Plato! you have paved the way,
>> With your confounded fantasies, to more
Immoral conduct by the fancied sway
>> Your system feigns o'er the controlless core
Of human hearts, than all the long array
>> Of poets and romancers.
>>> BYRON, *Don Juan*

15323. Out of Plato come all things that are still written and debated among men of thought. Great havoc makes he among our originalities.
>>> EMERSON, *Representative Men*

15324. Plato is philosophy and philosophy Plato,—at once the glory and the shame of mankind, since neither Saxon nor Roman have availed to add any idea to his categories.
>>> EMERSON, *Representative Men*

15325.
See there the olive grove of Academe,
Plato's retirement, where the Attic bird
Trills her thick-warbl'd notes the summer long.   MILTON,
>>> *Paradise Regained*

15326. Philosophy did not find Plato already a nobleman, it made him one.
>>> SENECA, *Epistulae ad Lucilium*

See also: 3322, 10237, 12423.

PLEASURE

Related Subjects: Amusement, Bliss, Comfort, Delight, Fun, Happiness, Laughter, Merriment, Sport.

15331. Pleasure must succeed to pleasure, else past pleasure turns to pain.   BROWNING, *La Saisiaz*

15332.
Chords that vibrate sweetest pleasure
Thrill the deepest notes of woe.
>>> BURNS, *Sensibility How Charming*

15333. People should be guarded against temptation to unlawful pleasures by furnishing them means of innocent ones.   W. E. CHANNING

15334.
You steal green apples from the Tree
Of Life, miscalling greenness pleasure.   LEE W. DODD,
>>> *To the Younger Generation*

15335. Any pleasure which takes and keeps the heart from God is sinful, and unless forsaken, will be fatal to the soul.   RICHARD FULLER

15336. If pleasure was not followed by pain, who would forbear it?
>>> SAMUEL JOHNSON, *The Idler*

15337. Life admits not of delays; when pleasure can be had, it is fit to catch it. Every hour takes away part

of the things that please us, and perhaps part of our disposition to be pleased.   SAMUEL JOHNSON,
Boswell: Life

15338. Short pleasure, long lament.
Proverb

15339. A pleasure is well paid for which is long expected.   *Proverb*

15340. Blunting the fine point of seldom pleasure.   SHAKESPEARE,
Sonnet LII

15341. In life there is nothing more unexpected and surprising than the arrivals and departures of pleasure. If we find it in one place to-day, it is vain to seek it there to-morrow. You cannot lay a trap for it.
ALEXANDER SMITH, *Dreamthorp*

15342. There are two things to aim at in life: first, to get what you want; and, after that, to enjoy it. Only the wisest of mankind achieve the second.
LOGAN PEARSALL SMITH,
Afterthoughts

15343. The Eastern monarch who proclaimed a reward to him who should discover a new pleasure, would have deserved well of mankind had he stipulated that it should be blameless.   RICHARD WHATELY

See also: 506, 523, 747, 1538, 2638, 3255, 5998, 6041, 7774, 10168, 14501, 16384, 17476, 19714, 20484, 21776.

PLOT, see Conspiracy

POETS AND POETRY

Related Subjects: Art, Authors, Ballad, Limericks, Literature, Sonnet, Writing.

15351.
O bards of rhyme and metre free,
My gratitude goes out to ye

For all your deathless lines—ahem!
Let's see now . . . . What is one of
them?   F. P. A. *Exchange*

15352.
In days of yore, the poet's pen
    From wing of bird was plundered,
Perhaps of goose, but now and then
    From Jove's own eagle sundered.
But now, metallic pens disclose
    Alone the poet's numbers;
In iron inspiration glows,
    Or with the poet slumbers.
JOHN QUINCY ADAMS, *The Pen*

15353.
You do poets and their song
A grievous wrong,
If your own soul does not bring
To their high imagining
As much beauty as they sing.
T. B. ALDRICH, *Appreciation*

15354.
Enamored architect of airy rhyme,
Build as thou wilt, heed not what
    each man says.
T. B. ALDRICH,
Enamored Architect of Airy Rhyme

15355. Poetry is simply the most beautiful, impressive and widely effective mode of saying things, and hence its importance.
MATTHEW ARNOLD, *Essays*

15356.
Poets are all who love, who feel
    great truths,
And tell them; and the truth of
    truths is love.
PHILIP J. BAILEY, *Festus*

15357. Poets are people who despise money except what you need for to-day.   J. M. BARRIE,
The Little White Bird

15358. Poetry fettered, fetters the human race. Nations are destroyed or flourish in proportion as their

poetry, painting, and music are destroyed or flourish.   BLAKE,
Jerusalem

15359. Poets ever fail in reading their own verses to their worth.

ELIZABETH B. BROWNING,
Lady Geraldine's Courtship

15360.
All poetry is difficult to read,
—The sense of it is anyhow.

BROWNING, *The Ring and the Book*

15361.
Thoughts may be
Over-poetical for poetry.

BROWNING, *Sordello*

15362.
And poets by their sufferings grow,
As if there were no more to do,
To make a poet excellent,
But only want and discontent.

SAMUEL BUTLER, *Fragments*

15363. He that works and *does* some Poem, not he that merely *says* one, is worthy of the name of Poet.

CARLYLE,
Introduction to Cromwell's Letters & Speeches

15364. A poet without love were a physical and metaphysical impossibility.   CARLYLE, *Burns*

15365. How does the poet speak to men, with power, but by being still more a man than they?

CARLYLE, *Burns*

15366. He who would write heroic poems should make his whole life a heroic poem.   CARLYLE,
Life of Schiller

15367. A vein of poetry exists in the hearts of all men.   CARLYLE,
Heroes & Hero-Worship

15368. There is a thing called poetical license.   CERVANTES,
Don Quixote

15369. Modesty is a virtue not often found among poets, for almost every one of them thinks himself the greatest in the world.

CERVANTES, *Don Quixote*

15370.
Most joyful let the Poet be;
It is through him that all men see.

W. E. CHANNING,
The Poet of the Old and New Times

15371. Free verse is like free love; it is a contradiction in terms.

G. K. CHESTERTON

15372. The more modern poets are quite capable of keeping the commas and leaving out the words.

G. K. CHESTERTON

15373. Good sense is the body of poetic genius, fancy its draper, motion its life, and imagination the soul.

COLERIDGE, *Biographia Literaria*

15374. A poem is not necessarily obscure, because it does not aim to be popular. It is enough if a work be perspicuous to those for whom it is written.   COLERIDGE,
Biographia Literaria

15375. I wish our clever young poets would remember my homely definitions of prose and poetry; that is, prose,—words in their best order; poetry,—the best words in their best order.   COLERIDGE,
Lectures on Shakespeare & Milton

15376.
There is a pleasure in poetic pains
Which only poets know.

COWPER, *The Task*

15377. If I read a book and it makes my whole body so cold no fire can ever warm me, I know that it is poetry. If I feel physically as if the top of my head were taken off, I

know that is poetry. These are the only ways I know it. Is there any other way? EMILY DICKINSON,
Brooks: New England: Indian Summer

15378.
Form is the Cage and Sense the Bird.
The Poet twirls them in his Mind,
And wins the Trick with both combined. AUSTIN DOBSON,
The Toyman

15379.
For that fine madness still he did retain
Which rightly should possess a poet's brain. MICHAEL DRAYTON

15380.
O gracious God! how far have we
Profan'd thy heavenly gift of poesy!
DRYDEN, *Elegy on Mrs. Killigrew*

15381. The verse of every young poet, however original he may afterwards grow, usually has plainly written across it the rhythmic signature of some great master.
HAVELOCK ELLIS,
The Dance of Life

15382. Poetry teaches the enormous force of a few words, and, in proportion to the inspiration, checks loquacity. EMERSON, *Parnassus*

15383. There are two classes of poets, —the poets by education and practice, these we respect; and poets by nature, these we love. EMERSON, *Parnassus*

15384.
Do you know,
Considering the market, there are more
Poems produced than any other thing?
No wonder poets sometimes have to seem

So much more business-like than business men
Their wares are so much harder to get rid of. ROBERT FROST,
New Hampshire

15385. There is only good and bad poetry.
GOETHE, *when asked about classic and romantic poetry.*

15386. I knew that if I could get [W. B.] Yeats on a horse I could put a new rhythm into English lyric verse. O. ST. J. GOGARTY,
As I Was Going Down Sackville Street

15387. It is not the statesman, the warrior, or the monarch that survives, but the despised poet, whom they may have fed with their crumbs, and to whom they owe all that they now are or have—a name.
HAWTHORNE, *Our Old Home*

15388. I know not if I deserve that a laurel wreath should one day be laid on my coffin. Poetry, dearly as I have loved it, has always been to me but a divine plaything. I have never attached any great value to Poetical fame; and I trouble myself very little whether people praise my verses or blame them. But lay on my coffin a sword for I was a brave soldier in the war of Liberation for humanity.
HEINE

15389.
A verse may find him who a sermon flies,
And turn delight into a sacrifice.
GEORGE HERBERT, *The Church Porch*

15390.
Vain was the chief's, the sage's pride!
They had no poet, and they died.
HORACE

15391. In every volume of poems something good may be found.
SAMUEL JOHNSON, *Boswell: Life*

15392. For a good poet's made, as well as born. BEN JONSON,
To the Memory of Shakespeare

15393. The poetry of earth is never dead. KEATS,
On the Grasshopper and Cricket

15394. Poetry should surprise by a fine excess, and not by singularity; it should strike the reader as a wording of his own highest thoughts, and appear almost a remembrance. KEATS

15395.
The young poet screams forever
About his sex and his soul.
JOYCE KILMER, *Old Poets*

15396.
The pleasantest sort of poet
Is the poet who's old and wise.
JOYCE KILMER, *Old Poets*

15397.
There is no peace to be taken
With poets who are young,
For they worry about the wars to be fought
And the songs that must be sung.
JOYCE KILMER, *Old Poets*

15398.
'Tis verse that gives
Immortal youth to mortal maids.
W. S. LANDOR, *Verse*

15399.
Great is the art of beginning, but greater the art is of ending;
Many a poem is marred by a superfluous verse. LONGFELLOW,
Elegiac Verse

15400.
And I believed the poets; it is they
Who utter wisdom from the central deep,
And, listening to the inner flow of things,
Speak to the age out of eternity.
LOWELL, *Columbus*

15401.
The newspaper poet's a commonplace fellow—
The humblest may know what his Poetry means.
But clearness is treason, and so, for this reason,
He never gets into the big magazines. DENIS MCCARTHY,
The Newspaper Poet

15402. Perhaps no person can be a poet, or even, can enjoy poetry, without a certain unsoundness of mind.
MACAULAY, *On Milton*

15403. We hold that the most wonderful and splendid proof of genius is a great poem produced in a civilized age. MACAULAY, *On Milton*

15404.
A poem should not mean
But be
ARCHIBALD MACLEISH: *Ars Poetica*

15405. Publishing a volume of verse is like dropping a rose-petal down the Grand Canyon and waiting for the echo. DON MARQUIS, *The Sun Dial*

15406. Poetry is what Milton saw when he went blind.
DON MARQUIS, *The Sun Dial*

15407. Anyone may be an honourable man, and yet write verse badly.
MOLIÈRE, *Le Misanthrope*

15408. Happy it is for mankind that Heaven has laid on few men the curse of being poets.
F. F. MOORE, *The Jessamy Bride*

15409. My definition of pure poetry, something that the poet creates outside of his own personality.

GEORGE MOORE,
Anthology of Pure Poetry

15410.
A regular poet published a book,
And an excellent book it was,
But nobody gave it a second look,
As nobody often does.

OGDEN NASH,
A Parable for Sports Writers

15411. Whatever your occupation may be and however crowded your hours with affairs, do not fail to secure at least a few minutes every day for refreshment of your inner life with a bit of poetry.

CHARLES E. NORTON

15412. Poetry comes fine spun from a mind at peace. OVID, *Tristia*

15413. Let us understand by poetry all literary production which attains the power of giving pleasure by its form, as distinct from its matter.

WALTER PATER, *The Renaissance*

15414. With me poetry has been not a purpose, but a passion; and the passions should be held in reverence: they must not—they can not at will be excited, with an eye to the paltry compensations, or the more paltry commendations, of mankind.

POE, *Poems: Preface*

15415. I would define, in brief, the Poetry of words as the Rhythmical Creation of Beauty. Its sole arbiter is Taste. POE, *The Poetic Principle*

15416.
While pensive poets painful vigils keep,
Sleepless themselves to give their readers sleep. POPE,
The Dunciad

15417.
I never indulge in poetics
Unless I am down with rheumatics.
QUINTUS ENNIUS

15418.
Ne'er
Was flattery lost on poet's ear;
A simple race! they waste their toil
For the vain tribute of a smile.
SCOTT, *The Lay of the Last Minstrel*

15419.
Call it not vain: they do not err
Who say, that when the poet dies,
Mute Nature mourns her worshipper,
And celebrates his obsequies.
SCOTT, *The Lay of the Last Minstrel*

15420. Neither rhyme nor reason.
SHAKESPEARE, *As You Like It*

15421. I would the gods had made thee poetical. SHAKESPEARE,
As You Like It

15422.
I had rather be a kitten and cry mew,
Than one of these same metre ballad-
mongers. SHAKESPEARE,
Henry IV

15423. I was not born under a rhyming planet. SHAKESPEARE,
Much Ado About Nothing

15424.
Not marble, nor the gilded monuments
Of princes, shall outlive this powerful rhyme. SHAKESPEARE,
Sonnet LV

15425.
Your monument shall be my gentle verse,
Which eyes not yet created shall o'erread;
And tongues to be your being shall rehearse,
When all the breathers of this world are dead;

You still shall live—such virtue hath
  my pen—
Where breath most breathes,—even
  in the mouths of men.
> SHAKESPEARE, *Sonnet LXXXI*

15426. The modest cough of a minor
poet.   BERNARD SHAW,
> *The Dark Lady of the Sonnets*

15427. Poetry is the record of the
best and happiest moments of the
happiest and best minds.
> SHELLEY, *A Defence of Poetry*

15428. Poets are the hierophants of
an unapprehended inspiration; the
mirrors of the gigantic shadows which
futurity casts upon the present.
> SHELLEY, *A Defence of Poetry*

15429. Poets are the unacknowledged
legislators of the world.
> SHELLEY, *A Defence of Poetry*

15430.
Of all the threads of rhyme
  Which I have spun,
I shall be glad if Time
  Save only one.
> FRANK D. SHERMAN, *His Desire*

15431. Sweet food of sweetly uttered
knowledge.
> SIR PHILIP SIDNEY,
> *Defence of Poesy*

15432.
You hope that we shall tell you that
  they found their happiness in fight-
  ing,
Or that they died with a song on
  their lips,
Or that we shall use the old familiar
  phrases
With which your paid servants please
  you in the Press:
But we are poets,
And shall tell the truth.
> OSBERT SITWELL, *Rhapsode*

15433. A poem round and perfect as
a star.   ALEXANDER SMITH,
> *A Life Drama*

15434.
Poets lose half the praise they should
  have got,
Could it be known what they dis-
  creetly blot.   EDMUND WALLER

15435. Old-fashioned poetry, but
choicely good.   IZAAK WALTON,
> *The Compleat Angler*

15436. The proof of a poet is that
his country absorbs him as affection-
ately as he has absorbed it.
> WALT WHITMAN,
> *Preface to Leaves of Grass*

15437. To have great poets, there
must be great audiences, too.
> WALT WHITMAN, *Notes Left Over*

15438. A poet can survive everything
but a misprint.   OSCAR WILDE,
> *The Children of the Poets*

15439. In spite of difference of soil
and climate, of language and manners, of laws and customs,—in spite
of things silently gone out of mind,
and things violently destroyed, the
Poet binds together by passion and
knowledge the vast empire of human
society, as it is spread over the whole
earth, and over all time.
> WORDSWORTH, *Lyrical Ballads*

15440. Poetry is the breath and finer
spirit of all knowledge; it is the impassioned expression which is in the
countenance of all Science.
> WORDSWORTH, *Lyrical Ballads*

See also: 185, 716, 1352, 2021, 2582,
2585, 2665, 4650, 6451, 9811, 9921,
10381, 10707, 11181, 13155, 13593,
13601, 14943, 15283, 20215, 21076.

POISON

Related Subjects: Death, Murder.

5441. Poison is poison though it comes in a golden cup.
THOMAS ADAMS

5442. Tobacco, coffee, alcohol, hashish, prussic acid, strychnine, are weak dilutions: the surest poison is time.
EMERSON, Society and Solitude

5443. The poisons are our principal medicines, which kill the disease, and save the life.
EMERSON, Conduct of Life

5444. The coward's weapon, poison.
PHINEAS FLETCHER, Sicelides

5445. Venom destroys venom.
LANGLAND, Piers Plowman

5446. A little poison now and then: that causeth pleasant dreams; and much poison at last for an easy death.
NIETZSCHE, Thus Spake Zarathustra

5447.
bought an unction of a mountebank,
So mortal that, but dip a knife in it,
Where it draws blood no cataplasm so rare,
Collected from all simples that have virtue
Under the moon, can save the thing from death
That is but scratch'd withal.
SHAKESPEARE, Hamlet

5448. Then, venom, to thy work.
SHAKESPEARE, Hamlet

5449. In poison there is physic.
SHAKESPEARE, Henry IV

5450. Sweet, sweet, sweet poison for the age's tooth.
SHAKESPEARE, King John

15451. They love not poison that do poison need.
SHAKESPEARE, Richard II

15452.
Let me have
A dram of poison, such soon-speeding gear
As will disperse itself through all the veins
That the life-weary taker may fall dead
And that the trunk may be discharg'd of breath
As violently as hasty powder fir'd
Doth hurry from the fatal cannon's womb.
SHAKESPEARE, Romeo & Juliet

See also: 1782, 1786, 4212, 8262, 9105, 19086.

POLAND

Related Subject: Europe.

15461. He smote the sledded Polacks on the ice.   SHAKESPEARE, Hamlet

15462.
The heart of Poland hath not ceased
To quiver, tho' her sacred blood doth drown
The fields, and out of every smouldering town
Cries to Thee.   TENNYSON, Poland

POLICE

Related Subjects: Crime, Law, Order.

15471.
Ah, take one consideration with another—
A policeman's lot is not a happy one!
W. S. GILBERT,
The Pirates of Penzance

15472. Policemen are soldiers who act alone; soldiers are policemen who act in unison.

HERBERT SPENCER, *Social Statics*

15473. A lidless watcher of the public weal.   TENNYSON, *The Princess*

15474. There were cries of "Coppers, coppers!" in the yard.

THOMAS TERRELL, *Lady Delmar*

15475. Cops, as a class, are exceptionally charitable. They're not the saving kind. They depend on their pensions to take care of them in their old age, so as they meet deserving cases while on duty, they do their best to help.

CAPT. C. W. WILLEMSE,
A Cop Remembers

15476. One of the commonest types of human failing is a desire on the part of certain individuals to share in the authority and glamour that surrounds the profession of the police officer. These people are known familiarly at the Station House as police buffs, and usually they are well to do men and women who get a great satisfaction out of possessing some kind of badge, license tag, or some insignia that will give them certain distinction in the public eye and instant recognition from a cop.

CAPT. C. W. WILLEMSE,
A Cop Remembers

See also: 12025.

POLICY

Related Subjects: Cunning, Plan.

15481. Policy consists in serving God in such a manner as not to offend the devil.   THOMAS FULLER

15482. It is not juggling that is to be blamed, but much juggling; for the world cannot be governed without it.

JOHN SELDEN, *Table Talk*

15483. Policy sits above conscience

SHAKESPEARE, *Timon of Athens*

See also: 1122, 6588, 9939, 10800, 13880.

POLITICS AND POLITICIANS

Related Subjects: Anarchy, Bribery, Democracy, Diplomacy, Election, Faction, Government, Majority, Office, Orator, Propaganda, Vote.

15491. Knowledge of human nature is the beginning and end of political education.   HENRY ADAMS,
The Education of Henry Adams

15492. Practical politics consists in ignoring facts.   HENRY ADAMS,
The Education of Henry Adams

15493. Modern politics is, at bottom, a struggle not of men but of forces.

HENRY ADAMS,
The Education of Henry Adams

15494. All political parties die at last of swallowing their own lies.

JOHN ARBUTHNOT

15495. The best political community is formed by citizens of the middle class. Those States are likely to be well administered in which the middle class is large, and larger if possible than both the other classes, or at any rate than either singly; for the addition of the middle class turns the scale and prevents either of the extremes from being dominant.

ARISTOTLE, *Politics*

15496. Politics is not all economics, but it is better illuminated by reference to that science than to any other. Certainly without economics, politics is an utter mystery.

CHARLES A. BEARD,
American Leviathan

5497. Realistically conceived a party is a union of people bent on getting possession of the organization authorized by the Constitution and employing its engines in making and enforcing laws which they hold to be just, expedient, or useful to their interests, as the case may be. Through the party their will to power is brought to a focus.
CHARLES A. BEARD,
American Leviathan

15498.
"Do you pray for the Senators, Dr. Hale?" someone asked the chaplain, Edward Everett Hale.
"No, I look at the Senators and pray for the country," he replied.
VAN WYCK BROOKS,
New England: Indian Summer

15499. An honest politician is one who, when he is bought, will stay bought.   SIMON CAMERON

15500. The attempt to turn a complex problem of the head into a simple moral question for the heart to answer, is of course a necessary part of all political discussions.
FRANK M. COLBY, *Essays*

15501. A politician thinks of the next election, a statesman, of the next generation.   J. F. CLARKE

15502. Politics, like economics, has its own laws, independent of morals.
CROCE

15503. Politicians are marvels of energy and principle when they're out of office, but when they get in, they simply run behind the machine.
GALSWORTHY, *Maid in Waiting*

15504. There's just one rule for politicians all over the world: Don't say in Power what you say in Opposition; if you do, you only have to carry out what the other fellows have found impossible.
GALSWORTHY, *Maid In Waiting*

15505.
Who, born for the universe, narrow'd his mind,
And to party gave up what was meant for mankind.
GOLDSMITH, *Retaliation*

15506. If parties in a republic are necessary to secure a degree of vigilance sufficient to keep the public functionaries within the bounds of law and duty, at that point their usefulness ends.
WILLIAM HENRY HARRISON,
Inaugural Address

15507. If you wish the sympathy of broad masses then you must tell them the crudest and most stupid things.
ADOLF HITLER, *Mein Kampf*

15508. The purification of politics is an iridescent dream.
J. J. INGALLS, *Epigram*

15509. A political party is not made to order. It is the slow development of powerful forces working in our social life. Sound ideas seize upon the human mind. Opinions ripen into fixed convictions. Masses of men are drawn together by common belief and organized about clearly defined principles. ROBERT M. LAFOLLETTE,
Political Philosophy

15510. Political institutions are a superstructure resting on an economic foundation.   LENIN

15511. People always have been and they always will be stupid victims of deceit and self-deception in politics, until they learn behind every kind of moral, religious, political, social phrase, declaration and promise to seek out the interests of this or that class or classes.   LENIN

15512. Those who would treat politics and morality apart will never understand the one or the other.

JOHN MORLEY, *Rousseau*

15513. Political campaigns are designedly made into emotional orgies which endeavor to distract attention from the real issues involved, and they actually paralyze what slight powers of cerebration man can normally muster.

JAMES H. ROBINSON,
The Human Comedy

15514. Never, never, you must never . . . remind a man at work on a political job that he may be president. It almost always kills him politically. He loses his nerve; he can't do his work; he gives up the very traits that are making him a possibility.

THEODORE ROOSEVELT, *to Lincoln Steffens*

15515. A politician, . . . one that would circumvent God.

SHAKESPEARE, *Hamlet*

15516. The nauseous sham goodfellowship our democratic public men get up for shop use.

BERNARD SHAW,
Back to Methuselah

15517. The partisan, when he is engaged in a dispute, cares nothing about the rights of the question, but is anxious only to convince his hearers of his own assertions.

SOCRATES, *Dialogues of Plato*

15518. It is dangerous to reason about politics and government; it is safer to go and see.

LINCOLN STEFFENS, *Autobiography*

15519. Political corruption is not a matter of men or classes or education or character of any sort; it is a matter of pressure. Wherever the pressure is brought to bear, society an government cave in. The problem then, is one of dealing with the pressure, of discovering and dealing wit the cause or the source of the pressure to buy and corrupt.

LINCOLN STEFFENS, *Autobiograph*

15520. And he gave it for his opinion, that whoever could make two ears of corn, or two blades of grass to grow upon a spot of ground wher only one grew before, would deserv better of mankind, and do more essential service to his country, tha the whole race of politicians put to gether. SWIFT, *Gulliver's Trave*

15521. I am not a politician, and m other habits are good.

ARTEMUS WARD,
Fourth of July Oratio

15522. True it is that politics make strange bedfellows.

CHARLES DUDLEY WARNER,
My Summer in a Garde

See also: 697, 3942, 3963, 3967, 454(4563, 6641, 10144, 10832, 1170; 20837.

POPPY

Related Subject: Flowers.

15531. The Poppy hath a charm fo pain and woe.

MARY A. BARR, *White Poppie*

15532.
Full-blown poppies, overcharged wit
    rain
Decline the head, and drooping kis
    the plain.   HOMER, *Ilia*

15533.
Through the dancing poppies stole
A breeze, most softly lulling to m
    soul.   KEATS, *Endymio*

15534.
In Flanders fields the poppies blow
Between the crosses, row on row.
JOHN McCRAE, *In Flanders Fields*

POPULARITY

Related Subjects: Applause, Esteem.

15541. So if you want people to like you . . . Be a good listener. Encourage others to talk about themselves.   DALE CARNEGIE,
How to Win Friends

15542. The tumultuous love of the populace must be seized and enjoyed in its first transports; there is no hoarding of it to use upon occasions; it will not keep.
LORD CHESTERFIELD,
Account of the Dutch Republic

15543. The popular breeze.
CICERO, *De Haruspicum Responsis*

15544. Popularity disarms envy in well-disposed minds. Those are ever the most ready to do justice to others, who feel the world has done them justice.   HAZLITT, *Characteristics*

15545. Popularity? It is glory's small change.   VICTOR HUGO, *Ruy Blas*

15546. To some men popularity is always suspicious. Enjoying none themselves, they are prone to suspect the validity of those attainments which command it.
G. H. LEWES, *Spanish Drama*

15547.
Honour, glory, and popular praise
Rocks whereon greatest men have oftest wreck'd.
MILTON, *Paradise Lost*

15548. When Fortune favors us, Popularity bears her company.
PUBLILIUS SYRUS, *Sententiae*

15549. Popularity is a crime from the moment it is sought; it is only a virtue where men have it whether they will or no.
SIR GEORGE SAVILLE,
Moral Thoughts and Reflections

15550.
All tongues speak of him, and the bleared sights
Are spectacled to see him.
SHAKESPEARE, *Coriolanus*

15551. That empty and ugly thing called popularity.   STEVENSON

See also: 1203, 13295.

POSSESSION

Related Subjects: Law, Property.

15561. Men would live exceedingly quiet if those two words, mine and thine were taken away.
ANAXAGORAS

15562. Unto every one that hath shall be given, and he shall have abundance; but from him that hath not shall be taken away even that which he hath.   *Bible: Matthew, xxv, 29*

15563. You cannot eat your cake and have your cake; and store's no sore.
CERVANTES, *Don Quixote*

15564. What a man has, so much he's sure of.   CERVANTES, *Don Quixote*

15565. Possession is eleven points in the law.
COLLEY CIBBER, *Woman's Wit*

15566. The use of the sea and air is common to all; neither can a title to the ocean belong to any people or private persons, forasmuch as neither nature nor public use and custom permit any possession thereof.
QUEEN ELIZABETH

15567. Much will have more.

EMERSON, *Society and Solitude*

15568. This, and this alone, I contend for—that he who makes should have; that he who saves should enjoy.

HENRY GEORGE, *Social Problems*

15569.
I can't, I trow,
Both eat my cake and have it too.

ROBERT HEATH, *Occasional Poems*

15570.
Bliss in possession will not last;
Remembered joys are never past;
At once the fountain, stream, and sea,
They were, they are, they yet shall be.

JAMES MONTGOMERY,
The Little Cloud

15571. Possession is the grave of bliss. No sooner do we own some great book than we want another.

A. EDWARD NEWTON,
Amenities of Book-Collecting

15572. An object in possession seldom attains the same charm that it had in pursuit.

PLINY THE YOUNGER

15573. Better to have than to wish.
Proverb

15574. It is better to have a little than nothing.

PUBLILIUS SYRUS, *Sententiae*

15575. It is Preoccupation with possession, more than anything else, that prevents men from living freely and nobly.   BERTRAND RUSSELL,
Principles of Social Reconstruction

15576. To have may be taken from us, to have had, never.

SENECA, *Epistulae ad Lucilium*

15577. An ill-favoured thing, sir, but mine own.

SHAKESPEARE, *As You Like It*

15578.
All things that are,
Are with more spirit chased than enjoy'd.   SHAKESPEARE,
The Merchant of Venice

15579.
            For it so falls out
That what we have we prize not to the worth
Whiles we enjoy it, but being lack'd and lost,
Why, then we rack the value; then we find
The virtue that possession would not show us
Whiles it was ours.
SHAKESPEARE,
Much Ado About Nothing

15580.
        They well deserve to have
That know the strong'st and surest way to get.
SHAKESPEARE, *Richard II*

15581. Things that I longed for in vain and things that I got—let them pass. Let me but truly possess the things I spurned and overlooked.

TAGORE, *Gitanjali*

15582. This is the happiest of mortals, for he is above everything he possesses.   VOLTAIRE, *Candide*

15583. The' ain't nothin' truer in the Bible 'n that sayin' thet them that has gits. E. N. WESTCOTT, *David Harum*

See also: 1069, 1486, 3040.

POSSESSIONS

Related Subjects: Miser, Property, Riches.

15591. I carry all my possessions with me.   BIAS

15592. As having nothing, and yet possessing all things.
Bible: 2 Corinthians, vi, 10

15593.
A man's best things are nearest him,
  Lie close about his feet.
    R. M. MILNES, *The Men of Old*

15594. Pains to get, care to keep,
fear to lose.   *Proverb*

15595. No possessions are good, but
by the good use we make of them;
without which wealth, power, friends,
and servants, do but help to make our
lives more unhappy.
    SIR WILLIAM TEMPLE

POSSIBILITY AND IMPOSSIBILITY

Related Subjects: Accident, Credulity, Difficulty, Probability.

15601. It is not a lucky word, this
same "impossible"; no good comes
of those who have it so often in their
mouths.   CARLYLE

15602.
And what's impossible can't be,
And never, never comes to pass.
    GEORGE COLEMAN,
        The Maid of the Moor

15603. One great difference between
a wise man and a fool is, the former
only wishes for what he may possibly
obtain; the latter desires impossibil-
ities.   DEMOCRITUS

15604. Few things are impossible to
diligence and skill.
    SAMUEL JOHNSON, *Rasselas*

15605. Few things are impossible in
themselves. It is not so much means,
as perseverance, that is wanting to
bring them to a successful issue.
    LA ROCHEFOUCAULD, *Maxims*

15606. Nothing is impossible; there
are ways that lead to everything, and
if we had sufficient will we should
always have sufficient means. It is

often merely for an excuse that we
say things are impossible.
    LA ROCHEFOUCAULD, *Maxims*

15607. "Impossible"—never let me
hear that foolish word again.
    MIRABEAU

15608. Impossible? The word "impossible" is not French.   NAPOLEON

15609. Impossible is a word only to
be found in the dictionary of fools.
    NAPOLEON

15610. You cannot make a silk purse
of a sow's ear.   *Proverb*

15611. Figs out of thistles.
    TENNYSON, *Idylls of the King*

See also: 1267, 1883, 1887, 2419,
2891, 3491, 6686, 8946, 13770.

POSTERITY

Related Subjects: Ancestry, Childhood, Heredity.

15621. We are always doing something for Posterity, but I would fain
see Posterity do something for us.
    ADDISON, *The Spectator*

15622. Not to the Past, but to the
future, looks true nobility, and finds
its blazon in posterity.
    BULWER-LYTTON,
        The Lady of Lyons

15623. He thinks posterity a pack-
horse, always ready to be loaded.
    DISRAELI

15624. The love of posterity is the
consequence of the necessity of death.
If a man were sure of living forever here, he would not care about
his offspring.
HAWTHORNE, *American Note Books*

15625.
What is thy body but a swallowing
  grave,

Seeming to bury that posterity
Which by the rights of time thou
　　needs must have,
If thou destroy them not in dark ob-
　　scurity?
　　SHAKESPEARE, *Venus and Adonis*

15626. Posterity gives to every man
his proper praise. TACITUS, *History*

15627. Posterity always establishes
men in their proper rank, pulling
down from their pedestals those who
have been lifted up through deceit,
in order to make place for others who
have the right to it. For this reason
the great ones who are unknown may
continue on their way in the conviction of eternal justice, which is often
tardy but always certain at the time
appointed.
　　ALBERT WOLFF, *The Figaro*

See also: 551, 2301, 5294.

POT

Related Subjects: Cooks and Cooking, Potter and Pottery.

15631. We'll find out a rich husband
to make you the pot boil.
　　SIR WILLIAM D'AVENANT,
　　　　　Play-House to be Let

15632. What's the use of watching?
A watched pot never boils.
　　MRS. GASKELL, *Mary Barton*

15633. Neither pot broken nor water
spilt.　　*Proverb*

15634. A pot that belongs to many is
ill stirred and worse boiled.
　　　　　Proverb

15635. One pot sets another boiling.
　　　　　Proverb

POTTER AND POTTERY

Related Subject: Pot.

15641.
No handycraft can with our art compare,
For pots are made of what we potters
are.　　*Anonymous*

15642.
Thy moist clay is pliant to command,
Unwrought, and easy to the potter's
　　hand:
Now take the mould; now bend thy
　　mind to feel
The first sharp motions of the form-
　　ing wheel.
　　DRYDEN, *Third Satire of Persius*

15643.
There's a joy without canker or cark,
　　There's a pleasure eternally new,
'Tis to gloat on the glaze and the
　　mark
Of china that's ancient and blue.
　　ANDREW LANG,
　　　　　Ballade of Blue China

15644. Every potter praises his own
pot, and more if it be broken.
　　　　　Proverb

15645. I am content to be a bric-a-
bracker and a Ceramiker.
　　MARK TWAIN, *A Tramp Abroad*

POVERTY

Related Subjects: Adversity, Beggar, Charity, Depression, Employment, Hunger, Misery, Misfortune,
Necessity, Want.

15650.
The worst of ills, and hardest to en-
　　dure,
　　Past hope, past cure,
Is Penury, who, with her sister-mate
Disorder, soon brings down the loft-
　　iest state,
　　And makes it desolate. ALCAEUS

15651. Poverty does not mean the possession of little, but the non-possession of much.   ANTIPATER

15652. Poverty is the parent of revolution and crime. ARISTOTLE, *Politics*

15653. The poor always ye have with you.   *Bible: John, xii, 8*

15654. Christ himself was poor. . . . And as he himself, so he informed his apostles and disciples, they were all poor, prophets poor, apostles poor.
ROBERT BURTON,
Anatomy of Melancholy

15655. Over the hill to the poorhouse I'm trudgin' my weary way.
WILL CARLETON,
Over the Hill to the Poor-House

15656.
Of all God's creatures, man
     Alone is poor.
MRS. THOMAS CARLYLE,
*To a Swallow Building
Under Our Eaves*

15657. Abolish poverty, and what would become of the race? Progress, development would cease.
ANDREW CARNEGIE,
Empire of Business

15658. I heartily subscribe to President Garfield's doctrine, that "The richest heritage a young man can be born to is poverty."
ANDREW CARNEGIE,
Empire of Business

15659. Wan iv th' shtrangest things about life is that th' poor, who need th' money th' most, ar-re th' very wans that niver have it.
F. P. DUNNE, *Poverty*

15660. Some great and noble sorrow may have the effect of drawing hearts together, but to struggle against destitution, to be crushed by care about shillings and sixpences—that must always degrade.
GEORGE GISSING, *New Grub Street*

15661.
Nor grandeur hear with a disdainful smile
     The short and simple annals of the poor.   THOMAS GRAY,
*Elegy Written in a Country
Churchyard*

15662. He is so poor that he could not keep a dog.
LONGUS, *Daphnis and Chloe*

15663. Poverty, the mother of manhood.   LUCAN, *The Civil War*

15664. If you are a poor man now, Almihanus, a poor man you will always be. Nowadays, riches are bestowed on no one but the rich.
MARTIAL

15665. Poverty is a soft pedal upon all branches of human activity, not excepting the spiritual.
H. L. MENCKEN, *A Book of Prefaces*

15666.
Rattle his bones over the stones!
He's only a pauper, whom nobody owns!   THOMAS NOEL,
The Pauper's Drive

15667. The child was diseased at birth, stricken with a hereditary ill that only the most vital men are able to shake off. I mean poverty—the most deadly and prevalent of all diseases.   EUGENE O'NEILL, *Fog*

15668. Better be poor and live, than rich and perish.   *Proverb*

15669. Better be poor than wicked.
Proverb

15670. Poverty is no sin.   *Proverb*

15671. As poor as Job.   *Proverb*

15672. There is God's poor, and the devil's poor; the first from Providence, the other from vice.   *Proverb*

15673. It is more easy to praise poverty than bear it.   *Proverb*

15674. He that is known to have no money has neither friends nor credit.   *Proverb*

15675. He bears poverty very ill who is ashamed of it.   *Proverb*

15676. A poor man has not many marks for fortune to shoot at.
    Proverb

15677.
When I hae a saxpence under my
    thumb,
Then I get credit in ilka town;
But when I am poor, they bid me gae
    by,
O, poverty parts good company.
    Scott, *The Abbot*

15678. It is not the man who has too little but the man who craves more, that is poor.   Seneca

15679.
A needy, hollow-eyed, sharp-looking
    wretch,
A living-dead man.
    Shakespeare,
    The Comedy of Errors

15680. Having nothing, nothing can he lose.   Shakespeare, *Henry VI*

15681.
Poor naked wretches, whereso'er you
    are,
That bide the pelting of this pitiless
    storm,
How shall your houseless heads and
    unfed sides,
Your looped and windowed ragged-
    ness, defend you
From seasons such as these?
    Shakespeare, *King Lear*

15682. Steep'd me in poverty to the very lips.   Shakespeare, *Othello*

15683.
Apothecary. My poverty, but not my will consents.
Romeo. I pay thy poverty, and not thy will.
    Shakespeare, *Romeo and Juliet*

15684. How apt the poor are to be proud. Shakespeare, *Twelfth Night*

15685. From a free society involuntary poverty will be banished.
    The end of involuntary poverty means the end of most prostitution and crime, and of all war between civilized peoples.   Upton Sinclair

15686.
"And wherefore do the poor com-
    plain?"
    The rich man asked of me—
"Come walk abroad with me," I said
    "And I will answer thee."
    Southey,
    The Complaints of the Poor

15687. We are sorry for the poor man, very sorry; and we will do almost anything for the poor man's relief. We will not only supply him with food sufficient to keep him on his legs, but we will teach and instruct him and point out to him the beauties of the landscape; we will discourse sweet music to him and give him abundance of good advice.
    Yes, we will do almost anything for the poor man but get off his back.
    Tolstoy

15688. He is now fast rising from affluence to poverty. Mark Twain,
    Henry Ward Beecher's Farm

15689. Poverty has advantages and disadvantages, yet notwithstanding poverty we risk it. The fishermen know that the sea is dangerous and the storm terrible, but they have never found those dangers sufficient reason for remaining ashore. They leave that philosophy to those who like it. Let the storm arise, the night descend, which is worse, danger or the fear of danger?   VAN GOGH, *Letters*

15690. When you sleep in your cloak there's no lodging to pay.
     G. J. WHYTE-MELVILLE,
         Boots and Saddles

See also: 420, 854, 2495, 2551, 2559, 3255, 3481, 4115, 4585, 5157, 5226, 9765, 11060, 14485, 14942, 18504, 19729.

POWER

Related Subjects: Ability, Advantage, Authority, Command, Dictatorship, Electricity, Energy, Force, Greatness, Influence, Machinery, Steam, Strength, Violence.

15691. The effect of power and publicity on all men is the aggravation of self, a sort of tumor that ends by killing the victim's sympathies.
     HENRY ADAMS,
   The Education of Henry Adams

15692. Power when wielded by abnormal energy is the most serious of facts.   HENRY ADAMS,
   The Education of Henry Adams

15693. Who holds a power but newly gained is ever stern of mood.
AESCHYLUS, *Prometheus Bound*

15694. Of the gods we believe, and of men we know, that by a necessary law of their nature they rule wherever they can. And it is not as if we were the first to make this law, or to act upon it; we found it existing before, and shall leave it to exist forever after us; all we do is to make use of it, knowing that you and every-

body else, having the same power as we have, would do the same as we do.
     Athenian envoys, upon the
       destruction of Melos.
       Durant: Life of Greece

15695. There are never wanting some persons of violent and undertaking natures, who, so they may have power and business, will take it at any cost.
                 BACON

15696. The powers that be are ordained of God.
     Bible: Romans, xiii, 1

15697. The arts of power and its minions are the same in all countries and in all ages. It marks its victim; denounces it; and excites the public odium and the public hatred, to conceal its own abuses and encroachments.   HENRY CLAY

15698. Power tends to corrupt, and absolute power corrupts absolutely. Great men are almost always bad.
     MANDELL CREIGHTON

15699. The alleged power to charm down insanity, or ferocity in beasts, is a power behind the eye.
     EMERSON, *Conduct of Life*

15700. Coal, iron and steam are the three co-operative powers of modern civilization.   J. W. HANSON,
     Wonders of the 19th Century

15701. The highest proof of virtue is to possess boundless power without abusing it.   MACAULAY,
   Review of Aikin's Life of Addison

15702.
Beware of the man who rises to power From one suspender.
     EDGAR LEE MASTERS,
       Spoon River Anthology

15703. I believe that . . . if a people wish to live they should develop a will to power, otherwise they vegetate, live miserably and become prey to a stronger people, in whom this will to power is developed to a higher degree. MUSSOLINI

15704.
Power, like a desolating pestilence,
Pollutes whate'er it touches.
SHELLEY, *Queen Mab*

15705.
The awful shadow of some unseen Power
Floats tho' unseen amongst us.
SHELLEY,
Hymn to Intellectual Beauty

15706. What do I care about the law? Haven't I got the power?
CORNELIUS VANDERBILT

15707.
Because the good old rule
Sufficeth them, the simple plan,
That they should take, who have the power,
And they should keep who can.
WORDSWORTH, *Rob Roy's Grave*

See also: 432, 662, 676, 774, 776, 1099, 1665, 1705, 3542, 8602, 8611, 11314, 15859, 18880, 19691, 21225, 21230, 21595.

PRAISE

Related Subjects: Admiration, Applause, Compliment, Fame, Flattery, Gratitude, Prayer.

15711. Let us now praise famous men. *Apocrypha: Ecclesiasticus*

15712. Praise is a debt we owe unto the virtues of others, and due unto our own from all whom malice hath not made mutes or envy stuck dumb.
SIR THOMAS BROWNE

15713.
There's no weapon that slays

Its victim so surely (if well aimed) as praise. BULWER-LYTTON,
Lucile

15714. Praise is the hire of virtue.
CICERO

15715. None knew thee but to love thee, nor named thee but to praise.
FITZ-GREENE HALLECK

15716.
Praise from a friend, or censure from a foe,
Are lost on hearers that our merits know. HOMER, *Iliad*

15717. Praise like gold and diamonds owes its value only to its scarity.
SAMUEL JOHNSON, *The Rambler*

15718. Usually we praise only to be praised. LA ROCHEFOUCAULD,
Maxims

15719. It is singular how impatient men are with over-praise of others, how patient with over-praise of themselves; and yet the one does them no injury, while the other may be their ruin. LOWELL,
Literary Remains of the Rev. Homer Wilbur

15720. That best of fame, a rival's praise. THOMAS MOORE,
Rhymes of the Road

15721.
The anxious and distrustful constantly
Require that their companions speak their praise,
Holding it as a gross discourtesy
If any disagree with them.
HELENE MULLINS,
Only the Self-Confident

15722. True praise takes root and spreads. *Proverb*

15723. To be commended by those who might blame without fear, gives great pleasure. *Proverb*

15724. They that value not praise, will never do anything worthy of it.
Proverb

15725. Faint praise is disparagement.
Proverb

15726. He that praiseth bestows a favour, he that detracts commits a robbery.   *Proverb*

15727. He that refuseth praise the first time does it because he would have it the second.   *Proverb*

15728. Even too much praise is a burden.   *Proverb*

15729. The greatest efforts of the race have always been traceable to the love of praise, as its greatest catastrophes to the love of pleasure.
RUSKIN, *Sesame and Lilies*

15730. You can tell the character of every man when you see how he receives praise.   SENECA

15731.
Who is it that says most which can say more
Than this rich praise,—that you alone are you?   SHAKESPEARE,
Sonnet LXXXIV

15732.
The love of praise, howe'er conceal'd by art,
Reigns more or less, and glows in ev'ry heart.   EDWARD YOUNG,
Love of Fame

See also: 625, 933, 1403, 1700, 2737, 3848, 8395, 14175, 19862, 21690.

PRAYER

Related Subjects: Devotion, Faith, God, Piety, Praise, Preachers, Religion.

15741. Lord, I shall be verie busie this day. I may forget Thee. . . . But doe not Thou forget me.
SIR JACOB ASTELEY, *Prayer before the battle of Newbury*

15742. People would be surprised to know how much I learned about prayer from playing poker.
MARY AUSTIN

15743. The effectual fervent prayer of a righteous man availeth much.
Bible: James, v, 16

15744. Do not pray for easy lives. Pray to be stronger men! Do not pray for tasks equal to your powers. Pray for powers equal to your tasks.
PHILLIPS BROOKS,
Twenty Sermons

15745.
Be not afraid to pray; to pray is right.
Pray, if thou canst, with hope, but ever pray,
Though hope be weak, or sick with long delay,
Pray in the darkness if there be no light.   HARTLEY COLERIDGE,
Prayer

15746.
He prayeth well who loveth well
Both man and bird and beast.
COLERIDGE, *The Ancient Mariner*

15747.
He prayeth best who loveth best
All things both great and small.
COLERIDGE, *The Ancient Mariner*

15748.
That saints will aid if men will call;
For the blue sky bends over all!
COLERIDGE, *Christabel*

15749.
If prayer do not aid me first,
That riseth up from heart which lives in grace
What other kind avails, not heard in heaven?   DANTE, *Purgatorio*

15750. Be not forgetful of prayer. Every time you pray, if your prayer is sincere, there will be new feeling and new meaning in it, which will give you fresh courage, and you will understand that prayer is an education.   DOSTOYEVSKY,
The Brothers Karamazov

15751. There can be prayers without words just as well as songs, I suppose. GEORGE DU MAURIER,
Trilby

15752. Old men's prayers for death are lying prayers, in which they abuse old age and long extent of life. But when death draws near, not one is willing to die, and age no longer is a burden to them.   EURIPIDES,
Alcestis

15753.
But I, when I undress me
  Each night, upon my knees
Will ask the Lord to bless me
  With apple pie and cheese!
          EUGENE FIELD,
Apple Pie and Cheese

15754. You pray in your distress and in your need; would that you might pray also in the fullness of your joy and in your days of abundance.
          KAHLIL GIBRAN, *The Prophet*

15755.
They who have steeped their souls in prayer
Can every anguish calmly bear.
          R. M. MILNES,
The Sayings of Rabia

15756.
          What in me is dark
Illumine, what is low raise and support;
That to the height of this great argument
I may assert eternal Providence,
And justify the ways of God to men.
          MILTON, *Paradise Lost*

15757.
Prayer is the soul's sincere desire,
  Uttered or unexpressed;
The motion of a hidden fire
  That trembles in the breast.
          JAMES MONTGOMERY,
What is Prayer?

15758.
Now I lay me down to sleep,
I pray the Lord my soul to keep;
If I should die before I wake,
I pray the Lord my soul to take.
          The New England Primer

15759. He who prays as he ought, will endeavor to live as he prays.
          ROBERT OWEN

15760.
Lord, for to-morrow and its needs,
  I do not pray;
Keep me, my God, from stain of sin,
  Just for to-day.
          SISTER MARY XAVIER,
Just for To-day

15761. Lord of Lords, grant us the good whether we pray for it or not, but evil keep from us, even though we pray for it.   PLATO

15762.
          We, ignorant of ourselves,
Beg often our own harms, which the wise powers
Deny us for our good; so find we profit
By losing of our prayers.
          SHAKESPEARE,
Antony and Cleopatra

15763.
My words fly up, my thoughts remain below:
Words without thoughts never to heaven go.   SHAKESPEARE,
Hamlet

15764. Give us grace and strength to forbear and to persevere. Give us courage and gaiety and the quiet mind,

spare to us our friends, soften to us
our enemies.   STEVENSON, *Prayer*

15765.
More things are wrought by prayer
Than this world dreams of. Where-
     fore, let thy voice
Rise like a fountain for me night and
     day.   TENNYSON,
             Idylls of the King

15766.
Great God, I ask thee for no meaner
   pelf
Than that I may not disappoint my-
     self,
That in my action I may soar as high
As I can now discern with this clear
     eye.   THOREAU, *A Prayer*

15767. We kneel, how weak! we rise,
how full of power!
       R. C. TRENCH, *Prayer*

15768.
Lord, what a change within us one
     short hour
Spent in Thy presence will prevail to
     make!   R. C. TRENCH, *Prayer*

15769. Whatever a man prays for, he
prays for a miracle. Every prayer
reduces itself to this: "Great God,
grant that twice two be not four."
           TURGENIEV, *Prayer*

15770.
Lord, in the morning thou shalt hear
My voice ascending high.
       ISAAC WATTS, *Psalm V*

15771. When the gods wish to punish
us they answer our prayers.
   OSCAR WILDE, *An Ideal Husband*

15772. The imperfect offices of prayer
and praise.   WORDSWORTH,
            The Excursion

See also: 953, 1234, 1417, 1750, 1890,
1898, 2059, 2443, 3815, 5667, 6179,
10087, 10208, 15498, 20195, 21431.

PREACHER AND PREACHING

**Related Subjects: Bible, Christi-
anity, Church, Eloquence, Funeral,
God, Orator, Prayer, Wedding.**

Preachers and Priests

15781.
Once have a priest for an enemy,
     good-bye
To peace.   SARA F. ADAMS,
            Vivia Perpetua

15782. As the caterpillar chooses the
fairest leaves to lay her eggs on, so
the priest lays his curse on the fairest
joys.   BLAKE, *Proverbs of Hell*

15783.
They said this mystery never shall
     cease:
The priest promotes war, and the
     soldier peace.   BLAKE,
            Gnomic Verses

15784.
     Mothers, wives, and maids,
These be the tools wherewith priests
     manage fools.   BROWNING,
            The Ring and the Book

15785. One great reason why clergymen's households are generally unhappy is because the clergyman is so
much at home and close about the
house.   SAMUEL BUTLER,
            The Way of All Flesh

15786.
     A priest,
A piece of mere church-furniture at
     best.   COWPER, *Tirocinium*

15787. The Lord opened unto me that
being bred at Oxford or Cambridge
was not enough to fit and qualify men
to be ministers of Christ.
         GEORGE FOX, *Journal*

15788. Nothing will mix and amalga-
mate more easily than an old priest

and an old soldier. In reality, they are the same kind of man. One has devoted himself to his country upon earth, the other to his country in heaven; there is no other difference.
VICTOR HUGO, Les Miserables

15789. In every country and in every age, the priest has been hostile to liberty. He is always in alliance with the despot, abetting his abuses in return for protection to his own.
JEFFERSON

15790. Avoid, as you would the plague, a clergyman who is also a man of business.   ST. JEROME

15791. The priest is always with the herd and against the individual.
HUGH KINGSMILL,
Matthew Arnold

15792. Vilify not your parish priest.
Proverb

15793. Beware of the forepart of a woman, the hind part of a mule, and all sides of a priest.   Proverb

15794. Bad priests bring the devil into the church.   Proverb

15795.
I won't take my religion from any
  man
who never works except with his
mouth and never cherishes any memory except
the face of the woman on the American
silver dollar.   CARL SANDBURG,
To a Contemporary Bunkshooter

15796. Every man is his own doctor of divinity, in the last resort.
STEVENSON, An Inland Voyage

15797. A little round, fat, oily man of God.   JAMES THOMSON,
The Castle of Indolence

15798. Priestly vestments show, in accentuated form, all the features that have been shown to be evidence of a servile status and a vicarious life.
THORSTEIN VEBLEN,
The Theory of the Leisure Class

Preaching

15799.
I preached as never sure to preach
  again,
And as a dying man to dying men.
RICHARD BAXTER,
Love Breathing Thanks and Praise

15800. He preaches well that lives well, quoth Sancho, that's all the divinity I understand.
CERVANTES, Don Quixote

15801. It is no part of the duty of a clergyman to preach upon subjects purely political, but it is not therefore his duty to avoid religious subjects which have been distorted into political subjects.
SYDNEY SMITH,
Lady Holland's Memoir

15802. Preaching has become a byword for long and dull conversation of any kind; and whoever wishes to imply, in any piece of writing, the absence of everything agreeable and inviting, calls it a sermon.
SYDNEY SMITH,
Lady Holland's Memoir

See also: 167, 401, 914, 1910, 4113, 7270, 16333, 16511, 18029.

PRECEDENT

Related Subjects: Custom, Judge, Law.

15811. Precedents deliberately established by wise men are entitled to great weight. They are evidence of truth, but only evidence. . . . But a solitary precedent . . . which has never

been re-examined, can not be conclusive.   HENRY CLAY

15812. A precedent embalms a principle.   DISRAELI

15813. One precedent creates another. They soon accumulate and
constitute law. What yesterday was
fact, to-day is doctrine.   JUNIUS

15814. Is not Precedent indeed a
King of Men?   SWINBURNE,
A Word from the Psalmist

See also: 19, 941.

PRECEPT, see Example

PREJUDICE

**Related Subjects: Bigotry, Con-
tempt, Fanaticism, Ignorance.**

15821. There are too few among us
who are willing to forget completely
what a particular person is a Negro,
a Jew, or a member of some nationality for which we have no sympathy,
and to judge him as an individual.
     FRANZ BOAS, *I Believe*

15822. He flattered himself on being
a man without any prejudices; and
this pretension itself is a very great
prejudice.   ANATOLE FRANCE,
The Crime of Sylvestre Bonnard

15823.
I ran against a Prejudice
   That quite cut off the view.
   CHARLOTTE GILMAN, *An Obstacle*

15824. Can it be only a coincidence
that the three races which have con-
tributed most to our popular song—
the Negro, the Irish, and the Jew—
should be the familiar examples of
oppressed nationalities, credited with
a fine intensity of inner life and with
passions less bridled than those of

the more conventional American
Anglo-Saxon?   ISAAC GOLDBERG,
Tin-Pan Alley

15825. No nation, no people, can long
endure in peace and safety if racial
and religious hatred and class bitterness set at naught Christian brotherhood.   CARDINAL HAYES

15826. A common prejudice should
not be found in one whose trade it is
to rectify error.
   SAMUEL JOHNSON, *Boswell: Life*

15827. All prejudices may be traced
back to the intestines. A sedentary
life is the real sin against the Holy
Ghost.   NIETZSCHE, *Ecce Homo*

15828.
All seems infected that th' infected
   spy,
As all looks yellow to the jaundic'd
   eye.   POPE, *Essay on Criticism*

15829. I will buy with you, sell with
you, talk with you, walk with you,
and so following; but I will not eat
with you, drink with you, nor pray
with you. What news on the Rialto?
     SHAKESPEARE,
The Merchant of Venice

15830.
I will feed fat the ancient grudge I
   bear him.
He hates our sacred nation; and he
   rails,
Even there where merchants most do
   congregate.   SHAKESPEARE,
The Merchant of Venice

15831.
Mislike me not for my complexion,
The shadow'd livery of the burnish'd
   sun.   SHAKESPEARE,
The Merchant of Venice

See also: 131, 677, 8384, 18902,
20014.

PREPAREDNESS

Related Subjects: Caution, Prevention, Prudence, Watch.

15841. The commonwealth of Venice in their armoury have this inscription: "Happy is that city which in time of peace thinks of war."
ROBERT BURTON,
Anatomy of Melancholy

15842. Forewarned, forearmed; to be prepared is half the victory.
CERVANTES, *Don Quixote*

15843. In all matters, before beginning, a diligent preparation should be made.   CICERO, *De Officiis*

15844. A man-of-war is the best ambassador. CROMWELL, *Carlyle: Life*

15845. Among other evils which being unarmed brings you, it causes you to be despised.
MACHIAVELLI, *The Prince*

15846.
For all your days prepare
  And meet them ever alike;
When you are the anvil, bear—
  When you are the hammer, strike.
EDWIN MARKHAM, *Preparedness*

15847. There is no record in history of a nation that ever gained anything valuable by being unable to defend itself. H. L. MENCKEN, *Prejudices*

15848. The first blow is as much as two.   *Proverb*

15849. One sword keeps another in the sheath.   *Proverb*

15850. A disarmed peace is weak.
Proverb

15851. He that prepares for ill, gives the blow a meeting, and breaks its stroke.   *Proverb*

15852. Have not thy cloak to make when it begins to rain.   *Proverb*

15853. He may hope for the best that's prepared for the worst.
Proverb

15854. A stitch in time saves nine.
Proverb

15855. A man surprised is half beaten.   *Proverb*

15856. Get thy spindle and thy distaff ready, and God will send the flax.   *Proverb*

15857. We should provide in peace what we need in war.
PUBLILIUS SYRUS, *Sententiae*

15858. We have had the lesson before us over and over again—nations that were not ready and were unable to get ready found themselves overrun by the enemy.
FRANKLIN D. ROOSEVELT,
Message to Congress, May 16, 1940

15859. Peace the offspring is of Power.   BAYARD TAYLOR,
A Thousand Years.

See also: 699, 5347, 8471, 14850, 20863.

THE PRESENT

Related Subject: Today.

15861.
  Every age
Appears to souls who live in 't (ask
  Carlyle)
Most unheroic.
ELIZABETH B. BROWNING,
Aurora Leigh

15862. Try to be happy in this very present moment; and put not off being so to a time to come; as though that time should be of another make from this, which is already come, and is ours.   THOMAS FULLER

15863. Since Time is not a person we can overtake when he is gone, let us honor him with mirth and cheerfulness of heart while he is passing.
GOETHE

15864. The future is purchased by the present.   SAMUEL JOHNSON

15865. Let us enjoy the fugitive hour. Man has no harbor, time has no shore, it rushes on and carries us with it.   LAMARTINE

15866. One realm we have never conquered—the pure present. One great mystery of time is terra incognita to us—the instant. The most superb mystery we have hardly recognized—the immediate, instant self. The quick of all the universe, of all creation, is the incarnate, carnal self.
D. H. LAWRENCE, *New Poems*

15867.
Trust no Future, howe'er pleasant!
Let the dead Past bury its dead!
Act,—act in the living present!
Heart within, and God o'erhead!
LONGFELLOW, *A Psalm of Life*

15868. Every man's life lies within the present; for the past is spent and done with, and the future is uncertain. MARCUS AURELIUS, *Meditations*

15869. Let ancient times delight other folk; I rejoice that I was not born till now; this age suits my nature.
OVID, *Art of Love*

15870. Past and to come seem best; things present worst.
SHAKESPEARE, *Henry IV*

15871. All the modern inconveniences.   MARK TWAIN,
Life on the Mississippi

15872.
The Present, the Present is all thou hast
For thy sure possessing;
Like the patriarch's angel hold it fast
Till it gives its blessing.
WHITTIER, *My Soul and I*

See also: 5608, 12991, 14689.

THE PRESS

Related Subjects: Books, Columnists, News, Printing, Propaganda.

15881. The stupendous Fourth Estate, whose wide world-embracing influences what eye can take in?
CARLYLE,
On Boswell's Life of Johnson

15882. Burke said there were Three Estates in Parliament; but, in the Reporters' Gallery yonder, there sat a Fourth Estate more important far than them all. It is not a figure of speech, or witty saying; it is a literal fact,—very momentous to us in these times.   CARLYLE,
Heroes & Hero-Worship

15883. Journalists have always been our most old-fashioned class, being too busy with the news of the day to lay aside the mental habits of fifty years before.   FRANK M. COLBY,
Constrained Attitudes

15884. Tilford Moots wuz over t' th' Henryville poor farm th' other day t' see an ole friend o' his thet used t' publish a newspaper thet pleased ever'buddy.   KIN HUBBARD

15885. An editor cannot always act as he would prefer. He is often obliged to bow to the wishes of the public in unimportant matters. Politics are the most important thing in life—for a newspaper.   IBSEN,
An Enemy of the People

15886. Newspaper publishing and business involvement on a large scale go hand in hand with the result that the press is becoming more and more a spokesman for special interests.

HAROLD L. ICKES,
America's House of Lords

15887. Local newspapers, those in the counties and smaller towns, may be affected by local friendships and prejudices and interests, but generally speaking, in the national field and with regard to·matters affecting the general welfare of the nation, they are sound at heart. This is a great consolation in these days of an arrogant, unscrupulous, and socially destructive, even if small, newspaper clique close to the apex of the economic pyramid.

HAROLD L. ICKES,
America's House of Lords

15888. The newspapers have a well-developed and thoroughly understood technique. They assert a monopoly of the right of criticism . . . Upon the head of the temerarious critic the thunderbolts of a Gutenbergian Jove will be hurled not only to annihilate him, if possible, but also to declare a savage warning to others who might be so rash as to question the truth or the finality of a newspaper utterance.   HAROLD L. ICKES,
America's House of Lords

15889. Publicists have long known both of the existence and the usefulness of this [newspaper] power. It has been used to elect and defeat candidates for public office, to destroy public confidence in administrative and legislative proposals, to stampede a nation into a prohibition hysteria and to reverse the majorities fourteen years later. The use as well as the misuse of information has made the power of suggestion the decisive force in world affairs. It can cause or prevent war. It can strengthen or destroy a democracy. It can build or wreck a nation.

HAROLD L. ICKES,
America's House of Lords

15890. American journalism is not merely a Big Business, it is a semi-monopolistic one. In many important cities the public has to depend upon one morning newspaper. In 1934, 82 per cent of all the dailies had a complete monopoly in their communities.   HAROLD L. ICKES,
America's House of Lords

15891. The liberty of the press is the Palladium of all the civil, political, and religious rights of an Englishman.   JUNIUS

15892. Newspapers always excite curiosity. No one ever lays one down without a feeling of disappointment.

CHARLES LAMB,
Detached Thoughts on Books and Reading

15893. All successful newspapers are ceaselessly querulous and bellicose. They never defend anyone or anything if they can help it; if the job is forced upon them, they tackle it by denouncing someone or something else.   H. L. MENCKEN, *Prejudices*

15894.
"The Press!—What is the Press?"
   I cried;
When thus a wondrous voice replied:
"In me all human knowledge dwells;
The oracle of oracles,
Past, present, future, I reveal,
Or in oblivion's silence seal;
What I preserve can perish never,
What I forego is lost forever."

JAMES MONTGOMERY, *The Press*

15895. The newspapers! Sir, they are the most villainous, licentious, abominable, infernal—Not that I ever read them! No, I make it a rule never to look into a newspaper.

SHERIDAN, *The Critic*

15896. A newspaper is indeed like a woman or a politician. When it is young, honest, and full of ideals, it is attractive, trusted, and full of the possibilities of power. Powerful men see this, see its uses, and so seek to possess it. And some of them do get and keep it, and they use, abuse, and finally ruin it.

LINCOLN STEFFENS,
Autobiography

15897. Of the Corporation of the Goosequill—of the Press, . . . of the fourth estate. . . . There she is—the great engine—she never sleeps. She has her ambassadors in every quarter of the world—her couriers upon every road. Her officers march along with armies, and her envoys walk into statesmen's cabinets. They are ubiquitous.   THACKERAY,
Pendennis

15898. A newspaper is a private enterprise, owing nothing to the public, which grants it no franchise. It is, therefore, "affected" with no public interest. It is emphatically the property of its owner who is selling a manufactured product at his own risk.
Wall St. Journal

15899. We have ceased to be a profession and are now an industry.
WILLIAM A. WHITE, *to American Society of Newspaper Editors.*

See also: 122, 5416, 5593.

PREVENTION

Related Subjects: Caution, Medicine, Preparedness, Safety.

15901. Preventives of evil are far better than remedies; cheaper and easier of application, and surer in result.   TRYON EDWARDS

15902. Prevention is the best bridle.
OWEN FELTHAM

15903. An ounce of prevention is worth a pound of cure.   *Proverb*

15904. Who would not give a trifle to prevent what he would give a thousand worlds to cure?
EDWARD YOUNG

15905. Laws act after crimes have been committed; prevention goes before them both.   J. G. ZIMMERMAN

PRICE

Related Subjects: Taxes, Worth.

15911.
For what is worth in anything
But so much money as 'twill bring?
SAMUEL BUTLER, *Hudibras*

15912. When God impelled me to set a price on my instruction in Christian Science Mind-healing, I could think of no financial equivalent for an impartation of a knowledge of that divine power which heals; but I was led to name three hundred dollars as the price for each pupil in one course of lessons at my College,—a startling sum for tuition lasting barely three weeks. This amount greatly troubled me. I shrank from asking it, but was finally led, by a strange providence, to accept this fee.

MARY BAKER EDDY

15913. My policy is to reduce the price, extend the operations and improve the article. You will notice that the reduction of price comes first. I have never considered any costs as fixed. Therefore I first reduce the price to a point where I believe more sales will result. Then we go ahead and try to make the

price. I do not bother about the costs. The new price forces the costs down.
HENRY FORD

15914. One of the ways of discovering what a cost ought to be is to name a price so low as to force everybody in the plant to the highest point of efficiency. The low price makes everybody dig for profits. I can make more discoveries concerning manufacturing and selling under this forced method than by any method of leisurely investigation.
HENRY FORD

15915. The way to spread a work is to sell it at a low price. No man will send to buy a thing that costs even sixpence, without an intention to read it. SAMUEL JOHNSON,
Boswell: Life

15916. The highest price we can pay for anything, is to ask it.
W. S. LANDOR,
Imaginary Conversations

15917. What we obtain too cheap, we esteem too lightly; it is dearness only that gives everything its value.
THOMAS PAINE,
The American Crisis

15918. A glutted market makes provision cheap. POPE,
Paraphrases from Chaucer

15919. Rare commodities are worth more than good. *Proverb*

15920. He that could know what would be dear, need be a merchant but one year. *Proverb*

15921. He is never likely to have a good thing cheap that is afraid to ask a price. *Proverb*

15922. A man may buy even gold too dear. *Proverb*

15923. Good cheap is dear at long run. *Proverb*

15924. Everything is worth what its purchaser will pay for it.
PUBLILIUS SYRUS, *Sententiae*

15925. I would not have given it for a wilderness of monkeys.
SHAKESPEARE,
The Merchant of Venice

15926. You pay a great deal too dear for what's given freely.
SHAKESPEARE, *The Winter's Tale*

See also: 2491, 2492, 2505, 2510, 2553, 4858, 10583, 14500.

PRIDE

Related Subjects: Appearance, Arrogance, Boasting, Conceit, Contempt, Dignity, Ostentation, Self-Respect, Superiority.

15931.
'T's pride, rank pride, and haughtiness of soul;
I think the Romans call it stoicism.
ADDISON, *Cato*

15932. Pride goeth before destruction, and an haughty spirit before a fall. *Bible: Proverbs, xvi, 18*

15933.
God laughs in heaven when any man
Says "Here I'm learned; this I understand;
In that, I am never caught at fault or doubt."
ELIZABETH B. BROWNING,
Aurora Leigh

15934.
As if true pride
Were not also humble!
BROWNING, *In an Album*

15935. They are proud in humility, proud in that they are not proud.
ROBERT BURTON,
Anatomy of Melancholy

15936.

Oh why should the spirit of mortal be proud?

Like a fast-flitting meteor, a fast-flying cloud,

A flash of the lightning, a break of the wave,

He passes from life to his rest in the grave.   BYRON, *Don Juan*

15937.

And the Devil did grin, for his darling sin

Is pride that apes humility.

COLERIDGE, *The Devil's Thoughts*

15938. Pride is ignorance; those assume most who have the least wisdom or experience; and they steal from their neighbor, because they have so little of their own.

MARY BAKER EDDY

15939. The bigger they come, the harder they fall. BOB FITZSIMMONS

15940.

It is the lofty pine that by the storm is oftener tossed; towers fall with heavier crash

Which higher soar.   HORACE, *Odes*

15941. Wounded vanity knows when it is mortally hurt; and limps off the field, piteous, all disguises thrown away. But pride carries its banner to the last.

HELEN HUNT JACKSON, *Ramona*

15942. Pride is equal in all men; and the only difference is in the means and manner of displaying it.

LA ROCHEFOUCAULD, *Maxims*

15943.

Rather than be less,

Car'd not to be at all.

MILTON, *Paradise Lost*

15944. I pray God to keep me from being proud. SAMUEL PEPYS, *Diary*

15945. How prudently we proud men compete for nameless graves, while now and then some starveling of Fate forgets himself into immortality.

WENDELL PHILLIPS

15946.

Of all the causes which conspire to blind

Man's erring judgment, and misguide the mind,

What the weak head with strongest bias rules,

Is pride, the never-failing vice of fools. POPE, *Essay on Criticism*

15947. He that is too proud to ask is too good to receive.   *Proverb*

15948. Insolence is pride when her mask is pulled off.   *Proverb*

15949. It is good pride to desire to be the best of men.   *Proverb*

15950. If pride were an art there would be many teachers.   *Proverb*

15951. As proud as a cock on his own dunghill.   *Proverb*

15952. As proud as a peacock.
        Proverb

15953. A proud look makes foul work in a fine face.   *Proverb*

15954. A proud mind and a poor purse are ill met.   *Proverb*

15955.

Look out how you use proud words.

When you let proud words go, it is not

Easy to call them back.

CARL SANDBURG, *Primer Lesson*

15956. Pride is an established conviction of one's own paramount worth in some particular respect; while vanity is the desire of rousing such a conviction in others. Pride works from within; it is the direct appreciation of oneself. Vanity is the desire to arrive at this appreciation indirectly, from without.

SCHOPENHAUER

15957. My pride fell with my fortunes.   SHAKESPEARE,
As You Like It

15958. Prouder than rustling in unpaid-for silk.   SHAKESPEARE,
Cymbeline

15959. I am very proud, revengeful, ambitious; with more offences at my beck, than I have thoughts to put them in, imagination to give them shape, or time to act them in.

SHAKESPEARE, *Hamlet*

15960.
He that is proud eats up himself;
Pride is his own glass, his own trumpet
His own chronicle.
SHAKESPEARE, *Troilus and Cressida*

15961.
My name is Ozymandias, king of kings:
Look on my works, ye Mighty, and despair!   SHELLEY, *Ozymandias*

15962.
Pride, when puffed up, vainly, with many things
Unseasonable, unfitting, mounts the wall,
Only to hurry to that fatal fall.
SOPHOCLES, *Oedipus Tyrannus*

15963. Pride is therefore pleasure arising from a man's thinking too highly of himself.   SPINOZA, *Ethics*

15964. There is such a thing as a man being too proud to fight.

WOODROW WILSON

See also: 417, 582, 793, 1099, 1181, 1467, 1635, 1801, 2495, 2621, 3121, 3130, 3152, 4809, 5021, 5852, 8178, 9406, 10105, 10108, 10111, 14392, 15390, 15684, 18931.

PRIEST, see Preacher

PRINCE

Related Subjects: Kings, Queen.

15971. Princes are like to heavenly bodies, which cause good or evil times, and which have much veneration but no rest.   BACON,
Of Empire

15972. Put not your trust in princes.
Bible: Psalms, cxlvi,

15973. Prince am I none, yet am princely born!
THOMAS DEKKER,
Shoemakers' Holiday

15974. The friendship of princes does not go beyond their convenience.
QUEEN ELIZABETH

15975. The Prince exists for the sake of the State; not the State for the sake of the Prince.   ERASMUS,
Adagia

15976. A prince without letters is a Pilot without eyes. All his government is groping.   BEN JONSON,
Explorata

15977. A prince has to have particular care that, to see and to hear him, he appears all goodness, integrity, humanity and religion, which last he ought to pretend to more than ordinarily. For everybody sees, but few understand; everybody sees how you appear, but few know what in reality you are, and those few dare not oppose the opinion of the multitude who have the majesty of their prince to defend them.
MACHIAVELLI, *The Prince*

15978. If the prince of a State love benevolence, he will have no opponent in all the empire.   MENCIUS

15979. Princes are lost by security, and preserved by prevention.
SIR WALTER RALEIGH

15980.
Yet in bestowing, madam,
He was most princely.
SHAKESPEARE, *Henry VIII*

15981. The princes among us are those who forget themselves and serve mankind.   WOODROW WILSON

See also: 5665.

PRINCIPLE

Related Subjects: Idea, Ideals, Philosophy.

15991. It is easier to fight for one's principles than to live up to them.
ALFRED ADLER

15992. I have linked my life with principles that will not die.
WILLIAM JENNINGS BRYAN

15993. Amid the pressure of great events, a general principle gives no help.   HEGEL

15994. Principles do not mainly influence even the principled; we talk on principle, but we act on interest.
W. S. LANDOR,
Imaginary Conversations

15995. Important principles may and must be flexible.   LINCOLN

15996.
Ez to my princerples, I glory
In hevin' nothin' o' the sort.
LOWELL, *The Biglow Papers*

15997. Flinch not, neither give up nor despair, if the achieving of every act in accordance with right principle is not always continuous with thee.
MARCUS AURELIUS, *Meditations*

15998. Search men's governing principles and consider the wise, what they shun and what they cleave to.
MARCUS AURELIUS, *Meditations*

15999. Principles have no real force except when one is well fed.
MARK TWAIN

16000.
Their feet through faithless leather meet the dirt;
And oftener chang'd their principles than shirt.   EDWARD YOUNG,
Epistle to Mr. Pope

See also: 155, 1070, 2816, 3112, 3813, 5282, 6947.

PRINTING

Related Subjects: Books, Ink, The Press.

16001. The art preservative of arts.
Anonymous

16002. The printing-press is either the greatest blessing or the greatest curse of modern times, one sometimes forgets which.   J. M. BARRIE,
Sentimental Tommy

16003. Ready-writing which we call Printing.   CARLYLE,
On Heroes & Hero-Worship

16004. He who first shortened the labor of Copyists by the device of *Movable Types* was disbanding hired Armies, and cashiering most Kings and Senates, and creating a whole new Democratic world; he had invented the Art of printing.
CARLYLE, *Sartor Resartus*

16005.
I am the printing-press, born of the mother earth. My heart is of steel, my

limbs are of iron, and my fingers are of brass.

I sing the songs of the world, the oratorios of history, the symphonies of all time.

I am the voice of today, the herald of tomorrow. I weave into the warp of the past the woof of the future. I tell the stories of peace and war alike.

I make the human heart beat with passion or tenderness. I stir the pulse of nations, and make brave men do better deeds, and soldiers die.

I am the laughter and tears of the world, and I shall never die until all things return to the immutable dust.

I am the printing-press.
ROBERT H. DAVIS,
I Am The Printing-Press

16006. Things printed can never be stopped; they are like babies baptized, they have a soul from that moment, and go on forever.
GEORGE MEREDITH

16007. All this I speak in print, for in print I found it.
SHAKESPEARE,
The Two Gentlemen of Verona

16008.
The jour printer with gray head and gaunt jaws works at his case,
He turns his quid of tobacco while his eyes blurr with the manuscript.
WALT WHITMAN, *Song of Myself*

See also: 1580.

PRISON

Related Subjects: Crime, Justice, Persecution, Punishment, Retribution.

16011. Prisons are built with stones of Law, brothels with bricks of Religion.   BLAKE, *Proverbs of Hell*

16012.
In durance vile here must I wake and weep,
And all my frowsy couch in sorrow steep.   BURNS,
Epistle from Esopus to Maria

16013.
As he went through Cold-Bath Fields he saw
A solitary cell;
And the Devil was pleased, for it gave him a hint
For improving his prisons in Hell.
COLERIDGE, *The Devil's Thoughts*

16014. Away with him to the deepest dungeon beneath the castle moat.
DICKENS, *Nicholas Nickleby*

16015. Give us, in mercy, better homes when we're a-lying in our cradles; give us better food when we're a-working for our lives; give us kinder laws to bring us back when we're a-going wrong; and don't set Jail, Jail, Jail afore us, everywhere we turn.   DICKENS, *The Chimes*

16016. When thee builds a prison, thee had better build with the thought ever in thy mind that thee and thy children may occupy the cells.
ELIZABETH FRY,
Report on Paris Prisons

16017. The black flower of civilized society, a prison.   HAWTHORNE,
The Scarlet Letter

16018.
Stone walls do not a prison make
Nor iron bars a cage;
Minds innocent and quiet take
That for an hermitage.
RICHARD LOVELACE,
To Althea from Prison

16019. Prison is a dreadful bore. But India is one vast prison.
JAWAHARLAL NEHRU

16020.

Nor stony tower, nor walls of beaten
　　brass,
Nor airless dungeon, nor strong links
　　of iron,
Can be retentive to the strength of
　　spirit.　　　　SHAKESPEARE,
　　　　　　　　　　　Julius Caesar

16021.

　　　Come, let's away to prison:
We two alone will sing like birds i'
　　the cage.　　　SHAKESPEARE,
　　　　　　　　　　　King Lear

16022. There, at the moated grange,
resides this dejected Mariana.
SHAKESPEARE, *Measure for Measure*

16023. Whilst we have prisons it
matters little which of us occupies the
cells.　　　　　　BERNARD SHAW,
　　　　　　　Maxims for Revolutionists

16024. The most anxious man in a
prison is the governor.
　　　　　　　　　　BERNARD SHAW,
　　　　　　　Maxims for Revolutionists

16025.

I know not whether Laws be right,
　Or whether Laws be wrong;
All that we know who lie in gaol
　Is that the wall is strong;
And that each day is like a year,
　A year whose days are long.
　　　　　　　　　　OSCAR WILDE,
　　　　　　The Ballad of Reading Gaol

16026.

This too I know—and wise it were
　If each could know the same—
That every prison that men build
　Is built with bricks of shame,
And bound with bars, lest Christ
　　should see
　How men their brothers maim.
　　　　　　　　　　OSCAR WILDE,
　　　　　　The Ballad of Reading Gaol

16027.

The vilest deeds like poison-weeds
　Bloom well in prison-air:
It is only what is good in Man
　That wastes and withers there:
Pale Anguish keeps the heavy gate
　And the Warder is Despair.
　　　　　　　　　　OSCAR WILDE,
　　　　　　The Ballad of Reading Gaol

See also: 1194, 6639.

PROBABILITY

Related Subjects: Accident, Credulity, Possibility.

16031. Fate laughs at probabilities.
　　　　　BULWER-LYTTON, *Eugene Aram*

16032.

Lest men suspect your tale untrue,
Keep probability in view.
　　　　　　　　　　JOHN GAY,
　　*The Painter who Pleased Nobody
　　　　　　　　　and Everybody*

16033. A thousand probabilities do
not make one truth.　　　*Proverb*

16034. Almost all human life depends on probabilities.
　　　　　　　　　VOLTAIRE, *Essays*

PROCRASTINATION

Related Subjects: Delay, Lateness, Neglect, Time, Tomorrow.

16041. Never leave that till to-morrow which you can do to-day.
　　　　　　　FRANKLIN, *Poor Richard*

16042.

procrastination is the
art of keeping
up with yesterday
　　DON MARQUIS, *archy and mehitabel*

16043. The next day is never so good
as the day before.
　　　　　PUBLILIUS SYRUS, *Sententiae*

16044.
Never do to-day what you can
Put off till to-morrow.
> W. B. RANDS, *Lilliput Levee*

16045. By and by is easily said.
> SHAKESPEARE, *Hamlet*

PRODIGALITY

Related Subjects: Excess, Extravagance, Waste.

16051. The younger son gathered all together, and took his journey into a far country, and there wasted his substance with riotous living.
> *Bible: Luke, xv, 13*

16052.
Squandering wealth was his peculiar art;
Nothing went unrewarded but desert,
Beggar'd by fools, whom still he found too late;
He had his jest, and they had his estate.
> DRYDEN,
> *Absalom & Achitophel*

16053. A princely mind will undo a private family.
> LORD HALIFAX,
> *Works*

16054. Free livers on a small scale; who are prodigal within the compass of a guinea.
> WASHINGTON IRVING,
> *The Stout Gentleman*

16055. On parchment wings his acres take their flight.
> SOAME JENYNS,
> *The Modern Fine Gentleman*

16056. We commonly say of a prodigal man that he is no man's foe but his own.
> BISHOP KING,
> *Lecture on Jonah*

16057. The prodigal robs his heir, the miser himself.
> *Proverb*

16058. Shall I keep your hogs and eat husks with them? What prodigal portion have I spent, that I should come to such penury?
> SHAKESPEARE, *As You Like It*

16059. Prodigals lately come from swine-keeping.
> SHAKESPEARE,
> *Henry IV*

16060.
How like the prodigal doth she return
With over-weather'd ribs!
> SHAKESPEARE,
> *The Merchant of Venice*

16061.
You must consider that a prodigal course
Is like the sun's; but not, like his, recoverable.
> SHAKESPEARE,
> *Timon of Athens*

16062. I have received my proportion, like the prodigious son.
> SHAKESPEARE,
> *The Two Gentlemen of Verona*

PROFIT

Related Subjects: Advantage, Business, Commerce, Compensation, Corporations, Dividends, Employment, Finance, Money, Reward.

16071. Gain not base gains; base gains are the same as losses.
> HESIOD, *Works and Days*

16072. What's none of my profit shall be none of my peril.
> *Proverb*

16073. Let him that receives the profit repair the inn.
> *Proverb*

16074. Every way makes my gain.
> SHAKESPEARE, *Othello*

16075. There is a crime here that goes beyond denunciation. There is a sorrow here that weeping cannot symbolize. There is a failure here that topples all our success. The fertile earth, the straight tree rows, the sturdy trunks, and the ripe fruit. And children dying of pellagra must die because a profit cannot be taken from an orange. And coroners must fill in the certificates—died of malnutrition—because the food must rot, must be forced to rot.

JOHN STEINBECK,
The Grapes of Wrath

See also: 344, 380, 398, 1477, 1991, 18007.

PROGRESS

Related Subjects: Discovery, Evolution, Future, Improvement, Invention, Pioneer, Science.

16081. The march of the human mind is slow.   BURKE,
Speech on Conciliation

16082. The struggle I had made to graduate taught me a great lesson—that it is by struggle that we progress. I learned concentration during that time I never thought I possessed.
ADMIRAL BYRD, *Exploring with Byrd*

16083. Almost everything that you believe now was scouted at and hissed scarcely a hundred years ago. Most acts of humanity that we practice today would have been despised and denied two hundred years ago. The world is moving and as it moves brutality is further off and humanity is nearer at hand. CLARENCE DARROW

16084. Progress has been much more general than retrogression.
DARWIN, *Descent of Man*

16085. So long as all the increased wealth which modern progress brings goes but to build up great fortunes, to increase luxury and make sharper the contrast between the House of Have and the House of Want, progress is not real and cannot be permanent. The reaction must come.
HENRY GEORGE,
Progress and Poverty

16086. All that is human must retrograde if it do not advance.
GIBBON, *Decline and Fall*

16087. The rung of a ladder was never meant to rest upon, but only to hold a man's foot long enough to enable him to put the other somewhat higher.   THOMAS HUXLEY,
On Medical Education

16088.
Those who first oppose a good work
Seize it and make it their own,
When the corner-stone is laid,
And memorial tablets are erected.
EDGAR LEE MASTERS,
Spoon River Anthology

16089. The test of our progress is not whether we add more to the abundance of those who have much; it is whether we provide enough for those who have too little.
FRANKLIN D. ROOSEVELT

16090. An' the on'y thing you got to look at is that ever' time they's a little step fo'ward, she may slip back a little, but she never slips clear back. You can prove that an' that makes the whole thing right. An' that means they wasn't no waste even if it seemed like they was. JOHN STEINBECK,
The Grapes of Wrath

16091.
Yet sometimes glimpses on my sight,
Through present wrong the eternal right;
And, step by step, since time began,
I see the steady gain of man.
WHITTIER,
The Chapel of the Hermits

See also: 5, 1375, 4108, 4125, 4126, 5423, 13393, 17062, 20383.

PROHIBITION

Related Subjects: **Abstinence, Liberty, Temperance.**

16101. Stolen waters are sweet, and bread eaten in secret is pleasant.
Bible: Proverbs, ix, 17

16102.
John Barleycorn got up again,
And sore surpris'd them all.
Burns, *John Barleycorn*

16103. Prohibition has made nothing but trouble.   Al Capone

16104.
Forbidden fruit a flavor has
    That lawful orchards mocks;
How luscious lies the pea within
    The pod that Duty locks!
Emily Dickinson, *Life*

16105. Vicious actions are not hurtful because they are forbidden, but forbidden because they are hurtful.
Franklin, *Autobiography*

16106. A law made to be habitually and openly violated is a frightful demoralizer of society. A law notoriously despised by many that appear as its public advocates, which takes many a vote from the same hand that an hour later is lifted trembling to the voter's lips with the draught that quiets at once his nerves and his conscience.   O. W. Holmes

16107. It is mighty difficult to get drunk on 2.75 per cent beer.
Herbert Hoover

16108. All I kin git out o' the Wickersham position on prohibition is that the distinguished jurist seems to feel that if we'd let 'em have it the problem o' keepin' 'em from gittin' it would be greatly simplified.
Kin Hubbard,
Abe Martin's Broadcast

16109. As for prohibition, it is going to be recorded as one of the results of the European War, foreseen by nobody.   Stephen Leacock,
The Woman Question

16110. Whether or not the world would be vastly benefited by a total banishment from it of all intoxicating drinks seems not now an open question. Three-fourths of mankind confess the affirmative with their tongues, and I believe all the rest acknowledge it in their hearts.   Lincoln

16111.
"Much sweeter," she saith, "more acceptable
Is drink, when it is stolen privily,
Than when it is taken in form avowable."   John Lydgate,
The Remedy of Love

16112.
So glister'd the dire Snake, and into fraud
Led Eve, our credulous Mother, to the Tree
Of Prohibition, root of all our woe.
Milton, *Paradise Lost*

16113. We are always striving for things forbidden, and coveting those denied us.   Ovid, *Art of Love*

16114. You cannot write on the banner of the Democratic party the skull and crossbones of an outlaw trade.
J. T. Robinson

16115. The only way you can fight booze is by ceasing to make life chronically painful for the masses.
Bernard Shaw

16116. Things forbidden have a secret charm.   Tacitus, *History*

16117. In the whole course of history, there's been no government that could alter the laws of nature. When by mere legislation man can stop fruit from fermenting of its own accord after it falls to the ground, he can talk about a law of prohibition. The very word destroys its meaning. You can't prohibit nature.

E. T. THURSTON,
Mr. Bottleby Does Something

16118. He found out a new thing—namely, that to promise not to do a thing is the surest way in the world to make a body want to go and do that very thing. MARK TWAIN,
The Adventures of Tom Sawyer

16119. Adam was but human—this explains it all. He did not want the apple for the apple's sake, he wanted it only because it was forbidden. The mistake was in not forbidding the serpent; then he would have eaten the serpent. MARK TWAIN,
Puddn'head Wilson's Calendar

16120. In all matters having to do with the personal habits and customs of large numbers of our people, we must be certain that the established processes of legal change are followed. WOODROW WILSON

PROMISE

Related Subjects: Debt, Oath, Vow.

16121. If we've promised them aught, let us keep our promise!
BROWNING,
The Pied Piper of Hamelin

16122. Promise is most given when the least is said.
GEORGE CHAPMAN,
Musoeus of Hero & Leander

16123. The Promised Land always lies on the other side of a wilderness. HAVELOCK ELLIS, *The Dance of Life*

16124. Failed the bright promise of your early day.
REGINALD HEBER, *Palestine*

16125. He that promises too much means nothing. *Proverb*

16126. When a man repeats a promise again and again, he means to fail you. *Proverb*

16127. He is poor indeed that can promise nothing. *Proverb*

16128. He loses his thanks who promises and delays. *Proverb*

16129. A promise against law or duty, is void in its own nature.
Proverb

16130. All promises are either broken or kept. *Proverb*

16131. A fair promise makes a fool merry. *Proverb*

16132. Be slow to promise, quick to perform. *Proverb*

16133. A man apt to promise is apt to forget. *Proverb*

16134. Never promise more than you can perform. PUBLILIUS SYRUS,
Sententiae

16135. He was ever precise in promise-keeping. SHAKESPEARE,
Measure for Measure

16136.
And though he promise to his loss,
He makes his promise good.
TATE & BRADY, *Psalms*

See also: 14610.

PROMPTNESS

Related Subjects: Haste, Rising, Speed.

16141. Promptness is the soul of business. LORD CHESTERFIELD

16142. Deliberate with caution, but act with decision and promptness.
C. C. COLTON

16143. The keen spirit seizes the prompt occasion; makes the thought start into instant action, and at once plans and performs, resolves, and executes. HANNAH MORE

16144. Punctuality is the soul of business. *Proverb*

16145. No sooner said than done— so acts your man of worth.
QUINTUS ENNIUS, *Annals*

16146.
Celerity is never more admir'd
Than by the negligent.
SHAKESPEARE, *Antony and Cleopatra*

16147. Better three hours too soon than a minute too late.
SHAKESPEARE,
The Merry Wives of Windsor

See also: 2605.

PROOF

Related Subject: Trials.

16151. Prove all things; hold fast that which is good.
Bible: 1 Thessalonians, v, 21

16152. The proof of the pudding is in the eating. CERVANTES,
Don Quixote

16153. You can not demonstrate an emotion or prove an aspiration.
JOHN MORLEY, *Rousseau*

16154. That which needs to be proved cannot be worth much.
NIETZSCHE,
The Twilight of the Idols

16155. Sir, he made a chimney in my father's house, and the bricks are alive at this day to testify it.
SHAKESPEARE, *Henry VI*

16156. Be sure of it; give me the ocular proof. SHAKESPEARE, *Othello*

16157. Some circumstantial evidence is very strong, as when you find a trout in the milk. THOREAU, *Journal*

See also: 1281, 1878, 1899, 3347, 12635.

PROPAGANDA

Related Subjects: Advertising, Democracy, Dictatorship, Government, Opinion, Politics, The Press, Radio.

16161. When teachers take up a text book in civics or economics they do not know to what extent vital parts of it have been "doctored" to suit private parties who expect to make profits out of "educating" the public to take their views of governmental policy. CHARLES A. BEARD,
American Leviathan

16162. The propagandist is a missionary. GEORGE CATLIN,
Propaganda as a Function of Democratic Government

16163. In both dictatorships and democracies propaganda is, as it always has been, an indispensable agent of social control. H. L. CHILDS,
Propaganda & Dictatorship

16164. Some of mankind's most terrible misdeeds have been committed under the spell of certain magic words or phrases.
JAMES BRYANT CONANT

16165. Slogans are both exciting and comforting, but they are also powerful opiates for the conscience.
JAMES BRYANT CONANT

16166.
Furious Propaganda, with her brand,
Fires the dry prairies of our wide
Waste Land;

Making the Earth, Man's temporal
station, be
One stinking altar to Publicity.
LEE W. DODD,
The Great Enlightenment

16167. If you wish to win the sympathy of broad masses then you must tell them the crudest and most stupid things. ADOLF HITLER,
Mein Kampf

16168. We live in a propaganda age. Public opinion no longer is formulated by the slow processes of what Professor John Dewey calls shared experience. In our time public opinion is primarily a response to propaganda stimuli.
Institute for Propaganda Analysis

16169. There are in our time societies which are not free. In these societies there are no competing propagandas. This freedom has already been lost, and, alas, lost partly through propaganda.
Institute for Propaganda Analysis

16170. If there is a right and a wrong in propaganda, it is to be found in the relation between means and ends, methods and purposes, and not in propaganda itself.
Institute for Propaganda Analysis

16171. If one assumes that propaganda is a method utilized for influencing the conduct of others on behalf of predetermined ends, it appears that every articulate person with a purpose is a propagandist.
Institute for Propaganda Analysis

16172. The study of propaganda goes to the heart of the most compelling popular, practical and scholarly issue of our time, which is the nature of the connection between what men think and how men live.
H. D. LASSWELL,
The Scope of Research on Propaganda & Dictatorship

16173. It is notorious that propaganda thrives where overt dissent flourishes.
H. D. LASSWELL,
The Scope of Research on Propaganda & Dictatorship

16174. Occasionally words must serve to veil the facts. But this must happen in such a way that no one become aware of it; or, if it should be noticed, excuses must be at hand, to be produced immediately. MACHIAVELLI

16175. Supporting springs from identification. To bring about identification is the goal of propaganda.
F. M. MARX,
State Propaganda in Germany

16176. Political propaganda has become the chief internal weapon of governments, and it is employed not only to persuade a sufficient number of people that a particular course of action is expedient or right, but to keep whole populations in a complete, and, it is apparently hoped, a perpetual emotional subjection.
A. B. WHITE, *The New Propaganda*

See also: 86, 18779.

PROPERTY

Related Subjects: Possession, Possessions.

16181. The soil was given to the rich and poor in common—wherefore, oh, ye rich, do you unjustly claim it for yourselves alone? Nature gave all things in common for the use of all; usurpation created private rights. Property hath no rights. The earth is the Lord's, and we are his offspring. The pagans hold earth as property. They do blaspheme God.
ST. AMBROSE

16182. Them that has china plates

themsels is the maist careful not to break the china plates of others.
J. M. BARRIE, *The Little Minister*

16183. Is it not lawful for me to do what I will with mine own?
Bible: Matthew, xx, 15

16184. Thieves respect property. They merely wish the property to become their property that they may more perfectly respect it.
G. K. CHESTERTON,
The Man Who Was Thursday

16185. The only things in life in which we can be said to have any property, are *our actions*.
C. C. COLTON

16186. Property has its duties as well as its rights.　DISRAELI, *Sybil*

16187. The bourgeoisie depends on one thing only—property.　HEINE

16188. Few rich men own their own property. The property owns them.
ROBERT INGERSOLL

16189. Taken generally, all our institutions and their working are conditioned by the property relations of any given society. The dominant ideas and principles of that society will be set by the way in which, in any moment, its property relations are working.　HAROLD J. LASKI, *I Believe*

16190. An ill-favoured thing, sir, but mine own.　SHAKESPEARE,
As You Like It

16191. Lord of thy presence and no land beside.　SHAKESPEARE,
King John

16192. The finest government cannot long endure when the tendency of the law is to create a rapid accumulation of property in the hands of a few, and to render the masses poor and dependent.　DANIEL WEBSTER

See also: 150, 1076, 2821, 6801 16374, 16624, 17207.

PROPHECY AND PROPHETS

Related Subjects: Astrology, Bible Future, Oracle.

16201. A prophet is not without honour, save in his own country, and in his own house.
Bible: Matthew, xiii, 5

16202. It has all the contortions of the sibyl without the inspiration.
BURKE, *Prior's Life of Burke*

16203. The best of prophets of the future is the past.　BYRON

16204. Thus in the beginning the world was so made that certain signs come before certain events.
CICERO, *De Divinatione*

16205. Ancestral voices prophesying war.　COLERIDGE, *Kubla Khan*

16206.
Thine was the prophet's vision, thine
The exaltation, the divine
Insanity of noble minds,
That never falters nor abates,
But labors and endures and waits,
Till all that it foresees it finds,
Or what it can not find creates!
LONGFELLOW, *Keramos*

16207. Prophets were twice stoned—first in anger; then, after their death with a handsome slab in the grave yard.　CHRISTOPHER MORLEY,
Where the Blue Begins

16208. Don't prophesy unless you know.　*Proverb*

16209.
O my prophetic soul!
My uncle!　SHAKESPEARE, *Hamlet*

16210.
If you can look into the seeds of time

And say which grain will grow and which will not.

SHAKESPEARE, *Macbeth*

See also: 6827, 10465, 11900, 12591.

PROSPERITY

Related Subjects: Fate, Fortune, Luck, Riches.

16211. Prosperity is not without many fears and distastes; and adversity is not without comforts and hopes.   BACON, *Of Adversity*

16212. Prosperity is the blessing of the Old Testament; adversity is the blessing of the New.   BACON, *Of Adversity*

16213.
Reverse cannot befall that fine Prosperity
Whose sources are interior.

EMILY DICKINSON,
The Single Hound

16214.
Prosperity could not be writ
In any book of destiny
For this red epitome
Of man's consistent cruelty
To man. Corruption, blight, and rust
Were its reward, and canker must
Set in. There were too many ghosts
Upon its lanes, too many hosts
Of dangling bodies in the wind,
Too many voices, choked and thinned,
Beseeching mercy on its air.

COUNTEE CULLEN, *Black Christ*

16215. You who are prosperous, don't forget that prosperity tends to harden.   B. C. FORBES,
Forbes' Epigrams

16216. Prosperity is just around the corner.   HERBERT HOOVER

16217. Whatever prosperous hour Providence bestows upon you, receive it with a thankful hand: and defer not the enjoyment of the comforts of life.   HORACE, *Epistles*

16218. Social prosperity means man happy, the citizen free, the nation great. VICTOR HUGO, *Les Miserables*

16219. Those calm, sunny seasons in the commercial world, which are known by the name of "times of unexampled prosperity."

WASHINGTON IRVING,
Wolfert's Roost

16220.
There is occasion for the vigilant
To fear for one who prospers, lest he fall.   SOPHOCLES, *Trachiniae*

16221. A comfortable career of prosperity, if it does not make people honest, at least keeps them so.

THACKERAY, *Vanity Fair*

16222.
There's a good time coming, it's almost here,
'Twas a long, long time on the way.
H. C. WORK, *Wake Nicodemus*

See also: 314, 316, 712, 3984, 8676, 10546, 13177.

PROSTITUTE, see Whore

PROTECTION

Related Subjects: Care, Insurance, Safety, Security, Tariff.

16231. As a hen gathereth her chickens under her wings.
Bible: Matthew, xxiii, 37

16232. Bind fast, find fast.   *Proverb*

16233. A bad padlock invites a picklock.   *Proverb*

See also: 669, 832, 9017, 10686.

PROTESTANTISM

Related Subjects: Calvinism, Christianity, Reformation, Religion.

16241. The German Protestant declared, "I have rights as against the church;" the Puritan Protestant, "I have rights as against the government;" the Independent, or American Protestant, "I have rights as against civil governments, church governments, and all mankind. These God gave me, and I will preserve." These were the three great strides which landed on Plymouth Rock.

H. W. BEECHER

16242. Protestantism makes the relation of a man to the Church to depend upon his relation to Christ; Romanism makes the relation of a man to Christ to depend on his relation to the Church. SCHLEIERMACHER

16243. Some one quoting the hackneyed sarcasm, that "between Protestantism and Romanism there is but a paper wall," the reply was, "True, but the whole Bible is printed on it."

H. L. WAYLAND

See also: 16974.

PROVERBS AND FAMILIAR SAYINGS

Related Subjects: Apothegms, Example, Platitude, Quotation, Wisdom.

16251. Despise not the discourse of the wise, but acquaint thyself with their proverbs; for of them thou shalt learn instruction.
Apocrypha: Ecclesiasticus

16252. Wise sayings are not only for ornaments. BACON, *Apothegms*

16253. Certainly apothegms are of excellent use. . . . They serve to be interlaced in continued speech. They serve to be recited upon occasion of themselves. They serve, if you take out the kernel of them and make them your own. BACON, *Apothegms*

16254. There is some degree of licentiousness and error in forming axioms. BACON, *Novum Organum*

16255. The genius, wit, and spirit of a nation are discovered in its proverbs. BACON, *Essays*

16256. Thou shalt become an astonishment, a proverb, and a byword, among all nations.
Bible: Deuteronomy, xxviii, 37

16257. He gave good heed, and sought out, and set in order many proverbs. *Bible: Ecclesiastes, xii, 9*

16258. I do not say a proverb is amiss when aptly and seasonably applied; but to be forever discharging them, right or wrong, hit or miss, renders conversation insipid and vulgar. CERVANTES, *Don Quixote*

16259. There is no proverb which is not true. CERVANTES, *Don Quixote*

16260. A proverb is a short sentence based on long experience.
CERVANTES, *Don Quixote*

16261. Most maxim-mongers have preferred the prettiness to the justness of a thought, and the turn to the truth. LORD CHESTERFIELD

16262. Never utter the truism, but live it among men. EMERSON,
Journal

16263. Don't you go believing in sayings, Picotee; they are all made by men, for their own advantage.
THOMAS HARDY, *Hand of Ethelberta*

16264.
The People's Voice the voice of God
we call;
And what are proverbs but the People's Voice?   JAMES HOWELL

16265. Pointed axioms and acute replies fly loose about the world, and are assigned successively to those whom it may be the fashion to celebrate.   SAMUEL JOHNSON,
Lives of the Poets

16266. In all pointed sentences, some degree of accuracy must be sacrificed to conciseness.   SAMUEL JOHNSON

16267. A proverb is no proverb to you till life has illustrated it.
KEATS, *Letters*

16268. Nothing is so useless as a general maxim.   MACAULAY, *Essays*

16269. Maxims are the condensed good sense of nations.
SIR JAMES MACKINTOSH

16270. A good maxim is never out of season.   *Proverb*

16271. The proverb is something musty.   SHAKESPEARE, *Hamlet*

16272. I can tell thee where that saying was born.   SHAKESPEARE,
Twelfth Night

16273. It is more trouble to make a maxim than it is to do right.
MARK TWAIN,
Pudd'nhead Wilson's New Calendar

See also: 963, 1607, 2353, 9408.

PROVIDENCE

Related Subjects: Destiny, Fate, God.

16281. Providence has a wild, rough, incalculable road to its end, and it is of no use to try to whitewash its huge, mixed instrumentalities, or to dress up that terrific benefactor in a clean shirt and white neckcloth of a student in divinity.   EMERSON,
Conduct of Life

16282. Any one thing in the creation is sufficient to demonstrate a Providence to an humble and grateful mind.
EPICTETUS, *Discourses*

16283.
Why doth IT so and so, and ever so,
This viewless, voiceless Turner of the
Wheel?   THOMAS HARDY,
The Dynasts

16284. Providence seldom vouchsafes to mortals any more than just that degree of encouragement which suffices to keep them at a reasonably full exertion of their powers.
HAWTHORNE,
The House of the Seven Gables

16285. Remember the wheel of Providence is always in motion; and the spoke that is uppermost will be under; and therefore mix trembling always with your joy.   PHILIP HENRY

16286. The lap of providence.
HUMPHREY PRIDEAUX,
Directions to Churchwardens

16287. Providence provides for the provident.   *Proverb*

16288.
There's a divinity that shapes our
ends,
Rough-hew them how we will.
SHAKESPEARE, *Hamlet*

16289. There's a special providence in the fall of a sparrow. If it be now, 'tis not to come; if it be not to come, it will be now; if it be not now, yet it will come: the readiness is all. Since no man has aught of what he leaves, what is 't to leave betimes?
SHAKESPEARE, *Hamlet*

16290.
> O God, thy arm was here:
> And not to us, but to thy arm alone,
> Ascribe we all!   SHAKESPEARE,
> > *Henry V*

16291.
> Arming myself with patience
> To stay the providence of some high
> > powers
> That govern us below.
> > SHAKESPEARE, *Julius Caesar*

16292.
> But He, that hath the steerage of my
> > course,
> Direct my sail!   SHAKESPEARE,
> > *Romeo and Juliet*

16293.
> A greater power than we can contra-
> > dict
> Hath thwarted our intents.
> > SHAKESPEARE, *Romeo and Juliet*

16294. Every drunken skipper trusts
to Providence. But one of the ways
of Providence with drunken skippers
is to run them on the rocks.
> BERNARD SHAW, *Heartbreak House*

16295. There are many scapegoats
for our sins, but the most popular is
providence.   MARK TWAIN,
> *More Tramps Abroad*

See also: 4, 1148, 2870, 3004, 3020,
3024, 3214, 8891, 10851, 16217.

PRUDENCE AND
IMPRUDENCE

Related Subjects: **Advice, Care,
Caution, Choice, Counsel, Danger,
Economy, Preparedness, Watch,
Wisdom.**

16301.
> > As the ancients
> Say wisely, have a care o' th' main
> > chance,

> And look before you ere you leap;
> For as ye sow, ye are like to reap.
> > SAMUEL BUTLER, *Hudibras*

16302. I tell you "put all your eggs
in one basket." It is easy to watch
and carry the one basket. It is trying
to carry too many baskets that breaks
most eggs in this country.
> ANDREW CARNEGIE,
> > *Empire of Business*

16303. 'Tis the part of a wise man
to keep himself to-day for to-morrow,
and not venture all his eggs in one
basket.   CERVANTES, *Don Quixote*

16304. Courage is a virtue only in
proportion as it is directed by prudence.   FENELON, *Telemachus*

16305.
> With more than a propitious gale,
> Take half thy canvas in.   HORACE

16306. Chance generally favors the
prudent.   JOUBERT, *Pensées*

16307. Have a care where there is
more sail than ballast.
> WILLIAM PENN, *Fruits of Solitude*

16308. Consider the little mouse, how
sagacious an animal it is which never
entrusts its life to one hole only.
> PLAUTUS, *Truculentus*

16309. The mouse that hath but one
hole is quickly taken.   *Proverb*

16310. Prudent cruelty is better than
foolish pity.   *Proverb*

16311. Prudent pauses forward business.   *Proverb*

16312. Don't buy a pig in a poke.
> *Proverb*

16313. A grain of prudence is worth
a pound of craft.   *Proverb*

16314. It is well to moor your bark
with two anchors.
> PUBLILIUS SYRUS, *Sententiae*

16315. It behooves a prudent person to make trial of everything before arms.   TERENCE, *Eunuchus*

See also: 736, 2284, 3006, 3888, 4484, 4774, 6689, 9577, 17799, 20161.

PRUDERY

Related Subjects: Censorship, Fastidiousness, Morality, Puritans, Reform.

16321. Perfect Love casts out Prudery together with Fear.
          RICHARD GARNETT,
             De Flagello Myrteo

16322.
Disdainful prudes, who ceaseless ply
The superb muscle of the eye.
    MATTHEW GREEN, *The Spleen*

16323. The peculiarity of prudery is to multiply sentinels, in proportion as the fortress is less threatened.
    VICTOR HUGO, *Les Miserables*

16324. Hence, far hence, ye prudes!
        OVID, *Art of Love*

16325. Will Honeycomb calls these over-offended ladies the outrageously virtuous. SIR RICHARD STEELE,
              The Spectator

16326. Prudery is a kind of avarice, the worst of all.   STENDHAL

PSYCHOANALYSIS

Related Subjects: Dreams, Psychology, Sanity and Insanity.

16331. A wonderful discovery—psychoanalysis. Makes quite simple people feel they're complex.
  S. N. BEHRMAN, *End of Summer*

16332. The uttered part of a man's life, let us always repeat, bears to the unuttered, unconscious part a small unknown proportion.   CARLYLE,
              Sir Walter Scott

16333. The best surgeon is he of the soul.   *Proverb*

16334.
And my imaginations are as foul
As Vulcan's stithy.
    SHAKESPEARE, *Hamlet*

See also: 1996, 5513, 6234, 6241, 6267, 10422, 13771, 17840.

PSYCHOLOGY

Related Subjects: Advertising, Dreams, Psychoanalysis, Sanity and Insanity.

16341. The psychiatrist, oriented in reality, recognizes that when the obstacles increase in the external conditions of living, the number of persons thrust beyond their capacity to adjust becomes greater; hence his interest joins that of the social scientist in bringing about changes in the social and economic life of the group to reduce the hazards of living.
             F. H. ALLEN

16342. A world of peace and freedom, from which the twin specters of war and insecurity will be banished, a world of equal opportunity . . . where children may lead healthy, happy lives and grow into useful, well adjusted citizens, where the personality is permitted to develop naturally and freely, where the individual is given a sense of personal worth and dignity and where his activities and ambitions are integrated with the development of group life—such is the goal toward which mental hygiene must strive.   ALBERT DEUTSCH,
    Treatment of the Mentally Ill In
                   America

16343. According as the man is, so must you humour him.
         TERENCE, *Adelphi*

See also: 1414, 1859, 2034, 10422, 10571, 10572, 10709, 13771, 13855, 17840, 19650.

THE PUBLIC, see The People

PUBLICITY, see Advertising

PUN

Related Subjects: **Epigram, Humor, Joke, Wit.**

16351. The seeds of punning are in the minds of all men, and though they may be subdued by reason, reflection, and good sense, they will be very apt to shoot up in the greatest genius.
ADDISON, *The Spectator*

16352. I think no innocent species of wit or pleasantry should be suppressed; and that a good pun may be admitted among the smaller excellencies of lively conversation.
JAMES BOSWELL,
Life of Samuel Johnson

16353. A man who could make so vile a pun would not scruple to pick a pocket. JOHN DENNIS,
The Gentleman's Magazine

16354. People that make puns are like wanton boys that put coppers on the railroad tracks.
O. W. HOLMES,
The Autocrat of the Breakfast-Table

16355. Far be it from me to insult the pun! I honour it in proportion to its merits—no more.
VICTOR HUGO, *Les Miserables*

16356. A pun is a pistol let off at the ear; not a feather to tickle the intellect. CHARLES LAMB,
Popular Fallacies

16357.
It often happens a bad pun
Goes farther than a better one.
W. S. LANDOR,
Last Fruit Off an Old Tree

16358. How every fool can play upon the word! SHAKESPEARE,
The Merchant of Venice

16359. I have mentioned puns. They are, I believe, what I have denominated them—the wit of words. They are exactly the same to words which wit is to ideas, and consist in the sudden discovery of relations in language. SYDNEY SMITH,
Sketches of Moral Philosophy

See also: 1661.

PUNISHMENT

Related Subjects: **Capital Punishment, Crime, Exile, Guilt, Hanging, Hell, Judgment Day, Justice, Law, Prison, Rebuke, Retribution.**

16361. The generality of men are naturally apt to be swayed by fear rather than by reverence, and to refrain from evil rather because of the punishment that it brings, than because of its own foulness.
ARISTOTLE, *Nicomachean Ethics*

16362. He that spareth his rod hateth his son. *Bible: Proverbs, xiii, 24*

16363. The public has more interest in the punishment of an injury, than he who receives it.
CATO THE CENSOR

16364. The object of punishment is the protection of society and the reformation of the offender.
GALSWORTHY

16365. If a man destroy the eye of another man, they shall destroy his eye. HAMMURABI,
*The Code of Hammurabi
King of Babylon*

16366. The whole of this procedure [solitary confinement] is cruel and barbarous, unworthy of a humane or

ivilized nation. To my knowledge,
t drives many men mad, and even
when it does not induce lunacy, men-
ally affects a large proportion of
those subjected to it.

H. B. MONTGOMERY

6367. Distrust all in whom the impulse to punish is powerful.

NIETZSCHE, *Thus Spake Zarathustra*

6368. He that spares the bad injures
he good.   *Proverb*

6369. Spare the rod, and spoil the
hild.   *Proverb*

6370. He that chastiseth one amend-
th many.   *Proverb*

6371. Like punishment and equal
ain, both key and key-hole. *Proverb*

6372. It is cruelty to the innocent
ot to punish the guilty.   *Proverb*

6373. Criminals are punished that
thers may be amended.   *Proverb*

6374.
Things have come to a heluva pass
When a man can't cudgel his own
    jack-ass.   HENRY WATTERSON

See also: 880, 1039, 3953, 5118,
5771, 17867, 20512, 21643.

PURITANS

Related Subjects: **Pilgrim Fathers,
Prudery.**

6381.
The Puritan through Life's sweet
    garden goes
To pluck the thorn and cast away the
    rose.   *Anonymous*

6382. It was a common saying
among the Puritans, "Brown bread
and the Gospel is good fare."

MATTHEW HENRY, *Commentaries*

16383. Puritanism, believing itself
quick with the seed of religious liberty, laid, without knowing it, the
egg of democracy.   LOWELL,
New England Two Centuries Ago

16384. The Puritan hated bear-
baiting, not because it gave pain to
the bear, but because it gave pleasure
to the spectators.   MACAULAY,
History of England

16385. What the Puritans gave the
world was not thought, but action.

WENDELL PHILLIPS

16386. A Puritan is a fanatical idealist to whom all stimulations of the
sense of beauty are abhorred; a philistine is a prosaic person who has no
ideals.   BERNARD SHAW,
Dramatic Opinions & Essays

See also: 1226.

PURITY AND IMPURITY

Related Subjects: **Blushing, Chastity, Cleanliness, Innocence, Perfection, Virtue.**

16391. Unto the pure all things are
pure.   *Bible: Titus, i, 15*

16392.
Like the stained web that whitens in
    the sun,
Grow pure by being purely shone
    upon.   THOMAS MOORE,
Lalla Rookh

16393.
My strength is as the strength of
    ten,
Because my heart is pure.

TENNYSON, *Sir Galahad*

16394.
Live pure, speak true, right wrong,
    follow the King—
Else, wherefore born?

TENNYSON, *Idylls of the King*

Impurity

16395. An impure man is every good man's enemy.　　H. W. Beecher

16396. 'To the pure all things are pure.' It may be the truth. But I sometimes wish Saint Paul had stated that hazardous truth in another form and declared that to the impure all things are impure.
Havelock Ellis, *The Art of Life*

16397. The man who tells me an indelicate story, does me an injury.
　　　　　　　　J. T. Fields

See also: 64, 2761, 6348.

PURPOSE

Related Subjects: Decision, End, Intention, Reason, Will.

16401. Purposeless activity may be a phase of death.　　Pearl Buck,
I Believe

16402. No good fish goes anywhere without a porpoise.
　　　　　Lewis Carroll,
　　　　　Alice in Wonderland

16403.
He trudg'd along unknowing what he sought,
And whistled as he went, for want of thought.　　Dryden,
　　　　　Cymon & Iphigenia

16404. Life has a value only when it has something as its object. Hegel

16405. Hedda's despair is that there are doubtless so many chances of happiness in the world, but that she cannot discover them. It is the want of an object in life that torments her.
Ibsen, *Hedda Gabler: Notes*

16406.
Show us not the aim without the way.
For ends and means on earth are so entangled

That changing one, you change the other too;
Each different path brings other ends in view. Ferdinand Lassale,
Franz von Sickingen

16407. I feel myself driven towards an end that I do not know. As soon as I shall have reached it, as soon as I shall become unnecessary, an atom will suffice to shatter me.
　　　　　Napoleon, *in Russia*

16408. Good purposes should be the directors of good actions, not the apology for bad.　　*Proverb*

16409. Drift is as bad as unthrift.
　　　　　　　　Proverb

16410. My purpose is, indeed, a horse of that colour.　　Shakespeare,
Twelfth Night

16411.
That no compunctious visitings of nature
Shake my fell purpose.
　　　　Shakespeare, *Macbeth*

16412. What, pray, is there to do with one's life in this twentieth century of ours except to take part in the struggle to build a world of security and peace?
　　　John Strachey, *I Believe*

16413.
Thy purpose firm is equal to the deed
Who does the best his circumstance allows
Does well, acts nobly; angels could do no more. Edward Young,
Night Thoughts

See also: 157, 1269, 2599, 2600, 2606, 2614, 2795, 3062, 4023, 4714, 8129, 9034, 9352, 9823, 11706, 20524.

Q

QUACK, QUACKERY

Related Subjects: Deceit, Doctor, Knave.

16421. Quackery gives birth to nothing; gives death to all things.
CARLYLE, *Heroes & Hero-Worship*

16422. One portion of our being is always playing the successful quack to the other.　　　　CARLYLE

16423.
　　　　Out, you imposters!
Quack salving, cheating mountebanks! your skill
Is to make sound men sick, and sick men kill.　　MASSINGER,
The Virgin-Martyr

16424. Quacks—not physicians.
THOMAS MOORE,
Ode to Rae Wilson

16425. Quackery has no friend like gullibility.　　　*Proverb*

16426. Quackery has no such friend as credulity.　　C. SIMMONS

16427. Nothing more strikingly betrays the credulity of mankind than medicine. Quackery is a thing universal, and universally successful. In this case it is literally true that no imposition is too great for the credulity of men.　　THOREAU

QUALITIES

Related Subjects: Character, Comparisons, Courage, Cowards, Honesty, Merit, Wickedness, Worth.

16431. The best is always good enough.　　ARNOLD BENNETT

16432. Wood burns because it has the proper stuff in it; and a man becomes famous because he has the proper stuff in him.　　GOETHE

16433. It is quality rather than quantity that matters.　　SENECA

16434. Come, give us a taste of your quality.　　SHAKESPEARE, *Hamlet*

16435.
That which ordinary men are fit for,
I am qualified in; and the best of me
　　is diligence.　　SHAKESPEARE,
King Lear
See also: 1072, 5376, 17913.

QUARRELING, QUARRELS

Related Subjects: Argument, Differences, Discord, Dueling.

16441.
Where two discourse, if the one's anger rise,
The man who lets the contest fall is wise.　　EURIPIDES,
Protesilaus

16442.
Those who in quarrels interpose
Must often wipe a bloody nose.
JOHN GAY, *The Mastiffs*

16443. Quarrels would not last long if the fault was only on one side.
LA ROCHEFOUCAULD, *Maxims*

16444. True disputants are like true sportsmen, their whole delight in the pursuit.　　POPE,
Thoughts on Various Subjects

16445. None but cats and dogs are allowed to quarrel in my house.
Proverb

16446. Keep aloof from quarrels; be neither a witness nor a party.
Proverb

16447. The Retort Courteous; . . . The Quip Modest; . . . The Reply Churlish; . . . The Reproof Valiant; . . . The Countercheck Quarrelsome; . . . The Lie with Circumstance; . . . The Lie Direct.   SHAKESPEARE,
As You Like It

16448.

Beware
Of entrance to a quarrel, but, being in,
Bear 't that the opposed may beware of thee.   SHAKESPEARE, *Hamlet*

16449. Thy head is as full of quarrels as an egg is full of meat.
SHAKESPEARE, *Romeo and Juliet*

16450. The test of a man or woman's breeding is how they behave in a quarrel.   BERNARD SHAW,
The Philanderer

16451. I won't quarrel with my bread and butter.   SWIFT,
Polite Conversation

See also: 856, 1162, 2297, 2696, 20449.

QUEEN

Related Subjects: Crown, Kings, Prince.

16461. Your queens are generally prosperous in reigning. BYRON,
Don Juan

16462. I know that I have but the body of a weak and feeble woman; but I have the heart of a King, and of a King of England, too.
QUEEN ELIZABETH

16463.

Our queen,
The imperial jointress to this warlike state.   SHAKESPEARE,
Hamlet

16464. I would not be a queen For all the world.   SHAKESPEARE,
Henry VIII.

See also: 17568.

QUESTION

Related Subjects: Curiosity, Inquiry, Riddle.

16471. Ask and learn.
Apocrypha: 1 Maccabees

16472. Every man ought to be inquisitive through every hour of his great adventure down to the day when he shall no longer cast a shadow in the sun. For if he dies without a question in his heart, what excuse is there for his continuance?
FRANK COLBY, *Essays*

16473. Them that asks no questions isn't told a lie.   KIPLING,
A Smuggler's Song

16474. He that makes a question where there is no doubt, must make an answer where there is no reason.
Proverb

16475. He that nothing questioneth nothing learneth.   *Proverb*

16476. It is not every question that deserves an answer.
PUBLILIUS SYRUS, *Sententiæ*

16477. I feel very strongly about putting questions; it partakes too much of the style of the day of judgment. You start a question, and it's like starting a stone. You sit quietly on the top of a hill; and away the stone goes, starting others.
STEVENSON, *Dr. Jekyll and Mr. Hyde*

16478.
No question is ever settled
Until it is settled right.
ELLA W. WILCOX,
Settle the Question Right

See also: 2498, 5434, 5948, 5956.

QUIET

Related Subjects: Calm, Peace, Rest, Serenity.

16481. Better is a dry morsel, and quietness therewith, than a house full of sacrifices with strife.
Bible: Proverbs, xvii, 1

16482. In quietness and confidence shall be your strength.
Bible: Isaiah, xxx, 15

16483. Study to be quiet.
Bible: 1 Thessalonians, iv, 11

16484. Quiet to quick bosoms is a hell. BYRON, *Childe Harold*

16485. He is as quiet as a lamb.
WILLIAM LANGLAND,
Piers Plowman

16486. Anything for a quiet life.
THOMAS MIDDLETON, *Title of play*

16487. A little with quiet Is the only diet. *Proverb*

16488. The holy time is quiet as a nun. WORDSWORTH,
It is a Beauteous Evening

See also: 2406.

QUOTATION

Related Subjects: Apothegms, Borrowing, Example, Platitude, Proverbs, Wisdom.

16491. That should be a warning to you never again to fall into the error of the would-be scholar—namely, quote second-hand.
BULWER-LYTTON, *My Novel*

16492. Appropriate things are meant to be appropriated. SAMUEL BUTLER

16493. With just enough of learning to misquote. BYRON,
English Bards & Scotch Reviewers

16494. Whoever in discussion adduces authority uses not intellect but memory. DA VINCI

16495. In literature quotation is good only when the writer whom I follow goes my way, and, being better mounted than I, gives me a cast.
EMERSON,
Quotation and Originality

16496. Quotations (such as have point and lack triteness) from the great old authors are an act of filial reverence on the part of the quoter, and a blessing to a public grown superficial and external.
LOUISE GUINEY

16497. If for the sake of a crowded audience you do wish to hold a lecture, your ambition is no laudable one, and at least avoid all citations from the poets, for to quote them argues feeble industry.
HIPPOCRATES, *Precepts*

16498. Classical quotation is the *parole* of literary men all over the world. SAMUEL JOHNSON,
Boswell: Life

16499.
Though old the thought and oft exprest,
'Tis his at last who says it best.
LOWELL, *For an Autograph*

16500. To be occasionally quoted is the only fame I care for.
ALEXANDER SMITH, *Dreamthorp*

16501. Quotations are best brought in to confirm some opinion controverted. SWIFT

16502.
Some for renown, on scraps of learning, dote,
And think they grow immortal as they quote. EDWARD YOUNG,
Love of Fame

R

RADIO

Related Subjects: Electricity, Propaganda.

16511. The main trouble with radio is preaching—preaching, not by ministers of the gospel, but by advertisers.   JAMES R. ADAMS,
More Power to Advertising

16512. No prediction of radio's future can be so wild, so fantastic, that even the most unimaginative engineer will dismiss it as impossible of realization.   WALDEMAR KAEMPFFERT

16513. The telegraph and the telephone have been called "space annihilators" in their day. Space annihilation indeed! We never really knew what the term meant until the time came when thousands listened at the same time to the voice broadcast through the ether just as if they were all in the same room. Patagonians, Eskimos, Chinese, Americans, Kaffirs, and Apaches are next-door neighbors. WALDEMAR KAEMPFFERT

16514. Governments soon learned that radio was easily their most effective medium of propaganda. The spoken word is more dramatic than cold type. . . . It can reach the illiterate as well as the literate. If shrewdly interwoven with entertainment, people will listen whether they like the message or not.
LAVINE & WECHSLER,
War Propaganda & the U. S.

16515. Though radio is already a nearly indispensable factor in our daily lives, it is as yet only an infant science whose mature power can only be guessed at in the light of what has already been achieved.
JOSEPH LEEMING,
Peaks of Invention

16516. The Radio Corporation of America sent a message consisting simply of the letter C around the world in five seconds.
JOSEPH LEEMING,
Peaks of Invention

16517. The World War hastened progress in radio development, as it did in the aircraft field. Wireless communication was a necessity to all governments, and each country did all in its power to hasten advances in the new art. JOHN A. MALONEY,
Great Inventors

RAGE

RAGE, see Anger

RAIN

Related Subjects: Clouds, Dew, Fog, Rainbow, Storm, Umbrella, Weather.

16521. Though it rain daggers with their points downward.
ROBERT BURTON,
Anatomy of Melancholy

16522.
It is not raining rain to me,
　It's raining daffodils;
In every dimpled drop I see
　Wild flowers on distant hills.
ROBERT LOVEMAN, *April Rain*

16523. It never rains but what it pours.   *Proverb*

16524.
All day the low-hung clouds have dropped
　Their garnered fullness down;
All day that soft gray mist hath wrapped
　Hill, valley, grove, and town.
CAROLINE SOUTHEY, *An April Day*

16525. I know Sir John will go, though he was sure it would rain cats and dogs.   SWIFT,
Polite Conversation

16526. The useful trouble of the rain.
TENNYSON, *Idylls of the King*

16527.
I am the Poem of Earth, said the voice of the rain,
Eternal I rise impalpable out of the land and the bottomless sea.
WALT WHITMAN,
The Voice of the Rain

See also: 1363, 2422, 6447, 8791.

RAINBOW

Related Subjects: Gold, Rain, Sun.

16531. Look upon the rainbow, and praise him that made it.
Apocrypha: Ecclesiasticus

16532.
Look, there's a rainbow now!
    See how that lovely rainbow throws
Her jewelled arm around
    This world, when the rain goes.
WILLIAM H. DAVIES, *The Rainbow*

16533.
God loves an idle rainbow,
No less than laboring seas.
RALPH HODGSON

16534.
There was an awful rainbow once in heaven:
We know her woof, her texture; she is given
In the dull catalogue of common things.
Philosophy will clip an angel's wings.
KEATS, *Lamia*

16535.
My heart leaps up when I behold
    A rainbow in the sky;

So was it when my life began,
So is it now I am a man,
So be it when I shall grow old,
    Or let me die! WORDSWORTH,
My Heart Leaps Up

16536.
The rainbow comes and goes,
And lovely is the rose.
WORDSWORTH,
Ode on Intimations of Immortality

16537. Understanding the rainbow is physics, but delight at the rainbow is morality!   LIN YUTANG,
I Believe

RAKE

Related Subjects: Dissipation, Vice, Villain.

16541.
He'd fly through the air with the greatest of ease,
This handsome young man on the flying trapeze;
His movements were graceful, all girls he could please,
    And my love he purloined away!
GEORGE LEYBOURNE,
The Man on the Flying Trapeze

16542. He was a rake among scholars and a scholar among rakes.
MACAULAY, *Essays*

16543. Women who like, and will have for a hero, a rake! how soon are you not to learn that you have taken bankrupts to your bosoms, and that the putrescent gold that attracted you is the slime of the Lake of Sin!
GEORGE MEREDITH, *Richard Feverel*

16544. A reformed rake makes the best husband.   *Proverb*

See also: 21620.

RANK

Related Subjects: Ancestry, Dignity, Name, Nobility, Office, Place, Titles.

16551. Rank is a great beautifier.
BULWER-LYTTON,
The Lady of Lyons

16552.
The rank is but the guinea's stamp,
  The man's the gowd for a' that.
BURNS, *Is There for Honest Poverty*

16553. Every error of the mind is the more conspicuous, and culpable, in proportion to the rank of the person who commits it.   JUVENAL

16554.
That in the captain's but a choleric word,
Which in the soldier is flat blasphemy.
SHAKESPEARE, *Measure for Measure*

See also: 12199.

RASHNESS

Related Subjects: Fool, Impulse.

16561. Rashness is the characteristic of ardent youth, and prudence that of mellowed age.   CICERO

16562. Rashness and haste make all things insecure. SIR JOHN DENHAM

16563. Rashness is the faithful but unhappy parent of misfortune.
THOMAS FULLER

16564. Every measure undertaken with temerity is liable to be perplexed with error, and punished by misfortune.   HERODOTUS, *Polymnia*

16565. Beware of rashness, but with energy and sleepless vigilance go forward and give us victories. LINCOLN

16566.
Though I am not splenetive and rash,
Yet have I in me something dangerous.   SHAKESPEARE, *Hamlet*

See also: 222, 295, 3906, 5235, 8128, 12304.

RAT

Related Subjects: Animal, Disease, Mouse.

16571.
Anything like the sound of a rat
Makes my heart go pit-a-pat!
BROWNING, *The Pied Piper*

16572. I smell a rat.
THOMAS MIDDLETON,
Blurt, Master-Constable

16573.
The very rats
Instinctively have quit it.
SHAKESPEARE, *The Tempest*

See also: 892, 2906.

RAVEN

Related Subjects: Birds, Black.

16581. Rarer even than a white raven.   JUVENAL, *Satires*

16582.
Ghastly, grim, and ancient Raven, wandering from the nightly shore,—
Tell me what thy lordly name is on the night's Plutonian shore?
Quoth the Raven, "Nevermore!"
POE, *The Raven*

16583. Bring up a raven and it will peck out your eyes.   *Proverb*

16584. The croaking raven doth bellow for revenge. SHAKESPEARE,
Hamlet

16585. Who will not change a raven for a dove?   SHAKESPEARE,
A Midsummer-Night's Dream

16586.

O, it comes o'er my memory,
As doth the raven o'er the infected
    house,
Boding to all.   SHAKESPEARE,
Othello

16587.

Did ever raven sing so like a lark,
That gives sweet tidings of the sun's
    uprise?   SHAKESPEARE,
Titus Andronicus

See also: 6207.

REACTION

Related Subjects: Impressions.

16591. Attack is the reaction. I never think I have hit hard unless it rebounds.   SAMUEL JOHNSON,
Boswell: Life

16592. Reaction is always equal and opposite to action; that is to say, the actions of two bodies upon each other are always equal and directly opposite.   SIR ISAAC NEWTON,
Third Law of Motion

See also: 100, 4159, 7327, 12549.

READING

Related Subjects: Books, Education, Library, Literature, Writing.

16601. Reading is to the mind what exercise is to the body. As by the one, health is preserved, strengthened and invigorated: by the other, virtue (which is the health of the mind) is kept alive, cherished and confirmed.   ADDISON

16602. If Russians knew how to read, they would write me off.
CATHERINE THE GREAT

16603. If I have not read a book before, it is, to all intents and purposes, new to me, whether it was printed yesterday or three hundred years ago.
HAZLITT, *On Reading New Books*

16604. When I take up a work that I have read before (the oftener the better) I know what I have to expect. The satisfaction is not lessened by being anticipated.   HAZLITT,
On Reading Old Books

16605. A man ought to read just as inclination leads him; for what he reads as a task will do him little good. A young man should read five hours in a day, and so may acquire a great deal of knowledge.
SAMUEL JOHNSON, *Boswell: Life*

16606. I cannot see that lectures can do so much good as reading the books from which the lectures are taken.   SAMUEL JOHNSON,
Boswell: Life

16607. He that I am reading seems always to have the most force.
MONTAIGNE, *Essay*

16608.
Some phrase that with the public took
Was all he read of any book.
HANNAH MORE,
Florio and His Friend

16609.
I divide all readers into two classes:
Those who read to remember and
    those who read to forget.
W. L. PHELPS

16610. Life being very short, and the quiet hours of it few, we ought to waste none of them in reading valueless books.   RUSKIN,
Sesame and Lilies

16611. Exceedingly well read.
SHAKESPEARE, *Henry IV*

16612.

He reads much;
He is a great observer, and he looks
Quite through the deeds of men.
SHAKESPEARE, *Julius Caesar*

16613.

Lord Summerhays: Reading is a dangerous amusement . . .

Tarleton: Why, man it's the beginning of education.

Lord Summerhays: On the contrary, it's the end of it. How can you dare teach a man to read until you've taught him everything else first?   BERNARD SHAW,
Misalliance

16614. Live always in the best company when you read.
SYDNEY SMITH,
Lady Holland's Memoir

16615. Books must be read as deliberately and reservedly as they were written.   THOREAU, *Walden*

See also: 206, 1391, 1991, 2025, 4750, 14428, 15360.

REAL ESTATE

Related Subjects: Business, Earth.

16621. The land shall not be sold for ever: for the land is mine; for ye are strangers and sojourners with me.
Bible: Leviticus, xxv, 23

16622.

Of this round earth whereon I stand,
I do not own one inch of land;
I shall not lose upon the day
When Gaffer Death drags me away.
ALICE BROWN, *Autolycus*

16623. Under all is the land. Upon its wise utilization and widely allocated ownership depend the survival and growth of free institutions and of our civilization. The Realtor is the instrumentality through which the land resource of the nation reaches its highest use and through which land ownership attains its widest distribution. He is a creator of homes, a builder of cities, a developer of industries and productive farms.
Code of Ethics:
National Assn. of Real Estate Boards

16624. No man shall be received into our commune who sayeth that the land may be sold. God's footstool is not property.
ST. CYPRIAN (200-258 A.D.)

16625. Think of the surface of a lake into which you drop a stone. That is the center of your operation. From that, there will run out ripples spreading in ever widening circles. Just so real estate has spread, or the people have spread over real estate in just about that way, always in an ever widening circle.
HARRY HALL, *Growth of New York*

16626. Make up your mind to buy at a time when other people are not buying freely—don't wait for a "boom." This takes courage but it pays profit.   W. B. HARMON

16627. Land is of fundamental importance as the basis of man's economic and social life.
W. C. HARRIS,
*The Annals: Amer. Acad. of
Polit. & Social Science*

16628. Increments in land values from the social point of view are unearned incomes, and . . . whenever society permits any individual to live on an unearned income, the goods and services he consumes actually are taken, although indirectly, from the other members of society.
W. N. LOUCKS,
*The Annals: Amer. Acad. of
Polit. & Social Science*

16629. There is an increasing purpose in the universe, and real estate gets all the benefit of it.

J. R. MURPHY,
Pointers in Real Estate

16630. It is rightfully contended that the owner of real estate is one who is more generally interested in the affairs of the city, or the community in which he lives, in the State, and in the Government generally. So, it really and truly makes for better citizenship.   J. R. MURPHY,
Pointers in Real Estate

16631. Real estate is one of the fundamental commodities. It has been bought, sold, mortgaged, and leased since the earliest days of history. Other commodities may be brought into use, become popular, and then disappear; but the land is underneath all.   N. L. NORTH, *Real Estate*

16632. All people must live somewhere.   N. L. NORTH, *Real Estate*

16633. Every person who invests in well-selected real estate in a growing section of a prosperous community adopts the surest and safest method of becoming independent, for real estate is the basis of wealth.

THEODORE ROOSEVELT

16634. The first man who, having enclosed a piece of ground, bethought himself of saying, *This is mine,* and found people simple enough to believe him, was the real founder of civil society.   ROUSSEAU

16635. You may buy land now as cheap as stinking mackerel.

SHAKESPEARE, *Henry IV*

16636. Now the difference between Wall Street and real estate is that you pick up the morning paper and you know if you are wiped out if you have stocks on margin. . . . With real estate there is nobody to tell us that we are wiped out. We may be wiped out and yet not know it.

R. E. SIMON, *Real Estate Appraisal*

16637. Mother Earth . . . is the greatest security in the world.

H. L. SIMPSON,
The Financing of Real Estate

16638.
The mortgage stones that covered her, by me
Removed, the land that was a slave is free.   SOLON

16639. It is a comfortable feeling to know that you stand on your own ground. Land is about the only thing that can't fly away.

ANTHONY TROLLOPE,
The Last Chronicle of Barset

16640. Broad acres are a patent of nobility; and no man but feels more of a man in the world if he have a bit of ground that he can call his own. However small it is on the surface, it is four thousand miles deep; and that is a very handsome property.

CHARLES DUDLEY WARNER,
My Summer in a Garden

See also: 16181, 16869.

REALISM AND REALITY

Related Subjects: Facts, Honesty, Life, Truth.

16641. It is a condition which confronts us—not a theory.

GROVER CLEVELAND

16642. Reality is something that happens. Nothing just exists in its own right. There is nothing behind nature, though there is infinitely more in nature than we know at present.

Our minds are real, but there was matter before there was mind.

J. B. S. HALDANE, *I Believe*

16643. It is not ill, but it is very well to be confronted with the ugly realities, the surviving savageries, that the smug hypocrisy of civilization denies; for 'til we recognize them we shall not abate them, or even try to do so.   W. D. HOWELLS,
Heroines of Fiction

16644. There is not a world of thought opposed to or interfering with a world of things: we have everywhere the same reality under different aspects. Nature is one as well as uniform.

SIR FREDERICK POLLOCK

16645. I am seeking only to face realities and to face them without soft concealments.

WOODROW WILSON

See also: 1186, 1216, 8234, 13220.

REASON

Related Subjects: **Argument, Cause, Intellectuals, Intelligence, Logic, Motive, Purpose.**

16651.
Whatever sceptic could inquire for,
For every why he had a wherefore.
SAMUEL BUTLER, *Hudibras*

16652. Every man's reason must be his guide. And I may as well expect that every man should be of my size and complexion so that he should reason just as I do.

LORD CHESTERFIELD

16653. I'll not listen to reason. . . . Reason always means what some one else has got to say.

MRS. GASKELL, *Cranford*

16654. To him who looks upon the

world rationally, the world in its turn presents a rational aspect. The relation is mutual.   HEGEL

16655. Human reason needs only to will more strongly than fate, and she is fate.   THOMAS MANN,
The Magic Mountain

16656. Always take the short cut; and that is the rational one. Therefore say and do everything according to soundest reason.

MARCUS AURELIUS, *Meditations*

16657.
Endued
With sanctity of reason.
MILTON, *Paradise Lost*

16658. A man always has two reasons for doing anything—a good reason and the real reason.

J. P. MORGAN

16659. Reason lies between the spur and the bridle.   *Proverb*

16660. If you will not hear reason, she will surely rap your knuckles.
Proverb

16661. There is a tendency among some thinkers of the present day to exalt intuition and to depreciate intellect. It is partly the outcome of the recent discoveries in psychology of Freud and his school. It comes partly from the teachings in philosophy of Nietzsche, Bergson and Croce. Political movements in Germany (Nazis) and Italy (Fascists) have brought this tendency into the world of practical affairs, and have given it a powerful influence in the shaping of events. . . . We see all around us what has been called "the retreat from Reason."

SIR HERBERT SAMUEL,
Belief and Action

16662. When a man has not a good reason for doing a thing, he has one good reason for letting it alone.
THOMAS SCOTT

16663. Man is a reasoning animal.
SENECA

16664. The "why" is plain as way to parish church.   SHAKESPEARE,
As You Like It

16665.
Now see that noble and most sover-
    eign reason,
Like sweet bells jangled, out of tune
    and harsh.   SHAKESPEARE,
Hamlet

16666.
Sure, he that made us with such large
    discourse,
Looking before and after, gave us
    not
That capability and godlike reason
To fust in us unused.
SHAKESPEARE, *Hamlet*

16667. Give you a reason on compulsion! If reasons were as plentiful as
blackberries, I would give no man a
reason upon compulsion, I.
SHAKESPEARE, *Henry IV*

16668. His reasons are as two grains
of wheat hid in two bushels of chaff:
you shall seek all day ere you find
them, and when you have them, they
are not worth the search.
SHAKESPEARE,
The Merchant of Venice

16669. This is the short and the
long of it.   SHAKESPEARE,
The Merry Wives of Windsor

16670. It is always right that a man
should be able to render a reason for
the faith that is within him.
SYDNEY SMITH,
Lady Holland's Memoir

16671.
I was promised on a time
To have reason for my rhyme;
From that time unto this season,
I received nor rhyme nor reason.
EDMUND SPENSER,
Promised Pension

See also: 72, 74, 114, 886, 1123, 1193, 1934, 2340, 3348, 3607, 7084, 10729, 10737, 12637, 14512, 21648.

REBELLION

**Related Subjects: Anarchy, Dis-
cord, Revolution.**

16681. Rebellion to tyrants is obedience to God.   *Anonymous*

16682.
The devil was the first o' th' name
From whom the race of rebels came.
SAMUEL BUTLER,
Miscellaneous Thoughts

16683. Men seldom, or rather never
for a length of time and deliberately,
rebel against anything that does not
deserve rebelling against.
CARLYLE, *Essays*

16684. A little rebellion now and
then is a good thing, and as necessary
in the political world as storms in
the physical.   JEFFERSON,
On Shays' Rebellion

16685.
O masters, lords and rulers in all
    lands,
How will the Future reckon with
    this Man?
How answer his brute question in
    that hour
When whirlwinds of rebellion shake
    the world?
How will it be with kingdoms and
    with kings—
With those who shaped him to the
    thing he is—

When this dumb terror shall reply
    to God,
After the silence of the centuries?
         EDWIN MARKHAM,
         The Man With the Hoe

16686.
Life was not gentle to him,
And the elements so mixed in him
That he made warfare on life,
In the which he was slain.
         EDGAR LEE MASTERS,
         Spoon River Anthology

16687. It doesn't take a majority to
make a rebellion; it takes only a few
determined leaders and a sound cause.
         H. L. MENCKEN, *Prejudices*

16688.
Quenching the flame of bold rebel-
    lion
Even with the rebels' blood.
         SHAKESPEARE, *Henry IV*

16689.
Rebellion in this land shall lose his
    sway,
Meeting the check of such another
    day.   SHAKESPEARE,
         Henry IV

16690. Rebellion, flat rebellion!
         SHAKESPEARE, *King John*

See also: 1814, 9505, 11641, 20053.

REBUKE

**Related Subjects: Criticism, Pun-
ishment, Scorn.**

16691. He who rebukes the world
is rebuked by the world.
         KIPLING, *Second Jungle Book*

16692. Reproof on her lip, but a
smile in her eye. SAMUEL LOVER,
         Rory O'More

16693. Woe to the house where there
is no chiding.   *Proverb*

16694. Reproof never does a wise
man harm.   *Proverb*

16695. Rebukes ought not to have
a grain more of salt than of sugar.
         Proverb

16696. Rebuke with soft words and
hard arguments.   *Proverb*

16697. Public reproof hardens
shame.   *Proverb*

16698. He that sharply chides is the
most ready to pardon.   *Proverb*

16699. Better a little chiding than a
great deal of heartbreak.
         SHAKESPEARE,
         The Merry Wives of Windsor

RECREATION

Related Subjects: Exercise, Sport.

16701. The bow cannot always
stand bent, nor can human frailty
subsist without some lawful recreation.   CERVANTES, *Don Quixote*

16702. Mingle your cares with pleasure now and then.
         DIONYSIUS CATO,
         Disticha de Moribus

16703. Recreation is not the highest
kind of enjoyment; but in its time
and place it is quite as proper as
prayer.   S. IRENAEUS PRIME

16704.
Sweet recreation barr'd, what doth
    ensue
But moody and dull melancholy,
Kinsman to grim and comfortless
    despair,
And at her heels a huge infectious
    troop
Of pale distemperatures, and foes to
    life?   SHAKESPEARE,
         The Comedy of Errors

16705. To walk abroad, and recreate yourselves.   SHAKESPEARE,
Julius Caesar

See also: 749.

REFINEMENT

Related Subjects: Breeding, Civilization, Courtesy, Culture, Manners.

16711. Refinement is the lifting of one's self upwards from the merely sensual, the effort of the soul to etherialize the common wants and uses of life.   H. W. BEECHER

16712. That alone can be called true refinement which elevates the soul of man, purifying the manners by improving the intellect.   COLERIDGE

16713. Refinement creates beauty everywhere. It is the grossness of the spectator that discovers anything like grossness in the object.   HAZLITT

16714. If refined sense and exalted sense be not so useful as common sense, their rarity, their novelty, and the nobleness of their objects make some compensation, and render them the admiration of mankind; as gold, though less serviceable than iron, acquires from its scarcity a value which is much superior.   DAVID HUME

16715. It is in refinement and elegance that the civilized man differs from the savage.   SAMUEL JOHNSON

16716. Too great refinement is false delicacy, and true delicacy is solid refinement.
          LA ROCHEFOUCAULD, *Maxims*

REFLECTION

Related Subjects: Consideration, Contemplation, Meditation, Memory, Mirror, Reverie, Thought.

16721. The next time you go out to a smoking party, young feller, fill your pipe with that 'ere reflection.
          DICKENS, *Pickwick Papers*

16722.
In vain sedate reflections we would make,
When half our knowledge we must snatch, not take.   POPE,
Moral Essays

16723. At last they came to where Reflection sits,—that strange old woman, who had always one elbow on her knee, and her chin in her hand, and who steals light out of the past to shed it on the future.
          OLIVE SCHREINER, *Dreams*

16724. But with the morning cool reflection came.   SCOTT,
Chronicles of the Canongate

16725. Till then, my noble friend, chew upon this.   SHAKESPEARE,
Julius Caesar

16726.
A soul without reflection, like a pile
Without inhabitant, to ruin runs.
          EDWARD YOUNG, *Night Thoughts*

See also: 472.

REFORM AND REFORMERS

Related Subjects: Bigotry, Censorship, Fanaticism, Improvement, Morality, Prudery, Reformation, Tolerance.

16731. It does not matter so much who holds the office. It is the reforms that are important.
          WILLIAM JENNINGS BRYAN

16732. In hope to merit heaven by making earth a hell.   BYRON,
Childe Harold

16733. Every reform however necessary, will by weak minds be carried

to an excess, that itself will need reforming.   COLERIDGE,
Biographia Literaria

16734. Turn over a new leaf.
THOMAS DEKKER,
The Honest Whore

16735. Be not angry that you cannot make others as you wish them to be, since you cannot make yourself as you wish you to be.
THOMAS À KEMPIS,
Of the Imitation of Christ

16736. It is easier to bear what's amiss, than go about to reform it.
Proverb

16737. The lunatic fringe in all reform movements.
THEODORE ROOSEVELT,
Autobiography

16738.
First Player. I hope we have reformed that indifferently with us, sir.
Hamlet. O, reform it altogether.
SHAKESPEARE, *Hamlet*

16739. I'll purge, and leave sack, and live cleanly.   SHAKESPEARE,
Henry IV

16740. All this struggling and striving to make the world better is a great mistake; not because it isn't a good thing to improve the world if you know how to do it, but because striving and struggling is the worst way you could set about doing anything.   BERNARD SHAW,
Cashel Byron's Profession

16741. There is an idea abroad among moral people that they should make their neighbors good. One person I have to make good, myself. But my duty to my neighbor is much more nearly expressed by saying that I have to make him happy if I may.
STEVENSON

16742. Nothing so needs reforming as other people's habits.
MARK TWAIN,
Pudd'nhead Wilson's Calendar

See also: 742, 1241, 3966, 4050, 6243, 10808, 11434, 16826.

REFORMATION

Related Subjects: Calvinism, Improvement, Protestantism, Reform

16751.
But 'tis the talent of our English nation,
Still to be plotting some new reformation.   DRYDEN,
Sophonisba

16752.
When doctrines meet with general approbation,
It is not heresy, but reformation.
DAVID GARRICK, *Epigram*

16753.
He bought a Bible of the new translation,
And in his life he show'd great reformation;
He walked mannerly and talked meekly;
He heard three lectures and two sermons weekly.
SIR JOHN HARRINGTON,
Of a Precise Tailor

16754. A true reformation must begin at the upper end.   *Proverb*

16755.
My reformation, glittering o'er my fault,
Shall show more goodly, and attract more eyes,
Than that which hath no foil to set it off.   SHAKESPEARE,
Henry IV

16756. Never came reformation in a flood.   SHAKESPEARE, *Henry V*

16757. Every generation needs re-generation.   C. H. SPURGEON,
Salt-Cellars

16758.
And ah for a man to arise in me,
That the man I am may cease to be!
TENNYSON, *Maud*

REGRET

Related Subjects: Disappointment,
Grief, Remorse, Sorrow.

16761. Regrets are the natural property of gray hairs.   DICKENS,
Martin Chuzzlewit

16762. The beginning of compunction is the beginning of a new life.
GEORGE ELIOT, *Felix Holt*

16763. Nor cast one longing, ling'ring look behind.
THOMAS GRAY, *Elegy Written in
a Country Church-yard*

16764.
    Thou wilt lament
Hereafter, when the evil shall be done
And shall admit no cure.
HOMER, *Iliad*

16765.
Familiar as an old mistake,
And futile as regret.
E. A. ROBINSON, *Bewick Finzer*

16766. O last regret, regret can die!
TENNYSON, *In Memoriam*

16767. To regret deeply is to live afresh.   THOREAU, *Journal*

See also: 13145.

RELIEF

Related Subjects: Charity, Comfort, Help.

16771. Continued dependence upon relief induces a spiritual and moral disintegration fundamentally destruc-tive to the national fibre. To dole out relief in this way is to administer a narcotic, a subtle destroyer of the human spirit.
FRANKLIN D. ROOSEVELT

16772.
For this relief much thanks; 'tis bitter cold,
And I am sick at heart.
SHAKESPEARE, *Hamlet*

RELIGION

Related Subjects: Belief, Bible,
Calvinism, Christ, Christianity,
Church, Consolation, Creeds, Devotion, Doctrine, Faith, God, Holiness, Monk, Prayer, Protestantism,
Righteousness, Salvation, Theology, Worship, Missionary.

16781. They that wait upon the Lord, shall renew their strength; they shall mount up with wings as eagles; they shall run, and not be weary; and they shall walk, and not faint.
Bible: Isaiah, xl, 31

16782. The writers against religion, whilst they oppose every system, are wisely careful never to set up any of their own.   BURKE

16783. One religion is as true as another.   ROBERT BURTON,
Anatomy of Melancholy

16784.
Petulant, capricious sects,
The maggots of corrupted texts.
SAMUEL BUTLER, *Hudibras*

16785.
With crosses, relics, crucifixes,
Beads, pictures, rosaries, and pixes,—
The tools of working our salvation
By mere mechanic operation.
SAMUEL BUTLER, *Hudibras*

16786. As I said before, I am really a great admirer of tangible religion, and am breeding one of my daughters a Catholic that she may have her hands full. It is by far the most elegant worship, hardly excepting the Greek mythology. What with incense, pictures, statues, altars, shrines, relics and the Real Presence, confession, absolution, there is something sensible to grasp at.   BYRON

16787. His religion, at best, is an anxious wish;—like that of Rabelais, "a great Perhaps." CARLYLE, *Burns*

16788. In Man, the positive content of religion is the instinctive sense—whether conscious or subconscious—of an inner unity and continuity with the world around. This is the stuff out of which religion is made.
EDWARD CARPENTER,
Pagan and Christian Creeds

16789. Religion must still be allowed to be a collateral security to Virtue.
LORD CHESTERFIELD, *Letters*

16790. To the man who has the religion of peace, the supreme value is love. To the man who has the religion of war, the supreme value is strife. G. LOWES DICKINSON,
The Choice Before Us

16791. By religion, then, I understand a propitiation or conciliation of powers superior to man which are believed to direct and control the course of nature and of human life.
SIR JAMES G. FRAZER,
The Golden Bough

16792. I would not make a fetish of religion and condone evil in its sacred name.   MAHATMA GANDHI

16793. Leave the matter of religion to the family altar, the church, and the private school, supported entirely by private contributions. Keep the

church and the State for ever separate.   ULYSSES S. GRANT

16794. I have no reason to doubt that the Lord loves the Shakers, but I don't believe he admires them.
J. G. HOLLAND

16795. It is the task of Rationalism to see that religion, this fundamental and important activity of man, shall neither be allowed to continue in false or inadequate forms, nor be stifled or starved, but made to help humanity in a vigorous growth that is based on truth and in constant contact with reality.
JULIAN HUXLEY,
Essays of a Biologist

16796. We, too, have our religion, and it is this: Help for the living, hope for the dead.
ROBERT INGERSOLL

16797. Religion, of which the rewards are distant, and which is animated only by faith and hope, will glide by degrees out of the mind unless it be invigorated and reimpressed by external ordinances, by stated calls to worship, and the salutary influence of example.
SAMUEL JOHNSON, *Life of Milton*

16798. For me and my kind the religious is lodged in the human.
THOMAS MANN, *I Believe*

16799. It can be of no importance to me of what religion my physician or my lawyer is; this consideration has nothing in common with the offices of friendship which they owe me.
MONTAIGNE, *Essays*

16800. Pop used to say about the Presbyterians, it don't prevent them committing all the sins there are but it keeps them from getting any fun out of it.

CHRISTOPHER MORLEY,
Kitty Foyle

16801. After coming in contact with a religious man, I always feel that I must wash my hands.

NIETZSCHE, *Ecce Homo*

16802. Religions, as they grow by natural laws out of man's life, are modified by whatever modifies his life. WALTER PATER,
The Renaissance

16803. Religion was not meant to curtail the enjoyments of the rich, but to keep the poor in their places, and to prevent the lower ones from rising above their stratum in life.

HERBERT PAUL, *Queen Anne*

16804. Religion is the best armour, but the worst cloak. *Proverb*

16805. It matters not what religion an ill man is of. *Proverb*

16806. A profitable religion never wanted proselytes. *Proverb*

16807. In order to be able to say that religious experience reveals reality, in order to be able to transform religious certitude into logical certainty, we are obliged to give an intellectual account of the experience. Hindu thought has no mistrust of reason. There can be no final breach between the two powers of the human mind, reason and intuition.

S. RADHAKRISHNAN

16808.
Religion beats me. I'm amazed at folk
Drinking the gospels in and never
  scratching
Their heads for questions.

SIEGFRIED SASSOON,
The Old Huntsman

16809. Religion is a great force—the only real motive force in the world; but what you fellows don't understand is that you must get at a man through his own religion and not through yours.

BERNARD SHAW, *Getting Married*

16810. Religious feeling is as much a verity as any other part of human consciousness; and against it, on the subjective side, the waves of science beat in vain. JOHN TYNDALL,
Fragments of Science

16811. I say the whole earth and all the stars in the sky are for religion's sake. WALT WHITMAN,
Starting from Paumanok

See also: 322, 940, 1321, 2013, 2711, 3031, 3474, 4144, 5046, 6144, 13629, 13631, 13632, 15037, 17618, 17826, 18257, 19180, 19186, 20292.

REMORSE

Related Subjects: Conscience, Despair, Regret, Repentance.

16821.
But, R-E-M-O-R-S-E!
The water-wagon is the place for me;
It is no time for mirth and laughter,
The cold, gray dawn of the morning
  after! GEORGE ADE,
The Sultan of Sulu

16822.
Last night at twelve I felt immense,
But now I feel like thirty cents.

GEORGE ADE, *The Sultan of Sulu*

16823.
Nor ear can hear nor tongue can tell
The tortures of that inward hell!

BYRON, *The Giaour*

16824.
Remorse is as the heart in which it
  grows;
If that be gentle, it drops balmy dews

Of true repentance; but if proud and
gloomy,
It is the poison tree, that pierced to
the inmost
Weeps only tears of poison.
          COLERIDGE, *Remorse*

16825. Remorse, the fatal egg by
Pleasure laid.   COWPER,
          The Mourning Bride

16826. Remorse begets reform.
          COWPER, *The Task*

16827. Remorse is memory awake.
          EMILY DICKINSON, *Poems*

16828.
Man, wretched man, whene'er he
stoops to sin,
Feels, with the act, a strong remorse
within.   JUVENAL, *Satires*

16829.
There are some people who are very
resourceful
At being remorseful,
And who apparently feel that the best
way to make friends
Is to do something terrible and then
make amends.
          OGDEN NASH, *Hearts of Gold*

16830. Remorse goes to sleep during
a prosperous period and wakes up in
adversity.   ROUSSEAU, *Confessions*

16831.
High minds, of native pride and
force,
Most deeply feel thy pangs, Remorse!
          SCOTT, *Marmion*

16832.
When thou shalt be disedged by
her
That now thou tirest on, how thy
memory
Will then be pang'd by me.
          SHAKESPEARE, *Cymbeline*

16833.
          Leave her to heaven
And to those thorns that in her bosom
lodge,
To prick and sting her.
          SHAKESPEARE, *Hamlet*

16834. I could accuse me of such
things that it were better my mother
had not borne me.
          SHAKESPEARE, *Hamlet*

16835.
The image of a wicked heinous fault
Lives in his eye: that close aspect of
his
Does show the mood of a much
troubled breast.
          SHAKESPEARE, *King John*

16836.
          Abandon all remorse;
On horror's head horrors accumulate.
          SHAKESPEARE, *Othello*

16837.
O that the vain remorse which must
chastise
Crimes doers, had but as loud a voice
to warn,
As its keen sting is mortal to avenge!
          SHELLEY, *The Cenci*

See also: 4714.

REPENTANCE

Related Subjects: Confession, Conscience, Guilt, Judgment Day, Remorse.

16841. I came not to call the righteous, but sinners to repentance.
          Bible: Matthew, ii, 17

16842. Now every repentance is not
a resurrection; it is rather a waking
out of a dream, than a rising to a
new life: Nay it is rather a startling
in our sleep, than any awaking at all,
to have a sudden remorse, a sudden
flash, and no constant perseverance.

Awake thou that sleepest, says the Apostle, out of the prophet: first *awake,* come to a sense of thy state, and then *arise from the dead,* says he, from the practice of dead works; and then, *Christ shall give thee light:* life, and strength to walk in new ways.   JOHN DONNE, *Sermons*

16843. Our repentance is not so much regret for the ill we have done as fear of the ill that may happen to us in consequence.
          LA ROCHEFOUCAULD, *Maxims*

16844. He said that in his whole life he most repented of three things: one was that he had trusted a secret to a woman; another, that he went by water when he might have gone by land; the third, that he had remained one whole day without doing any business of moment.
          PLUTARCH, *Lives*

16845. When men grow virtuous in their old age, they only make a sacrifice to God of the devil's leavings.
POPE, *Thoughts on Various Subjects*

16846. Repentance is the whip for fools.   *Proverb*

16847. Repentance is not to be measured by inches and hours.   *Proverb*

16848. Many there be, that buy nothing with their money but repentance.
          Proverb

16849. He that repents of a fault upon right grounds, is almost innocent.   *Proverb*

16850. Amendment is repentance.
          Proverb

16851.
The world will not believe a man repents;
And this wise world of ours is mainly right.   TENNYSON,
          Idylls of the King

See also: 137, 866, 886, 1840, 19616.

REPUBLIC, see Democracy

REPUTATION

Related Subjects: Calumny, Character, Fame, Greatness, Honor, Name.

16861. A good name is like a precious ointment; it filleth all around about, and will not easily away; for the odors of ointments are more durable than those of flowers.   BACON,
          Of Praise

16862. It is a maxim with me that no man was ever written out of reputation but by himself.
          RICHARD BENTLEY

16863.
Reputation said: "If once we sever,
Our chance of future meeting is but vain;
Who parts from me, must look to part for ever,
For Reputation lost comes not again."
          CHARLES LAMB,
          Love, Death, and Reputation

16864. He that regardeth not his reputation, despiseth virtue.
          Proverb

16865. A common blot is held no stain.   *Proverb*

16866. Beware of him who regards not his reputation.   *Proverb*

16867. Better be ill spoken of by one before all, than by all before one.
          Proverb

16868. No ruins are so irreparable as those of reputation.   *Proverb*

16869. Reputation is commonly measured by the acre.   *Proverb*

16870. Reputation is often got without merit, and lost without fault.
Proverb

16871. Reputation serves to virtue as light does to a picture.   *Proverb*

16872. Men take less care of their conscience than their reputation.
Proverb

16873. A wounded reputation is seldom cured.   *Proverb*

16874. A good reputation is more valuable than money.
Publilius Syrus, *Sententiae*

16875. I would to God thou and I knew where a commodity of good names were to be bought.
Shakespeare, *Henry IV*

16876.
Good name in man and woman, dear my lord,
Is the immediate jewel of their souls:
Who steals my purse steals trash; 'tis something, nothing;
'Twas mine, 'tis his, and has been slave to thousands;
But he that filches from me my good name,
Robs me of that which not enriches him,
And makes me poor indeed.
Shakespeare, *Othello*

16877. Reputation is an idle and most false imposition; oft got without merit, and lost without deserving.
Shakespeare, *Othello*

16878.
Reputation, reputation, reputation! Oh! I have lost my reputation. I have lost the immortal part of myself, and what remains is bestial.
Shakespeare, *Othello*

16879. They say a carpenter's known by his chips.   Swift,
Polite Conversation

See also: 1400, 2438, 2594, 6126, 11986, 17217, 19400.

RESEARCH

Related Subjects: Inquiry, Library, Study.

16881. Those hateful persons called Original Researchers.
J. M. Barrie, *My Lady Nicotine*

16882. Canst thou by searching find out God?   *Bible: Job, xi, 7*

16883. Ask, and it shall be given you; seek, and ye shall find; knock, and it shall be opened unto you.
Bible: Matthew, vii, 7

16884. We are as much gainers by finding a new property in the old earth as by acquiring a new planet.
Emerson, *Representative Men*

16885. We need the inspiration in many quarters for that character of scientific research where gold is not the principal reward.
N. M. Hopkins,
The Outlook for Research & Invention

16886. America now undoubtedly stands upon the golden threshold of her greatest era of industrial research, invention and development.
N. M. Hopkins,
The Outlook for Research & Invention

16887. It has been said that America has never been a nation of research in the profound scientific sense, but rather one of superficial invention. This statement has been resented, but more from patriotic impulse than from a careful analysis of the history and status of the subject.
N. M. Hopkins,
The Outlook for Research & Invention

16888. No engineer who has been to Germany and studied and traveled there can fail to appreciate that her great strength during the war lay in the foundation of her organized research.   N. M. HOPKINS,
The Outlook for Research & Invention

16889. The brief history of aviation since it first entered the realm of practicability furnishes a notable example of the efficacy of scientific research as an ally to the designer.
NAYLER & OWER, *Aviation of Today*

16890. Even today, almost every great institution for scientific research owes its being to some one man, who, as its founder or regenerator, breathed into it the breath of life.   SIMON NEWCOMB

16891.
Far must thy researches go
Wouldst thou learn the world to know.   SCHILLER,
Proverbs of Confucius

16892. Nothing is so difficult but that it may be found out by seeking.
TERENCE, *Heauton Timoroumenos*

See also: 7082.

RESENTMENT

Related Subjects: Anger, Indignation, Irritation.

16901. Resentment is a union of sorrow with malignity; a combination of a passion which all endeavor to avoid with a passion which all concur to detest.   SAMUEL JOHNSON

16902. Nothing on earth consumes a man more quickly than the passion of resentment.   NIETZSCHE,
Ecce Homo

16903. Resentment seems to have been given us by nature for defence, and for defence only; it is the safeguard of justice, and the security of innocence.   ADAM SMITH

See also: 4074, 5283.

RESERVE

Related Subjects: Conservatism, Dignity.

16911. Reserve is the truest expression of respect toward those who are its objects.   DE QUINCEY

16912. A reserved man is in continual conflict with the social part of his nature, and even grudges himself the laugh into which he is sometimes betrayed.   W. SHENSTONE

16913. Reserve is no more essentially connected with understanding, than a church organ with devotion, or wine with good nature.
W. SHENSTONE

16914. Persons extremely reserved are like old enamelled watches, which had painted covers that hindered your seeing what o'clock it was.
SIR ROBERT WALPOLE

See also: 6921.

RESIGNATION

Related Subjects: Calm, Humility, Meekness, Patience, Philosophy, Submission, Waiting.

16921. Now therefore keep thy sorrow to thyself, and bear with a good courage that which hath befallen thee.   *Apocrypha: 2 Esdras*

16922. Resignation! What a forlorn means of self-help! Yet it is the only one left to me.   BEETHOVEN

16923. Resignation is the rarest sort of courage.   Gustave Droz

16924. There is a certain satisfaction in feeling you are bearing with heroic resignation the irritating folly of others.   Jerome K. Jerome,
The Passing of the Third Floor Back

16925.
For after all, the best thing one can do
When it is raining, is to let it rain.
    Longfellow,
    Tales of a Wayside Inn

16926. There is no good in arguing with the inevitable. The only argument available with an east wind is to put on your overcoat.
    Lowell, *Democracy and Addresses*

16927.
All is best, though we oft doubt
What the unsearchable dispose
Of Highest Wisdom brings about.
    Milton, *Samson Agonistes*

16928. Bear, and blame not, what you cannot change.
    Publilius Syrus, *Sententiae*

16929. Things past redress are now with me past care.
    Shakespeare, *Richard II*

16930.
What's gone and what's past help
Should be past grief.
    Shakespeare, *The Winter's Tale*

See also: 2154, 2158, 3764.

RESISTANCE

Related Subjects: Defense, Defiance.

16931. I believe there is yet a spirit of resistance in this country, which will not submit to be oppressed; but I am sure there is a fund of good

sense in this country, which cannot be deceived.   Junius

See also: 693, 1837, 3297, 5632, 7527, 19557, 19566.

RESOLUTION AND IRRESOLUTION

Related Subjects: Courage, Decision, Earnestness, Fickleness, Firmness, Hesitation, Obstinacy, Perseverance, Zeal.

16941. I have aimed to assure them that knowledge can be obtained under difficulties; that poverty may give place to competency, that obscurity is not an absolute bar to distinction, and that a way is open to welfare and happiness to all who will resolutely and wisely pursue that way.
    Frederick Douglass,
    Autobiography

16942. Resolved, never to do anything which I should be afraid to do if it were the last hour of my life.
    Jonathan Edwards,
    Seventy Resolutions

16943. Bold resolution is the favourite of Providence.   *Proverb*

16944. In things that must be, it is good to be resolute.   *Proverb*

16945. He that gives time to resolve, gives time to deny, and warning to prevent.   *Proverb*

16946. Never tell your resolution beforehand.   John Selden,
    Table Talk

16947. I am tied to the stake, and I must stand the course.
    Shakespeare, *King Lear*

16948. When you rise in the morning, form a resolution to make the

day a happy one to a fellow-creature.
SYDNEY SMITH,
Lady Holland's Memoir

Irresolution

16949. Irresolution on the schemes of life which offer themselves to our choice, and inconstancy in pursuing them, are the greatest causes of all our unhappiness.   ADDISON

16950. Every man naturally persuades himself that he can keep his resolutions, nor is he convinced of his imbecility but by length of time and frequency of experiment.
SAMUEL JOHNSON,
Prayers & Meditations

16951. Irresolution frames a thousand horrors, embodying each.
J. MARTYN

See also: 69, 1024.

RESPECT

Related Subjects: Deference, Esteem, Honor, Virtue.

16961. Respect is what we owe; love, what we give.
PHILIP J. BAILEY, *Festus*

16962. There is no respect of persons with God.   *Bible: Romans, ii, 11*

16963. He removes the greatest ornament of friendship, who takes away from it respect. CICERO, *De Amicitia*

16964. A man's real life is that accorded to him in the thoughts of other men by reason of respect or natural love.   JOSEPH CONRAD,
Under Western Eyes

16965. Respect a man, he will do the more.   *Proverb*

16966.
That title of respect
Which the proud soul ne'er pays but to the proud.   SHAKESPEARE,
Henry IV

16967. I hold you as a thing ensky'd and sainted.   SHAKESPEARE,
Measure for Measure

16968. Is there no respect of place, persons, nor time in you?
SHAKESPEARE, *Twelfth Night*

16969.
Full twenty times was Peter feared,
For once that Peter was respected.
WORDSWORTH, *Peter Bell*

See also: 1226, 1934, 2566, 6028, 8834, 14609, 16911, 18062, 18283, 20323.

RESPONSIBILITY

Related Subjects: Authority, Burden, Care, Cause, Duty, Executives, Isolation, Obligation, Trust, Worry.

16971. Sin with the multitude, and your responsibility and guilt are as great and as truly personal, as if you alone had done the wrong.
TYRON EDWARDS

16972. Every person is responsible for all the good within the range of his abilities, and for no more, and none can tell whose sphere is the largest.   GAIL HAMILTON

16973. Responsibility's like a string we can only see the middle of. Both ends are out of sight.
WILLIAM McFEE,
Casuals of the Sea

16974. The feeling of a direct responsibility of the individual to God is almost wholly a creation of Protestantism.   J. S. MILL

16975. "Two things," said Immanuel
Kant, "fill me with awe: the starry
heavens, and the sense of moral re-
sponsibility in man."
JOHN TYNDALL,
Fragments of Science

16976. The most important thought
I ever had was that of my individual
responsibility to God.
DANIEL WEBSTER

See also: 2610, 3021, 7741.

REST

**Related Subjects: Bed, Calm,
Comfort, Contentment, Patience,
Quiet, Retirement, Sabbath, Sleep,
Wanderlust.**

16981. There is no rest for a messenger till the message is delivered.
JOSEPH CONRAD, *The Rescue*

16982.
Absence of occupation is not rest,
A mind quite vacant is a mind dis-
tress'd.   COWPER, *Retirement*

16983. The idle man does not know
what it is to enjoy rest. Hard work,
moreover, not only tends to give us
rest for the body, but, what is even
more important, peace to the mind.
SIR JOHN LUBBOCK,
The Pleasures of Life

16984. I have the feeling that once I
am at home again I shall need to
sleep three weeks on end to get rested
from the rest I've had!
THOMAS MANN,
The Magic Mountain

16985. For too much rest itself becomes a pain.   POPE,
The Odyssey of Homer

16986. Too much rest is rust.
SCOTT, *The Betrothed*

16987. Rest, rest, perturbed spirit!
SHAKESPEARE, *Hamlet*

16988. So may he rest; his faults lie
gently on him!   SHAKESPEARE,
Henry VIII

16989. Our foster-nurse of nature is
repose.   SHAKESPEARE, *King Lear*

16990. It is well to lie fallow for a
while.   MARTIN F. TUPPER,
Of Recreation

See also: 1955, 2862, 5059, 5541,
13523.

RETIREMENT

**Related Subjects: Concealment,
Rest, Retreat, Solitude.**

16991. He whom God hath gifted
with the love of retirement, possesses,
as it were, an extra sense.
BULWER-LYTTON

16992. A foundation of good sense,
and a cultivation of learning, are required to give a seasoning to retirement, and make us taste its blessings.
DRYDEN

16993. Don't think of retiring from
the world until the world will be sorry
that you retire. I hate a fellow whom
pride or cowardice or laziness drive
into a corner, and who does nothing
when he is there but sit and growl.
Let him come out as I do, and bark.
SAMUEL JOHNSON

16994. Let me caution persons
grown old in active business, not
lightly, nor without weighing their
own resources, to forego their customary employment all at once, for
there may be danger in it.
CHARLES LAMB,
The Superannuated Man

16995.

I could be well content
To entertain the lag-end of my life
With quiet hours.
SHAKESPEARE, *Henry IV*

16996. To judge rightly of our own worth we should retire from the world so as to see both its pleasures and pains in their proper light and dimensions—thus taking the heart from off this world and its allurements, which so dishonor the understanding as to turn the wisest of men into fools and children.   STERNE

RETREAT

Related Subjects: Defeat, Flight, Retirement, Solitude.

17001. It makes no difference if I burn my bridges behind me, since I never retreat.
FIORELLO H. LA GUARDIA

17002. A brave retreat is a brave exploit.   *Proverb*

17003.
Let us make an honourable retreat
With bag and baggage.
SHAKESPEARE, *As You Like It*

17004. When I retired from the rebel army in '61 I retired upon Louisiana in good order; at least in good enough order for a person who had not yet learned how to retreat according to the rules of war, and had to trust native genius.   MARK TWAIN,
Life on the Mississippi

See also: 8205.

RETRIBUTION

Related Subjects: Crime, Justice, Prison, Punishment.

17011. Whoso diggeth a pit shall fall therein.
Bible: Proverbs, xxvi, 27

17012.
The thorns which I have reap'd are of the tree
I planted; they have torn me, and I bleed,
I should have known what fruit would spring from such a seed.
BYRON, *Childe Harold*

17013. As he brews, so shall he drink.   BEN JONSON,
Every Man in His Humour

17014. He that sows iniquity shall reap sorrow.   *Proverb*

17015.
For 'tis the sport to have the enginer
Hoist with his own petar.
SHAKESPEARE, *Hamlet*

17016. The fool that eats till he is sick must fast till he is well.
G. W. THORNBURY,
The Jester's Sermon

REVENGE

Related Subjects: Anger, Crime, Cruelty, Enemy, Hatred, Malevolence, Murder, Passion.

17021. Revenge is a kind of wild justice, which the more man's nature runs to, the more ought law to weed it out.   BACON, *Of Revenge*

17022. Eye for eye, tooth for tooth, hand for hand, foot for foot.
Bible: Exodus, xxi, 24

17023. Vengeance is mine; I will repay, saith the Lord.
Bible: Romans, xii, 19

17024. Sweet is revenge—especially to women.   BYRON, *Don Juan*

17025. Vengeance is a dish that is best enjoyed cold.   GOEBBELS

17026.
But a man can never avenge himself
On the monstrous ogre Life.
                 EDGAR LEE MASTERS,
                    Spoon River Anthology

17027.
Revenge, at first though sweet,
Bitter ere long back on itself recoils.
                MILTON, *Paradise Lost*

17028. A woman always has her revenge ready.   MOLIÈRE, *Tartuffe*

17029. Men are more prone to revenge injuries, than to requite kindnesses.   *Proverb*

17030. Wait time and place to act thy
revenge, for it is never well done in
a hurry.   *Proverb*

17031. Revenge in cold blood is the
devil's own act and deed.   *Proverb*

17032. In taking revenge, a man is
but even with his enemy; but in passing it over, he is superior.   *Proverb*

17033. It costs more to revenge injuries than to bear them.
                THOMAS WILSON, *Maxims*

See also: 5342, 8409, 19696.

REVERIE

**Related Subjects: Contemplation,
Meditation, Reflection, Thought.**

17041. Thought is the labour of the
intellect, reverie is its pleasure.
                VICTOR HUGO, *Les Miserables*

17042.
    That inward eye
Which is the bliss of solitude.
                WORDSWORTH,
                I Wandered Lonely as a Cloud

17043.
In that sweet mood when pleasant
    thoughts

Bring sad thoughts to the mind.
                WORDSWORTH,
                Lines Written in Early Spring

17044.
    That blessed mood,
In which the burthen of the mystery,
In which the heavy and the weary
    weight
Of all this unintelligible world,
Is lightened.   WORDSWORTH

REVOLUTION

**Related Subjects: Anarchy,
Change, Chaos, Government, Rebellion, Socialism.**

17051. Inferiors revolt in order that
they may be equal, and equals that
they may be superior. Such is the
state of mind which creates revolutions.   ARISTOTLE, *Politics*

17052. Revolutions break out when
opposite parties, the rich and the
poor, are equally balanced, and there
is little or nothing between them:
for, if either party were manifestly
superior, the other would not risk an
attack upon them.   ARISTOTLE,
                    Politics

17053. All civilization has from time
to time become a thin crust over a
volcano of revolution.
                HAVELOCK ELLIS,
                Little Essays on Love and Virtue

17054.
By the rude bridge that arched the
    flood,
Their flag to April's breeze unfurled
Here once the embattled farmers
    stood,
And fired the shot heard round the
    world.   EMERSON,
                    Concord Hymn

17055. Let us remember that revolutions do not always establish free
dom.   MILLARD FILLMORE

17056. Revolutions are hot when factory chimneys are cold.
SAMUEL GRAFTON,
I'd Rather Be Right

17057. In spite of that section of the press which believes revolutions are caused by propaganda, it remains true in our day as in every day that revolutions are started by angry men.
SAMUEL GRAFTON,
I'd Rather Be Right

17058. A revolution, or anything that interrupts social order, may afford opportunities for the individual display of eminent virtues; but its effects are pernicious to general morality.
HAWTHORNE,
The Snow Image

17059. The conviction of the justification of using even most brutal weapons is always dependent on the presence of a fanatical belief in the necessity of the victory of a revolutionary new order on this globe. A movement which does not fight for such highest aims and ideals will therefore never take the ultimate weapon.
ADOLF HITLER,
Mein Kampf

17060. With a party of ten millions one can no longer make a revolution.
ADOLF HITLER, *Mein Kampf*

17061. I represent a party which does not yet exist; the party of revolution, civilization. This party will make the twentieth century. There will issue from it first, the United States of Europe, then the United States of the World.
VICTOR HUGO

17062. Would you realize what Revolution is, call it Progress; and would you realize what Progress is, call it Tomorrow.
VICTOR HUGO, *Les Miserables*

17063. A revolution conducted according to the rules of cricket is an absurdity.
ARTHUR KOESTLER,
Darkness at Noon

17064. If by the mere force of numbers a majority should deprive a minority of any clearly written constitutional right, it might, in a moral point of view, justify revolution—certainly would if such a right were a vital one.
LINCOLN

17065. The proletarians have nothing to lose but their chains. They have a world to win. Workers of the world, unite!
KARL MARX,
Manifesto of the Communist Party

17066. Of all the classes that stand face to face with the bourgeoisie today the proletariat alone is a really revolutionary class. The other classes decay and finally disappear in the race of modern industry; the proletariat is its special and essential product.
KARL MARX,
Manifesto of the Communist Party

17067.
In dim eclipse, disastrous twilight sheds
On half the nations, and with fear of change
Perplexes monarchs.
MILTON,
Paradise Lost

17068. Successful partisan warfare demands these fundamentals: fearlessness, swiftness, intelligent planning, mobility, secrecy, and suddenness and determination in action. Lacking any of these, it is difficult for partisans to win victories.
PENG TEH-HUAI,
Snow: Red Star Over China

17069. Revolutions are not made; they come.
WENDELL PHILLIPS

17070. Revolutions never go backward.   WENDELL PHILLIPS

17071. We are approaching a crisis and a century of revolution.

ROUSSEAU

See also: 5406, 14382.

REWARD

Related Subjects: Compensation, Dividends, Paradise, Payment, Profit.

17081.
Perhaps the reward of the spirit who tries
Is not the goal but the exercise.

E. V. COOKE, *Prayer*

17082. The reward of one duty is the power to fulfil another.

GEORGE ELIOT, *Daniel Deronda*

17083. What is vulgar, and the essence of all vulgarity, but the avarice of reward? 'Tis the difference of artisan and artist, of talent and genius, of sinner and saint.

EMERSON, *Conduct of Life*

17084. The reward of a thing well done, is to have done it.

EMERSON, *New England Reformers*

17085.
Those sweet rewards, which decorate the brave,
'Tis folly to decline.

SAMUEL JOHNSON

17086. Service without reward is punishment.   *Proverb*

17087. I never knew yet but rebuke and check was the reward of valour.

SHAKESPEARE, *Henry IV*

17088.
Not in rewards, but in the strength to strive,
The blessing lies.

J. T. TROWBRIDGE,
Twoscore and Ten

See also: 2131, 2141, 2626, 12185, 20605.

RICHES

Related Subjects: Avarice, Fortune, Gold, Jewel, Luxury, Mammon, Money, Possessions, Prosperity.

17091. An Embarrassment of Riches.

L. G. ALLAINVAL

17092. The superfluities of the rich are the necessaries of the poor. They who possess superfluities, possess the goods of others.   ST. AUGUSTINE

17093. Wealth maketh many friends.

Bible: Proverbs, xix, 4

17094. Riches certainly make themselves wings.

Bible: Proverbs, xxiii, 5

17095. He that maketh haste to be rich shall not be innocent.

Bible: Proverbs, xxviii, 20

17096. Where your treasure is, there will your heart be also.

Bible: Matthew, vi, 21

17097. It is easier for a camel to go through the eye of a needle, than for a rich man to enter into the kingdom of God.   *Bible: Matthew, xix, 24*

17098. Machiavel says virtue and riches seldom settle on one man.

ROBERT BURTON,
Anatomy of Melancholy

17099. You can only drink thirty or forty glasses of beer a day, no matter how rich you are.

COL. ADOLPHUS BUSCH

17100. The fostering and protection of large aggregations of wealth are the only foundation on which to build the prosperity of the whole people.

CALVIN COOLIDGE

17101. Riches have wings, and grandeur is a dream. COWPER, *The Task*

17102. Large was his wealth, but larger was his heart. DRYDEN, *Absalom & Achitophel*

17103. Wealth of itself, without the aid of philosophy, puts an end to puritanism and stoicism.
WILL DURANT, *The Life of Greece*

17104.
I care for riches to make gifts
To friends, or lead a sick man back to health
With ease and plenty. Else small aid is wealth
For daily gladness; once a man be done
With hunger, rich and poor are all as one. EURIPIDES, *Electra*

17105.
The loss of wealth is loss of dirt,
As sages in all times assert;
The happy man's without a shirt.
JOHN HEYWOOD, *Be Merry Friends*

17106. In all abundance there is lack. HIPPOCRATES, *Precepts*

17107.
As riches grow, care follows, and a thirst
For more and more. HORACE, *Odes*

17108.
Get place and wealth, if possible, with grace;
If not, by any means get wealth and place. HORACE

17109. The rich have become so unsocial that those who own property had rather throw their possessions into the sea than lend aid to the needy, while those who are in poorer circumstances would less gladly find a treasure than seize the possessions of the rich. ISOCRATES

17110. All riches come from iniquity, and unless one has lost another cannot gain. ST. JEROME

17111. It is better to live rich, than to die rich. SAMUEL JOHNSON, *Boswell: Life*

17112. You Can't Take It With You. KAUFMAN & HART, *Title of Play*

17113. Infinite riches in a little room. CHRISTOPHER MARLOWE, *The Jew of Malta*

17114. If you are poor now, Emilius, you will always be poor. Wealth is given today to none save the rich. MARTIAL, *Epigrams*

17115.
Whose wealth
Arithmetic cannot number.
MASSINGER, *The Roman Actor*

17116.
Let none admire
That riches grow in hell: that soil may best
Deserve the precious bane.
MILTON, *Paradise Lost*

17117.
Ormund: . . . But being rich isn't simply the opposite of being poor. It's not really worth much—being rich. Half the time there's a thick glass wall between you and most of the fun and friendliness of the world. There is something devilishly dull about most of the rich. Too much money seems to take the taste and color out of things. It oughtn't to do, but it does—damn it! J. B. PRIESTLEY, *I Have Been Here Before*

17118. Riches are like muck, which stink in a heap, but spread abroad, make the earth fruitful. *Proverb*

17119. Riches have made more men covetous, than covetousness hath made men rich.   *Proverb*

17120. Riches well got, and well used, are a great blessing.   *Proverb*

17121. God help the rich, the poor can beg.   *Proverb*

17122. Every one is kin to the rich man.   *Proverb*

17123. All strive to give to the rich man.   *Proverb*

17124. Abundance, like want, ruins many.   *Proverb*

17125. No good man ever grew rich all at once.   PUBLILIUS SYRUS, *Sententiae*

17126. Malefactors of great wealth.   THEODORE ROOSEVELT

17127. A great fortune is a great slavery.   SENECA

17128.
O, what a world of vile ill-favour'd faults
Looks handsome in three hundred pounds a year. SHAKESPEARE,
The Merry Wives of Windsor

17129.
Our purses shall be proud, our garments poor;
For 'tis the mind that makes the body rich.   SHAKESPEARE,
The Taming of the Shrew

17130. Many undeserving men are rich while their betters are poor. But we will not exchange what we are for what they have, since the one gift abides while the other passes from man to man.   SOLON

17131. If Heaven had looked upon riches to be a valuable thing, it would not have given them to such a scoundrel.   SWIFT, *Letter to Miss Vanhomrigh*

17132. No one goes to Hades with all his immense wealth.   THEOGNIS, *Maxims*

17133. That man is the richest whose pleasures are the· cheapest.   THOREAU, *Journal*

17134. Private information is practically the source of every large modern fortune.   OSCAR WILDE, *An Ideal Husband*

See also: 328, 390, 780, 931, 1817, 1820, 3061, 3257, 4115, 4118, 10553, 11060.

RIDDLE

Related Subject: Question.

17141. If ye had not ploughed with my heifer, ye had not found out my riddle.   *Bible: Judges, xiv, 18*

17142. It may well be doubted whether human ingenuity can construct an enigma of the kind which human ingenuity may not, by proper application resolve.   POE, *The Gold Bug*

17143. Much upon this riddle runs the wisdom of the world.   SHAKESPEARE, *Measure for Measure*

17144. You have not the Book of Riddles about you, have you?   SHAKESPEARE, *The Merry Wives of Windsor*

See also: 529, 3331, 4448, 21567.

RIDICULE, RIDICULOUSNESS

Related Subjects: Absurdities, Contempt, Foolishness, Irony, Mockery, Nonsense, Sarcasm, Satire.

17151. Neither will I make myself anybody's laughing-stock.   CERVANTES, *Don Quixote*

17152. I defy the wisest man in the world to turn a truly good action into ridicule. FIELDING, *Joseph Andrews*

17153. A man can stand very much in the cause of love: poverty, aunts, rivals, barriers of every sort,—all these only serve to fan the flame. But personal ridicule is a shaft that reaches the very vitals.
KENNETH GRAHAME,
The Golden Age

17154. We grow tired of everything but turning others into ridicule, and congratulating ourselves on their defects. HAZLITT, *The Plain Speaker*

17155. Ridicule often decides matters of importance more effectually, and in a better manner, than severity.
HORACE, *Satires*

17156. On the day of resurrection, those who have indulged in ridicule will be called to the door of Paradise, and have it shut in their faces. They will be called to another door, and again, on reaching it, will see it closed against them; and so on ad infinitum. *The Koran*

17157. The final test of truth is ridicule. . . . How loudly the barber-surgeons laughed at Harvey—and how vainly! What clown ever brought down the house like Galileo? Or Columbus? Or Jenner? Or Lincoln? Or Darwin? . . . They are laughing at Nietzsche yet. H. L. MENCKEN

17158. The sublime and the ridiculous are often so nearly related, that it is difficult to class them separately. One step above the sublime makes the ridiculous, and one step above the ridiculous makes the sublime again.
THOMAS PAINE, *Age of Reason*

17159. Ridicule is the test of truth.
Proverb

17160. Shall quips and sentences and these paper bullets of the brain awe a man from the career of his humour?
SHAKESPEARE,
Much Ado About Nothing

17161. There is no character, howsoever good and fine, but it can be destroyed by ridicule, howsoever poor and witless. MARK TWAIN,
Pudd'nhead Wilson's Calendar

See also: 413, 419, 1511, 3870, 4848.

RIGHT

Related Subjects: Justice, Morality, Principle, Virtue.

17171.
Here lies the body of William Jay,
Who died maintaining his right of
    way—
He was right; dead right, as he sped
    along,
But he's just as dead as if he were
    wrong. *Boston Transcript*

17172. Sir, I would rather be right than be President. HENRY CLAY

17173. He will hew to the line of right, let the chips fall where they may. ROSCOE CONKLING

17174.
But 'twas a maxim he had often tried,
That right was right, and there he
    would abide.
GEORGE CRABBE, *Tales*

17175.
I leave this rule for others when I'm
    dead,
Be always sure you're right—then go
    ahead.
DAVID CROCKETT, *Autobiography*

17176. To be engaged in opposing wrong affords, under the conditions of our mental constitution, but a slender guarantee for being right.

GLADSTONE,
Time and Place of Homer

17177. Let us have faith that right makes might; and in that faith let us to the end, dare to do our duty as we understand it. LINCOLN

17178.
I see the right, and I approve it too, Condemn the wrong, and yet the wrong pursue.

OVID, *Metamorphoses*

17179.
All nature is but art, unknown to thee;
All chance, direction, which thou canst not see;
All discord, harmony not understood;
All partial evil, universal good;
And spite of pride, in erring reason's spite,
One truth is clear, Whatever is, is right. POPE, *Essay on Man*

17180. As right as a ram's horn.
Proverb

17181. God defend the right!
SHAKESPEARE, *Henry VI*

17182. To do a great right, do a little wrong. SHAKESPEARE,
The Merchant of Venice

17183. The right is more precious than peace. WOODROW WILSON

See also: 774, 3596, 3910, 4337, 12913, 12914.

RIGHTEOUSNESS

Related Subjects: Bigotry, Morality, Religion, Salvation, Self-Righteousness, Virtue.

17191. Some people are so painfully good that they would rather be right than be pleasant. L. C. BALL

17192. One that feared God, and eschewed evil. *Bible: Job, i, 1*

17193. Create in me a clean heart, O God; and renew a right spirit within me. *Bible: Psalms, li, 10*

17194. A day in thy courts is better than a thousand. I had rather be a door-keeper in the house of my God, than to dwell in the tents of wickedness. *Bible: Psalms, lxxxiv, 10*

17195. The righteous shall flourish like the palm-tree: he shall grow like a cedar in Lebanon.
Bible: Psalms, xcii, 12

17196. Righteousness exalteth a nation. *Bible: Proverbs, xiv, 34*

17197. Strait is the gate, and narrow is the way. *Bible: Matthew, vii, 14*

17198. The quest for righteousness is Oriental, the quest for knowledge, Occidental.

SIR WILLIAM OSLER,
Life of Sir William Osler

17199. The righteous find peace, when the wicked feel torment.
Proverb

See also: 3667, 8202.

RIGHTS

Related Subjects: Democracy, Equality, Freedom, Justice, Liberty.

17201. Wherever there is a human being, I see God-given rights inherent in that being, whatever may be the sex or complexion.

W. L. GARRISON, *Life*

17202. The equal right of all men to the use of land is as clear as to their equal right to breathe the air—it is a right proclaimed by the fact of their existence. For we cannot suppose that some men have a right to be in this world, and others no right.

HENRY GEORGE

17203. All eyes are opened or opening to the rights of man. The general spread of the light of science has already laid open to every view the palpable truth, that the mass of mankind has not been born with saddles on their backs, nor a favored few booted and spurred, ready to ride them legitimately by the grace of God.

JEFFERSON

17204. Every man has by the law of nature a right to such a waste portion of the earth as is necessary for his subsistence.

SIR THOMAS MORE, *Utopia*

17205. We have no right to seize Sind [India], yet we shall do so, and a very advantageous, useful, humane piece of rascality it will be.

SIR CHARLES NAPIER

17206. Never exceed your rights, and they will soon become unlimited.

ROUSSEAU,
A Discourse on Political Economy

17207.
The rights of property are guarded
    by ten thousand laws and fort-
    resses.
The right of a man to live by his
    work—
    What is this right?
    And why does it clamor?
    And who can hush it
    so it will stay hushed?
    And why does it speak
    and though put down speak again
    with strength out of the earth?

CARL SANDBURG, *The People, Yes*

17208. What rights are his that dare not strike for them?

TENNYSON, *Idylls of the King*

See also: 698, 2461.

RISING

Related Subjects: Bed, Morning, Promptness, Sleep.

17211. Up roos the sonne, and up rose Emelye.

CHAUCER, *Canterbury Tales*

17212.
Early to bed and early to rise,
Makes a man healthy, wealthy, and
    wise.   FRANKLIN, *Poor Richard*

17213.
Get up, sweet Slug-a-bed, and see
The Dew bespangling Herbe and
    Tree.   ROBERT HERRICK,
    Corinna's Going a-Maying

17214. In the morning, when thou art sluggish at rousing thee, let this thought be present; "I am rising to a man's work."

MARCUS AURELIUS, *Meditations*

17215. He who doth not rise early never does a good day's work.

Proverb

17216. He rises o'er early that is hang'd ere noon.   *Proverb*

17217. Get a name to rise early, and you may lie all day.   *Proverb*

17218.
The day shall not be up so soon as I,
To try the fair adventure of to-
    morrow. SHAKESPEARE, *King John*

RISK

Related Subjects: Adventure, Boldness, Chance, Danger, Gambling, Speculation.

17221. Risk! Risk anything! Care no more for the opinions of others, for those voices. Do the hardest thing on earth for you. Act for yourself. Face the truth.

KATHERINE MANSFIELD, *Journals*

17222.

  I have set my life upon a cast,
And I will stand the hazard of the
 die.

   Shakespeare, *Richard III*

17223. Everything is sweetened by
risk.

   Alexander Smith, *Dreamthorp*

17224. 'Twould be as much as my life
was worth. Sterne, *Tristram Shandy*

See also: 168, 622, 2614, 4358, 10799.

RIVALRY

**Related Subjects: Competition,
Enemy, Envy, Jealousy, Opposition.**

17231. It is the privilege of posterity
to set matters right between those
antagonists who, by their rivalry for
greatness, divided a whole age.

     Addison

17232. In ambition, as in love, the
successful can afford to be indulgent
toward their rivals. The prize our
own, it is graceful to recognize the
merit that vainly aspired to it.

     C. N. Bovee

17233. Nothing is ever done beautifully which is done in rivalship; or
nobly, which is done in pride.

     Ruskin

17234. The finest woman in nature
should not detain me an hour from
you; but you must sometimes suffer
the rivalship of the wisest men.

    Sir Richard Steele,
     Letter to his wife

17235.

Of all the plagues a lover bears,
 Sure rivals are the worst.

   William Walsh, *Song*

See also: 15720.

RIVER

**Related Subjects: Fish, Sea, Ship,
Travel, Wanderlust, Water.**

17241.

  Thames and all the rivers of the
   kings
Ran into Mississippi and were
  drowned.

   Stephen Vincent Benet,
     John Brown's Body

17242. Are not Abana and Pharpar,
rivers of Damascus, better than all
the waters of Israel?

   Bible: 2 Kings, v, 12

17243. In rivers, the water that you
touch is the last of what has passed
and the first of that which comes: so
with time present.   Da Vinci

17244. Rivers are highways that
move on, and bear us whither we wish
to go.   Pascal, *Thoughts*

17245. Follow the river and you will
get to sea.   *Proverb*

17246. All rivers do what they can
for the sea.   *Proverb*

17247.

   I like rivers
Better than Oceans, for we see both
 sides.   E. A. Robinson

17248. There is a river in Macedon,
and there is also moreover a river at
Monmouth; . . . and there is salmons in both.

   Shakespeare, *Henry V*

17249. It is with rivers as it is with
people: the greatest are not always
the most agreeable nor the best to
live with.

  Henry Van Dyke, *Little Rivers*

17250. No matter how long the river,
the river will reach the sea.

    E. F. Ware, *The Blizzard*

See also: 13527.

ROAD

Related Subjects: Travel, Wanderlust.

17251. There is tolerable travelling
on the beaten road, run how it may;
only on the new road not yet levelled
and paved, and on the old road all
broken into ruts and quagmires, is
the travelling bad or impracticable.

CARLYLE,
On Boswell's Life of Johnson

17252.
I shall be telling this with a sigh
Somewhere ages and ages hence:
Two roads diverged in a wood, and
  I—
I took the one less travelled by.
And that has made all the difference.
ROBERT FROST, *The Road Not Taken*

17253.
Does the road wind up-hill all the
  way?
Yes, to the very end.
CHRISTINA ROSSETTI, *Up-Hill*

17254. 'Tis a long road knows no
turning.   SOPHOCLES, *Ajax*

See also: 4154, 10431, 17306.

ROBBER, see Thief

ROBIN

Related Subject: Birds.

17261.
A Robin Redbreast in a cage
Puts all heaven in a rage.
BLAKE,
The Marriage of Heaven and Hell

17262. The household bird, with the
red stomacher.   JOHN DONNE

17263.
Who killed Cock Robin?
  "I," said the Sparrow,

"With my bow and arrow,
  I killed Cock Robin."
Nursery Rhyme

17264.
Call for the robin-redbreast and the
  wren,
Since o'er shady groves they hover,
And with leaves and flowers do cover
The friendless bodies of unburied
  men.
JOHN WEBSTER, *The White Devil*

ROMANCE

Related   Subjects: Adventure,
Love, Mistress, Moon, Passion.

17271. Romance, like a ghost, eludes
touching. It is always where you
were, not where you are.
G. W. CURTIS, *Lotus-Eating*

17272. Romance and poetry, ivy, lichens, and wall-flowers, need ruin to
make them grow.
HAWTHORNE,
Preface: The Marble Faun

17273. Every form of human life is
romantic.   T. W. HIGGINSON,
A Plea for Culture

17274.
He loved the twilight that surrounds
The borderland of old romance.
LONGFELLOW,
Tales of a Wayside Inn

17275. To romance we owe the spirit
of adventure, the code of honour,
both masculine and feminine.
SANTAYANA,
The Genteel Tradition at Bay

17276. Tradition   wears   a   snowy
beard, romance is always young.
WHITTIER, *Mary Garvin*

17277. When one is in love, one always begins by deceiving oneself, and
one always ends by deceiving others.

That is what the world calls a romance.   OSCAR WILDE,
The Picture of Dorian Gray

17278.
Romance should never begin with
sentiment.
It should begin with science and end
with a settlement.
OSCAR WILDE, *An Ideal Husband*

17279. To say "mither" instead of
"mother" seems to many the acme of
romance.   OSCAR WILDE,
Romantic Poems & Ballads

17280. Nothing spoils a romance so
much as a sense of humour in the
woman.   OSCAR WILDE,
A Woman of No Importance

See also: 3629, 4444, 17304, 19312.

ROME AND THE ROMANS

**Related Subjects: Europe, Greece,
History, Italy.**

17281. When they are at Rome, they
do there as they see done.
ROBERT BURTON,
Anatomy of Melancholy

17282. O Rome! my country! city of
the soul!   BYRON, *Childe Harold*

17283. Rome? The city of all time,
and of all the world!
HAWTHORNE, *The Marble Faun*

17284. Rome was not built in a day.
Proverb

17285. It is hard to sit in Rome and
fight wi' the pope.   *Proverb*

17286. I am more an antique Roman
than a Dane.
SHAKESPEARE, *Hamlet*

17287. This was the noblest Roman
of them all.
SHAKESPEARE, *Julius Caesar*

17288. The last of all the Romans,
fare thee well!
SHAKESPEARE, *Julius Caesar*

See also: 2684, 2688, 2765, 2955,
3470, 6165, 14773.

ROSE

Related Subject: Flowers.

17291.
                Any nose
May ravage with impunity a rose.
BROWNING, *Sordello*

17292. But ne'er the rose without the
thorn.   ROBERT HERRICK, *The Rose*

17293. A Rose is sweeter in the
budde than full blowne.
JOHN LYLY,
Euphues & his England

17294.
'Tis the last rose of summer
    Left blooming alone.
THOMAS MOORE,
The Last Rose of Summer

17295.
The rose looks fair, but fairer we it
    deem
For that sweet odour which doth in
    it live. SHAKESPEARE, *Sonnet LIV*

See also: 423, 1536, 2521, 2958,
13665, 17713.

RUIN

**Related Subjects: Chaos, Decay,
Desolation, Failure, Fall, Misfortune.**

17301. All men that are ruined, are
ruined on the side of their natural
propensities.
BURKE, *On a Regicide Peace*

17302.
Stern Ruin's ploughshare drives elate,
    Full on the bloom.
BURNS, *To a Mountain Daisy*

17303. Men moralise among ruins.
DISRAELI, *Tancred*

17304.
There's a fascination frantic
In a ruin that's romantic.
W. S. GILBERT, *The Mikado*

17305. With ruin upon ruin, rout on rout.   MILTON, *Paradise Lost*

17306. The road to ruin is always in good repair; the travellers pay the expense of it.   *Proverb*

17307. Remains of rude magnificence.   SCOTT, *Marmion*

17308.
Thou art the ruins of the noblest man
That ever lived in the tide of times.
SHAKESPEARE, *Julius Caesar*

17309. Red ruin, and the breaking up of laws.
TENNYSON, *Idylls of the King*

See also: 11509, 16868, 17314.

RULE

Related Subjects: Dictatorship, Government, Grammar, Habit, Kings, Tyranny.

17311. Better no rule than cruel rule.
AESOP, *The Frogs Desiring a King*

17312. No rule is so general, which admits not some exception.
ROBERT BURTON,
Anatomy of Melancholy

17313.
For all a rhetorician's rules
Teach nothing but to name his tools.
SAMUEL BUTLER, *Hudibras*

17314. Resolv'd to ruin or to rule the state.
DRYDEN, *Absalom & Achitophel*

17315. He who rules must humor full as much as he commands.
GEORGE ELIOT

17316. No man ruleth safely but he that is willingly ruled.
THOMAS À KEMPIS,
Of the Imitation of Christ

17317. No ruler good save God.
Proverb

17318. He that hath a fellow-ruler, hath an over-ruler.   *Proverb*

17319. Ill can he rule the great, that cannot reach the small.
EDMUND SPENSER,
The Faerie Queene

See also: 745, 771, 1161, 3013, 10735, 15694.

RUMOR

Related Subjects: News, Scandal.

17321. She has a nice sense of rumor.
JOHN H. CUTLER

17322.
He's gone, and who knows how he may report
Thy words by adding fuel to the flame? MILTON, *Samson Agonistes*

17323. I believe there is nothing amongst mankind swifter than rumor.
PLAUTUS, *Fragments*

17324. Rumour is a great traveller.
Proverb

17325. In calamity any rumor is believed. PUBLILIUS SYRUS, *Sententiae*

17326.
I cannot tell how the truth may be;
I tell the tale as 'twas said to me.
SCOTT, *The Lay of the Last Minstrel*

17327.
Upon my tongues continual slanders ride,
The which in every language I pronounce,
Stuffing the ears of men with false reports.   SHAKESPEARE, *Henry IV*

17328.
Rumour doth double, like the voice
and echo,
The numbers of the fear'd.
                    SHAKESPEARE, *Henry IV*

RUST

**Related Subjects: Decay, Iron,
Water.**

17331. It is better to wear out than
to rust out.   BISHOP CUMBERLAND

17332. If I rest, I rust.
                    MARTIN LUTHER, *Maxims*

17333. I were better to be eaten to
death with rust than to be scoured to
nothing with perpetual motion.
                    SHAKESPEARE, *Henry IV*

17334. A sword, a spade, and a
thought should never be allowed to
rust.   JAMES STEPHENS,
                    The Crock of Gold

17335.
How dull it is to pause, to make an
end,
To rust unburnish'd, not to shine in
use.   TENNYSON, *Ulysses*

See also: 937, 9093, 14492, 16986.

S

SABBATH

Related Subjects: Church, Rest.

17341. There are many persons who
look on Sunday as a sponge to wipe
out the sins of the week.
                    H. W. BEECHER

17342. Sunday is the common
people's great Liberty day, and they
are bound to see to it that work does
not come into it.   H. W. BEECHER

17343. God's altar stands from Sunday to Sunday, and the seventh day
is no more for religion than any
other—it is for rest. The whole seven
are for religion, and one of them
for rest, for instruction, for social
worship, for gaining strength for the
other six.   H. W. BEECHER

17344. A world without a Sabbath
would be like a man without a smile,
like a summer without flowers, and
like a homestead without a garden.
It is the joyous day of the whole
week.   H. W. BEECHER

17345. Remember the sabbath day, to
keep it holy. Six days shalt thou labour, and do all thy work: But the

seventh day is the sabbath of the
Lord thy God: in it thou shalt not do
any work, thou, nor thy son, nor thy
daughter, thy manservant, nor thy
maidservant, nor thy cattle, nor thy
stranger that is within thy gates:
For in six days the Lord made heaven
and earth, the sea, and all that in
them is, and rested the seventh day:
wherefore the Lord blessed the sabbath day, and hallowed it.
                    Bible: Exodus, xx, 8-11

17346. The Sabbath was made for
man, and not man for the Sabbath.
                    Bible: Matthew, ii, 27

17347.
Of all the days that's in the week
I dearly love but one day,
And that's the day that comes be-
twixt
A Saturday and Monday.
    HENRY CAREY, *Sally in Our Alley*

17348. I feel as if God had, by giving the Sabbath, given fifty-two
springs in every year.   COLERIDGE

17349. There is a Sunday conscience,
as well as a Sunday coat; and those
who make religion a secondary con-

cern put the coat and conscience carefully by to put on only once a week.
DICKENS

17350.
Some keep the Sabbath going to church;
I keep it staying at home,
With a bobolink for a chorister,
And an orchard for a dome.
EMILY DICKINSON, *Nature*

17351. The Sunday is the core of our civilization, dedicated to thought and reverence. It invites to the noblest solitude and to the noblest society.
EMERSON

17352. Sunday is the golden clasp that binds together the volume of the week. LONGFELLOW

17353. Sunday is like a stile between the fields of toil, where we can kneel and pray, or sit and meditate.
LONGFELLOW

17354. He who ordained the Sabbath loves the poor. LOWELL

17355. The only ground, therefore, on which restrictions on Sunday amusements can be defended must be that they are religiously wrong; a motive of legislation which can never be too earnestly protested against.
J. S. MILL, *On Liberty*

17356. Without a Sabbath, no worship; without worship, no religion; and without religion, no permanent freedom. MONTALEMBERT

17357.
To-morrow our holy day comes,
Which our merciful Father has given,
That we may rest from our work
And prepare for His beautiful Heaven.
NANCY D. SPROAT,
Lullabies for Children

17358. The longer I live the more highly do I estimate the Christian Sabbath, and the more grateful do I feel to those who impress its importance on the community.
DANIEL WEBSTER

See also: 1453, 1907, 1911, 4064, 20031.

SACRIFICE

Related Subjects: Asceticism, Devotion, Hero, Martyr, Self-Denial, Worship.

17361. Greater love hath no man than this, that a man lay down his life for his friend. *Bible: John, xv, 13*

17362. It is a far, far better thing that I do, than I have ever done; it is a far, far better rest that I go to, than I have ever known.
DICKENS, *A Tale of Two Cities*

17363. The value of a sentiment is the amount of sacrifice you are prepared to make for it.
GALSWORTHY, *Windows*

17364. We can offer up much in the large, but to make sacrifices in little things is what we are seldom equal to.
GOETHE

17365. I am completely opposed to the idea of one generation sacrificing itself to those following it. History has always shown that to be a fool's bargain. JULES ROMAINS, *I Believe*

17366. Our virtues are dearer to us the more we have had to suffer for them. It is the same with our children. All profound affection admits a sacrifice. VAUVENARGUES

17367.
Too long a sacrifice
Can make a stone of the heart.
W. B. YEATS, *Easter, 1916*

See also: 907, 1243, 6370, 9691.

SADNESS, see Grief, Melancholy, Sorrow

SAFETY

Related Subjects: Caution, Danger, Insurance, Prevention, Protection, Security.

17371.
> Safe shall be my going,
> Secretly armed against all death's endeavor;
> Safe though all safety's lost, safe where men fall;
> And if these poor limbs die, safest of all.   RUPERT BROOKE, *Safety*

17372. The idea that you can purchase safety by throwing a small state to the wolves is a fatal delusion.
WINSTON CHURCHILL

17373. There is no right to strike against the public safety to anybody, anywhere, any time.
CALVIN COOLIDGE

17374. The coast was clear.
MICHAEL DRAYTON, *Nymphidia*

17375. That indeed were a world fit to perish, wherein the moralist had set up the ignoble maxim: Safety first.
HAVELOCK ELLIS,
Little Essays on Love and Virtue

17376. He that's secure is not safe.
FRANKLIN, *Poor Richard*

17377. A gifted small girl has explained that pins are a great means of saving life, "by not swallowing them."
C. E. MONTAGUE, *Dramatic Values*

17378.
The strongest tower has not the highest wall.

Think well of this, when you sit safe at home.   WILLIAM MORRIS,
The Earthly Paradise

17379. Better ride safe in the dark, says the proverb, than in daylight with a cut-throat at your elbow.
SCOTT, *Kenilworth*

17380. Be wary, then; best safety lies in fear.   SHAKESPEARE, *Hamlet*

17381. A ship in harbor is safe, but that is not what ships are built for.
J. A. SHEDD, *Salt from My Attic*

See also: 2235, 2592, 4287, 4911, 5459, 14171.

SAILOR

Related Subjects: Navy, Sea, Ship, War.

17391.
For if bold tars are Fortune's sport,
Still are they Fortune's care.
CHARLES DIBDIN, *The Blind Sailor*

17392. The wonder is always new that any sane man can be a sailor.
EMERSON, *English Traits*

17393. Your seamen are like your element, always tempestuous.
GEORGE FARQUHAR,
Sir Harry Wildaire

17394.
Now landsmen all, whoever you may be,
If you want to rise to the top of the tree,
If your soul isn't fettered to an office stool,
Be careful to be guided by this golden rule—
Stick close to your desks and never go to sea,
And you all may be Rulers of the Queen's Navee!
W. S. GILBERT, *H. M. S. Pinafore*

17395. Sailors should never be shy.
W. S. Gilbert, *H. M. S. Pinafore*

17396.
Of all the husbands on the earth,
The sailor has the finest berth,
For in 'is cabin he can sit
And sail and sail—and let 'er knit.
Wallace Irwin, *A Grain of Salt*

17397. There were gentlemen and there were seamen in the navy of Charles the Second. But the seamen were not gentlemen; and the gentlemen were not seamen.
Macaulay, *History of England*

17398. A white color is a disgrace in a sailor; he should be swarthy from the sea-water and the rays of the sun.   Ovid, *Art of Love*

17399.
Six days shalt thou labor and do all thou art able,
The seventh, holystone the deck and scrub the cable.
The Sailor's Catechism

17400. Tell that to the marines—the sailors won't believe it.
Scott, *Redgauntlet*

17401.
Like a drunken sailor on a mast;
Ready, with every nod, to tumble down
Into the fatal bowels of the deep.
Shakespeare, *Richard III*

17402. A seafaring man may have a sweetheart in every port; but he should steer clear of a wife as he would avoid a quicksand.
Smollett,
*The Adventures of Sir
Launcelot Greaves*

SAINT

Related Subjects: **Angel, Martyr, Paradise, Virtue.**

17411. Precious in the sight of the Lord is the death of his saints.
Bible: Psalms, cxvi, 15

17412. Every saint, as every man, comes one day to be superfluous.
Emerson, *Journals*

17413. A saint is a sceptic once in every twenty-four hours.
Emerson, *Journals*

17414. I don't like your way of conditioning and contracting with the saints. Do this and I'll do that! Here's one for t'other. Save me and I'll give you a taper or go on a pilgrimage.
Erasmus, *The Shipwreck*

17415.
Those Saints, which God loves best,
The Devil tempts not least.
Robert Herrick, *Temptation*

17416. The worst of madmen is a saint run mad.   Horace

17417. The way of this world is to praise dead saints and persecute living ones.   Nathaniel Howe

17418. 'Twould a saint provoke.
Pope, *Moral Essays*

17419. When it pleaseth not God, the saint can do little.   *Proverb*

17420. All are not saints that go to church.   *Proverb*

17421. The saint who works no miracles has few pilgrims. *Proverb*

17422. A young Saint an old Devil, (mark this, an old saying, and as true a one, as a young Whore an old Saint).   Rabelais·

17423. It is easier to make a saint out of a libertine than out of a prig.

SANTAYANA

17424.

O cunning enemy, that, to catch a
   saint,
With saints, dost bait thy hook!

SHAKESPEARE, *Measure for Measure*

17425. A saint may be defined as a person of heroic virtue whose private judgment is privileged.

BERNARD SHAW, *Saint Joan*

17426. The only difference between the saint and the sinner is that every saint has a past and every sinner has a future.   OSCAR WILDE,
   A Woman of No Importance

See also: 4259, 5686, 15748.

SALESMEN AND SALESMANSHIP

Related Subjects: **Advertising, Commerce, Competition.**

17431. You may be proud of your big plants. But unless you can twist this into a potent sales argument, you had better keep your pride to yourself. You want somebody to give you money, and not praise.

JAMES R. ADAMS,
   More Power to Advertising

17432. The concerns that are most successful are those that know the most about their prospective customers.   ROGER BABSON,
   Business Fundamentals

17433. Wholesaler or retailer, when your sales efforts are based on a statistical knowledge of your customer's business, when all wasted effort is eliminated by directing your energies straight to the concern or individual

with the buying power, then you are selling scientifically.

ROGER BABSON,
   Business Fundamentals

17434. To be sure it is possible to insist continually and obstinately that a person buy a particular thing and thus to produce the desired response. But such a technique is more likely to succeed if applied with finesse rather than by brute force. Most persons resent a blunt command. We like to feel that we are the captains of our souls and that we are doing what we please although, as a matter of fact, we probably are not doing so ten per cent of the time.

HAROLD E. BURTT,
   Psychology of Advertising

17435. It is desirable, on occasion, to scare a person into purchasing something. Everyone can be frightened by a wild animal or a revolver under appropriate circumstances, and if the advertisement is properly devised it is possible to arouse this same fear instinct: "Scare copy" is particularly appropriate in selling safety devices, things which are conducive to health, and some kinds of insurance.

HAROLD E. BURTT,
   Psychology of Advertising

17436. If a person can be induced to do something in connection with a product he is more likely to remember it. . . . The personal salesman has an advantage in that he can actually hand the prospect the egg beater to turn or induce him to step into the car and drive it.

HAROLD E. BURTT,
   Psychology of Advertising

17437. Salesmanship and advertising are twin sisters. It is hard to tell 'em apart.   ELBERT HUBBARD

17438. With so many legitimate methods of selling, why resort to the "take-a-chance" method, which is a species of gambling and against public policy?   I. E. LAMBERT,
Marquis of Queensbury Rules of Modern Business

17439. To them, the Romantic Hero was no longer the knight, the wandering poet, the cowpuncher, the aviator, nor the brave young district attorney, but the great sales-manager, who had an Analysis of Merchandizing Problems on his glass-topped desk, whose title of nobility was "go-getter", and who devoted himself and all his young samurai to the cosmic purpose of Selling—not of selling anything in particular, for or to anybody in particular, but pure Selling.
SINCLAIR LEWIS, *Babbitt*

17440. When I see a merchant overpolite to his customers, begging them to taste a little brandy and throwing half his goods on the counter,—thinks I, that man has an axe to grind.
CHARLES MINER,
Who'll Turn Grindstones

17441. Pleasing ware is half sold.
Proverb

17442. To things of sale a seller's praise belongs.   SHAKESPEARE,
Love's Labour's Lost

17443. For *completely* honorable methods of selling goods will necessitate honorable practices throughout the production process, because shoddy materials and bad workmanship must be misrepresented if they are to hold their own in the competitive field.   SHARP & FOX,
Business Ethics

17444. Everyone lives by selling something.   STEVENSON, *Beggars*

SALT

Related Subjects: Meat, Taste.

17451. Ye are the salt of the earth: but if the salt have lost his savour, wherewith shall it be salted?
Bible: Matthew, v, 13

17452. Salt of truth.
ELIZABETH B. BROWNING,
Aurora Leigh

17453. With a grain of salt.
CERVANTES, *Don Quixote*

17454. Salt seasons all things.
JOHN FLORIO, *Second Fruites*

17455. It is a foolish bird that stayeth the laying of salt on her tail.
JOHN LYLY,
Euphues & His England

17456. Not worth his salt.
PETRONIUS, *Satyricon*

17457. If you take away the salt, you may throw the flesh to the dogs.
Proverb

17458. Spilt salt is never all gathered.
Proverb

17459. We have some salt of our youth in us.   SHAKESPEARE,
The Merry Wives of Windsor

17460. Salt tears.   SHAKESPEARE,
A Midsummer-Night's Dream

See also: 2091, 8625.

SALVATION

Related Subjects: The Bible, Christ, Death, Eternity, God, Judgment Day, Paradise, Religion, Repentance, Righteousness.

17461. Work out your own salvation.
Bible: Philippians, ii, 12

17462.

If goodness lead him not, yet weariness

  May toss him to my breast.

      GEORGE HERBERT, *The Pulley*

17463. The whole structure of my
world would break down were I to
believe that another than myself could
give me salvation.

      EMIL LUDWIG, *I Believe*

17464.

When I can read my title clear

  To mansions in the skies,

I'll bid farewell to every fear,

  And wipe my weeping eyes.

      ISAAC WATTS,

      Hymns & Spiritual Songs

See also: 3275.

SANITY AND INSANITY

Related Subjects: Eccentricity,
Psychoanalysis, Psychology, Suicide.

17471. Clothed, and in his right
mind.   *Bible: Matthew, v, 15*

17472. He who would walk sanely
amid the opposing perils in the path
of life always needs a little optimism;
he also needs a little pessimism.

      HAVELOCK ELLIS,

      The Dance of Life

17473. One mad action is not enough
to prove a man mad.   *Proverb*

Insanity

17474. Babylon in all its desolation
is a sight not so awful as that of the
human mind in ruins.

      SCROPE DAVIES

17475. For many centuries the insane were regarded as demoniacs and
were consequently often handed over
to the exorcist or even to the execu-

tioner, when they were not completely abandoned. In later times they
were frequently treated as criminals
and paupers and as such came under
the supervision of penal and poor law
authorities.   ALBERT DEUTSCH,

    Treatment of the Mentally Ill in

              America

17476.

    There is a pleasure sure

In being mad which none but madmen know.   DRYDEN,

      The Spanish Friar

17477. No man is quite sane. Each
has a vein of folly in his composition
—a slight determination of blood to
the head, to make sure of holding
him hard to some one point which he
has taken to heart.   EMERSON

17478. Those whom God wishes to
destroy, he first deprives of their
senses.   EURIPIDES

17479. Insane people easily detect
the nonsense of other people.

      JOHN HALLAM

17480. Insanity is often the logic of
an accurate mind overtaxed.

      O. W. HOLMES,

  The Autocrat of the Breakfast-Table

17481. All power of fancy over reason is a degree of insanity.

      SAMUEL JOHNSON

17482. The difference between an insane man and a fool is, that a fool
from right principles draws a wrong
conclusion, while an insane person
draws a just inference from false
principles.   LOCKE

17483. The question is not yet settled,
whether madness is or is not the
loftiest intelligence—whether much
that is glorious—whether all that is
profound—does not spring from dis-

ease of thought—from moods of mind exalted at the expense of the general intellect.   POE, *Eleanora*

17484. If madness were pain, you'd hear outcries in every house.
Proverb

17485. As mad as a March hare.
Proverb

17486. Unemployment, overwork, congestion of population, child labor, and the hundred economic factors which increase the stress of living for the poor are often contributing factors in the production of mental disease.   T. W. SALMON

17487.
That he is mad, 'tis true; 'tis true 'tis pity;
And pity 'tis 'tis true.
SHAKESPEARE, *Hamlet*

17488. Oh! that way madness lies; let me shun that.
SHAKESPEARE, *King Lear*

17489. Mental disorder, as we ordinarily meet it, is a disorder of the individual as a social unit. It is not a purely individual affair like an infection, for instance, but is a disorder of the individual at the level of social adjustment.   WILLIAM A. WHITE

See also: 173, 863, 1205, 1320, 1487, 1917, 3224, 8858, 10054, 11554, 12894, 12965, 13326, 13982, 17416.

SARCASM

Related Subjects: Irony, Mockery, Ridicule, Satire.

17491. He that cometh to seek after knowledge with a mind to scorn and censure shall be sure to find matter for his humor, but none for his instruction.   BACON

17492. At the best, sarcasms, bitter irony, scathing wit, are a sort of sword-play of the mind. You pink your adversary, and he is forthwith dead; and then you deserve to be hung for it.   C. N. BOVEE

17493. Sarcasm I now see to be, in general, the language of the Devil; for which reason I have, long since, as good as renounced it.
CARLYLE, *Sartor Resartus*

17494. A true sarcasm is like a swordstick—it appears, at first sight, to be much more innocent, than it really is, till, all of a sudden, there leaps something out of it—sharp and deadly and incisive—which makes you tremble and recoil.
SYDNEY SMITH

See also: 1113, 12384.

SATAN, see Devil

SATIETY

Related Subject: Boredom.

17501. There is no sense of weariness like that which closes a day of eager and unintermitted pursuit of pleasure. The apple is eaten and the core sticks in the throat. Expectation has given way to ennui, and appetite to satiety.   C. N. BOVEE

17502. The feeling of satiety, almost inseparable from large possessions, is a surer cause of misery than ungratified desires.   DISRAELI, *Lothair*

17503. The best of things, beyond their measure, cloy.   HOMER, *Iliad*

17504.
Where's the eye, however blue,
Doth not weary? Where's the face
One would meet in every place?

Where's the voice, however soft,
One would hear so very oft?
                    KEATS, *Fancy*

17505. Often devotion to virtue arises from sated desire.
              LAURENCE HOPE,
I Arise and Go Down to the River

17506. Satiety comes of too frequent repetition; and he who will not give himself leisure to be thirsty can never find the true pleasure of drinking.
              MONTAIGNE, *Essays*

17507. Better go away longing than loathing.   *Proverb*

17508. Enough, with over-measure.
              SHAKESPEARE, *Coriolanus*

17509.
To loathe the taste of sweetness, whereof a little
More than a little is by much too much.   SHAKESPEARE, *Henry IV*

17510.
As a surfeit of the sweetest things
The deepest loathing to the stomach brings.   SHAKESPEARE,
          A Midsummer-Night's Dream

17511.
Spare diet is the cause love lasts,
For surfeits sooner kill than fasts.
              SIR JOHN SUCKLING,
                Against Absence

See also: 7325, 7864, 15340, 19265.

SATIRE

Related Subjects: Caricature, Humor, Irony, Mockery, Sarcasm.

17521. Lampoons and satires, that are written with wit and spirit, are like poisoned darts, which not only inflict a wound, but make it incurable.
              ADDISON

17522.
But satire, ever moral, ever new,
Delights the reader and instructs him, too,
She, if good sense refine her sterling page,
Oft shakes some rooted folly of the age.   BOILEAU, *Satires*

17523. Fools are my theme, let satire be my song.   BYRON,
English Bards & Scotch Reviewers

17524.
By satire kept in awe, they shrink from
Ridicule, though not from law.
                    BYRON

17525. True satire is not the sneering substance that we know, but satire that includes the satirist.
              FRANK M. COLBY, *Essays*

17526. Of a bitter satirist—Swift, for instance—it might be said, that the person or thing on which his satire fell shrivelled up as if the devil had spit on it.   HAWTHORNE

17527.
Satire's my weapon, but I'm too discreet
To run amuck, and tilt at all I meet.
                    HORACE

17528. In the present state of the world it is difficult not to write lampoons.   JUVENAL

17529.
Satire or sense, alas! can Sporus feel?
Who breaks a butterfly upon a wheel?
    POPE, *Epistle to Dr. Arbuthnot*

17530. Satires run faster than panegyrics.   *Proverb*

17531. Satire is a sort of glass, wherein beholders generally discover everybody's face but their own; which is the chief reason for the reception it meets in the world, and that so very few are offended with it.   SWIFT

17532. It is as hard to satirize well a man of distinguished vices, as to praise well a man of distinguished virtues.   SWIFT

17533. Satire! thou shining supplement of public laws.
EDWARD YOUNG

See also: 3282, 10651, 12384, 12385.

SAVAGERY

Related Subjects: Cruelty, Indian.

17541.
They led their wild desires to woods and caves,
And thought that all but savages were slaves.   DRYDEN,
Absalom & Achitophel

17542. Dirty savages, extemporizing from hand to mouth.   EMERSON,
Lectures

17543. This is the bloodiest shame, the wildest savagery.
SHAKESPEARE, *King John*

17544. A rude and savage man of Ind.   SHAKESPEARE,
Love's Labour's Lost

See also: 1597, 1654, 3465, 5596.

SAVING, see Thrift

SCANDAL

Related Subjects: Appearance, Calumny, Columnists, Curiosity, Meddler, News, Rumor, Tale.

17551. Tell it not in Gath, publish it not in the streets of Askelon.
Bible: 2 Samuel, i, 20

17552. Tattlers also, and busybodies, speaking things which they ought not.
Bible: 1 Timothy, v, 13

17553. Dead scandals form good subjects for dissection.   BYRON,
Don Juan

17554. In the case of scandal, as in that of robbery, the receiver is always thought as bad as the thief.
LORD CHESTERFIELD, *Letters*

17555.
Talk of unusual swell of waist
In maid of honour loosely laced.
MATTHEW GREEN, *The Spleen*

17556. Gossip is vice enjoyed vicariously.   ELBERT HUBBARD, *Philistine*

17557.
Knowing, what all experience serves to show,
No mud can soil us but the mud we throw.   LOWELL,
Epistle to George William Curtis

17558. It is at home, not in public, one washes one's dirty linen.
NAPOLEON

17559. You do not know it but you are the talk of all the town.
OVID, *Art of Love*

17560. Scandal has ever been the doom of beauty.   PROPERTIUS

17561. Gossips and tale-bearers set on fire all the houses they enter.
Proverb

17562. A lie has no legs, but a scandal has wings.   *Proverb*

17563. Her tea she sweetens, as she sips, with scandal.   SAMUEL ROGERS

17564. To babble and to talk is more tolerable and not to be endured.
SHAKESPEARE,
Much Ado About Nothing

17565. For greatest scandal waits on greatest state.   SHAKESPEARE,
The Rape of Lucrece

17566. Ladies, your most obedient.— Mercy on me! here is the whole set! a character dead at every word, I suppose. SHERIDAN, *The School for Scandal*

17567. Well, for my part, I believe there never was a scandalous tale without some foundation.

SHERIDAN, *School for Scandal*

17568. No scandal about Queen Elizabeth, I hope? SHERIDAN, *The Critic*

17569. Every man hath in his own life sins enough, in his own minde trouble enough: so that curiositie after the affairs of others cannot be without envy and an evil minde. What is it to me if my Neighbours Grandfather were a Syrian, or his Grandmother illegitimate, or that another is indebted five thousand pounds, or whether his wife be expensive?

JEREMY TAYLOR, *Holy Living*

17570.
Never yet
Was noble man but made ignoble talk. TENNYSON, *Idylls of the King*

17571.
Ye think the rustic cackle of your bourg
The murmur of the world!

TENNYSON, *Idylls of the King*

See also: 27, 10685.

SCHOLAR

Related Subjects: Culture, Education, Knowledge, Learning, School, Study, Teacher, University.

17581. We can make majors and officers every year, but not scholars.

ROBERT BURTON, *Anatomy of Melancholy*

17582. The world's great men have not commonly been great scholars, nor its great scholars great men.

O. W. HOLMES, *The Autocrat of the Breakfast-Table*

17583. Who robs a scholar, robs the public. *Proverb*

17584. Every good scholar is not a good schoolmaster. *Proverb*

17585. A scholar may be gulled thrice; a soldier but once. *Proverb*

17586. The classics have scarcely lost in absolute value as a voucher of scholastic respectability, since for this purpose it is only necessary that the scholar should be able to put in evidence some learning which is conventionally recognized as evidence of wasted time.

THORSTEIN VEBLEN, *The Theory of the Leisure Class*

17587.
Up! Up! my friend, and quit your books;
Or surely you'll grow double;
Up! up! my friend, and clear your looks;
Why all this toil and trouble?

WORDSWORTH, *The Tables Turned*

See also: 2339, 2796, 8292, 16491, 16542.

SCHOOL

Related Subjects: Books, Education, Grammar, Knowledge, Learning, Pedantry, Scholar, Study, Teacher, Teaching, University.

17591. The nation that has the schools has the future. BISMARCK

17592. "Reeling and Writhing, of course, to begin with," the Mock Turtle replied, "and the different branches of Arithmetic—Ambition,

Distraction, Uglification, and Derision." LEWIS CARROLL,
Alice in Wonderland

17593.
Better build schoolrooms for "the boy"
Than cells and gibbets for "the man."
ELIZA COOK,
A Song for the Ragged Schools

17594. The sounding jargon of the schools. COWPER, *Truth*

17595. There is now less flogging in our great schools than formerly, but then less is learned there; so that what the boys get at one end they lose at the other.
SAMUEL JOHNSON, *Boswell: Life*

17596.
Still sits the school-house by the road,
A ragged beggar sunning;
Around it still the sumachs grow
And blackberry vines are running.
WHITTIER, *In School Days*

See also: 2419, 5280, 7264, 7445.

SCIENCE

Related Subjects: **Alchemy, Astronomy, Electricity, Evolution, Industry, Invention, Knowledge, Learning, Machinery, Mathematics, Progress.**

17601. Science falsely so called.
Bible: 1 Timothy, vi, 20

17602. In science, address the few, in literature the many. In science, the few must dictate opinion to the many; in literature, the many, sooner or later, force their judgment on the few. BULWER-LYTTON, *Caxtonia*

17603. When one longs for a drink, it seems as though one could drink a whole ocean—that is faith; but when one begins to drink one can drink altogether two glasses—that is science. ANTON CHEKHOV

17604. In science we must be interested in things, not in persons.
MARIE CURIE, *Curie: Madame Curie*

17605. There were no patents. We were working in the interests of science. Radium was not to enrich anyone. Radium is an element. It belongs to all people.
MARIE CURIE, *Pierre Curie*

17606. The discoveries of Nobel—powerful explosives, have made it possible for men to achieve admirable things, but they are also a terrible means of destruction in the hands of those great criminals who draw nations into war. I am among those who believe with Nobel that humanity will obtain more good than evil from future discoveries.
PIERRE CURIE,
Address: Nobel Conference, 1903

17607. It is possible to conceive that in criminal hands radium might prove very dangerous, and the question therefore, arises whether it be to the advantage of humanity to know the secrets of nature, whether we be sufficiently mature to profit by them, or whether that knowledge may not prove harmful. PIERRE CURIE,
Address: Nobel Conference, 1903

17608. By your works you may be known. Your triumphs in the mechanical arts are the obverse of your failure in all that calls for spiritual insight. G. LOWES DICKINSON,
Letters from a Chinese Official

17609. I believe in the scientific spirit, but I dislike the scientific manner when it forsakes the ponderable for the imponderable values.
ELLEN GLASGOW, *I Believe*

17610. While bright-eyed Science watches round.
THOMAS GRAY, *Ode for Music*

17611. Science is vastly more stimulating to the imagination than are the classics. J. B. S. HALDANE, *Daedalus*

17612. The cultural claims of science rest on the social fact that the use and misuse of science intimately affects the everyday life of every citizen in a modern community.
LANCELOT HOGBEN,
Dangerous Thoughts

17613. Where the telescope ends, the microscope begins. Which of the two has the grander view?
VICTOR HUGO, *Les Miserables*

17614. The cradle of every science is surrounded by dead theologians as that of Hercules was with strangled serpents. THOMAS H. HUXLEY

17615. Science, particularly mathematics, though it seems less practical and less real than the news contained in the latest radio dispatches, appears to be building the one permanent and stable edifice in an age where all others are either crumbling or being blown to bits.
KASNER & NEWMAN,
Mathematics & the Imagination

17616. Thus, in a certain sense, the popularization of science is a duty to be performed, a duty to give courage and comfort to the men and women of good-will everywhere who are generally losing their faith in the life of reason. For most of the sciences the veil of mystery is gradually being torn asunder.
KASNER & NEWMAN,
Mathematics & the Imagination

17617. The rise of science has undoubtedly filled mankind with a new vision of, a new hope for, and a new effort toward a better human existence than the world has known in the past. If this is exalting the material

over the spiritual then she must again plead guilty. ROBERT A. MILLIKAN

17618. The next great task of Science is to create a religion for humanity.
JOHN MORLEY, *Essays*

17619. The scientist has always appealed to me because in the artistic world, which today lacks all standards, it is a relief to come across a mind which accepts nothing but fact and is even doubtful of that; which realizes that nothing can be established without constant experiment. Unlike literary people, scientists know what people are really like, and they accept humanity as it is, without that censoriousness which seems the main urge of many writers.
C. R. W. NEVINSON

17620. I chiefly owe to my illustrious teacher, Thomas Henry Huxley, the conviction that devotion to pure scientific research and fellowship with the scientific fraternity do not release one from his duty to his less fortunate fellow-men and to the community in which he lives.
HENRY F. OSBORN, *Evolution*

17621. In science the credit goes to the man who convinces the world, not to the man to whom the idea first occurs. SIR WILLIAM OSLER,
Life of Sir William Osler

17622. Science expresses in human terms our dynamic relation to surrounding reality.
SANTAYANA, *I Believe*

17623. Science is always wrong. It never solves a problem without creating ten more. BERNARD SHAW

17624. What is the sum of physical science? Compared with the comprehensible universe and with conceivable time, not to speak of infinity and eternity, it is the observation of a mere point, the experience of an instant.   GOLDWIN SMITH, *The Study of History*

17625. Science carries us into zones of speculation, where there is no habitable city for the mind of man.
STEVENSON, *Pulvis et Umbra*

17626. The development of modern science is secured not by the progress of any special branch of knowledge, but rather by the united efforts of various sciences and their mutual assistance in this striving forward.
SUN YAT-SEN,
Memoirs of a Chinese Revolutionary

17627. In all science error precedes the truth, and it is better it should go first than last. SIR ROBERT WALPOLE

17628. Science is even more changeable than theology. No man of science could subscribe without qualification to Galileo's beliefs, or to Newton's beliefs, or to all his own scientific beliefs of ten years ago.
ALFRED NORTH WHITEHEAD

See also: 1183, 1494, 1500, 2303, 2914, 2915, 3474, 4504, 5453, 5493, 7562, 7684, 8856, 9857, 20215, 20836, 21395.

SCORN

Related Subjects: **Anger, Contempt, Disgrace, Indifference, Rebuke, Shame, Superiority.**

17631. He will laugh thee to scorn.
Apocrypha: Ecclesiasticus

17632.
Of all the griefs that harass the distrest,
Sure the most bitter is a scornful jest.
SAMUEL JOHNSON, *London*

17633.
A dismal universal hiss, the sound
Of public scorn.
MILTON, *Paradise Lost*

17634. He despises me, I suppose, because I live in an alley: tell him his soul lives in an alley.
BEN JONSON, *of James I*

17635. Scorn at first makes after-love the more.   *Proverb*

17636. What! my dear Lady Disdain! are you yet living?
SHAKESPEARE,
Much Ado About Nothing

17637.
But, alas! to make me
A fixed figure for the time of scorn
To point his slow and moving finger
at!   SHAKESPEARE, *Othello*

See also: 800, 2496, 3394, 7007, 9612, 11951, 12323, 18218, 19757.

SCOTLAND AND THE SCOTCH

Related Subjects: **England, Thrift.**

17641.
The German heart is stout and true, the German arm is strong,
The German foot goes seldom back where armed foemen throng;
But never had they faced in field so stern a charge before,
And never had they felt the sweep of Scotland's broad claymore.
W. E. AYTOUN,
The Island of the Scots

17642. So much of what is great in Scotland has sprung from the closeness of the family ties.
J. M. BARRIE, *Margaret Ogilvy*

17643. Much may be made of a Scotchman if he be caught young.
SAMUEL JOHNSON, *Boswell: Life*

17644. The noblest prospect which a Scotchman ever sees, is the high-road that leads him to England.

SAMUEL JOHNSON, *Boswell: Life*

17645. My foot is on my native heath, and my name is MacGregor.

SCOTT, *Rob Roy*

17646. Stands Scotland where it did?

SHAKESPEARE, *Macbeth*

17647. That knuckle-end of England, —that land of Calvin, oat-cakes, and sulphur.   SYDNEY SMITH,
Lady Holland's Memoir

SCRATCHING

17651. Scratching is one of the pleasantest gratifications of nature, especially with the hand.

MONTAIGNE, *Essays*

17652. 'Tis better than riches to scratch when it itches.   *Proverb*

17653. Scratch my head, Peaseblossom.   SHAKESPEARE,
A Midsummer-Night's Dream

17654.
She loved not the savour of tar nor of pitch,
Yet a sailor might scratch her where'er she did itch.

SHAKESPEARE, *The Tempest*

17655. I would thou didst itch from head to foot and I had the scratching of thee.   SHAKESPEARE,
Troilus and Cressida

See also: 2893, 6771.

SCULPTURE

Related Subjects: Art, Painting.

17661.
I've seen much finer women, ripe and real,
Than all the nonsense of their stone ideal.   BYRON, *Don Juan*

17662.
A sculptor wields
The chisel, and the stricken marble grows
To beauty.
BRYANT, *The Flood of Years*

17663. The statue is then beautiful when it begins to be incomprehensible.   EMERSON, *Essays*

17664.
The more the marble wastes,
The more the statue grows.
MICHELANGELO

17665.
Where the statue stood
Of Newton with his prism and silent face,
The marble index of a mind forever
Voyaging through strange seas of thought, alone.
WORDSWORTH, *The Prelude*

See also: 181.

SEA, THE

Related Subjects: Fish, Navy, River, Sailor, Ship, Tide, Travel, Wanderlust, Water.

17671. They that go down to the sea in ships, that do business in great waters.   *Bible: Psalms, cvii, 23*

17672. Old ocean's gray and melancholy waste.   BRYANT, *Thanatopsis*

17673.
Roll on, thou deep and dark blue ocean, roll!
Ten thousand fleets sweep over thee in vain;
Man marks the earth with ruin,—his control
Stops with the shore.
BYRON, *Childe Harold*

17674.
He sinks into thy depths with bubbling groan,

Without a grave, unknell'd, uncof-
fin'd, and unknown.
               BYRON, *Childe Harold*

17675.
Thou glorious mirror, where the Al-
   mighty's form
Glasses itself in tempests.
               BYRON, *Childe Harold*

17676.
What are the wild waves saying,
   Sister, the whole day long,
That ever amid our playing
   I hear but their low, lone song?
               J. E. CARPENTER,
What Are the Wild Waves Saying

17677. The sea never changes and
its works, for all the talk of men, are
wrapped in mystery.
        JOSEPH CONRAD, *Typhoon*

17678. I have known the sea too long
to believe in its respect for decency.
        JOSEPH CONRAD, *Typhoon*

17679.
Of thousands, thou, both sepulchre
   and pall,
Old Ocean!   R. H. DANA,
             The Little Beach-Bird

17680. The Sea is as deepe in a
calme, as in a storme.
         JOHN DONNE, *Sermons*

17681.
The sea, unmated creature, tired and
   lone,
Makes on its desolate sands eternal
   moan.   F. W. FABER,
           The Sorrowful World

17682. I have a profound respect for
the sea as a moral teacher. No man
can be tossed about upon it without
feeling his impotence and insignificance. CHARLES B. FAIRBANKS,
           My Unknown Chum

17683. The sea possesses a power
over one's moods that has the effect

of a will. The sea can hypnotize. Nature in general can do so.
               IBSEN,
The Lady From the Sea: Notes

17684.
It keeps eternal whisperings around
   Desolate shores, and with its
     mighty swell
   Gluts twice ten thousand caverns.
           KEATS, *On the Sea*

17685.
Who hath desired the Sea?—the sight
   of salt water unbounded—
The heave and the halt and the hurl
   and the crash of the comber wind-
   hounded?   KIPLING,
         The Sea and the Hills

17686.
They went to sea in a sieve, they did;
   In a sieve they went to sea;
In spite of all their friends could say.
      EDWARD LEAR, *The Jumblies*

17687. There is nothing so desperately monotonous as the sea, and I no
longer wonder at the cruelty of pirates.   LOWELL, *Fireside Travels*

17688.
I must go down to the seas again, to
   the lonely sea and the sky,
And all I ask is a tall ship and a
   star to steer her by.
        JOHN MASEFIELD, *Sea-Fever*

17689.
And thou, vast ocean! on whose awful face
Time's iron feet can print no ruin-
   trace. ROBERT MONTGOMERY,
     The Omnipresence of the Deity

17690. He that would learn to pray,
let him go to sea.   *Proverb*

17691. Any one can hold the helm
when the sea is calm.
       PUBLILIUS SYRUS, *Sententiae*

17692.
An ocean is forever asking questions
And writing them aloud along the
    shore.   E. A. ROBINSON

17693.
Oh, where is the sea? the fishes cried,
As they swam its crystal clearness
    through.
    M. J. SAVAGE, *Where Is God?*

17694. Now would I give a thousand
furlongs of sea for an acre of barren
ground. SHAKESPEARE, *The Tempest*

17695.
Full fathom five thy father lies;
    Of his bones are coral made;
Those are pearls that were his eyes;
    Nothing of him that doth fade
But doth suffer a sea-change
    Into something rich and strange.
    SHAKESPEARE, *The Tempest*

17696. To unpathed waters, un-
dreamed shores. SHAKESPEARE,
    The Winter's Tale

17697.
I will go back to the great sweet
    mother,
    Mother and lover of men, the sea.
SWINBURNE, *The Triumph of Time*

17698. The moment the oceans of the
world become involved in war, that
moment the United States, the greatest oceanic power in the world, becomes involved. That has been recognized as true since the foundation
of this nation, from the time of
George Washington and his chief adviser, Alexander Hamilton, to that
of Franklin Delano Roosevelt.
DOROTHY THOMPSON, *On the Record*

17699.
Rocked in the cradle of the deep,
I lay me down in peace to sleep.
    EMMA WILLARD,
    The Cradle of the Deep

See also: 2205, 4881, 4902, 5533,
15566.

SEASONS, THE

**Related Subjects: Autumn, Spring,
Summer, Winter.**

17701. To every thing there is a season, and a time to every purpose under the heaven.
    Bible: Ecclesiastes, iii, 1

17702. While the earth remaineth,
seedtime and harvest, and cold and
heat, and summer and winter, and
day and night shall not cease.
    Bible: Genesis, vii, 22

17703.
Four Seasons fill the measure of the
    year;
There are four seasons in the mind of
    man. KEATS, *The Human Seasons*

17704. Every thing hath its time, and
that time must be watched. *Proverb*

17705.
At Christmas I no more desire a rose
Than wish a snow in May's new-
    fangled mirth;
But like of each thing that in season
    grows.   SHAKESPEARE,
    Much Ado About Nothing

See also: 5033, 5529, 20481.

SECRECY, SECRETS

**Related Subjects: Concealment,
Mystery, Obscurity.**

17711. Nothing is secret which shall
not be made manifest.
    Bible: Luke, viii, 17

17712. A sekret ceases tew be a sekret
if it iz once confided—it iz like a
dollar bill, once broken, it iz never
a dollar agin.
    JOSH BILLINGS, *Affurisms*

17713. When we desire to confine our words, we commonly say they are spoken under the rose.
SIR THOMAS BROWNE, *Vulgar Errors*

17714.
A secret's safe
'Twixt you, me, and the gate-post!
BROWNING, *The Inn Album*

17715. These are weighty secrets, and we must whisper them.
SUSAN COOLIDGE, *Secrets*

17716. Secret, and self-contained, and solitary as an oyster.
DICKENS, *A Christmas Carol*

17717. At no time are people so sedulously careful to keep their trifling appointments, attend to their ordinary occupations, and thus put a commonplace aspect on life, as when conscious of some secret that if suspected would make them look monstrous in the general eye.
HAWTHORNE, *The Marble Faun*

17718. Never suffer a thought to be harbored in your mind which you would not avow openly. When tempted to do anything in secret, ask yourself if you would do it in public. If you would not, be sure it is wrong.
JEFFERSON

17719.
Who shall doubt "the secret hid
Under Cheops' pyramid"
Was that the contractor did
Cheops out of several millions?
KIPLING, *A General Summary*

17720. Try your friend with a falsehood, and if he keep it a secret tell him the truth.   *Proverb*

17721. Do not speak of secret matters in a field that is full of little hills.
Proverb

17722. To him that you tell your secret you resign your liberty.
Proverb

17723. Thy secret is thy prisoner; if thou let it go, thou art a prisoner to it.   *Proverb*

17724. It is wise not to seek a secret, and honest not to reveal it.   *Proverb*

17725. Give it an understanding, but no tongue.   SHAKESPEARE, *Hamlet*

17726. Give thy thoughts no tongue.
SHAKESPEARE, *Hamlet*

17727. I will make a Star-chamber matter of it.   SHAKESPEARE,
The Merry Wives of Windsor

17728. There are no secrets better kept than the secrets that everybody guesses.   BERNARD SHAW,
Mrs. Warren's Profession

17729. If you wish to preserve your secret, wrap it up in frankness.
ALEXANDER SMITH, *Dreamthorp*

17730. Women, and young men, are very apt to tell what secrets they know, from the vanity of having been trusted.   LORD CHESTERFIELD,
Letters to His Son

17731. Man is God's secret, Power is man's secret, Sex is woman's secret.
JAMES STEPHENS, *The Crock of Gold*

17732. The man who has no secrets from his wife either has no secrets or no wife.   GILBERT WELLS

See also: 996, 2036, 2232, 3574, 4591, 14626.

SECURITY AND INSECURITY

Related Subjects: Certainty, Confidence, Dependence, Doubt, Freedom, Insurance, Protection, Safety, Surety.

17741. No one can build his security upon the nobleness of another person.   WILLA CATHER,
Alexander's Bridge

17742. The universal human yearning for something permanent, enduring, without shadow of change.
WILLA CATHER,
Death Comes for the Archbishop

17743. There is not much collective security in a flock of sheep on the way to the butcher.
WINSTON CHURCHILL

17744. The true security is to be found in social solidarity rather than in isolated individual effort.
DOSTOYEVSKY,
The Brothers Karamazov

17745. "Abundant living" means that each family would have an adequate supply of physical necessities and comforts, and sufficient leisure in which to enjoy them. Beyond that it means that each family should have the opportunity to share in the finer things of life. Culture cannot flourish amid privation and want; men must have physical security first.
MORDECAI EZEKIEL, *$2500 a Year*

17746.
I've often wish'd that I had clear,
For life, six hundred pounds a year;
A handsome house to lodge a friend,
A river at my garden's end,
A terrace walk, and half a rood
Of land set out to plant a wood.
HORACE

17747. He that is too secure is not safe. *Proverb*

See also: 1375, 2446, 3933, 4104, 4105, 5437, 5443, 7422, 7949, 16637.

SELF-CONFIDENCE

Related Subjects: Calm, Confidence, Courage, Superiority.

17751. They are most deceived that trust the most in themselves.
QUEEN ELIZABETH

17752. Self-trust is the essence of heroism. EMERSON, *Essays*

17753. Trust thyself: every heart vibrates to that iron string.
EMERSON, *Essays*

17754. Those who believe that they are exclusively in the right are generally those who achieve something.
ALDOUS HUXLEY, *Proper Studies*

17755. Self-confidence is the first requisite to great undertakings.
SAMUEL JOHNSON

17756. The promises of this world are for the most part vain phantoms, and to confide on one's self, and become something of worth and value, is the best and safest course.
MICHELANGELO

17757. Then where is truth, if there be no self-trust?
SHAKESPEARE, *The Rape of Lucrece*

17758. It is easy—terribly easy—to shake a man's faith in himself. To take advantage of that to break a man's spirit is devil's work.
BERNARD SHAW, *Candida*

17759. He lean'd not on his fathers, but himself.
TENNYSON, *Aylmer's Field*

17760. What a man thinks of himself, that it is which determines, or rather indicates, his fate. THOREAU, *Walden*

See also: 703, 1884, 1892, 3838, 6163.

SELF-CONTROL

Related Subjects: Abstinence, Conquest, Discipline, Moderation, Temperance, Temptation.

17761. One of the most important, but one of the most difficult things for a powerful mind is, to be its own master. A pond may lie quiet in a plain; but a lake wants mountains to compass and hold it in.   ADDISON

17762. He that is slow to anger is better than the mighty; and he that ruleth his spirit than he that taketh a city.   *Bible: Proverbs, xvi, 32*

17763. Conquer thyself. Till thou hast done this, thou art but a slave for it is almost as well to be subjected to another's appetite as to thine own.
        ROBERT BURTON,
        Anatomy of Melancholy

17764. Lord of himself,—that heritage of woe!   BYRON, *Lara*

17765. Over the times thou hast no power. To redeem a world sunk in dishonesty has not been given thee. Solely over one man therein thou hast a quite absolute, uncontrollable power. Him redeem and make honest.
        CARLYLE

17766.
Who to himself is law no law doth need,
Offends no law, and is a king indeed.
GEORGE CHAPMAN, *Bussy D'Ambois*

17767. No one who cannot master himself is worthy to rule, and only he can rule.   GOETHE

17768. Those who can command themselves, command others.
        HAZLITT

17769. No conflict is so severe as his who labors to subdue himself.
        THOMAS À KEMPIS,
        Of the Imitation of Christ

17770. He who reigns within himself and rules his passions, desires, and fears is more than a king.
        MILTON

17771. Rule lust, temper the tongue, and bridle the belly.   *Proverb*

17772. No man is free who cannot command himself.   PYTHAGORAS

17773. I will have a care of being a slave to myself, for it is a perpetual, a shameful, and the heaviest of all servitudes; and this may be done by uncontrolled desires.   SENECA

17774. Most powerful is he who has himself in his own power.   SENECA

17775.
Lord of himself, though not of lands;
And having nothing, yet hath all.
        SIR HENRY WOTTON,
        The Character of a Happy Life

See also: 861, 9192.

SELF-DEFENCE

17781.
        Self-defense is a virtue,
Sole bulwark of all right.
        BRYON, *Sardanapalus*

17782. Self-defence is Nature's eldest law.   DRYDEN,
        Absalom & Achitophel

17883. Self-preservation is the first law of nature.   *Proverb*

17884. Fear God and take your own part.   THEODORE ROOSEVELT

See also: 8072, 12483.

SELF-DENIAL

Related   Subjects: Asceticism, Fasting.

17791. Self-denial does not belong to religion as characteristic of it; it belongs to human life. The lower nature must always be denied when you are trying to rise to a higher sphere. It is no more necessary to be self-denying to be a Christian, than it is to be an artist, or an honest man, or a man at all in distinction from a brute. Of all joyous experiences there are none like those which spring from true religion.   H. W. BEECHER

17792. Self-denial is indulgence of a propensity to forego.
AMBROSE BIERCE, *Epigrams*

17793. Every personal consideration that we allow, costs us heavenly state. We sell the thrones of angels for a short and turbulent pleasure.
EMERSON

17794. Whoever will labor to get rid of self, to deny himself according to the instructions of Christ, strikes at once at the root of every evil, and finds the germ of every good.
FENELON

17795. Self-abnegation, that rare virtue, that good men preach and good women practice.   O. W. HOLMES

17796. The more a man denies himself, the more he shall obtain from God.   HORACE

17797. One secret act of self-denial, one sacrifice of inclination to duty, is worth all the mere good thoughts, warm feelings, passionate prayers in which idle people indulge themselves.
CARDINAL NEWMAN

17798. Teach self-denial, and make its practice pleasurable, and you can create for the world a destiny more sublime than ever issued from the brain of the wildest dreamer.
SCOTT

17799. Self denial is not a virtue: it is only the effect of prudence on rascality.   BERNARD SHAW,
Maxims for Revolutionists

17800. When you give, take to yourself. no credit for generosity, unless you deny yourself something in order that you may give. HENRY TAYLOR

17801. Self-denial is the shining sore on the leprous body of Christianity.
OSCAR WILDE

See also: 67, 69.

SELFISHNESS

Related Subjects: Avarice, Conceit, Gifts, Interest, Magnanimity, Misanthropy.

17811. It is the individual who is not interested in his fellow men who has the greatest difficulties in life and provides the greatest injury to others. It is from among such individuals that all human failures spring.
ALFRED ADLER, *Social Interest*

17812. People often grudge others what they cannot enjoy themselves.
AESOP, *The Dog in the Manger*

17813. I am convinced that we have a degree of delight, and that no small one, in the real misfortunes and pains of others.   BURKE,
On the Sublime and Beautiful

17814. The world will always be governed by self-interest. We should not try to stop this, we should try to make the self-interest of cads a little more coincident with that of decent people.
SAMUEL BUTLER, *Note Books*

17815. Selfishness is the greatest curse of the human race.
GLADSTONE

17816.
That man who lives for self alone
Lives for the meanest mortal known.
JOAQUIN MILLER,
Walker in Nicaragua

17817. We are here not to get all we can out of life for ourselves, but to try to make the lives of others happier.   SIR WILLIAM OSLER,
Life of Sir William Osler

17818. I love my friends well, but myself better.   *Proverb*

17819. He is a slave of the greatest slave, who serveth nothing but himself.   *Proverb*

17820. We have always known that heedless self-interest was bad morals; we know now that it is bad economics.
                    FRANKLIN D. ROOSEVELT

17821.
High though his titles, proud his name,
Boundless his wealth as wish can claim,—
Despite those titles, power, and pelf,
The wretch, concentred all in self,
Living, shall forfeit fair renown,
And, doubly dying, shall go down
To the vile dust from whence he sprung,
Unwept, unhonoured, and unsung.
SCOTT, *The Lay of the Last Minstrel*

17822.
Self-love, my liege, is not so vile a sin
As self-neglecting.
          SHAKESPEARE, *Henry V*

17823.
That sir which serves and seeks for gain,
And follows but for form,
Will pack when it begins to rain,
And leave thee in the storm.
          SHAKESPEARE, *King Lear*

17824. Next to the very young, I suppose the very old are the most selfish.   THACKERAY, *The Virginians*

17825. There's plenty of boys that will come hankering and gruvelling around when you've got an apple, and beg the core off you; but when *they've* got one, and you beg for the core, and remind them how you give them a core one time, they make a mouth at you, and say thank you

'most to death, but there ain't a-going to *be* no core.
MARK TWAIN, *Tom Sawyer Abroad*

17826. Selfishness is the only real atheism; aspiration, unselfishness, the only real religion.
          ISRAEL ZANGWILL,
          Children of the Ghetto

See also: 907, 3191, 4495, 12099, 19324.

SELF-KNOWLEDGE

Related Subjects: Conscience, Humility.

17831.
Oh wad some power the giftie gie us
To see oursels as others see us!
It wad frae monie a blunder free us,
          An' foolish notion.
                    BURNS, *To a Louse*

17832. He that knows himself, knows others; and he that is ignorant of himself, could not write a very profound lecture on other men's heads.
                    C. C. COLTON

17833.
We that acquaint ourselves with ev'ry zone,
And pass both topics, and behold each pole,
When we come home are to ourselves unknown,
And unacquainted still with our own soul.   SIR JOHN DAVIES,
          The Vanity of Human Learning

17834. When Thales was asked what was difficult, he said, "To know one's self." And what was easy, "To advise another."
          DIOGENES LAERTIUS, *Thales*

17835. Nothing will make us so charitable and tender to the faults of others, as, by self-examination, thoroughly to know our own. FENELON

17836. Self-knowledge is best learned, not by contemplation, but action. Strive to do your duty, and you will soon discover of what stuff you are made.   GOETHE

17837. An humble knowledge of thyself is a surer way to God than a deep search after learning.
THOMAS À KEMPIS,
Of the Imitation of Christ

17838. The highest and most profitable learning is the knowledge of ourselves. To have a low opinion of our own merits, and to think highly of others, is an evidence of wisdom. All men are frail, but thou shouldst reckon none so frail as thyself.
THOMAS À KEMPIS,
Of the Imitation of Christ

17839. One does not know—cannot know—the best that is in one.
NIETZSCHE, *Beyond Good and Evil*

17840.
Know then thyself, presume not God to scan;
The proper study of mankind is man.
POPE, *Essay on Man*

17841. He who knows himself best esteems himself least.   *Proverb*

17842. Every man is best known to himself.   *Proverb*

17843. The height of all philosophy is to know thyself; and the end of this knowledge is to know God. Know thyself, that thou mayest know God; and know God, that thou mayest love him and be like him. In the one thou art initiated into wisdom; and in the other perfected in it.
FRANCIS QUARLES

17844. Learn God, and thou shalt know thyself.   MARTIN F. TUPPER

17845.
Search thine own heart. What paineth thee
In others in thyself may be.
WHITTIER,
The Chapel of the Hermits

17846.
There is a luxury in self-dispraise;
And inward self-disparagement affords
To meditative spleen a grateful feast.
WORDSWORTH, *The Excursion*

See also: 317, 388, 2692, 5824, 9146.

SELF-LOVE, see Conceit

SELF-RELIANCE

Related Subjects: Courage, Dependence, Freedom, Security, Self-Confidence, Self-Respect.

17861.
Resolve to be thyself: and know, that he
Who finds himself, loses his misery.
MATTHEW ARNOLD, *Self-Dependence*

17862.
By thine own soul's law learn to live,
And if men thwart thee, take no heed,
And if men hate thee, have no care;
Sing thou thy song, and do thy deed,
Hope thou thy hope, and pray thy prayer.
PAKENHAM BEATTY, *Self-Reliance*

17863. Nothing can bring you peace but yourself. EMERSON, *Self-Reliance*

17864. The best lightning-rod for your protection is your own spine.
EMERSON

17865. If you would have a faithful servant, and one that you like, serve yourself.   FRANKLIN

17866. The man who cannot enjoy his own natural gifts in silence, and find his reward in the exercise of them, will generally find himself badly off.   GOETHE

17867.
It matters not how strait the gate,
   How charged with punishments the scroll,
I am the master of my fate;
   I am the captain of my soul.
                    W. E. HENLEY, *Invictus*

17868. A person under the firm persuasion that he can command resources virtually has them.   LIVY

17869. "Why don't you speak for yourself, John?"   LONGFELLOW,
   The Courtship of Miles Standish

17870. I am bigger than anything that can happen to me. All these things, sorrow, misfortune, and suffering, are outside my door. I am in the house and I have the key.
                    C. F. LUMMIS

17871. I have ever held it a maxim, never to do through another what it was possible for me to do myself.
                    MONTESQUIEU

17872. If ye would go up high, then use your own legs! Do not get yourselves *carried* aloft; do not seat yourselves on other people's backs and heads!   NIETZSCHE,
   Thus Spake Zarathustra

See also: 4, 4152, 9751, 9757.

SELF-RESPECT

Related Subjects: Pride, Self-Reliance, Superiority.

17881. The reverence of man's self, is, next to religion, the chiefest bridle of all vices.   BACON

17882. No more important duty can be urged upon those who are entering

the great theatre of life than simple loyalty to their best convictions.
                    E. H. CHAPIN

17883. If you want to be respected by others the great thing is to respect yourself. Only by that, only by self-respect will you compel others to respect you.   DOSTOYEVSKY,
   The Insulted and the Injured

17884. Self-respect, that corner stone of all virtue.   SIR JOHN HERSCHEL

17885. It may be no less dangerous to claim, on certain occasions, too little than too much. There is something captivating in spirit and intrepidity, to which we often yield as to a resistless power; nor can he reasonably expect the confidence of others who too apparently distrusts himself.
                    SAMUEL JOHNSON

17886. It is difficult to make a man miserable while he feels he is worthy of himself and claims kindred to the great God who made him. LINCOLN

17887.
Oft times nothing profits more
Than self-esteem, grounded on just
   and right. MILTON, *Paradise Lost*

17888. The pious and just honoring of ourselves may be thought the fountain-head from whence every laudable and worthy enterprise issues forth.   MILTON

17889. I care not so much what I am in the opinion of others as what I am in my own; I would be rich of myself and not by borrowing.
                    MONTAIGNE, *Essays*

17890.
One self-approving hour whole years
   outweighs
Of stupid starers and of loud huzzas:
And more true joy Marcellus exil'd
   feels

Than Caesar with a senate at his
  heels.   POPE, *Essay on Man*

17891. Above all things, reverence
yourself.   PYTHAGORAS

17892. So much is a man worth as
he esteems himself.   RABELAIS

17893. Every one stamps his own
value on himself. The price we challenge for ourselves is given us. Man
is made great or little by his own
will.   SCHILLER

17894. Be noble-minded! Our own
heart, and not other men's opinions
of us, forms our true honor.
    SCHILLER

17895. When thou hast profited so
much that thou respectest thyself,
thou mayest let go thy tutor. SENECA

17896. To have a respect for ourselves guides our morals; and to have
a deference for others governs our
manners.   STERNE

17897.
Self-reverence, self-knowledge, self-
  control,
These three alone lead life to sovereign power. TENNYSON, *Aenone*

See also: 293, 703, 21905.

SELF-RIGHTEOUSNESS

**Related Subjects: Bigotry, Com-
placency, Righteousness.**

17901. Regret not that which is past;
and trust not to thine own righteousness.   ST. ANTHONY

17902. Be not righteous overmuch.
    Bible: Ecclesiastes, vii, 16

17903. If there be ground for you to
trust in your own righteousness, then,
all that Christ did to purchase salvation, and all that God did to prepare
the way for it is in vain.
    JONATHAN EDWARDS

17904. Many religious people are
deeply suspicious. They seem—for
purely religious purposes, of course
—to know more about iniquity than
the Unregenerate.
    KIPLING, *Plain Tales*

17905. He that thinks too much of
his virtues, bids others think of his
vices.   *Proverb*

17906. Men who can hear the Decalogue and feel no self-reproach.
    WORDSWORTH,
    The Old Cumberland Beggar

SENSE, SENSES

**Related Subjects: Common Sense,
Delusion, Feeling, Illusion, Imagination, Instinct, Mind, Vision.**

17911. Take care of the sense and the
sounds will take care of themselves.
    LEWIS CARROLL,
    Alice in Wonderland

17912. Who would die a martyr to
sense in a country where the religion
is folly? CONGREVE, *Love for Love*

17913. Moral qualities rule the
world, but at short distances the
senses are despotic. EMERSON, *Essays*

17914. What thin partitions Sense
from Thought divide!
    POPE, *Essay on Man*

17915.
Good sense, which only is the gift of
  Heaven,
And though no science, fairly worth
  the seven.   POPE, *Moral Essays*

17916. He that overfeeds his senses
feasteth his enemies.   *Proverb*

17917. The wanton stings and motions of the sense.
SHAKESPEARE, *Measure for Measure*

See also: 393, 1325, 1353, 1786, 2136,
2887, 3274, 3880, 4585, 5222, 8853,
15373.

SENSITIVITY AND INSENSITIVITY

Related Subjects: Consideration, Delicacy, Feeling, Tact.

17921. Quick sensitiveness is inseparable from a ready understanding.   ADDISON

17922. Sensitiveness is closely allied to egotism. Indeed excessive sensitiveness is only another name for morbid self-consciousness. The cure for it is to make more of our objects, and less of ourselves.   C. N. BOVEE

17923. Where virtue is, sensibility is its ornament and becoming attire; but it, and all the amiable qualities may become, and too often have become the panders of vice, and the instruments of seduction.   COLERIDGE

17924. Sensibility would be a good portress, if she had but one hand; with her right she opens the door to pleasure, but with her left to pain.   C. C. COLTON

17925. Laughter and tears are meant to turn the wheels of the same machinery of sensibility; one is wind-power, and the other water-power; that is all.   O. W. HOLMES

17926. No, Sir; stark insensibility.   SAMUEL JOHNSON, *Boswell: Life*

17927. Sensibility is the power of woman.   LAVATER

17928. Sensibility is neither good nor evil in itself, but in its application. Under the influence of Christian principles it makes saints and martyrs; ill-directed, or uncontrolled, it is a snare, and the source of every temptation.   HANNAH MORE

17929. Too much sensibility creates unhappiness; too much insensibility leads to crime.   TALLEYRAND

SENSUALITY

Related Subjects: Dissipation, Vice.

17931. The body of a sensualist is the coffin of a dead soul.   C. N. BOVEE

17932. Sensuality is the grave of the soul.   W. E. CHANNING

17933. A youth of sensuality and intemperance delivers over a worn-out body to old age.   CICERO

17934. If sensuality be our only happiness, we ought to envy the brutes; for instinct is a surer, shorter, safer guide to such happiness than reason.   C. C. COLTON

17935. Sordid and infamous sensuality, the most dreadful evil that issued from the box of Pandora, corrupts the entire heart and eradicates every virtue.   FENELON

17936. When the cup of any sensual pleasure is drained to the bottom, there is always poison in the dregs.   JANE PORTER

17937. If sensuality were happiness, beasts were happier than men; but human felicity is lodged in the soul, not in the flesh.   SENECA

17938. I have never known a man who was sensual in his youth, who was high-minded when old.   CHARLES SUMNER

17939. All sensuality is one, though it takes many forms, as all purity is one. It is the same whether a man eat, or drink, or cohabit, or sleep sensually. They are but one appetite, and we only need to see a person do any one of these things to know how great a sensualist he is.   THOREAU

See also: 3162, 10924.

SENTIMENT, SENTIMENTAL-ITY, see Feeling

SEPARATION

Related Subjects: Absence, Exile, Parting.

17941. Who shall separate us from the love of Christ?

Bible: Romans, viii, 35

17942. The only solid and lasting peace between a man and his wife is doubtless a separation.

Lord Chesterfield

17943. The dearest friends are separated by impassable gulfs.

Emerson, *Essays*

17944. Life and these lips have long been separated.

Shakespeare, *Romeo and Juliet*

SERENITY

Related Subjects: Calm, Peace, Quiet.

17951.
Serene I fold my hands and wait,
  Nor care for wind or tide nor sea;
I rave no more 'gainst time or fate,
  For lo! my own shall come to me.

John Burroughs, *Waiting*

17952. If our hours were all serene, we might probably take almost as little note of them, as the dial does of those that are clouded.

Hazlitt, *On a Sun-Dial*

17953. The serenity of the wise is merely the art of imprisoning their agitation in the heart.

La Rochefoucauld, *Maxims*

17954.
The star of the unconquered will,
  He rises in my breast,

Serene, and resolute, and still,
  And calm, and self-possessed.

Longfellow, *The Light of Stars*

17955.
Serene will be our days and bright,
And happy will our nature be,
When love is an unerring light,
And joy its own security.

Wordsworth, *Ode to Duty*

See also: 520, 2336, 2390, 3202, 20711.

SERPENT

Related Subjects: Adam and Eve, Animal, Paradise.

17961. There's a snake in the grass.

Bacon, *Essays*

17962. Now the serpent was more subtil than any beast of the field which the Lord God had made.

Bible: Genesis, iii, 1

17963. Because thou hast done this, thou art cursed above all cattle, and above every beast of the field; upon thy belly shalt thou go, and dust shalt thou eat all the days of thy life.

Bible: Genesis, iii, 14

17964. And I will put enmity between thee and the woman, and between thy seed and her seed; it shall bruise thy head, and thou shalt bruise his heel. *Bible: Genesis, iii, 15*

17965. Put a snake in your bosom, and it will sting when it is warm.

Proverb

17966. When you see a snake, never mind where he came from. *Proverb*

17967. He that hath been bitten by a serpent is afraid of a rope. *Proverb*

17968. As old as a serpent. *Proverb*

17969. Where's my serpent of old Nile?

Shakespeare, *Antony and Cleopatra*

17970.
It is the bright day that brings forth
   the adder;
And that craves wary walking.
      SHAKESPEARE, *Julius Caesar*

17971.
We have scotch'd the snake, not
   kill'd it:
She'll close and be herself, whilst our
   poor malice
Remains in danger of her former
   tooth.   SHAKESPEARE, *Macbeth*

17972. Who sees the lurking serpent
steps aside.
SHAKESPEARE, *The Rape of Lucrece*

See also: 217, 5648, 6691, 16119.

SERVANT

**Related Subjects: Master, Service,
Servility.**

17981. Well done, thou good and
faithful servant.
      Bible: Matthew, xxv, 21

17982. One of the most considerable
advantages the great have over their
inferiors is to have servants as good
as themselves.
      CERVANTES, *Don Quixote*

17983.
Servant of God, well done! Well hast
   thou fought
The better fight.
      MILTON, *Paradise Lost*

17984. Few men have been admired
by their own domestics.
      MONTAIGNE, *Essays*

17985. A good servant should have
good wages.   *Proverb*

17986. Servants will not be diligent,
where the master's negligent.
      Proverb

17987. He that would be well served
must know when to change his servants.   *Proverb*

17988. Grandfather's servants are
never good.   *Proverb*

17989.
True servant's title he may wear,
   He only who has not
For his lord's gifts, how rich soe'er,
   His lord himself forgot.
      R. C. TRENCH, *The Split Pearls*

See also: 1811, 2383, 9332, 14275,
17865.

SERVICE

**Related Subjects: Courtesy, Favor,
Servant, Servility, Use.**

17991.
A service beyond all recompense
Weighs so heavy that it almost gives
   offense.   CORNEILLE, *Surena*

17992. I prefer death to lassitude. I
never tire of serving others.
      DA VINCI

17993. Pressed into service means
pressed out of shape.
      ROBERT FROST, *The Self-Seeker*

17994. The highest of distinctions is
service to others.   KING GEORGE VI

17995. He serves me most, who
serves his country best. HOMER, *Iliad*

17996.
   Thousands at his bidding speed,
And post o'er land and ocean without
   rest;
They also serve who only stand and
   wait.   MILTON, *On His Blindness*

17997. We are here to add what we
can *to,* not to get what we can *from,*
Life.   SIR WILLIAM OSLER,
      Life of Sir William Osler

17998. Nor are we to use living creatures like old shoes or dishes and throw them away when they are worn out or broken with service.

PLUTARCH, *Lives*

17999. First come, first served.
Proverb

18000. He who serves the public hath but a scurvy master.   *Proverb*

18001. He that serves everybody is paid by nobody.   *Proverb*

18002. He that looks for a requital, serves himself, not me.   *Proverb*

18003. Service is no heritage.
SHAKESPEARE,
All's Well that Ends Well

18004. It did me yeoman's service.
SHAKESPEARE, *Hamlet*

18005.
I have done the state some service, and they know 't;
No more of that.
SHAKESPEARE, *Othello*

18006.
     'Tis the curse of service,
Preferment goes by letter and affection,
And not by old gradation, where each second.
Stood heir to the first.
SHAKESPEARE, *Othello*

18007. He profits most who serves best.   A. F. SHELDON,
Motto For Rotary International

18008. The vocation of every man and woman is to serve other people.
TOLSTOY, *What Is to Be Done*

18009.
Enough if something from our hands
   have power
To live, and act, and serve the future
   hour.   WORDSWORTH,
Sonnet to the River Duddon

See also: 1, 396, 828, 1041, 1155, 1811, 2614, 2631, 4672, 9360, 12186, 14946, 17086, 18879, 20716.

SERVILITY

Related Subjects: Baseness, Cowards, Servant, Service.

18011. Always mistrust a subordinate who never finds fault with his superior.
CHURTON COLLINS, *Aphorisms*

18012. More vile Than is a slave in base servility.
SHAKESPEARE, *Henry VI*

18013. To dance attendance on their lordships' pleasures.
SHAKESPEARE, *Henry VIII*

18014. Away with slavish weeds and servile thoughts.
SHAKESPEARE, *Titus Andronicus*

See also: 1161.

SEXES, THE

Related Subjects: Love, Man, Woman.

18021. No improvement that takes place in either of the sexes, can be confined to itself; each is a universal mirror to each; and the respective refinement of the one, will be in reciprocal proportion to the polish of the other.   C. C. COLTON

18022. In company with several other old ladies of both sexes.
DICKENS, *Little Dorrit*

18023. It is the Man and Woman united that make the compleat human Being.   FRANKLIN

18024.
Amoebas at the start
   Were not complex;

They Tore themselves apart
  And started Sex.
              ARTHUR GUITERMAN, *Sex*

18025.
Breathes there a man with hide so
  tough
Who says two sexes aren't enough?
  SAMUEL HOFFENSTEIN, *The Sexes*

18026. A woman never forgets her
sex. She would rather talk with a man
than an angel, any day.
              O. W. HOLMES,
    The Poet at the Breakfast-Table

18027. Man is fire, and woman tow;
the devil comes and sets them in a
blaze.   *Proverb*

18028. The son of the female is the
shadow of the male.
              SHAKESPEARE, *Henry IV*

18029. As the French say, there are
three sexes,—men, women, and clergymen.   SYDNEY SMITH,
            Lady Holland's Memoir

See also: 1665.

SHADOW

**Related Subjects: Clouds, Dark-
ness, Light.**

18031. Beware lest you lose the substance by grasping at the shadow.
  AESOP, *The Dog and the Shadow*

18032. Shadow owes its birth to light.
              JOHN GAY

18033. Catch not at the shadow, and
lose the substance.   *Proverb*

18034. Every light has its shadow.
                          Proverb

18035.
          Hence, horrible shadow!
Unreal mockery, hence!
              SHAKESPEARE, *Macbeth*

18036.
By the apostle Paul, shadows to-night
Have struck more terror to the soul
  of Richard
Than can the substance of ten thou-
  sand soldiers.
              SHAKESPEARE, *Richard III*

18037.
I have a little shadow that goes in and
  out with me,
And what can be the use of him is
  more than I can see.
              STEVENSON, *My Shadow*

See also: 1195.

SHAKESPEARE, WILLIAM

18041.
But Shakespeare's magic could not
  copied be;
Within that circle none durst walk
  but he.   DRYDEN, *The Tempest*

18042. He [Shakespeare] was the
man who of all Modern, and perhaps
Ancient Poets, had the largest and
most comprehensive soul.
  DRYDEN, *Essay of Dramatic Poesy*

18043. How Shakespeare hated the
plain men! He knew too much about
them. He had to live too closely to
them when he was sidestepping the
Puritans, to whom he was a public
enemy.   O. ST. J. GOGARTY,
    As I Was Going Down Sackville St.

18044. A lively and lasting sense of
filial duty is more effectually impressed on the mind of a son or
daughter by reading King Lear, than
by all the dry volumes of ethics, and
divinity, that ever were written.
                          JEFFERSON

18045.
          Reader, look,
Not at his picture, but his book.
              BEN JONSON,
Comment on Shakespeare's Portrait

18046.

> Soul of the age!
> The applause, delight, the wonder of
>   our stage!
> My Shakespeare, rise! I will not lodge
>   thee by
> Chaucer or Spenser, or bid Beau-
>   mont lie
> A little further to make thee a room.
>   BEN JONSON,
>   *To the Memory of Shakespeare*

18047. He was not of an age but
for all time.   BEN JONSON,
     To the Memory of Shakespeare

18048. I loved the man [Shake-
speare] and do honor his memory, on
this side idolatry, as much as any.
         BEN JONSON, *Timber*

18049. The players have often mentioned it as an honor to Shakespeare,
that in his writing he never blotted
out a line. My answer hath been,
Would he had blotted a thousand.
         BEN JONSON, *Timber*

18050. Shakespeare is incarnated, uncompromising feudalism.
         WALT WHITMAN

See also: 182, 1405, 4752, 6902,
13409.

SHAME

**Related Subjects: Blushing, Con-
tempt, Disgrace, Scorn.**

18051.
Shame is the apprehension of a vision
Reflected from the surface of opin-
  ion—
The opinion of the public.
       ARISTOPHANES, *The Frogs*

18052.
Men the most infamous are fond of
  fame,
And those who fear not guilt yet start
  at shame.
   CHARLES CHURCHILL, *The Author*

18053. If yet, not lost to all the sense
of shame.   HOMER, *Iliad*

18054. He that shames let him be
shent.   *Proverb*

18055. He who has no shame has no
conscience.   *Proverb*

18056. Men may blush to hear what
they were not ashamed to act.
               Proverb

18057. He that despises shame wants
a bridle.   *Proverb*

18058. Ingenuous shame, once lost,
is never regained.
     PUBLILIUS SYRUS, *Sententiae*

18059. Shame may restrain what the
law does not prohibit.   SENECA

18060. Be not thy tongue thy own
shame's orator.   SHAKESPEARE,
       The Comedy of Errors

18061. Must I hold a candle to my
shames?   SHAKESPEARE,
       The Merchant of Venice

18062. The more things a man is
ashamed of, the more respectable he
is.   BERNARD SHAW,
       Man and Superman

See also: 211, 1223, 2924, 3826, 8980,
11561, 18263.

SHAW, GEORGE BERNARD

18071. If [Bernard] Shaw had died
like Keats at twenty-six, he would
never have been heard of.
     FRANK HARRIS, *Bernard Shaw*

18072. Voltaire called Swift a Rabelais *perfectionné;* I call you a Voltaire
perfected.
       ARCHIBALD HENDERSON,
         to Bernard Shaw

18073. It is perhaps no exaggeration
to claim for Shaw that he has

achieved a greater measure of fame during his own life time than has fallen to the lot of any playwright known to history. Bernard Shaw is a public institution, a popular one-man university, a twentieth century Bacon in broadcast.

ARCHIBALD HENDERSON,
Bernard Shaw

18074. The current popularity of Shaw is thus due, in considerable part, to the amusing antics of an ageless Punch controlled from behind the scenes by the hand of a genius—a serious thinker and moralist who chooses to put on his pantomimes to attract the unthinking multitude without their knowledge to the serious plays for which they serve as curtain-raisers. ARCHIBALD HENDERSON,
Bernard Shaw

18075. The fame of Bernard Shaw is in no small part the false notoriety of G.B.S.—the publicized vogue of a creature too fantastic to be other than an ingenious work of art.

ARCHIBALD HENDERSON,
Bernard Shaw

18076. [G.B.] Shaw is world pervasive, vocally transmissible with the speed of light, journalistically omnipresent.

ARCHIBALD HENDERSON,
Bernard Shaw

18077. Like the late poet, Paul Verlaine, there are days when Shaw wears his demon mask to frighten bores away.   J. G. HUNEKER

18078. I never struggled. I rose by sheer gravitation.   BERNARD SHAW

18079. My method is to take the utmost trouble to find the right thing to say, and then to say it with the utmost levity.   BERNARD SHAW,
Answers to Nine Questions

SHEEP AND SHEPHERD

Related Subject: Animal.

18081. The black sheep is a perilous beast.   *Anonymous*

18082. As sheep that have not a shepherd.   *Bible: 1 Kings, xxii, 17*

18083. He maketh me to lie down in green pastures: he leadeth me beside the still waters.
Bible: Psalms, xxiii, 2

18084. Other sheep I have, which are not of this fold: them also I must bring, and they shall hear my voice; and there shall be one fold and one shepherd.   *Bible: John, x, 16*

18085.
For kings have often fears when they
    do sup,
Where shepherds dread no poison in
    their cup.   ROBERT GREENE,
The Shepherd's Wife's Song

18086. He that will be made a sheep shall find wolves enough.
GABRIEL HARVEY

18087.
My name is Norval; on the Grampian
    hills
My father feeds his flocks; a frugal
    swain,
Whose constant cares were to increase his store,
And keep his only son, myself, at
    home.   JOHN HOME, *Douglas*

18088.
And every shepherd tells his tale
Under the hawthorn in the dale.
MILTON, *L'Allegro*

18089.
Baa, baa, black sheep,
Have you any wool?
Yes sir, yes sir, three bags full;
One for my master, one for my dame,
But none for the little boy who cries
    in the lane.   *Nursery Rhyme*

18090.
Little Bo-peep has lost her sheep,
　And can't tell where to find them;
Leave them alone, and they'll come
　　home,
　Wagging their tails behind them.
　　　　　　　　　　Nursery Rhyme

18091.
Mary had a little lamb,
. Its fleece was white as snow,
And everywhere that Mary went
　The lamb was sure to go.
　　　　　　　　　　Nursery Rhyme

18092.
The mountain sheep are sweeter,
But the valley sheep are fatter;
We therefore deemed it meeter
To carry off the latter.
　　　　　　　　T. L. Peacock,
　　　　　War Song of Dinas Vawr

18093.
Pleased to the last, he crops the flow-
　ery food,
And licks the hand just raised to shed
　his blood.　Pope, *Essay on Man*

18094. It is a foolish sheep that
makes the wolf his confessor.
　　　　　　　　　　　　Proverb

18095. He that makes himself a
sheep shall be eaten by the wolf.
　　　　　　　　　　　　Proverb

18096. Careless shepherds make
many a feast for the wolf.　*Proverb*

18097. One sheep follows another.
　　　　　　　　　　　　Proverb

18098. As good be hanged for a sheep
as a lamb.　　　　　　*Proverb*

18099. As mild as a lamb.　*Proverb*

18100.
Sleepest or wakest thou, jolly shep-
　herd?
　Thy sheep be in the corn;

And for one blast of thy minikin
　　mouth,
　Thy sheep shall take no harm.
　　　　　Shakespeare, *King Lear*

18101.
I am a tainted wether of the flock,
Meetest for death.
　　　　　　　　Shakespeare,
　　　　　The Merchant of Venice

18102.
Storm upon the mountain, night upon
　its throne!
And the little snow-white lamb left
　alone—alone!
Thomas Westwood, *The Pet Lamb*

See also: 1024, 2652, 3593, 16485,
21307.

SHELLEY, PERCY BYSSHE

18111. In his poetry, as well as in his
life, Shelley was indeed "a beautiful
and *ineffectual* angel, beating in the
void his luminous wings in vain."
　　　　　　Matthew Arnold,
　　　　　Literature and Dogma

18112.
Ah, did you once see Shelley plain,
　And did he stop and speak to you,
And did you speak to him again?
　How strange it seems and new!
　　　　Browning, *Memorabilia*

18113. Shelley? Ah! he is a pronounced case for the specialists. Any
man who could eat dry bread, drink
water, and write such angelic poetry
must have been quite mad. Admitted.
Would there were more Shelleys!
　　　　J. G. Huneker, *Essays*

18114.
You did not sing to Shelley such a
　　song
　As Shelley sang to you.
　　　　　　　　Sarah Piatt,
　　　　　A Word with a Skylark

18115. Mighty meat for little guests, when the heart of Shelley was laid in the cemetery of Caius Cestius!

FRANCIS THOMPSON, *Shelley*

18116. Byron asked me to preserve the skull [Shelley's] for him; but remembering that he had once used one as a drinking cup I was determined Shelley's should not be so profaned.

TRELAWNY

18117.
Knight-errant of the Never-ending
    Quest,
  And Minstrel of the Unfulfilled
    Desire;
  For ever tuning thy frail earthly
    lyre
To some unearthly music.

HENRY VAN DYKE, *Shelley*

18118.
'Tis no mean fortune to have heard
A singer who, if errors blurred
His sight, had yet a spirit stirred
  By vast desire,
And ardour fledging the swift word
  With plumes of fire.

WILLIAM WATSON,
Shelley's Centenary

SHIP

Related Subjects: Navy, River, Sailor, Sea, Shipwreck, Travel, Wanderlust, Water.

18121. We sailors are jealous for our vessels. Abuse us if you will, but have a care for what you may say of our ships. We alone are entitled to call them bitches, wet brutes, stubborn craft, but we will stand for no such liberties from the beach.

D. W. BONE, *Merchantmen-at-Arms*

18122. The ship, a fragment detached from the earth, went on lonely and swift like a small planet.

JOSEPH CONRAD,
The Nigger of the Narcissus

18123. Being in a ship is being in a jail, with the chance of being drowned.

SAMUEL JOHNSON, *Boswell: Life*

18124. That packet of assorted miseries which we call a Ship.

KIPLING, *The First Sailor*

18125. Ships fear fire more than water.   *Proverb*

18126. Great ships require deep waters.   *Proverb*

See also: 3651, 4351, 12735.

SHIPWRECK

Related Subjects: Ship, Storm.

18131. A common shipwreck is a consolation to all.   *Anonymous*

18132.
"We are lost!" the captain shouted,
  As he staggered down the stairs.

J. T. FIELDS, *Ballad of the Tempest*

18133.
He who has suffered shipwreck, fears
  to sail
Upon the seas, though with a gentle
  gale. ROBERT HERRICK, *Shipwreck*

18134.
And fast through the midnight dark
    and drear,
  Through the whistling sleet and
    snow,
Like a sheeted ghost, the vessel swept
  Tow'rds the reef of Norman's
    Woe.   LONGFELLOW,
    The Wreck of the Hesperus

18135. They make glorious shipwreck who are lost in seeking worlds.

LESSING

18136. He goes a great voyage, that goes to the bottom of the sea.

Proverb

See also: 5896.

SHOE

Related Subjects: Dress, Foot, Shoemaker, Walking.

18141. 'Tis the same to him who wears a shoe, as if the whole earth were covered with leather.

EMERSON, *Conduct of Life*

18142. We ought not to treat living creatures like shoes or pots and pans, which, when worn with use, we throw away.   PLUTARCH, *Lives*

18143. Now for good luck, cast an old shoe after me.   *Proverb*

18144. Better cut the shoe than pinch the foot.   *Proverb*

18145. Every shoe fits not every foot.   *Proverb*

18146. You cannot put the same shoe on every foot.

PUBLILIUS SYRUS, *Sententiae*

18147.

       And put
My clouted brogues from off my feet.

SHAKESPEARE, *Cymbeline*

18148. Those who wear the shoe know best where it pinches.

C. H. SPURGEON, *John Ploughman*

SHOEMAKER

Related Subject: Shoe.

18151. Him that makes shoes go barefoot himself.   ROBERT BURTON,
       Anatomy of Melancholy

18152. A man cannot make a pair of shoes *rightly* unless he do it in a devout manner.

CARLYLE, *Letter to Erskine*

18153. Brave shoemakers, all gentlemen of the gentle craft.

THOMAS DEKKER,
The Shoemakers' Holiday

18154. The shoemaker makes a good shoe because he makes nothing else.

EMERSON, *Letters and Social Aims*

18155.

Clogging up Miss	1.0
Mended up Miss	2
Toe capped Master	3
Turned up, clogged up and mended Maid	1.6
Lined, turned up and put a piece in Madam	4.6
Soleing and covering the Maid	6
Tapping Madam	6
Putting a piece in Madam	6
Stretching and easing little Master	7
Welting and stretching the Maid	10
Mending and patching the Cook	6

*English shoemaker's bill which dates
     from Nov. 1708 to Dec. 1709*
       Gogarty: *Going Native*

18156. Who is worse shod than the shoemaker's wife?   *Proverb*

18157. I am but, as you would say, a cobbler. . . . I am indeed, sir, a surgeon to old shoes; when they are in great danger I recover them. As proper men as ever trod upon neat's leather have gone upon my handiwork.   SHAKESPEARE, *Julius Caesar*

SICKNESS

Related Subjects: Disease, Doctors, Health, Hospital, Medicine.

18161. I reckon being ill as one of the great pleasures of life, provided one is not too ill and is not obliged to work till one is better.

SAMUEL BUTLER,
The Way of All Flesh

18162. While the sick man has life there is hope.   CICERO

18163. If there be a regal solitude, it is a sick bed.   CHARLES LAMB,
*Detached Thoughts on Books
& Reading*

18164. The sick man is a parasite of society. In certain cases it is indecent to go on living. To continue to vegetate in a state of cowardly dependence upon doctors and special treatments, once the meaning of life, the right to life, has been lost, ought to be regarded with the greatest contempt by society.   NIETZSCHE,
The Twilight of the Idols

18165. Once Antigonus was told his son was ill, and went to see him. At the door he met some young beauty. Going in, he sat down by the bed and took his pulse. "The fever," said Demetrius, "has just left me." "Oh, yes," replied the father, "I met it going out at the door."
PLUTARCH, *Lives*

18166. The purse of the patient protracts his cure.   *Proverb*

18167. The chamber of sickness is the chapel of devotion.   *Proverb*

18168. That sick man is not to be pitied, who hath his cure in his sleeve.
Proverb

18169. He who never was sick, dies the first fit.   *Proverb*

18170. He is in great danger, who being sick thinks himself well.
Proverb

18171.
How has he the leisure to be sick
In such a justling time?
SHAKESPEARE, *Henry IV*

18172.
This sickness doth infect
The very life-blood of our enterprise.
SHAKESPEARE, *Henry IV*

18173. I enjoy convalescence. It is the part that makes the illness worth while.   BERNARD SHAW,
Back To Methuselah

See also: 296, 5659, 12083.

SIGH

Related Subjects: Complaining, Melancholy, Mourning.

18181.
Make me to sigh when all my griefs
    are gone,
Happy the heart that sighed for such
    a one!
SAMUEL DANIEL, *I Must Not Grieve*

18182. Sigh'd and look'd, and sigh'd again.   DRYDEN, *Alexander's Feast*

18183. Implores the passing tribute of a sigh.   THOMAS GRAY,
*Elegy Written in a Country
Church-Yard*

18184.
Speed the soft intercourse from soul
    to soul,
And waft a sigh from Indus to the
    Pole.   POPE, *Eloisa to Abelard*

18185.
Oh, if you knew the pensive pleasure
    That fills my bosom when I sigh,
You would not rob me of a treasure
    Monarchs are too poor to buy.
SAMUEL ROGERS

18186. Sighs are the natural language of the heart.
THOMAS SHADWELL, *Psyche*

18187.
He raised a sigh so piteous and profound,
That it did seem to shatter all his bulk
And end his being.
SHAKESPEARE, *Hamlet*

18188. Sigh'd and look'd unutterable things.
JAMES THOMSON, *The Seasons*

SIGHT

Related Subjects: Appearance, Blindness, Eyes, Light, Vision.

18191. What you see, yet can not see over, is as good as infinite.

CARLYLE, *Sartor Resartus*

18192. To see sad sights moves more than hear them told.

SHAKESPEARE,
The Rape of Lucrece

18193. The sense of sight is indeed the highest bodily privilege, the purest physical pleasure, which man has derived from his Creator.

SYDNEY SMITH,
Lady Holland's Memoir

18194. Women and birds are able to see without turning their heads, and that is indeed a necessary provision, for they are both surrounded by enemies.

JAMES STEPHENS, *The Demi-Gods*

18195. The sight of you is good for sore eyes. SWIFT, *Polite Conversation*

18196. A picture may instantly present what a book could set forth only in a hundred pages.

TURGENIEV, *Fathers and Sons*

See also: 1733, 21899.

SILENCE

Related Subjects: Deafness, Sound.

18201. Even a fool, when he holdeth his peace, is counted wise.

Bible: Proverbs, xvii, 28

18202. Silence is deep as Eternity; speech is shallow as Time.

CARLYLE, *Sir Walter Scott*

18203. Silence is the unbearable repartée.   G. K. CHESTERTON

18204. Silence is a true friend who never betrays.   CONFUCIUS,
Analects

18205. When Silence speaks for Love she has much to say.

RICHARD GARNETT,
De Flagello Myrteo

18206. Silence gives consent.
GOLDSMITH, *The Good-Natur'd Man*

18207. A well-bred silence always at command.   W. E. HENLEY,
In Hospital

18208.
And silence, like a poultice, comes
To heal the blows of sound.
O. W. HOLMES, *The Music Grinders*

18209. Silence is the best resolve for him who distrusts himself.

LA ROCHEFOUCAULD, *Maxims*

18210. Be silent and safe—silence never betrays you.

J. B. O'REILLY, *Rules of the Road*

18211. Silence is a fine jewel for a woman, but it's little worn. *Proverb*

18212. Be silent, or speak something worth hearing.   *Proverb*

18213.
Silence in love bewrays more woe
    Than words, though ne'er so witty:
A beggar that is dumb, you know,
    May challenge double pity.

SIR WALTER RALEIGH,
The Silent Lover

18214. Silence more musical than any song.   CHRISTINA ROSSETTI, *Rest*

18215. The rest is silence.

SHAKESPEARE, *Hamlet*

18216.
I do know of these
That therefore only are reputed wise
For saying nothing.

SHAKESPEARE,
The Merchant of Venice

18217.
The silence often of pure innocence
Persuades when speaking fails.
SHAKESPEARE, *The Winter's Tale*

18218. Silence is ' the most perfect
expression of scorn.
BERNARD SHAW,
Back to Methuselah

18219. In silence also there's a worth
that brings no risk.
SIMONIDES, *Plutarch: Lives*

18220. He has occasional flashes of
silence, that make his conversation
perfectly delightful.
SYDNEY SMITH,
Lady Holland's Memoir

18221. Well-timed silence hath more
eloquence than speech.
MARTIN F. TUPPER, *Of Discretion*

18222. He knew the precise psycho-
logical moment when to say nothing.
OSCAR WILDE,
The Picture of Dorian Gray

18223.
The silence that is in the starry sky,
The sleep that is among the lonely
hills.   WORDSWORTH,
Song at the Feast of Brougham Castle

See also: 1045, 1448, 1600, 2751,
4170, 4605, 5227, 5265, 5933, 6556,
9514, 11728, 18763, 18765, 19341.

SIMPLICITY

Related Subjects: Brevity, Credulity, Innocence.

18231. This seemed as simple as running water; but simplicity is the most
deceitful mistress that ever betrayed
man.   HENRY ADAMS,
The Education of Henry Adams

18232.
Lost is our simplicity of times,

The world abounds with laws, and
teems with crimes.   *Anonymous*

18233. Elementary, my dear Watson.
CONAN DOYLE, *The Crooked Man*

18234. Oh, what a power has white
Simplicity!   KEATS

18235. Simplicity of character is no
hindrance to subtlety of intellect.
JOHN MORLEY, *Life of Gladstone*

18236. Beauty of style and harmony
and grace and good rhythm depend
on simplicity. PLATO, *The Republic*

18237. Simplicity is the Mean between Ostentation and Rusticity.
POPE, *Preface to Iliad (trans.)*

18238. Simplicity is an exact medium between too little and too much.
SIR JOSHUA REYNOLDS

18239. To see a thing and tell it in
plain words is the greatest thing a
soul can do.   RUSKIN

18240.
Great floods have flown
From simple sources.
SHAKESPEARE,
All's Well that Ends Well

18241. Our life is frittered away by
detail. . . . Simplify, simplify.
THOREAU, *Walden*

See also: 1695, 2401, 6743, 14406,
18897, 20244.

SIN AND SINNERS

Related Subjects: Adultery, Con-
fession, Conscience, Crime, Devil,
Error, Evil, Fall, Guilt, Hell, Lust,
Morality, Repentance, Temptation,
Vice, Virtue, Whore, Wickedness.

18251. Though your sins be as scarlet, they shall be white as snow.
Bible: Isaiah, i, 18

18252. He that is without sin among you, let him first cast a stone at her.
Bible: John, viii, 7

18253. The wages of sin is death.
Bible: Romans, vi, 23

18254.
Compound for sins they are inclined to,
By damning those they have no mind to.   SAMUEL BUTLER, *Hudibras*

18255. A private sin is not so prejudicial in this world as a public indecency.   CERVANTES, *Don Quixote*

18256. The sin they do by two and two they must pay for one by one.
KIPLING, *Tomlinson*

18257. What repels me particularly today in religion is its emphasis on sin. I have no consciousness of sin and no feeling of being damned.
LIN YUTANG, *I Believe*

18258.
Man-like is it to fall into sin,
Fiend-like is it to dwell therein,
Christ-like is it for sin to grieve,
God-like is it all sin to leave.
LONGFELLOW, *Sin*

18259. She gave me of the tree, and I did eat.   MILTON, *Paradise Lost*

18260. Who swims in sin shall sink in sorrow.   *Proverb*

18261. Many without punishment, none without sin.   *Proverb*

18262. The less the temptation, the greater the sin.   *Proverb*

18263. Auld sin, new shame.
Proverb

18264. Every sin carries its own punishment.   *Proverb*

18265. I hate the sin, but I love the sinner.   T. B. READ,
What a Word May Do

18266.
Commit
The oldest sins the newest kind of ways.   SHAKESPEARE, *Henry IV*

18267.
I am a man
More sinn'd against than sinning.
SHAKESPEARE, *King Lear*

18268. Some rise by sin, and some by virtue fall.   SHAKESPEARE,
Measure for Measure

18269. The sins of the father are to be laid upon the children.
SHAKESPEARE,
The Merchant of Venice

18270.
O! what authority and show of truth
Can cunning sin cover itself withal!
SHAKESPEARE,
Much Ado About Nothing

See also: 216, 224, 626, 634, 891, 996, 1546, 2059, 2173, 2243, 3111, 3163, 3311, 3342, 3583, 11708, 13575, 13911, 15670, 16828, 17426, 19004.

SINCERITY

Related Subjects: Candor, Honesty, Hypocrisy, Trust.

18271. It is often said it is no matter what a man believes if he is only sincere. But let a man sincerely believe that seed planted without ploughing is as good as with; that January is as favorable for seed-sowing as April; and that cockle seed will produce as good a harvest as wheat, and is it so?   H. W. BEECHER

18272. The whole faculties of man must be exerted in order to call forth noble energies; and he who is not earnestly sincere lives in but half his being, self-mutilated, self-paralyzed.
COLERIDGE

18273. Sincerity and truth are the basis of every virtue.

CONFUCIUS, *Analects*

18274. Sincerity is no test of truth —no evidence of correctness of conduct. You may take poison sincerely believing it the needed medicine, but will it save your life?

TRYON EDWARDS

18275. Sincerity is the, indispensable ground of all conscientiousness, and by consequence of all heartfelt religion. KANT

18276. True sincerity sends for no witness. *Proverb*

18277. The lady doth protest too much, methinks. SHAKESPEARE, *Hamlet*

18278. Before the world I must deal sincerely with you, however light a turn I may give my sincerity. I owe that to your dignity as an artist and to my profession. But in private I only want to please you, which makes me a liar and an actor.

BERNARD SHAW, *to Ellen Terry*

18279. Inward sincerity will of course influence the outward deportment; where the one is wanting, there is great reason to suspect the absence of the other. STERNE

See also: 1399, 6973, 8630.

SING, SINGING

Related Subjects: Art, Ballad, Melody, Music, Song, Voice.

18281.
No faith can last
That never sings.

LASCELLES ABERCROMBIE,
The Stream's Song

18282.
We have to sing, you see, here in the darkness
All men have to sing—poor broken things,
We have to sing here in the darkness in the roaring flood.
We have to find each other.
Have you courage tonight for a song?
Lift your voices. Come.

SHERWOOD ANDERSON,
Song of Industrial America

18283. Respect all such as sing when all alone! BROWNING, *Paracelsus*

18284. If a man cannot sing as he carries his cross he had better drop it.

HAVELOCK ELLIS

18285.
But in the mud and scum of things
There alway, alway something sings.

EMERSON, *Fragments*

18286. This is a fault common to all singers, that among their friends they never are inclined to sing when they are asked, unasked they never desist.

HORACE, *Satires*

18287.
God sent his Singers upon earth
With songs of sadness and of mirth.

LONGFELLOW, *The Singers*

18288. He sings several times faster than you'll tell money; he utters them as he had eaten ballads and all men's ears grew to his tunes.

SHAKESPEARE, *The Winter's Tale*

18289. Do not commit your poems to pages alone. Sing them, I pray you.

VERGIL, *Aeneid*

See also: 475, 715, 834, 3206, 3213.

SISTER

Related Subjects: Brother, Family.

18291.
My sister! my sweet sister! if a name

Dearer and purer were, it should be
thine. BYRON, *Epistle to Augusta*

18292. Never praise a sister to a
sister, in the hope of your compliments reaching the proper ears.
                    KIPLING, *Plain Tales*

18293.
For the Colonel's Lady an' Judy
    O'Grady
Are sisters under their skins!
                    KIPLING, *The Ladies*

18294.
For there is no friend like a sister,
In calm or stormy weather,
To cheer one on the tedious way,
To fetch one if one goes astray,
To lift one if one totters down,
To strengthen whilst one stands.
CHRISTINA ROSSETTI, *Goblin Market*

18295. A ministering angel shall my
sister be. SHAKESPEARE, *Hamlet*

18296. The weird sisters.
            SHAKESPEARE, *Macbeth*

See also: 838, 11274.

SKEPTICISM, see Doubt

SKILL

Related Subjects: Ability, Accuracy, Art, Craftsmanship, Genius,
Invention, Talent.

18301.
    'Tis God gives skill,
But not without men's hands: He
    could not make
Antonio Stradivari's violins
Without Antonio.
        GEORGE ELIOT, *Stradivarius*

18302. Skill to do comes of doing.
        EMERSON, *Society and Solitude*

18303. Skill makes love unending.
                OVID, *Art of Love*

18304. Let each man pass his days in
that wherein his skill is greatest.
                    PROPERTIUS

18305. All things require skill but an
appetite.   *Proverb*

18306. Skill and confidence are an
unconquered army.   *Proverb*

18307. Skill is stronger than strength.
                        Proverb

18308. Dexterity comes by experience.   *Proverb*

18309.
        To show our simple skill,
That is the true beginning of our
    end.   SHAKESPEARE,
        A Midsummer-Night's Dream

18310.
        Like an arrow shot
From a well-experienced archer hits
    the mark
His eye doth level at.
            SHAKESPEARE, *Pericles*

See also: 4362, 18970.

SKIN

Related Subjects: Body, Bone,
Flesh.

18311. A fair skin covers a crooked
mind.   *Proverb*

18312. It is good sleeping in a whole
skin.   *Proverb*

18313. My skin hangs about me like
an old lady's loose gown.
        SHAKESPEARE, *Henry IV*

18314. His silver skin laced with his
golden blood.   SHAKESPEARE,
                        Macbeth

18315. Your skins are whole.
                SHAKESPEARE,
        The Merry Wives of Windsor

SKULL

18316.

I'll not shed her blood;
Nor scar that whiter skin of hers
than snow,
And smooth as monumental alabaster.
SHAKESPEARE, *Othello*

See also: 11499.

SKULL

Related Subjects: Bone, Death, Head.

18321.

Remove yon skull from out the scatter'd heaps:
Is that a temple where a God may dwell?
Why ev'n the worm at last disdains her shatter'd cell!
Look on its broken arch, its ruin'd wall,
Its chambers desolate, and portals foul:
Yes, this was once Ambition's airy hall,
The dome of Thought, the palace of the Soul. BYRON, *Childe Harold*

18322. Alas, poor Yorick! I knew him, Horatio: a fellow of infinite jest, of most excellent fancy; he hath borne me on his back a thousand times; and now, how abhorred in my imagination it is! my gorge rises at it. Here hung those lips that I have kissed I know not how oft. Where be your gibes now? your gambols? your songs? your flashes of merriment, that were wont to set the table on a roar? Not one now, to mock your own grinning? quite chap-fallen? Now get you to my lady's chamber, and tell her, let her paint an inch thick, to this favour she must come.
SHAKESPEARE, *Hamlet*

See also: 11523, 18116.

SKY, see Heavens, The

SLANDER

Related Subjects: Abuse, Calumny, Injury, Insult, Lies, Malevolence, Offence.

18331. Slander, like Death, loves a shining mark.
CHARLES B. FAIRBANKS,
My Unknown Chum

18332. The sewing-circle—the Protestant confessional, where each one confesses, not her own sins, but the sins of her neighbors.
CHARLES B. FAIRBANKS,
My Unknown Chum

18333. When men speak ill of thee, live so as nobody may believe them.
PLATO

18334. At every word a reputation dies. POPE, *The Rape of the Lock*

18335. Slanderers are the devil's bellows, to blow up contention. *Proverb*

18336. To slander with a matter of truth. *Proverb*

18337. Such as give ear to slanderers, are worse than slanderers themselves. *Proverb*

18338. Jocular slanders often prove serious injuries. *Proverb*

18339. If you slander a dead man, you stab him in the grave. *Proverb*

18340. Defaming or slandering others is the greatest of all sins. *Proverb*

18341. He that flings dirt at another dirtieth himself most. *Proverb*

18342.

Was it a friend or foe that spread these lies?
Nay, who but infants question in such wise,
'Twas one of my most intimate enemies. ROSSETTI, *Fragment*

18343.
For slander lives upon succession
For ever housed where it gets pos-
   session.   SHAKESPEARE,
        The Comedy of Errors

18344.
                    Slander,
Whose edge is sharper than the
   sword, whose tongue
Outvenoms all the worms of Nile,
   whose breath
Rides on the posting winds and doth
   belie
All corners of the world.
        SHAKESPEARE, *Cymbeline*

18345. Done to death by slanderous
tongues.   SHAKESPEARE,
        Much Ado About Nothing

See also: 27, 3867, 7045, 20208.

SLAVERY

**Related Subjects: Despotism, Mas-
ter, Negro, Tyranny.**

18351. God has sent all men into the
world free, and nature has made no
man a slave.   ALCIDAMAS

18352. To think such breasts must
suckle slaves.   BYRON, *Don Juan*

18353. Beneath the favored middle
and upper classes is a large group
which exists in virtual slavery. It is
not the slavery of the past, however,
but the slavery of ignorance and lack
of training, the slavery to machines
which have not been properly related
to the needs of the men who run them,
and the slavery to outmoded institutions which have not yet been sup-
planted by those better adjusted to
modern industry and science.
        MORDECAI EZEKIEL, *$2500 a Year*

18354. Corrupted freemen are the
worst of slaves.   DAVID GARRICK

18355. I believe this government cannot endure permanently half slave
and half free.   LINCOLN

18356. My paramount object in this
struggle is to save the Union, and is
not either to save or destroy slavery.
If I could save the Union without
freeing any slave, I would do it; and
if I could do it by freeing all the
slaves, I would do it; and if I could
save it by freeing some and leaving
others alone, I would also do that.
        LINCOLN

18357.
They are slaves who fear to speak
For the fallen and the weak;
They are slaves who will not choose
Hatred, scoffing and abuse,
Rather than in silence shrink
From the truth, they needs must
   think;
They are slaves who dare not be
In the right with two or three.
        LOWELL, *Freedom*

18358. One made the observation of
the people of Asia that they were all
slaves to one man, merely because
they could not pronounce that syllable
No.   PLUTARCH

18359.
                    Mechanic slaves
With greasy aprons, rules, and ham-
   mers.
SHAKESPEARE, *Antony and Cleopatra*

18360. There is nothing to wonder at
in the Pyramids so much as the fact
that so many men could be found degraded enough to spend their lives
constructing a tomb for some ambitious booby, whom it would have been
manlier to have drowned in the Nile.
        THOREAU, *Walden*

18361. That execrable sum of all vil-
lainies, commonly called the Slave
Trade.   JOHN WESLEY, *Journal*

18362. Once fully enslaved, no nation, state, or city of this earth, ever afterward resumes its liberty.

WALT WHITMAN, *To the States*

See also: 1151, 2531, 2623, 3365, 3464, 4387, 4526, 5429, 6660, 6905, 6950, 7835, 13853, 13863, 17819.

SLEEP

Related Subjects: Bed, Dreams, Night, Rest, Rising.

18371. Sweet are the slumbers of the virtuous man.   ADDISON, *Cato*

18372. He went to bed and slept the sleep of the good-for-nothing, which, by an anachronism not a single songwriter has yet struck, is proven to be more sound than that of innocence.

BALZAC,
The Girl With the Golden Eyes

18373. It is vain for you to rise up early, to sit up late, to eat the bread of sorrows: for so he giveth his beloved sleep. *Bible: Psalms, cxxvii, 2*

18374. Yet a little sleep, a little slumber, a little folding of the hands to sleep.   *Bible: Proverbs, vi, 10*

18375. The sleep of a labouring man is sweet.   *Bible: Ecclesiastes, v, 12*

18376. In order to know when it is time to sleep I *never* look at my watch. I do that *only* mornings, to find out when it is time to get up.

BRAHMS
Schauffler: The Unknown Brahms

18377.
Sleep is a death; oh, make me try
By sleeping, what it is to die,
And as gently lay my head
On my grave, as now my bed!

SIR THOMAS BROWNE,
Religio Medici

18378. Sleep hath its own world, a boundary between the things misnamed death and existence.   BYRON

18379. Now blessings light on him that first invented this same sleep! It covers a man all over, thoughts and all, like a cloak; 'tis meat for the hungry, drink for the thirsty, heat for the cold, and cold for the hot. 'Tis the current coin that purchases all the pleasures of the world cheap; and the balance that sets the king and the shepherd, the fool and the wise man even.   CERVANTES, *Don Quixote*

18380.
Oh sleep! it is a gentle thing,
Beloved from pole to pole.
COLERIDGE, *The Ancient Mariner*

18381.
Care-charmer Sleep, son of the sable Night,
Brother to Death, in silent darkness born.   SAMUEL DANIEL, *To Delia*

18382. It is a common rule with primitive people not to waken a sleeper, because his soul is away and might not have time to get back.

SIR JAMES G. FRAZER,
The Golden Bough

18383. I cannot sleep a wink.
HORACE

18384. That indescribable expression peculiar to people who hope they have not been asleep, but know they have.
HELEN HUNT JACKSON, *Ramona*

18385. Preserve me from unseasonable and immoderate sleep.
SAMUEL JOHNSON,
Prayers and Meditations

18386. I never take a nap after dinner but when I have had a bad night; and then the nap takes me.
SAMUEL JOHNSON, *Boswell: Life*

18387.

Dear is my sleep, but more to be
    mere stone,
So long as ruin and dishonor reign:
To hear naught, to feel naught, is my
    great gain;
Then wake me not; speak in an
    undertone.   MICHELANGELO

18388. No small art is it to sleep: it
is necessary for that purpose to keep
awake all day.
NIETZSCHE, *Thus Spake Zarathustra*

18389.

Thank God for sleep!
And, when you cannot sleep,
Still thank Him that you live
To lie awake. JOHN OXENHAM,
    The Sacrament of Sleep

18390. One hour's sleep before midnight is worth two hours after.
    Proverb

18391. In sleep, what difference is
there between Solomon and a fool?
    Proverb

18392. He sleeps well who knows not
that he sleeps ill.
    PUBLILIUS SYRUS, *Sententiae*

18393.

The people sleep.
Ai! Ai! The people sleep.
Yet the sleepers toss in sleep
and an end comes of sleep
and the sleepers wake.
Ai! Ai! the sleepers wake!
  CARL SANDBURG, *The People, Yes*

18394.

          Weariness
Can snore upon the flint when resty
    sloth
Finds the down pillow hard.
    SHAKESPEARE, *Cymbeline*

18395. I have not slept one wink.
    SHAKESPEARE, *Cymbeline*

18396.

    O sleep, O gentle sleep,
Nature's soft nurse! How have I
    frighted thee,
That thou no more wilt weigh my
    eyelids down
And steep my senses in forgetful-
    ness?   SHAKESPEARE, *Henry IV*

18397. Winding up days with toil and
nights with sleep.
    SHAKESPEARE, *Henry V*

18398. Downy sleep, death's counterfeit.   SHAKESPEARE, *Macbeth*

18399.

Methought I heard a voice cry, "Sleep
    no more!
Macbeth does murder sleep!" the in-
    nocent sleep,
Sleep that knits up the ravell'd sleave
    of care,
The death of each day's life, sore
    labour's bath,
Balm of hurt minds, great nature's
    second course,
Chief nourisher in life's feast.
    SHAKESPEARE, *Macbeth*

18400.

Sleep shall neither night nor day
Hang upon his pent-house lid.
    SHAKESPEARE, *Macbeth*

18401.

    Not poppy, nor mandragora,
Nor all the drowsy syrups of the
    world,
Shall ever medicine thee to that sweet
    sleep
Which thou ow'dst yesterday.
    SHAKESPEARE, *Othello*

18402. A nap, my friend, is a brief
period of sleep which overtakes
superannuated persons when they endeavor to entertain unwelcome visitors or to listen to scientific lectures.
    BERNARD SHAW,
    Back to Methuselah

18403.
Thou hast been called, O sleep! the friend of woe;
But 'tis the happy that have called thee so.
SOUTHEY, *The Curse of Kehama*

18404.
Sleep is as nice as woman;
The more I court it, the more it flies me.   SIR JOHN SUCKLING,
The Tragedy of Brennoralt

18405. Sleep, Death's twin-brother.
TENNYSON, *In Memoriam*

18406.
Who can wrestle against Sleep?—
Yet is that giant very gentleness.
MARTIN F. TUPPER, *Of Beauty*

18407. Blessed barrier between day and day.   WORDSWORTH, *To Sleep*

18408. Tired nature's sweet restorer, balmy sleep!
EDWARD YOUNG, *Night Thoughts*

See also: 213, 521, 1022, 1094, 1374, 2073, 2868, 5017, 5080, 5108, 5122, 10206, 13983, 15758, 17699.

SMILE

Related Subjects: Charm, Cheerfulness, Good Humor, Laughter, Mouth.

18411. What sunshine is to flowers, smiles are to humanity. They are but trifles, to be sure; but, scattered along life's pathway, the good they do is inconceivable.   ADDISON

18412. An insincere grin? No. That doesn't fool anybody. We know it is mechanical and we resent it. I am talking about a real smile, a heart-warming smile, a smile that comes from within, the kind of a smile that

will bring a good price in the market place.   DALE CARNEGIE,
How To Win Friends

18413. You don't feel like smiling? Then what? Two things. First, force yourself to smile. If you are alone, force yourself to whistle or hum a tune or sing. Act as if you were already happy, and that will tend to make you happy.
DALE CARNEGIE,
How to Win Friends

18414. The social smile, the sympathetic tear.   THOMAS GRAY,
Education & Government

18415. With the smile that was childlike and bland,   BRET HARTE,
Plain Language from Truthful James

18416.
Eternal smiles his emptiness betray,
As shallow streams run dimpling all the way.
POPE, *Epistle to Dr. Arbuthnot*

18417. Better the last smile than the first laughter.   *Proverb*

18418.
Seldom he smiles, and smiles in such a sort
As if he mock'd himself, and scorn'd his spirit
That could be moved to smile at anything.
SHAKESPEARE, *Julius Caesar*

18419. Sunshine and rain at once; her smiles and tears.
SHAKESPEARE, *King Lear*

See also: 1676, 3282, 9322.

SMITH, see Blacksmith

SMOKING, see Tobacco

SMUGNESS, see Complacency

SNAIL

Related Subject: Animal.

18421.
The snail, which everywhere doth
    roam,
Carrying his own house still, still is at
    home.
JOHN DONNE, *To Sir Henry Wotton*

18422. The slow snail climbeth the
tower at last, though the swift swallow mount it sooner.
            JOHN LYLY, *Euphues*

18423.
    The snail, whose tender horns be-
        ing hit,
Shrinks backward in his shelly cave
    with pain,
And there, all smother'd up, in shade
    doth sit,
Long after fearing to creep forth
    again.
SHAKESPEARE, *Venus and Adonis*

SNAKE, see Serpent

SNEER

**Related Subjects: Contempt, Cyni-
cism, Insult.**

18431. There was a laughing devil in
his sneer.   BYRON, *The Corsair*

18432. I can't help it, I was born
sneering.
        W. S. GILBERT, *The Mikado*

18433. A sneer is the weapon of the
weak. Like other devil's weapons, it is
always cunningly ready to our hand,
and there is more poison in the handle
than in the point.   LOWELL

18434. Sir spokesman, sneers are
weakness veiling rage.
            GEORGE MEREDITH,
    A Ballad of Fair Ladies in Revolt

18435. Who can refute a sneer?
WILLIAM PALEY, *Moral Philosophy*

18436.
Damn with faint praise, assent with
    civil leer,
And without sneering, teach the rest
    to sneer.
        POPE, *Epistle to Dr. Arbuthnot*

18437. I fancy that it is just as hard
to do your duty when men are sneering at you as when they are shooting
at you.   WOODROW WILSON

See also: 19862.

SNEEZING

Related Subject: Nose.

18441. He's a friend at a sneeze; the
most you can get of him is a God
bless you.   *Proverb*

18442. He hath sneezed thrice; turn
him out of the hospital.   *Proverb*

SNOB

**Related Subjects: Club, Fop, In-
tellectuals, Society, Vanity.**

18451. Snobbery is the pride of those
who are not sure of their position.
            BERTON BRALEY

18452. To turn up his nose at his
father's customers.
            GEORGE ELIOT,
        The Mill on the Floss

18453. I attach but little value to
rank or wealth, but the line must be
drawn somewhere. A man in that station may be brave and worthy, but at
every step he would commit solecisms
that society would never pardon.
    W. S. GILBERT, *H. M. S. Pinafore*

18454. Snobbery is but a point in
time. Let us have patience with our
inferiors. They are ourselves of yesterday.

    ISAAC GOLDBERG, *Tin Pan Alley*

18455. We are all snobs of the Infinite, parvenus of the Eternal.

J. G. HUNEKER, *Iconoclasts*

18456. Ain't a snob a fellow as wants to be taken for better bred, or richer, or cleverer, or more influential than he really is?

CHARLES LEVER, *One of Them*

18457. He who meanly admires a mean thing is a Snob—perhaps that is a safe definition of the character.

THACKERAY, *Book of Snobs*

18458. A tuft-hunter is a snob, a parasite is a snob, the man who allows the manhood within him to be awed by a coronet is a snob. The man who worships mere wealth is a snob.

ANTHONY TROLLOPE,
Life of Thackeray

See also: 822, 1157, 6944, 19168.

SNOW

Related Subjects: Clouds, Frost, Ice, Weather, Winter.

18461.
"It snows!" cries the school-boy,
    "Hurrah!" and his shout
Is ringing through parlor and hall,
While swift as the wing of a swallow, he's out,
    And his playmates have answered
    his call. SARAH HALE, *It Snows*

18462. The pity of the snow, that hides all scars.

EDWIN MARKHAM,
Lincoln, The Man of the People

18463. You came as seasonably as snow in summer.   *Proverb*

18464. Whether you boil snow or pound it, you can have but water of it.
Proverb

18465. As white as the driven snow.
Proverb

18466.
    A little snow, tumbled about,
Anon becomes a mountain.

SHAKESPEARE, *King John*

18467. Where are the snows of yester-year? FRANÇOIS VILLON,
The Greater Testament

18468.
Like an army defeated
The snow hath retreated.

WORDSWORTH, *Written in March*

See also: 181, 3169.

SOCIALISM

Related Subjects: Capitalism, Fascism, Society.

18471. I am afraid to read radical books lest they should lead me perforce to radical conclusions and I should feel bound to sell all I have and give to the poor.

GAMALIEL BRADFORD

18472. In metaphysics I am content to be above the battle; in morals and politics, since there is a battle, I must be on the left, meaning by the left those who wish to participate in the adventure of a co-operative life for mankind. IRWIN EDMAN, *I Believe*

18473. The awakening of what the socialist vocabulary calls class consciousness in the working multitudes appears to us an important step forward if we regard it as the arousing of a consciousness of human dignity, rebuffed and humiliated, and of a consciousness of a vocation.

JACQUES MARITAIN, *I Believe*

18474. The socialist minister of the future must try to be as good a man at business for public ends as the ablest of the capitalists or managing directors are for private ends. It is essential that socialism should be sound public business as well as being healthy in its social morality.

HERBERT MORRISON

18475. But we must realize that the philosophy of Socialism has gradually permeated the entire structure of society the world over, and almost the only points in dispute are the pace and the methods of advance to its full realization. India will have to go that way, too, if she seeks to end her poverty and inequality, though she may evolve her own methods and may adapt the ideal to the genius of her race.   JAWAHARLAL NEHRU, *India and the World*

18476. Letting yourself be robbed is Americanism; defending yourself against robbery is Socialism.

UPTON SINCLAIR

SOCIETY

Related Subjects: **Capitalism, Club, Community, Conventionality, Custom, Environment, Fashion, Isolation, Snob, Socialism.**

18481. A society consists of a certain number of individuals living in a particular way in a particular place, at a particular time; nothing else.

W. H. AUDEN, *I Believe*

18482. Like unto nature, society, social nature, busies itself with insects, with the flowers of a day, with trifles, fancies, and, like it, also vomits fire and flame from its everlasting crater.

BALZAC, *The Girl With the Golden Eyes*

18483. Each sphere still throws its spawn into a superior one. The son of a rich grocer is made a notary, the son of a lumber merchant becomes a lawyer.   BALZAC, *The Girl With the Golden Eyes*

18484. None of us liveth to himself.

Bible: Romans, xiv, 7

18485. To stay experimentation in things social and economic is a grave responsibility. Denial of the right to experiment may be fraught with serious consequences to a nation. It is one of the happy incidents of the federal system that a single courageous state may, if its citizens choose, serve as a laboratory and try novel social and economic experiments without risk to the rest of the country.

JUSTICE BRANDEIS

18436. The democrat believes that society is built from the bottom, the aristocrat thinks society is suspended from the top. The democrat says: Legislate for all the people, for he believes that the prosperity of the masses will find its way up through the classes that rest upon the masses. The aristocrat, believing that society is suspended from the top, says, and he says it honestly—for he believes it: Legislate for the well-to-do and then be patient and wait until their prosperity leaks through to those below.

WILLIAM JENNINGS BRYAN

18487. The first condition of social happiness and prosperity must be the sense of the Common Life.

EDWARD CARPENTER, *Pagan & Christian Creeds*

18488.
While there is a lower class, I am in it.
While there is a criminal element, I am of it.
While there is a soul in jail, I am not free.   EUGENE V. DEBS

18489. An institution is the lengthened shadow of one man.

EMERSON, *Self-Reliance*

18490. Something is wrong when people suffer for food, clothing and shelter in the midst of abundant resources. Something is wrong when one-quarter or one-third of our workers cannot find work to do. Something is wrong when the family that grows cotton cannot afford clothing or mattresses, when the men who make automobiles cannot buy them, when the men who build houses cannot afford to live in even the cheapest new one.

MORDECAI EZEKIEL, *Jobs For All*

18491. Our whole social life is in essence but a long striving for the victory of justice over force.

GALSWORTHY

18492.
I owe a debt to society.
How much?
How much does society owe me?
A great deal too much.
Will it ever pay?
Never!
(Liberty, Equality, Fraternity)
PAUL GAUGUIN, *Intimate Journals*

18493. To educate men who must be condemned to poverty is to make them restive; to base on a state of most glaring social inequality political institutions under which men are theoretically equal, is to stand a pyramid on its apex.

HENRY GEORGE,
Progress and Poverty

18494. In almost every one, if not in every one, of the greatest political controversies of the last fifty years, whether they affected the franchise, whether they affected commerce, whether they affected religion, whether they affected the bad and abominable institution of slavery, or what subjects they touched, these leisured classes, these educated classes, these titled classes have been in the wrong.   GLADSTONE

18495. The great disasters of society are never started by subversives anyway. Subversives merely cash the check after good and patriotic, but mistaken, men have opened the account for them.

SAMUEL GRAFTON,
I'd Rather Be Right

18496. A terrible syllogism holds me in its clutches, and since I cannot refute the proposition that all men have the right to eat, I must submit to all the consequences. It has long been judged and condemned, this old social order. Let justice be done upon it! Let it be destroyed, this old world in which innocence perished and selfishness prospered, where man caused man to starve! Let it be wrecked from base to summit, this whited sepulchre full of lies and injustice! And blessed be the grocers who will make paper bags out of my poems for coffee or tobacco for the poor old women who in the present world of injustice perhaps have to go without such luxuries—*vivat justitia, pereat mundus!*

HEINE

18497. The three problems of the age—the degradation of man by poverty, the ruin of woman by starvation, and the dwarfing of childhood by physical and spiritual night.

VICTOR HUGO, *Les Miserables*

18498. The spirit of truth and the spirit of freedom—they are the pillars of society.

IBSEN, *Pillars of Society*

18499. I took with me certain simple criteria with which to measure. That which made for more life, for physical and spiritual health, was good; that which made for less life, which hurt, dwarfed and distorted life, was bad.   JACK LONDON,
People of the Abyss

18500. The history of all hitherto existing society is the history of class struggles.   KARL MARX, *Manifesto of the Communist Party*

18501. I believe, in fact, that the adventure of humanity is essentially an adventure of groups. It is also an adventure of individuals in conflict with groups or with each other.
JULES ROMAINS, *I Believe*

18502. But the eternal longing for a new order, a more just and more human order will never be suppressed. A thousand times extinguished it will leap into flame a thousand and one times.
ROMAIN ROLLAND, *I Will Not Rest*

18503. In spite of our efforts and in spite of our talk, we have not weeded out the overprivileged and we have not effectively lifted up the underprivileged. Both of these manifestations of injustice have retarded happiness.
FRANKLIN D. ROOSEVELT,
Message to Congress, Jan. 4, 1935

18504. Do not waste your time on social questions. What is the matter with the poor is Poverty. What is the matter with the rich is Uselessness.
BERNARD SHAW

18505. Every person who owes his life to civilized society and who has enjoyed since his childhood its very costly protections and advantages should appear at reasonable intervals before a properly qualified jury to justify his existence, which should be summarily and painlessly terminated if he fails to justify it and it develops that he is a positive nuisance and more trouble than he is worth. Nothing less will really make people responsible citizens.
BERNARD SHAW

18506. It is becoming almost impossible to doubt that unless we somehow manage to get together in a conscious effort to make things much better than they have ever been before, things will get intolerably worse.
JOHN STRACHEY, *I Believe*

18507. Morality, love, friendship and justice—all these are forms of expressing mutual aid. Mankind develops and progresses only on the condition that it obeys these fundamental laws, otherwise it perishes.
SUN YAT-SEN,
Memoirs of a Chinese Revolutionary

18508. Society is divided into two classes; the shearers and the shorn. We should always be with the former against the latter.   TALLEYRAND

18509. It seems clear to me that God designed us to live in society—just as He has given the bees the honey; and as our social system could not subsist without the sense of justice, He has given us the power to acquire that sense.   VOLTAIRE

Society in the fashionable sense

18510. Casual social intercourse is like dram-drinking, a mere stimulant that whips the nerves but does not nourish.   ALDOUS HUXLEY, *Essays*

18511.
            Society is no comfort
To one not sociable.
SHAKESPEARE, *Cymbeline*

18512. Society is commonly too cheap. We meet at very short intervals, not having had time to acquire any new value for each other.
THOREAU, *Walden*

18513.
                        There is
One great society alone on earth;

The noble living and the noble dead.
  WORDSWORTH, *The Prelude*

See also: 155, 241, 641, 695, 706, 1171, 1431, 1785, 2362, 3129, 3806, 3883, 4104, 4525, 4571, 4582, 5732, 7054, 9784, 12478, 16218, 21593, 22054.

SOCRATES

18521.
Socrates . . .
Whom, well inspir'd, the oracle pronounc'd
Wisest of men.   MILTON
See also: 3320, 3322, 3328.

SOLDIER

Related Subjects: Army, Conquerors, Discipline, War.

18531. As that great captain, Ziska, would have a drum made of his skin when he was dead, because he thought the very noise of it would put his enemies to flight. ROBERT BURTON,
  Anatomy of Melancholy

18532. If my soldiers were to begin to reflect, not one of them would remain in the ranks.
   FREDERICK THE GREAT

18533. The sex is ever to a soldier kind.
  POPE, *The Odyssey of Homer*

18534.
Ben Battle was a soldier bold,
 And used to war's alarms;
But a cannon-ball took off his legs,
 So he laid down his arms!
   THOMAS HOOD,
  Faithless Nellie Gray

18535.
It's Tommy this, an' Tommy that, an' "Chuck 'im out, the brute!"
But it's "Savior of 'is country," when the guns begin to shoot.
   KIPLING, *Tommy*

18536. Back of every soldier is a woman. EDGAR LEE MASTERS,
  Spoon River Anthology

18537. The blood of the soldier makes the glory of the general.
   Proverb

18538. Soldiers are martyrs to ambition. *Proverb*

18539.
Soldiers are citizens of death's grey land,
Drawing no dividend from time's tomorrows.
In the great hour of destiny they stand,
Each with his feuds, and jealousies, and sorrows.
Soldiers are sworn to action; they must win.
Some flaming, fatal climax with their lives,
Soldiers are dreamers; when the guns begin
They think of firelit homes, clean beds, and wives.
  SIEGFRIED SASSOON, *Dreamers*

18540.
And telling me, the sovereign'st thing on earth
Was parmaceti for an inward bruise;
And that it was great pity, so it was,
This villanous saltpetre should be digg'd
Out of the bowels of the harmless earth,
Which many a good tall fellow had destroy'd
So cowardly; and but for these vile guns,
He would himself have been a soldier.
  SHAKESPEARE, *Henry IV*

18541. Food for powder, food for powder; they'll fill a pit as well as better. SHAKESPEARE, *Henry IV*

18542. The professional military mind is by necessity an inferior and unimaginative mind; no man of high intellectual quality would willingly imprison his gifts in such a calling.
                    H. G. WELLS,
              The Outline of History

18543.
Who is the happy Warrior? Who is he
That every man in arms would wish
    to be?   WORDSWORTH,
  Character of the Happy Warrior

See also: 295, 338, 1127, 1372, 1582, 2796, 11251, 15472, 15788, 16554, 17585.

SOLITUDE

Related Subjects: Desolation, Hermit, Isolation, Meditation, Retirement, Retreat.

18551.
There is a solitude in seeing you,
Followed by your company when you
    are gone.
          WITTER BYNNER, *Lightning*

18552. Part of me remained forever at Latitude 80° 08' South: what survived of my youth, my vanity, perhaps, and certainly my skepticism. On the other hand I did take away something that I had not fully possessed before: appreciation of the sheer beauty and miracle of being alive, and a humble set of values. All this happened four years ago. Civilization has not altered my ideas. I live more simply now, and with more peace.   ADMIRAL BYRD, *Alone*

18553. In solitude, where we are least alone.   BYRON, *Childe Harold*

18554.
Alone, alone, all, all alone;
Alone on a wide, wide sea.
          COLERIDGE, *The Ancient Mariner*

18555.
So lonely 'twas, that God himself
Scarce seemed there to be.
          COLERIDGE, *The Ancient Mariner*

18556.
Oh for a lodge in some vast wilderness,
Some boundless contiguity of shade,
Where rumour of oppression and deceit,
Of unsuccessful or successful war,
Might never reach me more.
              COWPER, *The Task*

18557. Solitude, the safeguard of mediocrity, is to genius the stern friend.   EMERSON, *Conduct of Life*

18558. When you have shut your doors, and darkened your room, remember never to say that you are alone, for you are not alone; but God is within, and your genius is within,—and what need have they of light to see what you are doing?
          EPICTETUS, *Discourses*

18559. I was never less alone than when by myself.   GIBBON,
                    Decline & Fall

18560. The great source of terror to infancy is solitude.
          WILLIAM JAMES, *Psychology*

18561. Solitude is as needful to the imagination as society is wholesome for the character.   LOWELL

18562. The nurse of full-grown souls is solitude.   LOWELL, *Columbus*

18563.
For solitude sometimes is best society,
And short retirement urges sweet return.   MILTON, *Paradise Lost*

18564. Nature has presented us with a large faculty of entertaining ourselves alone; and often calls us to it, to teach us that we owe ourselves partly to society, but chiefly and mostly to ourselves.

MONTAIGNE, *Essays*

18565. The bonds that unite another person to ourself exist only in our mind. Memory as it grows fainter relaxes them, and notwithstanding the illusion by which we would fain be cheated and with which, out of love, friendship, politeness, deference, duty, we cheat other people, we exist alone. Man is the creature that cannot emerge from himself, that knows his fellows only in himself; when he asserts the contrary, he is lying.

MARCEL PROUST,
The Sweet Cheat Gone

18566. Better be alone than in bad company.   *Proverb*

18567. A solitary man is either a brute or an angel.   *Proverb*

18568. I might have been a gold-fish in a glass bowl for all the privacy I got.   SAKI, *Reginald*

18569. To be alone is the fate of all great minds—a fate deplored at times, but still always chosen as the less grievous of two evils.

SCHOPENHAUER

18570. My dismal scene I needs must act alone.   SHAKESPEARE,
Romeo and Juliet

18571.
I love tranquil solitude
   And such society
As is quiet, wise, and good.
SHELLEY,
Rarely, Rarely, Comest Thou

18572. One can acquire everything in solitude—except character.

STENDHAL

18573. I love to be alone. I never found the companion that was so companiable as solitude.   THOREAU

18574.
When from our better selves we have too long
Been parted by the hurrying world, and droop,
Sick of its business, of its pleasures tired,
How gracious, how benign, is Solitude.   WORDSWORTH, *The Prelude*

See also: 2304, 3452, 3687, 18668.

SON

Related Subject: Family.

18581. A wise son maketh a glad father.   *Bible: Proverbs, x, 1*

18582.
And all to leave what with his toil he won
To that unfeather'd two-legged thing, a son.   DRYDEN,
Absalom & Achitophel

18583. Gods! How the son degenerates from the sire!   HOMER, *Iliad*

18584.
Your work was waste? Maybe your share
Lay in the hour you laughed and kissed;
Who knows but that your son shall wear
The laurels that his father missed?
LAURENCE HOPE, *The Masters*

18585. He only half dies who leaves an image of himself in his sons.

GOLDONI, *Pamela*

18586. He that has but one hog, makes him fat, and he that has but one son, makes him a fool.   *Proverb*

18587. Had I a dozen sons, each in my love alike and none less dear than thine and my good Marcius, I had rather eleven die nobly for their country than one voluptuously surfeit out of action.

SHAKESPEARE, *Coriolanus*

18588. That thou art my son, I have partly thy mother's word, partly my own opinion, but chiefly a villainous trick of thine eye and a foolish hanging of thy nether lip, that doth warrant me. SHAKESPEARE, *Henry IV*

18589. A wayward son, spiteful and wrathful. SHAKESPEARE, *Macbeth*

18590. The boy was the very staff of my age, my very prop.

SHAKESPEARE, *The Merchant of Venice*

See also: 2264, 2444, 2565, 3236, 4941, 6337, 10615, 14226, 18028.

SONG

Related Subjects: Ballad, Harmony, Melody, Music, Sing.

18591.
Would you have your songs endure?
Build on the human heart.

BROWNING, *Sordello*

18592.
Perhaps it may turn out a sang,
Perhaps turn out a sermon.

BURNS, *Epistle to a Young Friend*

18593.
A tune is more lasting than the voice of the birds.
A song is more lasting than the riches of the world.

PADRAIC COLUM,
Polonius and the Ballad-Singer

18594. Songs without words are best.
GEORGE DU MAURIER, *Peter Ibbetson*

18595. Give me the making of the songs of a nation, and I care not who makes its laws. ANDREW FLETCHER

18596. What will a child learn sooner than a song? HORACE

18597.
The self-same song that found a path
Through the sad heart of Ruth, when, sick for home,
She stood in tears amid the alien corn;
The same that oft-times hath
Charm'd magic casements, opening on the foam
Of perilous seas, in faery lands forlorn. KEATS,
Ode to a Nightingale

18598. Odds life! must one swear to the truth of a song?
MATTHEW PRIOR, *A Better Answer*

18599.
Now, good Cesario, but that piece of song,
That old and antique song we heard last night:
Methought it did relieve my passion much,
More than light airs and recollected terms
Of these most brisk and giddy-paced times. SHAKESPEARE,
Twelfth Night

18600.
I had rather than forty shillings I had my
Book of Songs and Sonnets here.
SHAKESPEARE,
The Merry Wives of Windsor

18601. I would rather be remembered by a song than by a victory. I would rather build a fine sonnet than have built St. Paul's.
ALEXANDER SMITH, *Dreamthorp*

18602.
The song that nerves a nation's heart
Is in itself a deed. TENNYSON,
The Charge of the Heavy Brigade

See also: 2042, 2049, 3381, 3672.

SONNET

Related Subjects: Poets and Poetry.

18611.
The sonnet is a trunk, and you must pack
With care, to ship frail baggage far away;
The octet is the trunk; sestet, the tray;
Tight, but not overloaded, is the knack. CHRISTOPHER MORLEY,
Thoughts While Packing a Trunk

18612.
A sonnet is a moment's monument,—
Memorial from the Soul's eternity
To one dead deathless hour.
ROSSETTI, *The Sonnet*

18613. A torturer of phrases into sonnets. SCOTT, *Auchindrane*

18614. Will you then write me a sonnet in praise of my beauty?
SHAKESPEARE,
Much Ado About Nothing

18615. Deep-brain'd sonnets.
SHAKESPEARE,
A Lover's Complaint
18616.
Spare thou no pains; carve thought's pure diamond
With fourteen facets, scattering fire and light. J. A. SYMONDS,
The Sonnet

See also: 357, 2164, 18600.

SOPHISTRY

Related Subjects: Evasion, Excuse, Metaphysics, Philosophy.

18621. The juggle of sophistry consists, for the most part, in using a word in one sense in the premises, and in another sense in the conclusion. COLERIDGE

18622. To reason justly from a false principle is the perfection of sophistry, which it is more difficult to expose than to refute false reasoning. The proper way to expose its errors is to show that just and conclusive reasonings have been built on some false or absurd principle.
NATHANIEL EMMONS

18623. Some men weave their sophistry till their own reason is entangled. SAMUEL JOHNSON

18624. Sophistry, like poison, is at once detected and nauseated, when presented to us in a concentrated form; but a fallacy which, when stated barely in a few sentences, would not deceive a child, may deceive half the world, if diluted in a quarto volume.
RICHARD WHATELY

See also: 1129, 1131, 1446.

SORROW

Related Subjects: Consolation, Depression, Desolation, Despair, Grief, Loss, Melancholy, Mourning, Regret, Tears, Soul, Sympathy, Woe.

18631. Is it nothing to you, all ye that pass by? behold, and see if there be any sorrow like unto my sorrow.
Bible: Lamentations, i, 12

18632. I am lorn with-outen remedye. CHAUCER,
Canterbury Tales

18633. You cannot prevent the birds of sorrow from flying over your head, but you can prevent them from building nests in your hair.
Chinese Proverb
18634.
The path of sorrow, and that path alone,

Leads to the land where sorrow is
unknown.   COWPER,
*To an Afflicted Protestant Lady
in France*

18635. Sadness is a wall between
two gardens. KAHLIL GIBRAN,
Sand and Foam

18636. The sorrow for the dead is
the only sorrow from which we refuse to be divorced. Every other
wound we seek to heal, every other
affliction to forget; but this wound
we consider it a duty to keep open;
this affliction we cherish and brood
over in solitude.
WASHINGTON IRVING,
The Sketch-Book

18637. Hang sorrow! care'll kill a
cat.   BEN JONSON,
Every Man in His Humour

18638.
Into each life some rain must fall,
  Some days must be dark and
    dreary. LONGFELLOW,
        The Rainy Day

18639.
There is no flock, however watched
    and tended,
But one dead lamb is there!
There is no fireside, howsoe'er de-
    fended,
  But has one vacant chair!
    LONGFELLOW, *Resignation*

18640.
        There is no greater sorrow
Than to be mindful of the happy
    time
In misery. LONGFELLOW, *Inferno*

18641. Believe me, every man has
his secret sorrows, which the world
knows not, and oftentimes we call a
man cold when he is only sad.
        LONGFELLOW

18642.
This is life's sorrow:

That one can be happy only where
    two are;
And that our hearts are drawn to
    stars
Which want us not.
    EDGAR LEE MASTERS,
        Spoon River Anthology

18643. Sorrows remembered sweeten
present joy. ROBERT POLLOK,
        The Course of Time

18644. Better two losses than one
sorrow.   *Proverb*

18645. It is a curious thing in human
experience, but to live through a period of stress and sorrow with another human being creates a bond
which nothing seems able to break.
People can be happy together and
look back on their contacts very pleasantly, but such contacts will not make
the same kind of bond that sorrow
lived through together will create.
        ELEANOR ROOSEVELT

18646.
When sorrows come, they come not
    single spies,
But in battalions.
    SHAKESPEARE, *Hamlet*

18647. A countenance more in sorrow than in anger.
    SHAKESPEARE, *Hamlet*

18648. Affliction may one day smile
again; and till then, sit thee down,
sorrow!   SHAKESPEARE,
        Love's Labour's Lost

18649.
Give sorrow words; the grief that
    does not speak
Whispers the o'er-fraught heart and
    bids it break. SHAKESPEARE,
        Macbeth

18650.
Sorrow breaks seasons and reposing
    hours,

Makes the night morning, and the noontide night.

SHAKESPEARE, *Richard III*

18651.
 We look before and after,
  And pine for what is not;
 Our sincerest laughter
  With some pain is fraught;
Our sweetest songs are those that tell
 Of saddest thought.

SHELLEY, *To a Skylark*

18652.
   Each time we love,
We turn a nearer and a broader mark
To that keen archer, Sorrow, and he
 strikes. ALEXANDER SMITH,
     A Boy's Dream

18653. Sadness diminishes or hinders a man's power of action.

SPINOZA, *Ethics*

18654.
   Never morning wore
To evening, but some heart did
 break. TENNYSON, *In Memoriam*

18655. Where there is sorrow there is holy ground. OSCAR WILDE,
     De Profundis

See also: 1258, 1771, 2387, 2783, 2863, 2888, 9360, 9452, 10132, 11316, 11326, 14656, 21154.

SOUL

Related Subjects: Body, Eternity, Judgment Day, Life, Mind, Mortality, Salvation, Spirit.

18661. What is a man profited, if he shall gain the whole world, and lose his own soul?

Bible: Matthew, xvi, 26

18662. This night thy soul shall be required of thee.

Bible: Luke, xii, 20

18663. I should not dare to call my soul my own.

ELIZABETH B. BROWNING,
     Aurora Leigh

18664.
O God! it is a fearful thing
To see the human soul take wing
In any shape, in any mood.

BYRON, *The Prisoner of Chillon*

18665. Everywhere the human soul stands between a hemisphere of light and another of darkness on the confines of two everlasting hostile empires,—Necessity and Free Will.

CARLYLE, *Essays*

18666.
The soul of man is larger than the
 sky,
 Deeper than ocean, or the abysmal
  dark
Of the unfathomed center.

HARTLEY COLERIDGE,
    To Shakespeare

18667.
The soul selects her own society,
Then shuts the door.

EMILY DICKINSON, *Life*

18668.
The Soul's superior instants
 Occur to her alone.

EMILY DICKINSON,
    The Single Hound

18669.
Froba: Say, Nurse—in a hundred human beings, how many have got souls?
Nurse: It's difficult to say. So many people keep their souls locked up.

GALSWORTHY, *The Roof*

18670.
Out of the night that covers me,
 Black as the Pit from pole to pole,
I thank whatever gods may be
 For my unconquerable soul.

W. E. HENLEY, *Invictus*

18671.
Build thee more stately mansions, O
 my soul,

As the swift seasons roll!
Leave thy low-vaulted past!
Let each new temple, nobler than
    the last,
Shut thee from heaven with a dome
    more vast,
Till thou at length art free,
Leaving thine outgrown shell by
    life's unresting sea!
                    O. W. HOLMES,
            The Chambered Nautilus

18672.
A Soul of power, a well of lofty
    Thought
A chastened Hope that ever points
    to Heaven.   JOHN HUNTER,
            A Replication of Rhymes

18673.
Bards of Passion and of Mirth,
Ye have left your souls on earth!
Have ye souls in heaven too?
                    KEATS, *Ode*

18674. Great souls are portions of
Eternity.   LOWELL, *Sonnet VI*

18675.
Let not young souls be smothered out
    before
They do quaint deeds and fully flaunt
    their pride.
It is the world's one crime its babes
    grow dull,
Its poor are ox-like, limp and leaden
    eyed.
Not that they starve, but starve so
    dreamlessly,
Not that they sow, but that they sel-
    dom reap,
Not that they serve, but have no gods
    to serve,
Not that they die, but that they die
    like sheep.
                VACHEL LINDSAY,
                The Leaden-Eyed

18676.
I hold that when a person dies
    His soul returns again to earth;

Arrayed in some new flesh-disguise
    Another mother gives him birth.
With sturdier limbs and brighter
    brain
The old soul takes the roads again.
            JOHN MANSFIELD, *A Creed*

18677.
Passer by,
To love is to find your own soul
Through the soul of the beloved one.
            EDGAR LEE MASTERS,
                Spoon River Anthology

18678.
Now I, an under-tenant of the earth,
    can see
That the branches of a tree
Spread no wider than its roots.
And how shall the soul of a man
Be larger than the life he has lived?
            EDGAR LEE MASTERS,
                Spoon River Anthology

18679. You cannot hide the soul.
            HERMAN MELVILLE, *Moby Dick*

18680.
The soul that feeds on books alone—
I count that soul exceeding small
That lives alone by book and creed,—
A soul that has not learned to read.
                JOAQUIN MILLER,
                The Larger College

18681.
There was a little man, and he had a
    little soul;
And he said, Little Soul, let us try,
    try, try!   THOMAS MOORE,
                Little Man and Little Soul

18682. The soul of man is immortal
and imperishable.   PLATO,
                    The Republic

18683. It is with narrow-souled people as with narrow-necked bottles;
the less they have in them the more
noise they make in pouring out.
                    POPE,
            Thoughts on Various Subjects

18684. The soul is not where it lives, but where it loves. *Proverb*

18685. Little bodies have great souls. *Proverb*

18686. Would you damn your precious soul? Rabelais

18687. Every subject's duty is the king's; but every subject's soul is his own. Shakespeare, *Henry V*

18688. Now my soul hath elbow-room. Shakespeare, *King John*

18689. It's prudent to gain the whole world and lose your own soul. But don't forget that your soul sticks to you if you stick to it; but the world has a way of slipping through your fingers. Bernard Shaw,
Heartbreak House

18690.
The soul of man is like the rolling world,
One half in day, the other dipt in night;
The one has music and the flying cloud,
The other, silence and the wakeful stars. Alexander Smith,
Horton

18691.
The saddest thing that can befall a soul
Is when it loses faith in God and woman.
Alexander Smith, *A Life Drama*

18692.
For of the soule the bodie forme doth take:
For soule is forme, and doth the bodie make.
Edmund Spenser,
An Hymne in Honour of Beautie

18693. Casy! He talked a lot. Says one time he went out in the wilderness to find his own soul, an' he foun' he didn' have no soul that was his'n. Says he foun' he jus' got a little piece of a great big soul. Says a wilderness ain't no good, 'cause his little piece of a soul wasn't no good 'less it was with the rest, an' it was whole.
John Steinbeck,
The Grapes of Wrath

18694. No seed shall perish which the soul hath sown.
J. A. Symonds, *A Belief*

18695. Self is the only prison that can ever bind the soul.
Henry Van Dyke,
The Prison and the Angel

18696.
Of Christian souls more have been wrecked on shore
Than ever were lost at sea.
C. H. Webb,
With a Nantucket Shell

18697.
What do you suppose will satisfy the soul, except to walk free and own no superior?
Walt Whitman,
Laws for Creations

18698. I loaf and invite my soul.
Walt Whitman, *Song of Myself*

18699.
The windows of my soul I throw
Wide open to the sun.
Whittier, *My Psalm*

18700.
     The gods approve
The depth, and not the tumult, of the soul. Wordsworth,
Laodamia

18701.
Though inland far we be,
Our souls have sight of that immortal sea
Which brought us hither.
Wordsworth,
Ode on Intimations of Immortality

See also: 326, 333, 530, 732, 867, 1202, 1211, 1234, 1251, 1316, 1716, 1748, 1870, 2032, 2073, 2137, 2172, 2349, 2545, 2548, 2605, 3160, 3212, 3564, 3866, 3890, 4191, 4242, 4641, 4808, 5054, 5335, 6842, 9535, 10193, 12204, 14715, 14770, 16333, 16726, 17634, 17867, 18042, 18771, 19827, 19903, 21236.

SOUND

Related Subjects: Deafness, Ears, Echo, Noise, Silence, Voice.

18711. No sound is dissonant which tells of life.　　COLERIDGE,
This Lime-Tree Bower My Prison

18712. There is no sound but shall find some lovers, as the bitterest confections are grateful to some palates.
BEN JONSON, *Explorata*

18713. Not many sounds in life, and I include all urban and all rural sounds, exceed in interest a knock at the door.　CHARLES LAMB,
Valentine's Day

18714. Sonorous metal blowing martial sounds.　　MILTON,
Paradise Lost

18715. And empty heads console with empty sound.　　POPE,
The Dunciad

18716. Momentary as a sound.
SHAKESPEARE,
A Midsummer-Night's Dream

18717. Low, sweet, faint sounds, like the farewell of ghosts
SHELLEY, *Prometheus Unbound*

18718.
Sweet is every sound,
Sweeter thy voice, but every sound is sweet;
Myriads of rivulets hurrying thro' the lawn,

The moan of doves in immemorial elms,
And murmuring of innumerable bees.　TENNYSON, *The Princess*

18719. Sugar is not so sweet to the palate as sound to the healthy ear.
THOREAU, *Journal*

See also: 9543, 9693, 17911.

SPAIN AND THE SPANIARDS

Related Subjects: Europe.

18721. The Spaniard is a bad servant but a worse master.
THOMAS ADAMS, *Sermons*

19722. Oh, lovely Spain! renown'd romantic land!　　BYRON,
Childe Harold

18723.
Her soil has felt the foot-prints, and her clime
Been winnowed by the wings of Liberty.　THOMAS CAMPBELL,
Stanzas to the Memory of the Spanish Patriots

18724. There is no country in Europe which it is so easy to over-run as Spain; there is no country which it is more difficult to conquer.
MACAULAY

See also: 2885, 2886, 3282, 10873, 21383.

SPARROW

Related Subject: Birds.

18731.
I thought the sparrow's note from heaven,
Singing at dawn on the alder bough;
I brought him home, in his nest, at even;
He sings the song, but it cheers not now,
For I did not bring home the river and sky;—

He sang to my ear,—they sang to
my eye.
>   EMERSON, *Each and All*

18732.
He's cheerful in weather so bitterly
    cold
It freezes your bones to the
    marrow;
I'll admit he's a beggar, a gangster, a
    bum,
But I take off my hat to the
    sparrow.
>   MINNA IRVING, *The Sparrow*

18733.
The sparrows chirped as if they still
    were proud
Their race in Holy Writ should men-
    tioned be.   LONGFELLOW,
>   *The Birds of Killingworth*

SPECULATION

**Related Subjects: Gambling, Idea,
Risk, Theories, Thought.**

18741. A wise man was he who counselled that speculation should have
free course, and look fearlessly
toward all the thirty-two points of
the compass, whithersoever and howsoever it listed.   CARLYLE

18742. There is scarcely an instance
of a man who has made a fortune by
speculation and kept it.
>   ANDREW CARNEGIE,
>   *Empire of Business*

18743. The besetting evil of our age
is the temptation to squander and di-
lute thought on a thousand different
lines of inquiry.
>   SIR JOHN HERSCHEL

18744.
Thou hast no speculation in those
    eyes
Which thou dost glare with!
>   SHAKESPEARE, *Macbeth*

18745. More zeal and energy, more
fanatical hope and more intense
anguish have been expended over the
past century in efforts to "forecast"
the stock market than in almost any
other single line of human action.
>   R. D. SKINNER,
>   *Seven Kinds of Inflation*

18746.
What looks like swindling with a
    petty sum,
Is on a grand and speculative scale
Honest enough, so it be large enough.
>   WILLIAM W. STORY,
>   *Baron Fisco at Home*

18747. There are two times in a
man's life when he should not specu-
late: when he can't afford it and
when he can.   MARK TWAIN

See also: 17625.

SPEECH

**Related Subjects: Address, Con-
versation, Eloquence, Grammar,
Language, Lip, Mouth, Orator,
Talk, Tongue, Voice, Words.**

18751. Speech finely framed delighteth the ears.
>   *Apocrypha: 2 Maccabees*

18752. It is generally better to deal
by speech than by letter.
>   BACON, *Of Negotiating*

18753. My observation is that, generally speaking, poverty of speech is
the outward evidence of poverty of
mind.   BRUCE BARTON

18754. Though I say it that should
not say it.
>   BEAUMONT & FLETCHER,
>   *Wit at Several Weapons*

18755. Day unto day uttereth speech,
and night unto night showeth knowledge.
>   *Bible: Psalms, xix, 2*

18756. But let your communication be, Yea, yea; Nay, nay; for whatsoever is more than these cometh of evil. *Bible: Matthew, v, 37*

18757. They think that they shall be heard for their much speaking. *Bible: Matthew, vi, 7*

18758. Let your speech be always with grace, seasoned with salt. *Bible: Colossians, iv, 6*

18759. Let him now speak, or else hereafter for ever hold his peace. *Book of Common Prayer*

18760.
He said
Little, but to the purpose. BYRON, *Don Juan*

18761. To know how to say what others only know how to think is what makes men poets or sages; and to dare to say what others only dare to think makes men martyrs or reformers or both. ELIZABETH CHARLES, *Chronicles*

18762. As a vessel is known by the sound, whether it be cracked or not; so men are proved, by their speeches, whether they be wise or foolish. DEMOSTHENES

18763. Let thy speech be better than silence, or be silent. DIONYSIUS THE ELDER

18764.
What is the use of speech? Silence were fitter:
Lest we should still be wishing things unsaid. ERNEST DOWSON, *You Would Have Understood Me*

18765. We have medicines to make women speak; we have none to make them keep silence. ANATOLE FRANCE, *The Man Who Married a Dumb Wife*

18766. Monkeys, who very sensibly refrain from speech, lest they should be set to earn their livings. KENNETH GRAHAME, *The Golden Age*

18767. It is easier not to speak a word at all than to speak more words than we should. THOMAS À KEMPIS, *Of the Imitation of Christ*

18768. Speech is civilization itself. The word, even the most contradictory word, preserves contact—it is silence which isolates. THOMAS MANN, *The Magic Mountain*

18769. Oh, that men would learn that the true speaker is he who speaks only when he has something to say! PLUTARCH

18770. He that speaks, sows; he that hears, reaps. *Proverb*

18771. Speech is a mirror of the soul: as a man speaks, so is he. PUBLILIUS SYRUS, *Sententiae*

18772. Speech is the index of the mind. SENECA

18773. Well said: that was laid on with a trowel. SHAKESPEARE, *As You Like It*

18774. I will speak daggers to her, but use none. SHAKESPEARE, *Hamlet*

18775.
Mend your speech a little,
Lest you may mar your fortunes. SHAKESPEARE, *King Lear*

18776. He draweth out the thread of his verbosity finer than the staple of his argument. SHAKESPEARE, *Love's Labour's Lost*

18777.
Your fair discourse hath been as sugar,
Making the hard way sweet and delectable.   SHAKESPEARE,
Richard II

18778. She speaks, yet she says nothing.   SHAKESPEARE,
Romeo and Juliet

18779. Let any man speak long enough, he will get believers.
STEVENSON,
The Master of Ballantrae

See also: 147, 196, 660, 661, 2793, 3107, 4966, 5933, 6748, 9993, 10033.

SPEED

Related Subjects: Aviation, Haste, Promptness.

18781. In skating over thin ice our safety is our speed.   EMERSON,
Prudence

18782. To go as fast as a friar that is invited to dinner.   *Proverb*

18783. In the twinkling of an eye.
SHAKESPEARE,
The Merchant of Venice

See also: 1194, 1432, 16516.

SPIDER

18791.
Habitant of castle gray;
Creeping thing in sober way,
Visible sage mechanician,
Skilfulest arithmetician.
W. E. CHANNING, *The Spider*

18792.
I've lately had two spiders
Crawling upon my startled hopes—
Now though thy friendly hand has brushed 'em from me,
Yet still they crawl offensive to mine eyes:

I would have some kind friend to tread upon 'em.
COLLEY CIBBER,
Richard III (Adaptation)

18793.
Much like a subtle spider, which doth sit
In middle of her web, which spreadeth wide;
If aught do touch the utmost thread of it,
She feels it instantly on every side.
SIR JOHN DAVIES,
The Immortality of the Soul

18794.
"Will you walk into my parlour?" said the spider to the fly;
"'Tis the prettiest little parlour that ever you did spy."
MARY HOWITT,
The Spider and the Fly

18795.
The spider's touch, how exquisitely fine!
Feels at each thread, and lives along the line.   POPE, *Essay on Man*

18796. The spider lost her distaff, and is ever since forced to draw her thread through her tail.   *Proverb*

18797. When the spider is ranging in the different apartments of his web it is true that he only can weave so fine a thread; but it is in the power of the merest drone that has wings, to fly through and destroy it.
SIR RICHARD STEELE

See also: 611, 2183, 8232.

SPIRIT

Related Subjects: Angel, Courage, Ghost, Mind, Soul.

18801. Regard not them that have familiar spirits, neither seek after wizards, to be defiled by them.
Bible: Leviticus, xix, 31

18802. And when they shall say unto you, Seek unto them that have familiar spirits, and unto wizards that peep, and that mutter: should not a people seek unto their God? for the living to the dead? To the law and to the testimony: if they speak not according to this word, it is because there is no light in them.

Bible: Isaiah, viii, 19, 20

18803. Not of the letter, but of the spirit; for the letter killeth, but the spirit giveth life.

Bible: 2 Corinthians, iii, 6

18804. The great spirits that have gone before us can only survive as disembodied voices.   CARLYLE

18805. Spirit is now a very fashionable word; to act with spirit, to speak with spirit, means only to act rashly, and to talk indiscreetly. An able man shows his spirit by gentle words and resolute actions; he is neither hot nor timid.   LORD CHESTERFIELD

18806. A man of a right spirit is not a man of narrow and private views, but is greatly interested and concerned for the good of the community to which he belongs, and particularly of the city or village in which he resides, and for the true welfare of the society of which he is a member.   JONATHAN EDWARDS

18807.
Millions of spiritual creatures walk
    the earth
Unseen, both when we wake, and
    when we sleep.   MILTON,
                 Paradise Lost

18808.
Glendower. I can call spirits from the vasty deep.
Hotspur. Why, so can I, or so can any man;

But will they come when you do call for them?   SHAKESPEARE,
                 Henry IV

18809. High spirit in man is like a sword, which, though worn to annoy his enemies, yet is often troublesome to his friends: he can hardly wear it so inoffensively but it is apt to incommode one or other of the company; it is more properly a loaded pistol, which accident alone may fire and kill one.   W. SHENSTONE

18810.
Nothing in the world is single,
All things by a law divine
In one spirit meet and mingle.
    SHELLEY, *Love's Philosophy*

See also: 23, 654, 3274, 4817, 5750, 16987, 17193, 20954.

SPORT

Related Subjects: Amusement, Exercise, Fish, Fun, Hawk, Horse, Hunting, Merriment, Pleasure, Recreation, Swimming.

18811. I have known the time when a pugilistic encounter between two noted champions was almost considered in the light of a national affair; when tens of thousands of individuals, high and low, meditated and brooded upon it, the first thing in the morning and the last at night, until the great event was decided.
    GEORGE BORROW, *Lavengro*

18812.
Sport, that wrinkled Care derides,
And Laughter holding both his sides.
Come, and trip it, as you go,
On the light fantastic toe.
         MILTON, *L'Allegro*

18813.
To sport with Amaryllis in the shade,
Or with the tangles of Neaera's hair.
         MILTON, *Lycidas*

18814. There is a general adoration for purely destructive things such as State and Sport. One kills man, the other kills time. Sport is grossly encouraged by the State because it produces soldiers, destroys integrity, and encourages that reckless optimism which is the fundamental cause of gambling. In passing, although I have met all manner of men, I have never trusted a man who proclaimed himself a sportsman.
C. R. W. NEVINSON

18815. It was the saying of Bion, that though the boys throw stones at frogs in sport, yet the frogs do not die in sport but in earnest.
PLUTARCH, *Lives*

18816. It is a poor sport that is not worth the candle. *Proverb*

18817.
Then strip, lads, and to it, though
     sharp be the weather,
   And if, by mischance, you should
     happen to fall,
There are worse things in life than
     a tumble on heather,
   And life is itself but a game at
     football.   SCOTT, *Song*

See also: 2344, 2617, 2899, 4704.

SPRING

Related Subjects: April, Flowers, June, May, The Seasons.

18821. For, lo! the winter is past, the rain is over and gone; the flowers appear on the earth; the time of the singing of birds is come, and the voice of the turtle is heard in our land.
Bible: The Song of Solomon, ii,
11, 12

18822. And the spring comes slowly up this way.   COLERIDGE, *Christabel*

18823. When Spring unlocks the flowers to paint the laughing soil.
REGINALD HEBER,
7th Sunday after Trinity

18824.
     Now begins
The housewife's happiest season of
     the year,
The ground, already broken by the
     spade—
The beds, made level by the passing
     rake.   T. B. READ,
The New Pastoral

18825.
From you I have been absent in the
     spring,
When proud-pied April, dress'd in
     all his trim,
Hath put a spirit of youth in every-
     thing.   SHAKESPEARE,
Sonnet XCVIII

18826.
     O, wind,
If Winter comes, can Spring be far
   behind?   SHELLEY,
Ode to the West Wind

18827. When the hounds of spring are on winter's traces.
SWINBURNE, *Atalanta in Calydon*

18828. In the spring a young man's fancy lightly turns to thoughts of love.   TENNYSON, *Locksley Hall*

18829. Spring is a true reconstructionist.   HENRY TIMROD,
Spring's Lessons

18830.
Spring, with that nameless pathos in
     the air
Which dwells with all things fair,
Spring, with her golden suns and
     silver rain,
Is with us once again.
HENRY TIMROD, *Spring*

18831. The first day of spring is one thing, and the first spring day is another. The difference between them is sometimes as great as a month.   HENRY VAN DYKE,
Fisherman's Luck

See also: 1687, 6209, 6500.

SPYING

Related Subjects: Informer, Listening, Meddler, Treachery.

18841. Hearkners, we say, seldom hear good of themselves.
MATTHEW HENRY, *Commentaries*

18842. Listen at the key-hole, and you'll hear news of yourself.
Proverb

18843. He who peeps through a hole may see what will vex him.   *Proverb*

STAGE

Related Subjects: Acting, Drama, Tragedy.

18851. Things rarely go smooth at Rehearsal.   BROWNING,
Pacchiarotto

18852. Neither should the theatre in our country be regarded as a luxury. It is a necessity because in order to make democracy work the people must increasingly participate; they can't participate unless they understand; and the theatre is one of the great mediums of understanding.
HALLIE FLANAGAN, *Arena*

18853. In an age of terrific implications as to wealth and poverty, as to the function of government, as to peace and war, as to the relation of the artist to all these forces, the theatre must grow up. The theatre must become conscious of the implications of the changing social order, or the changing social order will ignore, and rightly, the implications of the theatre.
HALLIE FLANAGAN, *Arena*

18854. In the theatre . . . no one works alone.   JOHN GASSNER,
Introduction to Twenty Best Plays

18855. To say there is no American theatre at all is false, and to some degree silly. To say there is not yet an American theatre equal to the dramatic materials provided by the American environment and people, however, is very true, and to a small degree profound.
WILLIAM SAROYAN,
Introd.: My Heart's in the Highlands

18856. Not to go to the theatre is like making one's toilet without a mirror.   SCHOPENHAUER

18857.
All the world's a stage,
And all the men and women merely
   players.   SHAKESPEARE,
As You Like It

18858.
As in a theatre, the eyes of men,
After a well-graced actor leaves the
   stage,
Are idly bent on him that enters next,
Thinking his prattle to be tedious.
SHAKESPEARE, *Richard II*

18859. We will draw the curtain and show you the picture.
SHAKESPEARE, *Twelfth Night*

18860. On the stage we get the geniuses and the *hysteriques;* but the intermediate talents are drawn back from a profession in which brains and self-respect have no chance against emotional facility and neurotic sexuality.
BERNARD SHAW,
Dramatic Opinions & Essays

See also: 476, 13020, 19743.

STARS

Related Subjects: Astrology, Astronomy, The Heavens, Moon, Night, Universe.

18861. The stars, like measles, fade at last.
SAMUEL HOFFENSTEIN,
The Mimic Muse

18862.
The evening star,
Love's harbinger.   MILTON,
Paradise Lost

18863.
There's husbandry in heaven;
Their candles are all out.
SHAKESPEARE, *Macbeth*

18864.
Look how the floor of heaven
Is thick inlaid with patines of bright gold:
There's not the smallest orb which thou behold'st
But in his motion like an angel sings.
SHAKESPEARE,
The Merchant of Venice

18865. There was a star danced, and under that I was born.
SHAKESPEARE,
Much Ado About Nothing

18866. A man gazing on the stars is proverbially at the mercy of the puddles on the road.
ALEXANDER SMITH, *Dreamthorp*

18867. When sun is set the little stars will shine.
ROBERT SOUTHWELL,
Scorn Not the Least

18868.
Twinkle, twinkle, little star,
How I wonder what you are,
Up above the world so high,
Like a diamond in the sky.
JANE TAYLOR, *The Star*

See also: 487, 1274, 1521, 4027, 19820.

STATE

Related Subjects: Constitution, Government, Nation.

18871. States as great engines move slowly.   BACON,
Advancement of Learning

18872. I believe that those who profess horror at the intervention of the state for the protection of the weak lay themselves open to the suspicion that they wish to use their strength for the benefit of a portion for the oppression of the rest.
BISMARCK

18873. Always without exception, the most civilized State is the most aggressive.   J. G. FICHTE

18874. The state is at the bottom a product of the class struggle, serving to keep one particular class on top. This explains why the British Empire will commit suicide, as it is now doing, rather than risk a change in its class structure.
J. B. S. HALDANE, *I Believe*

18875. [The State] is the divine idea as it exists on earth . . . It is the absolute power on earth: it is its own end and object. It is the ultimate end which has the highest right against the individual.   HEGEL

18876. I believe that the State exists for the development of individual lives, not individuals for the development of the State.
JULIAN HUXLEY, *I Believe*

18877. The chief foundations of all states, new as well as old or composite, are good laws and good arms; and as there cannot be good laws where the state is not well armed, it follows that where they are well armed they have good laws.

MACHIAVELLI, *The Prince*

18878. As soon as any man says of the affairs of the State, "What does it matter to me?" the State may be given up for lost.   ROUSSEAU, *The Social Contract*

18879. As soon as public service ceases to be the chief business of the citizens, and they would rather serve with their money than with their persons, the State is not far from its fall.

ROUSSEAU, *The Social Contract*

18880. The State is Power. Of so unusual a type is its power, that it has no power to limit its power. Hence no treaty, when it becomes inconvenient, can be binding; hence the very notion of general arbitration is absurd; hence war is part of the Divine order. Small states must be contemptible, because they must be weak; success is the test of merit, power is its reward; and all nations get what they deserve.

TREITSCHKE

18881. For the race to get to this Modern State as a whole it had to get there as so many hundreds of millions of human beings, all individually aware of that as the general objective at which their lives aimed. The Modern State could not arrive as an empty form with all humanity left behind it. Every teacher, every writer, every talker, every two friends who talked together constituted a potential primary nucleus in a renascent social system. These nuclei had to be organized. Their existence had to be realized, and they had to be brought into effective cooperation.

H. G. WELLS,
The Shape of Things to Come

See also: 472, 657, 1153, 1155, 1583, 4248, 6619, 15975, 16793.

STATESMAN, STATESMANSHIP

Related Subjects: Diplomacy.

18891. The great difference between the real statesman and the pretender is, that the one sees into the future, while the other regards only the present; the one lives by the day, and acts on expediency; the other acts on enduring principles and for immortality.

BURKE

18892. What morality requires, true statesmanship should accept.   BURKE

18893. The three great ends for a statesman are, security to possessors, facility to acquirers, and liberty and hope to the people.   COLERIDGE

18894. It is curious that we pay statesmen for what they say, not for what they do, and judge them from what they do, not from what they say. Hence they have one code of maxims for professions, and another for practice, and make up their consciences as the Neapolitans do their beds, with one set of furniture for show and another for use.   C. C. COLTON

18895. The State, in choosing men to serve it, takes no notice of their opinions. If they be willing faithfully to serve it, that satisfies.   CROMWELL

18896. If I had wished to raise up a race of statesmen higher than politicians, animated not by greed or selfishness, by policy or party, I would familiarize the boys of the land with the characters of the Bible.

JOHN HALL

18897. The pose of simplicity which Mr. Baldwin affects ought to deceive no one; a simple man has never been prime minister of England. His pigs and his pipe are simply the technique

of propaganda. Like the orchid of Mr. Chamberlain or the ringlets of Disraeli, they create an image which the multitude can remember, and they give a satisfaction to innumerable followers who believe that a common interest in pigs and pipes is a permanent basis of political adequacy.
HAROLD J. LASKI

18898. Honest statesmanship is the wise employment of individual meannesses for the public good. LINCOLN

18899. The worth of a state, in the long run, is the worth of the individuals composing it.   J. S. MILL

18900. The minds of some of our statesmen, like the pupil of the human eye, contract themselves the more, the stronger light there is shed upon them.   THOMAS MOORE

18901. Statesmen are not only liable to give an account of what they say or do in public, but there is a busy inquiry made into their very meals, beds, marriages, and every other sportive or serious action. PLUTARCH

18902. Statesmen will care about popular prejudice as physicians will care about the diseased condition of their patients, which they want to ameliorate.   CARL SCHURZ,
Plea for Amnesty

See also: 501, 1375, 5412, 13597, 15501.

STATISTICS

Related Subjects: Facts, Index.

18911. Fundamental statistics are more important to the business man than those reflected in the figures on his own books, for fundamental conditions have more to do with his success.   ROGER BABSON,
Business Fundamentals

18912. There are three kinds of lies: lies, damned lies, and statistics.
Attributed to DISRAELI

18913. The methods of statistics are so variable and uncertain, so apt to be influenced by circumstance, that it is never possible to be sure that one is operating with figures of equal weight.   HAVELOCK ELLIS,
The Dance of Life

STEAM

Related Subjects: Machinery, Power.

18921.
Soon shall thy arm, unconquer'd steam! afar
Drag the slow barge, or drive the rapid car;
Or on wide-waving wings expanded bear
The flying chariot through the field of air.   ERASMUS DARWIN,
The Botanic Garden

18922. Steam is an apt scholar and a strong-shouldered fellow.
EMERSON, *Society and Solitude*

18923. Fulton knocked at the door of Napoleon with steam, and was rejected; and Napoleon lived long enough to know that he had excluded a greater power than his own.
HORATIO GREENOUGH

18924. Steam, that great civilizer.
FREEMAN HUNT,
American Merchants

18925. Steam engines are very human. Their very weaknesses are understandable. Steam engines do not flash back and blow your face in. They do not short-circuit and rive your heart with imponderable electric force. They have arms and lets and warm hearts and veins full of warm vapour. Give us steam every time. You know where you are with steam. WILLIAM McFEE, *A Six-hour Shift*

18926. The story of the steam engine in inextricably bound up with the name of James Watt. Watt's fame rests on his improvements which made the engine truly practical and efficient, rather than on the discovery of the first principle. JOHN A. MALONEY, *Great Inventors*

18927. What was probably the earliest design for a steam engine was nineteen hundred years old when Watt applied for his patent, for an Alexandrian Greek named Hero had built a crude steam turbine, although he made no further experiments. JOHN A. MALONEY, *Great Inventors*

STOICISM

Related Subjects: Courage, Endurance.

18931. 'Tis pride, rank pride, and haughtiness of soul; I think the Romans call it stoicism. ADDISON

18932. There are two ways of escaping from suffering; the one by rising above the causes of conflict, the other by sinking below them. The one is the religious method; the other is the vulgar, worldly method. The one is Christian elevation; the other is stoicism. H. W. BEECHER

18933. To feel for none is the true social art of the world's stoics—men without a heart. BYRON

18934. From forty to fifty a man is at heart either a stoic or a satyr. PINERO, *The Second Mrs. Tanqueray*

STOMACH, see Belly

STORM

Related Subjects: Clouds, Fog, Rain, Shipwreck, Snow, Thunder and Lightning, Weather, Wind.

18941.
The sky is changed,—and such a change! O night
And storm, and darkness! ye are wondrous strong,
Yet lovely in your strength, as in the light
Of a dark eye in woman! Far along,
From peak to peak, the rattling crags among,
Leaps the live thunder. BYRON, *Childe Harold*

18942. The seamen said it blew great guns. DICKENS, *David Copperfield*

18943.
Enclosed
In a tumultuous privacy of storm.
EMERSON, *The Snow-Storm*

18944. After a storm comes a calm. MATTHEW HENRY, *Commentaries*

18945. Small showers last long, but sudden storms are short. SHAKESPEARE, *Richard II*

18946. For many years I was self-appointed inspector of snow-storms and rain-storms, and did my duty faithfully. THOREAU, *Walden*

STORY, see Tale

STRAW

Related Subject: Grass.

18951. And Pharaoh commanded . . . Ye shall no more give the people straw to make brick, as heretofore: let them go and gather straw for themselves. *Bible: Exodus, v, 7*

18952. A drowning man catches at a straw. *Proverb*

18953. The last straw breaks the camel's back. *Proverb*

18954. Take a straw and throw it up into the air,—you may see by that which way the wind is.
JOHN SELDEN, *Table Talk*

STRENGTH

Related Subjects: **Ability, Firmness, Force, Health, Life, Might, Power.**

18961. Everything nourishes what is strong already. JANE AUSTEN, *Pride and Prejudice*

18962. And Delilah said to Samson, Tell me, I pray thee, wherein thy great strength lieth.
Bible: Judges, xvi, 6

18963. The race is not to the swift, nor the battle to the strong.
Bible: Ecclesiastes, ix, 11

18964. Few men during their lifetime come anywhere near exhausting the resources dwelling within them. There are deep wells of strength that are never used. ADMIRAL BYRD, *Alone*

18965. He could whip his weight in wildcats. EUGENE FIELD, *Modjesky as Cameel*

18966. Strength does not come from physical capacity. It comes from an indomitable will.
MAHATMA GANDHI

18967.
Lend me the stone strength of the past and I will lend you
The wings of the future, for I have them,
How dear you will be to me when I too grow old, old comrade.
ROBINSON JEFFERS,
To the Rock That Will Be a Cornerstone of the House

18968. More brawn than brain.
CORNELIUS NEPOS, *Epaminondas*

18969. A chain is no stronger than its weakest link. *Proverb*

18970. A man may be strong, and yet not mow well. *Proverb*

18971.
Think you I am no stronger than my sex,
Being so father'd and so husbanded?
SHAKESPEARE, *Julius Caesar*

18972.
The strength
Of twenty men.
SHAKESPEARE, *Romeo and Juliet*

See also: 311, 473, 481, 696, 1038, 1522, 1866, 1895, 2104, 2563, 2571, 2654, 3143, 3176, 3443, 5773, 7564, 16393, 16482, 20341, 20780.

STRIFE, see Discord, Quarreling

STUDY

Related Subjects: **Contemplation, Education, Inquiry, Knowledge, Learning, Library, Research, Scholar, School, Teaching.**

18981. Histories make men wise; poets, witty; the mathematics, subtile; natural philosophy, deep, moral, grave; logic and rhetoric, able to contend. BACON, *Of Studies*

18982. Reading maketh a full man, conference a ready man, and writing an exact man. BACON, *Of Studies*

18983.
When night hath set her silver lamp on high,
Then is the time for study.
PHILIP J. BAILEY, *Festus*

18984. Of making many books there is no end; and much study is a weariness of the flesh.
Bible: Ecclesiastes, xii, 12

18985.
> Exhausting thought,
> And hiving wisdom with each studi-
> ous year.   BYRON, *Childe Harold*

18986. Studious of elegance and ease.
> JOHN GAY, *Fables*

18987. As turning the logs will make a dull fire burn, so changes of studies a dull brain.   LONGFELLOW,
> *Drift-Wood*

18988. You are in some brown study.
> JOHN LYLY, *Euphues*

18989. Beholding the bright countenance of truth in the quiet and still air of delightful studies.   MILTON,
> *The Reason of Church Government*

18990. I'll talk a word with this same learned Theban. What is your study?
> SHAKESPEARE, *King Lear*

18991.
> What is the end of study? Let me know?
> Why, that to know, which else we should not know.
> Things hid and barr'd, you mean, from common sense?
> Ay, that is study's god-like recompense.   SHAKESPEARE,
> *Love's Labour's Lost*

18992.
> Study is like the heaven's glorious sun
> That will not be deep-searched with saucy looks;
> Small have continual plodders ever won,
> Save base authority from others' books.   SHAKESPEARE,
> *Love's Labour's Lost*

18993.
> So study evermore is overshot;
> While it doth study to have what it would
> It doth forget to do the thing it should,

> And when it hath the thing it hunteth most,
> 'Tis won as towns with fire, so won, so lost.   SHAKESPEARE,
> *Love's Labour's Lost*

18994. I am slow of study.
> SHAKESPEARE,
> *A Midsummer-Night's Dream*

18995. One of the best methods of rendering study agreeable is to live with able men, and to suffer all those pangs of inferiority which the want of knowledge always inflicts.
> SIDNEY SMITH

See also: 744, 1994, 4182, 17840.

STUPIDITY

Related Subjects: Awkwardness, Boredom, Ignorance, Superstition.

19001. Your true dull minds are generally preferred for public employ, and especially promoted to city honors; your keen intellects, like razors, being considered too sharp for common service.
> WASHINGTON IRVING,
> *Knickerbocker's History of New York*

19002. Dreadful things are just as apt to happen when stupid people control a situation as when definitely ill-natured people are in charge.
> DON MARQUIS,
> *Chapters for the Orthodox*

19003.
> Against stupidity the very gods
> Themselves contend in vain.
> SCHILLER, *The Maid of Orleans*

19004. There is no sin except stupidity.
> OSCAR WILDE,
> *The Critic as Artist*

See also: 414, 2011, 14206.

STYLE

Related Subjects: Dress, Fashion.

19011. Style is like happiness. Everyone recognizes it, everyone describes it, but no two people agree as to its exact nature.   HENRY S. CANBY

19012. Style is the dress of thoughts.
LORD CHESTERFIELD, *Letters*

19013. The infallible test of a blameless style: namely, its untranslatableness in words of the same language, without injury to the meaning.
COLERIDGE, *Biographia Literaria*

19014. That passage is what I call the sublime dashed to pieces by cutting too close with the fiery four-in-hand round the corner of nonsense.
COLERIDGE,
Lectures on Shakespeare & Milton

19015.
The style's the man, so books avow;
The style's the woman, anyhow.
O. W. HOLMES,
How the Old Horse Won the Bet

19016. Whose large style agrees not with the leanness of his purse.
SHAKESPEARE, *Henry VI*

19017.
I told him [Degas] about the painter Y., who had come to me in great excitement, exclaiming: "Well, I've found my true style at last!"
Said Degas: "Well, I'm glad I haven't found my style yet. I'd be bored to death."   A. VOLLARD,
Degas

19018. The whole purport of literature, which is the notation of the heart. Style is but the faintly contemptible vessel in which the bitter liquid is recommended to the world.
THORNTON WILDER,
The Bridge of San Luis Rey

SUBMISSION

Related Subjects: Conquest, Defeat, Deference, Humility, Meekness, Obedience, Resignation.

19021. The little Reed, bending to the force of the wind, soon stood upright again when the storm had passed over.   AESOP, *The Tree and the Reed*

19022. And whispering, "I will ne'er consent,"—consented.   BYRON,
Don Juan

19023. Has any benefit or progress ever been achieved by the human race by submission to organized and calculated violence? As we look back over the long story of the nations, we must see that, on the contrary, their glory has been founded upon the spirit of resistance to tyranny and injustice.
WINSTON CHURCHILL,
Blood, Sweat & Tears

19024. You cannot repeal a surrender.
CHARLES EVANS HUGHES

19025. It is no shame to yield to him that we must not oppose.   *Proverb*

SUBTLETY

Related Subjects: Cunning, Trickery.

19031. Subtlety will sometimes give safety, no less than strength; and minuteness has sometimes escaped, where magnitude would have been crushed. The little animal that kills the boa is formidable chiefly from its insignificance, which is incompressible by the folds of its antagonist.
C. C. COLTON

19032. Subtlety may deceive you; integrity never will.   CROMWELL

19033. Where more is meant than meets the ear.   MILTON,
Il Penseroso

19034. Subtility set a trap, and caught itself. *Proverb*

See also: 25, 3276, 17962.

SUCCESS

Related Subjects: Ambition, Conquerors, Victory.

19041. In public we say the race is to the strongest; in private we know that a lopsided man runs the fastest along the little side-hills of success.

FRANK M. COLBY,
Constrained Attitudes

19042.
Success is counted sweetest
By those who ne'er succeed.
EMILY DICKINSON, *Success*

19043. The secret of success is constancy to purpose. DISRAELI

19044. Be awful nice to 'em goin' up, because you're gonna meet 'em all comin' down. JIMMY DURANTE

19045.
We are waiting for you there—for you, the man!
Come up from the jostle as soon as you can;
Come up from the crowd there, for you are the man,
The man who comes up from the crowd. SAM W. FOSS,
The Man From the Crowd

19046. The success of any great moral enterprise does not depend upon numbers. W. L. GARRISON, *Life*

19047. Success, which touches nothing that it does not vulgarize, should be its own reward . . . the odium of success is hard enough to bear, without the added ignominy of popular applause.
CUNNINGHAME GRAHAM, *Success*

19048. Success is the sole earthly judge of the right and wrong.
ADOLF HITLER, *Mein Kampf*

19049. Success depends on three things: who says it, what he says, how he says it; and of these three things, what he says is the least important. JOHN MORLEY,
Recollections

19050. Whether the race of men on earth mounteth a loftier tower by justice, or by crooked wiles, my mind is divided in telling clearly. PINDAR

19051. Success is never blamed.
Proverb

19052. Success makes a fool seem wise. *Proverb*

19053. If a fool have success, it ruins him. *Proverb*

19054. It is a bad action that success cannot justify. *Proverb*

19055. Deserve success, and you shall command it. *Proverb*

19056. Nothing succeeds like success.
Proverb

19057. I have great success, but at what cost! At the expense of my health and my life. The enthusiasm of the applauding crowd passes into my blood, and sets me on fire. RACHEL

19058. Success or failure in business is caused more by mental attitude even than by mental capacities.
W. D. SCOTT

19059. Success in life means doing that thing than which nothing else conceivable seems more noble or satisfying or remunerative, and this enviable state I can truly say that I enjoy, for had I the choice I would be

nowhere else in the world than where I am.   ALAN SEEGER,
Letter from the Trenches

19060. Success consecrates the foulest crimes.   SENECA

19061. To succeed on your merits and then to maintain your position by following the same methods—this is honorable victory. And if it means monopoly it is a kind of monopoly which cannot be too warmly approved.   SHARP & FOX,
Business Ethics

19062. When a man returns home and finds for the moment nothing to struggle against, the vast resolve which has sustained him through a long and a difficult enterprise dies away, burning as it sinks in the heart; and thus the greatest successes are often accompanied by a peculiar melancholy.   H. M. STANLEY

19063. Success is a rare paint, hides all the ugliness.
    SIR JOHN SUCKLING,
The Tragedy of Brennoralt

19064. If the day and the night are such that you greet them with joy, and life emits a fragrance like flowers and sweet-scented herbs, is more elastic, more starry, more immortal,— that is your success.   THOREAU,
Walden

See also: 11, 1046, 1254, 1413, 2601, 2603, 3072, 3837, 3881, 4023, 5885, 6271, 9350, 9431, 9969, 15046, 20563, 21126.

SUFFERING

Related Subjects: Callousness, Compassion, Cruelty, Endurance, Hell, Martyr, Mercy, Misery, Pain.

19071. Generally speaking, men are too cowardly to be willing to undergo severe suffering, since they fear death and pain, but they highly prize being mentioned as having suffered.
    DIO CHRYSOSTOM

19072. In the shaping of our inner beliefs what we are made to suffer and to endure counts more than all we may glean in the realms of science.
    SIR ARTHUR KEITH, *I Believe*

19073. Know how sublime a thing it is to suffer and be strong.
    LONGFELLOW

19074. It is not true that suffering ennobles the character; happiness does that sometimes, but suffering, for the most part, makes men petty and vindictive.
    SOMERSET MAUGHAM,
The Moon and Sixpence

19075. We are healed of a suffering only by experiencing it to the full.
    MARCEL PROUST,
The Sweet Cheat Gone

19076.
Who alone suffers suffers most i' the mind,
Leaving free things and happy shows behind:
But then the mind much sufferance doth o'erskip,
When grief hath mates, and bearing fellowship.   SHAKESPEARE,
King Lear

19077. It is of no use reminding humanity of the sufferings of war. For the suffering is never more than that of the individual. It is not cumulative any more than the suffering of peace is cumulative—and it is infinitely more spectacular.
    I. A. R. WYLIE

See also: 15362, 18932.

SUICIDE

Related Subjects: **Death, Despair, Sanity and Insanity.**

19081. I think I will not hang myself to-day.   G. K. CHESTERTON,
A Ballade of Suicide

19082. The prevalence of suicide, without doubt, is a test of height in civilization; it means that the population is winding up its nervous and intellectual system to the utmost point of tension and that sometimes it snaps.   HAVELOCK ELLIS,
The Dance of Life

19083.
One more unfortunate,
  Weary of breath,
Rashly importunate,
  Gone to her death!
         THOMAS HOOD,
The Bridge of Sighs

19084. Nature puts upon no man an unbearable burden; if her limits be exceeded, man responds by suicide. I have always respected suicide as a regulator of nature.
       EMIL LUDWIG, *I Believe*

19085. a suicide is a person who has considered his own case and decided that he is worthless and who acts as his own judge jury and executioner and he probably knows better than anyone else whether there is justice in the verdict.   DON MARQUIS,
archy does his part

19086.
I know some poison I could drink;
  I've often thought I'd taste it;
But Mother bought it for the sink,
  And drinking it would waste it.
     EDNA ST. VINCENT MILLAY,
The Cheerful Abstainer

19087. The thought of suicide is a great consolation: by means of it one gets successfully through many a bad night.   NIETZSCHE,
Beyond Good & Evil

19088.
Razors pain you;
Rivers are damp;
Acids stain you;
And drugs cause cramp.
Guns aren't lawful;
Nooses give;
Gas smells awful;
You might as well live.
    DOROTHY PARKER, *Résumé*

19089.
       Against self-slaughter
There is a prohibition so divine
That cravens my weak hand.
    SHAKESPEARE, *Cymbeline*

19090.
O! that this too too solid flesh would
  melt,
Thaw and resolve itself into a dew;
Or that the Everlasting had not fix'd
His canon 'gainst self-slaughter!
     SHAKESPEARE, *Hamlet*

19091.
      O true apothecary!
Thy drugs are quick.
    SHAKESPEARE, *Romeo and Juliet*

19092. Man is a prisoner who has no right to open the door of his prison and run away.   SOCRATES, *Apology*

19093. A man should wait, and not take his own life until God summons him.   SOCRATES,
Dialogues of Plato

19094. Those who commit suicide are powerless souls, and allow themselves to be conquered by external causes repugnant to their nature.
      SPINOZA, *Ethics*

See also: 3872, 5244.

SUMMER

Related Subjects: August, Seasons.

19101.
Summer treads
On heels of Spring.   HORACE,
Odes

19102.
Summer is icumen in,
Lhude sing cuccu!
Groweth sed, and bloweth med,
And springth the wude nu—
Sing cuccu!
Attr. to JOHN OF DUNSTABLE,
Cuckoo Song

19103. This is very midsummer madness.   SHAKESPEARE,
Twelfth Night

19104. Shall I compare thee to a summer's day?   SHAKESPEARE,
Sonnet XVIII

19105. Steep thyself in a bowl of summertime.   VERGIL,
Minor Poems

See also: 1449, 1456, 1762.

SUN

Related Subjects: Day, Heavens, Moon, Rainbow, Sun-Dial, Sunrise, Sunset.

19111. Those who bring sunshine to the lives of others cannot keep it from themselves.
J. M. BARRIE, *A Window in Thrums*

19112.
The night has a thousand eyes,
    And the day but one;
Yet the light of the bright world dies,
    With the dying sun.
    F. W. BOURDILLON, *Light*

19113. The gay motes that people the sunbeams.
MILTON, *Il Penseroso*

19114. The brightest of all things, the sun, hath its spots.   *Proverb*

19115. They that walk much in the sun, will be tanned at last.   *Proverb*

19116. The sun is larger than it looks.
Proverb

19117. The sun with one eye vieweth all the world.
SHAKESPEARE, *Henry VI*

19118.
The self-same sun that shines upon his court
Hides not his visage from our cottage, but
Looks on alike.
SHAKESPEARE, *The Winter's Tale*

19119. Thank heavens, the sun has gone in, and I don't have to go out and enjoy it.
LOGAN PEARSALL SMITH,
Afterthoughts

See also: 702, 1330, 1332, 1451, 1719, 2522, 2549, 3494, 3523, 5056, 17211.

SUNDAY, see Sabbath

SUN-DIAL

Related Subjects: Sun, Time.

19121.
True as the needle to the pole,
Or as the dial to the sun.
        BARTON BOOTH, *Song*

19122.
True as the dial to the sun,
Although it be not shin'd upon.
        SAMUEL BUTLER, *Hudibras*

19123.
There stands in the garden of old St.
    Mark
    A sun dial quaint and gray.
It takes no heed of the hours which
    in dark
    Pass o'er it day by day.

It has stood for ages amid the flowers
   In that land of sky and song.
"I number none but the cloudless
   hours."
   Its motto the live day long.
              W. C. DOANE,
            Of a Sun Dial in Venice

19124.
Thou breathing dial! since thy day
   began
The present hour was ever mark'd
   with shade.   W. S. LANDOR

19125. I am moved by the light.
MAETERLINCK, *Measure of the Hours*

19126. I count only the hours that
are serene.   MAETERLINCK,
           Measure of the Hours
19127.
The Natural Clock-work, by the
   mighty ONE
Wound up at first, and ever since
   have gone.   *Sun Dial Motto*

SUNFLOWER

Related Subject: Flowers.

19131.
Light-enchanted sunflower, thou
Who gazest ever true and tender
On the sun's revolving splendour.
       CALDERON, *Magico Prodigioso*

19132.
The Sunflow'r, thinking 'twas for him
   foul shame
To nap by daylight, strove t'excuse
   the blame;
It was not sleep that made him nod,
   he said,
But too great weight and largeness
   of his head.
      ABRAHAM COWLEY, *Of Plants*

19133.
Spare for the sunflower, bright with
     yellow glow,
   To court the sky.
CAROLINE GILMAN, *To the Ursulines*

19134.
As the sunflower turns on her god
   when he sets,
The same look which she turn'd when
   he rose.   THOMAS MOORE,
*Believe Me if All Those Endearing
             Young Charms*

SUNRISE

**Related Subjects: Dawn, Morning,
Sun.**

19141. In every country the sun
riseth in the morning.   *Proverb*

19142.
   The heavenly-harness'd team
Begins his golden progress in the east.
       SHAKESPEARE, *Henry VI*

19143.
He fires the proud tops of the eastern
   pines
And darts his light through every
   guilty hole.
       SHAKESPEARE, *Richard II*

19144.
And yonder fly his scattered golden
   arrows,
And smite the hills with day.
BAYARD TAYLOR, *The Poet's Journal*

19145.
See how there,
   The cowled night
Kneels on the Eastern sanctuary-
   stair.   FRANCIS THOMPSON,
       A Corymbus for Autumn

19146.
But yonder comes the powerful King
   of Day,
Rejoicing in the East.
     JAMES THOMSON, *The Seasons*

19147. It is true, I never assisted the
sun materially in his rising; but,
doubt not, it was of the last importance only to be present at it.
          THOREAU, *Walden*

SUNSET

Related Subjects: Evening, Sun, Twilight.

19151.

Come watch with me the shaft of fire
   that glows
In yonder West: the fair, frail palaces,
The fading Alps and archipelagoes,
And great cloud-continents of sunset-
   sets.
            T. B. ALDRICH, *Sonnet*

19152.

Oft did I wonder why the setting sun
   Should look upon us with a blush-
      ing face:
Is't not for shame of what he hath
      seen done,
   Whilst in our hemisphere he ran
      his race?   LYMAN HEATH,
         On the Setting Sun

19153.

Down sank the great red sun, and in
   golden, glimmering vapors
Veiled the light of his face, like the
   Prophet descending from Sinai.
            LONGFELLOW, *Evangeline*

19154.

The setting sun, and music at the
   close,
As the last taste of sweets, is sweetest last.
            SHAKESPEARE, *Richard II*

19155. When the sun sets, who doth
not look for night?
            SHAKESPEARE, *Richard III*

19156.

   The sun was down,
And all the west was paved with sul-
   len fire.
I cried, "Behold! the barren beach of
   hell
At ebb of tide."
ALEXANDER SMITH, *A Life Drama*

See also: 857.

SUPERIORITY

Related Subjects: Confidence, Distinction, Pride, Scorn, Self-Confidence, Self-Respect.

19161.

He who ascends to mountain-tops,
   shall find
The loftiest peaks most wrapt in
   clouds and snow;
He who surpasses or subdues mankind
Must look down on the hate of those
   below.
            BYRON, *Childe Harold*

19162. Love alone renders us able to
endure superiority in others.
            GOETHE

19163. You may fail to shine in the
opinion of others both in your conversation and actions, from being superior, as well as inferior to them.
            GREVILLE

19164. When a person dies who does
any one thing better than any one else
in the world, it leaves a gap in society.
            HAZLITT, *Table Talk*

19165. I am the inferior of any man
whose rights I trample under foot.
Men are not superior by reason of
the accidents of race or color. They
are superior who have the best heart
—the best brain.
            ROBERT INGERSOLL, *Liberty*

19166. The superior man is the providence of the inferior. He is eyes for
the blind, strength for the weak, and
a shield for the defenseless. He stands
erect by bending above the fallen.
He rises by lifting others.
            ROBERT INGERSOLL, *Liberty*

19167.

Though I've belted you and flayed
   you,

By the livin' Gawd that made you,
You're a better man than I am, Gunga
   Din !

KIPLING, *Gunga Din*

19168.

My mother was a superior soul
   A superior soul was she
Cut out to play a superior role
   In the god-damn bourgeoisie.

   D. H. LAWRENCE, *Red-Herring*

19169. I am not in the roll of common men.

SHAKESPEARE, *Henry IV*

See also: 170, 1075, 1144, 1295, 3663,
3691, 6413, 8557.

SUPERSTITION

**Related Subjects: Belief, Fairies,
Ghosts, Gods and Goddesses, Ig-
norance, Imagination, Miracle,
Mystery, Mythology, Oracle,
Witch.**

19171. There is a superstition in
avoiding superstition, when men think
they do best if they go farthest from
the superstition,—by which means
they often take away the good as well
as the bad. BACON

19172. The master of superstition is
the people, and in all superstition
wise men follow fools. BACON

19173. As it addeth deformity to an
ape to be so like a man, so the simili-
tude of superstition to religion makes
it the more deformed. BACON

19174. Open biographical volumes
wherever you please, and the man
who has no faith in religion is the
one who hath faith in a nightmare
and ghosts. BULWER-LYTTON

19175. Superstition is a senseless
fear of God; religion the intelligent
and pious worship of the deity.

CICERO

19176. Superstitions are, for the most
part, but the shadows of great truths.

TRYON EDWARDS

19177. Superstition is the poetry of
life. It is inherent in man's nature;
and when we think it is wholly erad-
icated, it takes refuge in the strangest
holes and corners, whence it peeps
out all at once, as soon as it can do it
with safety. GOETHE

19178. We are all tattooed in our
cradles with the beliefs of our tribe;
the record may seem superficial, but
it is indelible. You cannot educate a
man wholly out of the superstitious
fears which were implanted in his
imagination, no matter how utterly
his reason may reject them.

O. W. HOLMES

19179. That the corruption of the
best thing produces the worst, is
grown into a maxim, and is commonly proved, among other instances,
by the pernicious effects of superstition and enthusiasm, the corruptions
of true religion. DAVID HUME

19180. Superstition is the only religion of which base souls are capable.

JOUBERT, *Pensées*

19181. Liberal minds are open to
conviction. Liberal doctrines are capable of improvement. There are
proselytes from atheism; but none
from superstition. JUNIUS

19182. Superstition always inspires
bitterness; religion, grandeur of
mind. The superstitious man raises
beings inferior to himself to deities.

LAVATER

19183. The greatest burden in the
world is superstition, not only of
ceremonies in the church, but of
imaginary and scarecrow sins at
home. MILTON

19184. I am at a loss to know whether it be my hare's foot which is my preservative, or my taking of a pill of turpentine every morning.

SAMUEL PEPYS, *Diary*

19185. Why is it that we entertain the belief that for every purpose odd numbers are the most effectual?

PLINY THE ELDER, *Natural History*

19186. Religion worships God, while superstition profanes that worship.

SENECA

19187.
But in the gross and scope of my opinion,
This bodes some strange eruption to our state.

SHAKESPEARE, *Hamlet*

19188.
And oftentimes, to win us to our harm,
The instruments of darkness tell us truths,
Win us with honest trifles, to betray 's
In deepest consequence.

SHAKESPEARE, *Macbeth*

19189. The child taught to believe any occurrence a good or evil omen, or any day of the week lucky, hath a wide inroad made upon the soundness of his understanding.

ISAAC WATTS

See also: 1203, 20200.

SURETY

Related Subjects: Certainty, Confidence, Insurance, Security.

19191. My son, if thou be surety for thy friend, if thou hast stricken thy hand with a stranger, Thou art snared with the words of thy mouth.

Bible: Proverbs, vi, 1, 2

19192. He that is surety for a stranger shall smart for it.

Bible: Proverbs, xxiv, 15

19193.
My son, if I, Hafiz, thy father, take hold of thy knees in my pain,
Demanding thy name on stamped paper, one day or one hour—refrain.
Are the links of thy fetters so light that thou cravest another man's chain? KIPLING,
Certain Maxims of Hafiz

19194. Be surety for another and harm is at hand. *Proverb*

19195.
One of the greatest in the Christian world
Shall be my surety.
SHAKESPEARE,
All's Well that Ends Well

19196.
But yet I'll make assurance doubly sure,
And take a bond of fate.
SHAKESPEARE, *Macbeth*

19197. Procure your sureties for your days of answer.

SHAKESPEARE, *Richard II*

19198. Have pity; I'll be his surety.
SHAKESPEARE, *The Tempest*

See also: 4513.

SUSPENSE

Related Subjects: Certainty, Doubt, Hesitation, Worry.

19201. Of all the conditions to which the heart is subject, suspense is one that most gnaws and cankers into the frame. One little month of suspense, when it involves death, we are told by an eye-witness, is sufficient to plough fixed lines and furrows in a convict of five-and-twenty,—sufficient to dash the brown hair with gray, and to bleach the gray to white.   BULWER-LYTTON

19202. But not long; for in the tedious minutes' exquisite interval— I'm on the rack; for sure the greatest evil man can know bears no proportion to this dread suspense.
    FROUDE

19203. Suspense, the only insupportable misfortune of life.
    HENRY ST. JOHN

19204. It is a miserable thing to live in suspense; it is the life of a spider.
    SWIFT,
    Thoughts on Various Subjects

See also: 8041.

SUSPICION

Related Subjects: Confidence, Contentment, Doubt, Jealousy, Trust.

19211.
For his mind
Had grown Suspicion's sanctuary.
    BYRON, *Childe Harold*

19212. Suspicion may be no fault, but shewing it is a great one.   *Proverb*

19213. Suspicion is the virtue of a coward.   *Proverb*

19214. At the gate where suspicion enters love goes out.   *Proverb*

19215. Something is rotten in the state of Denmark.
    SHAKESPEARE, *Hamlet*
19216.
Suspicion always haunts the guilty mind;
The thief doth fear each bush an officer.   SHAKESPEARE, *Henry VI*

See also: 1465, 2678, 2679, 3364, 4511, 4539, 4588, 4723, 11924, 17904, 20626.

SWALLOW

Related Subject: Birds.

19221. One swallow does not make spring.   ARISTOTLE, *Ethics*

19222. One swallow never makes a summer.
    CERVANTES, *Don Quixote*
19223.
The swallow is come!
The swallow is come!
 O, fair are the seasons, and light
Are the days that she brings,
With her dusky wings,
    And her bosom snowy white!
    LONGFELLOW, *Hyperion*
19224.
It's surely summer, for there's a swallow:
Come one swallow, his mate will follow,
The bird race quicken and wheel and thicken.   CHRISTINA ROSSETTI,
    A Bird Song
19225.
    The swallow sweeps
The slimy pool, to build his hanging house.
    JAMES THOMSON, *The Seasons*

SWAN

Related Subject: Birds.

19231. All our geese are swans.
    ROBERT BURTON,
    Anatomy of Melancholy

19232. The immortal swan that did her life deplore.
    GILES FLETCHER,
    Temptation and Victory of Christ
19233.
The swan in the pool is singing,
    And up and down doth he steer,
And, singing gently ever,
    Dips under the water clear.
    HEINE, *Book of Songs*

19234.
The swan, like the soul of the poet,
By the dull world is ill understood.
                    HEINE, *Early Poems*

19235.
There's a double beauty whenever a
    swan
Swims on a lake with her double
    thereon.   THOMAS HOOD,
                    Her Honeymoon

19236.
        The swan, with arched neck
Between her white wings mantling
    proudly, rows
Her state with oary feet.
                    MILTON, *Paradise Lost*

19237.
        The swan's down-feather,
That stands upon the swell at full of
    tide,
And neither way inclines.
SHAKESPEARE, *Antony and Cleopatra*

19238.
I am the cygnet to this pale faint
    swan,
Who chants a doleful hymn to his
    own death;
And, from the organ-pipe of frailty,
    sings
His soul and body to their lasting
    rest.
        SHAKESPEARE, *King John*

19239.
(Let music sound while he doth make
    his choice)
Then if he lose he makes a swan-
    like end.   SHAKESPEARE,
                    The Merchant of Venice

See also: 238, 3703, 4676.

SWEARING

**Related Subjects: Abuse, Curse,
Oath, Vow.**

19241. Thou shalt not take the name
of the Lord thy God in vain: for the
Lord will not hold him guiltless that
taketh his name in vain.
                    Bible: Exodus, xx, 7

19242.
Gret Swering is a thing abhominable,
And false swering is yet more reprev-
    able.
        CHAUCER, *Canterbury Tales*

19243.
I never use a big, big D.
What, never?
Hardly ever.   W. S. GILBERT,
                    H. M. S. Pinafore

19244.
    Unpack my heart with words,
And fall a-cursing, like a very drab.
        SHAKESPEARE, *Hamlet*

19245. That unmeaning and abominable custom, swearing.
                    WASHINGTON

See also: 893.

SWEAT

**Related Subjects: Effort, Labor,
Work.**

19251. In the sweat of thy face shalt
thou eat bread.
                    Bible: Genesis, iii, 19

19252. Which I have earned with
the sweat of my brows.
        CERVANTES, *Don Quixote*

19253.
His brow is wet with honest sweat,
    He earns whate'er he can,
And looks the whole world in the
    face,
    For he owes not any man.
                    LONGFELLOW,
                    The Village Blacksmith

19254.
    Falstaff sweats to death,
And lards the lean earth as he walks
    along.
        SHAKESPEARE, *Henry IV*

SWEETNESS

Related Subjects: Charm, Delight.

19261. I am glad that my Adonis hath a sweete tooth in his head.
JOHN LYLY,
Euphues and His England

19262. A wilderness of sweets.
MILTON, *Paradise Lost*

19263. He deserves not sweet, that will not taste of sour. *Proverb*

19264. Things sweet to taste prove in digestion sour.
SHAKESPEARE, *Richard II*

19265. Sweets grown common lose their dear delight.
SHAKESPEARE, *Sonnet CII*

19266.
Ah that such sweet things should be fleet,
Such fleet things sweet!
SWINBURNE, *Félise*

SWIMMING

Related Subjects: Bathing, Sport, Water.

19271.
Mother, may I go out to swim?
Yes, my darling daughter:
Hang your clothes on a hickory limb
But don't go near the water.
Anonymous

19272.
She gave me a good character,
But said I could not swim.
LEWIS CARROLL,
Alice in Wonderland

19273. I can swim like a fish.
JOHN FLETCHER, *The Sea-Voyage*

19274.
I read it in the story-book, that, for to kiss his dear,

Leander, swam the Hellespont,—and I will swim this here.
O. W. HOLMES,
The Ballad of the Oysterman

19275. Good swimmers are oftenest drowned. *Proverb*

19276. Good swimmers at length are drowned. *Proverb*

19277. Drown not thyself to save a drowning man. *Proverb*

19278. Little wanton boys that swim on bladders.
SHAKESPEARE, *Henry VIII*

19279. I can swim like a duck.
SHAKESPEARE, *The Tempest*

19280.
An unpractised swimmer plunging still,
With too much labour drowns for want of skill.
SHAKESPEARE, *The Rape of Lucrece*

19281. They care not whether they sink or swim.
THOMAS STARKEY, *England*

SWINE

Related Subject: Animal.

19291. Or shear swine, all cry and no wool.
SAMUEL BUTLER, *Hudibras*

19292. How Instinct varies in the grov'ling swine.
POPE, *Essay on Man*

19293.
The hog that ploughs not, nor obeys thy call,
Lives on the labours of this lord of all. POPE, *Essay on Man*

19294. It is ill to drive black hogs in the dark. *Proverb*

19295. Feed a pig, and you'll have a hog.   *Proverb*

19296. A hog upon trust, grunts till he's paid for.   *Proverb*

19297. A hog that's bemired, endeavours to bemire others.
Proverb

19298. A hog in armour is still but a hog.   *Proverb*

SWING, see Jazz

SWORD

Related Subjects: Dueling, Fight.

19301.
          Take away the sword;
States can be saved without it.
          BULWER-LYTTON, *Richelieu*

19302.
The trenchant blade, Toledo trusty,
For want of fighting was grown rusty,
And ate into itself, for lack
Of somebody to hew and hack.
          SAMUEL BUTLER, *Hudibras*

19303.
The sword within the scabbard keep,
And let mankind agree.
          DRYDEN, *The Secular Masque*

19304. The sword alone decides.
          PILSUDSKI

19305. It is a good blade that bends well.   *Proverb*

19306.
          Fully bravely hast thou fleshed
Thy maiden sword.
          SHAKESPEARE, *Henry IV*

See also: 1128, 2101, 9335, 10141, 15849.

SYMBOL, SYMBOLISM

Related Subject: Allegory.

19311. No passion, no idea can find

its final and strongest impression without the great symbol.
          EUGEN HADAMOVSKY,
          Nazi Director of Broadcasting

19312.
When I behold, upon the night's starr'd face,
Huge cloudy symbols of a high romance.
          KEATS, *When I Have Fears*

19313.
All things are symbols: the external shows
Of Nature have their image in the mind,
As flowers and fruits and falling of the leaves.
          LONGFELLOW, *The Harvest Moon*

19314. The word is a symbol, and its meaning is constituted by the ideas, images, and emotions, which it raises in the mind of the hearer.
          ALFRED NORTH WHITEHEAD,
          Symbolism

See also: 3413, 13782.

SYMPATHY

Related Subjects: Comfort, Consolation, Feeling, Grief, Help, Kindness, Pity, Sorrow, Understanding.

19321. Sympathy wanting, all is wanting. Personal magnetism is the conductor of the sacred spark that puts us in human communion, and gives us to company, conversation, and ourselves.   BRONSON ALCOTT

19322. There is no lack of sympathy in the world; only with sympathy one can't earn a warm meal as easily as without sympathy.
          BERT BRECHT, *A Penny for the Poor*

19323. Next to love, sympathy is the divinest passion of the human heart.
          BURKE

19324. All sympathy not consistent with acknowledged virtue is but disguised selfishness. COLERIDGE

19325. To rejoice in another's prosperity, is to give content to your own lot; to mitigate another's grief, is to alleviate or dispel your own. TRYON EDWARDS

19326. Our sympathy is cold to the relation of distant misery. GIBBON, *Decline & Fall*

19327. Whether I am on the winning or losing side is not the point with me: it is being on the side where my sympathies lie that matters, and I am ready to see it through to the end. ALAN SEEGER *Letter from the Trenches*

19328. There is a kind of sympathy in souls that fits them for each other; and we may be assured when we see two persons engaged in the warmths of a mutual affection, that there are certain qualities in both their minds which bear a resemblance to one another. SIR RICHARD STEELE

See also: 273, 1442.

SYSTEM

Related Subjects: Method, Order, Plan.

19331. My matured conclusion has been that no system is to be trusted, not even that of science, in any literal or pictorial sense; but all systems may be used and, up to a certain point, trusted as symbols. SANTAYANA, *I Believe*

19332. Our little systems have their day. TENNYSON, *In Memoriam*

See also: 160, 2761, 2811, 2813, 10434.

T

TACT

Related Subjects: Delicacy, Diplomacy, Gentleness, Sensitivity.

19341. Silence is not always tact, and it is tact that is golden—not silence. SAMUEL BUTLER

19342. 'Tis ill talking of halters in the house of a man that was hanged. CERVANTES, *Don Quixote*

19343. Tact consists in knowing how far to go too far. JEAN COCTEAU, *Call to Order*

19344. It is one of the greatest blessings that so many women are so full of tact. The calamity happens when a woman who has all the other riches of life just lacks that one thing. SIR WILLIAM OSLER, *Life of Sir William Osler*

19345. Talk to every woman as if you loved her, and to every man as if he bored you, and at the end of your first season you will have the reputation of possessing the most perfect social tact. OSCAR WILDE, *A Woman of No Importance*

See also: 856, 4161, 4185, 9484.

TAILOR

Related Subjects: Dress, Needle.

19351.
Sister, look ye,
How, by a new creation of my tailor's
I've shook off old mortality. JOHN FORD, *The Fancies Chaste and Noble*

19352. Be sure your tailor is a man of sense. O. W. HOLMES, *A Rhymed Lesson*

19353.
What a fine man
Hath your tailor made you! MASSINGER, *City Madam*

19354.
As if thou e'er wert angry
But with thy tailor! and yet that poor
shred
Can bring more to the making of a
man,
Than can be hoped from thee; thou
art his creature;
And did he not, each morning, new
create thee,
Thou'dst stink and be forgotten.
MASSINGER, *Fatal Dowry*

19355.
Get me some French tailor
To new-create you!
MASSINGER, *Renegade*

19356.
Th' embroider'd suit at least he
deem'd his prey;
That suit an unpaid tailor snatch'd
away.   POPE, *The Dunciad*

19357.
Thy gown? why, ay;—come, tailor,
let us see't
O mercy God! what masquing stuff is
here?
What's this? a sleeve? 'tis like a
demi-cannon:
What, up and down, carv'd like an
apple-tart?
Here's snip and nip and cut and slish
and slash
Like to a censer in a barber's shop:
Why, what i' devil's name, tailor,
call'st thou this!
SHAKESPEARE,
The Taming of the Shrew

TALE

Related Subjects: Fairies, Fiction,
Giant, Imagination, Mythology,
News, Scandal, Superstition.

19361.
Tell me the tales that to me were so
dear,
Long, long ago, long, long ago.
T. H. BAYLY, *Long, Long Ago*

19362. Story! God bless you! I have
none to tell, Sir.
GEORGE CANNING,
*The Friend of Humanity & the
Knife-Grinder*

19363. There are only two or three
human stories and they go on repeating themselves as fiercely as if they
had never happened before.
WILLA CATHER, *O Pioneers*

19364. A good storyteller is a person
who has a good memory and hopes
other people haven't.   IRVIN COBB

19365. The world hath just one tale
to tell, and it is very old, a little tale
—a simple tale—a tale that's easy
told: "There was a youth in Babylon
who greatly loved a maid!"
DON MARQUIS, *News from Babylon*

19366. A good tale is none the worse
for being twice told.   *Proverb*

19367. Tales of Robin Hood are
good enough for fools.   *Proverb*

19368. A good tale ill told is a bad
one.   *Proverb*

19369.
And so from hour to hour we ripe
and ripe
And then from hour to hour we rot
and rot;
And thereby hangs a tale.
SHAKESPEARE, *As You Like It*

19370.
I could a tale unfold whose lightest
word
Would harrow up thy soul, freeze thy
young blood,
Make thy two eyes, like stars, start
from their spheres,
Thy knotted and combined locks to
part,
And each particular hair to stand an
end,

Like quills upon the fretful porpen-
tine. SHAKESPEARE, *Hamlet*

19371.
   Little shall I grace my cause
In speaking for myself. Yet, by your
   gracious patience,
I will a round unvarnish'd tale de-
liver
Of my whole course of love.
SHAKESPEARE, *Othello*

19372. An honest tale speeds best being plainly told.
SHAKESPEARE, *Richard III*

19373. 'Tis a Chronicle of day by
day. SHAKESPEARE, *The Tempest*

19374. A sad tale's best for winter.
SHAKESPEARE, *The Winter's Tale*

See also: 1529, 2471, 2481, 3240,
3941, 4459, 4646, 4993, 5102, 10912,
13360, 19688.

TALENT

**Related Subjects: Ability, Genius,
Skill.**

19381. Doing easily what others find
difficult is talent; doing what is impossible for talent is genius.
AMIEL

19382. Great talents largely create
their own conditions. At least, they
may be said to crystallize tendencies
that exist in the air about them,—
tendencies that have gradually come
to exist,—of which lesser talents have
been unaware.
VAN WYCK BROOKS,
The Flowering of New England

19383. To each is given a certain inward talent, a certain outward environment of Fortune; to each, by
wisest combination of these two, a
certain maximum of capability.
CARLYLE, *Sartor Resartus*

19384. It always seemed to me a sort
of clever stupidity only to have one
sort of talent—like a carrier-pigeon.
GEORGE ELIOT

19385. Talent for talent's sake is a
bauble and a show. Talent working
with joy in the cause of universal
truth lifts the possessor to new power
as a benefactor. EMERSON

19386. Men of talent are men for occasions. HAZLITT

19387. Talent is the capacity of doing
anything that depends on application
and industry, it is a voluntary power,
while genius is involuntary.
HAZLITT

19388. There is no substitute for
talent. Industry and all the virtues are
of no avail. ALDOUS HUXLEY,
Point Counter Point

19389. Nature has concealed at the
bottom of our minds talents and abilities of which we are not aware. The
passions alone have the privilege of
bringing them to light, and of giving
us sometimes views more certain and
more perfect than art could possibly
produce.
LA ROCHEFOUCAULD, *Maxims*

19390. Talent is that which is in a
man's power; genius is that in whose
power a man is. LOWELL,
Rousseau and the Sentimentalists

See also: 2350, 2370, 2636, 3441,
3632, 4363, 4772, 10555, 14785,
21418.

TALK

**Related Subjects: Address, Con-
versation, Scandal, Speech, Vote.**

19391. You can't believe everything
you hear—but you can repeat it.
Anonymous

19392. In dinner talk it is perhaps allowable to fling on any faggot rather than let the fire go out.
J. M. BARRIE, *Tommy and Grizel*

19393. He that repeateth a matter separateth very friends.
Bible: Proverbs, xvii, 9

19394.
"The time has come," the Walrus said,
"To talk of many things:
Of shoes—and ships—and sealing-wax—
Of cabbages—and kings—
And why the sea is boiling hot—
And whether pigs have wings."
LEWIS CARROLL,
Through the Looking-Glass

19395. There's not the least thing can be said or done, but people will talk and find fault.
CERVANTES, *Don Quixote*

19396. Who think too little, and who talk too much.   DRYDEN,
Absalom & Achitophel

19397. They would talk of nothing but high life, and high-lived company, with other fashionable topics, such as pictures, taste, Shakespeare, and the musical glasses.   GOLDSMITH,
The Vicar of Wakefield

19398. Avoid the talk of men. For talk is mischievous, light, and easily raised, but hard to bear and difficult to escape. Talk never wholly dies away when voiced by many people.
HESIOD, *Works and Days*

19399.
There is so much good in the worst of us,
And so much bad in the best of us,
That it hardly behooves any of us
To talk about the rest of us.
Attributed to GOVERNOR EDWARD
HOCH, *of Kansas*

19400. What people say behind your back is your standing in the community.   E. W. HOWE,
Country Town Sayings

19401. Whom the disease of talking once possesseth, he can never hold his peace. Nay, rather than he will not discourse he will hire men to hear him.   BEN JONSON, *Timber*

19402. Then he will talk—good gods! how he will talk!
NATHANIEL LEE,
Alexander the Great

19403. Those whose conduct gives room for talk are always the first to attack their neighbours.
MOLIÈRE, *Tartuffe*

19404. The less men think, the more they talk.   MONTESQUIEU

19405.
They never taste who always drink;
They always talk who never think.
MATTHEW PRIOR,
Upon a Passage in the Scaligerana

19406. 'Tis no time to talk.
SHAKESPEARE, *Henry VI*

19407. Let it serve for table-talk.
SHAKESPEARE,
The Merchant of Venice

19408.
Iago. She was a wight, if ever such wight were,—
Desdemona. To do what?
Iago. To suckle fools and chronicle small beer.
Desdemona. O most lame and impotent conclusion!
SHAKESPEARE, *Othello*

19409. Talkers are no good doers.
SHAKESPEARE, *Richard III*

19410. A gentleman, nurse, that loves to hear himself talk, and will speak

more in a minute than he will stand to
in a month.   SHAKESPEARE,
Romeo and Juliet

19411. A man is like a phonograph
with half-a-dozen records. You soon
get tired of them all; and yet you
have to sit at table whilst he reels
them off to every new visitor.
BERNARD SHAW, *Getting Married*

19412. War talk by men who have
been in a war is always interesting;
whereas moon talk by a poet who has
not been in the moon is likely to be
dull.   MARK TWAIN,
Life on the Mississippi

19413. The only thing worse than being talked about is not being talked
about.   OSCAR WILDE

See also: 470, 504, 5851, 6748, 19654.

TASTE

Related Subjects: Delicacy, Salt.

19421. These questions of taste, of
feeling, of inheritance, need no settlement. Everyone carries his own inch-
rule of taste, and amuses himself by
applying it, triumphantly, wherever
he travels.   HENRY ADAMS,
The Education of Henry Adams

19422. A man that has a taste of musick, painting, or architecture, is like
one that has another sense, when compared with such as have no relish of
those arts. ADDISON, *The Spectator*

19423. I think I may define taste to
be that faculty of the soul which dis-
cerns the beauties of an author with
pleasure, and the imperfections with
dislike.   ADDISON

19424.
Happy is the man possessing
The superior holy blessing

Of a judgment and a taste
Accurate, refined and chaste.
ARISTOPHANES, *The Frogs*

19425.
What's one man's poison signor,
Is another's meat or drink.
BEAUMONT & FLETCHER,
Love's Cure

19426. Good taste is better than bad
taste, but bad taste is better than no
taste.   ARNOLD BENNETT

19427. Bad taste is a species of bad
morals.   C. N. BOVEE

19428. It may easily be maintained
that the many in most cases take their
taste from the few, and if this does
not hold with a writer's contemporaries, it is unfailing with posterity. If
a writer is to please the generations
that follow him, he can do it only by
securing the praise of those who by
taste and cultivation are qualified to
judge.   GAMALIEL BRADFORD,
American Portraits

19429. A truly elegant taste is generally accompanied with excellency
of heart.   FIELDING

19430. May not taste be compared to
that exquisite sense of the bee, which
instantly discovers and extracts the
quintessence of every flower, and disregards all the rest of it? GREVILLE

19431. Taste appreciates pictures:
connoisseurship appraises them.
A. W. & J. C. HARE,
Guesses at Truth

19432. The wild vicissitudes of taste.
SAMUEL JOHNSON

19433. Taste depends upon those
finer emotions which make the organization of the soul.
SIR JOSHUA REYNOLDS

19434. The greatest man is he who forms the taste of a nation; the next greatest is he who corrupts it.
SIR JOSHUA REYNOLDS

19435. Taste is, so to speak, the microscope of the judgment.
ROUSSEAU

19436. Though it make the unskilful laugh, cannot but make the judicious grieve. SHAKESPEARE, *Hamlet*

See also: 201, 527, 2554, 2675, 6721, 10412 12575, 15415 20238.

TAXES

Related Subjects: Duty, Government, Price.

19441. When more of the people's sustenance is exacted through the form of taxation than is necessary to meet the just obligations of Government and expenses of its economical administration, such exaction becomes ruthless extortion and a violation of the fundamental principles of a free Government.
GROVER CLEVELAND

19442. Idleness and pride tax with a heavier hand than kings and parliaments. If we can get rid of the former, we may easily bear the latter.
FRANKLIN,
Letter on the Stamp Act

19443. Taxes must neither apply to the laborer, nor to the soldier, nor to the poor, but only to the wealthy and rich. FREDERICK THE GREAT

19444. The delicate duty of devising schemes of revenue should be left where the Constitution has placed it —with the immediate representatives of the people.
WILLIAM HENRY HARRISON,
Inaugural Address

19445. When there is an income-tax, the just man will pay more and the unjust less on the same amount of income. PLATO, *The Republic*

19446. One sure way to determine the social conscience of a Government is to examine the way taxes are collected and how they are spent.
FRANKLIN D. ROOSEVELT

19447.
Cursed war and racking tax
Have left us scarcely raiment to our backs. SCOTT,
The Search After Happiness

19448. Men who prefer any load of infamy, however great, to any pressure of taxation, however light.
SYDNEY SMITH, *On American Debts*

19449. The schoolboy whips his taxed top; the beardless youth manages his taxed horse with a taxed bridle on a taxed road; and the dying Englishman, pouring his medicine, which has paid seven per cent, into a spoon that has paid fifteen per cent, flings himself back upon his chintz bed which has paid twenty-two per cent, and expires in the arms of an apothecary who has paid a license of a hundred pounds for the privilege of putting him to death.
SYDNEY SMITH,
Review of Seybert's Annals of the United States

See also: 2991, 3454, 10815.

TEA

19451. The hot water is to remain upon it [the tea] no longer than whiles you can say the Miserere Psalm very leisurely.
SIR KENELM DIGBY,
The Closet Opened

19452. There are few hours in life more agreeable than the hour dedicated to the ceremony known as afternoon tea.   HENRY JAMES,
The Portrait of a Lady

19453. Sassafras wood boiled down to a kind of tea, and tempered with an infusion of milk and sugar, hath to some tastes a delicacy beyond the China luxury.   CHARLES LAMB,
The Praise of Chimney-Sweepers

19454.
He came in
    When I was out
To borrow some tea
    Was why he came in,
And he went without;
So I was in
    And he was out.
JACK LONDON

19455. Thank God for tea! What would the world do without tea?—how did it exist? I am glad I was not born before tea.

SYDNEY SMITH,
Lady Holland's Memoir

TEACHER

Related Subjects: **Education, Grammar, Leader, Learning, Master, Pedantry, Scholar, School, Teaching, University.**

19461. A teacher affects eternity; he can never tell where his influence stops.   HENRY ADAMS,
The Education of Henry Adams

19462. The true teacher defends his pupils against his own personal influence. He inspires self-distrust. He guides their eyes from himself to the spirit that quickens him. He will have no disciple.

BRONSON ALCOTT, *Orphic Sayings*

19463. Brought up in this city at the feet of Gamaliel.
Bible: Acts, xxii, 3

19464. Arrogance, pedantry, and dogmatism are the occupational diseases of those who spend their lives directing the intellects of the young.
HENRY S. CANBY, *Alma Mater*

19465. And gladly wolde he lerne, and gladly teche.
CHAUCER, *The Canterbury Tales*

19466.
Charming women can true converts make,
We love the precepts for the teacher's sake.   GEORGE FARQUHAR,
The Constant Couple

19467. A teacher who can arouse a feeling for one single good action, for one single good poem, accomplishes more than he who fills our memory with rows on rows of natural objects, classified with name and form.   GOETHE, *Elective Affinities*

19468. University teachers, like the members of other professions, are, for the most part, mediocrities striving to be sublime; our business is to maximize their sublimity.
HAROLD J. LASKI

19469. No bubble is so iridescent or floats longer than that blown by the successful teacher.
SIR WILLIAM OSLER,
Life of Sir William Osler

19470. He that sits to work in the market-place shall have many teachers.   *Proverb*

19471. I am but a gatherer and disposer of men's stuff.
SIR HENRY WOTTON,
Preface to the Elements of Architecture

TEACHING

Related Subjects: Advice, Education, Grammar, Knowledge, Learning, Pedantry, Scholar, School, Study, Teacher, Universty.

19481. Woe to him who teaches men faster than they can learn.
WILL DURANT,
The Story of Philosophy

19482. The whole art of teaching is only the art of awakening the natural curiosity of young minds for the purpose of satisfying it afterwards.
ANATOLE FRANCE,
The Crime of Sylvestre Bonnard

19483. Let our teaching be full of ideas. Hitherto it has been stuffed only with facts.   ANATOLE FRANCE

19484. I care not what subject is taught if only it be taught well.
THOMAS H. HUXLEY

19485.
Men must be taught as if you taught them not,
And things unknown propos'd as things forgot.
POPE, *Essay on Criticism*

19486. Teaching others teacheth yourself.   *Proverb*

19487. Better untaught than ill taught.   *Proverb*

19488. He teacheth ill that teacheth all.   *Proverb*

19489.
Delightful task! to rear the tender thought,
To teach the young idea how to shoot.
JAMES THOMSON, *The Seasons*

See also: 86, 317, 1371, 3237, 3321, 4181, 13121, 13726, 16606.

TEARS

Related Subjects: Eyes, Grief, Joy, Pain, Sorrow.

19491. They that sow in tears shall reap in joy.   *Bible: Psalm, cxxvi, 5*

19492. To these crocodile tears, they will add sobs, fiery sighs, and sorrowful countenance.
ROBERT BURTON,
Anatomy of Melancholy

19493.
The drying up a single tear has more
Of honest fame than shedding seas of gore.   BYRON, *Don Juan*

19494. Heaven knows we need never be ashamed of our tears, for they are rain upon the blinding dust of earth, overlying our hard hearts.
DICKENS, *Great Expectations*

19495.
What precious drops are those
Which silently each other's track pursue,
Bright as young diamonds in their infant dew?
DRYDEN, *The Conquest of Granada*

19496. Waste not fresh tears over old griefs.   EURIPIDES, *Alexander*

19497.
        To see stand weeping by
A woman once embraced, will try
The tension of a man the most austere.   THOMAS HARDY,
The Contretemps

19498. The big round tear stands trembling in her eye.
HOMER, *Odyssey*

19499.
My tears must stop, for every drop
Hinders needle and thread.
THOMAS HOOD,
The Song of the Shirt

19500.
Thrice he assay'd, and thrice, in spite
  of scorn,
Tears, such as angels weep, burst
  forth.   MILTON, *Paradise Lost*

19501.
Give smiles to those who love you
  less,
But keep your tears for me.
           THOMAS MOORE,
      When Midst the Gay I Meet

19502.
The tear down childhood's cheek
  that flows,
Is like the dewdrop on the rose;
When next the summer breeze comes
  by,
And waves the bush, the flower is dry.
           SCOTT, *Rokeby*

19503.
         The big round tears
Coursed one another down his inno-
  cent nose
In piteous chase.
    SHAKESPEARE, *As You Like It*

19504.
What's Hecuba to him or he to Hec-
  uba,
That he should weep for her?
       SHAKESPEARE, *Hamlet*

19505. Like Niobe, all tears.
       SHAKESPEARE, *Hamlet*

19506. To weep is to make less the
depth of grief.
      SHAKESPEARE, *Henry VI*

19507. If you have tears, prepare to
shed them now.
      SHAKESPEARE, *Julius Caesar*

19508.
Let not women's weapons, water-
  drops,
Stain my man's cheeks.
      SHAKESPEARE, *King Lear*

19509. How much better is it to weep
at joy than to joy at weeping.
       SHAKESPEARE,
      Much Ado About Nothing

19510.
And if the boy have not a woman's
  gift
To rain a shower of commanded
  tears,
An onion will do well for such a shift.
       SHAKESPEARE,
      The Taming of the Shrew

19511.
O father! what a hell of witchcraft
  lies
In the small orb of one particular
  tear.   SHAKESPEARE,
      A Lover's Complaint

19512.
I could lie down like a tired child,
And weep away the life of care
Which I have borne and yet must
  bear.   SHELLEY,
      Stanzas Written in Dejection

19513.
Of all the languages of earth in which
  the human kind confer
The Master Speaker is the Tear: it
  is the Great Interpreter.
       RIDGELY TORRENCE,
      The House of a Hundred Lights

19514. I could not bear a mother's
  tears.   VERGIL, *Aeneid*

See also: 24, 495, 3711, 10619, 11457,
12922, 14581, 17460, 21660.

TEMPER

**Related Subjects: Ill-Nature, Tem-
perament.**

19521. He is a little chimney, and
heated hot in a moment.
       LONGFELLOW,
      The Courtship of Miles Standish

19522. It's my rule never to lose me temper till it would be dethrimental to keep it.   SEAN O'CASEY,
The Plough and the Stars

19523. The brain may devise laws for the blood, but a hot temper leaps o'er a cold decree.
SHAKESPEARE,
The Merchant of Venice

19524.
Why should a man, whose blood is warm within,
Sit like his grandsire cut in alabaster?
SHAKESPEARE,
The Merchant of Venice

19525.
High-stomach'd are they both, and full of ire,
In rage deaf as the sea, hasty as fire.
SHAKESPEARE, *Richard II*

19526. A little pot and soon hot.
SHAKESPEARE,
The Taming of the Shrew

TEMPERAMENT

Related Subjects: Art, Genius, Temper.

19531. It is often temperament which makes men brave and women chaste.
LA ROCHEFOUCAULD, *Maxims*

19532. There was no resisting the vortex of his temperament.
CHARLES LAMB, *Last Essays of Elia*

19533. Sensitive, swift to resent, but as swift in atoning for error.
LONGFELLOW,
The Courtship of Miles Standish

19534. You know the fiery quality of the duke. SHAKESPEARE, *King Lear*

19535.
Who can be wise, amazed, temperate and furious,
Loyal and neutral, in a moment?
SHAKESPEARE, *Macbeth*

19536.
These flashes on the surface are not he.
He has a solid base of temperament.
TENNYSON, *The Princess*

See also: 187, 1218, 3217, 4220, 10709, 19727.

TEMPERANCE

Related Subjects: Abstinence, Moderation, Prohibition, Self-Control.

19541. Temperance is a bridle of gold, and he that can use it aright is liker a God than a man; for as it will transform a beast to a man again, so it will make a man a God. BURTON

19542. Temperance puts wood on the fire, meal in the barrel, flour in the tub, money in the purse, credit in the country, contentment in the house, clothes on the children, vigor in the body, intelligence in the brain, and spirit in the whole constitution.
FRANKLIN

19543. Since the creation of the world there has been no tyrant like Intemperance, and no slaves so cruelly treated as his.
W. L. GARRISON, *Life*

19544. If temperance prevails, then education can prevail; if temperance fails, then education must fail.
HORACE MANN

19545. Temperance is the best physic.
Proverb

19546. Temperance and industry are man's true remedies; work sharpens his appetite and temperance teaches him to control it.   ROUSSEAU,
Emile, or Education

19547. No man ever repented that he

arose from the table sober, healthful, and with his wits about him.

JEREMY TAYLOR, *Sermons*

See also: 68, 70, 743, 5751, 9667.

TEMPTATION

Related Subjects: Abstinence, Bribery, Devil, Honesty, Self-Control, Sin, Whore.

19551. Greater is he who is above temptation than he who being tempted overcomes.

BRONSON ALCOTT, *Orphic Sayings*

19552. My son, if sinners entice thee, consent thou not.

Bible: Proverbs, i, 10

19553. Get thee behind me, Satan.

Bible: Matthew, xvi, 23

19554. Blessed is the man that endureth temptation; for when he is tried, he shall receive the crown of life. *Bible: James, i, 12*

19555. Resist the Devil, and he will flee from you. *Bible: James, iv, 7*

19556.
Why comes temptation, but for man to meet
And master and make crouch beneath his foot,
And so be pedestaled in triumph?

BROWNING,
The Ring and the Book

19557.
What's done we partly may compute,
But know not what's resisted.

BURNS,
Address to the Unco Guid

19558. Every man is to be had one way or another, and every woman almost any way.

LORD CHESTERFIELD

19559. I know, indeed, the evil of

that I purpose; but my inclination gets the better of my judgement.

EURIPIDES, *Medea*

19560.
Satan now is wiser than of yore,
And tempts by making rich, not making poor. POPE, *Moral Essays*

19561. He who avoids the temptation avoids the sin. *Proverb*

19562. Where a chest lies open, a reputed honest man may sin.

Proverb

19563. An open door may tempt a saint. *Proverb*

19564. All temptations are found either in hope or fear. *Proverb*

19565.
Ay me, how many perils doe enfold
The righteous man, to make him daily fall. EDMUND SPENSER,
The Faerie Queene

19566. I can resist everything except temptation. OSCAR WILDE,
Lady Windermere's Fan

19567. The only way to get rid of a temptation is to yield to it.

OSCAR WILDE,
The Picture of Dorian Gray

See also: 64, 217, 873, 3155, 4328, 4511, 5270, 9137, 21572.

TENDERNESS

Related Subjects: Affection, Care, Compassion, Friendship, Gentleness, Kiss, Love, Mercy.

19571. When death, the great reconciler, has come, it is never our tenderness that we repent of, but our severity. GEORGE ELIOT

19572. A tender-hearted and compassionate disposition, which inclines

men to pity and feel for the misfortunes of others, and which is, even for its own sake, incapable of involving any man in ruin and misery, is of all tempers of mind the most amiable; and though it seldom receives much honor, is worthy of the highest.
         FIELDING

19573. Tenderness, without a capacity of relieving, only makes the man who feels it more wretched than the object which sues for assistance.
         GOLDSMITH

19574. Tenderness is the repose of passion.   JOUBERT, *Pensées*

19575.
When thus the heart is in a vein
Of tender thought, the simplest strain
Can touch it with peculiar power.
       THOMAS MOORE,
         Evenings in Greece

19576. Tenderness is the repose of love.   ANTOINE DE RIVAROL

THANKSGIVING DAY

Related Subjects: Feast, Harvest, Holiday.

19581.
Over the river and through the wood;
To grandfather's house we'll go;
   The horse knows the way
   To carry the sleigh,
Through the white and drifted snow.
       LYDIA M. CHILD,
         Thanksgiving Day

19582.
This is the sum total of Thanksgiving lore:
Not to be thankful until you're tired of what you're being thankful for.
       OGDEN NASH,
   A Short Outline of Thanksgiving

See also: 865.

THEATRE, see Stage.

THEOLOGY

Related Subjects: Creeds, Doctrine, Religion.

19591. I have only a small flickering light to guide me in the darkness of a thick forest. Up comes a theologian and blows it out.   DIDEROT

19592. The broad ethics of Jesus were quickly narrowed to village theologies.   EMERSON, *Conduct of Life*

19593. The cure for false theology is mother-wit.   EMERSON,
         Conduct of Life

19594. Men are better than their theology. Their daily life gives it the lie.   EMERSON, *Essays*

19595. Theology is Anthropology.
         FEUERBACH,
      Wesen des Christenthums

19596. Theology is an attempt to explain a subject by men who do not understand it. The intent is not to tell the truth but to satisfy the questioner.
     ELBERT HUBBARD, *Philistine*

19597. Let us put theology out of religion. Theology has always sent the worst to heaven, the best to hell.
       ROBERT INGERSOLL,
         Myth and Miracle

See also: 2764, 13631, 17614.

THEORIES

Related Subjects: Facts, Idea, Philosophy, Speculation, Thought.

19601. In theory there is nothing to hinder our following what we are taught; but in life there are many things to draw us aside.
     EPICTETUS, *Discourses*

19602. Grey is the color of all theory.
GOETHE

19603. A favourite theory is a possession for life.   HAZLITT,
Characteristics

19604. My theory is to enjoy life, but the practice is against it.
CHARLES LAMB

19605. I have a paper afloat, with an electromagnetic theory of light, which, till I am convinced to the contrary, I hold to be great guns.
CLERK MAXWELL

19606. It is certainly not the least charm of a theory that it is refutable.
NIETZSCHE, *Beyond Good and Evil*

See also: 1219, 2025, 16641.

THIEF

Related Subjects: Crime, Honesty.

19611.
'Twas a thief that said the last kind word to Christ:
Christ took the kindness and forgave the theft.   BROWNING,
The Ring and the Book

19612. Small thieves be in towers fastened to wooden blocks; big ones strut about in gold and silver.
CATO THE CENSOR

19613.
When a felon's not engaged in his employment,
    Or maturing his felonious little plans,
His capacity for innocent enjoyment
Is just as great as any honest man's.   W. S. GILBERT,
The Pirates of Penzance

19614. A thief passes for a gentleman, when stealing has made him rich.   *Proverb*

19615. He that finds a thing steals it if he endeavors not to restore it.
Proverb

19616. The thief is sorry he is to be hanged, not that he is a thief.
Proverb

19617. The great thieves punish the little ones.   *Proverb*

19618. Save a thief from the gallows, and he'll be the first shall cut your throat.   *Proverb*

19619. Set a thief to catch a thief.
Proverb

19620. It is a shame to steal, but a worse to carry home.   *Proverb*

19621. All are not thieves that dogs bark at.   *Proverb*

19622. Rob me the exchequer.
SHAKESPEARE, *Henry IV*

19623. Every true man's apparel fits your thief.   SHAKESPEARE,
Measure for Measure

19624. Ships are but boards, sailors but men: there be land-rats and water-rats, water-thieves and land-thieves.   SHAKESPEARE,
The Merchant of Venice

19625. Flat burglary as ever was committed.   SHAKESPEARE,
Much Ado About Nothing

19626. The robb'd that smiles, steals something from the thief.
SHAKESPEARE, *Othello*

19627.
    I'll example you with thievery:
The sun's a thief, and with his great attraction
Rob's the vast sea; the moon's an arrant thief,
And her pale fire she snatches from the sun;

The sea's a thief whose liquid surge resolves
The moon into salt tears; the earth's a thief,
That feeds and breeds by a composture stolen
From general excrement, each thing's a thief.   SHAKESPEARE,
Timon of Athens

See also: 1095, 1717, 2508, 7738, 10601, 11137, 11715, 14226, 16184, 20801, 21153.

THIRST

Related Subjects: Desire, Drinking, Hunger.

19631.
The panting thirst that scorches in the breath
Of those that die the soldier's fiery death.   BYRON, *Lara*

19632.
Water, water, every where,
And all the boards did shrink;
Water, water, every where,
Nor any drop to drink.
COLERIDGE, *The Ancient Mariner*

19633.
Hunger is bitter, but the worst
Of human pangs, the most accursed
Of Want's fell scorpions, is Thirst.
ELIZA COOK, *Melaia*

19634.
The thirst that from the soul doth rise,
Doth ask a drink divine;
But might I of Jove's nectar sup,
I would not change for thine.
BEN JONSON

19635.
I drank at every vine.
The last was like the first.
I came upon no wine
So wonderful as thirst.
EDNA ST. VINCENT MILLAY, *Feast*

19636. He that can master his thirst is master of his health.   *Proverb*

19637. Go not to the pot for every thirst.   *Proverb*

19638. The thirsty drink in silence.
Proverb

19639. As dry as a bone.   *Proverb*

19640. He that goes to bed thirsty rises healthy.   *Proverb*

See also: 571, 4808, 6447, 6482.

THOUGHT

Related Subjects: Consideration, Contemplation, Idea, Intelligence, Meditation, Philosophy, Reflection, Reverie, Speculation, Theories.

19641.
If you strike
Upon a thought that baffles you, break off
From that entanglement and try another
So shall your wits be fresh to start again.   ARISTOPHANES,
The Clouds

19642.
It is much less what we do
Than what we think, which fits us for the future.
PHILIP J. BAILEY, *Festus*

19643.
Who can mistake great thoughts?
They seize upon the mind—arrest, and search,
And shake it.
PHILIP J. BAILEY, *Festus*

19644. As he thinketh in his heart, so is he.   *Bible: Proverbs, xxiii, 7*

19645.
Back of the beating hammer
By which the steel is wrought,

Back of the workshop's clamor
The seeker may find the Thought.
BERTON BRALEY, *The Thinker*

19646. Sickening thought itself engendereth corporal pain.
ROBERT BRIDGES,
The Testament of Beauty

19647. To most people nothing is more troublesome than the effort of thinking. SIR JAMES BRYCE,
Studies in History and Jurisprudence

19648. The dominant thought of youth is the bigness of the world, of age its smallness. As we grow older we escape from the tyranny of matter and recognise that the true centre of gravity is in the mind.
JOHN BUCHAN, *Pilgrim's Way*

19649. Thought alone is eternal.
BULWER-LYTTON, *Lucile*

19650. It is our less conscious thoughts and our less conscious actions which mainly mould our lives and the lives of those who spring from us. SAMUEL BUTLER,
The Way of All Flesh

19651.
                    I stood
Among them, but not of them; in a
  shroud
Of thoughts which were not their
  thoughts. BYRON, *Childe Harold*

19652. T h e lightning-spark of Thought, generated or say rather heaven-kindled, in the solitary mind, awakens its express likeness in another mind, in a thousand other minds, and all blaze up together in combined fire.   CARLYLE,
Sir Walter Scott

19653. It should be as easy to expel an obnoxious thought from your

mind as to shake a stone out of your shoe.   EDWARD CARPENTER,
A Visit to a Gnani

19654. "Really, now you ask me," said Alice, very much confused, "I don't think—"
"Then you shouldn't talk," said the Hatter.   LEWIS CARROLL,
Alice in Wonderland

19655. A New Thinker is only one who does not know what the old thinkers have thought.
FRANK M. COLBY

19656. Thinking in its lower grades is comparable to paper money, and in its higher forms it is a kind of poetry.   HAVELOCK ELLIS,
The Dance of Life

19657. The world's greatest thinkers have often been amateurs; for high thinking is the outcome of fine and independent living, and for that a professorial chair offers no special opportunities.
HAVELOCK ELLIS,
The Dance of Life

19658. To think is to act.
EMERSON, *Spiritual Laws*

19659. Second thoughts are ever wiser.   EURIPIDES, *Hippolytus*

19660. And to cease to think is but little different from ceasing to be.
FRANKLIN

19661. The secret thoughts of a man run over all things, holy, profane, clean, obscene, grave, and light, without shame or blame.
THOMAS HOBBES, *Leviathan*

19662. A man is not idle because he is absorbed in thought. There is a visible labour and there is an invisible labour.   VICTOR HUGO,
Les Miserables

19663. No thought which I have ever had has satisfied my soul.
RICHARD JEFFERIES,
The Story of my Heart

19664.
On the shore
Of the wide world I stand alone, and think
Till love and fame to nothingness do sink. KEATS, *When I Have Fears*

19665.
Cannon-balls may aid the truth,
But thought's a weapon stronger;
We'll win our battles by its aid;—
Wait a little longer.
CHARLES MACKAY,
The Good Time Coming

19666. If you make people think they're thinking, they'll love you. If you really make them think they'll hate you. DON MARQUIS,
The Sun Dial

19667.
It is thy very energy of thought
Which keeps thee from thy God.
CARDINAL NEWMAN,
Dream of Gerontius

19668. If there is anything that cannot bear free thought, let it crack.
WENDELL PHILLIPS

19669. It is for want of thinking that most men are undone. *Proverb*

19670.
The man who idly sits and thinks,
May sow a nobler crop than corn,
For thoughts are seeds of future deeds,
And when God thought—the world was born!
HARRY ROMAINE, *Inaction*

19671. There's something so beautiful in coming on one's very own inmost thoughts in another. In one way it's one of the greatest pleasures one has. OLIVE SCHREINER

19672.
There is nothing either good or bad,
But thinking makes it so,
SHAKESPEARE, *Hamlet*

19673.
Speak to me as to thy thinkings,
As thou dost ruminate, and give thy worst of thoughts
The worst of words.
SHAKESPEARE, *Othello*

19674.
Love's heralds should be thoughts
Which ten times faster glide than the sun's beams. SHAKESPEARE,
Romeo and Juliet

19675. Nimble thought can jump both sea and land.
SHAKESPEARE, *Sonnet XLIV*

19676. They are never alone that are accompanied with noble thoughts.
SIR PHILIP SIDNEY, *Arcadia*

19677. The world is not so much in need of new thoughts as that when thought grows old and worn with usage it should, like current coin, be called in, and, from the mint of genius, reissued fresh and new.
ALEXANDER SMITH, *Dreamthorp*

19678.
Thinking is but an idle waste of thought
And nought is everything, and everything is nought.
HORACE SMITH,
Rejected Addresses

19679. What thought can think, another thought can mend.
ROBERT SOUTHWELL, *Look Home*

19680. A penny for your thoughts.
SWIFT, *Polite Conversation*

19681.

The laws of being are the laws of thought.

Thought is conditioned by being; not being by thought.

GENEVIEVE TAGGARD

19682.

Though a man a thinking being is defined,

Few use the grand prerogative of mind.

How few think justly of the thinking few!

How many never think, who think they do!   JANE TAYLOR,

Essays in Rhyme

19683. Our great thoughts, our great affections, the truths of our life, never leave us. Surely they cannot separate from our consciousness, shall follow it whithersoever that shall go, and are of their nature divine and immortal.   THACKERAY

19684. To him whose elastic and vigorous thought keeps pace with the sun, the day is a perpetual morning.

THOREAU, *Walden*

19685. It is not given to any man, however endowed, to rise spontaneously into intellectual splendor without the parentage of antecedent thought.   JOHN TYNDALL,

Fragments of Science

19686. The brightest flashes in the world of thought are incomplete until they have been proved to have their counterparts in the world of fact.   JOHN TYNDALL,

Fragments of Science

19687.

But hushed be every thought that springs

From out the bitterness of things.

WORDSWORTH, *Elegiac Stanzas*

19688.

O Reader! had you in your mind

Such stores as silent thought can bring,

O gentle Reader! you would find

A tale in everything.

WORDSWORTH, *Simon Lee*

See also: 141, 154, 174, 574, 1142, 1211, 1409, 1527, 1864, 2323, 2330, 2420, 2476, 2788, 2793, 3089, 3936, 5931, 8228, 12457, 12631, 12971, 15763, 19404, 21444.

THREAT

Related Subjects: Abuse, Curse, Defiance, Injury, Insult, Violence, Warning.

19691. Threats without power are like powder without ball.

NATHAN BAILEY, *Dictionary*

19692. If it is not right to hurt, it is neither right nor wise to menace.

BURKE, *Speech*

19693. He threatens many that hath injured one.   BEN JONSON,

Fall of Sejanus

19694. His bark is worse than his bite.   *Proverb*

19695. Many a man threatens while he quakes for fear.   *Proverb*

19696. He who threateneth, hunteth after a revenge.   *Proverb*

19697. It is more easy to threaten than to kill.   *Proverb*

19698. There are more threatened than struck.   *Proverb*

19699. A man does not die of threats.

Proverb

19700.

There is no terror, Cassius, in your threats,

For I am arm'd so strong in honesty
That they pass by me as the idle
  wind,
Which I respect not.
      SHAKESPEARE, *Julius Caesar*

19701. I will tread this unbolted villain into mortar, and daub the walls of a jakes with him.
      SHAKESPEARE, *King Lear*

19702.
Before I be convict by course of law,
To threaten me with death is most
  unlawful.   SHAKESPEARE,
             Richard III

THRIFT

Related Subjects: Bargain, Economy, Scotland.

19711. Penny wise, pound foolish.
      ROBERT BURTON,
      Anatomy of Melancholy

19712. Gentlemen, it is the first hundred dollars saved which tells.
      ANDREW CARNEGIE,
      Empire of Business

19713. A little in one's own pocket is better than much in another man's purse. 'Tis good to keep a nest-egg. Every little makes a mickle.
      CERVANTES, *Don Quixote*

19714.
That though on pleasure she was
  bent,
  She had a frugal mind.
    COWPER, *History of John Gilpin*

19715. A penny saved is a penny got.   FIELDING, *The Miser*

19716. If thou shouldst lay up even a little upon a little, and shouldst do this often, soon would even this become great.   HESIOD,
      Works and Days

19717. Whatever you have, spend less.   SAMUEL JOHNSON,
      Boswell: Life

19718. The first years of man must provision for the last.
      SAMUEL JOHNSON, *Rasselas*

19719. Large enterprises make the few rich, but the majority prosper only through the carefulness and detail of thrift. He is already poverty-stricken whose habits are not thrifty.
      T. T. MUNGER

19720. Keep some till furthermore come.   *Proverb*

19721. Keep the wolf from the door.
      Proverb

19722. Take care of the pence, the pounds will take care of themselves.
      Proverb

19723. He that borrows an' bigs, make feasts an' thigs, drinks an' is na dry, these three are na thrifty.
      Proverb

19724. Better to say here it is than here it was.   *Proverb*

19725. If you keep a thing seven years, you are sure to find a use for it.   SCOTT, *Woodstock*

19726.
Thrift, thrift, Horatio! the funeral
  baked meats
Did coldly furnish forth the marriage tables.
      SHAKESPEARE, *Hamlet*

19727. Solvency is entirely a matter of temperament and not of income.
      LOGAN PEARSALL SMITH,
      Afterthoughts

19728.
Though small was your allowance,
  You saved a little store;

And those who save a little
   Shall get a plenty more.
        THACKERAY,
    The King of Brentford's
          Testament

19729. The doctrine of thrift for the poor is dumb and cruel, like advising them to try and lift themselves by their bootstraps. NORMAN THOMAS

See also: 564, 1468.

THRONE

Related Subjects: Crown, Kings.

19731. And in mercy shall the throne be established.   *Bible: Isaiah, xvi, 5*

19732.
The blood of beauty, wealth, and
   power—the heart-blood of a Queen,
The noblest of the Stuart race—the
   fairest earth has seen—
Lapped by a dog! Go think of it in
   silence and alone!
Then weigh against a grain of sand
   the glories of a throne.
   H. G. BELL, *Mary, Queen of Scots*

19733. The legs of the throne are the plough and the oar, the anvil and the sewing-machine.
        EMERSON, *Journals*

19734. Forbade to wade through slaughter to a throne.
        THOMAS GRAY,
   Elegy Written in a Country
         Church-yard

19735. The throne is but a piece of gilded wood covered with velvet.
        NAPOLEON

19736. A long train of these practices has at length unwillingly convinced me that there is something behind the throne greater than the King himself. WILLIAM PITT

19737. A doubtful throne is ice on summer seas.   TENNYSON,
     Idylls of the King

See also: 1182, 1749, 4373, 5173.

THUNDER AND LIGHTNING

Related Subjects: Electricity, Storm, Weather.

19741.
        Far along,
From peak to peak the rattling crags
   among
Leaps the live thunder!
     BYRON, *Childe Harold*

19742.
Loud roared the dreadful thunder,
The rain a deluge showers.
   ANDREW CHERRY, *Bay of Biscay*

19743. They will not let my play run; and yet they steal my thunder.
        JOHN DENNIS

19744.
The lightning flies, the thunder roars,
And big waves lash the frightened
   shores.   JOHN GAY,
   The Lady's Looking-Glass

19745. It must be done like lightning.   BEN JONSON,
   Every Man in his Humour

19746.
Thy thunder, conscious of the new
   command,
Rumbles reluctant o'er our fallen
   house.   KEATS, *Hyperion*

19747.
I saw the lightning's gleaming rod
Reach forth and write upon the sky
The awful autograph of God.
     JOAQUIN MILLER,
   The Ship in the Desert

19748.
        The thunder,
Wing'd with red lightning and impetuous rage,

Perhaps hath spent his shafts, and ceases now
To bellow through the vast and boundless deep.
MILTON, *Paradise Lost*

19749. When you can use the lightning, it is better than cannon.
NAPOLEON

19750. It's the thunder that frights, but the lightning that smites.
Proverb

19751. The thunderbolt hath but its clap. .
Proverb

19752. It is vain to look for a defence against lightning.
PUBLILIUS SYRUS, *Sententiae*

19753.
Loud o'er my head, though awful thunders roll,
And vivid lightnings flash from pole to pole,
Yet 'tis Thy voice, my God, that bids them fly,
Thy arm directs those lightnings through the sky.   SCOTT,
On a Thunderstorm

19754. If I had a thunderbolt in mine eye, I can tell who should down.   SHAKESPEARE,
As You Like It

19755.
Be thou as lightning in the eyes of France;
For ere thou canst report I will be there,
The thunder of my cannon shall be heard:
So hence! Be thou the trumpet of our wrath.   SHAKESPEARE,
King John

19756.
Sulphurous and thought-executing fires.

Vaunt-couriers to oak-cleaving thunderbolts.   SHAKESPEARE,
King Lear

19757.
You nimble lightnings, dart your blinding flames
Into her scornful eyes!
SHAKESPEARE, *King Lear*

19758.
     Merciful Heaven,
Thou rather with thy sharp and sulphurous bolt
Split'st the unwedgeable and gnarled oak
Than the soft myrtle.
SHAKESPEARE,
Measure for Measure

19759.
Are there no stones in heaven
But what serve for the thunder?
SHAKESPEARE, *Othello*

19760.
Too like the lightning, which doth cease to be
Ere one can say it lightens.
SHAKESPEARE, *Romeo and Juliet*

19761.
       The thunder,
That deep and dreadful organ-pipe, pronounc'd
The name of Prosper; it did bass my trespass.   SHAKESPEARE,
The Tempest

19762.
Thunder crumples the sky,
Lightning tears at it.
LEONORA SPEYER, *The Squall*

See also: 182, 1194, 7742, 8561, 21129.

TIDE

Related Subject: The Sea.

19771.
All night the thirsty beach has listening lain

With patience dumb,
Counting the slow, sad moments of
    her pain;
Now morn has come,
And with the morn the punctual tide
    again.   SUSAN COOLIDGE,
                    Flood-Tide

19772.
The western tide crept up along the
    sand,
    And o'er and o'er the sand,
    And round and round the sand,
    As far as eye could see
The rolling mist came down and hid
    the land:
    And never home came she.
         CHARLES KINGSLEY,
               The Sands o' Dee

19773.
The little waves, with their soft,
    white hands,
    Efface the footprints in the sands,
And the tide rises, the tide falls.
              LONGFELLOW,
    The Tide Rises, the Tide Falls

19774. Every tide hath its ebb.
                    Proverb

19775.
There is a tide in the affairs of men,
Which, taken at the flood, leads on to
    fortune;
Omitted, all the voyage of their life
Is bound in shallows and in miseries.
       SHAKESPEARE, *Julius Caesar*

19776.
Tide flowing is feared, for many a
    thing,
Great danger to such as be sick, it
    doth bring;
Sea ebb, by long ebbing, some respite
    doth give
And sendeth good comfort, to such
    as shall live.
         THOMAS TUSSER,
    500 Points of Good Husbandrie

See also: 19829.

TIGER

Related Subjects: Animal.

19781.
Tiger, tiger, burning bright
In the forests of the night,
What immortal hand or eye
Could frame thy fearful symmetry?
        BLAKE, *The Tiger*
    (Source of title of a novel by
               Max White)

19782. Who rides a tiger cannot dis-
mount.   *Chinese Proverb*

19783. Shun the companionship of
the tiger.   *Proverb*

19784. When did the tiger's young
ones teach the dam?
    SHAKESPEARE, *Titus Andronicus*

See also: 10178.

TIME

**Related Subjects: Age, Antiquity,
Day, Delay, Eternity, Hours, Late-
ness, Memory, Minute, Month,
Procrastination, Sun-Dial, Year.**

19791. I consider time as an immense
ocean, in which many noble authors
are entirely swallowed up.
    ADDISON, *The Spectator*

19792. Time as he grows old teaches
many lessons.   AESCHYLUS,
                 Prometheus

19793. Time does not become sacred
to us until we have lived it.
        JOHN BURROUGHS,
        The Spell of the Past

19794. There's a time for some
things, and a time for all things; a
time for great things, and a time for
small things.   CERVANTES,
                Don Quixote

19795.
The tyme, that may not sojourne,
But goth, and never may retourne,
As water that doun renneth ay,
But never drope retourne may.

CHAUCER,
The Romaunt of the Rose

19796.
Touch us gently, Time!
Let us glide adown thy stream
Gently,—as we sometimes glide
Through a quiet dream.

BARRY CORNWALL,
A Petition to Time

19797. I know that our inheritance is held in store for us by Time. I know there is a sea of Time to rise one day, before which all who wrong us or oppress us will be swept away like leaves. I see it, on the flow!

DICKENS, *The Chimes*

19798. It was the best of times, it was the worst of times, it was the age of wisdom, it was the age of foolishness, it was the epoch of belief, it was the epoch of incredulity, it was the season of Light, it was the season of Darkness, it was the spring of hope, it was the winter of despair.

DICKENS, *A Tale of Two Cities*

19799. Time is the image of eternity.

DIOGENES LAERTIUS, *Plato*

19800. It was a favourite expression of Theophrastus that time was the most valuable thing that a man could spend.

DIOGENES LAERTIUS,
Theophrastus

19801.
Time goes, you say? Ah no!
Alas, Time stays, *we* go.

AUSTIN DOBSON,
The Paradox of Time

19802. There is only one time in life for milk, only one time for youth;

we cannot postpone life or retrace its milestones, and what is once lost is lost forever.

HAVELOCK ELLIS,
The Art of Life

19803. Time dissipates to shining ether the solid angularity of facts.

EMERSON, *History*

19804. Time will explain it all. He is a talker, and needs no questioning before he speaks.

EURIPIDES, *Aeolus*

19805. The time God allots to each one of us is like a precious tissue which we embroider as we best know how.

ANATOLE FRANCE,
The Crime of Sylvestre Bonnard

19806. Remember that time is money.

FRANKLIN,
Advice to a Young Tradesman

19807. Dost thou love life? Then do not squander time, for that is the stuff life is made of.

FRANKLIN, *Poor Richard*

19808. As we advance in life, we acquire a keener sense of the value of time. Nothing else, indeed, seems of any consequence; and we become misers in this respect.

HAZLITT,
*The Feeling of Immortality
in Youth*

19809. Thursday come, and the week is gone.

GEORGE HERBERT,
Jacula Prudentum

19810.
Time, you old gipsy man,
Will you not stay,
Put up your caravan
Just for one day?

RALPH HODGSON,
Time, You Old Gipsy Man

19811.
Blood of the world, time stanchless
  flows;
The wound is mortal and is mine.
      ALDOUS HUXLEY, *Seasons*

19812. It is always the puzzle of the
nature of time that brings our
thoughts to a standstill. And if time
is so fundamental that an understanding of its true nature is for ever beyond our reach, then so also in all
probability is a decision in the age-
long controversy between determin-
ism and free-will.
      SIR JAMES JEANS,
      The Mysterious Universe

19813. That old bald cheater, Time.
      BEN JONSON, *The Poetaster*

19814.
      Time, that aged nurse,
Rock'd me to patience.
      KEATS, *Endymion*

19815.
The Moving Finger writes; and,
    having writ,
Moves on: nor all your piety nor Wit
  Shall lure it back to cancel half
    a Line,
Nor all your Tears wash out a Word
  of it.   OMAR KHAYYAM,
      Rubaiyat

19816.
    Time has laid his hand
Upon my heart, gently, not smiting
  it,
But as a harper lays his open palm
Upon his harp to deaden its vibra-
  tions.   LONGFELLOW,
      The Golden Legend

19817. Time has no divisions to mark
its passage, there is never a thunder-
storm or blare of trumpets to announce the beginning of a new month
or year. Even when a new century

begins it is only we mortals who ring
bells and fire off pistols.
      THOMAS MANN,
      The Magic Mountain

19818. Time cools, time clarifies; no
mood can be maintained quite unaltered through the course of hours.
      THOMAS MANN,
      The Magic Mountain

19819. Time is a sort of river of passing events, and strong is its current;
no sooner is a thing brought to sight
than it is swept by and another takes
its place, and this too will be swept
away.   MARCUS AURELIUS,
      Meditations

19820.
Stand still, you ever moving spheres
  of heaven,
That time may cease, and midnight
  never come.
      CHRISTOPHER MARLOWE,
      Faustus

19821. Time is a great legalizer, even
in the field of morals.
      H. L. MENCKEN,
      A Book of Prefaces

19822.
Oh glory, that we wrestle
  So valiantly with Time!
      R. M. MILNES, *The Eld*

19823.
      Whatever thing
The scythe of Time mows down.
      MILTON, *Paradise Lost*

19824. Go, sir, gallop, and don't forget that the world was made in six
days. You can ask me for anything
you like, except time.   NAPOLEON

19825. Time hath a taming hand.
      CARDINAL NEWMAN, *Persecution*

19826. Be ruled by time, the wisest
counsellor of all.   PLUTARCH,
      Lives

19827. Pythagoras, when he was asked what time was, answered that it was the soul of this world.
PLUTARCH

19828. The time which we have at our disposal every day is elastic; the passions that we feel expand it, those that we inspire contract it; and habit fills up what remains.
MARCEL PROUST,
Within a Budding Grove

19829. Time and tide wait for no man.
Proverb

19830. Every scrap of a wise man's time is worth saving.
Proverb

19831. Take time by the forelock.
Proverb

19832. He that has most time has none to lose.
Proverb

19833. As good have no time, as make no good use of it.
Proverb

19834. To repair the irreparable ravages of time.
RACINE, *Athalie*

19835.
Time will rust the sharpest sword,
Time will consume the strongest cord;
That which moulders hemp and steel,
Mortal arm and nerve must feel.
SCOTT, *Harold the Dauntless*

19836.
Ah! the clock is always slow;
It is later than you think.
ROBERT WILLIAM SERVICE,
It Is Later Than You Think

19837. The inaudible and noiseless foot of Time.
SHAKESPEARE,
All's Well that Ends Well

19838. Time travels in divers paces with divers persons. I'll tell you who Time ambles withal, who Time trots withal, who Time gallops withal, and who he stands still withal.
SHAKESPEARE, *As You Like It*

19839.
And then he drew a dial from his poke,
And looking on it with lack-lustre eye,
Says, very wisely, "It is ten o'clock:
Thus we may see," quoth he, "how the world wags."
SHAKESPEARE, *As You Like It*

19840. There's a time for all things.
SHAKESPEARE,
The Comedy of Errors

19841. But I will fit it with some better time.   SHAKESPEARE, *King John*

19842.
Come what come may,
Time and the hour runs through the roughest day.
SHAKESPEARE, *Macbeth*

19843.
What seest thou else
In the dark backward and abysm of time?   SHAKESPEARE,
The Tempest

19844.
Time hath, my lord, a wallet at his back,
Wherein he puts alms for oblivion.
SHAKESPEARE, *Troilus and Cressida*

19845. Thus the whirligig of time brings in his revenges.
SHAKESPEARE, *Twelfth Night*

19846.
Like as the waves make towards the pebbled shore,
So do our minutes hasten to their end.
SHAKESPEARE, *Sonnet LX*

19847. Time has fallen asleep in the afternoon sunshine.
ALEXANDER SMITH, *Dreamthorp*

19848.
Time goes by turns, and chances
　change by course,
From foul to fair, from better hap to
　worse.
　　　　ROBERT SOUTHWELL,
　　　　　　　Times Go by Turns

19849. The day before yesterday always has been a glamor day. The
present is sordid and prosaic. Time
colors history as it does a meerschaum
pipe.　　　VINCENT STARRETT,
　　　　　　　Buried Caesars

19850.
　If time be heavy on your hands,
Are there no beggars at your gate,
　Nor any poor about your lands?
Oh! teach the orphan-boy to read,
　Or teach the orphan-girl to sew.
TENNYSON, *Lady Clara Vere de Vere*

19851.
I know that age to age succeeds,
Blowing a noise of tongues and deeds,
A dust of systems and of creeds.
　　　　TENNYSON, *The Two Voices*

19852. As if you could kill time without injuring eternity.
　　　　THOREAU, *Walden*

19853. Time is but the stream I go
a-fishing in.　　THOREAU, *Walden*

19854. Time is infinite movement
without one moment of rest.
　　　　TOLSTOY, *War and Peace*

19855. It is later than you think.
　Traditional: Sun-dial inscription

19856. Wait, thou child of hope, for
Time shall teach thee all things.
　　　　MARTIN F. TUPPER,
　　　　　Of Good in Things Evil

See also: 33, 794, 1293, 1496, 1564,
1620, 2564, 2700, 3587, 3686, 4002,
4396, 5792, 7467, 8619, 9083, 15442,
15863, 20903, 22026.

TIMIDITY

Related Subjects: Awkwardness,
Cowardice, Embarrassment, Fear,
Humility, Inferiority, Meekness,
Submission.

19861. I went darkling, and whistling
to keep myself from being afraid.
　　　　DRYDEN, *Amphitryon*

19862.
Damn with faint praise, assent with
　civil leer,
And without sneering teach the rest
　to sneer;
Willing to wound, and yet afraid to
　strike,
Just hint a fault, and hesitate dislike.
　　　　ALEXANDER POPE,
　　　　　Epistle to Dr. Arbuthnot

19863. To the timid and hesitating
everything is impossible because it
seems so.　　　SCOTT, *Rob Roy*

19864. Who timidly requests invites
refusal.　　SENECA, *Hippolytus*

19865. But I am pigeon-liver'd, and
lack gall.　　SHAKESPEARE, *Hamlet*

19866. Thou wilt be as valiant as the
wrathful dove or most magnanimous
mouse.　　SHAKESPEARE, *Henry IV*

19867. The attempt and not the deed
Confounds us.　　SHAKESPEARE,
　　　　　　　　Macbeth

19868.
　O, these flaws and starts,
Impostors to true fear, would well
　become
A woman's story at a winter's fire,
Authorized by her grandam.
　　　　SHAKESPEARE, *Macbeth*

19869. Great empires are not maintained by timidity.　　TACITUS,
　　　　　　　　History

See also: 1194, 4357.

TITLES

Related Subjects: Name, Nobility, Rank.

19871. An earl by right, by courtesy a man. ALFRED AUSTIN, *The Season*

19872.
A successive title, long and dark,
Drawn from the mouldy rolls of
Noah's Ark. DRYDEN,
Absalom & Achitophel

19873. Such is their (the monarchs of Europe) passion for a long list of these splendid trifles, that I have known a German Prince with more titles than subjects, and a Spanish nobleman with more names than shirts. GOLDSMITH,
Citizen of the World

19874.
Stuck o'er with titles, and hung round with strings,
That thou mayst be by kings, or whores of kings. POPE,
Essay on Man

19875.
Knighthoods and honours, borne
As I wear mine, are titles but of scorn. SHAKESPEARE,
Cymbeline

19876.
What think you of a duchess? have you limbs
To bear that load of title?
SHAKESPEARE, *Henry VIII*

19877.
Now does he feel his title
Hang loose about him, like a giant's robe
Upon a dwarfish thief.
SHAKESPEARE, *Macbeth*

19878.
Nor never title yet so mean could prove,

But there was eke a mind which did that title love.
W. SHENSTONE,
The Schoolmistress

19879. I weigh the man, not his title;
'tis not the king's stamp can make the metal better or heavier.
WILLIAM WYCHERLEY,
The Plain-Dealer

TOAST

Related Subjects: Drinking, Feast.

19881.
Drink ye to her that each loves best!
And if you nurse a flame
That's told but to her mutual breast,
We will not ask her name.
THOMAS CAMPBELL, *Drink Ye to Her*

19882. I drink to the general joy of the whole table. SHAKESPEARE,
Macbeth

TOBACCO

19891.
O, finer far
Than fame, or riches, are
The graceful smoke-wreaths of this free cigar! GEORGE ARNOLD,
Beer

19892. A good cigar is as great a comfort to a man as a good cry to a woman. BULWER-LYTTON,
Darnley

19893. The man who smokes, thinks like a sage and acts like a Samaritan.
BULWER-LYTTON,
Night and Morning

19894. Tobacco, divine, rare, superexcellent tobacco, which goes far beyond all the panaceas, potable gold and philosopher's stones, a sovereign remedy to all diseases.
ROBERT BURTON,
Anatomy of Melancholy

19895.
Sublime tobacco! which from east to
     west
Cheers the tar's labour or the Turk-
     man's rest.   BYRON,
                 The Island

19896.
Pernicious weed! whose scent the fair
     annoys,
Unfriendly to society's chief joys;
Thy worst effect is banishing for
     hours
The sex whose presence civilizes
     ours.   COWPER, *Conversation*

19897. The wretcheder one is, the
more one smokes; and the more one
smokes, the wretcheder one gets—a
vicious circle.
     GEORGE DU MAURIER,
                 Peter Ibbetson

19898.
Tobacco is a dirty weed. I like it.
It satisfies no normal need. I like it.
It makes you thin, it makes you lean,
It takes the hair right off your bean.
It's the worst darn stuff I've ever
     seen. I like it.   G. L. HEMMINGER

19899. A lone man's companion, a
bachelor's friend, a hungry man's
food, a sad man's cordial, a wakeful
man's sleep, and a chilly man's fire
. . . there's no herb like unto it under
the canopy of heaven.
     CHARLES KINGSLEY, *Westward Ho*

19900. And a woman is only a
woman, but a good cigar is a smoke.
     KIPLING, *The Betrothed*

19901.
For thy sake, tobacco, I
Would do anything but die.
     CHARLES LAMB,
         A Farewell to Tobacco

19902. What this country needs is a
good five-cent cigar.
     THOMAS R. MARSHALL

19903. Attorney-General Seymour of
Virginia snorted at the establishment
of William and Mary College, which
was founded not only to inculcate
learning but to save souls. "Souls?"
he cried. "Damn your souls. Make
tobacco."   WERTENBAKER,
     Planters of Colonial Virginia

19904. Perfection is a thing so bother-
some that I often regret having cured
myself of using tobacco.
            EMILE ZOLA

TODAY

**Related Subjects: The Age, Mod-
ern, The Present.**

19911. Our age is superior to the middle ages only in so far as it has pro-
gressed beyond sham and formalism,
lofty pomp and hollow and dull dignity, and asks now to be shown things
just as they are.
         JOHN PETER ALTGELD

19912.
"The rule is, jam to-morrow, and
jam yesterday—but never jam *to-
day.*"
"It *must* come sometimes to 'jam
to-day,'" Alice objected.
"No, it can't," said the Queen. "It's
jam every *other* day: to-day isn't any
other day, you know."
     LEWIS CARROLL,
       Through the Looking-Glass

19913. Today is yesterday's pupil.
            FRANKLIN

See also: 929.

TOLERANCE

**Related Subjects: Bigotry, Fana-
ticism, Leniency, Magnanimity,
Opinion, Persecution, Reform.**

19921. For ye suffer fools gladly, seeing ye yourselves are wise.
     Bible: 2 Corinthians, xi, 19

19922.
Shall I ask the brave soldier, who fights by my side
In the cause of mankind, if our creeds agree?
Shall I give up the friend I have valued and tried,
If he kneel not before the same altar with me.   THOMAS MOORE,
Come, Send Round the Wine

19923. Those who preach race hatred and intolerance among us in such a world at war are traitors to our lonely democracy. They menace our moral unity. They divide our precious strength.   BISHOP SHEIL

See also: 698, 8605, 10667, 15154.

TOMB, see Grave, Monument

TOMORROW

Related Subjects: Future, Procrastination.

19931. Boast not thyself of to-morrow; for thou knowest not what a day may bring forth.
Bible: Proverbs, xxvii, 1

19932. Take therefore no thought for the morrow; for the morrow shall take thought for the things of itself. Sufficient unto the day is the evil thereof.   *Bible: Matthew, vi, 34*

19933. To-morrow to fresh woods, and pastures new.   MILTON, *Lycidas*

19934. My fatherland is not yesterday. It is tomorrow. And already the angelus of dawn has sounded.
ROMAIN ROLLAND, *I Will Not Rest*

19935.
To-morrow, and to-morrow, and to-morrow,
Creeps in this petty pace from day to day,

To the last syllable of recorded time;
And all our yesterdays have lighted fools
The way to dusty death.
     SHAKESPEARE, *Macbeth*

19936.
    If any
Count on two days, or any more, to come,
He is a fool; for a man has no morrow,
Till with good luck he has got through to-day.   SOPHOCLES,
       Trachiniae

19937. We know nothing of to-morrow; our business is to be good and happy to-day.   SYDNEY SMITH,
     Lady Holland's Memoir

See also: 929, 1236, 2593, 5053, 17218, 21861.

TONGUE

Related Subjects: Eloquence, Lip, Mouth, Speech, Voice.

19941. Keep thy tongue from evil, and thy lips from speaking guile.
     Bible: Psalms, xxxiv, 13

19942. The tongue can no man tame; it is an unruly evil.
     Bible: James, iii, 8

19943. The magic of the tongue is the most dangerous of all spells.
BULWER-LYTTON, *Eugene Aram*

19944. He who has little silver in his pouch must have the more silk on his tongue.   BULWER-LYTTON,
     The Last of the Barons

19945. No member needs so great a number of muscles as the tongue; this exceeds all the rest in the number of its movements.   DA VINCI

19946. He rolls it under his tongue as a sweet morsel.
MATTHEW HENRY, *Commentaries*

19947. The windy satisfaction of the tongue.   HOMER, *Odyssey*

19948. A sharp tongue is the only edge tool that grows keener with constant use.
WASHINGTON IRVING,
The Sketch-Book

19949. A good tongue has seldom need to beg attention.   *Proverb*

19950. The tongue of idle persons is never idle.   *Proverb*

19951. Confine your tongue, lest it confine you.   *Proverb*

19952. Birds are entangled by their feet, and men by their tongues.
Proverb

19953. Be aware of a fine tongue; 'twill sting mortally.   *Proverb*

19954. A bridle for the tongue is a necessary piece of furniture.
Proverb

19955. I would my horse had the speed of your tongue, and so good a continuer.   SHAKESPEARE,
Much Ado About Nothing

19956. A fluent tongue is the only thing a mother don't like her daughter to resemble her in.   SHERIDAN,
St. Patrick's Day

See also: 2437, 3941, 4416, 4462, 5101, 6422, 6427, 12175, 19968.

TOOTH

Related Subject: Mouth.

19961.
An aching tooth is better out than in,
To Lose a rotten member is a gain.
RICHARD BAXTER, *Hypocrisy*

19962. I am escaped with the skin of my teeth.   *Bible: Job, xix, 20*

19963. There shall be weeping and gnashing of teeth.
Bible: Matthew, xxii, 13

19964. Every tooth in a man's head is more valuable than a diamond.
CERVANTES, *Don Quixote*

19965.
The best of friends fall out, and so
His teeth had done some years ago.
THOMAS HOOD, *A True Story*

19966. In spite of my teeth.
THOMAS MIDDLETON,
A Trick to Catch the Old One

19967. Who hath aching teeth hath ill tenants.   *Proverb*

19968. The tongue is ever turning to the aching tooth.   *Proverb*

19969. By Isis, I will give thee bloody teeth.   SHAKESPEARE,
Antony and Cleopatra

19970. What! sigh for the toothache?
SHAKESPEARE,
Much Ado About Nothing

19971.
Being troubled with a raging tooth,
I could not sleep.
SHAKESPEARE, *Othello*

19972. With tooth and nail.
Traditional

See also: 226, 349, 6524.

TOWN

Related Subjects: Cities, Community, Village.

19981. God made the country, and man made the town.   COWPER,
The Task

19982. A small country town is not the place in which one would choose

to quarrel with a wife; every human being in such places is a spy.
SAMUEL JOHNSON, *Letters*

19983. Country in town.
MARTIAL, *Epigrams*

19984. This poor little one-horse town.   MARK TWAIN,
The Undertaker's Story

See also: 1512, 4262, 4324, 12856.

TRADE, see Commerce

TRADITION

19991. No one thinks of defending tradition in days that are making tradition, when people feel the past as a force of the present, an auxiliary, a ministrant, a helpmate. One not only defends tradition, one resorts to tradition to fill the void in oneself, when life runs low. And then one grasps only the forms of tradition. Only the husks of tradition remain in one's hands.   VAN WYCK BROOKS,
New England: Indian Summer

19992. It is not only what we have inherited from our fathers that exists again in us, but all sorts of old dead ideas and all kinds of old dead beliefs and things of that kind. They are not actually alive in us; but there they are dormant, all the same, and we can never be rid of them. Whenever I take up a newspaper and read it, I fancy I see ghosts creeping between the lines. There must be ghosts all over the world.   IBSEN, *Ghosts*

19993. Every tradition grows ever more venerable—the more remote is its origin, the more confused that origin is. The reverence due to it increases from generation to generation. The tradition finally becomes holy and inspires awe.
NIETZSCHE, *Human, All Too Human*

19994. The surface of the earth is soft and impressible by the feet of men; and so with the paths which the mind travels. How worn and dusty, then, how deep the ruts of tradition and conformity!   THOREAU, *Walden*

See also: 22063.

TRAGEDY

Related Subjects: Accident, Chance, Death, Drama, Fate, Misfortune.

20001. Nothing seems so tragic to one who is old as the death of one who is young, and this alone proves that life is a good thing.   ZOË AKINS,
The Portrait of Tiero

20002. The tragedy of a man who has found himself out.
J. M. BARRIE,
What Every Woman Knows

20003. That there should one man die ignorant who had capacity for knowledge, this I call a tragedy.
CARLYLE, *Sartor Resartus*

20004. There is nothing more tragic in life than the utter impossibility of changing what you have done.
GALSWORTHY, *Justice*

20005. Commonplace people dislike tragedy, because they dare not suffer and cannot exult. The truth and rapture of man are holy things, not lightly to be scorned. A carelessness of life and beauty marks the glutton, the idler, and the fool in their deadly path across history.
JOHN MASEFIELD,
The Tragedy of Nan

20006. Romantic plays with happy endings are almost of necessity inferior in artistic value to true tragedies. Not, one would hope, simply because they end happily; happiness in itself is certainly not less beautiful than grief; but because a tragedy in its great moments can generally afford to be sincere, while romantic plays live in an atmosphere of ingenuity and make-believe.

GILBERT MURRAY,
Preface to Iphigenia in Tauris

20007.
To wake the soul by tender strokes of art,
To raise the genius, and to mend the heart;
To make mankind, in conscious virtue bold,
Live o'er each scene, and be what they behold:
For this the Tragic Muse first trod the stage.   POPE,
Prologue to Addison's Cato

20008. A tragical plot may produce a comical conclusion.   *Proverb*

20009. In this world there are only two tragedies. One is not getting what one wants, and the other is getting it.   OSCAR WILDE,
Lady Windermere's Fan

See also: 5535.

TRANQUILLITY, see Quiet

TRAVEL

Related Subjects: **Distance, River, Road, Sea, Ship, Walking, Wanderlust.**

20011. See one promontory (said Socrates of old), one mountain, one sea, one river, and see all.
ROBERT BURTON,
Anatomy of Melancholy

20012. Journey over all the universe in a map, without the expense and fatigue of travelling, without suffering the inconveniences of heat, cold, hunger, and thirst.   CERVANTES,
Don Quixote

20013.
How much a dunce that has been sent to roam
Excels a dunce that has been kept at home!   COWPER,
The Progress of Error

20014. Foreign travel ought to soften prejudices, religious or political, and liberalize a man's mind; but how many there are who seem to have travelled for the purpose of getting up their rancour against all that is opposed to their notions.
CHARLES B. FAIRBANKS,
My Unknown Chum

20015. Oh! it is great to shake off the trammels of the world and of public opinion—to lose our importunate, tormenting, everlasting personal identity and become the creature of the moment, clear of all ties . . . to be known by no other title than *the Gentleman in the parlour!*
HAZLITT, *On Going a Journey*

20016. The soul of a journey is liberty to think, feel, do just as one pleases.   HAZLITT,
On Going a Journey

20017. They change their climate, not their disposition, who run beyond the sea.   HORACE, *Epistles*

20018. The traveler's-eye view of men and women is not satisfying. A man might spend his life in trains and restaurants and know nothing of humanity at the end. To know, one must be an actor as well as a spectator.
ALDOUS HUXLEY, *Essays*

20019. The use of travelling is to regulate imagination by reality, and instead of thinking how things may be, to see them as they are.

SAMUEL JOHNSON

20020. Whenever I prepare for a journey I prepare as though for death. Should I never return, all is in order. This is what life has taught me.

KATHERINE MANSFIELD

20021.
My heart is warm with the friends I make,
    And better friends I'll not be knowing;
Yet there isn't a train I wouldn't take
    No matter where It's going.

EDNA ST. VINCENT MILLAY, *Travel*

20022. A man travels the world over in search of what he needs and returns home to find it.

GEORGE MOORE, *The Brook Kerith*

20023. Discreet stops make speedy journeys.   *Proverb*

20024. Travel makes a wise man better, but a fool worse.   *Proverb*

20025. The fool wanders; the wise man travels.   *Proverb*

20026. A travelled man hath leave to lie.   *Proverb*

20027. When you are traveling abroad look not back at your own border.   PYTHAGORAS

20028. A man should know something of his own country, too, before he goes abroad.

STERNE, *Tristram Shandy*

20029. I pity the man who can travel from Dan to Beersheba and cry, "Tis all barren!"   STERNE,
A Sentimental Journey

20030. To travel hopefully is a better thing than to arrive.

STEVENSON, *Virginibus Puerisque*

20031. I always like to begin a journey on Sundays, because I shall have the prayers of the Church to preserve all that travel by land or by water.

SWIFT, *Polite Conversation*

20032. The swiftest traveller is he that goes afoot.   THOREAU, *Walden*

See also: 28, 2335, 3682, 5486, 10373, 12170, 14959.

TREACHERY

Related Subjects: Informer, Spying, Treason.

20041. No wise man ever thought that a traitor should be trusted.

CICERO, *Orationes in Verrem*

20042. Treachery, though at first very cautious, in the end betrays itself.   LIVY, *History*

20043.
Hast thou betrayed my credulous innocence
With vizor'd falsehood and base forgery?   MILTON, *Comus*

20044. Does not he to whom you betray another, to whom you were as welcome as to himself, know that you will at another time do as much for him?   MONTAIGNE, *Essays*

20045.
To say the truth, so Judas kiss'd his master,
And cried "all hail" whereas he meant all harm.

SHAKESPEARE, *Henry VI*

20046. *Et tu Brute!* Then fall, Caesar!

SHAKESPEARE, *Julius Caesar*

20047.

So Judas did to Christ: but he, in
twelve,
Found truth in all but one; I, in
twelve thousand, none.
SHAKESPEARE, *Richard II*

20048. Tellest thou me of "ifs"?
Thou art a traitor: Off with his head!
SHAKESPEARE, *Richard III*

See also: 5999.

TREASON

Related Subjects: Conspiracy, Heresy, Obedience, Treachery.

20051.

Is there not some chosen curse,
Some hidden thunder in the stores of
heaven,
Red with uncommon wrath, to blast
the man
Who owes his greatness to his country's ruin? ADDISON, *Cato*

20052.

This principle is old, but true as fate,
Kings may love treason, but the traitor hate. THOMAS DEKKER,
The Honest Whore

20053. Rebellion must be managed
with many swords; treason to his
prince's person may be with one
knife. THOMAS FULLER,
Holy & Profane State

20054.

Treason doth never prosper; what's
the reason?
Why, if it prosper, none dare call it
treason.
SIR JOHN HARRINGTON, *Epigrams*

20055.

The man who pauses on the paths of
treason,
Halts on a quicksand, the first step
engulfs him.
AARON HILL, *Henry V*

20056.

Tarquin and Caesar each had his Brutus, Charles the First his Cromwell,
and George the Third ["Treason!"
cried the Speaker]—*may profit by
their example!* If *this* be treason,
make the most of it!
PATRICK HENRY

20057.

Oh, for a tongue to curse the slave
Whose treason, like a deadly blight,
Comes o'er the councils of the brave,
And blasts them in their hour of
might!
THOMAS MOORE, *Lalla Rookh*

20058.

Though those that are betray'd
Do feel the treason sharply, yet the
traitor
Stands in worse case of woe.
SHAKESPEARE, *Cymbeline*

20059.

Treason is but trusted like the fox
Who, ne'er so tame, so cherish'd and
locked up,
Will have a wild trick of his ancestors. SHAKESPEARE, *Henry IV*

20060.

Some guard these traitors to the block
of death;
Treason's true bed and yielder up of
breath. SHAKESPEARE, *Henry IV*

20061.

Treason and murder ever kept together,
As two yoke-devils sworn to either's
purpose,
Working so grossly in a natural
cause,
That admiration did not hoop at them.
SHAKESPEARE, *Henry V*

20062.

Smooth runs the water where the
brook is deep;
And in his simple show he harbours
treason. SHAKESPEARE, *Henry VI*

20063.

Know, my name is lost;
By treason's tooth bare-gnawn and
canker-bit.

SHAKESPEARE, *King Lear*

See also: 1666, 2687, 11444, 20154.

TREE

Related Subjects: **Birds, Country,
Forest, Fruit, Garden, Nature, Oak,
Palm, Park, Pine, Willow.**

20071. He shall be as a tree planted
by the waters, and that spreadeth out
her roots by the river.

Bible: Jeremiah, xvii, 8

20072. The axe is laid unto the root
of the trees.   *Bible: Luke, iii, 9*

20073. He plants trees to benefit another generation.

CAECILIUS STATIUS, *Synephebi*

20074. I like trees because they seem
more resigned to the way they have
to live than other things do.

WILLA CATHER, *O Pioneers*

20075.
I think that I shall never see
A poem lovely as a tree.

JOYCE KILMER, *Trees*

20076.
Poems are made by fools like me,
But only God can make a tree.

JOYCE KILMER, *Trees*

20077. If a tree dies, plant another
in its place.   LINNAEUS

20078.
Woodman, spare that tree!
   Touch not a single bough!
In youth it sheltered me,
   And I'll protect it now.

MORRIS, *Woodman, Spare that Tree*

20079. He that plants trees loves
others besides himself.   *Proverb*

20080. The tree is no sooner down,
but every one runs for his hatchet.

Proverb

20081. A tree is known by its fruit.

Proverb

20082. Jock, when ye hae naething
else to do, ye may be aye sticking in
a tree; it will be growing, Jock, when
ye're sleeping.   SCOTT,
The Heart of Midlothian

20083. Except during the nine
months before he draws his first
breath, no man manages his affairs
as well as a tree does.

BERNARD SHAW,
Maxims for Revolutionists

20084. A man does not plant a tree
for himself, he plants it for posterity.

ALEXANDER SMITH, *Dreamthorp*

20085. I shall be like that tree,—I
shall die at the top.   SWIFT

20086.
He that planteth a tree is a servant
   of God,
He provideth a kindness for many
   generations,
And faces that he hath not seen shall
   bless him.

HENRY VAN DYKE,
The Friendly Trees

20087. A brotherhood of venerable
trees.   WORDSWORTH, *Sonnet*

See also: 826, 2104, 4252.

TRIALS

Related Subjects: **Adversity,
Courts of Law, Endurance, Judge,
Judgment, Jury, Justice, Law,
Lawyers, Martyr, Proof, Trouble.**

20091. Reckon any matter of trial to
thee among thy gains.

THOMAS ADAMS

20092. It is trial that proves one thing weak and another strong. A house built on the sand is in fair weather just as good as if builded on a rock. A cobweb is as good as the mightiest cable when there is no strain upon it.   H. W. BEECHER

20093. We are always in the forge, or on the anvil; by trials God is shaping us for higher things.
       H. W. BEECHER

20094. Trials are medicines which our gracious and wise physician prescribes, because we need them; and he proportions the frequency and weight of them to what the case requires. Let us trust in his skill, and thank him for his prescription.
       JOHN NEWTON

20095. That trial is not fair where affection is the judge.   *Proverb*

20096. He confesseth himself guilty, who refuseth to come to trial.
       Proverb

20097. Great trials seem to be a necessary preparation for great duties.
       EDWARD THOMSON

See also: 330, 2632, 8207.

TRICKERY

Related Subjects: Concealment, Cunning, Deceit, Flattery, Knave, Lies, Subtlety.

20101. It takes about a hundred years to tire this country of trickery—and we're fifty years overdue right now.   MAXWELL ANDERSON,
       Both Your Houses

20102.
She had a thousand jadish tricks,
Worse than a mule that flings and kicks. SAMUEL BUTLER, *Hudibras*

20103. In trickery, evasion, procrastination, spoliation, botheration, under false pretenses of all sorts, there are influences that can never come to good.   DICKENS, *Bleak House*

20104. Remember that all tricks are either knavish or childish.
       SAMUEL JOHNSON, *Boswell: Life*

20105. A trick to catch the old one.
       THOMAS MIDDLETON, *Title of Play*

20106. One trick needs a great many more to make it good.   *Proverb*

20107. I know a trick worth two of that.   SHAKESPEARE, *Henry IV*

20108.
       He coasts
And hedges his own way. But in this point
All his tricks founder.
       SHAKESPEARE, *Henry VIII*

20109. These are unsightly tricks.
       SHAKESPEARE, *King Lear*

20110.
       I have within my mind
A thousand raw tricks of these bragging Jacks,
Which I will practise.
       SHAKESPEARE,
       The Merchant of Venice

20111. If I be served such another trick, I'll have my brains ta'en out and buttered, and give them to a dog for a new-year's gift.
       SHAKESPEARE,
       The Merry Wives of Windsor

20112. He hath as many tricks as a dancing bear.
       SWIFT, *Polite Conversation*

See also: 1131, 14940, 1656, 3271, 5637.

TRIFLES

Related Subject: Little Things.

20121. This is not time for me to mind niceties, and spelling of letters. I have other fish to fry.
CERVANTES, *Don Quixote*

20122. Trifles make the sum of life.
DICKENS, *David Copperfield*

20123. Pleasant it is to trifle now and then.   HORACE

20124. At ev'ry trifle scorn to take offence.   POPE, *Essay on Criticism*

20125. Fall not out with a friend for a trifle.   *Proverb*

20126. For want of a nail the shoe is lost, for want of a shoe the horse is lost, for want of a horse the rider is lost.   *Proverb*

20127. Dispense with trifles.
SHAKESPEARE,
The Merry Wives of Windsor

20128. A snapper-up of unconsidered trifles.   SHAKESPEARE,
The Winter's Tale

20129. Trifles make up the happiness or the misery of mortal life. The majority of men slip into their graves without having encountered on their way thither any signal catastrophe or exaltation of fortune or feeling.
ALEXANDER SMITH, *Dreamthorp*

See also: 14989.

TROUBLE

Related Subjects: Adversity, Difficulty, Mischief, Trials.

20131. Man is born unto trouble, as the sparks fly upward.
Bible: Job, v, 7

20132. Some people are so fond of ill-luck that they run half-way to meet it.   DOUGLAS JERROLD,
Meeting Troubles Half-Way

20133. A trouble is a trouble, and the general idea, in the country, is to treat it as such, rather than to snatch the knotted cords from the hand of God and deal out murderous blows.
WILLIAM MCFEE,
Casuals of the Sea

20134.
there is always
a comforting thought
in time of trouble when
it is not our trouble
DON MARQUIS,
comforting thoughts

20135. If you should hear of any poor souls in trouble, let me know, that I may come to their assistance.
MICHELANGELO

20136. He that seeks trouble it were a pity he should miss it.   *Proverb*

20137. He that will have no trouble in this world must not be born in it.
Proverb

See also: 8131, 12407, 16103, 16526.

TROY

Related Subject: Greece.

20141. Troy owes to Homer what whist owes to Hoyle.
BYRON, *Don Juan*

20142. The Trojans became wise too late.   *Latin Proverb*

20143. Troy was not taken in a day.
Proverb

20144.
Had doting Priam check'd his son's desire,

Troy had been bright with fame and not with fire.   SHAKESPEARE, *The Rape of Lucrece*

20145. We were Trojans; Troy was.   VERGIL, *Aeneid*

20146. I am on the side of the Trojans. They fought for a woman.   OSCAR WILDE, *The Picture of Dorian Gray*

See also: 325, 6165.

TRUST AND DISTRUST

Related Subjects: Belief, Confidence, Credit, Credulity, Duty, Faith, Honesty, Obligation, Responsibility, Sincerity, Suspicion.

20151. Put your trust in God, my boys, and keep your powder dry.   COL. BLACKER, *Oliver's Advice*

20152. The man who trusts men will make fewer mistakes than he who distrusts them.   COUNT CAVOUR

20153. He was straight; you could trust him.   PETRONIUS, *Satyricon*

20154. In trust is treason.   *Proverb*

20155. It is an equal failing to trust everybody, and to trust nobody.   *Proverb*

20156. Trust thyself only, and another shall not betray thee.   *Proverb*

20157. For the trust reposed in me I will return the courage and the devotion that befit the time. I can do no less.   FRANKLIN D. ROOSEVELT, *First Inaugural Address*

Distrust

20158. Never trust a friend who deserts you at a pinch.   AESOP, *The Two Fellows and the Bear*

20159. A usurper always distrusts the whole world.   ALFIERI, *Polinice*

20160. What loneliness is more lonely than distrust?   GEORGE ELIOT, *Middlemarch*

20161.
When desperate ills demand a speedy cure,
Distrust is cowardice, and prudence folly.   SAMUEL JOHNSON, *Irene*

20162. A certain amount of distrust is wholesome, but not so much of others as of ourselves; neither vanity nor conceit can exist in the same atmosphere with it.   MME. NECKER

20163. He who trusteth not, is not deceived.   *Proverb*

20164. Distrust is the mother of safety, but must keep out of sight.   *Proverb*

20165. One can positively never be deceived if one mistrusts everything in the world, even one's own scepticism.   ARTHUR SCHNITZLER, *The Road to the Open*

20166.
Immortal gods, I crave no pelf;
I pray for no man but myself:
Grant I may never prove so fond,
To trust man on his oath or bond.   SHAKESPEARE, *Timon of Athens*

20167.
Three things a wise man will not trust,
The wind, the sunshine of an April day,
And woman's plighted faith.   SOUTHEY, *Madoc in Aztlan*

See also: 1592, 1653, 1864, 3087, 4948, 6870, 9035, 13226, 13603, 15972.

TRUTH

Related Subjects: Candor, Facts, Honesty, Lies, Realism.

20171. Pure truth cannot be assimilated by the crowd; it must be communicated by contagion.   AMIEL

20172. Great is truth and mighty above all things.
Apocrypha: 1 Esdras

20173. No pleasure is comparable to the standing upon the vantage-ground of truth.   BACON, *Of Truth*

20174. The contrary is probably just as true.   BEETHOVEN

20175. And ye shall know the truth, and the truth shall make you free.
Bible: John, viii, 32

20176.
A truth that's told with bad intent
Beats all the lies you can invent.
BLAKE, *Proverbs*

20177.
So absolutely good is truth, truth never hurts
The teller.
BROWNING, *Fifine at the Fair*

20178.
The truth was felt by instinct here,
—Process which saves a world of trouble and time.
BROWNING,
The Ring and the Book

20179. Fiction lags after truth, invention is unfruitful, and imagination cold and barren.   BURKE,
Speech on Conciliation with America

20180.
For truth is precious and divine,—
Too rich a pearl for carnal swine.
SAMUEL BUTLER, *Hudibras*

20181.
'Tis strange, but true; for truth is always strange,—
Stranger than fiction.
BYRON, *Don Juan*

20182. Nothing that was worthy in the past departs; no truth or goodness realized by man ever dies, or can die; but is all still here, and, recognized or not, lives and works through endless changes.
CARLYLE, *Sir Walter Scott*

20183. I must speak the truth, and nothing but the truth.
CERVANTES, *Don Quixote*

20184.
"Old things need not be therefore true,"
O brother men, nor yet the new.
A. H. CLOUGH

20185. Veracity does not consist in *saying,* but in the intention of *communicating* truth.   COLERIDGE,
Biographia Literaria

20186. It makes all the difference in the world whether one puts truth in the first place or in the second.
COLERIDGE

20187. Truth does not depart from human nature. If what is regarded as truth departs from human nature it may not be regarded as truth.
CONFUCIUS, *Analects*

20188.
For truth has such a face and such a mien,
As to be lov'd needs only to be seen.
DRYDEN,
The Hind & the Panther

20189. Great is truth. Fire cannot burn, nor water drown it.
DUMAS, *The Count of Monte Cristo*

20190. The truth does not vary be-

cause men forget or ignore or traduce
it.   IRWIN EDMAN, *I Believe*

20191. The highest compact we can
make with our fellow is,—"Let there
be truth between us two forever-
more."   EMERSON, *Conduct of Life*

20192. Truth and sincerity have a
certain distinguishing native lustre
about them which cannot be perfectly
counterfeited; they are like fire and
flame, that cannot be painted.
                        FRANKLIN

20193. Truth is the nursing mother
of genius. No man can be absolutely
true to himself, eschewing cant, compromise, servile imitation, and complaisance, without becoming original
for there is in every creature a fountain of life which, if not choked back
by stones and other dead rubbish,
will create a fresh atmosphere, and
bring to life fresh beauty.
                    MARGARET FULLER

20194. Dear, dear! Well, I always
say—when you once begin to tell the
truth, it don't do to stop sudden.
                GALSWORTHY, *The Show*

20195.
Truth from his lips prevail'd with
     double sway,
And fools, who came to scoff, re-
     main'd to pray.   GOLDSMITH,
               The Deserted Village

20196.
Dare to be true: nothing can need a
     lie;
A fault which needs it most, grows
     two thereby.
GEORGE HERBERT, *The Church Porch*

20197. Such truth as opposeth no
man's profit nor pleasure is to all men
welcome.
        THOMAS HOBBES, *Leviathan*

20198.
Urge him with truth to frame his fair
     replies;
And sure he will: for Wisdom never
     lies.   HOMER, *Odyssey*

20199.
Mine eyes have seen the glory of the
     coming of the Lord;
He is trampling out the vintage where
     the grapes of wrath are stored;
He hath loosed the fateful lightning
     of
     His terrible, swift sword;
     His truth is marching on.
          JULIA WARD HOWE,
          Battle Hymn of the Republic
          (Source of title of novel
               by John Steinbeck)

20200. It is the customary fate of
new truths to begin as heresies and to
end as superstitions.
          THOMAS H. HUXLEY,
          The Coming of Age of
          "The Origin of Species"

20201. Irrationally held truths may
be more harmful than reasoned errors.   THOMAS H. HUXLEY,
          The Coming of Age of
          "The Origin of Species"

20202. The dignity of truth is lost
with much protesting.
     BEN JONSON, *Catiline's Conspiracy*

20203.
Truth is the trial of itself
     And needs no other touch,
And purer than the purest gold,
     Refine it ne'er so much.
          BEN JONSON, *On Truth*

20204. The true way goes over a rope
which is not stretched at any great
height but just above the ground. It
seems more designed to make people
stumble than to be walked upon.
          FRANZ KAFKA,
          The Great Wall of China

20205. A forced truth, like a forced peace, has no enduring value.

SIR ARTHUR KEITH, *I Believe*

20206. The ultimate truth is penultimately always a falsehood. He who will be proved right in the end appears to be wrong and harmful before it.   ARTHUR KOESTLER,
Darkness at Noon

20207. The veracity which increases with old age is not far from folly.

LA ROCHEFOUCAULD, *Maxims*

20208. Truth is generally the best vindication against slander.

LINCOLN

20209. If the truth hurts most of us so badly that we don't want it told, it hurts even more grievously those who dare to tell it. It is a two-edged sword, often deadly dangerous to the user.

JUDGE BEN LINDSEY,
The Revolt of Modern Youth

20210. Truth is divided up into sectional compartments, presumably for greater ease of apprehension, so that a part often seems of more value than the whole. And the party walls are well safeguarded, only a few here and there are permeable. Permeability is generally regarded as dangerous, because liable to a leakage or inlet of heresy.   SIR OLIVER LODGE,
Demonstrated Survival

20211. If you suppress truth, if you hide truth, if you do not rise up and speak out in meeting, if you speak out in meeting without speaking the whole truth, then you are less true than truth.   JACK LONDON

20212. Great Truths are portions of the soul of man.

LOWELL, *Sonnet VI*

20213. Who speaks the truth stabs Falsehood to the heart.

LOWELL, *L'Envoi*

20214. Truth forever on the scaffold, Wrong forever on the throne.

LOWELL, *The Present Crisis*

20215. There is another way to truth: by the minute examination of facts. That is the way of the scientists: a hard and noble and thankless way. It is not the way of the great poet, the rare unreasonable who comes once in ten generations. He apprehends truth by power: the truth which he apprehends cannot be defined, save by greater power, and there is no greater power.

JOHN MASEFIELD, *Shakespeare*

20216.
Man with his burning soul
Has but an hour of breath
To build a ship of Truth
In which his soul may sail
Sail on the sea of death
For death takes toll
Of beauty, courage, youth,
Of all but Truth.

JOHN MASEFIELD, *Truth*

20217. If we say *truth,* we also say *freedom* and *justice;* if we speak of freedom and justice, we mean truth.

THOMAS MANN,
The Coming Victory of Democracy

20218. Truth uttered before its time is always dangerous.   MENCIUS

20219. The average man does not get pleasure out of an idea because he thinks it is true; he thinks it is true because he gets pleasure out of it.

H. L. MENCKEN

20220. Beholding the bright countenance of truth in the quiet and still air of delightful studies.

MILTON,
The Reason of Church Government

20221. Truth is as impossible to be soiled by an outward touch as the sunbeam.   MILTON,
Doctrine & Discipline of Divorce

20222. Though all the winds of doctrine were let loose to play upon the earth, so Truth be in the field, we do ingloriously, by licensing and prohibiting, to misdoubt her strength. Let her and Falsehood grapple: who ever knew Truth put to the worse in a free and open encounter?
          MILTON, *Areopagitica*

20223. I speak truth, not so much as I would, but as much as I dare; and I dare a little the more, as I grow older.   MONTAIGNE, *Essays*

20224. I do not know what I may appear to the world; but to myself I seem to have been only like a boy playing on the seashore, and diverting myself in now and then finding a smoother pebble or a prettier shell than ordinary, whilst the great ocean of truth lay all undiscovered before me.   SIR ISAAC NEWTON,
Brewster's Memoirs of Newton

20225. Truth never yet fell dead in the streets; it has such affinity with the soul of man, the seed however broadcast will catch somewhere and produce its hundredfold.
          THEODORE PARKER,
A Discourse of Matters Pertaining to Religion

20226. Truth stood on one side and Ease on the other; it has often been so.   THEODORE PARKER,
A Discourse of Matters Pertaining to Religion

20227. Truth often suffers more by the heat of its defenders, than from the arguments of its opposers.
WILLIAM PENN, *Fruits of Solitude*

20228. All men naturally have some love of truth.   *Proverb*

20229. Face to face, the truth comes out.   *Proverb*

20230. Follow truth too close at the heels 'twill strike out your teeth.
          Proverb

20231. Truth needs not many words; but a false tale a large preamble.
          Proverb

20232. Truth may be blamed, but shall never be shamed.   *Proverb*

20233. That must be true which all men say.   *Proverb*

20234. All truth is not to be told at all times.   *Proverb*

20235.
Great is truth and shall prevail,
Therefore must we weep and wail.
          LAURA E. RICHARDS,
The Mameluke and the Hospodar

20236. I believe that in the course of history—but only on condition that civilization is not interrupted by catastrophe—truth will be approached more and more closely.
          JULES ROMAINS, *I Believe*

20237. The only way I can argue impersonally for integrity and reality, truth and imagination, in art, in living, and in the theatre, is to argue specifically—with my own work as a basis for comparison.
          WILLIAM SAROYAN,
Introduction: My Heart's in the Highlands

20238. I regret very much that to speak the truth in our day appears to be bad taste. I find, however, that even at the risk of seeming to be a boor I must still say what I truly believe. I believe that time, with its in-

finite understanding, will one day for-
give me.   WILLIAM SAROYAN,
*Introduction: My Heart's in the
Highlands*

20239. While you live, tell truth and
shame the devil!
SHAKESPEARE, *Henry IV*

20240. The naked truth.
SHAKESPEARE, *Love's Labour's Lost*

20241.
Truth is truth
To the end of reckoning.
SHAKESPEARE, *Measure for Measure*

20242. Truth will come to light; mur-
der cannot be hid long.
SHAKESPEARE,
The Merchant of Venice

20243. Truth hath a quiet breast.
SHAKESPEARE, *Richard II*

20244.
And simple truth miscall'd simplicity,
And captive good attending captain
ill.   SHAKESPEARE, *Sonnet LXVI*

20245.
Most true it is that I have looked on
truth
Askance and strangely.
SHAKESPEARE, *Sonnet CX*

20246. Now is the time to pull ourselves together—to feel our muscle—
to realise the value of our strength
and pluck, and to tell the truth unashamed like men of courage and
character, not to shirk it like the official apologists of a Foreign Office
plot.
BERNARD SHAW, *to Lillah McCarthy*

20247. How awful to reflect that
what people say of us is true!
LOGAN PEARSALL SMITH,
Afterthoughts

20248. Mere white truth in simple
nakedness.   TENNYSON,
Idylls of the King

20249.
The golden guess
Is morning-star to the full round of
truth.   TENNYSON, *Columbus*

20250. Rather than love, than money,
than fame, give me truth.
THOREAU, *Walden*

20251. Analogy is milk for babes,
but abstract truths are strong meat.
MARTIN F. TUPPER, *Of Education*

20252. This is petrified truth.
MARK TWAIN,
A Complaint about Correspondents

20253. Truth is such a precious article let us all economize in its use.
MARK TWAIN

20254. I am all for truth. But The
Truth, in the Pauline sense of the
world, is as little to my liking as cya-
nide of potassium.
VAN LOON, *I Believe*

20255. Love truth, but pardon error.
VOLTAIRE, *Discours sur l'Homme*

20256. There are truths which are
not for all men, nor for all times.
VOLTAIRE

20257. There is nothing so powerful
as truth,—and often nothing so
strange.   DANIEL WEBSTER

20258.
Truths that wake,
To perish never. WORDSWORTH,
Ode on Intimations of Immortality

20259. I believe that in the end the
truth will conquer.
JOHN WYCLIFFE,
*A Short History of the English
People*

20260. If you shut up truth and bury it under the ground, it will but grow, and gather to itself such explosive power that the day it bursts through, it will blow up everything in its way.
EMILE ZOLA, *J'accuse*

20261. I know none of the people I accuse. I have never seen them. I bear them neither rancour nor hatred. They are no more to me than entities, spirits of social mischief. And the act I am performing here is but a revolutionary means to hasten the explosion of truth and justice.

I have but one passion—the truth —in the name of humanity which has suffered so much, and has a right to happiness. My flaming protest is but the cry of my heart. Then let them dare to force me into the Assize Court and hold the enquiry in broad daylight!

I am waiting.
EMILE ZOLA, *J'accuse*

See also: 315, 437, 938, 939, 979, 1116, 1121, 1126, 1176, 1193, 1270, 1420, 1580, 1693, 1696, 1865, 1881, 1895, 2585, 2750, 2762, 2871, 3037, 3067, 3175, 3295, 3328, 3362, 3551, 3604, 3805, 5815, 6091, 6097, 6161, 6169, 6978, 7109, 7111, 7174, 8531, 11034, 11041, 12176, 13633, 15165, 17157, 17487.

TURKEY AND THE TURKS

20271. The unspeakable Turk.
CARLYLE

20272. [The Ottoman Empire] has the body of a sick old man, who tried to appear healthy, although his end was near.   SIR THOMAS ROE

20273. Out-paramoured the Turk.
SHAKESPEARE, *King Lear*

TWILIGHT

Related Subjects: Evening, Sunset.

20281.
'Twas twilight, and the sunless day went down
    Over the waste of waters; like a veil,
Which, if withdrawn, would but disclose the frown
    Of one whose hate is mask'd but to assail.   BYRON, *Don Juan*

20282.
        Beauteous Night lay dead
Under the pall of twilight, and the love-star sickened and shrank.
GEORGE ELIOT, *Spanish Gypsy*

20283.
In the twilight of morning to climb to the top of the mountain,—
Thee to salute, kindly star, earliest herald of day,—
And to await, with impatience, the gaze of the ruler of heaven.—
Youthful delight, oh, how oft lur'st thou me out in the night.
GOETHE, *Venetian Epigrams*

20284. Sweet shadows of twilight! how calm their repose.
O. W. HOLMES,
Poems of the Class of '29

20285. Dim eclipse, disastrous twilight.   MILTON, *Paradise Lost*

20286.
Twilight, ascending slowly from the east,
Entwined in duskier wreaths her braided locks
O'er the fair front and radiant eyes of day;
Night followed, clad with stars.
SHELLEY, *Alastor*

20287.
Twilight and evening bell,
    And after that the dark.
TENNYSON, *Crossing the Bar*

20288.
Her eyes as stars of twilight fair,
Like twilight's too her dusky hair.
WORDSWORTH,
She Was a Phantom of Delight

See also: 487, 1733.

TYRANNY

Related Subjects: Censorship,
Cruelty, Despotism, Dictatorship,
Government, Kings, Persecution,
Rule, Slavery.

20291. Any excuse will serve a tyrant.
AESOP, *The Wolf and the Lamb*

20292. A tyrant must put on the appearance of uncommon devotion to religion. Subjects are less apprehensive of illegal treatment from a ruler whom they consider god-fearing and pious. On the other hand, they do less easily move against him, believing that he has the gods on his side.
ARISTOTLE, *Politics*

20293. Kings will be tyrants from policy, when subjects are rebels from principle.
BURKE,
Reflections on the Revolution in France

20294.
These men who do not die, but send to death,
These iron men whom mercy cannot bend
Beyond the lettered law; what when their breath
Shall suddenly and naturally end?
What shall their final retribution be,
What bloody silver then shall pay the tolls
Exacted for this legal infamy
When death indicts their stark immortal souls?
COUNTEE CULLEN,
Not Sacco and Vanzetti

20295. Tyranny is a habit capable of being developed, and at last becomes a disease.
DOSTOYEVSKY,
The House of the Dead

20296. The man and the citizen disappear for ever in the tyrant.
DOSTOYEVSKY,
The House of the Dead

20297.
Of all the tyrannies on human kind
The worst is that which persecutes the mind.
DRYDEN,
The Hind & the Panther

20298. With reasonable men, I will reason; with humane men I will plead; but to tyrants I will give no quarter, nor waste arguments where they will certainly be lost.
W. L. GARRISON, *Life*

20299. Excess of severity is not the path to order. On the contrary, it is the path to the bomb.
JOHN MORLEY, *Recollections*

20300. Tyranny, like hell, is not easily conquered; yet we have this consolation with us, that the harder the conflict, the more glorious the triumph.
THOMAS PAINE, *The Crisis*

20301.
For how can tyrants safely govern home,
Unless abroad they purchase great alliance?
SHAKESPEARE, *Henry VI*

20302. And the little screaming fact that sounds through all history: repression works only to strengthen and knit the repressed.
JOHN STEINBECK,
The Grapes of Wrath

20303. No matter what the dominant idea may be, whenever it has recourse to terror as the instrument for impos-

ing uniformity upon alien convictions, it is no longer idealism but brutality.
STEFAN ZWEIG, *The Right to Heresy*

See also: 776, 1384, 1385, 3424, 3435, 4155, 5419, 5425, 11481, 11621, 16681.

U

UGLINESS

Related Subject: Deformity.

20311. No man with a face capable of a hundred shades of expression can be ugly. J. G. HUNEKER

20312. Ugly women, finely dressed, are the uglier for it. *Proverb*

See also: 19063.

UMBRELLA

Related Subject: Rain.

20321.
We bear our shades about us; self-deprived
Of other screen, the thin umbrella spread,
And range an Indian waste without a tree. COWPER, *Task*

20322.
When my water-proof umbrella proved a sieve, sieve, sieve,
When my shiny new umbrella proved a sieve. ROSSITER JOHNSON,
A Rhyme of the Rain

20323. It is the habitual carriage of the umbrella that is the stamp of Respectability. The umbrella has become the acknowledged index of social position. STEVENSON,
Philosophy of Umbrellas

20324. Crusoe was rather a moralist than a pietist, and his leaf-umbrella is as fine an example of the civilized mind striving to express itself under adverse circumstances as we have ever met with. STEVENSON,
Philosophy of Umbrellas

See also: 702.

UNDERSTANDING AND MISUNDERSTANDING

Related Subjects: Error, Mistake, Perception, Sympathy.

20331. I shall light a candle of understanding in thine heart, which shall not be put out.
Apocrypha: 2 Esdras

20332. My understanding has forsook me, and is gone a wool-gathering. CERVANTES, *Don Quixote*

20333. The understanding is always the dupe of the heart.
LA ROCHEFOUCAULD, *Maxims*

20334. I want, by understanding myself to understand others. I want to be all that I am capable of becoming.
KATHERINE MANSFIELD

20335. Man's best candle is his understanding. *Proverb*

20336. He that would rightly understand a man, must read his whole story. *Proverb*

20337. The more we understand individual objects the more we understand God. SPINOZA

20338. The endeavor to understand is the first and only basis of virtue.
SPINOZA

20339. To understand is what is hard. Once one understands, action is easy.
SUN YAT-SEN

See also: 1191, 2473, 4640, 11312, 11394, 17725, 18852, 21385.

UNEMPLOYMENT, see Employment

UNHAPPINESS, see Happiness

UNION

Related Subjects: Club, Labor, Meeting, Unity, Wages.

20341. Union gives strength.
AESOP, *The Bundle of Sticks*

20342. When bad men combine, the good must associate; else they will fall one by one, an unpitied sacrifice in a contemptible struggle.
BURKE,
Thoughts on the Cause of the Present Discontent

20343. All for one, one for all, that is our device.
DUMAS, *The Three Musketeers*

20344.
All your strength is in your union.
All your danger is in discord;
Therefore be at peace henceforward,
And as brothers live together.
LONGFELLOW, *Song of Hiawatha*

20345. Not vain the weakest, if their force unite. POPE

20346. He spouted out some Scripture once. Says it's from the Preacher. Goes, "two are better than one, because they have a good reward for their labor. For if they fall, the one will lift up his fellow, but woe to him that is alone when he falleth, for he hath not another to help him up. Again, if two lie together, then they have heat: but how can one be warm alone? And if one prevail against him, two shall withstand him, and a three-fold cord is not quickly broken." JOHN STEINBECK, *The Grapes of Wrath*

The Federal Union

20347. Our Federal Union: it must be preserved. ANDREW JACKSON

20348. If we do not make common cause to save the good old ship of the Union on this voyage, nobody will have a chance to pilot her on another voyage. LINCOLN

Labor Unions

20349. The trust and the labor organizations cannot be described in the same language. The trust magnates have used their power to amass swollen fortunes, while no one will say that the labor organization has as yet secured for its members more than their share of the profits arising from their work. . . . In a trust a few men attempt to control the products of others; in a labor organization, the members unite for the protection of that which is their own, namely, their own labor, which, being necessary to their existence, is a part of them.
WILLIAM JENNINGS BRYAN

20350. The right to join labor unions is undisputed, and has been the subject of frequent affirmation in judicial opinions . . . the right to join them, as against coercive action to the contrary, may be the legitimate subject of protection in the exercise of the police authority of the states.
CHARLES EVANS HUGHES,
Opinion: Coppage vs. Kansas and Adair vs. U. S.

20351. The legality of collective action on the part of employees in order to safeguard their proper interests is not to be disputed. It has long been recognized that employees are entitled to organize for the purpose of securing the redress of grievances and to promote agreements with employers relating to rates of pay and conditions of work . . . Congress was not required to ignore this right of the employees but could safeguard it and seek to make their appropriative collective action an instrument of peace rather than of strife. Such collective action would be a mockery if representation were made futile by interference with freedom of choice.

CHARLES EVANS HUGHES,
Opinion: Texas and New Orleans RR. Co. vs. Brotherhood 281.

20352. The right of labor to organize has been recognized by the courts of this country since 1842. When Congress enacted the N.I.R.A. with its Section 7a guaranteeing to workers generally for the first time by Federal statute the right to organize and bargain collectively, free from interference of employers, millions of workers throughout America, oppressed and underpaid for many years, lifted up their hearts on reading those marvelous words, and for the first time in their lives stood erect and breathed the air of freedom.

CHARLTON OGBURN,
Before U. S. Senate Committee

20353. It is hereby declared to be the policy of the United States to remove obstructions to the free flow of commerce and to provide for the general welfare by encouraging the practice of collective bargaining, and by protecting the exercise by the worker of full freedom of association, self-organization, and designation of representatives of his own choosing, for the purpose of negotiating the terms and conditions of his employment or other mutual aid and or protection.

Declaration of Policy: National Labor Relations Act

20354. Denials of the right to bargain collectively lead also to strikes and other manifestations of economic strife, which create further obstacles to the free flow of commerce.

Declaration of Policy: National Labor Relations Act

20355. Equality of bargaining power between employers and employees is not attained when the organization of employers in the corporate and other forms of ownership association is not balanced by the free exercise by employees of the right to bargain collectively through representatives of their own choosing.

Declaration of Policy: National Labor Relations Act

See also: 656, 717, 4042, 11923, 18356.

UNITED STATES, see America

UNITY

Related Subjects: Loyalty, Patriotism, Union.

20361. United we stand, divided we fall.   AESOP,
The Four Oxen and the Lion

20362. Behold how good and how pleasant it is for brethren to dwell together in unity.
Bible: Psalms, cxxxiii, 1

20363. National unity can only be preserved upon a cause which is larger than the nation itself.

WINSTON CHURCHILL,
Blood, Sweat & Tears

20364. We must all hang together, or assuredly we shall all hang separately.
FRANKLIN

20365. *Mike McInerney:* Look now, Honor . . . It is what I often heard said, two to be better than one . . . Sure if you had an old trouser was full of holes . . . or a skirt . . .

wouldn't you put another in under it that might be as tattered as itself, and the two of them together would make some sort of a decent show?
LADY GREGORY,
The Workhouse Ward

29366. We mutually pledge to each other our lives, our fortunes, and our sacred honour. JEFFERSON,
Declaration of Independence

20367. Unite for the public safety, if you would remain an independent nation. NAPOLEON

20368. Weak things united become strong. *Proverb*

20369. One for all, or all for one we gage. SHAKESPEARE,
The Rape of Lucrece

20370. Men will find that they can prepare with mutual aid far more easily what they need, and avoid far more easily the perils which beset them on all sides, by united forces.
SPINOZA, *Ethics*

See also: 1931.

UNIVERSE

Related Subjects: Astronomy, God, The Heavens.

20371. Nothing is more certain than that worlds on worlds, and spheres on spheres, stretch behind and beyond the actually seen.
EDWARD CARPENTER,
The Drama of Love and Death

20372. We find the universe terrifying because of its vast meaningless distances, terrifying because of its unconceivably long vistas of time which dwarf human history to the twinkling of an eye, terrifying because of our extreme loneliness, and because of

the material insignificance of our home in space—a millionth part of a grain of sand out of all the seas in the world.
SIR JAMES JEANS,
The Mysterious Universe

20373. One Universe made up of all that is; and one God in it all, and one principle of Being, and one Law, the Reason, shared by all thinking creatures, and one Truth.
MARCUS AURELIUS, *Meditations*

20374. The world, and whatever that be which we call the heavens, by the vault of which all things are enclosed, we must conceive to be a deity, to be eternal, without bounds, neither created nor subject at any time to destruction. To inquire what is beyond it is no concern of man; nor can the human mind form any conjecture concerning it.
PLINY THE ELDER, *Natural History*

20375.
This truth within thy mind rehearse,
That in a boundless universe
Is boundless better, boundless worse.
TENNYSON, *The Two Voices*

See also: 150, 1322, 3026, 4925, 10534, 10536, 10539.

UNIVERSITY

Related Subjects: Education, Knowledge, Learning, Scholar, School, Teacher.

20381. Not long ago I asked a well known professor at one of the largest and best known universities in the East what, in his candid opinion, his university did for the many thousands of students who annually attended it. After a moment's thought he said that as far as he could see, the university turned out a standard-

ized, low grade mental product, much like an intellectual Ford factory.
JAMES TRUSLOW ADAMS,
Our Business Civilization

20382. The true University of these days is a Collection of Books.
CARLYLE, *Heroes & Hero-Worship*

20383.
"D'ye think th' colledges has much to do with th' progress iv th' wurruld?" asked Mr. Hennessy.
"D'ye think," said Mr. Dooley, "'tis th' mill that makes th' wather run?"   F. P. DUNNE,
Colleges and Degrees

20384. One of the benefits of a college education is to show the boy its little avail.
EMERSON, *Conduct of Life*

20385. A university may be a good hotel or an elegant cenotaph for an established science. The history of universities does not show that they are well equipped to serve as lying-in hospitals.   LANCELOT HOGBEN,
Dangerous Thoughts

20386. The college graduate is presented with a sheepskin to cover his intellectual nakedness.
ROBERT M. HUTCHINS

20387. A university that proposes to study matters of social constitution must expect to find true controversy within its halls in an age when these are a matter of profound dispute. If it is not prepared for the free competition of ideas, it is not, in the true sense, a university.
HAROLD J. LASKI, *I Believe*

20388. The business of a university is not the transformation of undergraduates into fountains of informa-

tion . . . Its business is the very different task of teaching the student how facts are converted into truth.
HAROLD J. LASKI

20389. If I were founding a university I would found first a smoking room; then when I had a little more money in hand I would found a dormitory; then after that, or more probably with it, a decent reading room and a library. After that, if I still had more money that I couldn't use, I would hire a professor and get some textbooks.   STEPHEN LEACOCK,
Oxford As I See It

20390.
Let us not burn the universities—yet,
After all, the damage they do might be worse . . .
Suppose Oxford had snared and disemboweled
Shakespeare! Suppose Harvard had rammed its buttermilk into Mark Twain!   H. L. MENCKEN

20391. Cauliflower is nothing but cabbage with a college education.
MARK TWAIN,
Pudd'nhead Wilson's Calendar

UNKINDNESS, see Kindness

USE, USEFULNESS

Related Subjects: Service, Worth.

20401. We often despise what is most useful to us.   AESOP,
The Hart and the Hunter

20402. Be useful where thou livest.
GEORGE HERBERT,
The Church Porch

20403. Nothing can have value without being an object of utility. If it

be useless, the labor contained in it is useless, cannot be reckoned as labor, and cannot therefore create value.
KARL MARX, *Capital*

See also: 981, 1199, 1397, 1865, 4968, 9490, 10815, 16268, 16526, 18504.

USURER, USURY

Related Subjects: **Borrowing, Credit, Debt, Interest.**

20411. A money-lender. He serves you in the present tense; he lends you in the conditional mood; keeps you in the subjunctive; and ruins you in the future.   ADDISON

20412. Usury is the taking of any interest whatever upon an unproductive loan.   HILAIRE BELLOC,
Economics for Helen

20413. Go not to a covetous old man, with any request, too soon in the morning, before he hath taken in that day's prey; for his covetousness is up before him, and he before thee, and he is in ill humor; but stay till the afternoon, till he be satiated upon some borrower.   THOMAS FULLER

20414. To borrow on usury brings sudden beggary.   *Proverb*

20415. To borrow on usance brings on a nuisance.   *Proverb*

V

VAGABOND

Related Subject: **Wanderlust.**

20421.
Oh, why don't you work like other men do?
How the hell can I work when there's no work to do?
Hallelujah, I'm a bum, hallelujah, bum again,
Hallelujah, give us a hand-out to revive us again.   *Anonymous,*
Hallelujah, I'm a Bum

20422. Are you not scared by seeing that the gypsies are more attractive to us than the Apostles?
EMERSON, *Journals*

20423. His house was known to all the vagrant train.   GOLDSMITH,
The Deserted Village

20424.
Whose furthest footstep never strayed
Beyond the village of his birth,
Is but a lodger for the night
In this old wayside inn of earth.

To-morrow he shall take his pack,
And set out for the ways beyond,
On the old trail from star to star,
An alien and a vagabond.
RICHARD HOVEY, *Envoy*

20425. The vagabond, when rich, is called a tourist.
PAUL RICHARD,
The Scourge of Christ

20426. You shall comprehend all vagrom men.   SHAKESPEARE,
Much Ado About Nothing

20427. Nature makes us vagabonds, the world makes us respectable.
ALEXANDER SMITH, *Dreamthorp*

20428.
Wealth I ask not, hope nor love,
Nor a friend to know me;
All I ask, the heavens above,
And the road below me.
STEVENSON, *The Vagabond*

20429.
I will sing, I will go, and never ask me why

I was born a rover and a passer-by.
RIDGELY TORRENCE, *Eye-Witness*

See also: 253.

VALENTINE

Related Subjects: Cupid, Love.

20431.
Muse, bid the Morn awake!
Sad Winter now declines,
Each bird both choose a mate;
This day's Saint Valentine's.
MICHAEL DRAYTON,
To His Valentine

20432.
Oft have I heard both youths and
virgins say,
Birds choose their mates, and couple
too, this day:
But by their flight I never can devine
When I shall couple with my Valen-
tine.   ROBERT HERRICK,
To His Valentine

20433.
Oh, if it be to choose and call thee
mine,
Love, thou art every day my Valen-
tine!   THOMAS HOOD,
For the Fourteenth of February

20434. Hail to thy returning festival,
old Bishop Valentine! Great is thy
name in the rubric, thou venerable
Archflamen of Hymen! Immortal
Go-Between; who and what manner
of person art thou? Art thou but a
name, typifying the restless principle
which impels poor humans to seek
perfection in union? or wert thou indeed a mortal prelate, with thy tip-
pet and thy rochet, thy apron on,
and decent lawn sleeves? Mysterious personage! like unto thee, assuredly, there is no other mitred father
in the calendar. CHARLES LAMB,
Essays of Elia: Valentine's Day

20435. By and by comes Mrs. Pierce,
with my name in her bosom for her
Valentine, which will cost me money.
SAMUEL PEPYS, *Diary*

20436.
To-morrow is Saint Valentine's day,
All in the morning betime.
And I a maid at your window,
To be your Valentine.
SHAKESPEARE, *Hamlet*

VALOR

**Related Subjects: Boldness, Chiv-
alry, Courage.**

20441. Valour would cease to be a
virtue, if there were no injustice.
AGESILAUS

20442. As much valour is to be found
in feasting as in fighting, and some
of our city captains and carpet
knights will make this good, and
prove it.   ROBERT BURTON,
Anatomy of Melancholy

20443. If I advance, follow me! If
I retreat, kill me. If I die, Avenge
me!   LA ROCHEJAQUELIN,
*To His Volunteers in the Revolt
of 1793 in La Vendée*

20444. To yield to the stronger is
valor's second prize.   MARTIAL,
On the Spectacles

20445. If all the world were just,
there would be no need of valour.
PLUTARCH, *Lives*

20446. Valour that parleys, is near
yielding.   *Proverb*

20447. In a false quarrel there is no
true valour.   *Proverb*

20448. He is as full of valour as of
kindness; Princely in both.
SHAKESPEARE, *Henry V*

20449. I have heard of some kind of men that put quarrels purposely on others to taste their valour.
SHAKESPEARE, *Twelfth Night*

20450.
There is no holier spot of ground
Than where defeated valor lies,
By mourning beauty crowned!
HENRY TIMROD,
*Ode, Decorating the Graves of
the Confederate Dead*

20451. Pluck takes us into a difficulty, nerve brings us out of it. Both are comprised in the noble quality we call valor.
G. J. WHYTE-MELVILLE,
Riding Recollections

See also: 325, 2129, 3156, 4484, 4490, 5090, 5941, 6357, 6934, 19866.

VALUE, see Worth

VANITY

Related Subjects: **Affectation, Boasting, Braggart, Conceit, Delusion, Dress, Elegance, Fame, Fashion, Flattery, Fop, Illusion, Mirror, Ornament, Ostentation, Peacock, Snob.**

20461. Every man at his best state is altogether vanity.
Bible: Psalms, xxxix, 3

20462. Surely men of low degree are vanity, and men of high degree are a lie; to be laid in the balance, they are altogether lighter than vanity.
Bible: Psalms, lxii, 9

20463. Vanity of vanities, ... all is vanity.   *Bible: Ecclesiastes, i, 2*

20464. All is vanity and vexation of spirit.   *Bible: Ecclesiastes, i, 14*

20465. What beats me is how chaps like us can be vain . . . If it were not ridiculous it would disgust me to hear my colleagues praise me so fulsomely to my face.   BRAHMS
Schauffler: The Unknown Brahms

20466. Even good men like to make the public stare.   BYRON, *Don Juan*

20467. Vanity plays lurid tricks with our memory.   JOSEPH CONRAD,
Lord Jim

20468.
Th' adorning thee with so much art
Is but a barb'rous skill;
'Tis like the pois'ning of a dart,
Too apt before to kill.
ABRAHAM COWLEY,
The Waiting Maid

20469.
The reason why fond women love to buy
Adulterate complexion: here 'tis read,—
False colours last after the true be dead.   THOMAS DEKKER,
*A Description of a Lady by
Her Lover*

20470. It has often been remarked that the breakfast-tables of people who avow themselves indifferent to what the Press may say of them are garnished by all the newspapers on the morning when there is anything to say.   GALSWORTHY,
The Silver Spoon

20471.
Lo, all our pomp of yesterday
Is one with Nineveh and Tyre!
KIPLING, *Recessional*

20472. How poor the human mind would be without vanity!
NIETZSCHE,
Human, All too Human

20473. *Glitter*—and in that one word how much of all that is detestable do we express!   POE,
Philosophy of Furniture

20474. She would rather be looked around at than up to.

PHIL ROBINSON

20475. Provided a man is not mad, he can be cured of every folly but vanity.   ROUSSEAU,
Emile, or Education

20476.
Take physic pomp;
Expose thyself to feel what wretches feel.   SHAKESPEARE,
King Lear

20477. It may easily come to pass that a vain man may become proud and imagine himself pleasing to all when he is in reality a universal nuisance.   SPINOZA, *Ethics*

20478. He had only one vanity, he thought he could give advice better than any other person.
MARK TWAIN,
The Man That Corrupted Hadleyburg

20479. Vanity as an impulse has without doubt been of far more benefit to civilization than modesty has ever been.   W. E. WOODWARD,
George Washington

See also: 266, 1144, 1243, 1373, 1514, 15142, 2222, 2313, 3401, 8976, 15941, 15956, 20623.

VARIETY

Related Subjects: Change, Fickleness, Novelty.

20481.
There is no season such delight can bring,
As summer, autumn, winter, and the spring.   WILLIAM BROWNE,
Variety

20482. Variety's the very spice of life.   COWPER, *The Task*

20483. Variety is the mother of Enjoyment.   DISRAELI, *Vivian Grey*

20484. No pleasure endures unseasoned by variety.
PUBLILIUS SYRUS, *Sententiae*

20485.
Age cannot wither her, nor custom stale
Her infinite variety.
SHAKESPEARE,
Antony and Cleopatra

See also: 6448.

VENGEANCE, see Revenge

VENUS

Related Subjects: Gods and Goddesses, Love, Mythology.

20491. Wot's the good o' callin' a young 'ooman a Wenus or a angel, Sammy?   DICKENS,
Pickwick Papers

20492.
Venus, thy eternal sway
All the race of men obey.
EURIPIDES, *Iphigenia at Aulis*

20493. Thou, O Venus, art sole mistress of the nature of things, and without thee nothing rises up into the divine realms of life, nothing grows to be lovely or glad.
LUCRETIUS, *De Rerum Natura*

20494.
Lo, she was thus when her clear limbs enticed
All lips that now grow sad with kissing Christ.   SWINBURNE,
Laus Veneris

VICE

Related Subjects: Corruption, Dissipation, Morality, Rake, Sensuality, Sin, Wickedness, Whore.

20501. One big vice in a man is apt

to keep out a great many smaller ones.   BRET HARTE,
To Men of Sandy Bar

20502. If individuals have no virtues, their vices may be of use to us.
JUNIUS

20503.
Saint Augustine! well hast thou said,
That of our vices we can frame
A ladder, if we will but tread
Beneath our feet each deed of shame.   LONGFELLOW,
The Ladder of Saint Augustine

20504. I prefer a comfortable vice to a virtue that bores.   MOLIÈRE

20505. I find that the best virtue I have has in it some tincture of vice.
MONTAIGNE, *Essays*

20506.
Vice is a monster of so frightful mien,
As to be hated needs but to be seen;
Yet seen too oft, familiar with her face,
We first endure, then pity, then embrace.   POPE, *Essay on Man*

20507. Cent per cent, do we pay for every vicious pleasure.   *Proverb*

20508. Vice is its own punishment and sometimes its own cure.
Proverb

20509. What maintains one vice would bring up two children.
Proverb

20510. Virtues all agree, but vices fight one another.   *Proverb*

20511. The maintaining of one vice costeth more than ten virtues.
Proverb

20512. As virtue is its own reward, so vice is its own punishment.
Proverb

20513. Every vice fights against nature.   *Proverb*

20514. Lordly vices require lordly estates.   *Proverb*

20515. All vice infatuates and corrupts the judgment.   *Proverb*

20516.
There is no vice so simple but assumes
Some mark of virtue on his outward parts.   SHAKESPEARE,
The Merchant of Venice

See also: 413, 746, 1241, 1291, 1463, 2225, 2492, 2967, 3871, 4583, 5396, 6301, 7307, 17532, 17556, 20630.

VICTORY

Related Subjects: Conquerors, Defeat, Self-Control, Success.

20521. Intellectual and moral victories are the only ones which do not leave the victor bankrupt and desolate in spirit when the goal is won.
A. E.

20522. Pyrrhus, when his friends congratulated to him his victory over the Romans under Fabricius, but with great slaughter of his own side, said to them, "Yes; but if we have such another victory, we are undone."
BACON, *Apothegms*

20523. He will swallow up death in victory; and the Lord God will wipe away tears from off all faces.
Bible: Isaiah, xxv, 8

20524. You ask, What is our aim? I can answer in one word: Victory— victory at all costs, victory in spite of all terror, victory however long and hard the road may be; for without victory there is no survival. Let that be realized; no survival for the British Empire; no survival for all that the British Empire has stood for.

WINSTON CHURCHILL,
Blood, Sweat & Tears

20525. Fields are won by those who believe in the winning.

T. W. HIGGINSON,
Americanism in Literature

20526. All victories are alike; defeat alone displays an individual profile.

J. G. HUNEKER, *Essays*

20527. You know, Hannibal, how to gain a victory, but not how to use it.

PLUTARCH, *Lives*

20528. They see nothing wrong in the rule that to the victors belong the spoils of the enemy.   W. L. MARCY

20529. May the great God, whom I worship, grant to my country and for the benefit of Europe in general, a great and glorious victory, and may no misconduct in anyone tarnish it, and may humanity after the victory be the predominant feature in the British fleet.   HORATIO NELSON, *Journal*

20530.
God how the dead men
Grin by the wall,
Watching the fun
Of the Victory Ball.

ALFRED NOYES,
A Victory Dance

20531. He that returns a good for evil obtains the victory.   *Proverb*

20532.
"But what good came of it at last?"
Quoth little Peterkin.
"Why, that I cannot tell," said he;
"But 'twas a famous victory."

SOUTHEY, *The Battle of Blenheim*

20533. Nothing except a battle lost can be half so melancholy as a battle won.   DUKE OF WELLINGTON,
Despatch

20534.
Others shall sing the song,
Others shall right the wrong,—
Finish what I begin,
And all I fail of win.

WHITTIER, *My Triumph*

See also: 2923, 4341, 4350, 5281, 5285, 14833.

VILLAGE

Related Subjects: **Cities, Community, Neighbor, Town.**

20541. If you would be known, and not know, vegetate in a village; if you would know, and not be known, live in a city.   C. C. COLTON

20542.
In every village marked with little
  spire,
Embowered in trees, and hardly
  known to fame.

W. SHENSTONE,
The Schoolmistress

20543.
A village is a hive of glass,
Where nothing unobserved can pass.

C. H. SPURGEON, *Salt-Cellars*

See also: 1905, 2071, 2104.

VILLAIN AND VILLAINY

Related Subjects: **Baseness, Evil, Knave, Malevolence, Rake, Wickedness.**

20551.
  He was the mildest manner'd man
That ever scuttled ship or cut a
  throat.   BYRON, *Don Juan*

20552. Sir, the gentleman soils the spot he stands upon.   HENRY CLAY

20553. A great bad man is worse than one of less talents, for he has the extended capability of doing harm.

GEORGE JAMES, *Richelieu*

20554. The villain still pursued her.
MILTON NOBLES, *The Phoenix*

20555. Where villainy goes before, vengeance follows later.   *Proverb*

20556.
O villain, villain, smiling, damned villain!
My tables,—meet it is I set it down,
That one may smile, and smile, and be a villain;
At least I'm sure it may be so in Denmark.   SHAKESPEARE,
Hamlet

20557. Some villain hath done me wrong.   SHAKESPEARE, *King Lear*

20558.
       I grant him bloody,
Luxurious, avaricious, false, deceitful,
Sudden, malicious, smacking of every sin
That has a name.
SHAKESPEARE, *Macbeth*

20559. The villainy you teach me I will execute, and it shall go hard, but I will better the instruction.
SHAKESPEARE,
The Merchant of Venice

20560. Barring that natural expression of villainy which we all have, the man looked honest enough.
MARK TWAIN, *A Mysterious Visit*

See also: 416, 632, 3941, 13813.

VIOLENCE

Related Subjects: Abuse, Curse, Energy, Force, Injury, Might, Power, Threat.

20561. Nine-tenths of mankind are more afraid of violence than of anything else.
WALTER BAGEHOT,
Biographical Studies

20562. Violence does even justice unjustly.   CARLYLE

20563. The very first essential for success is a perpetually constant and regular employment of violence.
ADOLF HITLER, *Mein Kampf*

20564. Nothing that is violent is permanent.   *Proverb*

20565. These violent delights have violent ends.   SHAKESPEARE,
Romeo and Juliet

See also: 1119, 8861.

VIOLET

Related Subject: Flowers.

20571. Those veiled nuns, meek violets.   THOMAS HOOD,
The Plea of the Midsummer Fairies

20572. Shrinking as violets do in summer's ray.
THOMAS MOORE, *Lalla Rookh*

20573. You pretty daughters of the Earth and Sun.
SIR WALTER RALEIGH,
The Shepherd to the Flowers

20574.
A violet in the youth of primy nature,
Forward, not permanent, sweet, not lasting,
The perfume and suppliance of a minute.   SHAKESPEARE, *Hamlet*

20575.
       Lay her i' the earth:
And from her fair and unpolluted flesh,
May violets spring!   SHAKESPEARE, *Hamlet*

20576.
       Who are the violets now
That strew the green lap of the new come spring?
SHAKESPEARE, *Richard II*

20577.

Violets dim,
But sweeter than the lids of Juno's
    eyes
Or Cytherea's breath.
    SHAKESPEARE, *The Winter's Tale*

20578.

A violet, by a mossy stone
Half hidden from the eye!
Fair as a star, when only one
Is shining in the sky.
           WORDSWORTH,
She Dwelt Among the Untrodden
                 Ways

VIRGIN AND VIRGINITY

**Related Subjects: Chastity, Honor,
Maid, Purity, Virtue.**

20581. You see me with child, and
you want me a virgin.
       CERVANTES, *Don Quixote*

20582.

Some say no evil thing that walks
    by night,
In fog or fire, by lake or moorish fen,
Blue meagre hag, or stubborn unlaid
    ghost,
That breaks his magic chains at cur-
    few time,
No goblin, or swart faery of the
    mine,
Hath hurtful power o'er true virgin-
    ity.   MILTON, *Comus*

20583.

Helena: Man is enemy to virginity;
    how may we barricado it against
    him?
Parolles: Keep him out.
           SHAKESPEARE,
    All's Well that Ends Well

20584. There was never virgin got
till virginity was first lost.
           SHAKESPEARE,
    All's Well that Ends Well

20585. Virginity breeds mites, much
like a cheese consumes itself to the
very paring, and so dies with feeding its own stomach. Besides, virginity is peevish, proud, idle, made of
self-love, which is the most inhibited
sin in the canon.
           SHAKESPEARE,
       All's Well that Ends Well

20586.

Young budding virgin, fair and fresh
    and sweet,
Whither away, or where is thy abode?
Happy the parents of so fair a child;
Happier the man, whom favourable
    stars
Allot thee for his lovely bed-fellow
           SHAKESPEARE,
      The Taming of the Shrew

20587. Virginity is a life of angels,
the enamel of the soul.
    JEREMY TAYLOR, *Holy Living*

20588. Beerbohm Tree said what we
have all wanted to say of the extra-
women in nearly every throne-room
and ball-room and school-room scene
since the theater began. "Ladies,"
said Tree, peering at them plaintively
through his monocle, "just a little
more virginity, if you don't mind."
       ALEXANDER WOOLLCOTT,
          Capsule Criticism

See also: 1081, 12248.

VIRTUE

**Related Subjects: Character, Chas-
tity, Decency, Excellence, Fidelity,
Honor, Innocence, Love, Modesty,
Morality, Repentance, Respectability, Righteousness, Saint, Sin, Virgin.**

20591. Virtue is like a rich stone,—
best plain set.   BACON, *Of Beauty*

20592. Virtue is like precious odours,
—most fragrant when they are incensed or crushed.   BACON,
Of Adversity

20593.
I think mankind by thee would be less bored
If only thou wert not thine own reward.
   JOHN KENDRICK BANGS,
A Hint to Virtue

20594. No better than you should be.
   BEAUMONT & FLETCHER,
The Coxcomb

20595. Whatsoever things are true, whatsoever things are honest, whatsoever things are pure, whatsoever things are lovely, whatsoever things are of good report; if there be any virtue, and if there be any praise, think on these things.
   Bible: Philippians, iv, 8

20596. Let us not be weary in welldoing: for in due season we shall reap, if we faint not.
   Bible: Galatians, vi, 9

20597. There is no road or ready way to virtue.
   SIR THOMAS BROWNE,
Religio Medici

20598. A virtue, to be serviceable, must, like gold, be alloyed with some commoner but more durable metal.
   SAMUEL BUTLER,
The Way of All Flesh

20599. Rags are royal raiment when worn for virtue's sake.
   BARKLEY CAMPBELL,
The White Slave

20600.
The firste vertu, sone, if thou wolt lere,
Is to restreyne and kepe wel thy tonge.   CHAUCER,
Canterbury Tales

20601.
Well may your hearts believe the truths I tell:
'Tis virtue makes the bliss, where'er we dwell.
   WILLIAM COLLINS,
Oriental Eclogues

20602. As a well-spent day brings happy sleep, so life well used brings happy death.   DA VINCI

20603. And virtue, though in rags, will keep me warm.   DRYDEN,
Imitation of Horace

20604. There are virtues which become crimes by exaggeration.
   DUMAS,
The Count of Monte Cristo

20605. The only reward of virtue is virtue.   EMERSON, *Friendship*

20606. Silver and gold are not the only coin; virtue too passes current all over the world.   EURIPIDES,
Oedipus

20607.
Only a sweet and virtuous soul,
Like seasoned timber, never gives.
   GEORGE HERBERT, *Virtue*

20608. Men are virtuous because women are; women are virtuous from necessity.   E. W. HOWE

20609. We need greater virtues to sustain good than evil fortune.
   LA ROCHEFOUCAULD, *Maxims*

20610. A man should *be* upright, not be *kept* upright.
   MARCUS AURELIUS, *Meditations*

20611.
       Most men admire
Virtue who follow not her lore.
   MILTON, *Paradise Regained*

20612. Sober, steadfast, and demure.
MILTON, *Il Penseroso*

20613.
Or, if Virtue feeble were,
Heav'n itself would stoop to her.
MILTON, *Comus*

20614.
Virtue could see to do what Virtue would
By her own radiant light, though sun and moon
Were in the flat sea sunk. And Wisdom's self
Oft seeks to sweet retired solitude,
Where, with her best nurse Contemplation,
She plumes her feathers, and lets grow her wings. MILTON,
Comus

20615. If everyone were clothed with integrity, if every heart were just, frank, kindly, the other virtues would be well-nigh useless, since their chief purpose is to make us bear with patience the injustice of our fellows.
MOLIÈRE, *Le Misanthrope*

20616. In the case of our multi-millionaires virtues must necessarily be "sterling virtues."
GUSTAVUS MYERS,
History of the Great American Fortunes

20617.
Be to her virtues very kind;
Be to her faults a little blind.
MATTHEW PRIOR,
An English Padlock

20618. He hath no mean portion of virtue that loveth it in another.
Proverb

20619. Who follow not virtue in youth, cannot fly sin in old age.
Proverb

20620. Virtue is its own reward.
Proverb

20621. Virtue is tied to no degrees of men.
Proverb

20622. Virtue which parleys, is near a surrender.
Proverb

20623. Virtue would not go far, if a little vanity walked not with it.
Proverb

20624. He that walketh with the virtuous is one of them. *Proverb*

20625. Virtue, though momentarily shamed, cannot be extinguished.
PUBLILIUS SYRUS, *Sententiae*

20626. Not that I mistrust her virtue, but—she is a woman. There lies the suspicion. RABELAIS

20627.
From lowest place when virtuous things proceed,
The place is dignified by the doer's deed. SHAKESPEARE,
All's Well that Ends Well

20628. Assume a virtue, if you have it not. SHAKESPEARE, *Hamlet*

20629. Virtue is bold and goodness never fearful. SHAKESPEARE,
Measure for Measure

20630.
Virtue itself turns vice, being misapplied;
And vice sometime's by action dignified. SHAKESPEARE,
Romeo and Juliet

20631.
Sir Toby. Dost thou think, because thou art virtuous, there shall be no more cakes and ale?
Clown. Yes, by Saint Anne, and ginger shall be hot i' the mouth too.
SHAKESPEARE, *Twelfth Night*

20632. Is it a world to hide virtues in? Shakespeare, *Twelfth Night*

20633. Virtue is the performance of pleasant actions.
James Stephens,
The Crock of Gold

20634.
Wearing the white flower of a blameless life,
Before a thousand peering littlenesses,
In that fierce light which beats upon a throne. Tennyson,
Idylls of the King

20635.
I think I could be a good woman if I had five thousand a year.
Thackeray, *Vanity Fair*

20636. The wicked are wicked, no doubt, and they go astray and they fall, and they come by their deserts; but who can tell the mischief which the very virtuous do?
Thackeray, *The Newcomes*

20637. There is never an instant's truce between virtue and vice.
Thoreau, *Walden*

20638. Good company and good discourse are the very sinews of virtue.
Izaak Walton,
The Compleat Angler

20639.
Some might suspect the nymph not over good—
Nor would they be mistaken, if they should. Edward Young,
Love of Fame

See also: 11, 66, 422, 819, 971, 1241, 1263, 1291, 1351, 1713, 1732, 1854, 2068, 2131, 2133, 2141, 2216, 2220, 2398, 2511, 2953, 3284, 3441, 3879, 4112, 4152, 4320, 4380, 4409, 4539, 4587, 4592, 5651, 6984, 7002, 12302,

15701, 16352, 17923, 20338, 20502, 20505.

VISION

Related Subjects: Angel, Blindness, Darkness, Dreams, Eyes, Fairies, Ghost, Illusion, Imagination, Sense, Sight.

20641. Where there is no vision, the people perish.
Bible: Proverbs, xxix, 18

20642. I have multiplied visions, and used similitudes.
Bible: Hosea, xii, 10

20643.
Earth's crammed with heaven,
And every common bush afire with God;
And only he who sees takes off his shoes—
The rest sit round it and pluck blackberries.
Elizabeth B. Browning,
Aurora Leigh

20644.
This is the very coinage of your brain:
This bodiless creation ecstasy
Is very cunning in.
Shakespeare, *Hamlet*

20645.
Is this a dagger which I see before me,
The handle toward my hand? Come, let me clutch thee:
I have thee not, and yet I see thee still.
Art thou not, fatal vision, sensible
To feeling as to sight? or art thou but
A dagger of the mind, a false creation,
Proceeding from the heat-oppressed brain? Shakespeare, *Macbeth*

20646. Vision is needed by the democracies. It is needed more than armaments!

DOROTHY THOMPSON,
Let the Record Speak

VISITORS, see Guests

VOICE

Related Subjects: Echo, Sing, Sound, Speech, Talk, Tongue, Words.

20651. A vast expenditure of human voice. ARISTOPHANES, *The Frogs*

20652.
The Devil hath not, in all his quiver's choice,
An arrow for the heart like a sweet voice. BYRON, *Don Juan*

20653. Apples, pears, and nuts spoil the voice. *Proverb*

20654.
Her voice was ever soft,
Gentle, and low, an excellent thing in woman. SHAKESPEARE,
King Lear

See also: 51, 2041, 2348, 6428.

VOTE AND VOTING

Related Subjects: Democracy, Election, Government, The People, Politics.

20661. Bad officials are elected by good citizens who do not vote.
Anonymous

20662. Your every voter, as surely as your chief magistrate, exercises a public trust. GROVER CLEVELAND

20663. Of this full emancipation of women, the political vote is assuredly not, as is rather commonly supposed in a land of party politics, the be-all and end-all; it as a symbol, whose practical importance—though considerable—is as nothing beside the fulfillment of the idea which it symbolizes. GALSWORTHY

20664.
The freeman, casting with unpurchased hand,
The vote that shakes the turret of the land. O. W. HOLMES,
Poetry, a Metrical Essay

20665. Ballots are the rightful and peaceful successors of bullets.
LINCOLN

20666.
They have such refined and delicate palates
That they can discover no one worthy of their ballots,
And then when some one terrible gets elected
They say, There, that's just what I expected! OGDEN NASH,
Election Day Is a Holiday

See also: 147, 2493, 2498.

VOW

Related Subjects: Oath, Promise, Swearing.

20671. Better is it that thou shouldest not vow, than that thou shouldest vow and not pay.
Bible: Ecclesiastes, v, 5

20672.
Vows with so much passion, swears with so much grace,
That 'tis a kind of heaven to be deluded by him.
NATHANIEL LEE,
Alexander the Great

20673.
Ease would recant
Vows made in pain, as violent and void. MILTON, *Paradise Lost*

20674. Vows made in storms are forgotten in calms. *Proverb*

20675.
'Tis not the many oaths that make
   the truth,
But the plain single vow that is vow'd
   true.   SHAKESPEARE,
      All's Well that Ends Well

20676. The vow that binds too
strictly snaps itself.
   TENNYSON, *Idylls of the King*

See also: 293, 5198.

VULGARITY

Related Subjects: Boasting, Ostentation.

20681. Vulgarity is an inadequate
conception of the art of living.
    MANDELL CREIGHTON,
      Life and Letters

20682. If a person has no delicacy,
he has you in his power.
   HAZLITT, *Literary Remains*

20683. That fellow would vulgarize
the day of judgment.
   DOUGLAS JERROLD, *A Comic Author*

20684. Be thou familiar, but by no
means vulgar.   SHAKESPEARE,
      Hamlet

20685.
So must the writer, whose productions should
Take with the vulgar, be of vulgar
   mould.   EDMUND WALLER,
      To Mr. Killigrew

20686. Vulgarity is simply the conduct of other people.
   OSCAR WILDE, *An Ideal Husband*

20687. Details are always vulgar.
    OSCAR WILDE,
    The Picture of Dorian Gray

See also: 95, 674, 8683, 11116,
17083.

W

WAGES

Related Subjects: Business, Depression, Employment, Industry, Inflation, Labor, Payment, Union, Work.

20691.
What have workers wanted through
   the ages?
Shorter hours and higher wages.
What have employers wanted for
   aye?
Longer hours and lower pay.
      F. P. A.,
     *The Diary of Our Own
     Samuel Pepys*

20692. The labourer is worthy of his
hire.   *Bible: Luke, x, 7*

20693. "A fair day's-wages for a fair
day's-work": it is as just a demand

as governed men ever made of governing. It is the everlasting right of
man.   CARLYLE, *Past and Present*

20694.
Question: Do you consider ten dollars a week enough for a longshoreman with a family to support?
Answer: If that's all he can get, and
he takes it, I should say it's
enough.   J. P. MORGAN,
    *Before the U. S. Commission on
    Industrial Relations.*

20695. From a bad paymaster get
what you can.   *Proverb*

20696. A good paymaster never
wants workmen.   *Proverb*

20697. Better sit idle than work for
nought.   *Proverb*

20698. Men work but slowly that have poor wages. *Proverb*

20699. If you pay not a servant his wages, he will pay himself. *Proverb*

20700. He that serves well need not be afraid to ask his wages. *Proverb*

20701. S'pose you got a job a work an' there's jus' one fella wants the job. You got to pay 'im what he asts. But s'pose they's a hunderd men wants that job. S'pose them men got kids an' them kids is hungry. S'pose a nickel'll buy at leas' sompin for the kids. An' you got a hunderd men. Jus' offer 'em a nickel—why, they'll kill each other fightin' for that nickel. JOHN STEINBECK,
The Grapes of Wrath

See also: 13249, 17985.

WAITING

Related Subjects: Delay, Expectation, Patience, Resignation.

20711. Serene I fold my hands and wait. JOHN BURROUGHS, *Waiting*

20712. Everything comes if a man will only wait. DISRAELI, *Tancred*

20713. Everything comes to him who hustles while he waits.
THOMAS A. EDISON

20714. Alas! all things come too late for those who wait.
J. G. HUNEKER, *Chopin*

20715. Learn to labor and to wait.
LONGFELLOW, *A Psalm of Life*

20716. They also serve who only stand and wait. MILTON,
On His Blindness

20717. Patient waiters are no losers.
Proverb

20718. Everything comes to those who can wait. RABELAIS

20719. I have no mockings or arguments; I witness and wait.
WALT WHITMAN, *Song of Myself*

See also: 17996.

WALKING

Related Subjects: Exercise, Foot, Leg, Shoe, Travel, Wanderlust.

20721.
I nauseate walking; 'tis a country diversion;
I loathe the country
CONGREVE, *The Way of the World*

20722. Walking is the best possible exercise. Habituate yourself to walk very far. JEFFERSON

20723. The humblest conveyances known as "Shanks's mare," and the 'Marrowbone Stage.'
G. A. SALA, *Twice Round the Clock*

20724.
I grant I never saw a goddess go;
My mistress, when she walks, treads on the ground.
SHAKESPEARE, *Sonnet CXXX*

See also: 1083, 16705.

WANDERLUST

Related Subjects: Rest, River, Road, Sea, Ship, Travel, Vagabond, Walking.

20731. Drop anchor anywhere and the anchor will drag—that is, if your soul is a limitless, fathomless sea, and not a dogpond.
ELBERT HUBBARD, *Epigrams*

20732.
Till a voice, as bad as Conscience, rang interminable changes

On one everlasting Whisper day
and night repeated—so:
"Something hidden. Go and find it.
Go and look behind the Ranges—
Something lost behind the Ranges.
Lost and waiting for you. Go!"
> KIPLING, *The Explorer*

20733.
The white moth to the closing vine,
The bee to the opened clover,
And the gipsy blood to the gipsy
blood
Ever the wide world over.
> KIPLING, *The Gipsy Trail*

20734.
You have heard the beat of the off-
shore wind,
And the thresh of the deep-sea rain;
You have heard the song—how long?
how long?
Pull out on the trail again!
> KIPLING, *The Long Trail*

20735.
It's little I know what's in my heart,
What's in my mind it's little I know,
But there's that in me must up and
start,
And it's little I care where my feet
go.
> EDNA ST. VINCENT MILLAY,
> *Departure*

20736.
I cannot rest from travel; I will drink
Life to the lees.   TENNYSON,
> *Ulysses*

WANT AND WANTS

Related Subjects: **Depression, Necessity, Poverty.**

20741. Socrates said, "Those who
want fewest things are nearest to the
gods."   DIOGENES LAERTIUS,
> *Socrates*

20742. How many things there are
that I do not want.   SOCRATES,
*On viewing the wares in the market
place.*

20743. "It is no good asking people
what they want," wrote De Windt.
"That is the error of democracy. You
have first to think out what they
ought to want if society is to be saved.
Then you have to tell them what they
want and see that they get it."
> H. G. WELLS,
> *Shape of Things to Come*

20744. Man wants but little, nor that
little long.   EDWARD YOUNG,
> *Night Thoughts*

See also: 1471, 3464, 9576, 20891.

WAR

Related Subjects: **Army, Conquerors, Death, Defense, Discord,
Enemy, Fight, Force, Imperialism, Kill, Navy, Sailor, Soldier,
Wounds.**

20751. It would be superfluous in me
to point out to your Lordship that
this is war.   CHARLES F. ADAMS

20752. This detestable [Civil] War is
not of our own choosing, and out of it
must grow consequences important to
the welfare of coming generations,
not likely to issue from a continuance
of peace.   CHARLES F. ADAMS,
> *Letter to his Son*

20753. You say there is neither glory
nor honor to be won in civil strife. I
answer, that it cannot be otherwise
than right for me to fight to maintain
that which my ancestors passed their
whole lives in establishing.
> CHARLES F. ADAMS JR.,
> *Letter to his Father*

20754.
>   My voice is still for war.
> Gods! can a Roman senate long debate
> Which of the two to choose, slavery
>   or death? ADDISON, *Cato*

20755. A rich man's war and a poor man's fight. *Anonymous*

20756.
> "It is eighteen years," I cried. "You must come no more.
> We know your names. We know that you are the dead.
> Must you march forever from France and the last, blind war?"
> *"Fool! From the next!"* they said.
> STEPHEN VINCENT BENET, *1936*

20757. There is no discharge in that war. *Bible: Ecclesiastes, viii, 8*

20758. Wars and rumours of wars.
Bible: Matthew, xxiv, 6

20759. There are only two things worth fighting for. One is defense of our homes. The other is the Bill of Rights. War for any other cause is simply a racket. The trouble with America is that the dollar gets restless when it earns only 6 per cent over here. It goes overseas to get 100 per cent. The flag follows the money—and the soldiers follow the flag.
GEN. SMEDLEY BUTLER

20760.
> The Assyrian came down like the wolf on the fold,
> And his cohorts were gleaming in purple and gold. BYRON,
> *The Destruction of Sennacherib*

20761. Battles, in these ages, are transacted by mechanism; with the slightest possible development of human individuality or spontaneity; men now even die, and kill one another, in an artificial manner.
CARLYLE, *The French Revolution*

20762. Nothing can be more disgraceful than to be at war with him with whom you have lived on terms of friendship. CICERO, *De Amicitia*

20763.
> But war's a game which were their subjects wise,
> Kings would not play at.
> COWPER, *The Task*

20764. Must there always be war? Of course it is hard to think that children are born into this world and men and women live for nothing else than to be slaughtered wholesale in a thousand ghastly ways.
CLARENCE DARROW

20765. You may fire when you are ready, Gridley. ADMIRAL DEWEY

20766. War is not "inevitable," but proceeds from definite and removable causes. G. LOWES DICKINSON,
The Choice Before Us

20767. All delays are dangerous in war. DRYDEN, *Tyrannic Love*

20768. War seldom enters but where wealth allures. DRYDEN,
The Hind & the Panther

20769. Monarchs ought to put to death the authors and instigators of war, as their sworn enemies and as dangers to their states.
QUEEN ELIZABETH

20770. So far as business and money are concerned, a country gains nothing by a successful war, even though that war involves the acquisition of immense new provinces.
HAVELOCK ELLIS,
The Task of Social Hygiene

20771. Do not men die fast enough without being destroyed by each other? FENELON, *Telemachus*

20772. The blood of a nation ought never to be shed except for its own preservation in the utmost extremity.
FENELON, *Telemachus*

20773. It simply is not true that war never settles anything.
JUSTICE FRANKFURTER

20774. In my opinion, there never was a good war or a bad peace.
FRANKLIN

20775. War scares are good; real wars will be better. Let there be no mistake about it. Arms dealers want war. They are hypocrites if they deny this. War is to them what milk is to a baby. They fatten on it. They fatten on it like pigs in corn.
JOHN GUNTHER, *Inside Europe*

20776.
"Yes; quaint and curious war is!
You shoot a fellow down
You'd treat if met where any bar is,
Or help to half-a-crown."
THOMAS HARDY, *The Man He Killed*

20777. My argument is that War makes rattling good history; but Peace is poor reading.
THOMAS HARDY, *The Dynasts*

20778. You furnish the pictures and I'll furnish the war.
WILLIAM RANDOLPH HEARST

20779. They wrote in the old days that it is sweet and fitting to die for one's country. But in modern war there is nothing sweet nor fitting in your dying. You will die like a dog for no good reason.
ERNEST HEMINGWAY,
Notes on the Next War

20780. The battle, sir, is not to the strong alone; it is to the vigilant, the active, the brave.   PATRICK HENRY

20781. As the nature of foul weather lieth not in a shower or two of rain but in an inclination thereto of many days together, so the nature of war consisteth not in actual fighting but in the known disposition thereto during all the time there is no assurance to the contrary. All other time is peace.   THOMAS HOBBES, *Leviathan*

20782. I think we shall find ourselves drifting into war with Germany.
COL. HOUSE,
to Pres. Wilson, June 16, 1915

20783. War is an abnormal state of society. Our intelligence should be directed toward the normal, toward peace and ways of creating and sustaining a peaceful existence.
Institute for Propaganda Analysis

20784. War is the most ghastly experience that can come to any country. And always it is the people—not the handful of men in positions of power—who must pay the full price. The price in dollars and cents. The price in dismembered families. The price in heart agonies. The price in bodily suffering. The price in numbed minds. The price in precious human lives. The price in putting together the nation's pieces, afterwards. Always it is the masses who pay.
ROBERT M. LAFOLLETTE

20785.
Ez fur war, I call it murder,—
   There you hev it plain an' flat;
I don't want to go no furder
   Than my Testyment fer that. . . .
LOWELL, *The Biglow Papers*

20786. A 'People's War', blazing up all over the country, will eventually prevent the victor from reaping the full fruits of his victory.
GENERAL LUDENDORFF,
The Nation at War, advising on German procedure if faced with a war on two fronts.

20787. We want no war of conquest. . . . War should never be entered upon until every agency of peace has failed.   WILLIAM McKINLEY

20788. I should like to put asterisks here, and then write: "It was in 1919 that I found myself once again a civilian." For it makes me almost physically sick to think of that nightmare of mental and moral degradation, the war.   A. A. MILNE, *Autobiography*

20789. The brazen throat of war.
MILTON, *Paradise Lost*

20790. My sentence is for open war.
MILTON, *Paradise Lost*

20791. Every war is a national calamity whether victorious or not.
GEN. VON MOLTKE

20792. War hath no fury like a noncombatant.   C. E. MONTAGUE, *Disenchantment*

20793. War alone keys up all human energies to their maximum tension and sets the seal of nobility on those peoples who have the courage to face it.   MUSSOLINI, *Fascism*

20794. Three cheers for war in general!   MUSSOLINI

20795. Speeches made to the people are essential to the arousing of enthusiasm for a war.   MUSSOLINI

20796. I still remember the effect I produced on a small group of Galla tribesmen massed around a man in black clothes. I dropped an aerial torpedo right in the center, and the group opened up like a flowering rose. It was most entertaining.
VITTORIO MUSSOLINI,
in an account of his adventures in Ethiopia.

20797. War involves in its progress such a train of unforeseen and unsupposed circumstances that no human wisdom can calculate the end. It has but one thing certain, and that is to increase taxes.
THOMAS PAINE,
Prospects on the Rubicon

20798. Don't cheer, boys; the poor devils are dying.
CAPT. J. W. PHILIP

20799. A man without one scar to show on his skin, that is smooth and sleek with ease and home-keeping habits, will undertake to define the office and duties of a general.
PLUTARCH, *Lives*

20800. War its thousands slays, Peace, its ten thousands.
BEILBY PORTEUS, *Death*

20801. War makes thieves, and peace hangs them.   *Proverb*

20802. War is death's feast. *Proverb*

20803. The fear of war is worse than war itself.   *Proverb*

20804. That war is only just which is necessary.   *Proverb*

20805. The surest way to prevent war is not to fear it.   JOHN RANDOLPH

20806. With supreme irony, the war to "make the world safe for democracy" ended by leaving democracy more unsafe in the world than at any time since the collapse of the revolutions of 1848.
JAMES H. ROBINSON,
The Human Comedy

20807. Also our present emergency and a common sense of decency make it imperative that no new group of war millionaires come into being in this nation as a result of the struggles abroad. The American people will not relish the idea of any American citizen growing rich and fat in an emergency of blood and slaughter and human suffering.

> FRANKLIN D. ROOSEVELT,
> *Fireside Chat, May 26, 1940*

20808.
(Ten thousand men and boys twist on their bodies in a red soak along a river edge,
Gasping of wounds, calling for water, some rattling death in their throats.)
Who by Christ would guess what it cost to move two buttons one inch on the war map here in front of the newspaper office where the freckle-faced young man is laughing to us?

> CARL SANDBURG, *Buttons*

20809. We are mad, not only individually, but nationally. We check manslaughter and isolated murders; but what of war and the much vaunted crime of slaughtering whole peoples? SENECA

20810.
When we, the Workers, all demand:
"What are we fighting for?" . . .
Then, then we'll end that stupid crime,
That devil's madness—War.

> R. W. SERVICE, *Michael*

20811.
In peace there's nothing so becomes a man
As modest stillness and humility;
But when the blast of war blows in our ears,
Then imitate the action of the tiger:
Stiffen the sinews, summon up the blood. SHAKESPEARE, *Henry V*

20812. Cry "Havoc!" and let slip the dogs of war. SHAKESPEARE,
Julius Caesar

20813.
> He is come to open
> The purple testament of bleeding war.
> SHAKESPEARE, *Richard II*

20814. Grim-visaged war hath smoothed his wrinkled front.
> SHAKESPEARE, *Richard III*

20815. Ever since Thucydides wrote his history, it has been on record that when the angel of death sounds his trumpet the pretences of civilization are blown from men's heads into the mud like hats in a gust of wind.
> SHAW, *Heartbreak House: Preface*

20816. If you made a poll of newspaper editors, you might find a great many who think that war is evil. But if you were to take a census among pastors of fashionable metropolitan churches—
> SIMEON STRUNSKY,
> *Professor Latimer's Progress*

20817. I am tired and sick of war. Its glory is all moonshine. It is only those who have neither fired a shot nor heard the shrieks and groans of the wounded who cry aloud for blood, more vengeance, more desolation. War is hell. GEN. SHERMAN

20818. War at best is barbarism.
> GEN. SHERMAN

20819. War is cruel and you cannot refine it. GEN. SHERMAN

20820. Consider war. Women bear children with much pain, and raise them with loving care, and then send them out, at the very prime of their lives, to be blown to pieces by shot and shell. Other men in factories, who might be making the means of human happiness—automobiles and radio sets and books and music—these men are making explosives to wipe out whole cities, and gasses to poison the inhabitants. In the late war we destroyed 30,000,000 human beings and $300,000,000,000 worth of treasure, the produce of a whole generation of useful toil.   UPTON SINCLAIR

20821. War loves to prey upon the young. SOPHOCLES, *Scyrian Women*

20822.
War never slays a bad man in its course,
But the good always!
SOPHOCLES, *Philoctetes*

20823. Give me the money that has been spent in war, and I will clothe every man, woman and child in an attire of which kings and queens would be proud. I will build a school-house in every valley over the whole earth. I will crown every hillside with a place of worship consecrated to the gospel of peace. CHARLES SUMNER

20824.
Heard the heavens fill with shouting, and there rain'd a ghastly dew
From the nations' airy navies grappling in the central blue.
TENNYSON, *Locksley Hall*

20825. All great wars, involving the major nations of men, are fought for peace. They are show-downs to determine the conditions under which hundreds of millions of men are to live their peace-time lives once the war is over.
DOROTHY THOMPSON, *On the Record*

20826. The Peloponnesus and Athens were both full of young men whose inexperience made them eager to take up arms. THUCYDIDES, *History*

20827. And so once more men will be made savage, fierce, and brutal, and love will wane in the world . . . And so once more the men who reaped profit from it all, will assert

with assurance that since there has been a war there must needs have been one, and that other wars must follow, and they will again prepare future generations for a continuance of slaughter, depraving them from their birth.   TOLSTOY,
The Coming of War

20828. It is said that God is always on the side of the heaviest battalions.
VOLTAIRE

20829. The real war will never get in the books. WALT WHITMAN,
Specimen Days

20830.
Beautiful that war and all its deeds of carnage must in time be utterly lost,
That the hands of the sisters Death and Night incessantly softly wash again and ever again, this soiled world.   WALT WHITMAN,
Reconciliation

20831.
Away with themes of war! away with War itself!
Hence from my shuddering sight, to never more return, that show of blacken'd, mutilated corpses!
That hell unpent, and raid of blood— fit for wild tigers, or for loptongued wolves—not reasoning men!
And in its stead speed Industry's campaigns.
With thy undaunted armies, Engineering!
Thy pennants, Labor, loosen'd to the breeze!
Thy bugles sounding loud and clear!
WALT WHITMAN

20832. As long as war is regarded as wicked, it will always have its fascination. When it is looked upon as vulgar, it will cease to be popular.
OSCAR WILDE, *The Critic as Artist*

20833. Today it is the duty of all citizens of a democracy to understand this business of fighting, for a People's War is the only effective answer to Totalitarian War.
TOM WINTRINGHAM,
New Ways of War

20834. It has happened several times in the past that a People's War has broken the most powerful military machine of the period.
TOM WINTRINGHAM,
New Ways of War

20835. The shape of war has changed, throughout history, principally in accordance with changes in civilian methods of production and transportation.
TOM WINTRINGHAM,
New Ways of War

20836. Faraday, the scientist, "inventing electricity," and Clausewitz, the military theorist, analysing war, were working at about the same time; Faraday's work—in its present form as the magneto and the wireless valve —has altered warfare more than the labours of Clausewitz, war's greatest scientist. TOM WINTRINGHAM,
New Ways of War

20837. War is not only a question of fighting; it is also a question of politics. In fact the classic definition of war, made by the greatest German military theorist, Clausewitz, is that war is a continuation of politics by other means.
TOM WINTRINGHAM,
New Ways of War

20838. Modern war makes imposed, arbitrary and automatic discipline and rigid tactics not only useless but harmful, unsuccessful.
TOM WINTRINGHAM,
New Ways of War

20839. Modern war makes voluntarily, understood and thinking discipline and elastic tactics based on initiative and independence, more valuable than ever before.
TOM WINTRINGHAM,
New Ways of War

20840. There is only one thing to do about bombers. That is stay in a hole and pay attention to your business. Your business, usually, is not with them, but with men and machines on the ground. Always remember that Hitler is trying to make you afraid— or is perhaps succeeding in making you afraid—simply by making various sorts of loud noise.
TOM WINTRINGHAM,
New Ways of War

20841.
One to destroy is murder by the law,
And gibbets keep the lifted hand in awe;
To murder thousands takes a specious name,
War's glorious art, and gives immortal fame.   EDWARD YOUNG,
Love of Fame

See also: 475, 694, 901, 1502, 2399, 2617, 2833, 3327, 3480, 3490, 3616, 5411, 5417, 6783, 6953, 7569, 11250, 12075, 12405, 13707, 15783, 16205.

WARMTH

Related Subjects: **Cheerfulness, Coal, Comfort, Fire, Friend.**

20851. Not so hot.
SHAKESPEARE, *The Winter's Tale*

20852. "Heat, ma'am!" I said; "it was so dreadful here, that I found there was nothing left for it but to take off my flesh and sit in my bones." SYDNEY SMITH,
Lady Holland's Memoir

See also: 1362, 7168.

WARNING

Related Subjects: Advice, Caution, Counsel, Danger, Recklessness, Safety, Threat.

20861.
I know the warning song is sung in vain,
That few will hear, and fewer heed the strain.   COWPER,
Expostulation

20862.
None pities him that's in the snare,
Who warned before, would not beware.   ROBERT HERRICK

20863. Forewarned is forearmed.
PLAUTUS, *Pseudolus*

20864.
For many men that stumble at the threshold
Are well foretold that danger lurks within.   SHAKESPEARE, *Henry VI*

WASHING

Related Subjects: Bathing, Cleanliness, Dirt, Water.

20871. Wash me, and I shall be whiter than snow. *Bible: Psalms, li, 7*

20872. Wash your hands often, your feet seldom, and your head never.
Proverb

20873. It will all come out in the wash.   *Proverb*

20874. I will wash my hands and wait upon you.   *Proverb*

20875. I wash, wring, brew, bake, scour, dress meat and drink.
SHAKESPEARE,
The Merry Wives of Windsor

See also: 2205, 2227, 4674.

WASHINGTON, GEORGE

20881.
Washington,
Whose every battle-field is holy ground,
Which breathes of nations saved, not worlds undone.   BYRON,
Don Juan

20882. Here you would know, and enjoy, what posterity will say of Washington. For a thousand leagues have nearly the same effect with a thousand years.   FRANKLIN,
Letter to Washington from the Court of France

20883. On the whole his character was, in its mass, perfect, in nothing bad, in few points indifferent; and it may truly be said that never did nature and fortune combine more perfectly to make a man great.
JEFFERSON

20884. A citizen, first in war, first in peace, and first in the hearts of his countrymen.   COL. HENRY LEE

20885.
Oh, Washington! thou hero, patriot sage,
Friend of all climes, and pride of every age!   THOMAS PAINE,
Washington

20886. The prevailin' weakness of most public men is to slop over. G. Washington never slopt over.
ARTEMUS WARD,
Fourth of July Oration

20887. As to pay, sir, I beg leave to assure the Congress that as no pecuniary consideration could have tempted me to accept this arduous employment at the expense of my domestic ease and happiness, I do not wish to make any profit from it.
WASHINGTON

20888. "George," said his father, "do you know who killed that beautiful little cherry tree yonder in the garden?" . . . Looking at his father with the sweet face of youth brightened with the inexpressible charm of all-conquering truth, he bravely cried out, "I can't tell a lie, Pa; you know I can't tell a lie. I did cut it with my hatchet." PARSON WEEMS,
The Life of George Washington

WASTE

Related Subjects: Economy, Excess, Extravagance, Futility, Idleness, Prodigality.

20891.
For wilful waste makes woeful want,
  And I may live to say,
Oh! how I wish I had the bread
That once I threw away!
Anonymous, The Crust of Bread

20892. Wherefore do ye spend money for that which is not bread? and your labour for that which satisfieth not?
Bible: Isaiah, lv, 2

20893. To what purpose is this waste?
Bible: Matthew, xxvi, 8

20894. Wasted his substance with riotous living. *Bible: Luke, xv, 13*

20895.
She saw two legs were lost on him
Who never meant to run.
GEORGE CANNING

20896. Waste not want not is my doctrine. CHARLES KINGSLEY,
Westward Ho!

20897. In my creed, waste of public money is like the sin against the Holy Ghost. JOHN MORLEY, *Recollections*

20898. Wilful waste brings woeful want. *Proverb*

20899. A man can never thrive who has a wasteful wife. *Proverb*

20900.
He that keeps not crust nor crumb,
Weary of all, shall want some.
SHAKESPEARE, *King Lear*

20901. We waste our lights in vain, like lamps by day.
SHAKESPEARE, *Romeo and Juliet*

20902.
          The remainder viands
We do not throw in unrespective sink
Because we now are full.
SHAKESPEARE, *Troilus and Cressida*

20903. The clock upbraids me with the waste of time.
SHAKESPEARE, *Twelfth Night*

See also: 433, 1706, 2633, 5028, 9576.

WATCH, WATCHFULNESS

Related Subjects: Attention, Caution, Interest, Preparedness, Prudence.

20911. Watchman, what of the night?
Bible: Isaiah, xxi, 11

20912.
For some must watch, while some must sleep:
So runs the world away.
SHAKESPEARE, *Hamlet*

20913. She watches him as a cat would watch a mouse. SWIFT,
Polite Conversation

Timepieces

20914. "Wal'r," said the captain, . . . "a parting gift, my lad. Put it back half an hour every morning, and about another quarter towards the afternoon, and it's a watch that'll do you credit." DICKENS,
Dombey & Son

20915.
Ever out of frame,
And never going aright, being a watch,
But being watch'd that it may still go right!   SHAKESPEARE,
Love's Labour's Lost

20916. And perchance wind up my watch.   SHAKESPEARE,
Twelfth Night

See also: 11109, 15632.

WATER

Related Subjects: Bathing, Dew, Fish, Island, River, Rust, Sea, Swimming, Washing.

20921. Unstable as water, thou shalt not excel.   *Bible: Genesis, xlix, 4*

20922. The noise of many waters.
Bible: Psalms xciii, 4

20923. As water spilt on the ground, which cannot be gathered up again.
Bible: 2 Samuel, xiv, 14

20924. The waters wear the stones.
Bible: Job, xiv, 19

20925.
Water, water, everywhere,
Nor any drop to drink.
COLERIDGE, *The Ancient Mariner*

20926. Everywhere water is a thing of beauty, gleaming in the dewdrop; singing in the summer rain; shining in the ice-gems till the leaves all seem to turn to living jewels; spreading a golden veil over the setting sun; or a white gauze around the midnight moon.   J. B. GOUGH,
A Glass of Water

20927.
Here's to old Adam's crystal ale,
Clear sparkling and divine,
Fair H$_2$O, long may you flow,
We drink your health (in wine).
OLIVER HERFORD,
Toast: Adam's Crystal Ale

20928. Water washes everything.
Proverb

20929.
In smooth water God help me; in rough water
I will help myself.   *Proverb*

20930. Dirty water does not wash clean.   *Proverb*

20931. Foul water will quench fire.
Proverb

20932. We never miss the water till the well runs dry.   *Proverb*

20933. Oil on troubled waters.
Proverb

20934. Still waters run deep.
Proverb

20935.
The waves settled placidly over his head,
And his last remark was a bubble.
INNES RANDOLPH, *A Fish Story*

20936.
Here's that which is too weak to be a sinner,
Honest water, which ne'er left man i' the mire.   SHAKESPEARE,
Timon of Athens

20937. Love's fire heats water, water cools not love.   SHAKESPEARE,
Sonnet CLIV

See also: 2201, 2442, 3495, 4906, 12933, 19632, 21328.

WATERLOO

Related Subjects: Conquerors, Defeat, Victory.

20941. Waterloo is a battle of the first rank won by a captain of the second.
VICTOR HUGO, *Les Miserables*

20942. Waterloo is not a battle; it is a change of front on the part of the Universe.
VICTOR HUGO, *Les Miserables*

20943. Every man meets his Waterloo at last. WENDELL PHILLIPS

20944. The battle of Waterloo was won on the playing fields of Eton.
DUKE OF WELLINGTON

WEAKNESS

Related Subjects: Coward, Decay, Failure, Faults.

20951.
He knows not how to wink at human frailty,
Or pardon weakness that he never felt. ADDISON, *Cato*

20952. The cord breaketh at last by the weakest pull. BACON, *Essays*

20953. All hands shall be feeble, and all knees shall be weak as water.
Bible: Ezekiel, vii, 17

20954. The spirit indeed is willing, but the flesh is weak.
Bible: Matthew, xxvi, 41

20955. Better make a weak man your enemy than your friend.
JOSH BILLINGS, *Affurisms*

20956. The concessions of the weak are the concessions of fear. BURKE

20957. People in general will much better bear being told of their vices and crimes than of their failings and weaknesses.
LORD CHESTERFIELD, *Letters*

20958. To be in the weakest camp is to be in the strongest school.
G. K. CHESTERTON, *Heretics*

20959. Throughout life, our worst weaknesses and meannesses are usu-ally committed for the sake of the people whom we most despise.
DICKENS, *Great Expectations*

20960. People who have no weaknesses are terrible; there is no way of taking advantage of them.
ANATOLE FRANCE,
The Crime of Sylvestre Bonnard

20961. Amiable weaknesses of human nature. GIBBON,
Decline & Fall

20962.
And the weak soul, within itself unblest,
Leans for all pleasure on another's breast. GOLDSMITH, *The Traveller*

20963. We are not weak if we make a proper use of those means which the God of Nature has placed in our power. PATRICK HENRY

20964. There are two kinds of weakness, that which breaks and that which bends.
LOWELL, *Among My Books*

20965. Men's weaknesses are often necessary to the purposes of life.
MAETERLINCK, *Joyzelle*

20966.
To be weak is miserable,
Doing or suffering.
MILTON, *Paradise Lost*

20967. Fine by defect, and delicately weak. POPE, *Moral Essays*

20968. Weak men had need be witty.
Proverb

20969. Every man has his weak side.
Proverb

20970. The weakest goes to the wall.
SHAKESPEARE, *Romeo and Juliet*

20971.
What 'twas weak to do
'Tis weaker to lament, once being done. SHELLEY, *The Cenci*

20972. We have unmistakable proof that throughout all past time, there has been a ceaseless devouring of the weak by the strong.
HERBERT SPENCER, *First Principles*

20973. You cannot run away from a weakness; you must some time fight it out or perish; and if that be so, why not now, and where you stand?
STEVENSON, *The Amateur Emigrant*

20974.
Weakness to be wroth with weakness! woman's pleasure, woman's pain—
Nature made them blinder motions bounded in a shallower brain.
TENNYSON, *Locksley Hall*

20975. I was weak as a rained-on bee.
RIDGELY TORRENCE,
The Tramp Sings

See also: 1031, 2222, 3073, 3996, 4711, 5373, 5478, 7466, 11785, 13505, 13886, 20886.

WEALTH, see Riches

WEATHER

Related Subjects: Clouds, Fog, The Heavens, Thunder and Lightning, Rain, Snow, Storm, Wind.

20981.
And altogether it's very bad weather,
And an unpleasant sort of a night!
R. H. BARHAM, *The Nurse's Story*

20982. When it is evening, ye say, It will be fair weather: for the sky is red. And in the morning, It will be foul weather today for the sky is red and lowering.
Bible: Matthew, xvi, 2-3

20983. I was born with a chronic anxiety about the weather.
JOHN BURROUGHS,
Is It Going to Rain?

20984. For the man sound in body and serene of mind there is no such thing as bad weather; every sky has its beauty, and storms which whip the blood do but make it pulse more vigorously.   GEORGE GISSING,
*The Private Papers of
Henry Ryecroft*

20985.
We will not woo foul weather all too soon,
Or nurse November on the lap of June.
THOMAS HOOD,
The Plea of the Midsummer Fairies

20986. When two Englishmen meet, their first talk is of the weather.
SAMUEL JOHNSON, *The Idler*

20987. The weather and my mood have little connection. I have my foggy and my fine days within me.
PASCAL, *Pensées*

20988.
To talk of the weather, it's nothing but folly,
For when it rains on the hill, it shines in the valley.   *Proverb*

20989. Change of weather is the discourse of fools.   *Proverb*

20990. In the old of the moon a cloudy morning bodes a fair afternoon.   *Proverb*

20991. If St. Swithin weep, that year the proverb says, the weather will be foul for forty days.   *Proverb*

20992. An evening red and a morning gray is a sign of a fair day.
Proverb

20993. A foul morn may turn to a fair day.   *Proverb*

20994.
It hain't no use to grumble and complain,

It's jest as easy to rejoice;
When God sorts out the weather and
   sends rain,
Why rain's my choice.
   JAMES WHITCOMB RILEY,
     Wet-Weather Talk

20995. I tax not you, you elements,
with unkindness.
   SHAKESPEARE, *King Lear*

20996. Many can brook the weather
that love not the wind.
SHAKESPEARE, *Love's Labour's Lost*

20997. What would have become of
us had it pleased Providence to make
the weather unchangeable? Think of
the state of destitution of the morning callers.   SYDNEY SMITH,
     Lady Holland's Memoir

20998. Plaguy twelve-penny weather.
   SWIFT

20999. There is a sumptuous variety
about New England weather that
compels the stranger's admiration—
and regret. . . . In the Spring I
have counted one hundred and thirty-
six different kinds of weather inside
of twenty-four hours. MARK TWAIN

21000. Everybody talks about the
weather, but nobody does anything
about it. CHARLES DUDLEY WARNER

See also: 1336.

WEDDING

Related Subjects: Bride, Courtship, Marriage, Preacher.

21001. If it were not for the Presents, an Elopement would be Preferable.   GEORGE ADE,
     Forty Modern Fables

21002. What therefore God hath
joined together, let not man put
asunder.   *Bible: Matthew, xix, 6*

21003. With this Ring I thee wed.
   Book of Common Prayer

21004. With all my worldly goods I
thee endow.
   Book of Common Prayer

21005. To have and to hold from this
day forward, for better, for worse,
for richer, for poorer, in sickness,
and in health, to love and to cherish,
till death us do part.
   Book of Common Prayer

21006.
Happiness untold awaits them
When the parson consecrates them.
   W. S. GILBERT, *Ruddigore*

21007.
For next to that interesting job,
The hanging of Jack, or Bill, or Bob,
There's nothing so draws a London
   mob
As the noosing of very rich people.
   THOMAS HOOD, *Miss Kilmansegg*

21008.
The voice that breathed o'er Eden,
   That earliest wedding-day,
The primal marriage blessing,
   It hath not passed away.
   JOHN KEBLE, *Holy Matrimony*

21009. Saw a wedding in the church;
and strange to see what delight we
married people have to see these poor
fools decoyed into our condition.
   SAMUEL PEPYS, *Diary*

21010. You've picked an unlucky
day for changing your name.
   PLAUTUS, *Asinaria*

21011. A man may weep upon his
wedding day.
   SHAKESPEARE, *Henry VIII*

21012. What God hath joined together no man shall ever put asunder: God will take care of that.
   BERNARD SHAW, *Getting Married*
See also: 1911.

WEED

Related Subjects: Flowers, Garden, Grass.

21021. Call us not weeds; we are flowers of the sea.
E. L. AVELINE, *The Mother's Fables*

21022. An ill weed grows apace.
GEORGE CHAPMAN,
An Humorous Day's Mirth

21023.
The flowers are loved, the weeds are spurned,
But for them both the suns are burned;
And when, at last, they fail the day,
The long night folds them all away.
J. V. CHENEY, *Weeds and Flowers*

21024. What I thought was a flower is only a weed, and is worthless.
LONGFELLOW,
Courtship of Miles Standish

21025.
A weed is no more than a flower in disguise,
Which is seen through at once, if love give a man eyes.
LOWELL, *A Fable for Critics*

21026. The richest soil, if uncultivated, produces the rankest weeds.
PLUTARCH, *Lives*

21027. He that bites on every weed must needs light on poison. *Proverb*

21028. One ill weed mars a whole mess of pottage. *Proverb*

21029.
Nothing teems
But hateful docks, rough thistles, kecksies, burs,
Losing both beauty and utility.
SHAKESPEARE, *Henry V*

21030.
Now 'tis the spring, and weeds are shallow-rooted;
Suffer them now and they'll o'ergrow the garden.
SHAKESPEARE, *Henry VI*

21031.
Burdocks, hemlock, nettles, cuckoo-flowers,
Darnel, and all the idle weeds that grow
In our sustaining corn.
SHAKESPEARE, *King Lear*

21032.
O thou weed,
Who art so lovely fair and smell'st so sweet
That the sense aches at thee, would thou hadst ne'er been born!
SHAKESPEARE, *Othello*

21033. Sweet flowers are slow and weeds make haste.
SHAKESPEARE, *Richard III*

21034. Lilies that fester smell far worse than weeds.
SHAKESPEARE, *Sonnet XCIV*

21035.
Once in a golden hour
I cast to earth a seed.
Up there came a flower,
The people said, a weed.
TENNYSON, *The Flower*

WEEPING, see Tears

WEIGHT

Related Subject: Fatness.

21041. A really busy person never knows how much he weighs.
E. W. HOWE, *Country Town Sayings*

21042. Good weight and measure is heaven's treasure. *Proverb*

21043. I have a kind of alacrity in sinking.   SHAKESPEARE, *The Merry Wives of Windsor*

See also: 2568.

WELCOME, see Hospitality

WEST

Related Subjects: East, North.

21051. Odd, how all dying things turn to the West, the region of questions. So mourners on the Nile consigned the mummied citizen to the mercies of the West and soldiers of the recent muddy mess in upper France "went West" to join Hiawatha, King Arthur and the ecstatic nun Petronilla who saw God descending from the West in the shape of a fish-hook to lift her virgin soul into bliss.
THOMAS BEER, *The Mauve Decade*

21052.
Out where the handclasp's a little
   stronger,
Out where the smile dwells a little
   longer,
   That's where the West begins.
ARTHUR CHAPMAN,
Out Where the West Begins

21053. Go West, young man, and grow up with the country.
HORACE GREELEY,
Hints Toward Reform

21054.
Where the prairies, like seas where the billows have rolled,
Are broad as the kingdoms and empires of old.
CHARLES MACKAY, *To the West*

21055.
Olivia: There lies your way, due west.
Viola: Then westward-ho!
SHAKESPEARE, *Twelfth Night*

21056. Go west, young man.
JOHN SOULE

See also: 8387.

WHEEL

Related Subjects: Automobile, Circles.

21061. Put your shoulder to the wheel.   AESOP,
Hercules and the Waggoner

21062. Their appearance and their work were as it were a wheel in the middle of a wheel.
Bible: Ezekiel, i, 16

21063. I'll put a spoke among your wheels.
JOHN FLETCHER, *The Mad Lover*

21064. The worst wheel of the cart makes the most noise.
FRANKLIN, *Poor Richard*

21065. I want to see the wheels go round.
JOHN HABBERTON, *Helen's Babies*

21066. The wheel has come full circle.   SHAKESPEARE, *King Lear*

See also: 3763.

WHITMAN, WALT

21071. We go to Whitman for his attitude toward life and the universe; we go to stimulate and fortify our souls; in short for his cosmic philosophy incarnated in a man.
JOHN BURROUGHS, *The Last Harvest*

21072. W. W. is the Christ of the modern world—he alone redeems it, justifies it, shows it divine.
JOHN BURROUGHS, *The Last Harvest*

21073. As Caesar Augustus found a Rome of brick and left it a Rome of marble, so Walt Whitman found the everyday world around us a world of familiar substance and left it a world aureoled in mystery.

B. DE CASSERES, *Philistine*

21074.
The American poet Whitman
Did little to assist the razor industry,
But he erected a plausible philosophy
Of indolence,
Which, without soft concealments,
He called *Loafing. . . .*
He was deficient in humour,
But he had a good time.

CHRISTOPHER MORLEY,
A Happy Life

21075. I sound my barbaric yawp over the roofs of the world.

WALT WHITMAN, *Song of Myself*

21076. No one will ever get at my verses who insists upon viewing them as a literary performance.

WALT WHITMAN,
A Backward Glance O'er Travel'd Roads

21077. Democracy's divine protagonist.

F. H. WILLIAMS, *Walt Whitman*

WHORE

Related Subjects: Lust, Sin, Temptation, Vice, Wickedness.

21081.
Who drives an ass and leads a whore,
Hath pain and sorrow evermore.

Anonymous

21082. For the lips of a strange woman drop as a honeycomb, and her mouth is smoother than oil: But her end is bitter as wormwood, sharp as a two-edged sword. Her feet go down to death; her steps take hold on hell.   *Bible: Proverbs, v, 3-5*

21083. Walk with stretched forth necks and wanton eyes, walking and mincing as they go.

Bible: Isaiah, iii, 16

21084.
The harlot's cry from street to street
Shall weave old England's winding-sheet,
The winner's shout, the loser's curse,
Dance before dead England's hearse.

BLAKE, *Auguries of Innocence*

21085.
For no man tells his son the truth
For fear he speak of sin;
And every man cries, "Woe, alas!"
And every man goes in.

DANA BURNET,
Sisters of the Cross of Shames

21086. Sampson with his strong Body, had a weak Head, or he would not have laid it in a Harlot's lap.

FRANKLIN, *Poor Richard*

21087.
Wanton look and twinkling,
Laughing and tickling,
Open breast and singing,
These without lying
Are tokens of whoring.

HAZLITT, *English Proverbs*

21088. In calling a prostitute an "unfortunate" the Victorians wished to imply that a prostitute was someone who had invested in the wrong stock, in spite of the advice of more experienced investors.

HUGH KINGSMILL, *Matthew Arnold*

21089. Once a whore, and ever a whore.   HENRY PARROT,
Laquei Ridiculosi

21090.
And thought the nation ne'er would thrive
Till all the whores were burnt alive.

MATTHEW PRIOR, *Paulo Purganti*

21091. A woman that paints puts up a bill that she is to let.   *Proverb*

21092. In silk and scarlet walks many a harlot.   *Proverb*

21093. A young whore, an old saint.   *Proverb*

21094.
No, he hath enjoy'd her:
She hath bought the name of whore thus dearly. . . .
She hath been colted by him.
    SHAKESPEARE, *Cymbeline*

21095.
I have heard I am a strumpet; and mine ear,
Therein false struck, can take no greater wound,
Nor tent to bottom that.
    SHAKESPEARE, *Cymbeline*

21096. Ever your fresh whore and your powder'd bawd.
SHAKESPEARE, *Measure for Measure*

21097. Your whores, sir, being members of my occupation, used painting.
SHAKESPEARE, *Measure for Measure*

21098. A common stale.
    SHAKESPEARE,
Much Ado About Nothing

21099.
A housewife that by selling her desires
Buys herself bread and clothes.
    SHAKESPEARE, *Othello*

21100.
Was this fair paper, this most goodly book,
Made to write "whore" upon?
    SHAKESPEARE, *Othello*

21101.
If to preserve this vessel for my lord
From any other foul unlawful touch
Be not to be a strumpet, I am none.
    SHAKESPEARE, *Othello*

21102.
I cannot say "whore":
It does abhor me now I speak the word;
To do the act that might the addition earn
Not the world's mass of vanity could make me.
    SHAKESPEARE, *Othello*

21103. This is the fruit of whoring.
    SHAKESPEARE, *Othello*

21104.
Be whores still;
And he whose pious breath seeks to convert you,
Be strong in whore, allure him, burn him up.
    SHAKESPEARE, *Timon of Athens*

21105. I never heard she was a naughty pack.
    SWIFT, *Polite Conversation*

21106. Indeed the profession she followed was one of those that emphasize the dim notion that lies at the back of many minds: the notion that we are not necessary to anyone, that attachments weave and unweave at the mercy of separation, satiety and experience. The loneliest associations are those that pretend to intimacy.
    THORNTON WILDER,
The Woman of Andros

21107.
When dying sinners, to blot out their score,
Bequeath the church the leavings of a whore.
    EDWARD YOUNG, *Love of Fame*

21108.
The whore is proud her beauties are the dread
Of peevish virtue, and the marriage-bed.
    EDWARD YOUNG, *Love of Fame*

See also: 1095, 3492, 7738, 8035, 13188.

WICKEDNESS

Related Subjects: Baseness, Character, Conscience, Error, Evil, Guilt, Knave, Malevolence, Morality, Perversity, Sin, Vice, Villainy, Whore.

21111. As saith the proverb of the ancients, Wickedness proceedeth from the wicked.
Bible: 1 Samuel, xxiv, 13

21112. Though wickedness be sweet in his mouth, though he hide it under his tongue. *Bible: Job, xx, 12*

21113. How oft is the candle of the wicked put out! and how oft cometh their destruction upon them! . . . They are as stubble before the wind, and as chaff that the storm carrieth away. *Bible: Job, xxi, 17, 18*

21114. I have seen the wicked in great power, and spreading himself like a green bay tree. Yet he passed away, and, lo, he was not: yea, I sought him, but he could not be found. *Bible: Psalms, xxxvii, 35, 36*

21115. The way of transgressors is hard. *Bible: Proverbs, xiii, 15*

21116. There is no peace, saith the Lord, unto the wicked.
Bible: Isaiah, xlviii, 22

21117. Let the wicked forsake his way, and the unrighteous man his thoughts. *Bible: Isaiah, lv, 7*

21118. Ye have ploughed wickedness, ye have reaped iniquity.
Bible: Hosea, x, 13

21119. Wide is the gate, and broad is the way, that leadeth to destruction.
Bible: Matthew, vii, 13

21120. The fine Felicity and flower of wickedness. BROWNING,
The Ring and the Book

21121. God bears with the wicked, but not forever.
CERVANTES, *Don Quixote*

21122. For never, never wicked man was wise. HOMER, *Odyssey*

21123. No man ever became extremely wicked all at once. JUVENAL

21124. The world loves a spice of wickedness. LONGFELLOW, *Hyperion*

21125.
All wickedness is weakness; that plea, therefore,
With God or man will gain thee no remission.
MILTON, *Samson Agonistes*

21126. The success of the wicked entices many more.
PHAEDRUS, *Fables*

21127. A wicked man is his own hell.
Proverb

21128. Woe be to the wicked, and woe be to them that cleave to them.
Proverb

21129. The wicked heart never fears God, but when it thunders. *Proverb*

21130. He that worketh wickedness by another is wicked himself.
Proverb

21131. Better dwell with a dragon than with a wicked woman. *Proverb*

21132. One man's wickedness may easily become all men's curse.
PUBLILIUS SYRUS, *Sententiae*

21133. No one is so wicked as to wish to appear wicked.
QUINTILIAN,
De Institutione Oratoria

21134. And now am I, if a man should speak truly, little better than one of the wicked.

SHAKESPEARE, *Henry IV*

21135.
What rein can hold licentious wickedness
When down the hill he holds his fierce career?

SHAKESPEARE, *Henry V*

21136. 'Cause I's wicked,—I is. I's mighty wicked, anyhow, I can't help it.   HARRIET BEECHER STOWE,
Uncle Tom's Cabin

See also: 1, 4013, 5650, 5945, 8813, 9683, 11445, 12891, 15669, 17199, 20636.

WIDOW

Related Subjects: Marriage, Wife.

21141. These widows, sir, are the most perverse creatures in the world.

ADDISON, *The Spectator*

21142. I caused the widow's heart to sing for joy. *Bible: Job, xxix, 13*

21143.
Honour is like a widow, won
With brisk attempt and putting on;
With ent'ring manfully, and urging,
Not slow approaches, like a virgin.

SAMUEL BUTLER, *Hudibras*

21144. Be wery careful o' vidders all your life.

DICKENS, *Pickwick Papers*

21145. I have heerd how many ord'-nary women one vidder's equal to, in pint o' comin' over you. I think it's five-and-twenty, but I don't rightly know vether it a'n't more.

DICKENS, *Pickwick Papers*

21146.
We'll play at widows, and we'll pass our time

Railing against the perfidy of man.

W. S. GILBERT,
Pygmalion and Galatea

21147. A widow of doubtful age will marry almost any sort of a white man.   HORACE GREELEY,
Letter to Dr. Griswold

21148. The shameless Chloe placed on the tombs of her seven husbands the inscription, "The work of Chloe." How could she have expressed herself more plainly?

MARTIAL, *Epigrams*

21149.
And I'd rather be bride to a lad gone down
Than widow to one safe home.

EDNA ST. VINCENT MILLAY, *Keen*

21150. And here do I see what creatures widows are in weeping for their husbands and then presently leaving off; but I cannot wonder at it, the cares of the world taking place of all other passions.

SAMUEL PEPYS, *Diary*

21151.
No crafty widows shall approach my bed;
Those are too wise for bachelors to wed.   POPE, *January and May*

21152. Be wary how you marry one that hath cast her rider, I mean a widow.   *Proverb*

21153. Who marries a widow and two daughters marries three thieves.
Proverb

21154. Sorrow for a husband is like a pain in the elbow, sharp and short.
Proverb

21155. A good occasion of courtship is when the widow returns from the funeral.   *Proverb*

21156. He who marries a widow will often have a dead man's head thrown in his dish.   *Proverb*

21157. A buxom widow must be either married, buried, or shut up in a convent.   *Proverb*

21158.
Tell him, in hope he'll prove a widower shortly,
I'll wear the willow garland for his sake.   SHAKESPEARE, *Henry VI*

21159.
Thou art a widow; yet thou art a mother,
And hast the comfort of thy children left thee.
        SHAKESPEARE, *Richard III*

21160. A married man can do anything he likes if his wife don't mind. A widower can't be too careful.
        BERNARD SHAW, *Misalliance*

21161.
He that would woo a maid must feign, lie and flatter,
But he that woos a widow must down with his britches and at her.
        NATHANIEL SMITH,
        Quakers' Spiritual Court

21162.
He first deceased; she for a little tried
To live without him, liked it not, and died.   SIR HENRY WOTTON,
        Upon the Death of Sir Albert Morton's Wife

See also: 13469, 15249.

WIFE

Related Subjects: **Family, Husband, Marriage, Mistress, Widow.**

21171. Every man who is high up loves to think that he has done it all himself; and the wife smiles, and lets it go at that.   J. M. BARRIE,
        What Every Woman Knows

21172. Whoso findeth a wife findeth a good thing.
        Bible: Proverbs, xviii, 22

21173. Giving honour unto the wife as unto the weaker vessel.
        Bible: 1 Peter, iii, 7

21174.
She is a winsome wee thing,
She is a handsome wee thing,
She is a lo'esome wee thing,
This sweet wee wife o' mine.
        BURNS,
        My Wife's a Winsome Wee Thing

21175. Every man, as the saying is, can tame a shrew but he that hath her.   ROBERT BURTON,
        Anatomy of Melancholy

21176. This flour of wyfly pacience.
        CHAUCER, *Canterbury Tales*

21177. Man's best possession is a sympathetic wife.
        EURIPIDES, *Antigone*

21178. She commandeth her husband, in any equal matter, by constant obeying him.
        THOMAS FULLER,
        Holy & Profane State

21179. He knows little who will tell his wife all he knows.
        THOMAS FULLER,
        Holy & Profane State

21180. I . . . chose my wife, as she did her wedding-gown, not for a fine glossy surface, but such qualities as would wear well.   GOLDSMITH,
        The Vicar of Wakefield

21181. She would have made a splendid wife, for crying only made her eyes more bright.   O. HENRY

21182.

Helmer: Before all else you are a wife and a mother.

Nora: That I no longer believe. I think that before all else I am a human being.

          IBSEN, *A Doll's House*

21183. I have known what it was to have a wife, and . . . I have known what it was to lose a wife.

     SAMUEL JOHNSON, *Boswell: Life*

21184. He that outlives a wife whom he has long loved, sees himself disjoined from the only mind that has the same hopes, and fears, and interest; from the only companion with whom he has shared much good and evil; and with whom he could set his mind at liberty, to retrace the past or anticipate the future.

     SAMUEL JOHNSON, *Boswell: Life*

21185. How much the wife is dearer than the bride.

LORD LYTTLETON, *An Irregular Ode*

21186. My wife, poor wretch.

         SAMUEL PEPYS, *Diary*

21187. Pittacus said, "Every one of you hath his particular plague, and my wife is mine; and he is very happy who hath this only."

          PLUTARCH, *Lives*

21188.

She who ne'er answers till a husband cools,

Or if she rules him, never shows she rules.   POPE, *Moral Essays*

21189. A good wife makes a good husband.   *Proverb*

21190. Many blame the wife for their own thriftless life.   *Proverb*

21191. Who hath a fair wife, needs more than two eyes.   *Proverb*

21192. The cunning wife makes her husband her apron.   *Proverb*

21193. Wives must be had, be they good or bad.   *Proverb*

21194. There is but one good wife in the world, and every man thinks he has her.   *Proverb*

21195. Ne'er seek a wife till ye ken what to do wi' her.   *Proverb*

21196. It is better to marry a quiet fool than a witty scold.   *Proverb*

21197. He that tells his wife news, is but lately married.   *Proverb*

21198. He that speaks ill of his wife dishonoureth himself.   *Proverb*

21199. He that loseth his wife and a farthing hath a great loss of a farthing.   *Proverb*

21200. He has great need of a wife that marries mamma's darling.   *Proverb*

21201. He has a great fancy to marry, that goes to the devil for a wife.   *Proverb*

21202. A fair wife without a fortune, is a fine house without furniture.   *Proverb*

21203. Choose a wife rather by your ear than your eye.   *Proverb*

21204. Better be a shrew than a sheep.   *Proverb*

21205. An obedient wife commands her husband.   *Proverb*

21206.

Long loved, long woo'd, and lately won,

My life's best hope, and now mine own.   SCOTT,

The Bridal of Triermain

21207.

You are my true and honourable wife,
As dear to me as are the ruddy drops
That visit my sad heart.
SHAKESPEARE, *Julius Caesar*

21208. A light wife doth make a heavy husband. SHAKESPEARE,
The Merchant of Venice

21209. Wives may be merry, and yet honest too. SHAKESPEARE,
The Merry Wives of Windsor

21210.

Such duty as the subject owes the prince,
Even such a woman oweth to her husband. SHAKESPEARE,
The Taming of the Shrew

21211.

Trusty, dusky, vivid, true,
With eyes of gold and bramble-dew,
Steel-true and blade-straight
The great artificer made my mate.
STEVENSON, *To My Wife*

21212. Try praising your wife, even if it does frighten her at first.
BILLY SUNDAY

21213. An ideal wife is any woman who has an ideal husband.
TARKINGTON

See also: 283, 395, 2161, 2390, 2678, 2679, 3175, 3185, 9471, 10471, 11230, 12329, 17402, 17732, 20899, 21598.

WILL

Related Subjects: Ambition, Choice, Decision, Desire, Firmness, Intention, Resolution.

21221. Where we are free to act, we are also free to refrain from acting, and where we are able to say No we are also able to say Yes.
ARISTOTLE, *Nicomachean Ethics*

21222.

The will is free;
Strong is the Soul, and wise, and beautiful:
The seeds of godlike power are in us still:
Gods are we, Bards, Saints, Heroes, if we will.
MATTHEW ARNOLD,
Sonnet: Written in Emerson's Essays

21223. Not my will, but thine, be done. *Bible: Luke, xxi, 42*

21224. I fall back on my favorite proverb, "Where there's a will there's a way."
BULWER-LYTTON, *The Caxtons*

21225. Will without power is like children playing at soldiers.
GEORGE CANNING, *The Rovers*

21226. The education of the will is the object of our existence.
EMERSON, *Society and Solitude*

21227. If we are not stupid or insincere when we say that the good or ill of man lies within his own will, and that all beside is nothing to us, why are we still troubled?
EPICTETUS, *Discourses*

21228. Two rules we should always have ready,—that there is nothing good or evil save in the will; and that we are not to lead events, but to follow them. EPICTETUS, *Discourses*

21229. To deny the freedom of the will is to make morality impossible.
FROUDE, *Short Studies*

21230. Will is power.
German Proverb

21231. The only way of setting the will free is to deliver it from wilfulness. A. W. & J. C. HARE,
Guesses at Truth

21232. People do not lack strength; they lack will.   VICTOR HUGO

21233. All theory is against the freedom of the will, all experience for it.
SAMUEL JOHNSON, *Boswell: Life*

21234. God is not willing to do everything, and thus take away our free will and that share of glory which belongs to us.
MACHIAVELLI, *The Prince*

21235. Where the willingness is great, the difficulties cannot be great.
MICHIAVELLI, *The Prince*

21236.
Do not let the will play gardener to
   your soul
Unless you are sure
It is wiser than your soul's nature.
EDGAR LEE MASTERS,
Spoon River Anthology

21237. The unconquerable will.
MILTON, *Paradise Lost*

21238.
Good he made thee, but to persevere
He left it in thy power, ordain'd thy
   will
By nature free, not overruled by Fate
Inextricable, or strict necessity.
MILTON, *Paradise Lost*

21239. Government of the will is better than increase of knowledge.
Proverb

21240. Will will have wilt, though will woe win.   *Proverb*

21241. Where the will is ready, the feet are light.   *Proverb*

21242. A man can surely do what he wills to do, but he cannot determine what he wills.   SCHOPENHAUER

21243.
Our wills and fates do so contrary
   run

That our devices still are overthrown.
SHAKESPEARE, *Hamlet*

21244. At war 'twixt will and will not.   SHAKESPEARE,
Measure for Measure

21245. He wants wit that wants resolved will.   SHAKESPEARE,
Two Gentlemen of Verona

21246.
What he will he does, and does so
   much
That proof is call'd impossibility.
SHAKESPEARE, *Troilus and Cressida*

21247. With will one can do anything.   SAMUEL SMILES, *Self-Help*

21248. Will was his guide, and grief led him astray.
EDMUND SPENSER,
The Faerie Queene

21249. You must take the will for the deed.
SWIFT, *Polite Conversation*

21250. And I compel all creatures to my will.   TENNYSON,
Idylls of the King

21251.
O, well for him whose will is strong!
He suffers, but he will not suffer
   long;
He suffers, but he cannot suffer
   wrong.   TENNYSON, *Will*

See also: 782, 2323, 2420, 5451, 7661, 10524, 15683, 15703, 16655, 17893, 18966.

WILL AND TESTAMENT

Related Subject: Inheritance.

21261. My sword I give to him that shall succeed me in my pilgrimage, and my courage and skill to him that can get it. My marks and scars I carry with me, to be a witness for me, that I have fought his battles who now will be my rewarder.

BUNYAN, *Pilgrim's Progress*

21262. Posthumous charities are the very essence of selfishness, when bequeathed by those who, when alive, would part with nothing.

C. C. COLTON

21263. A will is a solemn matter, even with men whose life is given up to business, and who are by habit mindful of the future.

WILLISTON FISH, *A Last Will*

21264. You give me nothing during your life, but you promise to provide for me at your death. If you are not a fool, you know what you make me wish for.   MARTIAL

21265.
But thousands die without or this or that,
Die, and endow a college or a cat.

POPE, *Moral Essays*

21266. A fat kitchen makes a lean will.   *Proverb*

21267. What thou givest after thy death, remember that thou givest it to a stranger, and most times to an enemy; for he that shall marry thy wife will despise thee, thy memory and thine, and shall possess the quiet of thy labors, the fruit which thou hast planted, enjoy thy love, and spend with joy and ease what thou hast spared and gotten with care and travail.   SIR WALTER RALEIGH

21268. Let's choose executors and talk of wills.

SHAKESPEARE, *Richard II*

WILLOW

Related Subject: Tree.

21271. We hanged our harps upon the willows in the midst thereof.

Bible: Psalms, cxxxvii, 2

21272.
Willow, in thy breezy moan,
I can hear a deeper tone;
Through thy leaves come whispering low,
Faint sweet sounds of long ago—
Willow, sighing willow!

MRS. HEMANS, *Willow Song*

21273. Willows are weak, yet they bind other wood.   *Proverb*

21274.
On a tree by a river a little tom-tit
Sang, "Willow, tit-willow, tit-willow!"
And I said to him, "Dicky-bird, why do you sit
Singing, 'Willow, tit-willow, tit-willow'?"

W. S. GILBERT, *The Mikado*

21275.
My mother had a maid call'd Barbara:
She was in love, and he she loved proved mad
And did forsake her: she had a song of "willow,"
An old thing 'twas, but it express'd her fortune,
And she died singing it.

SHAKESPEARE, *Othello*

21276.
The poor soul sat sighing by a sycamore tree,
Sing all a green willow;
Her hand on her bosom, her head on her knee,
Sing willow, willow, willow:
The fresh streams ran by her, and murmur'd her moans;

Sing willow, willow, willow;
Her salt tears fell from her, and
  soften'd the stones;
Sing willow, willow, willow.
        SHAKESPEARE, *Othello*

WIND

**Related Subjects: Clouds, Storm,
Weather, Zephyr.**

21281. The wind passeth over it, and
it is gone; and the place thereof shall
know it no more.
        Bible: Psalms, ciii, 15

21282. They have sown the wind, and
they shall reap the whirlwind.
        Bible: Hosea, viii, 7

21283. The wind bloweth where it
listeth.   *Bible: John, iii, 8*

21284.
          The wind
Sweeps the broad forest in its summer prime,
As when some master-hand exulting
  sweeps
The keys of some great organ.
      BRYANT, *Among the Trees*

21285.
Wind of the sunny south! oh, still
  delay
  In the gay woods and in the golden
    air,
  Like to a good old age released
    from care,
Journeying, in long serenity, away.
        BRYANT, *October*

21286. The way of the Wind is a
strange, wild way.
      INGRAM CROCKETT, *The Wind*

21287.
De win' can blow lak hurricane
  An' s'pose she blow some more
You can't get drown on Lac St.
  Pierre

So long you stay on shore.
      W. H. DRUMMOND,
  The Wreck of the "Julie Plante"

21288. He that will use all winds,
must shift his sail.
        JOHN FLETCHER,
    The Faithful Shepherdess

21289.
I hear the wind among the trees
Playing celestial symphonies;
I see the branches downward bent,
Like keys of come great instrument.
    LONGFELLOW, *A Day of Sunshine*

21290.
It's a warm wind, the west wind, full
  of birds' cries;
I never hear the west wind but tears
  are in my eyes.
For it comes from the west lands, the
  old brown hills,
And April's in the west wind, and
  daffodils.
  JOHN MASEFIELD, *The West Wind*

21291. The felon winds.
        MILTON, *Lycidas*

21292. The wind was a torrent of
darkness among the gusty trees.
  ALFRED NOYES, *The Highwayman*

21293. A little wind kindles, much
puts out the fire.   *Proverb*

21294. High winds blow on high
hills.   *Proverb*

21295. As the wind blows, you must
set your sail.   *Proverb*

21296. They who plough the sea do
not carry the winds in their hands.
    PUBLILIUS SYRUS, *Sententiae*

21297.
Who has seen the wind?
  Neither you nor I:

But when the trees bow down their
heads,
  The wind is passing by.
      CHRISTINA ROSSETTI,
      Who Has Seen the Wind?

21298. There is something in the
wind.   SHAKESPEARE,
      The Comedy of Errors

21299. Blow, winds, and crack your
cheeks! rage! blow!
      SHAKESPEARE, *King Lear*

21300. I tax not you, you elements,
with unkindness.
      SHAKESPEARE, *King Lear*

21301.
      Blow, wind! come, wrack!
At least we'll die with harness on our
back.   SHAKESPEARE, *Macbeth*

21302. Sits the wind in that corner?
      SHAKESPEARE,
      Much Ado About Nothing

21303.
I hear the little children of the wind
Crying solitary in lonely places.
      WILLIAM SHARP,
      Little Children of the Wind

21304.
O wild West Wind, thou breath of
  Autumn's being,
Thou, from whose unseen presence
  the leaves dead
Are driven, like ghosts from an en-
  chanter fleeing,
Yellow, and black, and pale, and hec-
  tic red,
Pestilence-stricken multitudes.
  SHELLEY, *Ode to the West Wind*

21305.
And wind, that grand old harper,
  smote
His thunder-harp of pines.
  ALEXANDER SMITH, *A Life Drama*

21306. You can't catch the wind in
a net.   C. H. SPURGEON,
      Ploughman's Pictures

21307. "God tempers the wind," said
Maria, "to the shorn lamb."
      STERNE, *A Sentimental Journey*

21308.
Sweet and low, sweet and low,
  Wind of the western sea,
Low, low, breathe and blow,
  Wind of the western sea!
      TENNYSON, *The Princess*

21309.
Wild as the winds, across the howling
  waste
Of mighty waters.
      JAMES THOMSON, *The Seasons*

See also: 4, 1364, 3380, 9290, 15208.

WINDOW

Related Subject: House.

21311.
Each window like a pill'ry appears,
With heads thrust thro' nail'd by the
  ears.   SAMUEL BUTLER, *Hudibras*

21312.
And diamonded with panes of quaint
  device
Innumerable, of stains and splendid
  dyes.
      KEATS, *The Eve of St. Agnes*

21313. Better keep yourself clean
and bright: you are the window
through which you must see the
world.   BERNARD SHAW,
      Maxims for Revolutionists

See also: 3398, 18699.

WINE

**Related Subjects: Ale and Beer,
Conviviality, Drinking, Grapes.**

21321. One that hath wine as a chain

about his wits, such an one lives no life at all. ALCAEUS, *Demetrius*

21322. How exceeding strong is wine! It causeth all men to err who drink it. *Apocrypha: 1 Esdras*

21323. On one occasion some one put a very little wine into a wine-cooler, and said that it was sixteen years old. "It is very small for its age," said Gnathaena. ATHENAEUS, *The Deipnosophists*

21324. Wine that maketh glad the heart of man. *Bible: Psalms, civ, 15*

21325. Wine is a mocker, strong drink is raging: and whosoever is deceived thereby is not wise. *Bible: Proverbs, xx, 1*

21326. Look not thou upon the wine when it is red, when it giveth his colour in the cup, when it moveth itself aright. At the last it biteth like a serpent, and stingeth like an adder. Thine eyes shall behold strange women, and thine heart shall utter perverse things. *Bible: Proverbs, xxiii, 31-33*

21327. Neither do men put new wine into old bottles: else the bottles break, and the wine runneth out, and the bottles perish: but they put new wine into new bottles, and both are preserved. *Bible: Matthew, ix, 17*

21328. Drink no longer water, but use a little wine for thy stomach's sake. *Bible: 1 Timothy, v, 23*

21329. Fill high the bowl with Samian wine! BYRON, *Don Juan*

21330. When asked what wine he liked to drink, he [Diogenes] replied, "That which belongs to another." DIOGENES LAERTIUS, *Diogenes*

21331. Some of the most dreadful

mischiefs that afflict mankind proceed from wine; it is the cause of disease, quarrels, sedition, idleness, aversion to labour, and every species of domestic disorders. FENELON, *Telemachus*

21332. From wine what sudden friendship springs! JOHN GAY, *The Squire & His Cur*

21333.
God made Man
  Frail as a bubble;
God made Love,
  Love made Trouble.
God made the Vine,
  Was it a sin
That Man made Wine
  To drown Trouble in?
OLIVER HERFORD, *A Plea*

21334. Inflaming wine, pernicious to mankind. HOMER, *Iliad*

21335. To-night with wine drown care. HORACE, *Odes*

21336. Upon the first goblet he read this inscription: Monkey wine; upon the second: lion wine; upon the third: sheep wine; upon the fourth: swine wine. These four inscriptions expressed the four descending degrees of drunkenness: the first, that which enlivens; the second, that which irritates; the third, that which stupefies; finally the last, that which brutalizes. VICTOR HUGO, *Les Miserables*

21337. Fill me with the old familiar Juice. OMAR KHAYYAM, *Rubaiyat*

21338.
  I wonder often what the Vintners buy
One half so precious as the stuff they sell. OMAR KHAYYAM, *Rubaiyat*

21339.
Bacchus, that first from out the purple grape

Crush'd the sweet poison of misused
wine.　　　　　MILTON, *Comus*

21340.
Come, send round the wine, and leave
　points of belief
To simpleton sages, and reasoning
　fools.　　　THOMAS MOORE,
　　　Come, Send Round the Wine

21341. Thanks be to God, since my
leaving drinking of wine, I do find
myself much better, and do mind my
business better, and do spend less
money, and less time lost in idle company.　　SAMUEL PEPYS, *Diary*

21342. Wine hath drowned more men
than the sea.　　　　　*Proverb*

21343. Bacchus hath drowned more
men than Neptune.　　　*Proverb*

21344. When the wine goes in,
strange things come out.
　　　SCHILLER, *The Piccolomini*

21345.
　Good wine needs neither bush not
　　preface
To make it welcome.
　　　SCOTT, *Perveril of the Peak*

21346. Good wine is a good familiar
creature if it be well used.
　　　SHAKESPEARE, *Othello*

21347. O thou invisible spirit of
wine! if thou hast no name to be
known by, let us call thee devil!
　　　SHAKESPEARE, *Othello*

See also: 75, 2450, 6011.

WINTER

Related Subjects: December, February, Frost, Ice, The Seasons,
Snow.

21351. Winter eateth what summer
getteth.　　　　　*Anonymous*

21352.
O Winter! bar thine adamantine
　doors:
The north is thine; there hast thou
　built thy dark,
Deep-founded habitation. Shake not
　thy roofs,
Nor bend thy pillars with thine iron
　car.　　　BLAKE, *To Winter*

21353. Winter lies too long in country towns; hangs on until it is stale
and shabby, old and sullen.
　　　WILLA CATHER, *My Antonia*

21354. But winter ling'ring chills the
lap of May.　　　GOLDSMITH,
　　　　　The Traveller

21355.
Oh the long and dreary Winter!
Oh the cold and cruel Winter!
　　　　LONGFELLOW,
　　　The Song of Hiawatha

21356. Winter lingered so long in the
lap of Spring, that it occasioned a
great deal of talk.　BILL NYE, *Spring*

21357.
Winter is icummen in,
Lhude sing Goddamm,
Raineth drop and staineth slop,
And how the wind doth ramm!
　　　Sing: Goddamm.
　　　EZRA POUND, *Ancient Music*

21358. Every mile is two in winter.
　　　　　　　Proverb

21359. A green winter makes a fat
churchyard.　　　　*Proverb*

21360. He that passeth a winter's day
escapes an enemy.　　　*Proverb*

21361. An early winter is a surly
winter.　　　　　*Proverb*

21362.
Here feel we but the penalty of
　Adam,

The seasons' difference, as the icy
   fang
And churlish chiding of the winter's
   wind,
Which, when it bites and blows upon
   my body,
Even till I shrink with cold, I smile
   and say,
"This is no flattery."
      SHAKESPEARE, *As You Like It*

21363.
Quake in the present winter's state
   and wish
The warmer days would come.
      SHAKESPEARE, *Cymbeline*

21364. Winter's not gone yet, if the
wild-geese fly that way.
      SHAKESPEARE, *King Lear*

21365.
When icicles hang by the wall,
   And Dick the shepherd blows his
     nail,
And Tom bears logs into the hall,
   And milk comes frozen home in
     pail,
When blood is nipp'd and ways be
   foul,
Then nightly sings the staring owl,
      Tu-whit;
Tu-who, a merry note,
While greasy Joan doth keel the pot.
SHAKESPEARE, *Love's Labour's Lost*

21366. Winter tames man, woman
and beast.   SHAKESPEARE,
     The Taming of the Shrew

21367.
   Winter, which being full of care
Makes summer's welcome thrice more
   wish'd, more rare.
      SHAKESPEARE, *Sonnet LVI*

21368. Be like the sun and the meadow, which are not in the least concerned about the coming winter.
      BERNARD SHAW,
     An Unsocial Socialist

21369. If Winter comes, can Spring
be far behind?   SHELLEY,
     Ode to the West Wind

21370.
      Thus Winter falls,
A heavy gloom oppressive o'er the
   world,
Through Nature shedding influence
   malign,
And rouses up the seeds of dark disease.
      JAMES THOMSON, *The Seasons*

21371. Such a winter eve. Now for a
mellow fire, some old poet's page, or
else serene philosophy.
      THOREAU, *Journal*

See also: 498, 1762.

WISDOM

**Related Subjects: Apothegms,
Caution, Discretion, Example, Experience, Intelligence, Learning,
Oracle, Perception, Proverbs, Prudence, Quotation, Wit.**

21381. As you know our role in life
has always been to be wiser than
anyone else, and the consciousness of
that is the only reward we are likely
to get from it.   HENRY ADAMS,
     Letter

21382. Wise men, though all laws
were abolished, would lead the same
lives.   ARISTOPHANES

21383. It hath been an opinion that
the French are wiser than they seem,
and the Spaniards seem wiser than
they are; but howsoever it be between
nations, certainly it is so between
man and man.   BACON,
     Of Seeming Wise

21384. Wisdom crieth without; she
uttereth her voice in the streets.
     Bible: Proverbs, i, 20

21385. Wisdom is the principal thing; therefore get wisdom; and with all thy getting get understanding. *Bible: Proverbs, iv, 7*

21386. Wisdom is better than rubies. *Bible: Proverbs, viii, 11*

21387. A wise man is strong; yea, a man of knowledge increaseth strength. *Bible: Proverbs, xxiv, 5*

21388. One wise man's verdict outweighs all the fools'.
Browning,
Bishop Blougram's Apology

21389. A man doesn't begin to attain wisdom until he recognizes that he is no longer indispensable.
Admiral Byrd, *Alone*

21390.
A sadder and a wiser man
He rose the morrow morn.
Coleridge, *The Ancient Mariner*

21391.
Defer not till to-morrow to be wise,
To-morrow's sun to thee may never rise. Congreve,
Letter to Cobham

21392. It takes a wise man to discover a wise man.
Diogenes Laertius, *Xenophanes*

21393. In order to have wisdom we must have ignorance.
Theodore Dreiser, *I Believe*

21394. All human wisdom is summed up in two words,—wait and hope.
Dumas,
The Count of Monte Cristo

21395. Science and philosophy, in the history of states, reach their height after decadence has set in; wisdom is a harbinger of death.
Will Durant, *The Life of Greece*

21396.
Go where he will, the wise man is at home,
His hearth the earth,—his hall the azure dome. Emerson,
Wood-Notes

21397.
If, as they say, some dust thrown in my eyes
Will keep my talk from getting over-wise,
I'm not the one for putting off the proof.
Let it be overwhelming.
Robert Frost, *Dust in the Eyes*

21398. Wisdom is never dear, provided the article be genuine.
Horace Greeley

21399.
The wisdom of mankind creeps slowly on,
Subject to every doubt that can retard
Or fling it back upon an earlier time.
Richard Horne, *Orion*

21400. They are wise in their generation who have discovered that intellectual pleasure is the most satisfying and the most enduring.
Somerset Maugham,
Books and You

21401. A little too wise, they say, do ne'er live long.
Thomas Middleton, *The Phoenix*

21402.
     To know
That which before us lies in daily life
Is the prime wisdom.
Milton, *Paradise Lost*

21403. The wealth of mankind is the wisdom they leave.

J. B. O'Reilly, *Rules of the Road*

21404. Not by years but by disposition is wisdom acquired.

PLAUTUS, *Trinummus*

21405. A wise man may look ridiculous in the company of fools.

Proverb

21406. Wisdom is a good purchase, though we pay dear for it. *Proverb*

21407. Wisdom don't always speak in Greek and Latin. *Proverb*

21408. The wise hand doth not all the foolish tongue speaketh. *Proverb*

21409. Some are wise, and some are otherwise. *Proverb*

21410. An ounce of wisdom is worth a pound of forecast. *Proverb*

21411. He that is a wise man by day is no fool by night. *Proverb*

21412. He that is not handsome at twenty, nor strong at thirty, nor rich at forty, nor wise at fifty, will never be handsome, strong, rich, or wise.

Proverb

21413. He bids fair to grow wise who has discovered that he is not so.

PUBLILIUS SYRUS, *Sententiae*

21414. 'Tis wise to learn; 'tis God-like to create. J. G. SAXE,

The Library

21415.
Unlearn'd, he knew no schoolman's subtle art,
No language, but the language of the heart.
By nature honest, by experience wise,
Healthy by temperance, and by exercise. POPE,

Epistle to Dr. Arbuthnot

21416. So wise so young, they say, do never live long.

SHAKESPEARE, *Richard III*

21417.
For to be wise, and love,
Exceeds man's might; that dwells with gods above.

SHAKESPEARE,
Troilus and Cressida

21418. God give them wisdom that have it; and those that are fools, let them use their talents.

SHAKESPEARE, *Twelfth Night*

21419.
Though a man be wise,
It is no shame for him to live and learn. SOPHOCLES, *Antigone*

21420. The fewer the things in which we are wise, the more value we set, of course, on our wisdom and the more irritating becomes the stupidity of our fellows in the field where we are wise. CLARENCE STREIT,

Union Now

21421. Knowledge comes, but wisdom lingers. TENNYSON,

Locksley Hall

21422. Immortal gods! how much does one man excel another! What a difference there is between a wise person and a fool! TERENCE,

Eunuchus

21423. Be wise to-day; 'tis madness to defer. EDWARD YOUNG,

Night Thoughts

21424.
Be wise with speed;
A fool at forty is a fool indeed.

EDWARD YOUNG, *Love of Fame*

WISH

Related Subjects: Desire, Hope, Will.

21431. Every wish is like a prayer—with God.

ELIZABETH B. BROWNING,
Aurora Leigh

21432. Men whose dearest wishes are fixed on objects wholly out of their own power, become in all cases more or less impatient and prone to anger.

COLERIDGE, *Biographia Literaria*

21433.
All her commands were gracious, sweet requests.
How could it be then, but that her requests
Must need have sounded to me as commands? COLERIDGE, *Zapolya*

21434. Most men let their wishes run away with them. They have no mind to stop them in their career, the motion is so pleasing.

LORD HALIFAX, *Works*

21435. The evil wish is most evil to the wisher. HESIOD,
Works and Days

21436. When I wish I was rich, then I know I am ill.

D. H. LAWRENCE, *Riches*

21437. I wish I knew the good of wishing. H. S. LEIGH,
A Day for Wishing

21438. You have wished it so, you have wished it so, George Dandin, you have wished it so.

MOLIÈRE, *George Dandin*

21439. We live, not as we wish to but as we can. MENANDER,
The Lady of Andros

21440. Wishes never filled the bag.
Proverb

21441. If wishes were horses, beggars might ride. *Proverb*

21442. Wishers were ever fools.
SHAKESPEARE,
Antony and Cleopatra

21443. Your heart's desires be with you! SHAKESPEARE, *As You Like It*

21444. Thy wish was father, Harry, to that thought. SHAKESPEARE,
Henry IV

21445.
Take this in good part, whatsoever thou be,
And wish me no worse than I wish unto thee. THOMAS TUSSER,
Five Hundred Points of Good Husbandrie

21446. We cannot wish for that we know not. VOLTAIRE, *Zaire*

21447.
Wishing, of all employments, is the worst;
Philosophy's reverse, and health's decay!
EDWARD YOUNG, *Night Thoughts*

21448.
Like our shadows,
Our wishes lengthen as our sun declines. EDWARD YOUNG,
Night Thoughts

See also: 64, 164, 1259, 1333, 15573.

WIT

Related Subjects: Cleverness, Conversation, Epigram, Humor, Joke, Laughter, Originality, Pun, Wisdom.

21451. The monuments of wit survive the monuments of power.
BACON, *Essex's Device*

21452. Wit needs leisure, and certain inequalities of position.
BALZAC, *The Imaginary Mistress*

21453. Aristotle said melancholy men of all others are most witty.
ROBERT BURTON,
Anatomy of Melancholy

21454.
We grant, although he had much wit,
He was very shy of using it.
SAMUEL BUTLER, *Hudibras*

21455. Good wits jump; a word to the wise is enough.
CERVANTES, *Don Quixote*

21456. Don't put too fine a point to your wit for fear it should get blunted. CERVANTES, *Don Quixote*

21457.
Wit will shine
Through the harsh cadence of a rugged line. DRYDEN,
To the Memory of Mr. Oldham

21458. No task's too steep for human wit. HORACE, *Odes*

21459.
There still remains, to mortify a wit,
The many-headed monster of the pit.
HORACE

21460. The greatest fault of a penetrating wit is to go beyond the mark.
LA ROCHEFOUCAULD, *Maxims*

21461. In the midst of the fountain of wit there arises something bitter, which stings in the very flowers.
LUCRETIUS, *De Rerum Natura*

21462. Impropriety is the soul of wit. SOMERSET MAUGHAM,
The Moon and Sixpence

21463. A witty woman is a treasure; a witty beauty is a power.
GEORGE MEREDITH,
Diana of the Crossways

21464. The well of true wit is truth itself. GEORGE MEREDITH,
Diana of the Crossways

21465. Have you summoned your wits from wool-gathering?
THOMAS MIDDLETON,
The Family of Love

21466. You see him in travail to produce *bons mots.* MOLIÈRE,
Le Misanthrope

21467.
You beat your pate, and fancy wit will come;
Knock as you please, there's nobody at home. POPE, *An Empty House*

21468. A wit with dunces, and a dunce with wits. POPE,
The Dunciad

21469. Many that are wits in jest, are fools in earnest. *Proverb*

21470. It is wit to pick a lock, and steal a horse, but wisdom to let it alone. *Proverb*

21471. Use your wit as a buckler, not as a sword. *Proverb*

21472. Quick wits are generally conceited. *Proverb*

21473. Better a witty fool than a foolish wit. *Proverb*

21474. As much wit as three folks, two fools and a madman. *Proverb*

21475. After wit is everybody's wit. *Proverb*

21476. Wit and wisdom are born with a man. JOHN SELDEN,
Table Talk

21477. Brevity is the soul of wit.
SHAKESPEARE, *Hamlet*

21478. They have a plentiful lack of wit. SHAKESPEARE, *Hamlet*

21479. I am not only witty in myself but the cause that wit is in other men. SHAKESPEARE, *Henry IV*

21480. There's a skirmish of wit between them.   SHAKESPEARE,
Much Ado About Nothing

21481. Wit consists in knowing the resemblance of things which differ, and the difference of things which are alike.   MME. DE STAËL

21482. That is as well said as if I had said it.   SWIFT, *Polite Conversation*

21483. A witty saying proves nothing.   VOLTAIRE,
Le Diner du Comte de Boulainvilliers

See also: 504, 523, 731, 854, 1563, 1952, 2480, 3637, 6307, 7586, 8199, 13245, 13342, 14622, 20968.

WITCH, WITCHCRAFT

Related Subjects: Bigotry, Fanaticism, Superstition.

21491. I have ever believed, and do now know, that there are Witches: they that are in doubt of these . . . are obliquely and upon consequence a sort, not of Infidels, but Atheists.
SIR THOMAS BROWNE,
Religio Medici

21492.
They are neither man nor woman—
They are neither brute nor human,
    They are Ghouls!
            POE, *The Bells*

21493. They that burn you for a witch lose all their coals.   *Proverb*

21494.
An' all us other children, when the
    supper things is done,
We set around the kitchen fire an'
    has the mostest fun
A-list'nin' to the witch tales 'at Annie
    tells about

An' the gobble-uns 'at gits you
Ef you Don't Watch Out!
        JAMES WHITCOMB RILEY,
                Little Orphant Annie

21495. Aroint thee, witch, aroint thee!   SHAKESPEARE, *King Lear*

21496.
                    What are these,
So wither'd, and so wild in their attire;
That look not like the inhabitants o' th' earth,
And yet are on 't?
            SHAKESPEARE, *Macbeth*

21497.
Double, double, toil and trouble;
Fire burn and cauldron bubble.
            SHAKESPEARE, *Macbeth*

21498. How now, you secret, black, and midnight hags!
            SHAKESPEARE, *Macbeth*

21499. Saw you the weird sisters?
            SHAKESPEARE, *Macbeth*

21500.
The foul witch Sycorax, who with age and envy
Was grown into a hoop.
        SHAKESPEARE, *The Tempest*

21501. It is beyond all question or dispute that magic words and ceremonies are quite capable of most effectually destroying a whole flock of sheep, if the words be accompanied by a sufficient quantity of arsenic.
            VOLTAIRE

See also: 5201, 12904, 13017, 19511.

WOE

Related Subjects: Adversity, Grief, Misery, Mourning, Sorrow.

21511. Here is woe's self, and not the mask of woe.
            T. B. ALDRICH, *Andromeda*

21512. But we are all the same—the fools of our own woes!

MATTHEW ARNOLD,
Empedocles on Etna

21513.
Thus do extremest ills a joy possess,
And one woe makes another woe seem less.

MICHAEL DRAYTON,
England's Heroical Epistles

21514.
Sure there's a lethargy in mighty woe,
Tears stand congeal'd and cannot flow, . . .
Like Niobe we marble grow
    And petrify with grief.

DRYDEN, *Threnodia Augustalis*

21515. Thus woe succeeds a woe, as wave a wave. ROBERT HERRICK,
Sorrows Succeed

21516.
Weep on! and, as thy sorrows flow,
I'll taste the luxury of woe.

THOMAS MOORE, *Anacreontic*

21517.
Lift not the festal mask!—enough to know,
No scene of mortal life but teems with mortal woe. SCOTT,
The Lord of the Isles

21518.
But I have that within which passeth show;
These but the trappings and the suits of woe. SHAKESPEARE, *Hamlet*

21519.
One woe doth tread upon another's heel,
So fast they follow.

SHAKESPEARE, *Hamlet*

21520.
            O, woe is me,
To have seen what I have seen, see what I see! SHAKESPEARE,
Hamlet

21521.
The man that makes his toe
When he his heart should make
Shall of a corn cry woe,
    And turn his sleep to wake.

SHAKESPEARE, *King Lear*

21522.
    My grief lies all within;
And these external manners of laments
Are merely shadows to the unseen grief
That swells with silence in the tortured soul. SHAKESPEARE,
Richard II

21523.
    All these woes shall serve
For sweet discourses in our time to come. SHAKESPEARE,
Romeo and Juliet

21524.
Woe, woe, and woe upon woe!

SOPHOCLES, *Ajax*

See also: 41, 222, 2174, 2176, 8015, 8161.

WOLF

Related Subject: Animal.

21531. This ravening fellow has a wolf in 's belly.

BEAUMONT & FLETCHER,
Women Pleased

21532. There is the meekness of the clergyman. There spoke the wolf in sheep's clothing. FIELDING, *Amelia*

21533. Who is bred among wolves will learn to howl.

JOHN FLORIO,
Second Fruites

21534. You've cried "Wolf!" till, like the shepherd youth, you're not believed when you do speak the truth. J. R. PLANCHÉ, *Extravaganza*

21535. The wolf finds a reason for taking the lamb. *Proverb*

21536. A wolf will never make war against another wolf. *Proverb*

21537. Wolves lose their teeth but not their nature. *Proverb*

21538. Who's afraid of the big bad wolf? ANN RONELL, *Title & Refrain of Song Popularized in Walt Disney's Three Little Pigs*

21539. The wolf from the door. JOHN SKELTON, *Colyn Cloute*

See also: 1024, 1036, 3080.

WOMAN

Related Subjects: Beauty, Coquetry, Man, The Sexes.

21541. If we mean to have heroes, statesman and philosophers, we should have learned women. ABIGAIL ADAMS, *Brooks: Flowering of New England*

21542. The woman who is known only through a man is known wrong. HENRY ADAMS, *The Education of Henry Adams*

21543. The woman that deliberates is lost. ADDISON, *Cato*

21544.
Too lightly opened are a woman's ears;
Her fence downtrod by many trespassers. AESCHYLUS, *Agamemnon*

21545. Ye must know that women have dominion over you: do ye not labour and toil, and give and bring all to the woman? *Apocrypha: 1 Esdras*

21546. With women the heart argues, not the mind. MATTHEW ARNOLD, *Merope*

21547. Women love the lie that saves their pride, but never an unflattering truth. GERTRUDE ATHERTON, *The Conqueror*

21548. No matter how hard a man may labour, some woman is always in the background of his mind. She is the one reward of virtue. GERTRUDE ATHERTON, *The Conqueror*

21549.
It is folly to tell women truth!
They would rather live on lies, so they be sweet. PHILIP J. BAILEY, *The Devil's Advice on Lovemaking*

21550. There are feelings which women guess in spite of the care men take to bury them. BALZAC, *Colonel Chabert*

21551.
The way to fight a woman is with your hat. Grab it and run. JOHN BARRYMORE

21552. Women, deceived by men, want to marry them; it is a kind of revenge as good as any other. BEAUMANOIR

21553. It is better to dwell in a corner of the housetop, than with a brawling woman in a wide house. *Bible: Proverbs, xxi, 9*

21554. A continual dropping in a very rainy day and a contentious Woman are alike. *Bible: Proverbs, xxvii, 15*

21555. Woman would be more charming if one could fall into her arms without falling into her hands.
AMBROSE BIERCE, *Epigrams*

21556. You are not permitted to kill a woman who has injured you, but nothing forbids you to reflect that she is growing older every minute. You are avenged 1440 times a day.
AMBROSE BIERCE, *Epigrams*

21557. It would be interesting to figure out just how many foot-pounds of energy men have saved themselves, since the creation of the world, by keeping up the pretense that a special knack is required for washing dishes and for dusting, and that the knack is wholly feminine.
HEYWOOD BROUN, *Holding a Baby*

21558. It is not easy for any woman to lose her identity in the shadow of a great man and it is worse when she has to play a supporting role to a husband of distinctly minor quality.
HEYWOOD BROUN, *Wife of Lot*

21559. A woman's always younger than a man at equal years.
ELIZABETH B. BROWNING,
Aurora Leigh

21560.
Auld Nature swears the lovely dears
 Her noblest work she classes, O;
Her 'prentice han' she tried on man,
 And then she made the lasses, O!
BURNS, *Green Grow the Rashes*

21561. Women wear the breeches.
ROBERT BURTON,
Anatomy of Melancholy

21562. I heard a man say that brigands demand your money or your life, whereas women require both.
SAMUEL BUTLER, *Note Books*

21563. Her stature tall,—I hate a dumpy woman. BYRON, *Don Juan*

21564.
The world was sad, the garden was a wild,
And man, the hermit, sigh'd—till woman smiled.
THOMAS CAMPBELL,
Pleasures of Hope

21565. The expression a woman wears on her face is far more important than the clothes she wears on her back. DALE CARNEGIE,
How to Win Friends

21566. Demonstrations of love are never altogether displeasing to women, and the most disdainful, in spite of all their coyness, reserve a little complaisance in their hearts for their admirers. CERVANTES,
Don Quixote

21567. What man has assurance enough to pretend to know thoroughly the riddles of a woman's mind, and who could ever hope to fix her mutable nature?
CERVANTES, *Don Quixote*

21568. There is no proved intellectual inferiority in woman, or any evidence for delimiting her activities to a specific sphere. STUART CHASE,
Are Radicals Crazy?

21569. We shall find no fiend in hell can match the fury of a disappointed woman. COLLEY CIBBER,
Love's Last Shift

21570.
The wind and clouds, now here, now there,
 Hold no such strange dominion
As woman's cold, perverted will,
 And soon estranged opinion.
JOHN CLARE, *When Lovers Part*

21571. No woman is ever completely deceived. JOSEPH CONRAD,
Under Western Eyes

21572.
The Woman tempted me—and tempts me still!
Lord God, I pray You that she ever will!   E. V. COOKE, *Adam*

21573. American women have the best figures, French women have the most charm, and Italian women the most vivacity.   EVE CURIE

21574. Woman, the creature of an hour.   DANTE, *Purgatory*

21575. There is something about a roused woman, especially if she add to all her other strong passions, the fierce impulses of recklessness and despair, which few men like to provoke.   DICKENS, *Oliver Twist*

21576. She's the ornament of her sex.
DICKENS,
The Old Curiosity Shop

21577. In a word, I have never yet been able to find one consideration, one argument, or suggestion in favor of man's right to participate in civil government which did not equally apply to the right of woman.
FREDERICK DOUGLASS,
Autobiography

21578.
She hugg'd the offender, and forgave the offence:
Sex to the last.   DRYDEN,
Cymon & Iphigenia

21579. It is often woman who inspires us with the great things that she will prevent us from accomplishing.   DUMAS

21580. I'm not denying the women are foolish: God Almighty, made 'em to match the men.
GEORGE ELIOT

21581.
Though little dangers they may fear,
When greater dangers men environ

Then women show a front of iron;
And, gentle in their manner, they
Do bold things in a quiet way.
THOMAS ENGLISH, *Betty Zane*

21582. Woman is woman's natural ally.   EURIPIDES, *Alope*

21583.
O woman, perfect woman! what distraction
Was meant to mankind when thou wast made a devil!
JOHN FLETCHER,
Monsieur Thomas

21584.
Though woman never can be man,
By change of sex and a' that,
To social rights, 'gainst class and clan,
Her claim is just, for a' that,
For a' that, and a' that,
Her Eden slip, and a' that,
In all that makes a living soul
She matches man, for a' that.
W. L. GARRISON, *An Autograph*

21585.
'Tis woman that seduces all mankind;
By her we first were taught the wheedling arts.   JOHN GAY,
The Beggar's Opera

21586. The Eternal Feminine draws us on.   GOETHE, *Faust*

21587.
Women are our sub-conscious selves,
Materializations from our souls.
O. ST. J. GOGARTY

21588. A modest woman, dressed out in all her finery, is the most tremendous object of the whole creation.   GOLDSMITH,
She Stoops to Conquer

21589.
When lovely woman stoops to folly,
And finds too late that men betray,

What charm can soothe her melancholy?
What art can wash her guilt away.
GOLDSMITH,
The Vicar of Wakefield

21590. Let men tremble to win the hand of woman, unless they win along with it the utmost passion of her heart. HAWTHORNE,
The Scarlet Letter

21591.
Ermined and minked and Persian-lambed,
Be-puffed (be-painted, too, alas!)
Be-decked, be-diamonded—be-damned!
The women of the better class.
OLIVER HERFORD,
The Women of the Better Class

21592.
Oh woman, woman! when to ill thy mind
Is bent, all hell contains no fouler fiend. HOMER, *Odyssey*

21593. A woman cannot be herself in the society of the present day, which is an exclusively masculine society, with laws framed by men and with a judicial system that judges feminine conduct from a masculine point of view. IBSEN,
A Doll's House: Notes

21594. There are two kinds of spiritual law, two kinds of conscience, one in man and another, altogether different, in woman. They do not understand each other; but in practical life the woman is judged by man's law, as though she were not a woman but a man. IBSEN,
A Doll's House: Notes

21595. Sir, nature has given woman so much power that the law cannot afford to give her more.
SAMUEL JOHNSON

21596. I am very fond of the company of ladies. I like their beauty; I like their delicacy, I like their vivacity, and I like their silence.
SAMUEL JOHNSON

21597. The endearing elegance of female friendship.
SAMUEL JOHNSON, *Rasselas*

21598.
Maids must be wives and mothers to fulfil
The entire and holiest end of woman's being. FRANCES KEMBLE,
Woman's Heart

21599. The silliest woman can manage a clever man; but it needs a very clever woman to manage a fool!
KIPLING, *Plain Tales*

21600.
Oh, the years we waste and the tears we waste
And the work of our head and hand
Belong to the woman who did not know . . .
And did not understand.
KIPLING, *The Vampire*

21601. The female of the species is more deadly than the male.
KIPLING,
The Female of the Species

21602. The first proof a man gives of his interest in a woman is by talking to her about his own sweet self. If the woman listens without yawning, he begins to like her. If she flatters the animal's vanity, he ends by adoring her. KIPLING,
Under the Deodars

21603. An' I learned about women from 'er. KIPLING, *The Ladies*

21604. A woman's guess is much more accurate than a man's certainty. KIPLING, *Plain Tales*

21605. O men, respect women who have borne you.   *The Koran*

21606.
As unto the bow the cord is,
So unto the man is woman,
Though she bends him, she obeys him,
Though she draws him, yet she follows,
Useless each without the other!
LONGFELLOW,
The Song of Hiawatha

21607. I'm opposed to women drivers on moral grounds.
CHIEF OF POLICE MCCLELLAND,
Long Beach, Cal.

21608. The females of all species are most dangerous when they appear to retreat.   DON MARQUIS,
A Farewell

21609. A woman can forgive a man for the harm he does her, but she can never forgive him for the sacrifices he makes on her account.
SOMERSET MAUGHAM,
The Moon and Sixpence

21610. A woman is necessarily an evil, and he is a lucky man who catches her in the mildest form.
MENANDER

21611.
In argument with men a woman ever
Goes by the worse, whatever be her cause.
For want of words, no doubt, or lack of breath!   MILTON,
Samson Agonistes

21612.
Ladies, whose bright eyes
Rain influence, and judge the prize.
MILTON, *L'Allegro*

21613.
My only books
Were woman's looks,
And folly's all they've taught me.
THOMAS MOORE,
The Time I've Lost in Wooing

21614. Nature intended women to be our slaves; and it is only because of our distorted outlooks that they venture to describe themselves as our rulers. . . . What a mad idea to demand equality for women! They are our property, we are not theirs . . . They belong to us, just as a tree which bears fruit belongs to the gardener.   NAPOLEON,
Ludwig: Napoleon

21615. In revenge and in love woman is more barbarous than man.
NIETZSCHE, *Beyond Good & Evil*

21616. God created woman. And boredom did indeed cease from that moment—but many other things ceased as well! Woman was God's *second* mistake.   NIETZSCHE,
The Antichrist

21617.
O woman! lovely woman! Nature made thee
To temper man: we had been brutes without you.
THOMAS OTWAY, *Venice Preserved*

21618.
What mighty ills have not been done by woman!
Who wast betrayed the Capital?—A woman!
Who lost Mark Antony the world?—A woman!
Who was the cause of a long ten years' war,
And laid at last old Troy in ashes?—Woman!

Destructive, damnable, deceitful woman! THOMAS OTWAY,
The Orphan

21619. It is a great consolation to reflect that, among all the bewildering changes to which the world is subject, the character of woman cannot be altered.
COVENTRY PATMORE,
Bad Morality Is Bad Art

21620.
Men, some to business, some to pleasure take;
But every woman is at heart a rake.
POPE, *Moral Essays*

21621. Most women have no characters at all. POPE, *Moral Essays*

21622. Woman's at best a contradiction still. POPE, *Moral Essays*

21623. Let women spin, and not preach. *Proverb*

21624. Women conceal all that they know not. *Proverb*

21625. Women in mischief are wiser than men. *Proverb*

21626. A woman that loves to be at the window, is like a bunch of grapes on the highway. *Proverb*

21627. A woman is to be from her house three times; when she is christened, married and buried. *Proverb*

21628.
For when a woman is left too much alone,
Sooner or later she begins to think;
And no man knows what then she may discover.
E. A. ROBINSON, *Tristram*

21629. Women and elephants never forget an injury. SAKI, *Reginald*

21630. You never so much want to be happy with a woman as when you know that you're ceasing to care for her. ARTHUR SCHNITZLER, *Anatole*

21631.
O woman! in our hours of ease,
Uncertain, coy, and hard to please,
And variable as the shade
By the light quivering aspen made;
When pain and anguish wring the brow,
A ministering angel thou!
SCOTT, *Marmion*

21632. A woman is a dish for the gods. SHAKESPEARE,
Antony and Cleopatra

21633.
Do you not know I am a woman?
When I think, I must speak.
SHAKESPEARE, *As You Like It*

21634. Frailty, thy name is woman!
SHAKESPEARE, *Hamlet*

21635. One that was a woman, sir; but, rest her soul, she's dead.
SHAKESPEARE, *Hamlet*

21636. O tiger's heart wrapp'd in a woman's hide. SHAKESPEARE,
Henry VI

21637.
She's beautiful and therefore to be wooed,
She is a woman, therefore to be won.
SHAKESPEARE, *Henry VI*

21638. How hard it is for women to keep counsel. SHAKESPEARE,
Julius Caesar

21639. There was never yet fair woman but she made mouths in a glass. SHAKESPEARE, *King Lear*

21640. A child of our grandmother Eve, a female; or, for thy more sweet understanding, a woman.
SHAKESPEARE,
Love's Labour's Lost

21641.
For where is any author in the world
Teaches such beauty as a woman's
    eye?
Learning is but an adjunct to our-
    self.   SHAKESPEARE,
             Love's Labour's Lost

21642.
From women's eyes this doctrine I
    derive;
They sparkle still the right Prome-
    thean fire;
They are the books, the arts, the
    academes,
    That show, contain, and nourish
        all the world.
             SHAKESPEARE,
             Love's Labour's Lost

21643. The pleasing punishment that
women bear.   SHAKESPEARE,
             Measure for Measure

21644.
We cannot fight for love, as men may
    do;
We should be woo'd and were not
    made to woo. SHAKESPEARE,
     A Midsummer-Night's Dream

21645.
Was ever woman in this humour
    wooed?
Was ever woman in this humour
    won? SHAKESPEARE, *Richard III*

21646.
A woman moved is like a fountain
    troubled,
Muddy, ill-seeming, thick, bereft of
    beauty.   SHAKESPEARE,
        The Taming of the Shrew

21647.
Let still the woman take
An elder than herself: so wears she to
    him,
So sways she level in her husband's
    heart;

For, boy, however we do praise our-
    selves,
Our fancies are more giddy and un-
    firm,
More longing, wavering, sooner lost
    and worn,
Than women's are.
        SHAKESPEARE, *Twelfth Night*

21648.
I have no other but a woman's rea-
    son;
I think him so, because I think him
    so.   SHAKESPEARE,
      The Two Gentlemen of Verona

21649.
Have you not heard it said full oft,
A woman's nay doth stand for
    naught?   SHAKESPEARE,
       Sonnets to Sundry Notes
                of Music

21650. Women upset everything.
When you let them into your life,
you find that the woman is driving
at one thing and you're driving at another.   BERNARD SHAW, *Pygmalion*

21651. A woman should be seen, not
heard.   SOPHOCLES, *Ajax*

21652.
What will not woman, gentle woman
    dare,
When strong affection stirs her spirit
    up?   SOUTHEY, *Madoc in Wales*

21653. A wise woman never yields
by appointment. It should always be
an unforeseen happiness.
             STENDHAL

21654. Women are wiser than men
because they know less and understand more. JAMES STEPHENS,
            The Crock of Gold

21655. Something depressing comes
on the mind when it has been too

extensively occupied with the female
sex.   JAMES STEPHENS,
In the Land of Youth

21656.
Women are the baggage of life: they
are
Troublesome, and hinder us in the
great march.
And yet we cannot be without 'em.
SIR JOHN SUCKLING,
The Tragedy of Brennoralt

21657. Woman is the lesser man.
TENNYSON, *Locksley Hall*

21658.
For men at most differ as heaven and
earth,
But women, worst and best, as heaven
and hell.   TENNYSON,
Idylls of the King

21659. I know the disposition of
women: when you will, they won't;
when you won't, they set their hearts
upon you of their own inclination.
TERENCE, *Eunuchus*

21660. The book of female logic is
blotted all over with tears, and Justice in their courts is forever in a passion. THACKERAY, *The Virginians*

21661. Women like not only to conquer, but to be conquered.
THACKERAY, *The Virginians*

21662. When I have one foot in the
grave I will tell the truth about
women. I shall tell it, jump into my
coffin, pull the lid over me, and say,
"Do what you like now."
TOLSTOY, *Diary*

21663. A woman changes when she
loves and is loved. When there is nobody who cares for her she loses her
spirits and the charm is gone. Love
draws out what is in her and on it
her development decidedly depends.

Nature must have its free course,
must go its normal way; what a
woman wants is to be with one man
and with him forever. That is not
always possible, but when it is otherwise it is against nature.
VAN GOGH, *Letters*

21664.
Blonde or brunette, this rhyme ap-
plies,
Happy is he who knows them not.
FRANÇOIS VILLON,
The Greater Testament

21665.
If woman lost us Eden, such
As she alone restore it.
WHITTIER, *Among the Hills*

21666. Men always want to be a
woman's first love. That is their
clumsy vanity. We women have a
more subtle instinct about things.
What we like is to be a man's last
romance.   OSCAR WILDE,
A Woman of No Importance

21667. All women used to be owned
by men. Formerly they ruled us by
physical force—now by financial
force.   JESSE L. WILLIAMS,
Why Marry?

21668.
The reason firm, the temperate will,
Endurance, foresight, strength, and
skill;
A perfect woman, nobly planned,
To warn, to comfort, and command.
WORDSWORTH,
She Was a Phantom of Delight

See also: 212, 266, 318, 391, 404,
438, 455, 459, 461, 733, 1351, 1396,
1521, 1669, 2003, 2437, 2438, 2529,
2856, 3141, 3143, 3151, 3157, 3476,
4294, 4421, 4819, 5188, 5646, 5932,
6011, 6305, 7492, 8199, 8282, 8646,
12096, 12580, 19466, 19900, 20654.

WONDER

Related Subjects: **Admiration, Credulity, Miracle.**

21671. Wonder—which is the seed of knowledge.   BACON,
Advancement of Learning

21672. Things too wonderful for me, which I knew not.
Bible: Job, xlii, 3

21673. There be three things which are too wonderful for me, yea, four which I know not; The way of an eagle in the air; the way of a serpent upon a rock; the way of a ship in the midst of the sea; and the way of a man with a maid.
Bible: Proverbs, xxx, 18, 19

21674. Has a man done wondering at women?—there follow men, dead and alive, to wonder at. Has he done wondering at men?—there's God to wonder at.   BROWNING,
Pippa Passes

21675. Wonder is the basis of Worship.   CARLYLE, *Sartor Resartus*

21676. The man who cannot wonder, who does not habitually wonder . . . is but a pair of spectacles, behind which there is no Eye.
CARLYLE, *Sartor Resartus*

21677. The world will never starve for wonders; but only for want of wonder.   G. K. CHESTERTON,
A Century of Progress Exposition

21678. Peace, it's wonderful!
FATHER DIVINE

21679. Wonder is the daughter of ignorance.   JOHN FLORIO,
First Fruites

21680. Wonders will never cease.
DAVID GARRICK, *Correspondence*

21681. Indeed, what is there that does not appear marvellous when it comes to our knowledge for the first time? How many things, too, are looked upon as quite impossible until they have been actually effected?
PLINY THE ELDER, *Natural History*

21682. A nine days' wonder.
Proverb

21683. Nay, I'll speak that which you will wonder at.   SHAKESPEARE,
All's Well that Ends Well

21684. O, wonderful, wonderful, and most wonderful wonderful! and yet again wonderful, and after that out of all hooping.   SHAKESPEARE,
As You Like It

21685.
Whilst I am bound to wonder, I am bound
To pity too.   SHAKESPEARE,
Cymbeline

21686.
This man so complete
Who was enroll'd 'mongst wonders.
SHAKESPEARE, *Henry VIII*

21687.
Can such things be,
And overcome us like a summer's cloud,
Without our special wonder?
SHAKESPEARE, *Macbeth*

21688. You shall see wonders.
SHAKESPEARE,
The Merry Wives of Windsor

21689. I was struck all of a heap.
SHERIDAN, *The Duenna*

21690. Wonder is involuntary praise.
EDWARD YOUNG, *The Revenge*

21691.
We nothing know, but what is marvellous;

Yet what is marvellous, we can't believe.　EDWARD YOUNG,
Night Thoughts

See also: 431, 1307, 6022, 21873.

WOODS, see Forest

WOOING, see Courtship

WORDS

Related Subjects: Boasting, Conversation, Deeds, Eloquence, Grammar, Language, Speech, Voice, Writing.

21701. No one means all he says, and yet very few say all they mean, for words are slippery and thought is viscous.　HENRY ADAMS,
The Education of Henry Adams

21702. Words are the physicians of a mind diseased.　AESCHYLUS,
Prometheus

21703.
What things have we seen
Done at the Mermaid! heard words that have been
So nimble and so full of subtile flame
As if that every one from whence they came
Had meant to put his whole wit in a jest,
And resolved to live a fool the rest
Of his dull life.
FRANCIS BEAUMONT,
Letter to Ben Jonson

21704. How forcible are right words!
Bible: Job, vi, 25

21705. A word spoken in due season, how good is it!
Bible: Proverbs, xv, 23

21706. A word fitly spoken is like apples of gold in pictures of silver.
Bible: Proverbs, xxv, 11

21707. Heaven and earth shall pass away, but my words shall not pass away.　*Bible: Matthew, xxiv, 35*

21708. In the beginning was the Word, and the Word was with God, and the Word was God.
Bible: John, i, 1

21709. And this I say, lest any man should beguile you with enticing words.　*Bible: Colossians, ii, 4*

21710.
Tender pauses speak
The overflow of gladness, when words are all too weak.
BRYANT, *The Damsel of Peru*

21711. There are a lot of words in this world, and many of them are lying around loose.　WHIT BURNETT,
The Literary Life & the Hell With It

21712.
But words are things, and a small drop of ink
Falling like dew upon a thought, produces
That which makes thousands, perhaps millions, think.
BYRON, *Don Juan*

21713. Be not the slave of Words.
CARLYLE, *Sartor Resartus*

21714. "When I use a word," Humpty-Dumpty said, "it means just what I choose it to mean—neither more nor less."
LEWIS CARROLL,
Through the Looking-Glass

21715. Words are but empty thanks.
COLLEY CIBBER, *Woman's Wit*

21716. Polysyllabic (or what the common people call, *dictionary*) words.　COLERIDGE,
Biographia Literaria

21717. Thou art a Retailer of Phrases, and dost deal in Remnants of Remnants. Congreve, *The Way of the World*

21718. Although words exist for the most part for the transmission of ideas, there are some which produce such violent disturbance in our feelings that the role they play in the transmission of ideas is lost in the background. Einstein

21719.
And don't confound the language of the nation
With long-tailed words in *osity* and *ation*. J. H. Frere,
The Monks and the Giants

21720. Words are wise men's counters,—they do but reckon by them; but they are the money of fools.
Thomas Hobbes, *Leviathan*

21721. But words once spoke can never be recall'd. Horace,
Ars Poetica

21722.
Men ever had, and ever will have, leave
To coin new words well suited to the age,
Words are like leaves, some wither ev'ry year,
And ev'ry year a younger race succeeds. Horace, *Ars Poetica*

21723. Dictionaries are like watches; the worst is better than none, and the best cannot be expected to go quite true. Samuel Johnson

21724. How many honest words have suffered corruption since Chaucer's days! Thomas Middleton,
No Wit, no Help, Like a Woman's

21725. His words, like so many nimble and airy servitors, trip about him at command. Milton,
Apology for Smectymnuus

21726.
His words, replete with guile,
Into her heart too easy entrance won.
Milton, *Paradise Lost*

21727. Democritus said, words are but the shadows of actions.
Plutarch

21728.
Words are like leaves; and where they most abound,
Much fruit of sense beneath is rarely found. Pope, *Essay on Criticism*

21729. Deliver your words not by number but by weight. *Proverb*

21730. Ill words are bellows to a slackening fire. *Proverb*

21731. Good words are worth much, and cost little. *Proverb*

21732. An acute word cuts deeper than a sharp weapon. *Proverb*

21733.
Oh, many a shaft at random sent
Finds mark the archer little meant!
And many a word, at random spoken,
May soothe or wound a heart that's broken! Scott,
The Lord of the Isles

21734. Syllables govern the world.
John Selden, *Table Talk*

21735. Whose words all ears took captive. Shakespeare,
All's Well that Ends Well

21736. Answer me in one word.
Shakespeare, *As You Like It*

21737.
Polonius. What do you read, my lord?
Hamlet. Words, words, words.
Shakespeare, *Hamlet*

21738. Men of few words are the best men. Shakespeare, *Henry V*

21739

'Tis well said again;
And 'tis a kind of good deed to say well:
And yet words are no deeds.

SHAKESPEARE, *Henry VIII*

21740.

Zounds! I was never so bethump'd with words
Since I first call'd my brother's father dad.   SHAKESPEARE,
King John

21741.

Here are a few of the unpleasant'st words
That ever blotted paper!

SHAKESPEARE,
The Merchant of Venice

21742. Charm ache with air, and agony with words.

SHAKESPEARE,
Much Ado About Nothing

21743.

I understand a fury in your words,
But not the words.

SHAKESPEARE, *Othello*

21744. How long a time lies in one little word!   SHAKESPEARE,
Richard II

21745. A word and a blow.

SHAKESPEARE, *Romeo and Juliet*

21746. These words are razors to my wounded heart.   SHAKESPEARE,
Titus Andronicus

21747. Words pay no debts.

SHAKESPEARE,
Troilus and Cressida

21748.

For deeds doe die, how ever noblie donne,
And thoughts of men do as themselves decay,

But wise wordes taught in numbers for to runne,
Recorded by the Muses, live for ay.

EDMUND SPENSER,
The Ruines of Time

21749. Large divine and comfortable words.   TENNYSON,
Idylls of the King

21750. A powerful agent is the right word. Whenever we come upon one of those intensely right words in a book or a newspaper the resulting effect is physical as well as spiritual, and electrically prompt.

MARK TWAIN,
Essay on William Dean Howells

21751. They spell it Vinci and pronounce it Vinchy; foreigners always spell better than they pronounce.

MARK TWAIN,
The Innocents Abroad

21752. Many a treasure besides Ali Baba's is unlocked with a verbal key.

HENRY VAN DYKE

21753.

If any words of mine,
Through right of life divine,
Remain, what matters it
Whose hand the message writ?

WHITTIER, *An Autograph*

21754.

Honied words like bees,
Gilded and sticky, with a little sting.

ELINOR WYLIE, *Pretty Words*

See also: 165, 971, 1162, 1871, 2307, 2472, 2475, 3314, 11315, 15763, 19314.

WORK

Related Subjects: Business, Deeds, Effort, Employment, Industry, Labor, Occupation, Sweat, Wages.

21761.

Work and pray, live on hay,

You'll get pie, in the sky,
When you die—
It's a lie!   *Anonymous,*
          Song of the I.W.W.

21762.
He works and blows the coals
And has plenty of other irons in the
fire.   Aristophanes,
          The Acharnians

21763. Thou renderest to every man
according to his work.
          Bible: Psalms, lxii, 12

21764. Establish thou the work of our
hands upon us; yea, the work of our
hands establish thou it.
          Bible: Psalms, xc, 17

21765. Every man's work shall be
made manifest.
          Bible: 1 Corinthians, iii, 13

21766. A workman that needeth not
to be ashamed.
          Bible: 2 Timothy, ii, 15

21767. Everyone has a mass of bad
work in him which he will have to
work off and get rid of before he can
do better—and indeed, the more lasting a man's ultimate good work, the
more sure he is to pass through a
time, and perhaps a very long one, in
which there seems very little hope for
him at all. We must all sow our
spiritual wild oats.
          Samuel Butler,
          The Way of All Flesh

21768. All work is as seed sown; it
grows and spreads and sows itself
anew.   Carlyle,
          On Boswell's Life of Johnson

21769. All work, even cotton-spin-
ning, is noble; work is alone noble.
. . . A life of ease is not for any man,
nor for any god.   Carlyle,
          Past and Present

21770. The ass will carry his load, but
not a double load; ride not a free
horse to death.   Cervantes,
          Don Quixote

21771.
Work thou for pleasure—paint, or
    sing, or carve
The thing thou lovest, though the
    body starve—
Who works for glory misses oft the
    goal;
Who works for money coins his very
    soul.
Work for the work's sake, then, and
    it may be
That these things shall be added unto
    thee.   Kenyon Cox, *Work*

21772.
Work, and thou wilt bless the day
    Ere the toil be done;
They that work not, can not pray,
    Can not feel the sun.
          J. S. Dwight, *Rest*

21773. The time will come when
every kind of work will be judged by
two measurements: one by the product itself, as is now done, and the
other by the effect of the work on the
producer.   A. H. Eaton

21774. Cecil's saying of Sir Walter
Raleigh, "I know that he can toil terribly," is an electric touch.
          Emerson, *Representative Men*

21775. Toil, says the proverb, is the
sire of fame.   Euripides, *Licymnius*

21776. Work is the meat of life,
pleasure the dessert.
          B. C. Forbes, *Forbes' Epigrams*

21777. Work is love made visible.
And if you cannot work with love but
only with distaste, it is better that
you should leave your work and sit at
the gate of the temple and take alms
of those who work with joy.
          Kahlil Gibran, *The Prophet*

21778. You do de pullin', Sis Cow, en I'll do de gruntin'.

> JOEL CHANDLER HARRIS,
> *Uncle Remus*

21779. Thank God every morning when you get up that you have something to do that day which must be done, whether you like it or not. Being forced to work, and forced to do your best, will breed in you temperance and self-control, diligence and strength of will, cheerfulness and content, and a hundred virtues which the idle never know.

> CHARLES KINGSLEY, *Letter*

21780. By the work one knows the workman.   LA FONTAINE, *Fables*

21781.
Who first invented work, and bound
   the free
And holiday-rejoicing spirit down
To that dry drudgery at the desk's
   dead wood?   CHARLES LAMB,
> *Work*

21782. My father taught me to work; he did not teach me to love it.
> LINCOLN

21783.
No man is born into the world whose
   work
Is not born with him; there is always
   work
And tools to work withal, for those
   who will;
And blessèd are the horny hands of
   toil.   LOWELL,
> *A Glance Behind the Curtain*

21784. At the end of work, you may judge of the workman.   *Proverb*

21785. Account not that work slavery that brings in penny savory.
> *Proverb*

21786. It is working that makes a workman.   *Proverb*

21787. Not to oversee workmen, is to leave them your purse open.
> *Proverb*

21788. A bad workman quarrels with his tools.   *Proverb*

21789. All work and no play makes Jack a dull boy.   *Proverb*

21790. In order that people may be happy in their work, these three things are needed: They must be fit for it: They must not do too much of it: And they must have a sense of success in it.   RUSKIN,
> *Pre-Raphaelitism*

21791. Work consists of whatever a body is *obliged* to do, and Play consists of whatever a body is not obliged to do.   MARK TWAIN,
> *The Adventures of Tom Sawyer*

21792.
This is my work; my blessing, not my
   doom;
Of all who live, I am the one by whom
This work can best be done in the
   right way.   HENRY VAN DYKE,
> *The Three Best Things*

21793. Work alone will efface the footsteps of work.   WHISTLER

See also: 1214, 1232, 1838, 1931, 2128, 2246, 3005, 3021, 3206, 9474, 12288.

WORLD AND WORLDLINESS

Related Subjects: Cosmopolitanism, Cynicism, Earth, The Heavens, Mammon.

21801.
O World, be nobler, for her sake!
   If she but knew thee what thou art,
What wrongs are borne, what deeds
   are done
In thee, beneath thy daily sun,
   Know'st thou not that her tender
     heart

For pain and very shame would
break?
O World, be nobler, for her sake!
LAURENCE BINYON,
O World, Be Nobler

21802.
Do what you will, this world's a
fiction
And is made up of contradiction.
BLAKE

21803. This world, and the wrong it
does.   BROWNING,
Old Pictures in Florence

21804. It is so easy to get lost in the
world.   JOHN BURROUGHS

21805. If the world will be gulled, let
it be gulled.   ROBERT BURTON,
Anatomy of Melancholy

21806. I have not loved the world, nor
the world me.   BYRON,
Childe Harold

21807.
This world nis but a thurghfare full
of wo,
And we ben pilgrimes, passing to and
fro;
Deeth is an ende of every worldly
sore.   CHAUCER,
Canterbury Tales

21808. To me it seems as if when God
conceived the world, that was poetry;
He formed it, and that was sculpture;
He varied and colored it, and that was
painting; and then, crowning all, He
peopled it with living beings, and that
was the grand divine, eternal drama.
CHARLOTTE CUSHMAN

21809. It's a mad world. Mad as Bed-
lam.   DICKENS, *David Copperfield*

21810. The world is a wheel, and it
will all come round right.
DISRAELI, *Endymion*

21811.
Good-bye, proud world! I'm going
home;
Thou art not my friend and I'm not
thine.   EMERSON, *Good-bye*

21812. That cold accretion called the
world, which, so terrible in the mass,
is so unformidable, even pitiable, in
its units.   THOMAS HARDY,
Tess of the D'Urbervilles

21813. The world is nothing but a
great desire to live and a great dissatisfaction with living. HERACLITUS

21814.
Let the world slide, let the world go;
A fig for care, and a fig for woe!
If I can't pay, why I can owe,
And death makes equal the high and
low.   JOHN HEYWOOD,
Be Merry Friends

21815. The axis of the earth sticks
out visibly through the centre of each
and every town or city.
O. W. HOLMES,
The Autocrat of the Breakfast-Table

21816.
This world is very odd to see,
We do not comprehend it;
But in one fact we all agree,
God won't, and we can't, mend it.
A. H. CLOUGH, *Dipsychus*

21817. The chess-board is the world,
the pieces are the phenomena of the
universe, the rules of the game are
what we call the laws of Nature. The
player on the other side is hidden
from us. We know that his play is
always fair, just, and patient. But also
we know, to our cost, that he never
overlooks a mistake, or makes the
smallest allowance for ignorance.
THOMAS H. HUXLEY, *Lay Sermons*

21818. The whole drift of my education goes to persuade me that the

world of our present consciousness is only one out of many worlds of consciousness that exist.

WILLIAM JAMES,
The Varieties of Religious Experience

21819. The world is merely a bridge; ye are to pass over it, and not to build your dwellings upon it.
Agrapha: The Unwritten Sayings of Jesus

21820. This world, where much is to be done and little to be known.
SAMUEL JOHNSON,
Prayers and Meditations

21821.
Deign on the passing world to turn thine eyes,
And pause a while from learning to be wise. SAMUEL JOHNSON,
The Vanity of Human Wishes

21822.
The world in all doth but two nations bear,—
The good, the bad; and these mixed everywhere.
ANDREW MARVELL, *The Loyal Scot*

21823.
O world, I cannot hold thee close enough!
Thy winds, thy wide gray skies!
Thy mists, that roll and rise!
Thy woods, this autumn day, that ache and sag
And all but cry with color.
EDNA ST. VINCENT MILLAY,
God's World

21824. The world, dear Agnes, is a strange affair. MOLIÈRE,
L'École des Femmes

21825. But, good God! what an age is this, and what a world is this! that a man cannot live without playing the knave and dissimulation.
SAMUEL PEPYS, *Diary*

21826. The world is a great book, of which they that never stir from home read only a page. *Proverb*

21827. The world is a net; the more we stir in it, the more we are entangled. *Proverb*

21828. Be wisely worldly, be not worldly wise.
FRANCIS QUARLES, *Emblems*

21829. Then I began to think that it is very true which is commonly said, that the one half of the world knoweth not how the other half liveth.
RABELAIS

21830.
Great wide, beautiful, wonderful world,
With the wonderful waters round you curled,
And the wonderful grass upon your breast,
World, you are beautifully drest.
W. B. RANDS, *The Child's World*

21831. There is no more mistaken path to happiness than worldliness, revelry, high life. SCHOPENHAUER

21832. O, how full of briers is this working-day world!
SHAKESPEARE,
As You Like It

21833.
O God! O God!
How weary, stale, flat and unprofitable
Seem to me all the uses of this world.
SHAKESPEARE, *Hamlet*

21834. This goodly frame, the earth, seems to me a sterile promontory; this most excellent canopy, the air, look you, this brave o'er-hanging firmament, this majestical roof fretted with golden fire, why, it appears no other thing to me than a foul and pestilent congregation of vapours.
SHAKESPEARE, *Hamlet*

21835. I'll tell the world.
SHAKESPEARE, *Measure for Measure*

21836.
I hold the world but as the world,
Gratiano,—
A stage, where every man must play
a part;
And mine a sad one.
SHAKESPEARE,
The Merchant of Venice

21837.
I'll put a girdle round about the earth
In forty minutes.
SHAKESPEARE,
A Midsummer-Night's Dream

21838. The world is not thy friend
nor the world's law.
SHAKESPEARE, *Romeo and Juliet*

21839. Let the world slide.
SHAKESPEARE,
The Taming of the Shrew

21840.
O brave new world,
That has such people in't!
SHAKESPEARE, *The Tempest*

21841.
Me seemes the world is runne quite
out of square,
From the first point of his appointed
course,
And being once amisse growes daily
Wourse and wourse.
EDMUND SPENSER,
The Faerie Queene

21842. There was all the world and
his wife.   SWIFT,
Polite Conversation

21843.
For why is all around us here
As if some lesser god had made the
world,
But had not force to shape it as he
would?   TENNYSON,
Idylls of the King

21844.
That man's the best Cosmopolite
Who loves his native country best.
TENNYSON, *Hands All Round*

21845. The world is a comedy to
those that think, a tragedy to those
who feel.   HORACE WALPOLE

21846. I look upon all the world as my
parish.   JOHN WESLEY

21847.
It is a very good world to live in,
To lend or to spend, or to give in;
But to beg or to borrow, or to get a
man's own,
It is the very worst world that ever
was known.   JOHN WILMOT,
Epigram

21848.
The world is too much with us; late
and soon,
Getting and spending, we lay waste
our powers:
Little we see in Nature that is ours.
WORDSWORTH,
The World is too Much With Us

See also: 534, 574, 585, 2797, 2882,
3035, 3112, 3243, 3563, 4378, 8693,
8734, 9732, 10435, 10892, 12582,
14487, 18661, 18689, 18857, 20632,
21124.

WORM

Related Subject: Earth.

21851.
The loving worm within its clod
Were diviner than a loveless God.
BROWNING, *Christmas-Eve*

21852. Worms wind themselves into
our sweetest flowers.
COWPER, *The Task*

21853.
Fear not then, thou child infirm;
There's no god dare wrong a worm.
EMERSON, *Essays*

21854.
"I do not want to be a fly,
I want to be a worm!"
CHARLOTTE GILMAN, *A Conservative*

21855. I cannot but think that he who finds a certain proportion of pain and evil inseparably woven up in the life of the very worms, will bear his own share with more courage and submission.   THOMAS H. HUXLEY

21856. Your worm is your only emperor for diet; we fat all creatures else to fat us, and we fat ourselves for maggots.   SHAKESPEARE, *Hamlet*

21857. The smallest worm will turn, being trodden on.
SHAKESPEARE, *Henry VI*

See also: 7043, 11255.

WORRY

Related Subjects: Agitation, Burden, Care, Patience, Responsibility, Suspense.

21861. There are two days in the week about which and upon which I never worry. Two carefree days, kept sacredly free from fear and apprehension. One of these days is Yesterday. . . . And the other day I do not worry about is Tomorrow.
R. J. BURDETTE, *The Golden Day*

21862.
O fond anxiety of mortal men!
How vain and inconclusive arguments
Are those, which make thee beat thy
wings below!   DANTE, *Paradise*

21863. I have never yet met a healthy person who worried very much about his health, or a really good person who worried much about his own soul.   J. B. S. HALDANE

21864. Worry is interest paid on trouble before it becomes due.
DEAN INGE

21865. I have lost everything, and I am so poor now that I really cannot afford to let anything worry me.
JOSEPH JEFFERSON

21866. There is little peace or comfort in life if we are always anxious as to future events. He that worries himself with the dread of possible contingencies will never be at rest.
SAMUEL JOHNSON

21867. Worry, the interest paid by those who borrow trouble.
GEORGE W. LYON

21868. The bow too tensely strung is easily broken.
PUBLILIUS SYRUS, *Sententiae*

21869. Cudgel thy brains no more about it.   SHAKESPEARE, *Hamlet*

21870.
Tell me, sweet lord, what is't that
takes from thee
Thy stomach, pleasure, and thy
golden sleep?   SHAKESPEARE,
Henry IV

WORSHIP

Related Subjects: Church, Devotion, God, Gods, Idolatry, Love, Meeting, Religion, Sacrifice.

21871. Where two or three are gathered together in my name, there am I in the midst of them.
Bible: Matthew, xviii, 20

21872.
He wales a portion with judicious
care,
And "Let us worship God!" he says,
with solemn air.   BURNS,
The Cotter's Saturday Night

21873. Worship is transcendent wonder.   CARLYLE,
Heroes & Hero-Worship

21874.

Go! kneel a worshipper at Nature's
shrine!
For you her fields are green, and fair
her skies!
For you her rivers flow, her hills
arise!   J. R. DRAKE,
The Culprit Fay

21875. And what greater calamity can
fall upon a nation than the loss of
worship.   EMERSON

21876. The various modes of worship
which prevailed in the Roman world
were all considered by the people as
equally true; by the philosopher as
equally false; and by the magistrate
as equally useful.   GIBBON,
Decline and Fall

21877. Devotional contact makes a
worshipping throng as different from
the same numbers praying apart as a
bed of coals is from a trail of scattered cinders.   O. W. HOLMES

21878. O unbelievers, I will not worship that which ye worship; nor will
ye worship that which I worship . . .
Ye have your religion, and I my religion.   *The Koran*

21879. And learn there may be worship without words!   LOWELL,
My Cathedral

21880. Every one's true worship was
that which he found in use in the
place where he chanced to be.
MONTAIGNE, *Essays*

21881. Where it is a duty to worship
the sun it is pretty sure to be a crime
to examine the laws of heat.
JOHN MORLEY, *Voltaire*

21882. Pompey bade Sylla recollect
that more worshipped the rising than
the setting sun. PLUTARCH'S, *Lives*

21883.

They that worship God merely from
fear,
Would worship the devil too, if he
appear.   *Proverb*

21884. We have found in this terrible age that if the concept of God is
removed from men's lives a vacuum
is created, and that vacuum is
promptly filled by a Hitler or a Stalin.
The instinct to worship is hardly less
strong than the instinct to eat.
DOROTHY THOMPSON,
Speech, May 6, 1941

See also: 17356, 21675.

WORTH

**Related Subjects: Appearance,
Character, Deserving, Excellence,
Honesty, Merit, Price, Qualities,
Use.**

21891. Outside show is a poor substitute for inner worth.   AESOP,
The Fox and the Mask

21892. It is not what he has, nor even
what he does, which directly expresses the worth of a man, but what
he is.   AMIEL, *Journal*

21893. Of whom the world was not
worthy.   *Bible: Hebrews, xi, 38*

21894. The by-product is sometimes
more valuable than the product.
HAVELOCK ELLIS,
Little Essays on Love and Virtue

21895. A man passes for that he is
worth. What he is engraves itself on
his face in letters of light.
EMERSON, *Essays*

21896. The "value" or "worth" of
a man, is, as of all other things, his
price; that is to say, so much as would
be given for the use of his power.
THOMAS HOBBES, *Leviathan*

21897.
Farewell! I did not know thy worth;
But thou art gone, and now 'tis
    priz'd;
So angels walk'd unknown on earth,
But when they flew were recogniz'd.
    THOMAS HOOD, *To an Absentee*

21898.
Slow rises worth, by poverty de-
    press'd:
But here more slow, where all are
    slaves to gold,
Where looks are merchandise, and
    smiles are sold.
    SAMUEL JOHNSON, *London*

21899. Worth seeing? yes; but not
worth going to see.
    SAMUEL JOHNSON, *Boswell: Life*

21900. Life is continually weighing
us in very sensitive scales, and telling every one of us precisely what
his real weight is to the last grain
of dust.   LOWELL,
    *On a Certain Condescension
        in Foreigners*

21901.
We cheat ourselves in cheating worth
    of wonder.
Not the unwitting dead
But we who leave the praise unsaid
    are plundered.
    ARCHIBALD MACLEISH

21902. Ye are worth thy weight of
gold.   HENRY MEDWALL, *Nature*

21903. Worthy things happen to the
worthy.   PLAUTUS, *Paenulus*

21904. It is no good hen, that cackles
in your house and lays in another's.
    Proverb

21905. So much is a man worth as he
esteems himself.   RABELAIS

21906. When we assert that this or
that has "value," we are giving ex-

pression to our emotions, not to a fact
which would still be true if our personal feelings were different.
    BERTRAND RUSSELL

21907. Worth is by worth in every
rank admired.
    RICHARD SAVAGE,
        Epistle to Aaron Hill

21908. They are worthy To inlay
heaven with stars.
    SHAKESPEARE, *Cymbeline*

21909. I could have better spared a
better man.
    SHAKESPEARE, *Henry IV*

21910. I am not worth this coil that's
made for me.
    SHAKESPEARE, *King John*

21911.
Let there be some more test made of
    my metal,
Before so noble and so great a figure
Be stamp'd upon it.
    SHAKESPEARE, *Measure for Measure*

21912. They are not China dishes,
but very good dishes.
    SHAKESPEARE, *Measure for Measure*

21913. They are but beggars that
can count their worth.
    SHAKESPEARE, *Romeo and Juliet*

21914.
    A man of worth
In his own household will appear up-
    right
In the state also.
    SOPHOCLES, *Antigone*

21915. All good things are cheap: all
bad are very dear.
    THOREAU, *Journal*

21916. There buds the promise of
celestial worth.
    EDWARD YOUNG, *The Last Day*

See also: 1655, 2065, 4858, 10861.

WOUNDS

Related Subjects: Blood, Cruelty, Injury, War.

21921.
For want of timely care
Millions have died of medicable
wounds.   JOHN ARMSTRONG,
Art of Preserving Health

21922. I was wounded in the house of my friends.
Bible: Zechariah, xiii, 6

21923. To tear open a wound.
CICERO, *De Lege Agraria*

21924. They that are afraid of wounds must not come near a battle.
JOHN CLARKE, *Paroemiologia*

21925. Fools, through false shame, conceal their open wounds.
HORACE, *Epistles*

21926. Wounds cannot be cured unless probed and dressed.
LIVY, *History*

21927. His breast was covered with honorable wounds. PLUTARCH, *Lives*

21928. A wound heals but the scar remains.   *Proverb*

21929. Small wounds, if many, may be mortal.   *Proverb*

21930. Search not a wound too deep, lest thou make a new one.   *Proverb*

21931. A green wound is soon healed.   *Proverb*

21932. His cicatrice, an emblem of war, here on his sinister cheek.
SHAKESPEARE,
All's Well that Ends Well

21933. With a wound. I must be cured.   SHAKESPEARE,
Antony and Cleopatra

21934.
The wound that bred this meeting here
Cannot be cured by words.
SHAKESPEARE, *Henry VI*

21935.
Open thy gate of mercy, gracious God!
My soul flies through these wounds to seek out Thee.
SHAKESPEARE, *Henry VI*

21936.
Show you sweet Caesar's wounds, poor, poor dumb mouths,
And bid them speak for me.
SHAKESPEARE, *Julius Caesar*

21937. What wound did ever heal but by degrees?
SHAKESPEARE, *Othello*

21938.
Iago: What, are you hurt, lieutenant?
Cassio: Ay, past all surgery.
SHAKESPEARE, *Othello*

21939. He jests at scars, that never felt a wound.   SHAKESPEARE,
Romeo and Juliet

21940.
Romeo. Courage, man; the hurt cannot be much.
Mercutio. No, 'tis not so deep as a well, nor so wide as a churchdoor; but 'tis enough, 'twill serve.
SHAKESPEARE, *Romeo and Juliet*

21941. He in peace is wounded, not in war.   SHAKESPEARE,
The Rape of Lucrece

WRITING

Related Subjects: Authors, Books, Fiction, Grammar, Ink, Language, Letters, Literature, Pen, Poets, Words.

21951. I always write only half-

sentences, and the reader himself must supply the other half. BRAHMS

21952. In every man's writings, the character of the writer must lie recorded. CARLYLE, *Goethe*

21953. It is not the hand, but the understanding of a man, that may be said to write.
CERVANTES, *Don Quixote*

21954. Men have lost sight of distant horizons. Nobody writes of humanity, for civilization; they write for their country, their sect; to amuse their friends or annoy their enemies.
NORMAN DOUGLAS, *South Wind*

21955. I have the conviction that excessive literary production is a social offence.
GEORGE ELIOT, *Life and Letters*

21956. All the conventional rules of the construction of speech may be put aside if a writer is thereby enabled to follow more closely and lucidly the form and process of his thought. HAVELOCK ELLIS,
The Dance of Life

21957. As a man lives and thinks, so will he write. GALSWORTHY

21958. You that intend to write what is worthy to be read more than once, blot frequently: and take no pains to make the multitude admire you, content with a few judicious readers.
HORACE, *Satires*

21959. The mob of gentlemen who wrote with ease. HORACE

21960. A bad book is as much of a labour to write as a good one; it comes as sincerely from the author's soul. ALDOUS HUXLEY,
Point Counter Point

21961. An old tutor of a college said to one of his pupils: Read over your composition, and wherever you meet with a passage which you think is particularly fine, strike it out.
SAMUEL JOHNSON, *Boswell: Life*

21962. Perhaps no man ever thought a line superfluous when he wrote it. We are seldom tiresome to ourselves.
SAMUEL JOHNSON

21963. Who casts to write a living line, must sweat. BEN JONSON,
To the Memory of Shakespeare

21964. A good many young writers make the mistake of enclosing a stamped, self-addressed envelope, big enough for the manuscript to come back in. This is too much of a temptation to the editor.
RING LARDNER,
How to Write Short Stories

21965. The writers who have nothing to say are the ones you can buy; the others have too high a price.
WALTER LIPPMANN,
A Preface to Politics

21966. Atmosphere stands always for the elimination of the artist. Get your good strong phrases, fresh and vivid; write intensively, not exhaustively or lengthily; don't narrate—paint! draw! build! *Create!* Better one thousand words that are builded than a whole book of mediocre spun-out, dashed-off stuff. Damn you! Forget you! And then the world will remember you!
JACK LONDON, *to Cloudesley Johns*

21967. Look, then, into thine heart, and write! LONGFELLOW,
Voices of the Night

21968. He does not write at all whose poems no man reads. MARTIAL

21969. We do not write as we want to but as we can.
SOMERSET MAUGHAM

21970.
True ease in writing comes from art, not chance,
As those move easiest who have learn'd to dance.
POPE, *Essay on Criticism*

21971. The great majority of novelists write from a shallow inkwell. They but scratch the surface of reality. . . . I know scarcely a single writer who, throughout a work of any size, comes to grips with life like an athlete, hand to hand,—who embraces the entire mass of reality, his chosen prey, in the net of his spiritual and intellectual perception.
ROMAIN ROLLAND

21972.
I once did hold it, as our statists do,
A baseness to write fair.
SHAKESPEARE, *Hamlet*

21973. Devise, wit; write, pen; for I am for whole volumes in folio.
SHAKESPEARE, *Love's Labour's Lost*

21974.
You write with ease to show your breeding,
But easy writing's curst hard reading.
SHERIDAN

21975. In composing, as a general rule, run your pen through every other word you have written; you have no idea what vigor it will give your style.
SYDNEY SMITH,
Lady Holland's Memoir

21976. As to the Adjective; when in doubt, strike it out.
MARK TWAIN,
Pudd'nhead Wilson's Calendar

21977.
The only work about writing—
It's a very terrible thing—
Is wrapping your stuff and stamping it
And tying it up with string.
MARGARET WIDDEMER, *Confessions*

See also: 592, 1641, 2662.

WRONGS

Related Subjects: Cruelty, Error, Injury, Mistake, Sin.

21981.
Some kind of wrongs there are, which flesh and blood
Cannot endure.
BEAUMONT & FLETCHER,
The Little French Lawyer

21982. The wrong was his who wrongfully complain'd.
COWPER, *Hope*

21983.
My ear is pain'd,
My soul is sick with every day's report
Of wrong and outrage with which earth is fill'd. COWPER, *The Task*

21984.
Wrongs do not leave off there where they begin,
But still beget new mischiefs in their course. SAMUEL DANIEL,
The History of the Civil War

21985. You cannot do wrong without suffering wrong.
EMERSON, *Essays*

21986. For every social wrong there must be a remedy. But the remedy can be nothing less than the abolition of wrong.
HENRY GEORGE, *Social Problems*

21987. He knew he had the wrong end of the stick.
GABRIEL HARVEY, *Letter-Book*

21988. He wrought no wrong in deed or word to any man.
HOMER, *Odyssey*

21989. A wrong-doer is often a man that has left something undone, not always he that has done something.
MARCUS AURELIUS, *Meditations*

21990. A passionate wrong cries ever till judgment comes.
JOHN MASEFIELD, *The Wild Swan*

21991. The wrong way always seems the more reasonable.
GEORGE MOORE,
The Bending of the Bough

21992. It is hard to suffer wrong and pay for it too.   *Proverb*

21993. Wrong has no warrant.
Proverb

21994. By bearing old wrongs you provoke new ones.
PUBLILIUS SYRUS, *Sententiae*

21995. He hath done me wrong.
SHAKESPEARE, *Henry VI*

21996.
Wrongs, unspeakable, past patience,
Or more than any living man could bear.
SHAKESPEARE, *Titus Andronicus*

21997. I didn't come on the wrong side of the blanket.
SMOLLETT, *Humphrey Clinker*

See also: 3283, 17178.

X, Y, Z

YEAR

Related Subjects: Month, Time.

22001. Six years—six little years— six drops of time.
MATTHEW ARNOLD, *Mycerinus*

22002.
Years have hardier tasks
Than listening to a whisper or a sigh.
STEPHEN VINCENT BENET
The Golden Corpse

22003. A thousand years in thy sight are but as yesterday when it is past, and as a watch in the night.
Bible: Psalms, xc, 4

22004. We spend our years as a tale that is told.   *Bible: Psalms, xc, 9*

22005. The days of our years are threescore years and ten; and if by reason of strength they be fourscore years, yet is their strength labour and sorrow; for it is soon cut off, and we fly away.   *Bible: Psalms, xc, 10*

22006.
Lament who will, in fruitless tears,

The speed with which our moments fly;
I sigh not over vanished years,
But watch the years that hasten by.
BRYANT, *The Lapse of Time*

22007.
Lib'ral in all things else, yet Nature here
With stern severity deals out the year.   COWPER, *Table Talk*

22008. The wonderful year.
DRYDEN

22009. We do not count a man's years until he has nothing else to count.   EMERSON

22010. The years teach much which the days never know.
EMERSON, *Essays*

22011. A year is no contemptible portion of this mortal existence.
GIBBON, *Miscellaneous Works*

22012. Sad, sad to think that the year is all but done.
CHARLES KINGSLEY, *The Starlings*

22013. Nothing is swifter than the years.   OVID, *Metamorphoses*

22014. Years know more than books.
Proverb

22015. I will not let the years run over me like a Juggernaut car.
THOREAU, *Journal*

22016.
I do not think seventy years is the time of a man or woman, . . .
Nor that years will ever stop the existence of me, or any one else.
WALT WHITMAN,
Who Learns My Lesson Complete?

22017.
The years like great black oxen tread the world
And God, the herdsman, goads them on behind.   W. B. YEATS,
The Countess Cathleen

See also: 505, 4965, 13491.

YESTERDAY

Related Subjects: History, Memory, Past.

22021. How long ago it may seem since yesterday!
J. M. BARRIE, *Sentimental Tommy*

22022.
He seems
To have seen better days, as who has not
Who has seen yesterday?
BYRON, *Werner*

22023. The public only takes up yesterday as a stick to beat today.
JEAN COCTEAU, *A Call to Order*

22024.
These poor Might-Have-Beens,
These fatuous, ineffectual Yesterdays!   W. E. HENLEY,
To James McNeill Whistler

22025.
And all our yesterdays have lighted fools
The way to dusty death.
SHAKESPEARE, *Macbeth*

22026. O, call back yesterday, bid time return!
SHAKESPEARE, *Richard II*

22027. Yesterday will not be called again.
JOHN SKELTON, *Magnyfycence*

22028.
Whose yesterdays look backwards with a smile
Nor, like the Parthian, wound him as they fly.
EDWARD YOUNG, *Night Thoughts*

See also: 3046, 16042, 19935, 20471, 21861.

YOUTH

Related Subjects: Age, Beauty, Boy, Charm, Childhood, Enthusiasm, Love.

22031. Young men have a passion for regarding their elders as senile.
HENRY ADAMS,
The Education of Henry Adams

22032. Young men are fitter to invent than to judge, fitter for execution than for counsel, and fitter for new projects than for settled business.   BACON, *Of Youth and Age*

22033. Rejoice, O young man, in thy youth.   *Bible: Ecclesiastes, xi, 9*

22034. Remember now thy Creator in the days of thy youth.
Bible: Ecclesiastes, xii, 1

22035. Youth is the only season for enjoyment, and the first twenty-five years of one's life are worth all the rest of the longest life of man, even

though those five-and-twenty be spent in penury and contempt, and the rest in the possession of wealth, honours, respectability.

GEORGE BORROW, *The Romany Rye*

22036.
In the lexicon of youth, which fate reserves
For a bright manhood, there is no such word
As "fail."

BULWER-LYTTON, *Richelieu*

22037.
In sorrow he learned this truth—
One may return to the place of his birth,
He cannot go back to his youth.

JOHN BURROUGHS, *The Return*

22038. To me it seems that youth is like spring, an over-praised season—delightful if it happen to be a favoured one, but in practice very rarely favoured and more remarkable, as a general rule, for biting east winds than genial breezes.

SAMUEL BUTLER,
The Way of All Flesh

22039.
To ride, shoot straight, and speak the truth—
This was the ancient Law of Youth.
Old times are past, Old days are done;
But the law runs true, O little son!

C. T. DAVIS, *For a Little Boy*

22040. The young man walks by himself, fast but not fast enough, far but not far enough (faces slide out of sight, talk trails into tattered scraps, footsteps tap fainter in alleys); he must catch the last subway, the streetcar, the bus, run up the gangplanks of all the steamboats, register at all the hotels, work in the cities, answer the want-ads, learn the trades,

take up the jobs, live in all the boarding-houses, sleep in all the beds. One bed is not enough, one job is not enough, one life is not enough. At night, head swimming with wants, he walks by himself alone. No job, no woman, no house, no city.

JOHN DOS PASSOS, *U. S. A.*

22041. The young are prodigal of life from a superabundance of it; the old are tenacious on the same score, because they have little left, and cannot enjoy even what remains of it.

HAZLITT,
The Feeling of Immortality in Youth

22042. There is a feeling of Eternity in youth, which makes us amends for everything. To be young is to be as one of the Immortal Gods.

HAZLITT,
The Feeling of Immortality in Youth

22043. No young man believes he shall ever die.   HAZLITT,
The Feeling of Immortality in Youth

22044. When the brisk minor pants for twenty-one.   HORACE

22045. Andrew Carnegie, when asked on one occasion whether he was not worried for fear some of the young men he was training would take his place, shook his head and replied, "All that worries me is that they won't."   WALTER HOVING,
Your Career in Business

22046. Towering in the confidence of twenty-one.

SAMUEL JOHNSON, *Boswell: Life*

22047.
Young blood must have its course, lad,
And every dog his day.

CHARLES KINGSLEY, *Water Babies*

22048. Youth had been a habit of hers for so long, that she could not part with it. KIPLING, *Plain Tales*

22049. I do beseech you to direct your efforts more to preparing youth for the path and less to preparing the path for youth.

JUDGE BEN LINDSEY

22050.

I say to you
That the much-sought prize of eternal
    youth
Is just arrested growth.

EDGAR LEE MASTERS,
Spoon River Anthology

22051.
Would you be young again?
    So would not I—
One tear to memory given,
    Onward I'd hie.

CAROLINA OLIPHANT,
Would You Be Young Again?

22052. Pension never enriched a young man.   *Proverb*

22053. If youth knew what age would crave, it would both get and save.
Proverb

22054. The temper of our youth has become more restless, more critical, more challenging. Flaming youth has become a flaming question. And youth comes to us wanting to know what we may propose to do about a society that hurts so many of them.

FRANKLIN D. ROOSEVELT,
Address, April 13, 1936

22055. I never knew so young a body with so old a head.

SHAKESPEARE,
The Merchant of Venice

22056. Young in limbs, in judgement old.   SHAKESPEARE,
The Merchant of Venice

22057. Youth is a wonderful thing. What a crime to waste it on children.
BERNARD SHAW

22058.

The flower
Of our young manhood.

SOPHOCLES, *Oedipus Tyrannus*

22059. Youth is wholly experimental.
STEVENSON,
A Letter to a Young Gentleman

22060. In the brave days when I was twenty-one.

THACKERAY, *The Garret*

22061. The youth gets together his materials to build a bridge to the moon, or, perchance, a palace or temple on the earth, and, at length, the middle-aged man concludes to build a woodshed with them.

THOREAU, *Journal*

22062.
Youth, large, lusty, loving—Youth,
    full of grace, force, fascination,
Do you know that Old Age may come
    after you, with equal grace, force,
    fascination?

WALT WHITMAN,
Youth, Day, Old Age and Night

22063. The Youth of America is their oldest tradition. It has been going on now for three hundred years.

OSCAR WILDE

22064.
Bliss was it in that dawn to be alive,
But to be young was very heaven.

WORDSWORTH, *The Prelude*

22065.
    Many are our joys
In youth, but oh! what happiness to
    live
When every hour brings palpable ac-
    cess
Of knowledge, when all knowledge is
    delight,
And sorrow is not there!

WORDSWORTH, *The Prelude*

22066.

A youth to whom was given
So much of earth—so much of
heaven.
WILLIAM WORDSWORTH, *Ruth*

See also: 664, 1033, 1120, 1494, 1499,
1672, 2263, 3068, 3974, 4861, 5143,
8277, 9214, 11764, 14302, 15170,
17824, 19648, 20619, 20826.

ZEAL

Related Subjects: **Ambition, Aspiration, Earnestness, Energy, Enthusiasm, Industry, Resolution.**

22071. If our zeal were true and genuine we should be much more angry with a sinner than a heretic.
ADDISON, *The Spectator*

22072. A zeal of God, but not according to knowledge.
Bible: Romans, x, 2

22073. It is good to be zealously affected always in a good thing.
Bible: Galatians, iv, 18

22074. Zeal without knowledge is the sister of folly.
DAVIES OF HEREFORD, *School of Folly*

22075. I do not love a man who is zealous for nothing.
GOLDSMITH, *Vicar of Wakefield*

22076.

His zeal
None seconded, as out of season
judg'd,
Or singular and rash.
MILTON, *Paradise Lost*

22077.

Zeal then, not charity, became the
guide,
And Hell was built on spite, and
Heav'n on pride.
POPE, *Essay on Man*

22078. I have more zeal than wit.
POPE, *Imitation of Horace*

22079. We are often moved with passion, and we think it to be zeal.
THOMAS À KEMPIS,
Of the Imitation of Christ

22080. Zeal without knowledge is frenzy.   *Proverb*

22081. Zeal without knowledge is fire without light.   *Proverb*

22082. Zeal is fit only for wise men, but is found mostly in fools. *Proverb*

22083.

I see you stand like greyhounds in
the slips,
Straining upon the start.
SHAKESPEARE, *Henry V*

22084. Not too much zeal.
TALLEYRAND

See also: 15173.

ZEPHYR

Related Subject: **Wind.**

22091.

Where the light wings of Zephyr, oppress'd with perfume,
Wax faint o'er the gardens of Gúl in her bloom.
BYRON, *The Bride of Abydos*

22092.

Let Zephyr only breathe,
And with her tresses play.
W. H. DRUMMOND, *Phoebus, Arise*

22093.

And on the balmy zephyrs tranquil
rest
The silver clouds.
KEATS, *Oh! How I Love*

22094.

Zephyr with Aurora playing,
As he met her once a-Maying,

There on beds of violets blue,
And fresh-blown roses wash'd in dew,
Fill'd her with thee, a daughter fair,
So buxom, blithe, and debonair.

MILTON, *L'Allegro*

22095.

Soft o'er the shrouds aerial whispers
  breathe,

That seem'd but zephyrs to the train
  beneath.

POPE, *The Rape of the Lock*

22096.

As gentle
As zephyrs blowing below the violet,
Not wagging his sweet head.

SHAKESPEARE, *Cymbeline*

ACKNOWLEDGMENTS

Grateful acknowledgments are due to the many authors and publishers, selections from whose publications are included in this book. Some of these are listed below. To list them all would encumber this book unreasonably. If any required acknowledgements have been omitted or any rights overlooked, it is by accident, and forgiveness is desired.

D. Appleton-Century Company, for an excerpt from Berton Braley's "Hurdy-Gurdy on Olympus."

The Bobbs-Merrill Company, for an excerpt from "A Cedar Box" by Robert Nathan.

Doubleday, Doran and Company, Inc., for excerpts from the works of Joyce Kilmer and F. P. A. and from "Mountain Against Mountain" by Arthur D. Ficke.

E. P. Dutton and Company, Inc., for excerpts from "Lyric Laughter" and "Death and General Putnam and 101 other Poems" by Arthur Guiterman.

Farrar and Rinehart, for excerpts from the works of Lizette Woodworth Reese.

Stephen Vincent Benet and Farrar & Rinehart, for excerpts from "Ballads and Poems", copyright 1918, 1920, 1923, 1925, 1927, 1929, 1930, 1931; "Nightmare at Noon", copyright 1940 and "Burning City", copyright 1935, by Stephen Vincent Benet.

Harcourt Brace and Company, for excerpts from "Smoke and Steel" by Carl Sandburg, from "Selected Poems" by Louis Untermeyer and from "The Hollow Men" by T. S. Eliot.

Harper & Brothers, for excerpts from the works of E. B. White and Countee Cullen.

Henry Holt and Company, for excerpts from the works of Carl Sandburg, Robert Frost and Walter de la Mare.

Alfred A. Knopf, Inc., for excerpts from "The Dream Keeper" by Langston Hughes and from "The Patient to the Doctor" by Witter Bynner.

J. B. Lippincott Company, for excerpts from "Poems" by Christopher Morley.

Little, Brown and Company, for excerpts from "The Poems of Emily Dickinson", ed. by Martha Dickinson Bianchi and Alfred Leete Hampson, and excerpts from "The Face is Familiar" and other works of Ogden Nash.

Liveright Publishing Corporation, for excerpts from "Poems in Praise of Practically Nothing" by Samuel Hoffenstein.

Longmans, Green and Company, Inc., for excerpts from the works of Sarah Piatt.

The Macmillan Company, for excerpts from the works of Padraic Colum, Sara Teasdale, James Stephens, W. B. Yeats, Laurence Binyon and Vachel Lindsay.

Virgil Markham for excerpts from the works of Edwin Markham.

Edgar Lee Masters for excerpts from "Spoon River Anthology."

Edna St. Vincent Millay and Harper and Brothers for excerpts from "A Few Figs from Thistles", copyright 1918, 1919, 1922; "The Harp Weaver and Other Poems", copyright 1920, 1921, 1922, 1923; "Second April", copyright 1921; "Renascence and Other Poems", copyright 1917; and "Poems Selected for Young People," copyright 1929, all by Miss Millay.

Random House, for excerpts from the works of Robinson Jeffers.

The Reilly and Lee Company, for excerpts from Edgar A. Guest.

Charles Scribner's Sons, for excerpts from the works of Edwin Arlington Robinson, Robert Louis Stevenson, Henry Van Dyke, Struthers Burt, Alan Seeger and George Santayana.

The Viking Press, Inc., for excerpts from "Not So Deep As A Well" by Dorothy Parker.

INDEX OF AUTHORS